GARDENS

OF ENGLAND AND WALES
OPEN FOR CHARITY

1998

**A GUIDE TO 3,500 GARDENS
THE MAJORITY OF WHICH ARE NOT NORMALLY
OPEN TO THE PUBLIC**

D1385154

THE NATIONAL GARDENS SCHEME CHARITABLE TRUST
HATCHLANDS PARK, EAST CLANDON, GUILDFORD, SURREY GU4 7RT
TEL 01483 211535   FAX 01483 211537
Reg Charity No: 279284

Charity *(Auschar)*
bred by David Austin 1997

The new David Austin rose to celebrate the 70th anniversary of the National Garden Scheme

Charity, pictured here and on the cover of this book, is a magnificent soft apricot-yellow variety of true Old Rose character – and David Austin Roses is pleased to contribute a 10% royalty donation to the NGS, for each Charity rose sold by April 1999.

To reserve your roses telephone our Order Line 01902 376377 immediately.

Send off now for David Austin's FREE Handbook of Roses – 88 pages of colour photographs, rose descriptions, and many interesting and helpful rose growing tips – *over 900 varieties, including all of David Austin's unique 'English Rose' introductions, which can also be seen at our superb rose gardens in Shropshire.*

DAVID AUSTIN ROSES
David Austin Roses Limited
Bowling Green Lane, Albrighton, Wolverhampton WV7 3HB
Catalogue Line: 01902 376376 Order Line: 01902 376377

Contents

The gardens listed alphabetically in counties, each prefaced
by a diary of opening dates

©The National Gardens Scheme 1998

Published by the National Gardens Scheme, Hatchlands Park, East Clandon,
Guildford, Surrey GU4 7RT

Editor: The Director, National Gardens Scheme

Cover illustration of the rose 'Charity' raised by David Austin Roses

A catalogue record for this book is available from the British Library.

Typeset in Linotron Bell Centennial by Land & Unwin (Data Sciences) Limited, Bugbrooke.

Text printed and bound by Wm Clowes Ltd, Beccles.

Cover and illustrations printed by George Over Limited, Rugby.

Trade Distributor: Seymour, Windsor House, 1270 London Road, Norbury, London, SW16 4DH.

ISBN 0-900558-30-X   ISSN 1365-0572

Carr Sheppards and the National Gardens Scheme

We are very glad to renew our sponsorship of the 'Yellow Book' for the fifth year. As very old-established private client stockbrokers, we are keen supporters of tradition and excellence, particularly in the gentle activity of gardening – a pastime much loved by many of our clients and staff.

The vision, patience and hard work which goes into your gardens have parallels in the way we continue to advise our clients in these turbulent and sometimes inexplicable times. For this reason we are very proud to be associated with you and we hope our happy relationship will continue for many years.

Fred Carr

Fred Carr, Chief Executive

CARR SHEPPARDS

A message from the Chairman

For over 70 years the National Gardens Scheme
has been raising money for its beneficiaries by
opening gardens of quality and interest to the
public. Thanks to the support of visitors and the
great generosity of Garden Owners the sums
raised have continued to increase. This year we
are delighted to extend our giving to three
additional beneficiaries: Crossroads, Help the
Hospices and Marie Curie Cancer Care.

The Chairman and Council of The National
Gardens Scheme wish to express their deep
gratitude to all those whose very generous
support makes it possible for the Scheme to
help so many worthwhile charities. We hope
that you will enjoy visiting many of the beautiful
gardens listed in this book and then recommend
them to others.

Daphne Foulsham

The National Gardens Scheme

- *What is the National Gardens Scheme?*

A charity founded in 1927 which raises money by opening gardens to the public.

- *How is the money raised?*

Owners generously open their gardens to the public on specific days and money is raised from entry charges plus the sales of teas and plants.

- *How many gardens are there and where are they?*

3,500 spread throughout England and Wales.

- *Who are the main beneficiaries?*

The Scheme provides financial assistance to the charities listed on page 13.

- *How much money is donated to the charities supported?*

In 1997 over £1.3 million.

- *How can I help?*

The more gardens you visit the more the National Gardens Scheme will raise for charity.

Patron, President and Council of The National Gardens Scheme Charitable Trust

Get the most out of your garden with the help of the Royal Horticultural Society

Whatever your gardening experience, there are times when having some expert advice would be very useful. Membership of the RHS is like having a panel of experts on hand whenever you need it. From practical advice in *The Garden* magazine to instructional model gardens and inspirational flower shows – there's something for every gardener. If you're already a member, then you'll know how much enjoyment you get from your membership. So why not give a gift of membership to a fellow garden lover.

Help protect Britain's gardening heritage

As Britain's Gardening Charity, we rely entirely on membership subscriptions to enable us to continue our important work in science, education and conservation. From training gardeners who now help to run some of the world's most beautiful gardens, to maintaining the world's most complete horticultural library, the RHS is ensuring that gardening remains exciting and alive.

The RHS is not only the world's premier gardening organisation, it is your key to a world of gardening delights throughout the year.

Ten good reasons to join today

1. Save £5 by joining – or enrolling a friend – today.

2. Free monthly magazine *The Garden* delivered to your door.

3. Free unlimited access for you and a guest to RHS Gardens Wisley, Rosemoor and Hyde Hall.

4. Free unlimited access for you to a further 24 beautiful gardens.

5. Reduced price tickets and members' only days to the Chelsea Flower Show and the RHS Great Summer Flower Show at Hampton Court Palace.

6. Reduced price tickets to BBC Gardeners' World Live, Scotland's National Gardening Show, and the Malvern Spring and Autumn Shows.

7. Free entry to monthly Westminster Flower Shows

8. Free gardening advice from Britain's experts

9. Privileged access to over 250 talks and demonstrations throughout the UK

10. Free seeds from RHS Garden Wisley

Simply complete the form below today to save £5

Gardens of England and Wales – Special RHS Membership Offer

Code 1098

☐ I would like to enjoy membership at the special reduced rate of £28, saving £5 (normal price of membership £33)

☐ I enclose a cheque made payable to The Royal Horticultural Society for £28

PLEASE COMPLETE IN BLOCK CAPITALS

Title . . . . .Initials . . . . .Surname . . . .

Address . . . .

. . . .

Postcode .Daytime Tel. No. . . . .

Please return your completed form and cheque to: RHS Membership Department, 80 Vincent Square, London SW1P 2PE. Offer expires 31 October 1998. Please allow 28 days for delivery of your membership pack. If you would like to give a gift of RHS membership, simply complete this form with your details and attach a separate sheet with your friend's name and address and return with your cheque to the RHS at the address above.

Beneficiaries

The National Gardens Scheme provides financial support to the following:

- **The Queen's Nursing Institute** – for the welfare of elderly and needy district nurses

- **County Nursing Associations** – for support to retired and needy nurses

- **The Nurses' Welfare Service** – for assistance to nurses in personal difficulty

- **Macmillan Cancer Relief** – for the provision and training of Macmillan cancer nurses

- **Marie Curie Cancer Care** – for the care of people with cancer

- **Help the Hospices** – for support to the hospice movement throughout the country

- **Crossroads** – for practical support and respite care for carers

- **The Gardens Fund of the National Trust** – and for the education and training of gardeners through NGS bursaries

- **The Gardeners' Royal Benevolent Society** – for assistance to retired gardeners

- **The Royal Gardeners' Orphan Fund** – for assistance to the orphans of gardeners

- **Additional Charities Nominated by Owners (ACNO)** – about 1000 in total

- **Other charities as decided from time to time by Council**

Royal Gardens

SANDRINGHAM HOUSE AND GROUNDS Norfolk

By gracious permission of Her Majesty The Queen, the House and grounds at Sandringham will be open on the following days: from April 9 to October 4 inclusive daily. Please note that the **house only** will be **closed** to the public from 22 July to 6 August inclusive and that the house and grounds will be closed from July 27 to August 5 inclusive. Coach drivers and visitors are advised to confirm these closing and opening dates nearer the time. Picnicking and dogs are not permitted inside the grounds.

Hours

Sandringham House: 11 to 4.45; museum: 11 to 5 and grounds: 10.30 to 5.

Admission Charges

House, grounds and museum: adults £4.50, OAPs £3.50, children £2.50. Grounds and museum only: adults £3.50, OAPs £3.00; children £2.00. Advance party bookings will be accepted. There are reductions in admission fees for pre-paid parties. Free car and coach parking.

Sandringham Church

Subject to weddings, funerals and special services, when the grounds are open as stated above, opening times will be 11-5 April to October. At other times of the year the church is open by appointment only.

Sandringham Flower Show

Wednesday 29th July 1998.

Enquiries

The Public Access Manager, Estate Office, Sandringham or by telephone 9-1, 2-4.30 Monday to Friday inclusive on King's Lynn 772675.

FROGMORE GARDENS Berkshire

By gracious permission of Her Majesty The Queen, Frogmore Gardens, Windsor Castle, will be open from 10.00 am-7.00 pm (last admission 6.00 pm) on **Wednesday May 20**. Entrance to gardens and mausoleum through Long Walk gate. Coaches by appointment only: apply to the National Gardens Scheme, Hatchlands Park, East Clandon, Guildford, Surrey, GU4 7RT (Telephone 01483 211535) stating whether you are interested in a morning or afternoon visit. Admission £2.50, accompanied children free of charge. Dogs, other than guide dogs, not allowed.

Visitors are requested kindly to refrain from entering the grounds of the Home Park. Light refreshments will be available. Also open:

Royal Mausoleum

Included in admission charge for gardens.

Frogmore House

Open in aid of the Royal Collection Trust. Entrance only from Frogmore Gardens. Admission £3.20 (adults), £2.20 (over 60's), £1.10 (8–16 year olds). Children under the age of 8 not admitted. Regrettably, the House is not suitable for wheelchairs.

National Trust Gardens

Certain gardens opened by The National Trust are opened in aid of the The National Gardens Scheme on the dates shown in this book. National Trust Members are requested to note that where a National Trust property has allocated an opening day to the National Gardens Scheme which is one of its normal opening days, members can still gain entry on production of their National Trust membership card (although donations to the Scheme will be welcome). However, where the day allocated is one on which the property would not normally be open, then the payment of the National Gardens Scheme admission fee will be required.

Elizabeth Shaw™

Elizabeth Shaw Chocolates are delighted to support the evening openings of the National Gardens Scheme during 1998.

Best known for their top quality Mint Crisps, Elizabeth Shaw has a long tradition of making fine chocolates. Their range now includes liqueur truffles and other specialities.

What could be more appropriate than to sample an Elizabeth Shaw chocolate in a lovely British Garden?

Elizabeth Shaw looks forward to welcoming you at an evening opening soon!

General Information and Symbols

¶ Opening for the first time.

❀ Plants/produce for sale if available.

♿ Gardens with at least the main features accessible by wheelchair.

✗ No dogs except guide dogs.

There are three categories of garden in the National Gardens Scheme which open regularly to the public. They are indicated as follows:

● These gardens advertise their own dates in this publication although they do not nominate specific days for the NGS. Not all the money collected by these gardens comes to the NGS but they do make a guaranteed contribution.

■ These gardens nominate specific days for the NGS and advertise their own dates in this publication.

▲ These gardens open regularly to the public but they do not advertise their own dates in this publication. For further details, contact the garden directly.

Additional Charities Nominated by Owner (ACNO) Where the owners of private gardens (not normally open to the public) have nominated some other cause to receive an agreed share from the admission money, the name of the other cause is included in the descriptive entry as (ACNO to ....) with an ® or © to indicate whether it is a Registered Charity or a Charitable Cause.

Tea When this is available at a garden the information is given in capitals, e.g. TEAS (usually with home-made cakes) or TEA (usually with biscuits). There is, of course, an extra charge for any refreshments available at a garden. TEAS in aid of ... is used where part or all the proceeds go to another organisation.

Open by appointment Please do not be put off by this notation. The owner may consider his garden too small to accommodate the numbers associated with a normal opening or, more often, there may be a lack of car parking. The minimum size of party is either stated in the garden description or can be found out when making the appointment. If the garden has normal open days, the entrance fee is as stated in the garden description.

Coach parties Please, by appointment only unless stated otherwise.

Photographs Photographs taken in a garden may not be used for sale or reproduction without the prior permission of the garden owner.

Lavatories Private gardens do not normally have outside lavatories. Regrettably, for security reasons, owners have been advised not to admit visitors into their houses to use inside lavatories.

Children All children must be accompanied by an adult.

Distances and sizes In all cases these are approximate.

Maps The maps in this book are designed to help visitors by showing the approximate locations of gardens within each county. The locations are not necessarily precise, particularly where gardens are in clusters. Detailed directions to each garden can be found in the garden descriptions.

The ENGLISH GARDEN

PHOTOGRAPHIC · WORKSHOPS

THE ENGLISH GARDEN MAGAZINE, *in association with* PENTAX *and the* NATIONAL GARDENS SCHEME, *invites readers to take part in its programme of one day photographic workshops.* **PENTAX**

Sponsored by PENTAX and in association with the NATIONAL GARDENS SCHEME, THE ENGLISH GARDEN magazine has invited four leading garden photographers - **Jerry Harpur, Lu Jeffery, Andrew Lawson and Clive Nichols** - to pass on expert advice to readers at **four one-day workshops** to be held in April and September at glorious gardens around the country. All are open under the NATIONAL GARDENS SCHEME and each has been chosen by the photographer who knows the garden well.

APRIL
The Old Rectory, Burghfield, Berkshire - *22 April*

Photographer: Clive Nichols has three times been voted Garden Photographer of the Year; he also runs seminars on garden photography in London and Bath.

The NGS Yellow Book says of The Old Rectory: 'Medium sized garden with herbaceous and shrub borders, hellebores and lilies, unusual plants collected by the owner from Japan and China, and old fashioned cottage plants.'

Rosemoor, Great Torrington, Devon - *30 April*

Photographer: Andrew Lawson. A keen gardener who trained as an artist and taught himself photography, Andrew brings a specialist eye to plant and garden photography.

The NGS Yellow Book says of Rosemoor: 'The Royal Horticultural Society's first regional centre. Rhododendrons, ornamental trees and shrubs, a dwarf conifer collection, 2,000 roses, alpine beds, two colour themed gardens, a herb garden, a potager, 200 metres of herbaceous border, a bog garden, cottage garden, plantsman's garden and a fruit and vegetable garden.'

SEPTEMBER
Thatched Farm, Radbourne, Derbyshire - *2 September*

Photographer: Lu Jeffery's work includes house interiors as well as gardens, so it's not surprising that she believes gardens need small, shapely rooms 'like a theatrical set'.

The NGS Yellow Book says of Thatched Farm: 'The garden and courtyard surround a seventeenth century listed farmhouse set in tranquil parkland. Many unusual plants are grown from seed collected from around the world. There are Mediterranean and island beds, raised alpine beds, trees, shrubs and herbaceous perennials, two ponds and a bog garden.'

Saling Hall, Great Saling, Essex - *17 September*

Photographer: Jerry Harpur is the winner of The Garden Writers' Guild Photographic Award for 1995 and 1996 and is the Garden Writers' Guild Garden Photgrapher of the Year for 1997. His work aims to capture the atmosphere of the garden.

The NGS Yellow Book says of Saling Hall: 'Twelve acres including a walled garden, a small park with fine trees, an extensive new collection of unusual plants with an emphasis on trees and water gardens.'

THE WORKSHOPS

- Each workshop is limited to 20 people.
- One of our four professional photographers will offer instruction and supervise photography.
- The latest *Pentax* range will be available on loan for you to try on the day.
- Representatives from *Pentax* will be on hand to offer additional technical expertise.
- All film used on the day is provided free and will be developed free of charge by *Pentax*.

- *THE ENGLISH GARDEN* One Day Workshops cost £80 per person per day.
- A buffet lunch and refreshments are included in the price.
- All participants will receive a gift bag containing a discount voucher for the purchase of a *Pentax* camera, a photography guide, lens cloth, a 1998 copy of the *NGS Yellow Book*, secateurs, an *ENGLISH GARDEN* jottings book and other goodies.

- In addition, the best photographs taken by participants will be featured in a future edition of *THE ENGLISH GARDEN*.
- The organisers reserve the right to cancel a workshop in the event of bad weather.

For further information on *THE ENGLISH GARDEN's* Photographic Workshops, please telephone 01189 771677.

"Shropshire – where's Shropshire?"

"Somewhere between Rutland and Somerset…"

WHAT'S THE SECRET, SHROPSHIRE?

IF YOU WANT to find out how Shropshire manages to grow such a variety of rare, magnificent gardens, you'll have to dig deeper than the sub-soil. For this county is built on rocks from ten out of the twelve known geological periods – the smallest area in the world with so many. On this foundation we blossom and bloom with diversity and intensity.

Most of these delightfully different cultivated plots are listed below, starting on page 269. When you have chosen the ones to visit, you'll need to know where to stay and details of special bargain offers; all in the pages of our lovely new brochure, for free.

Call 0870 6010532 (24 hrs) now, or write to: Shropshire Tourism (GEW) Craven Arms, Shropshire SY7 8DU, for your copy.

Curious fact: when you journey from *Hawkstone* to *Hodnet Hall* you have to go through *Paradise*.

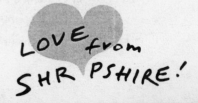

LOVE from SHR PSHIRE!

The Counties of England and Wales

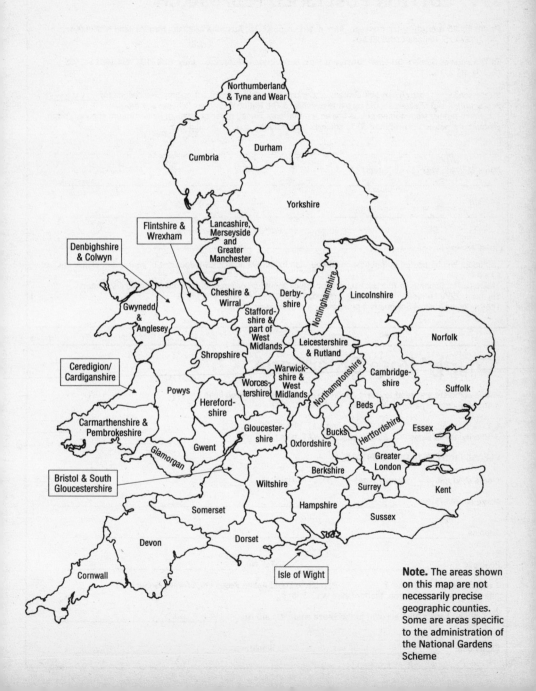

Note. The areas shown on this map are not necessarily precise geographic counties. Some are areas specific to the administration of the National Gardens Scheme

Gardens of England and Wales
OPEN FOR CHARITY
1999 EDITION PUBLISHED FEB/MARCH

Price: £5.75 including UK postage. Airmail to Europe £6.75; Australia A$20.00; New Zealand NZ$24.00; USA US$20.75; Canada CDN$ 22.50

To The National Gardens Scheme, Hatchlands Park, East Clandon, Guildford, Surrey, GU4 7RT. Tel 01483 211535 (Fax 01483 211537)

Please send _____ copy/copies of *Gardens of England and Wales* for which I enclose PO/cheque for _____
Postal orders and cheques should be made payable to The National Gardens Scheme and crossed.
If sending money from abroad please use an international money order or sterling, dollar or euro cheques; other cheques are not acceptable. Add $2 to cheques for clearance.

_____

Name Mr/Mrs/Miss (Block letters)

_____

Address

_____

_____

The books will be posted on publication. If you wish to receive an acknowledgement of your order, please enclose an s.a.e.
Trade terms Supplies of this book on sale or return should be ordered direct from our trade distributors:
Seymour, 1270 London Road, Norbury, London, SW16 4DH (Tel 0181-679 1899)
The National Gardens Scheme is a registered charity, number 279284.

'Charity' Rose Order Form

Please complete and send to David Austin Roses Ltd, Bowling Green Lane
Albrighton, Wolverhampton WV7 3HB. Tel 01902 373931

| 1 'Charity' shrub rose | £9.95 including VAT, plus £3.95 p&p |
| 3 'Charity' shrub roses | £25.50 including VAT, plus £3.95 p&p |

PLEASE PRINT IN BLOCK CAPITALS

Please send me _____ Charity roses   Date _____

Name Mr/Mrs/Miss _____

Address _____

Postcode _____   Tel. No. _____

I enclose cheque/PO value £ _____ Payable to David Austin Roses Ltd, Bowling Green Lane
Albrighton, Wolverhampton, Staffordshire WV7 3HB

or debit my Access/Visa account to the above amount. Card No. _____

Expiry date _____   Signature _____

ENGLAND

Bedfordshire

Hon County Organiser: Mr & Mrs C Izzard, Broadfields, Keysoe Row East, Bedford MK44 2JD
Hon County Treasurer: Mr Clive Thomas, FCCA, 21 Park Drive, Little Paxton, St Neots, Cambs PE19 4NS

DATES OF OPENING

Regular openings
For details see garden description

King's Arms Path Garden, Ampthill
Toddington Manor, Toddington

By appointment only
For telephone numbers and other details see garden descriptions. Private visits welcomed

The Old Stables, Hockliffe

March 14 Saturday
Swiss Garden, nr Biggleswade
March 29 Sunday
Broadfields, Keysoe Row East
April 5 Sunday
Broadfields, Keysoe Row East
April 12 Sunday
88 Castlehill Rd, Middle End, Totternhoe

King's Arms Path Garden, Ampthill
April 19 Sunday
Woburn Abbey, Woburn
April 26 Sunday
Howard's House, Cardington
May 5 Tuesday
Seal Point, Luton
May 10 Sunday
The Manor House, Stevington
May 24 Sunday
88 Castlehill Rd, Middle End, Totternhoe
Milton House, nr Bedford
May 25 Monday
88 Castlehill Rd, Middle End, Totternhoe
June 2 Tuesday
Seal Point, Luton
June 14 Sunday
Yelden Gardens, Yelden
June 21 Sunday
Goldington & Putnoe Gardens
The Manor House, Stevington

June 27 Saturday
Toddington Manor, Toddington
June 28 Sunday
Howard's House, Cardington
July 5 Sunday
Woburn Abbey, Woburn
July 7 Tuesday
Seal Point, Luton
July 12 Sunday
88 Castlehill Rd, Middle End, Totternhoe
Grove Lodge, 6 Deepdale, Potton
July 13 Monday
88 Castlehill Rd, Middle End, Totternhoe
July 18 Saturday
Broadfields, Keysoe Row East
July 26 Sunday
Crosshall Manor, St Neots
August 4 Tuesday
Seal Point, Luton
September 1 Tuesday
Seal Point, Luton
September 19 Saturday
Swiss Garden, nr Biggleswade

DESCRIPTIONS OF GARDENS

Broadfields, Keysoe Row East &✿ (Mr & Mrs Chris Izzard) Leave Bedford on Kimbolton Rd B660 approx 8½m. Turn R at Keysoe Xrds by White Horse public house ½m on R. 3 acres; herbaceous borders; spring bulbs, summer bedding, fuchsias; mature trees; shrubs; vegetable and fruit gardens. TEAS. *Adm £2 Chd 50p. Suns March 29, April 5 (2-6) Sat July 18 (2-6). Private visits (garden societies etc) welcome, please* **Tel 01234 376326**

88 Castlehill Road, Totternhoe ⚘✿ (Chris & Carole Jell) Middle End. 2m W of Dunstable, R turn off B489 Aston-Clinton Rd. Fronting main rd approx ½m through village. ¾-acre, S sloping on limestone and clay, entirely created by owners. Interesting design of small gardens within a garden. Diverse planting managed in a natural and artistic way to create great peace and beauty. Old roses, clematis and herbaceous for scent and form. Aquilegeas good in May. TEAS. *Adm £2 Chd free. Suns May 24, July 12; Mons May 25, July 13 (2-6). Also private visits of small groups, please* **Tel 01525 220780**

Crosshall Manor, Eaton Ford &✿ (Mr V Constantine) Crosshall. Just off A1 on the B1048 NW of St Neots. C18 manor house situated in 1½ acres of formal lawned gardens with mature trees, mixed borders, shrubs, large pond, terrace, pools with fall fountains; formal rose gardens, pergolas, pots, trough plantings and other features. TEAS. *Adm £2 Chd 50p. Sun July 26 (2-6)*

¶**Goldington and Putnoe Gardens** & Please park in St Mary's Church car park for both gardens and cross Church Lane by light controlled crossing. Teas at church in aid of St Mary's Church Roof Fund. *Combined adm £2. Sun June 21 (2-6)*

¶**62 Church Lane, Goldington** (Mr & Mrs R S Burn)

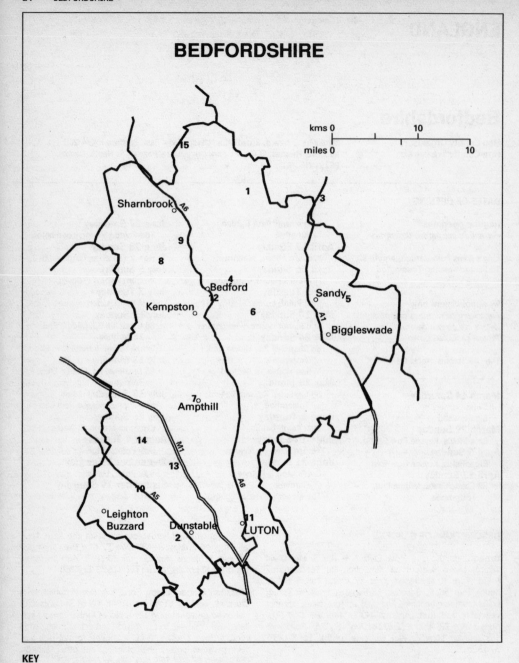

BEDFORDSHIRE

KEY

1. Broadfields
2. 88 Castlehill Rd
3. Crosshall Manor
4. Goldington & Putnoe Gardens
5. Grove Lodge

6. Howard's House
7. King's Arms Path Garden
8. The Manor House
9. Milton House
10. The Old Stables

11. Seal Point
12. Swiss Garden
13. Toddington Manor
14. Woburn Abbey
15. Yelden Gardens

North of Goldington Green off A428 (Goldington Rd) Bedford. Wedge shaped plot of approx ⅓-acre. Garden developed by present owners, incl shrubs, rose arches, small pond and rock garden. Fruit trees and vegetable plots

¶30 The Ridgeway ⚹ (Mr & Mrs Edward Peck) Smallish suburban garden of awkward shape, space fully utilised. SE front garden grass with small borders. Rear garden lawned and bordered by flower gardens leading to secluded rear section with circular arbour. A do-it-yourself garden with mobile walls for easy change of design

Grove Lodge, Potton ❀ (Peter Wareing & Jean Venning) 6 Deepdale. 2m E of Sandy on 1042 towards Potton, past RSPB Reserve, downhill to Xrds. L at 'Locomotive' - lane to TV mast; first house on R. 1½-acre sandy hillside garden; conifers; heathers, shrubs, incl rhododendrons, climbing roses, herbaceous border, orchard with wild flowers, rockery banks with pond. TEAS and plant sale. *Adm £1.50 Chd 50p. Sun July 12 (2-6). Private visits welcome for parties of 12 and over, please* Tel 01767 261298

Howard's House, Cardington & (Humphrey Whitbread Esq) 2m SE of Bedford. Large walled flower and vegetable gardens; flowering cherries and clematis, mature trees. *Adm £1.50 Chd 50p. Suns April 26, June 28 (2-6)*

■ Kings Arms Path Garden, Ampthill & ⚹❀ Ampthill Town Council (Mrs N W Hudson) Free parking in town centre. Entrance opp old Market Place, Ampthill, down Kings Arms Yard. Small woodland garden of about 1½ acres created by plantsman the late William Nourish. Trees, shrubs, bulbs and many interesting collections. Maintained since 1987 by 'The Friends of the Garden.' Tea at adjacent Bowling Club or nearby tea shops. *Adm £1 Chd 25p. Suns Feb 15 (2-4), May 24, June 21, Aug 23, Oct 10 (2.30-5). For NGS Easter Sun April 12 (2.30-5). Private group visits welcome, please* Tel 01525 402030/403945

The Manor House, Stevington ⚹❀ (Kathy Brown) Church Rd. 5m NW Bedford off A428 through Bromham. Home of garden writer and designer specialising in 'garden recipes'. Features seasonal and long term containers, many incl bulbs and bedding, herbs and edible flowers, roses, succulents and grasses; also a formal French style garden, long wisteria walk, cottage garden, spring bulbs and wild flowers in orchard and grasslands; old roses and herbaceous plants. No photography. TEAS in aid of St Mary's. *Adm £2 Chd 50p. Guided tours available. Suns April 19, July 19 (2-6). For NGS Suns May 10, June 21 (2-6). Private parties welcome, please* Tel 01234 822064

Milton House, nr Bedford &❀ (Mr & Mrs Clifton Ibbett) N of Bedford on the A6. The drive to the house is on the R, S of the village of Milton Ernest. Formal, terrace and sunken gardens set in large grounds with lakes and waterfall. TEAS in aid of All Saints Parish Church, Milton Ernest. *Adm £2 Chd 50p. Sun May 24 (2-6)*

The Old Stables, Dunstable ⚹❀ (Mr & Mrs D X Victor) 3m N of Dunstable. From A5 in Hockliffe, W on A4012. Turn R after ¼m (signposted Church End), then L at

Church. Follow lane for ½m and take field track on R. 2 acres incl walled garden. Alpines, mixed herbaceous and shrub borders, oxalis, hardy geraniums, erodiums, dianthus, saxifrages, euphorbias, deutzias and clematis. *Adm £2 Chd £1. Private visits welcome, (individuals or groups) please* Tel 01525 210633

Seal Point, Luton ⚹❀ (Mrs Danae Johnston) 7 Wendover Way. In NE Luton, turning N off Stockingstone Rd into Felstead Way. A small sloping exciting town garden with unusual herbaceous plants, climbers and trees; water features, topiary cats and bonsai; beds representing yin and yang; original ornaments, grasses, ferns. Featured on TV 'Look East' 1996. TEA by arrangement. *Adm £2 Chd under 14 free. Tues May 5, June 2, July 7, Aug 4, Sept 1 (2-8). Private visits welcome, also small groups, please* Tel 01582 611567

Swiss Garden, Biggleswade &⚹❀ (Bedfordshire County Council) Old Warden. Signposted from A1 and A600. 2m W Biggleswade, next door to the Shuttleworth Collection. 9 acre landscape garden set out in 1830s alongside a further 10 acres native woodland with lakeside picnic area. Garden includes many tiny buildings, footbridges, ironwork features and intertwining ponds. Romantic landscape design highlighted by daffodils, rhododendrons and old rambling roses in season. *Adm £2.50 Concessions and Chd £1.25 (ACNO to Friends of the Swiss Garden®). Sats March 14, Sept 19 (1.30-5)*

■ Toddington Manor, Toddington &❀ (Sir Neville & Lady Bowman-Shaw) Exit 12 M1. Signs in village. Gardens restored completely by present owners. Pleached Lime walk with herbaceous and hosta borders. Walled garden, greenhouses and herb garden. Wild garden, delphinium and peony borders. Good walks in woods round lake. Cricket matches at weekends. Rare Breeds of Livestock and Vintage tractor collection. Gift Shop and tea room. Dogs welcome on leads. *Adm £3.75 OAP's £3 Chd £2 Group rates. Open May 1-July 31, Wed-Sat (11-5) (Closed Sun, Mon & Tues) Aug 1st-31st Sat and Sun (11-5) (Closed Mon-Fri). For NGS Sun June 27 (11-5)*

Woburn Abbey, Woburn ⚹ (The Marquess of Tavistock) Woburn Abbey is situated 1½m from Woburn Village, which is on the A4012 almost midway from junctions 12 and 13 of the M1 motorway. 22 acres of private garden originally designed by Wyattville, with recent restoration of the The Duchess' rose garden. Unique hornbeam maze with C18 temple by Chambers. TEAS. *Adm £1 Chd free. Suns April 19 (gardens), Sun July 5 (11-5) (gardens)*

Yelden Gardens ⚹ Beds/Northants border, 14m N of Bedford, 4m S of Rushden. Adjacent to A6 and A45. Cream teas and plants from gardens for sale in aid of St Mary's Church. *Adm £2.50 Chd free. Sun June 14 (2-6)*
    The Old Rectory (Mr & Mrs P Rushton) 2.5 acres of established gardens. Many fine trees. Ornamental pond. Herb garden. Shrubberies. Woodland walk
    The Manor (Mr & Mrs P Laughton) 2.5 acres. Formal rose garden surrounding fish pond. Shrubberies leading to tennis court. Herbaceous borders. Ornamental vegetable garden. Natural pond. Orchard

Berkshire

Hon County Organiser: Bob Avery Esq, 'Jingles', Derek Rd., Maidenhead, SL6 8NT
Tel 01628 627580

Asst Hon County Organisers: (NW) Mrs C M J Povey, Bussock Mayne, Snelsmore Common, Newbury
Tel 01635 248347
(SW) Mrs P P A Meigh, Fishponds, West Woodhay, Nr Newbury
Tel 01488 668269
(Central) Mrs M A Henderson, 'Ridings', Kentons Lane, Wargrave, RG10 8PB
Tel 01734 402523
(E) Mrs J Bewsher, Arcturus, Church Road, Bray SL6 1UR
Tel 01628 622824

Hon County Treasurer: Bob Avery Esq

DATES OF OPENING

Regular openings
For details see garden description

Englefield House, Theale
The Old Rectory, Burghfield, nr
  Reading
Swallowfield Park, nr Reading
Waltham Place, White Waltham

By appointment only
*For telephone numbers and other
details see garden descriptions.
Private visits welcomed*

Donnington Grove Country Club,
  Donnington

March 15 Sunday
Foxgrove, Enborne, nr Newbury
March 29 Sunday
Welford Park, nr Newbury
April 5 Sunday
Kirby House, Inkpen
Odney Club, Cookham
West Woodhay House, Inkpen
April 13 Monday
Foxgrove, Enborne, nr
  Newbury
Swallowfield Park, nr Reading
April 19 Sunday
Blencathra, Finchampstead
Folly Farm, nr Reading
The Old Rectory, Farnborough,
  Wantage
April 26 Sunday
The Harris Garden, Whiteknights,
  Reading
Little Harwood, Pinkney's Green,
  Maidenhead
Whiteknights, The Ridges,
  Finchamstead
April 29 Wednesday
The Old Rectory, Burghfield, nr
  Reading

May 3 Sunday
Alderwood House, Greenham
  Common
Bussock Wood, Snelsmore
  Common, nr Newbury
Simms Farm House, Mortimer, nr
  Reading
May 4 Monday
Fox Hill, Inkpen
Simms Farm House, Mortimer, nr
  Reading
May 5 Tuesday
Bloomsbury, Padworth
  Common
May 9 Saturday
Englefield House, Theale
May 10 Sunday
Hurst Gardens, nr Reading
Scotlands, Cockpole Green, nr
  Wargrave
Summerfield House, Crazies Hill,
  nr Wargrave
May 17 Sunday
Foxgrove, Enborne, nr Newbury
The Old Rectory, Farnborough,
  Wantage
May 20 Wednesday
Frogmore Gardens, Windsor
May 21 Thursday
Meadow House, nr Newbury
May 24 Sunday
Blencathra, Finchampstead
Little Bowden, Pangbourne
Old Rectory Cottage, nr
  Pangbourne
Stone House, Brimpton
May 25 Monday
Folly Farm, nr Reading
May 31 Sunday
Aldermaston Park, Aldermaston
Sunningdale Park, Ascot
June 2 Tuesday
Bloomsbury, Padworth
  Common
June 4 Thursday
Meadow House, nr Newbury

June 7 Sunday
Alderwood House, Greenham
  Common
Bear Ash, Hare Hatch, nr
  Wargrave
Braywood House, Windsor Forest
Old Rectory Cottage, nr
  Pangbourne
Sonning Village Gardens
June 13 Saturday
Eton College, Windsor
June 14 Sunday
Bloomsbury, Padworth
  Common
June 18 Thursday
Meadow House, nr Newbury
June 21 Sunday
Basildon Park, Lower Basildon
Chieveley Manor, nr Newbury
Folly Farm, nr Reading
Kirby House, Inkpen
Peasmore Gardens
Waltham Place, White Waltham
West Woodhay House, Inkpen
June 24 Wednesday
Rooksnest, Lambourn
June 28 Sunday
The Old Rectory, Farnborough,
  Wantage
Woolley Park, nr Wantage
July 5 Sunday
Old Rectory Cottage, nr
  Pangbourne
Stone House, Brimpton
July 7 Tuesday
Bloomsbury, Padworth Common
July 9 Thursday
Meadow House, nr Newbury
July 12 Sunday
Inkpen House, Hungerford
Stanford Dingley Village Gardens
Swallowfield Park, nr Reading
July 19 Sunday
Priory House, Sunningdale
July 23 Thursday
Meadow House, nr Newbury

BERKSHIRE

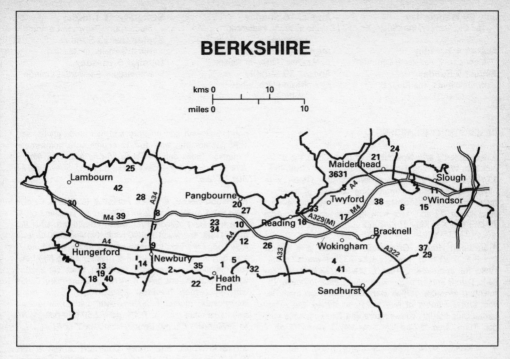

KEY

1. Aldermaston Park
2. Alderwood House
3. Bear Ash
4. Blencathra
5. Bloomsbury
6. Braywood House
7. Bussock Wood
8. Chieveley Manor
9. Donnington Grove Country Club
10. Englefield House
11. Eton College
12. Folly Farm
13. Fox Hill
14. Foxgrove, Enborne
15. Frogmore Gardens
16. The Harris Garden
17. Hurst Gardens
18. Inkpen House
19. Kirby House
20. Little Bowden
21. Little Harwood
22. Meadow House
23. Stanford Dingley Village Gardens
24. Odney Club
25. The Old Rectory, Farnborough
26. The Old Rectory, Burghfield
27. Old Rectory Cottage
28. Peasmore Gardens
29. Priory House
30. Rooksnest
31. Scotlands
32. Simms Farm House
33. Sonning Village Gardens
34. Stanford Dingley Village Gardens
35. Stone House
36. Summerfield House
37. Sunningdale Park
38. Waltham Place
39. Welford Park
40. West Woodhay House
41. Whiteknights
42. Woolley Park

The maps in this book are designed to help visitors by showing the approximate locations of gardens within each county. The locations are not necessarily precise, particularly where gardens are in clusters. Detailed directions to each garden can be found in the garden descriptions.

Scotland's Gardens Scheme

The National Gardens Scheme has a similar but quite separate counterpart in Scotland. Called Scotland's Gardens Scheme, it raises money for the Queen's Nursing Institute (Scotland), the Gardens Fund of the National Trust for Scotland and over 160 registered charities nominated by Garden Owners. The Handbook is available (£3.75 incl p&p) from Scotland's Gardens Scheme, 31 Castle Terrace, Edinburgh, EH1 2EL.

July 29 Wednesday
The Old Rectory, Burghfield, nr
   Reading
August 4 Tuesday
Bloomsbury, Padworth Common
August 9 Sunday
Whiteknights, The Ridges,
   Finchamstead

August 16 Sunday
Bloomsbury, Padworth
   Common
August 20 Thursday
Meadow House, nr Newbury
August 30 Sunday
Waltham Place, White
   Waltham

September 1 Tuesday
Bloomsbury, Padworth Common
September 13 Sunday
Hurst Gardens, nr Reading
October 6 Tuesday
Bloomsbury, Padworth Common

DESCRIPTION OF GARDENS

Aldermaston Park, Newbury &✿ (Blue Circle Industries plc) 10m W; Reading 10m E; Basingstoke 8m off A340 S. 137 acres, surrounding Victorian Mansion (1849) with modern offices making interesting contrast of architecture. Fine trees; specimen rhododendrons and shrubs; large lawns; 11-acre lake with lakeside walk. TEA. *Adm £2 Chd free. Sun May 31 (1-4.30)*

Alderwood House, Greenham Common ✿✿ (Mr & Mrs P B Trier) S of Newbury take A339 towards Basingstoke for approx 3m. Turn L towards New Greenham Park. Turn R immed before gate along track to house. Interesting 2½-acre garden started in 1904. On many levels with a number of rare trees and shrubs. Old roses, herbaceous border, conservatory and fine vegetable garden. TEAS. *Adm £1 Chd 50p. Suns May 3, June 7 (2-6)*

▲ **Basildon Park, Reading** &✿✿ (Lady Iliffe; The National Trust) Lower Basildon. Between Pangbourne and Streatley, 7m NW of Reading on W of A329. Private garden designed and planted by Lady Iliffe with help of Lanning Roper. Mainly old roses but other interesting plants constantly being added by owner. Lunches. TEAS in NT house. *Adm to Garden only NT members 50p non members £1 Chd free. For NGS Sun June 21 (1-5.30)*

Bear Ash, Hare Hatch ✿✿ (Lord & Lady Remnant) 2m E of Wargrave. ½m N of A4 at Hare Hatch, between Reading and Maidenhead. 2 acres charming garden overlooking lake in parkland; silver and gold planting; shrub and specie roses. Wild flower meadow, small herb garden. TEAS. *Adm £2 Chd free. Sun June 7 (2-6)*

Blencathra, Finchampstead &✿ (Dr & Mrs F W Gifford) Entrance from private drive at the NW end of the Ridges on B3348. Parking on joint private drive or The Ridges. Disabled passengers may alight near the house. 11-acre garden which present owners started in 1964, laid out and maintained with minimum of help. Many varied mature trees; lawns; heathers; rhododendrons; azaleas; wide range of conifers; three small lakes and stream; bog areas and spring bulbs. Interesting throughout year. TEAS. *Adm £2 Chd free. Suns April 19, May 24 (2-6); private visits welcome,* **Tel 0118 9734563**

Bloomsbury, Padworth Common ✿✿ (Mr & Mrs M J Oakley) Rectory Rd. ½ way between Reading and Newbury. From A4, take Padworth Lane at The Courtyard Hotel. 20-acre farm now grazing and gardens with plant nursery, begun from scratch 9yrs ago. Woodland beds in small orchard, roses in mixed borders, white garden. Paddock area with irises and kniphofias, leading to large

polytunnel with conservatory and half-hardy plants, etc. TEAS. Interesting walk to C11 church with home-made lemonade (Suns only). *Adm £1.50 Chd free. Tues May 5, June 2, July 7, Aug 4, Sept 1, Oct 6 (11-4), Suns June 14, Aug 16 (2-6)*

Braywood House, Windsor Forest ✿ (Michael & Carolyn Pawson) 4 m SW of Windsor. B3022 past Legoland on R. Turn R at next roundabout. Turn R immed into Drift Rd. After 1½m Braywood House on R. Parking opp on L at New Lodge. Parking for disabled only at house. Young 7-acre garden. Planned, planted & maintained by Mrs Pawson. Small arboretum with specimen trees contrasting with several ancient oaks. A Victorian Churchyard C1866 with interesting historical associations; Spring walk, shady walk, mulberry garden, pond garden, woodland walk, vegetable garden. TEAS. *Adm 1.50 Chd free (ACNO to St Michael's Church, Bray®). Sun June 7 (2-6)*

Bussock Wood, Snelsmore Common ✿ (Mr & Mrs W A Palmer) 3m N of Newbury. On B4494 Newbury-Wantage Rd. Bluebells, fine trees and views; sunken garden with lily pond. Early Briton Camp. TEAS in aid of St James the Less, Winterbourne. Plants for sale. *Adm £1 Chd 10p. Sun May 3 (2-5.30)*

Chieveley Manor, nr Newbury &✿✿ (Mr & Mrs C J Spence) 5m N of Newbury. Take A34 N pass under M4, then L to Chieveley. After ½m L up Manor Lane. Large garden with fine views over stud farm. Walled garden containing borders, shrubs & rose garden. Listed house (not open). TEAS. *Adm £1 Chd free (ACNO to St Mary's Church, Chieveley®). Sun June 21 (2-6)*

Donnington Grove Country Club, Donnington (Shi-Tennoji Int Ltd) Leave M4 at Junction 13; take A34 to Newbury. Leave A34 at 1st junction, turn R then L towards Donnington Castle for 2m. Cross 1st mini roundabout. At 2nd, turn R into Grove Rd. From Hungerford take the A4 Bath Rd, turn L at Oxford Rd B4494 and L into Grove Rd. Buddhist Temple and water garden set within 25-acre walled English garden, being centrepiece of approx 80 acres of C18 country parkland. Lake, river and woodland walks. The temple garden contains fish ponds and wide selection of rhododendrons and azaleas. The remaining garden is laid out to herbaceous borders, shrubs and lawns. TEA. *By appt please,* **Tel 01488 638298** *Head Gardener, Charles Robins*

● **Englefield House, nr Theale** &✿✿ (Sir William and Lady Benyon) Entrance on A340. 7 acres of woodland garden with interesting variety of trees; shrubs; stream and water garden; formal terrace with fountain and borders. Commercial garden centre in village. Deer park.

Part of garden suitable for wheelchairs. Home made TEAS and refreshments. Long Gallery NGS days only. *Adm £2 Chd free under 12 yrs (ACNO to St Mark's Church®). Open every Mon all yr and Tues, Weds, Thurs from April 1 to July 31 incl (10-6). For NGS Sat May 9 (2-6). Private parties for House and Garden welcome, please* Tel 01734 302221

Eton College Gardens, Windsor &%& (Provost & Fellows) Stations: Windsor ¾m Eton ½m. Bus: Green Line 704 & 705 London-Windsor 1m. Luxmoore's Garden is an island garden created by a housemaster about 1880; reached by beautiful new bridge; views of college and river. Provost's and Fellows' Gardens adjoin the ancient buildings on N and E sides. Parking off B3022 Slough to Eton rd, signposted. TEAS in aid of Datchet PCC. *Combined adm £1 Chd 20p. Sat June 13 (2-6)*

Folly Farm, Sulhamstead &% (The Hon Hugh & Mrs Astor) 7m SW of Reading. A4 between Reading/Newbury (2m W of M4 exit 12); take rd marked Sulhamstead at Mulligans Restaurant. One of the few remaining gardens where the Lutyens architecture remains intact. Garden, laid out by Gertrude Jekyll, has been planted to owners' taste, bearing in mind Jekyll and Lutyens original design. Raised white garden, sunken rose garden; spring bulbs; herbaceous borders; ilex walk; avenues of limes, yew hedges, formal pools. House (not open). TEAS. *Adm £1.50 Chd free (ACNO to West Berkshire Relate®). Sun April 19, Mon May 25, Sun June 21 (2-6)*

Fox Hill, Inkpen && (Mrs Martin McLaren) Between Hungerford and Newbury, turn off A4 at sign saying Kintbury and Inkpen. Drive into Kintbury. Turn L by shop onto Inkpen Rd. After approx 1m, turn R at Xrds. After passing village signpost saying Inkpen, turn 1st L down bridle rd. Garden 2nd on L. Car park in field. 3-acre garden, spring blossom, tulips, bulbs and fritillaries: many interesting shrubs: small formal garden: duck pond and canal with water plants. Home made TEAS. *Adm £1 Chd free. Mon May 4 (2-6)*

Foxgrove, Enborne &% (Miss Audrey Vockins) 2½m SW of Newbury. From A343 turn R at 'The Gun' 2m from town centre. Bus: AV 126, 127, 128; alight Villiers Way PO 1m. 1-acre garden with adjoining nursery (Foxgrove Plants); interesting foliage plants, troughs, raised beds, spring bulbs, naturalised in orchard; snowdrop species and varieties; peat bed. New 40yd ditch and bank garden. Collection of daphnes (30+). Cyclamen and colchicums in the autumn. TEAS. *Adm £1.50 Chd free. Sun March 15, Mon April 13, Sun May 17 (2-6)*

Frogmore Gardens, Windsor &% (by gracious permission of Her Majesty The Queen) Windsor Castle; entrance via Park St gate into Long Walk (follow AA signs). Visitors are requested kindly to keep on the route to the garden and not stray into the Home Park. Station and bus stop; Windsor (20 mins walk from gardens); Green Line bus no 701, from London. Limited parking for cars only (free). 30 acres of landscaped gardens rich in history and beauty. Large lake, fine trees, lawns, flowers and flowering shrubs. The Royal Mausoleum, within the grounds, will also be open free of charge. Refreshment tent adjoining Frogmore House. **Coaches by appointment only** (apply to NGS, Hatchlands Park, East Clandon, Guildford, Surrey GU4 7RT enc. s.a.e. or **Tel 01483 211535** stating am or pm). *Adm £2.50 Chd free. Wed May 20 (10.30-7; last adm 6)*

The Harris Garden & Experimental Grounds &%& (University of Reading, School of Plant Sciences) Whiteknights, Reading RG6 6AS. Off A327, Shinfield Rd, 1½m S of Reading Town Centre. Turn R just inside Pepper Lane entrance to University campus. 12-acre research and teaching garden extensively redeveloped since 1989. Rose gardens; herbaceous borders, winter garden, herb garden etc. Flowering cherry circle, new in 1995. Jungle garden in 1996 and Gold garden started in 1997. Extensive glasshouses. Many plants labelled. TEAS in aid of Friends of The Harris Garden. *Adm £1.50 Chd free. Sun April 26 (2-6)*

Hurst Gardens, nr Reading & On the A321 between Twyford and Wokingham. Both gardens are in the village of Hurst but quite a distance apart. They offer an interesting contrast in age, size and approach. TEAS at Hurst Lodge only. *Combined adm £2 Chd free (ACNO to Helen House Childrens Hospice®). Suns May 10, Sept 13 (2-5.30)*
 Hurst Lodge & (Mr & Mrs Alan Peck) Large 5-acre old garden which has been cared for by members of the same family for over 75 yrs. It features lawns and mature trees, a recently created rockery, pond and bog garden, a formal parterre, a walled garden with herbaceous borders, a large kitchen garden as well as camellias, azaleas, rhododendrons, magnolias, flowering cherries, a variety of Japanese maples and bulbs
 Reynolds Farm (Mr & Mrs Christopher Wells) This is a small wild garden for all seasons with an interesting collection of plants. Designed to get a quart out of a pint pot, and, what is more, without killing yourself while doing it. Much use made of foliage as to size shape and colour also an instant peat garden designed to defeat moles, ask me and I will tell you how. Luckily my weed tolerance exceeds that of my amanuensis this gets me some vituperation but cuts down on kneeling

Inkpen House, Inkpen && (Mr & Mrs David Male) Lower Green. Between Newbury and Hungerford; turn off A4 at sign marked Kintbury and Inkpen. Drive into Kintbury. Turn L by shop onto Inkpen Rd. After approx 1m turn R at Xrds. After passing sign marked Inkpen take R fork signposted Lower Inkpen. After red telephone kiosk on R take 2nd turn on L marked C13 Ch. Car park in field on L. 4-acre garden laid out at beginning of C18 in the Versailles style with formal planting of avenues and bosquets. Pleached lime walk and walled kitchen garden. TEAS. *Adm £1.50 Chd free. Sun July 12 (2-6)*

Kirby House, Inkpen &&& (Richard Astor Esq) Turn S off A4 to Kintbury; L at Xrds in Kintbury (by Corner Stores) towards Combe. 2m out of Kintbury, turn L immed beyond Crown & Garter PH, house and garden at bottom of hill. 6 acres in beautiful setting. Formal rose borders, replanted herbaceous border in kitchen garden, newly planted colour theme border between yew buttress hedges. C18 Queen Anne house (not open). TEAS at West Woodhay House. *Combined adm with* **West Woodhay House** *£2.50 Chd free (ACNO to St Swithins Church®). Suns April 5, June 21 (2-6)*

Little Bowden, Pangbourne ＆❀ (Geoffrey Verey Esq) 1½m W of Pangbourne on Pangbourne-Yattendon Rd. Large garden with fine views; woodland walk, azaleas, rhododendrons, bluebells. Heated swimming pool 50p extra. TEAS. *Adm £2 Chd free. Sun May 24 (2.30-6)*

Little Harwood, Pinkneys Green ❀ (David & Margaret Harrold) From Maidenhead take A308 towards Marlow. At Pinkneys Green turn R into Winter Hill Rd signposted to Winter Hill & Cookham Dean. Where rd forks continue on main rd towards Cookham Dean, now Choke Lane. 500yds along Choke Lane you reach a Z bend & SLOW sign. Turn immed L through iron gates & up drive. 2 acres of mature formal & informal terraced gardens, incl water garden, rock garden, herbaceous border & herb bed. Large specimen trees and clipped yew & hawthorn hedges. 13 acres of bluebell woodland walk. TEAS. *Adm £1.50 Chd free (ACNO to Compassion in World Farming®). Sun April 26 (2-6)*

▲**Meadow House, nr Newbury** ＆❀❀ (Mr & Mrs G A Jones) Ashford Hill is on the B3051 8m SE of Newbury. Take turning at SW end of village signposted Wolverton Common. Meadow House on R approx 300yds along lane. Approx 1¾-acre plantsman's garden with nursery. Pond with waterside planting; mixed shrub and herbaceous borders. Many unusual plants. *Adm £2 Chd free. Open for NGS Thurs May 21, June 4, 18, July 9, 23, Aug 20 (10-5). Private visits welcome by appt, please* **Tel 0118 9816005**

North Ecchinswell Farm, Newbury see Hampshire

Odney Club, Cookham ＆❀ (John Lewis Partnership) Car park in grounds. 120 acres; lawns, garden and meadows on R Thames; specimen trees. Cream TEAS River Room. *Adm £2 Chd free (ACNO to Sue Ryder Foundation Nettle-bed®). Sun April 5 (2-6)*

The Old House, Silchester see Hampshire

Old Meadows, Silchester see Hampshire

■ **The Old Rectory, Burghfield** ＆❀❀ (Mr A R Merton) 5m SW of Reading. Turn S off A4 to Burghfield village; R after Hatch Gate Inn; entrance on R. Medium-sized garden; herbaceous and shrub borders; roses, hellebores, lilies, many rare and unusual plants collected by owner from Japan and China; old-fashioned cottage plants; autumn colour. Georgian house (not open). TEAS. *Adm £2 Chd free. Open last Wed in month Feb to Oct incl (11-4). For NGS Weds April 29, July 29 (11-4)*

The Old Rectory, Farnborough ❀❀ (Mr & Mrs Michael Todhunter) 4m SE of Wantage. From B4494 Wantage-Newbury Rd, 4m from Wantage turn E at sign for Farnborough. Outstanding garden with unusual plants: fine view; old-fashioned roses, arboretum; collection of small flowered clematis; herbaceous borders. New boule garden. Four big beds. Beautiful house (not open) built

C1749. Near church with John Piper window in memory of John Betjeman who lived at The Old Rectory. Teas in village. *Adm £2 Chd free (ACNO to Farnborough PCC®). Suns April 19, May 17, June 28 (2-6). Private visits by written appt*

Old Rectory Cottage, Tidmarsh ❀ (Mr & Mrs A W A Baker) ½m S of Pangbourne, midway between Pangbourne and Tidmarsh on A340 turn E down narrow lane; L at T-junction. 2-acre cottage garden and wild garden with small lake bordered by R. Pang. Unusual plants, spring bulbs, roses climbing into old apple trees, ferns, hellebores and lilies. White doves and golden pheasants. Featured on TV and in many gardening books. *Adm £2 Chd free (ACNO to BBONT®). Suns May 24, June 7, July 5 (2-6)*

Peasemore Gardens 7m N of Newbury on A34 to M4 junction 13. N towards Oxford then immed L signed Chievely. Through Chievely and onto Peasemore approx 3½m or B4494 from Newbury 6m R signposted Peasemore. TEAS at The Old Rectory. *Combined adm £2 Chd free. Sun June 21 (2-6)*

> **The Old Rectory, Peasemore** ＆❀ (Mr & Mrs I D Cameron) Georgian house with fine trees in lovely setting. Shrub roses, peonies, rose garden, herbaceous border & new double mixed borders, 3 acre wild flower meadow
>
> **Paxmere House** ＆❀ (The Marchioness of Lansdowne) Opp The Old Rectory. 4-acre cottage garden. Roses, shrubs, etc
>
> **Peasmore House** ＆ (Mr & Mrs Richard W Brown) Past 3 thatched cottages on R entering Peasemore. Garden on R behind flint and brick wall. 2½ acres traditional garden with lovely trees, shrubs and roses with extensive views over arable downland

Priory House, Sunningdale ❀❀ (Mr & Mrs John Leigh) Take turning opp Waitrose, Ridgemount Rd, Priory Rd 1st L. Free parking at Sunningdale BR Station. Courtesy bus to garden at regular intervals. No parking at Priory House or in Priory Rd. 2¼ acre garden designed in 1930s by Percy Cane planted for yr-round interest and colour. Ornamental pond, large lawn with shrub borders, yew hedges and rare trees. Perennial borders, heathers, vegetable garden, new rose garden; rhododendrons and azaleas with impressive hostas by stream. Mature camellias, fine shrubs and conifers. *Adm £2.50 Chd free (ACNO to Make-A-Wish Foundation UK®). Sun July 19 (2-6)*

Rooksnest, Lambourn Woodlands ❀ (Dr & Mrs M D Sackler) Earls Court Farm. Situated approx 3m from the A338 (Wantage) Rd along the B4000. Nearest village, Lambourn. Rooksnest signposted on the B400 in both directions, ie whether approaching from Lambourn or from the A338. Approx 10-acre exceptionally fine traditional English garden. Recently restored with help from Arabella Lennox-Boyd. Incl terraces; rose garden; lilies; herbaceous borders, herb garden; many specimen trees and fine shrubs. TEA. *Adm £1.50 Chd free. Wed June 24 (2-5)*

The National Gardens Scheme is a charity which traces its origins back to 1927. Since then it has raised over £18 million for charitable purposes.

Scotlands, Wargrave &❀ (Mr Michael & The Hon Mrs Payne) In centre of triangle formed by A4130 (was A423) E of Henley-on-Thames, the A321 to Wargrave and the A4 at Knowl Hill - midway between Warren Row Village and Cockpole Green. 4 acres; clipped yews; shrub borders; grass paths through trees to woodland and pond-gardens with Repton design rustic summer house. Rocks with waterfall and new gazebo. Featured in Good Gardens Guide & several garden books. Teas at Summerfield House. *Combined adm with* **Summerfield House,** *Crazies Hill £3 Chd free. Sun May 10 (2-6). Private parties welcome, please* **Tel 01628 822648**

Simms Farm House, Mortimer &❀❀ (The Rev His Hon. Christopher & Mrs Lea) 6m SW of Reading. At T-junction on edge of village, from Grazeley, turn R uphill approx 1m; L by church into West End Rd; at next Xrd L down Drury Lane; R at T-junction. 1-acre garden with mixed shrub borders, small rockery; bog garden; formal pond; unusual plants. Lovely view. TEA. *Adm £1.50 Chd free. Sun, Mon May 3, 4 (2-6). Private visits welcome, please* **Tel 01189 332360**

Sonning Village Gardens ❀ 4m E of Reading in Sonning Lane off the A4 (9m W of Maidenhead off the A4) 400m heading N along Sonning Lane. School found on L. TEAS. *Combined adm £2 Chd free. Sun June 7 (2-6).*
    Reading Blue Coat School (Headmaster) The school is in 45 acres of fields and woods with paths running down to the R Thames and Sonning Lock. The garden consists mainly of annual bedding, roses and shrubs mixed with trees eg magnolias in Magnolia Walk
    South Hill (Mr & Mrs Tomlinson) Entrance opp Reading Blue coat School. 5 acres of lawns; specimen trees beautifully planted with shrubs; walled garden
    Thatched Cottage & (Dr & Mrs G Bailey) 4 acres shrub borders, lawns, specimen trees, drifts of spring flowers

Stanford Dingley Village Gardens &❀❀ Village on the Pang River, 5m from M4 junction 12. Take A4 then A340 and turn to Bradfield go through Bradfield College junction and take 1st L after bridge. Follow Back Lane into Stanford Dingley N end and turn S (L) to church, pub, bridge and gardens. Many footpaths, field parking at Bradfield Farm. At least three other village gardens. *Combined adm £2 Chd free. Sun July 12 (2-6)*
    Bradfield College (The Headmaster) (Through main gate to W of junction). A small new garden laid out by Jane Fearnley Whittingstall. Access to grounds and College Chapel
    Bradfield Farm & (Mr & Mrs Newton) ½-acre wide variety of plants. Further 5-acres mixed broadleaf planting in 1990. *Private visits by appt Tel 01734 744113*
    The Mill (Mrs P Stinton) Interesting and unusual wild garden with bog area, adjoining village green. Recently restored to former glory
    Mill Cottage (Mr A Roberts) Pretty, small cottage garden to both front and rear, bordering River Pang

Stone House, Brimpton &(Mr & Mrs Nigel Bingham) 6m E of Newbury. Turn S off A4 at junction by Coach & Horses, signed Brimpton & Aldermaston. ½m W of T-junction by War Memorial signed Newbury. Medium-sized garden in attractive park; naturalised bulbs; rhododendrons; water garden; extensive collection plants and shrubs, walled kitchen garden; picnic area. TEA. *Adm £1 Chd free (ACNO to St Peter's Church, Brimpton®). Suns May 24, July 5 (2-6)*

Summerfield House, Crazies Hill ❀ (Mr & Mrs R J S Palmer) Crazies Hill. Midway between Henley-on-Thames and Wargrave. 2m E of Henley on A423, take turn at top of hill signed Cockpole Green, then turn R at Green. Garden opp village hall. 7 acres, herbaceous and shrub borders, many recently planted rare trees, large working greenhouse. 1½-acre lake plus 20 acres parkland. House (not open) formerly Henley Town Hall, originally constructed in 1760 in centre of Henley and moved at end of C19. TEAS. *Combined adm with* **Scotlands** *£3 Chd free. Sun May 10 (2-6)*

Sunningdale Park, Ascot ❀ (Civil Service College) 1½m E of Ascot off A329 at Cannon Inn or take Broomhall Lane off A30 at Sunningdale. Over 20 acres of beautifully landscaped gardens designed by Capability Brown. Terrace garden and victorian rockery designed by Pulham incl cave and water features. Lake area with paved walks; extensive lawns with specimen trees and flower beds; impressive massed rhododendrons. Beautiful 1m woodland walk. Limited access for wheelchairs. Cream TEAS. *Adm £2.50 Chd free. Sun May 31 (2-5)*

■ **Swallowfield Park** &❀ (Country Houses Association) 5m S of Reading off B3349, entrance nr village hall. Level grounds of 25 acres which incl a large walled garden and herbaceous borders, rose beds, vegetable gardens, massed rhododendrons and many specimen trees. There are wide lawns and gravel paths, with a small lake and a wooded walk to the R Loddon. Visit dogs' graves. The distinguished house (open) was built in 1689 for Lord Clarendon. *Adm £2.50 Chd free (ACNO to Country Houses Association®). Weds, Thurs May 1 to Sept 30. Parties welcome, please* **Tel 01189 883815.** *Home-made TEAS. For NGS Easter Mon April 13, Sun July 12 (2-5)*

Waltham Place, White Waltham &❀ (Mr & Mrs N Oppenheimer) 3½m S of Maidenhead. Exit 8/9 on M4, the A423(M) or M40 exit 4 then A404 to A4 Maidenhead exit and follow signs to White Waltham. L at church, situated at top of hill. From the S B3024 to White Waltham. 20 acres of organic gardens with bluebell woodland and lake. Specimen trees incl splendid weeping beech and atlas cedar, herbaceous borders with planting immune to rabbits. Traditional walled garden with hot border, japanese, butterfly and iris gardens. Part of a self sufficient organic farm with kitchen garden. Dried Flowers, plants and home-made cream TEAS (June 21 & Aug 30 only). *Adm £2.50 Chd 50p (ACNO to other charities). Suns June 21, Aug 30 (2-7). Weds during April to Sept (2-5)*

Welford Park &❀ (Mrs J H Puxley) 6m NW of Newbury on Lambourn Valley Rd. Entrance on Newbury/Lambourn Rd (fine gates with boot on top). Spacious grounds; spring flowers; walk by R. Lambourn. Queen Anne house (not open). TEAS. *Adm £2 Chd free (ACNO to Welford Church Council®). Sun March 29 (2-4.30)*

West Silchester Hall, Silchester, nr Reading see Hampshire

West Woodhay House, Newbury ✿ (H Henderson Esq) 6m SW of Newbury. From Newbury take A343. At foot of hill turn R for East Woodhay and Ball Hill. 3½m turn L for West Woodhay. Go over Xrds in village, next fork R past Church. Gate on L. Parkland; large garden with bulbs, roses, shrubs, lake, woodland garden. Large walled kitchen garden, greenhouses and new lakes and arboretum planted 1997. TEAS. *Combined adm £2.50 Chd 25p (ACNO to West Woodhay Church®) to include* **Kirby House**. *Suns April 5, June 21 (2-6)*

Whiteknights, Finchampstead ✿✿✿ (Mr & Mrs P Bradly) Midway along Finchampstead Ridges on B3348 between Finchampstead War Memorial and Crowthorne Station. 2½ acres, lawns, dwarf conifers, interesting plantings, fruit and vegetable garden. Japanese water garden. Mediterranean garden and new Chinese garden. Tudor Life in Miniature Exhibition. As seen in The Times and on TV 'Grass Roots'. TEAS in aid of West Berkshire Hospital Charity Childrens Fund. *Adm £2 Chd 50p. Suns April 26, Aug 9 (2-5.30). Private visits and parties welcome, please* **Tel 01189 733274**

Woolley Park ✿✿ (Mr & Mrs Philip Wroughton) 5m S of Wantage on A338 turn L at sign to Woolley. Large park, fine trees and views. Two linked walled gardens beautifully planted. Teas close to Old Rectory, Farnborough. *Adm £1. Sun June 28 (2-6)*

The *National Gardens Scheme* is pleased to invite you to a special Evening Opening at

The Royal Botanic Gardens, Kew

during Chelsea Week
Thursday, May 21st
6.30–9pm

Enjoy the glorious late spring at Kew at an exclusive Evening Opening. Two of the major glasshouses will be open, with staff available to explain their collections and Kew's work.

Admission: £4 Adults, £2 Children,
in aid of the National Gardens Scheme
(as this is a fund-raising event, admission fee also applies to Season Ticket holders and Friends of the Royal Botanic Gardens, Kew)
Refreshments available

Kew is easily reached via the Kew Gardens station (London Underground District Line, and by rail from North London on Silverlink). Also from Kew Bridge station (South West Trains). By road the Gardens are located just south of Kew Bridge on the A307, Kew Road.

Entry by Victoria Gate Only, on the Kew Road, opposite Lichfield Road.

Bristol and South Gloucestershire

Hon County Organiser:	Mrs Mary Bailey, Quakers, Lower Hazel, Rudgeway, Bristol BS35 3QP Tel 01454 413205
Assistant Hon County Organisers:	Dr Margaret Lush, Hazel Cottage, Lower Hazel, Rudgeway, Bristol BS35 3QP Tel 01454 412112
	Mrs Amanda Osmond, Church Farm House, Hawkesbury, nr Badminton, S Glos GL9 1BN Tel 01454 238533
County Leaflet:	Mrs Jean Damey, 2 Hawburn Close, Bristol BS4 2PB Tel 0117 9775587
Hon County Treasurer:	J K Dutson Esq., The Firs, Rockhampton, Nr Berkeley, Glos GL13 9DY Tel 01454 413210

DATES OF OPENING

Regular Openings
For details see garden description

Jasmine Cottage, Clevedon
Pearl's Garden, Coalpit Heath

By appointment only
For telephone numbers and other details see garden descriptions. Private visits welcomed

10 Linden Road, Clevedon
The Manor House, Walton-in-Gordano
University of Bristol Botanic Garden

February 23 Monday
The Urn Cottage, Charfield
March 29 Sunday
19 Derricke Road, Stockwood
March 30 Monday
The Urn Cottage, Charfield
April 5 Sunday
Failand Court, Lower Failand
April 12 Sunday
Algars Manor & Algars Mill, Iron Acton
April 13 Monday
Algars Manor & Algars Mill, Iron Acton
April 18 Saturday
The Brake, Tockington
Old Down House, Tockington
April 19 Sunday
The Brake, Tockington
Old Down House, Tockington
April 22 Wednesday
Emmaus House, Clifton
April 27 Monday
The Urn Cottage, Charfield
May 7 Thursday
Jasmine Cottage, Clevedon
May 10 Sunday
Hazel Cottage, Lower Hazel
May 14 Thursday
Jasmine Cottage, Clevedon

May 17 Sunday
Algars Manor & Algars Mill, Iron Acton
May 20 Wednesday
Emmaus House, Clifton
Highview, Portishead
May 21 Thursday
Jasmine Cottage, Clevedon
May 24 Sunday
Jasmine Cottage, Clevedon
Pearls Garden, Coalpit Heath
Petty France Hotel, Badminton
May 25 Monday
Pearls Garden, Coalpit Heath
The Urn Cottage, Charfield
May 28 Thursday
Jasmine Cottage, Clevedon
May 31 Sunday
Barum, Clevedon
Highview, Portishead
Rock House, Elberton
June 4 Thursday
Jasmine Cottage, Clevedon
June 6 Saturday
19 Derricke Road, Stockwood
June 7 Sunday
Clifton Gardens, Bristol
Old Rectory, Stanton Prior
The Old Vicarage, Hill, nr Berkeley
June 11 Thursday
Jasmine Cottage, Clevedon
June 13 Saturday
Heneage Court, Falfield
June 14 Sunday
Brooklands, Burnett
Heneage Court, Falfield
Highview, Portishead
Tranby House, Whitchurch, Bristol
June 17 Wednesday
Brooklands, Burnett
Emmaus House, Clifton
Highview, Portishead
June 18 Thursday
Jasmine Cottage, Clevedon
June 21 Sunday
Badminton House, Badminton
Doynton House
Dyrham Park, Chippenham

University of Bristol Botanic Garden
June 25 Thursday
Jasmine Cottage, Clevedon
June 27 Saturday
Frenchay Gardens, Bristol
June 28 Sunday
Canok Garth, Clevedon
Frenchay Gardens, Bristol
Highview, Portishead
Jasmine Cottage, Clevedon
June 30 Tuesday
Bristol Zoo Gardens, Clifton (Evening)
July 2 Thursday
Jasmine Cottage, Clevedon
July 8 Wednesday
Highview, Portishead
July 9 Thursday
Jasmine Cottage, Clevedon
July 12 Sunday
Barum, Clevedon
Hawkesbury Gardens
Highview, Portishead
July 15 Wednesday
Emmaus House, Clifton
July 16 Thursday
Jasmine Cottage, Clevedon
July 19 Sunday
19 Derricke Road, Stockwood
Petty France Hotel, Badminton
Tranby House, Whitchurch, Bristol
July 23 Thursday
Jasmine Cottage, Clevedon
July 25 Saturday
Highview, Portishead
July 26 Sunday
Highview, Portishead
July 30 Thursday
Jasmine Cottage, Clevedon
August 1 Saturday
Camers, Old Sodbury
August 2 Sunday
Camers, Old Sodbury
August 5 Wednesday
Highview, Portishead
August 6 Thursday
Jasmine Cottage, Clevedon

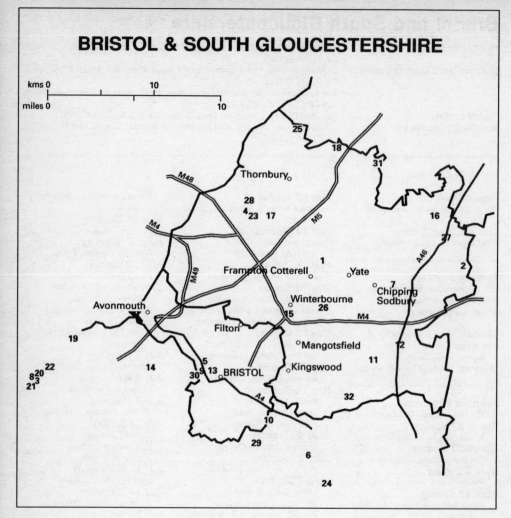

BRISTOL & SOUTH GLOUCESTERSHIRE

KEY

1. Algars Manor & Algars Mill
2. Badminton House
3. Barum
4. The Brake
5. Bristol Zoo Gardens
6. Brooklands
7. Camers
8. Canok Garth
9. Clifton Gardens
10. 19 Derricke Road
11. Doynton House
12. Dyrham Park
13. Emmaus House
14. Failand Court
15. Frenchay Gardens
16. Hawkesbury Gardens
17. Hazel Cottage

18. Heneage Court
19. Highview
20. Jasmine Cottage
21. 10 Linden Road
22. The Manor House
23. Old Down House
24. Old Rectory
25. The Old Vicarage
26. Pearls Garden
27. Petty France Hotel
28. Rock House
29. Tranby House
30. University of Bristol Botanic
    Garden
31. The Urn Cottage
32. West Tyning

The maps in this book are designed to help visitors by showing the approximate locations of gardens within each county. The locations are not necessarily precise, particularly where gardens are in clusters. Detailed directions to each garden can be found in the garden descriptions.

August 13 Thursday
Jasmine Cottage, Clevedon
August 15 Saturday
Highview, Portishead
August 16 Sunday
19 Derricke Road, Stockwood
Highview, Portishead
Tranby House, Whitchurch,
Bristol
August 19 Wednesday
Highview, Portishead
August 20 Thursday
Jasmine Cottage, Clevedon

August 26 Wednesday
Emmaus House, Clifton
August 27 Thursday
Jasmine Cottage, Clevedon
August 30 Sunday
Highview, Portishead
University of Bristol Botanic
Garden
September 9 Wednesday
Highview, Portishead
September 12 Saturday
Old Down House, Tockington
West Tyning, Beach

September 13 Sunday
Highview, Portishead
Old Down House, Tockington
West Tyning, Beach
September 19 Saturday
19 Derricke Road, Stockwood
Highview, Portishead
September 27 Sunday
The Urn Cottage, Charfield
September 28 Monday
The Urn Cottage, Charfield
October 19 Monday
The Urn Cottage, Charfield

DESCRIPTIONS OF GARDENS

Algars Manor & Algars Mill, Iron Acton 9m N of Bristol. 3m W of Yate/Chipping Sodbury. Turn S off Iron Acton bypass B4059, past village green, 200yds, then over level Xing (Station Rd). Outdoor teas at Algars Manor (weather permitting). *Combined adm £1.50 Chd 20p. Easter Sun, Mon April 12, 13; Sun May 17 (2-6)*
    Algars Manor ❀ (Dr & Mrs J M Naish) 3-acre woodland garden beside R Frome; mill-stream; native plants mixed with azaleas, rhododendrons, camellias, magnolias, eucalyptus. Picnic areas. Early Jacobean house (not open) and old barn. Featured in NGS video 3. *Private visits also welcome* **Tel 01454 228372**
    Algars Mill (Mr & Mrs J Wright) entrance via Algars Manor. 2-acre woodland garden beside R Frome; spring bulbs, shrubs; early spring feature of wild Newent daffodils. 300-400 yr old mill house (not open) through which mill-race still runs

Badminton House, Badminton ♿❀ (The Duke of Beaufort) 5m E of Chipping Sodbury. Large garden designed 13 years ago. Still in the process of being created. Mixed and herbaceous borders; many old-fashioned and climbing roses; conservatories and orangery; walled kitchen garden recreated in Victorian style ¼m from house with a new glasshouse. TEAS. *Adm £1.50 OAPs/Chd £1 under 10 free. Sun June 21 (2-6)*

¶**Barum, Clevedon** ⚶❀ (Marian & Roger Peacock) 50 Edward Rd. 12m W of Bristol (M5 junction 20). Follow signs to the seafront and pier, cont N on B3124, past Walton Park Hotel, turn R at St Mary's Church up Channel Rd, over X-rds, turn L into Edward Rd at top. Delightful ⅓-acre garden, in a protected position gently sloping to the SE, on shallow soil overlaying limestone bedrock. Crammed with a large collection of unusual varieties of trees, shrubs and climbers incl several species from subtropical regions and the southern hemisphere. Veg patch. This gives yr-round display providing something for everyone to enjoy. *Adm £1.50 Chd free. (ACNO to League of Friends of Clevedon Cottage Hospital ®). Suns May 31, July 12 (2-6). Private visits welcome, please* **Tel 01275 341584**

The Brake, Tockington (Mr & Mrs D C J Skinner) Vicarage Lane. 10m N of Bristol. From A38 turn L signposted Tockington/Olveston after bridging M4. R at triangle in Tockington and L 50yds on - Old Down Hill. L at top of hill then immediate R. Alternatively follow brown signs to Oldown. Fine views of Severn Estuary and both bridges. Long mixed borders with emphasis on plants and shrubs that thrive on dry, exposed hillside; woodland walk with interesting ground cover, bulbs, cyclamen. *Combined adm with* **Old Down House** *£1.50 Chd free (ACNO to BRACE®). Sat, Sun April 18, 19 (2-6)*

Bristol Zoo Gardens ♿⚶ From the M5, take A4018 via junction 17 or A4 via junction 18, then follow brown elephant signs. These signs can also be followed from the city centre. Please use main entrance on A4176 (Clifton Down). The zoo is a 12-acre garden with something for everyone, from interesting bedding and herbaceous borders to a rose garden, rock garden, large lake and numerous trees and shrubs. Gardens established in 1835. Sorry no guide dogs. TEAS in aid of Zoological Society. *Adm £2 Chd £1. Tues June 30 (6-8)*

Brooklands, Burnett ♿⚶❀ (Mr & Mrs Patrick Stevens) 2m S Keynsham on B3116. Turn R into Burnett Village. 1½-acre garden; mature trees and variety of ornamental shrubs; rose garden; herbaceous border; extensive planting of shrub roses and clematis; fine views of distant Mendip Hills. TEAS (on Sun in aid of St Michael's Church, Burnett). *Adm £1.50 Chd free. Sun June 14, Wed June 17 (2-6)*

Camers, Old Sodbury ❀ (Mr & Mrs A G Denman) Entrance in Chapel Lane off A432 at Dog Inn. Approx 2 acres, parterre, walled garden, shrubberies, herbaceous and orchard recreated in mature setting. Lovely views. TEAS. *Adm £1.50 Chd 50p. Sat, Sun Aug 1, 2 (2-6)*

Canok Garth, Clevedon ♿ (Mr & Mrs Peter Curtis) 9 Channel Rd. 12m W of Bristol (Junction 20 off M5). Follow signs to seafront and pier, continue N on B3124 past Walton Park Hotel, turn R at St Mary's Church. ½-acre garden with a little of everything. Herbaceous border, interesting shrubs and trees, annuals, lawns, fruit and vegetables. Fairly intensively cultivated, but with ample room for grandchildren. *Adm £1 Chd free. Sun June 28 (2-6)*

Evening Opening (see also garden descriptions)
Bristol Zoo Gardens   June 30   6–8pm

Clifton Gardens, Bristol ✗ Close to Clifton Suspension Bridge. *Combined adm £1.50 Chd 25p. Sun June 7 (2-5.30)*

9 Sion Hill ❀ (Mr & Mrs R C Begg) Entrance from Sion Lane. Small walled town garden, densely planted; climbing & herbaceous plants; herb garden; old roses

16 Sion Hill ᕃ (Drs Cameron and Ros Kennedy) Entrance via green door in Sion Lane, at side of No 16. Small pretty town garden with pond, several interesting shrubs and trees

17 Sion Hill ᕃ (Mr & Mrs Philip Gray) Entrance from Sion Lane. Town garden with trees and shrubs. TEAS

19 Derricke Rd, Stockwood, Bristol ✗❀ (Myra & David Tucker) A37 Wells Rd. At Whitchurch T-lights (Black Lion) turn into Staunton Lane whch runs into Stockwood Lane. Over 2 white roundabouts then 2nd L and 1st R. One of the smaller gardens in the book but densely planted and extremely colourful corner plot now 5 yrs old. Trees, shrubs, bulbs, grasses, ferns, herbaceous perennials, ornaments, pots, baskets and small pond. *Adm £1 (not suitable for children). Sats June 6, Sept 19, Suns March 29, July 19, Aug 16 (2-dusk). Private visits welcome, please* **Tel 01275 542727**

Doynton House, Doynton ᕃ❀ (Mrs C E Pitman) 8m E of Bristol 7m N of Bath, ¾m NE of A420 at E end of Wick. Mature, old-fashioned 2-acre garden with herbaceous borders, shrubs and lawns. TEAS. *Adm £1.50 Chd free. Sun June 21 (2-6)*

▲Dyrham Park, Chippenham ᕃ✗❀ (The National Trust) 8m N of Bath. 12m E of Bristol. Approached from Bath-Stroud Rd (A46), 2m S of Tormarton interchange with M4 exit 18. Situated on W side of late C17 house. Herbaceous borders, yews clipped as buttresses, ponds and cascade, Parish Church set on terrace. Niches and carved urns. Long lawn to old West entrance. Deer Park. TEAS in aid of NT. *Adm incl Deer Park £2.80 Chd £1.40. For NGS Sun June 21 (11-5.30)*

Emmaus House, Clifton Hill ✗❀ (Sisters of La Retraite) From Clifton Downs down to Clifton Village to bottom of Regent St on R. 1½-acre with Victorian walled kitchen, fruit, formal herb and Zen gardens. Rose and herbaceous borders, lawns, secret garden, ponds with fountains and fine views towards Dundry. Bristol in Bloom winner 1997. TEAS in aid of Enid Davies Memorial Trust. *Adm £1.50 OAPS £1 Chd free. Weds April 22, May 20, June 17, July 15, Aug 26 (10.30-4.30). Private visits welcome by prior arrangement, weekdays only April-Sept please,* **Tel 0117 9079950**

Failand Court, Lower Failand ᕃ❀ (Mr & Mrs B Nathan) 6m SW of Bristol. Take B3128 from Bristol towards Clevedon. Past Long Ashton Golf Club, over T lights in Failand. 2nd turning R to Lower Failand. Or M5 junction 19 towards Bristol. 1st R through Portbury, turn L into Failand Lane. 1m to top of hill. Turn L past church first R. Park in Oxhouse Lane. 1¼-acre mature garden originally landscaped by Sir Edward Fry. Further developed by Miss Agnes Fry. Interesting trees, shrubs and vegetable garden. TEAS. *Adm £1.50 Chd free. Sun April 5 (2-5)*

Frenchay Gardens ✗❀ 5m N of Bristol. From M32 take Exit 1 towards Downend. Follow signs towards Frenchay Hospital. At t-lights turn R, take 1st turn L into Beckspool Rd. Take 1st R into Malmains Drive with limited parking. TEAS in aid of Frenchay Church at Lluestowen, Bristol Rd. *Combined adm £2.50 Chd 25p. Sat, Sun June 27, 28 (2-6)*

6 Malmains Drive ᕃ (Robert & Karen Smith) Approx ⅓ acre incl coach house. Paved areas with bubble fountain. A variety of planted tubs and containers. Rockery with conifers and heathers

13 Malmains Drive (Mr & Mrs J R West) ⅔-acre with rose garden, conifer and heather beds, sunken garden, herbaceous borders and mature shrubs, fruit and vegetable garden

29 Malmains Drive ᕃ (Mr & Mrs G E Bayley) Approx ⅓-acre. Long narrow garden with established trees creating areas for shade loving plants leading to an open area with summerhouse. Access to neighbour's garden with fish and water features

33 Malmains Drive ᕃ❀ (Mr & Mrs Eric White) ⅓-acre plantsman's garden designed by owners since 1983 for low maintenance with unusual trees and shrubs. A yr-round garden split up into different planting areas - mixed shrub and perennial borders, heather bed with grasses, wild area, rock garden plus container planting. *Private visits also welcome, please* **Tel 0117 9574403**

¶46 Malmains Drive ᕃ✗ (Mr & Mrs P G Mayall) Suburban garden with shrubs, herbaceous plants and containers

Lluestowen ᕃ (Mrs B Wiltshire) Bristol Rd. 1-acre old established spacious garden with a specimen tulip tree and other unusual trees. Many flowering cherries and pine trees. Paved courtyard with moongate entrance. Large area of strawberry beds

¶34 Penn Drive ᕃ✗ (Mr & Mrs P G Veale) 100 yds past Malmains Drive, turn L, follow rd to end. ⅙-acre suburban garden with mature trees a large Fremontodendron, mixed borders, gravel garden, vegetables and fruit, wild garden

Hawkesbury Gardens Turn off A46 to Hawkesbury Upton - drive through the village. *Combined adm £2 Chd free. Sun July 12 (2-6)*

¶Church Farm House ✗❀ (Mr & Mrs R N Osmond) Turn L by the pond and drive down the hill. Country garden in unique setting opp historic church (open). TEAS in aid of St Mary's Church

¶Hawkesbury Home Farm ✗ (Sir John & Lady Jenkinson) Park by the pond. A walled garden with old roses and a fine collection of shrubs

Hazel Cottage, Lower Hazel ✗❀ (Dr & Mrs Brandon Lush) 700yds W of Rudgeway from A38; 10m N of Bristol. ½-acre cottage garden in rural setting with wide variety of plants and shrubs incl alpines and some unusual varieties. TEAS in aid of BRACE. *Adm £1.50 Chd 50p. Sun May 10 (2-5)*

Heneage Court, Falfield ❀ (Mrs M Durston) Exit M5 at junction 14, turn R on to A38, 1st R into Heneage Lane. From Bristol, A38 through Almondsbury to Falfield. From Gloucester A38 to Falfield. A well-established 3½-acre garden, large lawn with flower beds, shrubs and lily pond, small orchard, fruit and vegetable garden. Walled rose garden with small fish pond leading to swimming pool, garden of roses and rock garden, new planting of trees. Terrace overlooking 2 trout lakes. TEAS. *Adm £1.50 OAP's £1 Chd free (ACNO to CLIC®). Sat, Sun June 13, 14 (2-5)*

Highview, Portishead ⚘ (Mike & Mary Clavey) From Bristol take the A369 (10m) M5 Junction 19. At Portishead take the Nore Rd (Coast Rd) for 1½m, pass garden centre, take 2nd L into Hill Crest Rd and L to bottom of private drive. Please park in Hillcrest Rd. 1-acre garden made from scratch by owners since 1987. Large collection of heathers, variety of plants in mixed borders. Herbaceous and rockery plants, rose bed, water features. Alpine bed, various wooden pergolas. Outstanding Channel views. Approach to house and garden on slope. Home-made TEAS. *Adm £1.50 Chd free. Weds May 20, June 17, July 8, Aug 5, 19, Sept 9, Sats July 25, Aug 15, Sept 19; Suns May 31, June 14, 28, July 12, 26, Aug 16, 30 Sept 13 (2-5.30). Also private visits welcome, please* **Tel 01275 849873**

Jasmine Cottage, Clevedon ⚘❀ (Mr & Mrs Michael Redgrave) 26 Channel Rd. 12m W of Bristol (junction 20 off M5). Follow signs to seafront and pier, continue N on B3124, past Walton Park Hotel, turn R at St Mary's Church. Medium-sized garden created by owners from a wooded shelter belt for interest in all seasons. Rose pergola and gazebo, island beds with mixed planting, large collection of clematis, unusual climbers and tender perennials a speciality. Plants propagated from the garden available in small nursery. Toilet facilities. TEAS on Thurs only, for pre-booked parties only with minimum 10. *Adm £1.50 Chd free. Suns May 24, June 28 (2-5.30). Every Thurs May 7 to Aug 27 (2-5.30). Private visits welcome April to Sept, please* **Tel 01275 871850**

10 Linden Road, Clevedon ❀ (Ruth & William Salisbury) Coming from the seafront, head up Alexandra Rd opp the pier, cross the roundabout. Linden Rd is between the Midland and Barclays Banks. No 10 is 150yds on the R. A very small but richly planted seaside town garden. Over 400 different species of trees, shrubs and plants grow in 3 areas, the largest being 35′ × 40′. After 10 yrs this area is being redesigned and visitors are welcome to share the changes with owners as they develop the garden. Visitors should therefore not expect manicured perfection! *Adm £1 Chd free. Open by appt Jan to Oct, please* **Tel 01275 874694**

The Manor House, Walton-in-Gordano ⚘⚘❀ (Mr & Mrs Caryl Wills and Mr & Mrs Simon Wills) 2m NE of Clevedon. Entrance on N side of B3124, Clevedon to Portishead Rd, just by houses on roadside nearest Clevedon. Clevedon-Portishead buses stop in village. 4-acres; trees, shrubs, herbaceous and bulbs mostly labelled. *Adm £2, Acc chd under 14 free (ACNO to St Peter's Hospice, Bristol®). Open by appt only all year, please* **Tel 01275 872067**

Old Down House, Tockington ⚘❀ (Mr & Mrs Robert Bernays) 10m N of Bristol. Follow brown Tourist Board signs to Oldown from A38 at Alveston. 5 acres divided into small formal and informal gardens by hedges and walls; topiary, shrubs; extensive lawns; rock garden; fine trees (weeping beeches, etc). Herbaceous borders, semi-wild areas with spring and autumn cyclamen; fine views to Severn and Welsh hills. TEAS. *Combined adm with* **The Brake** *£1.50 Chd free (ACNO to BRACE®). Sat, Sun April 18, 19; Adm £1 Sept 12, 13 (2-6). Private parties welcome, please* **Tel 01454 413605**

The Old Rectory, Stanton Prior ⚘❀ (Lt Col & Mrs Patrick Mesquita) 6m from Bath on A39 Wells Rd; at Marksbury turn L to Stanton Prior. 1-acre garden next to Church, in beautiful countryside with medieval pond and many interesting features incl knot garden, apple and pear arches; rose pergola and productive vegetable garden. TEAS. *Adm £1.50 Chd free. Sun June 7 (2-6). Parties by appt all yr, please* **Tel 01761 471942**

The Old Vicarage, Hill, nr Berkeley ⚘⚘❀ (Dr & Mrs A Longstaff) 2m N of Thornbury. At Whitfield on A38 take B4061. Turn R at Upper Morton and follow signposts to Rockhampton then Hill. Old Vicarage on R after entrances to Church and Hill Court. Set against the backdrop of the small aboretum of Hill Court and the charming tiny Church of St Michael, this Victorian vicarage garden has in recent yrs been largely redesigned and replanted. Features incl a part-walled brick-pathed potager, with moon gate. Unusual herbaceous plants and shrubs, 2 ponds, one in a small mediterranean garden, the other next to the herb garden. TEAS. *Adm £1.50 Chd free. Sun June 7 (11-5)*

Crossroads

Crossroads is a charity which cares for carers. The National Gardens Scheme is delighted to include it in its list of beneficiaries. Some facts and figures:

- One in 7 of the adult population is caring for a relative or friend.

- Most of the carers are women.

- 20% of carers say they never get a break and 65% of carers say their health has suffered as a result of caring responsibilities.

- **Crossroads** employs over 4,000 staff who support and provide respite care for the carers.

- **Crossroads** supports 28,000 carers and provides nearly 3 million care hours per year.

- The contribution of carers saves tax payers over £30 billion per year.

■ **Pearl's Garden, Coalpit Heath** ៦⚘ (Pearl & Doug Watts) Take Downend (Westerleigh Rd) to Tormarton Rd past Folly Public House over motorway and garden is 500yds on L. From junction 18 on M4, turn N on the A46 and almost immed L signposted Pucklechurch. After 5½m the garden is on R shortly before bridge over motorway. 2-acre 'mini estate' mature trees; herb and terrace gardens; statuary amusing and formal; 100 different hollies. Designed and built by owners since 1966 with water features and peafowl. Plenty of seats. TEAS. *Adm £1.50 Chd free. Each Sun in May and June. For NGS Sun, Mon May 24, 25 (12-5). Ploughman's Lunch available. Also private visits welcome May and June, please* **Tel 01179 562953**

Petty France Hotel, Badminton ៦⚘ (W J Fraser Esq) On A46 5m N exit 18 M4. Edge of Badminton Estate. Chipping Sodbury 5m. 2 acres of mature shrubs and trees incl specimen cedar, 200-yr-old yew hedge, medlar and tulip trees. Vegetable garden and herbs. Many spring flowers and shrubs. TEAS. *Adm £1.50 Chd free. Suns May 24, July 19 (2-5). Private parties also welcome, please* **Tel 01454 238361**

Rock House, Elberton ⚘ (Mr & Mrs John Gunnery) From Old Severn Bridge on M48 take B4461 to Alveston. In Elberton, take 1st turning L to Littleton-on-Severn and turn immed R. 1-acre walled garden undergoing improvement. Pond and old yew tree. Mixed borders. Cottage garden plants. *Adm £1 Chd free (ACNO to St John's Church, Elberton®). Sun May 31 (2-6)*

Tranby House, Whitchurch, Bristol ⚘ (Jan Barkworth) Norton Lane. ½m S of Whitchurch Village. Leave Bristol on A37 Wells Rd, through Whitchurch Village 1st turning on R, signposted Norton Malreward. 1¼-acre informal garden, designed and planted to encourage wildlife. Wide variety of trees, shrubs, and flowers; ponds and wild flower meadow. Plants and pressed flower cards for sale in aid of The Wildlife Trust. Partly suitable for wheelchairs. TEA. *Adm £1.50 Chd free. Suns June 14, July 19, Aug 16 (2-5.30)*

University of Bristol Botanic Garden ៦⚘ Bracken Hill, North Rd, Leigh Woods, 1m W of Bristol via Clifton. Cross suspension bridge, North Rd is 1st R. As featured on Gardeners World 1993, 1994 and 1995, Superintendent Nicholas Wray, (presenter). 5-acre garden supporting approx 4,500 species; special collections incl cistus, hebe, ferns, salvia and sempervivum, plus many native plants. Range of glasshouses and large Pulhams rock garden. TEAS. *Adm £1 Chd 50p (ACNO to Friends of Bristol University Botanic Garden®). Private visits welcome all year, please* **Tel 01179 733682.** *For NGS Suns June 21, Aug 30 (11-5)*

The Urn Cottage, Charfield ៦⚘ (Mr A C & Dr L A Rosser) 19 Station Road, Wotton-under-Edge, Glos GL12 8SY. 3m E of M5 exit 14. In Charfield turn off main road at The Railway Tavern, then 400yds on L: short walk from parking. Family garden, created from scratch by owners since 1982 surrounding stone built cottage with Cotswold views. Richly planted with schemes differing in character from sunbaked flagstones to streamside shade. Experiments in plant association incl colour, foliage, grasses, groundcover, with always an emphasis on well behaved plants, continuity of interest and wildlife. TEAS in aid of CLIC and 'Send a Cow'. *Adm £1.50 Chd 30p. Mons Feb 23 (10-12) March 30 (2-5) April 27 (10-12) May 25 (2-6) Sun Sept 27 (2-5) Mons Sept 28, Oct 19 (10-12). Parties by appt all year*

West Tyning, Beach ៦⚘ (Mr & Mrs G S Alexander) From Bath (6m) or Bristol (7m) on A43l. From Bitton village turn N up Golden Valley Lane, signposted Beach. Continue up lane for 2m to Wick–Upton Cheyney Xrds, turn R towards Upton Cheyney for 200yds. Parking in nearby field. 1¼-acre garden; roses and clematis over a series of pergolas which separate and join different areas; lawns with curved mixed borders in both sun and shade; woodland with ferns, hellebores and other shade plants; rough grass with fruit and shrubs; rock garden and vegetable garden. Cream TEAS with home-made cakes by Bitton WI. *Adm £1.50 Chd free. Sat, Sun Sept 12, 13 (2-6). Groups of 10 or more welcome by appt, please* **Tel 01179 322294**

SYMBOLS USED IN THIS BOOK (See also Page 17)

¶   Opening for the first time.

⚘   Plants/produce for sale if available.

៦   Gardens with at least the main features accessible by wheelchair.

⚘   No dogs except guide dogs.

●   These gardens advertise their own dates in this publication although they do not nominate specific days for the NGS. Not all the money collected by these gardens comes to the NGS but they do make a guaranteed contribution.

■   These gardens nominate specific days for the NGS and advertise their own dates in this publication.

▲   These gardens open regularly to the public but they do not advertise their own dates in this publication. For further details, contact the garden directly.

Buckinghamshire

Hon County Organiser:	Mrs Sue Wright, Brudenell House, Quainton, Aylesbury HP22 4AW Tel 01296 655250
Assistant Hon County Organisers:	Mrs Angela Sanderson, Wellfield House, Cuddington, Aylesbury HP18 OBB (supplies) Tel 01844 291626
	Mrs Joy Try, Favershams Meadow, Mumfords Lane, Gerrards Cross, SL9 8TQ Tel 01753 882733
Hon County Treasurer:	Dr H Beric Wright

DATES OF OPENING

Regular openings
For details see garden description

Turn End, Haddenham

By Appointment only
For telephone numbers and other details see garden descriptions. Private visits welcomed

Blossoms, nr Great Missenden
Hall Barn, Beaconsfield
Harewood, Chalfont St Giles
Old Farm, Brill
Wichert, Ford, nr Aylesbury

Private visits (incl parties)
See individual entries

February 22 Sunday
Great Barfield, High Wycombe
March 8 Sunday
Springlea, Seymour, Marlow
Waddesdon Dairy Water Garden, nr Aylesbury
March 15 Sunday
Campden Cottage, Chesham Bois
April 5 Sunday
Campden Cottage, Chesham Bois
Great Barfield, High Wycombe
Springlea, Seymour, Marlow
Walmerdene, Buckingham
The White House, Denham Village
April 12 Sunday
Overstroud Cottage, Gt Missenden
Turn End, Haddenham
April 19 Sunday
Long Crendon Gardens, Thame
The Old Vicarage, Padbury
6 Oldfield Close, Little Chalfont
April 24 Friday
Waddesdon Dairy Water Garden, nr Aylesbury
April 26 Sunday
Nether Winchendon House, nr Aylesbury
6 Oldfield Close, Little Chalfont
Whitewalls, Marlow

May 3 Sunday
Campden Cottage, Chesham Bois
The Manor House, Bledlow, nr Princes Risborough
Overstroud Cottage, Gt Missenden
Springlea, Seymour, Marlow
May 4 Monday
Gracefield, Lacey Green
Turn End, Haddenham
Winslow Hall, nr Buckingham
May 10 Sunday
Ascott, nr Leighton Buzzard
Cliveden, Taplow
Fressingwood, Little Kingshill
Oaklands, Main Street, Weston Turville
Peppers, Great Missenden
May 17 Sunday
Chalfont St Giles Gardens
Cublington Gardens
Favershams Meadow, Gerrards Cross
Quainton Gardens, Aylesbury
May 24 Sunday
Cuddington Gardens, nr Thame
Sheredon, Longwick
May 25 Monday
The Manor Farm, Little Horwood, Winslow
May 27 Wednesday
Cuddington Gardens, nr Thame
May 31 Sunday
Brill Gardens, Brill
June 7 Sunday
Abbotts House, Winslow
Campden Cottage, Chesham Bois
Olney Gardens, Olney
Overstroud Cottage, Gt Missenden
Springlea, Seymour, Marlow
June 10 Wednesday
Dorneywood Garden, Burnham
Oaklands, Main Street, Weston Turville
June 14 Sunday
East & Botolph Claydon Gardens
Olney Gardens, Olney
Whitchurch Gardens, Whitchurch
June 16 Tuesday
Stowe Landscape Gardens, Buckingham

June 17 Wednesday
59 The Gables, Haddenham
June 18 Thursday
Cublington Gardens
June 21 Sunday
Chilton Gardens, Nr Thame
Favershams Meadow, Gerrards Cross
Hillesden House, Buckingham
Long Crendon Gardens
The Manor House, Bledlow, nr Princes Risborough
The Manor House, Hambleden
June 24 Wednesday
59 The Gables, Haddenham
Kingsbridge, Steeple Claydon
June 25 Thursday
Old Manor Farm, Cublington
June 26 Friday
Waddesdon Dairy Water Garden, nr Aylesbury
June 27 Saturday
Bucksbridge House, Wendover
June 28 Sunday
Aylesbury Gardens. Aylesbury
Bucksbridge House, Wendover
Cheddington Gdns, Leighton Buzzard
Gipsy House, Great Missenden
Kingsbridge, Steeple Claydon
Tythrop Park, Kingsey, Thame
July 1 Wednesday
Dorneywood Garden, Burnham
14 The Square, Brill
July 5 Sunday
Great Barfield, High Wycombe
Overstroud Cottage, Gt Missenden
Sheredon, Longwick
Springlea, Seymour, Marlow
July 8 Wednesday
14 The Square, Brill
July 12 Sunday
Campden Cottage, Chesham Bois
Great Horwood and Singleborough Gardens
Watercroft, Penn
Weir Lodge, Chesham
July 15 Wednesday
14 The Square, Brill

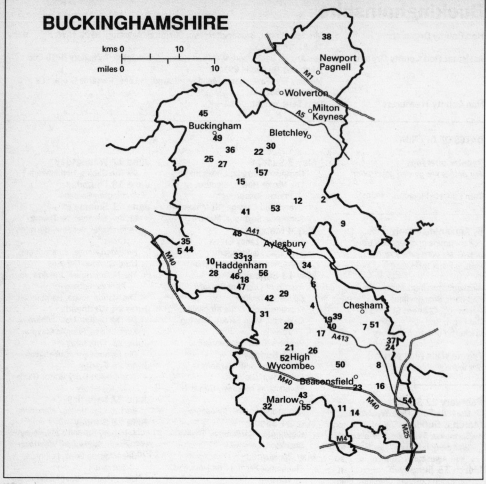

BUCKINGHAMSHIRE

kms 0   10
miles 0   10

38
Newport
Pagnell
Wolverton
Milton
Keynes
45
Buckingham
49
Bletchley
36
25   27
25
22   30
57
15
41   53   12   2
9
48   A41
Aylesbury
35
5 44
10 Haddenham
33 13
28   46 18   56
47
42   29
31   4
20   19 39
40
17   A413   7 51
37
24
21   26
52 High
Wycombe
50   8
Beaconsfield
23   16
Marlow   43
32   55   11 14
M4

Chesham

KEY

1. Abbotts House
2. Ascott
3. Aylesbury Gardens
4. Blossoms
5. Brill Gardens
6. Bucksbridge House
7. Campden Cottage
8. Chalfont St Giles Gardens
9. Cheddington Gdns
10. Chilton Gardens
11. Cliveden
12. Cublington Gardens
13. Cuddington Gardens
14. Dorneywood Garden
15. East & Botolph Claydon Gardens
16. Favershams Meadow
17. Fressingwood
18. 59 The Gables
19. Gipsy House
20. Gracefield

21. Great Barfield
22. Great Horwood and
    Singleborough Gardens
23. Hall Barn
24. Harewood
25. Hillesden House
26. Hughenden Manor
27. Kingsbridge
28. Long Crendon Gardens
29. Lower Icknield Farm
    Nurseries
30. The Manor Farm
31. The Manor House, Bledlow
32. The Manor House, Hambleden
33. Nether Winchendon House
34. Oaklands
35. Old Farm
36. The Old Vicarage
37. 6 Oldfield Close
38. Olney Gardens

39. Overstroud Cottage
40. Peppers
41. Quainton Gardens
42. Sheredon
43. Springlea
44. 14 The Square
45. Stowe Landscape Gardens
46. Turn End
47. Tythrop Park
48. Waddesdon Dairy Water
    Garden
49. Walmerdene
50. Watercroft
51. Weir Lodge
52. West Wycombe Park
53. Whitchurch Gardens
54. The White House
55. Whitewalls
56. Wichert
57. Winslow Hall

July 19 Sunday
Hughenden Manor, High Wycombe
The White House, Denham Village
Whitewalls, Marlow

July 22 Wednesday
14 The Square, Brill

July 26 Sunday
Lower Icknield Farm Nurseries, Kimble
Nether Winchendon House, nr Aylesbury
Quainton Gardens, Aylesbury

July 29 Wednesday
14 The Square, Brill

August 1 Saturday
Dorneywood Garden, Burnham

August 2 Sunday
Dorneywood Garden, Burnham
Springlea, Seymour, Marlow

August 5 Wednesday
14 The Square, Brill

August 9 Sunday
Campden Cottage, Chesham Bois

August 12 Wednesday
14 The Square, Brill

August 16 Sunday
Ascott, nr Leighton Buzzard

August 19 Wednesday
14 The Square, Brill

August 21 Friday
Waddesdon Dairy Water Garden, nr Aylesbury

August 23 Sunday
Peppers, Great Missenden

August 26 Wednesday
14 The Square, Brill

September 6 Sunday
Campden Cottage, Chesham Bois
Overstroud Cottage, Gt Missenden
Springlea, Seymour, Marlow

West Wycombe Park, West Wycombe

September 13 Sunday
Cliveden, Taplow
Turn End, Haddenham

September 20 Sunday
Whitewalls, Marlow

September 27 Sunday
Gipsy House, Great Missenden
Great Barfield, High Wycombe
Walmerdene, Buckingham

September 30 Wednesday
59 The Gables, Haddenham

October 4 Sunday
Campden Cottage, Chesham Bois
59 The Gables, Haddenham

1999
February 21 Sunday
Great Barfield, High Wycombe

DESCRIPTIONS OF GARDENS

¶**Abbotts House, Winslow** &⚘❀ (Mrs Jane Rennie) 9m N of Aylesbury on A413, into Winslow. Town centre parking. Pedestrian access off Church Walk, opp the W door of St Laurence's Church. ¼-acre walled Victorian kitchen garden. Renovated and replanted 9yrs ago. Herbaceous borders, herb and vegetable beds, fruit pergola, wall fruit and shrubs, greenhouse. TEAS and % of plant sales in aid of local charities. *Adm £1.20 Chd free. Sun June 7 (2-6). Private visits welcome, please* **Tel 01296 712326**

▲**Ascott, Wing** &⚘ (Sir Evelyn and Lady de Rothschild; The National Trust) 2m SW of Leighton Buzzard, 8m NE of Aylesbury via A418. Bus: 141 Aylesbury-Leighton Buzzard. A garden combining Victorian formality with early C20 natural style and recent plantings to lead it into the C21. Terraced lawns with specimen and ornamental trees; panoramic views to the Chilterns. Naturalised bulbs, mirror image herbaceous borders. Impressive topiary incl box and yew sundial and Planet garden. Special opening of S border, May only. *Adm (incl NT members) £4 Chd £2 Under 5 free. For NGS Suns May 10, Aug 16 (2-6). Last adm 5pm*

¶**Aylesbury Gardens** ⚘❀ ¾m SE of Aylesbury centre. Four well designed interesting town gardens off A413. Parking. Teas in aid of PTA, at Grange School. *Combined adm £2.50 Chd free. Sun June 28 (2-6)*
   ¶**63 Highbridge Rd** (Mr & Mrs H A Goodair) A cottage garden with a fine collection of unusual and rare plants, many being variegated. Also large collection of clematis. Patio with many containers
   ¶**2 Spenser Road** (Mr & Mrs G A Brown) Medium-sized town garden with 60ft Victorian greenhouse. Herbaceous borders, ornamental pond and many trees from seed
   ¶**90 Walton Way** (Mr & Mrs R Lewis-Smith) Established garden incorporating a wide variety of perennials many of which are tender. Attractive wildlife pond with marginal plants and a larger pond with koi
   ¶**7 Westminster Drive** (Mr & Mrs B J Ferguson) Formal town garden with interesting features incl mixed borders, shrubs and annuals. Pergola with hanging baskets, also vegetable parterre and new pond

Blossoms, Cobblers Hill &⚘ (Dr & Mrs Frank Hytten) 2½m NW of Great Missenden. [Map ref SP874034]. 4-acre garden begun as hill-top fields, plus 1-acre beechwood. Lawns, old apple orchard, small lake, water, scree and patio gardens, troughs. Large areas of bluebells, wild daffodils, fritillaria and other spring bulbs. Flowering cherries, large climbing roses and many interesting trees incl small collections of acer, eucalyptus and salix; foliage effects throughout the year. TEAS. *Adm £1.50. Private visits only, please* **Tel 01494 863140**

Brill Gardens &⚘❀ 7m N of Thame. Turn off B4011, or turn off A41 at Kingswood, both signed Brill. C17 windmill open (2.30-5.30). Teas in village hall in aid of WI. *Combined adm £2.50 Chd free. Sun May 31 (2-6)*
   ¶**Brill House** (Mr & Mrs J D Drysdale) Approx ½-acre; lawns, shrubs, small formal garden, herbaceous border. Wonderful views
   Leap Hill (Mr & Mrs R E Morris-Adams) Thame Rd, approx 1m from Brill centre. 2 acres of roses, shrubs, herbaceous and spring bulbs, pond. Bog area and rockery, vegetable garden and new woodland area. A windy garden to manage
   The Old Vicarage (Mr & Mrs Peter Toynbee) The Square. ¾-acre partly walled garden with areas of interest in both sun and shade. Small formal potager, children especially welcome

By Appointment Gardens. These owners do not have a fixed opening day usually because they cannot accommodate large numbers or have insufficient parking space.

Bucksbridge House, Wendover &%❀ (Mr & Mrs J Nicholson) Heron Path. ½m S of Wendover. Chapel Lane is 2nd turn on L off A413 towards Amersham. House is on L at bottom of lane. Georgian house with established 2-acre garden; large herbaceous border, unusual shrubs, roses, laburnum arches, an ornamental vegetable garden and 2 well stocked greenhouses. TEAS in aid of St Mary's Church. *Adm £1.50 Chd free. Sat, Sun June 27, 28 (2-6)*

Campden Cottage, Chesham Bois %❀ (Mrs P Liechti) 51 Clifton Rd, signed from A416 midway between Amersham on the Hill and Chesham nr pedestrian lights. Car park signed on main rd. ½-acre plantsman's garden of yr-round interest; fine collection of unusual and rare plants. Hellebores in March. Teas Old Amersham. No push chairs. *Adm £1.50 Acc chd free. Suns March 15, April 5, May 3, June 7, July 12, Aug 9, Sept 6, Oct 4 (2-6). Also by appt for parties with TEAS. No coaches. Please* **Tel 01494 726818**

Chalfont St Giles Gardens %❀ Off A413. TEAS in aid of Iain Rennie Hospice. *Combined adm £3 for 2 or 3 gardens or £1.50 per garden Chd free. Sun May 17 (2-6)*
   Concordia (Mrs D E Cobb) 76 Deanway. Parking in Deanway. A small challenging garden on a difficult sloping site. Herbaceous and shrub borders; rock garden; fruit trees; collection of epiphytic orchids
   Halfpenny Furze (Mr & Mrs R Sadler) Mill Lane. From London take A413 signed Amersham. Mill Lane is ¼m past mini roundabouts at Chalfont St Giles. Limited parking in Mill Lane. 1-acre plantsman's garden on clay: part woodland (rhododendrons, azaleas, acers, magnolias, cercis, cercidiphyllum) part formal (catalpa, cornus, clerodendrum, unusual shrubs, roses and mixed borders). TEAS. *Parties welcome by arrangement, please* **Tel 01494 872509**
   North Down (Mr & Mrs J Saunders) From Halfpenny Furze, short uphill walk L into Dodds Lane. Garden is 250yds on R. Limited parking in Dodds Lane. Approx ¾-acre garden with vistas and interest throughout yr. Mixed beds of perennials, unusual plants, shrubs, incl rhododendrons, azaleas, acers; spring bulbs; clematis and other climbers; sempervivums; patio with water feature. *Parties welcome by arrangement, please* **Tel 01494 872928**

Cheddington Gardens %❀ 11m E of Aylesbury; turn off B489 at Pitstone. 7m S of Leighton Buzzard; turn off B488 at Cheddington Station. Teas in the Methodists Chapel or on the green. *Combined adm £2 Chd free (ACNO to Methodist Chapel and St Giles Church, Cheddington®). Sun June 28 (2-6)*
   Chasea (Mr & Mrs A G Seabrook) Medium-sized garden; assorted tubs and baskets; 2 pools backing onto rockeries; conifers; perennials and bedding
   Cheddington Manor (Mr & Mrs H Hart) 3½-acres; small lake and moat in informal setting, roses, herbaceous borders, and interesting mature trees
   Rose Cottage (Mr & Mrs D G Jones) ¼-acre cottage garden planted for all yr interest with accent on colour; old roses; small scree area with unusual plants, conservatory; vegetable parterre and a camomile seat, the design is constantly changing

21 Station Road (Mr & Mrs P Jay) ½-acre informal garden with wildflower conservation area; herbaceous and shrub borders; herbs and kitchen garden

Chilton Gardens, nr Thame &%❀ 3m N of Thame. In Long Crendon turn off B4011 follow signs to Chilton; village has C18 mansion house C12-C16 church, parking available. TEAS in aid of church. *Combined adm £2 Chd free. Sun June 21 (2-6)*
   The Old School House (Mr & Mrs John Rolfe) Working cottage garden; with extensive views
   The Old Vicarage (Mr & Mrs G Rosenthal) Approx ½-acre walled garden; mature trees, mixed borders, vegetable garden; plants for shady areas
   Signpost Cottage (Mr & Mrs George Baker) Approx ⅔-acre colourful village garden behind C17 thatched cottage. Bright containers on terrace

▲**Cliveden, Taplow** &% (The National Trust) 2m N of Taplow. A number of separate gardens within extensive grounds, first laid out in the C18 incl water garden, rose garden; topiary; herbaceous borders; woodland walks and views of the Thames. Suitable for wheelchairs only in part. TEAS. *Adm grounds only £4.80 Parties £4.20 Chd £2.40. For NGS Suns May 10, Sept 13 (11-6)*

Cublington Gardens &%❀ From Aylesbury take Buckingham Rd (A413). At Whitchurch (4m) turn R to Cublington. TEAS in aid of Royal National Rose Society 2000 Appeal. *Combined adm £2.50 Chd free. Sun May 17, Thurs June 18 (2-6)*
   Old Manor Farm (Mr & Mrs N R Wilson) Reads Lane. Large country garden divided into knot and yellow gardens, ¼-acre 'old' roses, herbaceous borders; swimming pool, ha ha, walled vegetable garden and new gravel garden. *Also open Thurs June 25 Adm £2 Chd free. Private visits and parties welcome, please* **Tel 01296 681279**
   The Old Rectory (Mr & Mrs J Naylor) 2-acre country garden with herbaceous border, rosebeds, shrubs and mature trees; vegetables; ponds, climbing plants

Cuddington Gardens, nr Thame &%❀ 3½m NE Thame or 5m SW Aylesbury off A418. TEAS in aid of Darby and Joan and Village Hall Restoration Fund. Parking Dadbrook House and The Old Rectory. *Combined adm £2 Acc chd free. Sun, Wed May 24, 27 (2-6)*
   Dadbrook House (Mr & Mrs G Kingsbury) 3-acre S-facing garden with three terraces which descend to a small lake. Mown paths lead from a formal rose parterre and elaborate knot through mature trees to a fantasy garden with willow sculptures and naturalized bulbs. Behind the house, a walled decorative herb and vegetable garden with pleached hornbeam and box edging
   The Old Rectory (Mr & Mrs R J Frost) Former Victorian rectory with stunning views over Winchendon valley. 2-acre garden bounded by mature trees, laid out as a 'country garden' of borders, island beds, paved garden with fish pond and pavilion. Recent planting designed to provide continuity of colour throughout the yr. Not suitable for wheelchairs

Tyringham Hall (Mr & Mrs Ray Scott) Water and bog garden, patios and lawns surround mediaeval house. Dell with well and waterfall. TEAS

Wellfield House (Mr & Mrs C S Sanderson) ½-acre garden surrounding Victorian house. Mixed borders for all-yr colour; shaded areas; terrace with rockery and small water feature. Newly planted area for flowering trees and wildlife. TEAS

▲**Dorneywood Garden, Burnham** ఉ ౹∜ ౹⊛ (The National Trust) Dorneywood Rd. From Burnham village take Dropmore Rd, and at end of 30mph limit take R fork into Dorneywood Rd. Dorneywood is 1m on R. From M40 junction 2, take A355 to Slough then 1st R to Burnham, 2m then 2nd L after Jolly Woodman signed Dorneywood Rd. Dorneywood is about 1m on L. 6-acre country house garden on several levels with herbaceous borders, greenhouse, rose, cottage and kitchen gardens. TEAS. *Adm £2.50 Chd under 15 free.* Open **by written appt only** *on Weds June 10, July 1, Sat Aug 1, Sun Aug 2 (2-5). Apply to the Secretary, Dorneywood Trust, Dorneywood, Burnham, Bucks SL1 8PY*

East & Botolph Claydon Gardens ఉ ౹∜ ⊛ 2 and 3m SW of Winslow. Follow signs to Claydons. Teas in village hall in aid of WI and Church funds. *Combined adm £2.50 Chd free. Sun June 14 (2-6)*

    Ashton (Mr & Mrs G Wylie) Botyl Rd, Botolph Claydon. ⅓-acre plot on clay with superb views on site of former barnyard. Mixed beds of shrubs and herbaceous plants

    The Emerald (Mr & Mrs J P Elder) St Mary's Rd, E Claydon. ¾-acre garden with mature trees; shrub and perennial beds. Rockery banks using sleepers and brickwork. Gravelled and paved area in front of house with pond and planting. Vegetable garden with raised beds using sleepers

    1 Emerald Close (Mr & Mrs L B Woodhouse) E Claydon. Small garden with collection of deciduous and coniferous bonsai

    ¶**Inglenooks** (Mr & Mrs D Polhill) ½-acre garden. Under development since 1994. Surrounding a C17 thatched cottage

    Littleworth Farm (Mrs M O'Halloran) Verney Junction. Main features of the ½-acre are walled herbaceous and formal kitchen gardens

    The Old Vicarage (Mr & Mrs N Turnbull) Church Way, E Claydon. ¾-acre on clay, started in 1991 and aiming at yr-round interest

    The Pump House (Mr & Mrs P M Piddington) St Mary's Rd, E Claydon. ¾-acre, trees, shrubs, borders, herbs, fishpond

Favershams Meadow, Gerrards Cross ఉ ౹∜ ⊛ (Mr & Mrs H W Try) 1½m W Gerrards Cross on A40. Turn N into Mumfords Lane opp lay-by with BT box. Garden ¼m on R. 1½-acres with mixed herbaceous, knot, parterre and separate blue and white gardens. Roses on part C16 house and in David Austin rose garden. Brick paved vegetable area. All maintained to a high standard. TEAS in aid of Open Door Community Church, Uxbridge. *Adm £2 Chd free. Suns May 17, June 21 (2-6). Group visits welcome, May, June, July, please* **Tel 01753 882733**

¶**Fressingwood, Little Kingshill** ఉ ౹∜ (Mr & Mrs J & M Bateson) A413 Amersham to Aylesbury. L at Chiltern hospital, sign Gt and Little Kingshill. 1st L Nags Head Lane. Turn R under railway bridge and 1st L New Rd, continue to top, off New Rd into Hare Lane, 1st house on R. ½-acre garden with all yr-round colour. Shrubbery, small formal garden, pergolas with wisteria and clematis. Landscaped terrace. Formal lily pond and bonsai collection. Many interesting features. TEAS in aid of Children in Distress. *Adm £1 Chd free. Sun May 10 (2-6)*

59 The Gables, Haddenham ఉ ⊛ (Mrs A M Johnstone) Off A418 6m W of Aylesbury, 3m E of Thame. Travelling S along Churchway, The Gables is 2nd turning L after Miles' Garage. This small garden (60′ × 35′) is planted for all yr interest and incl Bonsai, ferns, a mini pond and many unusual plants. New small gravel area with grasses. Teas available at nearby inn. *Adm £1 Chd under 10 free. Weds June 17, 24, Sept 30 (2-5); Sun Oct 4 (2-6)*

Gipsy House, Gt Missenden ౹∜ (Mrs F Dahl) A413 to Gt Missenden. From High St turn into Whitefield Lane, continue under railway bridge. Large Georgian house on R. York stone terrace, pleached lime walk to writing hut; shrubs, roses, herbs, small walled vegetable garden, orchard, gipsy caravan and maze for children. Limited access for wheelchairs. Teas locally. *Adm £1.50 Chd 50p (ACNO to Roald Dahl Foundation®). Suns June 28, Sept 27 (2-5)*

Gracefield, Lacey Green ఉ ⊛ (Mr & Mrs B Wicks) Take A4010 High Wycombe to Aylesbury Rd. Turn R by Red Lion at Bradenham, up hill to Walters Ash; L at T-junction for Lacey Green. Brick and flint house on main rd beyond church facing Kiln Lane. 1½-acre mature garden; unusual plants, orchard, soft fruit, shrub borders, rockery; sink gardens. Two ponds. Ploughman's lunches, TEAS and plants in aid of local Macmillan Nurses Group. *Adm £1.50 Chd free. Bank Hol Mon May 4 (11.30-5). Parties welcome by written appt May to Aug*

Great Barfield, Bradenham ఉ ౹∜ ⊛ (Richard Nutt Esq) A4010 4m NW of High Wycombe 4m S of Princes Risborough. Park on green. 1½-acre garden, designed as informal background for unusual plants. Feb snowdrops,

---

Remember that every time you visit a National Gardens Scheme garden you are helping to raise money for:

The Queen's Nursing Institute
County Nursing Associations
The Nurses' Welfare Service
Macmillan Cancer Relief
Marie Curie Cancer Care
Help the Hospices
Crossroads
The Gardens Fund of the National Trust
The Gardeners' Royal Benevolent Society
The Royal Gardeners' Orphans Fund
Additional Charities Nominated by Owners
Other charities as decided from time to time by Council

hellebores, willows and bulbs; April unique pulmonarias and bergenias, naturalised red trilliums. July old-fashioned and climbing roses, lilies; Sept autumn colour incl colchicum and sorbus berries. National collections of iris unguicularis, leucojum. TEAS. *Adm £1.50 Chd under 16 free (ACNO to NCCPG®). Suns Feb 22 (2-5), April 5 (2-5.30), July 5 (2-6), Sept 27 (2-5). Private visits welcome, please* Tel 01494 563741. *Provisional first opening in 1999 Sun Feb 21*

Great Horwood and Singleborough Gardens ⅋⅋❀ 2m N of Winslow, on B4033. Teas in Village Hall and at Stagsden in aid of Church Restoration Appeal. *Combined adm £2.50 Chd free. Sun July 12 (2-6)*
   2 Greenway (Mrs Peggy Weare) Great Horwood. Small garden full of colour
   ¶**Little Rafters** (Mr & Mrs G W Berrey) Great Horwood. Small cottage garden, well stocked with shrubs, climbers and perennials. Paved area with water feature and colourful containers
   6 Nash Road (Mrs Liz Whitehall) Great Horwood. Garden with many 'rooms'. Large perennial and herbaceous borders
   ¶**The Old Dairy** (Mr & Mrs D Lowen) Great Horwood. From farmyard to old cottage garden with rose walk and herbaceous borders in 4yrs
   Old Vine Cottage (Mr & Mrs M Alford) Singleborough. C15 thatched cottage with secluded back garden and terrace with pond and rockery
   Stagsden (Mr & Mrs B A Nicholson) Singleborough. ¾-acre garden with trees and open views. Numerous shrub and herbaceous beds, vegetable plot, greenhouse and barn. All grown without mains water

Hall Barn, Beaconsfield (The Dowager Lady Burnham & The Hon Mrs Farncombe) Lodge gate 300yds S of Beaconsfield Church in town centre. One of the original gardens opening in 1927, still owned by the Burnham family. Unique landscaped garden of great historical interest, laid out in the 1680's. Vast 300-yr-old curving yew hedge. Formal lake. Long avenues through the Grove to a temple, classical ornament or statue. Obelisk with fine carvings in memory of Edmund Waller's grandson who completed the garden about 1730. *Garden open* by written appointment only. *Applications to The Hon Mrs Farncombe, Hall Barn, Beaconsfield, Buckinghamshire HP9 2SG*

¶**Harewood, Chalfont St Giles** ⅋⅋ (Mr & Mrs John Heywood) Burtons Lane. From A404 Amersham-Rickmansworth Rd, in Little Chalfont Village turn S down Burtons Lane. Harewood is 1m on R, opp beechwood. New ½-acre garden on site of old orchard being developed for yr-round interest with low maintenance by former owners of Harewood, Harewood Rd. Wide variety of hardy plants and shrubs; climbers, sink gardens, and small wild flower meadow in orchard. Cream TEAS. *Adm £1 Chd free. Private visits welcome, please* Tel 01494 763553

Hillesden House, Hillesden ⅋⅋❀ (Mr & Mrs R M Faccenda) 3m S of Buckingham. By superb Perpendicular Church 'Cathedral in the Fields'; lawns, shrubberies; rose, alpine and foliage gardens; interesting clipped hedges;

conservatory; surrounded by park with red deer and highland cattle. Large lakes with ornamental duck and carp. Views over countryside. TEAS in aid of Hillesden Church. *Adm £2 Chd under 12 free. Sun June 21 (2-6)*

▲**Hughenden Manor, High Wycombe** ⅋⅋❀ (The National Trust) 1½m N of High Wycombe on W side of Great Missenden Rd A4128. Mary Anne Disraeli's colour schemes inspire Spring and Summer bedding. Unusual conifers, planted from photographs taken at time of Disraeli's death. Walled garden (not usually open) with herbs and Victorian fruit varieties. Old English apple orchard with picnic area. Beech woodland walks. Herbaceous border re-planting spring 1998. Tearoom. *Adm House & Garden £3.80 Chd £1.90 Family £9.50. Adm garden only £1 Chd 50p. For NGS Sun July 19, Garden (12-5), House (1-5). Last adm 4.30.* Timed tickets for entry to Manor

Kingsbridge, Steeple Claydon ⅋❀ (Mr & Mrs T Aldous) 3m S of Buckingham. Halfway between Padbury and Steeple Claydon. Xrds with sign to 'Kingsbridge Only'. 3-acre garden with ha ha, stream, mixed borders and gazebo and a further 1-acre shrubbery created 10 yrs ago. Cream TEAS in aid of Claydon Parish Rooms Appeal. *Adm £1.50 Chd free. Wed June 24, Sun June 28 (2-6)*

Long Crendon Gardens ⅋❀ 2m N of Thame B4011 to Bicester. TEAS. *Combined adm £2.50 Chd free (ACNO to Long Crendon Charities®)*
Sun April 19 (2-6)
   Barry's Close (Mr & Mrs R Salmon) 2 acres of sloping garden with interesting collection of trees and shrubs. Herbaceous border; spring fed pools and water garden
   Manor House (Sir William & Lady Shelton) turn R by church; house through wrought iron gates. 6 acres; lawns sweep down to 2 ornamental lakes, each with small island; walk along lower lake with over 20 varieties of willow; fine views towards Chilterns. House (not open) 1675. TEAS
   The Old Crown (Mr & Mrs R H Bradbury) 100yds past Chandos Inn. 1 acre on steep SW slope. Old-fashioned and other roses and climbers. Flowering shrubs, herbaceous plants. Spring bulbs, assorted colourful containers in summer; 2 vegetable patches
   Springfield Cottage (Mrs Elizabeth Dorling) 6 Burts Lane. ¼-acre very secluded, mature garden. Foliage predominating all yr with primroses, bluebells, herbaceous borders, flowering shrubs and many clematis
   Windacre (Mr & Mrs K Urch) 62 Chilton Rd, next to Primary School. 1-acre; roses, interesting shrubs, herbaceous plants, lenten roses, main features sunken lawns, conifers and trees. Cream TEAS
Sun June 21 (2-6)
   Braddens Yard (Mr & Mrs P Simpson) ½-acre walled garden, largely created over past 7 yrs. Collection of roses, herbaceous and climbing plants. Arched walk with clematis, honeysuckle and roses; pond; small bothy garden. Cake stall
   Croft House (Cdr & Mrs Peter Everett) Thame Rd. In Square. White wrought iron railings. ½-acre walled garden; plants and shrubs of botanical interest especially to flower arrangers. TEAS

8 Ketchmere Close (Mr & Mrs A Heley) Colourful split level garden with extensive views. Wide range of shrubs, conifers, rockery and water feature
The Old Crown (Mr & Mrs R H Bradbury) Description with April opening

¶**Lower Icknield Farm Nurseries, Kimble** (Mr & Mrs J Baldwin) 2m N of Princes Risborough on B4009 between Longwick and Kimble, opp Askett turn. 1½-acres with mixed borders mostly planted for late summer colour with a wide variety of hardy and tender perennials incl argyranthemums, penstemon, diascia and salvias, also display borders with some unusual annuals. Teas at Swan Inn. *Adm £1 Chd free. Sun July 26 (11-5)*

The Manor Farm, Little Horwood ⅍❀ (Mr & Mrs Peter Thorogood) 2m NE Winslow signed off A413. 5m E Buckingham and 5m W Bletchley S off A421. Hilltop farmhouse garden on acid clay, laid out and replanted 1986. Wide range of alpines and plantsman's plants for yr-round interest in colour, form and foliage; good roses, pergola, 100' hosta border, herbaceous, wild flower meadow, damp garden, lovely views. Cream TEAS in aid of Great Horwood WI. *Adm £2 Chd free. Mon May 25 (2-6). Private visits welcome May to Sept, please* **Tel 01296 714758**

The Manor House, Bledlow ⍋❀ (The Lord & Lady Carrington) ½m off B4009 in middle of Bledlow village. Station: Princes Risborough, 2½m. Paved garden, parterres, shrub borders, old roses and walled kitchen garden. House (not open) C17 & C18. Water and species garden with paths, bridges and walkways, fed by 14 chalk springs. Also 2-acre garden with sculptures and landscaped planting. Partly suitable wheelchairs. TEA in aid of Bledlow Church May, TEAS June. *Adm £3 Chd free. Suns May 3, June 21 (2-6); also private visits welcome May to Sept by written application (2-4.30)*

The Manor House, Hambleden ⍋ (Maria Carmela, Viscountess Hambleden) NE of Henley-on-Thames, 1m N of A4155. Conservatory; shrubs and old-fashioned rose garden. Tea at Hambleden Church. *Adm £1.50 Chd 20p. Sun June 21 (2-6)*

▲**Nether Winchendon House, Nether Winchendon** ⅍⍋❀ (Mr & Mrs R Spencer Bernard) 5m SW of Aylesbury; 7m from Thame. Picturesque village, beautiful church. 5 acres; fine trees, variety of hedges; naturalised spring bulbs; shrubs; herbaceous borders. Tudor manor house (not open) home of Sir Francis Bernard, last British Governor of Massachusetts. TEA weather permitting. *Adm £1.50 Chd under 15 free. For NGS Suns April 26, July 26 (2-5.30). Private visits welcome by written application*

Oaklands, Weston Turville ⅍⍋❀ (Mr & Mrs Roy Brunswick) 35 Main St. 2m SE of Aylesbury. Turn off A413 or A41 onto B4544. Garden is opp Five Bells Inn (car park). Secluded mature ½-acre offering something for everyone. Flower borders, incl some of the 100 varieties of clematis in the garden, surround the bog garden and duck jacuzzi, a haven for visiting birds and animals. The magic grotto and fairy paths are a delight to children and lead to the apiary where bee demonstrations can be

seen, weather permitting. TEAS in aid of 14th Vale of Aylesbury Venture Sea Scouts. *Adm £1.20 Chd free. Sun May 10 (2-5.30) Wed June 10 (2-5)*

Old Farm, Brill ⍋ (Dr & Mrs Raymond Brown) South Hills, off Windmill St. 7m N of Thame. Turn off B4011, (Thame to Bicester), or turn off A41 at Kingswood, both signed to Brill. C17 windmill open Suns 2.30-5.30. ½-acre established garden around 3 terraces; old shrub roses; secluded position with high open views over Otmoor; kitchen garden, soft fruit, many plants grown from seed incl S African annuals and rarer species. *Private visits welcome, June, July and August, please* **Tel 01844 238232**

The Old Vicarage, Padbury ⍋⍋❀ (Mr & Mrs H Morley-Fletcher) 2m S of Buckingham on A413 follow signs in village. 2½ acres on 3 levels; flowering shrubs and trees. Display collection of hebes, geometric vegetable garden; pond and sunken garden; parterre. TEAS in aid of League of Friends of Buckingham Hospital. *Adm £1.50 Chd free. Sun April 19 (2-6)*

6 Oldfield Close, Little Chalfont ⍋❀ (Mr & Mrs Jolyon Lea) 3m E of Amersham. Take A404 E through Little Chalfont, turn 1st R after railway bridge, then R again into Oakington Ave. Plantsman's ⅙-acre garden of borders, peat beds, rock plants, troughs and small alpine house. Over 2,000 species and varieties of rare plants. Plant stall and tea in aid of Bethany Village Leprosy Society, in India. *Adm £1 Chd free. Suns April 19, 26 (2-5). Private visits welcome all yr, please* **Tel 01494 762384**

¶**Olney Gardens** ⅍⍋❀ On A509 5m N of Newport Pagnell and 12m S of Wellingborough. Please park in Market Place, Cattle Market car park or High St. Churchyard Nature Trail. Teas in Parish Church in aid of heating fund. *Combined adm £2 Chd 50p. Suns June 7, 14 (2-6)*
　　¶**Cowper & Newton Museum** (Trustees of the Cowper Memorial Museum) Market Place. The walled flower garden is being restored to incl only plants up to 1800, many of which were mentioned by poet William Cowper. Adjacent summer house garden, maintained by Mr & Mrs Charles Knight, in style of Victorian kitchen garden with organic new and old unusual vegetables. Border of herbs and medicinal plants
　　¶**The Old Vicarage** (Dr & Mrs John Wallace) Church St. Walled C17 town garden recreated since 1993 with wide long herbaceous border. Trimmed yew hedge separates gravel sun area with wall fruits and vines from lawn and specimen Cedrus labanus. Pyrus canteclor underplanted with iris and lily; extensive pergola with climbing roses and clematis. S front has raised bed of old shrub roses and cistus. Grade II Vicarage (not open) was home of Revd John Newton, co-writer with Cowper of the Olney Hymns (Amazing Grace)

Overstroud Cottage, Frith Hill ⍋❀ (Mr & Mrs J Brooke) The Dell. Turn E off A413 at Gt Missenden onto B485 Frith Hill to Chesham. White Gothic cottage set back in layby 100yds up hill on L. Parking on R at Church. Artistic chalk garden on 2 levels. Potager featured in Joy Larkcom's 'Creative Vegetable Gardening'; snowdrops, narcissi, hellebores, primulas, pulmonarias, geraniums, species roses, clematis and lily pond. Not suitable for children or push chairs. Teas at Parish Church. *Adm £1.50 Chd 50p. Suns April 12, May 3, June 7 (Church Flower Festival), July 5, Sept 6 (2-6). Parties welcome by appt, please* Tel 01494 862701

Peppers, Gt Missenden &⚭❀ (Mr & Mrs J Ledger) 4 Sylvia Close. A413 Amersham to Aylesbury Rd. At Great Missenden by-pass turn at sign Great & Little Kingshill (Chiltern Hospital). After 400yds turn L, Nags Head Lane. After 300yds turn R under railway bridge. Sylvia Close 50yds on R. Approx 1 acre. Wide variety of plants, shrubs, trees, incl uncommon conifers, collection of acers, unusual containers, herbaceous borders all yr colour. TEAS. Donation from plant sale and teas to Workaid. *Adm £1 Chd free. Suns May 10, Aug 23 (10-5). Private visits welcome, please* Tel 01494 864419

Quainton Gardens 7m NW of Aylesbury. Nr Waddesdon turn off A41
Sun May 17 (2-6) &❀ TEAS. *Combined adm £2.50 Chd free*
  Brudenell House (Dr & Mrs H Beric Wright) Opp Church. Productive 2½ acres with unusual trees, long herbaceous and mixed borders, sweet peas, large water feature, wooden sculptures, fruit and vegetables. TEAS in aid of NGS May, Quainton Sports Club, July
  Capricorner (Mrs G Davis) Small garden planted for yr-round interest with many scented plants; semi-wild area with trees
  Hatherways (Mr & Mrs D Moreton) A cottage garden as featured in 'The Garden' with old-fashioned roses and clematis; interesting and unusual shrubs, herbaceous plants and a ditch garden. *Private visits welcome May and June, please* Tel 01296 655224
  Messengers Cottage (Mr D Burn) 36 Lower Street. Small, S-facing rear garden with mixture of curved herbaceous and shrub borders. Raised vegetable and flower beds
  Thorngumbald (Mr & Mrs J Lydall) Lots of garden in a small space incl old-fashioned plants, organically grown; small pond, conservatory; attempts to encourage wild life
Sun July 26 (2-6) &❀ TEAS. *Combined adm £2.50 Chd free*
  Brudenell House (Description with May opening)
  Capricorner (Description with May opening)
  Cross Farmhouse (Mr & Mrs E Viney) 1-acre garden on hillside with old farm pond. Mixed shrub and herbaceous planting emphasising shape, texture and colour of foliage. Fine view and buildings
  Messengers Cottage (Description with May opening)
  Thorngumbald (Description with May opening)

Sheredon, Longwick &❀ (Mr & Mrs G Legg) Thame Rd. Between Princes Risborough and Thame on A1429 next to Longwick PO. 1-acre plantsman's garden. Fish pond with bog plants. Old English and modern roses. Collection of perennial plants. Arches leading to orchard, vegetables, berries and fruits. Chickens and aviary. TEAS (July only). *Suns May 24, July 5 (11-5.30). Private and horticultural groups welcome, please* Tel 01844 346557

Springlea, Seymour Plain &⚭❀ (Mr & Mrs M Dean) 1m from Marlow, 2½m from Lane End off B482. From Lane End pass Booker airfield; in 1m L at pillar-box on grass triangle. ⅓-acre flower arrangers' garden for colour and foliage. Spring bulbs, azaleas, rhododendrons, unusual trees, shrubs. Rockery, pond, waterfall, bog garden, hostas. Arched walkway with over 240 clematis. 60' herbaceous border against brick wall with many climbers, plants labelled throughout garden. TEAS by WI (not March or April). *Adm £1.50 Chd free. Suns March 8 (1-5), April 5, May 3, June 7, July 5, Aug 2, Sept 6 (1-6). Private visits March to October, please* Tel 01628 473366

14 The Square, Brill (Mrs Audrey Dyer) 7m N of Thame. Turn off B4011 (Thame to Bicester), or turn off A41 at Kingswood, both signed to Brill. Secret paved garden behind small terraced cottage packed with plants for yr-round interest, some in pots handbuilt by owner. TEAS. *Adm £1 Chd free. Weds July and August (2-5). Small parties welcome, please* Tel 01844 237148

▲**Stowe Landscape Gardens, Buckingham** (The National Trust) 3m NW of Buckingham via Stowe Ave. Follow brown NT signs. One of the supreme creations of the Georgian era; the first, formal layout was adorned with many buildings by Vanbrugh, Kent and Gibbs; in the 1730s Kent designed the Elysian Fields in a more naturalistic style, one of the earliest examples of the reaction against formality leading to the evolution of the landscape garden; miraculously, this beautiful garden survives; its sheer scale must make it Britain's largest work of art. Conducted tours available. TEAS. *Adm £4.40 Chd free. For NGS Tues June 16 (10-5). Last adm 4pm*

■**Turn End, Haddenham** ❀ (Peter Aldington) Townside. Haddenham turn off A418. At Rising Sun take Townside. Architect's own house and garden. 1 acre but space used to create an illusion of size. Series of enclosed gardens, sunken or raised, sunny or shady, each different yet harmonious, contrast with lawns, borders and glades. Spring bulbs, iris, old roses and climbers. House courtyard with fish pool. Featured internationally in glossies. TEAS in aid of Haddenham 3rd World Link. *Adm £1.50 Chd 50p. Weds in June and July 1 (10-4). For NGS Sun April 12, Mon May 4, Sun Sept 13 (2-6). Groups by appt at other times, please* Tel 01844 291383/291817

Tythrop Park, Kingsey &❀ (Mr & Mrs Jonathan Marks) 2m E of Thame, via A4129; lodge gates just before Kingsey. 4 acres. Replanting of wilderness. Walled kitchen garden, fully productive. Muscat and black (Muscat) d'Hamburg vine propagated from vine at Hampton Court 150 yrs ago in vine house. Arboretum. Parterre to S of Carolean house (not open). TEAS. *Adm £1.50 Chd free (ACNO to NCH Action for Children®). Sun June 28 (2-6)*

▲**Waddesdon Dairy Water Garden** ⚭❀ (The Alice Trust) Off A41 between Aylesbury and Bicester on Waddesdon Estate. Private garden restored by Lord Rothschild, with naturalistic outcrops of Pulham rock, cascading water, still ponds and intricate planting which provide overwhelming drama. The Manor gardens (National Trust), make innovative use of trees and shrubs coupled with flamboyant displays of high Victorian bedding. Refreshments at restaurant. *Adm Water Garden £1 Chd 50p; odm Manor Gardens £3 Chd £1.50, NT members free (10-5). For NGS Sun March 8, Fris April 24, June 26, Aug 21 (2-5)*

Walmerdene, Buckingham &&& (Mr & Mrs M T Hall) 20 London Rd. From Town Centre take A413 (London Rd). At top of hill turn R. Park in Brookfield Lane. Cream house on corner. Medium town garden, unusual plants mostly labelled; species and hybrid hellebores; bulbs; herbaceous; euphorbias; climbing, shrub and species roses; clematis. Sink garden, rill garden, 2 ponds, white and yellow border; 2 greenhouses. TEAS Sept only. *Adm £1 Acc chd free. Suns April 5 (2-5), Sept 27 (2-6). Private visits, for groups and individuals, welcome in June for roses, please* Tel 01280 817466

Watercroft, Penn & (Mr & Mrs P Hunnings) 3m N of Beaconsfield on B474, 600yds past Penn Church. Medium-sized garden on clay; white flowers, culinary herb garden planted 1993, rose walk, weeping ash; kitchen garden; pond, wild flower meadow. New Italian garden with yew hedges. C18 house, C19 brewhouse (not open). Cream TEAS in aid of Holy Trinity Church, Penn. *Adm £1.50 Chd 30p. Sun July 12 (2-6)*

Weir Lodge, Chesham &&& (Mr & Mrs Mungo Aldridge) Latimer Rd. 1m SE of Chesham. Turn L from A416 along Waterside at junction of Red Lion St and Amersham Rd. From A404 Rickmansworth-Amersham Rd turn R at signpost for Chenies and go for 4m. Parking at Weir House Mill (McMinns). ¾-acre garden on bank of R. Chess. Recovered from dereliction in 1983 by owners. Stream and ponds with planted banks. Gravelled terrace with sun loving plants. Assorted containers; mixed beds. Mature trees, incl fine beeches in adjoining paddock. TEAS in aid of Chesham Society. *Adm £1 Chd free. Sun July 12 (2-6)*

▲**West Wycombe Park, West Wycombe** & (Sir Francis Dashwood; The National Trust) 3m W of High Wycombe on A40. Bus: from High Wycombe and Victoria. Landscape garden; numerous C18 temples and follies incl Temple of the Winds, Temple of Venus, Temple of Music. Swan-shaped lake with flint bridges and cascade. *Adm (grounds only) £2.50 Chd £1.25 (incl NT members). For NGS Sun Sept 6 (2-5)*

Whitchurch Gardens &&& 4m N of Aylesbury on A413. TEAS. *Combined odm £2.50 Chd free. Sun June 14 (2-6)*
    ¶**Badgers** (Mr & Mrs J E Bellamy) Secluded, peaceful garden with many trees, shrubs and garden seats. Fishpond under weeping willow
    Mullions (Dr & Mrs L I Holmes-Smith) ⅓-acre picturesque cottage garden behind C17 cottage. 2 ponds and garden on 3 terraces
    The Old Cottage (Mr Roger Gwynne-Jones) ¾-acre cottage garden with herbaceous border, herb garden and wild area. Views over Vale of Aylesbury
    Priory Court (Mr & Mrs Ian Durrell) Approx ⅔-acre split level garden with rose beds, shrubbery and herbaceous borders. Part newly planted for shade and redesigned area after removal of swimming pool

Quenington House (Mr & Mrs D F Ryder Richardson) 7 High Street. Paved terrace with rose beds leads to lawn. Lovely views; secret and herb gardens
Yew Tree Cottage (Mr & Mrs B S Foulger) 3 tier garden with fish pond, patios and small wooded area, the whole offering sanctuary for wildlife. Panoramic views over the Vale of Aylesbury

The White House, Denham Village && (Mr & Mrs P G Courtenay-Luck) Approx 3m NW of Uxbridge, signed from A40 or A412; nearest station Denham Green. Underground Uxbridge. Parking in village rd. The White House is in centre of village. 6 acres formal garden and 11-acre paddock. Garden being restored to former glory; rejuvenation of old yew hedges. R Misbourne meanders through lawns containing shrubberies, flower beds, orchard and rose garden. Large walled Italian and vegetable garden and restored Victorian greenhouses. Cream TEAS in aid of St Mary's Church, Denham Village. *Adm £2 Acc chd free. Suns April 5, July 19 (2-5)*

Whitewalls, Marlow && (Mr W H Williams) Quarry Wood Rd. From Marlow town centre cross over bridge. 1st L white garden wall, 3rd house on L. Thames-side garden approx ½-acre with spectacular view of weir. Large lily pond, interesting planting of trees, shrubs and herbaceous perennials. Many colourful containers. Sight of large conservatory with exotic plants. Teas available in Marlow. *Adm £1.50 Chd free (ACNO to Crossroads, Wycombe District®). Suns April 26, July 19, Sept 20 (2-5.30). Private visits and parties welcome, please* Tel 01628 482573

Wichert, Ford && (Mr & Mrs C Siggers) 5m SW of Aylesbury, 5m ENE of Thame. From Aylesbury A418 towards Thame. L at Bugle Horn into Portway. After 3m L into Ford. Approx 100yds beyond Xrds L into drive immed after Old Bakehouse. Approx 1½ acres developed into separate gardens since 1990. Silver and Pearl, shade, fern, kitchen and pavement gardens; maze, pond and wild garden with indigenous British trees. *Adm £1 Chd free. Private visits welcome, please* Tel 01296 748431

Winslow Hall, Winslow & (Sir Edward & Lady Tomkins) On A413 10m N of Aylesbury, 6m S of Buckingham. Free public car park. Winslow Hall (also open), built in 1700, designed by Christopher Wren, stands in a beautiful garden with distant perspectives, planted with many interesting trees and shrubs. In spring, blossom, daffodils and the contrasting foliage of trees combine to make the garden particularly attractive. TEAS. *Adm house & garden £3 garden only £1.50 Chd free. Bank Hol Mon May 4 (2-6)*

Regular openings. Open throughout the year. They are listed at the beginning of the Diary Section.

By Appointment Gardens. These owners do not have a fixed opening day usually because they cannot accommodate large numbers or have insufficient parking space.

Cambridgeshire

Hon County Organisers:

South: Lady Nourse, Dullingham House, Dullingham, Newmarket CB8 9UP
Tel 01638 508186

North: Mrs M Holmes, Manor House, Alwalton, Peterborough, PE7 3UU
Tel 01733 233435

Assistant Hon County Organisers: John Drake Esq., Hardwicke House, High Ditch Road, Fen Ditton, Cambridge
South: CB5 8TF Tel 01223 292246

Mrs M Gould, The Grange, Church Road, Easton, Nr Huntingdon PE18 OTU
Tel 01480 891043

North: Mr G Stevenson, 'Pennard', 1a The Village, Orton Longueville, Peterborough
PE2 7DN Tel 01733 391506

Hon County Treasurers
(South Cambridgeshire):   John Drake, Esq
(North Cambridgeshire):   Malcolm Holmes, Esq

DATES OF OPENING

Regular openings
For details see garden description

Childerley Hall, Dry Drayton
The Crossing House, Shepreth
Docwra's Manor, Shepreth
Elgood's Brewery Gardens, Wisbech
The Manor, Hemingford Grey

By appointment only
*For telephone numbers and other
details see garden descriptions.
Private visits welcomed*

Mill House, North End, Bassingbourn

March 29 Sunday
Bainton House, Stamford
Barton Gardens, Cambridge
Tadlow House, Tadlow
April 5 Sunday
Chippenham Park, nr Newmarket
Trinity College Fellows' Garden,
Cambridge
April 11 Saturday
Moonrakers, Whittlesford
Padlock Croft, West Wratting
Weaver's Cottage, West Wickham
April 12 Sunday
Netherall Manor, Soham, Ely
April 13 Monday
Padlock Croft, West Wratting
Weaver's Cottage, West Wickham
April 17 Friday
Wimpole Hall, Royston
April 19 Sunday
Docwra's Manor, Shepreth
Downing College, Cambridge
April 26 Sunday
Cambridge University Botanic
Garden

May 2 Saturday
Scarlett's Farm, West Wratting
May 3 Sunday
Leckhampton, Cambridge
May 4 Monday
Ely Gardens
Scarlett's Farm, West Wratting
May 10 Sunday
Docwra's Manor, Shepreth
Netherall Manor, Soham, Ely
Tadlow House, Tadlow
Tetworth Hall, nr Sandy
May 23 Saturday
Hyset, Horseheath
Padlock Croft, West Wratting
Scarlett's Farm, West Wratting
Weaver's Cottage, West Wickham
May 24 Sunday
Fen Ditton Gardens
Tetworth Hall, nr Sandy
May 25 Monday
Hyset, Horseheath
Padlock Croft, West Wratting
Scarlett's Farm, West Wratting
Weaver's Cottage, West Wickham
May 31 Sunday
Island Hall, Godmanchester
June 7 Sunday
Ramsey Gardens, nr Huntingdon
June 14 Sunday
Ely Gardens
Madingley Hall, Cambridge
June 20 Saturday
Hyset, Horseheath
Padlock Croft, West Wratting
Weaver's Cottage, West Wickham
June 21 Sunday
Alwalton Gardens
Elgood's Brewery Gardens,
Wisbech
Grantchester Gardens,
Grantchester

Haslingfield Gardens
Horningsea & Waterbeach
Gardens
Impington Gardens
Inglethorpe Manor, nr Wisbech
Shingay Gardens
Sutton Gardens, nr Ely
Whittlesford Gardens
June 24 Wednesday
Alwalton Gardens
June 28 Sunday
1 Chapel Hill, Haslingfield
Clare College, Fellows Garden,
Cambridge
83 High Street, Harlton
Melbourn Bury, Royston
Melbourn Lodge, Royston
The Old Post Office, Brington
Swaffham Bulbeck Gardens
West Wratting Park, West
Wratting
July 4 Saturday
Emmanual College Garden &
Fellows' Garden
July 5 Sunday
Greystones, Swaynes Lane,
Comberton
Nuns Manor, Frog End, Shepreth
July 11 Saturday
21 Lode Road, Lode
July 12 Sunday
Anglesey Abbey, Cambridge
King's College Fellows' Garden,
Cambridge
21 Lode Road, Lode
Newnham College, Cambridge
Orton Longueville Gardens
Shingay Gardens
July 19 Sunday
Chippenham Park, nr
Newmarket
Great Stukeley Gardens

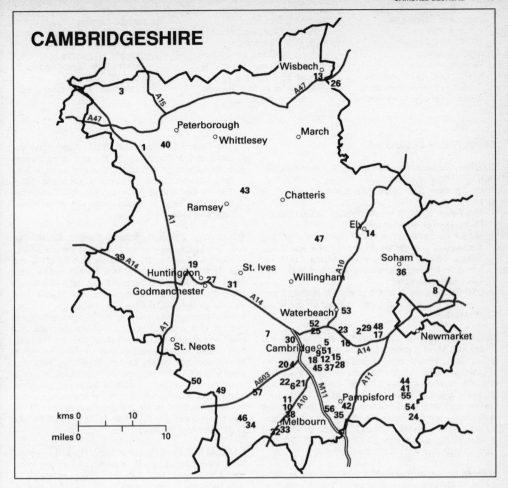

CAMBRIDGESHIRE

KEY

1. Alwalton Gardens
2. Anglesey Abbey
3. Bainton House
4. Barton Gardens
5. Cambridge University Botanic Garden
6. 1 Chapel Hill
7. Childerley Hall
8. Chippenham Park
9. Clare College
10. The Crossing House
11. Docwra's Manor
12. Downing College
13. Elgood's Brewery Gardens
14. Ely Gardens
15. Emmanual College Garden & Fellows' Garden
16. Fen Ditton Gardens
17. Swaffham Bulbeck Gardens
18. Grantchester Gardens

19. Great Stukeley Gardens
20. Greystones
21. Haslingfield Gardens
22. 83 High Street
23. Horningsea & Waterbeach Gardens
24. Hyset
25. Impington Gardens
26. Inglethorpe Manor
27. Island Hall
28. King's College Fellows' Garden
29. 21 Lode Road
30. Madingley Hall
31. The Manor
32. Melbourn Bury
33. Melbourn Lodge
34. Mill House
35. Moonrakers
36. Netherall Manor
37. Newnham College

39. The Old Post Office
40. Orton Longueville Gardens
41. Padlock Croft
42. Pampisford Gardens
43. Ramsey Gardens
44. Scarlett's Farm
45. Selwyn College
46. Shingay Gardens
47. Sutton Gardens
48. Swaffham Bulbeck Gardens
49. Tadlow House
50. Tetworth Hall
51. Trinity College Fellows' Garden
52. Unwins Seeds Trial Grounds
53. Horningsea & Waterbeach Gardens
54. Weaver's Cottage
55. West Wratting Park
56. Whittlesford Gardens
57. Wimpole Hall

Pampisford Gardens, nr
Cambridge
Whittlesford Gardens

July 25 Saturday
Hyset, Horseheath
Padlock Croft, West Wratting
Scarlett's Farm, West Wratting
Weaver's Cottage, West Wickham

August 8 Saturday
Padlock Croft, West Wratting
August 9 Sunday
Anglesey Abbey, Cambridge
Netherall Manor, Soham, Ely
August 15 Saturday
Unwins Seeds Trial Grounds,
Histon, Cambridge

August 16 Sunday
Netherall Manor, Soham, Ely
Selwyn College, Cambridge
September 26 Saturday
Scarlett's Farm, West Wratting
October 18 Sunday
Chippenham Park, nr Newmarket

DESCRIPTIONS OF GARDENS

Alwalton Gardens, Alwalton ✵ 4m W of Peterborough, next to E of England showground. Parking at Village Hall. TEAS. *Combined adm £2 Chd free. Sun, Wed June 21, 24 (2-6)*
> **The Forge** ⅄ (Mr & Mrs M Watson) Cottage garden. Creative use of re-cycled materials
> **Manor House** ✿ (Mr & Mrs M Holmes) Walled garden divided into garden 'rooms' by yew and beech hedges. Borders and topiary surrounding C17 farmhouse (not open). Developing woodland walk with views over Nene valley
> **Oak Cottage** (Mr & Mrs J Wilson) Behind C17 cottage, a small, secluded garden planted for scent and atmosphere

▲ **Anglesey Abbey, Cambridge** ⅄✵ (The National Trust) 6m NE of Cambridge. From A14 turn N on to B1102 through Stow-cum-Quy. 100 acres surrounding an Elizabethan manor created from the remains of a priory founded in reign of Henry I. Garden created during last 70 years; avenues of beautiful trees; groups of statuary; hedges enclosing small intimate gardens; daffodils and 4,400 white and blue hyacinths (April); magnificent herbaceous borders (June). Lunches & TEAS. *Adm house and garden £6.80; garden only £3.40 Chd £1.70. For NGS Suns July 12, Aug 9 (11-5.30). Last adm 4.30*

Bainton House, nr Stamford ⅄ (Maj William & Hon Mrs Birkbeck) B1443 Stamford-Helpston rd. Turn N at Bainton Church into Tallington rd. ¼m on L. 2 acres. Spring flowers, spinney and wild garden. TEAS in aid of St Mary's Church. *Adm £1.50 Chd 50p. Sun March 29 (2-5.30)*

Barton Gardens, Cambridge 3½m SW of Cambridge. Take A603, in village turn R for Comberton Rd. Delightful group of gardens of wide appeal and expertise. Gift and plant stalls. Teas in village hall. *Combined adm £1.50 Chd 50p (ACNO to GRBS®). Sun March 29 (2-5)*
> **Farm Cottage** ⅄✵ (Dr R M Belbin) 18 High St. Cottage garden with water feature. Courtyard garden
> **The Gables** ⅄ (P L Harris Esq) 11 Comberton Rd. 2-acre old garden, mature trees, ha-ha, spring flowers
> **14 Haslingfield Road** ⅄ (J M Nairn Esq) Orchard, lawns, mixed domestic
> **Kings Tythe** ⅄ (Maj C H Thorne) Comberton Road. Small domestic garden; good through way to larger gardens of **Town's End** and **The Gables**
> **31 New Road** ⅄ (Dr D Macdonald) Cottage garden
> **Orchard Cottage, 22 Haslingfield Road** ⅄ (Mr J Blackhurst) Interesting mixed domestic. ½-acre garden with raised vegetable beds

> **The Seven Houses** ⅄✵✿ (GRBS) Small bungalow estate on L of Comberton Rd. 1½-acre spring garden; bulbs naturalised in orchard. Colourful summer borders. Gift stall. Sale of seeds, plants, bric a brac stall
> **Town's End** ⅄✵ (B R Overton Esq) 15a Comberton Rd. 1-acre; lawns, trees, pond; extensive views. Raised vegetable beds

¶**Cambridge University Botanic Garden, Cambridge** ⅄✵ Cory Lodge. Approx ¾m to the S of the city centre. Entrance via Bateman St, off Trumpington Rd (A10) and Hills Rd (A604). Five minutes from railway station; walk down Station Rd to Hills Rd, turn R and within 20yds turn L into Bateman St. Car parking available on adjacent rds. 40-acre garden with diverse plant collections of international repute grown primarily for their scientific value and set in a beautiful landscape of mature trees and wildflower meadows. Notable features incl: a winter garden; limestone and sandstone rock gardens; an Alpine House; lake and stream garden. Systematic beds displaying over 81 different families of flowering plants; a woodland garden; and glasshouse range incl a tropical house. April is an excellent time for late spring bulbs; flowering trees and shrubs, the woodland garden and the wild flower meadows. TEA. *Adm £1.50 OAPS £1 Chd £1 (5-17). Sun April 26 (10-6)*

1 Chapel Hill, Haslingfield ✵ (Mr & Mrs A R King) 5m SW of Cambridge along A10. A garden with mature trees, shrubs and roses. Also many herbaceous perennials, a large patio and 2 ponds. *Adm £1 Chd free. Sun June 28 (2-6)*

Childerley Hall, Dry Drayton ✵ (Mr & Mrs John Jenkins) 6m W of Cambridge on A428 opp. Caldecote turn. 4 acres of mixed planting with special emphasis on shrub roses. *Adm £2 Chd free. Private visits welcome May 16 to June 30, please* **Tel 01954 210271**

Chippenham Park, Chippenham ⅄✿ (Mr & Mrs Eustace Crawley) 5m NE of Newmarket, 1m off A11. 3½m of walled park landscaped by Mr Eames and Mr Lapidge to incl "a beautiful sheet of water ¾m long, small stretches of canal existing from the old formal garden, 2 lines of lime trees on each side of the park said to represent the Anglo-Dutch and French fleets at the Battle of La Hogue in May 1692". Restored C18 dovecote. 7-acre garden with borders of unusual and rare shrubs, trees and perennials. Daffodils by the lake in spring, summer borders and dramatic autumn colour. Many specialist Plant Stalls. Refreshments. *Adm £2 Chd free (ACNO to St Margaret's Church, Chippenham®). Suns April 5, July 19, Oct 18 (11-5)*

Clare College, Fellows' Garden, Cambridge *&* (Master & Fellows) The Master and Fellows are owners of the Fellows' Garden which is open; the Master's garden (nearby) is not open to the public. Approach from Queen's Rd or from city centre via Senate House Passage, Old Court and Clare Bridge. 2 acres; one of the most famous gardens on the Cambridge Backs. TEAS. *Adm £1.50 Chd under 13 free. Sun June 28 (2-6). Private visits welcome, please* Tel **01223 333 222**

The Crossing House, Shepreth & (Mr & Mrs Douglas Fuller and Mr John Marlar) Meldreth Rd. 8m SW of Cambridge. ½m W of A10. King's Cross-Cambridge railway runs alongside garden. Small cottage garden with many old-fashioned plants grown in mixed beds in company with modern varieties; shrubs, bulbs, etc, many alpines in rock beds and alpine house. *Collecting box. Open daily, dawn till dusk. Parties by appt, no coaches, please* Tel **01763 261071**

■ **Docwra's Manor, Shepreth** &*&&* (Mrs John Raven) 8m SW of Cambridge. ½m W of A10. Cambridge-Royston bus stops at gate opposite the War Memorial in Shepreth. 2½-acres of choice plants in series of enclosed gardens. TEA April 19, May 10 only, in aid of Shepreth Church Funds. *Adm £2 Chd free. All year Wed, Fri (10-4), Suns April 5, May 3, June 7, July 5, Aug 2, Sept 6, Oct 3 (2-5). Proceeds for garden upkeep. Also private visits welcome by appt, please* Tel **01763 261473.** *For NGS Suns April 19, May 10 (2-6)*

Downing College, Cambridge &*&* (The Master & Fellows of Downing College) Regent Street. Centre of Cambridge opp the University Arms Hotel to the S of Parkers's Piece. Approach from Regent St only. Fine example of 16-acre garden in a classical setting. Wilkins' Greek revival buildings frame wide lawns and paddock. Mature and newly planted rare trees. Unusual view of the Roman Catholic Church. Master's garden. Fellows' garden and walled rose garden with period roses. TEAS. *Adm £1.50 Chd 50p (ACNO to The Paget Gorman Society®). Sun April 19 (2-6)*

■ **Elgood's Brewery Gardens, Wisbech** &❀ (Brewery Gardens Ltd) In the town of Wisbech on the N brink of the R Nene approx 1m W of the town centre. A garden of approx 4 acres established in the Georgian era has been restored around many of the original 200 yr-old specimen trees. Features incl lawns, a lake, rockery, rose and herb gardens and maze under construction. TEAS. *Adm £2 OAPS/Chd £1.50. April 19 to Sept 27, Wed to Sun and Bank Hols. For NGS Sun June 21 (1.30-5.30)*

Ely Gardens &*&❀* 16m N of Cambridge on A10. *(ACNO to Old Palace Sue Ryder Home®)*
Mon May 4 (2-5) *Combined adm £1 Chd 50p*
  The Old Fire Engine House Restaurant and Gallery (Mr & Mrs R Jarman) Delightful walled country garden with mixed herbaceous borders and wild flowers. Situated just W of the Cathedral. TEAS
  The Old Palace 1½ acres with duck pond in fine setting next to Cathedral. 2 borders planted with C17 plants and other interesting mixed borders. Superb trees, oldest and largest oriental plane tree in the country

Sun June 14 (2-5.30) *Combined adm £3 Chd 50p single garden £1*
  Belmont House, 43 Prickwillow Rd ❀ (Mr & Mrs P J Stanning) Designed ½-acre garden with interesting and unusual plants
  Queen's Hall (Mr & Mrs R H Youdale) In Cathedral Close. Recently re-created in theme of "medieval garden" using as much as possible plants available pre 1600
  Rosewell House, 60 Prickwillow Road (Mr & Mrs A Bullivant) Well stocked garden with emphasis on perennial planting and splendid view of cathedral and surrounding fenland
  The Bishop's House (The Rt Rev the Bishop of Ely & Mrs Sykes) To R of main Cathedral entrance. Walled garden, former cloisters of monastery. Mixed herbaceous, box hedge, rose and kitchen garden
  31 Egremont St (Mr & Mrs J N Friend-Smith) A10 Lynn Rd out of Ely. 2nd L. Approx 1 acre. Lovely views of cathedral, mixed borders, cottage garden. Ginkgo tree, tulip tree and many other fine trees
  The Old Palace Description with May opening. TEAS
  48 St Mary's Street (Mr J Hardiment) Formal walled garden with a wide variety of beautiful and unusual plants

Emmanuel College Garden & Fellows' Garden, Cambridge &*&* in centre of Cambridge. Car parks at Parker's Piece and Lion Yard, within 5 mins walk. One of the most beautiful gardens in Cambridge; buildings of C17 to C20 surrounding 3 large gardens with pools; also herb garden; herbaceous borders, fine trees inc Metasequoia glyptostroboides. On this date access allowed to Fellows' Garden with magnificent Oriental plane and more herbaceous borders. Teashops in Cambridge. *Adm £1 Chd free. Sat July 4 (2.30-5.30). Private visits welcome, please* Tel **01223 334241**

Fen Ditton Gardens *&❀* 3½m NE of Cambridge. From A14 Cambridge-Newmarket rd turn N by Borough Cemetery into Ditton Lane; or follow Airport sign from bypass. Teas in church hall. *Combined adm £2 Chd 50p (ACNO to Cambridgeshire Gardens Trust©). Sun May 24 (2-5.30)*
  Hardwicke House *&❀* (Mr J Drake) 2 acres designed to provide shelter for plants on exposed site; divided by variety of hedges; species roses; rare herbaceous plants; home of national collection of aquilegias, collection of plants grown in this country prior to 1650. Please park in road opposite. Large sale of plants in aid of NGS; rare aquilegias from National Collection; foliage plants and rare herbaceous plants. **Exceptional rare plant sale for NGS.** *Private visits welcome by appt, please* Tel **01223 292246**
  The Old Stables (Mr & Mrs Zavros) Large informal garden; old trees, shrubs and roses; many interesting plants, herbs and shrubs have been introduced. House (not open) converted by owners in 1973 from C17 stables. *Private visits welcome by appt, please* Tel **01223 292507**

The National Gardens Scheme is a registered charity (No 279284). Its aim is to raise money for selected beneficiaries by opening gardens of quality and interest to the public.

The Rectory (Revd & Mrs L Marsh) Small rectory garden. Largely mediterranean flowers, extensive range of climbers, trompe l'oeil. Intensive organic vegetable garden which supplies household throughout the year, incl 34′ long decorative arch support for beans, sugar peas, spaghetti marrows, cucumbers and tomatoes

Grantchester Gardens ❀ 2m SW of Cambridge. A10 from S, L at Trumpington (Junction 11, M11). M11 from N, L at Junction 12. Madrigal Singers will be performing at the Old Vicarage. Craft Fair at Manor Farm, quality handmade goods; wooden toys; pottery, stained glass. TEAS. *Combined adm £2.50 Chd 50p (ACNO to Grantchester Church®). Sun June 21 (2-6)*

   Home Grove ৬ (Dr & Mrs C B Goodhart) 1-acre mature, orchard-type garden with specimen trees and shrub roses. Lawns with children's play area. Carefully planned kitchen garden

   North End House (Mr & Mrs A Frost) 1 acre, shrub and herbaceous borders; old-fashioned roses; water garden and rockery. Small conservatory

   The Old Vicarage ৬⚘ (Lord & Lady Archer) 2½ acres; house dating from C17; informal garden laid out in mid C19 with C20 conservatory; lawn with fountain; ancient mulberry tree; many other interesting trees; small lake with bridge; beyond garden is wilderness leading to river bank bordered by large old chestnut trees immortalised by Rupert Brooke, who lodged in the house 1910–1912

¶**Great Stukeley Gardens** 2m N of Huntingdon on B1043. Parking at village hall, Owl End and at the Church. Teas at Wytchwood. *Combined adm £2.50 Chd 50p. Sun July 19 (1.30-5.30)*

   Wytchwood, Owl End ❀ (Mr & Mrs David Cox) 1½-acre brightly planted borders of perennials, annuals and shrubs, lawns and ponds leading to 1 acre of wild plants and grasses set among Rowan and Birch trees

   ¶**29 Park View** ⚘❀ (Carole & Forbes Smith) Approx ⅓ acre plant enthusiasts garden in a country setting. Still developing

   ¶**The Old Vicarage** ৬ (Mr Michael N Bone) Approx 1½-acres of newly landscaped garden incl natural pond and small orchard area planted with mixture of climbing and herbaceous plants in a relaxed setting next to village church

Greystones, Swaynes Lane, Comberton ৬⚘❀ (Dr & Mrs Lyndon Davies) 5m W of Cambridge. From M11 take exit 12 and turn away from Cambridge on A603. Take first R B1046 through Barton to Comberton; follow signs from Xrds. Plantswoman's garden of approx ½ acre attractively planted with wide range of flowering plants framed by foliage and shrubs. Gravel bed and troughs. Water feature. TEAS. *Adm £1.50 Chd 50p (ACNO to St Marys Church, Comberton®). Sun July 5 (2-5.30). Private visits welcome, please* **Tel 01223 264159**

Haslingfield Gardens ⚘ 5m SW of Cambridge along A10. Turn R in Harston. 1½m to car park. Teas in aid of village society and detailed directions at Haslingfield Village Hall. *Combined adm £1.50 Chd free. Sun June 21 (2-6)*

   15 Back Lane (Mr & Mrs H Wiseman) On a slight slope, garden is a mixture of lawn, copse, paths,

perennials and shrubs aiming at yr-round interest

1 Chapel Hill (Mr & Mrs A R King) See separate entry. *Also open Sun June 28 (2-6)*

Rowan Cottage ৬ (Mrs Doble) A small patio garden with plants in pots

¶**36 Badcock Road** (Mr & Mrs Day) Arches filled with roses and clematis, borders, alpine bed, water features

¶**44 Cantelupe Road** (Mr & Mrs M Coles) A small garden with herbaceous perennials, shrubs and roses with a view of open spaces

¶**7 Church Street** (Mr & Mrs Leeson) ½-acre cottage garden on side of hill with some old trees, etc

¶**Goreway** (Mr & Mrs Ridgeon) A garden made from paddocks converted to lawns and single planting

¶**Wyont House** (Mr & Mrs D Rutherford) Mixed planting with a variety of perennials, shrubs plus a small pond

83 High Street, Harlton ৬⚘❀ (Dr Ruth Chippindale) 7m SW of Cambridge. A603 (toward Sandy); after 6m turn L (S) for Harlton. ⅓-acre interesting design which includes many different features, colours and a wide diversity of plants. TEAS. *Adm £1 Chd free (ACNO to Harlton Church Restoration Fund®). Sun June 28 (2-6). Private visits welcome, please* **Tel 01223 262170**

Horningsea and Waterbeach Gardens ⚘ TEAS. *Combined adm £2 Chd 50p (ACNO to Village Church®). Sun June 21 (2-5.30)*

   15 Abbots Way, Horningsea (Don & Sally Edwards) 4m NE of Cambridge from A1307 Cambridge Newmarket Rd. Turn N at borough cemetery to Horningsea or take B1047 N from A14. 1-acre developing plantswoman's garden on old flood bank of R Cam; overlooking river and water meadows. Spring and natural pond, newly built pergola. Clematis and solomon's seal amongst fine collection of rare and unusual plants, shrubs and trees. Entrance to car park and garden signposted nr village hall; no access to garden via Abbots Way

   92 Bannold Road, Waterbeach (Mr & Mrs R L Guy) Plantsman's tiny garden. Over 300 plants in 150 varieties. Clematis, shrubs, grasses

   32 Station Road, Waterbeach ৬❀ (Mr & Mrs B D Reeve) Visitors please park at station or village green. Small S facing enclosed garden. Large variety of interesting plants, conservatory with selection of vines ·

Hyset, Cardinals Green (Mr & Mrs S Agnew) A1307 between Linton and Haverhill. On opp side of bypass A1307 to Horseheath Village. Take turning signed 'The Camps'. Hyset is 2nd on R. ⅓-acre garden being developed by professional plantsman/horticulturist. Interesting range of herbaceous, shrubs, climbers and alpines. Attractive water feature displaying host of plants and insect life. Poly tunnel growing range of salads. *Combined adm £2 Chd 50p with* **Padlock Croft, Scarletts Farm and Weaver's Cottage**. *Sat May 23, Mon May 25, Sats June 20, July 25 (2-6). Private visits welcome, please* **Tel 01223 892982**

Impington Gardens ⚘ 2m N of Cambridge City. Very close to A14. Leave the A14 at the B1049 junction signposted to Histon and Cottenham (large roundabout).

Take first L into Cambridge Rd, go round bollards, in 1 min Highfield Rd is 1st L, a cul-de-sac. Please park in the Cambridge Rd. TEAS. *Combined adm £2 Chd free. Sun June 21 (2-6). Private visits welcome, please* **Tel 01223 233307**

5 Highfield Road (B Butcher) Medium-sized garden laid to lawn and general flower beds, conifers and roses

13 Highfield Road & (Mr & Mrs R J McCombie) Informal mixed planting borders, vegetables, fruit trees and lawn. ½-acre

23 Highfield Road ❀ (Mr & Mrs W Ward) Narrow winding paths through a well stocked medium-sized cottage garden; 2 small ponds

Inglethorpe Manor &❀❀ (Mr & Mrs Roger Hartley) Emneth, near Wisbech. 2m S of Wisbech on A1101. 200yds on L beyond 40mph derestriction sign. Entrance opp Ken Rowe's Garage. Large garden with interesting mature trees, lawns, mixed and herbaceous borders, shrub roses, rose walk and water garden. Victorian house (not open). TEAS in aid of NSPCC. *Adm £1.50 Chd free. Sun June 21 (2-6)*

Island Hall, Godmanchester ❀ (Mr Christopher & The Hon Mrs Vane Percy) Godmanchester. In centre of Godmanchester next to free car park, 1m S of Huntingdon (A1) 15m NW of Cambridge (A14). 3-acre grounds, important mid C18 mansion (not open). Tranquil riverside setting with mature trees in an area of Best Landscape. Chinese bridge over Saxon mill race to an embowered island with wild flowers. Garden restored over the last 13 yrs to a mid C18 formal design, with box hedging, clipped hornbeams, parterres, topiary and good vistas over borrowed landscape, punctuated with C18 wrought iron and stone urns. TEAS. *Adm £2 Chd free. Sun May 31 (1-5)*

King's College Fellows' Garden, Cambridge &❀ Fine example of a Victorian garden with rare specimen trees. Colour booklet available £1.50, free leaflet describing numbered trees. TEAS. *Adm £1 Chd free. Sun July 12 (2-6)*

Leckhampton, Cambridge &❀ (Corpus Christi College) 37 Grange Rd. Grange Rd is on W side of Cambridge and runs N to S between Madingley Rd (A1303) and A603; drive entrance opp Selwyn College. 10 acres; originally laid out by William Robinson as garden of Leckhampton (Civic Trust Award); formal lawns, rose garden, small herbaceous beds; extensive wild garden with bulbs, cowslips, prunus and fine specimen trees. TEAS. *Adm £1.50 Chd free. Sun May 3 (2-6)*

21 Lode Road, Lode ❀ (Richard P Ayres) Take B1102 from Stow cum Quy roundabout NE of Cambridge at junction with A14. Lode is 2m from roundabout. Small garden adjoining C15 thatched cottage designed by the owner (head gardener at Anglesey Abbey NT). Planted with bold groups of herbaceous plants complimenting a fine lawn and creating an element of mystery and delight. TEAS. *Adm £1 Chd 50p (ACNO to Lode Church®). Sat, Sun July 11, 12 (11-5)*

Madingley Hall Cambridge ❀ (University of Cambridge) 4m W, 1m from M11 Exit 13. C16 Hall set in 7½ acres of attractive grounds. Features incl landscaped walled garden with hazel walk, borders in individual colours and rose pergola. Meadow, topiary and mature trees. TEAS. *Adm £1.50 Chd free (ACNO to Madingley Church Restoration Fund®). Sun June 14 (2.30-5.30)*

●**The Manor, Hemingford Grey** ❀ (Mr & Mrs P S Boston) 4m E of Huntingdon off A14. Entrance to garden by small gate off river towpath. No parking at house except disabled by arrangement with owners. Park in village. Garden designed and planted by author Lucy Boston, surrounds C12 manor house on which her Green Knowe Books were based (House only open by prior appt). 4 acres with topiary; over 200 old roses and large herbaceous borders with mainly scented plants. Enclosed by river, moat and wilderness. *Adm to garden £1 Chd 50p. Open daily (10-6 sunset in winter) 10% takings to NGS, rest to preservation of house.* **Tel 01480 463134**

Melbourn Bury, Royston &❀❀ (Mr & Mrs Anthony Hopkinson) 2¼m N of Royston; 8m S of Cambridge; off the A10 on edge of village, Royston side. 5 acres; small ornamental lake and river with wildfowl; large herbaceous border; fine mature trees with wide lawns and rose garden. TEAS. *Combined adm with* **Melbourn Lodge** *£2 Chd free. Sun June 28 (2-6)*

Melbourn Lodge, Royston &❀❀ (J R M Keatley Esq) Melbourn 3m N of Royston, 8m S of Cambridge. House in middle of Melbourn village. 2-acre garden maintained on 9 hrs work per week in season. C19 grade II listed house (not open). TEAS at Melbourn Bury. *Combined adm with* **Melbourn Bury** *£2 Chd free. Sun June 28 (2-6)*

Mill House, North End, Bassingbourn &❀❀ (Anthony & Valerie Jackson) Fen Road. On the NW outskirts of Bassingbourn 1m from Church, on the rd to Shingay. Take North End at the war memorial in the centre of Bassingbourn which is just W of the A1198, 2m N of Royston (do not take Mill Lane). Garden created out of open countryside by garden designer owners. Clever use of walls, pergolas, water and varying land levels provide a backdrop for many very fascinating plants notably viticella clematis, giving interest and colour throughout the year. *Private and group visits welcome by appt in June and July, please* **Tel 01763 243491**

Moonrakers, Whittlesford (Mr & Mrs K Price) Royston Road. Off A505 between Whittlesford Station and M11 junction 10, 7m S of Cambridge. 1½ acres wildlife garden, with old espalier apple trees in kitchen garden surrounded by hedgerows, trees, shrubs and pond. *Adm £1. Sat April 11 (2-6). Private visits welcome, please* **Tel 01223 832087**. *Also open as* **Whittlesford Gardens** *Suns June 21, July 19*

Netherhall Manor, Soham ❀ (Timothy Clark) Enter Soham from Newmarket, Tanners Lane is 2nd R 100yds after cemetery. Enter Soham from Ely, Tanners Lane is 2nd L after War Memorial. 1-acre walled garden incl courtyard featured on Geoffrey Smiths 'World of Flowers' and 'Gardeners World'. April-Crown Imperials, Victorian hyacinths and old primroses. May-florists ranunculus (picotee and bizarre), and tulips (rose, bizarre, byblomen). Also during Aug formal beds of Victorian pelargoniums, calceolarias, fuchsia, lobelias and heliotropes, an organic seasonal kitchen garden. *Adm £1 Chd 50p. Suns April 12, May 10, Aug 9, 16 (2-5)*

Newnham College, Cambridge &🅰🐕❀ (The Principal & Fellows of Newnham College) Entrance from Newnham Walk. Can be approached from Sidgwick Ave or Newnham Walk, Cambridge. From City Centre via Queen's Rd or Silver St. Parking on street or College car parks. Unsuspected haven in busy city. 18 acres of Victorian and Edwardian gardens, encircled by Basil Champney's buildings. Herbaceous borders, nut walk, summer house and memorial mound. Sunken rose garden with lily pond and fountain; observatory. TEAS. *Adm £1.50 Chd free (ACNO to Newnham College Development Trust®). Sun July 12 (2-6)*

Nuns Manor, Shepreth &🐕❀ (Mr & Mrs J R L Brashaw) Frog End. 8m SW of Cambridge 300yds from A10 Melbourn-Shepreth Xrds. C16 farmhouse surrounded by delightful 2-acre garden, designed, created and maintained by owners. A plantsman's garden with interesting plants in mixed and herbaceous borders and large pond. Featured in The English Garden. Owners unusual homegrown plants for sale. TEA in aid of Shepreth Church. *Adm £1.50 Chd free. Sun July 5 (2-5.30); also group visits by appt April to Sept, please Tel 01763 260313*

The Old Post Office, Brington ❀ (The Hon Mrs Sue Roe) nr Huntingdon. Turn off A14 onto B660 northbound approx 7m W of junction with A1. Then follow signs to Brington. In Brington go towards Old Weston. Last house on L. A packed cottage garden with plenty of unusual plants. Approx ¾-acre. The boundary between garden and countryside is deliberately left blurred to encourage wildlife. Pond, small wild flower meadow. TEA. *Adm £1.50 Chd 50p. Sun June 28 (2-6). Private visits at weekends welcome April to Sept by appt, please Tel 01832 710223*

Orton Longueville Gardens, Peterborough 🐕 Off 605 Oundle Rd, 2½m E of intersection with A1 after junction with Nene Parkway. TEAS at The Old School. *Combined adm £2 Chd 50p. Sun July 12 (1-5)*
   Hemingdale &🐕 (Mr & Mrs John Wilkinson) A cottage garden, incl material for flower arranging, vegetables and herbs
   The Old School (Dr & Mrs Ross Gordon) A converted 1853 village school, playground, school master's house and garden. Formal layout with informal planting of ⅓-acre gardens in picturesque village
   Pennard 🐕 (Mr & Mrs G Stevenson) Garden developed during the past 4 yrs, featuring shrubs, herbaceous beds and arches supporting varieties of rose, honeysuckle and clematis. *Private visits also welcome weekdays, please Tel 01733 391506*

Padlock Croft, West Wratting &🐕❀ (Mr & Mrs P E Lewis) From dual carriageway on B1207 between Linton and Horseheath take turning N (Balsham W Wratting); Padlock Road is at entry to village. Plantsman's organic garden of ⅔-acre, home of the National Campanula Collection; mixed borders, troughs, alpine house etc incl rare plants; rock and scree gardens; succulents; potager with raised beds. *Adm £1 Combined adm £2 Chd 50p with* **Hyset, Scarletts Farm** *and* **Weaver's Cottage.** *Sats, Mons April 11, 13, May 23, 25; Sats June 20, July 25, Aug 8 (2-6). Private visits also welcome, weekdays, please* **Tel 01223 290383**

Pampisford Gardens &🐕❀ 8m S of Cambridge on A505. TEAS at the Old Vicarage in aid of RDA. *Combined adm £2.50 Chd free. Sun July 19 (2-5.30)*
   Beech Corner (Dr & Mrs B E Bridgland) 22 Church Lane. Rear garden has been planned as a small paved courtyard leading round into mini woodland
   The Dower House (Dr & Mrs O M Edwards) 7 High Street. Medieval house surrounded by well designed and interesting garden
   Glebe Crescent A group of pensioners houses with very colourful small gardens
   The Old Vicarage (Mr & Mrs Nixon) Next to Church in village. 2½-acres; mature trees; shrub and herbaceous borders with good ground cover plants; small Victorian style conservatory planted with rare species

Ramsey Gardens, nr Huntingdon. TEAS. *Combined adm £2 Chd free. Sun June 7 (2-6)*
   The Elms, Ramsey Forty Foot (Mr & Mrs K C Shotbolt) From Ramsey travel through Ramsey Forty Foot, just before bridge over drain, turn R, 300yds on R. Large water garden beautifully landscaped with shrubs, water lilies, ferns and large tank koi carp. Mirror carp, golden orfe in lakes. 2-acres full of unusual plants; spring flowers. *Also by appt, please* **Tel 01487 812601**
   ¶**First Cottage** (Mr Richard Fort) Adjacent to 'The Elms' 150′ × 40′ garden with herbaceous border, shrub beds, miniature steam railway around ornamental pond and rockery
   77 Great Whyte 🐕 (Mr & Mrs H Holden) Cottage garden 55′ × 45′ well stocked with trees, shrubs and flowers, many interesting plants and features. *At other times by appt, please Tel 01487 812529*

Scarlett's Farm, West Wratting &%* (Mr & Mrs M Hicks) Padlock Rd. From dual carriageway on A1307 between Linton and Horseheath taking turning N (W Wratting 3½); Padlock Road is at entry to village. Scarlett's Farm at end of Padlock Road. ⅓-acre mixed country garden, incl formal but irregular parterre, full of colourful ornamentals, small nursery attached. TEAS. *Adm £1, Chd 50p. Combined adm £2 Chd 50p with* **Hyset,** *and* **Padlock Croft.** *Sats, Mon May 2, 4, 23, 25; July 25, Sept 26 (2-6).* **Tel 01223 290812**

¶**Selwyn College, Cambridge** &% (The Master and Fellows) Grange Road. Situated ½m W of the city centre. Selwyn College can be entered from Grange Rd which runs parallel with Queens Rd, known locally as 'The Backs'. Unusual, exotic and an original approach to the use of plants in the recreation of this Victorian garden combine to make this a most exciting garden to visit, particularly in late summer when the circular border is simply stunning. A great many unusual plants. The garden has been renovated over the past 2 yrs and a pond, fernery and damp garden are planned for 1998. Enjoy. TEAS. *Adm £2 Chd free under 14. Sun Aug 16 (2-5.30)*

¶**Shingay Gardens** % 12m W of Cambridge, 3m beyond A603 junction with A1198. TEAS and parking at South Farm. *Combined adm £2.50 (ACNO to CAMVET). Suns June 21, July 12 (2-6)*
   South Farm *% (Mr P Paxman) Grounds of 10 acres, ringed by shelter planting surround farm house of Tudor origins and courtyard of listed farm buildings, home to rare breed poultry collection. Woodland, wild meadow, bog and water gardens contrast with more formal plantings, an exotic conservatory and large kitchen garden with more than 100 unusual varieties and species. Featured in Kitchen Garden magazine
   Private Nature Reserve (Herr Wentzel) 8 mins walk from South Farm (or drive) centred on 3 acre lake with remarkable naturally established wild flowers, aquatic birds, dragonflies and butterflies
   Brook Cottage (Mr & Mrs Charvil) 4 mins walk from South Farm. A countryman's cottage garden. Abundant year long mixed colour, spilling over boundary stream, inter-mixed with traditional vegetables and poultry

Sutton Gardens, nr Ely &%* 6m W of Ely on A142, turn L at roundabout into village. Teas at 5 Church Lane in aid of Sutton WI. *Single garden £1, Combined adm £2.50 Chd free. Sun June 21 (2-6)*
   1 Church Lane &* (Miss B M & Miss B I Ambrose) Small garden near church with unusual trees, shrubs, climbers, perennials and alpines. Greenhouse, raised beds, troughs and tubs. Border for shade-loving plants
   51 High Street * (Mr A Wilkinson & Mr A Scott) A cottage style garden with terraced borders. Conservatory with vine, cacti and gloriosa lilies
   7 Lawn Lane &* (Mr & Mrs R Kybird) Small garden with many hanging baskets and containers; fuchsias, penstemons, hardy geraniums, roses and clematis. Patio on two levels with pergola and water feature
   8 Lawn Lane * (Mr & Mrs H J Fortin) Small garden closely planted and colourful, with rockery, formal pool, terrace and curved lawns on 2 levels. Secluded vegetable corner. Meticulously cared for by plantaholic

Trinity Cottage, 36 High Street %* (Anna & Archie McOustra) Blending of small scale mixed plantings in an irregular ¼-acre cottage garden setting, unusual shrubs intermingling with herbaceous plants particularly hardy geraniums, incl ponds, rockery and vegetable garden

Swaffham Bulbeck Gardens * 8m E of Cambridge off B1102 past Anglesey Abbey. TEAS in aid of St Mary's Church, Swaffham Bulbeck. *Combined adm £1.50 Chd free. Sun June 28 (2-6)*
   Lordship Cottage (Dr & Mrs M Touriss) Beautiful cottage garden to one of the oldest houses in the village (near recreation ground)
   The Priest's House (Mr & Mrs R Jones) 1 acre garden (plus 1 acre paddock) of herbaceous borders, rose beds and soft fruit (opp Church)
   Martin House (Prof & Mrs L Sealy) Station Rd. New garden with Chinese influence, designed and made by Mrs Sealy. Herb garden
   The Merchant's House, Commercial End & (Mr & Mrs H L S Bevington) 1-acre walled gardens to C17 house originally used for canal-based merchanting business. Potager, orchard, old roses, mixed herbaceous borders
   The Old Rectory &* (Mr & Mrs J Few-Mackay) High Street next to church. English rectory garden
   2 Station Road * (Mr & Mrs C Rice) Small formal garden
   Stocks Hill House * (Mr & Mrs D Butler) Small informal garden with herbaceous borders

Tadlow House, Tadlow &% (Mr & Mrs Andrew Parkinson) 3½m W of Arrington on N side of B1042 adjacent to church. 2½-acre garden with spring flower walks and blossom incl tulips, narcissi, anemone blanda and fritillaria. New plantings incl recently designed water garden, parterre and circle gardens; interesting shrubs and trees. Adjacent C13 church with William Butterfield's C19 restoration. TEA in aid of Tadlow Church. *Adm £1.50 Chd free. Suns March 29, May 10 (2-5.30)*

Tetworth Hall * (Lady Crossman) 4m NE of Sandy; 6m SE of St Neots off Everton-Waresley Rd. Large woodland and bog garden; rhododendrons; azaleas, unusual shrubs and plants; fine trees. Queen Anne house (not open). TEA. *Adm £2 Chd free (ACNO to Waresley Church®). Suns May 10, 24 (2-6). Private visits welcome April 15 to June 15, please* **Tel 01767 650212**

Trinity College, Fellows' Garden, Cambridge &% Queen's Road. Garden of 8 acres, originally laid out in the 1870s by W B Thomas; lawns with mixed borders, shrubs, specimen trees. Drifts of spring bulbs. *Adm £1 Chd free. Sun April 5 (2-6)*

Unwins Seeds Ltd, Histon % (Mr & Mrs David Unwin) Impington Lane. 3m N of Cambridge, 1m off A14 on B1049. Follow signs for Histon and Cottenham. At traffic lights nr Rose & Crown in centre of Histon, turn R into Impington Lane. Trial grounds of approx 6 acres where 4,500 varieties of annuals, biennials, perennials and vegetables from seed are assessed. Many new and experimental strains are on show. The company uses the trials to determine the garden worth of new varieties and monitor the trueness to type of strains it already lists. TEA. *Adm £1.50 Chd under 14 free. Sat Aug 15 (12-5)*

Weaver's Cottage, West Wickham (Miss Sylvia Norton) Streetly End. On A1307 between Linton and Haverhill turn N at Horseheath towards W Wickham. Weaver's Cottage is 8th on R after 40 sign. ½-acre garden exuberantly planted for fragrance with spring bulbs; shrubs; herbaceous; climbers; old roses. Newly created sunken and scree gardens. NCCPG Lathyrus Collection. *Combined adm £2 Chd 50p with* **Padlock Croft** *Sat April 11, Mon April 13, also with* **Hyset** *and* **Scarlett's Farm** *Sats May 23, June 20, July 25, Mon May 25 (2-6). Private visits welcome, please* **Tel 01223 892399**

West Wratting Park &✗❀ (Mr & Mrs Henry d'Abo) 8m S of Newmarket. From A11, between Worsted Lodge and Six Mile Bottom, turn E to Balsham; then N along B1052 to West Wratting; Park is at E end of village. Georgian house (orangery shown), beautifully situated in rolling country, with fine trees; rose and herbaceous gardens. TEA. *Adm £2 Chd free. Sun June 28 (2-7)*

Whittlesford Gardens ❀ 7m S of Cambridge. 1m NE of Junction 10 of the M11 and A505. TEAS. Flowers in P church. *Combined adm £2 (ACNO to the 2 Churches). Sun July 19 (2-6)*
   The Guildhall ✗ (Dr P & Dr M Spufford) North Road. Medieval building (not open), small knot garden. *June 21 only*
   Cherrytree Cottage ✗ (Mr & Mrs J Eastwood) Easy maintenance, organic garden, fishpond. Lots of pretty places to sit and enjoy. *June 21, July 19*
   13 West End ✗ (Mr & Mrs C Taylor) Interesting range of climbers, ground cover plants, in small paved garden, pond. *June 21 only*
   15 West End (Mr & Mrs A Watson) Small garden with herbaceous beds and ornamental pond. *June 21, July 19*
   21 West End (Mr & Mrs G Jezierski) Cottage garden with herbaceous beds, shrubs, pond and vegetable area. *Sun June 21 only*
   23 Newton Road & (Mr & Mrs F Winter) Cottage garden, herbaceous plants, shrubs, fish pond. Allotment consisting of all veg, fruit, flowers and bird avery. *July 19 only*
   5 Parsonage Court &✗ (Mrs L Button) Please park on main road. Trees, shrubs and large pond. *June 21 only*
   Brook Cottage ✗ (R Marshall Esq & Ms J Lewis) Newton Road. Small untidy peaceful cottage garden bordered by stream. *July 19 only*

11 Scotts Garden ✗ (Mr & Mrs M Walker) Shady walled garden, shrub borders. Plants for sale. *June 21, July 19*
12 Swallow Croft (Miss J Woodley) Colourful garden of mixed shrubs and hanging baskets and tubs. *July 19*
Moonrakers (Mr & Mrs K Price) 1½ acres wildlife garden espalier apple trees, shrubs and pond. *June 21, July 19*

▲**Wimpole Hall, Arrington** &✗ (National Trust) 5m N of Royston signed off A603 to Sandy 7m from Cambridge or off A1198. Part of 350-acre park. First sight of reinstatement of Victorian Parterres on N lawns. Rose garden and fine trees, marked walks in park. National Collection of Walnuts. Massed plantings of daffodil. Lunches & TEA. *Adm £2 Chd £1. For NGS Fri April 17 (10.30-5)*

Marie Curie Cancer Care

Marie Curie Cancer Care is a charity which cares for people with cancer. The National Gardens Scheme is delighted to include it in its list of beneficiaries. Some facts and figures:

- More than 250,000 people in Britain develop cancer every year. Almost 160,000 people die from the disease annually, the second biggest killer after heart disease.

- **Marie Curie Nurses** provide over 1.3 million hours a year of practical nursing care at home. The service is available day or night, 365 days a year, to patients and their families without charge.

- **Marie Curie Centres** cared for more than 4,600 patients in 1996/97.

- **Marie Curie Cancer Care** operates a research institute which investigates the underlying causes of cancer.

Carmarthanshire & Pembrokeshire

See separate Welsh section on page 370

Ceredigion/Cardiganshire

See separate Welsh section on page 373

Cheshire & Wirral

Hon County Organiser: Nicholas Payne Esq, The Mount, Whirley, Macclesfield SK11 9PB
Tel 01625 426730

Assistant Hon County Organisers: Mrs T R Hill, Salterswell House, Tarporley CW6 OED
Tel 01829 732804
Mrs N Whitbread, Lower Huxley Hall, Hargrave, Chester CH3 7RJ
Tel 01829 781481

DATES OF OPENING

Regular openings
For details see garden description

Arley Hall & Gardens, Northwich
Norton Priory, Runcorn
Peover Hall, Knutsford
Rode Hall, Scholar Green
Stonyford Cottage, Cuddington

By appointment only
*For telephone numbers and other
details see garden descriptions.
Private visits welcomed*

Rosewood, Puddington
2 Stanley Road, Heaton Moor
Willow Cottage, Prestbury

April 5 Sunday
The Well House, Tilston
April 12 Sunday
Orchard Villa, Alsager
April 13 Monday
Thornton Manor, Thornton Hough
April 19 Sunday
Briarfield, Burton
Cranberry Cottage, Smallwood
Poulton Hall, Poulton Lancelyn
85 Warmingham Rd, Coppenhall
April 26 Sunday
37 Bakewell Road, Hazel Grove
Willaston Grange, Willaston
May 10 Sunday
Lyme Park, Disley
The Quinta Garden and
Arboretum, Swettenham
Rode Hall, Scholar Green
Tushingham Hall, Whitchurch
May 11 Monday
Beeston House, Bunbury
May 16 Saturday
Peover Hall, Knutsford
May 17 Sunday
37 Bakewell Road, Hazel Grove
Bolesworth Castle, Tattenhall
Hare Hill Gardens, Over Alderley
Haughton Hall, Bunbury
35 Heyes Lane, Timperley
Orchard Villa, Alsager
Peover Hall, Knutsford

May 20 Wednesday
35 Heyes Lane, Timperley
Reaseheath, Nantwich
May 22 Friday
St Davids House, Noctorum
(evening opening)
May 24 Sunday
Dorfold Hall, Nantwich
Snelson House, Snelson
May 25 Monday
Ashton Hayes, Chester
May 27 Wednesday
Reaseheath, Nantwich
May 31 Sunday
Henbury Hall, nr Macclesfield
Manley Knoll, Manley
The Stray, Neston
June 3 Wednesday
Dunge Valley Gardens,
Kettleshulme
The Quinta Garden and
Arboretum, Swettenham
Reaseheath, Nantwich
June 6 Saturday
Arley Hall & Gardens, Northwich
Bank House, Bickerton
June 7 Sunday
Bank House, Bickerton
Little Moreton Hall, Congleton
Stonyford Cottage, Cuddington
June 10 Wednesday
Dunge Valley Gardens,
Kettleshulme
Reaseheath, Nantwich
June 12 Friday
Orchard Villa, Alsager
June 13 Saturday
The Old Parsonage, Arley Green
June 14 Sunday
37 Bakewell Road, Hazel Grove
Norton Priory, Runcorn
The Old Parsonage, Arley Green
5, Pine Hey, Neston
85 Warmingham Rd, Coppenhall
13 Yew Tree Cottages, Compstall
June 17 Wednesday
Reaseheath, Nantwich
June 21 Sunday
Cherry Hill, Malpas
Greenhills Farm Gardens, Lower
Whitley

The Mount, Higher Kinnerton
Ness Cottage, Mollington
The Well House, Tilston
June 22 Monday
Tatton Park, Knutsford
June 24 Wednesday
Reaseheath, Nantwich
June 28 Sunday
Burton Village Gardens
July 1 Wednesday
Reaseheath, Nantwich
July 4 Saturday
17 Poplar Grove, Sale
July 5 Sunday
37 Bakewell Road, Hazel Grove
Free Green Farm, Lower Peover
73 Hill Top Avenue, Cheadle
Hulme
17 Poplar Grove, Sale
Poulton Hall, Poulton Lancelyn
13 Yew Tree Cottages,
Compstall
July 8 Wednesday
Reaseheath, Nantwich
July 11 Saturday
Bridgemere Garden World
July 12 Sunday
The Mount, Whirley
Wood End Cottage, Whitegate
July 15 Wednesday
Cholmondeley Castle Garden,
Malpas
Reaseheath, Nantwich
Warrington Gardens
July 19 Sunday
Sandymere, Cotebrook
July 22 Wednesday
Reaseheath, Nantwich
July 29 Wednesday
Reaseheath, Nantwich
August 2 Sunday
Bluebell Cottage, Dutton
August 5 Wednesday
Capesthorne, Macclesfield
August 16 Sunday
Dunham Massey, Altrincham
Orchard Villa, Alsager
August 23 Sunday
Lyme Park, Disley
September 13 Sunday
1 Woodpecker Drive, Northwich

CHESHIRE & WIRRAL

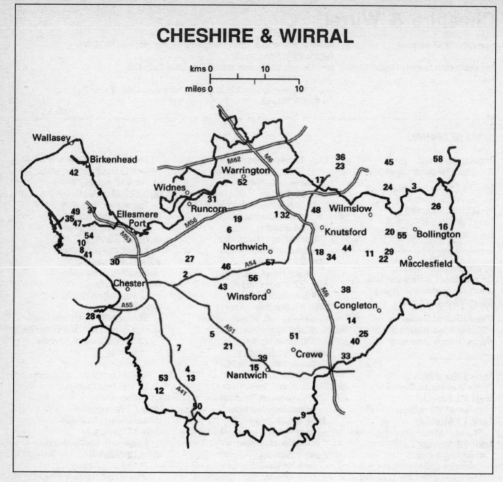

KEY

1. Arley Hall & Gardens
2. Ashton Hayes
3. 37 Bakewell Road
4. Bank House
5. Beeston House
6. Bluebell Cottage
7. Bolesworth Castle
8. Briarfield
9. Bridgemere Nurseries Ltd
10. Burton Village Gardens
11. Capesthorne
12. Cherry Hill
13. Cholmondeley Castle Garden
14. Cranberry Cottage
15. Dorfold Hall
16. Dunge Valley Gardens
17. Dunham Massey
18. Free Green Farm
19. Greenhills Farm Gardens
20. Hare Hill Gardens

21. Haughton Hall
22. Henbury Hall
23. 35 Heyes Lane
24. 73 Hill Top Avenue
25. Little Moreton Hall
26. Lyme Park
27. Manley Knoll
28. The Mount, Higher
    Kinnerton
29. The Mount, Whirley
30. Ness Cottage
31. Norton Priory
32. The Old Parsonage
33. Orchard Villa
34. Peover Hall
35. 5, Pine Hey
36. 17 Poplar Grove
37. Poulton Hall
38. The Quinta Garden &
    Arboretum

39. Reaseheath
40. Rode Hall
41. Rosewood
42. St Davids House
43. Sandymere
44. Snelson House
45. 2 Stanley Road
46. Stonyford Cottage
47. The Stray
48. Tatton Park
49. Thornton Manor
50. Tushingham Hall
51. 85 Warmingham Rd
52. Warrington Gardens
53. The Well House
54. Willaston Grange
55. Willow Cottage
56. Wood End Cottage
57. 1 Woodpecker Drive
58. 13 Yew Tree Cottages

DESCRIPTIONS OF GARDENS

■ **Arley Hall & Gardens, Northwich** &❀ (The Viscount Ashbrook) Well signed from M6 junctions 19 & 20 & M56 junctions 9 & 10. 12 acres; twin herbaceous borders, avenue of quercus Ilex trees, walled gardens; azaleas, rhododendrons; woodland garden. Lunches. Gift shop. Specialist plant nursery. TEA. *Adm Gardens & Grounds only £3.60, OAP £3 Chd under 16 £1.80. Hall £2.50 Extra chd £1.20 (ACNO to St Lukes Cheshire Hospice®). Easter to Sept (12-5) Tues to Sun & Bank Hols. Hall open days vary throughout season, last adm to gardens 4.30. For NGS Sat June 6 (12-4.30).* **Tel 01565 777353.** *Arley Garden Festival Sat, Sun June 27, 28 (10-5)*

Ashton Hayes, Chester ✄ (Mrs J Searle) Midway between Tarvin and Kelsall on A54, take B5393 N to Ashton and Mouldsworth. Approach to Ashton Hayes can be seen halfway between Ashton and Mouldsworth. The ¾m drive is beside former lodge. About 12 acres, incl arboretum and ponds. Predominantly a valley garden of mature trees and flowering shrubs. Great variety of azaleas and rhododendrons; notable embothrium. TEAS. *Adm £2 OAPs £1.50 Chd 50p (ACNO to Church of St John the Evangelist, Ashton Hayes®). Mon May 25 (2-6)*

37 Bakewell Road, Hazel Grove ✄ (Mr & Mrs H Williams) From Manchester on A6 following signs to Buxton, bear R at Rising Sun Public House, Hazel Grove. Taking the Macclesfield Rd (A523) take 1st R (Haddon Rd) then 1st L into Bakewell Rd. Small suburban garden 17yds × 6½yds heavily planted with azaleas, rhododendrons (several rare and unusual varieties), hydrangeas; pool and waterfall. Excellent example of how much can be planted in a small area. TEA. *Adm £1.50 Chd free. Suns April 26, May 17, June 14, July 5 (11-6). Private visits by appt* **Tel 01625 260592**

¶**Bank House, Bickerton** ❀ (Dr & Mrs M A Voisey) 11m S of Chester on A41 turn L at Broxton roundabout to Nantwich on A534. Take 5th R (1.8m) to Bickerton. Take 2nd R into Goldford Lane. Bank House is then 0.9m on L. 1½-acre garden situated at the foot of Bickerton Hill, below the sandstone trail. This has sheltered, terraced borders stocked with a wide range of shrubs, trees and herbaceous plants, and a productive vegetable garden. Field parking. TEAS. *Adm £2 Chd 50p (ACNO to Age Concern® (Malpas Day Centre)). Sat, Sun June 6, 7 (2-6)*

Beeston House, Bunbury &✄❀ (Mr & Mrs B S Jenkins) Off A49 3m S of Tarporley, 10m N of Whitchurch. Turn W at Bunbury Xrds large brown sign for Beeston Castle, 100yds from A49. 3 acres of traditional English country garden, rhododendrons, azaleas, flowering shrubs, foliage plants and herbaceous borders all designed to create all-year-round interest. TEAS. *Adm £2 Acc chd 50p (ACNO to Tarporley War Memorial Hospital®). Sun May 11 (2-6)*

Bluebell Cottage, Dutton &✄❀ (R L & D Casey) Lodge Lane. From M56 (junction 10) take A49 Whitchurch Rd for 3m, turn R on A533 towards Runcorn at traffic lights. Lodge Lane is the 1st turning L approx 1.5m. 1½-acre garden with ave of young trees leading to canal. The cottage garden has been developed into a series of rooms.

Large lawn areas with herbaceous borders. Adjacent is a 3-acre wild flower meadow, bluebell woodland and nursery. TEAS in aid of Cheshire Wildlife Trust. *Adm £2 Chd 50p. Sun Aug 2 (1-5.30). Private visits welcome, please* **Tel 01928 713718**

Bolesworth Castle, Tattenhall &❀ (Mr & Mrs A G Barbour) Enter by lodge on A41 8m S of Chester or 1m N of Broxton roundabout. Landscape with rhododendrons, shrubs and borders. Woodland walk replanted 1993/7. TEAS. *Adm £2.50 Chd free (ACNO to Harthill & Burwardsley Churches®). Sun May 17 (2-5.30)*

Briarfield, Burton ✄❀ (Peter & Liz Carter) 9m NW of Chester. Turn off A540 at Burton Xrds (traffic lights) and follow road for 1m to Burton village centre. Free car parking. 1½-acres of rare trees and shrubs, many spring flowering. Mixed borders with spring bulbs, erythroniums a speciality. Set against National Trust woodland background. *Adm £2 Chd free. Sun April 19 (2-6)*

▲**Bridgemere Garden World, Bridgemere** &✄ On A51 7m S of Nantwich, 1m N of Woore. Follow brown tourist signs from Nantwich. The Garden Kingdom television gardens, over 22 gardens showing many different styles of plant grouping. Plus the recreated Bridgemere Garden World prize winning exhibition gardens from Garden Festivals, Chelsea Flower Show Gold Medal gardens and the garden where the Gardeners' Diary television programme is filmed. Coffee shop and restaurant on site. *Adm £1.50 OAPs and Chd over 8yrs £1. For NGS Sat July 11 (10-6)*

Burton Village Gardens ✄❀ 9m NW of Chester. Turn off A540 at Willaston-Burton Xrds (traffic lights) and follow rd for 1m to Burton. Free parking. Teas at Village Hall in aid of Clare House Children's Hospice. *Combined adm £3 Chd free. Sun June 28 (2-6)*
> **Bank Cottage** (Mr & Mrs J R Beecroft) Small, very colourful, mixed cottage garden with old roses backing on to cricket ground
> **Briarfield** ❀ (Mr & Mrs P Carter) About an acre of rare trees and shrubs, colourful mixed borders together with fruit and vegetable garden in woodland setting. Short woodland trail to
> **Lynwood** ❀ (Mr & Mrs P M Wright) On the fringe of the village on the Neston Road. ½-acre garden with shrub borders; rockery, pond with waterfall, pergola and arbour with climbers

▲**Capesthorne, Macclesfield** & (Mr & Mrs W A Bromley-Davenport) 5m W of Macclesfield. 7m S of Wilmslow on A34. Varied garden; daffodil lawn; azaleas, rhododendrons; herbaceous border, arboretum and lake. Georgian chapel and memorial garden. TEAS and light lunches. Free car park. *Adm garden £2.50 OAPs £2 Chd £1. For NGS Wed Aug 5 (12-6).* **Tel 01625 861221**

Evening Opening (see also garden descriptions)

St David's House, Noctorum   May 22 5.30–8.30pm

Cherry Hill, Malpas ♿🐕 (Mr & Mrs Miles Clarke) 2m W of Malpas signed from B5069 to Chorlton. Massed bulbs in spring; walks through pine woods and rhododendrons to trout lake; walled garden, herbaceous borders, shrub roses. Ornamental vegetable garden. TEAS in attractive house overlooking Welsh mountains. Cricket ground. *Adm £2 Chd 50p. Sun June 21 (2-5.30)*

▲**Cholmondeley Castle Garden, Malpas** ♿🐕 (The Marchioness of Cholmondeley) Situated off A41 Chester/Whitchurch rd and A49 Whitchurch/Tarporley rd. Romantically landscaped gardens full of variety. Azaleas, rhododendrons, flowering shrubs; rare trees; herbaceous borders and water garden. Lakeside picnic area; rare breeds of farm animals, incl llamas; gift shop. Ancient private Chapel in the park. Tearoom offering light lunches etc. TEAS. *Adm gardens only £2.50 OAPs £2 Chd 75p. For NGS Wed July 15 (12-5).* Tel **01829 720383** *or* **720203**

¶**Cranberry Cottage, Smallwood** ♿🐕 (Paula & Malcolm Bright) From A50 at public house 'Legs of Man' turn into Back Lane. From A34 turn to Smallwood to public house 'Blue Bell'; thereafter signed. ¾-acre country cottage garden planted with rare bulbs. Spring flowering shrubs; clematis, azaleas, rhododendrons and viburnums. Magnolias and a variety of blossom trees. TEA. *Adm £2 Chd 50p. Sun April 19 (12-6)*

▲**Dorfold Hall, Nantwich** 🐕🐾 (Mr & Mrs Richard Roundell) 1m W of Nantwich on A534 between Nantwich and Acton. 18-acre garden surrounding C17 house with formal approach; lawns and recently planted herbaceous borders; spectacular spring woodland garden with rhododendrons, azaleas, magnolias and bulbs. TEAS in aid of Acton Parish Church. *Adm £2 Chd 75p. For NGS Sun May 24 (2-5.30)*

▲**Dunge Valley Gardens, Kettleshulme** 🐕🐾 (Mr & Mrs David Ketley) Take B5470 rd from Macclesfield. Kettleshulme is 8m from Macclesfield. Turn R in village signed Dunge Valley Gardens. Surrounded by romantic hills and set in 5 acres, at 1000ft, this is the highest garden in Cheshire; woodland, streams, bog gardens, herbaceous borders, species rhododendrons, magnolias, acers and meconopsis plus roses. TEAS. *Adm £2.50 Chd 50p. For NGS Weds June 3, 10 (10.30-6).* Tel **01663 733787**

▲**Dunham Massey, Altrincham** ♿🐕🐾 (The National Trust) 3m SW of Altrincham off A56. Well signed. Garden over 20 acres, on ancient site with moat lake, mount and orangery. Mature trees and fine lawns with extensive range of shrubs and herbaceous perennials suited to acid sand, many planted at waterside. Set in 350 acres of deer park. TEAS. *Adm £3 Chd free NGS day only (car entry £2.80). For NGS Sun Aug 16 (11-5)*

Free Green Farm, Lower Peover ♿🐾 (Sir Philip & Lady Haworth) Free Green Lane connects the A50 with the B5081. From Holmes Chapel take A50 past the Drovers Arms. L into Free Green Lane, farm is on R. From Knutsford take A50, turn R into Middlewich Lane (B5081), turn L into Broom Lane, turn L into Free Green Lane, farm is on L. 2-acre garden with pleached limes; herbaceous borders; ponds and new parterre. Parking in field

behind house (sign posted) not in lane. British woodland for conservation. TEAS in aid of Cancer Research Campaign. *Adm £2 Chd 50p. Sun July 5 (2-6)*

Greenhills Farm Gardens, Lower Whitley ♿🐕🐾 (Mr & Mrs Peter Johnson) From M56 take A49 S. In 1m turn R signed Dutton (Grimditch Lane), 1st L, Greenhills Lane go to end. From S go up A49 towards Warrington, turn L 1m before M56 signed Dutton etc. Approx. 1½-acre of yr-round interest. Shrubs, herbaceous borders, roses, fruit and specimen trees and a small lake have made a beautifully landscaped garden. TEAS by the Red Cross. *Adm £2 Chd 50p. Sun June 21 (2-5.30)*

▲**Hare Hill Gardens, Over Alderley** ♿🐾 (The National Trust) Between Alderley Edge and Prestbury, turn off N at B5087 at Greyhound Rd [118:SJ85765]. Attractive spring garden featuring a fine display of rhododendrons and azaleas. A good collection of hollies and other specimen trees and shrubs. The 10-acre garden includes a walled garden which hosts many wall shrubs including clematis and vines. The borders are planted with agapanthus and geraniums. Partially suitable for wheelchairs. *Adm £2.50 Chd £1.25. For NGS Sun May 17 (10-5.30)*

Haughton Hall, Bunbury 🐕 (Mr & Mrs R J Posnett) Tarporley. 5m NW of Nantwich off A534 Nantwich/Wrexham Rd, 6m SE of Tarporley via A49. Medium-sized garden; species of rhododendron, azaleas, shrubs, rock garden; lake with temple; waterfall. Collection of ornamental trees. Home-made TEAS. *Adm £2 Chd 50p. Sun May 17 (2-6)*

Henbury Hall, nr Macclesfield ♿🐾 (Mr & Mrs Sebastian de Ferranti) 2m W of Macclesfield on A537 rd. Turn down School Lane, Henbury at Blacksmiths Arms: East Lodge on R. Large garden with lake, beautifully landscaped and full of variety. Azaleas, rhododendrons, flowering shrubs, rare trees, herbaceous borders. TEAS in aid of East Cheshire Hospice. *Adm £2 Chd £1 (ACNO to Drugwatch®). Sun May 31 (2-5)*

35 Heyes Lane, Timperley 🐕 (Mr & Mrs David Eastwood) Heyes Lane is a turning off Park Rd (B5165) 1m from the junction with the A56 Altrincham-Manchester rd 1½m N of Altrincham. Or from A560 turn W in Timperley Village for ¼m. Newsagents shop on corner. A small suburban garden 30' × 90' on sandy soil maintained by a keen plantswoman member of the Organic Movement (HDRA). An all yr round garden; trees; small pond; greenhouses; 16 kinds of fruit with a good collection of interesting and unusual plants. *Adm £1.50 incl TEA Chd free. Sun May 17, Wed May 20 (2-5)*

73 Hill Top Avenue, Cheadle Hulme 🐾 (Mr & Mrs Martin Land) Turn off A34 (new by-pass) at roundabout signed Cheadle Hulme (B5094). Take 2nd turn L into Gillbent Rd, signposted Cheadle Hulme Sports Centre. Go to end, small roundabout, turn R into Church Rd. 2nd rd on L is Hill Top Ave. From Stockport or Bramhall turn R/L into Church Rd by The Church Inn. Hill Top Ave is first rd on R. ⅙-acre plantswoman's garden. Plantings of herbaceous, shrub and climbing roses, clematis, pond and damp area, shrubs and small trees. TEAS. *Adm £2 Chd* *free (ACNO to Arthritis & Rheumatism Council®). Sun July 5 (2-6)*

▲**Little Moreton Hall, Congleton** ♿✦❀ (The National Trust) On A34, 4m S of Congleton. 1½-acre garden surrounded by a moat, next to finest example of timber-framed architecture in England. Herb and historic vegetable garden, orchard and borders. Knot garden. Adm includes entry to the Hall with optional free guided tours. Wheelchairs and electric mobility vehicle available. Picnic lawns. Shop and restaurant serving coffee, lunches and teas. TEAS. *Adm £4 Chd £2. For NGS Sun June 7 (12-5.30 last admission 5)*

▲**Lyme Park, Disley** ♿✦ (The National Trust) 6m SE of Stockport just W of Disley on A6 rd. 17-acre garden retaining many original features from Tudor and Jacobean times; high Victorian style bedding; a Dutch garden; a Gertrude Jekyll style herbaceous border; an Edwardian rose garden, a Wyatt orangery and many other features. Also rare trees, a wild flower area and lake. TEAS. Donations to NGS. *Adm £3.30 per car to estate, £2 Chd £1 to gardens. For NGS Suns May 10, Aug 23 (11-4.45)*

Manley Knoll, Manley ♿❀ (Mrs D G Fildes) NE of Chester. Nr Mouldsworth. B5393. Quarry garden; azaleas and rhododendrons. TEAS. *Adm £2 Chd free. Sun May 31 (2-6). Private visits welcome for parties 20 to 30, please* **Tel 01928 740226**

The Mount, Higher Kinnerton ♿✦ (Mr & Mrs J Major) 6m W of Chester, L off A5104 just after it crosses A55. Approx 2½-acre garden with mature trees; shrubs and lawns; kitchen garden, variety of perennial plants. A lot of reorganising and planting has taken place over the last 12 months. The garden has been featured in a Japanese Coffee Table Book and Cheshire Life. TEAS in aid of Home Farm Trust. *Adm £2 Chd free. Sun June 21. Private parties welcome, please* **Tel 01244 660275.** *Best months June and July*

The Mount, Whirley ♿✦❀ (Mr & Mrs Nicholas Payne) About 2m due W of Macclesfield along A537 rd. Opp Blacksmiths Arms at Henbury, go up Pepper St, turn L into Church Lane, then Andertons Lane in 100yds. The Mount is 200yds on L. The garden is approx 2 acres and has interesting trees including eucryphia nymansensis, fern leaved beech and sciadopitys. Shrubberies; herbaceous border; swimming pool and short vista of Irish Yews. TEAS. *Adm £2 Chd 50p. Sun July 12 (2-5.30). Parties welcome, please* **Tel 01625 426730**

¶**Ness Cottage, Mollington** ♿✦❀ (Brian & Sue Harris) Off the A540, 5 miles N of Chester and ¼m S of A55. ½-acre garden of all-round interest; lawns herbaceous borders, ponds and water features plus patio areas. Wildlife garden also with camomile lawn. TEAS in aid of Jarman Ward, West Cheshire Hospital. *Adm £1.50 Chd free. Sun June 21 (2-5.30) also private visits welcome for parties, please Tel 01244 880122 after 6pm*

■ **Norton Priory, Runcorn** ♿❀ (The Norton Priory Museum Trust Ltd) Tudor Road, Manor Park. From M56 Junction 11 turn for Warrington and follow signs. From Warrington take A56 for Runcorn and follow signs. 16 acres of gardens; Georgian summerhouses; rock garden and stream glade; 3-acre walled garden of similar date (1760s) recently restored. Fruit training; rosewalk; colour borders; herb garden, cottage garden. Priory remains also open. TEA. *Combined adm £3 Chd £1.70. Daily April to October (12-5) weekends and bank hols (12-6) Nov to March (12-4) (Walled garden closed Nov-Feb). For NGS Sun June 14 (12-6).* **Tel 01928 569895**

The Old Parsonage, Arley Green ♿❀ (The Viscount & Viscountess Ashbrook) 5m NNE of Northwich and 3m Great Budworth; M6 junctions 19, 20 and M56 junction 10. Follow signposts to Arley Hall and Gardens and notices to Old Parsonage which lies across park at Arley Green. 2-acre garden yew hedges, herbaceous and mixed borders, shrub roses, climbers, woodland garden and pond, with unusual young trees and foliage shrubs. Waterplants, rhododendrons, azaleas, meconopsis. TEAS in aid of Red Cross June 13, NGS June 14. *Adm £2 Chd under 16 £1 (ACNO to Save the Children®). Sat, Sun June 13, 14 (2-6)*

Orchard Villa, Alsager ♿❀ (Mr & Mrs J Trinder) 72 Audley Rd. At traffic lights in Alsager town centre turn S towards Audley, house is 300yds on R beyond level Xing. Long and narrow, this ⅓-acre has been planted by enthusiastic plant collectors and features spring bulbs, hellebores, alpines, irises, grasses and other herbaceous perennials. TEAS. *Adm £2 Chd free. Sun April 12 (12-4.30), Sun May 17 (1.30-5), Fri June 12 (2-8), Sun Aug 16 (1.30-5) also private visits welcome, please* **Tel 01270 874833**

■ **Peover Hall, Knutsford** ♿✦ (Randle Brooks Esq) Over Peover. 3m S of Knutsford on A50, L at Whipping Stocks down Stocks Lane. Lodge gates off Blackden Lane signed to Church. 15-acres. 5 walled gardens: lily pond, rose, herb, white and pink gardens; C18 landscaped park, moat, C19 dell, rhododendron walks, large walled kitchen garden, Church walk, purple border, blue and white border, pleached lime avenues, fine topiary work. Dogs in park only. TEAS. *Adm £2 Chd £2. Mons & Thurs (2-5) May to Oct. NOT Bank Hols. Other days by appt for parties. For NGS Sat, Sun May 16, 17 (2-6)*

5 Pine Hey, Neston ♿✦❀ (Mr & Mrs S J Clayton) Take A540 rd. Turn off at Shrewsbury Arms traffic lights towards Neston. Turn R at T-junction drive through Neston past cross on the L, then fork L at traffic lights and continue along Leighton Rd, Pine Hey is on L. The garden covers approx ¾ acre. It is laid out informally and incl a copse, water garden, lawns and herbaceous garden. Featured on Granada TV in 1996/7. TEAS in aid of Wirral Methodist Housing Association. *Adm £1.50 Chd free (ACNO to Wirral Methodist Housing Association®). Sun June 14 (2-5). Private parties welcome, please* **Tel 0151 3363006**

17 Poplar Grove, Sale ✦❀ (Gordon Cooke Esq) From the A6144 at Brooklands Station turn down Hope Rd. Poplar Grove 3rd on R. This recently enlarged town garden has been created by the owner who is a potter and landscape designer. It has a special collection of unusual plants in an artistic setting with many interesting design features and details. *Adm £1.50 Chd 75p (ACNO to North Manchester General Hospital®). Sat, Sun July 4, 5 (2-6)*

Poulton Hall, Poulton Lancelyn ❀ (The Lancelyn Green Family) 2m from Bebington. From M53, exit 4 towards Bebington; at traffic lights (½m) R along Poulton Rd; house 1m on R. 2½ acres; lawns, ha-ha, wild flower meadow, shrubbery, walled gardens with sculptures relating to the books of Roger Lancelyn Green. Cream TEAS. *Adm £2 Chd 20p. Suns April 19, July 5 (2-6)*

The Quinta Garden and Arboretum, Swettenham ᵭ♨ (Sir Bernard Lovell & The Cheshire Wildlife Trust) Turn E off A535 at Twemlow (Yellow Broom Café) and follow signs to Swettenham. 40-acre garden, arboretum and nature reserve with a collection of rare trees and shrubs leading to walks overlooking the Dane Valley and down to Swettenham Brook. A site of special interest (SSSI) and biological importance. TEA. *Adm £2 Acc chd free. Sun May 10, Wed June 3 (10-sunset)*

Reaseheath, Nantwich ᵭ♨❀ (Reaseheath College) 1½m N of Nantwich on the A51. The Gardens of 12 acres used as a teaching resource, are based on a Victorian Garden containing many mature trees of horticultural interest. There are glasshouses; model fruit, rose, woodland lakeside and bog gardens and extensive shrub borders and lawns. New garden centre now open to the public 7 days per week. TEA. *Adm £2. Weds May 20, 27, June 3, 10, 17, 24, July 1, 8, 15, 22, 29 (2-4.30). Parties welcome, please* **Tel 01270 625131; Fax 01270 625665 steved@reaseheath.ac.uk**

■ **Rode Hall, Scholar Green** ❀ (Sir Richard & Lady Baker Wilbraham) [National Grid reference SJ8157] 5m SW of Congleton between A34 and A50. Nesfield's terrace and rose garden with view over Humphrey Repton's landscape is a feature of Rode gardens, as is the Victorian wild garden with a grotto and the walk to the lake past the old Stew pond. Other attractions include a restored ice house and working walled kitchen garden. TEAS. *Adm £2 Chd £1 (ACNO to All Saints Odd Rode Parish Church®). Tues, Weds, Thurs & Bank Hols March 31 to Sept 24 (2-5). For NGS Sun May 10 (1.30-5)*

Rosewood ❀ (Mr & Mrs C E J Brabin) Puddington. 6m N of Chester turn L (W) off Chester to Hoylake A540 to Puddington. Telephone for precise directions. 1-acre garden incl small wood, pond with bogside species, rhododendron, magnolia and azalea species and hybrids; many unusual trees. Most of the new plantings are grown from seed by owner. TEAS by arrangement. *Adm £2 Chd free. Open by appt only to groups or individuals.* **Tel 0151 353 1193**

¶**St Davids House, Noctorum** (Ian Mitchell Esq) 3.2m S from Birkenhead Town Hall. From there A553 then A502 through Claughton village. After 2 sets of lights, 1st L (Noctorum Lane). After Xrds, St Davids Lane is 1st on R. Victorian garden of 1½ acres currently being restored. Azaleas, rhododendrons, herbaceous borders, rock garden and pool. *Adm £2 Chd 50p. Fri May 22 (5.30-8.30)*

¶**Sandymere, Cotebrook** ᵭ♨❀ (John & Alex Timpson) On A54 about 300yds W of traffic lights at Xrds of A49/A54. A large, beautifully landscaped garden with lakes, woodland walks, terraces, undulating lawns and mixed borders. TEAS. *Adm £2.50 OAPs £1.50 Chd free. Sun July 19 (2-5.30)*

¶**Snelson House, Snelson** ᵭ♨❀ (Mr & Mrs Malcolm Taylor) Pepper Street is nearly opp 'The Egertons Arms' public house on the A537 W of Chelford. Towards Knutsford. A 2-acre garden with pond, waterfall, laburnum walk, rhododendrons and azaleas. Spacious lawns bordered by interesting shrubs and herbaceous plants. Scree area, rarities: ginkgo, walnut tree, fig. TEAS in aid of Cancer Research. *Adm £2 Chd 50p. Sun May 24 (2-5.30)*

2 Stanley Road, Heaton Moor ♨❀ (Mr G Leatherbarrow) Approx 1½m N of Stockport. Follow Heaton Moor Rd off A6. Stanley Rd on L. 1st house on R. Tiny town garden with all year interest, packed with interesting plants, creating a secret cottage garden atmosphere. Old species and English roses, clematis, hardy geraniums, ivies, varied evergreens, daphnes, hellebores, delphiniums, mixed herbaceous; ponds. Max no. of visitors 2 — no room for more. Not suitable for less agile. TEA. *Adm £2 Chd 75p. Private visits welcome Feb to end Sept, please* **Tel 0161 442 3828 :http://www.maigold.demon.co.uk**

■**Stonyford Cottage, Cuddington** ᵭ♨❀ (Mr & Mrs Anthony Overland) 6m W of Northwich. Turn R off A556 (Northwich to Chester). At Xrds ¾m past A49 junction (signpost Norley-Kingsley). Entrance in ½m on L. The gardens feature a 'Monet' style pool with bridges to an island, woodland walk and damp garden. Listed in Good Gardens Guide and shown on BBC Gardeners World. Adjacent nursery, unusual plants for sale. TEAS in aid of Special Olympics (Cheshire) *Adm £2 Chd 50p. April to Sept, Wed, Sun and Bank Hols (12-5.30). For NGS Sun June 7 (1.30-5.30). Private visits and parties welcome, please* **Tel 01606 888128**

The Stray, Neston ᵭ♨❀ (Mr & Mrs Anthony Hannay) Approx 10m NW of Chester. ½m NW of Shrewsbury Arms (traffic lights). Turn off A540 into Upper Raby Rd. After ³⁄₁₀m turn R into unmade lane and The Stray is immediately on the L. 1½ acres of newly planted shrubs, herbaceous and mixed borders. Interesting colour schemes and unusual plants. Replanting commenced in 1991. A chance to see a new garden maturing. TEAS in aid of RNLI. *Adm £2 Chd 50p. Sun May 31 (2-5)*

▲**Tatton Park, Knutsford** ᵭ♨❀ (Cheshire County Council: The National Trust) Well sign-posted on M56 junction 7 and from M6 junction 19. 2½m N of Knutsford. Features include orangery by Wyatt, fernery by Paxton, Japanese, Italian and rose gardens. Greek monument and African hut. Hybrid azaleas and rhododendrons, swamp cypresses, tree ferns, tall redwoods, bamboos and pines. TEAS. *Adm £2.80 Group £2.30 Chd £1.80. For NGS Mon June 22 (10.30-5)*

Thornton Manor, Thornton Hough ❀ (The Viscount Leverhulme) Wirral. From Chester A540 to Fiveway Garage; turn R on to B5136 to Thornton Hough village. From

Birkenhead B5151 then on to B5136. From M53, exit 4 to Heswall; turn L after 1m. Bus: Woodside-Parkgate; alight Thornton Hough village. Large garden of yr-round interest. TEAS. *Free car park. Adm £2 OAPs £1 Chd 50p. Easter Bank Hol Mon April 13 (12-7)*

Tushingham Hall, Whitchurch (Mr & Mrs P Moore Dutton) 3m N of Whitchurch. Signed off A41 Chester-Whitchurch Rd; Medium-sized garden in beautiful surroundings; bluebell wood alongside pool; ancient oak, girth 26ft. TEAS. *Adm £2 Chd 50p (ACNO to St Chad's Church, Tushingham®). Sun May 10 (2-5.30)*

85 Warmingham Road, Coppenhall &❀ (Mr & Mrs A Mann) Approx 3m N of Crewe town centre on the road between Leighton Hospital and Warmingham Village. Close by White Lion Inn, Coppenhall. ⅓-acre plantsman's garden, with shrubs, perennial borders, raised beds, troughs, rock garden, peat garden, pond and greenhouse with cacti and succulents. Speciality alpines. TEAS. *Adm £2 Chd free. Suns April 19, June 14, (1-5). Private visits welcome March to Sept, please* **Tel 01270 582030**

¶**Warrington Gardens** *Combined adm £2 Chd 50p. Wed July 15 (11-6). Gardens 5 minutes walk from each other*

  ¶**68 Cranborne Avenue** &❀ (Mr & Mrs J Carter) From Stockton Heath N on A49 over swing bridge. L at 2nd set of lights into Gainsborough Road. 4th L into Cranbourne Ave. A small garden of elegant design approx 235 sq yds with apple trees, shrubs and perennials, pond, pergola and statuary

  62 Irwell Road & (Mr & Mrs D Griffiths) From Stockton Heath, N on A49 over swing bridge on to Wilderspool Causeway. L at 2nd set of lights into Gainsborough Rd. 2nd R into Irwell Rd. No 62 approx halfway down on R. Approx 1m from Warrington town centre. A small cottage garden approx 150 sq yds where colour and scent combine with sounds of trickling water and wind chimes to create a tranquil oasis in the midst of suburbia. As seen on TV's 'Surprise Gardeners'. TEAS

The Well House, Tilston & (Mrs S H French-Greenslade) nr Malpas. 12m S of Chester on A41, 1st turn R after Broxton roundabout, L on Malpas Rd through Tilston. House and antique shop on L. Field parking signed. 1-acre cottage garden, bridge over natural stream, many bulbs, herbs and shrubs. TEAS. *Adm £2 Chd 25p (ACNO to Cystic Fibrosis Trust®). Suns April 5, June 21 (2-5.30). Private visits by appt March-July, please* **Tel 01829 250332**

Willaston Grange, Willaston ⅄ (Sir Derek and Lady Bibby) A540 Chester to West Kirby until opposite the Elf Garage. Proceed down B5151 Hadlow Rd, towards Willaston. Borders, rock garden, vegetable garden, orchard, about 3 acres. Special feature - woodland walk. TEAS. *Adm £1.50 OAPs £1 Chd free. Sun April 26 (2-6)*

Willow Cottage, Prestbury & (Mrs Martin Tolson) Straight behind the Admiral Rodney Public House in Prestbury. An intensively planted small cottage garden of less than ¹⁄₁₀-acre. *Adm £2 Chd £1. Private visits (max of 10) welcome May to July (2.30-5), please* **Tel 01625 828697**

Wood End Cottage, Whitegate &❀ (Mr & Mrs M R Everett) Turn S off A556 (Northwich by-pass) at Sandiway P/O lights after 1.7m turn L to Whitegate village; opp. school follow Grange Lane for 300yds. ½-acre plantsman's garden sloping to a natural stream. Mature trees, many clematis, herbaceous, raised beds, shade and moisture loving plants. Large plant stall. TEAS. *Adm £2 Chd 50p (ACNO to David Lewis Centre for Epilepsy®). Sun July 12 (2-6); also by appt, please* **Tel 01606 888236**

¶**1 Woodpecker Drive, Northwich** &❀ (Mr & Mrs D Scott) Turn off A556 at A533 to Northwich. After 1st traffic lights, 1st R. Limited parking. ⅓-acre plantswoman's surburban garden with unusual and interesting plants. Heavily planted herbaceous borders incl shrubs. Good late colour. Selection of shrubby Lonicera. TEA. *Adm £1.50 Chd 50p (ACNO to British Diabetic Association®). Sun Sept 13 (1.30-5)*

¶**13 Yew Tree Cottages, Compstall** & (Mike & Sylvia Murphy) 6m E of Stockport, off B6104 between Marple and Romiley. Follow Etherow Country Park sign. Turn into village, take 2nd L after 'Anchor Arms' public house. Parking restricted but within walking distance of village car parks. ⅓-acre cottage garden set in an elevated position. Large collection of hardy perennials, roses, old and new, clematis penstemons, hardy geraniums, shrubs and more. TEA. *Adm £1.50 Chd 50p. Suns June 14, July 5 (11.30-5.30). Private visits also welcome mid May to August, please* **Tel 0161 427 7142**

Cornwall

Hon County Organiser:	G J Holborow Esq, Ladock House, Ladock, Truro TR2 4PL
	Tel 01726 882274
Assistant Hon County Organisers:	Mrs D Morison, Boskenna, St Martin, Manaccan, Helston TR12 6BS
	Tel 01326 231210
	Mrs Richard Jerram, Trehane, Trevanson, Wadebridge PL27 7HP
	Tel 01208 812523
	Mrs Michael Latham, Trebartha Lodge, North Hill, Launceston PL15 7PD
	Tel 01566 782373
	Mrs Michael Trinick, Newton House, Lanhydrock, Bodmin PL30 4AH
	Tel 01208 72543
	Mrs Mark Benson, Primrose Cottage, St Martin, Helston TR12 6BU
	Tel 01326 231112
Leaflets/Yellow Books:	Mr & Mrs Michael Cole, Nansawsan House, Ladock, Truro TR2 4PW
	Tel 01726 882392
Publicity:	Mrs Elizabeth Ann Waldron-Yeo, Pembre, Trelill Bodmin, PL30 3HZ
	Tel 01208 850793
Hon County Treasurer:	Mrs Cynthia Bassett, 5 Athelstan Park, Bodmin, PL31 1DS
	Tel 01208 73247

DATES OF OPENING

Regular openings

Bosvigo House, Truro
Carwinion, Mawnan Smith
Flambards Victorian Village Garden,
   Helston
Headland, Polruan
Heligan Gardens, Pentewan
The Japanese Garden and Bonsai
   Nursery, St Mawgan
Ken Caro, Bicton, nr Liskeard
Lanterns, nr Mylor
Paradise Park, Hayle
Pencarrow, Bodmin
Prideaux Place, Padstow
Probus Gardens, Truro
Trebah, Mawnan Smith
Tregrehan, Par
Trevarno Gardens, Helston
Trewithen, nr Truro

By appointment only

Carnowall, Black Rock, Praze
Chyverton, Zelah
Furzeball, Pont
Trevegean, Heamoor

March 15 Sunday
   Trengwainton, Penzance
March 22 Sunday
   Ince Castle Gardens, Saltash
April 5 Sunday
   Bodwannick, Nanstallon
   Penjerrick Garden, Budock
   Tremeer Gardens, St Tudy
April 11 Saturday
   Glendurgan, Mawnan Smith

April 12 Sunday
   Trelissick, Feock
April 13 Monday
   Moyclare, Liskeard
April 19 Sunday
   Ince Castle Gardens, Saltash
   St Michael's Mount, Marazion
April 26 Sunday
   Estray Parc, Penjerrick
   Lamorran House, St Mawes
   Polgwynne, Feock
May 1 Friday
   The Japanese Garden & Bonsai
      Nursery, St Mawgan
May 3 Sunday
   Estray Parc, Penjerrick
   High Noon, Ladock
   Ladock House, Ladock
   Pinetum. Harewood
   Tregrehan, Par
May 4 Monday
   Moyclare, Liskeard
May 7 Thursday
   Headland, Polruan
May 10 Sunday
   Boconnoc, Lostwithiel
   Bodwannick, Nanstallon
   Hallowarren, Carne
   Ince Castle Gardens, Saltash
   Wynlands, Manaccan
May 15 Friday
   Cotehele, Saltash
May 17 Sunday
   Bodellan Farmhouse, Porthcurno
   Lanhydrock, Bodmin
   Nansawsan House, Ladock
   Trenance, Launceston
May 21 Thursday
   Headland, Polruan

May 24 Sunday
   Carclew Gardens,
      Perran-ar-Worthal
May 25 Monday
   Moyclare, Liskeard
May 28 Thursday
   Headland, Polruan
May 31 Sunday
   Peterdale, Millbrook
   Pinetum. Harewood
   Roseland House, Chacewater
   Tregenna Castle, St Ives
June 7 Sunday
   Creed House, Creed
   Ince Castle Gardens, Saltash
   Newton House, Lanhydrock
June 14 Sunday
   Hallowarren, Carne
   The Hollies, Grampound, nr Truro
   Newton House, Lanhydrock
   Wynlands, Manaccan
June 21 Sunday
   Bodwannick, Nanstallon
   Long-Cross Victorian Garden,
      Trelights, St Endellion
   Scawn Mill, nr Liskeard
   Tregilliowe Farm, Ludgvan
June 24 Wednesday
   Antony, Torpoint
June 28 Sunday
   Roseland House, Chacewater
   Water Meadow, Luxulyan
July 5 Sunday
   Bodellan Farmhouse, Porthcurno
July 7 Tuesday
   The Japanese Garden & Bonsai
      Nursery, St Mawgan
July 12 Sunday
   Bonython, Helston

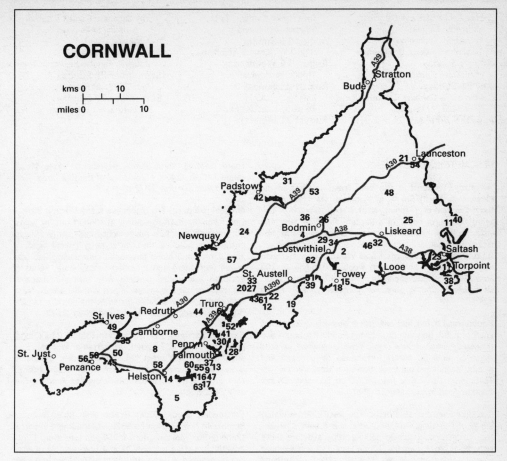

CORNWALL

kms 0   10

miles 0   10

KEY

1. Antony
2. Boconnoc
3. Bodellan Farmhouse
4. Bodwannick
5. Bonython
6. Bosvigo House
7. Carclew Gardens
8. Carnowall
9. Carwinion
10. Chyverton
11. Cotehele
12. Creed House
13. Estray Parc
14. Flambards Victorian Village
    Garden
15. Furzeball
16. Glendurgan
17. Hallowarren
18. Headland
19. Heligan Gardens
20. High Noon
21. Higher Truscott

22. The Hollies
23. Ince Castle Gardens
24. The Japanese Garden &
    Bonsai Nursery
25. Ken Caro
26. Kingberry
27. Ladock House
28. Lamorran House
29. Lanhydrock
30. Lanterns
31. Long-Cross Victorian
    Garden
32. Moyclare
33. Nansawsan House
34. Newton House
35. Paradise Park
36. Pencarrow
37. Penjerrick Garden
38. Peterdale
39. Pine Lodge Gardens
40. Pinetum
41. Polgwynne

42. Prideaux Place
43. Probus Gardens
44. Roseland House
45. St Michael's Mount
46. Scawn Mill
47. Trebah
48. Trebartha
49. Tregenna Castle
50. Tregilliowe Farm
51. Tregrehan
52. Trelissick
53. Tremeer Gardens
54. Trenance
55. Trenarth
56. Trengwainton
57. Trerice
58. Trevarno Gardens
59. Trevegean
60. Treviades Gardens
61. Trewithen
62. Water Meadow
63. Wynlands

Ince Castle Gardens, Saltash
Kingberry, Bodmin
Trenance, Launceston
Treviades Gardens, Constantine
July 19 Sunday
Tregilliowe Farm, Ludgvan
July 26 Sunday
Pine Lodge Gardens, Cuddra
Scawn Mill, nr Liskeard
August 9 Sunday

Ince Castle Gardens, Saltash
Pinetum, Harewood
August 16 Sunday
Higher Truscott, St Stephens
August 19 Wednesday
Trerice, nr Newquay
August 23 Sunday
Kingberry, Bodmin
Trenarth, Constantine
August 31 Monday

The Japanese Garden & Bonsai
Nursery, St Mawgan
Moyclare, Liskeard
September 6 Sunday
Bodellan Farmhouse, Porthcurno
September 20 Sunday
Paradise Park, Hayle
September 27 Sunday
Trebartha, nr Launceston

DESCRIPTIONS OF GARDENS

▲**Antony, Torpoint** ⚹ (National Trust: Trustees of the Carew Pole Trust) 5m W of Plymouth via Torpoint car ferry; 2m NW of Torpoint, N of A374; 16m SE of Liskeard; 15m E of Looe. In a Repton landscape with fine vistas to the R Lynher. Features a formal courtyard, terraces, ornamental Japanese pond and knot garden. **Antony Woodland Garden and Woods:** an established woodland garden and natural woods extending to 100 acres. TEAS. *Woodland garden adm £2.50. Combined Gardens adm £3 Chd ½ price. For NGS Wed June 24 (1.30-5.30)*

Boconnoc, Lostwithiel ⟠⚹ (Mr & Mrs J D G Fortescue) 2m S of A390. On main rd between middle Taphouse and Downend garage, follow signs. Privately owned gardens covering some 20 acres, surrounded by parkland and woods. Magnificent old trees, flowering shrubs and views. TEAS. *Adm £1.50 Chd free (ACNO to Boconnoc Church Window Fund®). Sun May 10 (2-6)*

Bodellan Farmhouse, Porthcurno ⚹ (Richard B Webb) 9m W of Penzance. On L at 30mph speed limit signs before Porthcurno. Roadside parking 100yds before these signs or at beach Carpark (10min walk). ⅔-acre exposed coastal garden on 5 levels. Rock shrubbery, ornamental ponds, sunken garden, views. Garden linked with legends of C6 Saint. Try dousing the earth energies. Teas in Porthcurno. *Adm £2 Chd free (ACNO to Tibet House Trust® July 5, Sept 6). Suns May 17, July 5, Sept 6 (2-5.30) Private visits welcome, please* **Tel 01736 810225**

Bodwannick, Nanstallon (P M & W M Appleton) 2½m W Bodmin. Turn at Bodmin Trailer Centre (A30) signposted Nanstallon, L at Xrds signposted Hoopers Bridge then sharp R. Approx 1-acre compact garden incl water garden, herbaceous, granite Cornish cross, roses, shade garden and shrubs. Over 50 varieties of daffodils and narcissus. Cream TEAS. *Adm £1.50 Chd free (ACNO to F.L.E.E.T.). Suns April 5, May 10, June 21 (2-6). Private visits welcome, please* **Tel 01208 831427**

Bonython, Helston ⟠ (Mr Robert & The Hon Mrs Lyle) Cury Cross Lanes. 5m S of Helston. From A3083 Helston-Lizard Rd L at Wheel Inn. Entrance 300yds on R. Bonython family recorded from 1277. Nothing remains of the mediaeval house, present fabric impressive example C18 granite construction (house not open). 10 acres surrounding gardens with walled garden, incl newly planted herb and vegetable garden, herbaceous borders, new or-chard planting, shrub roses, developing water garden round 2 lakes. Cream TEAS in aid of the Red Cross. *Adm £2 Chd free. Sun July 12 (2-6)*

● **Bosvigo House, Truro** ⚹⚘ (Mr & Mrs M Perry) Bosvigo Lane. ¾m from Truro centre. At Highertown, nr Sainsbury roundabout, turn down Dobbs Lane. After 500yds, entrance to house is on L, after nasty L-hand bend. 3-acre garden still being developed surrounding Georgian house (not open) and Victorian conservatory. Series of enclosed and walled gardens with mainly herbaceous plants for colour and foliage effect. Woodland walk. Many rare plants. Partly suitable for wheelchairs. *Adm £2 Chd 50p. Open Weds to Sats March to end Sept (11-6)*

Carclew Gardens, Perran-an-Worthal ⚹ (Mrs Chope) nr Truro. From A39 turn E at Perran-ar-Worthal. Bus: alight Perran-ar-Worthal 1m. Large garden, rhododendron species; terraces; ornamental water. TEAS. *Adm £2 Chd 50p (ACNO to Barristers Benevolent Fund®). Sun May 24 (2-5.30)*

Carnowall, Black Rock, Praze ⚹⚘ (Rod & Penny Smith) 5m N of Helston on B3297, take turning at Farms Common to T-junction, turn L 150 yds turn sharp L into private lane. (Map ref: 665 341). A fine example of what can be grown well at an altitude of 500′. 1½-acre garden created from fields by present owners and still developing. Enclosed gardens interconnected by sunken gravel paths, raised beds, colourful herbaceous borders, trees, shrubs and much use of local stone. Original water-colours for sale. Cream TEAS. *Adm £2. Private visits welcome mid May to mid Aug except Sats, please* **Tel 01209 831757**

● **Carwinion, Mawnan Smith** ⚘ (Mr H A E Rogers) via Carwinion Rd. An unmanicured or permissive valley garden of some 10 acres with many camellias, rhododendrons and azaleas flowering in the spring. Apart from an abundance of wild flowers, grasses, ferns etc, the garden holds the premier collection of temperate bamboos in the UK. TEAS April to Oct (2-5.30). *Adm £2 Chd free. Open daily throughout the year (10-5.30). Private visits welcome, please* **Tel 01326 250258**

Chyverton, Zelah (Mr N T Holman) N of Truro. Entrance ¾m SW of Zelah on A30. Georgian landscaped garden with lake and bridge (1770); large shrub garden of great beauty; outstanding collection magnolias, acers, camellias, rhododendrons, primulas, rare and exotic trees and shrubs. Visitors personally conducted by owner. *Adm*

£3.50 (parties over 20 persons by arrangement Adm £3) Chd under 16 free. Private visits welcome for parties under 5 weekdays March to June by appt, please write or **Tel 01872 540324**

▲Cotehele, Saltash ♿✂❀ (The National Trust) 2m E of St Dominick, 4m from Gunnislake (turn at St Ann's Chapel); 8m SW of Tavistock; 14m from Plymouth via Tamar Bridge. Terrace garden falling to sheltered valley with ponds, stream and unusual shrubs. Fine medieval house (one of the least altered in the country); armour, tapestries, furniture. Dogs in wood only and on lead. Lunches and TEAS. *Adm garden, grounds & mill £2.80 Chd half price. For NGS Fri May 15 (11-5)*

▲Creed House, Creed ❀ (Mr & Mrs W R Croggon) From the centre of Grampound on A390. Take rd signposted to Creed. After 1m turn L opp Creed Church and the garden is on L. Parking in lane. 5-acre landscaped Georgian Rectory garden. Tree collection; rhododendrons; sunken alpine and formal walled herbaceous gardens. Trickle stream to ponds and bog. Natural woodland walk. Restoration began 1974 – continues and incl recent planting. TEAS. *Adm £2 Chd free. For NGS Sun June 7 (2-5.30).* **Tel 01872 530372**

Estray Parc, Penjerrick (Mr & Mrs J M Williams) Leave Penjerrick main entrance on R follow the rd towards Mawnan Smith until entrance to The Home Hotel on L. Directly opp turn R and follow the signs. In 1983 most of this 3-acre garden was a bramble thistle-infested field. A considerable variety of plants have been introduced and continuous grass cutting has produced passable sloping lawns interspersed by a large collection of trees and shrubs. *Adm £1.50 OAPs £1 Chd over 13 50p (ACNO to Pediatric Appeal®). Suns April 26, May 3 (2-6)*

● Flambards Victorian Village Garden, Helston ♿✂❀ From A394 follow official brown and white signs to Flambards, located on A3083. A well designed and maintained 20-acre site providing an excellent family day out. Interesting sections by very colourful award winning bedding displays and hanging baskets. Mature trees, named shrubs of varied and striking foliage. Many exciting activities. Recreation of a Victorian village and several exhibitions illustrating wartime Britain, Cornwall at war and the history of Aviation. Wheelchairs available. Cafeteria. *Open most days Easter to end Oct (10.30-5). Please* **Tel 24hr info 01326 564093**

Furzeball, Pont ♿✂ (Phyllis & Eric Milner Kay) 1½m Fowey-Bodinnick Ferry. [Nat. Grid Ref: SX145527]. No access for coaches. 1-acre sheltered cottage garden. Outstanding views over countryside. Garden designed to exploit natural features: summer annuals and perennials, rhododendrons and azaleas, springs, small water garden, gunnera, ferns etc. Lawns, fruit trees, vegetables, also wild flower sanctuary. All areas connected by footpath/steps made from local stone. Visitors conducted by owners. *Adm £2.50. May 20 to June 28, (11-5) closed Mons and Tues. Preferably by appt, please* **Tel 01726 870600**

> **The National Gardens Scheme** is a registered charity (No 279284). Its aim is to raise money for selected beneficiaries by opening gardens of quality and interest to the public.

▲Glendurgan, Mawnan Smith ✂❀ (The National Trust), take rd to Helford Passage, 5m SW of Falmouth. Follow NT signposts. Walled garden, laurel maze, giants stride, valley with specimen trees, bluebells and primulas running down to Durgan fishing village on R Helford. Large car park. Lunches and TEAS. *Adm £3.20 Chd half price. For NGS Sat April 11 (10.30-5.30)*

Hallowarren, Carne ✂ (Mr & Mrs Mark Osman) 1m out of the centre of Manaccan village. Down hill past Inn on R, follow signpost to Carne. House on R. Parking nearby or signposted. Approx 1½ acres set in a beautiful wooded valley bordering a gentle stream. Happy mixture of wilderness and cultivation, cottage garden with old roses, lilies and kitchen herbs, unusual shrubs and trees. TEAS in Manaccan Village Hall in aid of St Anthony Church. *Combined adm with* **Wynlands** *£2 Chd free. Suns May 10, June 14 (2-5.30)*

■ Headland, Polruan ✂ (Jean & John Hill) Battery Lane. Passenger ferry from Fowey and 10min walk up the hill. Or follow signs to Polruan (on East of Fowey Estuary) ignore first car park, turn L for second car park (overlooking harbour) turn L (on foot) down St Saviour's Hill. 1¼-acre cliff garden with sea on 3 sides; mainly plants which withstand salty gales but incl sub-tropical. Cove for swimming. Cream TEAS. *Adm £1.50 Chd £1. Open every Thurs May 6 to 13 Aug. For NGS Thurs May 7, 21, 28 (2-6)*

●Heligan Gardens, Pentewan ♿❀ (Mr Tim Smit) From St Austell take B3273 signposted Mevagissey, follow signs. Heligan Gardens is the scene of the largest garden restoration project undertaken since the war. Of special interest in this romantic Victorian garden are; the fern ravine, 4 walled gardens with peach houses, vineries, melon grounds, a splendid collection of Bee boles, crystal grotto, Italian garden with a pool, an Elizabethan beacon 'Mount' and a large tropical Japanese valley garden. All are connected by an intricate web of over 2½m of ornamental footpaths, most unseen for more than half a century. TEAS and light refreshments. *Adm £4.50 OAPs £4 Chd £2. Open every day (10-6). Groups welcome,* **Tel 01726 844157**

High Noon, Ladock ♿ (R E Sturdy) 7m E of Truro on A39. 3½ acres ornamental trees, rhododendrons, camellias, and magnolias, 15yrs old; rose garden; daffodils; lawns; formal pool; S-facing slope with good views. *Combined adm with* **Ladock House** *£2 Chd free. Sun May 3 (2-5.30)*

Higher Truscott, St Stephens ♿✂❀ (Mr & Mrs J C Mann) 3m NW of Launceston between St Stephens and Egloskerry. Signposted. Yr-round elevated garden of 1 acre in a natural setting. Trees, shrubs, climbers, herbaceous plants and alpines (many unusual). Splendid views. Ornamental vegetable garden. TEAS. *Adm £1.50 Chd free. Sun Aug 16 (2-6)*

The Hollies, Grampound, nr Truro 占必恭 (Mr J & Mrs N B Croggon) In centre of village on Truro-St Austell rd. 2-acre garden of unusual design; unusual mixed planting of trees, shrubs and alpines. TEAS. *Adm £1 Chd free. Sun June 14 (2.30-5). Coach and private parties welcome by appt.* Tel 01726 882474

Ince Castle Gardens, Saltash 占 (Viscount & Patricia, Viscountess Boyd of Merton) 3m SW of Saltash. From A38 at Stoketon Cross take turn signed Trematon, then Elmgate. 5 acre garden, woodlands, borders, orchard, bulbs and shell house. TEAS. *Adm £2 Chd free. Suns March 22 (ACNO to Primrose Appeal), April 19 (ACNO Cornwall Historic Churches®), May 10 (ACNO Cornwall Garden Soc®), June 7 (ACNO St Johns®), July 12 (ACNO Children's Hospice SW®), Aug 9 (St Stephens, Saltash®) (2-5)*

¶■The Japanese Garden and Bonsai Nursery, St Mawgan 占必恭 (Robert and Stella Hore). 6m E of Newquay, 1.5m from North coast. 'Japanese Garden'. Rd signs from A3059 and B3276. Authentic Japanese Garden set in 1 acre: water garden, stroll garden, zen garden, bamboo grove. Japanese Maples, azaleas, rhododendrons and ornamental grasses in abundance etc. Bonsai nursery - adjacent to garden - entrance free. *Adm £2.50 Chd £1 Group rate for ten or more £2 (ACNO to St Mawgan School 7 July) (ACNO to St Mawgan Church 31 Aug). Open 7 days a week (not 25-27 Dec and 1 Jan). For NGS Fri May 1, Tues July 7, Mon Aug 31 (10-6 Last entry to garden 5)*

●Ken Caro, Bicton, nr Liskeard 必恭 (Mr & Mrs K R Willcock) Pensilva 5m NE of Liskeard. From A390 to Callington turn off N at Butchers Arms, St Ive; take Pensilva Rd; at next Xrds take rd signed Bicton. 2 acres mostly planted in 1970, with a further 2-acre extension in 1993; well-designed and labelled plantsman's garden; rhododendrons, flowering shrubs, conifers and other trees; herbaceous. Panoramic views. Collection of aviary birds. Featured in NGS video 2. *Adm £2 Chd 50p. April 12 to June 30 every Sun, Mon, Tues, Wed; Tues & Weds only July & Aug (2-6).* Tel 01579 362446

Kingberry, Bodmin 恭 (Dr & Mrs M S Stead) N-side of town, 100yds uphill from East Cornwall Hospital. Ltd parking on hill, otherwise car parks in town centre. Approx 1-acre garden. Herbaceous borders, formal lawns, gravel terrace, ornamental pond, original stone walls, orchard and conservatory, some interesting perennials. A surprising haven in centre of Bodmin. TEAS. *Adm £1.50 Chd free. Suns July 12, Aug 23 (2-6)*

Ladock House, Ladock 占 (Mr G J & Lady Mary Holborow) 7m E of Truro on A39. Car park and entrance by church. Georgian old rectory with 4 acres of lawns, rhododendrons, camellias and azaleas with woodland garden. All planted during last 20yrs. TEAS in aid of Ladock Church. *Combined adm with* **High Noon** *£2 Chd free (ACNO to Ladock Church®). Sun May 3 (2-5.30)*

Lamorran House, St Mawes 必恭 (Mr & Mrs Dudley-Cooke) Upper Castle Rd. First turning R after garage; signposted to St Mawes Castle. House ½m on L. Parking in rd. 4-acre sub-tropical hillside garden with beautiful views to St Anthonys Head. Extensive water gardens in Mediterranean and Japanese settings. Large collection of rhododendrons, azaleas, palm trees, cycads, agaves and many S hemisphere plants and trees. *Adm £2.50 Chd free. Open Weds and Fri April through Sept. For NGS Sun April 26 (10-5).* Tel 01326 270800

▲Lanhydrock, Bodmin 占必恭 (The National Trust) 2½m on B3268. Station: Bodmin Parkway 1¾m. Large-sized garden; formal garden laid out 1857; shrub garden with good specimens of rhododendrons and magnolias and fine views. Lunches and TEAS. House closed Mondays. *Adm garden only £3.10 Chd half price. For NGS Sun May 17 (11-5.30; last adm to house 5)*

●Lanterns, Mylor 恭 (Mrs I Chapman) 1m NE of Mylor. From Mylor follow the Restronguet Passage/Pandora Inn rd signs, Lanterns is on the RH-side before reaching the waterfront. ½-acre mature garden in natural setting planted by owners. Wide variety of shrubs, bulbs, herbaceous perennials, climbers, conservatory/greenhouse plants. Interesting in any season; small streams and dry areas; waterside walks. Owner always pleased to advise on plants and planting. *Collecting box (ACNO to Children's Hospice SW®). Open every day throughout the year (11am-dusk)*

▲Long Cross Victorian Gardens, Trelights, St Endellion 占恭 (Mr & Mrs Crawford) 7m N of Wadebridge on B3314. Charm of this garden is mazelike effect due to protecting hedges against sea winds; views of countryside and sea scapes (Port Isaac and Port Quin Bays) Garden specially designed to cope with environment of Cornwall's N Coast. Lunches and cream TEAS, coffee, evening meal. *Adm £1.25 Chd 25p. For NGS Sun June 21 (10.30-6.30). Private visits welcome for parties of 25 and over, please* Tel 01208 880243

¶Moyclare, Liskeard 占必 (Major & Mrs Henslowe) Lodge Hill. ½m from Liskeard centre on St Keyne Duloe road (B3254) 200yds past station on L. This garden was started in 1927, extended to one acre in 1936, and planted with many rare specimen trees and shrubs. *Adm £2 Chd free. Mons April 13, May 4, 25, Aug 31 (2-6)*

Nansawsan House, Ladock 占必恭 (Mr & Mrs Michael Cole) 7m E of Truro on B3275(A39). Parking at Falmouth Arms or Parish Hall. 1½ acres, part of a once larger Victorian garden. Rhododendrons, camellias, shrubs, trees and borders. CREAM TEAS in aid of Ladock Church. *Adm £1.50 Chd free. Sun May 17 (2-5). Also by appt* 01726 882392

Newton House, Lanhydrock 占必 (Mrs Michael Trinick) 3½m SE of Bodmin on W bank of R. Fowey nr Respryn Bridge. Follow signs to Lanhydrock and Respryn. Surrounded by woods in the beautiful valley of the R. Fowey. 3 acres of old-fashioned walled garden, lawns, shrubs, herbaceous border and old shrub roses, fruit, vegetables and orchard. TEAS. *Adm £2 Chd free (ACNO to Lanhydrock Church®). Suns June 7, 14 (2-6)*

■ **Paradise Park, Hayle** ᏪᏪᏪ (Mr Michael Reynolds) Follow the A30 to Hayle, go to St Ives/St Erth roundabout then follow official brown and white signs to Paradise Park. The 2-acre walled garden is part of the 14 acres opened in 1973 as 'The rare and endangered birds breeding centre'. Much effort has been expended to make the gardens a suitable setting for a bird breeding collection of international importance. The World Parrot Trust is based here. Walled garden with pergolas, trellis and gazebos; climbing roses, clematis, lilies and passiflora are featured. TEAS. *Open throughout the yr from 10am to 5pm.* Cafe in Park. *Adm £5.50 Chd £3.50 (ACNO to World Parrot Trust®). For NGS Sun Sept 20 (10-5)*

●**Pencarrow, Bodmin** ᏪᏪ (Molesworth-St Aubyn Family) 4 miles N.W. Bodmin, signed off the A389. 50 acres of formal and woodland gardens laid out in the 1840's by Sir William Molesworth Bt. Marked walks past the Victorian Rockery, Italian and American Gardens, Lake and Ice House. Over 650 different varieties of rhododendrons, also an Internationally known specimen conifer collection. *House, Tearooms and Craft Centre open Sun to Thurs. 1.30-5 Easter Sun to Oct 15. Adm garden only £2 Chd free. Gardens open daily from 1 April*

▲**Penjerrick Garden, Budock** ᏪᏪ (Rachel Morin) 3m SW of Falmouth between Budock/Mawnan Smith, opp. Penmorvah Manor Hotel. Parking along drive verge. Coaches outside gate. 15-acre subtropical garden, home to important rhododendron hybirds Penjerrick/Barclayi. The upper garden with sea view contains rhododendrons, camellias, magnolias, bamboos, tree ferns and magnificent trees. Across a bridge a luxuriant valley features ponds in a wild primeval setting. *Adm £1.50 Chd 50p (ACNO to RUKBA). For NGS Sun April 5 (11.30-4.30). Tours* Tel 01872 870105

Peterdale, Millbrook ᏪᏪ (Mrs Ann Mountfield) St John's Rd. From Skinners Garage follow rd to mini roundabout and turn L. Straight ahead up St John's Rd Peterdale sign next to gate on wall. Last house on L. A plantsperson's garden featured on TV and Practical Garden, also Gardener's World magazine won Best Family Garden 1995. *Adm £2 Chd free. Sun May 31 (2-6). Groups of 20 or less by written application* Tel 01752 823364

Pine Lodge Gardens, Cuddra ᏪᏪᏪ (Mr & Mrs R H J Clemo) On A390 E of St Austell between Holmbush and Tregrehan. Follow signs. 30-acre estate comprises gardens within a garden. The wide range of some 5,500 plants all of which are labelled, have been thoughtfully laid out using original designs and colour combinations to provide maximum interest for the garden lover. In addition to rhododendrons, magnolias, camellias, herbaceous borders with many rare and tender plants, marsh gardens, tranquil fish ponds, lake within the park, pinetum. TEAS. *Adm £3 Chd £1.50. Sun July 26 (1-5). Also open for groups of 20 or more by appt all year* Tel 01726 73500

Pinetum, Harewood ᏪᏪᏪ (Mr & Mrs G R Craw) Calstock 6m SW of Tavistock. From A390 Tavistock-Callington Rd proceed towards Calstock. After 1m follow sign to Calstock Parish Church. At church continue straight on.

3rd house on R. Walkways meander through 2-acre pinetum full of maturing, uncommon, specimen trees of botanical and ornamental intrigue interspersed with shrubs, plants and garden features for yr-round colour and interest. TEAS. *Adm £1.50 Chd free. Suns May 3, 31; Aug 9 (2-5.30)*

Polgwynne, Feock ᏪᏪ (Mrs P Davey) 5m S of Truro via A39 (Truro-Falmouth rd) and then B3289 to 1st Xrds: straight on ½m short of Feock village. 3½-acre garden and grounds. Fruit and vegetable garden, woodlands extending to shore of Carrick Roads; magnificent Ginkgo Biloba (female, 12' girth) probably the largest female ginkgo in Britain; other beautiful trees; many rare and unusual shrubs. Lovely setting and view of Carrick Roads. TEAS. *Adm £2 Chd free. Sun April 26 (2-5).* **Tel 01872 862612**

●**Prideaux Place, Padstow** Ᏺ (Mr & Mrs Prideaux-Brune) On the edge of Padstow follow brown signs for Prideaux Place, from ring rd (A389). Surrounding Elizabethan house the present main grounds were laid out in the early C18 by Edmund Prideaux. Ancient deer park with stunning views over Camel estuary; Victorian woodland walks currently under restoration. Restored sunken formal garden. A garden of vistas. Cream TEAS. *Adm £2 Chd £1. Easter Sunday to mid-Oct (1.30-5); Bank Hols (11-5)*

Probus Gardens, Truro ᏪᏪᏪ (Cornwall County Council) On E side of Probus village at the Trewithen roundabout. Clearly signed. 7½-acre garden started from a green field site in the early 1970's, to serve the needs of the local community as a centre for horticulture. Explains many aspects of gardening with displays of annuals, herbaceous perennials, shrubs, trees, conifers and hedges. Annually, different trials are grown. A place to get ideas. TEAS. *Adm £2.80 Chd free. Daily April 1 to Oct 4 Mons to Fris Oct 5 to 18 Dec; 1999 Jan 4 to April 7 (10-4)*

Roseland House, Chacewater Ᏺ (Charlie & Liz Pridham) 4m W of Truro, at Truro end of main st. Parking in village car park (100yds) or surrounding rds. 1-acre garden subdivided by walls and trellises hosting a wide range of climbers. Mixed borders of unusual plants, Victorian conservatory and greenhouse extend the gardening yr. TEAS. *Adm £1.50 Chd free. Tues June, July (1-6). Suns May 31, June 28 (2-5).* **Tel 01872 560451**

▲**St Michael's Mount, Marazion** ᏪᏪ (The Rt Hon Lord St Levan; The National Trust) ½m from shore at Marazion by Causeway; otherwise by ferry. Flowering shrubs; rock plants, castle walls; fine sea views. TEAS. *Adm Castle & gardens £3.90, Chd £1.95 (under 16). For NGS Sun April 19 (10.30-5.30) last entrance 4.45*

Scawn Mill, nr Liskeard ᏪᏪ (Mrs A Ball & Dr Julian Ball) From the A38 at the E end of Dobwalls take the signpost to Duloe, Herodsfoot and Looe for 1½ m. Turn R at sign for Scawn and continue for 1m down to the river. Water lily lake lying beside the West Looe River terraced with azaleas, black pines and Japanese maples. Walks beside primulas, herbaceous border and Japanese garden. ½m walk through newly planted woodland with spectacular wild flowers. Public footpath following West Looe River to Herodsfoot. TEAS. *Adm £1.50 Chd free. Suns June 21, July 26 (2-5.30)*

●**Trebah, Mawnan Smith** ❀ (Trebah Garden Trust) 4m from Falmouth. Follow tourism signs from Hillhead Roundabout on A39 approach to Falmouth. Parking (free)/access for coaches. 25-acre S facing ravine garden, planted in 1820's. Extensive collection rare/mature trees/shrubs incl glades huge tree ferns 100 yrs old and sub-tropical exotics. Hydrangea collection covers 2½ acres. Water garden, waterfalls, rock pool stocked with mature Koi Carp. Magical garden for plantsman/artist /family. Play area/trails for children. Use private beach. Coffee Shop. *Adm £3.20 OAPs £3 Chd and disabled £1. Special group and winter prices. RHS members free. Open every day throughout year (10.30-5 last admission).* **Tel 01326 250448**

Trebartha, nr Launceston (The Latham Family) North Hill, SW of Launceston. Nr junction of B3254 & B3257. Wooded area with lake surrounded by walks of flowering shrubs; woodland trail through fine woods with cascades and waterfalls; American glade with fine trees. No coaches. TEAS. *Adm £1.50 Chd 50p. Sun Sept 27 (2-5.30)*

¶**Tregenna Castle, St Ives** &❀ Leave A30 West Hayle, A3074 to St Ives. After Carbis Bay entrance signs to Tregenna Castle L-hand side. Magnificent setting overlooking St Ives Bay. A garden mix within 72 acre estate incl a re-discovered woodland garden and a newly created sub-tropical walled garden. Cream TEAS. *Adm £1.50 Chd 50p (ACNO to RNLI®). Sun May 31 (10-dusk)*

Tregilliowe Farm, Ludgvan &❀ (Mr & Mrs J Richards) Penzance-Hayle A30 Rd from Penzance turn R at Crowlas Xrds. After approx 1m turn sharp L on to St Erth Rd. 2nd farm lane on R. 2-acre garden still developing. Herbaceous beds with wide range of perennials and new grasses bed. Raised Mediterranean bed. TEAS June in aid of St Julia's Hospice. July in aid of Save the Children. *Adm £1.50 Chd free. Suns June 21, July 19 (2-6).* **Tel 01736 740654**

■**Tregrehan, Par** &❀❀ (Mr T Hudson) Entrance on A390 opp Britannia Inn 1m W of St Blazey. Access for cars and coaches. Garden largely created since early C19. Woodland of 20 acres containing fine trees, award winning camellias raised by late owner and many interesting plants from warm temperate climes. Show greenhouses a feature containing softer species. TEA. *Adm £2.50 Chd free. Mid March to mid June daily. Not open Easter Sunday. For NGS Sun May 3 (10.30-5)*

▲**Trelissick, Feock** &❀❀ (The National Trust; Mr & Mrs Spencer Copeland) 4m S of Truro, nr King Harry Ferry. On B3289. Planted with tender shrubs; magnolias, camellias and rhododendrons with many named species characteristic of Cornish gardens. Fine woodlands encircle the gardens through which a varied circular walk can be enjoyed. Superb view over Falmouth harbour. Georgian house (not open). Lunches and TEAS. *Adm £4 Chd half price. Car park £1.50 refundable. For NGS Sun April 12 (12.30-5.30)*

Tremeer Gardens St Tudy, 8m N of Bodmin; W of B3266, all rds signed. 7-acre garden famous for camellias and rhododendrons with water; many rare shrubs. *Adm £1 Chd 50p. Sun April 5 (2-5).* **Tel 01208 850313**

Trenance, Launceston &❀ (Mr & Mrs J Dingle) Follow signs for Leisure Centre along Dunheved Rd. At College end of rd take sharp L bend and immed after this take another L turning into Windmill Hill. Trenance is approx 200yds on L. A 2-acre garden for all seasons. A wide variety of trees and shrubs incl rhododendrons, camellias, azaleas, acers and magnolias; heathers and conifers, ballard hellebores, 60 varieties hardy geraniums, primulas, herbaceous borders, roses and clematis with several smaller gardens within the main garden. TEA. *Adm £1.50 Chd 50p. Suns May 17, July 12 (2-5.30)*

Trenarth, Constantine ❀ (Mrs L M Nottingham) High Cross. Nearest main rds A39, A394 Truro, Falmouth, Helston. 1½m E of Constantine, 2m W of Mawnan Smith, 1½m S of Treverva. Nearest landmark High Cross Garage. From Treverva with garage on L take lane to L, then immed R down dead-end lane. Trenarth is ½m at end of lane. Diverse 2-acre gardens round old farmhouse. Courtyard, conservatory, C18 garden walls, yew hedging, herbaceous and rockery beds, shrub borders, new croquet lawn, orchard and woodland walk to Helford River. Extensively replanted during past 4 yrs, with further wilderness areas awaiting reclamation. TEAS. *Adm £1.50 Chd free. Sun Aug 23 (2-5)*

▲**Trengwainton, Penzance** &❀❀ (The National Trust) 2m N W of Penzance, ½ mile West of Heamoor on Penzance-Morvah rd (B3312), ½m off St Just rd (A3071) The garden of mainland Britain perhaps most favoured for the cultivation of exotic shrubs and trees. Plantsman's delight. *Adm £3 Chd half price. For NGS Sun March 15 (10.30-5.30)*

▲**Trerice, nr Newquay** &❀❀ (The National Trust) Newlyn East 3m SE of Newquay. From Newquay via A392 and A3058; turn R at Kestle Mill (NT signposts). The summer-flowering garden is unusual in content and layout and there is an orchard planted with old varieties of fruit trees. A small museum traces the history of the lawn mower. Lunches & TEAS. Children's Garden Trail. *Adm house & garden £4. For NGS Wed Aug 19 (11-5.30)*

●**Trevarno Gardens, Helston** &❀ (Mr M Sagin & Mr N Helsby) Sithney Helston. Signed from Crowntown on the B3303, 3m NW of Helston. Set within beautiful and historic Trevarno Estate dating back to 1296, one of Cornwall's most romantic and secret woodland gardens covering 40 acres. Extensive collection of rare shrubs, specimen trees, walled gardens, mysterious rockeries, grotto, enchanting lake, cascade and fountains and abundant wildlife; now subject of major restoration and replanting programme. TEAS. *Adm £3 OAPs £2.50 Chd under 14 £1.25, under 5 free. Open daily (10.30-5) Jan 1 to Dec 24. Evening functions, by arrangement* **Tel 01326 574274**

Trevegean, Heamoor ❀ (Mr & Mrs E C Cousins) 9 Manor Way. Take Penzance by-pass; take first L off roundabout towards Treneere and Heamoor. Sharp R turn for Manor way. ⅓-acre divided into series of enclosed areas; planting some formal, informal, topiary garden, shrubs and perennials; connected by brick and slab paths some edged with box. TEAS. *Adm £1 Chd free (ACNO to St Julias®). By appt only April to end of June*

Treviades Gardens, Constantine &⚘ Off the Falmouth to Constantine R at High Cross - 1m on the Falmouth side of Constantine and N of Port Navas. At High Cross, turn to Port Nevas. The gardens are on the L going down hill. Travelling from the Truro area follow the A39. Use the Penryn by-pass. At Hillhead Roundabout, follow the signs to Constantine. Cream TEAS. *Combined adm £2 Chd free (ACNO to Cornwall Children's Hospital Appeal®). Sun July 12 (2-5.30)*
    Treviades Barton (Mr & Mrs M J Ford) Series of walled gardens, each one with own character (i.e. roses in one); vegetable garden and small arboretum
    Treviades Wollas (Mrs P M Watson) S facing medium-sized garden in two parts - leading down to small water garden fed by two springs

●**Trewithen, Truro** &⚘ (Mr A M J Galsworthy) ½m E Probus. Entrance on A390 Truro-St Austell Rd. Signposted. Large car park. Internationally renowned garden of 30 acres laid out by Maj G Johnstone between 1912 & 1960 with much of original seed and plant material collected by Ward and Forrest. Famed for towering magnolias and rhododendrons; wide range of own hybrids.

Flatish ground amidst original woodland park. TEAS. *Adm £2.80 Chd £1.50 Group £2.50. Mon to Sat March 1 to Sept 30, Suns April-May only (10-4.30). Special arrangements for coaches.* **Tel 01726 883647**

Water Meadow, Luxulyan ✗ (Philip & Rose Lamb) 5m NW of St Austell, 6m S of Bodmin. [Map ref SX 052582.] Park in village street between church and school. Turn by church, garden 200yds downhill on L. 1½-acre garden on sloping site with Grade II listed grotto. Large pond with streamside and waterside planting and bog garden with extensive primula, astilbe, gunnera, arum lilies etc. Gravel garden surrounded by roses & herbaceous planting. Specimen trees and shrubs with mixed borders. Cream TEAS in aid of WI. *Adm £1.50 Chd free. Sun June 28 (2-5) also by appt please* **Tel 01726 851399**

Wynlands, Manaccan ✗⚘ (Mr & Mrs Henry Towner) W of Manaccan take Manaccan rd from Newtown St Martin. Approx 1¼m Wynlands on L. Lay-by in front. Parking in field opp farm and in lay-by. [OS ref: SW 753243]. ½-acre garden designed for maximum wind protection and yr-round interest, by owner in the last 10 yrs. Wide variety of trees, shrubs and bulbs. Old fashioned, climbing, and new English roses, delphiniums and herbaceous perennials. Japanese corner, conservatory, greenhouse, vegetable and fruit garden. Small orchard. *Combined adm with* **Hallowarren** *£2 Chd free. Suns May 10, June 14 (2-5.30)*

Help the Hospices

Help the Hospices is a charity which supports the hospice movement throughout the country. The National Gardens Scheme is delighted to include it in its list of beneficiaries. Some facts:

- **Help the Hospices** is the only national charity helping all providers of hospice and palliative care for the terminally ill.

- **Help the Hospices'** priority is to support all measures to improve patient care for all life-threatening conditions.

- **Help the Hospices** receives no government funding.

- **Help the Hospices** principally supports the voluntary hospices as they receive relatively little government funding.

- **Help the Hospices** support is mainly in direct response to applications from voluntary hospices, usually for training.

- **Help the Hospices** funds training for the NHS and nursing home staff in patient care for the terminally ill as well as funding its own initiatives in training, research, hospice management and team leadership.

- **Help the Hospices** pays special attention to training in communication skills for staff and volunteers.

Cumbria

Hon County Organiser: (South)	Mrs R E Tongue, Paddock Barn, Winster, Windermere LA23 3NW
Assistant Hon County Organiser: (North West)	Mrs E C Hicks, Scarthwaite, Grange-in-Borrowdale, Keswick CA12 5UQ
Assistant Hon County Organiser: (North East)	Mrs Lavinia Howard, Deer Park Lodge, Johnby, Penrith CA11 0UU
Hon County Treasurer:	Derek Farman Esq, Mill House, Winster, Windermere LA23 3NW

DATES OF OPENING

Regular openings
For details see garden description

Brockhole, Windermere
Holker Hall & Gdns, Cark-in-Cartmel
Hutton-in-the-Forest, Penrith
Levens Hall, Kendal
Marton House, Long Morton, nr
    Appleby
Mirehouse, Keswick
Winderwath, nr Penrith

By appointment only
*For telephone numbers and other
details see garden descriptions.
Private visits welcomed*

Langholme Mill, Woodgate, Lowick
    Green, nr Carlisle
The Mill House, Sebergham
Scarthwaite, Grange-in-Borrowdale
Wood Hall, Cockermouth

April 19 Sunday
    Levens Brow, Kendal
April 20 Monday
    Levens Hall, Kendal
April 26 Sunday
    Marton House, Long Marton
May 2 Saturday
    Copt Howe, Chapel Stile
May 3 Sunday
    Copt Howe, Chapel Stile
    Dallam Tower, Milnthorpe
    The Nook, Helton, nr Penrith
    Rydal Mount, Eskdale Green, nr
        Gosforth
    Stagshaw, Ambleside
May 4 Monday
    Copt Howe, Chapel Stile
May 6 Wednesday
    Rydal Mount, Eskdale Green, nr
        Gosforth
May 9 Saturday
    Acorn Bank, Temple Sowerby, nr
        Penrith
May 10 Sunday
    Winderwath, nr Penrith
May 13 Wednesday
    Browfoot, Skelwith

St Annes, Great Langdale
May 14 Thursday
    Browfoot, Skelwith
    St Annes, Great Langdale
May 17 Sunday
    Matson Ground, Windermere
May 23 Saturday
    Copt Howe, Chapel Stile
May 24 Sunday
    Copt Howe, Chapel Stile
    Fell Yeat, Kirkby Lonsdale
    Galesyke, Wasdale
    Halecat, Witherslack
    High Beckside Farm, Cartmel
May 25 Monday
    Copt Howe, Chapel Stile
    Galesyke, Wasdale
May 27 Wednesday
    Brackenburn, Manesty
    Browfoot, Skelwith
    High Rigg,
        Grange-in-Borrowdale
    St Annes, Great Langdale
    Windy Hall, Windermere
May 28 Thursday
    Browfoot, Skelwith
    St Annes, Great Langdale
May 30 Saturday
    Mirehouse, Keswick
May 31 Sunday
    Blakeholme Wray, Newby
        Bridge
    Browfoot, Skelwith
    40 Fairfield Lane, Barrow in
        Furness
    Hazelmount, Thwaites
    Lindeth Fell Country House,
        Bowness-on-Windermere
    Palace How, Brackenthwaite,
        Loweswater
June 7 Sunday
    Stagshaw, Ambleside
    Station House, Lamplugh
June 10 Wednesday
    Brockhole, Windermere
June 13 Saturday
    Acorn Bank, Temple Sowerby, nr
        Penrith
    Bush Green Cottage, Broughton
        in Furness
    Tomarobandy, Bitterlees

June 14 Sunday
    Bush Green Cottage, Broughton
        in Furness
    40 Fairfield Lane, Barrow in
        Furness
    Fell Yeat, Kirkby Lonsdale
    Greystones, Embleton
    Tomarobandy, Bitterlees
June 17 Wednesday
    Fell Yeat, Kirkby Lonsdale
    Holker Hall Gardens,
        Cark-in-Cartmel
June 20 Saturday
    Rannerdale Cottage,
        Buttermere
June 21 Sunday
    Dallam Tower, Milnthorpe
    Hutton-in-the-Forest, Penrith
    Marton House, Long Marton
    Rannerdale Cottage,
        Buttermere
June 27 Saturday
    Sizergh Castle, Kendal
June 28 Sunday
    The Brown House, Maryport
July 5 Sunday
    Askham Hall, Penrith
    Charney Well, Grange over
        Sands
    Matson Ground, Windermere
    Yew, Bowness-on-Windermere
July 8 Wednesday
    Brockhole, Windermere
July 11 Saturday
    Acorn Bank, Temple Sowerby, nr
        Penrith
    Bush Green Cottage, Broughton
        in Furness
July 12 Sunday
    Beckfoot Mill, Duddon Bridge,
        Broughton in Furness
    The Brown House, Maryport
    Bush Green Cottage, Broughton
        in Furness
    High Cleabarrow, Windermere
July 19 Sunday
    Dallam Tower, Milnthorpe
    Halecat, Witherslack
    Hutton-in-the-Forest, Penrith
July 26 Sunday
    38 English Street, Longtown

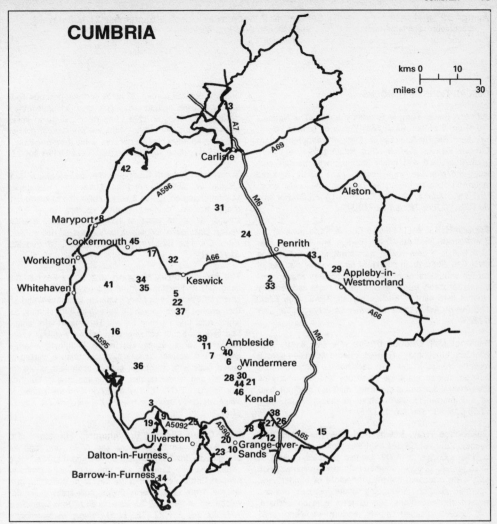

CUMBRIA

kms 0   10
miles 0   30

KEY

1. Acorn Bank
2. Askham Hall
3. Beckfoot Mill
4. Blakeholme Wray
5. Brackenburn
6. Brockhole
7. Browfoot
8. The Brown House
9. Bush Green Cottage
10. Charney Well
11. Copt Howe
12. Dallam Tower
13. 38 English Street
14. 40 Fairfield Lane
15. Fell Yeat
16. Galesyke

17. Greystones
18. Halecat
19. Hazelmount
20. High Beckside Farm
21. High Cleabarrow
22. High Rigg
23. Holker Hall & Gdns
24. Hutton-the-Forest
25. Langholme Mill
26. Levens Brow
27. Levens Hall
28. Lindeth Fell Country House
29. Marton House
30. Matson Ground
31. The Mill House
32. Mirehouse

33. The Nook
34. Palace How
35. Rannerdale Cottage
36. Rydal Mount
37. Scarthwaite
38. Sizergh Castle
39. St Annes
40. Stagshaw
41. Station House
42. Tomarobandy
43. Winderwath
44. Windy Hall
45. Wood Hall
46. Yews

August 30 Sunday
Rydal Mount, Eskdale Green, nr Gosforth

September 2 Wednesday
Rydal Mount, Eskdale Green, nr Gosforth

September 21 Monday
Levens Hall, Kendal

DESCRIPTIONS OF GARDENS

▲**Acorn Bank, Temple Sowerby** ♿✿❦ (The National Trust) 6m E of Penrith on A66; ½m N of Temple Sowerby. Bus: Penrith-Appleby or Carlisle-Darlington; alight Culgaith Rd end. Medium-sized walled garden; fine herb garden; orchard and mixed borders; wild garden with woodland/riverside walk leading to a partly restored watermill open to the public. Dogs on leads only woodland walk. *Adm £2.20 Chd £1.10 Family £5.80. For NGS Sats May 9, June 13, July 11 (10-5)*

Askham Hall ✿❦ (The Earl & Countess of Lonsdale) 5m S of Penrith. Turn off A6 for Lowther and Askham. Askham Hall is a pele tower, incorporating C14, C16 and early C18 elements in courtyard plan. Formal outlines of garden with terraces of herbaceous borders and original topiary, probably from late C17. Shrub roses and recently created herb garden. Kitchen garden. TEAS. *Adm £1.50 Chd free (ACNO Askham & Lowther Churches®). Sun July 5 (2-5)*

Beckfoot Mill, Duddon Bridge ✿❦ (Mr & Mrs J M Atkinson) Broughton in Furness. ⅔-acre woodland garden recently created in dell with beck flowing through into R Duddon. Choice plantings of shrubs and perennials on steep banks. Surrounds converted mill; use made of disued mill machinery. Paths steep in places. TEAS. *Adm £1.50 Chd 50p. Sun July 12 (2-5)*

Blakeholme Wray, Newby Bridge ✿ (Mr & Mrs W T Rooney) [Grid Ref GR 384 895] Blakeholme Wray is 2m N of Newby Bridge on A592. Limited disabled parking. 4 acres garden, 22 acres woodland. An outstanding position with lawns sweeping down to the shore of Windermere. Informal planting is ongoing under present owners: massed rhododendrons and azaleas, damson orchard, wild orchids, bluebell carpets, ancient woodland walk, abundant wildlife. Partially suitable for wheelchairs. TEA. *Adm £2 Chd free. Sun May 31 (12-5)*

Brackenburn, Manesty (Prof & Mrs D C Ellwood) Take rd signed Portinscale and Grange off A66. Follow all signs for Grange. Garden is 1½ acres on the mountainside on RH-side of rd 3½m from A66. The Garden has wonderful views of Lake Derwentwater. There are several water features planted for damp acid conditions with many rhododendrons, azaleas, ferns and primulas. Brackenburn is the former home of author Sir Hugh Walpole. *Adm £1.50 Acc chd free (ACNO to Scottish terrier emergency care scheme®). Wed May 27 (11-5)*

■**Brockhole, Windermere** ♿ (Lake District National Park) 2m NW of Windermere on A591 between Windermere and Ambleside. 10 acres formal gardens, designed by Thomas Mawson. Acid soils and mild aspect, many unusual or slightly tender plants, shrub roses, herbaceous borders, scented garden. 20 acres informal grounds, wide variety of trees and shrubs. Picnic area, adventure playground, boat trips on Lake Windermere. Dogs on leads. Restaurant and tea rooms. *Adm free (Multi-tariff parking available, season ticket for car park. Daily April 6 to Nov 1; for NGS Wed June 10, July 8 (10-5).* **Tel 015394 46601**

Browfoot, Skelwith Bridge ❦ (Trevor Woodburn) Ambleside on A593 2½m from Ambleside. Re-vamped woodland garden approx 2 acres; collection of rhododendrons, azaleas, conifers, natural rockery, many other shrubs; delightful views of Loughrigg and the Brathay Valley. Unsuitable for wheelchairs, dogs on leads. *Adm £1.50 Chd free. Wed, Thurs May 13, 14; 27, 28; Sun May 31 (11-5)*

The Brown House, Maryport ✿❦ (Celia Eddy & Tim Longville) At junction of A596 and A594, at main Maryport traffic lights by St Mary's Church, turn into Wood St, then immed R into Church St. Take 3rd L into Fleming St, which runs into Fleming Sq and Fleming Pl with ample free parking. Small walled garden behind Victorian townhouse on Solway coast. Enthusiasts imagining a larger garden and warmer climate have crammed a warren of raised beds with a cottage garden profusion of old favourites and tender rarities. Garden featured in Cumbria Life Sep/Oct 1997. TEAS. *Adm £1.50 Chd free (ACNO to West Cumbria Hospice at Home®). Suns June 28, July 12 (1-5)*

Bush Green Cottage, Broughton-in-Furness ♿✿❦ (Mr & Mrs James Haunch) On A595 on edge of Broughton. ½m from Foxfield on RH-side. Approx 1-acre cottage garden. Streams and pool. Originally Crossing Keepers Cottage on Furness Railway; large collection geraniums. Wide variety hardy plants; new areas under development. *Adm £1.50 Acc chd under 12 free. Sats, Suns June 13, 14; July 11, 12 (11-5). Private visits welcome from June onwards, please* **Tel after 8pm (except Mons) 01229 716 724**

¶**Charney Well, Grange over Sands** ✿ (Christopher Holliday & Richard Roberts) Follow Cartmel signs at Crown Hill roundabout in centre Grange. Turn R at Midland Bank then 1st L, garden 100yds on L. Public Car Park, Hampsfell Rd. S facing ½-acre steep hillside site specializing in exotic species and yr-round foliage interest re-planted over last 10yrs. Incl a garden walled on three sides where tender and sub-tender species flourish. Almost a hundred phormiums, many shrubs, climbers etc. of interest to plantsman. Magnificent views over Morecambe Bay. TEAS. *Adm £2 Chd free. Sun July 5 (10.30-4)*

Copt Howe ❦ (Professor R N Haszeldine) Chapel Stile. Great Langdale. 2-acre plantsman's garden. Views Langdale Pikes. Extensive collections of acers (especially Japanese), camellias, azaleas, rhododendrons, quercus, fagus, rare shrubs, trees, unusual perennials; herbaceous and bulbous species; alpines, trough gardens; rare dwarf and large conifers; Expedition plants from Far East. Featured by the media, gardening magazines. Cream TEAS May 3, 24. *Adm £2 OAP £1.50 Chd free. Sat, Sun, Mon May 2, 3, 4; 23, 24, 25 (11-5). Also by appt, please* Tel **015394 37685**

Dallam Tower, Milnthorpe & (Brigadier & Mrs C E Tryon-Wilson) 7m S of Kendal. 7m N of Carnforth, nr junction of A6 and B5282. Station: Arnside, 4m; Lancaster, 15m. Medium-sized garden; natural rock garden, waterfalls, rambler roses and rose beds; wood walks, lawns, shrubs. C19 cast iron orangery. Dogs on leads. *Adm £1 Chd free. Suns May 3, June 21, July 19 (2-5)*

38 English Street, Longtown &❀ (Mr & Mrs C Thomson) Carlisle. M6 junction 44, A7 for 6m into Longtown. 300yds on L next door to Annes Hairdressers. Entrance through open archway. Terraced house garden. Red sandstone and water features; containers and troughs, pergola and herbaceous. TEA. *Adm £1.50 Acc chd free (ACNO to Cat Protection League®). Sun July 26 (2-5). Private visits and parties welcome, please* Tel **01228 791364**

¶**40 Fairfield Lane, Barrow-in-Furness** &❀ (Mr & Mrs Malcolm Needham) Approach Barrow on A590 and turn L at sign to Furness General Hospital. Turn R at mini roundabout, L at first lights, and then R opp public house. House L at top of the hill. ½-acre garden with good mixture of unusual shrubs, perennials and alpines. Collection of cacti and succulents in greenhouse, small pond and fruit/vegetable garden. *Adm £1.50 Chd under 12 free (ACNO to St Mary's Hospice®). Suns May 31, June 14 (1-5). Also open by appt, please* Tel **01229 834859**

Fell Yeat, Casterton, nr Kirkby Lonsdale &❀ (Mr & Mrs O S Benson) Approx 1m E of Casterton Village on the rd to Bull Pot. Leave A65 at Devils Bridge, follow A683 for a mile, take the R fork to High Casterton at the golf course, straight across at two sets of Xrds, the house is immediately on the L about ¼m from no through rd sign. 1-acre informal country garden with mixed borders, herbaceous, old roses, small fernery, herb garden and small pond and is building up the National Collection of Ligularias. TEAS Suns only, Tea Wed only in aid of Holy Trinity Church, Casterton. *Adm £1.50 Chd 20p. Suns, Wed May 24, June 14, 17 (1.30-5)*

Galesyke, Wasdale &❀ (Christine & Mike Mckinley) From the N enter Gosforth and follow signposts to Nether Wasdale. Pass through Nether Wasdale, following signs to the Lake and Wasdale Head. After approx ¾m, entrance on R. From the S head towards Santon Bridge turn off A595 at Holmbrook or approach from Eskdale. Turn R at Santon Bridge following signs to Wasdale Head. Approx 3m to entrance. Secluded landscaped riverside garden of approx 1½ acres containing a variety of mature trees and flowering shrubs. Riverside meadow and secluded woodlands walks. TEAS. *Adm £1.50 Chd under 12 free. Sun, Mon May 24, 25 (11.30-5)* Tel **019467 26267**

Greystones, Embleton &❀ (Mr D Cook). Just off A66, 4m E of Cockermouth, 2m W of Bassenthwaite Lake. Take turning marked 'Wythop Mill' with watermill sign. Lane 200yds on R. 1-acre of mostly new garden being developed on various levels around mature trees, with shrubs, herbaceous beds and borders, woodland garden, ponds, scree, spring bulbs. Organic fruit and vegetable beds. Teas at Wythop Mill ½m. *Adm £1 Chd free. Sun June 14 (2-5) Private visits welcome (mid/late April usually good), please* Tel **017687 76375**

▲**Halecat, Witherslack** &❀❀ (Mrs Michael Stanley) 10m SW of Kendal. From A590 turn into Witherslack following the Halecat brown signs. L in township at another brown sign and L again, signpost 'Cartmel Fell'; gates on L [map ref. 434834]. Medium-sized garden; mixed shrub and herbaceous borders, terrace, sunken garden; gazebo; daffodils and cherries in Spring, over 70 different varieties of hydrangea; beautiful view over Kent estuary to Arnside. Nursery garden attached. TEA. *Adm £1.50 Chd free. For NGS Suns May 24, July 19 (2-5). Also private parties welcome, please* Tel **015395 52229**

Hazelmount, Thwaites, Millom &❀❀ (Mrs J Barratt) 2m from Broughton-in-Furness off A595 up hill after crossing Duddon River Bridge. 5-acre woodland garden, small lake with stream and water garden; spring display of species rhododendrons, azaleas and flowering shrubs. Mature trees and exceptional views of Duddon Estuary and sea. Cream TEAS. Dogs on lead. *Adm £1.50 Chd free. Sun May 31 (2-5.30)*

High Beckside Farm, Cartmel &❀ (Mr & Mrs P J McCabe) 1¼m N of Cartmel. Take the Haverthwaite Rd, R at the village shop in the square. A newly created conservation area, a wild garden with ponds, waterfalls, waterfowl; flowering bushes and a number of rare trees. An arboretum in the very early stages of formation. 11 acres of wild flowers on a hillside with fine views. A small house garden and scree garden. Approx ¼m from house

---

Scotland's Gardens Scheme

The National Gardens Scheme has a similar but quite separate counterpart in Scotland. Called Scotland's Gardens Scheme, it raises money for the Queen's Nursing Institute (Scotland), the Gardens Fund of the National Trust for Scotland and over 160 registered charities nominated by Garden Owners. The Handbook is available (£3.75 incl p&p) from Scotland's Gardens Scheme, 31 Castle Terrace, Edinburgh, EH1 2EL.

to conservation area. Stout shoes. TEA. *Adm £1.50 Chd 25p. Sun May 24 (1-5). Private visits welcome, please* Tel **015395 36528**

High Cleabarrow &✗❀ (Mr & Mrs R T Brown) 3m SE of Windermere off B5284 Crook to Kendal Rd (nr Windermere Golf Course). 2-acre garden owner designed and planted comprising mixed borders, island beds, formal rose garden, old-fashioned roses, pond with waterside planting, many unusual plants. Large collection of geraniums, hostas and hydrangeas. Woodland area under development. TEAS. *Adm £1.50 Chd 50p. Sun July 12 (1.30-5.30)*

High Rigg, Grange-in-Borrowdale (Miss B Newton) From Keswick take B5289 to Grange; cross rd bridge, suitable for mini-buses. House ½m on L. ¾-acre fellside garden with mixed shrub/herbaceous border, rock and bog gardens. Rhododendrons, azaleas and many other shrubs and trees. *Adm £1.50 Acc chd free. Wed May 27 (11-5)*

■ **Holker Hall, Cark-in-Cartmel** &✗❀ (Lord & Lady Cavendish) 4m W of Grange-over-Sands. 12m W of M6 (junction 36). Magnificent formal and woodland gardens world-class. Exotic trees, shrubs, ancient oaks, beech walk with a stunning display of rhododendrons, azaleas, magnolias and camellias. Summer garden, rose garden elliptical garden. A limestone cascade. National Collection of styracaceae. Wildflower meadow. Largest slate sundial in world. Deer park, adventure playground, gift shop cafe. Holker Garden Festival May 29, 30, 31. *Adm £3.15 gardens only. Garden tours arranged. Open Sun-Fri April 1 to Oct 30 (10-6) last admission 4.30pm. For NGS Adm £2.50 Chd £1.75. Wed June 17 (6.30-9)*

■ **Hutton-in-the-Forest, Penrith** (Lord Inglewood) 5m NW of Penrith. 3m from exit 41 of M6. Magnificent grounds with C18 walled flower garden, terraces and lake. C19 Low garden, specimen trees and topiary; woodland walk and dovecote. Mediaeval House with C17, C18 and C19 additions. TEAS. *Adm £2 gardens, grounds, £3.50 house, gardens & grounds Chd free gardens, grounds £1.50 house & garden & grounds. Gardens and grounds open daily all year except Sats (11-5). House open (1-4). Tearoom (12-4.30). Easter Fri, Sun, Mon; then Thurs, Fris, Suns and Bank Hols May 1 to Oct 4. For NGS Suns June 21, July 19 (11-5)*

Langholme Mill, Woodgate, Lowick Green ✗ (Dr W E Gill) On the A5092 Greenodd to Workington rd 3m from Greenodd on a short stretch of dual carriageway. Park in front of the house. Approx ¾-acre of woodland garden with a beck running the length of it. Camellias, dwarf rhododendrons smaller rhododendrons, yak species and hybrids Japanese azaleas and azaleas; acers, bamboos, hostas, astilbes and waterside plants. *Adm £1.50 Chd under 12 free. Private visits welcome please write or* Tel **01229 885215**

Levens Brow, Kendal ✗ (Mr & Mrs O R Bagot) 5m S of Kendal on A6. Junction 36 on M6. 1½-acre garden, mixed borders. Trees and shrubs bordered on 2 sides by Levens Park. Delightful spring garden, extensive plantings narcissus, fritillary, anemone and blossom trees. Large collection hellebores orientalis hybrids. Local limestone walling and rockeries of character. *Adm £1.50 Chd 50p (ACNO to NSPCC®). Sun April 19 (11.30-5)*

■ **Levens Hall, Kendal** &✗❀ (C H Bagot Esq) 5m S of Kendal on A6; exit 36 from M6. 10 acres incl topiary garden and 1st ha-ha laid out by M Beaumont in 1694. Magnificent beech circle; formal bedding; herbaceous borders. Superb panelling, plasterwork in Elizabethan mansion, added to C13 pele tower. Steam collection. Wheelchairs garden, shop and tea room only. *Adm House & Garden £5.20 Chd £2.80 Garden only £3.80 Chd £2.10. Reduction for groups April 1 to Oct 15. Gift shop, tearoom, children's play and picnic areas. Sun, Mon, Tues, Wed, Thurs house (12-4.30) grounds (10.30-5), Steam collection (2-5). Closed Fri & Sat. For NGS Mons April 20, Sept 21 (10.30-5)*

Lindeth Fell Country House Hotel, Bowness-on-Windermere & (Air Commodore & Mrs P A Kennedy) 1m S of Bowness on A5074. 6-acres of lawns and landscaped grounds on the hills above Lake Windermere, probably designed by Mawson around 1907; conifers and specimen trees best in spring and early summer with a colourful display of rhododendrons, azaleas and Japanese maples; grounds offer splendid views to Coniston mountains. Top terrace suitable for wheelchairs. TEAS in hotel £1. *Adm £1.50 Chd free. Sun May 31 (1-5). Also private parties welcome, please* Tel **01539 443 286**

■ **Marton House, Long Marton** ✗ (Mr & Mrs M S Hardy-Bishop) Turn off A66 2m W of Appleby signposted Long Marton. Follow rd through village under bridge. Car park on R after house. A 6½-acre walled garden. Magnificent Cedar of Lebanon, woodland walk, rose garden. Italian garden leading to small lake, ducks, glorious pennine views. Cream TEAS in aid of Eden Animal Rescue & Friends of Long Marton School. *Adm £2 Chd 50p. Open daily April to Oct (10-5). For NGS Suns April 26, June 21 (1-5)*

Matson Ground, Windermere &❀ (Matson Ground Trust) From Kendal turn R off B5284 signposted Heathwaite, 100yds after Windermere Golf Club. Garden is on L after ½m. From Bowness turn L onto B5284 from A5074. After ¾m turn L at Xrds. Garden on L ¾m along lane. Stream flows through ornamental garden to large pond in the wild garden of spring bulbs, later wild flowers. Azaleas, rhododendrons, large mixed shrub/herbaceous borders, topiary work. New white garden, spring/summer border, camomile lawn on terrace. ½-acre walled organic kitchen garden, greenhouses and dovecote. 2-acre woodland. Dogs on leads. TEAS. *Adm £1.50 Chd 50p. Suns May 17, July 5 (1-5)*

Evening Opening (see also garden descriptions)

Holker Hall, Cartmel   June 17 6.30–9 pm

Regular openings. Open throughout the year. They are listed at the beginning of the Diary Section.

The Mill House, Sebergham ✿❀ (Mr & Mrs R L Jefferson) Take junction 41 off M6 A5305 Penrith to Wigton Rd into Sebergham turning to L into an easily missed lane just before bridge over river Caldew. 200 yds up lane, after bungalow take L fork in drive. Available parking. 2-acre garden set in secluded valley around the water mill; features millstream and pond, a large herbaceous border and a gravel garden; fruit and vegetable garden. Wildflower meadow walks to river (new this year). *Adm £1.50 Chd free. Open May to July 14. Private visits welcome by appt, please* **Tel 01697 476472**

¶■ **Mirehouse, Keswick** ♿❀ (James Spedding) 3½m N of Keswick on A591 signed at A66 roundabout outside Keswick. The oldest elements are the avenue of Scots Pine planted in 1786 and the walled garden. In the early C19 the area between the house and Bassenthwaite Lake was landscaped. The terracing and colonnade behind the house are Victorian. Garden being gradually restored. New and interesting varieties of flowering shrubs are regularly added to the fine collection. The walled garden has been replanted with bee plants. Teas available in neighbouring tea room. *Adm £1.50 Chd 80p (ACNO to The Calvert Trust®). April-Oct daily (10.5.30). For NGS Sat May 30 (10-5.30)*

The Nook, Helton ♿❀ (Mr & Mrs P Freedman) Penrith N 5m from B5320, take signs to Askham-Haweswater. Turn R into Helton. ½-acre terraced rock garden, beds and tubs, alpines, ornamental pool, goldfish, bog plants, fruit and herb garden; magnificent views over R Lowther and parkland. Homemade provisions and cakes for sale. TEAS. *Adm £1.50 Chd free. Sun May 3 (11-4)*

Palace How, Brackenthwaite ♿✿❀ (Mr & Mrs A & K Johnson) Loweswater, 6m SE of Cockermouth on B5292 and B5289 or from Keswick 10m over Whinlatter Pass, through Lorton village, follow signs for Loweswater. Established damp garden set in lovely situation amongst mountains. Unusual trees and shrubs, especially rhododendrons and acers. Pond with bog plants; candelabra primulas; Himalayan poppies, roses and alpines. Cream teas at Loweswater Village Hall in aid of NSPCC. *Adm £2 Chd free. Sun May 31 (11-5). Private visits and parties welcome, please* **Tel 01900 85648**

Rannerdale Cottage, Buttermere ❀ (The McElney Family) 8m S of Cockermouth, 10m W of Keswick. ½-acre cottage garden with beck and woodland walk overlooking Crummock Water, splendid mountain views. Herbaceous, shrubs, roses, perennial geraniums, tree peonies, pond with fish. TEAS. *Adm £1.50 Chd free. Sat, Sun June 20, 21 (11-5)*

Rydal Mount, Holmrook ❀ (Don & Toni Richards) Eskdale Green, nr Gosforth. Turn off A595 where signed 6m to Eskdale Green. Turn sharp R opp Eskdale Stores. 2nd house on R. 1½-acre garden on natural rock facing SW. Heathers and tree heaths with shrubs and small trees favouring acid soil; eucalyptus and American blueberrys; water garden. Blueberry TEAS. *Adm £1 Chd free (ACNO to West Cumbria Hospice at Home®). Suns, Weds May 3, 6; Aug 30, Sept 2 (2-5). Also private visits welcome, please* **Tel 019467 23267**

St Annes, Great Langdale ❀ (Mr & Mrs R D Furness) 5m from Ambleside on B5343. Follow signs for Langdale/Old Dungeon Ghyll. At Skelwith Bridge take R hand fork and at Elterwater take R hand. Through Chapel Stile, ¾m on L hand side travelling W. 3-acre partial woodland with established variety of conifers and trees, azaleas and rhododendrons. Establishing wild flower area. Natural rock faces with alpines, streams and rocky paths. Magnificent views Langdales. Partially suitable for wheelchairs. TEAS. *Adm £1.50 Chd free. Wed, Thurs May 13, 14; 27, 28 (11-4.30). Open for groups by appt, please* **Tel 015394 37271**

Scarthwaite, Grange-in-Borrowdale ✿ (Mr & Mrs E C Hicks) From Keswick take B5289 to Grange; cross on road bridge, suitable for mini buses, house ¼m on L. ¼m walk from far side of bridge for coach parties. Ferns, cottage garden plants and many others closely packed into ⅓ acre. *Adm £1.50 Acc chd free. Open Easter until end August by appt. Private visits and parties welcome, please* **Tel 017687 77233**

▲**Sizergh Castle, nr Kendal** ♿✿❀ (The National Trust) Close to and W of the main A6 trunk road, 3m S of Kendal. Approach road leaves A6 close to and S of A6/A591 interchange. ⅔-acre Limestone Rock Garden largest owned by the National Trust; collection of Japanese maples, dwarf conifers, hardy ferns, primulas, gentians, perennials and bulbs; water garden, aquatic plants; on castle walls shrubs and climbers, many half-hardy; south garden with specimen roses, lilies, shrubs and ground cover. Wild flower areas, herbaceous border, crab apple orchard with spring bulbs, 'Dutch' garden. *Castle & gdn adm £3.30 Chd £1.70; Gdn adm £2 Chd £1. For NGS Sat June 27 (12.30-5.30)*

▲**Stagshaw, nr Ambleside** (The National Trust) ½m S of Ambleside. Turn E off A 591, Ambleside to Windermere rd. Bus 555 Kendal-Keswick alight Waterhead. Woodland gdn incl fine collection of rhododendrons and azaleas. Ericaceous trees & shrubs incl magnolias, camellias, embothriums. Views over Windermere. *Adm £1.30 Chd 60p. For NGS Suns May 3, June 7 (10-5.30)*

Station House, Lamplugh ♿❀ (Mr & Mrs G H Simons) Wright Green. Lamplugh approx 6m from Workington, Whitehaven and Cockermouth signposted off A5086 Lilyhall-Workington from Cockermouth-Egremont Rd ½m under disused railway line. From Workington-Whitehaven A595 at Leyland roundabout take rd signposted Branthwaite-Loweswater. 2-acre garden created over site of disused railway line and station. Features shrubs and trees; vegetable and fruit garden. Morning coffee/TEAS. *Adm £1 Chd 50p. Sun June 7 (10.30-4.30)*

Tomarobandy, Blitterlees ✿❀ (Mr & Mrs Tom Wrathall) nr Silloth. On Silloth-Maryport Rd, B5300, centre of village on W side of rd. (Parking behind Tom Wrathall's service station). 1½-acre coastal garden, compartmented by windbreaks to form a series of twelve themed gardens. Wide variety of plants for yr-round interest. Teas at Rosebarn Restaurant in village. *Adm £2 Acc chd free. Sat, Sun June 13, 14 (10-4)*

■ **Winderwath, nr Penrith** ✗❀ (Miss Jane Pollock) 5m E of Penrith N of A66. Mature garden laid out at end of C19 with interesting trees and borders. Recently established rock garden; many specialist alpines. Surplus plants and secondhand garden tools for sale. Picnic area. TEA. *Adm £2 Acc chd free. 1 March to 31 Oct Mon-Fri (10-4). For NGS Sun May 10 (1-5)*

Windy Hall, Windermere ✗ (Diane & David Kinsman) Crook Road. 8m from Kendal on B5284 up Linthwaite Country House Hotel driveway. 3 to 4-acre garden maintained by owners and developed from wilderness in 16 yrs. Woodland, herbaceous, alpine, and kitchen gardens. Wide variety of plants, especially rhododendrons, camellias, magnolias, sorbus, hydrangeas and many climbers. NCCPG collections of Aconitum, Aruncus and Filipendula. Waterfowl gardens and rarebreed sheep. TEAS. *Adm £1.50 Chd 25p. Wed May 27 (10-6). Private visits and parties by appt, please* **Tel 015394 46238**

Wood Hall, Cockermouth ❀ (Mr & Mrs W Jackson) Entrance to drive in large lay-by ¼m N (towards Carlisle) off the A595/A594 roundabout nr Cockermouth. A 5½-acre Thomas Mawson garden, with terraces, walls, small feature gardens, lawns, woods and paths. Venerable trees and newer planting. Alpines, shrubs and herbaceous plants. Partially suitable for wheelchairs. *Adm £1.50 and Acc chd free. Private visits and parties welcome, please* **Tel 01900 823585**

Yews, Bowness-on-Windermere ✗❀ (Sir Oliver & Lady Scott) Middle Entrance Drive, 50yds. Medium-sized formal Edwardian garden; fine trees, ha-ha, herbaceous borders; greenhouses. Bog area being developed, Bamboo, Primula, Hosta. TEAS. *Adm £1.50 Chd free (ACNO to Marie Curie Cancer Care®). Sun July 5 (2-5.30)*

Marie Curie Cancer Care

Marie Curie Cancer Care is a charity which cares for people with cancer. The National Gardens Scheme is delighted to include it in its list of beneficiaries. Some facts and figures:

- More than 250,000 people in Britain develop cancer every year. Almost 160,000 people die from the disease annually, the second biggest killer after heart disease.

- **Marie Curie Nurses** provide over 1.3 million hours a year of practical nursing care at home. The service is available day or night, 365 days a year, to patients and their families without charge.

- **Marie Curie Centres** cared for more than 4,600 patients in 1996/97.

- **Marie Curie Cancer Care** operates a research institute which investigates the underlying causes of cancer.

SYMBOLS USED IN THIS BOOK (See also Page 17)

¶   Opening for the first time.

❀   Plants/produce for sale if available.

&   Gardens with at least the main features accessible by wheelchair.

✗   No dogs except guide dogs.

●   These gardens advertise their own dates in this publication although they do not nominate specific days for the NGS. Not all the money collected by these gardens comes to the NGS but they do make a guaranteed contribution.

■   These gardens nominate specific days for the NGS and advertise their own dates in this publication.

▲   These gardens open regularly to the public but they do not advertise their own dates in this publication. For further details, contact the garden directly.

Denbighshire and Colwyn

See separate Welsh section on page 376

Derbyshire

Hon County Organiser: Mr & Mrs R Brown, 210 Nottingham Rd, Woodlinkin, Langley Mill, Nottingham
NG16 4HG Tel 01773 714903

Hon County Treasurer: Mrs G Nutland, 4 Sadler Close, Adel, Leeds LS16 8NN

DATES OF OPENING

Regular openings
For details see garden description

Fir Croft, Calver, nr Bakewell
Lea Gardens, nr Matlock
Renishaw Hall, nr Sheffield

By appointment only
*For telephone numbers and other
details see garden descriptions.
Private visits welcomed*

Birchfield, Ashford in the Water
Corner Cottage, Osmaston-
  by-Ashbourne
Darley House, Darley Dale
Fanshawe Gate Hall,
  Holmesfield
Rock House, Nether Heage

April 4 Saturday
Castle Farm, Melbourne
April 5 Sunday
Bowbridge House, Mackworth
Castle Farm, Melbourne
April 11 Saturday
Castle Farm, Melbourne
April 12 Sunday
Castle Farm, Melbourne
32 Heanor Road, Codnor
Radburne Hall, Radburne
April 19 Sunday
Field House Farm, Rosliston, nr
  Burton-on-Trent
April 22 Wednesday
Bluebell Arboretum, Smisby
Field House Farm, Rosliston, nr
  Burton-on-Trent
April 26 Sunday
Bluebell Arboretum, Smisby
Fir Croft, Calver, nr Bakewell
The Riddings, Kirk Ireton
May 3 Sunday
Cherry Tree Cottage, Hilton
May 4 Monday
Cherry Tree Cottage, Hilton
May 10 Sunday
Bath House Farm, Ashover
Broomfield College, Morley
57 Portland Close, Mickleover
May 13 Wednesday
Bluebell Arboretum, Smisby

May 17 Sunday
Bluebell Arboretum, Smisby
Fir Croft, Calver, nr Bakewell
The Limes, Apperknowle
May 24 Sunday
Dam Farm House, Ednaston
Dove Cottage, Clifton, Ashbourne
Field House Farm, Rosliston, nr
  Burton-on-Trent
286 Handley Rd, New Whittington
Monksway, Tideswell
May 25 Monday
Field House Farm, Rosliston, nr
  Burton-on-Trent
May 26 Tuesday
Shatton Hall Farm, Bamford
May 28 Thursday
Gamesley Fold Cottage, Glossop
May 30 Saturday
Duffield House, Breaston
May 31 Sunday
Bowbridge House, Mackworth
Cherry Tree Cottage, Hilton
Fir Croft, Calver, nr Bakewell
Thatched Farm, Radbourne
June 4 Thursday
Kedleston Hall, Derby
June 7 Sunday
Birchwood Farm, Portway
Green Farm Cottage, Offcote,
  Ashbourne
The Old Slaughterhouse, Shipley
  Gate
Yew Tree Bungalow, Thatchers
  Lane, Tansley
June 14 Sunday
Fir Croft, Calver, nr Bakewell
Gamesley Fold Cottage, Glossop
32 Heanor Road, Codnor
210 Nottingham Road, Woodlinkin
57 Portland Close, Mickleover
White Gate, Arleston Meadows
June 17 Wednesday
Bluebell Arboretum, Smisby
June 21 Sunday
334 Belper Road, Stanley
  Common
Bluebell Arboretum, Smisby
Cashel, Kirk Ireton
Dove Cottage, Clifton, Ashbourne
Field House Farm, Rosliston, nr
  Burton-on-Trent
Thatched Farm, Radbourne
White Gate, Arleston Meadows

June 24 Wednesday
Field House Farm, Rosliston, nr
  Burton-on-Trent
June 27 Saturday
46 Long Meadow Road, Alfreton
June 28 Sunday
Cherry Tree Cottage, Hilton
Fields Farm, Codnor
Fir Croft, Calver, nr Bakewell
Gamesley Fold Cottage, Glossop
Monksway, Tideswell
Yew Tree Bungalow, Thatchers
  Lane, Tansley
July 5 Sunday
Bowbridge House, Mackworth
286 Handley Rd, New
  Whittington
32 Heanor Road, Codnor
Lea Hurst, Holloway
23 Mill Lane, Codnor
Monksway, Tideswell
July 8 Wednesday
Oaks Lane Farm, Brockhurst
July 11 Saturday
Bath House Farm, Ashover
Monksway, Tideswell
July 12 Sunday
Bath House Farm, Ashover
Field House Farm, Rosliston, nr
  Burton-on-Trent
The Gardens at Dobholme
  Fishery, Marsh Lane
Hardwick Hall, Doe Lea
274 Heanor Road, Ilkeston
The Limes, Apperknowle
Oaks Lane Farm, Brockhurst
Stainsborough Hall, Hopton, nr
  Wirksworth
Yew Tree Bungalow, Thatchers
  Lane, Tansley
July 15 Wednesday
Field House Farm, Rosliston, nr
  Burton-on-Trent
July 18 Saturday
Monksway, Tideswell
Tissington Hall, nr Ashbourne
July 19 Sunday
334 Belper Road, Stanley
  Common
Dam Farm House, Ednaston
Dove Cottage, Clifton, Ashbourne
Fields Farm, Codnor
The Limes, Apperknowle
159 Longfield Lane, Ilkeston

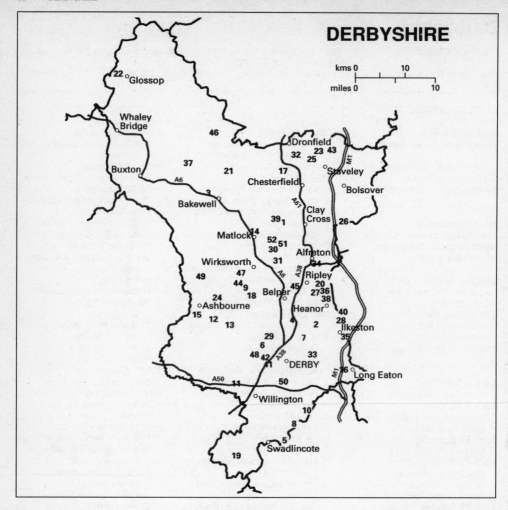

DERBYSHIRE

KEY

1. Bath House Farm
2. 334 Belper Road
3. Birchfield
4. Birchwood Farm
5. Bluebell Arboretum
6. Bowbridge House
7. Broomfield College
8. Calke Abbey
9. Cashel
10. Castle Farm
11. Cherry Tree Cottage
12. Corner Cottage
13. Dam Farm House
14. Darley House
15. Dove Cottage
16. Duffield House
17. Fanshawe Gate Hall
18. Field Farm

19. Field House Farm
20. Fields Farm
21. Fir Croft
22. Gamesley Fold
23. The Gardens at Dobholme
    Fishery
24. Green Farm Cottage
25. 286, Handley Rd
26. Hardwick Hall
27. 32 Heanor Road, Codnor
28. 274 Heanor Road, Ilkeston
29. Kedleston Hall
30. Lea Gardens
31. Lea Hurst
32. The Limes
33. Locko Park
34. 46 Long Meadow Road
35. 159 Longfield Lane

36. 23 Mill Lane
37. Monksway
38. 210 Nottingham Road
39. Oaks Lane Farm
40. The Old Slaughterhouse
41. 57 Portland Close
42. Radburne Hall
43. Renishaw Hall
44. The Riddings
45. Rock House
46. Shatton Hall Farm
47. Stainsborough Hall
48. Thatched Farm
49. Tissington Hall
50. White Gate
51. Yew Tree Bungalow,
    Tansley
52. Yew Tree Farm, Tansley

Her Majesty Queen Elizabeth the Queen Mother is Patron of the National Gardens Scheme. She is holding a bouquet which includes the rose 'Charity' bred specially for the 70th anniversary of the National Gardens Scheme by David Austin Roses   *Photograph courtesy of QNI*

Tapeley Park, **Instow** in **Devon** is one of the larger gardens in the Scheme and features an Italianate garden with stunning coastal views
Photograph by Andrew Lawson

Right: **The White House, Keyworth** in **Nottinghamshire** which specialises in tender and half-hardy plants
Photograph by Clive Boursnell

Below: Ponds and streams are an important feature in the woodland garden at **The Old Rectory, Litton Cheney** home of the County Organiser of **Dorset**
Photograph by Brian Chapple

Left: Aquilegias bloom at **10 Lawn Road, London**, one of the smaller gardens in the National Gardens Scheme. *Photograph by Rosalind Simon*

Below: Ornamental fountains at **The Manor House, Stevington, Bedfordshire** *Photograph by Kathy Brown*

The Brown House, Maryport, is one of the Scheme's most northerly gardens in **Cumbria**
Photograph by Val Corbett

Surrounding countryside enhances the view from **Dam Farm House**, **Ashbourne**, in **Derbyshire**
Photograph by Rosalind Simon

Right: **Macmillan Cancer Relief** is the main beneficiary of the National Gardens Scheme. Here a Macmillan nurse plays with her young patient
Photograph courtesy of Macmillan Cancer Relief

Below: A brilliant display of colour in Christopher Lloyd's garden at **Great Dixter**, **Northiam, Sussex**
Photograph by Jonathan Buckley

Left: The owners photographed these beautiful hellebores in the garden at **Ridleys Cheer**, **Mountain Bower**, **Wiltshire**
Photograph by Antony Young

Below: A quiet corner in the award-winning garden at **Sun House**, **Long Melford**, **Suffolk**
Photograph by Marcus Harpur

July 22 Wednesday
Bluebell Arboretum, Smisby
July 23 Thursday
Birchwood Farm, Portway
July 25 Saturday
Monksway, Tideswell
July 26 Sunday
Bluebell Arboretum, Smisby
Locko Park, Spondon
159 Longfield Lane, Ilkeston
The Riddings, Kirk Ireton
Shatton Hall Farm, Bamford
Yew Tree Bungalow,
  Tansley
Yew Tree Farm, Tansley

July 29 Wednesday
Calke Abbey, Ticknall
August 2 Sunday
Field Farm, Kirk Ireton
32 Heanor Road, Codnor
August 9 Sunday
23 Mill Lane, Codnor
August 16 Sunday
Dove Cottage, Clifton, Ashbourne
August 23 Sunday
White Gate, Arleston Meadows
August 26 Wednesday
Bluebell Arboretum, Smisby
August 30 Sunday
Bluebell Arboretum, Smisby

August 31 Monday
Tissington Hall, nr Ashbourne
September 20 Sunday
The Riddings, Kirk Ireton
September 23 Wednesday
Bluebell Arboretum, Smisby
September 27 Sunday
Bluebell Arboretum, Smisby
Broomfield College, Morley
October 21 Wednesday
Bluebell Arboretum, Smisby
October 25 Sunday
Bluebell Arboretum, Smisby

DESCRIPTION OF GARDEN

Bath House Farm, Ashover ᴴᴸ (Mr & Mrs Hetherington) 4½m N of Matlock on A632 Chesterfield Rd. Take 1st R after leaving village of Kelstedge and next R at T-junction. The garden has extensive views over the valley and features heathers, mixed borders, rare shrubs and trees around the central feature of ponds, streams and waterfall. New features include a pergola, woodland stream and rhododendrons plus an indoor tropical rainforest planting! TEAS. *Adm £1.50 for Sunday May 10 (10.30-4.30). Also indoor flower festival (with refreshments throughout the day). On July 11, 12 (10.30-4.30) admission garden only £1.50, Garden and house £3. For private view, sorry no coaches* **Tel 01246 590562**

¶334 Belper Road, Stanley Common ᴴᴸᴱ (Gill & Colin Hancock) 7m N of Derby, 3m W of Ilkeston on the A609, ¾m from the Rose and Crown Xrds (A608). ¾-acre garden. Large herbaceous island bed, shrub borders, pergolas, kitchen garden. Small water features and a natural wildlife pond. TEAS. *Adm £1.50 Chd free. Suns June 21, July 19 (2-5)*

Birchfield, Ashford in the Water ᴸ (Brian Parker) Dukes Drive. 2m NW of Bakewell on A6 to Buxton. Beautifully situated terraced garden of approx ¾ acre. Designed for all-yr-round colour, it contains a wide variety of shrubs and perennials, bulbs, water and scree gardens. Areas of copse with wild flowers are being developed in adjacent field. TEA. *Adm £1 Chd free (ACNO to Matlock and District Mencap Society®). Private visits welcome from individuals as well as groups April to Sept, please* **Tel 01629 813800**

Birchwood Farm, Portway ᴸᴱ (Stuart & Janet Crooks) 5m N Derby. From A38 take B6179 by Little Chef through Little Eaton till first Xrds. Turn L then R over railway crossing and take rd to Holbrook. Car parking in field at top of drive. ⅓-acre garden enclosed within old brick and stone walls. This garden is for plant enthusiasts. The wide range of herbaceous plants incl hardy geraniums, penstemons, silver plants, campanulas, delphiniums, English roses and pond. Private nursery adjacent. TEA. *Adm £1.50 Chd free. Sun June 7, Thurs July 23 (2-5.30). Private visits also welcome, please* **Tel 01332 880685**

Bluebell Nursery & Woodland Garden, Smisby ᴴᴸᴱ (Robert & Suzette Vernon) From the A511 Burton on Trent to Ashby-de-la-Zouch Rd, turn for Smisby by the Mother Hubbard Inn, 1m NW of Ashby. Arboretum is on L after ½m Annwell Lane. 5-acre young Arboretum planted in the last 6 yrs incl many specimens of rare trees and shrubs. Bring wellingtons in wet weather. TEA. *Adm £1 Chd free (ACNO to MENCAP®). Suns April 26, May 17, June 21, July 26, Aug 30, Sept 27, Oct 25; Weds April 22; May 13, June 17, July 22, Aug 26, Sept 23, Oct 21 (10-5). Private visits welcome, please* **Tel 01530 413700**

Bowbridge House, Mackworth ᴴᴸ (Richard & Jennifer Wood) On A52 Derby to Ashbourne Rd 3m W of Derby Ring Rd, on S side, just past the Little Chef. 4½-acre garden originally laid out in 1762 by William Eames. Extensively informally replanted since 1978 by present owners with rare and unusual trees, shrubs, climbers and herbaceous plants. Flowering sized magnolia campbelli; paulownia, numerous rhododendrons, shrub roses, 3 conservatories, ponds and vegetable garden. TEA. *Adm £1.50 Chd free. Suns April 5, May 31, July 5 (2-5.30)*

Broomfield College, Morley ᴴᴸᴱ On A608, 4m N of Derby and 6m S of Heanor. Landscaped garden of 10 ha; shrubs, trees, rose collection, herbaceous borders; glasshouses; walled garden under restoration; garden tours and advice; demonstrations of seasonal garden tasks, crafts, carvery lunches, refreshments. *Adm £1 Chd free. Suns May 10, Sept 27 (10.30-4.30)*

▲Calke Abbey, Ticknall ᴴᴸ (The National Trust) 9m S of Derby on A514 between Swadlincote and Melbourne. Extensive walled gardens constructed in 1773. Divided into flower garden, kitchen garden and physic garden. Restoration commenced in 1987. Surrounding the walled garden the pleasure ground has been re-fenced and replanting is underway. Phase 1 of orangery restoration just completed. Phase 2 subject to further fundraising. Lunches and TEAS. *Adm £2.20 Chd £1. For NGS Wed July 29 (11-5)*

Cashel, Kirk Ireton ᴱ (Anita & Jeremy Butt) Turn off B5023 (Duffield-Wirksworth rd). 2m S of Wirksworth. Follow rd to Kirk Ireton take sharp R turn at church corner.

Follow lane for 200 metres. Garden on R, car parking 50 metres beyond the house. 2½ acres of gradually developing garden situated on a sloping site with views of the Ecclesbourne Valley. Many interesting trees, plants and shrubs. TEAS in aid of local church. *Adm £1.50 Chd free. Sun June 21 (2-5). Private visits welcome, please* **Tel 01335 370495**

¶**Castle Farm, Melbourne** &❀ (Mr & Mrs John Blunt) From Melbourne Market Place turn into Potter St (side of Melbourne Hotel) continue down into Castle Square. Castle Farm Garden faces across the square. 1 acre farmhouse garden on site of Melbourne Castle with some ruins remaining. Herbaceous borders. Herb garden and Old Roses Garden. Ornamental pond and bog garden. Large orchard. Vegetable garden with greenhouses and tree nursery. TEAS. *Adm £1.50 Chd free (ACNO to Sustrams (Bristol) and Macmillan Nurses). Sats, Suns April 4, 5, 11, 12 (2-5)*

Cherry Tree Cottage, Hilton &❀ (Mr & Mrs R Hamblin) 7m W of Derby, turn off the A516 opp The Old Talbot Inn in village centre. Parking - small public car park in Main St. A plant lover's C18 garden, about ⅓-acre with herbaceous borders; herb garden; scree garden. Many unusual and interesting plants; specie aquilegias, old dianthus. Featured on 'Gardeners World' and in several gardening magazines. *Adm £1 Chd free. Suns May 3, 31, June 28, Mon May 4 (2-5). Groups welcome by appt weekdays April, May, June only. Visitors also welcome to see snowdrops and hellebores early spring. Please* **Tel 01283 733778**

Corner Cottage, Osmaston-by-Ashbourne &❀ (Alan & Lynn Poulter) 2½m SE of Ashbourne in centre of village ½m off A52. Plantlovers' garden of ½ acre in unspoiled Victorian estate village, aiming to provide seasonal variety and colour around every corner. Pond and bog garden, rockery, alpines, irises, formal walled garden, shrubs, herbaceous borders and annuals. *Adm £1.50 Chd free. Private visits of 8 or more welcome March to Sept please* **Tel 01335 346112**

■**Dam Farm House, Ednaston** &❀❀ (Mrs J M Player) Yeldersley Lane, Ednaston, 5m SE of Ashbourne on A52, opp Ednaston Village turn, gate on R 500yds. 3-acre garden which has been extended to incl a young arboretum. Beautifully situated. Contains mixed borders, scree. Unusual plants have been collected many are propagated for sale. TEAS (some Suns). *Adm £2 Chd free. Suns June 21, Aug 16 (1.30-4.30). For NGS Suns May 24, July 19 (1.30-4.30). Private visits and groups welcome April 1 to Oct 31 by appt, please* **Tel 01335 360291**

Darley House, Darley Dale &❀❀ (Mr & Mrs G H Briscoe) 2m N of Matlock. On A6 to Bakewell. 1½ acres; originally set out by Sir Joseph Paxton in 1845; being restored by present owners; many rare plants, trees; balustrade and steps separating upper and lower garden, a replica of Haddon Hall. As featured on BBC 'Gardeners World'. Picture Gallery. Plants and extensive range of seeds available. TEA. *Adm £1.50 Chd free. Open by appt from May 1 to Sept 30 for private visits and groups not exceeding 15, please* **Tel 01629 733341**

Dove Cottage, Clifton &❀ (Anne and Stephen Liverman) 1½m SW of Ashbourne. ¾-acre garden by R Dove extensively replanted and developed since 1979. Emphasis on establishing collections of hardy plants and shrubs incl alchemillas, alliums, berberis, geraniums, euphorbias, hostas, lilies, variegated and silver foliage plants inc astrantias. Plantsmans garden featured on Channel 4 'Garden Club', 'Good Garden Guide' and 'Gardeners World Cottage Garden 1995'. TEA. *Adm £1.50 Chd free (ACNO to British Heart Foundation®). Suns May 24, June 21, July 19, Aug 16 (1-5). Private visits welcome, please* **Tel 01335 343545**

Duffield House, Breaston &❀ (Dr & Mrs R N Wilson) Blind Lane. Turn off A6005 opp Church and park in the Green. Walk 100yds to L. ¼ acre, newly developed. Gravel gardens, ponds, herbaceous and shrub borders. TEA in aid of Treetops Hospice. *Adm £1 Chd free. Sat May 30 (2-5)*

Fanshawe Gate Hall, Holmesfield &❀ (Mr & Mrs John Ramsden) Situated on the edge of the Peak National Park. 1m E of Holmesfield Village. Follow B6054 towards Owler Bar. 1st R turn after Robin Hood Inn. Marked Old Hall on OS map. C13 seat of the Fanshawe family. Old-fashioned cottage-style garden approx 2 acres. Many stone features, fine C16 dovecote. Upper walled garden with herbaceous, shrub, variegated and fern plantings, water features, climbers, rose beds, terracing and lawns. Lower courtyard with knot garden and herb border. *Adm £1.50 Chd free. Private visits only by appt, please* **Tel 0114 2890391**

Field Farm, Kirk Ireton ❀ (Graham & Irene Dougan) At top of Main St Kirk Ireton turn L signed Blackwall. On sharp RH bend of Blackwall Lane, find Field Lane, single track without passing places. Field Farm 400m parking in field. 1½-acre hilltop garden with informal planting of trees, shrubs, alpines, roses and herbaceous borders, colourful display of containers in yard. TEA in aid of local WI. *Adm £1.50 Chd free. Sun Aug 2 (2-5). Private and group visits welcome by appt May to Sept, please* **Tel 01335 370958**

Field House Farm, Rosliston &❀❀ (Keith & Judy Thompson) From junction 11 (M42) take A444 NW to Castle Gresley. Turn to Linton and Rosliston. From A38 turn E at Barton Turns fly-over to Walton-on-Trent then follow signs to Rosliston. Farm is signed up drive between Rosliston and Coton-in-the-Elms. An artistic plant collector's ¾-acre garden. 2 ponds, 'dry' bog garden, secret garden, stone garden, wildlife garden, hardy geraniums, hostas and penstemons. TEAS. *Adm £1 Chd free. Suns April 19, May 24, June 21, July 12, Weds April 22, June 24, July 15, Mon May 25 (2-6). Private visits of 10 or over welcome, please* **Tel 01283 761472**

¶**Fields Farm, Codnor** &❀❀ (Mr & Mrs Graham Woolley) 300yds from Codnor Market Place on A6007. Towards Heanor. Approx 1-acre garden with mixed herbaceous borders, shrubs, climbers, hostas, small pond, separate water feature, pergola, small Mediterranean garden. TEAS for 3rd Codnor Scout Group. TEAS. *Adm £1.50 Chd free. Suns June 28, July 19 (2-5)*

■ **Fir Croft, Calver** ❀❀ (Dr Furness) Froggatt Rd, via Sheffield. 4m N of Bakewell; at the junction of B6001 with B6054 adjacent to the 'power' garage. Plantsman's garden; rockeries; water garden and nursery; extensive collection (over 2000 varieties) of alpines, conifers, incl over 600 sempervivums, 500 saxifrages and 350 primulas. Tufa and scree beds. *Collection box. Nursery opens every Sat, Sun, Mon (1-5) March to Dec. Adjacent garden for NGS Suns April 26, May 17, 31, June 14, 28 (2-5)*

Gamesley Fold Cottage, Glossop ❀❀ (Mr & Mrs G Carr) Off Glossop-Marple Rd nr Charlesworth, turn down the lane directly opp St Margaret's School, Gamesley. White cottage at the bottom. Old-fashioned cottage garden down a country lane with lovely views of surrounding countryside. A spring garden planted with herbaceous borders, wild flowers and herbs in profusion to attract butterflies and wildlife. Featured in Good Housekeeping and Good Gardens Guide. TEAS. *Adm £1.50 Chd free. Thurs May 28, Suns June 14, 28 (11-4). Groups welcome May and June, please Tel 014578 67856*

¶**The Gardens of Dobholme Fishery, Troway** ❀ (Paul & Pauline Calvert) Halfway along B6056, Dronfield to Eckington, 2½m from each. Coming from Dronfield turn L at Blackamoor Head Inn for Troway. Follow signs in village. Situated in the beautiful conservation area of the Moss Valley. Developed on a sloping site of approx 2 acres around fishing ponds only 5yrs ago. The garden is designed to encourage wildlife planted in a wild, natural look. Heavy clay with many springs, stone quarried from the site is widely used to pave the pond sides. Sloping uneven terrain. *Adm £1.50 Chd free. Sun July 12 (2-5)*

Grafton Cottage, Barton-under-Needwood See Staffordshire

Green Farm Cottage, Offcote nr Ashbourne ❀❀ (Mr & Mrs Peter Bussell) 1½m NE of Ashbourne on T-junction Bradley-Kniveton-Ashbourne. Take Wirksworth Rd out of Ashbourne (B5035) and follow Offcote sign (approx 1¼m from main rd). ⅓-acre plantsman's garden featured in 'Your Garden' and 'Derbyshire Life'. Constructed from a wilderness in 1978. Flower-filled terraces, lawns, spring bulbs and a variety of perennials, incl hellebores, shrubs and trees; greenhouse, soft fruit and small orchard area. TEA and plants in aid of Ashbourne Animal Welfare. *Adm £1 Acc chd free. Sun June 7 (2-5). Private visits welcome April to Aug, please Tel 01335 343803*

¶**286 Handley Road, New Whittington** ❀ (E J Lee) From A6135, take B6052 through Eckington and Marsh Lane 3m. Turn L at Xrds signed Whittington, then 1m. From Coal Aston (Sheffield), take B6056 towards Chesterfield to give way sign, then 1m. From Chesterfield, take B6052. ⅓-acre sloping site. Herbaceous borders, rock garden, alpines, streams, pools, bog gardens, alpine house. Acers, bamboos, ferns, eucalyptus, euphorbias, grasses, conifers. 1400 plants permanently labelled, garden plan displayed, plant location guide available. TEA. *Adm £1.50 Chd free (ACNO to Sheffield Botanical Gardens Trust®). Suns May 24, July 5 (2-6). Private parties by appt, written application please*

▲**Hardwick Hall, Doe Lea** ❀❀ (The National Trust) 8m SE of Chesterfield. S of A617. Grass walks between yew and hornbeam hedges; cedar trees; herb garden; herbaceous and rose borders. Finest example of Elizabethan house in the country. Restaurant in Old Kitchens. TEAS on days the Hall is open. *Adm hall and garden £6 Chd £3 garden only £2.75 Chd £1. For NGS Sun July 12 (12-5.30 last entry 4.30)*

32 Heanor Road, Codnor ❀❀ (Mr & Mrs Eyre) 300yds from Codnor market place (clock tower) on A6007 towards Heanor. Down lane at side of shop. Parking in adjacent field with way out on to A610 Nottingham to Ripley Rd. 1½-acre garden with yr-round interest has been constructed over many yrs from its origins as a market garden. Lawns, variety of trees, camellias, flowering shrubs, mixed borders, scree, rockery; 2 ponds and pergola, arbour and stepping pond. TEA. *Adm £1.50 Chd free. Suns April 12, June 14, July 5, Aug 2 (2-5). Coach parties and private visits welcome, please Tel 01773 746626*

¶**274 Heanor Road, Ilkeston** ❀ (Mr & Mrs G Seagrave) On A6007, 2m from Heanor towards Ilkeston, opp Ilkeston Hospital. Large all yr-round garden, with over 40 different varieties of conifers, 70 different shrubs, ornamental trees, rockery, pergola, greenhouse. Varieties of soft, top and stone fruit, vegetables. 'Beautiful Erewash' joint 2nd 1997. TEA. *Adm £1.50 Chd free. Sun July 12 (2-5.30)*

▲**Kedleston Hall, Kedleston** ❀❀ (The National Trust) 3m NW of Derby. Signed from junction of A38/A52. 12-acre garden. A broad open lawn, bounded by a ha-ha, marks the C18 informal garden. A formal layout to the W was introduced early this century when the summerhouse and orangery, both designed by George Richardson late C18, were moved to their present position. The gardens are seen at their best during May and June when the azaleas and rhododendrons are one mass of colour. The Long Walk, a woodland walk of some 3m, is bright with spring flowers. Guided walk of gardens and Long Walk at 2pm. TEA. *Adm £2 Chd £1. For NGS Thurs June 4 (11-6)*

● **Lea Gardens** ❀❀ (Mr & Mrs Tye) Lea, 5m SE of Matlock off A6. A rare collection of rhododendrons, azaleas, kalmias, alpines and conifers in a delightful woodland setting. Light lunches, TEAS, home-baking. Coaches by appt. *Adm £3 Chd 50p daily, season ticket £4. Daily March 20 to July 5 (10-7)*

Lea Hurst (Residential Home), Holloway ❀❀ (Royal Surgical Aid Society) 6m SE of Matlock off A6, nr Yew Tree Inn, Holloway. Former home (not open) of Florence Nightingale. Large garden consisting of rose beds, herbaceous borders, shrubberies incl varieties, ornamental pond, wildlife garden, all set in beautiful countryside. TEAS in aid of RSAS. *Adm £1.50 Chd under 16 free. Sun July 5 (2-5)*

The Limes, Apperknowle ❀❀ (Mr Roy Belton) 6m N of Chesterfield; on A61 taking the Dronfield, Unstone turn off to Unstone, turn R at Unstone school for 1m to Apperknowle; 1st house past Unstone Grange. Bus; Chesterfield or Sheffield to Unstone. 2½-acre garden with herbaceous borders, lily ponds, roses and flowering shrubs, hundreds of naturalised daffodils. Massed bedding of pansies and polyanthus in the spring, geraniums and bedding plants in the summer. Lavender Maze. Large natural pond with ducks and geese. Nature trail over 5 acres. TEAS. *Adm £1 Chd 25p. Suns May 17, July 12, 19 (2-6).* **Tel 01246 412338**

Locko Park, Spondon ✿ 6m NE of Derby. From A52 Borrowash bypass, 2m N via B6001, turn to Spondon. Large garden; pleasure gardens; rose gardens. House by Smith of Warwick with Victorian additions. Chapel, Charles II, with original ceiling. TEA. *Adm £1 Chd 30p. Sun July 26 (2-5)*

159 Longfield Lane, Ilkeston ❀✿ (David & Diane Bennett) (Stanton side) off Quarry Hill, opp Hallam Fields Junior School. A house in a garden described by visitors as an artist's garden, a large, informal over-flowing garden that works for its owners with fruit, shrubs, flowers, two small fish ponds and a conservatory. A strong emphasis on texture, colour and lots of unexpected corners. Home-made TEAS. *Adm £1 Chd free. Sun July 19 (2-5.30). Private visits of 6 and under welcome, May to July, please* **Tel 01159 325238**

46 Long Meadow Road, Alfreton ♿❀✿ (Rosemary Townsend) A38 Derby/M1. Take A61 Chesterfield and Matlock exit. At roundabout towards Alfreton through traffic light, past Swan and Salmon public house on R. Take next R, just before the church into Long Meadow Rd. Walled garden, jointly managed between 2 houses. Mainly cottage garden type with vegetable and fruit area and 2 ponds. Approx ¼-acre. Live music will be performed by students from the local Music Centre (not pop music). TEAS. *Adm £1 Chd free (ACNO to Avema Trust®). Sat June 27 (2-5). For other dates,* **Tel 01773 521612**

23 Mill Lane, Codnor ♿❀✿ (Mrs S Jackson) 12m NW of Nottingham. A610 Ripley 10m N of Derby, A38 Ripley. 2 car parks nearby. Lawns, herbaceous borders, small pond, waterfall; fruit trees; clematis. Amber Valley 'Best Kept Garden' competition 3rd 1997. TEA. *Adm £1 Chd free. Suns July 5, Aug 9 (11-6). Private visits also welcome June to Sept, please* **Tel 01773 745707**

Monksway, Tideswell (Mr & Mrs R Porter) Summer Cross. Tideswell is situated 9m N of Buxton on the B6049. Turn up Parke Rd, between newsagent and greengrocer, off Queen St. Take a L turn at the top and then 1st R onto Summer Cross. Monksway is fourth semi-detached house on L. Well stocked gently sloping garden 1000′ above sea level containing perennial and shrub borders, rose, conifer, alpine scree beds and aviary. Limited parking. *Adm £1 Chd free. Suns May 24, June 28, July 5, Sats July 11, 18, 25 (1-5). Private visits welcome, please* **Tel 01298 871687**

210 Nottingham Rd, Woodlinkin (Mr & Mrs R Brown) Nr Codnor; A610. ½-acre; collections of old, modern shrub and climbing roses; shrubs; trees. TEA. *Adm £1.50 Chd free. Sun June 14 (2-5)*

Oaks Lane Farm, Brockhurst ❀✿ (Mr & Mrs J R Hunter) Ashover nr Chesterfield. At Kelstedge 4m from Matlock on A632 Chesterfield Rd, just above Kelstedge Inn, turn L up Kelstedge Lane, then turn R ½m, garden is 150yds on R. ¾-acre informal plantsman's garden in beautiful situation with herbaceous borders, natural streams and pond. Small bog garden. Many varieties of hostas, euphorbia and old-fashioned roses. Spring bulbs and hellebores. Partially suitable for wheelchairs. TEA. *Adm £1.50 Chd free. Wed and Sun July 8, 12 (1-5). Open by appt May 1 to Aug 31, please* **Tel 01246 590324**

The Old Slaughterhouse, Shipley Gate ❀✿ (Robert & Joyce Peck) 1m S of Eastwood, take Church St from Sun Inn traffic lights, and over A610, L to narrow rd to Shipley Gate; parking near Shipley Lock (Erewash Canal) and Shipley Boat Inn. ¾-acre garden, created from overgrown tip; 200-yrs-old stone aqueduct, trees, ponds, cottage garden plants, scree garden; walks in Erewash Valley. TEA. *Adm £1 Chd free. Sun June 7 (2-6). Private visits welcome, please* **Tel 01773 768625**

57 Portland Close, Mickleover ❀✿ (Mr & Mrs A L Ritchie) Approx 3m W of Derby, turn R off B5020 Cavendish Way then 2nd L into Portland Close. Small plantsman's garden, wide variety of unusual bulbs, alpines and herbaceous plants. Special interest in sink gardens, hostas, named varieties of primulas (single and double); auriculas (show, border, alpine and doubles), violas and hardy geraniums. Featured in 'Good Garden Guide'. *Adm £1 Chd free under 16. Suns, May 10, June 14 (2-5). Private visits also welcome of 10 and over, please* **Tel 01332 515450**

Radburne Hall, Radburne ❀ (Mrs J W Chandos-Pole) Radburne, 5m W of Derby. W of A52 Derby-Ashbourne rd; off Radburne Lane. Large landscape garden; large display of daffodils; shrubs; formal rose terraces; fine trees and view. Hall (not open) is 7-bay Palladian mansion built c1734 by Smith of Warwick. Ice-house in garden. *Adm £1 Chd 50p. Sun April 12 (2.30-6)*

● **Renishaw Hall, Renishaw** ♿✿ (Sir Reresby & Lady Sitwell) Renishaw Hall is situated equidistant 6m from both Sheffield and Old Chesterfield on A616 2m from its junction with M1 at exit 30. Italian style garden with terraces, old ponds, yew hedges and pyramids laid out by Sir George Sitwell c1900. Interesting collection of herbaceous plants and shrubs; nature trail; museum; lakeside walk. Shop provides wine, souvenirs, antiques; also Art Galleries. TEAS. *Adm £3 OAPs £2 Chd £1. Every Fri, Sat, Sun and Bank Hol Mons April 10 to Sept 13 (10.30-4.30). Private parties of 20 and over welcome, please* **Tel 01777 860755**

The Riddings Farm, Kirk Ireton ❀✿ (The Spencer Family) Between Ashbourne and Wirksworth. Leave Kirk Ireton via Gorsey Lane (close to Barley Mow). Turn L at T-junction onto Broom Lane. 1st R into Hays Lane. Informal hillside garden about ¾ acre, created since 1979, with lovely views over Carsington Water. Carpets of primulas and daffodils, then rhododendrons, hardy geraniums, shrub roses, hydrangeas and fuchsias. New wildlife pond. Unusual plants propogated for adjacent nursery. TEAS in aid of Ashbourne Animal Welfare. *Adm £1 Chd free. Suns April 26, July 26, Sept 20 (2-5). Private visits welcome, please* **Tel 01335 370331**

Rock House, Nether Heage, nr Belper 👜⚘❀ (Ann Taylor) [Map ref. 365566.] 11m N of Derby. From the A38 at Ripley W to Heage 3m. From the A6 at Belper N to Heage 3m. From Heage to Nether Heage W on Ambergate Rd ½m. From A6 at Ambergate E to Nether Heage 1½m. Medium-size garden (approx 400 sq yds) informal cottage style. Hundreds of varieties of perennials, shrubs, trees and climbers. It reflects owners artistic skills and love of plants and wildlife. Partly accessible to wheelchair users. *Adm £1 Chd free. Private visits welcome afternoons and evenings June to Sept incl, please* **Tel 01773 852804**

Shatton Hall Farm, Bamford (Mr & Mrs J Kellie) 3m W of Hathersage, take A625 from Hathersage, turn L to Shatton, after 2m (opp High Peak Roses). After ½m turn R through ford drive ½m and house is on L over cattle grids. ½-acre garden with its ancient yew tree and C16 farmhouse in picturesque scenery is still being developed and contains many unusual plants and shrubs. Informal plantings incl large natural water garden. Access to extensive woodland and streamside walks. TEAS. *Adm £1.50 Chd 50p. Tues May 26, Sun July 26 (1.30-5) Private visits welcome April to September, please* **Tel 01433 620635**

Stainsborough Hall, Hopton nr Wirksworth 👜❀ (Mr & Mrs Twogood) On B5035 Wirksworth to Ashbourne Rd. 1½m W of Wirksworth take L turning to Kirk Ireton, house ¼m. The stone house and buildings merge delightfully with lawns, shrubs, roses and flower beds designed informally on different levels to provide meandering walks. Covering some 2 acres, the garden incl many young trees, shrubs, herbaceous borders and rose beds. A duck pond with a variety of domestic ducks adds to the tranquillity of the scene. Cream TEAS. *Adm £1 Chd free. Sun July 12 (2-6)*

Thatched Farm, Radbourne 👜⚘❀ (Mr & Mrs R A Pegram) Exit A52 Derby-Ashbourne rd. 2m N of Derby Ring Road. A 2-acre plant lover's garden. The garden and courtyard surround a C17 listed farmhouse. Mediterranean and island beds, troughs and alpines in raised beds, wild garden. Trees, shrubs and herbaceous perennials, extensive collection of tender perennials. 2 ponds and bog garden. Home-made cream TEAS. *Adm £1.50 Chd free (ACNO to RELATE® May 31 & Parkinsons Disease Soc® June 21). Suns May 31, June 21 (2-6). Private parties, min 12, also welcome, please* **Tel 01332 824507**

Tissington Hall, nr Ashbourne ⚘❀ (Sir Richard & Lady FitzHerbert) N of Ashbourne. E of A515. Large garden; roses, herbaceous borders. Tea available in village at The Old Coach House (party bookings on 01335 350501 with tour of gardens possible). Please park considerately. *Adm £1 Chd free. Sat July 18, Mon Aug 31 (2-5). Parties by written appt only on other days*

White Gate, Arleston Meadows ⚘ (Mrs Judy Béba-Thompson) Derby. From A5111 (Ring rd), take Sinfin turn at Foresters' Leisure Park. Follow Arleston signs for 2½m. At Xrds turn L into Wragley Way. From A5132 nr Barrow-upon-Trent take Sinfin turn, 1m and L into Wragley Way. Park in Wragley Way, garden signed through cutting. Very small romantic garden, designed by owner, over 70 varieties of rose and clematis; tiny White Garden; colour-themed scented borders on alkaline clay. TEAS in aid of WI. *Adm £1.50 Acc chd free. Suns June 14, 21, Aug 23 (1.30-5.30). Private visits and groups welcome May to September, please* **Tel 01332 763653**

Yew Tree Bungalow, Tansley ⚘❀ (Jayne Conquest) Thatchers Lane. 2m W of Matlock on A615, 2nd R after Tavern at Tansley. ½-acre informal plantswoman's garden, with herbaceous borders, vegetable and herb gardens. Incl hardy geraniums, herbaceous potentillas and campanulas. TEAS in aid of Chesterfield Cancer Services Appeal. *Adm £1 Chd free. Suns June 7, 28 July 12, 26 (2-6)*

¶**Yew Tree Farm, Tansley** ⚘❀ (Mrs Avril Buckley) 2m W of Matlock on A615, 2nd R after 'Tavern at Tansley'. 1 acre country garden with stream-fed pond and terrace area. Stocked with hostas, ferns, astilbes, roses, topiary. Ornamental and productive potager. Orchard with free-range poultry. Garden 'rooms' of herbaceous perennials, wild area and gold and purple themed shrubbery. TEAS. *Adm £1 Chd free. Sun July 26 (1.30-5)*

Crossroads

Crossroads is a charity which cares for carers. The National Gardens Scheme is delighted to include it in its list of beneficiaries. Some facts and figures:

- One in 7 of the adult population is caring for a relative or friend.

- Most of the carers are women.

- 20% of carers say they never get a break and 65% of carers say their health has suffered as a result of caring responsibilities.

- **Crossroads** employs over 4,000 staff who support and provide respite care for the carers.

- **Crossroads** supports 28,000 carers and provides nearly 3 million care hours per year.

- The contribution of carers saves tax payers over £30 billion per year.

Devon

Hon County Organisers:	Michael & Sarah Stone, The Cider House, Buckland Abbey, Yelverton PL20 6EZ Tel 01822 853285
Assistant County Organisers:	
North Devon	Mervyn T Feesey Esq., Woodside, Higher Raleigh Rd, Barnstaple EX31 4JA Tel 01271 43095
East Devon	Mrs Ruth Charter, Ravenhill, Long Dogs Lane, Ottery St Mary EX11 1HX Tel 01404 814798
North-East Devon	Mrs Diane Rowe, Little Southey, Northcott, Nr Cullompton EX15 3LT Tel 01884 840545
Central Devon	Miss Elizabeth Hebditch, Bibbery, Higher Bibbery, Bovey Tracey TQ13 9RT Tel 01626 833344
South Devon	Mrs Juliet Sutton-Scott-Tucker, Riversbridge, Dartmouth, Devon TQ6 OLG Tel 01803 770372
Torbay	Mrs Sheila Blake, Higher Homefield, Sherford, Kingsbridge TQ7 2AT Tel 01548 531229
South-West Devon	Mrs Shirin Court, Westpark, Yealmpton, Nr Plymouth PL8 2HP Tel 01752 880236
Exeter	Mrs Margaret Lloyd, Little Cumbre, 145 Pennsylvania Road, Exeter EX4 6OZ Tel 01822 855377
Publicity	Mrs Julie Moore, Moorland Barton, Green Lane, Yelverton, Devon PL20 6BW Tel 01822 855377
Hon Treasurer	Mrs Julia Tremlett, Bickham House, Kenn, nr Exeter EX6 7XL Tel 01392 832671

DATES OF OPENING

Regular openings
For details see garden description

Avenue Cottage, Ashprington
Burrow Farm Garden, Dalwood
Docton Mill & Gardens, Hartland
The Downes, Monkleigh
Flete, Ermington
The Garden House, Yelverton
Hill House, nr Ashburton
Lukesland, Ivybridge
Marwood Hill, Nr Barnstaple
Plant World, nr Newton Abbot
Pleasant View Nursery, Nr Newton
  Abbot
Rosemoor Garden, Great Torrington
Rowden Gardens, Brentor
Tapeley Park & Gardens, Instow

By appointment only
*For telephone numbers and other
details see garden descriptions.
Private visits welcomed*

Barton House, Nymet Rowland
Clovelly Court, Clovelly
The Gate House, Lee, Ilfracombe
Hayne Old Manor,
  Moretonhampstead
The Moorings, nr Lyme Regis
The Old Rectory, Woodleigh
Orchard Cottage, Exmouth
Spillifords, nr Tiverton

Sweet Chestnut, Bovey Tracey
96 Wasdale Gardens, Plymouth
Weetwood, nr Honiton
Westpark, Yealmpton

February 22 Sunday
  Little Cumbre, Exeter
  Yonder Hill, Colaton Raleigh
March 2 Monday
  Docton Mill and Garden
March 8 Sunday
  Yonder Hill, Colaton Raleigh
March 15 Sunday
  Bickham House, Kenn, nr Exeter
  Gorwell House, nr Barnstaple
  The Pines, Salcombe
  Wood Barton, Kentisbeare
March 18 Wednesday
  Bickham House, Kenn, nr Exeter
March 19 Thursday
  Greenway Gardens, Churston
  Ferrers
March 22 Sunday
  Fast Rabbit Farm, Ash, Dartmouth
  Membland Villa, Newton Ferrers
  38 Phillipps Avenue, Exmouth
  Yonder Hill, Colaton Raleigh
March 29 Sunday
  Fast Rabbit Farm, Ash, Dartmouth
  Higher Knowle, nr Bovey Tracey
  38 Phillipps Avenue, Exmouth
  The Pines, Salcombe
  Rock House Garden, Chudleigh

March 30 Monday
  Dippers, Shaugh Prior, Nr
  Plymouth
April 4 Saturday
  Shobrooke Park Gardens,
  Crediton
  Sutton Mead, Moretonhampstead
April 5 Sunday
  Higher Knowle, nr Bovey Tracey
  38 Phillipps Avenue, Exmouth
  Saltram House, Plymouth
  Sunnybrook Cottage, Luffincott
  Sutton Mead, Moretonhampstead
  Yonder Hill, Colaton Raleigh
April 6 Monday
  Docton Mill and Garden
April 9 Thursday
  38 Phillipps Avenue, Exmouth
April 10 Friday
  Yonder Hill, Colaton Raleigh
April 11 Saturday
  Yonder Hill, Colaton Raleigh
April 12 Sunday
  Bundels, Sidbury
  The Downes, Monkleigh
  Fast Rabbit Farm, Ash, Dartmouth
  Higher Knowle, nr Bovey Tracey
  Kingston House, Staverton
  Meadowcroft, Plympton
  The Pines, Salcombe
  Yonder Hill, Colaton Raleigh
April 13 Monday
  Ash Thomas & Brithem Bottom
  Gardens

Dippers, Shaugh Prior, Nr
  Plymouth
1 Feebers Cottage, Westwood
Higher Knowle, nr Bovey Tracey
Membland Villa, Newton Ferrers
Yonder Hill, Colaton Raleigh

April 15 Wednesday
St Olaves, Murchington

April 19 Sunday
Andrew's Corner, nr Okehampton
Bickham House, Kenn, nr Exeter
Coleton Fishacre, Kingswear
Gorwell House, nr Barnstaple
Higher Knowle, nr Bovey Tracey
Inglewood, Newton Ferrers
Killerton Garden, Broadclyst
Rowden House, Noss Mayo
Sunnybrook Cottage, Luffincott

April 22 Wednesday
Bickham House, Kenn, nr Exeter

April 23 Thursday
Greenway Gardens, Churston
  Ferrers

April 26 Sunday
Castle Drogo, Drewsteignton
Fast Rabbit Farm, Ash, Dartmouth
Hartland Abbey, nr Bideford
Higher Knowle, nr Bovey Tracey
Knightshayes Gardens, nr
  Tiverton
The Pines, Salcombe
Rock House Garden, Chudleigh
Yonder Hill, Colaton Raleigh

April 30 Thursday
Greenway Gardens, Churston
  Ferrers
Meadowcroft, Plympton

May 2 Saturday
Cleave House, Sticklepath
Mothecombe House, Holbeton
The Old Rectory, East
  Portlemouth

May 3 Sunday
Andrew's Corner, nr Okehampton
Broadhembury House,
  Broadhembury
Bundels, Sidbury
Cleave House, Sticklepath
Fast Rabbit Farm, Ash,
  Dartmouth
Hamblyn's Coombe, Dittisham
Higher Knowle, nr Bovey Tracey
The Lodge, Hartley Avenue,
  Mannamead
Mothecombe House, Holbeton
The Old Glebe, Eggesford
The Old Rectory, East
  Portlemouth
38 Phillipps Avenue, Exmouth
Starveacre, nr Axminster
Sunnybrook Cottage, Luffincott
Topsham Gardens, nr Exeter
Wrangaton House, Wrangaton
Wylmington Hayes, nr Honiton

Yonder Hill, Colaton Raleigh

May 4 Monday
Broadhembury House,
  Broadhembury
Docton Mill and Garden
Hamblyn's Coombe, Dittisham
Higher Knowle, nr Bovey Tracey
Holywell, Bratton Fleming
Membland Villa, Newton Ferrers
The Old Glebe, Eggesford
The Old Rectory, East
  Portlemouth
Topsham Gardens, nr Exeter
Wrangaton House, Wrangaton
Wylmington Hayes, nr Honiton
Yonder Hill, Colaton Raleigh

May 6 Wednesday
Lukesland, Ivybridge
Pleasant View Nursery, Nr
  Newton Abbot
St Olaves, Murchington

May 7 Thursday
Little Cumbre, Exeter

May 10 Sunday
Arlington Court, nr Barnstaple
Fast Rabbit Farm, Ash, Dartmouth
Gorwell House, nr Barnstaple
Higher Knowle, nr Bovey Tracey
Hillside Gardens, Knowle
Inglewood, Newton Ferrers
Lukesland, Ivybridge
Meadowcroft, Plympton
Rowden House, Noss Mayo
Saltram House, Plymouth
Wylmington Hayes, nr Honiton

May 16 Saturday
Ottery St Mary Gardens
Shobrooke Park Gardens, Crediton

May 17 Sunday
Bickham House, Kenn, nr Exeter
The Cider House, Yelverton
Coleton Fishacre, Kingswear
1 Feebers Cottage, Westwood
Half Moon House, Manaton
Higher Knowle, nr Bovey Tracey
Membland Villa, Newton Ferrers
The Orchard, Kenn
Ottery St Mary Gardens
38 Phillipps Avenue, Exmouth
The Pines, Salcombe
Sunnybrook Cottage, Luffincott
Wood Barton, Kentisbeare
Woodside, Barnstaple
Wylmington Hayes, nr Honiton

May 20 Wednesday
Bickham House, Kenn, nr Exeter
Pleasant View Nursery, Nr
  Newton Abbot

May 23 Saturday
Little Upcott Gardens, Marsh
  Green
Monks Aish, South Brent
Withleigh Farm, nr Tiverton
Wolford Lodge, nr Honiton

May 24 Sunday
Andrew's Corner, nr Okehampton
Broadhembury House,
  Broadhembury
Bundels, Sidbury
Fast Rabbit Farm, Ash, Dartmouth
Higher Knowle, nr Bovey Tracey
Lee Ford, Budleigh Salterton
Little Upcott Gardens, Marsh
  Green
Monks Aish, South Brent
The Old Glebe, Eggesford
The Old Mill, Blakewell
Withleigh Farm, nr Tiverton
Wylmington Hayes, nr Honiton
Yonder Hill, Colaton Raleigh

May 25 Monday
Alswood, George Nympton
Ash Thomas & Brithem Bottom
  Gardens
Bicton College of Agriculture
Broadhembury House,
  Broadhembury
Dippers, Shaugh Prior, Nr
  Plymouth
Higher Knowle, nr Bovey Tracey
Holywell, Bratton Fleming
Little Upcott Gardens, Marsh Green
Membland Villa, Newton Ferrers
The Old Glebe, Eggesford
Yonder Hill, Colaton Raleigh

May 30 Saturday
Beatlands Farm, Metcombe
Dartington Hall Gardens, nr
  Totnes
Dicot, nr Chardstock
Pleasant View Nursery, Nr
  Newton Abbot

May 31 Sunday
Andrew's Corner, nr Okehampton
Beatlands Farm, Metcombe
Dartington Hall Gardens, nr
  Totnes
Dicot, nr Chardstock
Emmerford Cottage, Stoodleigh
Fast Rabbit Farm, Ash, Dartmouth
1 Feebers Cottage, Westwood
Higher Knowle, nr Bovey Tracey
Higher Spriddlestone, Brixton, nr
  Plymouth
Overbecks, Salcombe
38 Phillipps Avenue, Exmouth
Pleasant View Nursery, Nr
  Newton Abbot
Southcombe House,
  Widecombe-in-the-Moor
Starveacre, nr Axminster
Sunnybrook Cottage, Luffincott
Wylmington Hayes, nr Honiton

June 1 Monday
Docton Mill and Garden

June 3 Wednesday
Pleasant View Nursery, Nr
  Newton Abbot

June 4 Thursday
Little Cumbre, Exeter
June 6 Saturday
Beatlands Farm, Metcombe
Bovey Tracey Gardens
Newton Abbot Gardens
Skerraton, Dean Prior
June 7 Sunday
Beatlands Farm, Metcombe
Bovey Tracey Gardens
Broadhembury House,
   Broadhembury
Higher Spriddlestone, Brixton, nr
   Plymouth
Hillside Gardens, Knowle
Holywell, Bratton Fleming
Little Upcott Gardens, Marsh
   Green
The Lodge, Hartley Avenue,
   Mannamead
Meadowcroft, Plympton
Membland Villa, Newton Ferrers
Newton Abbot Gardens
38 Phillipps Avenue, Exmouth
Skerraton, Dean Prior
Topsham Gardens (Grove Hill only)
Whitechapel Manor, Nr South
   Molton
Wylmington Hayes, nr Honiton
Yonder Hill, Colaton Raleigh
June 8 Monday
Dippers, Shaugh Prior, Nr
   Plymouth
June 10 Wednesday
Bicton College of Agriculture
Little Upcott Gardens, Marsh
   Green
Scypen, Ringmore
Stone Lane Gardens, Nr Chagford
June 13 Saturday
Beatlands Farm, Metcombe
June 14 Sunday
Andrew's Corner, nr Okehampton
Beatlands Farm, Metcombe
Castle Drogo, Drewsteignton
The Downes, Monkleigh
Fast Rabbit Farm, Ash, Dartmouth
1 Feebers Cottage, Westwood
Gidleigh Gardens
Gorwell House, nr Barnstaple
Heddon Hall, Parracombe
Kingston House, Staverton
The Old Mill, Blakewell
The Old Parsonage, Warkleigh
38 Phillipps Avenue, Exmouth
Riversbridge, nr Dartmouth
Rowden Gardens, Brentor
Scypen, Ringmore
Southcombe House,
   Widecombe-in-the-Moor
Sunnybrook Cottage, Luffincott
Wylmington Hayes, nr Honiton
June 15 Monday
Rowden Gardens, Brentor

June 17 Wednesday
Cleave House, Sticklepath
June 20 Saturday
Barton House, Nymet Rowland
Bundels, Sidbury
Webbery Gardens, Alverdiscott
June 21 Sunday
Ash Thomas & Brithem Bottom
   Gardens
Barton House, Nymet Rowland
Bickham House, Kenn, nr Exeter
Bundels, Sidbury
Cadhay, Ottery St Mary
Cleave House, Sticklepath
Glebe Cottage, nr Warkleigh
Half Moon House, Manaton
Kerscott House, Nr Swimbridge
Little Upcott Gardens, Marsh
   Green
Membland Villa, Newton Ferrers
Mothecombe House, Holbeton
Overbecks, Salcombe
38 Phillipps Avenue, Exmouth
Priors, Abbotskerswell
Riversbridge, nr Dartmouth
Webbery Gardens, Alverdiscott
Woodside, Barnstaple
Wylmington Hayes, nr Honiton
Yonder Hill, Colaton Raleigh
June 24 Wednesday
Lower Coombe Farm
Bickham House, Kenn, nr Exeter
Bicton College of Agriculture
Bundels, Sidbury
Little Upcott Gardens, Marsh
   Green (Evening)
June 26 Friday
Pleasant View Nursery, Nr
   Newton Abbot
June 27 Saturday
Bundels, Sidbury
Rose Marie Cottage, Brixham
Shobrooke Park Gardens, Crediton
June 28 Sunday
Alswood, George Nympton
Blackhall Manor, South Taunton
Bundels, Sidbury
Cadhay, Ottery St Mary
Fast Rabbit Farm, Ash, Dartmouth
1 Feebers Cottage, Westwood
Flete, Ermington, Ivybridge
Knightshayes Gardens, nr Tiverton
Little Southey, Culm Valley, nr
   Culmstock
Little Upcott Gardens, Marsh
   Green
38 Phillipps Avenue, Exmouth
Priors, Abbotskerswell
Rose Marie Cottage, Brixham
Sunnybrook Cottage, Luffincott
Wembury House, Wembury
Whitechapel Manor, Nr South
   Molton
Wylmington Hayes, nr Honiton

June 29 Monday
Little Southey, Culm Valley, nr
   Culmstock
July 1 Wednesday
Sunrise Hill, Withleigh
July 2 Thursday
Westfield Lodge, Budleigh
   Salterton
July 3 Friday
Court Hall, North Molton
July 4 Saturday
Rose Marie Cottage, Brixham
Westfield Lodge, Budleigh
   Salterton
July 5 Sunday
Arlington Court, nr Barnstaple
Dunsford Gardens, Dunsford
Hillside Gardens, Knowle
Killerton Garden, Broadclyst
Rose Marie Cottage, Brixham
Rowden Gardens, Brentor
Yonder Hill, Colaton Raleigh
July 6 Monday
Barton House, Nymet Rowland
Docton Mill and Garden
Rowden Gardens, Brentor
July 8 Wednesday
Little Upcott Gardens, Marsh
   Green
Stone Lane Gardens, Nr Chagford
July 10 Friday
Pleasant View Nursery, Nr
   Newton Abbot
July 12 Sunday
Ash Thomas & Brithem Bottom
   Gardens
The Cider House, Yelverton
Court Hall, North Molton
Fast Rabbit Farm, Ash, Dartmouth
1 Feebers Cottage, Westwood
Gorwell House, nr Barnstaple
Heddon Hall, Parracombe
Membland Villa, Newton Ferrers
Portington, nr Lamerton
Priors, Abbotskerswell
Sunnybrook Cottage, Luffincott
July 15 Wednesday
The Garden House, Yelverton
July 18 Saturday
Monteverde, Old Feniton
July 19 Sunday
Andrew's Corner, nr Okehampton
Bickham House, Kenn, nr Exeter
Blackhall Manor, South Taunton
Glebe Cottage, nr Warkleigh
The Lodge, Hartley Avenue,
   Mannamead
Monteverde, Old Feniton
38 Phillipps Avenue, Exmouth
Portington, nr Lamerton
Woodside, Whimple, nr Exeter
Yonder Hill, Colaton Raleigh
July 22 Wednesday
Bickham House, Kenn, nr Exeter

Little Upcott Gardens, Marsh
Green (Evening)
Oare Manor Cottage, Oare, Lynton
Sunrise Hill, Withleigh
July 24 Friday
Pleasant View Nursery, Nr
Newton Abbot
July 25 Saturday
Dicot, nr Chardstock
July 26 Sunday
Alswood, George Nympton
Dicot, nr Chardstock
Hole Farm, Nr Bickington
Kerscott House, Nr Swimbridge
Little Upcott Gardens, Marsh
Green
Membland Villa, Newton Ferrers
Oare Manor Cottage, Oare, Lynton
July 27 Monday
Fardel Manor, nr Ivybridge
July 29 Wednesday
The Old Mill, Blakewell
Pleasant View Nursery, Nr
Newton Abbot
August 2 Sunday
Hillside Gardens, Knowle
Longham, Coryton, nr Lydford
Gorge
Yonder Hill, Colaton Raleigh
August 3 Monday
Docton Mill and Garden
August 5 Wednesday
Little Upcott Gardens, Marsh
Green
Stone Lane Gardens, Nr
Chagford
August 9 Sunday
Little Upcott Gardens, Marsh
Green
August 12 Wednesday
The Garden House,
Yelverton
Pleasant View Nursery, Nr
Newton Abbot

August 16 Sunday
Bickham House, Kenn, nr Exeter
Bicton College of Agriculture
Membland Villa, Newton Ferrers
38 Phillipps Avenue, Exmouth
Rowden Gardens, Brentor
Woodside, Whimple, nr Exeter
August 17 Monday
Rowden Gardens, Brentor
August 19 Wednesday
Bickham House, Kenn, nr Exeter
Little Upcott Gardens, Marsh
Green
Sunrise Hill, Withleigh
August 21 Friday
Pleasant View Nursery, Nr
Newton Abbot
August 23 Sunday
Fast Rabbit Farm, Ash,
Dartmouth
Little Upcott Gardens, Marsh
Green
Yonder Hill, Colaton Raleigh
August 24 Monday
Yonder Hill, Colaton Raleigh
August 26 Wednesday
Pleasant View Nursery, Nr
Newton Abbot
August 30 Sunday
Alswood, George Nympton
Kerscott House, Nr Swimbridge
August 31 Monday
Membland Villa, Newton Ferrers
September 2 Wednesday
Stone Lane Gardens, Nr Chagford
September 4 Friday
Pleasant View Nursery, Nr
Newton Abbot
September 6 Sunday
1 Feebers Cottage, Westwood
Flete, Ermington, Ivybridge
Hillside Gardens, Knowle
38 Phillipps Avenue, Exmouth
Rowden Gardens, Brentor

Yonder Hill, Colaton Raleigh
September 7 Monday
Docton Mill and Garden
Rowden Gardens, Brentor
September 9 Wednesday
Pleasant View Nursery, Nr
Newton Abbot
September 13 Sunday
Gorwell House, nr Barnstaple
Rock House Garden, Chudleigh
September 16 Wednesday
Pleasant View Nursery, Nr
Newton Abbot
September 20 Sunday
Ash Thomas & Brithem Bottom
Gardens
Bickham House, Kenn, nr Exeter
1 Feebers Cottage, Westwood
Membland Villa, Newton Ferrers
Rock House Garden, Chudleigh
Yonder Hill, Colaton Raleigh
September 23 Wednesday
Bickham House, Kenn, nr Exeter
September 27 Sunday
Gidleigh Gardens
October 4 Sunday
Fast Rabbit Farm, Ash, Dartmouth
The Old Mill, Blakewell
Yonder Hill, Colaton Raleigh
October 5 Monday
Docton Mill and Garden, Hartland
October 11 Sunday
1 Feebers Cottage, Westwood
Gorwell House, nr Barnstaple
October 18 Sunday
Yonder Hill, Colaton Raleigh
October 25 Sunday
Starveacre, nr Axminster
November 8 Sunday
Rock House Garden, Chudleigh
February 21 Sunday
Little Cumbre, Exeter
February 22 Monday 1999
Yonder Hill, Colaton Raleigh

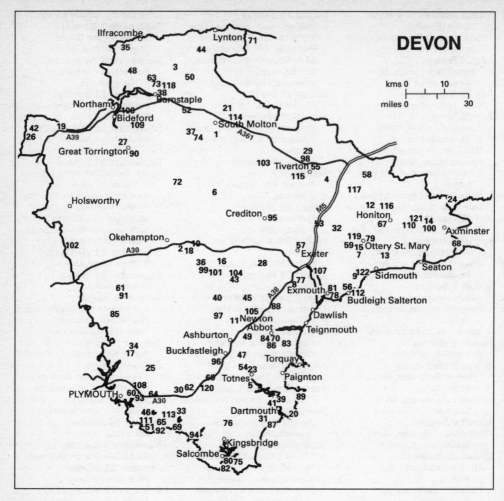

DEVON

kms 0   10

miles 0   30

KEY

DESCRIPTIONS OF GARDENS

Alswood, George Nympton ♿✿❀ (Bob & Marjorie Radford) 2m S of S Molton, halfway between the villages of George Nympton and Alswear. Ample parking, 2-acre developing garden, enthusiastically designed and maintained by owners; set in rural area with panoramic views of the Crooked Oak Valley. Many unusual specimen trees and shrubs. Well established spectacular herbaceous, erica and aquatic areas, pond and stream, unique architectural features. Plants and cream TEAS in aid of George Nympton Church Fund. *Adm £1.50 Chd free. Bank Hol Mon May 25, Suns June 28, July 26, Aug 30 (2-5.30)*

Andrew's Corner, Belstone ♿✿❀ (H J & Mr & Mrs R J Hill) 3m E of Okehampton signed to Belstone. Parking restricted but may be left on nearby common. Plantsman's garden 1,000ft up on Dartmoor, overlooking Taw Valley; wide range unusual trees, shrubs, herbaceous plants for year round effect incl alpines, rhododendrons, bulbs, dwarf conifers; well labelled. TEAS. *Adm £1.50 Chd free. Suns April 19; May 3, 24, 31; June 14; July 19 (2.30-6); also private visits welcome, please* **Tel 01837 840332**

▲Arlington Court, Arlington ♿✿ (The National Trust) Nr Barnstaple. 7m NE of Barnstaple on A39. Rolling parkland and woods with lake. Rhododendrons and azaleas; fine specimen trees; small terraced Victorian garden with herbaceous borders and conservatory. Regency house containing fascinating collections of objet d'art. Carriage collection in the stables, carriage rides. Restaurant. *Adm garden only £2.80 Chd £1.40. For NGS Suns May 10, July 5 (11-5.30)*

Ash Thomas and Brithem Bottom Gardens ✿ 5m SE of Tiverton, 2m S of Halberton. Take A361 from junction 27 on M5 signed Tiverton but leave in ½m signed Halberton. In 3m turn L signed Ash Thomas. 1st garden 1m. A

route map to each garden will be available on open days. TEAS and toilet at Greenlands only. *Combined adm £1.50 Chd 50p. Mons April 13, May 25, Sun June 21, Wed June 24 (Lower Coombe farm only) Suns July 12, Sept 20 (2-6)*

  Greenlands (Dr & Mrs J P Anderson) Ash Thomas. ⅓-acre garden in open rural setting with far-reaching views. Alpine beds and troughs, herbaceous borders, roses and rustic screening, spring bulbs, annuals, herbs, fruit garden, vegetable plot, pond and wild areas. Parking. TEAS. *(ACNO to St Francis Hospital, Katete, Zambia®). Private visits also welcome March to Sept, please* **Tel 01884 821257**

  Lower Coombe Farm (Mr & Mrs M Weekes) Brithem Bottom. Large cottage garden with an interesting selection of plants, old roses and a ditch garden situated behind C17 farmhouse. Parking in farmyard

Avenue Cottage, Ashprington ♿ (Mr R J Pitts & Mr R C H Soans) A381 from Totnes to Kingsbridge. 3m SE Totnes, from centre of village uphill past church for 400yds, drive on R. 11 acres of garden with woodland. Part of listed C18 landscape. Secluded valley site undergoing re-creation. Large collection of young and mature plants. Guided tours and tea by prior arrangement. *Adm £1.50 Chd 25p. Collecting box. Tues to Sat March 31 to Sept 26 (11-5). Private visits also welcome, please* **Tel 01803 732769.** *No coaches*

Barton House, Nymet Rowland ✿❀ (Mr and Mrs A T Littlewood) 9m NW of Crediton. Follow signs to Nymet Rowland from A377 at Lapford or B3220 at Aller Bridge. Garden opposite C15 church. 1-acre garden designed and maintained by owners. Beautiful views to Dartmoor. Individual areas developed with varied character. Herbs; pond; herbaceous; yew garden; ferns, grotto, roses and fountain pool. Teas in village hall for St Bartholomew's Church. *Adm £1 Chd 50p. Sat, Sun June 20, 21 (2-6)*

Beatlands Farm, Metcombe ♿✿❀ (Mr & Mrs D E Pounce) Nr Tipton St John. 2½m S of Ottery St Mary. [SYO892]. 50yds N of Tipton Church take LH turn up Metcombe Vale for ½m. Instead of sharp R at Z bend, bear L up private rd. Secluded 2-acre garden surrounding C17 farmhouse. Streams, waterways, large ponds and wide variety of planting for colour and foliage effect. Streamside walk through woodland. Productive vegetable garden. *Adm £2 Chd 50p. Due to ¼m narrow drive and limited parking regret no admission without prior appt, please* **Tel 01404 812968**. *Sats, Suns May 30, 31, June 6, 7, 13, 14 (2-dusk)*

Bickham House, Kenn ♿✿❀ (Mr & Mrs John Tremlett) 6m W of Exeter 1m off A38. Leave dual carriage-way at Kennford Services, follow signs to Kenn. 1st R in village, follow lane for ¾m to end of no-through rd. Ample parking. No shade for dogs. 5-acre garden in peaceful wooded valley. Lawns, mature trees and shrubs; naturalised bulbs, mixed borders. Conservatory, small parterre, pond garden; 1-acre walled kitchen garden; lake. Cream TEAS. *Adm £1.50 Chd 50p. Suns, Weds March 15, 18, April 19, 22, May 17, 20, June 21, 24, July 19, 22, Aug 16, 19, Sept 20, 23 (2-5). Private visits welcome by appt* **Tel 01392 832671**

Bicton College of Agriculture, East Budleigh ♿✿❀ Use Sidmouth Lodge entrance, ½ way between Budleigh Salterton and Newton Poppleford on B3178. Parking at top of drive. Renowned monkey puzzle avenue; walled garden; glasshouses. Rich variety of plants in beds and borders, laid out for teaching and effect. National collections agapanthus & pittosporum; ½m arboretum with magnolias, cherries, camellias. TEAS. *Adm £2 Chd free (ACNO to Bicton Overseas Agricultural Trust®). Mon May 25; Weds June 10, 24; Sun Aug 16 (10.30-4.30). Gardens also open daily throughout year, except Christmas day (10.30-5). Parties welcome, please* **Tel 01395 562353**

Blackhall Manor, South Tawton ✿❀ (Roger & Jacqueline Yeates) 6m E of Okehampton. Leave A30 at either Whiddon Down or Okehampton signed Sticklepath for 4m. South Tawton 2m N of Sticklepath. Small cottage garden around C16 thatched listed former farmhouse. Parking in village square. Walk through churchyard into garden. TEAS. *Adm £1.50 Chd 50p. Suns June 28, July 19 (2-6). Private visits welcome, please* **Tel 01837 840171**

Bovey Tracey Gardens Gateway to Dartmoor. A382 midway Newton Abbot to Moretonhampstead. TEAS. *Combined adm £2. Sat, Sun June 6, 7 (2-6)*
¶**2 Devon House Drive** ❀ (Mr & Mrs L Miskin) Near entrance to Coombe Cross Hotel, few yds beyond Higher Bibbery. Interesting variety of roses. Herbaceous borders with contrasting colours and shapes. Interested in organic and companion planting. Fruit trees, herbs and vegetable areas
Beavers Lea (Mr & Mrs D A Pook) Higher Bibbery. Cul-de-sac behind Coombe Cross Hotel. B3344 to Chudleigh Knighton. A very small garden on a sloping site. Shrubs, evergreens and herbaceous plants
Bibbery ❀ (Misses E & A Hebditch) Higher Bibbery. B3344 to Chudleigh Knighton. Cul-de-sac behind Coombe Cross Hotel. Plantspersons small garden,

sheltered corners harbouring interesting shrubs and tender plants. TEAS. *Also private visits welcome, please* **Tel 01626 833344**
Church View ❀ (Mr & Mrs L Humphreys) East Street. B3344 opp St Peter & St Paul's Church. Small garden, but many unusual plants, incl secluded vegetable area. Disabled parking
Lamorran (Sally & Andrew Morgan) Furzeleigh Lane 30yds up from Bovey Hosp entrance, limited parking at bottom of lane. Hillside garden with moorland views, mixed planting includes herbaceous, alpine and vegetables
Pineholm ✿❀ (Dr & Mrs A A Baker) High Close. B3344 to Chudleigh Knighton. 1st L past Coombe Cross Hotel. Wild garden with stream. Wide variety of fruit incl vines, figs and citrus
Sunnyside (Mr & Mrs J D Green) Hind Street. Nr town centre off A382. Opp Baptist Church. Well established enclosed garden; trees and shrubs; herbaceous and colourful conservatory; productive vegetable area. Parking nearby

Broadhembury House, Broadhembury ❀ (Mr & Mrs W Drewe) 5m equidistant on A373 from Honiton-Cullompton signed Broadhembury. 2-acre informal garden in C16 picturesque thatched village. A spring garden with rhododendrons and azaleas, daffodils and bluebells. Ample parking in village square. TEAS. *Adm £1.50 Chd 50p (ACNO to Muscular Dystrophy Group®). Suns, Mons May 3, 4, 24, 25; Suns June 7 (2-5). Larger groups welcome by appt during May and June, please* **Tel 01404 841326**

Bundels, Sidbury ♿ (Alan & Barbara Softly) Ridgway. From Sidmouth B3175 turn left at free Car Park in Sidbury. From Honiton A375, turn right. Garden 100yds up Ridgway on left. 1½-acre organic garden incl small wood and pond set round C16 thatched cottage (not open); over 100 varieties of old-fashioned and other shrub roses. Typical cottage garden with accent on preservation of wild life. Teas in village. Dogs on lead. *Adm £1.50 Acc chd free. Suns April 12, May 3, 24 (2-5.30); Sats, Suns June 20, 21, 27, 28; Wed June 24 (10-12 2-5.30). By appt May and June, please* **Tel 01395 597312**

●**Burrow Farm Garden, Dalwood** ♿❀ (Mr & Mrs John Benger) Between Axminster and Honiton. From A35 3½m W of Axminster turn N at Taunton X then keep L towards Stockland, garden ½m on R. Secluded 6 acre garden of informal design with many unusual shrubs and herbaceous plants. Pergola walk with shrub roses. Woodland with rhododendrons and azaleas, ponds and large bog garden. Terraced courtyard featuring later flowering plants. Coffee, light lunches, cream TEAS. *Adm £2.50 Chd 50p. April 1 to Sept 30 daily (10-7), please* **Tel 01404 831285**

Cadhay, Ottery St Mary ♿❀ (Oliver William-Powlett) 1m NW of Ottery St. Mary on B3176. Ample parking. Tranquil 2-acre garden in lovely setting between the Elizabethan Manor House (not open) and ancient stew ponds. Carefully planned double herbaceous borders particularly colourful in summer. Small part-walled water garden features, roses and clematis. *Adm £1.50 Chd 50p. Suns June 21, 28 (2-5)*

▲**Castle Drogo, Drewsteignton** &&❀ (The National Trust) W of Exeter, S of A30. Medium-sized garden with formal beds and herbaceous borders; shrubs, woodland walk overlooking Fingle Gorge. Wheelchair available. Plant centre. Restaurant. Tea room. *Adm gardens only £2.40 Chd £1.20. For NGS Suns April 26, June 14 (10.30-5.30)*

The Cider House, Buckland Abbey &&❀ (Mr & Mrs M J Stone) Yelverton. From A386 Plymouth-Tavistock, follow NT signs to Buckland Abbey. At Xrds before Abbey entrance turn N signed Buckland Monachorum. Drive 200yds on L, or short walk for visitors to Abbey. Peaceful and secluded garden with restrained planting complementing mediaeval house, part of a Cistercian monastery. Terrace borders and herbs, former Abbey walled kitchen garden with fruit, vegetables and flowers. Unspoilt aspect over wooded valley surrounded by NT land. Cream TEAS. *Adm £1.50 Chd 50p. Suns May 17, July 12 (2-6)*

Cleave House, Sticklepath &❀ (Ann & Roger Bowden) 3½m E of Okehampton on old A30 towards Exeter. Cleave House on left in village, on main road just past small right turn for Skaigh. ½-acre garden with mixed planting for all season interest. National Collection of hostas with 600 varieties, 200 of these are for sale. Partially suitable for wheelchairs. *Adm £1 Chd free (ACNO to NCCPG). Wed June 17; Sat May 2; Suns May 3, June 21 (10.30-5). Private visits also welcome April to Oct, please* **Tel 01837 840481**

Clovelly Court, Clovelly &❀ (The Hon Mrs Rous) 11m W of Bideford. A39 Bideford to Bude turn at Clovelly Cross Filling Station, 1m lodge gates and drive straight ahead. 25 acres parkland with beautiful open views through woodlands towards sea. 1-acre walled garden with borders, fruit and vegetables. Restored Victorian glasshouses. Medieval Manor adjacent C14 Church nr coastline. Free parking in drive. Directions at Garden entrance, nursery adjacent dark stained doors in Church Path. *Adm £1 Chd 20p (ACNO to NSPCC®). Private visits and coach parties welcome May 1 to Sept 30 (2-5), please* **Tel 01237 431200**

▲**Coleton Fishacre, nr Kingswear** &❀ (The National Trust) 2m NE of Kingswear. The 8-ha garden was created by Rupert and Lady Dorothy D'Oyly Carte between 1925-1948. Re-established and developed by NT since 1983. Wide range of tender and uncommon trees and shrubs in spectacular coastal setting. Refreshments and light lunches. Unusual plants for sale. *Adm £3.50 Chd £1.70. For NGS Suns April 19, May 17 (10.30-5.30)*

Court Hall, North Molton &❀ (Mr & Mrs C Worthington) 2½m N from A361 Barnstaple-Tiverton rd. In N Molton drive up the hill into the square with church on your L take the only drive beside the old school buildings and Court Hall is just round the bend. A small south facing walled garden; large conservatory; rose, clematis, honeysuckle arbours surround a swimming pool garden with tender plants, rock wall and table; adjoining vegetable garden. *Adm £1.50 Chd 50p. Fri July 3, Sun July 12 (2.30-6)*

▲**Dartington Hall Gardens, Dartington** &❀ (Dartington Hall Trust) Approx 1½m NW of Totnes. From Totnes take A384, turn R at Dartington Parish Church. 28-acre garden around C14 Hall. Mediaeval tiltyard, herbaceous border, small Japanese garden designed in 1990. *Adm (donation) £2.00 recommended. For NGS Sat, Sun May 30, 31 (dawn to dusk). Guided tours for parties of 10 or more £4 each*

Dicot, Chardstock &❀ (Mr & Mrs F Clarkson) Axminster to Chard A358 at Tytherleigh to Chardstock. R at George Inn, L fork to Hook, R to Burridge, 2nd house on L. 3-acre enthusiasts garden, trees, unusual shrubs and conifers, bog orchids in June. Stream, mixed borders, fish pool, features. TEAS. *Adm £1.50 Chd 75p. Sats, Suns May 30, 31 July 25, 26 (2-5.30). Private visits also welcome, please* **Tel 01460 220364**

Dippers, Shaugh Prior &❀ (Mr & Mrs R J Hubble) 8m NE of Plymouth. Garden 100yds down lane opp church near top of village. Park in village. No parking in lane. ¾-acre informal garden. Emphasis on foliage contrast with collection of dwarf rhododendrons, dwarf conifers and shrubs together with herbaceous and heathers. Extensive collection of alpines, in raised beds and troughs. NCCPG National Collection of dianthus. *Adm £1.50 Chd free (ACNO to Woodside Animal Welfare Trust®). Mons March 30, April 13, May 25, June 8 (1-5)*

■ **Docton Mill and Garden, Lymebridge** ❀ (Mr & Mrs M G Bourcier) nr Hartland. Follow brown flower signs from Hartland or West Country Inn on A39. Less than 1m from the sea, nestling in one of Devon's outstanding beauty spots. A garden for all seasons (depicted on BBC, ITV and Channel 4 Garden party). A restored Mill surrounded by 8 acres of gardens, created around the original mill streams, encompassing an exceptional bog garden, orchard and natural woodland. Devon cream TEAS at mill. *Adm £2.50 Chd 50p. Daily March 1 to Oct 31 (10-5). For NGS 1st Monday each month. Parties by arrangement* **Tel 01237 441369**

The Downes, Monkleigh &❀ (Mr & Mrs R C Stanley-Baker) 4½m S of Bideford; 3m NW of Torrington. On A386 to Bideford turn left (W) up drive, ¼m beyond layby. 15 acres with landscaped lawns; fine views overlooking fields and wood lands in Torridge Valley; many unusual trees and shrubs; small arboretum; woodland walks. Featured in Homes and Gardens June 1993. TEA Sats, Suns only. *Adm £2 Chd 20p. Daily April 12 to June 14 (all day). Private visits also welcome by appt June to Sept, please* **Tel 01805 622244**

Dunsford Gardens, Dunsford TEAS at Sowton Mill. *Combined adm £2.50 £1.50 per garden, Chd free. Sun July 5 (2-6)*
 ¶**Honeyway Farm** &❀ (B S & G E Hearson) From Exeter B3212 (Moretonhampstead) W for 6m reaching Two Crosses crossroads at top of steep hill turn R, garden ½m on L. 2 acres very subject to winds from SE and SW. Extensive rocks, views, paths winding to new outlooks. Shrubs and herbaceous perennials, new island beds being established. Ponds with goldfish and lilies. Yr-round interest. Woodland walks around new plantations (deciduous and conifer), dogs off leash

here at owners risk. *(ACNO Devon Air Ambulance®)*

Sowton Mill ❀ (A Cooke and S Newton) From Dunsford take B3193 S for ½m. Entrance straight ahead off sharp R bend by bridge. From A38 N along Teign Valley for 8m. Sharp R after humpback bridge. 4 acres laid out around former mill, leat and river. Part woodland, ornamental trees and shrubs, mixed borders and scree. Yr-round interest. TEAS. *Adm £1.50 Chd free (ACNO to Cygnet Training Theatre®). Private visits also welcome, please* **Tel 01647 252347**

Emmerford Cottage, Tiverton (Mr & Mrs M J Bassano) N of Tiverton take A396, from roundabout L in 2½m signed Stoodleigh, R in ½m at 'weak bridge' signed Cove. House ¼m on L. 3½-acres, begun in 1989 lies in its own woodland setting in the Exe Valley, has a wide variety of plants and trees set in various situations where plants 'get on together'. Shrub and herbaceous borders round the house, shrub roses on terrace, sloping azalea and rhododendron woodland with stream and pond features. A new arboretum is taking shape. No toilets. *Adm £1.50 Chd free (ACNO to CHICKS®). Sun May 31 (2-6). Private parties (up to 10) also welcome, please* **Tel 01398 351287**

Fardel Manor, Ivybridge ઠ☀❀ (Dr A G Stevens) 1¼m NW of Ivybridge; 2m SE of Cornwood; 200yds S of railway bridge. 5-acre, all organic garden, maintained with conservation and wildlife in mind. Partly reticulated. 2½ acres developed over past 12 years with stream, pond and lake. Also, small courts and walled gardens around C14 Manor, with orangery, herbaceous borders, formal pond and shrub garden. TEAS. *Adm £1.50 Chd 50p (ACNO to Frame®). Mon July 27 (11-4.30)*

Fast Rabbit Farm, Ash Cross ઠ❀ (Mr & Mrs Mort) 1½m from Dartmouth off the A3122 Dartmouth-Totnes rd pass park and ride. Turn L at Rose Cottage. Opp direction, from Totnes or Kingsbridge, pass Woodland Park on R, drive past Norton Park on L turn R at Rose Cottage. Garden created in sheltered valley with natural stream. Several ponds and lake; partially wooded; rockery; extensively planted; extends 12 acres plus new woodland planting and walks created through woodland at head of valley. Small specialist nursery open daily. Car park. Some level walks. 'Invalids' please phone prior to visit. TEAS. *Adm £1.50 Chd 50p. Suns March 22, 29, April 12, 26, May 3, 10, 24, 31, June 14, 28, July 12, Aug 23, Oct 4 (11-5). Parties welcome by appt, please* **Tel 01803 712437**

1 Feebers Cottage, Westwood ઠ☀❀ (Mr & Mrs M J Squires) 2m NE of Broadclyst from B3181 (formerly A38) Exeter-Taunton, at Dog Village bear E to Whimple, after 1½m fork left for Westwood. A modern cottage garden, a little of everything set in ¾ of an acre, with a maze of pathways; specialising in plants which tolerate heavy clay soil (alpines in raised beds) and a section of plants introduced by Amos Perry. Nursery. Cream TEAS Sun June 28 only, tea and biscuits on other days. *Adm £1 Chd free. Mon April 13 and Suns May 17, 31 June 14, 28 (Cream TEAS), July 12, Sept 6, 20, Oct 11 (2-6). Private visits welcome, please* **Tel 01404 822118**

■ **Flete** ✄ (Country Houses Association) Ermington, 2m W of Modbury on A379 Plymouth-Kingsbridge rd. Entrance adjacent to Sequers Bridge. 15 acres of gardens overlooking R Erme and valley. Landscaped in 1920's by Russell Page and incl an Italian garden and water garden which Lawrence of Arabia helped to construct. Many fine trees and shrubs. Interesting cobbled terrace to W face of original Tudor manor. *Adm £2 Chd £1 (ACNO to Country Houses Assoc®). House and gardens open every Weds, Thurs pm May to end Sept. For NGS Sun June 28, Sept 6 (2-5) when TEAS will be available.* **Tel 01752 830308**

■ **The Garden House, Buckland Monachorum** ✄❀ (The Fortescue Garden Trust) Yelverton. W of A386, 10m N of Plymouth. 8-acre garden, incl a romantic, terraced walled garden surrounding the ruins of a C16 vicarage. Also incl an acer glade, spring garden, rhododendron walk, herbaceous glade, cottage garden and quarry garden. Coaches and parties by appt only, wide range of plants for sale. TEAS. *Adm £3.50 Chd £1 (Share to NGS®). March 1 to Oct 31 daily. For NGS Weds July 15, Aug 12 (10.30-5)*

The Gate House, Lee ✄ (Mr & Mrs D Booker) Lee Coastal Village 3m W of Ilfracombe. Park in village car park. Take lane alongside The Grampus public house. Garden is 50yds past inn buildings. Peaceful streamside garden with a range of habitats; bog garden (National Collection of Rodgersia), woodland, herbaceous borders, patio garden with semi-hardy 'exotics'. 2¼ acres, where no chemicals are used, only a few minutes walk from the sea and dramatic coastal scenery. Good food at the Grampus. *Collecting box. Open most days (9-12) (2-4). Please* **Tel 01271 862409** *to check especially in Aug*

Gidleigh Gardens From A30 take A382 for Mortonhampstead via Whiddon Down. In 100yds R to Gidleigh for 4m. Entrances adjacent C15 Church. Home made TEAS at Castle Farm. *Combined adm £2 Chd £1. Suns June 14, Sept 27 (2-5.30)*

   Castle House ✄ (Mr & Mrs M Hardy) Hillside gardens around remains of mediaeval castle. Plantings amongst granite stones and water cascades link the gardens to the Dartmoor landscape

   Castle Farm ✄ (Mr & Mrs M Bell) A natural garden in one of Dartmoor's sheltered combes; stream, waterfalls and pools. Streamside walk in 6 acre wild valley. Views to deer forest and Castle Drogo

■ **Glebe Cottage, Warkleigh** ✄❀ (Mrs Carol Klein) 1m N Chittlehamholt on B3227. Garden featured on TV, 5 times Chelsea Gold Medal winners. 1-acre cottage garden with extensive collections of plants for different situations (C4 Wild about the Garden). Wide variety of plants available from adjoining nursery. Open Tues, Wed, Thurs, Fri mornings. *Adm £1.50 Chd free. For NGS Suns June 21, July 19*

Gorwell House, Barnstaple ઠ❀ (Dr J A Marston) 1m E of Barnstaple centre, on Bratton Fleming rd, drive entrance between two lodges on left. 4 acres of trees and shrubs, rare and tender, walled garden; mostly created since 1982; grotto; small temple; summer house with views across estuary to Hartland Point. TEAS (except March 15, April 19, Oct 11). *Adm £1.50. Suns March 15, April 19, May 10, June 14, July 12, Sept 13, Oct 11 (2-6)*

Greenway Gardens, Churston Ferrers ❀ (Mr & Mrs A A Hicks) 4m W of Brixham. From B3203, Paignton-Brixham, take rd to Galmpton, thence towards Greenway Ferry. 30 acres; old-established garden with mature trees; shrubs; rhododendrons, magnolias and camellias. Recent plantings; commercial shrub nursery. Woodland walks by R Dart. Limited parking, partly suitable for wheelchairs. Plants in adj nursery not in aid of NGS. TEA and biscuits. *Adm £1.50 Chd 50p. Thurs March 19, April 23, 30 (11-5).* **Tel 01803 842382**

¶**Half Moon House, Manaton** ✦ (Noel Welch & the National Trust). From Bovey Tracey take the B3387 (passing the entrance to park on R) for ¼m then bear R to Manaton (signed) for approx 4m. Car park at church with donation box and Half Moon House (not open), a thatched Devon longhouse, at the far end of the village green. Formal enclosed garden, a recreation of the old mediaeval Marian garden, surrounded by woodland with extensive views over Dartmoor National Park and magnificent granite outcrops throughout (approx 25 acres). The woodland leads to Manaton Rocks viewpoint and is carpeted with bluebells in spring. TEAS. *Adm £1.50 Chd 50p. Suns May 17, June 21 (2.30-6)*

Hamblyn's Coombe, Dittisham (Robert & Bridget McCrum) From Red Lion Inn follow The Level until it forks R up steep private road. Car park at top. 10 min pretty walk to 7-acre garden with stunning views, sloping steeply to R Dart. Extensive planting with unusual design features accompanying Bridget McCrum's stone carvings and bronzes. Wildflower meadow and woods. TEAS. *Adm £1.50 Chd free. Sun, Mon May 3, 4 (2-6). Private visits also welcome by appt, please* **Tel 01803 722228**

▲**Hartland Abbey, Hartland** &❀ (Sir Hugh & Lady Stucley) Turn off A39 W of Clovelly Cross. Follow signs to Hartland through town on rd to Stoke and Quay. Abbey 1m from town on right. 2 woodland shrubberies with camellias, rhododendrons; azalea and rare plants; wildflower walk through woods to remote Atlantic cove; walled gardens. Wheelchairs only on lawns around Abbey. TEAS. *Adm £2 Chd 50p (ACNO to St Necton's Church, Hartland®). For NGS Sun April 26 (2-5.30).* **Tel 01237 441264 (The Administrator)**

Hayne Old Manor, Moretonhampstead ❀ (Mr & Mrs R L Constantine) ¼m S of Moretonhampstead on A382. 5 acres with lake and walled garden, shrubs and herbaceous borders. Recent landscaping and new plantings, extensive views. Plant stall in aid of NABC. Cream TEAS. *Adm £1.50 Chd free. Private visits welcome by appt*

Heddon Hall, Parracombe ❀ (Mr & Mrs W H Keatley) 10m NE of Barnstaple off A39. 400yds N up hill from village centre. Entrance to drive on R. Ample parking 200yds. Garden of former rectory on edge of Exmoor extending to 3 acres. Walled garden with formal layout and herbaceous beds; sheltered flower garden; semi shaded S sloping shrubbery with paths leading down to natural stream and water garden. Cream TEAS. *Adm £1.50 Chd 50p. Suns June 14, July 12 (2-5.30)*

Higher Knowle, Lustleigh (Mr & Mrs D R A Quicke) 3m NW of Bovey Tracey A382 towards Moretonhampstead; in 2½m L for Lustleigh; in ¼m L/R; in ¼m steep drive L. 3-acre woodland garden around stone house built in 1914 with Lutyens style features. On steep hillside with spectacular views over Bovey valley to Dartmoor, sheltered garden usually avoids late frosts and is home to tender plants. The old oak wood is carpeted with primroses and bluebells among giant boulders with mature Asiatic magnolias in late March followed by camellias, new hybrid magnolias, rhododendrons/azaleas, and embothriums. *Adm £2 Chd free (ACNO to Moretonhampstead Hospital Improvement Appeal). Suns March 29; April 5, 12, 19, 26; May 3, 10, 17, 24, 31; Mons April 13, May 4, 25 (2-6). Private visits welcome, please* **Tel 01647 277275**

Higher Spriddlestone, Brixton & (Mr & Mrs David Willis) Nr Plymouth. A379 5m E from Plymouth, S at Otter Nurseries sign, ¾m to top of hill, R opp Spriddlestone sign, entrance 50yds on L. 1½-acre organic garden designed for shelter, low maintenance and wildlife. Climbing and scented plants. Produce, flowers and foliage for the house. Cream TEAS. *Adm £1.50 Chd free. Suns May 31, June 7 (2-5). Private visits also welcome, please* **Tel 01752 401184**

Hill House Nursery & Gardens, Landscove &❀ (Mr & Mrs R Hubbard) Follow brown signs from A384 Buckfastleigh to Totnes rd. Old Vicarage beside church, both designed by John Loughborough Pearson, architect of Truro Cathedral. The 3-acre garden was the subject of 'An Englishman's Garden' by Edward Hyams, a previous owner. Also featured in 'English Vicarages and Their Gardens' and several times on TV. A fine collection of plants in adj nursery. TEAS, picnic area. *Adm collection box. Open all year. Tea Room March 1 to Oct 4 (11-5)*

¶**Hillside Gardens, Knowle** ❀ (R Gardner & Mrs C Garner) 2.2m N of the Braunton traffic lights on the A361 Main rd to Ilfracombe. Please use N entrance by house. Garden has been developed over the past 4yrs and is fast maturing. The 1¾ acre site contains specimen trees, island beds of trees and shrubs, heather beds, wild flower area, orchard and kitchen garden. Overlooking the Caen Valley, there is also a 4 acre conservation area with well defined paths. *Adm £1 Chd free. Suns May 10, June 7, July 5, Aug 2, Sept 6 (2-6)*

Hole Farm, Farlacombe & (Rev Ian Graham-Orlebar) A383 Ashburton to Newton Abbot rd 3m NE from Ashburton signed Gale, Burne, Woodland. 1m at top of hill, lane on R to Hole Farm. 1½-acre valley garden, with woodland, wild garden, 2 ponds, herbaceous borders and bog areas. Old farm and buildings (not open). TEAS. *Adm £2 Chd 50p. Sun July 26 (2-5)*

Holywell, Bratton Fleming ✦ (Mr Ray Steele) 7m NE of Barnstaple. Turn W beside White Hart Inn (opp White Hart Garage) signed Village Hall. At 300yds fork L for Rye Park. Entrance drive ¼m at sharp L. Parking at house. Garden on edge of Exmoor in woodland setting of mature trees, in all about 25 acres. Stream, ponds and borders. Woodland walk to Lower River meadow and old Lynton

Railway Track. *Adm £1.50 Chd free. Mons May 4, 25, Sun June 7 (2-5.30). Private visits welcome, please* Tel 01598 710213

Inglewood, Newton Ferrers ✿❀ (Major & Mrs Stevenson) 10m E of Plymouth. A374 Plymouth to Kingsbridge. At Yealmpton S to Newton Ferrers. At the green Xrds R into Parsonage Rd and along Court Rd for ¾m. Entrance on L. Unusual situation overlooking R Yealm. Steep garden. Recently reconstructed, with many terraces. Colour selection of plants and shrubs. TEAS. *Adm £1.50 Chd free. Suns April 19, May 10 (2-5)*

Kerscott House, Swimbridge ♿✿❀ (Mrs Jessica Duncan) Barnstaple-South Molton (former A361) 1m E of Swimbridge, R at top of hill, immediate fork L, 100yds on L, 1st gate past house. Developing 6-acre garden surrounding C16 farmhouse in peaceful rural setting. Ornamental trees, wide selection of shrubs, herbaceous and tender perennials, ponds and bog garden. Living willow constructions. 2½ acres new woodland planted 1995. *Adm £1 Chd 50p. Suns June 21, July 26, Aug 30 (2-6). Private visits also welcome during July, please* Tel 01271 830943

▲**Killerton Garden, Broadclyst** ♿✿❀ (The National Trust) 8m N of Exeter. Via B3181 Cullompton Rd (formerly A38), fork left in 7m on B3185. Garden 1m follow NT signs. 8ha of spectacular hillside gardens with naturalised bulbs sweeping down to large open lawns. Delightful walks through fine collection of rare trees and shrubs; herbaceous borders. Wheelchair and 'golf' buggy with driver available. Restaurant. Tea room, plant centre. *Adm gardens only £3.50 Chd £1.70. For NGS Suns April 19, July 5 (10.30-5.30)*

Kingston House, Staverton ♿✿ (Mr & Mrs M R Corfield) 4m NE of Totnes. A384 Totnes to Buckfastleigh, from Staverton, 1m due N of Sea Trout Inn, follow signs to Kingston. George II 1735 house grade II *. Gardens are being restored in keeping with the period. Walled garden, rose garden, herbaceous borders, pleached limes and hornbeams, vegetable garden. Unusual formal garden with santolinas, lavender and camomile. Cream TEAS. *Adm £1.50 Chd 50p (ACNO to Animals in Distress, Ipplepen®). Suns April 12, June 14 (2-6). Private parties over 20 welcome by arrangement, please* Tel 01803 762235. No coaches

▲**Knightshayes Gardens, Tiverton** ♿✿❀ (The National Trust) 2m N of Tiverton. Via A396 Tiverton-Bampton; turn E in Bolham, signed Knightshayes; entrance ½m on left. Large 'Garden in the Wood', 20ha of landscaped gardens with pleasant walks and views over the Exe valley. Choice collections of unusual plants, incl acers, birches, rhododendrons, azaleas, camellias, magnolias, roses, spring bulbs, alpines and herbaceous borders; formal gardens; Wheelchair available. Restaurant, plant centre. *Adm garden only £3.50 Chd £1.70. For NGS Suns April 26, June 28 (11-5.30)*

Lee Ford, Budleigh Salterton ♿❀ (Mr & Mrs N Lindsay-Fynn) Knowle. A recently landscaped formal and woodland garden with extensive display of spring bulbs, camellias, rhododendrons, azaleas and magnolias. Traditional walled vegetable garden. Ornamental conservatory and Adam pavilion. TEAS and charity stalls. *Adm £2 OAPs £1.50 Chd £1 Special rate for groups 20 or more £1.50 (ACNO to the Lindsay-Fynn Trust®). Sun May 24 (1.30-5.30); also by prior appt for parties of 20 or more (Light refreshments available)* Tel 01395 445894

Little Cumbre, Exeter ✿❀ (Dr & Mrs John Lloyd) At top of Pennsylvania Rd, 50yds below telephone kiosk on same side. Extensive views to Dartmoor and the Exe Estuary. ½-acre mixed shrub and herbaceous garden and ½ acre of woodland, newly acquired. Galanthus, hellebores, clematis and small ornamental trees with interesting bark. Ample parking in rd. *Adm £2 Chd 50p. Suns Feb 22, May 7, June 4. 1999 Sun Feb 21 (2-5)*

Little Southey, Northcott ♿✿❀ (Mr & Mrs S J Rowe) Nr Culmstock. Uffculme to Culmstock rd, through Craddock then turn R at 6'6 restriction sign, Little Southey ½m on L. Culmstock to Uffculme turn L at de-restriction sign to Blackborough, 1st R at Xrds to Northcott. House on R. Garden surrounding C17 farmhouse. Wide variety of plants grown for yr-round interest. Limited parking if wet. Plant sale partly in aid of NCCPG June 28 only. TEAS. *Adm £1.50 Chd free. Sun June 28 (2-6); Mon June 29 (2-6)*

Little Upcott Gardens, Marsh Green ♿✿❀ (Mr & Mrs M Jones) Signposted off A30 Exeter to Honiton rd 4m E of M5 junction 29. Also signposted off B3180. Garden signposted from Marsh Green. Informal 2-acre garden. Sensitive combination of plant styles and colour and unusual varieties of conifers, shrubs, perennials and alpines, some for sale. The original cottage garden is also open and a water feature with ornamental ducks. Seats available and assistance given to disabled incl partially sighted, by prior arrangement. Parties welcomed with cream teas, available by appt. TEAS. *Adm £1.50 Chd 50p (ACNO to Cats Protection League, Ottery Branch®). Mons, Weds, Sat, Sun May 23, 24, 25, 27, June 7, 10, 14, 21, 28; July 8, 12, 26; Aug 5, 9, 19, 23 (1.30-5.30); Weds June 24, July 22 (5.30-9). Brochure with other opening times available on request, please* Tel 01404 822797

The Lodge, Mannamead ♿❀ (Mr & Mrs M H Tregaskis) Hartley Ave, Plymouth. 1½m from City Centre via Mutley Plain. Turn right at Henders Corner into Eggbuckland Rd, 3rd right at Tel kiosk to end of cul de sac. ½-acre S sloping aspect with variety of citrus fruits, olives, unusual shrubs, conifers, camellias and ground cover plants. Large vegetable area. Former L.A. Nursery with range of lean-to glasshouses for fruit and tender subjects. Featured on BBC TV 'Out and About' 1997. TEA. *Adm £1.50 Acc chd free (ACNO to St. Luke's Hospice®). Suns May 3, June 7, July 19 (2-5.30). Private visits also welcome, please* Tel 01752 220849

Evening Opening (see also garden descriptions)

Little Upcott Gardens, Marsh Green
June 24, July 22 5.30pm–9pm

Longham, Coryton ✿✿ (Jennie Hale & Andrew Osborne) Nr Lydford Gorge. A30, turn onto A386 Tavistock. 5m to Dartmoor Inn, signed to Lyford, past Lydford Gorge (NT). 3m R for Chillaton, 500yds R to Liddaton, downhill to Liddaton Cross, sharp R, 400yds over railway bridge, immed R into T sign rd, ½m downhill, L over small bridge, signed Longham Farm. Follow short track to the cottage. Ample parking. Small cottage garden with colourful mass herbaceous planting, ornamental grasses, shrubs, unusual perennials and climbers, vegetable garden, raised beds and polytunnel. Beautiful rural setting in wooded valley. TEAS. *Adm £1 Chd 50p. Sun Aug 2 (2-6). Private visits by appt, please* **Tel 01822 860287**

■ **Lukesland, Ivybridge** (Mr & Mrs B N Howell) 1½m N of Ivybridge on Harford Rd, E side of Erme valley. 15 acres of flowering shrubs, wild flowers and rare trees with pinetum in Dartmoor National Park. Beautiful setting of small valley around Addicombe Brook with lakes, numerous waterfalls and pools. Extensive and unusual collection of large and small leaved rhododendrons and one of the largest magnolia campbellii in country. Partially suitable for wheelchairs. TEAS. *Adm £2.50 Chd free. Suns, Weds, April 19 to June 17. Bank Hol Mons May 4, 25. For NGS Wed May 6, Sun May 10 (2-6). Coaches on application only,* **Tel 01752 893390**

●**Marwood Hill, Marwood** ✿ (Dr J A Smart) 4m N of Barnstaple signed from A361 Barnstaple-Braunton rd and B3230 Barnstaple to Ilfracombe Rd. Outside Guineaford village, opp Marwood church. 20-acre garden with 3 small lakes. Extensive collection of camellias under glass and in open; daffodils, rhododendrons, rare flowering shrubs, rock and alpine scree; waterside planting; bog garden; many clematis; Australian native plants. National Collections astilbe, iris ensata, tulbaghia. Partially suitable for wheelchairs. Plants for sale between 11-5. Teas in Church Room (Suns & Bank Hols or by prior arrangement for parties). *Adm £2 Acc chd under 12 free. Daily except Christmas Day (dawn-dusk)*

Meadowcroft, Plympton &✿ (Mrs G Thompson) 1 Downfield Way. From Plymouth L at St Mary's Church roundabout, along Glen Rd, 3rd R into Downfield Drive; garden on immed R. From A38, Plympton turn-off L at 1st roundabout, R at 2nd down Hillcrest Drive and Glen Rd, L at bottom of hill, before Dillons and into Downfield Drive, garden on immed R. 2-acre country garden in urban area, rhododendrons, azaleas, fruit, bog garden, mixed borders, spring bulbs, interesting trees. TEAS. *Adm £1.50 Chd free. Sun April 12, Thurs April 30, Suns May 10, June 7 (2-5)*

Membland Villa, Newton Ferrers ✿✿ (Mr & Mrs Jack Hockaday) 10m E of Plymouth. A374 Plymouth-Kingsbridge. At Yealmpton, S to Newton Ferrers. Follow signs. Late C19 house, part of the Revelstoke Estate, built by Edward Baring. Charming country garden, filled with many varied and unusual plants incl old roses, climbers etc. TEAS served in the conservatory. Small exhibition of wildlife paintings. Extensive Bluebell wood, spectacular in season. TEAS. *Adm £1.50. Suns March 22, May 17, June 7, 21, July 12, 26, Aug 16, Sept 20; Mons April 13, May 4, 25, Aug 31 (1-5). Parties of 10 or more welcome, but please write for booking.* **Tel 01752 872626**

Monks Aish, South Brent ✿✿ (Capt & Mrs M J Garnett) 1m W of South Brent, near the hamlet of Aish, off B3372 W of village. Follow signposts to Aish. After going under Aish railway bridge up hill, 3rd house on L next to Great Aish. [Grid Ref 688603.] A very attractive 1-acre garden with stream, a little different from most with varieties of shrubs, trees, flowers, fruit and vegetables. TEAS. *Adm £2 Chd under 12 50p (ACNO to The Missions to Seamen®). Sat, Sun May 23, 24 (2-5). Private visits welcome, please* **Tel 01364 73102**

¶**Monteverde, Old Feniton** ✿✿ (Mr & Mrs D C Harvey) From A30 4m W of Honiton, turn N at Fenny Bridges and follow signs. Enthusiast's large garden developing from old pasture, round modern bungalow. Varied shrubs, herbaceous plants and bulbs. Perfume, colour-coordination, and mini nature reserve. Stream, waterfalls, large pool, bog garden and potager. TEAS. *Adm £1.50 Chd 50p (ACNO to Friends of Kew®). Sat, Sun July 18, 19 (2-5.30)*

The Moorings, Rocombe (Mr & Mrs A Marriage) Uplyme, 2m NW of Lyme Regis. From Lyme Regis, about 1m on A3070, turn R signposted Rocombe, over Xrds, take narrow lane signposted Rocombe 4th house on R, drive beyond house. From Axminster, straight at Hunters Lodge then fork R twice, straight at Xrds and R again. ¾m on L. 3-acre peaceful woodland garden, developed since 1965, on hillside with terraced paths, overlooking unspoilt countryside. Fine trees incl many species eucalyptus, unusual pines, nothofagus; flowering shrubs; daffodils and other spring flowers, ground cover, many ferns, autumn colour. *Adm £1 Chd free. Private visits welcome, please* **Tel 01297 443295**

Mothecombe House, Holbeton &✿ (Mr & Mrs A Mildmay-White) SE of Plymouth 10m. From A379, between Yealmpton and Modbury, turn S for Holbeton. Continue 2m to Mothecombe. Queen Anne house (not open). Walled gardens, herbaceous borders. Orchard with spring bulbs; camellia walk and flowering shrubs. Bog garden; streams and pond; bluebell woods leading to private beach. Teas at beach car park, Old School tea house. *Adm garden £2 Chd free. Sat, Sun May 2, 3, June 21 (2-5.30). Parties welcome by appt, please* **Tel 01752 830444**

Newton Abbot Gardens Old Totnes Road, 1m S of Newton Abbot off the A381, opp Bradley Manor (NT). 3 suburban gardens with views of Wolborough Hill and church. Parking in rd. TEAS. *Combined adm £1.50 Chd 50p. Sat, Sun June 6, 7 (2-5)*

    Fieldfare ✿ (Mr & Mrs M Bishop) Large garden, still being developed with beds of heathers, spring borders, roses, shrubs, herbs, and herbaceous plants. Climbers, pond, soft fruit and new Japanese garden. TEAS

    The Mount ✿✿ (Mr & Mrs R Lea) Landscaped garden with mixed planting amongst established shrubs and trees. Paved area surrounded by bulbs, herbaceous plants, and flowering shrubs. Steps to lower lawn and summerhouse with herbaceous border and climbers. Hosta border and newly planted gravel garden

    Le Cateau ✿ Approx ⅓-acre cottage style garden with large weeping willow and natural pond

Oare Manor Cottage, Oare ✿ (Mr & Mrs J Greenaway) 6m E of Lynton off A39. R after County Gate to Oare. 50yds from Oare Church, immortalized in R D Blackmore's 'Lorna Doone'. Sheltered cottage garden in the romantic Oare Valley. Old-fashioned herbaceous borders. Featured on ITV Westcountry. Fine views of the moor. Parking in lower field or opp church. TEA. *Adm £1.50 Chd 50p (ACNO to Anti-Slavery International®). Weds, Sun July 22, 26 (2-6). Private visits welcome, please* **Tel 01598 741242**

The Old Glebe, Eggesford ⅏✿ (Mr & Mrs Nigel Wright) 4m SW of Chulmleigh. Turn S off A377 at Eggesford Station (½-way between Exeter & Barnstaple), cross railway and River Taw, drive straight uphill (signed Brushford) for ¾m; turn right into bridle path. 7-acre garden of former Georgian rectory with mature trees and several lawns, courtyard, walled herbaceous borders, bog garden and small lake; emphasis on species and hybrid rhododendrons and azaleas, 750 varieties. Rhododendrons for sale. TEAS. *Adm £2 Chd £1 (ACNO to The Abbeyfield Chulmleigh®). Suns, Mon Bank Hols May 3, 4, 24, 25 (2-6).* **Tel 01769 580632**

The Old Mill, Blakewell ✿ (Mr & Mrs Shapland) Muddiford, nr Barnstaple. ½m past hospital off B3230 to Ilfracombe at Blakewell Fisheries. Follow signs to Mill (grade II) at end of lane. 4-acre south sloping garden started in 1989 set in beautiful countryside. Unusual trees, conifers and shrubs. A Lavender walk, vegetable plot, orchard and ponds. Lime tree avenue leading to Folly and secret Japanese style garden. Lower garden, rockpool, with large waterfall and ample parking in field. *Suns May 24, June 14, Oct 4 (11-5), Wed July 29 (11-8). Private visits also welcome, please* **Tel 01271 375002**

The Old Parsonage, Warkleigh ✿❀ (Mr & Mrs Alex Hill) 4m SW South Molton on B3226 past Clapworthy Mill (Hancocks Cider) R at stone barn signs to Warkleigh. From S through Chittlehamholt then 2nd R at War Memorial. Telephone kiosk marked on OS landranger sheet 180. 1-acre garden around former C16 Parsonage. Herbaceous border at entrance; enclosed stepped terraced garden behind house with wide range of plants and raised beds. Hillside above planted with trees and shrubs for all seasons interest. Cream TEAS. *Adm £1.50 Chd 50p (ACNO to NCCPG®). Sun June 14 (2-5.30). Private visits welcome, please* **Tel 01769 540329**

The Old Rectory, East Portlemouth (Mr & Mrs C W L Barwell) Opp Salcombe. From A379 Kingsbridge to Dartmouth R at Frogmore over bridge towards E Portlemouth for 5m. Through village to estuary, R for 200yds, entrance on L. Or from Salcombe, passenger ferry to E Portlemouth, L for ½m. Former rectory in 3-acre garden on Salcombe estuary with lovely views of Southpool Creek. Landscaped and walled gardens with camellias, magnolias, viburnums. Herbaceous and mixed borders with roses and tender plants in walled garden. TEAS. *Adm £1.50 Chd free. Sat, Sun, Mon May 2, 3, 4 (11-5).* **Tel 01548 842670**

The Old Rectory, Woodleigh ⅏✿ (Mr & Mrs H E Morton) Nr Loddiswell. 3½m N of Kingsbridge E off Kingsbridge-Wrangaton Rd at Rake Cross (1m S of Loddiswell). 1½m to Woodleigh. Secret garden of trees, shrubs and naturalised bulbs with emphasis on rhododendrons, camellias and magnolias in spring and hydrangeas in Autumn. Chemical free. Maintained by owner. *Adm £2 Chd 50p. Private visits usually welcome at any time, please* **Tel 01548 550387**

The Orchard, Kenn ❀ (Mrs Hilda M Montgomery) 5m S of Exeter off A38. ¾ acre; mostly rare trees; variety of conifers, azaleas, camellias, rhododendrons, many shrubs; fishponds and flowerbeds. Masses of spring bulbs. Ample parking nr Church. *Adm £1 Chd 50p. Sun May 17 (2-5.30) please* **Tel 01392 832530**

Orchard Cottage, Exmouth ⅏✿ (Mr & Mrs W K Bradridge) 30, Hulham Rd. From Exeter A376 L into Hulham Road, just before 1st set of traffic lights. Entrance lane between Nos 26 and 32 Hulham Rd, opp lower end of Phillips Avenue. ¼-acre typical cottage garden. Parking in Hulham Road or Phillips Avenue. *Adm £1 Chd free. By appt only, please* **Tel 01395 278605** *(2.30-5.30)*

Ottery St Mary Gardens Maps available at each garden. *Combined adm £1.50 Chd 50p. Sat, Sun May 16, 17 (2-6)*
¶**Bramblemore** ✿ (June & Tony Jones) After turning into Longdogs Lane from Sidmouth Rd, Orchard Close is 2nd turning L. Please park in L Lane not the Close. A ½-acre garden developed over the last 4yrs from scratch on idiosyncratic lines; concerned mainly with variation of shape and colour. Pond area, wooded enclave and vegetable patch. Teas as no 5
Little Ash Farm ⅏ (Sadie & Robert Reid) Fenny Bridges. Situated on A30, next to Esso Garage at Fenny Bridges. Park in layby. Developing ½-acre garden, trees, shrubs, large pond and borders with integrated vegetables. Handmade furniture workshop
Ravenhill ⅏✿❀ (Ruth & Guy Charter) Longdogs Lane. Take Sidmouth Rd from town square, 200yds up Tip Hill turn L up narrow Longdogs Lane, 5th house on R. Medium-sized garden with a wide variety of unusual plants. South aspect, country views; pond; keen NCCPG propagator. *(ACNO to NCCPG®)*
10 Slade Close ✿❀ (Betty & Jenny Newell) From town centre take rd towards Seaton. Turn R into Slade Rd, then L into Slade Close and R again. Small garden, mixed shrubs, spring flowers, small pond, scree garden

▲**Overbecks, Sharpitor** ✿ (The National Trust) 1½m SW of Salcombe. From Salcombe or Malborough follow NT signs. 2.4ha garden with rare plants and shrubs; spectacular views over Salcombe Estuary. Tea room same days as museum 12-4.15. *Adm garden only £2.60 Chd £1.30. For NGS Suns May 31, June 21 (10-8 sunset if earlier)*

38 Phillipps Avenue, Exmouth ✿❀ (Mr & Mrs R G Stuckey) From Exeter, turn L into Hulham rd just before 1st set of traffic lights, 1st L in Phillipps Avenue (ample parking). Small, highly specialised alpine and rock garden containing extensive collection of rock plants and minature shrubs, many rare and unusual; scree bed; troughs. National NCCPG Helichrysum collection. Small alpine nursery. Teashops Exmouth. *Adm £1 Chd free. Suns*

March 22, 29, April 5, 9, May 3, 17, 31; June 7, 14 (ACNO to NCCPG®), 21, 28, July 19, Aug 16, Sept 6. Private visits also welcome, please **Tel 01395 273636**

The Pines, Salcombe &. (R A Bitmead) Main Rd. At junction of Devon and Sandhills rds; lower entrance and parking Sandhills rd. All seasons ¾-acre S facing garden; fine coastal views to Sharpitor Headland and N Sands Valley. Informal garden of surprises; many interesting and unusual shrubs, trees; water gardens; bulbs, camellias, azaleas, heathers. *Adm £2 Chd free. Suns March 15, 29, April 12, 26, May 17 (11-5). Private visits also welcome all year, please* **Tel 01548 842198**

Plant World, Newton Abbot ❀ (Ray & Lin Brown) St. Mary Church Rd. Follow brown signs from A380 Penn Inn Roundabout. Car park on L past aquatic centre. 4-acre Hillside Garden, laid out as a map of the world with native plants. Alpines, especially primulas and gentians, shrubs, herbaceous. Himalayan and Japanese gardens. Comprehensive cottage garden with hardy geraniums, campanulas. 3 National Primula Collections. Seen on BBC Gardeners World June 1993. Rare and unusual plants sold in adjacent nursery. Picnic area, viewpoint over Dartmoor and Lyme Bay. Collecting box. *Adm £1 Chd under 12 free. Easter to end of Sept every day but Wed (9.30-5)*

Pleasant View Nursery, Two Mile Oak &.⚘ (Mr & Mrs B D Yeo) Nr Denbury. 2m from Newton Abbot on A381 to Totnes. R at Two Mile Oak Public House signed Denbury. ¾m on L. Large car park. 2-acre plantsman's garden with a wide range of choice and uncommon shrubs giving colour all season. Additional 2-acre field planted with individual specimen shrubs. National Collections of Abelia and Salvia. Plants for sale in adjoining nursery (see advert). *Adm £1.50 Chd 25p. Sat, Sun May 30, 31 (2-6). Every Wed and Fri, May to Sept incl (2-5). Parties welcome by appt, please* **Tel 01803 813388**

Portington, Lamerton (Mr & Mrs I A Dingle) From Tavistock B3362 to Launceston. ¼m beyond Blacksmiths Arms, Lamerton, fork L (signed Chipshop). Over Xrds (signed Horsebridge) first L then L again (signed Portington). From Launceston R at Carrs Garage and R again (signed Horsebridge), then as above. Garden in peaceful rural setting with fine views over surrounding countryside. Mixed planting with shrubs and borders; woodland walk to small lake. TEAS. *Adm £1.50 Chd 20p (ACNO to St Luke's Hospice®). Suns July 12, 19 (2-5.30)*

Priors, Abbotskerswell &.⚘ (Mrs Hunloke) 1½m SW of Newton Abbot on Totnes-Newton Rd, signposted Abbotskerswell. Garden at bottom of village. ⅓-acre enclosed colourful garden, long, wide, herbaceous borders, old shrub roses; unusual plants. *Adm £1 Chd 50p. Suns June 21, 28, July 12 (2-5.30)*

Riversbridge, Dartmouth &.❀ (Mr & Mrs Sutton-Scott-Tucker) ½m inland from Blackpool sands and signed from A3122. Small walled gardens adjoining farmyard in lovely unspoilt valley with ponds and stream; herbaceous plants, roses and some unusual shrubs. TEAS. *Adm £1.50 Chd free. Suns June 14, 21 (2-6)*

Rock House Garden, Chudleigh ❀ (Mrs D M & B Boulton) Station Hill. A38 Exeter to Plymouth signed Chudleigh. S edge of town. Entrance at Rock Nursery. Garden in ancient bishop's palace quarry with massive limestone rock. Delights for all seasons. Rare and unusual trees and shrubs. Massed daffodils in spring. Autumn brings one of the finest displays of cyclamen. Cave and ponds with Koi and Orfe. Walk with spectacular views of Dartmoor and access to Chudleigh rock, glen and waterfall. *Adm £1.50 Chd £1. Suns March 29, April 26, Sept 13, 20, Nov 8 (9.30-5.0)*

Rose Marie Cottage, Brixham ❀ (Howard & Rosemarie East) 42 Rea Barn Rd. From Brixham Town Centre take Darmouth rd, in approx ¼m turn L at t-lights (or R if coming from Dartmouth). Garden is 150yds on L. Small secluded walled garden. Rose arbour; clematis; herbaceous borders. TEAS. *Sats, Suns June 27, 28 July 4, 5 (11-4)*

●**Rosemoor Garden, Great Torrington** &.⚘❀ (The Royal Horticultural Society) 1m SE of Great Torrington on B3220 to Exeter. 40-acre plantsman's garden; rhododendrons (species and hybrid), ornamental trees and shrubs; dwarf conifer collection, species and old-fashioned roses, scree and raised beds with alpine plants, arboretum. 2000 roses in 200 varieties, two colour theme gardens, herb garden, potager, 200 metres of herbaceous border, a large stream and bog garden, cottage garden, foliage and plantsman's garden and a fruit and vegetable garden. Facilities for the disabled. *Adm £3.20 Chd £1 Groups £2.50 per person. Open daily all year (10-6 April to Sept. 10-5 Oct to March) (Share to NGS®).* **Tel 01805 624067**

■ **Rowden Gardens, Brentor** &.⚘❀ (Mr & Mrs John Carter) 4m N of Tavistock. From A386 through Lydford village, or take Brentor Rd from Tavistock. Between 'Mucky Duck' and 'Brentor' Inns take rd signed Liddaton. Entrance 300yds on R. Tranquil 1-acre plantsman's garden begun in 1986 by author/lecturer John Carter. Featured in Practical Gardening '95. Ponds displaying water-lilies and many unusual aquatics. Bog gardens, grass walk, plantings of crocosmia, dierama, ligularia, ranunculus, rheums. Huge collection damp loving iris incl new introductions and unique home-bred varieties. 2 NCCPG national collections. Plants for sale in adjoining nursery. Cream teas in Lydford. *Adm £1.50 Chd free. Suns, Mons June 14, 15, July 5, 6, Aug 16, 17, Sept 6, 7 (10-5). Private visits welcome, please* **Tel 01822 810275**

Rowden House, Noss Mayo ❀ (Mr & Mrs T Hill) 10m E of Plymouth. A374 Plymouth to Kingsbridge. At Yealmpton S to Noss Mayo. At church follow signs to Stoke Beach for 1m. Entrance on R. Grade II listed farmhouse with ½-acre garden in rural setting. Developed over past 10 yrs. Exposed to salt-laden winds. Spring-fed pond. Interesting collection of plants. *Adm £1.50 Chd free. Suns April 19, May 10 (2-5.30)*

St Olaves, Murchington ⚘ (Mr & Mrs R Padley) 1m W of Chagford. A382 1m S of Whiddon Down signpost Throwleigh and Gidleigh, then signs to Murchington and to garden. Garden converted, restored and replanted since 1971. Romantic landscape views over the Upper Teign Valley. Fine old trees and many younger ones, incl a collection of modern magnolia hybrids. Massive granite retaining walls. On S-facing slope down which a cascade falls to the river. *Adm £2 Chd 50p (ACNO to Devon Gardens Trust®). Weds April 15, May 6 (2-5.30). Also private visits always welcome for magnolias and camellias mid March to May, please* **Tel 01647 433415**

▲**Saltram House, Plympton** ⅋⊛ (The National Trust) 3m E of Plymouth, S of A38, 2m W of Plympton. 4ha with fine specimen trees; spring garden; rhododendrons and azaleas. C18 orangery and octagonal garden house. George II mansion with magnificent plasterwork and decorations, incl 2 rooms designed by Robert Adam. Wheelchair available. Restaurant. *Adm gardens only £2.60 Chd £1.30. For NGS Suns April 5, May 10 (10.30-5.30)*

Scypen, Ringmore ⅋⊛ (Mr & Mrs John Bracey) From A379 Plymouth-Kingsbridge S at Harraton Cross on B3392. R at Pickwick Inn. Park in Journey's End car park on L opp church. ½-acre coastal garden, integrating design, landscaping and mixed planting for year-round effect and to take advantage of lovely views. Salt and wind tolerant plants; silver garden; chamomile and thyme lawns. Featured on BBC Westcountry programme for NGS 70th Anniversary. TEAS. *Adm £1 Chd 25p. Wed, Sun June 10, 14 (2-5)*

Shobrooke Park Gardens, Crediton ⅋⊛ (Dr & Mrs J R Shelley) 1m NE Crediton on A3072. 15-acre woodland gardens with daffodils, rhododendrons and roses. Laid out in mid C19 with extensive Portland Stone terraces with views over the park and ponds. Restoration in an early stage with help from The Countryside Commission. TEAS. *Adm £2 Chd free. Sats April 4, May 16, June 27 (2-5)*

Skerraton, Dean Prior ⅋⊛ (Mr & Mrs M Ogle) 3m SW of Buckfastleigh. A38 ½m W of Buckfastleigh signed Dean. Follow signs to Skerraton for 2½m. 2 acres, 800' up on Dartmoor with views across South Hams to sea. Woodland area with azaleas, camellias and rhododendrons. Stream with marginal plants. Formal area with island and mixed borders. Pool. Most plants labelled. Dartmoor ponies and foals in paddocks and stables by house. TEAS. *Adm £2.50 Chd free (ACNO to Dean Prior Parish Church®). Sat, Sun June 6, 7 (2-6)*

¶**Southcombe House, Widecombe-in-the-Moor** 6m W of Bovey Tracey, house marked on Landranger OS map 191. After village church take rd SW for 200yds then sharp R signposted Southcombe up steep hill. House is 200yds on L. Pass house and park on L, alternatively park in public car park in village and walk. 5-acre SE facing garden, recently planted arboretum and developing wild flower meadow on steep slope at 900ft above sea level with fine views to nearby tors. Primarily of interest to wild flower enthusiasts. Teas in village. *Adm £2 Chd free. Suns May 31, June 14 (2-5.30)*

Spillifords, Lower Washfield (Dr Gavin Haig) Tiverton can be reached on A396 Tiverton to Bampton. Turn L over iron bridge signposted Stoodleigh. L again after crossing bridge marked Washfield and L again on hill following Washfield sign. The bridge is approx 2m from link rd roundabout. Spillifords is 1st house on L after Hatswell. Parking for 30 cars by annexe on same side as house. 1½-acre wildlife and wild flower garden. On steeply sloping bank of R Exe (unsuitable for disabled) wild flowers, butterflies, birds and other wildlife abound in an ideal arboreal and riverside environment. TEAS. *Adm £2 Chd £1. Guided tours by appointment only. Weds, Sats pm April to Aug (3-6). Please* **Tel 01884 255353**

Starveacre, Dalwood ⊛ (Mr and Mrs Bruce Archibold) Leave Axminster on A35 travelling W. After 3m (Shute Xrds) turn R at staggered Xrds follow signs to Dalwood and go through village, over stream, round sharp L bend. Follow road, ignoring L turn, up steep hill and at top turn L. Under pylons and up hill. Car park on L. A plantsman's garden of 5 acres on a hillside facing S and W with superb views. Mixed plantings of rhododendrons, camellias, conifers, acers and magnolias. TEAS. *Adm £2 Chd free. Suns May 3, 31, Oct 25 (2-5)*

■ **Stone Lane Gardens, Chagford** ⊛ (Kenneth & June Ashburner) Stone Farm, Chagford. On NE edge of Dartmoor National park. From A30 signed Moretonhampstead, through Whiddon Down (A382) for ¼m, then signed Drewsteignton. After 1½m, 2nd R into Stone Lane. Parking on L. 5-acre arboretum featuring streams and pond with National Collections of wild-origin birch and alder. Sculpture exhibition 'mythic' garden June-Sept. TEAS. No coaches. *Adm £2.50 Gardens open daily June to Sept. For NGS Weds June 10, July 8, Aug 5, Sept 2 (2-6). Private visits, please* **Tel 01647 231311**

Sunnybrook, Luffincott ⅋⊛ (Bill & Jean Wonnacott) A388 ½-way between Holsworthy and Launceston signed Luffincott at lay-by, cottage 1m on L. Small cottage garden with pond and short walk through adjacent old coppice wood. Bluebells, wild flowers and native ferns in spring. Shrubs and perennial planting around cottage and pond. Numerous containers. Cream TEAS. Ample parking. *Adm £1.50 Chd 50p (ACNO to Save the Children Fund®). Suns April 5, 19, May 3, 17, 31, June 14, 28, July 12 (2-6). Private visits also welcome, please* **Tel 01409 271380**

Sunrise Hill, Withleigh ⅋⊛ (Chris & Sharon Britton) 3m W of Tiverton on B3137 rd to Witheridge and South Molton. Garden reached through Withleigh Nurseries, situated at E end of village. 1½ acres of colourful garden incl 40m 'Rainbow' border, unusual plants, shrubs, lawns and new plantings. Plants for sale at adjacent nursery (on open days 10% of sales to Uranch House). TEAS in aid of Uranch House. *Adm £1.50 Chd free. Weds July 1, 22, Aug 19 (2-5.30). Parties welcome by appt, please* **Tel 01884 253351**

¶**Sutton Mead, Moretonhampstead** ⅋⅋ (Edward & Miranda Allhusen) ½m N Moretonhampstead. Leave village towards Chagford and turn R beside speed restriction sign. 3-acre garden with views of Dartmoor. Rhododendrons and azaleas, ponds, new woodland garden currently being cleared and replanted, mixed spring bulbs and primroses, borders, vegetable garden. TEAS. *Adm £1.50 Chd free. Sat, Sun April 4, 5 (2-5)*

Sweet Chestnut, Bovey Tracey ✗ (P Thompson) Whisselwell Lane. From Bovey Tracy, follow Haytor Rd to Edgemoor Hotel. Sharp L opp hotel, then 1st R, signed Whisselwell Farm. Last house on R. 1-acre woodland garden. Rhododendrons and camellias in abundance and other ericaceous plants and ground cover. Good yr-round planting and autumn colour with list available on request. *Adm £1.50 Chd 25p. Private visits welcome, please* **Tel 01626 833280**

● **Tapeley Park & Gardens, Instow** ♿❀ (Hector Christie) A39 Barnstaple-Bideford drive entrance and lodge 1m S of Instow. Italianate garden with stunning coastal views to the atlantic and Lundy Island. The terraces with long wall borders shelter many herbaceous and tender plants, replanted under the guidance of Mary Keen and Carol Klein. Walled kitchen and vegetable garden with long greenhouse for tender plants and grapes. Ice and shell houses. Lunches & cream TEAS. *Adm £2.80 OAP £2.30 Chd £1.80 (ACNO to NGS®). Good Fri to Oct 30 daily except Sats (10-5)*

Topsham Gardens ♿❀ 4m from Exeter. Free parking in Holman Way car park. Teas at 20 Monmouth Ave. *Adm £1 each garden Chd free. Sun, Mon May 3, 4 (2-6)*
  4 Grove Hill (Margaret and Arthur Boyce) Off Elm Grove Rd, opp junction with Station Rd. A small town garden with some rare plants, troughs and screes with alpine plants and unusual bulbs. *Also open Sun June 7*
  20 Monmouth Avenue (Anne & Harold Lock) Access to Monmouth Ave by footpath on the L after leaving Holman Way car park. ⅓-acre level garden, wide range of unusual plants and shrubs giving year round effect, mixed curved borders, herbaceous, shrubs and bulbs incl a collection of hardy geraniums and alliums. Some old-fashioned roses. Featured on TV 'Gardens For All'. TEAS. *Private visits also welcome, please* **Tel 01392 873734**

96 Wasdale Gardens, Estover ✗❀ (David & Colleen Fenwick) Plymouth. Outskirts of city. From A38 Forder Valley Junction, follow Forder Valley Rd (old A38), R into Novorossisk Rd, L into Miller Way, L at 3rd mini roundabout into Keswick Crescent, 1st L into Wasdale Gardens. Car park next to 102 Wasdale Gardens, follow path along top of car park past nos 95 and 94. Small council house garden with large diversity of unusual plants, mostly herbaceous. NCCPG Nat Cols Crocosmia and Chasmanthe, as seen on TV. Recycled materials used in garden design. *Adm £1 Chd 50p. Visits welcome by appt June 1 to Sept 1, please* **Tel 01752 785147**

Webbery Gardens, Alverdiscott ✗❀ Approx 2½m E of Bideford. Either from Bideford (E The Water) along the Alverdiscott Rd or from the Barnstaple to Torrington Rd B3232. Take the rd to Bideford at Alverdiscott and pass through Stoney Cross. TEA. *Combined adm £2 Chd free. Sat, Sun June 20, 21 (2-6)*
  Little Webbery (Mr & Mrs J A Yewdall) Parking next door field. Approx 3-acre garden with two large borders near the house with lawns running down a valley; pond, mature trees on either side and fields below, separated by 2 Ha Has. Walled garden with box hedging, partly used for fruit, vegetables, and incl a greenhouse; lawns; rose garden and trellises; shrubs and climbing plants. A tennis court below and a lake beyond
  Little Webbery Cottage (Mr & Mrs J A Yewdall) Parking and entrance as for Little Webbery. Self contained cottage garden with wide selection of flowering plants and shrubs incl pergolas with roses, clematis and jasmine
  Webbery Garden Cottage (Mr & Mrs J Wilson) Long tree-lined drive. Herbaceous borders, specimen shrubs, roses. Special feature is old walled garden housing traditional vegetables, fruit and flowers; with small vineyard. TEA

Weetwood, Offwell ♿ (Mr & Mrs J V R Birchall) 2m from Honiton. Turn S off A35 (signed Offwell), at E end of Offwell. 1-acre all seasons garden; rhododendrons, azaleas, shrubs, ornamental pools, rock gardens, collection of dwarf conifers. Teashops Honiton. *Adm £1 Chd 20p (ACNO to SSAF®). Private visits usually welcome spring, summer & autumn, please* **Tel 01404 831363**

Wembury House, Wembury ♿✗ (Mr & Mrs N Hanbury) 3m SE of Plymouth. A379 Plymouth to Kingsbridge signed Wembury at Elburton roundabout. 2m sharp R at 30mph sign. Follow lane for 200yds, R over cattle grid by Pink Lodge. Set within high walls of former Tudor mansion, giving protection to a wide range of trees and shrubs. 3 large box-edged beds of iceberg roses in front of Victorian orangery and with herbaceous borders either side of the Gerogian house. Steps leading up to Tudor perimeter ramparts. TEAS. *Adm £1.50 Chd 50p (ACNO to The Primrose Appeal, Derriford Hospital®). Sun June 28 (2-6)*

¶**Westfield Lodge, Budleigh Salterton** ✗❀ (Michael & Jill Miller) B3179 from Exeter to Budleigh Salterton. Turn L at only traffic lights in town, follow rd round. Pass Normans on the L, next turning R. A surprising ¾ acre within, and overlooking, the town. Established garden with good bones, and well-stocked borders, at very different levels. *Adm £1.50 Chd 50p. Thurs, Sat July 2, 4 (2-5.30)*

Westpark, Yealmpton ✗ (Mr & Mrs D Court) 7m E of Plymouth; on Kingsbridge Rd (A379) Xrds centre of village, turn S on Newton Ferrers rd; park end of Torr Lane. An old-fashioned rambling 2-acre garden in peaceful country setting. Year round colour and variety. Rose pergola, mulberry (1907), unusual species of shrubs, climbers and naturalized bulbs, woodland with cyclamen, ferns, rocky outcrop. Vegetable garden. TEAS. *Adm £1.50 Chd 30p (ACNO to St Bartholomew's Church®). Garden by appt mid Feb to mid Sept, please* **Tel 01752 880236**

Whitechapel Manor, South Molton ♿ (Mrs Margaret Aris) 3m NE of South Molton. A361 Tiverton to Barnstaple. At South Molton roundabout, exit N signed Whitechapel for 1m, ¾m drive through woodland. Grade I listed Elizabethan manor countryside hotel, on edge of Exmoor in tranquil woodland and pasture setting. Terraced gardens, clipped yew enclosures. Herbaceous borders and walled orchard. Woodland walk. Cream TEAS. Lunches. *Adm £2 Chd 50p. Suns June 7, 28 (2-6), please* **Tel 01769 573377**

Withleigh Farm, Withleigh village ✿ (T Matheson) 3m W of Tiverton on B3137, 10yds W of 'Withleigh' sign, entrance to drive at white gate. Peaceful undisturbed rural setting with valley garden, 15 years in making; stream, pond and waterside plantings; bluebell wood walk under canopy of mature oak and beech; wild flower meadow, primroses and daffodils in spring, wild orchids. TEA. *Adm £1.50 Chd 50p (ACNO to Cancer & Arthritis Research®). Sat, Sun May 23, 24 (2-5). Private visits also welcome, please* Tel 01884 253853

Wolford Lodge, Dunkeswell ও (The Very Rev. the Dean of Windsor and Mrs Patrick Mitchell) Take Honiton to Dunkeswell rd. After 4m up hill go L at Limer's Cross. Drive ½m down small hill on L at white railings and entrance gate and lodge. 4 acres semi-woodland with massed rhododendrons, azaleas and camellias. Distant views to S over unspoilt Devon countryside. Woodland walks. *Adm £1.50 OAP/Chd £1. Sat May 23 (2-6)*

Wood Barton, Kentisbeare ও✿✿ (Mr & Mrs Richard Horton) 3m from M5 exit 28. A373 Cullompton to Honiton rd. 2m turn L signed Goodiford for 1m and turn L again at White Cottages. Farm drive, 100yds R. Bull on sign. [Landranger 192. Lat 09 Long 05/06.] 2 acres woodland garden planted 50yrs with species trees on S facing slope. Magnolias, azaleas, camellias, rhododendrons, acers; several ponds and water feature. Autumn colour. TEAS. *Adm £1 Chd 50p (ACNO to Action Research®). Suns March 15, May 17 (2-6). Also private visits by appt* Tel 01884 266285

Woodside, Barnstaple ✕ (Mr & Mrs Mervyn Feesey) Higher Raleigh Rd. A39 to Hospital and Lynton, turn R 300yds above fire station. Semi-woodland, S sloping with intensive shrub planting and many ornamental grasses, sedges, bamboos and monocots (Author of RHS Handbook on Ornamental Grasses). Parts of garden are shaded and peaceful, offering protection to unusual and tender shrubs. Special interest in New Zealand flora. Raised beds and troughs, variegated, acid loving shrubs, ornamental trees and conifers, all with emphasis on form and colour of foliage. *Adm £1.50 Chd 50p. Suns May 17, June 21 (2-5.30)*

Woodside, Whimple ✕ (Mr & Mrs E J Braund) Just off A30 rd between Honiton and Exeter. Turn N opp the B3180 turning for Exmouth. 1st L, house 1st on L, signposted Exeter 9m. Honiton 7m. ¾-acre garden 500′ above sea level. Large variety of herbaceous plants, shrubs and roses. Colourful throughout the summer. TEA incl in adm. *Adm £1.50 Chd free. Suns July 19, Aug 16 (2-5.30). Private visits welcome by appt June to end Aug, please* Tel 01404 822340

¶**Wrangaton House, Wrangaton** ও✿ (Surgeon Captain & Mrs R L Travis) Midway between Ivybridge and S Brent. ½m N of A38. From Exeter leave A38 at Wrangaton Cross, cross over to N of A38 and proceed westward ½m. From Plymouth leave A38 at Ivybridge and take Exeter rd for 3m. Both directions turn N up Blacksmith Lane. Wrangaton House is ¼m on L past the thatched cottage. 3 acres mature garden to mellow manor house on southern slopes of Dartmoor. Large pool; water

plants; streams; rhododendrons; azaleas; camellias and bulbs. Adjacent bluebell wood of 1½ acres. Beautiful situation. TEAS. *Adm £2 Chd free (ACNO to RNLI®). Sun, Mon May, 3, 4 (2-5)*

●**Wylmington Hayes, Wilmington** ✕✿ (Mr and Mrs P Saunders) 5½m NE of Honiton on A30, turn R. Signposted Stockland 3m, Axminster 10m, after 3½m entrance gates on R (before Stockland TV Station) or from A35 3½m W of Axminster turn N nr Shute Garage on to Stockland Road for 3m, entrance on L nr TV mast. 83 acres of reclaimed gardens created 1911 and woodlands with spectacular hybrid rhododendrons, azaleas, magnolias, camellias, acers. Lakes, ponds, topiary, arboretum, woodland walks with wildlife. Collection of ornamental and domestic waterfowl including black swans. Scottish Country Dancing June 7, 21. Steel Force Band June 14; Accordian Music June 28. TEAS. *Adm £3 Chd £1. Suns, Bank Hol Mons May 3, 4, 10, 17, 24, 31, June 7, 14, 21, 28 (2-5). Coaches & parties by appt please* Tel 01404 831751

Yonder Hill, Colaton Raleigh ও✕✿ (Mrs M H Herbert) On B3178 between Newton Poppleford and Colaton Raleigh take turning signed to Dotton, then immed R into small lane. ¼m 1st house on R. Ample car parking. Interesting and unusual plants and ideas in a stunningly beautiful, tranquil, 2 acre garden planted to compliment and harmonise with outstanding natural surroundings. Wheelchair access to all parts. Toilet facilities. Wheelchair available. DIY TEA. *Adm £1 Chd 50p. Suns Feb 22, March 8, 22, April 5, Fri-Mon April 10, 11, 12, 13, Sun April 26, Suns, Mons May 3, 4, 24, 25, Suns June 7, 21, July 5, 19, Aug 2, 23, Mon Aug 24, Suns Sept 6, 20, Oct 4, 18. Mon Feb 22 1999. Visitors welcome on other days. Please,* Tel 01395 567541

By Appointment Gardens. These owners do not have a fixed opening day usually because they cannot accommodate large numbers or have insufficient parking space.

Dorset

Hon County Organiser: Mrs Hugh Lindsay, The Old Rectory, Litton Cheney, Dorchester DT2 9AH
Tel 01308 482383 Fax 01308 482261
Assistant Hon County Organisers: Miss Jane Bennett, The Maples, Fontmell Magna, Shaftesbury SP7 0PF
Tel 01747 811766
Mrs Raymond Boileau, Rampisham Manor, Dorchester DT2 0PT
Tel 01935 83612
Stanley Cherry Esq., Highbury, Woodside Rd, West Moors, Ferndown BH22 0LY
Tel 01202 874372
Walter Ninniss Esq, 52 Rossmore Road, Parkstone, Poole BH12 3NL
Tel 01202 740913
Publicity: Mrs S Henwood, The Old Rectory, West Compton, Dorchester DT2 0EY
Tel & Fax 01300 320007
Hon County Treasurer: Michael Gallagher Esq, 6 West Street, Chickerell, Weymouth DT3 4DY

DATES OF OPENING

Regular openings
For details see garden description

Abbotsbury Gardens, nr Weymouth
Athelhampton House & Gardens
Chiffchaffs, Bourton
Compton Acres Gardens, Poole
Cranborne Manor Garden, Cranborne
Heatherwood, Ashington Wimborne
Horn Park, Beaminster
Ivy Cottage, Ansty
Kingston Maurward Garden,
 Dorchester
Knoll Gardens and Nursery,
 Hampreston
Leigh Farm, Halstock
Mapperton Gardens, nr Beaminster
Minterne, nr Cerne Abbas
Parnham, Beaminster
Snape Cottage, Bourton
Stapehill Abbey, Wimborne
Star Cottage, Wimborne
Sticky Wicket, Buckland Newton
Thornhill Park, Stalbridge
Upwey Wishing Well, Upwey

By appointment only
*For telephone numbers and other
details see garden descriptions.
Private visits welcomed*

Fernhill Cottage, Witchampton
Highbury, West Moors
Little Platt, Plush
Moulin Huet, West Moors
Wall Farm, Broadwindsor

March 15 Sunday
 Welcome Thatch, Witchampton
March 22 Sunday
 Aurelia Gardens, West Moors
 Langebride House, Long Bredy

Mews Cottage, Portland
78 Wakeham, Portland
Witchcroft, Southwell, Portland
March 29 Sunday
 Stour House, Blandford
April 1 Wednesday
 Cranborne Manor Garden,
  Cranborne
 Edmondsham House, Cranborne
April 5 Sunday
 Bexington, Lytchett Matravers
 Fernhill House, Witchampton
 Frankham Farm, Ryme
  Intrinseca
 Langebride House, Long Bredy
 Welcome Thatch, Witchampton
April 8 Wednesday
 Edmondsham House, Cranborne
April 10 Friday
 Aurelia Gardens, West Moors
April 12 Sunday
 Aurelia Gardens, West Moors
 Boveridge Farm, Cranborne
 Cartref, Stalbridge
 Chiffchaffs, Bourton
 Deans Court, Wimborne Minster
 Horn Park, Beaminster
 1 Manor Close, Stratton
 Manor Orchard, Stratton
 Old Rectory, Litton Cheney
 Snape Cottage, Bourton
April 13 Monday
 Ashley Park Farm, Damerham
 Aurelia Gardens, West Moors
 Deans Court, Wimborne Minster
 Edmondsham House, Cranborne
April 15 Wednesday
 Edmondsham House, Cranborne
 1 Manor Close, Stratton
 Manor Orchard, Stratton
April 18 Saturday
 Glebe Cottage, Woodsford
 Knitson Old Farmhouse, nr
  Swanage

April 19 Sunday
 Cothayes House & Vine Cottage
 The Manor House, Hinton-St-Mary
April 22 Wednesday
 Edmondsham House, Cranborne
April 25 Saturday
 Millmead, Winterborne Stickland
April 26 Sunday
 Corfe Barn, Broadstone
 Friars Way, Upway
 The Old Mill, Spetisbury
 24a Western Avenue, Poole
April 28 Tuesday
 Clent Cottage, Ryall
 Honeybrook, Osmington
April 29 Wednesday
 Edmondsham House, Cranborne
 Rampisham Manor, Rampisham
May 2 Saturday
 29 Filleul Road, Sandford Woods
May 3 Sunday
 Boveridge Farm, Cranborne
 Chiffchaffs, Bourton
 29 Filleul Road, Sandford Woods
 46 Roslin Road South,
  Bournemouth
May 6 Wednesday
 Leigh Farm, Halstock
 Rampisham Manor, Rampisham
May 7 Thursday
 Friars Way, Upway
May 10 Sunday
 34 Avon Avenue, Avon Castle
 Bexington, Lytchett Matravers
 Frankham Farm, Ryme Intrinseca
 Glebe House, East Lulworth
 7 Highfield Close, Corfe Mullen
 Honeybrook, Osmington
 Welcome Thatch, Witchampton
May 14 Thursday
 Friars Way, Upway
May 16 Saturday
 Knitson Old Farmhouse, nr
  Swanage

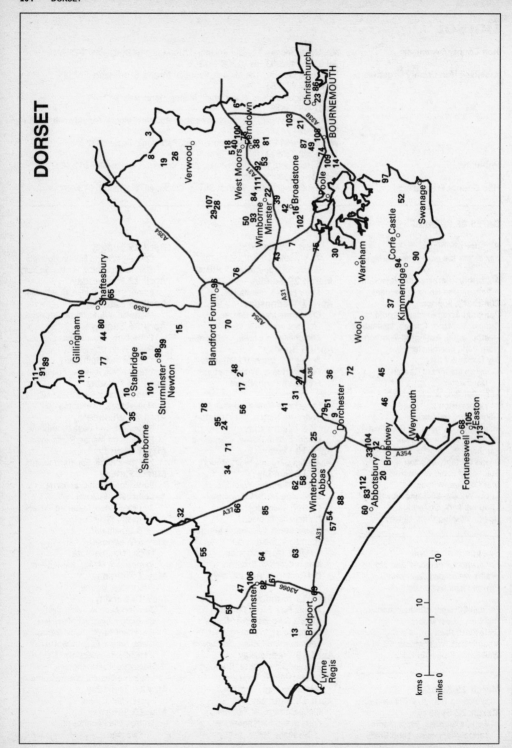

DORSET

KEY

1. Abbotsbury Gardens
2. Aller Green
3. Ashley Park Farm
4. Athelhampton House & Gardens
5. Aurelia Gardens
6. 34 Avon Avenue
7. Bexington
8. Boveridge Farm
9. Came Home Farm
10. Cartref
11. Chiffchaffs
12. 7 Church St
13. Clent Cottage
14. Compton Acres Gardens
15. Coombe Cottage
16. Corfe Barn
17. Cothayes House & Vine Cottage
18. Cottesmore Farm
19. Cranborne Manor Garden
20. Crickhollow
21. 2 Curlew Road
22. Deans Court
23. 28 Denmead Road
24. Domineys Yard
25. Dymonds Folly
26. Edmondsham House
27. Farriers
28. Fernhill Cottage
29. Fernhill House
30. 29 Filleul Road
31. 4 Flower Cottage
32. Frankham Farm
33. Friars Way
34. The Friary
35. Frith House
36. Glebe Cottage
37. Glebe House
38. 2 Greenwood Avenue
39. Heatherwood
40. Highbury
41. Higher Melcombe
42. 7 Highfield Close
43. Highwood Garden
44. Hilltop Cottage
45. Holworth Farmhouse
46. Honeybrook
47. Horn Park
48. Ivy Cottage
49. 80 Keith Road
50. Kingston Lacy
51. Kingston Maurward Gardens
52. Knitson Old Farmhouse
53. Knoll Gardens and Nursery
54. Langebride House
55. Leigh Farm
56. Little Platt
57. Litton Cheney Gardens
58. 1 Manor Close
59. The Manor Farmhouse
60. The Manor House, Abbotsbury
61. The Manor House, Hinton-St-Mary
62. Manor Orchard
63. Mappercombe Manor
64. Mapperton Gardens
65. Mayo Farm
66. Melbury House
67. Melplash Court
68. Mews Cottage
69. Midsummer's Cottage
70. Millmead
71. Minterne
72. Moigne Combe
73. Moulin Huet
74. The Old Coach House
75. The Old Farmhouse
76. The Old Mill
77. The Old Rectory, Fifehead Magdalen
78. The Old Rectory, Pulham
79. The Old Vicarage
80. The Orchard
81. Orchard House
82. Parnham
83. Portesham House
84. The Priest's House Museum & Garden
85. Rampisham Manor
86. Red House Museum & Gdns
87. 46 Roslin Road South
88. The Scented Garden
89. Silton House
90. Smedmore
91. Snape Cottage
92. Stapehill Abbey
93. Star Cottage
94. Steeple Manor
95. Sticky Wicket
96. Stour House
97. Studland Bay House
98. Sturminster Newton Gardens
99. Sweetwell
100. Tara
101. Thornhill Park
102. Three Bays
103. Throop Mill Cottage
104. Upwey Wishing Well
105. 78 Wakeham
106. Wall Farm
107. Welcome Thatch
108. Wentworth College
109. 24a Western Avenue
110. Weston House
111. Wimborne Minster Model Town & Gardens
112. 2 Winters Lane
113. Witchcroft

Remember that every time you visit a National Gardens Scheme garden you are helping to raise money for:

The Queen's Nursing Institute
County Nursing Associations
The Nurses' Welfare Service
Macmillan Cancer Relief
Marie Curie Cancer Care
Help the Hospices
Crossroads
The Gardens Fund of the National Trust
The Gardeners' Royal Benevolent Society
The Royal Gardeners' Orphans Fund
Additional Charities Nominated by Owners

Studland Bay House, nr Swanage
May 17 Sunday
Ashley Park Farm, Damerham
Boveridge Farm, Cranborne
Cartref, Stalbridge
2 Curlew Road, Bournemouth
Domineys Yard, Buckland Newton
Friars Way, Upwey
Moigne Combe, nr Dorchester
Smedmore, Kimmeridge
Star Cottage, Wimborne
Studland Bay House, nr Swanage
May 21 Thursday
Friars Way, Upwey
May 24 Sunday
34 Avon Avenue, Avon Castle
Came Home Farm, Dorchester
Deans Court, Wimborne Minster
The Friary, Hilfield
Glebe House, East Lulworth
Highwood Garden, Wareham
Manor Farmhouse, Little Windsor
Mews Cottage, Portland
Moigne Combe, nr Dorchester
46 Roslin Road South,
   Bournemouth (Evening)
78 Wakeham, Portland
May 25 Monday
Came Home Farm, Dorchester
Deans Court, Wimborne Minster
Horn Park, Beaminster
May 26 Tuesday
Clent Cottage, Ryall
The Friary, Hilfield
May 27 Wednesday
Came Home Farm, Dorchester
   (Evening)
The Friary, Hilfield
May 28 Thursday
Friars Way, Upwey
May 30 Saturday
The Manor House, Abbotsbury
May 31 Sunday
Ashley Park Farm, Damerham
7 Church St, Upwey, Weymouth
Corfe Barn, Broadstone
Crickhollow, Portesham
2 Greenwood Avenue, Ferndown
Highwood Garden, Wareham
Holworth Farmhouse, Holworth
The Manor House, Abbotsbury
Orchard House, Ferndown
Thornhill Park, Stalbridge
Weston House, Buckhorn Weston
June 3 Wednesday
Crickhollow, Portesham
Leigh Farm, Halstock
June 4 Thursday
Friars Way, Upwey
June 6 Saturday
29 Filleul Road, Sandford Woods
June 7 Sunday
Dymonds Folly, Charminster
Farriers, Puddletown

29 Filleul Road, Sandford Woods
4 Flower Cottage, Lower
   Waterston
Honeybrook, Osmington
80 Keith Road, Talbot Woods
Kingston Lacy, nr Wimborne
   Minster
Litton Cheney Gardens
Mappercombe Manor, Powerstock
The Old Rectory, Fifehead
   Magdalen
Portesham House, Portesham
46 Roslin Road South,
   Bournemouth
Snape Cottage, Bourton
Welcome Thatch, Witchampton
Wimborne Minster Model Town &
   Gardens
June 9 Tuesday
Litton Cheney Gardens
June 10 Wednesday
Mappercombe Manor, Powerstock
The Orchard, Blynfield Gate, nr
   Shaftesbury
June 11 Thursday
Friars Way, Upwey
June 13 Saturday
Red House Museum & Gdns,
   Christchurch
Tara, West Moors
June 14 Sunday
Ashley Park Farm, Damerham
Bexington, Lytchett Matravers
Cothayes House & Vine Cottage
28 Denmead Road, Iford
Friars Way, Upwey
2 Greenwood Avenue, Ferndown
7 Highfield Close, Corfe Mullen
Mayo Farm, Shaftesbury
Midsummer's Cottage, Bridport
Orchard House, Ferndown
Portesham House, Portesham
Silton House, Silton
Sturminster Newton Gardens
Tara, West Moors
Throop Mill Cottage
June 16 Tuesday
The Scented Garden, Littlebredy
June 17 Wednesday
The Orchard, Blynfield Gate, nr
   Shaftesbury
June 18 Thursday
Friars Way, Upwey
June 20 Saturday
Tara, West Moors
June 21 Sunday
Coombe Cottage, Shillingstone
Cranborne Manor Garden,
   Cranborne
Fernhill House, Witchampton
Frankham Farm, Ryme Intrinseca
Holworth Farmhouse, Holworth
Manor Farmhouse, Little Windsor
The Manor House, Hinton St Mary

The Old Vicarage, Stinsford
Star Cottage, Wimborne
Sticky Wicket, Buckland Newton
Sweetwell, Fiddleford
Tara, West Moors
June 23 Tuesday
The Scented Garden, Littlebredy
June 25 Thursday
Dymonds Folly, Charminster
Friars Way, Upwey
June 28 Sunday
7 Church St, Upwey, Weymouth
Coombe Cottage, Shillingstone
Corfe Barn, Broadstone
Dymonds Folly, Charminster
Mews Cottage, Portland
The Priest's House Museum &
   Garden, Wimborne
Steeple Manor, nr Wareham
78 Wakeham, Portland
Weston House, Buckhorn Weston
Witchcroft, Southwell, Portland
June 30 Tuesday
Clent Cottage, Ryall
The Scented Garden, Littlebredy
July 1 Wednesday
Leigh Farm, Halstock
July 4 Saturday
29 Filleul Road, Sandford Woods
July 5 Sunday
Chiffchaffs, Bourton
29 Filleul Road, Sandford Woods
7 Highfield Close, Corfe Mullen
80 Keith Road, Talbot Woods
46 Roslin Road South,
   Bournemouth
Thornhill Park, Stalbridge
Wimborne Minster Model Town
   & Gardens
July 7 Tuesday
The Scented Garden, Littlebredy
July 8 Wednesday
The Orchard, Blynfield Gate, nr
   Shaftesbury
July 12 Sunday
Bexington, Lytchett Matravers
Cottesmore Farm, West Moors
28 Denmead Road, Iford
Domineys Yard, Buckland Newton
Higher Melcombe, Melcombe
   Bingham
1 Manor Close, Stratton
Manor Orchard, Stratton
Star Cottage, Wimborne
Stour House, Blandford
2 Winters Lane, Portesham
July 14 Tuesday
The Scented Garden, Littlebredy
July 18 Saturday
Knitson Old Farmhouse, nr
   Swanage
July 19 Sunday
2 Curlew Road, Bournemouth
Friars Way, Upwey

2 Greenwood Avenue, Ferndown

July 21 Tuesday
The Scented Garden, Littlebredy

July 22 Wednesday
1 Manor Close, Stratton
Manor Orchard, Stratton
The Orchard, Blynfield Gate, nr
Shaftesbury

July 26 Sunday
7 Church St, Upwey, Weymouth
Farriers, Puddletown
Hilltop Cottage, Woodville
Melplash Court, nr Bridport
Mews Cottage, Portland
Red House Museum & Gdns,
Christchurch
Snape Cottage, Bourton
78 Wakeham, Portland
24a Western Avenue, Poole
Witchcroft, Southwell, Portland

July 28 Tuesday
Clent Cottage, Ryall

July 29 Wednesday
Hilltop Cottage, Woodville

August 1 Saturday
Three Bays, Beacon Hill

August 2 Sunday
Chiffchaffs, Bourton
Frith House, Stalbridge
Hilltop Cottage, Woodville
The Old Rectory, Pulham
Three Bays, Beacon Hill

August 5 Wednesday
Hilltop Cottage, Woodville
Leigh Farm, Halstock
The Old Rectory, Pulham

August 8 Saturday
Knitson Old Farmhouse, nr
Swanage

August 9 Sunday
Bexington, Lytchett Matravers
Hilltop Cottage, Woodville
Knitson Old Farmhouse, nr
Swanage
Thornhill Park, Stalbridge

August 16 Sunday
The Old Coach House,
Bournemouth
Stour House, Blandford
2 Winters Lane, Portesham

August 23 Sunday
7 Church St, Upwey,
Weymouth
Coombe Cottage, Shillingstone
Leigh Farm, Halstock
Mews Cottage, Portland
Sticky Wicket, Buckland Newton

August 25 Tuesday
Clent Cottage, Ryall

August 30 Sunday
Aller Green, Ansty
Deans Court, Wimborne
Minster
Ivy Cottage, Ansty

August 31 Monday
Aurelia Gardens, West Moors
Deans Court, Wimborne Minster

September 6 Sunday
Crickhollow, Portesham
The Old Farmhouse, Organ Ford
Wimborne Minster Model Town &
Gardens

September 10 Thursday
Friars Way, Upwey

September 13 Sunday
Bexington, Lytchett Matravers

September 16 Wednesday
Leigh Farm, Halstock
The Orchard, Blynfield Gate, nr
Shaftesbury

September 19 Saturday
Wentworth College,
Bournemouth

September 20 Sunday
Aurelia Gardens, West Moors
Deans Court, Wimborne Minster
Friars Way, Upwey

September 26 Saturday
Millmead, Winterborne Stickland

September 27 Sunday
Mews Cottage, Portland
Snape Cottage, Bourton

September 29 Tuesday
Clent Cottage, Ryall

October 6 Tuesday
Clent Cottage, Ryall

October 7 Wednesday
Edmondsham House, Cranborne
Leigh Farm, Halstock

October 14 Wednesday
Edmondsham House, Cranborne

October 18 Sunday
Aurelia Gardens, West Moors

October 21 Wednesday
Edmondsham House, Cranborne

October 28 Wednesday
Edmondsham House, Cranborne

DESCRIPTIONS OF GARDENS

● **Abbotsbury Gardens, nr Weymouth** &❀ (Ilchester Estates) From B3157 Weymouth-Bridport, 200yds W of Abbotsbury village. 20 acres; uniquely mild Mediterranean-type climate, started in 1760 and considerably extended in C19; much replanting during past few years; very fine collection of rhododendrons, camellias, azaleas; wide variety of unusual and tender trees and shrubs. Peacocks. Children's play area, woodland trail, aviaries and plant centre. Partly suitable for wheelchairs. TEAS. *Adm £4.20 OAPs £3.50 Chd £1.30, Family £9 Reduced rate in winter (For party rate* **Tel 01305 871387***). Easter to Oct 31 (10-6), Nov to Feb (10-dusk)*

Aller Green, Ansty ❀ (A J Thomas Esq) Aller Lane, 12m N of Dorchester. From Puddletown take A354 to Blandford; After public house, take 1st L down Long Lane signed Dewlish and Cheselbourne; through Cheselbourne to Ansty then 1st R before Fox Inn down Aller Lane. 1-acre typical Dorset cottage garden; unusual trees, shrubs and perennials in old orchard setting and many perennials grown for Autumn Colour. Teas at **Ivy Cottage.** *Combined adm with* **Ivy Cottage** *£2.50 Chd 50p (ACNO to the Red Cross®). Sun Aug 30 (2-5.30)*

Ashley Park Farm, Damerham &❀ (David Dampney Esq) Follow yellow signs off B3078, immediately W of village, 5m from Fordingbridge. Gardens of 5 acres with woodland walks. Arboretum with many interesting trees, eucalyptus grove; wild flower meadow. Many exciting plants for south facing walls, borders. Growing collection of ferns. TEAS. *Adm £1.50 Chd free (ACNO to Damerham Church®). Mon April 13, Suns May 17, 31, June 14 (2-5.30). (See also* **Boveridge Farm***). Private visits welcome, please* **Tel 01725 518 200**

● **Athelhampton House & Gardens, Dorchester** &❀❀ (Patrick Cooke Esq) 5m E of Dorchester on A35. The Gardens dating from 1891 incl the Great Court with 12 giant yew topiary pyramids overlooked by two terraced pavilions. This glorious Grade I architectural garden is full of vistas and surprises with spectacular fountains and River Piddle flowing through it. C15 Manor house. Conservatory restaurant serving lunches and cream teas. *Adm House & Gardens £4.80, OAPs £4.50, Chd £1.50. Gardens only adults & OAPs £3 Chd free. Reduced rates for groups. Open March 1 to Nov 1 Daily (except Sats). Also Suns in winter.* **Tel 01305 848363**

Aurelia Gardens, West Moors &⚶☸ (Mr & Mrs Robert Knight) Newman's Lane. N of village off B3072 Bournemouth-Verwood rd. Emphasis on coloured foliage and plumage. Heathers, dwarf conifers, grasses and alpines. Five rare breeds of poultry: white crested blue polands, partridge wyandottes, dark brahmas, salmon faverolles and buff cochins. Large natural wildlife pond. Featured on TV. 5-acre level grounds, incl nursery. Free parking. *Adm £1. Not suitable for children. Fri April 10, Suns March 22, April 12, Sept 20, Oct 18. Mons April 13, Aug 31 (10-4)*

¶**34 Avon Avenue, Ringwood** &⚶☸ (Mr & Mrs Robert Ives) Avon Castle. Avon Ave is E off Hurn/Matchams Lane, most readily approached from Boundary Lane, turning NE over bridge over A338 (Spur Rd). Garden of ¾-acre. A pleasant prospect of vistas designed and maintained by owners over seventeen yrs. A foliage garden of yr-round interest in rooms, with rare and unusual shrubs and herbaceous plants. Collections of conifers, rhododendrons and azaleas, hellebores and alliums. Specimen Juniperus 'Pfitzerana Aurea'. Vegetable and fruit garden. TEAS. *Adm £1 Chd 50p (ACNO to RNLI® May 10 and The Soroptomists® May 24). Suns May 10, 24 (2-5.30)*

Bexington, Lytchett Matravers &⚶☸ (Mr & Mrs Robin Crumpler) In Lime Kiln Rd, opp old School at W end of village. Colourful garden of ½-acre maintained by owners, with mixed borders of many interesting and unusual plants, shrubs and trees. Bog garden of primulas and hostas etc. Four rockeries of alpines, with walkways over bog area connecting two lawns, making a garden of interest from spring bulbs to autumn colour. Cream TEAS & plant stall for Alzheimer's Disease Society & gardening charities. *Adm £1 Chd 20p. Suns April 5, May 10, June 14, July 12, Aug 9, Sept 13 (2-6). Group visits welcome by appt, please* **Tel 01202 622068**

Boveridge Farm, Cranborne ⚶ (Mr & Mrs Michael Yarrow) Leave Cranborne on Martin Rd, thence take 2nd R Boveridge Farm. A plantsman's garden of 2 acres on 3 levels, part chalk and part acid; with lawns around old farmhouse, formerly manor house of the Hooper family; in rural surroundings with fine views. Fern bank and many rare and interesting trees and shrubs. Specimen acer 'Brilliantissimum', prunus 'Shidare Yoshino', prunus 'Pendula Rubra', Paulownia tomentosa. Teas at **Ashley Park**, Damerham (next village 3m). *Adm £1 Chd free (ACNO to Cranborne Village Hall Appeal©). Suns April 12, May 3, 17 (2-5). (See also* **Ashley Park Farm***). Group visits welcome by appt, please* **Tel 01725 517241**

¶**Came Home Farm, Dorchester** &⚶☸ (John & Kathy Loveridge) 1½m E of Dorchester on A352 Dorchester to Wareham Rd, opp Came Lodge. Approx ⅔ acre cottage garden. Freedraining gravel overlying chalk. Self-seeding encouraged, to form drifts of different colours throughout late spring and early summer. Wild plants intermingle with unusual cultivated plants. Style always evolving naturally rather than planned. Ponds and plants attract many wild birds and animals. TEAS. *Adm £1.50 Chd free (ACNO to Raleigh International Trust®). Sun, Mon May 24, 25 (2-6), Wed May 27 (6-9)*

▲**Cartref, Stalbridge** ⚶☸ (Nesta Ann Smith) Station Rd. From A30, S at Henstridge for 1m. Turn L opp Stalbridge PO, house 80yds on R. Free car park nearby. A plantsman's garden approx ¼-acre, cottage garden and unusual plants. Small woodland area with choice shade-loving plants. Small potager, organically grown. TEA. *Adm £2 Chd free. For NGS Suns April 12, May 17 (10-5). Private visits by appt please* **Tel 01963 363705**

■ **Chiffchaffs, Chaffeymoor** ⚶☸ (Mr & Mrs K R Potts) Leave A303 (Bourton by pass) at junction signposted Gillingham, Blandford and Bourton at W end of Bourton village. A garden for all seasons with many interesting plants, bulbs, shrubs, herbaceous border, shrub roses. Attractive walk to woodland garden with far-reaching views across the Blackmore Vale. Nursery open Tues-Sat and on garden open days. *Adm £2 Chd 50p (ACNO to St Michael's Church, Penselwood®). Open April 5 to Sept 30, 1st and 3rd Sun each month, Bank Holiday weekends, Weds & Thurs. For NGS Suns April 12, May 3, July 5, Aug 2 plus 10% of all receipts (2-5.30). Private visits and coaches by appt please* **Tel 01747 840841**

187 Christchurch Road, Ringwood See Hampshire

7 Church Street, Upwey &⚶☸ (Ann & Gordon Powell) ½m from bottom of Ridgeway Hill on A354 Dorchester-Weymouth rd turn R B3159 (Bridport rd) L turn at bottom of hill. Please park on rd except disabled. 3 acres incl beds laid out for colour theming of foliage and flowers, vegetable garden and established woodland. Teas at Wishing Well. *Adm £1.50 Chd free. Suns May 31, June 28, July 26; Aug 23 (2-6). Group visits by appt, please* **Tel 01305 812303**

¶**Clent Cottage, Ryall** ⚶☸ (S Huggins & T Farnden) 7m W of Bridport on A35. Turn R opp garage as you enter Morcombelake, signed Ryall. 1½m narrow lane. Considerable parking on main Rd please, space limited, and walk to garden. If you are potty about plants then savour this 1½ acre plantsman's garden still under development. Designed with unusual and exciting perennials for yr-round colour, small vineyard and orchard. *Adm £1.50 Chd free. Tues April 28, May 26, June 30, July 28, Aug 25, Sept 29 (10.30-4), Oct 6 (11-3)*

● **Compton Acres Gardens, Poole** &⚶☸ Canford Cliffs Road. Sign from Bournemouth and Poole. Wilts & Dorset Buses 147, 150, 151. Yellow Buses nos 11 & 12 stop at entrance. Gardens with Japanese and Italian influences, rock and water, heather dell, woodland walk and sub-tropical glen. Magnificent bronze and marble statuary. Large selection of plants and stoneware garden ornaments. Refreshments available. Large free car/coach park. *Adm £4.75 OAPs £3.70 Chd £1. March 1 to Oct 31 daily. 10-6 last admission 5.15pm.* **Tel 01202 700778**

Coombe Cottage, Shillingstone ☸ (Mike & Jennie Adams) Blandford Rd. 5m NW of Blandford on A357 next to PO Stores on main rd. Parking advised in Gunn Lane. ⅓-acre plantsman's cottage garden, enclosed by walls and hedges, with a catholic mix of herbaceous and woody perennials, climbers, bulbs and self-seeding annuals (many unusual), in broad, mostly rectangular borders, some of them colour co-ordinated. Small formal vegetable plot. TEAS. *Adm £1 Chd free. Suns June 21, 28, Aug 23 (2-6)*

Corfe Barn, Broadstone ⚘⚘ (John & Kathleen McDavid) Corfe Lodge Rd. From main roundabout in Broadstone W along Clarendon Rd, ¾m N into Roman Rd, after 50yds W into Corfe Lodge Rd. ⅔ acre on three levels on site of C19 lavender farm. Informal country garden with much to interest both gardeners and flower arrangers. Parts of the original farm have been incorporated in the design. A particular feature of the garden is the use made of old walls. TEAS. *Adm 50p Chd 25p. Suns April 26, May 31, June 28 (2-5)*

¶**Cothays House & Vine Cottage** ⚘ 6m off A354 Blandford/Dorchester rd. Leave at Milton Arms in Winterbourne Whitechurch and follow signs for Milton Abbey, pass Abbey and through Hilton village. At top of hill turn R and follow signs for The Fox. Pass the public house on L and for Cothayes take 1st R at Ansty/Melcombe Park Farm. House on L after ¾m, Vine Cottage is ¼m on R after old petrol pumps. TEAS at Cothays in aid of Village Hall. *Combined adm £2. Suns April 19, June 14 (11-5)*

  ¶**Cothays House, Ansty** (Pat & David Wells) Tranquil 2-acre garden on sloping land with streams linking ponds; variety of trees and woodland walks. Shrubs and perennials combine to provide colourful borders with stream banks hosting wet loving plants

  ¶**Vine Cottage** (Mrs Wendy Jackson) Small cottage garden with emphasis on interesting and unusual perennials and a wealth of containers

¶**Cottesmore Farm, West Moors** ⚘⚘ (Mr & Mrs Paul Guppy) Newmans Lane. N of village off B3072 Bournemouth and Verwood Rd. The owners, late of High Hollow, Corfe Mullen, an NGS garden seen on TV, offer visitors the chance of seeing their new garden in the making. Theme of unusual plants. Display garden, also comprising breeds of bantams and chickens, with seven enclosures of guinea pigs and rabbits, in all making an acre of considerable interest incl indigenous wild flowers. Parking in field. *Adm 50p Chd 25p (ACNO to Cats Protection League®). Sun July 12 (2-5)*

■ **Cranborne Manor Garden, Cranborne** ⚘⚘ (The Viscount & Viscountess Cranborne) 10m N of Wimborne on B3078. Beautiful and historic garden laid out in C17 by John Tradescant and enlarged in C20, featuring several gardens surrounded by walls and yew hedges: white garden, herb and mount gardens, water and wild garden. Many interesting plants, with fine trees and avenues. *Adm £3 OAPs £2 Chd 50p (ACNO to African Medical and Research Foundation®). Weds March to Sept incl (9-5). For NGS Wed April 1 (9-5), Sun June 21 (10-5)*

¶**Crickhollow, Portesham** ⚘ (James & Daphne Mortimore) From Dorchester take A35 W. L at Winterbourne Abbas and follow signs to Portesham. L onto B3157 signed Weymouth and 2nd L after 1½m. Thatched cottage 400yds on L. ½-acre charming cottage garden with orchard, vegetables, shrubs, mixed borders, roses, 3 greenhouses and artist's studio. *Adm £1.50 Chd 50p. Sun May 31, Wed June 3 (2-6), Sun Sept 6 (2-5.30)*

2 Curlew Road, Bournemouth ⚘⚘⚘ (Mr & Mrs Gerald Alford) Strouden Park. From Castle Lane West turn S into East Way, thence E into Curlew Rd. Small town garden 150' × 30' divided into rooms and linked by arches. Conifers, acers, rhododendrons, clematis; spring and summer bedding; three water features. Seen on Pebble Mill '94 and Grass Roots '95. Placed 3rd in Garden of Excellence '97, Bournemouth in Bloom. The owners are seriously disabled and their garden is thus of especial interest to other disabled people. *Adm £1 Chd 30p. Suns May 17, July 19 (2-6). Private visits welcome of 2 or more please* Tel 01202 512627

▲**Deans Court, Wimborne** ⚘⚘⚘ (Sir Michael & Lady Hanham) Just off B3073 in centre of Wimborne. 13 acres; partly wild garden; water, specimen trees, free roaming peacocks. House (open by written appt) originally the Deanery to the Minster. Herb garden with over 200 species and walled kitchen garden. Chemical free plants and produce for sale. Free car parking. Morning coffee/TEAS. *Adm £2 OAPs £1.50 Chd 50p. For NGS Suns April 12, May 24, Aug 30, Sept 20 (2-6). Mons April 13, May 25, Aug 31 (10.30-6). Other openings refer Wimborne T I C.* Tel 01202 886116

¶**28 Denmead Road, Iford** ⚘⚘ (Mrs D Riggs) From Christchurch Rd turn E at Iford roundabout into Iford Lane, then 3rd R and 1st L. Newly designed town garden 100' × 35', with cottage style planting, incl old-fashioned roses and many unusual perennials. Small herb garden, trellis and arbour with roses and clematis, all lovingly tended. Many containers creatively planted. Front garden planted with drought resisting plants. *Adm 80p Chd free. Suns June 14, July 12 (2-5)*

Domineys Yard, Buckland Newton ⚘⚘⚘ (Mr & Mrs Gueterbock) Dorchester and Sherborne 11m. 2m E A352 or take B3143. Take 'no through rd' between church and 'Gaggle of Geese'. Entrance 200 metres on L. Park and picnic in field with alder lined stream and recent tree planting, or in lane if wet. 2½-acre all seasons garden on chalk, clay and greensand surrounds C17 thatched cottage. Developed since 1961. Unusual plants, shrubs, trees. Kitchen garden. Heated swimming pool. TEAS. *Adm £1.50 Chd 50p (ACNO to Pulham Church Repairs®). Suns May 17, July 12 (2-6). Private visits welcome, please* Tel 01300 345295

¶**Dymonds Folly, Charminster** ⚘ (John & Barbara Askew) A352 Dorchester - Cerne Abbas. On R ½m N of the Xrds in centre of Charminster. Public car park outside Three Compasses inn just W of the Xrds. Parking for disabled only at the house. The ½-acre garden is informally planted with a wide variety of perennials. It consists of a walled area, a colonized vegetable garden and a small frontage on to the River Cerne. TEAS in aid of Dorset victim support. *Adm £1.50 Chd free. Sun June 7, Thurs June 25, Sun June 28 (2-5.30)*

The National Gardens Scheme is a charity which traces its origins back to 1927. Since then it has raised over £18 million for charitable purposes.

Edmondsham House, nr Cranborne &✿❀ (Mrs Julia Smith) Edmondsham, off B3081 between Cranborne and Verwood. Large garden; spring bulbs, trees, shrubs; walled garden with herbaceous border; vegetables and fruit; grass cockpit. Early church nearby. TEAS Weds only. *Adm £1 Chd 50p under 5 free (ACNO to PRAMA®). Mon April 13, Weds April 1, 8, 15, 22, 29, Oct 7, 14, 21, 28 (2-5); also private visits and parties welcome, please* **Tel 01725 517207**

Farriers, Puddletown &❀ (Mr & Mrs P S Eady) 16 The Moor. On the A354 Puddletown-Blandford rd opp the rd to Piddlehinton, close to the Blue Vinney public house, Dorchester 5m. ⅓-acre informal country garden with much to interest gardeners and flower arrangers, designed and maintained by owners; shrubs, herbaceous, dahlias, sweet peas, vegetable plot, greenhouse with collection streptocarpus, pond. Park in village. *Joint opening with* **Flower Cottage** *on June 7 only. Adm £1 each garden Chd free also July 26 (2-6). Private visits welcome, please* **Tel 01305 848634**

Fernhill Cottage, Witchampton ✿❀ (Miss Shirley Forwood) Next to Fernhill House, directions as below. Small thatched cottage garden, uncommon perennials and old-fashioned cottage plants. *Adm 50p Chd free. Parties and private visits welcome, please* **Tel 01258 840321** *evenings*

Fernhill House, Witchampton &✿❀ (Mrs Henry Hildyard) 3½m E of Wimborne B3078 L to Witchampton then L up Lower St. (Blandford rd) house on R 200yds. Spring bulbs and blossom, roses and herbaceous borders, woodland walk with water garden and shrubs. Teas in aid of Village Hall, June 21. *Adm £1 Chd free (ACNO to Joseph Weld Hospice Trust®). Suns April 5, June 21 (2-5). Plants for sale at Gardener's Fair July 5. Parties by appt, please* **Tel 01258 840105**

¶29 Filleul Road, Sandford Woods, Wareham &✿❀ (Sylvia & Richard Preston) Turn N off A351 opp Gulf Petrol Stn, then R into Filleul Rd. A small ⅔-acre colourful summer garden, partly suitable for wheelchairs, maintained by owners. Lawns, shrubs, dwarf conifers, herbaceous plantings. Pool, bog garden and cottage plant border. Foliage plants are a special interest for flower arranging. TEAS. *Adm £1 Chd free. Sats, Suns May 2, 3, June 6, 7, July 4, 5; Sats (2-6) Suns (11-4)*

4 Flower Cottage, Lower Waterston &❀ (Audrey Penniston) From Puddletown on the B3142 take the rd between Blue Vinney public house and Old's Garage on way to Piddletrenthide. ⅓-acre cottage garden, with herbaceous borders, scree, fernery and vegetables. TEAS. *Joint opening with* **Farriers** *Adm £1 (each garden) Chd free (ACNO to Dewlish Parish Church®). Sun June 7 (2-6). Private visits welcome, please* **Tel 01305 848694**

Frankham Farm, Ryme Intrinseca &✿ (Mr & Mrs R G Earle) A37 Yeovil-Dorchester; 3m S of Yeovil turn E at Xrds with garage; drive ¼m on L. 2 acres started in 1960s; plantsman's garden with shrubs, trees, spring bulbs, clematis, roses, vegetables and fruit; extensive wall planting. Recently planted unusual hardwoods. TEAS

in aid of Ryme Church. *Adm £1.50 Chd free. Suns April 5, May 10, June 21 (2-5.30)*

Friars Way, Upwey ✿❀ (Les & Christina Scott) Church Street. On B3159 Martinstown Rd (opp church car park). C17 thatched cottage. ¾-acre hillside cottage garden. A plantsman's paradise. 'Garden Rooms' have been cleverly created, affording a surprise around every corner. Featured on TV. TEAS at Wishing Well. *Adm £1.50 Chd 50p. Suns April 26, May 17, June 14, July 19, Sept 20. Every Thurs May/June and Sept 10 (2.30-6). Private visits and parties welcome, please* **Tel 01305 813243**

The Friary, Dorchester (The Society of St Francis) Hilfield. A352 from Dorchester to Minterne Magna, 1st L after village, 1st turning on R signed The Friary. From Yeovil turn off A37 signed Batcombe, 3rd turning on L. A small woodland garden begun in 1950's then neglected. Reclamation began in 1984. The Secret Garden has a number of mature trees, rhododendrons, azaleas, magnolias, camellias and other choice shrubs with a stream on all sides crossed by bridges (stout shoes recommended). TEA. *Adm £1 Chd free. Sun, Tue, Wed May 24, 26, 27 (2-5). The Friary is happy to receive visitors every day apart from Monday*

Frith House, Stalbridge &❀ (Urban Stephenson Esq) Between Milborne Port & Stalbridge, 1m S of A30. Turn W nr PO in Stalbridge. 4 acres; self-contained hamlet: lawns; 2 small lakes; woodland walks. Terrace in front of Edwardian house, mature cedars; flower borders, excellent kitchen garden. TEAS. *Adm £1.50 Chd free. Sun Aug 2 (2-6). Groups welcome by appt, please* **Tel 01963 250 232**

Glebe Cottage, Woodsford (Mr F K Fletcher) Take Wareham Rd W out of Dorchester. Follow signs to Crossways and L fork to Woodsford after passing under light controlled bridge. Entrance ¼m after Woodsford Castle on L and labelled Woodsford House. Drive forks to Glebe Cottage. Approach from E by taking sign to Woodsford at Moreton/Woodsford Cross Rd on B3390. Camellias, mostly in woodland setting. 1½-acre garden with rhododendrons and azaleas and many varieties of trees. TEAS. *Adm £1 Chd 50p. Sat April 18 (2-6)*

Glebe House, East Lulworth &❀ (Mr & Mrs J G Thompson) 4m S of Wool, 6m W of Wareham. Take Coombe Keynes Rd to East Lulworth. Glebe House just to E of Weld Arms and War Memorial. Shrub garden with lawns; walks and terrace, 2 acres with interesting and varied planting, wide variety of shrubs. TEAS. *Adm £1.25 Chd free (ACNO to Wool & Bovington Cancer Relief®). Suns May 10, 24 (2-6)*

2 Greenwood Avenue, Ferndown ❀ (Mr & Mrs P D Stogden) Off Woodside Rd which is between Ringwood Rd (A348) and Wimborne Rd (C50 ex-A31), E of town centre. ⅓-acre designed and maintained by owners. An interesting and informal garden, with accent on herbaceous plants; many rare and unusual. Hostas, sempervivums and penstemons are a special interest of the owners. Soft fruits and vegetable garden. Arbour and pergola. Dogs must be kept on leads. TEAS. *Adm £1 Acc chd free. Suns May 31, June 14, July 19 (11-5)*

Heatherwood, Ashington ✗ (Mr & Mrs Ronald Squires) 1m S of Wimborne. Leave A349 Wimborne-Poole rd at Merley Bridge, signed Ashington, into Merley Park Rd. Garden is ¾m on L. ½-acre garden created by present owners from original woodland. Main theme of the garden is heathers (800 in 50 varieties), conifers (300 in 30 varieties), azaleas and acers. Large lawn with ornamental pool and rockery. Featured on TV's 'That's Gardening' and 'Grass Roots'. Car park at adjacent nursery. *Collection box. Daily except Dec 24 to Jan 1 (9-5, Suns 9.30-12)*

Highbury, West Moors ♿✗❀ (Stanley Cherry Esq) 8m N of Bournemouth. In Woodside Rd, off B3072 Bournemouth-Verwood rd; last rd at N end of West Moors village. Woodland garden of ½ acre in mature setting surrounding interesting Edwardian house (1909 listed). Unusual plants and shrubs with ground cover. Weather station. Seen on T.V. TEAS in orchard when fine. *House and garden, organised parties Adm £1 (incl TEA); Otherwise by appt. Garden only 75p (2-6). April to Sept Tel 01202 874372*

Higher Melcombe, Melcombe Bingham ❀ (Lt Col J M Woodhouse) 11m NE of Dorchester. From Puddletown A354 to Blandford. After ½m follow signs to Cheselbourne then to Melcombe. At Xrds in Melcombe Bingham follow signpost 'Private rd to Higher Melcombe'. From Sturminster Newton signs to Hazelbury Bryan, Ansty, past Fox Inn to Melcombe Bingham Xrds. 1½-acre garden, many annuals. Fine views and setting outside Elizabethan house. Parking adjoining field. TEAS in chapel. *Adm £1. Sun July 12 (1.30-5)*

7 Highfield Close, Corfe Mullen ✗❀ (Mr & Mrs Malcolm Bright) From Wareham Rd turn E in Hanham Rd, thence ahead into Highfield Close. Colourful ⅓-acre summer garden designed and made by owners over 15yrs. Bedding plants, fuchsias and pelargoniums interplanted with shrubs; fish pond and ornamental pool. Much to interest gardeners in a small area. TEAS. *Adm 75p Chd free (ACNO to Friends of the Hadleigh Practice, Corfe Mullen©). Suns May 10, June 14, July 5 (2-5)*

Highwood Garden, Wareham ✗ (H W Drax Esq) Charborough Park, 6m E of Bere Regis behind long wall. Enter park by any lodge on A31; follow signpost to Estate Office, then Highwood Garden. Large garden with rhododendrons and azaleas in woodland setting. TEAS. *Adm £2 Chd £1 (7-16 yrs) (ACNO to Red Post Parish©). Suns May 24, 31 (2.30-6)*

Hilltop Cottage, Stour Provost ✗❀ (Mr & Mrs Emerson) approx 5m N Sturminster Newton on B3092 turn R at Stour Provost Xrds, signed Woodville. After 1¼m a thatched cottage on the RH-side. Parking in lane outside. Well established cottage garden now being extended with a wealth of different and interesting perennials. Very colourful and inspirational with misty blue views over Blackmore Vale. Incl a small nursery. TEAS. *Adm £1 Chd free. Suns July 26, Aug 2, 9, Weds July 29, Aug 5 (2-6)*

Holworth Farmhouse, Holworth ✗❀ (Anthony & Philippa Bush) 7m E of Dorchester, 1m S of A352. Follow signs to Holworth up the hill, past duck pond on R. After 250yds turn L to C16 Grade II farmhouse on side of hill with magnificent views. Partially walled and terraced garden uses hedges to show what can be done to protect a wide variety of herbaceous plants, shrubs and old roses from the effects of strong and persistent winds. Also a wildlife pond, potager and badger wood. TEAS in aid of Joseph Weld Hospice & 'Fight for Sight'. *Adm £2 Chd free. Suns May 31, June 21 (2-6). Private visits and parties welcome at other times, please Tel 01305 852242*

Honeybrook, Osmington ✗❀ (Allan & Gill Howarth) 4m E of Weymouth on A353. Parking only at The Sunray large car park. Proceed down Chapel Lane into Village st and turn R into Church Lane. Garden 500yds from public house. Views of the White Horse and village from this informal ⅓-acre terraced hillside garden constructed and maintained since 1991 by present owners. Feature pond with waterfall, an abundance of colour spring and early summer but planted to give yr-round interest. TEAS. *Adm £1 Chd free. Tues April 28, Suns May 10, June 7 (2-5)*

■ **Horn Park, Beaminster** ♿❀ (Mr & Mrs John Kirkpatrick) On A3066 1½m N of Beaminster on L before tunnel. Large garden; magnificent view to sea; listed house built by pupil of Lutyens in 1910 (not open). Plantsman's garden worth visiting at all seasons; many rare plants and shrubs in terraced, herbaceous, rock and water gardens. Woodland garden and walks in bluebell woods. Good autumn colouring. Wild flower meadow with 164 varieties incl orchids. TEAS, toilet, ample parking. *Adm £3 Chd under 16 free. Open Sun - Thurs incl, (2-6) April to Oct 31. For NGS Easter Sun April 12, Bank Hol Mon May 25 (2-6) Tel 01308 862212*

■ **Ivy Cottage, Ansty** ✗❀ (Anne & Alan Stevens) Aller Lane, 12m N of Dorchester. A354 from Puddletown to Blandford; After pub take 1st L down Long Lane signed Dewlish-Cheselbourne, through Cheselbourne to Ansty 6 miles from Puddletown, then 1st R before Fox Inn, down Aller Lane. 1½-acre excellent plantsman's garden specialising in unusual perennials, moisture-loving plants; specimen trees and shrubs; well laid out vegetable garden. TEAS Sun Aug 30. *Combined adm with **Aller Green** £2.50 Chd 50p. Also every Thurs April to Oct incl Adm £2 (Share to NGS®) (10-5). For NGS Sun Aug 30 (ACNO to Red Cross®) (2-5.30). Tel 01258 880053*

¶ **80 Keith Road, Talbot Woods** (Howard Collin) W of N end of Glenferness Ave turn into Roslin Road South and follow rd round into Keith Rd. Enclosed town garden of approx ¼ acre redesigned in the last six years round an existing cedar tree. Divided by hedges and shrub planting into areas of differing mood. Plantings range from rhododendrons to Kiftsgate style roses climbing along walls and over the summerhouse, in addition to mixed plantings in box hedged borders. *Combined adm with **46 Roslin Rd** £1.50 Chd 50p. Suns June 7, July 5 (1.30-5)*

By Appointment Gardens. These owners do not have a fixed opening day usually because they cannot accommodate large numbers or have insufficient parking space.

▲**Kingston Lacy, Wimborne Minster** &⚘❀ (The National Trust) 1½m W of Wimborne Minster on the Wimborne-Blandford rd B3082. The setting landscaped in the C18, to W J Bankes's Kingston Lacy House. Magnificent trees planted over 175 years by Royal and famous visitors; avenue of limes and cedars; 9 acres of lawn; Dutch garden; sunken garden laid out to 1906 plans. A Victorian Fernery, extensive collection of rhododendrons and azaleas, National Collections of anemone nemorosa and convallaria. TEAS and lunches in aid of NT. *Adm House & Garden £6, Gardens £2.50, Chd half price. For NGS Sun June 7 (11.30-6)*

■ **Kingston Maurward Gardens** &⚘❀ 1m E of Dorchester. Follow brown Tourist Information signs. National collections of penstemons and salvias. Classic Georgian mansion set in 35 acres of gardens laid out in C18 with 5-acre lake. Terraces and gardens divided by hedges and stone balustrades. Stone features and interesting plants. Elizabethan walled garden laid out as demonstration. Nature and tree trails. Animal park. Restaurant. *Adm £3.75 Chd £2. Open March 14 to Oct 31 daily (10-5.30). Private visits and guided tours welcome, please* **Tel 01305 264738** *(Mike Hancock)*

Knitson Old Farmhouse, Knitson ⚘❀ (Rachel & Mark Helfer) Signposted L off A351 Knitson, approx 1m W of Swanage 3m E of Corfe Castle. Ample parking in yard or in adjacent level field. Approx 1 acre of mature cottage garden. Herbaceous borders, rockeries, climbers, shrubs – many interesting cultivars. Large organic kitchen garden, orchard. Purbeck Woodcraft Exhibition. TEAS in aid of F.A.R.M. Africa. *Adm £1.50 Chd 50p. Sats April 18, May 16, July 18, Sat, Sun Aug 8, 9 (2-5). Private visits and parties welcome, please* **Tel 01929 422836**

●**Knoll Gardens and Nursery, Hampreston** &⚘❀ (Neil Lucas, Esq) 2½m W of Ferndown, ETB brown signs from A31. Wide collection of trees, shrubs and herbaceous plants, continually being expanded. Under new ownership since 1994. Water gardens with waterfalls, pools and streams; mixed borders and woodland setting. NCCPG collections of phygelius and deciduous ceanothus. Licensed tea rooms and visitor centre with gift/ bookshops and garden accessories, to which entry is free. Large car park. Many plants shown available in adjacent nursery. TEAS. *Adm £3.40 OAP's £2.90 Students £2.40 Chd £1.70. Group rates on application. Daily, April 1 to Oct 31 (10-5.30); March Wed to Sun (10-4)*

Langebride House, Long Bredy ❀ (Mrs John Greener) ½-way Bridport and Dorchester, S off A35, well signed. Substantial old rectory garden with many designs for easier management. 200-yr-old beech trees, pleached limes, yew hedges, extensive collections of spring bulbs, herbaceous plants, flowering trees and shrubs. TEA in aid of Joseph Weld House. *Adm £1.50 Chd free. Suns March 22, April 5 (2-5). Private visits welcome March to end July* **Tel 01308 482257**

¶■ **Leigh Farm, Halstock** ⚘❀ (Mr & Mrs L J Lauderdale) Leave A37 Yeovil-Dorchester rd 2m S of Yeovil to Sutton Bingham and Halstock continue 3½m to Halstock. R at Post Office continue 1¾m on R. 1 acre young, expanding

plantsman's garden, being developed by former owners of Ashtree Cottage, Kilmington. Ponds, herbaceous borders, trees, shrubs and roses in beautiful rural setting. Garden and Nursery open Tues and Weds, March to October. *Adm £2 Chd 50p (ACNO to Woodgreen Animal Shelters®). For NGS Weds May 6, June 3, July 1, Aug 5, Sept 16, Oct 7 (10-5). Sun Aug 23 (2-6)*

Little Platt, Dorchester (Sir Robert Williams) Plush, 9m N of Dorchester by B3143 to Piddletrenthide, then 1½m NE by rd signed Plush & Mappowder, 1st house on L entering Plush. 1-acre garden created from a wilderness since 1969; interesting collection of ornamental trees and flowering shrubs, incl several daphnes, spiraeas and viburnums; spring bulbs, hellebores, numerous hardy geraniums and unusual perennials. *Adm £1.50 Chd 50p. Private visits welcome March to Aug* **Tel 01300 348320**

Litton Cheney Gardens 1m S of A35, 10m Dorchester, 6m Bridport. Small village in the beautiful Bride Valley. '97 opening featured on Westcountry TV - Autumn '97. TEAS in Church Hall in aid of the Church. *Combined adm £2.50 Chd 50p. Sun June 7, Tues June 9 (2-6)*

> **2 Litton Hill** ⚘❀ (Patricia & Malcolm Munro) New garden on difficult site; ⅕ acre; shallow soil overlying chalk. S facing with steep slopes. Showing plants that flourish on chalk; plants of interest to dyers
> **The Old Rectory** ❀ (Mr & Mrs Hugh Lindsay) Small walled garden, partly paved and with a prolific quince tree. A steep path leads to 4 acres of natural woodland with many springs, streams and 2 small lakes; mostly native plants, and many primulas. Wild flower lawn; (stout shoes recommended). Featured in House and Garden, May '97. TEAS in aid of Red Cross on 12 April. *Adm £2 Chd free. Also open Easter Sun April 12 (2-5.30). Private visits welcome April to June, please* **Tel 01308 482383**

Macpenny Woodland Garden & Nurseries, Bransgore See Hampshire

1 Manor Close, Stratton & (Mr & Mrs W A Butcher) 3m NW of Dorchester off A37 to Yeovil, turn into village, gardens signed at Church. ⅕-acre plantsman's garden. Alpines at front. To the rear interesting shrubs, and herbaceous beds. *Combined adm with* **Manor Orchard** *£1.50 Chd free. Suns, Weds April 12, 15; July 12, 22 (2-5.30)*

Manor Farmhouse, Little Windsor ⚘❀ (Mr & Mrs E Hornsby) 4m NW of Beaminster; 1m from Broadwindsor. From A3066 turn off at Mosterton, signed Drimpton. 3 acres landscaped gardens; pond and water garden; with primulas and orchids; unusual trees and shrubs. TEA. *Adm £1.50 Chd free. Suns May 24, June 21 (2-6). Private visits welcome please,* **Tel 01308 868491**

The Manor House, Abbotsbury ⚘❀ (Mr & Mrs Robert Harris) Equidistant (9m) from Dorchester, Weymouth and Bridport. The Manor House is in Church St opp St Nicholas Church. Park in the public carpark by the Swan Inn. No parking by The Manor House. The gardens extending to 2½ acres were designed in 1988 by Ian Teh. They feature 4 inter-connecting ponds surrounded by herbaceous borders, a herb garden and abundance of roses. The gardens lie below St Catherine's chapel with views of the sea. TEAS. *Adm £2 Chd free. Sat, Sun May 30, 31 (2.30-6)*

The Manor House, Hinton St Mary &⚘❀ (Mr & Mrs A Pitt-Rivers) 1m NW of Sturminster Newton on B3092. Next to Church in Hinton St Mary. 5-acre garden with views over Blackmore Vale. Spring bulbs, trees and shrubs, yew and box hedges, pleached lime walk, lots of roses. Major alterations made in 1992 and 1996. C15 Tithe Barn. TEA. *Adm £2. Suns April 19, June 21 (2-6)*

Manor Orchard, Stratton &❀ (Mr & Mrs G B David) 3m NW of Dorchester off A37 to Yeovil, turn into village, gardens signed at Church. 1-acre garden planted for yr-round interest. Spring bulbs, herbaceous and shrub borders, lawns, pond, roses, vine. Kitchen garden with fruit tunnel and topiary. Cream TEAS (Suns only). DIY teas on Weds. *Combined adm with* **1 Manor Close** *£1.50 Chd free. Suns, Weds April 12, 15; July 12, 22 (2-5.30)*

●**Mapperton Gardens, nr Beaminster** &⚘❀ (The Earl & Countess of Sandwich) 6m N of Bridport off A35. 2m SE of Beaminster off B3163. Descending valley gardens beside one of Dorset's finest Grade I manor houses (C16-C17). Magnificent walks and views. Fish ponds, orangery, formal Italian-style borders and topiary; specimen trees and shrubs; car park. Upper levels only suitable for wheelchairs. Gift shop with plants and terracota pots. TEAS. House open to group tours by prior appt **Tel 01308 862645**. *Adm garden £3 Chd £1.50, under 5 free. March to Oct incl daily (2-6)*

¶**Mappercombe Manor, Powerstock** ❀ (Cdr & Mrs William Crutchley) 4m NE of Bridport. From A35 at Bridport take A3066 towards Beaminster. Turn R at Kings Head. At T-junction turn R towards Loders. Next L to Nettlecombe. After 3m, keeping straight, entrance on RH side. Monks rest house with stew pond and dovecote. S facing gardens on 4 levels with ancient monastic route. Approx 2½ acres. Apart from walls and pillars and mature trees garden has been mostly replanted; mixed borders and young trees and shrubs in last ten years. TEAS and plants in aid of Powerstock Hut. *Adm £2 Chd free. Sun, Wed June 7, 10 (2-6)*

¶**Mayo Farm, Shaftesbury** &❀ (Robin & Trish Porteous) ½m E of Shaftesbury on B3081. An informal farmhouse garden with beautiful views overlooking The Blackmore Vale. Walled areas with ponds, herbaceous and mixed borders, a small orchard and further pathways through trees and wild flowers. An 'English garden' which includes a small nursery, soft fruit and Christmas trees. Created over the last ten years by its owners. TEAS. *Adm £2 Chd 50p. Sun June 14 (2-6)*

Melbury House ⚘❀ 6m S of Yeovil. Signed on Dorchester-Yeovil rd. 13m N of Dorchester. Large garden; very fine arboretum; shrubs and lakeside walk; beautiful deer park. Garden only. TEAS. *Adm £2 OAPs/Chd £1 (ACNO to Macmillan Cancer Relief®). Thurs May 14, 28, June 11, 25; July 9, 30 (2-5). Private visits welcome for parties of 15 max, please* **Tel 01935 83699** (*Andrew Clark*)

Melplash Court, Melplash &❀ On A3066 between Beaminster and Bridport, just N of Melplash. Turn W and enter between field gates next to big gates and long ave of chestnut trees. While the gardens as they exist today were originally designed by Lady Diana Tiarks they continue to evolve and consist of park planting, bog garden, croquet lawn and adjacent borders. Formal kitchen garden and herb garden, ponds, streams and lake; new borders and areas of interest are added and opened up each year. TEAS in aid of Melplash Church. *Adm £2 Chd free. Sun July 26 (2-6)*

Merebimur, Mockbegger, nr Ringwood See Hampshire

Mews Cottage, Portland ⚘❀ (Mr & Mrs P J Pitman) 34 Easton Street. Situated in the 1st village on the top of the Island, 50yds past the Punchbowl Inn on the L. Park in the main st and follow signs. Small cottage style garden, with a pond and a good mix of herbaceous plants and unusual shrubs, incl crinodendron hookerianum and callistemon. In spring a good collection of hellebore and spring bulbs. In summer a National Collection of Penstemon (180+ named varieties incl many alpine varieties). Autumn colour is achieved with a large collection of nerine bowdenii. TEAS. *Adm £1 Chd free. Suns March 22, May 24, June 28, July 26, Aug 23, Sept 27 (2-5)*

Midsummer's Cottage, Bridport (S New) 65 South Street. From A35 to town centre turn into South St at Clock Tower. Park in street or nearby car park. Next door but one to Woodman Inn on L by red telephone box. Imaginative, 16′ × 50′, town garden planted with roses, herbaceous plants and climbers, with green formal area and water feature. Summerhouse designed by owner. Also 'Borrowed Landscape' feature. An example of what can be achieved in a small area. *Adm 75p. Sun June 14 (11-4)*

¶**Millmead, Winterborne Stickland** &⚘❀ (Michele Barker) 4m SW of Blandford Forum. After 'Shire Horse', turn R down West St, signed Winterborne Houghton. 1st L after 30mph sign. Although only started in 1990, the garden, which has been designed and constructed by its owners, already has a well established feel. Within ⅓ acre, they have created a beautiful formal country garden on different levels, divided into separate 'rooms', each with its own character. The emphasis is on structure and planting, with many new and unusual plants. *Adm £2 Chd 50p. Sats April 25, Sept 26 (2-5)*

● **Minterne, Minterne Magna** (The Lord Digby) On A352 Dorchester-Sherborne rd. 2m N Cerne Abbas; woodland garden set in a valley landscaped in the C18 with small lakes, cascades and rare trees; many species and hybrid rhododendrons and magnolias tower over streams and water plants. *Adm £3 Acc chd and parking free. Open daily March 28 to Nov 10 (10-7)*

Moigne Combe, nr Dorchester (Maj-Gen H M G Bond) 6m E of Dorchester. 1½m N of Owermoigne turn off A352 Dorchester-Wareham rd. Medium-sized garden; wild garden and shrubbery; heathers, azaleas, rhododendrons etc; woodland paths and lake walk. Tea the Post Office, Kit Lane, Owermoigne. *Adm £1 1st chd 25p thereafter 10p. Suns May 17, 24 (2-5)*

Moulin Huet, West Moors ⅍⅍❀ (Harold Judd Esq) 15 Heatherdown Rd. 7m N of Bournemouth. Leave A31 at West Moors Garage into Pinehurst Rd, take 1st R into Uplands Rd, then 3rd L into Heatherdown Rd. thence into cul-de-sac. ⅓-acre garden made by owner from virgin heathland after retirement. Considerable botanical interest; collections of 90 dwarf conifers and bonsai; many rare plants and shrubs; alpines, sink gardens, rockeries, wood sculpture. TV 'Gardeners' World'. *Adm 75p Chd free. Two Suns in May, see local press. Private visits and parties welcome March to Oct, please* **Tel 01202 875760**

Oakdene, Sandleheath See Hampshire

¶**The Old Coach House, Bournemouth** ⅍ (Mrs Honor Beesley) From Surrey Rd turn N into Prince of Wales Rd. There is no parking allowed in this section of road. ¼-acre garden recently arranged in terraces overlooking the Upper Central Gardens and the Bourne stream. The garden has been planted over the last 4yrs with perennials, hardy fuschia, penstemons, hostas, plox etc and shrubs, magnolias, elaeagnus and weigela etc. *Adm £1 Acc chd free (ACNO to Green Island Trust®). Sun Aug 16 (2-6)*

The Old Farmhouse, Organford ⅍❀ (Mr & Mrs D J Palmer) From A35, 1m W of The Baker's Arms roundabout, take the rd S to Organford. ½-acre garden with typical Georgian fronted old Dorset farmhouse. Date of layout is unknown but has been retained with additional planting, incl the unconventional design of the rear walled garden. Planting incl robust old-fashioned perennials, herbs, shrubs, with a vegetable and fruit area. TEAS. *Adm £1 Chd free. Sun Sept 6 (2.30-5)*

The Old Mill, Spetisbury ⅍⅍❀ (The Rev & Mrs J Hamilton-Brown) Spetisbury Village opposite school on A350 3m SE of Blandford. 2 acres mainly water garden by R Stour; choice trees and plants, Caltha Collection, spring bulbs and hellebores. *Adm £2 Chd free. Sun April 26 (2-5). Individuals and parties by appt, please* **Tel 01258 453939**

The Old Rectory, Fifehead Magdalen ⅍❀ (Mrs Patricia Lidsey) 5m S of Gillingham just S of the A30. Medium-sized garden with interesting shrubs and perennials; pond; grandchildren's garden; plant stall. TEAS in aid of St Mary Magdalen. *Adm £1 Chd free. Sun June 7 (2-6) also private visits welcome, please* **Tel 01258 820293**

The Old Rectory, Litton Cheney see Litton Cheney Gardens

The Old Rectory, Pulham, Dorchester ⅍❀ (Mr & Mrs N Elliott) On B3143 turn E at Xrds in Pulham. 13m N of Dorchester, Sherborne and Sturminster Newton both 8m. 3 acres with mature trees and shrubs; herbaceous borders, shrub roses, clematis, beautiful terrace, pots, lawns, yew hedges and fine view towards Bulbarrow. 2 ponds and recently planted 4½ acre wood with shrubs and mown rides. *Adm £2 Chd free. Sun, Wed Aug 2, 5 (2-6)*

The Old Vicarage, Stinsford ⅍❀ (Mr & Mrs Antony Longland) Off roundabout at E end of Dorchester bypass A35. Follow signs for Stinsford Church 400yds. 1¼ acres

incl an Italianate garden, herbaceous and mixed borders with unusual plants and shrubs, nearly 200 roses, lawns, terraces with exuberant pots, and fruit. Thomas Hardy, C Day Lewis and Cecil Hanbury, creator of gardens at La Mortola and Kingston Maurward, commemorated in church next door. TEAS. *Adm £2 Chd 50p. Sun June 21 (2-6). Private group visits welcome, please* **Tel 01305 265827**

The Orchard, Blynfield Gate ⅍❀ (Mr & Mrs K S Ferguson) 2m W of Shaftesbury on the rd to Stour Row. From Shaftesbury take B3091 to St James's Church then onto the Stour Row rd. A 3-acre country garden, orchard and native meadow developed since 1981. Lawns and paths link formal, informal and wild areas. Colourful mixed borders and island beds with a wide variety of plants, several chosen for their intermingling qualities and lengthy flowering period. Hedgebanks of hardy geraniums, interesting trees and shrubs, small natural pond and plenty of seats. Home-made TEAS. *Adm £2 to incl descriptive guide Chd free (ACNO to Red Cross®). Weds June 10, 17; July 8, 22; Sept 16 (2-6)*

¶**Orchard House, Ferndown** ⅍⅍❀ (Mr & Mrs John Norris) 6 Aldridge Rd. From Parley Xrds continue N on A347 (New Rd), after ½m turn R into Gold Links Rd, thence 2nd R into Lone Pine Drive and 1st L into Aldridge Rd. Colourful ½-acre garden carefully maintained by owners. Spring and summer bulbs, herbaceous plants and ground cover, hostas, perennial geraniums. Roses, pool and small vegetable garden. Greenhouse and conservatory dahlias. Many plants are labelled with new plants always being added. TEAS. *Adm £1 Chd free (ACNO to Osborne Day Centre for MS®). Suns May 31, June 14 (11-4)*

● **Parnham, Beaminster** ⅍ (Mr & Mrs John Makepeace) ½m S of Beaminster on A3066, 5m N of Bridport. 14 acres including grand herbaceous borders, intimate courtyard garden, formal terraces; topiary, spring fed water rills overlooked by gazebos to the south; recognised by English Heritage as very important 1910 period. Riverside walk, many unusual plants and fine old trees. House dates from 1540. Grade 1 listed. Also John Makepeace furniture workshops. Childrens play area. Tree trail. Restaurant, coffee, lunches. TEAS. *Adm to whole site £5 Chd 5-15 £2. Suns, Tues, Weds, Thurs, Bank Hols Easter or April to end Oct (10-5).* **Tel 01308 862204**

Portesham House, Portesham ⅍⅍❀ (Mrs G J Romanes) 7m W of Weymouth on coast rd, B3157 to Bridport. From Dorchester take A35 W, turn L in Winterborne Abbas and follow signs to Portesham; parking in village. Home of Admiral Sir Thomas Masterman Hardy, with 300-yr-old mulberry tree; 2 acres of family garden with modern dry stone walling, old walls and recent plantings by stream. Tree paeonies, herbaceous paeonies, unusual trees and shrubs. Teas at Millmead Country Hotel. *Adm £1.50 Chd free. Suns June 7, 14 (2-5.30). For early flowering tree paeonies in May please,* **Tel 01305 871300**

Potters Cot, Hightown Hill, nr Ringwood. See Hampshire

▲The Priest's House Museum and Garden, Wimborne ర్ ✗ (The Priest's House Museum Trust) 23 High St. Public car parks nearby. Old 'borough plot' garden of ½ acre, at rear of local museum, in historic town house. Extending to mill stream and containing many unusual plants, trees and exhibits. Tea-room daily. *Adm £2 Family £5 OAP/Students £1.60 Chd 90p. For NGS Sun June 28 (2-5).* Tel 01202 882533

Pumpkin Patch, Ringwood. See Hampshire

Rampisham Manor, Rampisham ✗❀ (Mr & Mrs Boileau) 9m S of Yeovil take A37 to Dorchester. 7m turn R signed Evershot follow signs to Rampisham. 11m NW Dorchester take A37 to Yeovil, L A356 signed Crewkerne; at start of wireless masts R to Rampisham. 3-acre garden. Mixture of formal and flowing planting in rural setting, spring bulbs, English roses amongst shrubs, vegetables, grasses bed, hedged walks, water and new woodland garden. TEAS. *Adm £1.50 Chd 50p. Weds April 29, May 6 (2-5). Private visits welcome, please* Tel 01935 83612

▲Red House Museum and Gardens, Christchurch ర్ ❀ (The Hampshire Museum Service) Quay Road. Tranquil setting in heart of town's conservation area. Gardens of ½ acre developed from early 1950's to complement Museum; plants of historic interst; herb garden, rose border and woodland walk. Gardens used as gallery display area for sculpture exhibitions. Admission to Museum and Art Gallery included. *Adm £1 OAP/Chd 60p (under 5 free). For NGS Sat June 13 (10-4), Sun July 26 (2-4)*

46 Roslin Road South, Bournemouth ✗❀ (Dr & Mrs Malcolm Slade) W of N end of Glenferness Ave in Talbot Woods area of Bournemouth. Plantswoman's ⅓-acre walled town garden planted with many unusual and rare plants. Sunken gravel garden with collection of grasses, surrounded by colourful mixed borders. Features include many well planted containers, raised octagonal alpine bed, rose pergola leading to enclosed patio, kitchen garden and greenhouses. *Adm 80p Chd free. Mon May 3 (1.30-5), special evening opening Sun May 24 (6-8.30). Combined adm with* 80 Keith Rd *£1.50 Chd 50p. Suns June 7, July 5 (1.30-5)*

The Scented Garden, Littlebredy ✗❀ (Chris & Judy Yates) 10m equidistant Dorchester and Bridport. 1½m S off the A35. Park on Littlebredy village green by round bus shelter. 400yd walk to garden (not ideal for the disabled). 1-acre Victorian walled garden, in tranquil setting, being lovingly restored. Old roses and stately delphiniums form the backbone to the mixed, colour themed beds and borders, which contain many unusual plants. Display bed containing National Collection of lavender (over 60). *Adm £1 Chd 20p (ACNO to Littlebredy Church®). Tues June 16, 23, 30 July 7, 14, 21 (2.30-8)*

¶Silton House, Silton ✗❀ (Mr & Mrs A Corlett) 4m NW of Gillingham, take B3095 from Gillingham. Turn L at Milton Lodge Hotel and continue towards Bourton. Turn L to Silton Church just before A303 bypass at Bourton. House next to church limited parking outside church. 2¼-acre garden. 200-year-old copper beech, ancient mulberry. Garden developing in rooms divided by mature beech and new yew hedging and topiary. Long hot border against wall. Gravel garden and new flower garden. Orchard with spring bulbs. TEAS. *Adm £1.50 Chd 50p. Sun June 14 (2-5)*

Smedmore, Kimmeridge ర్❀ (Dr Philip Mansel) 7m S of Wareham. Turn W off A351 (Wareham-Swanage) at sign to Kimmeridge. 2 acres of colourful herbaceous borders; display of hydrangeas; interesting plants and shrubs; walled flower gardens; herb courtyard. House also open for NGS. *Adm £2 Chd £1. Sun May 17 (2-5). Private visits welcome by appt, please* Tel 01929 480719 *(Mr T Gargett)*

■ Snape Cottage, Chaffeymoor ✗❀ (Ian & Angela Whinfield) At W end of Bourton. Opp Chiffchaffs. ½-acre plantsman's country garden full of old-fashioned and uncommon perennials, most labelled. Organically managed and planted for yr-round interest with large collections of snowdrops, hellebores, pulmonarias, auriculas, geraniums, dianthus, iris, penstemon and asters. Special emphasis on plant history and nature conservation. Beautiful views, wildlife pond. *Adm £1.50 Chd free. Feb 15, 22 March 22. Every Sun and Wed April to Sept (closed Aug). For NGS Suns April 12, June 7, July 26, Sept 27 (2-5). Parties welcome by appt, please* Tel 01747 840330 *(evenings only)*

Spinners Boldre See Hampshire

● Stapehill Abbey, Ferndown ర్✗❀ Wimborne Rd West. 2½m W of Ferndown on the old A31, towards Wimborne, ½m E of Canford Bottom roundabout. Early C19 Abbey, its gardens and estate restored and renovated to lawns, herbaceous borders; rose and water gardens; Victorian cottage garden; lake and Victorian greenhouse. Mature trees. Busy working Craft Centre; Countryside Museum featuring the National Tractor Collection, all under cover. Refreshments available in former refectory throughout the day. Licensed coffee shop. Large free car/coach park. *Adm £4.80 OAPs £4.40 Chd £3.30. Open daily Easter to Sept (10-5); Oct to Easter (10-4), except Mons and Tues. Closed Dec 20 to Feb 3.* Tel 01202 861686

■ Star Cottage, Cowgrove ✗❀ (Lys de Bray) 8 Roman Way, Cowgrove, nr Wimborne. Leave B3082 at Wimborne Hospital, along Cowgrove Rd for approx 1½m to Roman Way on R. Created in 1992 from a field, the garden is another 'living library' of RHS gold medallist and author Lys de Bray, whose botanical paintings are on permanent exhibition in her working studio, open all the year at weekends and bank holidays. *Adm £1.50 Chd £1. Open Sats & Suns all year. Easter to end Oct (2-6). End Oct to end March (2-4). For NGS Suns May 17, June 21, July 12. Private visits arranged* Tel 01202 885130

Steeple Manor, Steeple ర్✗❀ (Mr Julian & the Hon Mrs Cotterell) 5m SW of Wareham in Isle of Purbeck. Take Swanage rd from Wareham, and follow signs to Steeple. A beautiful garden designed by Brenda Colvin 1920's round C16/17 Purbeck stone manor house (not open); lovely setting in folds of Purbeck hills in small hamlet next to ancient church, specially decorated for the occasion. Approx 5 acres, the garden includes walls, hedges, ponds, stream, bog garden and meadow, collection old roses; many interesting plants and shrubs for the plantsman. Parts suitable for wheelchairs. Free parking. Cream TEAS. *Adm £2.50 (includes written guide) Chd under 16 free. Sun June 28 (1.30-6)*

■ **Sticky Wicket, Buckland Newton** 杏❀❀ (Peter & Pam Lewis) 11m from Dorchester and Sherborne. 2m E of A352 or take B3143 from Sturminster Newton. T-junction midway Church, School and Gaggle of Geese public house. 1½-acre colourist and conservationist's garden created since 1987, unusual designs, well documented, showing wild life interest; fragrant cottage garden planting with many perennials and herbs. TEAS. *Adm £2.50 Chd £1. Every Thurs June 4 to Sept 24 incl (10.30-8). For NGS Suns June 21, Aug 23 (2-6). Groups only by appt, please* **Tel 01300 345476**

Stour House, Blandford 杏❀❀ (T S B Card Esq) East St. Enter Blandford from the ring rd by the B3082 from Wimborne. 200yds along East St (one-way) on the L. 2½-acre town garden, half on a romantic island in R Stour reached by a remarkable bridge; bulbs; borders well planted with perennials and many rare shrubs; river views. TEAS in aid of Blandford Parish Church, July. *Adm £1 Chd 20p (ACNO to Blandford Parish Church®). Suns March 29 (2-5) July 12, Aug 16 (2-6)*

Studland Bay House, Studland 杏❀ (Mrs Pauline Ferguson) On B3351 5m E of Corfe Castle. Through village, entrance on R after Studland Bay House. Ample parking (no coaches). From Bournemouth, take Sandbanks ferry, 2½m, garden on L after Knoll House Hotel. 6-acre spring garden overlooking Studland Bay. Planted in 1930's on heathland; magnificent rhododendrons, azalea walk, camellias, magnolias, ferns and stream; recent drainage and replanting, garden suitable for wheelchairs. Cream TEAS in aid of Swanage Hospital. *Adm £2 Chd free. Sat, Sun May 16, 17 (2-5)*

Sturminster Newton Gardens 杏❀ Off A357 between Blandford and Sherborne take turn opp Nat West Bank. Park in car park or behind Stourcastle Lodge. Walk down Penny St for **Ham Gate** and Goughs Close for **Stourcastle Lodge**. TEAS at **Ham Gate**. *Combined adm £2 Chd free. Sun June 14 (2-6). Parties by appt, please* **Tel 01258 472462** *or* **01258 472320**

> **Ham Gate** (Mr & Mrs H E M Barnes) Informal 2-acre garden with shrubs, trees, lawns running down to R Stour, pleasant woodland views across water meadows, over the last few years Pam Lewis of Sticky Wicket has helped redesign the garden
>
> **Stourcastle Lodge** (Jill & Ken Hookham-Bassett) S facing secluded cottage garden, with a wide selection of interesting herbs, perennials and shrubs, a dovecote and water features

¶**Sweetwell, Fiddleford** ❀❀ (Mrs Ann R Hay) 1½m from Sturminster Newton on A357 towards Blandford. Sharp R-hand corner with Fiddleford Inn on L. Turn L up lane at the inn, 6th house on L. Some parking, overflow in free car park along lane at Fiddleford Mill. C16 timbered thatched cottage in 1 acre garden, created from derelict site in 1981. Shrub and herbaceous borders, stone garden, old roses, pond. TEAS. *Adm £1.50 Chd free. Sun June 21 (2-5)*

Tara, West Moors 杏❀ (Mr & Mrs W H Adams) 66 Elmhurst Rd. 7m N of Bournemouth. Leave A31 at Gulf Garage into Pinehurst Rd and take 4th R into Elmhurst Rd. Carefully tended garden 130' × 40' lawns with island beds. Bridge over bog garden with water features, statuary, ivy topiary and bonsai. Featured in Amateur Gardening and Garden News, the garden is also used in its advertising by an organic fertiliser manufacturer. Plants, Teas and other stalls in aid of animal charities. *Adm 75p Chd 25p. Sats, Suns June 13, 14; 20, 21 (10-4.30)*

■ **Thornhill Park, Stalbridge** ❀❀ (Richard and Cary Goode) 1m S of Stalbridge on A357. Gates opposite T junction. Go down drive for ¾m. 6-acre garden surrounding C18 house built by Sir James Thornhill. Garden currently being re-established and extended by Cary Goode, a professional Garden Designer. Incl formal and informal areas of planting in various colour themes, several ponds, walled garden, nut walk, willow garden and woodland. TEAS. *Adm £2 Chd 50p. Fris (10-5) and Suns (2-5) April to Sept (Share to NGS®). For NGS (ACNO to Dorset Gardens Trust®) Suns May 31, July 5, Aug 9 (2-5)*

Three Bays, Beacon Hill 杏❀ (Mr & Mrs Christopher Garrett) 8, Old Wareham Rd, (nr Limberlost junction with A350). 1½m SW of Corfe Mullen. Garden of ¼ acre made and maintained by owners. There is a Japanese flavour to the garden, with stone lanterns, dovecot and water features. New rose garden 1993. Shrubs and herbaceous borders with much use of sloping site. TEAS. *Adm £1 Chd 50p (ACNO to Cancer Research Campaign®). Sat, Sun Aug 1, 2. Private visits welcome for parties of 40 and over, please* **Tel 01202 623352**

Throop Mill Cottage, Throop 杏 (Dr & Mrs James Fisher) 4m N of Bournemouth Square. Ring Rd (Castle Lane B3060) to Broadway PH. Broadway Lane becomes Throop Rd in ¾m. Thatched cottage next to Throop Mill. 1-acre riverside garden with landscape features such as a ha-ha. Developing collection of ferns in a small valley. TEAS. *Adm £1 Chd 50p. Sun June 14 (2-5.30)*

¶● **Upwey Wishing Well and Water Garden, Upwey** 杏❀❀ (Mrs Vivien Harrison) 3m N of Weymouth on B3159 and just off Dorchester to Weymouth Rd (A354). A tranquil, well-stocked water garden, with ponds (¼ acre). The large natural spring, which is the source of the River Wey is known as the Wishing Well and is an ancient monument. A fine show of bog primulas in May/June. Huge gunneras and unusual foliage plants provide a unique and exotic setting. TEAS and lunches. *Entrance through cafe, adm free but donations welcomed for National Gardens' charities. Open daily April to Sept (10.30-6), Wed to Sun March, Oct-Dec (10.30-6)*

¶**78 Wakeham, Portland** ❀❀ (Mr & Mrs M A Osmond) Wakeham is a long, wide, rd leading from the village of Easton at the top of the island. No 78 is a 3 storey house 300yds along, on the R-hand side. Newly created garden (over last 3yrs). Approx 60' × 60' in size. Mixture of shrubs and perennials. Interesting features incl patio, rockery, pond, cottage garden area and kitchen garden. *Adm £1 Chd free. Suns March 22, May 24, June 28, July 26. Private visits by appt,* **Tel 01305 821299**

Wall Farm, Broadwindsor (Cdr & Mrs P Corson) 1m from Broadwindsor on B3164 Axminster rd. Turn L behind Tin Hut. Very narrow lane, beware tractors. Parking limited. 4-acre garden surrounding C17 thatched farmhouse in a hidden valley. Garden in the making, started 6 yrs ago and being continued by present owners. A mass of spring bulbs and bluebells. Herbaceous borders, small hedged garden. Stream and bog garden and another pond in the making. A flower arranger's garden. Yr-round interest. *Adm £1.50 Chd free. Private weekday visits April to Sept welcome, please* **Tel 01308 868203**

Welcome Thatch, Witchampton ⚲❀ (Mrs Diana Guy) 3½m E of Wimborne, B3078 L to Witchampton, thence through village past church & shop to last but one on R. Please avoid parking close village centre. Listed thatched cottage. Enthusiast's garden (⅔ acre) with unusual plants of interest from spring to autumn, ranging from the exotic and tender to hardy perennials and shrubs. Large collection of hardy geraniums. Hellebores for sale. TEAS. *Adm £1 Chd free. Suns March 15, April 5, May 10, June 7 (2-5.30). Private parties welcome by appt, please* **Tel 01258 840894**

¶**Wentworth College, Bournemouth** ⚲ (Wentworth Milton Mount Ltd) 250yds from the beach and Boscombe Overcliff Dr. 3m E of Bournemouth town centre; off A35, off Beechwood Ave. Originally the seaside estate of Lord Portman, Wentworth Lodge was built in 1872. The main Victorian house has gradually been extended to accommodate the needs of Wentworth College. Formal gardens have been restored to reflect their origins. The grounds also incl woodland with mature specimen trees and rhododendrons in approx 3 acres. TEAS. *Adm £1.50 Chd free. Sat Sept 19 (2-5)*

24a Western Avenue, Poole ⚲ (Mr & Mrs Peter Jackson) Central in Branksome Park, ½m from Compton Acres. Award winning 1-acre part Mediterranean, part English garden close to sea. Formal areas incl lawns, cherry tree walk, rose garden, herbaceous beds, topiary and courtyard with tender wall plants. Tree ferns, drimys, bamboo and camellias flourish. Sunny banks are planted with eucalyptus, acacias, and a collection of callistemons, agaves, yuccas and other drought resistant plants. *Adm £1.50 Chd free. Suns April 26, July 26 (2-6)*

Weston House, Buckhorn Weston ⚲❀ (Mr & Mrs E A W Bullock) 4m W of Gillingham and 4m SE of Wincanton. From A30 turn N to Kington Magna, continue towards Buckhorn Weston and after railway bridge take L turn towards Wincanton. 2nd on L is Weston House. 1 acre plus fields; old and English roses; herbaceous and mixed borders backed by old walls with climbers. Small woodland and wild flower areas; wild-life pond; lawns and view of Blackmore Vale. TEAS in aid of Buckhorn Weston Parish Church. *Adm £1.50 Chd free. Suns May 31, June 28 (2-6)*

▲**Wimborne Minster Model Town & Gardens** ⚲⚲❀ (The Wimborne Minster Model Town Trust). King St 200yds W of Minster, opp public car park. 1½-acre

grounds with ¹⁄₁₀ scale models of the town in early fifties, surrounded by landscaped gardens. Herbaceous borders, alpines, herbs, heather and rose gardens, with many rare and unusual plants, with pools and fountain, making a colourful pleasure garden. Visitors' and exhibition centres. Many seats and views over Stour valley. Refreshments daily. *Adm £2.50 OAPs £2 Chd £1 (3-15) under 3 free. For NGS Suns June 7, July 5, Sept 6 (10-5).* **Tel 01202 881924**

2 Winters Lane, Portesham ⚲❀ (Mr & Mrs K Draper) 7m W of Weymouth on coast rd, B3157 to Bridport. From Dorchester take A35 W, turn L in Winterborne Abbas and follow signs to Portesham. Winters Lane is signed to Coryates. ¼-acre garden with ponds and water features, small herb garden; container garden. 50 varieties of clematis, wishing well and miniature village; (most plants labelled). Featured in 'The Water Garden' May 95. Teas at Orchard House July 12 only. *Adm 75p Chd free. Suns July 12, Aug 16 (2-6). Private visits and parties welcome June and July, please* **Tel 01305 871316**

Witchcroft, Southwell ⚲❀ (Mr & Mrs Rowland & Pamela Reynolds) 1 Sweet Hill Rd, Southwell, Portland. Follow the signs for Portland Bill (A354). 'Witchcroft' is the bungalow 300yds on L, past Eight Kings public house in the village of Southwell. Small cottage garden with pond, shrubs, and herbaceous borders and open rural views. Spring bulbs and hellebores, in summer new and old-fashioned roses. Park in main st. TEAS in aid of Cancer and Leukaemia in Childhood Trust. *Adm £1 Chd free. Suns March 22, June 28, July 26 (2-5)*

SYMBOLS USED IN THIS BOOK

(See also Page 17)

¶ Opening for the first time.

❀ Plants/produce for sale if available.

& Gardens with at least the main features accessible by wheelchair.

⚲ No dogs except guide dogs.

● These gardens advertise their own dates in this publication although they do not nominate specific days for the NGS. Not all the money collected by these gardens comes to the NGS but they do make a guaranteed contribution.

■ These gardens nominate specific days for the NGS and advertise their own dates in this publication.

▲ These gardens open regularly to the public but they do not advertise their own dates in this publication. For further details, contact the garden directly.

County Durham

Hon County Organiser: Mrs Ian Bonas, Bedburn Hall, Hamsterley, Bishop Auckland DL13 3NN
Tel 01388 488231

DATES OF OPENING

Regular openings
For details see garden description

Raby Castle, Staindrop

April 13 Monday
Birkheads Cottage Garden &
Nursery, Sunniside
April 19 Sunday
Wycliffe & Hutton Magna Gardens
April 26 Sunday
Barningham Park, Barnard Castle

May 3 Sunday
Croft Hall, Darlington
Whorlton Village Gardens
May 4 Monday
Birkheads Cottage Garden &
Nursery, Sunniside
May 24 Sunday
Westholme Hall, Winston
June 7 Sunday
Ravensford Farm, Hamsterley
June 21 Sunday
Birkheads Cottage Garden &
Nursery, Sunniside

10 The Chesters, Ebchester
June 28 Sunday
The Gainford Gardens
Low Walworth Hall, Darlington
17 The Lyons, Hetton-Le-Hole
July 5 Sunday
Westholme Hall, Winston
July 12 Sunday
Broomshiels Hall, Satley
August 23 Sunday
Bedburn Hall, Hamsterley
August 30 Sunday
Westholme Hall, Winston

DESCRIPTIONS OF GARDENS

Barningham Park, Barnard Castle ❀ (Sir Anthony Milbank) 6m S. Turn S off A66 at Greta Bridge or A66 Motel via Newsham. Woodland walks, trees and rock garden. House (not open) built 1650. Home-made cream TEAS. *Adm £2.50 Chd 50p (under 14). Sun April 26 (2-5). Also by appt for parties, please* **Tel 01833 621202**

Bedburn Hall, Hamsterley &❀ (Ian Bonas Esq) 9m NW of Bishop Auckland. From A68 at Witton-le-Wear, turn off W to Hamsterley; turn N out of Hamsterley-Bedburn and down 1m to valley. From Wolsingham on B6293 turn off SE for 3m. Medium-sized garden; terraced garden on S facing hillside with streams; lake; woodland; lawns; rhododendrons; herbaceous borders; roses. TEAS. *Adm £2 Chd 50p. Sun Aug 23 (2-6)*

▲**Birkheads Cottage Garden & Nursery, Sunniside, Whickham, Tyne and Wear** ⚹❀ (Christine Liddle) From A1M N or S take A692 or A693 on to A6076 rd between Sunniside and Stanley. Birkheads Nursery is signed 1m S of Tanfield Steam Railway. 1m from sign. Look out for the beehive! Over 4,000 different hardy plants in garden of 2.5 acres incl pond, formal topiary garden, rockeries, gravel garden, herbaceous borders. Newly planted wildflower garden set in open countryside. Beautiful views. *Adm £1.50 Chd 50p. For NGS Mons April 13, May 4, June 21 (10-5). Parties welcome, at other times by appt, please* **Tel 01207 232262**

¶**Broomshiels Hall, Satley** & (Mr & Mrs Cook) 1m N of Tow Lane on the A68 turn off to Satley. Approx 1m turn R at Lodge entrance to main house. Approx 2 acres of country garden incl rose garden, shrubbery walk, small lake and formal potager. TEAS. *Adm £2 Chd free. Sun July 12 (2-6)*

10 The Chesters, Ebchester &❀ (Dianne Allison) Nr Consett. S end of village on A694, signed, 2m from Consett. Small 'cottage-style' garden, as seen on 'Gardeners World', with the National Collection of Polemoniums among a wide variety of plants. National Trust woodland walk nearby for dog walking etc. Lectures and group visits by appointment. TEAS. *Adm £1 Chd free/donation. Sun June 21 (2-5)*

Croft Hall, Darlington &⚹ (Mr & Mrs Trevor Chaytor Norris) Croft Village lies 3m S of Darlington on A167 to Northallerton and 6m from Scotch Corner. Croft Hall is 1st house on R as you enter the village from Scotch Corner. Square yellow Georgian. 3 acres incl lawn with avenue of red may, water garden with temple, shrubbery bank, herb and knot gardens, long herbaceous border sheltered by magnificent yew hedge. TEAS. *Adm £2 Chd 50p. Sun May 3 (2-6)*

The Gainford Gardens, Gainford &❀ On A67, 8m W of Darlington; 8m E of Barnard Castle. One of the loveliest villages in the county, lying around a large tranquil green between A67 and R Tees. Georgian flavour predominates. TEAS. *Combined adm £2 Chd free (ACNO to St Mary's Parish Church®). Sun June 28 (2-6)*
    14 Academy Gardens (Mr & Mrs G Taylor)
    35 Academy Gardens (Mr & Mrs M Metcalf)
    No 1 Balmer Hill (Mr & Mrs R W Holmes)
    No 2 Balmer Hill (Mr & Mrs A D Best)
    No 3 Balmer Hill (Mrs J R Pennell)
    ¶**No 4 Balmer Hill** (Mr & Mrs H Finan)
    7 High Row (Peter & Merope Pease)
    24 Low Green (Mrs M P Ferens)
    2 Piggy Lane (Mr & Mrs J G Ormston)

Low Walworth Hall, Darlington &❀ (Mr & Mrs Worrall) 3½m W on Staindrop Rd. B6279 (½m drive). Old walled garden; herbaceous borders, shrubs, roses; trout rearing

DURHAM

KEY

1. Barningham Park
2. Bedburn Hall
3. Birkheads Cottage Garden & Nursery
4. Broomshiels Hall
5. 10 The Chesters
6. Croft Hall
7. The Gainford Gardens
8. Low Walworth Hall
9. 17 The Lyons
10. Raby Castle
11. Ravensford Farm
12. Westholme Hall
13. Whorlton Village Gardens
14. Wycliffe & Hutton Magna Gardens

Scotland's Gardens Scheme

The National Gardens Scheme has a similar but quite separate counterpart in Scotland. Called Scotland's Gardens Scheme, it raises money for the Queen's Nursing Institute (Scotland), the Gardens Fund of the National Trust for Scotland and over 160 registered charities nominated by Garden Owners. The Handbook is available (£3.75 incl p&p) from Scotland's Gardens Scheme, 31 Castle Terrace, Edinburgh, EH1 2EL.

pond. Small Japanese garden. Interesting and varied shrubs and greenhouse plants for sale. Homemade cream TEAS. *Adm £2 Chd 50p. Sun June 28 (2-5.30). Also by appt, please* Tel 01325 468004

17 The Lyons, Hetton Le Hole ⚇❀ (Jim & Eileen Manwaring) From A1 to A690 towards Sunderland, turn R to Hetton Le Hole. At New Inn roundabout take B1285, ½m to Hetton Lyons Park. From A19 take B1285 through Murton, 1½m to Hetton Lyons Park. White cottage opp park entrance. Approx ½-acre S facing garden, with lawns, shrubbery, roses, vegetables and herbaceous borders with a wide variety of plants. Pond and greenhouses. TEAS. *Adm £1 Chd 50p (ACNO to St Nicholas Church®). Sun June 28 (2-6). Private visits welcome please* Tel 0191 5263769

● **Raby Castle, Staindrop** ⚇❀ (The Rt Hon The Lord Barnard) NW of Darlington. 1m N of Staindrop on A688. Buses: 75, 77 Darlington-Barnard Castle; 8 Bishop Auckland-Barnard Castle; alight Staindrop, North Lodge, ¼m. Walled garden; informal garden with ericas; old yew hedges; shrub and herbaceous borders; roses. Castle open. Horse-drawn carriages and fire engines. Tearoom. *Adm Castle Gardens and carriages £4 OAPs £3 Chd £1.50. Family ticket £10 (2 adults, 2-3 Chd) Gardens & carriages only £1.50 OAPs/Chd £1. Open all Bank Hols; Sat to Wed May, June; Wed and Sun July to end Sept*

Ravensford Farm, Hamsterley ⚇❀ (Mr & Mrs J Peacock) 9m NW of Bishop Auckland. From A68 at Witton-le-Wear turn off W to Hamsterley. Go through village and turn L just before tennis courts. 2½-acre garden created since 1986 from a field containing a mass of nettles and thistles, and 1 ancient apple tree. There is now a small wood, 2 ponds, a sunken garden, a rhododendron walk and mixed borders containing flowering shrubs, roses and herbaceous perennials. TEAS. *Adm £1.50 Chd 50p. Sun June 7 (2-6)*

Westholme Hall, Winston ⚇❀ (Mr & Mrs J H McBain) 11m W of Darlington. From A67 Darlington-Barnard Castle, nr Winston turn N onto B6274. 5 acres of gardens and grounds laid out in 1892 surround the Jacobean house (not open). Rhododendrons, flowering shrubs, mixed borders, old-fashioned rose garden. The croquet lawn leads on to an orchard, stream and woodland. Home made TEAS in tea rooms. *Adm £2 Chd 50p. Suns May 24, July 5, Aug 30 (2-6)*

Whorlton Village Gardens, Barnard Castle ❀ A67 from Darlington, westwards for 12m, turn L at sign to Whorlton. A group of gardens in a small attractive village above the Tees. TEAS. *Adm £2 Chd 50p (ACNO to Whorlton Village Community Assoc®). Sun May 3 (2-5)*

Wycliffe Gardens and Hutton Magna From Scotch Corner 8m NW on A66. Turn R to Thorpe and Wycliffe. TEAS. *Combined adm £2 Chd 50p. Sun April 19 (2-5)*
  Orchard Cottage ⚇ (Miss C Scrope) ¼-acre cottage garden
  The Nest (Mr & Mrs J Usher) ¼-acre riverside garden featuring magnolias
  The Old Vicarage (Mr & Mrs D Raw) Garden contemporary to house specialising in hellebore, primula and spring bulbs

---

Help the Hospices

Help the Hospices is a charity which supports the hospice movement throughout the country. The National Gardens Scheme is delighted to include it in its list of beneficiaries. Some facts:

- **Help the Hospices** is the only national charity helping all providers of hospice and palliative care for the terminally ill.

- **Help the Hospices'** priority is to support all measures to improve patient care for all life-threatening conditions.

- **Help the Hospices** receives no government funding.

- **Help the Hospices** principally supports the voluntary hospices as they receive relatively little government funding.

- **Help the Hospices** support is mainly in direct response to applications from voluntary hospices, usually for training.

- **Help the Hospices** funds training for the NHS and nursing home staff in patient care for the terminally ill as well as funding its own initiatives in training, research, hospice management and team leadership.

- **Help the Hospices** pays special attention to training in communication skills for staff and volunteers.

Essex

Hon County Organiser:	Mrs Judy Johnson, Saling Hall, Great Saling, Braintree CM7 5DT
	Tel 01371 850243
Assistant Hon County Organisers:	Mrs Jill Cowley, Park Farm, Great Waltham, Chelmsford CM3 1BZ (Publicity)
	Tel 01245 360871
	Mrs Rosie Welchman, The Old Rectory, Little Sampford, CB10 2QT
	01799 586230
Hon County Treasurer:	Eric Brown Esq, 107 Castle Street, Saffron Walden CB10 1BQ

DATES OF OPENING

Regular openings
For details see garden description

Beth Chatto Gardens, Elmstead
 Market
Gardens of Easton Lodge, Great
 Dunmow
Feeringbury Manor, Feering
Glen Chantry, Wickham Bishops
Hyde Hall, Rettendon
Marks Hall Estate, Coggeshall
Marsh Lane, Harlow
Volpaia, Hockley
Wickham Place Farm, Wickham
 Bishops

By appointment only
*For telephone numbers and other
details see garden descriptions.
Private visits welcomed*

Olivers, Colchester
Reed House, Great Chesterford

February 15 Sunday
 Writtle College, Writtle
March 29 Sunday
 Glen Chantry, Wickham Bishops
 The Magnolias, Brentwood
 St Mary's Hall, Great Bentley
April 5 Sunday
 The Magnolias, Brentwood
April 12 Sunday
 Glen Chantry, Wickham Bishops
 Lower Dairy House, Nayland
 Park Farm, Great Waltham
April 13 Monday
 Lower Dairy House, Nayland
 Park Farm, Great Waltham
April 16 Thursday
 Wickham Place Farm, Wickham
 Bishops
April 19 Sunday
 Lower Dairy House, Nayland
 The Magnolias, Brentwood
 Saling Hall Lodge, Great Saling
April 23 Thursday
 Wickham Place Farm, Wickham
 Bishops

 Woodpeckers,
 Burnham-on-Crouch
April 26 Sunday
 Lower Dairy House, Nayland
 The Magnolias, Brentwood
April 30 Thursday
 Wickham Place Farm, Wickham
 Bishops
 Woodpeckers,
 Burnham-on-Crouch
May 3 Sunday
 Glen Chantry, Wickham Bishops
 Lower Dairy House, Nayland
 Park Farm, Great Waltham
 Rose Cottage, Theydon Bois
May 4 Monday
 Glen Chantry, Wickham Bishops
 Lower Dairy House, Nayland
 Park Farm, Great Waltham
 Rose Cottage, Theydon Bois
May 6 Wednesday
 Saling Hall, Great Saling
May 7 Thursday
 Wickham Place Farm, Wickham
 Bishops
 Woodpeckers,
 Burnham-on-Crouch
May 10 Sunday
 Hobbans Farm, Bobbingworth
 Lower Dairy House, Nayland
 The Magnolias, Brentwood
 Rose Cottage, Theydon Bois
 Saling Hall Lodge, Great Saling
May 13 Wednesday
 Saling Hall, Great Saling
May 14 Thursday
 Wickham Place Farm, Wickham
 Bishops
 Woodpeckers,
 Burnham-on-Crouch
May 15 Friday
 Perrymans, Boxted
May 17 Sunday
 Lower Dairy House, Nayland
 The Magnolias, Brentwood
 Rose Cottage, Theydon Bois
 Shore Hall, Cornish Hall End
May 20 Wednesday
 Saling Hall, Great Saling
 Shore Hall, Cornish Hall End

May 21 Thursday
 Wickham Place Farm, Wickham
 Bishops
May 22 Friday
 Perrymans, Boxted
May 23 Saturday
 Edelweiss, Hornchurch
May 24 Sunday
 Edelweiss, Hornchurch
 Glen Chantry, Wickham Bishops
 Hobbans Farm, Bobbingworth
 Lower Dairy House, Nayland
 Park Farm, Great Waltham
 Rose Cottage, Theydon Bois
May 25 Monday
 Glen Chantry, Wickham
 Bishops
 Little Sampford Gardens
 Lower Dairy House, Nayland
 Park Farm, Great Waltham
 Rose Cottage, Theydon Bois
May 27 Wednesday
 Saling Hall, Great Saling
May 28 Thursday
 Wickham Place Farm, Wickham
 Bishops
 Woodpeckers,
 Burnham-on-Crouch
May 29 Friday
 Perrymans, Boxted
May 31 Sunday
 Saling Hall Lodge, Great Saling
June 3 Wednesday
 Marks Hall Estate, Coggeshall
 (eve)
 Saling Hall, Great Saling
June 4 Thursday
 Wickham Place Farm, Wickham
 Bishops
June 5 Friday
 Perrymans, Boxted
June 7 Sunday
 Folly Faunts House, Goldhanger
 Glen Chantry, Wickham
 Bishops
 Lower Dairy House, Nayland
 The Magnolias, Brentwood
 The Old Rectory, Boreham
 Park Farm, Great Waltham
 Rose Cottage, Theydon Bois

June 8 Monday
Park Farm, Great Waltham
June 10 Wednesday
Saling Hall, Great Saling
June 11 Thursday
Wickham Place Farm, Wickham
  Bishops
Woodpeckers, Burnham-on-Crouch
June 12 Friday
Perrymans, Boxted
June 13 Saturday
Stamps & Crows, Layer Breton
  Heath
June 14 Sunday
8 Dene Court, Chelmsford
The Dower House, Castle
  Hedingham
Fanners Farm, Great Waltham
6 Fanners Green, Great Waltham
Hobbans Farm, Bobbingworth
Lower Dairy House, Nayland
Rose Cottage, Theydon Bois
Stamps & Crows, Layer Breton
  Heath
June 15 Monday
Fanners Farm, Great Waltham
6 Fanners Green, Great Waltham
June 17 Wednesday
Saling Hall, Great Saling
Stamps & Crows, Layer Breton
  Heath
June 18 Thursday
Wickham Place Farm, Wickham
  Bishops
June 21 Sunday
Clavering Gardens
Fountain Farm, Ardleigh
Lower Dairy House, Nayland
Rose Cottage, Theydon Bois
Shore Hall, Cornish Hall End
Woolards Ash, Hatfield Broad
  Oak
June 22 Monday
Fountain Farm, Ardleigh
June 24 Wednesday
Saling Hall, Great Saling
June 25 Thursday
Shore Hall, Cornish Hall End
Wickham Place Farm, Wickham
  Bishops
Woodpeckers,
  Burnham-on-Crouch
June 27 Saturday
Edelweiss, Hornchurch
June 28 Sunday
8 Dene Court, Chelmsford
Edelweiss, Hornchurch

Hobbans Farm, Bobbingworth
Littlebury Gardens
The Magnolias, Brentwood
The Old Vicarage, Rickling
St Mary's Hall, Great Bentley
Saling Hall, Great Saling
Saling Hall Lodge, Great Saling
Schluck, Cranham
July 1 Wednesday
Saling Hall, Great Saling
July 2 Thursday
Wickham Place Farm, Wickham
  Bishops
Woodpeckers,
  Burnham-on-Crouch
July 5 Sunday
Barnards, Sible Hedingham
Barnards Farm, West Horndon
Lower Dairy House, Nayland
78 Monkswood Avenue, Waltham
  Abbey
Rose Cottage, Theydon Bois
July 8 Wednesday
Saling Hall, Great Saling
July 9 Thursday
Wickham Place Farm, Wickham
  Bishops
July 12 Sunday
Hobbans Farm, Bobbingworth
Lower Dairy House, Nayland
78 Monkswood Avenue, Waltham
  Abbey
Rose Cottage, Theydon Bois
July 15 Wednesday
Horkesley Hall, Little Horkesley
Saling Hall, Great Saling
July 16 Thursday
Wickham Place Farm, Wickham
  Bishops
July 18 Saturday
Amberden Hall, Widdington
July 19 Sunday
Amberden Hall, Widdington
8 Dene Court, Chelmsford
The Magnolias, Brentwood
Park Farm, Great Waltham
Rose Cottage, Theydon Bois
Wickets, Langley Upper Green
July 20 Monday
Park Farm, Great Waltham
July 22 Wednesday
Saling Hall, Great Saling
July 23 Thursday
Wickham Place Farm, Wickham
  Bishops
July 25 Saturday
Edelweiss, Hornchurch

July 26 Sunday
Edelweiss, Hornchurch
Hobbans Farm, Bobbingworth
Schluck, Cranham
July 29 Wednesday
Saling Hall, Great Saling
July 30 Thursday
Wickham Place Farm, Wickham
  Bishops
August 2 Sunday
Wickets, Langley Upper Green
August 9 Sunday
Hobbans Farm, Bobbingworth
The Magnolias, Brentwood
August 16 Sunday
Rose Cottage, Theydon Bois
August 19 Wednesday
Horkesley Hall, Little Horkesley
August 22 Saturday
Edelweiss, Hornchurch
August 23 Sunday
Edelweiss, Hornchurch
Hobbans Farm, Bobbingworth
August 30 Sunday
The Magnolias, Brentwood
Rose Cottage, Theydon Bois
August 31 Monday
Rose Cottage, Theydon Bois
September 3 Thursday
Wickham Place Farm, Wickham
  Bishops
September 6 Sunday
Barnards Farm, West Horndon
Deers, Clavering
Glen Chantry, Wickham
  Bishops
Hobbans Farm, Bobbingworth
September 10 Thursday
Wickham Place Farm, Wickham
  Bishops
September 13 Sunday
Rose Cottage, Theydon Bois
September 17 Thursday
Wickham Place Farm, Wickham
  Bishops
September 20 Sunday
Glen Chantry, Wickham Bishops
Hobbans Farm, Bobbingworth
The Magnolias, Brentwood
September 24 Thursday
Wickham Place Farm, Wickham
  Bishops
October 18 Sunday
Writtle College, Writtle
October 25 Sunday
The Magnolias, Brentwood

Regular openings. Open throughout the year. They are listed at the beginning of the Diary Section.

By Appointment Gardens. These owners do not have a fixed opening day usually because they cannot accommodate large numbers or have insufficient parking space.

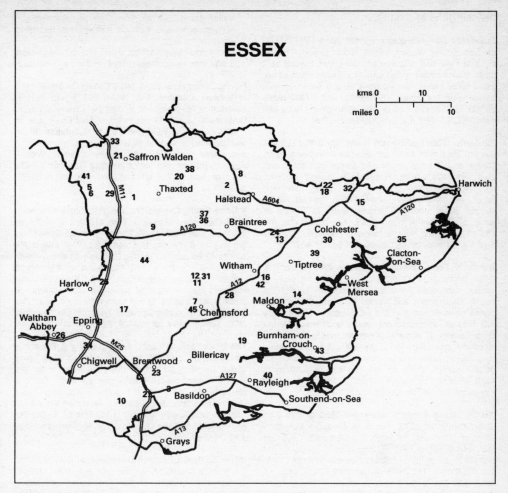

ESSEX

KEY

1. Amberden Hall
2. Barnards, Sible Hedingham
3. Barnards Farm, West Horndon
4. Beth Chatto Gardens
5. Clavering Gardens
6. Deers
7. 8 Dene Court
8. The Dower House
9. Gardens of Easton Lodge
10. Edelweiss
11. Fanners Farm
12. 6 Fanners Green
13. Feeringbury Manor
14. Folly Faunts House
15. Fountain Farm
16. Glen Chantry
17. Hobbans Farm

18. Horkesley Hall
19. Hyde Hall
20. Little Sampford
21. Littlebury Gardens
22. Lower Dairy House
23. The Magnolias
24. Marks Hall Estate
25. Marsh Lane
26. 78 Monkswood Avenue
27. 171A Moor Lane
28. The Old Rectory
29. The Old Vicarage
30. Olivers
31. Park Farm
32. Perrymans
33. Reed House
34. Rose Cottage
35. St Mary's Hall
36. Saling Hall

37. Saling Hall Lodge
38. Shore Hall
39. Stamps & Crows
40. Volpaia
41. Wickets
42. Wickham Place Farm
43. Woodpeckers
44. Woolards Ash
45. Writtle College

The maps in this book are designed to help visitors by showing the approximate locations of gardens within each county. The locations are not necessarily precise, particularly where gardens are in clusters. Detailed directions to each garden can be found in the garden descriptions.

DESCRIPTIONS OF GARDENS

Amberden Hall, Widdington ઠ&❀ (Mr & Mrs D Lloyd) 6m from Saffron Walden. E off B1383 nr Newport. Follow signs to Mole Hall Wildlife Park. Drive ½m beyond park on R. Medium-sized walled garden with collection of unusual hardy plants, shrubs, ivy allée and secret garden. Raised vegetable garden. TEAS on Sun. *Adm £2 Chd 50p (ACNO to St Mary's Church and Widdington Village Hall Rebuilding Fund®). Sat, Sun July 18, 19 (2-6)*

Barnards, Sible Hedingham ઠ&❀ (Mr & Mrs Leonard Ratcliff) 1½m from A604, on Hedingham-Wethersfield rd. Garden on L. Formal plantsman's garden of 3 acres, created since 1994 with an Elizabethan 'Forthright'. Parterre. Mediterranean/Edible garden. Lime walk. Evergreen 'Mondrian' garden. Farm pond. Rough area of old-fashioned shrub roses and grasses. Walks to 5 acres of newly planted native trees. TEAS. *Adm £2.50 Chd free (ACNO to Halstead Hospital League of Friends®). Sun July 5 (2-5.30). Parties by appt, please* **Tel 01787 462293**

Barnards Farm, West Horndon ઠ&❀ (Bernard & Sylvia Holmes) On A128, 2km S of A127. An evolving garden from open fields around Georgian house (not open), Essex pylons and framed by barns. Partially designed to be viewed from the air. Aviators welcome. Life size bronzes, sculptured pots and a brick maze. Herbaceous borders, 17 hectares of grounds, ponds, developing woodland, arboretum, malus collection, Japanese garden, long avenue, water course, parterre, and ornamental vegetable garden. Open air religious service 5.30 to 6. TEAS. *Adm £2 Chd free (ACNO to St Francis Church West Horndon®). Suns July 5, Sept 6 (2-5.30)*

●**Beth Chatto Gardens, Elmstead Market** &❀ (Mrs Beth Chatto) On A133, ¼m E of Elmstead Market. 5 acres of attractively landscaped garden with many unusual plants, shown in wide range of conditions from hot and dry to water garden. Books available by Beth Chatto The Dry Garden, The Damp Garden, Beth Chatto's Garden Notebook, The Green Tapestry. Adjacent nursery open. *Adm £2.50 Chd free. March 1 to Oct 31, every Mon to Sat but closed Bank Hols (9- 5); Nov 1 to end of Feb every Mon to Fri but closed Bank Hols (9-4). Parties by appt*

Clavering Gardens, Clavering ઠ❀ On B1038 7m N of Bishops Stortford. Turn W off B1383 (old A11) at Newport. TEAS in Cricket Pavilion on village green in aid of Clavering Cricket Club. *Adm £3 Chd free. Sun June 21 (1.30-6)*

¶**April Cottage** (Mr & Mrs N C Harris) Small cottage garden with old-fashioned perennials and roses, raised alpine bed

Brooklands (Mr & Mrs John Noble) Walled garden, herbaceous and shrub borders, rustic rose trellis, arboretum. Extended garden planting in old orchard; 1½ acres

Clavering Court (Mr & Mrs S R Elvidge) Approx 1½ acres, fine trees, shrubs and borders. Walled garden, Edwardian greenhouse

Deers (Mr & Mrs S Cooke) Parking in yard next to house. For details see separate entry

Piercewebbs (Mr & Mrs B R William-Powlett) Old

walled garden, shrubs, lawns, ha ha, yew and stilt hedges, pond and trellised rose garden. Extensive views

Shovellers (Miss J & Miss E Ludgate) Stickling Green. 3-acre extended cottage garden, orchard and meadow

Deers, Clavering ઠ (Mr & Mrs S Cooke) On B1038 7m N of Bishop's Stortford. Turn W off B1383 (old A11) at Newport; nr Fox & Hounds, in centre of Clavering, turn to Langley and take 2nd L (on bend), to Ford End, house on R ¾m along lane. Parking in yard next to house. Shrub and herbaceous borders; ponds; old roses in formal garden; walled vegetable garden; flower meadow; trees. 4 acres. *Combined adm with* **Clavering Gardens** *£3 Chd free. Sun June 21 (1-5.30). Also open alone Sun Sept 6 (2-5). Adm £2.50 Chd free*

8 Dene Court, Chelmsford &❀ (Mrs Sheila Chapman) W of Chelmsford (Parkway). Take A1060 Roxwell Rd for 1m. Turn R at traffic lights into Chignall Rd, Dene Court 3rd exit on R. Parking in Chignall Rd. Well maintained and designed compact garden (250 sq yds) circular lawn surrounded by many unusual plants incl wide variety of clematis. Ferns and grasses; ornamental well; 3 pergolas; rose and clematis covered perimeter wall. Featured in Essex Homes and Living and Garden News. *Adm £1 Chd 50p (ACNO to Audrey Appleton Trust for the Terminally Ill®). Suns June 14, 28, July 19 (2-5.30)*

The Dower House, Castle Hedingham &❀ (Mr & Mrs John Allfrey) on B1058. 5m from Halstead A1017 (was A604). 1m NE of Sible Hedingham. Follow signs to Hedingham Castle. Garden 50yds from entrance. Terraced plantsman's garden of 1½ acres overlooking Tudor church and village. Mixed borders developed since 1987 with flower arranging in mind. TEAS. *Adm £1.50 Chd free (ACNO to St Nicholas Church, Castle Hedingham®). Sun June 14 (2-6)*

●**The Gardens of Easton Lodge, Great Dunmow** ઠ❀ (Mr & Mrs B Creasey) Brown heritage signs from A120, W of Dunmow. 1½m N of Dunmow. Home of 'Darling Daisy', Countess of Warwick, who in 1903 commissioned Harold Peto to lay out Italian and Japanese Gardens. Abandoned 1950; major restoration since 1993 incl brick and cobble courtyard, ponds, C18th dovecote, conservatory and pavilion. Work started on sunken Italian Garden. History Exhibition. Cream TEAS. *Adm £3 OAPs £2.70 Chd under 12 free (ACNO to Five Parishes®). Sats, Suns, Bank Hols April 10 to Oct 31 (11-6). Private visits welcome, please* **Tel 01371 876979**

Edelweiss, Hornchurch (Joan H Hogg, Pat F Lowery) 20 Hartland Rd. From Romford E along the A124 past Tesco on L, turn R into Albany Rd opp church on corner of Park Lane on the L. Go to the bottom of Albany Rd, humps all the way, turn L at the end into Hartland Rd. Small town garden 200' × 25'. Laid out to maximise small narrow plot and featuring many containers, baskets, seasonal bedding and mixed borders. Home-made produce. Narrow access and steps not suitable for pushchairs. Cream TEAS. *Adm £1 Chd free. Sats, Suns May 23, 24, June 27, 28, July 25, 26, Aug 22, 23 (3-6). Private visits welcome, June-Aug please* **Tel 01708 454610**

Fanners Farm, Great Waltham &% (Mr & Mrs P G Lee) 4m N of Chelmsford. In Great Waltham turn into South Street by pine shop opp inn/restaurant. Garden 1¼m on R. Informal garden of approx 2 acres surrounding C14 house (not open). Secret rose garden, 2 ponds, conservatory and 'potager'. Small collection of vintage and classic cars. TEAS. *Adm £1 Chd free. Sun, Mon June 14, 15 (2-6)*

6 Fanners Green, Great Waltham &%❀ (Dr & Mrs T M Pickard) 4m N of Chelmsford. In Great Waltham turn into South Street by pine shop opp inn/restaurant. Garden 1¼m on R. A 15-yr-old small country garden of ⅓ acre divided into different formal areas with informal planting. Herb garden and conservatory. *Adm £1 Chd free. Sun, Mon June 14, 15 (2-6)*

Feeringbury Manor, Feering & (Mr & Mrs G Coode-Adams) Coggeshall Rd, between Coggeshall and Feering. 7-acre garden bordering R Blackwater. Many unusual plants incl wide variety of honeysuckles, clematis, old-fashioned roses; rare bog-loving plants, border, ponds and stream; small Victorian water wheel. Featured in The Passionate Gardener. *Adm £2 Chd free (ACNO to Colchester and District Visual Arts Trust®). Weekdays April 6 to July 31 (8-1) closed weekends and Bank Hols. Private visits welcome, please* **Tel 01376 561946**

Folly Faunts House, Goldhanger &❀ (Mr & Mrs J C Jenkinson) On B1026 between Colchester and Maldon. 5-acre garden around an C18 manor house (not open) created since 1963. Garden is divided into 7 different compartments each with a wide variety of unusual plants, shrubs and trees. Formal and informal water gardens. 20 acres of park and woodland, planted in 1988, is divided into 3 double avenues. Large car park. TEAS. *Adm £2 Chd £1. Sun June 7 (2-5). Parties of 12 or more by appt, please* **Tel 01621 788213**

¶**Fountain Farm, Ardleigh** &% (Mr & Mrs C P Tootal) [OS Ref 040295], 4m NE of Colchester. Follow signs towards Ardleigh from Crown roundabout (at A12/A120 junction) to Wick Lane. House is 1m on L, 1m W of Ardleigh Xrds. Please park on rd by reservoir. 5 acres on bank of Ardleigh Reservoir. 3 areas of formal garden, herb garden, vegetables, mature trees and 5-yr old wildflower meadow, copse and native hedging established under Countryside Commission Scheme. TEAS. *Adm £1.50 Chd 50p. Sun, Mon June 21, 22 (2-6)*

■ **Glen Chantry, Wickham Bishops** &%❀ (Mr & Mrs W G Staines) 1½m SE of Witham. Take Maldon Rd from Witham and 1st L to Wickham Bishops. Cross narrow bridge over R Blackwater. Turn immed L up track by side of Blue Mills. 3-acre garden, emphasis on mixed borders, unusual perennials and shrub roses. Limestone rock gardens, ponds, formal specialist white garden, foliage beds with grasses and hostas; plant nursery. TEAS in aid of local charities. *Adm £1.50 Chd 50p. Fris, Sats April 4-Oct 16 (10-4) DIY TEAS). For NGS Suns Mar 29, April 12; May 3, 24; June 7; Sept 6, 20; Mons May 4, 25 (2-5). Also parties by appt, please* **Tel 01621 891342**

Hobbans Farm, Bobbingworth %❀ (Mrs Ann Webster) Ongar. N of A414 between Ongar 'Four Wantz' roundabout and N Weald 'Talbot' roundabout just past Blake Hall Gardens. 1st farm entrance on R after St Germain's Church. Mature, romantic informal garden, set in 1½ acres divided into several parts surrounding C15 farmhouse. Unusual plants; clematis, old roses, small herb and sink gardens. Set in pastures with fine views. TEAS in aid of Local Charities. *Adm £1.50 Chd free. Suns May 10, 24, June 14, 28, July 12, 26, Aug 9, 23, Sept 6, 20 (2-6)*

Horkesley Hall, Little Horkesley & (Mr & Mrs Richard Eddis) Colchester. Little Horkesley is W of A134, 3m N of Colchester. House marked on map just beyond church. A young garden of approx 5 acres within the setting of a classical house, 2 old fishponds and some fine old trees around the perimeter. Its creation began in 1990/91 and the emphasis is on shrubs and trees chosen for colour and effect, incl some which are unusual and rare. *Adm £2 Chd £1 (ACNO to Co-workers of Mother Theresa®). Weds July 15, Aug 19 (2-5); also by appt, please* **Tel 01206 272067**

●**Hyde Hall Garden, Rettendon** &%❀ (Royal Horticultural Society) 7m SE of Chelmsford; 6m NE of Wickford. Signed from A130. 20-acre garden with flowering trees, shrubs, perennials, and spring bulbs. Large temperate glass house and small, alpine house. Collection of modern and shrub roses. Nat. Collection malus and viburnum. Large formal pond; enlarged lower pond and new bridge. Thatched Barn Restaurant, (licensed). *Adm £3 Chd 70p 6-16 Chd under 6 free. Parties 10+ £2.50. Open every day between March 25 and October 31. March to Aug (11-6), Sept, Oct (11-5)*

¶**Little Sampford, nr Saffron Walden** %❀ B1053 9m E of Saffron Walden, 4m W/NW of Finchingfield. TEAS in aid of Sampford's Churches. (Flower Festival at Gt Sampford Church). *Combined adm £2 Chd free. Mon May 25 (2-6)*
> ¶**The Grange** (Mr & Mrs C P Robinson) A mature garden renovated 6 years ago which surrounds an C18 house (not open). Herbaceous and mixed borders, rose beds, new shrub planting and small courtyard garden. Woods and charming view over River Pant
> ¶**The Old Rectory** (Mr & Mrs H Welchman) 2½-acres of formal gardens, with 5 acre ancient wild flower meadow. Many mature trees typical of Rectory gardens, large mixed borders, two ponds, roses, recently planted shrubs and trees, all aimed to produce a long season of interesting colour

Littlebury Gardens %❀ 2m from Saffron Walden, opp Littlebury church on B1383 1m N of Audley End House, entrance in Littlebury Green Rd. TEAS. *Combined adm £1.50 Chd free. Sun June 28 (2-5.30)*
> **Granta House** & (Mr & Mrs R A Lloyd) Old walled garden of 2 acres; unusual shrubs, herbaceous plants and roses, plants in dry areas; courtyard
> **North House** (Dr & Mrs B G Sanders) opp Granta House. Mixed borders, herb garden, roses, ornamental vegetable garden created by artists over 10 yrs

Lower Dairy House, Nayland &⚘❀ (Mr & Mrs D J Burnett) 7m N of Colchester off A134. Turn L at bottom of hill before Nayland village into Water Lane, signed to Little Horkesley. Garden ½m on L past farm buildings. Plantsman's garden approx 1½ acres. Natural stream with waterside plantings; rockery and raised beds; lawns; herbaceous borders; roses. Many varieties of shrubs and ground cover plants. Spring bulbs and blossom. Tudor House (not open). Teas in village. *Adm £1.50 Chd 50p. Suns, Bank Hol Mons April 12, 13, 19, 26; May 3, 4, 10, 17, 24, 25; June 7, 14, 21; July 5, 12 (2-6). Also private visits welcome, please* **Tel 01206 262220**

The Magnolias, Brentwood ⚘❀ (Mr & Mrs R A Hammond) 18 St John's Ave. From A1023 turn S on A128; after 300yds R at traffic lights; over railway bridge; St John's Ave 3rd on R. ½-acre informal garden with particular appeal to plantsmen; good collection spring bulbs; ground-cover; trees and shrubs incl maples, rhododendrons, camellias, magnolias and pieris. Koi ponds and other water interests. Featured on Garden Club. *Adm £1.50 Chd 50p. Suns March 29; April 5, 19, 26; May 10, 17; June 7, 28; July 19; Aug 9, 30; Sept 20; Oct 25 (10-5). Parties by appt March to Oct incl, please* **Tel 01277 220019**

■¶**Marks Hall, Coggeshall** &❀ (Thomas Phillips Price Trust) Off the A120 (follow signs), N of picturesque village of Coggeshall, 8m W of Colchester. A fledgling Arboretum of 100 acres with ornamental lakes, walled garden, cascades and mature avenues of oaks, limes and horse chestnuts. The collection of shrubs and trees is being established on a geographical theme, which incl areas such as Japan and Gondwanaland. Large areas of ancient woodland provide peace and tranquility. Disabled buggy. TEAS. *Adm £3 per car. April 4 to Oct 31, Tues to Fri (10.30-4.30), Sats, Suns, Bank Hol Mons (10.30-6). For NGS Wed June 3 (6-9)*

●**Marsh Lane, Harlow** & (The Gibberd Garden Trust) Marsh Lane is a narrow turning off B183 Rd (to Hatfield Heath), approx 1m E of the junction with A414. Look for 'Garden Open' sign on L. 7-acre C20 garden designed by Sir Frederick Gibberd, on side of small valley. Terraces, wild garden, landscaped vistas, pools and streams, 'Roman Temple', moated log 'castle', gazebo, tree house and large collection of modern sculpture. TEAS. *Adm £3 Concessions £2 Chd free. Suns Easter Sun to end of Sept (2-6). Weekday parties by appt, please* **Tel 01279 442112**

¶**78 Monkswood Avenue, Waltham Abbey** ❀ (Julie Farrey) Junction 26 M25. Monkswood Ave is at the traffic lights in Waltham Abbey town centre. Garden 75′ × 60′. Cottage style with unusual perennials, wild flowers and shrubs. Informal in design with a wild life pond and water feature. Small gravel area containing sun-loving plants. TEAS. *Adm £1 Chd free. Suns July 5, 12 (12-6)*

The Old Rectory, Boreham &⚘❀ (Sir Jeffery & Lady Bowman) 4m NE of Chelmsford. Take 1137 to Boreham Village, turn into Church Rd at Red Lion Public House. ½m along on R opp church. 2½-acre garden with ponds, stream, interesting trees and shrubs, herbaceous borders and kitchen garden. TEAS. *Adm £1.50 Chd free. Sun June 7 (2-6)*

The Old Vicarage, Rickling &⚘ (Mr & Mrs James Jowitt) 7m S from Saffron Walden: from Newport take B1038 W, after 2m, turn L to Rickling. The Old Vicarage is on the L after 1m. 2-acre garden divided by mature yew hedges, interesting 'hot' borders, herbaceous and mixed borders; rose garden, shrubbery, new herb garden. TEAS in aid of Rickling Church. *Adm £2 Chd 50p. Sun June 28 (2-6)*

Olivers, Colchester &⚘❀ (Mr & Mrs D Edwards) 3m SW of Colchester, between B1022 & B1026. Follow signs to zoo and continue 1m towards Colchester. Turn R at roundabout (Cunobelin Way) and R into Olivers Lane. From Colchester via Maldon Rd turn L at roundabout, R into Olivers Lane. C18 house (not open) overlooks Roman R valley, surrounded by terrace and yew-backed borders; closely planted with unusual plants. Lawns; 3 lakes; meadow; woodland with fine trees underplanted with shrubs incl rhododendrons and old roses; spring bulbs and bluebells. *Adm £2 Chd free. Parties and private visits by appt, please* **Tel 01206 330575**

Park Farm, Great Waltham ⚘❀ (Mrs J E M Cowley & Mr D Bracey) Take B1008 N from Chelmsford through Broomfield Village. On Little Waltham bypass turn L into Chatham Hall Lane signed Howe Street; Park Farm ½m on L. 2 acres of garden in separate 'rooms' formed by yew hedges with climber-obscured old farmhouse and dairy in centre. Many different species of bulbs; shrubs; roses and herbaceous perennials; designing still proceeding with new projects underway. TEAS. *Adm £1.25 Chd 50p. Suns April 12, May 3, 24, June 7, July 19; Mons April 13, May 4, 25, June 8, July 20 (2-6). Parties by appt, please* **Tel 01245 360871**

Perrymans, Boxted &⚘❀ (Mr & Mrs H R J Human) 4m NE from Colchester Station to Boxted Cross. Follow Dedham Rd, drive entrance on R 200yds past village shop. 7-acre undulating garden created from scratch since 1970, lakes, rose garden, borders, spring bulbs and selection of old and new trees; small vegetable garden. Refreshments in aid of the Museum of Garden History. *Adm £2 Chd 50p. Fris May 15, 22, 29, June 5, 12 (10.30-4). Private visits welcome, any number, please* **Tel 01206 272297**

Reed House, Great Chesterford &⚘ (Mrs W H Mason) 4m N of Saffron Walden and 1m S of Stump Cross, M 11. On B184 turn into Great Chesterford High St. Then L at Crown & Thistle public house into Manor Lane. ¾-acre garden developed in the last 12 years with collection of unusual plants. Featured in Essex Homes and Living. *Adm £1.50. Open by appt, please* **Tel 01799 530312**

Rose Cottage, Theydon Bois ⚘❀ (Anne & Jack Barnard) 42 Blackacre Rd. 2m S of Epping on B172. At pedestrian crossing turn into Poplar Row (opp Bull inn).

Evening Opening (see also garden descriptions)

Marks Hall, Coggeshall   June 3   6–9 pm

Pass village pond, turn 2nd R. Garden at top of hill on R. Small romantic garden 35' × 130', on a sloping site on verges of Epping Forest. Designed in compartments incl woodland, sundial, cottage and fountain gardens. Luxuriant planting; small collection of old-fashioned and new English roses; cottage garden; unusual plants, herbs and bulbs. TEAS. *Adm £1 Chd free. Suns May 3, 10, 17, 24; June 7, 14, 21; July 5, 12, 19; Aug 16, 30; Sept 13; Mons May 4, 25, Aug 31 (2-6).* **Tel 01992 814619**

¶**St Mary's Hall, Great Bentley** ⚘❀ (Mrs Mary Fox) Take A133 to Clacton. Turn R after Little Chef to Gt Bentley (Shair Lane). ½m bear L over railway bridge. After 250yds bear R, gardens are ½m on R. 1m from village centre, 10m from Colchester and Clacton. 10 acres surrounding Georgian House (not open), several 'rooms' and courtyards with walled gardens. Parkland display of daffodils and several box-hedged formal parterres. Many roses incl Princess of Wales. Home-grown seasonal bedding plants, mixed herbaceous borders, walkways, terraces, gazebo, orchard, vegetable garden and stocked ponds. TEAS. *Adm £2 Chd free. Suns March 29, June 28 (2-6)*

Saling Hall, Great Saling ♿⚘ (Mr & Mrs H Johnson) 6m NW of Braintree. Turn N off A120 between Braintree and Dunmow at the Saling Oak. 12 acres; walled garden dated 1698; small park with fine trees; extensive new collection of unusual plants with emphasis on trees; water gardens. Hugh Johnson is 'Tradescant' of the RHS. TEAS Sun only. *Adm £2 Chd free (ACNO to St James's Church, Great Saling®). Weds in May, June, July (2-5). Sun June 28 with* **Saling Hall Lodge** *Combined adm £2.50 (2-6). Parties by appt on weekdays. Written application, please*

Saling Hall Lodge, Great Saling ♿⚘❀ (Mr & Mrs K Akers) 6m NW of Braintree. Turn N off A120 between Braintree and Dunmow at the Saling Oak. Drive at end of village on L, please park in village. Well-designed and maintained ½-acre garden with pond, limestone rock garden, small peat garden, tufa bed and sinks. As seen on Channel 4 and Anglia TV. TEAS. *Adm £1 Chd free. Suns April 19, May 10, 31 (2-5). Combined adm with* **Saling Hall** *£2.50 Sun June 28 (2-6)*

¶**Schluck, Cranham** ⚘❀ (Mr & Mrs W Taylor) 171A Moor Lane. Leave M25 junction 29. Join A127 E to Romford. From A127 take slip rd to Upminster, turning L into Hall Lane. At mini roundabout turn L into Avon Rd. Bottom of Avon Rd (past shops) turn R (Front Lane) 4th turning L into Moor Lane. Or 346 bus from Upminster station. ½-acre informal plantsman's garden, created since 1986 and designed as separate areas. Large selection of shrubs, trees and perennials, small alpine collection, vegetable area, 3 large ponds (1 Koi, 2 wildlife), many interesting features. TEAS. *Adm £1 Chd 50p. Suns June 28, July 26 (12-6). Private visits welcome, please* **Tel 01708 221085**

Shore Hall, Cornish Hall End ⚘❀ (Mr & Mrs Peter Swete) nr Braintree. 2½m NE of Finchingfield. ½m W of Cornish Hall End on Gt Sampford Rd. Long drive with poplars. 3½-acre garden surrounding C17 house (not open) with several enclosed formal areas and interesting

shrubs. 100-yr-old box hedges enclose formal beds planted with herbaceous and old roses; rose garden surrounding lily ponds; newly planted ornamental vegetable and fruit garden and many young rare trees. TEAS in aid of local charity Suns only. *Adm £2 Chd free. Suns May 17, June 21, Wed May 20, Thurs June 25 (2-6). Parties by appt weekdays, May to July, please* **Tel 01799 586411**

Stamps and Crows, Layer Breton Heath ♿❀ (Mr & Mrs E G Billington) 5½m S of Colchester on B1022 take L fork signed Birch and Layer Breton. On R side of Layer Breton Heath. 2½ acres of moated garden surrounding C15 farmhouse (not open). Herbaceous borders, mixed shrubs, old roses and good ground cover. Recently created bog garden and dovecote. TEAS (Sun only). *Adm £1.50 Chd free (ACNO to St. Mary's Church, Layer Breton®). Sat, Sun, Wed June 13, 14, 17 (2-6). Parties by appt, please* **Tel 01206 330220**

●**Volpaia, Hockley** ⚘❀ (Mr & Mrs D Fox) 54 Woodlands Rd. 2¾m NE of Rayleigh. B1013 Rayleigh-Rochford, turn S from Spa Hotel into Woodlands Rd. On E side of Hockley Woods. 1 acre containing many exotic trees, rhododendrons, camellias and other shrubs. Carpets of wood anemones and bluebells in spring, underplanting is very diverse, especially with woodland, liliaceous plants and ferns. TEA. *Adm £1 Chd 30p (ACNO to Essex Group of NCCPG®). All Thurs & Suns from April 12 to June 21 (2.30-6). Also private visits welcome, please* **Tel 01702 203761**

Wickets, Langley Upper Green ♿⚘ (Mr & Mrs D Copeland) 11m N of Bishops Stortford. Turn W off B1383 (old A11) at Newport. After 5m turn R off B1038 at Clavering, signed Langley. Upper Green is 3m further on. Last house on R of cricket green. Cottage garden and paddock with long views. 1½ acres. Newly planted in 1990. Island beds, herbaceous borders, rose borders, hanging baskets, ponds. Highest village in Essex, windy site. TEAS. *Adm £1 Chd free. Suns July 19, Aug 2 (2-5.30)*

¶**Wickham Place Farm, Wickham Bishops** ♿⚘❀ (Mr & Mrs K Kittle) 2½m SE of Witham nr R Blackwater on B1018. Take B1018 from Witham towards Maldon. After going under A12 take 2nd L (Station Road) to Wickham Bishops. 1st house on L. 2-acre walled garden with further 12 acres of woodland. Huge climbers, roses and wisterias cascade down into wide borders filled with shrubs, perennials and bulbs. Planted for yr round colour on light dry soil. Knot garden and natural pond. Mixed woodland with rabbit resistant shrubs and bulbs alongside wide paths. TEA. *Adm £1.50 Chd 50p (ACNO to Farleigh Hospice®). Thurs April 16 to July 30 and Sept 3 to 24 (10-4)*

Woodpeckers, Burnham-on-Crouch ♿⚘❀ (Mr & Mrs N J Holdaway & Mrs L M Burton) Mangapp Chase. B1010 to Burnham-on-Crouch. Just beyond town sign turn L into Green Lane. Turn L after ½m. Garden 200yds on R. 1½ acres. Planted with old 'cottage' favourites as well as newer varieties of roses, shrubs and herbaceous perennials. 'Potager', rose walk, new pond all set amongst mature trees. TEAS. *Adm £1 Chd 50p. Thurs April 23, 30; May 7, 14, 28; June 11, 25; July 2 (12-6). Parties welcome by appt, please* **Tel 01621 782137**

¶**Woolards Ash, Hatfield Broad Oak** ✗ (Mr & Mrs M Le Q Herbert) 6½m SE of Bishops Stortford. From Hatfield Broad Oak follow B183 N (towards Takeley). After ¾m take 1st R (signed to Taverners Green and Broomshawbury), then 2nd R to Woolards Ash. 2½ acres of subtly-planted borders divided by beech and yew hedges. Mature trees, shrubs and old roses set in pastoral landscape. TEAS. *Adm £2 Chd 50p. Sun June 21 (2-6)*

▲**Writtle College, Writtle** &❀ Lordship Rd. On A414 W of Chelmsford, nr Writtle village, clearly signed. Approx 15 acres; informal lawns, tree collection, good autumn tints, mixed borders, alpines, formal 'Victorian' garden, aromatic garden. Small gardens designed and built by students undergoing training, bedding trial area, heather garden, ornamental and landscaped glasshouses. Extensive range of bulbs and winter flowering shrubs. TEA. *Adm £2 Chd free. For NGS Suns Feb 15, Oct 18 (10-4)*

Flintshire & Wrexham, Glamorgan

See separate Welsh section on pages 380 and 383

The *National Gardens Scheme* is pleased to invite you to a special Evening Opening at

The Royal Botanic Gardens, Kew
during Chelsea Week
Thursday, May 21st 6.30–9pm

Enjoy the glorious late spring at Kew at an exclusive Evening Opening. Two of the major glasshouses will be open, with staff available to explain their collections and Kew's work.

Admission: £4 Adults, £2 Children, in aid of the National Gardens Scheme (as this is a fund-raising event, admission fee also applies to Season Ticket holders and Friends of the Royal Botanic Gardens, Kew) Refreshments available

Kew is easily reached via the Kew Gardens station (London Underground District Line, and by rail from North London on Silverlink). Also from Kew Bridge station (South West Trains). By road the Gardens are located just south of Kew Bridge on the A307, Kew Road.

Entry by Victoria Gate Only, on the Kew Road, opposite Lichfield Road.

Gloucestershire (North & Central)

Hon County Organiser:	Mrs Stella Martin, Dundry Lodge, France Lynch, Stroud GL6 8LP
	Tel 01453 883419
Assistant Hon County Organisers:	Mrs Barbara Adams, Warners Court, Charfield, Wotton under Edge GL12 8TG
	Mrs Jennie Davies, Applegarth, Alstone, nr Tewkesbury GL20 8JD
	Mrs Lisa Fellows, The Holme House, Jubilee Road, Mitcheldean GL17 0EE
	Mr Tony Marlow, Greenedge, 32 Dr Browns Road, Minchinhampton GL6 9BT
	Miss Anne Palmer, 10, Vineyard Street, Winchcombe GL54 5LP
	Mrs Catherine Watson, Colnpen House, Winson, Cirencester GL7 5EN
Hon County Treasurer:	Mr Graham Baber, 11 Corinium Gate, Cirencester GL7 2PX

DATES OF OPENING

Regular openings
For details see garden description

Barnsley House
Batsford Arboretum, nr
   Moreton-in-Marsh
Bourton House Garden,
   Bourton-on-the-Hill
Cerney House, North Cerney
Cinderdine Cottage, Dymock, nr
   Newent
Cowley Manor, nr Cheltenham
Ewen Manor, nr Cirencester
Green Cottage, Lydney
Hunts Court, North Nibley, nr Dursley
Kiftsgate Court, nr Chipping
   Campdent
Lydney Park Spring Gardens, Lydney
Mill Dene, Blockley
Misarden Park, Miserden, nr
   Cirencester
The Old Chapel, nr Stroud
The Old Manor, Twyning,
   Tewkesbury
Painswick Rococo Garden, Painswick
Rodmarton Manor, nr Cirencester
Sezincote, nr Moreton-in-Marsh
Snowshill Manor, nr Broadway
Stanway House, nr Winchcombe
Sudeley Castle Gardens, Winchcombe
Tinpenny Farm Fiddington
Trevi Garden, Hartpury, nr
   Gloucester

By appointment only
*For telephone numbers and other
details see garden descriptions.
Private visits welcomed*

Amai Yume Teien, Blockley
Camp Cottage, Highleadon, nr
   Newent
Cotswold Farm, Cirencester
Orchard Cottage, Gretton, nr
   Winchcombe
Spring Tyning, Coaley

February 1 Sunday
Home Farm, Huntley, nr Newent
February 5 Thursday
Cinderdine Cottage, Dymock, nr
   Newent
February 10 Tuesday
Cinderdine Cottage, Dymock, nr
   Newent
February 12 Thursday
Cinderdine Cottage, Dymock, nr
   Newent
February 15 Sunday
Cinderdine Cottage, Dymock, nr
   Newent
Minchinhampton Gardens
February 17 Tuesday
Cinderdine Cottage, Dymock, nr
   Newent
February 19 Thursday
Cinderdine Cottage, Dymock, nr
   Newent
February 22 Sunday
Cinderdine Cottage, Dymock, nr
   Newent
February 23 Monday
The Old Rectory, Duntisbourne
   Rous, nr Cirencester
March 1 Sunday
Cinderdine Cottage, Dymock, nr
   Newent
Green Cottage, Lydney
Home Farm, Huntley, nr Newent
March 3 Tuesday
Cinderdine Cottage, Dymock, nr
   Newent
March 8 Sunday
Green Cottage, Lydney
March 15 Sunday
Green Cottage, Lydney
March 22 Sunday
Green Cottage, Lydney
Cinderdine Cottage, Dymock, nr
   Newent
March 24 Tuesday
Cinderdine Cottage, Dymock, nr
   Newent
March 29 Sunday
Brockweir Gardens, Chepstow

Green Cottage, Lydney
Westonbirt Gardens at
   Westonbirt School
April 5 Sunday
Cinderdine Cottage, Dymock, nr
   Newent
Home Farm, Huntley, nr Newent
Misarden Park, Miserden, nr
   Cirencester
Stanway House, nr Winchcombe
Trevi Garden, Hartpury, nr
   Gloucester
April 6 Monday
The Old Rectory, Duntisbourne
   Rous, nr Cirencester
April 7 Tuesday
Cinderdine Cottage, Dymock, nr
   Newent
April 11 Saturday
Ashley Manor, nr Tetbury
April 12 Sunday
Beverston Gardens, nr Tetbury
Cinderdine Cottage, Dymock, nr
   Newent
The Glebe House, Shipton Moyne
Hodges Barn, nr Tetbury
Trench Hill, Sheepscombe
Trevi Garden, Hartpury, nr
   Gloucester
April 13 Monday
Ashley Manor, nr Tetbury
Beverston Gardens, nr Tetbury
Cinderdine Cottage, Dymock, nr
   Newent
Trench Hill, Sheepscombe
Trevi Garden, Hartpury, nr
   Gloucester
April 19 Sunday
Cinderdine Cottage, Dymock, nr
   Newent
Clover House, Winson, nr
   Cirencester
Minchinhampton Gardens
Upton Wold, nr
   Moreton-in-Marsh
April 21 Tuesday
Cinderdine Cottage, Dymock, nr
   Newent

April 26 Sunday
Abbotswood, Stow-on-the-Wold
Blockley Gardens
Brockweir Gardens, Chepstow
Lydney Park Spring Gardens,
   Lydney
Pigeon House, Southam, nr
   Cheltenham
Southrop Manor, nr Lechlade
Sudeley Castle Gardens,
   Winchcombe
Trevi Garden, Hartpury, nr
   Gloucester
May 2 Saturday
Barnsley House, nr Cirencester
May 3 Sunday
Ampney Knowle, Barnsley, nr
   Cirencester
Brook Farm, Newent
Cinderdine Cottage, Dymock, nr
   Newent
Eastcombe, Bussage and
   Brownshill Gardens
Ewen Manor, nr Cirencester
Green Cottage, Lydney
Hidcote Manor Garden, Chipping
   Campden
Mill Dene, Blockley
Millend House, nr Newland,
   Coleford
Trevi Garden, Hartpury, nr
   Gloucester
May 4 Monday
Cinderdine Cottage, Dymock, nr
   Newent
Eastcombe, Bussage & Brownshill
   Gardens
Millend House, nr Newland,
   Coleford
Trevi Garden, Hartpury, nr
   Gloucester
May 5 Tuesday
Cinderdine Cottage, Dymock, nr
   Newent
May 6 Wednesday
Lydney Park Spring Gardens,
   Lydney
May 9 Saturday
Kiftsgate Court,nr Chipping
   Campden
May 10 Sunday
Abbotswood, Stow-on-the-Wold
Batsford Arboretum, nr
   Moreton-in-Marsh
Cerney House Gardens, North
   Cerney
Green Cottage, Lydney
Home Farm, Huntley, nr Newent
Oxleaze Farm, Filkins, Lechlade
Snowshill Manor, nr Broadway
Southrop Manor, nr Lechlade
May 11 Monday
The Old Rectory, Duntisbourne
   Rous, nr Cirencester

May 13 Wednesday
Rookwoods, Waterlane, nr Bisley
May 17 Sunday
Green Cottage, Lydney
Millend House, nr Newland,
   Coleford
Stowell Park, nr Northleach
Trevi Garden, Hartpury, nr
   Gloucester
May 20 Wednesday
Vale House, Hidcote Boyce
May 24 Sunday
Boddington Manor, Boddington
   Nr Cheltenham
Cinderdine Cottage, Dymock, nr
   Newent
Eastington Gardens, nr
   Northleach
Green Cottage, Lydney
Mill Dene, Blockley
Millend House, nr Newland,
   Coleford
The Red House, Staunton, nr
   Gloucester
Trevi Garden, Hartpury, nr
   Gloucester
Willow Lodge, nr Longhope,
   Gloucester
May 25 Monday
Brackenbury, Coombe, nr
   Wotton-under-Edge
The Bungalow, nr Newent
Cinderdine Cottage, Dymock, nr
   Newent
Eastington Gardens, nr Northleach
Millend House, nr Newland,
   Coleford
The Red House, Staunton, nr
   Gloucester
Trevi Garden, Hartpury, nr
   Gloucester
Willow Lodge, nr Longhope,
   Gloucester
May 26 Tuesday
Cinderdine Cottage, Dymock, nr
   Newent
May 28 Thursday
Bourton House Garden,
   Bourton-on-the-Hill
May 31 Sunday
Brockweir Gardens, Chepstow
Green Cottage, Lydney
Stanway House, nr Winchcombe
Tetbury Gardens
June 3 Wednesday
Green Cottage, Lydney
June 6 Saturday
Barnsley House, nr Cirencester
June 7 Sunday
Burnside, Prestbury
Cinderdine Cottage, Dymock, nr
   Newent
The Glebe House, Shipton Moyne
Green Cottage, Lydney

Hodges Barn, nr Tetbury
Home Farm, Huntley, nr Newent
13 Merestones Drive, Cheltenham
Millend House, nr Newland, Coleford
Pigeon House, Southam, nr
   Cheltenham
Trevi Garden, Hartpury, nr
   Gloucester
Willow Lodge, nr Longhope,
   Gloucester
June 8 Monday
Willow Lodge, nr Longhope,
   Gloucester
June 9 Tuesday
Cinderdine Cottage, Dymock, nr
   Newent
June 10 Wednesday
Green Cottage, Lydney
Vale House, Hidcote Boyce
June 13 Saturday
The Bungalow, nr Newent
The Old House, Burleigh
June 14 Sunday
Alderley Grange, Alderley
25 Bowling Green Road,
   Cirencester
Chalford Gardens, nr Stroud
The Chestnuts, Minchinhampton
Green Cottage, Lydney
Hillesley House, nr
   Wotton-under-Edge
Humphreys End House,
   Randwick, nr Stroud
Hunts Court, North Nibley, Nr
   Dursley
Icomb Place, nr
   Stow-on-the-Wold
Oxleaze Farm, Filkins, Lechlade
Pitt Court, North Nibley, Dursley
The Red House, Staunton, nr
   Gloucester
Southrop Manor, nr Lechlade
June 17 Wednesday
Green Cottage, Lydney
June 18 Thursday
Church Cottage, Stinchcombe, nr
   Dursley
Rockcliffe, nr Lower Swell
June 20 Saturday
Trevi Garden, Hartpury, nr
   Gloucester
June 21 Sunday
Blockley Gardens,
   Moreton-in-Marsh
Cinderdine Cottage, Dymock, nr
   Newent
Grange Farm, Evenlode, nr
   Moreton in Marsh
Green Cottage, Lydney
Hunts Court, North Nibley, Nr
   Dursley
13 Merestones Drive, Cheltenham
Millend House, nr Newland,
   Coleford

Pitt Court, North Nibley, Dursley
Sunningdale, nr
  Westbury-on-Severn
Trevi Garden, Hartpury, nr
  Gloucester
Willow Lodge, nr Longhope,
  Gloucester
Witcombe Gardens, nr Gloucester
June 22 Monday
The Old Rectory, Duntisbourne
  Rous, nr Cirencester
Willow Lodge, nr Longhope,
  Gloucester
June 23 Tuesday
Cinderdine Cottage, Dymock, nr
  Newent
June 24 Wednesday
Oxleaze Farm, Filkins, Lechlade
Southrop Manor, nr Lechlade
Vale House, Hidcote Boyce
June 25 Thursday
Bourton House Garden,
  Bourton-on-the-Hill
Rockcliffe, nr Lower Swell
Sunningdale, nr
  Westbury-on-Severn
June 27 Saturday
Hullasey House, Tarlton, nr
  Cirencester
The Old House, Burleigh
June 28 Sunday
Beverston Gardens, nr Tetbury
25 Bowling Green Road,
  Cirencester
Brackenbury, Coombe, nr
  Wotton-under-Edge
Brockweir Gardens, Chepstow
Hullasey House, Tarlton, nr
  Cirencester
Hunts Court, North Nibley, Nr
  Dursley
Mill Dene, Blockley
Misarden Park, Miserden, nr
  Cirencester
Pitt Court, North Nibley, Dursley
Quenington Gardens, nr
  Fairford
Stanton Gardens, Broadway
Stowell Park, nr Northleach
Sunningdale, nr
  Westbury-on-Severn
Willow Lodge, nr Longhope,
  Gloucester
Withington Gardens, nr
  Cheltenham
June 29 Monday
Beverston Gardens, nr Tetbury
Hullasey House, Tarlton, nr
  Cirencester
Willow Lodge, nr Longhope,
  Gloucester
July 1 Wednesday
Moor Wood, Woodmancote, nr
  Cirencester

July 2 Thursday
Rockcliffe, nr Lower Swell
July 4 Saturday
Mill Dene, Blockley (Evening)
July 5 Sunday
Broad Campden Gardens, nr
  Chipping Campden
Cinderdine Cottage, Dymock, nr
  Newent
Great Rissington Farm, Cheltenham
Hunts Court, North Nibley, Nr
  Dursley
Millend House, nr Newland,
  Coleford
Sezincote, nr Moreton-in-Marsh
Sunningdale, nr
  Westbury-on-Severn
Willow Lodge, nr Longhope,
  Gloucester
July 6 Monday
Willow Lodge, nr Longhope,
  Gloucester
July 7 Tuesday
Cinderdine Cottage, Dymock, nr
  Newent
July 8 Wednesday
Rookwoods, Waterlane, nr Bisley
July 12 Sunday
25 Bowling Green Road,
  Cirencester
The Bungalow, nr Newent
Campden House, Chipping
  Campden
Hunts Court, North Nibley, Nr
  Dursley
The Red House, Staunton, nr
  Gloucester
Willow Lodge, nr Longhope,
  Gloucester
July 13 Monday
Willow Lodge, nr Longhope,
  Gloucester
July 15 Wednesday
Daylesford House, nr
  Stow-on-the-Wold
July 16 Thursday
Sunningdale, nr
  Westbury-on-Severn
July 18 Saturday
22 St Peter's Road, Cirencester
Trevi Garden, Hartpury, nr
  Gloucester
July 19 Sunday
25 Bowling Green Road,
  Cirencester
Cinderdine Cottage, Dymock, nr
  Newent
Cowley Manor, nr Cheltenham
Millend House, nr Newland,
  Coleford
22 St Peter's Road, Cirencester
Sunningdale, nr
  Westbury-on-Severn
Trench Hill, Sheepscombe

Trevi Garden, Hartpury, nr
  Gloucester
July 21 Tuesday
Cinderdine Cottage, Dymock, nr
  Newent
July 23 Thursday
Sunningdale, nr
  Westbury-on-Severn
July 26 Sunday
25 Bowling Green Road,
  Cirencester
Brackenbury, Coombe, nr
  Wotton-under-Edge
Brockweir Gardens, Chepstow
Sunningdale, nr Westbury-on-Severn
Trench Hill, Sheepscombe
Willow Lodge, nr Longhope,
  Gloucester
July 27 Monday
Willow Lodge, nr Longhope,
  Gloucester
July 30 Thursday
Bourton House Garden,
  Bourton-on-the-Hill
August 2 Sunday
25 Bowling Green Road,
  Cirencester
Cinderdine Cottage, Dymock, nr
  Newent
Millend House, nr Newland,
  Coleford
Minchinhampton Gardens
Trevi Garden, Hartpury, nr
  Gloucester
August 3 Monday
Minchinhampton Gardens
August 4 Tuesday
Cinderdine Cottage, Dymock, nr
  Newent
August 9 Sunday
Willow Lodge, nr Longhope,
  Gloucester
August 10 Monday
Willow Lodge, nr Longhope,
  Gloucester
August 15 Saturday
Kiftsgate Court,nr Chipping
  Campden
August 16 Sunday
Millend House, nr Newland,
  Coleford
Westonbirt Gardens at
  Westonbirt School
Willow Lodge, nr Longhope,
  Gloucester
August 17 Monday
Willow Lodge, nr Longhope,
  Gloucester
August 23 Sunday
Cinderdine Cottage, Dymock, nr
  Newent
August 25 Tuesday
Cinderdine Cottage, Dymock, nr
  Newent

GLOUCESTERSHIRE (NORTH & CENTRAL)

KEY

1. Abbotswood
2. Alderley Grange
3. Amai Yume Teien
4. Ampney Knowle
5. Ashley Manor
6. Barnsley House
7. Batsford Arboretum
8. Beverston Gardens
9. Blockley Gardens
10. Boddington Manor
11. Bourton House Garden
12. 25 Bowling Green Road
13. Brackenbury
14. Broad Campden Gardens
15. Brockweir Gardens
16. Brook Farm
17. The Bungalow
18. Burnside
19. Camp Cottage
20. Campden House
21. Cerney House Gardens
22. Chalford Gardens
23. The Chestnuts
24. Church Cottage
25. Cinderdine Cottage
26. Clover House
27. Cotswold Farm
28. Cowley Manor
29. Daylesford House
30. Eastcombe

31. Eastington Gardens
32. Ewen Manor
33. The Glebe House
34. Grange Farm
35. Great Rissington Farm
36. Green Cottage
37. Hidcote Manor Garden
38. Hillesley House
39. Hodges Barn
40. Home Farm
41. Hullasey House
42. Humphreys End House
43. Hunts Court
44. Icomb Place
45. Kiftsgate Court
46. Lydney Park Spring
    Gardens
47. 13 Merestones Drive
48. Mill Dene
49. Millend House
50. Minchinhampton Gardens
51. Misarden Park
52. Moor Wood
53. The Old Chapel
54. The Old House
55. The Old Manor
56. The Old Rectory
57. Orchard Cottage
58. Oxleaze Farm
59. Painswick Rococo Garden

60. Park Farm
61. Pigeon House
62. Pitt Court
63. Quenington Gardens
64. The Red House
65. Rockcliffe
66. Rodmarton Manor
67. Rookwoods
68. 22 St Peter's Road
69. Sezincote
70. Snowshill Manor
71. Southrop Manor
72. Spring Tyning
73. Stanton Gardens
74. Stanway House
75. Stowell Park
76. Sudeley Castle Gardens
77. Sunningdale
78. Tetbury Gardens
79. Tinpenny Farm Fiddington
80. Trench Hill
81. Trevi Garden
82. Upton Wold
83. Vale House
84. Westbury Court Garden
85. Westonbirt Gardens at
    Westonbirt School
86. Willow Lodge
87. Witcombe Gardens
88. Withington Gardens

August 27 Thursday
Bourton House Garden,
Bourton-on-the-Hill
August 29 Saturday
Rodmarton Manor, nr Cirencester
August 30 Sunday
Brockweir Gardens, Chepstow
Eastington Gardens, nr Northleach
Millend House, nr Newland, Coleford
Trevi Garden, Hartpury, nr
Gloucester
August 31 Monday
Brackenbury, Coombe, nr
Wotton-under-Edge
Brockweir Gardens, Chepstow
Eastington Gardens, nr Northleach
Millend House, nr Newland,
Coleford

Trevi Garden, Hartpury, nr
Gloucester
September 6 Sunday
Brook Farm, Newent
Cinderdine Cottage, Dymock, nr
Newent
Park Farm, Alderley
Westbury Court Garden,
Westbury-on-Severn
Westonbirt Gardens at
Westonbirt School
September 8 Tuesday
Cinderdine Cottage, Dymock, nr
Newent
September 13 Sunday
Green Cottage, Lydney
Sudeley Castle Gardens,
Winchcombe

September 20 Sunday
Green Cottage, Lydney
September 24 Thursday
Bourton House Garden,
Bourton-on-the-Hill
September 27 Sunday
Brockweir Gardens, Chepstow
October 4 Sunday
Cowley Manor, nr Cheltenham
October 29 Thursday
Bourton House Garden,
Bourton-on-the-Hill

1999 February
Cinderdine Cottage, Dymock, nr
Newent. Tues 9, 16, Thurs 11,
18, Suns 14, 21 (12-5)

DESCRIPTIONS OF GARDENS

Abbotswood, Stow-on-the-Wold (Dikler Farming Co) nr Lower Swell. Several acres of massed plantings of spring bulbs, heathers, flowering shrubs and rhododendrons in dramatic, landscaped hillside stream gardens; fine herbaceous planting in elegant formal gardens with lily pond, terraced lawn and fountain created by Sir Edwin Lutyens. TEAS. Car park free. *Adm £2 Chd free. Suns April 26, May 10 (1.30-6)*

Alderley Grange, Alderley &⚹ (Mr Guy & the Hon Mrs Acloque) 2m S of Wotton-under-Edge. Turn NW off A46, Bath-Stroud rd, at Dunkirk. Walled garden with fine trees, roses; herb gardens and aromatic plants. *Adm £2 Chd free. Sun June 14 (2-6). Private groups by written request welcome during June*

Amai Yume Teien (Garden of Sweet Dreams), Blockley ⚹ (Mr Tim Brown) On the Chipping Campden rd almost opp St Georges Hall and the School. A unique example of a Japanese kare sansui teien (dry landscape garden) set in the improbable context of an old Cotswold village. The garden is a small rectangle within a 25sq metre space bounded by two interesting types of Japanese fencing. It is crossed by rectilinear paths (an example of mino ishi) which create five sub-rectangles. Looks interesting in all weathers. *Adm £1 Chd 50p (ACNO to London Lesbian and Gay Switchboard®). Private visits welcome usually last Sun of each month at 11.30, please* **Tel 01386 701026**

Ampney Knowle, nr Cirencester ⚹ (Mr & Mrs Richard Pile) 4m NE Cirencester B4425 ¼m S of Barnsley on Ampney Crucis rd. Medium-sized garden, created by present owners, around C18 farmhouse with plant packed terrace; walled gardens, mixed borders with choice and less known plants and old shrub roses. Atmospheric woodland garden with indigenous wild flowers and 40-acre bluebell wood. TEAS in aid of Royal British Legion Women's Section. *Adm £2 Chd free. Sun May 3 (12-6). Private visits welcome, please* **Tel 01285 740230**

Ashley Manor, nr Tetbury ⚹ (Mr & Mrs M J Hoskins) On A433, turn R through Culkerton to Ashley. Old garden next to church redesigned by present owners and imaginatively planted. Mature yew hedges divide 4 separate gardens and are the backdrop to a collection of clematis, shrub roses and herbaceous plants. Kitchen garden. TEA. *Adm £1.50 Chd free (ACNO to Ashley Church®). Sat April 11, Mon April 13 (2-5)*

■ **Barnsley House, Barnsley** &⚹✿ (Mr Charles Verey) 4m NE of Cirencester on B4425. Mature garden created and cared for by Rosemary Verey, with interesting collection of shrubs and trees; ground cover; herbaceous borders; pond garden; laburnum walk; knot and herb gardens; formal kitchen garden; C18 summer houses. C17 house (not open). *Adm £3 Chd free (no charge Dec and Jan). Mons, Weds, Thurs & Sats (10-6). Parties by appt only* **Tel 01285 740281.** *For NGS (ACNO to Barnsley Church®). Sats May 2, June 6 (2-6)*

■ **Batsford Arboretum, nr Moreton-in-Marsh** &✿ (The Batsford Foundation Registered Charity No 286712) Off A44. Arboretum and wild gardens; over 1500 named trees (many rare) and shrubs; magnolias, flowering cherries, bulbs; beautiful views from Cotswold escarpment. House not open. TEAS at Garden Centre. *Adm £3 OAPs £2.50 Chd 11-15 £2.50 under 10 free. Open daily, March 1 to Nov 5 (10-5). Oct 1 to Nov Adm £3.50 OAPs £3 Chd 11-15 £3. For NGS Sun May 10 (2-5)*

Beverston Gardens ✿ 2m W of Tetbury on A4135 rd to Dursley
  Beverston Castle (Mrs L Rook) Overlooked by romantic C12-C15 castle ruin, the overflowingly planted paved terrace leads from C17 house across moat to sloping lawn with spring bulbs in abundance and full herbaceous and shrub borders. Large walled kitchen garden and greenhouses. TEAS, Sundays. *Adm £1.50 OAPs & Chd £1 (ACNO to Cotswold Home Appeal Burford®). Suns, Mons April 12 (2-6) 13 (11-6), June 28 (2-6), June 29 (11-6)*
  Orchard Cottage &✿ (Mr & Mrs H L Pierce) On corner by memorial hall. ⅔-acre space used to the full with mixed borders, trees, shrubs, climbers, ferns and other shady plants, together with kitchen garden, wall and cordon fruit and herb interest in sheltered back garden. *Adm £1 Chd free. Sun, Mon June 28, 29 (2-6)*

Blockley Gardens ✖️❀ NW of Moreton-in-Marsh. A44 Moreton-Broadway; turning E. Popular Cotswold hillside village with great variety of high quality gardens, some walking necessary and some gardens not safe for small children. TEAS at St George's Hall in aid of Blockley WI and Blockley Ladies Choir. *Combined adm £3 single garden £1 Chd free. Suns April 26, June 21 (2-6)*

    Colebrook House
    Grange Cottage (Mrs J Moore) *Sun April 26 only*
    Holly House (Simon Ford & Robert Ashby)
    Malvern Mill (Mr & Mrs J Bourne)
    Mill Dene (Mr & Mrs B S Dare) *For additional openings and full description see main entry*
    The Old Silk Mill (Mr & Mrs A Goodrick-Clarke) (Very dangerous for children.) *Sun June 21 only*
    Pear Trees (Mrs J Beckwith) *also by appt*

Boddington Manor, Boddington ✿❀ (Robert Hitchins Ltd) 3m W of Cheltenham off the A4019 Cheltenham to Tewkesbury rd. After crossing the M5 motorway take first turning L which is signed to Boddington. Old garden sympathetically restored since 1985 incl wild flower woodland walk, mature specimen trees, extensive lawns and lakes; established Pinetum and bog garden. New planting of acers, birches, liquidambars, in meadow setting. Neogothic manor house (not open). 'Gardening with Nature Fair'. Cream TEAS. *Adm £1.50 Chd free. Sun May 24 (11-5)*

■ **Bourton House Garden, Bourton-on-the-Hill** ✖️❀ (Mr & Mrs R Paice) 2m W of Moreton-in-Marsh on A44. Intensively planted 3 acres with topiary, knot garden, potager, colour and herbaceous borders, water features and C16 Tithe Barn. Imaginative containers, vast range of unusual plants incl tender and half hardy; providing lots of late season interest; a plantsman's paradise. *Adm £3 Chd free. Every Thurs & Fri May 28 to Oct 23. Also Bank hols Sun, Mon May 24, 25 Aug 30, 31 (12-5). For NGS last Thurs of every month. May to Oct (12-5). Parties of 20 minimum welcome, please* **Tel 01386 700121**

25 Bowling Green Road, Cirencester ❀ (Fr John & Susan Beck) Take A417 to Gloucester just to traffic lights, cross or turn R into The Whiteway then 1st L to no 25 on R of rd bend. Please respect neighbours' driveways, no pavement parking. Uncontrollable enthusiasts' ever-growing semi-detached corner plot plant home. Wide range of perennials, daylilies (130+ varieties), roses, geraniums, clematis etc. Featured in Historic Houses, Castles and Gardens 1997 and 1998, Japanese language edition of NGS yellow book. *Adm £1.25 Chd under 16 free. Suns June 14, 28, July 12, 19, 26, Aug 2 (2-5). Private visits welcome June to Aug, please* **Tel 01285 653778**

Brackenbury, Coombe ❀ (Mr & Mrs Peter Heaton) 1m NE of Wotton-under-Edge. From Wotton Church ½m on Stroud rd B4058 turn R (signed Coombe); from Stroud on B4058, 300yds past Wotton-under-Edge sign turn L, (signed Coombe). Garden on R. ⅔-acre plantsman's terraced garden with multi-layer planting; foliage a special feature. Well stocked mixed borders, cottage garden, pool; 1000 different hardy perennials and 200 different shrubs. Vegetables on deep-bed system. National Collection of Erigerons June and July. Home-made TEAS. *Adm*

£1.50 Chd free (ACNO to Cotswold Care Hospice®). Mon May 25, Suns June 28, July 26, Mon Aug 31 (2-6)

Broad Campden Gardens ✿❀ 5m E of Broadway 1m SE of Chipping Campden. Big group of gardens of wide appeal and expertise: large and small, old and new, formal and informal, within picturesque popular village with meandering stream. Teas in aid of Village Hall. *Combined adm £3 Chd free. Sun July 5 (2-6). Free car park. Coach parties please* **Tel 01386 840467**

    The Angel House (Mr & Mrs Bill Boddington) Angel Lane
    Briar Hill House (Sir Geoffrey and Lady Ellerton)
    The Farthings (Mr & Mrs John Astbury)
    Halfpenny Cottage (Mr & Mrs Kenneth Jones)
    Hillside (Mr John Wilkinson)
    The Malt House (Mr & Mrs Nick Brown)
    Manor Barn (Mr Michael Miles & Mr Christopher Gurney) Angel Lane
    Oldstones (Mr & Mrs Hugh Rolfe) Angel Lane
    Pinders (Mr & Mrs Ian Dunnett)
    Sharcomb Furlong (Mr & Mrs Basil Hasberry)
    Withy Bank (Mr & Mrs Jim Allen)
    Wold Cottage (Mr & Mrs James Jepson)
    Wyldlands (Mr & Mrs John Wadey)

Brockweir Gardens ✿✖️❀ (2m Tintern Abbey) From A466 Chepstow to Monmouth rd, cross R Wye to Brockweir, ¾m uphill take L turning to Coldharbour. Also from B4228 at Hewelsfield Xrds. TEAS in aid of Marie Curie Cancer Care and RSPCA at Laurel Cottage. *Adm £1 each garden. Suns March 29, April 26, May 31, June 28, July 26, Aug 30, Sept 27 (Laurel Cottage only), Mon Aug 31 (2-6)*

    Laurel Cottage ✿✖️ (David & Jean Taylor) Informal 1-acre cottage garden with lovely views over Offas Dyke. Dry stone walling creates gardens within a garden with lawns, herbaceous flowers and spring bulbs. Interesting selection of unusual shrubs and plants. *Also open Sept 27. Private visits welcome all year, please* **Tel 01291 689565**
    Threeways (Iorrie & Gwen Williams) Also on foot from Laurel Cottage. 2-acre garden with unusual shrubs and trees. Small woodland area, bog garden and stream. Formal area with water feature and well stocked herbaceous borders

¶**Brook Farm, Newent** ✿❀ (Mr & Mrs A Keene) 1m S of Newent off B4216 Newent to Huntley Rd, turning R into Bousdon Lane at the end of speed limit signs. 1-acre garden recently created out of an old farmyard and filled with unusual perennials. Stream and walks in 5 acres of woodland. TEA. *Adm £1.50 Chd free. Suns May 3, Sept 6 (2-6)*

The Bungalow, nr Newent ✖️❀ (Mrs Sue Clive) Birches Lane off B4215, ½-way between Newent and Dymock, signposted Botloes Green and Pool Hill. The Bungalow is first on L on edge of Three Choirs Vineyard. Park in orchard. ½-acre garden created and maintained by professional working woman at weekends. Full of interest, incl 2 water features, sitting areas, pergolas and arches, formal and informal planting of herbaceous and wild flowers, herbs and fruit, merging into an orchard, with fine view over the Malvern Hills. TEAS. *Adm £1.50 Chd free (ACNO to Downs Syndrome Assoc®). Mon May 25, Sat June 13, Sun July 12 (2-6)*

Burnside, Prestbury ❀ (Mr & Mrs John Anton-Smith) Burnside is 300yds E of B4632, up Mill Lane, in the village of Prestbury which is 2m NE of Cheltenham. 1½-acre working garden specialising in plant-breeding of hellebores, pulsatillas, geraniums, erodiums and other plants, and production of unusual herbaceous plants. Stock beds, large rockery, stream. *Adm £1 Chd free (ACNO to NCCPG Glos Group®). Sun June 7 (2-6). Private visits welcome, please* **Tel 01242 244645**

Camp Cottage, Highleadon ✿❀ (Les Holmes & Sean O'Neill) nr Newent. 6m NW of Gloucester. From Glos take A40 Ross rd, turn R onto B4215 Newent rd, 3-4m along turn R at sign for Upleadon. The cottage is about 100yds up lane on L hand side. A much publicised plant lover's garden around C17 thatched cottage. About 1 acre overflowing with old roses, climbing plants, snowdrops, hellebores and many unusual plants from all over the world mostly grown from seed and cuttings. Pergola, arches and short shrubland walk. TEA. *Adm £1 Chd 50p. Due to long illness, no regular openings. Please* **Tel 01452 790352** *betwen 6 and 7 for further details*

Campden House ✿❀ (Mr & Mrs Philip Smith) Chipping Campden. Drive entrance on Chipping Campden to Weston Subedge rd, about ¼m SW of Campden. 2-acre garden featuring mixed borders of plant and colour interest around Manor House and C17 Tithe Barn. Set in fine parkland in hidden valley. TEAS and plant stall in aid of Marie Curie Cancer Care. *Adm £2 Chd free. Sun July 12 (2-6)*

■ **Cerney House Gardens, North Cerney** ✿❀ (Sir Michael & Lady Angus) 4m N of Cirencester on A435 Cheltenham rd. Turn L opp Bathurst Arms, past church up hill, pillared gates on R. Romantic walled garden filled with old-fashioned roses and herbaceous borders. There is a working kitchen garden with a scented garden and well-labelled herb garden. Spring bulbs in abundance all around the wooded grounds. TEAS. *Adm £3 Chd £1 (free on NGS day). Tues, Weds, Fris, April to Sept (2-6). For NGS Sun May 10 (2-6). Private visits welcome, please* **Tel 01285 831300/831205**

Chalford Gardens ✿ 4m E of Stroud on A419 to Cirencester. Gardens are high above the Chalford Vale and reached on foot by steep climb from car park on main rd or from High St. *Combined adm £3 Chd free. Sun June 14 (2-5)*
  Marle Hill House (Mike & Leslie Doyle-Davidson) 1-acre newly reclaimed Victorian woodland garden, containing a number of interlinked secret, formal and natural areas on terraced hillside
  The Old Chapel (F J & F Owen) For description see separate entry. *Garden also open with Art Exhibition in studio Sat-Fri June 13-19, Mon-Sun June 22-28 (10-5) Adm £2 (50% to NGS)*
  The Rock House (Mr & Mrs George Edwards) 1-acre, S facing old garden. Dramatic 40' cliff and cave provide backdrop for climbing roses, clematis, shrubbery, rockery, lawn and herbaceous borders. *Private visits welcome (May to July) by appt* **Tel 01453 886363**

The Chestnuts, Minchinhampton ✿❀ (Mr & Mrs E H Gwynn) From Nailsworth by Avening rd (B4014) L Weighbridge Inn ¼m up hill. From Minchinhampton 1m via New Rd or Well Hill. This peaceful ⅔-acre walled garden with lovely views offers an interesting mix of shrubs, bulbs, roses, clematis, rock garden, pool garden and wildflower lawn. ⅔-acre arboretum, with many unusual trees and shrubs. *Adm £2 Chd free (ACNO to Glos Wildlife Trust®). Sun June 14 (2-6)*

Church Cottage, Stinchcombe ✿❀ (Mr & Mrs David Leach) Off A38, 5m NW of Dursley. Peacefully situated next to the church. A plant lover's cottage garden of about ¼-acre planted since 1992 and still evolving. Good variety of hardy plants. Please use car park. *Adm £1 Chd free. Thurs June 18 (1.30-5.30). Private visits and small groups welcome, June and July please* **Tel 01453 542116**

Cinderdine Cottage, Dymock, nr Newent ✿❀ (John & Daphne Chappell) Cottage ¾m on R of lane signed Ryton/Ketford. Country garden for all seasons. Unusual snowdrop collection; hellebores, pulmonarias and other spring flowering plants. Large herbaceous borders summer and early autumn. TEA at Cinderdine Cottage. *Adm £1 Chd free (ACNO to St Mary's Church, Dymock®). Thurs Feb 5, 12, 19, Tues Feb 10, 17, Sun Feb 15, 22, Suns March 1, 22, April 5, 12, 19, May 3, 24 June 7, 21, July 5, 19, Aug 2, 23, Sept 6. Tues Mar, 3, 24, April 7, 21, May 5, 26, June 9, 23, July 7, 21, Aug 4, 25, Sept 8. Mons April 13, May 4, 25 (12-5). 1999 Tues Feb 9, 16, Thurs 11, 18, Suns 14, 21. Parties welcome Feb to Sept, please* **Tel 01531 890265**

Clover House, Winson (Mrs H Kemble) Winson lies approx 7 miles NW of Cirencester. Take the A433 Cirencester/Bibury Rd from Cirencester, turn L just before Bibury signposted Ablington/Winson. On entering Winson Clover House is 1st house on R. Well-established garden of approx 12 acres with a river garden fronting the R Coln. Daffodils & Narcissi are a spring feature of the garden. *Adm £2 Chd free. Sun April 19 (2-6.30)*

Cotswold Farm, Cirencester ✿ (Major & Mrs P D Birchall) 5m N of Cirencester on A417. From Cirencester turn L sign-posted Duntisbourne Abbots/Services, then immed R and under underpass. Private drive straight ahead. From Gloucester turn L sign-posted Duntisbourne, Abbots/Services past Centurion garage. Private drive on L. Cotswold garden in lovely position on different levels with a terrace designed by Norman Jewson in 1938; shrubs and trees, mixed borders, alpine border, shrub roses. *Adm £2 Chd free. Private parties welcome by appt with adequate notice mid June to mid Aug, please* **Tel 01285 653856**

■ **Cowley Manor, Cowley** ❀ nr Cheltenham. SE of Cheltenham off A435. 50 acres of Victorian landscaped grounds with lakes and Italianate terraces and cascade (awaiting restoration) provide a setting for innovatory herbaceous planting by Noël Kingsbury inspired by contemporary German and Dutch design. Lakeside walk. 3rd yr of a garden returning to life after a period of neglect. No dogs at weekends. TEAS in aid of Alzheimers Disease

Society. *Adm £2.50 Chd free. Every day except Mon & Fri from March 1 to Oct 30. For NGS Suns July 19, Oct 4 (2-6). Teas and plants NGS days only*

Daylesford House, Daylesford &% (Sir Anthony & Lady Bamford) Between Stow-on-the-Wold and Chipping Norton off A436. Magnificent lakeside and wooded walks amidst unusual shrubs and trees. Large decorative formal fruit and vegetable walled garden with orchid house, peach house and working glasshouses. Trellised rose garden on raised terrace. Grounds immed around Grade 1 house not open. Visitors should note this is a very large garden with substantial distances to be walked. No cameras. *Adm £3 Chd free. Wed July 15 (2-5.30). No coach parties NGS days. Limited private visits by arrangement, please contact Secretary, Daylesford House GL56 OYH*

Eastcombe, Bussage & Brownshill Gardens 3m E Stroud. 2m N of A419 Stroud to Cirencester on turning signposted to Bisley and Eastcombe. Cream TEAS at Eastcombe Village Hall. *Combined adm £2.75 Chd free incl adm to art exhibition (of pottery, watercolour and pastel Cotswold landscape paintings) by John Bailey (ACNO to Glos Macmillan Cancer Service®, and Cotswold Care Day Hospice®). Sun, Mon May 3, 4 (2-6)*
Eastcombe:
Brewers Cottage & (Mr & Mrs T G N Carter) Hillside garden with a small hidden courtyard
¶**Covilon Cottage, Manor Farm Lane** & (Mr & Mrs W E Hunt) Unspoilt cottage garden with flowers, fruit and vegetable plot
18 Farmcote Close & (Mr & Mrs K Chalmers) Small garden planned for retirement
21 Farmcote Close &% (Mr & Mrs R Bryant) Interesting perennials, bulbs, shrubs and old roses. Trained fruit
Fidges Hill House (Mr & Mrs R Lewis) Secluded and lovely view. No car access, please park in village. Steep descent
Highlands (Mr & Mrs J Page) Small, tranquil and colourful cottage garden
Vatch Rise &% (Mr & Mrs R G Abbott) Interesting bulbous plants, alpines and unusual perennials. Plantsman's garden
Brownshill:
Beechcroft & (Mr & Mrs R H Salt) Mature trees, shrubs, borders, vegetables, fruit, conservatory and wild area
Bovey End (Sir Norman & Lady Wakefield) A large, informal garden sloping steeply; many trees and shrubs
Bussage:
Pine Corner (Mr & Mrs W Burns-Brown) ¾-acre terraced garden. Spring bulbs, shrubs, alpines; water feature
Redwood % (Mr & Mrs D F Collins) Terraced garden with 3 ponds and unusual plants. Hundreds of plants for sale. *Private visits welcome April to July, please* **Tel 01453 882595**

Eastington Gardens, nr Northleach (A40). Charming Cotswold village with lovely views. 2 gardens of traditional appeal. TEAS at **Middle End**. *Combined adm £1.50 Chd free (ACNO to Northleah Church Fund®). Suns, Mons May 24, 25, Aug 30, 31 (2-6)*

Middle End (Mr & Mrs Owen Slatter) Medium-sized garden of general interest. Ample parking at house
Yew Tree Cottage (Mr M Bottone) Small garden packed with hardy plants for sun and shade. Ample parking in village

■ **Ewen Manor, nr Cirencester** &% (Lady Gibbs) Via A429 3m from Cirencester turn at signpost Ewen 1m. Profusely planted series of gardens with architectural features, yew hedges, pattern mown lawn, terrace and containers, lily pool, cedar trees over 200yrs old and woodland area all around. Georgian Cotswold manor (not open). TEAS Sun only. *Adm £2 Chd free. Tues, Wed, Thurs May 5 to July 9 (11-4.30) (Share to NGS®). For NGS Sun May 3 (ACNO to Cotswold Care Hospice®) (2-6). Private visits welcome, please* **Tel 01285 770206**

¶**The Glebe House, Shipton Moyne** &% (Mr & Mrs Richard Boggis-Rolfe) In Shipton Moyne 2½m S of Tetbury. Next to church. Medium-sized garden surrounding the Old Rectory. Mixture of formal and informal planting. Double herbaceous border. Walled kitchen garden, mown walks through young orchard & newly planted woodland with bulbs. TEAS. *Adm £2.50 Chd free under 10. Suns April 12, June 7 (2-6)*

Grange Farm, Evenlode, nr Moreton in Marsh % (Lady Aird) Evenlode 3m from Moreton-in-Marsh and Stow-on-the-Wold. E of the A429 Fosseway and 1½m from Broadwell. This medium-sized atmospheric garden continues to be developed and the C17 rose-covered house and ancient apple trees provide a wonderful setting for the water garden, wide lawns, grass steps and extensive plantings. Lots of places to sit, vegetable patch and croquet lawn. TEAS. *Adm £2 Chd free (ACNO to Evenlode Church®). Sun June 21 (11-6). Private visits welcome, please* **Tel 01608 650607**

¶**Great Rissington Farm, Cheltenham** % (The Hon John & Mrs Donovan) 4m SE of Stow on the Wold, 6m NW of Burford off A424 on Barrington Rd. Turn at North Lodge (nr Barn Business Centre), pass farm buildings to bottom of lane. C16 Cotswold house with 2 acres, 4 small walled gardens filled with a large collection of roses and herbaceous plants. Wide border on edge of lawn has bold planting of large shrubs. Small spinney being replaced with interesting new trees and shrubs. Exciting young garden with great potential complemented by marvellous views over surrounding countryside. TEAS. *Adm £1 Chd free (ACNO to Motor Neurone®). Sun July 5 (2-6)*

Green Cottage, Lydney &% (Mr & Mrs F Baber) Approaching Lydney from Gloucester DO NOT TAKE BY-PASS, keep to A48 through Lydney. Leaving Lydney turn R into narrow lane at de-limit sign. Garden 1st R. Shady parking. 1¼-acre country garden planted for seasonal interest and wildlife. Mature trees, planted stream and woodland banks, bog garden, cottage flowers. Herbaceous paeonies (200), featured throughout garden incl National Reference Collection of rare Victorian and Edwardian cultivars. Hellebores March, NRC Paeonies June, others May. *Adm £1.50 Chd free. Suns March 1, 8, 15, 22, 29 (1-4), May 3, 10, 17, 24, 31 June 7, 14, 21, Sept 13, 20 (2-6) Weds June 3, 10, 17 (1-5).* **Tel 01594 841918**

▲**Hidcote Manor Garden, Chipping Campden** &✿ (The National Trust) Series of formal gardens, many enclosed within superb hedges, incl hornbeam on stems. Many rare trees, shrubs, plants. Coffee, lunches and teas. *Adm £5.50 Chd £2.70. For NGS Sun May 3 (11-6)*

Hillesley House, Hillesley ✿ (Mr & Mrs J Walsh) 3m from Wotton-under-Edge on rd to Hawkesbury Upton and the A46. Recently revived garden in 4 acres surrounding Tudor house (not open); walled garden, borders in sun and shade, roses. Innovative perennial plantings by Noël Kingsbury offer interesting ideas. TEAS. *Adm £2 Chd free. Sun June 14 (2-6)*

Hodges Barn, Shipton Moyne &✿ (Mrs C N Hornby) 3m S of Tetbury on Malmesbury side of village. Very unusual C15 dovecote converted into a family home. Cotswold stone walls act as host to climbing and rambling roses, clematis, vines and hydrangeas; and together with yew, rose and tapestry hedges they create the formality of the area around the house; mixed shrub and herbaceous borders, shrub roses and a water garden; woodland garden planted with cherries, magnolias and spring bulbs. Featured in RHS 'The Garden' May 1996. Teas in Village Hall. *Adm £2.50 Chd free. Mons, Tues, Fris April 1 to Aug 19 (2-5). For NGS Suns April 12, June 7 (2-6). Adjoining garden of Hodges Farmhouse also open for NGS by kind permission of Mrs Clive Lamb*

Home Farm, Huntley (Mrs T Freeman) On B4216 ½m from the A40 in Huntley travelling towards Newent. Set in elevated position with exceptional views. 1m walk through woods and fields to show carpets of spring flowers. Enclosed garden wth fern border, sundial and heather bed. Herbaceous borders. White and mixed shrub borders. Stout footwear advisable in winter. *Adm £1.50 Chd free. Suns Feb 1, March 1, April 5, May 10, June 7 (2-5). Private visits welcome, please* **Tel 01452 830209**

Hullasey House, Tarlton &✿ (Jonathan & Gail Taylor) Midway between Cirencester and Tetbury off A433. Medium-sized Cotswold garden with exceptional views. Stone walls, many old roses, gravel gardens round the house. Walled herb and fruit potager; walled mixed shrub/herbaceous garden. *Adm £2 Chd free (ACNO to Tarlton Church®). Sat, Sun, Mon June 27, 28, 29 (2-5). Other Mons by appt* **Tel 01285 770132**

Humphreys End House, Randwick &✿ (Mr & Mrs J W A Hutton) 2m W of Stroud, follow signs to Cashes Green and Randwick (M5 junction 13). Map Ref [SO 832061]. Different areas of contrasting mood and interesting planting in 1-acre garden surrounding listed C16 farmhouse. Wildlife pond, herbs, old roses, grasses. Organic vegetable garden. TEAS. *Adm £1.50 Chd free. Sun June 14 (2-6). Private visits welcome on Fris in May, June, July, please* **Tel 01453 765401**

■ **Hunts Court, North Nibley, nr Dursley** &✿✿ (Mr & Mrs T K Marshall) 2m NW of Wotton-under-Edge. From Wotton B4060 Dursley rd turn R in Nibley at Black Horse; fork L after ¼m. Unusual shrubs, 450 varieties old roses, large collection of penstemons in peaceful 2½-acre gar-

den with lawns set against tree clad hills and Tyndale monument. Superb views. House (not open) possible birth place of William Tyndale. Picnic area. Home-made TEAS by local charities (Suns only). *Adm £1.50 Chd free. Garden and Nursery open Tues-Sat all year ex Aug; also Bank Hol Mons, May 4, 25. For NGS Suns June 14, 21, 28; July 5, 12 (2-6);* **Tel 01453 547440**

Icomb Place, nr Stow-on-the-Wold &✿ (Mr & Mrs T L F Royle) 4m S of Stow after 2m on A424 Burford rd turn L to Icomb village. 100-year-old sizeable garden extensively restored. Featuring woodland walk through mature & young trees in arboretum; rhododendrons & azaleas; grotto; pools, stream and water garden; parterre; lawned garden with extensive views. C14 manor house (not open). TEAS. *Adm £2 Chd £1 (ACNO to Deus Laudamus Trust®). Sun June 14 (2-6)*

■ **Kiftsgate Court, nr Chipping Campden** &✿ (Mr & Mrs J G Chambers) adjacent to Hidcote Nat Trust Garden. 1m E of A46 and B4081. Magnificent situation and views; many unusual plants and shrubs; tree paeonies, hydrangeas, abutilons, species and old-fashioned roses, incl largest rose in England, R.filipes Kiftsgate. TEAS (April 28 to Sept 1). Lunches June and July. Buses by appt. *Adm £3.50 Chd £1. Suns, Weds, Thurs & Bank Hols Mons April 2 to Sept 28 (2-6). Also Suns, Weds, Thurs, Sats in June & July (12-6). For NGS (ACNO to Sue Ryder Home, Leckhampton Court®) Sats May 9, Aug 15 (2-6).* **Tel 01386 438777**

■ **Lydney Park Spring Gardens, Lydney** ✿ (Viscount Bledisloe) On A48 Gloucester-Chepstow rd between Lydney & Aylburton. Drive is directly off A48. 8 acres of extensive valley garden with many varieties of rhododendron, azaleas and other flowering shrubs; trees and lakes. Garden round house; magnolias and daffodils (April). Roman Temple Site and Museum. Deer park with fine trees. TEAS; also picnic area (in park). *Adm £2.40 Weds £1.40 (Acc chd & cars free). Easter Sun & Mon; Every Sun, Wed & Bank Hol from Sun March 29 to June 14. Every day May 25 to May 31 (11-6). For NGS Sun April 26, Wed May 6 (11-6).* **Tel 01594 842844**

13 Merestones Drive, Cheltenham &✿ (Mr Dennis Moorcraft) Merestones Drive is a turning off The Park reached by following signs to Gloscat (a technical college). Nearest main rd is A46 from Stroud. Town garden shaded by large trees; hostas and ferns a speciality; many unusual plants; scree garden; small brook. TEAS. *Adm £1.50 Chd 50p. Suns June 7, 21 (2-6). Private visits welcome, please* **Tel 01242 578678**

■ **Mill Dene, Blockley** &✿ (Mr & Mrs B S Dare) School Lane. Limited parking. From A44, Bourton-on-the-Hill, turn Blockley. 1.3m down hill turn L cul-de-sac behind 30mph sign. 2½-acre garden with steep lawned terraces, stream and mill-pool in a frost pocket. Potager; grotto and trompe l'oeil. Dangerous for young children. Home-made TEAS. *Adm £2 Chd 50p. Open Mon to Fri (2-5.30) April 1 to Sept 30 and Bank Hols. For NGS Suns May 3, 24 June 28 (2-5.30). Sat July 4 (6.30-8.30) 'Scents of a Summer Evening' £3.50 incl one glass wine. Also open with* **Blockley**

Gardens. *Private visits welcome all yr, please* **Tel 01386 700457**

Millend House, Coleford ❀ (Mr & Mrs J D'A Tremlett) 1½m SW out of Coleford on the Newland rd, centre of Coleford clocktower signposted (Newland 2m). Magnificently located; the 2-acre hillside garden contains many unusual herbaceous plants and shrubs, both shade and sun loving, many of which are for sale. There are also scree and fern beds, a gazebo, ornamental pond, small vegetable and soft fruit garden, and a walk round a 200yr-old wood. TEAS in aid of Glos Macmillan Nurses. *Adm £1.50 Chd free. Suns, Mons, May 3, 4, 17, 24, 25; June 7, 21, July 5, 19; Aug 2, 16, 30, 31 (2-6). Private groups welcome May 1 to Sept 30, please* **Tel 01594 832128**

Minchinhampton Gardens, Minchinhampton ♿❀❀ 4m SE Stroud. From Market Sq down High St 100yds; then R at Xrds; 300yds turn L. Cream TEAS except Feb TEA in aid of Minchinhampton Centre for the Elderly. *Combined adm £2 Chd free. Suns Feb 15, April 19, Aug 2, Mon Aug 3 (12-4.30)*
    Lammas Park (Mr & Mrs P Grover) Lawns, herbaceous borders, wild garden, restored 'hanging gardens'
    St Francis (Mr & Mrs Peter Falconer) Garden made in old park round modern Cotswold stone house. Fine beech avenue; terraced garden; trough gardens; bonsai trees; unusual plants; giant snowdrops (spring); C18 ice-house. Picnickers welcome. *Also private visits welcome, please* **Tel 01453 882188**

■ **Misarden Park, Miserden** ♿❀❀ (Maj M T N H Wills) 6m NW of Cirencester. Follow the signs off the A417 or B4070 from Stroud. Spring flowers, shrubs, fine topiary (some designed by Sir Edwin Lutyens) and herbaceous borders within a walled garden; roses; fine specimen trees; C17 manor house (not open) standing high overlooking Golden Valley. New water feature planned for 1998. Garden Nurseries open daily except Mons. TEAS in aid of Miserden School PTA. *Adm £3 Chd free. April 1 to Sept 30 every Tues, Wed & Thurs (9.30-4.30). For NGS (ACNO to Cobalt Unit®). Suns April 5, June 28 (2-6).* **Tel 01285 821303**

Moor Wood, Woodmancote ❀ (Mr & Mrs Henry Robinson) 3½m from Cirencester turn L off A435 to Cheltenham at North Cerney signed 'Woodmancote 1¼m': entrance in village on L beside lodge with white gates. 2 acres of shrub, orchard and wildflower gardens in isolated valley setting. Holder of the National Collection of rambler roses. TEA. *Adm £2 Chd free. Wed July 1 (2-6). Private visits, please* **Tel 01285 831397**

The Old Chapel ❀ (F J & F Owen) 4m E of Stroud on A419 to Cirencester. Above Chalford Vale, steep climb from car park on main rd, up Marle Hill. 1-acre Victorian chapel garden on precipitous hillside. A tiered tapestry of herbaceous borders, formal potager, small orchard, pond and summer house, old roses. Gothic pergola and rose tunnel, many unusual plants all laid out on terraced S-facing Marle Cliff. Garden open with Art Exhibition in studio. *Adm £2 Chd free (50% to NGS). Sat to Fri June 13 to 19, Mon to Sun June 22 to 28 (10-5). Also in conjunction with* **Chalford Gardens** *Sun June 14 (2-5)*

¶**The Old House, Burleigh** ❀ (Lady McMahon) Near Minchinhampton, 4m SE of Stroud. From A419 take a Minchinhampton turn off at Gliding Club (3m to the garden) or at Brimscombe (1m) and follow signs. Old country garden, on several levels and with areas of differing character, surrounds C17 Cotswold stone house. Restoration and development now in 7th yr. Terraces threaded with narrow paths through old herbaceous paeonies, many old-fashioned roses. Unusual shrubs and trees recently built folly and stream garden. *Adm £2 Chd free (ACNO to Council for the Protection of Rural England®). Sats June 13, 27 (12-5). Private visits welcome by written appt only*

The Old Manor, Twyning ♿❀❀ (Mrs Joan Wilder) 3m N of Tewkesbury via A38 to Worcester; follow sign to Twyning; garden opposite T-junction at top end of village. 2-acre walled garden. Unusual shrubs, trees, herbaceous, alpines; two areas of developing arboretum; sunken garden; terrace plantings; troughs. Field walks for picnics. Small nursery, all stock from garden. *Adm £2 Acc chd free (ACNO to GRBS® & RGOF®). Every Mon (except Bank Hols) March to Oct (2-5, or dusk if earlier) Private visits welcome by appt except Suns incl winter months, please* **Tel 01684 293516** *evenings*

The Old Rectory, Duntisbourne Rous ❀ (Charles & Mary Keen) NW of Cirencester at Daglingworth take valley rd for the Duntisbournes. After ½m no through rd joins from R at entrance to Old Rectory. Writer and designer's own 1½-acre Cotswold family garden in the making, now in its 6th yr. Featured in recent book. Beautiful setting nr Saxon church. Planted for atmosphere and all-yr-interest, this small garden has ten distinct areas and moods. Winter flowers, tender plants and unusual pelargoniums a speciality. *Adm £2 Chd free. Mons Feb 23, April 6 (11-4), May 11, June 22 (11-5). Private visits for groups of 10 or more, by WRITTEN APPT ONLY welcome. Charges negotiable*

Orchard Cottage, Gretton ❀ (Mr Rory Stuart) 2m N of Winchcombe. Up Duglinch Lane beside Bugatti Inn. Approx 300yds up lane turn R after magnolia grandiflora. Approx 1½-acres. Romantically overplanted, owner-maintained garden, created largely by the late Mrs Nancy Saunders. Always some interest. Teas in Winchcombe. *Adm £1.50. Open all year, by appt only* **Tel 01242 602491**

¶**Oxleaze Farm, Filkins, Lechlade** ♿❀❀ (Mr & Mrs Charles Mann) 5m S of Burford, 3m N of Lechlade off A361 to the W (signed Barringtons) then 2nd L and signed. A medium-sized 'developing garden', combining formality and informality with mixed borders, shrub borders, vegetable potager and decorative fruit cage, with recently added pond and sunken garden. A series of 'garden rooms' surround the central lawn, with reflective corners giving the visitor a chance to enjoy the enthusiasm of this typical Cotswold garden. *Adm £1.50 Chd free. Suns May 10, June 14; Wed June 24 (2-6). Private visits welcome*

Evening Opening (see also garden descriptions)

Mill Dene, Blockley	July 4	6.30–8.30pm

● **Painswick Rococo Garden** ❀ (Painswick Rococo Garden Trust Reg No 299792) ½m outside village on B4073. Unique C18 garden from the brief Rococo period combining contemporary buildings, vistas, ponds, kitchen garden and winding woodland walks. Coach House restaurant for coffee, lunches. 'Present Collection' shop. *Adm £2.90 OAP £2.60 Chd £1.50 (Share to NGS®). Jan 14 to Nov 30. Weds to Suns and Bank Hol. July and Aug daily. Restaurant open Weds to Suns (11-5).* **Tel 01452 813204**

Park Farm, Alderley ♿❀ (Mr & Mrs A J V Shepherd) 1½m S from Wotton-under-Edge, just before village. The lake with its waterside plants and large Koi carp is the pivotal attraction in a scenically designed 2½-acre garden also offering maturing herbaceous borders, young trees and a new rose garden. TEAS in aid of Alderley Church Fund. *Adm £2 Chd free. Sun Sept 6 (2-6)*

Pigeon House, Southam ❀❀ (Mr & Mrs Julian Taylor) Southam Lane. 3m from Cheltenham off B4632 toward Winchcombe. Revitalised 2-acre garden surrounding C14 manor house. Small lake and bubbling water garden with fish and bog plants. Wide range of flowering shrubs and borders designed to create multitude of vistas and plant interest. TEAS in aid of Southam Church of the Ascension. *Adm £1.50 Chd free. Suns April 26, June 7 (2-6)*

Pitt Court, North Nibley ♿❀❀ (Mr & Mrs M W Hall) Turn off the B4060 at North Nibley past the Black Horse Inn into Barrs Lane. Continue for approx ¾m. A small garden of about ⅓ acre, making interesting and ingenious use of paving, stones and brick for walls, steps and beds as settings for increasing collection of smaller trees, conifers, shrubs and herbaceous plants. Separate lawn and alpine area. Limited car parking. Teas at **Hunts Court** open nearby with plenty of parking (½m). *Adm £1 Chd free. Suns June 14, 21, 28 (2-6)*

Quenington Gardens, nr Fairford ♿❀❀ E of Cirencester. Peaceful Cotswold riverside village with church renowned for Norman doorways. 6 welcoming gardens offer wide range of style, content and character. TEAS in aid of The Home Farm Trust at **The Old Rectory**. *Combined adm £2.50 Chd free. Sun June 28 (2-6)*

    Apple Tree Cottage (Mrs P Butler-Henderson) Small cottage garden. Interesting conservatory
    Court Farm (Mr & Mrs Frank Gollins) Part of historic grounds of Knights Hospitallers. Woodland walk
    Mawley Field (Mr & Mrs N Collins) Mixed herbaceous borders, rose garden, kitchen garden
    Old Post House (Mrs D Blackwood) A small terraced garden, plant-filled and colourful
    The Old Rectory (Mr & Mrs David Abel-Smith) Picturesque riverside garden. Extensive organic vegetable garden
    Pool Hay (Mr & Mrs A W Morris) Small is beautiful. Picturesque riverside cottage garden

The Red House, Staunton, nr Gloucester ♿❀ (Mr & Mrs W K Turner) Pillows Green, on A417 from Staunton Xrds ½m off B4208. Split level 2 acre organic and wildlife garden with herbaceous borders; rockery and terrace with containers; parterre; also flower meadow. C17 House open by appt. Garden designed and maintained by owners. All plants for sale grown from garden stock. TEA. *Adm £1.50 Chd free (ACNO to Glos Wildlife Trust®). Sun, Mon May 24, 25; Suns June 14, July 12 (2-6). Private visits welcome, please* **Tel 01452 840505**

Rockcliffe, nr Lower Swell ❀❀ (Mr & Mrs Simon Keswick) On B4068. From Stow-on-the-Wold turn R into drive 1½m from Lower Swell. 5-acre garden incl herbaceous borders, pink and white and blue gardens, rose terrace, walled kitchen garden and orchard. TEAS in aid of local schools. *Adm £2 Chd under 15 free. Thurs June 18, 25, July 2 (10-6)*

■ **Rodmarton Manor, Cirencester** ♿❀ (Mr & Mrs Simon Biddulph) Between Cirencester and Tetbury off A433. 8-acre garden of this fine Arts and Crafts house is a series of 'outdoor rooms' each with its own distinctive character. Leisure garden, winter garden, troughery, topiary, hedges, lawns, rockery, containers, wild garden, kitchen garden; snowdrops and magnificent herbaceous borders. *Adm £2.50 Acc chd free. Every Wed April 15 to Aug 26 (2-5) and every Sat May 16 to Aug 29 (2-5). For NGS a snowdrop day and Sat Aug 29. Private group visits welcome at other times, please* **Tel 01285 841253 or Fax 01285 841298**

Rookwoods, Waterlane ❀ (Mr & Mrs R Luard) 5m E of Stroud. Between Sapperton and Bisley. Turn down 'No Through Rd' in Waterlane then follow signs. 3-acre well structured garden with herbaceous borders to colour themes. Pleached Whitebeam around pool area. Wide variety of old-fashioned and modern climbing and shrub roses (labelled), water gardens and outstanding views. TEAS. *Adm £1.50 Chd free. Weds May 13, July 8 (2-6). Coaches by appt. Private visits welcome May and July, please* **Tel 01452 770747**

¶**22 St Peter's Road, Cirencester** (Hugh & Jean Dickinson) Off Cricklade St turn R into Ashcroft Rd then L then R. A small town garden completely redesigned and replanted in 1997. Good structure, and plantings of mixed annuals, perennials and shrubs. Of interest to those wanting quick results. Partially suitable for wheelchairs. *Adm £1 Chd 50p. Sat, Sun July 18, 19 (11.30-4.30)*

■ **Sezincote, nr Moreton-in-Marsh** ❀ (Mr & Mrs David Peake) Turn W along A44 towards Evesham; after 1½m (just before Bourton-on-the-Hill) take turn L, by stone lodge with white gate. Exotic oriental water garden by Repton and Daniell with lake, pools and meandering stream, banked with massed perennial plants of interest. Large semi-circular orangery, formal Indian garden, fountain, temple and unusual trees of vast size in lawn and wooded park setting. House in Indian manner designed by Samuel Pepys Cockerell. TEAS (NGS day only). *Adm £3 Chd £1 under 5 free. Open every Thurs Fri & Bank Hols (except Dec) (2-6). For NGS Sun July 5 (2-6)*

▲**Snowshill Manor, nr Broadway** ❀ (The National Trust) Small terraced garden in which organic and natural methods only are used. Highlights include tranquil ponds, old roses, old-fashioned flowers and herbaceous borders rich in plants of special interest. House contains collections of fine craftmanship incl musical instruments, clocks, toys, bicycles. Grounds, ticket office, restaurant and shop open 12 noon. TEAS. *Adm house & gdn £5.50 Chd £2.75 Garden only £2.50, Chd £1.25. Family ticket £13.70. For NGS Sun May 10 (12-5)*

Southrop Manor, nr Lechlade &*%* (Mr & Mrs G MacEchern) 2m E of Fairford off A417, or 2m W off A361 before Lechlade. Large riverside garden enjoying a new period of revitalisation and replanting. Of special interest is a formal stew pond garden, lime avenue and yew hedges, informal soft-coloured borders (clematis, roses abound) and a small walled garden of herbs, box hedging, roses and unusual flowers. Also woodland, spring bulbs and sweeping lawns. Redevelopment still in progress. *Adm £2 Chd free. Suns April 26, May 10, June 14, Weds June 24 (2-6). Parties by appt during May and June*

¶**Spring Tyning, Dursley** *%* (Mrs Sally Whittal) 2m NNW of Uley on the Cotswold Escarpment between Coaley & Uley. 2-acre garden with panoramic views over the Severn Valley planted in a naturalistic way to blend with unspoilt landscape; some structure and formality around the house. Many banks planted for interest and ground cover. Plantsman's garden incl dell, raised pond, landscaped tennis court and planted dry areas. Spring bulbs and colour through to September with many plants labelled. Refreshments available. *Adm £2 Chd free (ACNO to Save the Children Fund®). Private visits welcome by written appt*

Stanton Gardens, Broadway &*%* One of the most picturesque and unspoilt C17 Cotswold villages with many gardens to explore (21 open in 1997) ranging from charming cottage to large formal gardens of appeal to visitors of all tastes. Plant and produce stalls. Car park free. TEAS from 3-5.30. *Adm £2.50 Chd free. Sun June 28 (2-6) (ACNO to Stanton Church and village hall®). For information, please* **Tel 01386 584212**

■**Stanway House, nr Winchcombe** (Lord Neidpath) 1m E of B4632 Cheltenham-Broadway rd on B4077 Toddington to Stow-on-the-Wold rd. 20 acres of planted landscape in early C18 formal setting. Arboretum, historic pleasure grounds with specimen trees incl pinetum; remains of ornamental canal and cascade; chestnut and oak avenue; folly. Striking C16 manor with gatehouse, tithe barn and church. Tea at The Bakehouse, Stanway. *Adm grounds only £1 Chd 50p; House and grounds £3.50 OAPs £3 Chd £1. Also house open Tues & Thurs June to Sept (2-5). For NGS (ACNO to The Garden History Society®) Suns April 5, May 31 (2-5).* **Tel 01386 584469**

Stowell Park, Northleach &*%* (The Lord & Lady Vestey) Off Fosseway A429 2m SW of Northleach. Large garden, lawned terraces with magnificent views over the Coln Valley. Fine collection of old-fashioned roses and herbaceous plants, with a pleached lime approach to the House. Two large walled gardens contain vegetables, fruit, cut flowers and ranges of greenhouses, also a long rose pergola and wide, plant-filled borders divided into colour sections. House (not open) originally C14 with later additions. TEAS. Plant sales May 17 only. *Adm £2 Chd free. Sun May 17 (ACNO to St Michael's Church, Yauworth®). Sun June 28 (ACNO to The Royal British Legion®) (2-5)*

■**Sudeley Castle Gardens, Winchcombe** *%* (Lord and Lady Ashcombe) The 8 individual gardens around C15 Castle incl the Queen's Garden, with old-fashioned roses, perennials, herbs, Tudor Knot Garden with water features and recently opened Victorian Kitchen garden. Also formal pools, spring bulbs and fine trees in extensive grounds. Specialist plant centre. Restaurant. *Adm gardens and Emma Dent exhibition £4 OAPs £3.20 Chd £1.80. Open daily March 1 to 31 (10.30-4.30) April 1 to Oct 31 (10.30-5.30). For NGS Suns April 26, Sept 13 (10.30-5.30). TEAS. Group tours of gardens can be booked please,* **Tel 01242 602308**

Sunningdale, nr Westbury-on-Severn &*%* (Mr J Mann Taylor) Grange Court. Turn off A48 in Chaxhill. [OS map ref. SO727 164]. ¾-acre sanctuary of sumptuous spectacles and shrubby seclusions for solitude and study. Stimulate your sensorium with this symbiosis of serendipity and strategy. Savour the scented sensations of a spectrum saturated with species seldon seen. A significant speciality is the NCCPG colletion of *Phlomis*. No sleaze or scandal. *Adm £1.50 Chd 50p. Suns June 21, 28, July 5, 19, 26; Thurs June 25, July 16, 23 (2-5). Private visits welcome, please* **Tel 01452 760268**

Tetbury Gardens, Tetbury. *Combined adm £2.50 Chd free. Sun May 31 (2-6)*
> **The Chipping Croft** *%* (Dr & Mrs P W Taylor) At bottom of Chipping Hill approached from market place. 2-acre, secluded, walled town garden on three levels, with mature trees, shrubs, herbaceous borders, rose beds and unusual plants; spring blossom and bulbs. A series of formal gardens, incl fruit and vegetable/flower potager all informally planted; also a water garden. C17 Cotswold house (not open). TEAS in aid of Action Research. *Private visits by arrangement welcome, please* **Tel 01666 503570**
> **The Old Stables** (Brigadier and Mrs J M Neilson) Enter New Church St B3124 from Long St at Xrds signed to Stroud and Dursley. Turn L at Fire station into Close Gardens. Small walled garden on two levels in old stable yard of a town house. Flowering shrubs; clematis; bonsai; water garden; paved area with alpines in troughs

¶**Tinpenny Farm, Fiddington** &*%* (E S Horton) 2½m SE of Tewkesbury. From the roundabout at junction 9 of the M5 take the A46 exit towards Evesham. Just after the traffic lights turn R to Fiddington 1½m along turn R to Walton Cardiff. First house on R. Interesting collection of plants finding a new home in a largish garden 'in the making' on thick clay. This is 1st year of opening, garden started in 1997. *Adm £1 Chd free. Weds all year; Bank Holiday Mons; 2nd Sun in month; parties by appt (12-5)*

¶**Trench Hill, Sheepscombe** &*%* (Celia & Dave Hargrave) c. ½m from Painswick on A46 to Cheltenham turn R to Sheepscombe. Approx 1½m (before reaching village) turn L by telegraph poles, Trench Hill top of lane. 2 to 3 acres set in a small woodland with panoramic views. Variety of herbaceous and mixed borders, rose garden, extensive vegetable plots, wildflower areas, plantings of spring bulbs, a woodland walk, small pond, waterfall and new larger reservation pond. Run on organic principles. TEAS. *Adm £1.50 Chd free (ACNO to Sheepscombe Village Hall). Sun, Mon April 12, 13 (11-5); Suns July 19, 26 (11-6). Private visits welcome* Tel **01452 814 306**

Trevi Garden, Hartpury &☆❀ (Gilbert & Sally Gough) 5m NW of Gloucester via A417. In village turn by War Memorial. 1 acre of gardens within a garden; winding water garden; new terraced alpine garden; clematis walk, shrubberies, herbaceous borders, collections of hardy geraniums/ penstemons, diascias and epimediums. Garden for the connoisseur. TEAS. *Adm £1.50 Chd free (ACNO to Gurkha Welfare Trust®) (June 20, 21 only ACNO to CRACK Cancer Campaign®). Suns, Mons April 5, 12, 13, 26; May 3, 4, 17, 24, 25; June 7, 20, 21; Aug 2, 30, 31; Clematis weekend Sat, Sun July 18, 19; also open every 2nd, 4th Thurs March 26 to Sept 24 (2-6); coaches/ groups by appt on other dates* Tel **01452 700370**

Upton Wold, nr Moreton-in-Marsh ☆❀ (Mr & Mrs I R S Bond) On A44 1m past A424 junction at Troopers Lodge Garage. Ever developing and changing garden architecturally and imaginatively laid out around C17 house with commanding views. Yew hedges; old shrub roses; herbaceous walk; some unusual plants and trees; vegetable garden; pond garden and woodland garden. Cream TEAS. *Adm £3 Chd free. Sun April 19 (10-6). Private visits (£4) welcome May to July, please* Tel **01386 700667**

¶**Vale House, Hidcote Boyce** ☆❀ (Miss B C Muir) On rd from Chipping Campden to NT Hidcote Manor and Kiftsgate Court gardens (see entries) on the edge of Hidcote Boyce. Garden designed and planted from 1972 by daughter of Kiftsgate's creator. Series of small gardens within windbreak hedges allowing superb views to Bredon Hill. Unusual and interesting colour themed plantings. Partially suitable for wheelchairs. *Adm £2 Chd free (ACNO Moreton in Marsh Hospital®). Weds May 20, June 10, June 24 (2-5). Open by appt May and June* Tel **01386 438228**

▲**Westbury Court Garden, Westbury-on-Severn** &☆ (The National Trust) 9m SW of Gloucester on A48. Formal Dutch style water garden, earliest remaining in England; canals, summer house, walled garden; over 100 species of plants grown in England before 1700. *Adm £2.70 Chd £1.35. For NGS Sun Sept 6 (11-6)*

Westonbirt Gardens at Westonbirt School & 3m S of Tetbury. A433 Tetbury-Bristol. 22 acres. Formal Victorian Italian garden, terraced pleasure garden, rustic walks, lake redredged & stocked with carp. Rare, exotic trees and shrubs. Tea at Hare & Hounds Hotel, Westonbirt ½m, (to book tea room for parties Tel **01666 880233**). *Adm £2 Chd 25p (ACNO to Westonbirt Church Organ Appeal®). Suns March 29, Aug 16, Sept 6 (2-5.30)*

Willow Lodge, nr Longhope &☆❀ (Mr & Mrs John H Wood) on A40 between May Hill & Longhope 10m W of Gloucester, 6m E of Ross-on-Wye. Plantsman's garden with unusual and rare plants with colour themed herbaceous borders, shrubs, an alpine walk, stream and pools, several greenhouses, organic vegetable garden, young arboretum with over 300 trees and shrubs from around the world, and wild flowers in the 4-acre grounds. Plants labelled. Ample parking. TEAS. *Adm £1 Chd free. Suns, Mons May 24, 25; June 7, 8, 21, 22, 28, 29; July 5, 6, 12, 26, 27; Aug 9, 10, 16, 17 (2-6). Groups and private visits especially welcome between May and Aug, please* Tel **01452 831211**

Witcombe Gardens, nr Gloucester & From Gloucester (crossing of A46 & A417) towards Witcombe (signed). For Gt Witcombe Gdns turn R at 12 Bells Inn (¼m). For Court Farm House straight on for ½m. Strawberry cream TEAS at Court Farm House in aid of Witcombe and Bentham Village Hall. *Combined adm £2 Chd free. Sun June 21 (2-6)*

    Church Cottage ☆❀ (Sir Christopher & Lady Lawson) Great Witcombe. More than 2 acres of country garden with shrubs, trees and lawns. Stream and two ponds. Rose arbour. Old clipped yews. Further beds of roses, herbaceous borders, and several seats for resting. Soft drinks

    Court Farm House ❀ (Mr & Mrs Andrew Hope) Little Witcombe. An informal family garden of 1 acre. Shrubs, roses, herbaceous perennials and self-seeding annuals; pond, pergola; wild garden, rock garden, herb garden, scree bed; children welcome

    Witcombe Park ☆ (Mrs W W Hicks Beach) Great Witcombe. A plant connoisseur's medium-sized garden set in beautiful Cotswold scenery. Richly planted borders, flowering shrubs, roses; walled garden, cottage garden area and sunken water garden; C17 gazebo

Withington Gardens 8m E of Cheltenham, S of A40 in hidden Cotswold valley. TEAS at Halewell in aid of St Michaels and All Angels' Church. *Combined adm £2.50 Chd free. Sun June 28 (2-6)*

    Halewell (Mrs Elizabeth Carey-Wilson) Grade II listed part C15 house (not open) with 4 acres of terraced garden, incl topiary, leading down to lakeside walk

    Keepers Cottage (Mr E C Housego) ¾-acre cottage garden on edge of village with lovely views

    The Old House (Mr & Mrs John Holmes-Smith) Plantsman's Cotswold stone terraced garden of 1 acre with shrubbery; small pond; herbaceous borders and an abundance of roses. Secret garden in yellow and white

    Withington Court (Mr & Mrs Jonathan Carr) Elegant setting with fine C18 listed house (not open). 5 acres incl paddock running down to R Coln. Trees, old clipped yew. Borders being gradually replanted

Gwent and Gwynned

See separate Welsh sections on pages 386 and 390

Hampshire

Hon County Organiser:	Mrs A R Elkington, Little Court, Crawley nr Winchester SO21 2PU Tel 01962 776365 Central West Hampshire
Assistant Hon County Organisers:	North-West: M H Walford Esq, Little Acre, Down Farm Lane, Headbourne Worthy, Winchester SO23 7LA
	North: Mrs C Oldale, Little Coopers, Coopers Hill, Eversley, RG27 0QA
	North-East: Mrs E Powell, Broadhatch House, Bentley, Nr Farnham GU10 5JJ
	Central-East: Mrs W F Richardson, Hill House, Old Alresford SO24 9DY
	East: Mrs D Hart Dyke, Hambledon House, Hambledon PO7 4RU
	South: Mrs H Sykes, The Cottage, 16 Lakewood Rd, Chandlers Ford SO53 1ES
	South-West: Mrs A Dickens, 2 Victoria Place, Lymington SO41 3TD
	West: C K Thornton Esq, Merrie Cottage, Woodgreen, Nr Fordingbridge SP6 2AT
Hon County Treasurer:	S Every Esq, The White House, Crawley, Winchester SO21 2PR

DATES OF OPENING

Regular openings
For details see garden description

Alverstoke Crescent Garden, Gosport
Apple Court & Apple Court Cottage, Lymington
Braxton Gardens, Milford-on-Sea
Exbury Gardens, Southampton
Furzey Gardens, Minstead
Sir Harold Hillier Gardens & Arboretum, Ampfield
Houghton Lodge, Stockbridge
The Little Cottage, Lymington
Little Court, Crawley
Longthatch, Warnford
Longstock Park & Water Gardens, Stockbridge
Macpenny Nurseries, Bransgore
Mottisfont Abbey, Romsey
2 Warren Farm Cottages, West Tytherley

February 7 Saturday
Brandy Mount House, Alresford
February 22 Sunday
Little Court, Crawley
February 23 Monday
Little Court, Crawley
February 24 Tuesday
Little Court, Crawley
March 1 Sunday
Little Court, Crawley
March 8 Sunday
Longthatch, Warnford
March 15 Sunday
Brandy Mount House, Alresford
Little Court, Crawley
Longthatch, Warnford
The White Cottage, Beech
March 16 Monday
Little Court, Crawley
The White Cottage, Beech

March 22 Sunday
Heathlands, Locks Heath
Longthatch, Warnford
Sowley House, Sowley
March 25 Wednesday
Hayden Barn Cottage, Warnford
Old Meadows, Silchester
March 29 Sunday
Bramley Lodge, Fyfield
Durmast House, Burley
Fernlea, Chilworth
April 5 Sunday
Abbey Cottage, Itchen Abbas
Crawley Gardens, nr Winchester
East Lane, Ovington
Fairfield House, Hambledon
Harcombe House, Ropley
Little Barn, Woodgreen
April 6 Monday
Crawley Gardens, nr Winchester
April 7 Tuesday
Chalkwood, Ropley
April 10 Friday
187 Christchurch Road, Ringwood
April 12 Sunday
Bramdean House, Bramdean
Brandy Mount House, Alresford
187 Christchurch Road, Ringwood
The Cottage, Chandlers Ford
Paddocks Way, Brook
Weir House, Alresford
April 13 Monday
Beechenwood Farm, Odiham
Bramdean House, Bramdean
187 Christchurch Road, Ringwood
The Cottage, Chandlers Ford
April 16 Thursday
Little Court, Crawley
April 19 Sunday
Hayden Barn Cottage, Warnford
Hinton Ampner, Alresford
Houghton Lodge, Stockbridge
Longthatch, Warnford
The Old House, Silchester

April 20 Monday
Houghton Lodge, Stockbridge
April 26 Sunday
Abbey Road Gardens
Bracken Cottage, Greatham
Fernlea, Chilworth
53 Ladywood, Eastleigh
60 Lealand Road, Drayton
Norsebury Gardens, Stoke Charity
North Ecchinswell Farm, Newbury
Shalden Park House, Shalden
April 27 Monday
Norsebury Gardens, Stoke Charity
May 3 Sunday
Abbey Cottage, Itchen Abbas
Coles, Privett
The Cottage, Chandlers Ford
Greenfingers, Milton
Hordle Walhampton, Lymington
Little Court, Crawley
The Old House, Silchester
Rumsey Gardens, Clanfield
Vernon Hill House, Bishop's Waltham
May 4 Monday
Abbey Cottage, Itchen Abbas
Coles, Privett
The Cottage, Chandlers Ford
Croft Mews, Botley
Hambledon House, Hambledon
Vernon Hill House, Bishop's Waltham
May 5 Tuesday
Chalkwood, Ropley
Little Court, Crawley
May 8 Friday
Rotherfield Park, East Tisted (Evening)
May 9 Saturday
Coles, Privett
Rotherfield Park, East Tisted
May 10 Sunday
Bluebell Cottage, Froxfield

Bramdean House, Bramdean
Brandy Mount House, Alresford
Coles, Privett
The Dower House, Dogmersfield
Eversley Gardens
Heathlands, Locks Heath
Spinners, Boldre
Tylney Hall Hotel, Rotherwick
319 Warsash Road, Titchfield
May 13 Wednesday
Birches, E Wellow
May 14 Thursday
Birches, E Wellow
Rowans Wood, Ampfield
May 16 Saturday
3 St.Helens Road, Hayling Island
May 17 Sunday
Birches, E Wellow
The Dower House, Dogmersfield
Fairfield House, Hambledon
Forde's Cottage, Oakshott
Hayden Barn Cottage, Warnford
The Old House, Silchester
Paddocks Way, Brook
Pylewell Park, Lymington
3 St.Helens Road, Hayling Island
South End House, Lymington
Waldrons, Brook
2 Warren Farm Cottages, West
Tytherley
May 18 Monday
2 Warren Farm Cottages, West
Tytherley
May 23 Saturday
Hayling Island Gardens
Potters Cot, Ringwood
May 24 Sunday
Bracken Cottage, Greatham
Bramshaw Lodge, Bramshaw
Fernlea, Chilworth
Hambledon House, Hambledon
Hayling Island Gardens
Longthatch, Warnford
Monxton Gardens
Potters Cot, Ringwood
Pumpkin Patch, Ringwood
Pylewell Park, Lymington
Romsey Gardens
Valentine Cottage, Newnham
Warwick House, Wickham
West Silchester Hall, Silchester
May 25 Monday
Bramshaw Lodge, Bramshaw
Longthatch, Warnford
Monxton Gardens
Pumpkin Patch, Ringwood
West Silchester Hall, Silchester
May 27 Wednesday
Birches, E Wellow
Robins Return, Tiptoe
May 28 Thursday
Birches, E Wellow
Rowans Wood, Ampfield
(Evening)

May 30 Saturday
Coles, Privett
Froyle Cottage Gardens, nr Alton
May 31 Sunday
Birches, E Wellow
1 Brook Cottages, East Meon
Coles, Privett
Flintstones, Durley
Froyle Cottage Gardens, nr Alton
The Old House, Silchester
Romsey Gardens
Rowans Wood, Ampfield
June 1 Monday
Flintstones, Durley
June 2 Tuesday
Harfield Farm House, Curdridge
The Little Cottage, Lymington
June 3 Wednesday
Birches, E Wellow
The Vyne, Sherborne St John
(Evening)
June 4 Thursday
Birches, E Wellow
Harfield Farm House, Curdridge
June 7 Sunday
Birches, E Wellow
Bluebell Cottage, Froxfield
The Garden House, Lymington
Maurys Mount, West Wellow
North Ecchinswell Farm,
Newbury
Tylney Hall Hotel, Rotherwick
The White Cottage, Beech
June 8 Monday
The White Cottage, Beech
June 9 Tuesday
Apple Court and Apple Court
Cottage, Lymington
The Little Cottage, Lymington
Spinners, Boldre
June 13 Saturday
93 Holly Hill, Bassett
Little Brook, Milford-on-Sea
Woodside Cottage, Milford-on-Sea
June 14 Sunday
Applecroft, Woodgreen
Beechenwood Farm, Odiham
Bramdean House, Bramdean
Bramdean Lodge, Alresford
Clibdens, Chalton
Closewood House, Denmead
Cranbury Park, Otterbourne
Croft Mews, Botley
93 Holly Hill, Bassett
53 Ladywood, Eastleigh
Merrie Cottage, Woodgreen
Vernon Hill House, Bishop's
Waltham
Warwick House, Wickham
June 15 Monday
Applecroft, Woodgreen
Clibdens, Chalton
Croft Mews, Botley
Merrie Cottage, Woodgreen

June 16 Tuesday
The Little Cottage, Lymington
June 17 Wednesday
Closewood House, Denmead
Hayden Barn Cottage, Warnford
Robins Return, Tiptoe
White House, Romsey
June 18 Thursday
White House, Romsey
June 19 Friday
White House, Romsey
June 21 Sunday
Appletrees, Burridge
Chilland, Martyr Worthy
Chilland Ford, Martyr Worthy
Clibdens, Chalton
Crawley Gardens
Crookley Pool, Horndean
Droxford Gardens
Hinton Ampner, Alresford
Longstock Park, nr Stockbridge
Oakdene, Sandleheath
The Old Rectory, West
Tytherley
Warwick House, Wickham
West Green House, Hartley
Wintney
Westbrook House, Holybourne
June 22 Monday
Appletrees, Burridge
Broadhatch House, Bentley
Chilland, Martyr Worthy
Chilland Ford, Martyr Worthy
Clibdens, Chalton
Crawley Gardens, nr Winchester
Crookley Pool, Horndean
March End, Sherfield English
June 23 Tuesday
The Little Cottage, Lymington
Oakdene, Sandleheath
June 24 Wednesday
Broadhatch House, Bentley
June 27 Saturday
Brandy Mount House, Alresford
Fritham Lodge, Lyndhurst
Robins Return, Tiptoe
June 28 Sunday
Abbey Road Gardens
Brook Cottage, Bishops Waltham
Conholt Park, Chute
Fairfield House, Hambledon
60 Lealand Road, Drayton
March End, Sherfield English
Marycourt, Odiham
Mottisfont Abbey, Romsey
The Old Vicarage, Appleshaw
Pumpkin Patch, Ringwood
Shalden Park House, Shalden
Valentine Cottage, Newnham
Waldrons, Brook
June 29 Monday
Broadhatch House, Bentley
Brook Cottage, Bishops Waltham
March End, Sherfield English

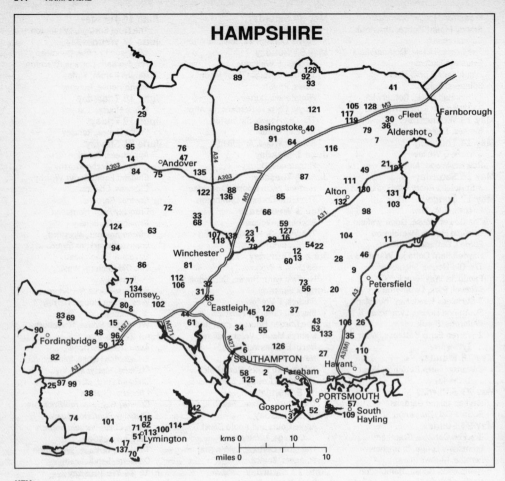

HAMPSHIRE

KEY

1. Abbey Cottage
2. Abbey Road Gardens
3. Alverstoke Crescent Garden
4. Apple Court
5. Applecroft
6. Appletrees
7. Beechenwood Farm
8. Birches
9. Bluebell Cottage
10. Bohunt Manor
11. Bracken Cottage
12. Bramdean House
13. Bramdean Lodge
14. Bramley Lodge
15. Bramshaw Lodge
16. Brandy Mount House
17. Braxton Gardens
18. Broadhatch House
19. Brook Cottage
20. 1 Brook Cottages
21. Bury Court

22. Chalkwood
23. Chilland
24. Chilland Ford
25. 187 Christchurch Road
26. Clibdens
27. Closewood House
28. Coles
29. Conholt Park
30. Copperfield
31. The Cottage
32. Cranbury Park
33. Crawley Gardens
34. Croft Mews
35. Crookley Pool
36. The Dower House
37. Droxford Gardens
38. Durmast House
39. East Lane
40. 8 Elbow Corner
41. Eversley Gardens
42. Exbury Gardens

43. Fairfield House
44. Fernlea
45. Flintstones
46. Forde's Cottage
47. Forest Edge
48. Fritham Lodge
49. Froyle Cottage Gardens
50. Furzey Gardens
51. The Garden House
52. Greenfingers
53. Hambledon House
54. Harcombe House
55. Harfield Farm House
56. Hayden Barn Cottage
57. Hayling Island Gardens
58. Heathlands
59. Hill House
60. Hinton Ampner
61. 93 Holly Hill
62. Hordle Walhampton
63. Houghton Lodge

64. Jasmine Lodge
65. 53 Ladywood
66. Lake House
67. 60 Lealand Road
68. Little Court
69. Little Barn
70. Little Brook
71. The Little Cottage
72. Longstock Park
73. Longthatch
74. Macpenny Nurseries
75. Malt Cottage
76. Mandelieu
77. March End
78. Martyr Worthy Manor
79. Marycourt
80. Maurys Mount
81. Merdon Manor
82. Merebimur
83. Merrie Cottage
84. Monxton Gardens
85. Moth House
86. Mottisfont Abbey
87. Moundsmere Manor
88. Norsebury House
89. North Ecchinswell Farm

90. Oakdene
91. Oakley Manor
92. The Old House
93. Old Meadows
94. The Old Rectory
95. The Old Vicarage
96. Paddocks Way
97. Potters Cot
98. Pullens
99. Pumpkin Patch
100. Pylewell Park
101. Robins Return
102. Romsey Gardens
103. Rose Cottage
104. Rotherfield Park
105. Rotherwick Gardens
106. Rowans Wood
107. Rozelle Close
108. Rumsey Gardens
109. 3 St.Helens Road
110. Setters Green
111. Shalden Park House
112. Sir Harold Hillier Gardens & Arboretum
113. South End House
114. Sowley House

115. Spinners
116. Tunworth Old Rectory
117. Tylney Hall Hotel
118. Ulvik
119. Valentine Cottage
120. Vernon Hill House
121. The Vyne
122. Wades House
123. Waldrons
124. 2 Warren Farm Cottages
125. 319 Warsash Road
126. Warwick House
127. Weir House
128. West Green House
129. West Silchester Hall
130. Westbrook House
131. Wheatley House
132. The White Cottage
133. White Cottage, Beech
134. White House, Hambledon
135. White Windows
136. Wonston Lodge
137. Woodside Cottage
138. The Worthys Gardens

June 30 Tuesday
Chalkwood, Ropley
The Little Cottage, Lymington
July 1 Wednesday
Bracken Cottage, Greatham
Broadhatch House, Bentley
Warwick House, Wickham
July 5 Sunday
Copperfield, Dogmersfield
Durmast House, Burley
Greenfingers, Milton
Marycourt, Odiham
Moth House, Alresford
Moundsmere Manor, Preston Candover
Tunworth Old Rectory, nr Basingstoke
Vernon Hill House, Bishop's Waltham
The Vyne, Sherborne St John
July 7 Tuesday
The Little Cottage, Lymington
July 8 Wednesday
Crookley Pool, Horndean
Marycourt, Odiham
Robins Return, Tiptoe
July 11 Saturday
Apple Court and Apple Court Cottage, Lymington
1 Brook Cottages, East Meon
Merebimur, Mockbeggar
Potters Cot, Ringwood
12 Rozelle Close, Littleton
Weir House, Alresford

July 12 Sunday
Abbey Cottage, Itchen Abbas
Bramdean House, Bramdean
Bramdean Lodge, Alresford
Broadhatch House, Bentley
Forde's Cottage, Oakshott
Forest Edge, Andover Down
Hambledon House, Hambledon
Lake House, Northington
Longthatch, Warnford
Malt Cottage, Upper Clatford
Mandelieu, Andover
Merebimur, Mockbeggar
Old Meadows, Silchester
Potters Cot, Ringwood
Rose Cottage, Kingsley Common
Rotherwick Gardens
12 Rozelle Close, Littleton
Weir House, Alresford
West Silchester Hall, Silchester
The White Cottage, Beech
White Windows, Andover
July 13 Monday
Broadhatch House, Bentley
Hambledon House, Hambledon
Rose Cottage, Kingsley Common
The White Cottage, Beech
White Windows, Andover
July 14 Tuesday
The Little Cottage, Lymington
July 18 Saturday
93 Holly Hill, Bassett

Ulvik, Winchester
July 19 Sunday
Chilland, Martyr Worthy
93 Holly Hill, Bassett
Martyr Worthy Gardens
Pumpkin Patch, Ringwood
Tylney Hall Hotel, Rotherwick
Ulvik, Winchester
Wades House, Barton Stacey
2 Warren Farm Cottages, West Tytherley
July 20 Monday
Chilland, Martyr Worthy
Ulvik, Winchester
2 Warren Farm Cottages, West Tytherley
July 21 Tuesday
The Little Cottage, Lymington
Wades House, Barton Stacey
July 25 Saturday
8 Elbow Corner, Basingstoke
July 26 Sunday
8 Elbow Corner, Basingstoke
Fernlea, Chilworth
Jasmine Lodge, Kempshott
Paddocks Way, Brook
12 Rozelle Close, Littleton
July 28 Tuesday
The Little Cottage, Lymington
July 29 Wednesday
Old Meadows, Silchester
Robins Return, Tiptoe
August 1 Saturday
8 Elbow Corner, Basingstoke

August 2 Sunday
Bohunt Manor, Liphook
8 Elbow Corner, Basingstoke
Hill House, Old Alresford
Jasmine Lodge, Kempshott
Oakley Manor, Oakley
West Silchester Hall,
  Silchester
The White Cottage, Beech

August 3 Monday
West Silchester Hall,
  Silchester
The White Cottage, Beech

August 4 Tuesday
Hill House, Old Alresford
The Little Cottage, Lymington
The Worthys Gardens

August 5 Wednesday
Bury Court, Bentley

August 6 Thursday
Bury Court, Bentley

August 9 Sunday
Abbey Road Gardens
Bramdean House, Bramdean
Bramdean Lodge, Alresford
Brook Cottage, Bishops Waltham
Little Court, Crawley
93 Holly Hill, Bassett
60 Lealand Road, Drayton
Merdon Manor, Hursley

August 10 Monday
Brook Cottage, Bishops
  Waltham
Little Court, Crawley

August 11 Tuesday
The Little Cottage, Lymington

August 12 Wednesday
Old Meadows, Silchester

August 16 Sunday
Conholt Park, Chute
2 Warren Farm Cottages, West
  Tytherley

August 17 Monday
2 Warren Farm Cottages, West
  Tytherley

August 18 Tuesday
The Little Cottage, Lymington

August 25 Tuesday
The Little Cottage, Lymington

August 26 Wednesday
Old Meadows, Silchester

August 29 Saturday
Pullens, West Worldham

August 30 Sunday
Abbey Cottage, Itchen Abbas
Longthatch, Warnford

August 31 Monday
Abbey Cottage, Itchen Abbas
Pumpkin Patch, Ringwood

September 1 Tuesday
The Little Cottage, Lymington

September 6 Sunday
Forde's Cottage, Oakshott
Hambledon House, Hambledon
93 Holly Hill, Bassett
White Cottage, Hambledon

September 7 Monday
Hambledon House, Hambledon
White Cottage, Hambledon

September 8 Tuesday
The Little Cottage, Lymington

September 9 Wednesday
Robins Return, Tiptoe

September 12 Saturday
Hinton Ampner, Alresford

September 13 Sunday
Bramdean House, Bramdean
Bramdean Lodge, Alresford
Hinton Ampner, Alresford
Little Court, Crawley
Rotherfield Park, East Tisted

September 14 Monday
Little Court, Crawley

September 15 Tuesday
The Little Cottage, Lymington

September 20 Sunday
Paddocks Way, Brook
2 Warren Farm Cottages, West
  Tytherley
White Windows, Andover
Wonston Lodge, Wonston

September 21 Monday
2 Warren Farm Cottages, West
  Tytherley

September 22 Tuesday
The Little Cottage, Lymington

September 23 Wednesday
Setters Green, Rowlands Castle
White Windows, Andover

September 27 Sunday
Setters Green, Rowlands Castle

September 29 Tuesday
The Little Cottage, Lymington

September 30 Wednesday
Setters Green, Rowlands Castle

October 7 Wednesday
Bury Court, Bentley

October 8 Thursday
Bury Court, Bentley

October 10 Saturday
Weir House, Alresford
Wheatley House, Kingsley
  Bordon

October 11 Sunday
Coles, Privett
2 Warren Farm Cottages, West
  Tytherley
Wheatley House, Kingsley
  Bordon

October 12 Monday
2 Warren Farm Cottages, West
  Tytherley

1999
February 6 Saturday
Brandy Mount House, Alresford

February 21 Sunday
Little Court, Crawley

February 22 Monday
Little Court, Crawley

February 23 Tuesday
Little Court, Crawley

Regular   Openings. Open throughout the year. They are listed at the beginning of the Diary Section.

DESCRIPTIONS OF GARDENS

Abbey Cottage, Itchen Abbas &⚘❀ (Colonel P J Daniell) Rectory Lane. 1m E of Itchen Abbas on B3047. An inspiring 1½-acre walled garden and meadow on alkaline soil, designed and created on different levels, and maintained by owner. Trees, hedges and walls provide a strong framework within which a wide range of plants flourish and provide yr-round interest. TEA. *Adm £1.50 Chd free (ACNO to Itchen Abbas Church®). Sun April 5, Sun, Mon May 3, 4, Sun July 12, Sun, Mon Aug 30, 31 (12-5)*

Abbey Road Gardens From M27 Junction 9 travel on A27 towards Fareham. At top of hill past Titchfield Gyratory, turn L at traffic lights into Highland Rd. Take 4th turning R into Blackbrook Rd. Abbey Rd is 4th turning on L. Featured in Portsmouth News Aug 97. *Combined adm £1.50 Chd free. Suns April 26, June 28, Aug 9 (11-5)*
  80 Abbey Road ⚘❀ (Brian & Vivienne Garford) Very small garden with extensive collection of herbs and plants of botanical and historical interest. 2 small ponds, miniscule meadow area, but no lawn. Many original ideas for small gardens
  86 Abbey Road ⚘❀ (Tricia & Don Purseglove) Small

garden started in 1991. Mixed planting and trellis work for breezy position. Small vegetable plot and patio garden with fish pond. TEA

Alverstoke Crescent Garden, Gosport & (Gosport Borough Council) From A32 and Gosport follow signs for Stokes Bay then Alverstoke Village. Crescent is off Anglesey Road. Recreated Regency garden, being partnership between council and community, opp Grade II Regency Crescent. Terrace walk with series of small scenes. Central area, site of old bath house, has grassy bays and inlets, shrubs and old roses, authentic plants of the period. Private guided visits, **Tel 01705 586403.** *Daily. Donations to No 21 The Crescent*

■ **Apple Court & Apple Court Cottage, Lymington** ※❀ (Mrs D Grenfell, Mr R Grounds & Mrs M Roberts) From the A337 between Lymington and New Milton turn N into Hordle Lane at the Royal Oak at Downton Xrds. 1½-acres within former walled Victorian kitchen garden. 3 Nat Ref Collections incl small leafed hosta. Hostas and daylilies. Theatrical white garden, modern grassery, fern path. Specialist nursery. Adjoining small cottage garden with variegated catalpa. Featured in BBC 'Gardeners World', Telegraph and 'The Gardener's Guide' to Growing Hostas'. *Adm £2 Chd 50p. Thurs to Mons Feb 1 to Thurs Oct 31; every day July to Aug (10-1) (2-5). For NGS Tues June 9 (9.30-1); Tues July 11 (2-5)*

Applecroft, Woodgreen ※ (Mr & Mrs J B Milne) Brook Lane, Woodgreen. 3m N of Fordingbridge on A338 turn E to Woodgreen. Turn R at Horse and Groom and R again along the edge of the common. Park on common and walk down through 5-barred gate. Small garden. Distant view to the SW over the Avon Valley. Mixed planting incl annuals and vegetables in the cottage style. Shady arbour and pond. TEA (Mon). *Adm £1 Chd free. Sun, Mon June 14, 15 (2-6)*

¶**Appletrees, Burridge** ※❀ (Kath & Ray Butcher) From A27 take A3051. Park Gate to Botley Rd on L after 1½m. If you approach from Botley on A3051 Appletrees is 2m on R. Flower arrangers ⅓ acre garden densely planted with perennials, good foliage. Large patio with sinks and containers. Many winding paths and seats, small pond and waterfall. *Adm £1.50 Sun, Mon June 21, 22 (2-5.30)*

Ashley Park Farm. See Dorset

Beechenwood Farm, Odiham &❀ (Mr & Mrs M Heber-Percy) Hillside. Turn S into King St. from Odiham High St. Turn L after cricket ground for Hillside. Take 2nd turn R for Roke after 1m. Modern house ½m. Garden in many parts incl woodland garden, rock garden, pergola, conservatory, herb garden with exuberant planting, belvedere with spectacular views over Odiham. Newly planted 8 acre wood (open from 1pm for picnics). WI TEAS. *Adm £2 Chd free. Easter Mon April 13; Sun June 14 (2-6); also private visits welcome March to July, please* **Tel 01256 702300**

¶**Birches, East Wellow** &※❀ (Mr & Mrs J Vinnicombe) Turn R off A36, 2m N of M27. Good access and parking for disabled. ¾-acre on acid soil. Mature setting with new planting. Large and expanding collection of plants,

most, incl shrubs, propagated by owners. Plants listed by bed. TEA in period gazebo. *Adm £1.50 Chd free. Weds May 13, 27, June 3, Thurs May 14, 28, June 4, (11-4.30); Suns May 17, 31, June 7 (2-6)*

Bluebell Cottage, Froxfield ※ (Mr & Mrs T Clarke) Broadway. 3½m NW of Petersfield. Between top of Stoner Hill and Froxfield Green. Take sign to Froxfield off A272 and follow yellow signs. 1-acre incl natural woodland with prolific bluebells and ferns. Mixed borders, kitchen garden with raised beds and greenhouse. Conservatory, pool. *Adm £1.50 Chd free. Suns May 10, June 7 (2-6)*

Bohunt Manor, Liphook &※ (Lady Holman) On old A3 in 30m area in Liphook nr station. Flowering shrubs, herbaceous borders, lakeside and woodland walks, rhododendrons, bulbs, wild flowers and vegetable garden. Tame waterfowl will eat out of children's hands. Specimen trees. About ¾hr to walk round, lake 3½ acres. *Adm £1.50 OAP £1 Chd free. Sun Aug 2 (10-6)*

Bracken Cottage, Greatham ※❀ (Mr & Mrs Day) Petersfield Rd. On A325 halfway between Petersfield and Farnham. On the RH-side 100yds S of the village PO and store. ⅓-acre cottage garden. Developed since 1987 on 3 levels by use of walling. Mixed borders intensively planted with the aim of providing yr-round foliage interest combined with herbaceous plants. Small pond and vegetable garden. TEAS. *Adm £1.50 Chd free. Suns April 26, May 24, Wed July 1 (2-6). Private visits welcome, please* **Tel 01420 538680**

Bramdean House, Bramdean ※ (Mr & Mrs H Wakefield) In village on A272. 6½ acres carpets of spring bulbs. Walled garden with famous herbaceous borders, 1-acre working kitchen garden, large collection of unusual plants. Featured TV Grassroots programme and many gardening books. TEAS. *Adm £2 Chd free (ACNO to Bramdean Parish Church®). Mon April 13, Suns April 12, May 10, June 14, July 12, Aug 9, Sept 13 (2-5); also private parties by appt, please* **Tel 01962 771214 Fax 01962 771095**

Bramdean Lodge, Bramdean & (Hon Peter & Mrs Dickinson) In village, on A272 (car park and TEAS as for Bramdean House). Disabled use Wood Lane entrance and park in yard. 1¾ acres around Victorian Gothic house. Walled garden. Borders densely planted. Style evolved rather than planned. Many oddities. Over 100 varieties of clematis, and 400 of roses, all labelled. *Adm £1.50 Chd free. Suns June 14, July 12, Aug 9, Sept 13 (3-6). Private parties welcome, please* **Tel 01962 771324**

Bramley Lodge, Fyfield &※❀ (Mrs J D Ward) From Weyhill roundabout take Thruxton Rd. In 150yds turn R signed Fyfield. Continue ¾m under bridge 100yds on R. Long 1-acre garden framed and sheltered by old railway embankment, with many shrubs in curving beds, underplanted with drifts of spring bulbs; ponds and bog garden, lime tolerant heathers and conifers. Plants in aid of St Peter in the Wood Church, Appleshaw. TEAS. *Adm £1.50 Acc chd free. Sun March 29 (2-5)*

Bramshaw Lodge, Bramshaw &✿❀ (Dr, Mrs & Miss Couchman) Lyndhurst. 2m from junction 1 on M27 on B3079. On L past Bramshaw Village Hall. Victorian garden of 1½ acres, circa 1850, with mature trees, rhododendrons and azaleas and expanding shrub and herbaceous planting surrounded by natural forest. TEAS. *Adm £2 Chd free. Sun, Mon May 24, 25 (2-6)*

Brandy Mount House, Alresford &❀ (Mr & Mrs M Baron) From centre, first R in East St before Sun Lane. Please leave cars in Broad St. 1-acre informal plantsman's garden, spring bulbs, hellebores, species geraniums, snowdrop collection, daphne collection, European primulas, herbaceous and woodland plants. Daphnes featured in Week-end Mail March 1997. TEAS March 15, April 12, May 10, June 27. *Adm £1.50 Chd free. Sat Feb 7 (11-4); Suns March 15, April 12, May 10, Sat June 27 (2-5) 1999 Sat Feb 6 (11-4)*

Braxton Gardens, Milford-on-Sea &✿❀ (J D M Aldridge) Braxton Courtyard. 3m W of Lymington. From A337 at Everton take turning to Milford-on-Sea, 70yds on L is Lymore Lane. Turn into Lane and gardens are at Braxton courtyard on L. Attractive courtyard with raised lily pool and dovecote. Restored C19 barn leading into formal walled garden. Knot garden, nursery. TEA. (dog rings & water provided). *Donations. Open 9-5 March 15-Oct 31 Sat and Sun (10-5). Limited opening hours in winter please enquire,* **Tel 01590 642008**

Broadhatch House, Bentley &✿❀ (Bruce & Lizzie Powell) 4m NE of Alton. Turn off A31 (Bentley by-pass), right through village up School Lane. R to Perrylands, after 300yds drive on R. 3½ acres, divided by yew hedges into old-fashioned rose gardens, double herbaceous and shrub borders, with walled garden and incl wide range of perennials and flowering shrubs. TEA. *Adm £2 Chd free (ACNO to Bentley Recreation Ground Charity®). Mons, Wed June 22, 24, 29 Wed, Sun, Mon July 1, 12, 13 (2-6). Also private visits welcome in mid June/July, please* **Tel 01420 23185**

¶**Brook Cottage, Bishops Waltham** &✿❀ (Pam & Ken Simcock) From Bishops Waltham, take B3035 to Botley and exactly ½m small lane on R (Brooklands Farm Lane) 3rd drive on L. 1-acre garden surrounded by open countryside. Great variety of plants with stream, ponds and water plants. Container planting and secret garden with oriental theme. *Adm £1.50 Chd free. Suns, Mons June 28, 29 Aug 9, 10 (1-6)*

1 Brook Cottages, East Meon ❀ (Mr & Mrs D Stapley) Petersfield. Off A272 at Langrish turn L for East Meon. Turn L in front of church. Follow rd round L into the High Street. Brook Cottage is just past Izaak Walton Public House. ⅓-acre with over 300 herbs. Small areas with herbs for wines and liqueurs. Open knot of culinary and physic herbs. Chamomile seat and covered way of scented climbers. Medical astrology garden and circular serenity. Featured on TV Grass Roots 1996 also Gardeners World. Dyes, crafts, etc. *Adm £1.50. Sun May 31, Sat July 11 (2-6). Private visits welcome, please* **Tel 01730 823376**

¶▲**Bury Court, Bentley** &✿❀ (John Coke) 1m N of Bentley on the Crondall Rd. New garden designed in co-operation with Piet Oudolf, created out of an old farmyard. Currently the only pure example of the continental 'naturalistic' style, making heavy use of grasses in association with perennials selected for an extended season of interest. TEAS. *Adm £2 Chd 50p. For NGS Weds, Thurs Aug 5, 6 (10-dusk) Oct 7, 8 (10-6)*

Chalkwood, Ropley &✿❀ (Mr & Mrs Ian Shield) Stapley Lane. From Alresford on A31 turn R to Petersfield. Stapley Lane 1½m on R. Chalkwood ½m on L. 2 acres developed entirely by owner. Plantsmen's garden, woodland areas, pond, wildflowers. Parking in paddock. *Adm £1.50 Chd free. Tues April 7, May 5, June 30 (2-5.30) Private visits welcome, please* **Tel 01962 772209**

Chilland, Martyr Worthy & (Mr & Mrs John Impey) Midway between Winchester and Alresford on B3047. 4-acre garden with stream at bottom overlooking R Itchen watermeadows with woods and farmland beyond. Large collection of mature shrubs planned for their yr-round colour effects. Many fine trees incl huge plane and ancient mulberry, nutwalk, spring bulbs, clematis and herbaceous borders. *Adm £1.50 Chd free. Sun, Mon June 21, 22 with adjacent* **Chilland Ford Garden** *Sun July 19 with* **Martyr Worthy Gardens.** *Also open Mon July 20 (2-6)*

Chilland Ford, Martyr Worthy ✿ (Mr & Mrs D R Cooper) Midway between Winchester and Alresford on B3047. A small, romantic, riverside garden with many climbing plants. *Adm £1.50 Chd free. Sun, Mon June 21, 22 (2-6) with* **Chilland**

187 Christchurch Road, Ringwood &✿❀ (Mr & Mrs C S Fryer) S of Ringwood on B3347, approx ¾m from the A31 turn off into Ringwood, follow signs for Kingston-Sopley. Across 3 roundabouts look L for police station. 187 4th turning L past it. Parking in Willow Dr 3rd L and in service rd by house. Small garden packed with many interesting plants, gravelled front garden with many variety of houseleeks, also pulsatillas, hardy geraniums, grasses, ferns and evergreens. TEAS. *Adm £1 incl chd. Fri, Sun, Mon April 10, 12, 13 (1.30-4.30)*

¶**Clibdens, Waterlooville** ✿ (Mrs Jacqueline Budden) Chalton is 6m S of Petersfield. Turn L off A3 N of Horndean then directly R to Chalton. Clibdens is the 1st house on L in the village. 1-acre surrounding farm with fine views to Windmill Hill. Recently developed garden on chalk with interesting collection of shrubs and plants, incl gravel garden. TEAS. *Adm £1.50 Chd free Sun, Mon June 14, 15, 21, 22 (2-6). By appt June and July, please* **Tel 01705 592172**

Closewood House, Denmead & (Mrs Peter Clowes) Take Closewood Rd to the W of the B2150 between Waterlooville and Denmead. L at T-junction after ½m. Signs to car park after 300 metres. 1½ acre garden with good collection of scented roses and flowering shrubs. Also 3 acre field recently planted with over 100 different trees. Car park. TEAS (Sun) TEA (Wed). *Adm £2 Chd free. Sun June 14, Wed June 17 (2-6)*

●**Coles, Privett** ⚇❀ (Mrs Tim Watkins) Nr Alton and Petersfield. Approx 6m NW of Petersfield between Privett and High Cross. From A32, S of Alton between East Tisted and West Meon Hut, turn E to Froxfield at Pig and Whistle/Lawns inn, after ½m turn L at T-junction and continue for ¾m, entrance on L. 26 acres specialising in rhododendrons and azaleas, set amongst mixed woodland with rare specimens. Walks, clearings and decorative ponds, spring bluebells; autumn leaf colours. TEAS. *Adm £3, OAP £2.50 Chd 50p (Share to NGS). Sat May 9, 30, Suns, May 3, 10, 31, Oct 11, Mon, May 4 (2-5.30). Private visits Tel 0171 493 2008*

Compton Lodge, Farnham see under Surrey

Conholt Park, Chute ⚇ (Caroline Tisdall) Andover. Turn N off A342 Andover-Devizes rd at Weyhill Church. 5m N through Clanville and Tangley Bottom. Turn L at Conholt (Marked on ordinance survey) ½m on R, just off Chute causeway. 10 acres surrounding Regency House, Rose, 'Calor', winter, and secret gardens. 1½-acre walled garden with potager, berry wall, rare fruit orchard, white border, hardy geraniums and allium collections. On farm unusual animals incl bison and shire horses. TEAS. *Adm £2.50 Chd free. Suns June 28, Aug 16 (12-5). Also by appt,* Tel 01264 730335

Copperfield, Dogmersfield ⚇❀ (Mr & Mrs John Selfe) Turn N off Odiham-Farnham A287 to Dogmersfield. Turn L by Queens Public House. Set in 1½ acres. A true plantsman's garden; with vast beds displaying a wide range of plants and ornamental trees incl many rare and unusual varieties. Designed by nurseryman owner to provide spectacular yr-round colour and a stunning water feature. A camomile lawn and woodland walk. TEAS. *Adm £2 Chd free (ACNO to the Samantha Dickson Research Trust®). Sun July 5 (12-5)*

The Cottage, Chandler's Ford ⚇❀ (Mr & Mrs H Sykes) 16 Lakewood Rd. Leave M3 at junction 12, follow signs to Chandler's Ford. At The King Rufus on Winchester Rd, turn R into Merdon Ave, then 3rd rd on L. ¾-acre garden planted for yr-round interest with spring colour from bulbs, camellias, rhododendrons, azaleas and magnolias. Woodland, conifers, herbaceous borders, bog garden, ponds, fruit and vegetable garden. Bantams. TEAS. *Adm £1.50 Chd 10p (ACNO to British Heart Foundation®). Suns, Mons April 12, 13; May 3, 4 (2-6)*

Cranbury Park, Otterbourne ⚇❀ (Mr & Mrs Chamberlayne-Macdonald) 5m S of Winchester. 2m N of Eastleigh; main entrance on old A33 between Winchester-Southampton, by bus stop at top of Otterbourne Hill. Entrances also in Hocombe Rd, Chandler's Ford. Extensive pleasure grounds laid out in late C18 and early C19; fountains; rose garden; specimen trees; lakeside walk. Family carriages and collection of prams will be on view. TEAS. *Adm £2 Chd 50p (ACNO to Church of St Denys, Chilworth®). Sun June 14 (2-6) last admission 5pm*

Crawley Gardens 5m NW of Winchester, off A272 or A3049 Winchester-Stockbridge Rd. Parking at top of village nr the church. TEAS Sun only. *Combined adm £2.50 Chd free. Sun, Mon April 5, 6, June 21, 22 (2-5.30)*

Glebe House ⚇ (Lt-Col & Mrs John Andrews) 1½-acres. Shrubs incl eucalyptus collection

Lithend ⚇⚇❀ (Mrs F L Gunner) 5m NW of Winchester off A272 in Crawley village; small cottage garden

Little Court ⚇⚇❀ (Professor & Mrs A R Elkington) Other dates: see separate entry

Manor Lodge ⚇⚇❀ (Mr & Mrs K Wren) Crawley, nr Winchester. Signposted from A272 and near the village pond. Chalk walled garden with large collection of old and modern climbing and shrub roses. Many clematis. Thatched summer house. Lily pond. Spring bulbs. Hellebores, euphorbias and many shrubs. Cream TEAS in aid of St Mary's Crawley. Parking in rd only

Paige Cottage ⚇ (Mr & Mrs T W Parker) 1 acre of traditional English country garden incl grass tennis court and walled Italian style swimming pool; roses climbing into apple trees

Croft Mews, Botley ⚇⚇❀ (Captain & Mrs W T T Pakenham) 2m N of Botley on B3354, on L under trees (M27 exit 7). A recently created garden about 2 acres with much older buildings and walls, in grounds of old country house. Walled garden, lawns and mixed borders, woodland area, kitchen garden. Many interesting ideas and features incl new ha ha with views over meadows. TEAS in aid of NSPCC (Sun only). *Adm £1.50 Chd free. Mon May 4, Sun June 14 (2-6) Mon June 15 (11-5). Private visits for groups May to Aug (no coaches)* Tel 01703 692425

Crookley Pool, Horndean ⚇⚇❀ (Mr & Mrs F S K Privett) Turn up Blendworth Lane by the main bakery from the centre of Horndean. House 200yds before church on L. Off the A3 5m S of Petersfield. 2-acre garden surrounded by parkland. Mixed borders of unusual plants and roses, with a special interest in colour and plants for hot dry situations. Wisteria and rose covered walls and pergolas. Walled kitchen garden. TEAS. *Adm £2 Chd free. Sun, Mon June 21, 22, Wed July 8 (2-5.30)*

The Dower House, Dogmersfield ⚇ (Mr Michael Hoare) Turn N off A287. 6-acre garden including bluebell wood with large and spectacular collection of rhododendrons, azaleas, magnolias and other flowering trees and shrubs; set in parkland with fine views over 20-acre lake. TEAS. *Adm £2 Chd free. Suns May 10, 17 (2-6)*

Droxford Gardens 4½m N of Wickham on A32 approx mid-way between Alton-Portsmouth. TEAS. *Combined adm £3 or £1 each garden Chd 50p. Sun June 21 (2-6)*

The Mill House ⚇❀ (Mrs C MacPherson) Garden of 2 acres; shrubs, climbing roses and rose garden, herbaceous borders, pond, mill stream, orchard, vegetable garden. Car park

Park View Cottage ⚇ (Mrs F V D Aubert) Small town garden, flowers, shrubs and very small wooded walk. Car park

¶**The Grove House** (Mr & Mrs J Hooper) Just out of village centre on the Swanmore Rd. 50yds from junction with A32. Approx 2 acres of neglected garden undergoing restoration. Wild flower meadow, grass tennis court and 1920s thatched pavillion, vegetable garden and herbaceous borders. Car park

Durmast House, Burley &❀ (Mr & Mrs P E G Daubeney) 1m SE of Burley, nr White Buck Hotel. 4-acre garden designed by Gertrude Jekyll in 1907 in the process of being restored from the original plans. Formal rose garden edged with lavender, 130-yr-old Monterey pine, large choisya, Victorian rockery, lily pond, coach-house, large wisteria and Jekyll herbaceous border. TEAS. *Adm £1.50 Chd 50p (ACNO to Delhi Commonwealth Women's Assoc Clinic®). Suns March 29, July 5 (2-5). Private parties welcome, please* **Tel 01425 403527**

East Lane, Ovington (Sir Peter & Lady Ramsbotham) A31 from Winchester towards Alresford. Immed after roundabout 1m W of Alresford, small sign to Ovington turn sharp L up incline, down small country rd to Ovington. East Lane is the only house on L, 500yds before Bush Inn. 4 acres, spring bulbs, mixed herbaceous and shrubs; woodland plantings; walled rose garden. Terraced water garden. Ample parking. *Adm £2 Chd free. Sun April 5 (2-5.30)*

8 Elbow Corner, Basingstoke & (Mr & Mrs M Penfold) Off Church Square, Basingstoke. Car park opp Anvil Theatre, Churchill Way in the centre of Basingstoke. Walk via Lower Church St to Elbow Garden, adjacent to St Michael's Church. A short terrace of houses covered with hanging baskets, with small front gardens planted with annuals to give a blaze of colour. A winner of Basingstoke in bloom competition. TEA. *Adm £1.50 Chd 50p. Sats, Suns July 25, 26 Aug 1, 2 (10-5)*

Eversley Gardens ❀ On the B3016 signposted from A30 just W of Blackbushe Airport and from the B3272 E of the cricket ground at Eversley Cross. Large car park clearly signposted at nearby Westfield Farm. *Combined adm £2.50 Chd free (ACNO to the Samantha Dickson Research Trust®). Sun May 10 (2-6)*
   Kiln Copse (Mr & Mrs J Rowse) 8 acres; wide variety of spring flowering bulbs, bluebell wood and foxgloves. Good collection of rhododendrons, azaleas and roses; lake-side with bog-side plants, large mixed borders, round garden with gazebo and plants climbing into the trees
   Little Coopers (Mr & Mrs J K Oldale) A woodland walk meanders through bluebells, rhododendrons, azaleas and many unusual shrubs, labelled. Shaded by mature trees, water and bog garden with ponds and stream, then extensive lawn leading to Mediterranean and rose gardens. Small Japanese garden. Featured on TV. *Private parties welcome, please* **Tel 01252 872229**

● **Exbury Gardens, Southampton** &❀ (Exbury Gardens Trust) Exbury, off B3054 3m SE of Beaulieu off A326. 200 acres of landscaped woodland gardens with rhododendrons, azaleas, magnolias and camellias. Rock garden, cascades, river walk, rose gardens, heather gardens, seasonal trails and walks. Luncheon and teas. *Spring Season: Sun March 1 to mid April Adm £3.30 OAPs £2.80 Chd (10-15) £2.20 mid April to mid June £4.80, OAPs £4.30 Weds/Thurs £3.80 Chd £3.80. Mid June - mid July £3.30 OAPs £2.80 Chd £2.20. Summer garden (53 acres) mid July - mid Sept £2.20 OAPs & Chd £1.70. Autumn garden (200 acres) mid Sept - Nov £2.80 OAPs £2.20 Chd £1.70*

Fairfield House, Hambledon ❀❀ (Mrs Peter Wake) 10m SW of Petersfield. Hambledon village. 5-acre informal garden on chalk, with extensive walls, fine mature trees; large collection of shrubs and climbing roses mixed with wide variety of small trees and interesting perennials. Adjacent car park and wild flower meadow. Featured in 'A Heritage of Roses' by Hazel Le Rougetel, 'The Rose Gardens of England' by Michael Gibson, 'The Latest Country Gardens' by George Plumptre. TEAS. *Adm £2 Chd free. Suns April 5, May 17, June 28 (2-6). Also private visits welcome anytime by appt; suitable for groups, please* **Tel 01705 632431**

Fernlea, Chilworth ❀❀ (Mr & Mrs P G Philip) From Winchester on M3 take exit 14 to Southampton A33 at roundabout follow A27 to Romsey and Chilworth at Clump Inn turn L follow Manor Rd into Chilworth. Dr over motorway bridge turn R. Fernlea last house on L. 15-acre wildlife garden natural habitat, woodland walks, also many Mediterranean plants within informal planting, formal beds around house and newly created kitchen garden. Some plants and seasonal produce for sale. Picnics welcome. TEAS. *Adm £1.50 Chd free. Suns March 29, April 26, May 24, July 26 (12-5)*

Flintstones, Durley & (June & Bill Butler) Sciviers Lane. From M3 junction 11 follow signs Marwell Zoo. From B2177 turn R opp Woodman Inn. From M27 junction 7 follow signs Fair Oak Durley turn L at Robin Hood. ¾-acre on clay developed over 5yrs, with raised beds and close tapestry effect of texture and colour. TEA. *Adm £1.50 Chd free. Sun, Mon May 31, June 1 (2-6)*

¶**Fordes Cottage, Oakshott** &❀❀ (Miss L & Dr J Edwards) Hawkley. At A3 roundabout turn S to W Liss. At 'Spread Eagle' turn R 'Hawkley'. After 2m at top of steep hill turn L 'Colemore'. Straight on past green, down hill, after ⅓m turn L 'Oakshott'. Garden is 200yds on L. A multi-season organic garden of 2 acres with excellent views. Walled garden, cottage plantings, peat bank, alpines, old roses and fruit. Wild flower area encouraging wildlife and natural predators. Well labelled. *Adm £1.50 Chd 50p. Suns May 17, July 12, Sept 6 (2-6). Visits welcome, please* **Tel 01730 827 330**

Forest Edge, Andover Down &❀❀ (Annette & David Beeson) On the B3400 Andover to Whitchurch rd. A 1-acre conservationist's garden. Surrounding house is a traditional garden, where herbaceous plants, shrubs and climbers blend into the surrounding trees and hedges; also gravel scree. Beyond is the wild garden with a variety of natural and semi-natural habitats for flora and fauna, each managed to encourage different plants and animals. Pond for frogs, newts and dragonflies. Clouds of butterflies some yrs. *Adm £1.50 Chd free. Sun July 12 (2-6)*

Evening Openings (see also garden descriptions)		
Rotherfield Park, East Tisted	May 8	5–8pm
Rowans Wood, Ampfield	May 28	6–8.30pm
The Vyne, Sherborne St John	June 3	7pm

Fritham Lodge, Lyndhurst ♿❀ (Christopher and Rosie Powell) Fritham. 3m NW of M27 junction 1 Cadnam. Follow signs to Fritham. Parking in field. Set in heart of New Forest in 18 acres; with 1-acre old walled garden round Grade II listed C17 house originally one of Charles II hunting lodges. Parterre of old roses, potager with wide variety of vegetables, herbs and fruit trees, pergola, herbaceous and blue and white mixed borders, ponds, walk across hay meadows to woodland and stream. TEAS. *Adm £1.50 Chd free. Sat June 27 (2-5)*

¶**Froyle Cottage Gardens, nr Alton** ♿❀ Access to Lower Froyle from A31 between Alton and Farnham. At Bentley, follow signs from Lower Froyle to Upper Froyle. Six cottage gardens in Upper and Lower Froyle. 'The village of Saints', each garden approx ⅓ acre, comprising mixed borders, unusual plants, vegetables, water features, climbers and container planting. Flower arrangers garden. TEAS. *Combined adm £2 Chd free. Sat, Sun May 30, 31 (2-6)*

● **Furzey Gardens, Minstead** ♿✄❀ (Furzey Gardens Charitable Trust) 8m SW of Southampton. 1½m SW of A31/M27 junction; 3½m NW of Lyndhurst. 8 acres of informal shrub garden; collections of azalea, rhododendron and heathers; lake; fernery; summer and winter flowering trees and shrubs. Restored C16 cottage. Will Selwood Gallery (limited opening in winter) with refreshments. *Adm £3 OAPs £2.50 Chd £1.50 Families £8 March to Oct. £1.50 OAPs £1 Chd 50p Families £3 winter (ACNO to Minstead Training Project and other charities). Daily except Christmas (10-5; dusk in winter).* **Tel 01703 812464**

The Garden House, Lymington ❀ (Mr & Mrs C Kirkman) Off Lymington High St opp Woolworths. Unusual herbaceous, grasses, house leeks, agaves and shrubs, interspersed with a riot of annuals, and 2 ponds in ¾ acre. Prime example of close boscage. TEAS with extravagant portions of clotted cream. *Adm £1.50 Chd free (ACNO to the Worshipful Company of Gardeners' Charitable Trust®). Sun June 7 (2-6)*

Greenfingers, Milton ❀ (St James's Hospital) Locks Way. From A27 or M27 take A2030 into Portsmouth, at traffic lights rd curves R. Continue to Velder Ave until roundabout. Take L turn into Milton Rd (A288) hospital is signposted top of Locksway Rd 8th rd from roundabout. Greenfingers Horticulture Training Therapy centre is signposted in hospital grounds. ⅔-acre approx. Display beds of all kinds, incl vegetables, nature and ornamental ponds, polytunnels and greenhouses. TEA. *Adm £1 Chd free. Suns May 3, July 5 (11-5)*

Hambledon House, Hambledon ✄❀ (Capt & Mrs David Hart Dyke) 8m SW of Petersfield. In village centre behind George Hotel. 2-acre partly walled plantsman's garden. Large borders filled with wide variety of unusual shrubs and plants. Hidden, secluded areas reveal surprise views of garden and village rooftops. TEAS. *Adm £2 Chd free. Mon May 4, Sun May 24, Suns, Mons July, 12, 13, Sept 6, 7 (2-6); also private visits and groups welcome, please* **Tel 01705 632380**

Harcombe House, Ropley (Mr & Mrs G Bearman) Park Lane. E of Alresford. Leave A31 Alton-Winchester Rd at The Anchor, Ropley. After ½m take 1st R Park Lane. 12-acre garden; rose garden; herbaceous borders; spring bulbs; flowering shrubs, small water garden; good views. *Adm £1.50 Chd free. Sun April 5 (2-6)*

Harfield Farm House, Curdridge ✄ (Mr & Mrs P Cartwright) On B3035 from Bishops Waltham to Botley 1st entrance L on the brow of the hill. 1½ acres surrounding C17 farmhouse and C18 barns; walled garden with mixed shrub and herbaceous border espalier apple walk. Courtyard, with original planting for low maintenance in different compartments and levels. TEAS. *Adm £1.50 Chd 50p. Tues, Thurs June 2, 4 (2-6) also by appt* **Tel 01489 784244**

Hayden Barn Cottage, Warnford ♿✄❀ (Captain & Mrs Broadbent) Take A32. Opp George and Falcon public house take single track rd signposted to Clanfield. Go ¾m. Red brick cottage on L. Parking through garden not in narrow lane or drive. To avoid congestion please arrive during 1st half of any hour. 1-acre garden on several levels developed entirely by owners. Herbaceous and mixed borders, rockery, shrubberies and good spring colour set off by extensive brick and flint walling, terraces and grassy banks. No coaches. TEAS. *Adm £1.50 Chd free. Weds March 25, June 17, Suns April 19, May 17 (1-5)*

Hayling Island Gardens ♿❀ From A27 Havant/Hayling Island. Roundabout, travel S 2m, turn R into West Lane continue for 1m. TEAS. *Sat, Sun May 23, 24 (11-6)*
¶**Broomhill** ✄ (Mrs Ann Legge) On L 2-acre garden with mature trees, shrubs rhododendrons and herbaceous borders surrounding a croquet lawn. Small wildlife pond and rockeries. Vegetable plot, copse with wild orchids. TEAS. *Adm £1.50 Chd free*
Littlewood (Steven and Sheila Schrier) 163 West Lane. Littlewood is on R in a wood, opp Broomhill 2½-acre woodland garden protected from the sea winds by multi barrier hedge. Woodland walk and access to Hayling Billy harbour trail. Rhododendrons, azaleas, camellias and many other shrubs. Pond, bog garden watered from roof of comfortable conservatory with many house plants. 'Tree' house in woods and propagating greenhouse. Picnickers welcome. Easy access for elderly and wheelchair bound. *Adm £1.50 Chd free*

Heathlands, Locks Heath ♿❀ (Dr & Mrs John Burwell) 47 Locks Rd. Locks Rd runs due S from Park Gate into Locks Heath. No 47 is 1m down on the RH-side [Grid Ref 513 069]. 1-acre garden designed & developed by the owner since 1967. Yr-round interest against a background of evergreens and mature trees. Spring bulbs, rhododendrons, paulownias. cyclamen, ferns and some less usual plants. Topiary, small herbaceous border and scree bed. National Collection of Japanese anemones. TEAS. *Adm £1.50 Chd free. Suns March 22, May 10 (2-5.30)*

The National Gardens Scheme is a charity which traces its origins back to 1927. Since then it has raised over £18 million for charitable purposes.

Hill House, Old Alresford & (Maj & Mrs W F Richardson) From Alresford 1m along B3046 towards Basingstoke, then R by church. 2 acres with large old-fashioned herbaceous border and shrub beds, set around large lawn; kitchen garden. TEAS. *Adm £1.50 Chd free. Sun, Tue Aug 2, 4 (2-5.30)*

● **Sir Harold Hillier Gardens and Arboretum, Ampfield** &*&* Jermyns Lane. Situated between Ampfield and Braishfield, 3m NE of Romsey. Signposted from A3090 (A31) and A3057. 184-acres containing the finest collection of hardy trees and shrubs in the UK. Home to 11 National Collections. Wonderful spring and autumn colour with guided tours at 2pm every Suns and Weds in May and Oct. TEAS and light lunches. *Adm April to Oct £4 OAP £3.50 Chd £1 (Group rate 10+ £3); Nov to March £3, OAP £2.50 Chd £1. Daily April 1 to Oct 31 (10.30-6); Nov 1 to March 31 (10.30-5 or dusk)*

▲**Hinton Ampner, Alresford** &*&* (The National Trust) S on Petersfield-Winchester Rd A272. 1m W of Bramdean village. 12-acre C20 shrub garden designed by Ralph Dutton. Strong architectural elements using yew and box topiary, with spectacular views. Bold effects using simple plants, restrained and dramatic bedding. Orchard with spring wild flowers and bulbs within formal box hedges; magnolia and philadelphus walks. Dell garden made from chalk pit. Shrub rose border dating from 1950s. Chosen for 'Alan Titchmarsh's favourite gardens'. TEAS. *Adm £3 Chd £1.50. For NGS Suns April 19, June 21. Sat, Sun Sept 12, 13 (1.30-5)*

¶**193 Holly Hill, Bassett** &*&* (Mrs Myra Burville) 2½m N Southampton. M3 exit 14. Take the avenue towards Southampton. At the 1st roundabout, go right around, and back up the avenue, 1st L, 1st L again, approx 400m on L. ⅓-acre developed over 10yrs. Closely planted for foliage effect. Mixed shrubs and perennials. Wildlife and fishponds. Baskets, containers and pots containing hostas and mediterranean plants. 2nd in best private garden, Southampton in Bloom 1997. TEAS. *Adm £1.50 Chd 50p (ACNO to British Diabetic Association®). Sat, Sun June 13, 14, July 18, 19, Suns Aug 9, Sept 6 (2-6)*

Hordle Walthampton, Lymington (Hordle Walthampton School) 1m E of Lymington on the Beaulieu Rd. 97 acres of woodland, lakes and formal gardens. TEAS. *Adm £2 Chd 50p (ACNO to Hordle Walhampton School Trust®). Sun May 3 (2-6)*

■ **Houghton Lodge, Stockbridge** &*&* (Captain M W Busk) 1½m S of Stockbridge A30 on rd to Houghton. Landscape pleasure grounds surround C18 cottage ornée overlooking the tranquil beauty of R Test. Topiary, 'Peacock' garden, herb and walled garden, greenhouses, fuchsia collection. Hydroponicum; horticulture without soil. Location of filming 'Oscar Wilde'. TEA. *Adm £2.50 Chd free. Daily March 1 to Sept 30 except Weds (2-5), Sats, Suns, Bank Hols (10-5). For NGS Sun, Mon April 19, 20 (10-5)*

Jasmine Lodge, Kempshott & (Nigel & Linda Murgatroyd) Jasmine Rd, Basingstoke. From M3, junction 7, follow Basingstoke signs. At Kempshott roundabout turn L into Heather Way, then immed R into Jasmine Rd. Park on rd away from bend. Front and back gardens each 30' × 70'. Basingstoke in Bloom winner 1996. Over 5,000 summer bedding plants in carpet bedding, baskets and containers. Featured in Amateur Gardening Oct 1996. *Adm £1.50 Chd free (ACNO to St Michael's Hospice, Basingstoke). Suns July 26, Aug 2 (11-5)*

53 Ladywood, Eastleigh *&* (Mr & Mrs D Ward) Leave M3 junction 12. Follow signs to Eastleigh. R at roundabout into Woodside Ave, 2nd R into Bosville. Ladywood is 5th on R. Park in Bosville. 45' × 45', developed by owners over 8 yrs, giving many ideas for small gardens. On Grass Roots and Garden Party 1996, in Gardeners' World magazine 1997. Over 1500 different plants labelled. Rustic fences give vertical space for clematis and climbing roses. Hardy geraniums, pulmonarias, and foliage plants. Afternoon TEAS. *Adm £1.50 Chd 75p. Suns April 26, June 14 (11-5.30). Private visits April 1 to Aug 31 Tues afternoons,* **Tel 01703 615389**

Lake House, Northington &*&* (Lord & Lady Ashburton) Alresford. 4m N of Alresford off B3046. Follow English heritage signs to The Grange, then directions. 2 large lakes in Candover valley set off by mature woodland with waterfalls, abundant bird life, long landscaped vistas. 1½-acre walled garden, mixed borders, long herbaceous border, rose pergola leading to moon gate. Formal kitchen garden, flowering pots, conservatory and greenhouses. Picnicking by lakes. TEAS. *Adm £2.50 Chd free (ACNO to Friends of St John's Church, Northington®). Sun July 12 (11-5). Group visits welcome, please* **Tel 01962 734820**

Landford Lodge, nr Salisbury see Wiltshire

60 Lealand Road, Drayton &*&* (Mr F G Jacob) 2m from Cosham E side of Portsmouth. Old A27 (Havant Rd) between Cosham and Bedhampton. Small prize winning garden created and designed by owner since 1969. Featured in National Gardening Magazines. Exotic plants with rockery, ponds, dwarf conifers and collection of grasses, cacti and other exotics in greenhouse. TEAS. *Adm £1 Chd free. Suns April 26, June 28, Aug 9 (11-5). Also private visits welcome, please* **Tel 01705 370030**

Little Barn Garden & Barnhawk Nursery &*&* (Drs R & V A Crawford) Woodgreen. 3m NE of Fordingbridge via A338. Turn E to Woodgreen; bear L in village; R immed past Horse and Groom, continue for 1¼m. 2½ acres of mature informal garden with all-yr interest in form, colour and texture; rhododendron, azalea, camellia, magnolia, acer and collector's plants with peat, scree, rock, woodland, bog and water area. *Adm £1.50 Chd free. Sun April 5 (2-6). Also private visits welcome, please* **Tel 01725 512213**

Little Brook, Milford-on-Sea *&* (Mrs J Spenser) Lymore Lane. 4m W of Lymington off A337. Immed on joining B3058 turn L into Lane for ½m, Little Brook on L. A summer garden of approx ¼-acre, situated on a gentle S facing slope. Stocked with an abundance of perennials, shrubs and self seeded annuals. TEAS. *Adm £1 Chd free (ACNO to SPANA®). Sat June 13 (11-5)*

The Little Cottage, Lymington ⚡ (Lyn & Peter Prior) On N fringe of Lymington on A337, opp Toll House Inn. Formal town garden arranged in seven harmoniously colour schemed rooms; soft colours surround cottage and match the interior decor; elsewhere strong and vibrant colours are used to dramatic effect. Box edging, topiary, gazebos, arbours and tender plants in pots and urns form subtle pictures. Artists and photographers are welcome. *Adm £2 (unsuitable for children). Tues June to Sept (10-1 & 2-6).* **Tel 01590 679395**

Little Court, Crawley ⚡⚡❀ (Prof & Mrs A R Elkington) 5m NW of Winchester off A272 or A3049 in Crawley village; 300yds from either village pond or church. 1½ acres prolific bulbs, perennials and climbers in related colours. Victorian kitchen garden, bantams and geese, with view to downs. Illus in 'Planting Companions' and 'The Perfect Country Garden'. TEAS Suns only. *Adm £2 Combined with* **Crawley Gardens** *£2.50. Suns, Mons, Tues Feb 22, 23, 24, March 1, 15, 16, Sun, Mon, Thur April 5, 6, 16 (2-5.30); May 3, 5, June 21, 22, Aug 9, 10, Sept 13, 14 (2-5.30); Feb 21, 22, 23 (1999). Also by appt, please* **Tel 01962 776365**

■ **Longstock Park Gardens, nr Stockbridge** ⚡⚡ (Leckford Estate Ltd; Part of John Lewis Partnership) 3m N. From A30 turn N on to A3057; follow signs to Longstock. Famous water garden with extensive collection of aquatic and bog plants set in 7 acres of woodland with rhododendrons and azaleas. A walk through the park leads to an arboretum, herbaceous border and nursery. Featured in several TV programmes and gardening books. Plants and Teas at adjacent garden centre. TEAS in aid of local churches. *Adm £3 Chd 50p. 1st and 3rd Sunday in month April to Sept. For NGS Sun June 21 (2-5)*

■ **Longthatch, Warnford** ⚡⚡❀ (Mr & Mrs P Short) Lippen Lane. 1m S of West Meon on A32 turn R from N or L from S at George & Falcon, 100yds turn R at T-junction, continue for ¼m; thatched C17 house on R. Parking opp. 3½-acre plantsman's garden on R Meon. Rare trees and shrubs. Part of the National Collection of Helleborus. Fine lawns, herbaceous borders, island beds, alpine and bog gardens. Spring fed ponds with riverside plantings and a damp woodland area with hellebores, primulas and shade loving plants. Featued on 'Grass Roots' and Sky TV 1997. *Adm £2 Chd free. Every Weds March 4 to Aug 26 (10-5). For NGS Suns March 8, 15, 22, April 19; Sun, Mon May 24, 25; July 12, Aug 30 (2-5). Private visits by Societies and individuals welcome. please* **Tel 01730 829285**

Macpenny Woodland Garden & Nurseries, Bransgore ❀ (Mr & Mrs T M Lowndes) Burley Road. Midway between Christchurch and Burley. From Christchurch via A35, at Cat and Fiddle turn left; at Xrds by The Crown, Bransgore turn R and on ¼m. From A31 (travelling towards Bournemouth) L at Picket Post, signed Burley; through Burley to Green Triangle then R for Bransgore and on 1m beyond Thorney Hill Xrds. 17 acres; 4-acre gravel pit converted into woodland garden; many unusual plants. Large selection shrubs and herbaceous plants available. *Collecting box. Daily except Dec 25 & 26 and Jan 1 (Mons-Sats 9-5; Suns 2-5)*

Malt Cottage, Upper Clatford ⚡ (Mr & Mrs Richard Mason) From the Andover-Stockbridge or Andover-Salisbury Rd. Park behind village hall. Opposite Crook & Shears Public House, 6 acres developed by designer owners. Formal garden blending into natural water meadows with ¼m chalk stream. Lakes, bog garden; uncommon trees and shrubs. TEA available in aid of another charity. *Adm £2 Chd free. Sun July 12 (2-5)*

¶**Mandelieu, Picket Piece** ⚡ (Mr & Mrs R Bateman) From B3400 Andover to Whitchurch Rd turn NE at Harwood garage into 'Oxdrove'. L at tee. 400yds on L opp 'Andover Patio Centre'. ½-acre owner designed shrub garden with many unusual plants, selected for yr-round texture and colour. Recently extended. Fish and wildlife ponds. TEA. *Adm £1.50 Chd free. Sun July 12 (2-6)*

▲**March End, Sherfield English** ⚡⚡❀ (Dr David & Mrs Joan Thomas) 5m W of Romsey on the A27 Salisbury rd, at X-rds, turn N into Branches Lane, 1st R Doctor's Hill, 1st house on R. 1-acre totally organic garden on free-draining acid sandy soil surrounding C16 thatched cottage. Large vegetable garden of 4 foot beds with different mulches and green manures. S facing garden wall with kiwi, peach, fig and grape under covered walk. Garden with many insect-attractant flowers. *Adm £1.50 Chd 50p (ACNO to the Romsey Opportunity Group®). For NGS Mons, Sun June 22, 28, 29 (2-6). Private visits welcome, please* **Tel 01794 340255**

Martyr Worthy Gardens ⚡ Midway between Winchester and Alresford on B3047. Gardens joined by Pilgrims Way through Itchen Valley, approx ½m. Teas in Village Hall in aid of village hall. *Adm £2 Chd free. Sun July 19 (2-6)*
> **Chilland** (Mr & Mrs John Impey) see separate entry. *(Also open Sun, Mon June 21, 22, Mon July 20)*
> **Manor House** (Cdr & Mrs N J Rivett-Carnec) Large garden, roses, mixed borders, lawns, shrubs and fine trees, next to C12 church

Marycourt, Odiham ⚡ (Mr & Mrs M Conville) 2m S of Hartley Wintney on A30 or Exit 5 on M3; In Odiham High St. 1-acre garden and paddocks. Old garden roses; shrubs; ramblers dripping from trees. Silver/pink border, long shrubaceous and colourful herbaceous borders; hosta beds and delphinium planting. Dry stone wall with alpines thriving. Grade II starred house. *Adm £2 Chd free. Suns June 28, July 5 (2-6); Wed July 8 (all day) also group visits welcome, please* **Tel 01256 702100**

Maurys Mount, West Wellow ⚡❀ (Dr & Mrs P Burrows) Slab Lane. On A 36 midway between Salisbury and Southampton, Slab Lane is a turning between the roundabout and Red Rover Inn on A36 in West Wellow. An Edwardian style garden created over 3 generations of family. 10-acres of woodland, garden and paddocks incl young arboretum, conservatory, formal herb and kitchen gardens and mature trees incl 300yr old oak. Woodland walk with pond, orchard and wild-flower meadow. Jacob sheep, ducks, geese, hens and horses. TEAS in aid of Imperial Cancer Research Fund. *Adm £2 Chd 50p. Sun June 7 (2-5)*

Meadow House, nr Newbury See Berkshire

Merdon Manor, Hursley &⚹❀ (Mr & Mrs J C Smith) SW of Winchester. From A3090 Winchester-Romsey, at Standon turn on to rd to Slackstead; on 1.5m. 5 acres with panoramic views; herbaceous and rose borders; small secret walled water garden as seen on TV. Ha-ha and sheep. TEAS. *Adm £2 Chd 25p. Sun Aug 9 (2-6); also private visits welcome, please* **Tel 01962 775215 or 775281**

Merebimur, Mockbeggar &⚹❀ (Mr & Mrs C Snelling) 3m N of Ringwood on the A338, turn E to Mockbeggar at The Old Beams Inn. Turn L at the next small Xrds and next L into New Rd. Limited parking at garden but parking on verge opp the end of New Rd with very short walk. ½-acre owner maintained garden with pond, lawns, pergola and mixed borders with many unusual plants. TEA. *Adm £1.50 Chd free. Sat, Sun July 11, 12 (10-5). Private visits welcome, please* **Tel 01425 473116**

Merrie Cottage, Woodgreen &⚹ (Mr & Mrs C K Thornton) 3m N of Fordingbridge on A338 turn E to Woodgreen. Fork R at PO towards Godshill. Entrance 200 yds on L. Limited parking for disabled or park on common and walk down footpath. The irregular sloping shape offers vistas with a profusion of iris and primulas in May and June, followed by seed-grown lilies and wide variety of moisture lovers. No hard landscape or colour theme but interest is held throughout yr. TEAS (Sun) TEA (Mon at **Applecroft**). TEAS on private visits for Treloar Trust. *Adm £2 Chd free. Sun, Mon June 14, 15 (2-6). Private visits welcome, please* **Tel 01725 512273**

Monxton Gardens &⚹❀ 3m W of Andover, between A303 and A343; parking at Field House. TEAS in village hall in aid of Church. *Combined adm £2.50 Chd free. Sun, Mon May 24, 25 (2-5.30)*
>   **Bec House** &⚹ (Mr & Mrs Anthony Rushworth-Lund) Old rectory garden with spring bulbs and mature trees; rose garden, croquet lawn, orchard and new water garden
>   **Field House** (Dr & Mrs Pratt) 2-acre garden made by owners with an air of tranquillity, winding paths, 2 ponds with frogs, herbaceous borders, foliage and kitchen garden, car park
>   **Hutchens Cottage** (Mr & Mrs R A Crick) ¾-acre cottage garden with old roses, clematis, shrubs, mature trees, small orchard; mixed thyme patch and kitchen garden
>   **White Gables** (Mrs & Mrs D Eaglesham) Cottage style garden of ⅓ acre, leading down to Pill Hill Brook. Interesting shrubs, old roses and herbaceous plants

Moth House, Alresford (Mrs I R B Perkins) Brown Candover is on B3046 from Alresford to Basingstoke. 5m from Alresford, just past village green on L. 2-acre garden. Gold and silver garden. Herbaceous borders and shrub walk. Speciality roses. TEAS. *Adm £2 Chd free. Sun July 5 (11-6)*

▲**Mottisfont Abbey & Garden, Romsey** &⚹❀ (The National Trust) Mottisfont, 4½m NW of Romsey. From A3057 Romsey-Stockbridge turn W at sign to Mottisfont. 4 wheelchairs and battery car service available at garden.

30 acres; originally a C12 Priory; landscaped grounds with spacious lawns bordering R Test; magnificent trees; remarkable ancient spring pre-dating the Priory; walled garden contains NT's famous collection of old-fashioned roses. Lunch and tea available in the Abbey. *Adm £5 Chd £2.50. For NGS Sun June 28 (12-8.30), last adm 7.30 pm*

Moundsmere Manor, Preston Candover &⚹ (Mr & Mrs Andreae) 6m S of Basingstoke on B3046. Drive gates on L just after Preston Candover sign. Authentic Edwardian garden designed by Reginald Blomfield incl period greenhouse in full use. Formal rose garden and long herbaceous borders, unusual mature specimen trees and superb views over the Candover Valley. Coaches by appt. *Adm £2 Chd £1. Sun July 5 (2-5)*

Norsebury House, Stoke Charity ⚹❀ (Mr & Mrs M Goranson) Nr Winchester. Just S of A30 and W of A34 2m from Sutton Scotney. Follow signs to Stoke Charity and Hunton. 64 acres incl paddocks. Fine views, garden in many sections incl topiary, rose garden, pergola, vines, ponds, pots, orchard, poultry, greenhouse. TEA. *Adm £2 Chd free. Sun, Mon April 26, 27 (2-6)*

North Ecchinswell Farm, Newbury &❀ (Mr & Mrs Robert Henderson) Turn S off A339 Newbury-Basingstoke rd. House 1m from turning (sign-posted Ecchinswell and Bishops Green) on LH-side. Approx 6-acre garden incl 1 acre of shrub borders, with many roses, around house. Small arboretum leading to woodland. Walks with stream and small lake; carpets of wild flowers incl bluebells; bog plants, and shrubs. TEAS. *Adm £2 Chd free. Suns April 26, June 7 (ACNO to Ecchinswell Village Hall Appeal®). (2-5.30). Private parties welcome, please* **Tel 01635 268244**

Oakdene, Sandleheath &⚹❀ (Mr & Mrs Christopher Stanford) Just into Sandleheath on the B3078, 1m from Fordingbridge on the RH-side immed beyond small church. Garden of nearly 2 acres with over 300 roses of all types incl rambler covered long pergola, 'white' and 'red' herbaceous beds, orchard with free-range hens, flower-bordered productive organic kitchen garden, dovecotes with resident doves. Cream TEAS in aid of St George's Church, Damerham. *Adm £2 Chd free. Sun June 21, Tue June 23 (2-5.30). Private visits welcome, please* **Tel 01425 652133**

Oakley Manor, Oakley &⚹❀ (Mr & Mrs Priestley) Rectory Rd. 5m W of Basingstoke. From Basingstoke towards Whitchurch on B3400 turn L Station Rd and follow signs. Bus 55a, 55b Basingstoke to Oakley. Large 5-acre garden surrounded by open farmland with comprehensive planting incl a conservation area. Mature trees, shrubs, perennials and annuals. Thatched Wendy House. TEA. Free parking at the Manor. *Adm £2 Chd free. Sun Aug 2 (2-5.30)*

The Old House, Silchester &❀ (Mr & Mrs M Jurgens) Bramley Road, next to Roman Museum. Queen Anne rectory with large garden dating from 1920s with pergola, dell, ponds, spring bulbs, woodland carpeted with bluebells, well labelled collection of rhododendrons, camellias, azaleas, specimen trees and shrubs; easy walk to

Roman town and medieval church. TEAS in aid of St Mary the Virgin Church, Silchester. *Adm £2 Chd 50p. Suns April 19, May 3, 17, 31 (2-6). Private parties welcome March to June, please* **Tel 01189 700240**

Old Meadows, Silchester &⚘ (Dr & Mrs J M Fowler) Off A340 between Reading and Basingstoke. 1m S of Silchester on rd to Bramley, signed at Xrds. 5 acres including walled potager, fine display of spring bulbs, new shrubs. Herbaceous borders, meadow walk. TEAS. *Adm £2 Chd free (ACNO to Basingstoke North Hampshire Medical Fund®). Wed March 25 (2-4), Sun July 12 (2-6), Weds July 29, Aug 12, 26 (2-4). Private visits welcome, July to Aug, please* **Tel 01256 881450**

The Old Rectory, West Tytherley (Mr & Mrs C Vincent) 10m E of Salisbury; 10m NW of Romsey, from A30 4½m W of Stockbridge take turn signed W Tytherley/Norman Court. In village take turning signed to Norman Court School. Queen Anne house, Grade II listed (not open). Lake and rockery, waterfall with bridges, gazebo, rope pergola walk. Traditional walled kitchen garden. In all 140 acres, incl thoroughbred stud with mares and foals. TEAS. *Adm £2 Chd 50p (ACNO to Jonathan Conville Memorial Trust®). Sun June 21 (2-6)*

The Old Vicarage, Appleshaw ⚘ (Sir Dermot & Lady De Trafford) Take A342 Andover to Marlborough Rd, turn to Appleshaw 1m W of Weyhill, fork L at playing field, on L in village by clock. 2-acre walled garden mature trees, bush and rambler roses, shrub borders, shrubs and trees in grass; fruit and herb garden with box hedges. TEAS. *Adm £1.50 Chd free (ACNO to St Peter in the Wood Church, Appleshaw®). Sun June 28 (2-5)*

Paddocks Way, Brook &⚘ (Ken & Janet Elcock) 1m W from junction 1 M27 on B3079 turn L into Canterton Manor Drive before Green Dragon. Country garden of ¾ acre, maintained solely by plant loving owners. Mixed borders and island beds containing spring bulbs and unusual herbaceous perennials, grasses and shrubs grown for flower and foliage effect. Kitchen garden with vegetables, fruit, greenhouse and frames. TEAS. *Adm £1.50 Chd 50p. Suns April 12 (2-5), May 17, July 26 (11-5.30), Sept 20 (2-5). Also private visits and societies welcome, please* **Tel 01703 813297**

Potters Cot, Ringwood ⚘ (Mr & Mrs M G Smith) Hightown Hill. Approaching from Southampton. A31 past Picket Post 1st L over two cattle grids. From Bournemouth to Picket Post, then underpass to Hightown 1st L. Farm Cottage with extensive views, 2½ acres on acid soil. Specimen bulbs, lilies, roses, annuals and herbaceous borders, flowing shrubs. 7yr old arboretum planted for foliage effect. Small working kitchen garden. TEAS. *Adm £2 Chd £1. Sat, Sun May 23, 24 (2-6), Sat, Sun, July 11, 12 (2-6)*

Pullens, West Worldham &⚘ (Mr & Mrs R N Baird) From Alton take B3006 SE on the Selborne Rd. After 2½m turn L to W Worldham. By church turn R. Pullens 100yds on R behind wall. Approx 1-acre plantsman's garden on greensand surrounded by hedges and walls. Particular emphasis on colour and yr-round interest. Tranquil

atmosphere. Featured on Channel 4 TV. TEAS. *Adm £1.50 Chd free. Sat Aug 29 (2-6)*

Pumpkin Patch, Ringwood ⚘ (Richard & Jenny Henry) 41 Seymour Rd. From junction with A31 take A338 Salisbury turn R after 400yds sharp L after garage into Northfield Rd 3rd R Seymour Rd. ½-acre garden positively invites you up the garden path! Densely planted mixed shrubs, climbers and herbaceous. Glass houses hold varied collections of plants incl succulents, orchids and other exotics. TEAS. *Adm £1.50 Chd free (ACNO to Cystic Fibrosis Trust®). Suns, Mons May 24, 25, June 28, July 19, Aug 31 (11-5)*

Pylewell Park, Lymington &⚘ (The Lord Teynham) 2½ m E beyond IOW car ferry. Large garden of botanical interest; good trees, flowering shrubs, rhododendrons, lake, woodland garden. *Adm £2.50 Chd 50p (ACNO to Wessex Regional Medical Oncology Unit®). Suns May 17, 24 (2-5.30). Private visits welcome, please* **Tel 01590 673010**

Robins Return, Tiptoe &⚘ (Mr & Mrs J Ingrem) 2m NE of New Milton. Take B3055, at Xrds by Tiptoe Church, turn into Wootton Rd (signposted to Wootton). Garden 400yds on L. ⅔-acre garden. Wisteria pergola (35yds long). Box edgings; ornamental pool and rock gardens. Fern garden. Wall with trained fruit trees and flowering shrubs, greenhouses, organic kitchen garden. TEA. *Adm £1.50 Chd free (ACNO to The Evangelical Aid Relief (Tear Fund)®). Weds May 27, June 17, Sat June 27, Weds July 8, 29, Sept 9 (2-5)*

Marie Curie Cancer Care

Marie Curie Cancer Care is a charity which cares for people with cancer. The National Gardens Scheme is delighted to include it in its list of beneficiaries. Some facts and figures:

- More than 250,000 people in Britain develop cancer every year. Almost 160,000 people die from the disease annually, the second biggest killer after heart disease.

- **Marie Curie Nurses** provide over 1.3 million hours a year of practical nursing care at home. The service is available day or night, 365 days a year, to patients and their families without charge.

- **Marie Curie Centres** cared for more than 4,600 patients in 1996/97.

- **Marie Curie Cancer Care** operates a research institute which investigates the underlying causes of cancer.

¶Romsey Gardens ⚘ Centre of Romsey nr Abbey. *Combined adm £1.50 Chd free. Suns May 24, 31*
¶King Johns Garden (Test Valley Council) Historic garden planted with material available up to 1700 with many herbs next to C13 listed house *(10-4)*. TEAS
¶4 Mill Lane (Miss J Flindall) Small long floriferous town garden *(11-5.30)*

Rose Cottage, Kingsley Common ⚘✿ (Ian & Julia Elliot) On B3004, 5m E of Alton. Park on green below church or in public house carpark. 150yds down the track on R. Sheltered ½-acre garden with distinctive areas. Cottage-style herbaceous borders, range of conifers and trees, ornamental pond and rockery, rose garden, grass and bamboo feature, productive kitchen garden and large attractive patio with tubs and baskets. TEAS. *Adm £1.50 Chd free (ACNO to All Saints Church). Sun, Mon July 12, 13 (2-6)*

Rotherfield Park, East Tisted ⚘ (Sir James & Lady Scott) 4m S of Alton on A32. Picturesque 12-acre garden incl 1-acre walled garden with trained fruit trees. Ice house. Garden starred as Manderley in the 1997 television film of Rebecca. Picnic in the park (Sat/Sun only) from noon. TEAS in aid of local churches. *Adm £2 Chd £1. Fri May 8 (5-8), Sat, Sun May 9, Sept 13 (2-5)*

Rotherwick Gardens, Hook ♿✿ 2½m N of Hook. M3 exit 5 or M4 exit 11 via B3349. TEAS. *Adm £2 Chd free (ACNO to Whitewater School®). Sun July 12 (2-6)*
¶Whitewater School Children's chequerboard garden and nature pond developed as a learning resource and featured in 'The Garden' Oct 1997
No 1 Wogsbarne Cottages (Mr & Mrs Whistler) Cottage garden with flowers, vegetables and ornamental pond
The Ricks (Mr & Mrs J J Morris) 1 acre garden herbaceous border, shrubs and vegetables

Rowans Wood, Ampfield ♿⚘✿ (Mrs D C Rowan) Straight Mile, on A3090 (S side) (was A31); 2m E of Romsey. 2m W of Potters Heron Hotel. Parking on service Rd. Woodland garden developed since 1962 and planted for yr-round interest. Camellias, rhododendrons, flowering trees, spring bulbs followed by azaleas, hostas and other perennials. TEAS. *Adm £2 Chd free (ACNO to Winchester & Romsey Branch RSPCA®). Thurs, Sun May 14, 31 (2-6), Thurs May 28 (6-8.30 with wine). Parties welcome, mid April to early June, please* Tel 01794 513072

12 Rozelle Close, Littleton ⚘ (Margaret & Tom Hyatt) Turn E off Winchester to Stockbridge Rd to Littleton. Rozelle Close is near Running Horse public house. ⅓-acre spectacular display of herbaceous and 10,000 bedding plants; tubs; troughs; hanging baskets; 2 ponds; 3 greenhouses; vegetables. *Donations (ACNO to Littleton and Harestock New Memorial Hall®). Suns July 12, 26, Sat July 11 (9.30-5.30)*

Rumsey Gardens, Clanfield ♿⚘ (Mr & Mrs N R Giles) 117 Drift Rd. 6m S of Petersfield. Turn off A3 N of Horndean, signed Clanfield. Planting of garden from a corn-field began during 1956 in poor shallow chalk soil. Acid beds have been constructed enabling lime hating shrubs and plants to be grown. Rock garden, heather beds, pools and bog gardens have been laid out. Collection of cotoneasters. TROBI/NCCPG. *Adm £1.50 Chd 50p. Sun May 3 (11-5). Private visits by societies welcome, please* Tel 01705 593367

3 St Helens Road, Hayling Island ♿⚘✿ (Mr & Mrs Norman Vaughan) From Beachlands on seafront, turn R 3rd turning on R into Staunton Avenue, then 1st L. Parking in drive. ⅓-acre ornamental garden with conifers in variety. Interesting trees and shrubs; water garden; old roses; fine lawns. Thatched summer house and well. Prizewinning garden featured in 'Amateur Gardening'. TEAS. *Adm £1. Sat, Sun May 16, 17 (11-5)*

Setters Green, Rowlands Castle ⚘✿ (Jonathan & Jenna Lyn Dicks) 40 Links Lane, N of Havant. Take the B2149 for about 3m, fork R to Rowlands Castle. Turn L before the village green and L again. Parking 1st R in the recreation ground or in the lane. A contemporary garden of ⅔-acre with a backdrop of mature trees. Pond, pergola and abundant mixed planting with shrubs. Feature grasses and perennials to give form and texture through the seasons. Teas in village. *Adm £1.50 Chd 50p. Sun Sept 27, Wed Sept 23, 30 (2-5)*

Shalden Park House, Shalden ♿✿ (Mr & Mrs Michael Campbell) Take B3349 from either Alton or M3 intersection 5. Turn W at Xrds by The Golden Pot Public House marked Herriard, Lasham, Shalden. Garden is ¼m on L. 4-acre woodland garden with extensive views. Pond with duckhouse. Walled kitchen garden. Herbaceous borders. Beds of annuals. Glasshouses. Embryonic arboretum with wild flower walk. Lunchtime picnickers welcome. TEAS. *Adm £1.50 Chd free (ACNO to The Red Cross®). Suns April 26, June 28 (2-6)*

South End House, Lymington ♿⚘✿ (Mr & Mrs Peter Watson) At town centre, turn S opp St Thomas Church 70yds, or park behind Waitrose and use walkway. Walled town garden to Queen Anne house. ¼-acre, architecturally designed as philosophers' garden. Pergolas, trellises and colonnade attractively planted with vines, clematis, wisteria and roses, combine with sculpted awnings to form 'outdoor rooms', enhanced by fountains, music and lights. TEAS. *Adm £1.50 Chd free. Sun May 17 (2-5.30). Private groups welcome, by arrangement, please* Tel 01590 676848

Sowley House, Sowley ♿✿ (Mr & Mrs O Van Der Vorm) At Lymington follow signs to I.O.W. ferry. Continue E on this rd past the ferry nearest to the Solent for 3m until Sowley pond on L. Sowley House is opp the pond. Beautiful setting overlooking Solent and I.O.W. of 19 acres at high tide and 52 acres at low tide, stream walk, wild garden with drifts of primroses and violets. Helleborus collection, woodland and walled herb garden with varied planting; roses, clematis. TEA. *Adm £2 Chd free. Sun March 22 (2-5). Private visits welcome, (no coaches) please* Tel 01590 626231

▲**Spinners, Boldre** ⚘❀ (Mr & Mrs P G G Chappell) Signed off the A337 Brockenhurst-Lymington Rd (do not take sign to Boldre Church). Azaleas, rhododendrons, magnolias, hydrangeas, maples etc interplanted with a wide range of choice herbaceous plants and bulbs. Nursery specialises in the less common and rare hardy shrubs and plants. *Adm £1.50 Chd under six free. For NGS Sun May 10, Tues June 9 (with Apple Court) (10-5).* Tel 01590 673347

Tunworth Old Rectory ⅛⚘❀ (The Hon Mrs Julian Berry) 5m SE of Basingstoke. 3m from Basingstoke turn S off A30 at sign to Tunworth. Garden laid out with yew hedges, enclosing different aspects of the garden i.e. swimming pool, double rose and mixed border; ruby wedding garden; pleached hornbeam walk; lime avenue, ornamental pond, interesting trees incl beech lined walk to church. TEAS. *Adm £2 OAP £1 Chd free (ACNO to All Saints Church Tunworth®). Sun July 5 (2-5.30)*

Tylney Hall Hotel, Rotherwick ⚘❀ From M3 Exit 5 Via A287 and Newnham, M4 Exit 11 via B3349 and Rotherwick. Large garden. 67 acres surrounding Tylney Hall Hotel with extensive woodlands and fine vistas now being fully restored with new plantings; fine avenues of Wellingtonias; rhododendron and azaleas; Italian Garden; lakes; large water and rock garden and dry stone walls originally designed with assistance of Gertrude Jekyll. Plants for sale June 7 only. TEA. *Adm £2 Chd free. Suns May 10, June 7, July 19 (10-6)*

¶**Ulvik, Winchester** ⅛⚘ (Mr & Mrs G G Way) 1m N Winchester. 5th house on L in Harestock Rd off A3049 (old A272). A long ½-acre. Varied planting with bamboo and fern collections, grass, gravel bed. Many shrubs and perennial plants. Show standard vegetables on 4' bed system. Cold drinks. *Adm £1.50 Chd 50p. Sat, Sun, Mon July 18, 19, 20 (2-6)*

Valentine Cottage, Newnham ⅛⚘❀ (Mr & Mrs Brown) Newnham Rd. From Hook follow A30 towards Basingstoke. After approx 1m at The Dorchester Arms turn R into School Lane signed Newnham. At the end of School Lane turn L into Newnham Rd and 200yds on the R is the car park at Village Hall. 25yd walk along Newnham Rd to Valentine Cottage. An exuberant cottage garden of ⅔ acre, developed over last 6yrs specialising in clematis, roses and laid out into individual smaller gardens. TEAS. *Adm £1.50 Chd 50p. Suns May 24, June 28 (2-6). Also private visits welcome, please* Tel 01256 762049

Vernon Hill House, Bishop's Waltham ❀ (Mr & Mrs F C Fryer) ½m N of Bishop's Waltham roundabout, turn off B3035 into Beeches Hill and follow garden signs. Peaceful 6-acre garden. Fine trees, far-reaching views. Small individual gardens, some colour co-ordinated. New mediterranean double border with tender and sub-tropical plants. Wild spring garden; kitchen garden. TEA. *Adm £2 Chd free. Sun, Mon May 3, 4; Suns June 14, July 5 (2-7); also private parties May to late July,* Tel 01489 892301

▲**The Vyne, Sherborne St John** ⅛⚘ (The National Trust) 4m N of Basingstoke. Between Sherborne St John and Bramley. From A340 turn E at NT signs. 17 acres

with extensive lawns, lake, fine trees, herbaceous border. Garden tour starting at 2.30. Gardeners available to answer questions. TEAS. *Adm £2.50 Chd £1.25. For NGS Sun July 5 (12.30-5.30). Also Evening Garden Tour and Buffet, Wed June 3 (7pm) Cost £12 person (limited to 75) for details* Tel 01256 881337

¶**Wades House, Barton Stacey** ⅛⚘ (Mr & Mrs Antony Briscoe) Midway between A303 and A30 near Andover. House is approached from S entrance to village. 2-acres on chalk with spectacular views, large herbaceous borders, over 300 roses, kitchen garden, many containers with diverse planting. TEAS. *Adm £1.50 Chd free. Sun, Tues July 19, 21 (2-5)*

Waldrons, Brook ⅛⚘❀ (Major & Mrs J Robinson) Lyndhurst. 1m W from exit 1 M27 (on A3079). 1st house L past the Green Dragon public house and directly opp the Bell Inn. A C18 listed cottage with a conservatory, in a garden of 1 acre, containing a herbaceous border, shrubs and flower beds created around old orchard trees. Small duck pond (free roaming call ducks); herb garden, arbour, rose trellis, raised alpine garden and a small stable yard. TEAS. *Adm £1.50. Suns May 17, June 28 (2-5)*

2 Warren Farm Cottages, West Tytherley ⚘❀ (Dr & Mrs J G Mitchell) 2m NW of West Tytherley via A30 (Salisbury-Stockbridge Rd) 2m E Lopcombe Corner, 4.5m W Stockbridge take turn S signed West Tytherley. 3rd house on R, 1.9m. Please park along rd. Tiny cottage garden with vegetables interplanted and in pots. Hardy geraniums, hostas, pulmonarias and poppies. Late season interest. Lounging cats. Country Homes and Interiors, Cottage Garden Supplement 1998. *Adm £1. Suns, Mons May 17, 18 (geranium-hosta weekend) (10-6), July 19, 20, Aug, 16, 17, Sept 20, 21, Oct 11, 12. Every Fri May 1 to Sept 25 (10-6).* Tel 01980 863101

¶**319 Warsash Road, Titchfield** (Sheila & Asley Powell) Off A27 at Park Gate down Locks Rd, at end turn L into Warsash Rd, 319 is on L-hand side. Small garden long narrow and subdivided, designed for all-yr effect incl phormiums, heathers, ivies and irises. *Adm £1 Chd free (ACNO to British Heart Foundation®). Sun May 10 (2-6)*

Warwick House, Wickham ⚘❀ (Mrs Lucy Marson) 2½m N of Fareham on A32. Park in square or signed car park. Warwick House is in Bridge St. Turn R at the end of the square furthest from the Winchester Rd. Teas available in the Square. ⅛-acre intimate walled town garden with interesting and contrasting planting. Paved courtyard, troughs. Ornamental vegetable and herb garden. *Adm £1.50 Chd free. Suns May 24, June 14, 21; Wed July 1 (11-5). Private visits between May 1 and July 31* Tel 01329 832313

¶**Weir House, Alresford** ⅛ (Mr & Mrs G Hollingbery) From Alresford go down Broad St (B3046) past 'Globe' public house. Take 1st L (signed Abbotstone). Park in field as signed (150yds). 3-acre garden with newly planted herbaceous border. 'Flow' garden planted May '97 in modern style. 1 acre kitchen garden, pond, river walks, large lawn. Plethora of old and new spring bulbs. Restored 'Vulcan Rams' operating irrigation. October opening will incl garden lighting after dark. TEA, July 11, 12. *Adm £2 Chd free (ACNO to CPRE®). Sun April 12 (2-5), Sat, Sun July 11, 12 (2-6), Sat Oct 10 (4-7)*

▲West Green House, Hartley Wintney &⚹ (Ms Marylyn Abbott, National Trust) Turn N off the A30 at Pheonix Green (about 1m W of Hartley Wintney) at Thackhams Lane from where signed. A ruined large walled garden recently restored. Enter through topiaried Alice in Wonderland garden to an herbaceous garden enclosed in box borders. A potager radiates from fruit cages. Parterre, green theatre, orangery. TEAS. *Adm £3 Chd £1. For NGS Sun June 21 (11-4)*

West Silchester Hall, Silchester &❀ (Mrs Jenny Jowett) Bramley Rd, Silchester. Off A340 between Reading and Basingstoke (signed from centre of village). 1½ acres, plantsman artist's garden, a good collection of herbaceous plants, rose and shrub borders, rhododendrons and many acid loving plants, small pond and bog garden, and interesting display of half hardies, kitchen garden, and owner maintained. Exhibition of botanical paintings. TEAS. *Adm £2. Suns May 24, July 12, Aug 2, Mons May 25, Aug 3 (2-6). Parties by appt March-Sept, please* **Tel 01189 700278**

Westbrook House, Holybourne ⚹❀ (Andrew Lyndon-Skeggs) Howards Lane. Turn off A31 at roundabout immed to NE of Alton towards Holybourne/Alton 1st R to Holybourne. 1st L up Howards Lane. House on R. 2½ acres with continuing design and development. Mature trees and impressive formal planting of shrubs and herbaceous with 'maze' garden leading to orchard, woodland, stream and unexpected view. Featured in Country Life. Cream TEAS. *Adm £2 Chd free. Sun June 21 (2.30-5.30)*

Wheatley House, Kingsley Bordon &⚹❀ (Mr & Mrs Michael Adlington) Wheatley is a small hamlet between Binsted and Kingsley 4m E of Alton, 5m SW of Farnham. From Alton follow signs to Holybourne and Binsted. At end of Binsted turn R signed Wheatley. ¾m down lane on the L. Magnificent setting with panoramic views over fields and forests. Sweeping mixed borders, shrubberies, roses and rockery. 1½ acres, designed by the artist-owner, with particular emphasis on colour and form. TEAS in Barn. *Adm £1.50 Chd 50p (ACNO to Red Cross®). Sat, Sun Oct 10, 11 (11.30-5.30)*

The White Cottage, Beech &⚹❀ (Mr & Mrs P Conyers) 35 Wellhouse Rd. Leave Alton on Basingstoke Rd A339. After approx 1m turn L to Medstead and Beech. Wellhouse Rd is 2nd turning on R. Parking at village hall at bottom of rd, limited parking at house. 1-acre chalk garden with a wide range of unusual shrubs and plants; many hardy geraniums, hellebores and bulbs. Conservatory with exotics, large collection of carnivorous plants featured on TV, pond and scree bed. TEA. *Adm £1.50 Chd free. Suns, Mons March 15, 16 (11-5), June 7, 8, July 12, 13, Aug 2, 3 (11-6). Private visits welcome, please* **Tel 01420 89355**

White Cottage, Hambledon ⚹ (Mr & Mrs A W Ferdinando) Speltham Hill, 'tween 'George' and shop. Park in street or at hill-top. See an ancient cottage small, climbers clinging to its wall. Gain garden, hillside very steep; two-fifty steps to help you peep at covered ground, plants large and small, alpines, shrubs, trees dwarf and tall. A tea-house of the East afar provides a hide, alas no char. Dragons, bridges, pagoda too pools and fish, vista and view. *Donations. Sun, Mon Sept 6, 7 (2-6)*

White House, Romsey &⚹ (A Burn) The Frenches. Take A27 towards Whiteparish. After 3m turn L at Shootash Xrds, turn immed R entrance ½m on R. 1-acre sloping country garden with distant view. Borders with varied plant collection, also hidden corners; winding paths to wild pond and bog garden, enclosed swimming pool, formal pond. Pergolas and trellis with many roses and clematis. TEA. *Adm £1.50 Chd free. Wed, Thurs, Fri June 17, 18, 19 (11-5.30)*

White Windows, Long Parish &⚹❀ (Mr & Mrs B Sterndale-Bennett) Longparish. E of Andover off A303 to village centre on B3048. ⅔-acre with unusual range of hardy perennials, trees and shrubs planted for yr-round foliage interest and colour blendings in garden rooms, incl many hellebores, hardy geraniums and euphorbias. Garden featured on TV and in books and magazines. TEAS (Suns only). *Adm £2 Chd free. Sun, Mon July 12, 13, Sun Sept 20, Wed Sept 23 (2-6). Private visits welcome Weds April to Sept, please* **Tel 01264 720222**

Wonston Lodge, Wonston & (Mr & Mrs N J A Wood) A34 or A30 to Sutton Scotney. At War Memorial turn to Wonston-Stoke Charity; ¾m in Wonston centre. 3 acres. Pond with aquatic plants and ornamental ducks; shrub roses; clematis; topiary. TEAS. *Adm £2 Chd free. Sun Sept 20 (2-6)*

Woodside Cottage, Milford-on-Sea ❀ (Mr & Mrs G England) 4m W of Lymington off A337. After ½m turn R into Manor Rd (almost opp Milford School), 400yds R into George Rd, 5th house on R. An informal, closely planted cottage garden of approx ¼-acre with two small ponds. Wide range of perennials, some unusual, incl salvias, geraniums and grasses, many grown from seed. Owner gardens by "where can I find space for this" philosophy, some unusual combinations result. Also potted plant collections and interesting plants from seed. TEAS. *Adm £1 Chd free. Sat June 13 (11-5). Private visits welcome Tues mid May to mid July, please* **Tel 01590 642291**

The Worthys Gardens *Combined adm £2. Tues Aug 4 (2-5)*
   22 Springvale Road ⚹ (Mr & Mrs Fry) Kingsworthy. N end of Springwell Rd. Kingsworthy almost opp Dairiall's shop. ¾-acre. Magnolias, snowdrops, crocuses and daffodils. From late June; a comprehensive display of agapanthus Headbourne hybrids being Lewis Palmer's stock: he lived nearby. Sept for drifts of cyclamen, heathers and fine display of foliage. *Private visits welcome, please* **Tel 01962 882288**
Little Acre (Mr M Walford) Headbourne Worthy. Just off S end of Springvale, in Down Farm Lane. 1½-acre trees and shrubs planted by owner, for foliar effect and low maintenance. New 'Fastigate Orchard'. TEA

Herefordshire

Hon County Organiser:	Lady Curtis, 30 Witherington Road, London N5 1PP
Assistant County Organisers:	Mr & Mrs Roger Norman, Ivy Croft, Ivington Green, Leominster HR6 OJN Tel 01568 720344
	Dr J A F Evans, The Lawns, Nunnington, Hereford HR1 3NJ Tel 01432 850664
Hon County Treasurer:	Mr M Robins, Bursar, Royal National College for the Blind, College Road, Hereford HR8 2AN

DATES OF OPENING

Regular openings
For details see garden description

Abbey Dore Court, nr Hereford
Arrow Cottage, Weobley
Bryan's Ground, Stapleton
Kingstone Cottages, Ross-on-Wye
Kyrle House, Peterstow
Lingen Nursery & Garden, Lingen
The Nest, Moreton
The Picton Garden, Colwall
Stockton Bury, Kimbolton
Strawberry Cottage, Hamnish

By appointment only
For telephone numbers and other details see garden descriptions. Private visits welcomed

Well Cottage, Blakemere

April 5 Sunday
Grantsfield, nr Kimbolton
Lower Hope, Ullingswick
April 12 Sunday
Arrow Cottage, nr Weobley
April 19 Sunday
Stone House, Scotland
April 26 Sunday
Brilley Court, nr Whitney-on-Wye
Dinmore Manor, Wellington
Stockton Bury, Kimbolton
May 3 Sunday
Strawberry Cottage, Hamnish
May 9 Saturday
The Nest, Moreton
May 15 Friday
Strawberry Cottage, Hamnish
May 16 Saturday
Lingen Nursery & Garden, Lingen
May 17 Sunday
Lingen Nursery & Garden, Lingen
Stone House, Scotland
Torwood, Whitchurch
May 24 Sunday
Kingstone Cottages, Ross-on-Wye
May 28 Thursday
Strawberry Cottage, Hamnish
May 30 Saturday
Bryan's Ground, Stapleton

May 31 Sunday
Ash Farm, Much Birch
Caves Folly Nursery, Colwall
Elmbury, Hereford
Frogmore, Pontshill
Longacre, Colwall
The Nest, Moreton
June 7 Sunday
The Bannut, Bringsty
How Caple Court, How Caple
Lower Hope, Ullingswick
Strawberry Cottage, Hamnish
Whitfield, Wormbridge
June 14 Sunday
Haynstone Orchard, Preston on Wye
Mansel House, Mansel Lacy
Moccas Court, nr Hereford
Torwood, Whitchurch
June 15 Monday
Coddington Vineyard, Coddington
June 18 Thursday
Strawberry Cottage, Hamnish
June 20 Saturday
Hergest Croft Gardens, Kington
Overcourt Garden Nursery, Sutton St Nicholas
June 21 Sunday
Elton Hall, Elton
Mansel House, Mansel Lacy
Overcourt Garden Nursery, Sutton St Nicholas
Stone House, Scotland
June 23 Tuesday
Croft Castle, Kingsland
June 26 Friday
Strawberry Cottage, Hamnish
June 28 Sunday
Berrington Hall, Leominster
Brilley Court, nr Whitney-on-Wye
July 5 Sunday
Bryan's Ground, Stapleton
July 12 Sunday
The Bannut, Bringsty
Lingen Nursery & Garden, Lingen
Lower Hope, Ullingswick
Strawberry Cottage, Hamnish
Torwood, Whitchurch
July 17 Friday
Strawberry Cottage, Hamnish
July 19 Sunday
Elton Hall, Elton

Grantsfield, nr Kimbolton
The Marsh Country Hotel, Eyton
July 25 Saturday
The Nest, Moreton
Wych & Colwall Horticulture Society Show, Colwell Green
July 26 Sunday
Arrow Cottage, nr Weobley
Caves Folly Nursery, Colwell
The Nest, Moreton
Strawberry Cottage, Hamnish
August 2 Sunday
Bringsty Gardens
August 7 Friday
Strawberry Cottage, Hamnish
August 8 Saturday
The Nest, Moreton
August 9 Sunday
Arrow Cottage, nr Weobley
August 16 Sunday
Brook House, Colwall
Coddington Vineyard, Coddington
Elton Hall, Elton
Strawberry Cottage, Hamnish
Torwood, Whitchurch
August 20 Thursday
Strawberry Cottage, Hamnish
August 23 Sunday
Lingen Nursery & Garden, Lingen
August 29 Saturday
Monnington Court, Hereford
August 30 Sunday
The Bannut, Bringsty
Monnington Court, Hereford
The Nest, Moreton
Strawberry Cottage, Hamnish
August 31 Monday
Monnington Court, Hereford
September 3 Thursday
Strawberry Cottage, Hamnish
September 13 Sunday
The Bannut, Bringsty
Strawberry Cottage, Hamnish
Torwood, Whitchurch
October 4 Sunday
Stockton Bury, Kimbolton
October 11 Sunday
Dinmore Manor, Wellington
Lower Hope, Ullingswick

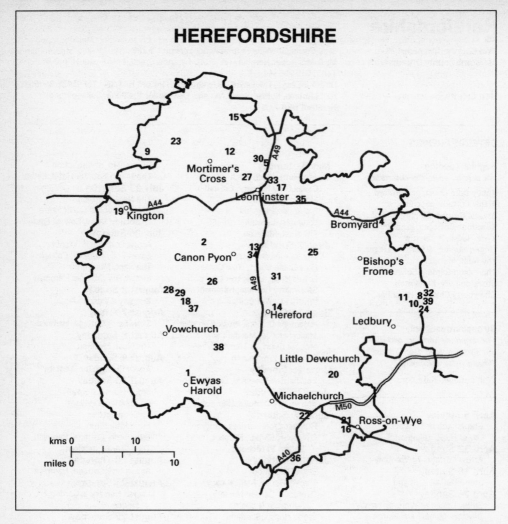

HEREFORDSHIRE

KEY

The maps in this book are designed to help visitors by showing the approximate locations of gardens within each county. The locations are not necessarily precise, particularly where gardens are in clusters. Detailed directions to each garden can be found in the garden descriptions.

DESCRIPTIONS OF GARDENS

● **Abbey Dore Court, nr Hereford** &*❀ (Mrs C L Ward) 11m SW of Hereford. From A465 midway Hereford-Abergavenny turn W, signed Abbey Dore; then 2½m. 6 acres bordered by R Dore of rambling and semi formal garden with unusual shrubs, perennials and clematis in large borders. Pond, rock garden and newly planted trees. River walk with ferns and hellebores leading to borders, planted for foliage colour. Small nursery selling mainly herbaceous perennials. Coffee, lunch and TEAS (11-5). *Adm £2 Chd 50p (ACNO to Mother Theresa®). Sat March 1 to Sun Oct 18 daily except Weds (11-6)*

■ **Arrow Cottage, nr Weobley** *❀ (Mr & Mrs L Hattatt) From Weobley take unclassified rd direction Wormsley (Kings Pyon/Canon Pyon). After 1m, turn L signposted Ledgemoor. 2nd R (no through rd). 1st house on L. Design is at its most stylish in this 2-acre plant lover's garden. Colour-themed enclosures, old roses, clematis, a formal 170ft rill and natural stream create mystery and delight at every turn. Featured on Channel 4 1997 and in all major garden guides. Unusual plants for sale. Regret no children. TEAS. *Adm £2. Wed-Fri, Suns, April to Sept. For NGS Suns April 12, July 26, Aug 9 (2-5)*

Ash Farm, Much Birch *❀ (David & Alison Lewis) From Hereford take A49 S to Much Birch (approx 7m). After the Pilgrim Hotel take 1st turning R at Xrds into Tump Lane. Garden is on L. Ample parking. Small walled farmhouse garden and ½-acre new garden created from old fold yard for all-yr interest over past 9 yrs. Small trees, herbaceous borders, blue and white borders. TEA. *Adm £1.50 Chd free. Sun May 31 (2-6)*

The Bannut, Bringsty &❀ (Daphne & Maurice Everett) 3m E of Bromyard on A44 Worcester Rd. (½m E of entrance to National Trust, Brockhampton). 1-acre garden, with mixed borders, island beds of trees, shrubs and herbaceous plants and small damp garden. Double border in shades of pink, blue, silver, yellow and white formal garden are recent additions. Colourful heather garden designed around Herefordshire cider mill. There is also an unusual knot garden with water feature. Walls, pergola, and terraces around house are used to display interesting plants and climbers. TEAS. *Adm £1.50 Chd free. Suns June 7, July 12, Aug 30, Sept 13 (2-5). Groups by appt, please* Tel 01885 482206

▲**Berrington Hall, Leominster** &* (The National Trust) 3m N of Leominster on A49. Signposted. Bus Midland Red (W) x 92, 292 alight Luston, 2m. Extensive views over Capability Brown Park; formal garden; wall plants, unusual trees, camellia collection, herbaceous plants, wisteria. Woodland walk, rhododendrons, walled garden with apple collection. Light lunches and TEAS. *Adm house & garden £4 Chd £2. Grounds only £1.80. For NGS Sun June 28 (12.30-6)*

Regular openings. Open throughout the year. They are listed at the beginning of the Diary Section'.

Brilley Court, nr Whitney-on-Wye &* (Mr & Mrs D Bulmer) 6m E Hay-on-Wye. 1½m off main A438 Hereford to Brecon Rd signposted to Brilley. Medium-sized walled garden, spring and herbaceous. Valley stream garden; spring colour. Ornamental kitchen garden. Large quantity of roses. Wonderful views. TEAS by appt only. *Adm £1.50 Chd 50p (ACNO to CRMF®). Suns April 26, June 28 (2-6). Also by appt, please* Tel 01497 831467

Bringsty Gardens *❀ 3m E of Bromyard via A44 10m W of Worcester; Bringsty Common. Both gardens at S of rd. TEAS on Terrace at Brookside. *Combined adm £2 Chd free. Sun Aug 2 (2-5.30). Parties and private visits welcome* Tel 01885 821835
    Brookside (Mr & Mrs John Dodd) Turn down track by large oak tree. Cottage with 2-acre garden. Specimen trees and shrubs in grass sloping to lake. Mixed beds with all yr interest
    ¶**Wittanacre** (Mr & Mrs Stephen Dodd) behind Wintergreen Nurseries. New garden with range of unusual and interesting plants

Brook House, Colwall & (Mr J Milne) 3m SW Malvern and 3m E of Ledbury on B2048. ½-way between Malvern/Ledbury via Wyche Cutting; opp Oddfellows Hotel. Water garden; flowering trees and shrubs; walled garden. Old Herefordshire farmhouse with mill stream. *Adm £1.50 Chd 50p. Sun Aug 16 (2-6). Private visits welcome, please* Tel 01684 540283

■ **Bryan's Ground, Stapleton** &♨❀ (David Wheeler & Simon Dorrell) between Kinsham and Stapleton. 12m NW of Leominster. At Mortimers Cross take B4362 signed Presteigne. At Combe, follow signs. 3-acre Edwardian garden. Home of Hortus, The International Garden Journal. Yew and box topiary, parterres, formal herb garden, partly walled kitchen garden. Flower and shrub borders with 'Sulking House'. Shrubbery with spring bulbs, 'Heritage' apple orchard, lighthouse and Edwardian greenhouse. Featured in New York Times and The Observer. TEAS. *Adm £2 Chd 50p. Sats, Suns, Mons May 23 to Sept 21. For NGS Sat May 30, Sun July 5 (2-5)*

Caves Folly Nursery, Colwell &♨ (Mr Leaper & Mrs Evans) Evendine Lane, off Colwall Green. B4218 between Malvern and Ledbury. Car parking at Caves Folly. Small nursery established 13 yrs specialising in herbaceous and alpine plants, some unusual. All plants are grown organically. Recently planted herbaceous borders, solar powered fountains and display garden. TEAS. *Combined adm with* **Longacre** *£1.50 Chd free. Sun May 31 (2-6). Also open Sun July 26. Adm £1 Chd free (2-5)*

Coddington Vineyard, Coddington & (Drs Denis & Ann Savage) nr Ledbury. From Ledbury take Bromyard rd, 1st R after railway bridge signposted Wellington Heath, turn R at next T-junction (oak tree on island) and follow signs to Coddington. Vineyard signposted. 5 acres incl 2-acre vineyard, listed threshing barn and cider mill. Garden and vineyard planted 1985 with terraces, woodland, pond and stream. Interesting trees and shrubs. Wine tasting incl in *Adm £2 Chd free. Suns June 15, Aug 16 (2-6)*

▲**Croft Castle, Kingsland** &♨ (The National Trust) 5m NW of Leominster. On B4362 (off B4361, Leominster-Ludlow). Large garden; borders; walled garden; landscaped park and walks in Fishpool Valley; fine old avenues. Special garden open for NGS (Castle closed). *Adm £1 Chd 50p. For NGS Tues June 23 (1.30-4.30)*

▲ **Dinmore Manor, Wellington** &♨❀ (R G Murray Esq) Hereford 6m N of Hereford. Route A49. Bus: Midland Red Hereford-Leominster, alight Manor turning 1m. Spectacular hillside location. A range of impressive architecture dating from C14-20. Chapel; cloisters; Great hall (Music Room) and extensive roof walk giving panoramic views of countryside and beautiful gardens below; stained glass. TEAS for NGS. *Adm £3 Acc chd under 14 free (ACNO to St John Ambulance®). For NGS Suns April 26, Oct 11 (10-5.30)*

Elmbury, Hereford ♨❀ (Mrs E Haines) 98 Aylestone Hill. ¾m NE of city centre on A4103 Worcester rd. ½-acre garden on sloping site containing alpine and scree beds, herbaceous borders, 2 pools with water plants, several raised peat beds containing meconopsis, camellias and rhododendrons are a special feature. TEAS. *Adm £1.50 Chd free. Sun May 31 (2-5.30)*

¶**Elton Hall, Elton** &♨❀ (Mr James Hepworth) 6m SW of Ludlow. From Ludlow take 1st turn R after crossing Ludford bridge, signed Wigmore/Burrington. 5-acre garden being developed. Georgian house (not open) former home of Thomas Andrew Knight, founder of (later Royal)

Horticultural Society. Apple orchard includes C18 Elton varieties. Walled herb garden, decorative kitchen garden. Herbaceous borders with unusual perennials. Nuttery, wild flower meadow, Victorian greenhouse, tortoise castle, gothic temple and Moorish sheep palace. NCCPG Echinacea Collection. Featured in Gardens Illustrated 1998. TEA. *Adm £2 Chd free. Suns June 21, July 19, Aug 16 (2-6). Clubs, societies welcome*

The Elms School see Wych & Colwall Horticultural Society Show

Frogmore, Pontshill &♨❀ (Sir Jonathan & Lady North) 4m SE of Ross-on-Wye. 1m S of A40 through Pontshill. 2-acre garden with fine mature trees and many unusual young trees and shrubs. Mixed borders specialising in hardy geraniums. Nut walk and ha ha. Mown walk along stream and to spinney. TEAS in aid of Hope Mansel Church. *Adm £2 Chd free. Sun May 31 (2-6)*

Grantsfield, nr Kimbolton &♨❀ (Col & Mrs J G T Polley) 3m NE of Leominster. A49 N from Leominster, turn R to Grantsfield. Car parking in field; not coaches which must drop and collect visitors in the village. Minibus acceptable. Contrasting styles in gardens of old stone farmhouse; wide variety of unusual plants and shrubs, old roses, climbers; herbaceous borders; superb views. 1-acre orchard and kitchen garden with flowering and specimen trees. Spring bulbs. TEAS. *Adm £1.50 Chd free (ACNO to Hammish Church and St John Ambulance®). Suns April 5, July 19 (2-5.30). Private visits welcome April to end Sept, please Tel 01568 613338*

Haynstone Orchard, Preston on Wye ♨❀ (Valerie Thomas) Take A438 from Hereford W to Brecon. After approx 7m Preston on Wye signed L. Once in village take Blakemere Rd and garden is 250yds on L. Approx 2-acre country garden with mixed borders planted over last 4 yrs to give yr-round interest. Many old roses, yew enclosures and lime walk. Small woodland area currently being developed. TEAS. *Adm £1.50. Sun June 14 (2-6). Visitors by appt, please Tel 01981 500579*

▲**Hergest Croft Gardens, Kington** &❀ (W L Banks Esq) ½m off A44 on Welsh side of Kington, 20m NW of Hereford: Turn L at Rhayader end of bypass; then 1st R; gardens ¼m on L. 50 acres of garden owned by Banks' family for 4 generations. Edwardian garden surrounding house; Park wood with rhododendrons up to 30ft tall; old-fashioned kitchen garden with spring and herbaceous borders. One of finest private collections of trees and shrubs; selected to hold National Collections maples and birches. Hergest Croft celebrated its centenary in 1996. TEAS. *Adm £2.50 Chd under 15 free (ACNO to NCCPG®). For NGS Sat June 20 (1.30-6.30). Tel 01544 230160*

▲**How Caple Court, How Caple** ❀ (Mrs Peter Lee) 5m N of Ross on Wye 10m S of Hereford on B4224; turn R at How Caple Xrds, garden 400 yds on L. 11 acres. Edwardian gardens set high above R Wye in park and woodland; formal terraces: yew hedges, statues and pools; sunken Florentine water garden under restoration; woodland walks; herbaceous and shrub borders, shrub roses, mature trees: Mediaeval Church with newly restored C16

Diptych. Nursery. TEAS. *Adm £2.50 Chd £1.25. For NGS Sun June 7 (10-5).* **Tel 01989 740626**

Kingstone Cottages, Ross-on-Wye ✂❀ (Michael & Sophie Hughes) A40 Ross-Gloucester, turn L at Weston Cross to Bollitree Castle, then L to Rudhall. Informal 1½-acre cottage garden containing National Collection of old pinks and carnations and other unusual plants. Terraced beds, ponds, grotto, summerhouse, lovely views. Separate parterre garden containing the Collection. Featured in 'Bloom' Ch 4, Jan 1998. *Adm £1 Chd free. Mons to Fris May 4 to July 3 (9-4); Sun May 24 (10-5). Private visits welcome, please* **Tel 01989 565267**

Kyrle House, Peterstow ✂ (Miss Alison Barber) From Ross-on-Wye take A49 N to Peterstow approx ½m. Garden on L 50yds past Yew Tree Inn. 1⅓-acre country garden started from scratch in 1993 by present owners. Formal cottage style linked by a series of rooms. Many herbaceous borders, small sunken garden, herb garden, pergola and pool garden, small grotto, and secret garden. Organic vegetable garden and fruit house, Victorian conservatory. Rare breed poultry. TEAS. *Adm £1.50 open Sun May 31 to Sun Aug 30 (2-6). Private visits welcome, please* **Tel 01989 768412**

■ **Lingen Nursery & Garden, Lingen** ♿✂❀ (Mr Kim Davis) Off B4362 E from Presteigne, 3m opposite Chapel in village. Specialist alpine and herbaceous nursery and general garden, rock garden and herbaceous borders, peat bed, raised screes and Alpine House. Stock beds incl a large collection of show auriculas. 2 acres of developing garden. Unusual plants with labelling. Nursery. Catalogue available. National collection of iris sibirica and herbaceous campanula held for NCCPG. TEAS. *Adm £1.50 Chd free. Feb-Oct every day (10-6). For NGS Sat, Suns May 16, 17; July 12; Aug 23 (2-6). Coach parties by appt* **Tel 01544 267720**

Longacre, Colwall ♿✂ (Mr D Pudsey & Mrs H Pudsey) Evendine Lane, off Colwall Green. Between Malvern and Ledbury, off B4218. 1½-acre garden developed since 1970. Emphasis on multi-season trees and shrubs planted to create vistas across lawns, down paths and along avenues. TEAS and car parking at Caves Folly Nursery. *Combined adm with* **Caves Folly Nursery** *£1.50 Chd free. Sun May 31 (2-6)*

Lower Hope, Ullingswick ♿✂❀ (Mr & Mrs Clive Richards) From Hereford take A465 N to Bromyard. After 6m turn L at Burley Gate on A417 signed Leominster. Approx 2m take 3rd turning on R signed Lower Hope and Pencombe, 0.6m on LH-side. 5-acre garden facing S and W. Herbaceous borders, rose walks and gardens, laburnum tunnel, Mediterranean garden, water garden incl bog gardens, streams and ponds. Conservatories with exotic species of orchids, bougainvilleas and other rare plants. Prize-winning herd of pedigree Hereford cattle and flock of pedigree Suffolk sheep. TEAS. *Adm £2 Chd £1. Suns April 5, June 7, July 12, Oct 11 (2-6)*

¶**Mansel House, Mansel Lacey** ♿✂❀ (Mrs D Davenport) 7m W of Hereford on A438. After Wyevale Garden Centre take the next R for Creden Hill on A480. Continue through Creden Hill and after approx 2m take a R-hand turn for Mansel Lacy. The house is opposite the church. A well established garden of 4 acres surrounded by mature trees. Sweeping lawns and stream, old fashioned roses; a rose and clematis walk and herbaceous borders. TEAS. *Adm £2 Chd under 12 free (ACNO to The Haven Trust®). Suns June 14, 21 (2-6)*

The Marsh Country Hotel, Eyton ✂❀ (Mr & Mrs Martin Gilleland) 2m NW of Leominster. Signed Eyton and Lucton off B4361 Richard Castle Rd. A 1½-acre garden created over the past 9 yrs. Herbaceous borders, small orchard, lily pond, herb garden and stream with planted banks and rose walk. Vegetable plot. Landscaped reed bed sewage treatment system. Featured on Channel 4 'Garden Party' 1997. C14 timbered Great Hall listed grade II* (not open). TEAS. *Adm £1.50 Chd 50p. Sun July 19 (2-5)*

Moccas Court, nr Hereford ♿ (Trustees of Baunton Trust) 10m W of Hereford. 1m off B4352. 7-acres; Capability Brown park-land on S bank of R. Wye. House designed by Adam and built by Keck in 1775. Teas in village hall. *Adm house & garden £2 Chd £1 (ACNO to Moccas Church®). Sun June 14 (2-6). By appt for groups of 20 or over, please* **Tel 01981 500381**

Monnington Court, Hereford ♿ A438 to Monnington-on-Wye Lane. 20 acres, lake, river, sculpture garden (Mrs Bulmer is sculptor Angela Conner). Famous mile long avenue of pines and yews, favourite of Sir John Betjeman and in Kilvert's Diary. Foundation Farm of British Morgan Horse, living replicas of statues in Trafalgar Square, etc, cider press. C13 Moot Hall, C15 C17 house. TEAS/Barbecue 11-6.30. Horse display 3.30. *Adm house, garden, display £6 Chd £3.50. Garden, display only £4.50 Chd £3 (ACNO to British Morgan Horse Foundation Farm©). Sat, Sun, Mon Aug 29, 30, 31 (10.30-6.30). Private visits by appt, please* **Tel 01981 500698**

■ **The Nest, Moreton** ♿✂❀ (Mrs Sue Evans) N from Leominster on A49 for 3m; turn L in village of Ashton for Moreton, Eye and Luston. 1m down rd and signpost on L 'Eye Veterinary Clinic'. 1530 timber-framed Yeoman's house. Drive flanked by old canal and new chestnut trees. Established fruit garden and a new potager. Southerly aspect is lawned with rockery and shrubberies. Informal summer flower garden and fountain. Bog garden with a variety of lobelias, ferns and primulas. TEAS. *Adm £1.50 Chd free (ACNO to Eye Parish Church®). Every Sat, Sun in May and Aug, July 11, 12. For NGS Sat, Sun May 9, 31, July 25, 26, Aug 8, 30 (2-5)*

Overcourt Garden Nursery, Sutton St Nicholas ♿✂❀ (Mr & Mrs P Harper) 3m N of Hereford. Turn L at Xrds in village towards Marden for ¼m. Grade II C16 house once a vicarage and school house, with connections to Crusader Knights of St John. Views to the Black Mountains. 1½-acre garden developed over the last 5yrs with large shrub and flower borders. Wide range of unusual plants for sale in nursery. TEAS in aid of village playing field. *Adm £1.50 Chd free. Sat, Sun June 20, 21 (2-6). Private visits welcome, please* **Tel 01432 880845**

● **The Picton Garden, Colwall** &⌀❀ (Mr & Mrs Paul Picton) Walwyn Rd. 3m W of Malvern on B4218. 1½-acres W of Malvern Hills. A plantsman's garden. Moist and shade gardens. Roses with scented old and modern varieties. Mature interesting shrubs. Large herbaceous borders full of colour from early summer. NCCPG collection of asters, (Michaelmas Daisies), gives a tapestry of colour from late Aug through Sept and Oct. *Adm £2 Chd free. April 1 to Aug 30, Wed to Sun (2.15-5.30); Aug 31 to Oct 20 daily (10-5.30); Oct 21 to Oct 31 Wed to Sun (10-5). Groups of 10 or more welcome, please* **Tel 01684 540416**

¶■ **Stockton Bury, Kimbolton** &⌀❀ (Mr Raymond G Treasure) 2m N of Leominster on the A49. Turn R onto the A4112 Kimbolton Rd. The gardens are 300yds on the R. A superb, sheltered, 4-acre garden with a very long growing season giving colour and interest all-yr long. An extensive collection of plants, many rare and unusual set amongst Mediaeval buildings, a real kitchen garden. Pigeon house, Tithe Barn, cider press, ruined Chapel and rill, all surrounded by unspoilt countryside. Home grown plants for sale. *Adm £2.50. Open April to October, Wed, Thurs, Fri, Sat, Sun and Bank Hols (2-6). For NGS Suns April 26, Oct 4 (2-6)*

Stone House, Scotland ❀ (Peter & Sheila Smellie) Wellington. A49 6m N of Hereford, end of dual carriageway, turn L for Westhope. ¾m turn R up narrow track. Parking ¼m. Parking difficult in wet conditions. 1-acre S sloping garden with magnificent views over countryside. Winding paths traverse the bank and terraced areas which contain a wide selection of unusual shrubs and herbaceous plants. Children welcome. *Adm £1.50 Chd 50p. Suns April 19, May 17, June 21 (1-6). Private visits welcome, please* **Tel 01432 830470**

■ **Strawberry Cottage, Hamnish** ⌀❀ (Mr & Mrs M R Philpott) 3m E of Leominster. A44 E from Leominster, turn L at 1st Xrds to Hamnish. A 2-acre cottage garden created by the present owners. Part on steep slope with large rockeries. 300 roses. Mixed and herbaceous borders. Beds with single colour themes. Pond, wild garden and kitchen garden. Spectacular views. Featured on BBC TV (Wales). TEAS. *Adm £2 Chd free. Garden open every*

Thurs, Fris, Suns and Bank Hol Mons April 26 to Sept 13. *For NGS Suns, Thurs, Fris May 3, 15, 28, June 7, 18, 26, July 12, 17, 26, Aug 7, 16, 20, 30, Sept 3, 13 (11-5). Private visits welcome, please* **Tel 01568 760319**

Torwood, Whitchurch &⌀❀ (Mr & Mrs S G Woodward) Ross-on-Wye. A40 turn to Symonds Yat W. Interesting cottage garden adjacent to village school and roundabout. Shrubs, conifers, herbaceous plants, etc. Featured by Central TV and in several books. TEAS. *Adm £1 Chd free (ACNO to Hodgkins Disease & Lymphoma Assoc®). Suns May 17, June 14, July 12, Aug 16, Sept 13 (2-6). Private visits welcome all year, please* **Tel 01600 890306**

Well Cottage, Blakemere & (R S Edwards Esq) 10m due W of Hereford. Leave Hereford on A465 (Abergavenny) rd. After 3m turn R towards Hay B4349 (B4348). At Clehonger keep straight on the B4352 towards Bredwardine. Well Cottage is on L by phone box. ¾-acre garden of mixed planting plus ½ acre of wild flower meadow suitable for picnics. There is a natural pool with gunnera and primulae. Good views over local hills and fields. Featured in Diana Saville's book 'Gardens for Small Country Houses' and Jane Taylor's 'The English Cottage Garden'. *Adm £1.50 OAPS £1 Chd free. Private visits welcome May to Aug, please* **Tel 01981 500475**

Whitfield, Wormbridge &❀ (G M Clive Esq) 8m SW of Hereford on A465 Hereford-Abergavenny Rd. Parkland, large garden, ponds, walled kitchen garden, 1780 gingko tree, 1½m woodland walk with 1851 Redwood grove. Picnic parties welcome. TEAS. *Adm £2 Chd £1 (ACNO to St John Ambulance®). Sun June 7 (2-6). Private visits welcome, please* **Tel 0198 121 202**

●**Wych & Colwall Horticultural Society Show, Colwall Green** &❀ (L A C Ashley, Headmaster) The Elms School. Medium-sized garden, herbaceous borders, fine views of Malvern Hills. Interesting exhibits of perennials, shrubs and crafts. Classes for flowers, vegetables, art & handicrafts. Professional Horticultural displays. TEAS. *Adm to show and garden £1 Chd 10p (Share to NGS®). Sat July 25 (2-5.30)*

SYMBOLS USED IN THIS BOOK (See also Page 17)

¶	Opening for the first time.
❀	Plants/produce for sale if available.
&	Gardens with at least the main features accessible by wheelchair.
⌀	No dogs except guide dogs.
●	These gardens advertise their own dates in this publication although they do not nominate specific days for the NGS. Not all the money collected by these gardens comes to the NGS but they do make a guaranteed contribution.
■	These gardens nominate specific days for the NGS and advertise their own dates in this publication.
▲	These gardens open regularly to the public but they do not advertise their own dates in this publication. For further details, contact the garden directly.

Hertfordshire

Hon County Organiser:	Mrs Edward Harvey, Wickham Hall, Bishop's Stortford CM23 1JQ
Assistant Hon County Organisers:	Mr Michael Beldebos, The Spinney, 6 High Elm, Harpenden AL5 2JU
	Mrs Hedley Newton, Moat Farm House Much Hadham SG10 6AE
	Mrs Leone Ayres, Patmore Corner, Albury, Ware SG11 2LY
Hon County Treasurer:	Mrs Rösli Lancaster, Manor Cottage, Aspenden, Nr Buntingford SG9 9PB

DATES OF OPENING

Regular openings
For details see garden description

Benington Lordship, nr Stevenage
Capel Manor Gardens, Enfield
The Manor House, Ayot St Lawrence

By Appointment Only
For telephone numbers and other details see garden descriptions. Private visits welcomed

207 East Barnet Road, New Barnet
94 Gallants Farm Road, East Barnet
1 Gernon Walk, Letchworth

April 5 Sunday
Holwell Manor, nr Hatfield
Pelham House, Brent Pelham
April 13 Monday
23 Wroxham Way, Harpenden
April 19 Sunday
The Abbots House, Abbots Langley
St Paul's Walden Bury, Hitchin
May 4 Monday
23 Wroxham Way, Harpenden
May 10 Sunday
St Paul's Walden Bury, Hitchin
May 17 Sunday
Cockhamsted, Braughing
Hunton Park, Hunton Bridge
West Lodge Park, Hadley Wood
May 24 Sunday
Great Sarratt Hall, Rickmansworth
Queenswood School, Hatfield
Street Farm Cottage, Bovingdon

May 25 Monday
Queenswood School, Hatfield
May 31 Sunday
Ashridge Management College, Berkhamsted
20 Park Avenue South, Harpenden
June 7 Sunday
Hunton Park, Hunton Bridge
May Cot, Knebworth
St Paul's Walden Bury, Hitchin
Wickham Hall, Bishop's Stortford
June 14 Sunday
Cockhamsted, Braughing
Hill House, Stanstead Abbots
The Gardens of Mackerye End, Harpenden
Shaw's Corner, Ayot St Lawrence
23 Wroxham Way, Harpenden
Wynches & Little Wynches, Much Hadham
June 20 Saturday
Tanglewood, Tring
June 21 Sunday
The Barn, Serge Hill, Abbots Langley
May Cot, Knebworth
Micklefield Hall, Rickmansworth
Moor Place, Much Hadham
Serge Hill, Abbots Langley
Thundridge Hill House, nr Ware
June 27 Saturday
Benington Lordship, nr Stevenage
June 28 Sunday
Bayford Village Gardens
Benington Lordship, nr Stevenage
Childwick Green
The Manor House, Ayot St Lawrence
Rothamsted Manor, Harpenden

July 4 Saturday
Lamer Hill, Wheathampstead
July 5 Sunday
The Abbots House, Abbots Langley
Hunton Park, Hunton Bridge
3 Mansion House Farm, Abbots Langley
The Mill House, Tewin, Nr Welwyn
Ragged Hall, Nr Hemel Hempstead
July 12 Sunday
Waterdell House, Croxley Green
July 19 Sunday
20 Park Avenue South, Harpenden
Putteridge Bury
Street Farm Cottage, Bovingdon
Temple Dinsley Garden, Preston
23 Wroxham Way, Harpenden
August 30 Sunday
The Abbots House, Abbots Langley
August 31 Monday
23 Wroxham Way, Harpenden
September 6 Sunday
Hunton Park, Hunton Bridge
20 Park Avenue South, Harpenden
September 13 Sunday
High Elms Gardens
23 Wroxham Way, Harpenden
September 27 Sunday
Knebworth House, Stevenage
October 11 Sunday
Capel Manor Gardens, Enfield
October 25 Sunday
West Lodge Park, Hadley Wood

DESCRIPTIONS OF GARDENS

The Abbots House, Abbots Langley &⚹❀ (Dr & Mrs Peter Tomson) 10 High Street, Abbots Langley NW of Watford (5m from Watford). Junction 20 M25, junction 6 M1. Parking in free village car park. 1¾-acre garden with interesting trees; shrubs; mixed borders; bog garden; sunken garden; ponds; conservatory. Nursery featuring plants propagated from the garden. TEAS. *Adm £2 Chd free (ACNO to Breakespeare School®). Suns April 19, July 5, Aug 30 (2-5). Also at other times by appt Tel 01923 264946*

Ashridge Management College & 3m N of Berkhamsted. Approx 200 acres. The pleasure gardens designed by Repton and modified by Wyatville. Rosary, Italian garden, skating pond, Armorial garden, grotto. Avenues of trees from Victorian period with Rhododendron walk. TEAS. *Adm £2 Chd £1. Sun May 31 (2-6)*

The Barn, Abbots Langley ⚹❀ (Tom Stuart-Smith and family) ½m E of Bedmond in Serge Hill Lane. 1-acre plantsman's garden. Small sheltered courtyard planted with unusual shrubs and perennials, contrasts with more open formal garden with views over wild flower meadow.

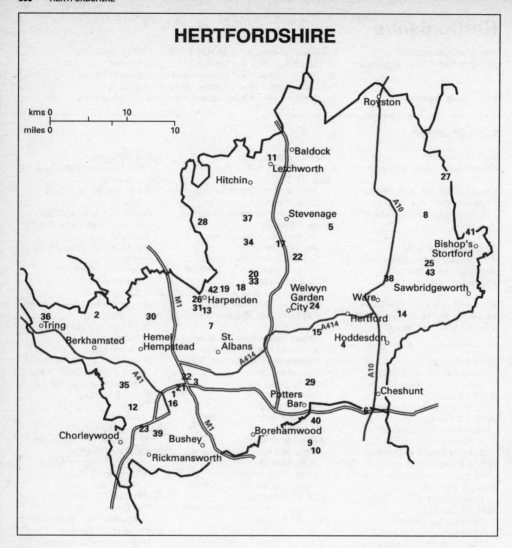

HERTFORDSHIRE

kms 0 ___ 10
miles 0 ___ 10

Royston

°Baldock
11 °Letchworth
Hitchin°
27
Stevenage
28   37   5   8
34   17   22
Bishop's
Stortford
20   25
33   43
42 19 18
26° Harpenden   Welwyn   38
31 13   Garden   Ware°   Sawbridgeworth
36   2   30   7   City 24   Hertford   14
Tring°   Berkhamstead°   Hemel°   St.   15 A414   Hoddesdon°   4
Hempstead   Albans   A414
A41   32 3   29
35   21   Potters   Cheshunt°
1   Bar°   A10
12   16   6
23 39   M1   40   Borehamwood
Chorleywood°   Bushey°   9
°Rickmansworth   10

KEY

1. The Abbots House
2. Ashridge Management College
3. The Barn
4. Bayford Village Gardens
5. Benington Lordship
6. Capel Manor Gardens
7. Childwick Green
8. Cockhamsted
9. 207 East Barnet Road
10. 94 Gallants Farm Road
11. 1 Gernon Walk
12. Great Sarratt Hall
13. High Elms Gardens
14. Hill House
15. Holwell Manor

16. Hunton Park
17. Knebworth House
18. Lamer Hill
19. The Gardens of Mackerye
    End
20. The Manor House
21. 3 Mansion House Farm
22. May Cot
23. Micklefield Hall
24. The Mill House
25. Moor Place
26. 20 Park Avenue South
27. Pelham House
28. Putteridge Bury
29. Queenswood School

30. Ragged Hall
31. Rothamsted Manor
32. Serge Hill
33. Shaw's Corner
34. St Paul's Walden Bury
35. Street Farm Cottage
36. Tanglewood
37. Temple Dinsley Garden
38. Thundridge Hill House
39. Waterdell House
40. West Lodge Park
41. Wickham Hall
42. 23 Wroxham Way
43. Wynches & Little
    Wynches

Teas at Serge Hill. *Combined adm £3 with* **Serge Hill** *(ACNO to Tibet Relief Fund UK®). Sun June 21 (2-5)*

Bayford Village Gardens Day &⚘❀ (off B158 between Hatfield and Hertford). 14 village gardens open. Ploughman's lunch, bars, home-made teas. Marked walks. A very interesting range of both large and small gardens for this popular bi-annual event. Bands will be playing in several gardens. Refreshments at all gardens. *Combined adm £4 Chd 50p. (ACNO to St Mary's Church, and Village School®). Sun June 28 (11.30-5)*
    Bayfordbury (Rialto Homes Plc) 14 acres of grounds with specimen trees incl original cedar trees brought into the country as seed by the Rev Uvedale of Enfield Place in 1754
    The Manor House (Mr & Mrs David Latham) Ancient garden with ornamental lake, many specimen trees, walled garden, John of Gaunt 900yr old oak tree
    Bayford House (Mr & Mrs Robert Wilson Stephens) Extensive lawns, old cedars and other specimen trees, shrubs and herbaceous borders. Walled kitchen garden
    The Warren House (Mr & Mrs Neville Hudson) Mature garden with extensive views, ornamental lake with island and cascade
    Bayford Hall (Mr & Mrs George Rowley) Rose garden, ornamental pond, acre of wild garden, peacocks, guinea fowl

■ **Benington Lordship** ⚘❀ (Mr & Mrs C H A Bott) Benington. 5m E of Stevenage, in Benington Village. Hilltop garden on castle ruins overlooking lakes. Amazing April display of scillas, rose garden, hidden rock/water garden, spectacular borders, ornamental kitchen garden, nursery. *Adm £2.60 Chd free (ACNO to St Peters Church®). Spring and Summer Bank Hol Mons, Weds April to Sept 30 (12-5). Suns April to Aug 31, Sun Oct 18 (2-5). For NGS TEAS and Floral Festival in Church adjoining garden. Sat, Sun June 27, 28 (12-6). Private visits of 20 and over, please* **Tel 01438 869668**

■ **Capel Manor Gardens** & (Horticultural & Environmental Centre) Bullsmoor Lane, Enfield, Middx. 3 mins from M25 junction M25/A10. 30 acres of historical and modern theme gardens, Japanese garden, large Italian style maze, rock and water features. 5 acre demonstration garden run by Gardening Which? Walled garden with rose collection and woodland walks. TEAS. *Adm £4 OAP £3.50 Chd £2. Open daily (10-5.30 - check for winter opening times). For NGS (ACNO to Horticultural Therapy©) Sun Oct 11 (10-5). For other details* **Tel 0181 3664442**

Childwick Green Midway between St Albans and Harpenden on A1081. Entrance through wrought iron gates signposted St Mary's Church. Teas at Forge Cottage. *Combined adm £2 Chd 50p (ACNO to The National Autistic Society®). Sun June 28 (2-6)*
    Forge Cottage (Cindy & Stan Andrews) ⅓-acre plantsman's garden. Informal with rockery and pond, troughs and containers, mixed herbaceous and shrub beds, pergolas with roses and clematis. Exhibition of paintings and plant stall

¶**10 Childwick Green** (Bob & Catherine Kay) Cottage garden covering ½ acre with mature yew and cupressus hedges, vine, peach and apricot trees with other eye catching features. Idyllic setting

Cockhamsted, Braughing &⚘❀ (Mr & Mrs David Marques) 2m E of village towards Braughing Friars (7m N of Ware). 2 acres; informal garden; shrub roses surrounded by open country. Island with trees surrounded by water-filled C14 moat. TEAS in aid of Leukaemia Research. *Adm £2 Chd free. Suns May 17, June 14 (2-6)*

207 East Barnet Road, New Barnet ⚘❀ (Margaret Arnold) M25 junction 24 then A111 to Cockfosters. Underground stations High Barnet or Cockfosters. On bus route 84A and 307. This is a delightful example of a minute courtyard garden. High fences are covered with clematis, honeysuckle and passion flowers, roses and vines scramble over an arch above a seat. Small pond with goldfish and water plants. Many interesting and unusual plants mainly in pots. *Adm £1 Chd 50p. Private visits welcome, please* **Tel 0181 440 0377**

94 Gallants Farm Road ⚘❀ (Mr & Mrs John Gething) East Barnet. M25 junction 24 then A111 to Cockfosters. Underground stations High Barnet, Cockfosters or Arnos Grove. On bus route 84a and 307. Small town garden 50' x 30' approx, designed to give variety of views of hidden rooms. The mixed planting of trees, shrubs and perennials is constantly changing as new plants are acquired and others outgrow their allotted space. Fishpond, rockery, obelisks and a plethora of pots provide plenty of interest. TEA. *Adm £1 Chd 50p. Private visits welcome (parties max. 16) please* **Tel 0181 368 4261**

1 Gernon Walk, Letchworth (First Garden City) ⚘ (Miss Rachel Crawshay) Tiny town garden, 100' long but only 8' wide in middle, planned and planted since 1984 for yr-round and horticultural interest. *Collecting box. Private visits only, please* **Tel 01462 686399**

Great Sarratt Hall, Rickmansworth &⚘❀ (H M Neal Esq) Sarratt, N of Rickmansworth. From Watford N via A41 (or M1 Exit 5) to Kings Langley; and left (W) to Sarratt; garden is 1st on R after village sign. 4 acres; herbaceous and mixed shrub borders; pond, moisture-loving plants and trees; walled kitchen garden; rhododendrons, magnolias, camellias; new planting of specialist conifers and rare trees. TEAS. *Adm £2 Chd free (ACNO to Courtauld Institute of Art Fund®). Sun May 24 (2-6)*

High Elms Gardens, Harpenden &❀ On B487 (Redbourn Lane) off A1081 St Albans to Harpenden Rd. TEAS. *Combined adm £2 Chd 50p (ACNO to Multiple Sclerosis Society®). Sun Sept 13 (2-5)*
    ¶**9 High Elms** (Mrs P Gordon) New ⅓-acre garden begun in Aug '96. Woodland area with bulbs; herbaceous borders, shrubs, rockery, scree garden, pergola and gazebo
    The Spinney, 6 High Elms (Tina & Michael Belderbos) ½-acre garden planted since 1980 featuring gardens within a garden incl a recently designed sunken herb garden

Hill House, Stanstead Abbotts, nr Ware ఉ&ఉ (Mr & Mrs R Pilkington) From A10 turn E on to A414; then B181 for Stanstead Abbotts; left at end of High St, garden 1st R past Church. Ample car parking. 8 acres incl wood; species roses, herbaceous border, water garden, conservatory, woodland walks. Lovely view over Lea Valley. Unusual plants for sale. Home-made TEAS. *Adm £2 Chd 50p (ACNO to St Andrews Parish Church of Stanstead Abbotts®). Sun June 14 (2-5.30). Private visits welcome, please Tel 01920 870013*

Holwell Manor, nr Hatfield ఉ&ఉ&ఉ (Mr & Mrs John Gillum) On W side of B1455, short lane linking A414 with B158 between Hatfield (3m) and Hertford (4m). B1455 joins the A414 roundabout and is signposted Essendon. Holwell is 500yds from this roundabout. Natural garden with large pond fed by hydraulic ram powered fountain, mature trees, river walks; approx 2-3 acres. Island in pond covered with daffodils and narcissi in spring. TEAS. *Adm £2 Chd 50p. Sun April 5 (2-5.30)*

Hunton Park, Hunton Bridge nr Abbots Langley ఉ 1m S of Junction 20 off M25 and 3m N of Watford. On exiting from Junction 20 follow signs to Watford (A41), turn L at traffic lights after ½m signposted Abbots Langley. Follow Bridge Rd for ½m up hill and Hunton Park is to be found on the RH-side. 22 acres of terraced lawns, gardens, pond and woodlands incl mature trees and ancient yews. First established in the 1840s the gardens comprise herbaceous borders, heather gardens, woodland plants and rose garden. A picnic area is provided. TEA. *Adm £2 Chd free. Suns May 17, June 7, July 5, Sept 6 (1-5).* **Tel 01923 261511**

▲**Knebworth House, Knebworth** ఉ&ఉ (The Lord Cobbold) 28m N of London; direct access from A1(M) at Stevenage. Station and Bus stop: Stevenage 3m. Historic house, home of Bulwer Lytton; Victorian novelist and statesman. Knebworth's magnificent gardens, laid out by Lutyens in 1908, have benefited from 15 years of restoration and embellishment. Lutyens' pollarded lime avenues, Gertrude Jekyll's herb garden, the newly restored maze, yew hedges, roses and herbaceous borders are key features of the formal gardens with peaceful woodland walks beyond. Cafeteria and TEAS. *Adm £2 Chd £1.50. For NGS Sun Sept 27 (11-5.30)*

Lamer Hill, Wheathampstead ఉ&ఉ (Mrs M Flory) 1m N of Wheathampstead on B651 to Lower Gustard Wood. Turn R opp entrance to Mid-Herts Golf Club up private rd to start of wood. Old 4-acre garden re-designed during last 12 yrs; so many areas reaching maturity. Variety of trees, mature and new incl pleached hornbeams. Mixed borders; woodland walk. Partially suitable for wheelchairs. TEAS. *Adm £2 Acc chd under 10 free. Sat July 4 (2-5.30)*

The Gardens of Mackerye End, Harpenden ఉ&ఉ A1 junction 4, follow signs for Wheathampstead then Luton. Gardens ½m from Wheathampstead on R. M1 junction 10 follow Lower Luton Rd (B653) to Cherry Tree Inn. Turn L following signs to Mackerye End. Coffee, lunches and TEAS. *Adm £2.50 OAP £1.50 Chd £1. Sun June 14 (11-5)*

Mackerye End House ఉ (Mr & Mrs David Laing) A 1550 Grade 1 manor house set in 11 acres of gardens and park. Front garden set in framework of formal yew hedges with a long border and a fine C17 tulip tree. Victorian walled garden now divided into smaller sections; path maze; cutting garden; quiet garden; vegetables. W garden enclosed by pergola walk of old English roses and vines

Hollybush Cottage (Mr & Mrs John Coaton) Delightful cottage garden around this listed house

Eightacre (Mr & Mrs J Walker) 2-acre garden incl shrub and herbaceous beds, wild life pond, raised vegetable beds, greenhouse and orchards

■ **The Manor House, Ayot St Lawrence** ఉ&ఉ (Mrs Andrew Duncan) Bear R into village from Bride Hall Lane, ruined Church on L and the Brocket Arms on R. On L at bend there is a pair of brick piers leading to drive. Go through green iron gates. The Manor house is on your L. New garden, with formal garden, mixed borders and nut grove, large walled garden and orchard. TEAS NGS day only. *Adm £2 OAP/Chd £1 (under ten free) Suns July 12, Aug 16, Mon Aug 31 (2-6). By appt for parties, please* **Tel 01438 820943**. *For NGS Sun June 28 (2-6)*

3 Mansion House Farm, Abbots Langley (Peter & Sue Avery) Sited about 150yds from small roundabout in Abbots Langley on the Watford to Leverstock Green rd. M25 junction 20 or M1 junction 6. ½-acre garden with perennial borders and rose garden. Large dewpond with water lilies and other aquatic plants; garden seats are strategically placed. *Adm £1.50 Chd free (ACNO to Friends of St Lawrence®). Sun July 5 (2-5)*

May Cot, Knebworth ఉ&ఉ (Richard & Juliet Penn-Clark) 100 Pondcroft Rd. Running parallel to and W of B197 in Knebworth Village. Small cottage garden 100′ × 20′ planted in 1993 incl immature knot garden, old and English roses. Small potager started 1995 at No.98, incl in adm charge. *Adm £1 Chd 50p. Sun June 7, 21. Private visits welcome, please* **Tel 01438 816988**

¶**Micklefield Hall, Rickmansworth** ఉ (Mr & Mrs Richard Edmonds) 4½m due W of Watford and 1m from exit 18 of the M25. Solesbridge Lane/Sarratt Rd. Located 3m N of Rickmansworth, this large country garden, 3½ acres, with fine views, features shrub borders, orchard, extensive double herbaceous borders leading to a summer house and pond shaded by a 500yr old oak tree. New rose walk under construction. Kitchen garden. Irrigation system fed by rainwater from disused slurry pit. TEAS. *Adm £2 Chd 50p (ACNO to Macmillan Cancer Relief Hertfordshire®). Sun June 21 (2-6)*

The Mill House, Tewin, nr Welwyn ఉ&ఉ&ఉ (Dr and Mrs R V Knight) 3½m W of Hertford and 3½m E of Welwyn on B1000. Parking at Archers Green which is signposted on B1000. On the banks of the R Mimram. Approx 20 acres; mature gardens incl fine hedges, woodlands, many rare trees labelled, shrub and herbaceous borders, spring fed water gardens, with an abundance of wildlife in a lovely valley setting. Plants and TEAS in aid of Isabel Hospice. *Adm £2 Chd under 10 free. Sun July 5 (2-6)*

Moor Place, Much Hadham &❀ (Mr & Mrs Bryan Norman) Entrance either at war memorial or at Hadham Cross. 2 C18 walled gardens. Herbaceous borders. Large area of shrubbery, lawns, hedges and trees. 2 ponds. Approx 10 acres. TEAS. *Adm £2.50 Chd 50p. Sun June 21 (2-5.30)*

Myddelton House see London

20 Park Avenue South, Harpenden &❀ (Miss Isobel Leek) Off A1081 turn W by The Cock Inn and War Memorial up Rothamsted Ave; 3rd on L. ½-acre plantsman's garden with trees, shrub and herbaceous borders, alpine gravel bed, 2 ponds and bog garden planted for yr-long interest and colour; aviary. Plants and TEAS. *Adm £1.50 Chd 50p. Suns May 31, July 19, Sept 6 (2-5.30). Private visits welcome, please* **Tel 01582 621671**

Pelham House, Brent Pelham &❀ (Mr David Haselgrove & Dr Sylvia Martinelli) On E side of Brent Pelham on B1038. When travelling from Clavering immed after the village sign. 3½-acre informal garden on alkaline clay started by present owners in 1986. Plenty of interest to the plantsman. Wide variety of trees and shrubs especially birches and oaks. Bulb frames, raised beds with alpines and acid-loving plants and small formal area with ponds. Many daffodils and tulips. TEAS. *Adm £2 Chd free (ACNO to Brent Pelham Church®). Sun April 5 (2-5)*

Putteridge Bury ❀ (University of Luton) On A505 Hitchin/ Luton rd 2m NE of Luton on S side of dual carriageway. Gertrude Jekyll's plans for the rose garden and mixed border have been faithfully restored by the Herts Gardens Trust and are maintained by the University. Edwin Lutyens' reflecting pool and massive yew hedges are important features. Wide lawns, mature trees and new specimens make this an enjoyable garden to visit. Combined with nearby Temple Dinsley it provides an insight into garden design by Lutyens and Jekyll. TEAS. *Adm £2 Chd £1 (ACNO to Herts Gardens Trust®). Sun July 19 (10-5)*

Queenswood School, Hatfield &❀ Shepherds Way. From S: M25 junction 24 signposted Potters Bar. In ½m at lights turn R onto A1000 signposted Hatfield. In 2m turn R onto B157. School is ½m on the R. From N: A1000 from Hatfield. In 5m turn L onto B157. 120 acres informal gardens and woodlands. Rhododendrons, fine specimen trees, shrubs and herbaceous borders. Glasshouses; fine views to Chiltern Hills. Picnic area. Lunches and TEAS. *Adm £2 OAPS/Chd £1. Sun, Mon May 24, 25 (11-6)*

¶Ragged Hall, nr Hemel Hempstead &❀ (Mr & Mrs Anthony Vincent) Gaddesden Row. 4m N of Hemel Hempstead. Take A4146 to Water End. Turn R up hill for 2m, turn R at T-junction. House is 3rd L, ⅓m. Garden of 1½ acres. Mixed borders. Some unusual plants. Enclosed rose garden with old and new roses. Potager with vegetables and flowers. TEAS in aid of Gt Gaddesden Church. *Adm £1.50 Chd 50p. Sun July 5 (2-6)*

Rothamsted Manor, Harpenden &❀ (Rothamsted Experimental Station) 5m N of St Albans, 1m from Harpenden. Turn off A1081 at roundabout. Junction with B487 toward Redbourn. Immed take R diagonal rd across Hatching Green. 6-acre formal gardens with fine topiary, rose garden and large herbaceous border surrounding C17 house, former home of Sir John Lawes, set in parkland. Concert band of local school will play. Tours of Rothamsted ecological and agricultural experiments from 1843, extra charge. TEAS. *Adm £2 Chd £1 (ACNO to Lawes Agricultural Trust®). Sun June 28 (2-5)*

St Paul's Walden Bury, Hitchin & (Simon Bowes Lyon and family) on B651 5m S of Hitchin; ½m N of Whitwell. Formal woodland garden listed Grade 1. Laid out about 1730, influenced by French tastes. Long rides and avenues span about 40 acres, leading to temples, statues, lake and ponds. Also more recent flower gardens and woodland garden with rhododendrons, azaleas and magnolias. Dogs on leads. TEAS. *Adm £2 Chd 50p (ACNO to St Pauls Walden Church®). Suns April 19, May 10, June 7 (2-7). Lakeside concert July. Also other times by appt adm £5* **Tel 01438 871218** *or* **871229**

Serge Hill, Abbots Langley ❀ (Murray & Joan Stuart-Smith) ½m E of Bedmond. The house is marked on the OS map. Regency house in parkland setting with fine kitchen garden of ½ acre. A range of unusual wall plants, mixed border of 100yds. New small courtyard garden and wall garden planted with hot coloured flowers. TEAS. *Combined adm £3 with* **The Barn** *(ACNO to Herts Garden Trust®). Sun June 21 (2-5)*

¶Shaw's Corner, Ayot St Lawrence &❀ (The National Trust) At SW end of village, 2m NE of Wheathampstead; approx 2m from B653. Approx 4 acres with richly planted borders, orchard, small meadow, wooded areas and views over the Hertfordshire countryside. An historical garden, belonging to George Bernard Shaw from 1906 until his death in 1950. Hidden among the trees is the revolving summerhouse where Shaw retreated to write. TEAS. *Adm £1.50 Chd 75p. Sun June 14 (1-5)*

Street Farm Cottage, Bovingdon &❀ (Mrs Penelope Shand) Marked on OS map; on rd between Bovingdon and Chipperfield exactly 1m from the Chesham Rd entrance to Bovingdon High St. Approx 3 acres comprising extensive lawns, long herbaceous borders. A large pond with an island surrounded by decorative shrubs and boasting beautiful water lilies and various miscanthas. Also raised beds, island beds and shrubberies with unusual plants in an attractive sylvan setting. A miniature paved garden enclosed by a yew hedge with tiny clipped box hedges surrounding several beds. *Adm £2 OAPS £1.50 Chd free (ACNO to The Blue Cross®). Suns May 24, July 19 (11-5)*

General Information and Symbols. For general information on the use of this book and a key to the symbols see Page 17.

¶**Tanglewood, Tring** ⌖⌖ (Mr & Mrs E Page) Nursery garden. E of Tring High St. Turn L at roundabout, then R into Mortimer Hill. Nursery gardens is 1st L. Free parking in town or on Mortimer Hill. Mature trees give this small garden a woodland effect. Mixed planting with shrubs and perennials, rose arches, rock garden with small pool. Planted for yr-round interest. TEAS. *Adm £1.50 Chd 50p. Sat June 20 (2-5). Also by appt,* **Tel 01442 823659**

Temple Dinsley, Preston (Princess Helena College) Nr Hitchin. B656 Hitchin/Welwyn Garden City rd. Turn off just S of St Ippolits, signed Preston and Princess Helena College. The Herts Gardens Trust and the College are re-storing this important Edwin Lutyens garden which sur-rounds an altered Queen Anne house. Edwardian rose garden pergolas and architectural features are sur-rounded by lawns and trees. This evocative garden dem-onstrates the skill of Lutyens' designs and is an interesting counterpart to the gardens at Putteridge Bury. TEAS. *Adm £2 Chd £1 (ACNO to Princess Helena Col-lege®). Sun July 19 (10-5). Private visits welcome, please* **Tel 01462 432100**

Thundridge Hill House, Ware ⌖⌖ (Mr & Mrs Christopher Melluish) ¾m from The Sow & Pigs Inn off the A10 down Cold Christmas Lane 2m from Ware to the N. [Map Ref: OS 814 359] Well-established garden of approx 2½ acres; good variety of plants and shrubs incl old roses. Fine views down to Rib Valley. TEAS in aid of St Mary's Thundridge Parish Funds. *Adm £2 Chd 50p. Sun June 21 (2-5)*

Waterdell House, Croxley Green ⌖⌖⌖ (Mr & Mrs Peter Ward) 1½m from Rickmansworth. Exit 18 from M25. Direction R'worth to join A412 towards Watford. From A412 turn left signed Sarratt, along Croxley Green, fork right past Coach & Horses, cross Baldwins Lane into Little Green Lane, then left at top. 1½-acre walled gar-den systematically developed over more than 40 years: mature and young trees, topiary holly hedge, herbaceous borders, modern island beds of shrubs, old-fashioned roses, vegetable, fruit and pond gardens. TEAS £1. *Adm £2 OAPs/Chd £1.50. Sun July 12 (2-6) and private visits welcome by appt yr round, please* **Tel 01923 772775**

West Lodge Park, Hadley Wood ⌖ (Trevor Beale Esq) Cockfosters Rd. On A111 between Potters Bar and South-gate. Exit 24 from M25 signed Cockfosters. The 10-acre Beale Arboretum consists of over 700 varieties of trees and shrubs, incl national plant collections of eleagnus and hornbeam cultivars, with a good selection of conifers, oaks, maples and mountain ash. A network of paths has been laid out, and most specimens are labelled. Lunch or teas can be booked in West Lodge Park hotel in the grounds. *Adm £2 Chd free. Suns May 17 (2-5); Oct 25 (12-4). Organised parties anytime by appt* **Tel 0181 440 8311**

Wickham Hall, Bishop's Stortford ⌖⌖⌖ (Mr & Mrs Ted Harvey) 1m NW of Bishop's Stortford. From A120 roundabout W of Bishop's Stortford take exit as for town. Wickham Hall drive is 300yds on LH-side. 1-acre garden surrounding Elizabethan farm house. Mixed borders of shrubs and old-fashioned roses. Large walled garden. **The Dovecote** (Mr & Mrs D Whiffen) Delightful small cottage garden with many interesting plants. TEAS. *Com-bined adm £2 Chd 50p. Sun June 7 (2-6)*

23 Wroxham Way, Harpenden ⌖⌖ (Mrs M G M Easter) NE Harpenden A1081 and B652 Station Rd or B653 Lower Luton Rd and Station Rd to Coldharbour Lane, L into Ox Lane, then 1st L. Plantsman's garden 70' × 35'. Sloping site with steps and walls. Large mixed border at front. Planted for yr-round interest. Galanthus, crocus, hellebo-rus, diascia, old dianthus; geranium; penstemon; alpine scree; herbs; camomile lawn. National Collection of Thy-mus. *Adm £1 (ACNO to Gt Ormond St Children's Hospi-tal®). Mons April 13 (2-5), May 4, Aug 31, Suns June 14, July 19, Sept 13 (2-5.30). Private visits welcome, please* **Tel 01582 768467**

¶**Wynches and Little Wynches, Much Hadham** B180, Much Hadham direction Ware. Turn R 500yds after Jolly Waggoners public house under old railway bridge. TEAS. *Combined adm £2.50 Chd £1 (ACNO to NSPCC®). Sun June 14 (2-6)*
¶**Wynches** ⌖⌖ (Mr Michael S Ross-Collins) The gar-den is approx 4 acres with mature woodland contain-ing many beautiful specimen trees. The 2 ponds feature in the recent scheme to construct a unique par 3 golf course within the 16 acres of the property with-out interfering with the garden
¶**Little Wynches** ⌖⌖⌖ (Mr & Mrs M Lock) 2 acre in-formal garden and meadow, trees, mixed borders of shrubs, herbaceous plants and old-fashioned roses

---

Isle of Wight

Hon County Organiser: Mrs John Harrison, North Court, Shorwell PO30 3JG
Hon County Treasurer: Mrs R Hillyard, The Coach House, Duver Rd, St Helens, Ryde PO33 1XY

DATES OF OPENING

By appointment only
For telephone numbers and other details see garden descriptions. Private visits welcomed

Fountain Cottage, Bonchurch
Highwood, Cranmore
Old Barn, Shalfleet
Owl Cottage, Mottistone
Waldeck, Brighstone
Westport Cottage, Yarmouth

April 12 Sunday
Kings Manor, Freshwater
April 19 Sunday
Gatcombe House, Gatcombe
April 26 Sunday
Woolverton House, St Lawrence
May 3 Sunday
Badminton, Clatterford Shute, Carisbrooke
May 24 Sunday
Northcourt Gardens, Shorwell
June 14 Sunday
Northcourt Gardens, Shorwell

June 17 Wednesday
Mottistone Manor Garden, Mottistone
June 21 Sunday
Hamstead Grange, Yarmouth
June 28 Sunday
Pitt House, Bembrige
July 5 Sunday
Ashknowle House, Whitwell, Ventnor
August 16 Sunday
Crab Cottage, Shalfleet
August 23 Sunday
Nunwell House, Brading

DESCRIPTIONS OF GARDENS

Ashknowle House, Whitwell *⚲❀* (Mr & Mrs K Fradgley) The turn for Ashknowle Lane is from the Ventnor Rd in Whitwell close to the church. The lane is unmarked and unmade. Cars can be left in the village but parking is provided in the grounds. A 3-acre mature but developing garden with trees, shrubs and lawned areas. Of special interest is the vegetable garden with glasshouses and raised beds. The garden has recently been extended by a further acre of young trees. TEA. *Adm £1.50 Chd free. Sun July 5 (2-5)*

Badminton, Clatterford Shute *❀* (Mr & Mrs G S Montrose) Parking in Carisbrooke Castle car park. Public footpath in corner of car park leads down to the garden. ¾-acre garden with natural chalk stream. Mixed borders planted by owners during last 21 yrs, for all-yr interest. Lovely views. Continuing development of parts of the garden. *Adm £1.50 Chd 25p. Sun May 3 (2-5)*

Crab Cottage, Shalfleet *⚲❀* (Mrs Peter Scott) Turn past New Inn into Mill Rd. Go through NT gates. The entrance is first on L. Please park cars in car park before going through NT gates. Less than 5 mins walk. 1.1-acre 6-yr-old garden with good views. Croquet lawn, pond and walled garden. TEA. *Adm £1.50 Chd free (ACNO to St Michael, Shalfleet®). Sun Aug 16 (2-5.30)*

¶**Fountain Cottage, Bonchurch** *⚲* (Mr & Mrs Dodds) Situated at junction of Bonchurch Village Rd, Trinity Rd and St Boniface Rd. Attractive S facing victorian cottage situated in 2 acres with ponds, stream and natural fountain. TEA. *Adm £2 Chd free. Private visits by appt, please* **Tel 01983 852435**

> **By Appointment Gardens.** These owners do not have a fixed opening day usually because they cannot accommodate large numbers or have insufficient parking space.

¶**Gatcombe House, Gatcombe** *⚲⚲* (Mr & Mrs C Scott) 3m SW of Newport. Large park and woodland with ornamental trees, shrubs and lake. Listed C18 house (not open), Norman Church. TEAS. *Adm £1.50 (ACNO to Gatcombe Church®). Sun April 19 (2-5)*

Hamstead Grange, Yarmouth *⚲* (Mr & Mrs Tom Young) Hamstead Drive. Entrance to 1½m drive on A3054 between Shalfleet and Ningwood. Rose garden with shrubs, lawns and trees and new water garden. 3 acres with superb views of Solent. Swimming pool. TEAS in aid of local charities. *Adm £1.50 Chd 20p. Sun June 21 (2.30-5)*

Highwood, Cranmore *⚲❀* (Mr & Mrs Cooper) Cranmore Ave is approx halfway between Yarmouth and the village of Shalfleet on the A3054. From Yarmouth the turning is on the L hand side, opp a bus shelter 3m out of Yarmouth on an unmade rd. 10-acre site with several acres under cultivation. A garden for all seasons and plant enthusiasts. Pond, woodland area with hellebores, borders and island beds. TEA. *Adm £1.50 Chd free. Private visits welcome, please* **Tel 01983 760550**

Kings Manor, Freshwater *⚲⚲❀* (Mrs Jamie Sheldon) Head E out of Yarmouth over R Yar Bridge. Approx 1m turn L at top of Pixleys Hill. Entrance on L at top of next hill. 3-acre informal garden with shrubs and spring bulbs and frontage onto marshes. Special features - views of estuary and saltings - formal garden around lily pond. TEAS. *Adm £1.50 Chd free (ACNO to Angels International®). Sun April 12 (2.30-5)*

▲**Mottistone Manor Garden, Mottistone** (The National Trust) 8m SW Newport on B3399 between Brighstone and Brook. Medium-sized formal terraced garden, backing onto Medieval and Elizabethan manor house, set in wooded valley with fine views of English Channel. *Adm £2 Chd £1. For NGS Wed June 17 (2-5.30)*

ISLE OF WIGHT

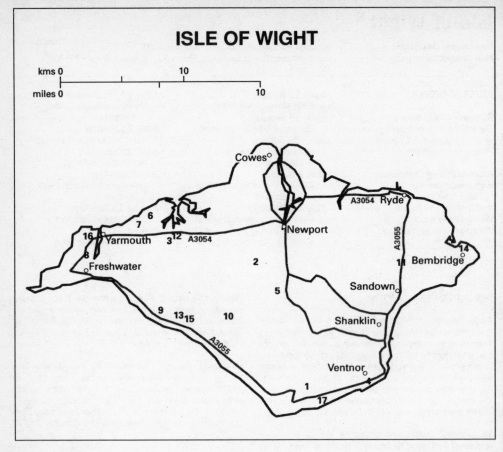

kms 0   10

miles 0   10

Cowes°

A3054 Ryde

Newport

A3055

16 Yarmouth   3 12   A3054

8   Freshwater

7 6

2

Bembridge 14

11

Sandown°

5

9 13 15   10

Shanklin°

A3055

Ventnor°

1

17

KEY

1. Ashknowle House
2. Badminton
3. Crab Cottage
4. Fountain Cottage
5. Gatcombe House
6. Hamstead Grange

7. Highwood
8. Kings Manor
9. Mottistone Manor Garden
10. Northcourt Gardens
11. Nunwell House

12. Old Barn
13. Owl Cottage
14. Pitt House
15. Waldeck
16. Westport Cottage
17. Woolverton House

Northcourt Gardens, Shorwell ё꘎ (Mrs C D Harrison, Mr & Mrs J Harrison) On entering Shorwell from Carisbrooke entrance on R. 15 acres incl bathhouse, walled kitchen garden, stream planted with candelabra primulas and bog plants. Garden rises to mediterranean terraces and new sub-tropical garden with sea views. Collection of 76 hardy geraniums. Jacobean Manor House. TEAS. *Adm £2 Chd 25p. Suns May 24, June 14 (2-5.30)*

Nunwell House, Brading ꘎꘎ (Col & Mrs J A Aylmer) 3m S of Ryde; signed off A3055 in Brading into Coach Lane. 5 acres beautifully set formal and shrub gardens with exceptional view of Solent. House developed over 5 centuries, full of architectural interest. Coaches by appt

only. TEAS. *Adm £1.50 Chd 20p; House £2 Chd 30p extra. Sun Aug 23 (2-5)*

¶**Old Barn, Shalfleet** ꘎꘎ (Mrs M Hampton) Take the rd to Newtown, E of Shalfleet. Corf Lane 1st on L. 1¼-acre attractive spring garden. Also 2 herbaceous borders, shrubs and bog garden. *Adm £1.50. By appt March-July, ring before 10,* **Tel 01983 531420**

Owl Cottage, Mottistone ё꘎ (Mrs A L Hutchinson) Hoxall Lane. 9m SW of Newport, from B3399 at Mottistone turn down Hoxall Lane for 200yds. Interesting cottage garden, view of sea. Plant sale. TEA incl in *Adm £2 Chd free. Visits by appointment Tues, Wed, Thurs, May,*

June and July. Parties max 30 (2.30-5.30), please **Tel 01983 754220** after 6pm

Pitt House, Bembridge &⚘ (L J Martin Esq) E of Bembridge Harbour. Enter Bembridge Village, pass museum and take 1st L into Love Lane. Continue down lane (5 min walk) as far as the bend; Pitt House is on L. Enter tall wrought iron gates. If coming by car enter Ducie Ave 1st L before museum. Pitt House at bottom of ave, on the R. Parking in lane. Approx 4 acres with varied aspects and points of interest. A number of sculptures dotted around the garden; also victorian greenhouse, mini waterfall and 4 ponds. TEAS. *Adm £1.80 Chd 50p. Sun June 28 (10.30-5)*

Waldeck, Brighstone ⚘⚘ (Mr & Mrs G R Williams) 8m SW of Newport. Take Carisbrooke-Shorwell rd, then B3399 to Brighstone. Through village centre, turn R off main rd into Moor Lane. Limited parking in lane. ¾-acre garden informally planted to provide some colour and interest from trees, shrubs and perennial plants throughout the year. Special emphasis placed on foliage and shade tolerant plants such as acers, ferns, hostas, etc. Teas available. *Adm £1.50 Chd free (ACNO to Society for the Blind®). Private and group visits welcome by appt from May 24 until July 31, please* **Tel 01983 740430**

Westport Cottage, Tennyson &⚘ (M Fisher & K Sharp) Tennyson Close off Tennyson Rd. ½-acre walled working garden. Semi-hardy and unusual plants. TEA. *Adm £1.50 Chd 25p (ACNO to St Mary's Hospital League of Friends©). Private visits welcome, especially garden groups, flower arrangers. Talks and meals by arrangement, please* **Tel 01983 760751**

Woolverton House, St Lawrence (Mr & Mrs S H G Twining) 3m W of Ventnor; Bus 16 from Ryde, Sandown, Shanklin. Flowering shrubs, bulbs, fine position. Homemade TEAS. **51st yr of opening for NGS**. *Adm £1.50 Chd 25p (ACNO to St Lawrence Village Hall®). Sun April 26 (2-5)*

The *National Gardens Scheme* is pleased to invite you to
a special Evening Opening at

The Royal Botanic Gardens, Kew
during Chelsea Week
Thursday, May 21st 6.30–9pm

Enjoy the glorious late spring at Kew at an exclusive Evening Opening. Two of the major glasshouses will be open, with staff available to explain their collections and Kew's work.

Admission: £4 Adults, £2 Children,
in aid of the National Gardens Scheme
(as this is a fund-raising event, admission fee also applies to Season Ticket holders and Friends of the Royal Botanic Gardens, Kew)
Refreshments available

Kew is easily reached via the Kew Gardens station (London Underground District Line, and by rail from North London on Silverlink). Also from Kew Bridge station (South West Trains). By road the Gardens are located just south of Kew Bridge on the A307, Kew Road.

Entry by Victoria Gate Only, on the Kew Road, opposite Lichfield Road.

Kent

Hon County Organiser:	Mrs Valentine Fleming, Stonewall Park, Edenbridge TN8 7DG
Assistant Hon County Organisers:	Mrs Jeremy Gibbs, Upper Kennards, Leigh, Tonbridge TN11 8RE
	Mrs Nicolas Irwin, Hoo Farmhouse, Minster, Ramsgate CT12 4JB
	Mrs Richard Latham, Stowting Hill House, nr Ashford TN25 6BE
	Miss E Napier, 447 Wateringbury Road, East Malling ME19 6JQ
	Mrs M R Streatfeild, Hoath House, Chiddingstone Hoath, Edenbridge TN8 7DB
	Mrs Simon Toynbee, Old Tong Farm, Brenchley TN12 7HT
Hon County Treasurer:	Valentine Fleming Esq, Stonewall Park, Edenbridge TN8 7DG

DATES OF OPENING

Regular openings
For details see garden descriptions

Beech Court Gardens, Challock
Church Hill Cottage, Charing Heath
Doddington Hall, nr Sittingbourne
Finchcocks, Goudhurst
Goodnestone Park, Wingham, nr
 Canterbury
Great Comp, Borough Green
Groombridge Place, Groombridge
Hault Farm, Waltham, nr Canterbury
Hever Castle, nr Edenbridge
Higham Park, Bridge
Hole Park, Rolvenden
Marle Place, Brenchley
Mount Ephraim, Hernhill, Faversham
Penshurst Place, Penshurst
The Pines Garden & Bay Museum, St
 Margaret's Bay
Riverhill House, Sevenoaks
Rock Farm, Nettlestead
Squerryes Court, Westerham
Yalding Organic Gardens, Yalding

By appointment only
*For telephone number and other
details see garden descriptions.
Private visits welcomed*

Cares Cross, Chiddingstone Hoath
Greenways, Single Street, nr Downe
43 Layhams Road, W Wickham
Oswalds, Bishopsbourne
The Pear House, Sellindge
Saltwood Castle, nr Hythe
Tanners, Brasted

February 22 Sunday
Goodnestone Park, Wingham, nr
 Canterbury
190 Maidstone Road, Chatham
February 26 Thursday
Broadview Gardens, Hadlow
 College
March 1 Sunday
Great Comp, Borough Green

March 8 Sunday
Great Comp, Borough Green
Weeks Farm, Egerton Forstal
March 15 Sunday
Great Comp, Borough Green
March 22 Sunday
Church Hill Cottage, Charing
 Heath
Cobham Hall, Cobham
Godinton Park, nr Ashford
Goodnestone Park, Wingham, nr
 Canterbury
2 Thorndale Close, Chatham
Withersdane Hall, Wye
March 29 Sunday
Church Hill Cottage, Charing
 Heath
Godinton Park, nr Ashford
Hault Farm, Waltham, nr
 Canterbury
Jessups, Markbeech
190 Maidstone Road, Chatham
April 4 Saturday
Great Maytham Hall, Rolvenden
April 5 Sunday
Church Hill Cottage, Charing
 Heath
Mere House, Mereworth
Owl House, Lamberhurst
Sissinghurst Place Gardens,
 Sissinghurst
Spilsill Court, Staplehurst
2 Thorndale Close, Chatham
39 Warwick Crescent, Borstal, nr
 Rochester
April 6 Monday
Sissinghurst Place Gardens,
 Sissinghurst
April 7 Tuesday
Sissinghurst Place Gardens,
 Sissinghurst
April 12 Easter Sunday
Church Hill Cottage, Charing
 Heath
Edenbridge House, Edenbridge
Higham Park, Bridge, nr
 Canterbury
Hole Park, Rolvenden
Longacre, Selling

The Pines Garden & Bay
 Museum, St Margaret's Bay
Weald Cottage, Edenbridge
Weeks Farm, Egerton Forstal
April 13 Easter Monday
Church Hill Cottage, Charing
 Heath
Crittenden House, Matfield
Longacre, Selling
Sotts Hole Cottage, Borough
 Green
Weald Cottage, Edenbridge
Yalding Gardens
April 19 Sunday
Coldham, Little Chart, Forstal
Godmersham Park, Godmersham
Hole Park, Rolvenden
Lodge House, Smeeth
Marle Place, Brenchley
Stoneacre, Otham
Swan Oast, Stilebridge, Marden
2 Thorndale Close, Chatham
Torry Hill, nr Sittingbourne
April 20 Monday
Groombridge Place, Groombridge
April 22 Wednesday
Riverhill House, Sevenoaks
Sissinghurst Garden, Sissinghurst
Westview, Hempstead, Gillingham
April 25 Saturday
Pett Place, Charing
April 26 Sunday
Bradbourne House, East Malling
Coldharbour Oast, Tenterden
Copton Ash, Faversham
Longacre, Selling
Mount Ephraim, Hernhill,
 Faversham
Olantigh, Wye
Pett Place, Charing
St Michael's Gardens, Roydon,
 Peckham Bush
Stonewall Park, Edenbridge
Swan Oast, Stilebridge, Marden
Westview, Hempstead,
 Gillingham
May 2 Saturday
The Beehive, Lydd
Rock Farm, Nettlestead

May 3 Sunday
The Beehive, Lydd
Church Hill Cottage, Charing
 Heath
Copton Ash, Faversham
Edenbridge House, Edenbridge
Goudhurst Gardens
Hault Farm, Waltham, nr
 Canterbury
Hole Park, Rolvenden
Ladham House, Goudhurst
Longacre, Selling
Old Place Farm, High Halden
Swan Oast, Stilebridge, Marden
2 Thorndale Close, Chatham
39 Warwick Crescent, Borstal, nr
 Rochester
Weald Cottage, Edenbridge
Withersdane Hall, Wye
May 4 Monday
The Beehive, Lydd
Church Hill Cottage, Charing
 Heath
Copton Ash, Faversham
Crittenden House, Matfield
Longacre, Selling
Weald Cottage, Edenbridge
May 6 Wednesday
Penshurst Place, Penshurst
Rock Farm, Nettlestead
May 9 Saturday
Rock Farm, Nettlestead
May 10 Sunday
Charts Edge, Westerham
Church Hill Cottage, Charing
 Heath
Finchcocks, Goudhurst
Hole Park, Rolvenden
Luton House, Selling
Meadow Wood, Penshurst
Swan Oast, Stilebridge, Marden
May 13 Wednesday
Riverhill House, Sevenoaks
Rock Farm, Nettlestead
Waystrode Manor, Cowden
Westview, Hempstead, Gillingham
May 15 Friday
Great Maytham Hall, Rolvenden
May 16 Saturday
25 Crouch Hill Court, Lower
 Halstow
Emmetts Garden, Ide Hill
Rock Farm, Nettlestead
May 17 Sunday
Bilting House, nr Ashford
Brenchley Gardens
Brookers Cottage, Shipbourne
Ladham House, Goudhurst
Larksfield, Crockham Hill
Larksfield Cottage, Crockham Hill
Longacre, Selling
New Barns House, West Malling
Owl House, Lamberhurst
The Red House, Crockham Hill

St Michael's Gardens, Roydon,
 Peckham Bush
Sea Close, Hythe
2 Thorndale Close, Chatham
Town Hill Cottage, West Malling
Westview, Hempstead, Gillingham
May 20 Wednesday
Edenbridge House, Edenbridge
Rock Farm, Nettlestead
May 22 Friday
Kypp Cottage, Biddenden
May 23 Saturday
25 Crouch Hill Court, Lower
 Halstow
Kypp Cottage, Biddenden
Rock Farm, Nettlestead
May 24 Sunday
Charts Edge, Westerham
Church Hill Cottage, Charing
 Heath
Doddington Place, nr
 Sittingbourne
Hall Place, Leigh, Tonbridge
Hole Park, Rolvenden
Kypp Cottage, Biddenden
Longacre, Selling
Oxon Hoath, nr Hadlow
The Pines Garden & Bay
 Museum, St Margaret's Bay
The Silver Spray, Sellindge
Sutton Valence Gardens
Waystrode Manor, Cowden
Weald Cottage, Edenbridge
May 25 Monday
Beech Court Gardens, Challock
Church Hill Cottage, Charing
 Heath
Forest Gate, Pluckley
Kypp Cottage, Biddenden
Longacre, Selling
Scotney Castle, Lamberhurst
The Silver Spray, Sellindge
Weald Cottage, Edenbridge
May 26 Tuesday
Kypp Cottage, Biddenden
May 27 Wednesday
Kypp Cottage, Biddenden
Rock Farm, Nettlestead
Waystrode Manor, Cowden
May 28 Thursday
Kypp Cottage, Biddenden
May 30 Saturday
25 Crouch Hill Court, Lower
 Halstow
Old Buckhurst, Markbeech
Rock Farm, Nettlestead
May 31 Sunday
Copton Ash, Faversham
Hole Park, Rolvenden
Kypp Cottage, Biddenden
Larksfield, Crockham Hill
Larksfield Cottage, Crockham Hill
190 Maidstone Road, Chatham
Marle Place, Brenchley

Old Buckhurst, Markbeech
The Red House, Crockham Hill
2 Thorndale Close, Chatham
Thornham Friars, Thurnham
June 1 Monday
Kypp Cottage, Biddenden
June 2 Tuesday
Kypp Cottage, Biddenden
June 3 Wednesday
Doddington Place, nr
 Sittingbourne
Knole, Sevenoaks
Kypp Cottage, Biddenden
Rock Farm, Nettlestead
The Silver Spray, Sellindge
Sissinghurst Garden, Sissinghurst
Westview, Hempstead, Gillingham
June 4 Thursday
Kypp Cottage, Biddenden
Penshurst Place, Penshurst
June 6 Saturday
25 Crouch Hill Court, Lower
 Halstow
Rock Farm, Nettlestead
The Silver Spray, Sellindge
June 7 Sunday
Abbotsmerry Barn, Penshurst
Kypp Cottage, Biddenden
Little Trafalgar, Selling
Longacre, Selling
Nettlestead Place, Nettlestead
Old Buckhurst, Markbeech
Ramhurst Manor, Leigh,
 Tonbridge
Westview, Hempstead, Gillingham
June 8 Monday
Kypp Cottage, Biddenden
June 9 Tuesday
Kypp Cottage, Biddenden
June 10 Wednesday
Doddington Place, nr
 Sittingbourne
Kypp Cottage, Biddenden
Rock Farm, Nettlestead
Upper Pryors, Cowden
June 11 Thursday
Kypp Cottage, Biddenden
June 13 Saturday
25 Crouch Hill Court, Lower
 Halstow
Haydown, Great Buckland, nr
 Cobham
Rock Farm, Nettlestead
June 14 Sunday
Abbotsmerry Barn, Penshurst
Edenbridge House, Edenbridge
Goudhurst Gardens
Hartlip Gardens
Kypp Cottage, Biddenden
Lullingstone Castle, Eynsford
Maycotts, Matfield
Old Buckhurst, Markbeech
Pevington Farm, Pluckley
Puxted House, Brenchley

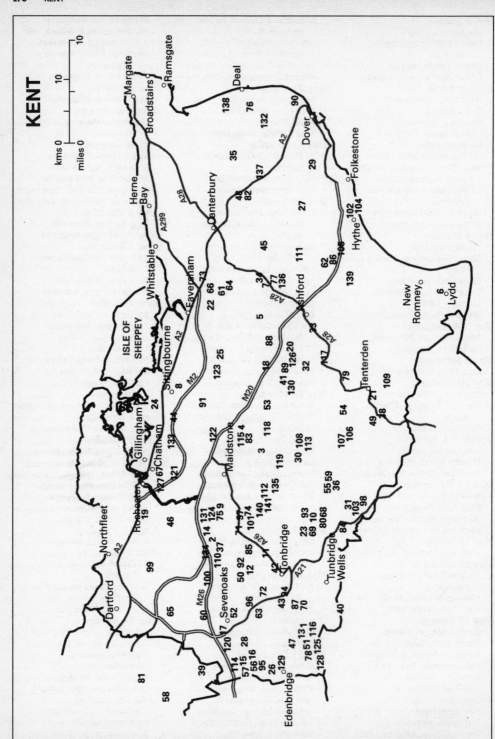

KENT

kms 0
miles 0

10

10

Margate
Broadstairs
Ramsgate

Herne
Bay

Whitstable

ISLE OF
SHEPPEY

Sittingbourne

Gillingham
Chatham

Rochester

Northfleet

Dartford

Sevenoaks

Tonbridge

Tunbridge
Wells

Edenbridge

Faversham

Canterbury

Maidstone

Deal

Dover

Folkestone

Hythe

New
Romney

Lydd

Ashford

Tenterden

138
76
132
35
90
29
27
104
102
139
6
109
82
45
48
5
37
73
66
61
64
22
34
77
136
88
126 20
32
89
41
130
53
54
49
48
21
79
118
108
106
107
113
30
119
3
135
112
55 59
36
93
10
103
98
31
84
68
80
69
23
140
141
10174
75 9
124
131
14
2
37
110
85
12
92
50
96
72
63
52
70
87
43
44
40
60
65
99
46
19
21
67
133
24
8
91
123 25
122
115 4
83
100
17
120
28
15
16
56
95
26
114
57
81
58
39
129
47
78 51
125
128
116
85
62
86
111
37
24
5
22

A299
A28
A2
A2
A28
A28
M2
M20
M26
M20
M2
A26
A21
M20
A2
A2
A28
N7
N7

KEY

1. Abbotsmerry Barn
2. Aldon House
3. Amber Green Farmhouse
4. Battel Hall
5. Beech Court Gardens
6. The Beehive
7. Bilting House
8. 185 Borden Lane
9. Bradbourne House Gardens
10. Brenchley Gardens
11. Broadview Gardens
12. Brookers Cottage
13. Cares Cross
14. Cedar House
15. Charts Edge
16. Chartwell
17. Chevening
18. Church Hill Cottage
19. Cobham Hall
20. Coldham
21. Coldharbour Oast
22. Copton Ash
23. Crittenden House
24. 25 Crouch Hill Court
25. Doddington Place
26. Edenbridge House
27. Elham Gardens
28. Emmetts Garden
29. Everden Farmhouse
30. Field House
31. Finchcocks
32. Forest Gate
33. Godinton Park
34. Godmersham Park
35. Goodnestone Park
36. Goudhurst Gardens
37. Great Comp Charitable Trust
38. Great Maytham Hall
39. Greenways
40. Groombridge Place Gardens
41. Groome Farm
42. 115 Hadlow Road
43. Hall Place
44. Hartlip Gardens
45. Hault Farm
46. Haydown
47. Hever Castle
48. Higham Park
49. Hole Park
50. Ightham Mote
51. Jessups
52. Knole

53. Knowle Hill Farm
54. Kypp Cottage
55. Ladham House
56. Larksfield
57. Larksfield Cottage
58. 43 Layhams Road
59. Little Combourne Farmhouse
60. Little Oast
61. Little Trafalgar
62. Lodge House
63. Long Barn
64. Longacre
65. Lullingstone Castle
66. Luton House
67. 190 Maidstone Road
68. Marle Place
69. Maycotts
70. Meadow Wood
71. Mere House
72. Mill House
73. Mount Ephraim
74. Nettlestead Place
75. New Barns House
76. Northbourne Court
77. Olantigh
78. Old Buckhurst
79. Old Place Farm
80. Old Tong Farm
81. Orchard Cottage
82. Oswalds
83. Otham Gardens
84. Owl House
85. Oxon Hoath
86. The Pear House
87. Penshurst Place
88. Pett Place
89. Pevington Farm
90. The Pines Garden & The Bay Museum
91. Placketts Hole
92. Plaxtol Gardens
93. Puxted House
94. Ramhurst Manor
95. The Red House
96. Riverhill House
97. Rock Farm
98. Rogers Rough
99. Rose Cottage
100. St Clere
101. St Michael's Gardens
102. Saltwood Castle

103. Scotney Castle
104. Sea Close
105. The Silver Spray
106. Sissinghurst Garden
107. Sissinghurst Place Gardens
108. Slaney Cottage
109. Smallhythe Place
110. Sotts Hole Cottage
111. South Hill Farm
112. Southover
113. Spilsill Court
114. Squerryes Court
115. Stoneacre
116. Stonewall Park Gardens
117. Street Cottage
118. Sutton Valence Gardens
119. Swan Oast
120. Tanners
121. 2 Thorndale Close
122. Thornham Friars
123. Torry Hill
124. Town Hill Cottage
125. Upper Pryors
126. Walnut Tree Gardens
127. 39 Warwick Crescent
128. Waystrode Manor
129. Weald Cottage
130. Weeks Farm
131. Went House
132. West Studdal Farm
133. Westview
134. Whitehill
135. Whitehurst
136. Withersdane Hall
137. Womenswold Gardens
138. Worth Gardens
139. Wyckhurst
140. Yalding Gardens
141. Yalding Organic Gardens

The maps in this book are designed to help visitors by showing the approximate locations of gardens within each county. The locations are not necessarily precise, particularly where gardens are in clusters. Detailed directions to each garden can be found in the garden descriptions.

Scotland's Gardens Scheme

The National Gardens Scheme has a similar but quite separate counterpart in Scotland. Called Scotland's Gardens Scheme, it raises money for the Queen's Nursing Institute (Scotland), the Gardens Fund of the National Trust for Scotland and over 160 registered charities nominated by Garden Owners. The Handbook is available (£3.75 incl p&p) from Scotland's Gardens Scheme, 31 Castle Terrace, Edinburgh, EH1 2EL.

St Michael's Gardens, Roydon,
Peckham Bush (Evening)
The Silver Spray, Sellindge
Sotts Hole Cottage, Borough
Green
2 Thorndale Close, Chatham
Torry Hill, nr Sittingbourne
Went House, West Malling
Whitehill, Wrotham
Withersdane Hall, Wye

June 15 Monday
Kypp Cottage, Biddenden

June 16 Tuesday
Kypp Cottage, Biddenden

June 17 Wednesday
Edenbridge House, Edenbridge
(Evening)
Kypp Cottage, Biddenden
Rock Farm, Nettlestead
Smallhythe Place, Tenterden

June 18 Thursday
Forest Gate, Pluckley (Evening)
Kypp Cottage, Biddenden

June 20 Saturday
25 Crouch Hill Court, Lower
Halstow
Little Combourne Farmhouse,
Curtisden Green
Rock Farm, Nettlestead
Yalding Organic Gardens

June 21 Sunday
Brookers Cottage, Shipbourne
Coldham, Little Chart, Forstal
Kypp Cottage, Biddenden
Little Combourne Farmhouse,
Curtisden Green
Little Trafalgar, Selling
Long Barn, Weald, Sevenoaks
Longacre, Selling
Mill House, Hildenborough
Olantigh, Wye
Plaxtol Gardens
Rogers Rough, Kilndown
St Clere, Kemsing
Sea Close, Hythe
Sissinghurst Place Gardens,
Sissinghurst
South Hill Farm, Hastingleigh

June 22 Monday
Kypp Cottage, Biddenden
Sissinghurst Place Gardens,
Sissinghurst

June 23 Tuesday
Kypp Cottage, Biddenden
Sissinghurst Place Gardens,
Sissinghurst (**Evening**)

June 24 Wednesday
Brooke's Cottage, Shipbourne
Ightham Mote, Ivy Hatch
Kypp Cottage, Biddenden
Old Tong Farm, Brenchley
(Evening)
Rock Farm, Nettlestead
Waystrode Manor, Cowden

June 25 Thursday
Kypp Cottage, Biddenden
Southover, Hunton

June 27 Saturday
Beech Court Gardens, Challock
25 Crouch Hill Court, Lower
Halstow
Elham Gardens
Pett Place, Charing
Rock Farm, Nettlestead
Womenswold Gardens

June 28 Sunday
Cedar House, Addington
Church Hill Cottage, Charing Heath
Kypp Cottage, Biddenden
Old Tong Farm, Brenchley
Otham Gardens
Pett Place, Charing
Street Cottage, Bethersden
Swan Oast, Stilebridge, Marden
2 Thorndale Close, Chatham
39 Warwick Crescent, Borstal, nr
Rochester
Waystrode Manor, Cowden
Went House, West Malling
Womenswold Gardens
Wyckhurst, Aldington

June 29 Monday
Kypp Cottage, Biddenden

June 30 Tuesday
Kypp Cottage, Biddenden

July 1 Wednesday
Kypp Cottage, Biddenden
Rock Farm, Nettlestead
Wyckhurst, Aldington

July 2 Thursday
Kypp Cottage, Biddenden

July 3 Friday
Weald Cottage, Edenbridge
(Evening)

July 4 Saturday
25 Crouch Hill Court, Lower
Halstow
Rock Farm, Nettlestead

July 5 Sunday
Cedar House, Addington
Charts Edge, Westerham
Longacre, Selling
Marle Place, Brenchley
Northbourne Court, nr Deal
Placketts Hole, Bicknor, nr
Sittingbourne
Rose Cottage, Hartley
South Hill Farm, Hastingleigh
Waystrode Manor, Cowden
Weald Cottage, Edenbridge
Worth Gardens

July 8 Wednesday
Chartwell, Westerham
Rock Farm, Nettlestead
The Silver Spray, Sellindge

July 11 Saturday
25 Crouch Hill Court, Lower
Halstow

Rock Farm, Nettlestead
The Silver Spray, Sellindge

July 12 Sunday
Aldon House, Offham
Battel Hall, Leeds, Maidstone
Bilting House, nr Ashford
Cobham Hall, Cobham
Edenbridge House, Edenbridge
Groome Farm, Egerton
115 Hadlow Road, Tonbridge
Little Oast, Otford
Little Trafalgar, Selling
Old Tong Farm, Brenchley
Sea Close, Hythe
Swan Oast, Stilebridge, Marden
Walnut Tree Gardens, Little Chart

July 15 Wednesday
Haydown, Great Buckland, nr
Cobham (Evening)
Rock Farm, Nettlestead
Sissinghurst Garden, Sissinghurst
Torry Hill, nr Sittingbourne
(**Evening**)

July 18 Saturday
25 Crouch Hill Court, Lower
Halstow
Rock Farm, Nettlestead

July 19 Sunday
Long Barn, Weald, Sevenoaks
Longacre, Selling
Rogers Rough, Kilndown
Squerryes Court, Westerham
Walnut Tree Gardens, Little
Chart

July 22 Wednesday
Rock Farm, Nettlestead
Squerryes Court, Westerham

July 24 Friday
Great Maytham Hall, Rolvenden

July 25 Saturday
25 Crouch Hill Court, Lower
Halstow
Rock Farm, Nettlestead
Swan Oast, Stilebridge, Marden
(Evening)

July 26 Sunday
Amber Green Farmhouse, Chart
Sutton
Copton Ash, Faversham
Little Trafalgar, Selling
Slaney Cottage, Staplehurst
Spilsill Court, Staplehurst
Swan Oast, Stilebridge, Marden
Walnut Tree Gardens, Little Chart

July 29 Wednesday
185 Borden Lane, Sittingbourne
Rock Farm, Nettlestead

August 1 Saturday
25 Crouch Hill Court, Lower
Halstow

August 2 Sunday
Amber Green Farmhouse, Chart
Sutton
185 Borden Lane, Sittingbourne

Chevening, nr Sevenoaks
Field House, Staplehurst
115 Hadlow Road, Tonbridge
190 Maidstone Road, Chatham
Orchard Cottage, Bickley
Sotts Hole Cottage, Borough
 Green
Walnut Tree Gardens, Little Chart
August 5 Wednesday
Knole, Sevenoaks
August 8 Saturday
25 Crouch Hill Court, Lower
 Halstow
August 9 Sunday
Little Trafalgar, Selling
Sea Close, Hythe
Swan Oast, Stilebridge, Marden
Walnut Tree Gardens, Little Chart
August 15 Saturday
25 Crouch Hill Court, Lower
 Halstow
August 22 Saturday
25 Crouch Hill Court, Lower
 Halstow
Swan Oast, Stilebridge, Marden
 (Evening)
August 23 Sunday
Beech Court Gardens, Challock
Coldharbour Oast, Tenterden
Mount Ephrain, Hernhill,
 Faversham
Swan Oast, Stilebridge, Marden
West Studdal Farm, nr Dover
August 26 Wednesday
The Silver Spray, Sellindge
August 29 Saturday
25 Crouch Hill Court, Lower
 Halstow
August 30 Sunday
Church Hill Cottage, Charing
 Heath

Copton Ash, Faversham
115 Hadlow Road, Tonbridge
Knowle Hill Farm, Ulcombe
Little Trafalgar, Selling
Longacre, Selling
The Pines Garden & Bay
 Museum, St Margaret's Bay
The Silver Spray, Sellindge
Swan Oast, Stilebridge, Marden
Withersdane Hall, Wye
August 31 Monday
Church Hill Cottage, Charing
 Heath
Copton Ash, Faversham
Little Trafalgar, Selling
Longacre, Selling
The Silver Spray, Sellindge
September 5 Saturday
25 Crouch Hill Court, Lower
 Halstow
Old Buckhurst, Markbeech
September 6 Sunday
Broadview Gardens, Hadlow
 College
Doddington Place, nr
 Sittingbourne
Old Buckhurst, Markbeech
September 9 Wednesday
Doddington Place, nr
 Sittingbourne
September 12 Saturday
25 Crouch Hill Court, Lower
 Halstow
September 13 Sunday
Finchcocks, Goudhurst
Goodnestone Park, Wingham, nr
 Canterbury
Hault Farm, Waltham, nr
 Canterbury
Longacre, Selling
Nettlestead Place, Nettlestead

Sotts Hole Cottage, Borough
 Green
Weeks Farm, Egerton Forstal
Yalding Organic Gardens
September 19 Saturday
25 Crouch Hill Court, Lower
 Halstow
Great Maytham Hall, Rolvenden
September 20 Sunday
Copton Ash, Faversham
Little Trafalgar, Selling
September 23 Wednesday
Edenbridge House, Edenbridge
September 26 Saturday
25 Crouch Hill Court, Lower
 Halstow
September 27 Sunday
Edenbridge House, Edenbridge
Stoneacre, Otham
September 30 Wednesday
Whitehurst, Chainhurst, Marden
October 4 Sunday
Everden Farmhouse, Alkham
Ladham House, Goudhurst
Sea Close, Hythe
October 7 Wednesday
Sissinghurst Garden, Sissinghurst
Whitehurst, Chainhurst, Marden
October 11 Sunday
Hole Park, Rolvenden
Owl House, Lamberhurst
October 18 Sunday
Hole Park Rolvenden
Mere House, Mereworth
October 19 Monday
Groombridge Place, Groombridge
October 25 Sunday
Beech Court Gardens, Challock
Copton Ash, Faversham
November 1 Sunday
Great Comp, Borough Green

DESCRIPTIONS OF GARDENS

Abbotsmerry Barn, Penshurst ✿❀ (Margaret & Keith Wallis) Salmans Lane. Between Penshurst and Leigh on B2176: 200yds N of Penshurst turn L, 1m down lane with speed ramps. 5-acre garden with widely varied planting on S-facing slope overlooking the Eden valley. TEAS. *Adm £2 Acc chd free (ACNO to James House Hospice Trust©). Suns June 7, 14 (2-5.30)*

Aldon House, Offham ᴊ (Mr & Mrs Robert Fawssett) Aldon Lane, 2m W of West Malling. Turn S from A20 into Aldon Lane, entrance 1st L after railway bridge. 1-acre traditional garden with wide range of shrubs, herbaceous and foliage plants, young trees. *Adm £1.50 Acc chd free. Sun July 12 (2-6)*

Amber Green Farmhouse, Chart Sutton ✿❀ (Mr & Mrs J Groves) 7m SE of Maidstone. Turn W off A274 onto B2163, in 1m turn L at Chart Corner, next R is Amber

Lane, house ½m W. C16 listed weatherboarded farmhouse (not open) in 1-acre garden. Enchanting cottage garden with hardy perennials, old fashioned climbing and shrub roses, two natural ponds, shrub beds, bog plants. Chart Sutton Best Kept Village in West Kent 1997. *Adm £1.50 Acc chd free. Suns July 26, Aug 2 (2-5.30)*

Battel Hall, Leeds, Maidstone ᴊ ✿ (John D Money Esq) From A20 Hollingbourne roundabouts take B2163 S (signed Leeds Castle), at top of hill take Burberry Lane, house 100yds on R. Garden of approx 1 acre created since 1954 around medieval house; roses, herbaceous plants, shrubs and ancient wisteria. TEAS. *Adm £2 Chd £1 (ACNO to Macmillan Fund for Cancer Relief®). Sun July 12 (2-6)*

■ **Beech Court Gardens, Challock** ᴊ✿❀ (Mr & Mrs Vyvyan Harmsworth) W of crossroads A251/A252, off the Lees. An oasis of beauty and tranquillity in 10 acres of woodland garden surrounding medieval farmhouse; large collection of rhododendrons, azaleas, viburnums, roses, summer borders, fine collection of trees especially acers, giving colour and interest at all seasons. Picnic area, pets, crafts, children's trail, area for visually impaired people. TEAS. *Adm £2.50, OAP £2.30 Chd £1, under 5 free. Open every day March 28-Nov 1 (Mon-Thurs 10-5.30; Fri-Sun 12-6). For NGS Mon May 25 (10-5.30); Sat June 27, Suns Aug 23, Oct 25 (12-6)*

The Beehive, Lydd ᵴ♨ (C G Brown Esq) 10 High Street. S of New Romney on B2075, in centre of Lydd opp Church. Small walled garden, tucked behind village street house dating from 1550, with many varieties of plants. There are paths and cosy corners in this cottage garden with pond and pergola; a pool of seclusion; the busy world outside unnoticed passes by. Teas usually available in the church. *Adm £1.50 Acc chd free (ACNO to Horder Centre for Arthritis, Crowborough®). Sat, Sun, Mon May 2, 3, 4 (2.30-5)*

Bilting House ᵴ♨♧ (John Erle-Drax Esq) A28, 5m NE of Ashford, 9m from Canterbury. Wye 1½m. Old-fashioned garden with ha-ha; rhododendrons, azaleas; shrubs. In beautiful part of Stour Valley. TEAS. *Adm £2 Chd £1 (ACNO to BRCS®). Suns May 17, July 12 (2-6)*

185 Borden Lane, Sittingbourne ᵴ♨ (Mr & Mrs P A Boyce) ½m S of Sittingbourne. 1m from Sittingbourne side of A2/A249 junction. Small informal garden with many varieties of fuchsia; hardy perennials; shrubs; pond; fruit, vegetable and herb garden. Home-made TEAS. *Adm £1 Acc chd free. Wed July 29, Sun Aug 2 (1.30-5); also private visits welcome, please Tel 01795 472243*

Bradbourne House Gardens, East Malling ᵴ (East Malling Trust for Horticultural Research & Horticulture Research International) 4m W of Maidstone. Entrance is E of New Road, which runs from Larkfield on A20 S to E Malling. The Hatton Fruit Garden consists of demonstration fruit gardens of particular interest to amateurs, in a walled former kitchen garden and incl intensive forms of apples and pears. Members of staff available for questions. TEAS. *Adm £2.50 (incl entry to ground floor of House) Acc chd free. Sun April 26 (2-5)*

Brenchley Gardens 6m SE of Tonbridge. From A21 1m S of Pembury turn N on to B2160, turn R at Xrds in Matfield signed Brenchley. *Combined adm £2.50 Acc chd free. Sun May 17 (2-6)*

    Holmbush ᵴ♨ (Brian & Cathy Worden Hodge) 1½-acre informal garden, mainly lawns, trees and shrub borders, planted since 1960

    Portobello (Barry M Williams Esq) 1½ acres, lawn, trees, shrubs incl azaleas and shrub roses; walled garden. House (not open) built by Monckton family 1739

    Puxted House ᵴ♧ (P J Oliver-Smith Esq) 1½ acres with rare and coloured foliage shrubs, water and woodland plants. Alpine and rose garden all labelled. Present owner cleared 20yrs of brambles in 1981 before replanting. TEAS. *Also opening on June 14*

Broadview Gardens, Hadlow College, Hadlow ᵴ♨♧ On A26 9m SW of Maidstone and 4m NE of Tonbridge. 9 acres of ornamental planting in attractive landscape set-

ting; island beds with mixed plantings, rock garden, lake and water gardens; series of demonstration gardens incl oriental, Italian and cottage gardens. TEAS in aid of local charities. *Adm £2 Acc chd (under 16) free. Thurs Feb 26 (hellebores); Sun Sept 6 (10-5)*

Brookers Cottage, Shipbourne ᵴ♨ (Ann & Peter Johnson) Back Lane. 3m N of Tonbridge, 5m E of Sevenoaks just off A227. Plantsman's garden with over 1,000 plants, mostly labelled. ⅔-acre garden with natural pond, scree bed, herbaceous borders and island beds; large collection of hardy geraniums (cranesbills); small fruit and vegetable patch. *Adm £1.50 Chd 50p. Suns May 17, June 21; Wed June 24 (2-6)*

Cares Cross, Chiddingstone Hoath ᵴ♨ (Mr & Mrs R L Wadsworth) [Ordnance Survey Grid ref. TQ 496 431.] Landscaped garden around C16 house (not open). Dramatic views to N Downs over fields with old oaks, restored hedgerows, wildfowl lake and vineyard. Garden features old roses; water garden; innovative ground cover; rare shrubs and trees; speciality American plants. *Adm £3 (incl glass of Kentish wine). By appt only to groups of 5-20, weekdays and evenings only mid May to end July. Write to Mrs R L Wadsworth, Cares Cross, Chiddingstone Hoath, Kent TN8 7BP*

Cedar House, Addington ᵴ♨ (Mr & Mrs J W Hull) Trottiscliffe Road, 1½m W of West Malling. Turn N from A20 into Trottiscliffe Road, continue for about ½m, garden on R. ½-acre garden with wide range of trees, shrubs and perennials. Emphasis also on old roses and foliage plants for yr-round interest. TEAS. Share to Concern for Chernobyl Children. *Adm £1.50 Acc chd free. Suns June 28, July 5 (2-6)*

Charts Edge, Westerham ᵴ♨ (Mr & Mrs John Bigwood) ½m S of Westerham on B2026 towards Chartwell. 7-acre hillside garden being restored by present owners; large collection of rhododendrons, azaleas & magnolias; specimen trees & newly-planted mixed borders; Victorian folly; walled vegetable garden; rock garden. Fine views over N Downs. TEAS. *Adm £2 Chd free (ACNO to BHS Dressage Group©). Suns May 10, 24, July 5 (2-6)*

▲**Chartwell, nr Westerham** (The National Trust) 2m S of Westerham, fork L off B2026 after 1½m, well signed. 12-acre informal gardens on a hillside with glorious views over Weald of Kent. Fishpools and lakes together with red-brick wall built by Sir Winston Churchill, the former owner of Chartwell. The avenue of golden roses given by the family on Sir Winston's golden wedding anniversary will be at its best. Self-service restaurant serving coffee, lunches and teas. *Adm to garden only £2.50 Chd £1.25. For NGS Wed July 8 (11-4.30)*

Chevening, nr Sevenoaks ᵴ (By permission of the Board of Trustees of Chevening Estate and The Secretary of State for Foreign and Commonwealth Affairs) 4m NW of Sevenoaks. Turn N off A25 at Sundridge traffic lights on to B2211; at Chevening Xrds 1½m turn L. 27 acres with lawns and woodland garden, lake, maze, formal rides, parterre. TEAS in aid of Kent Church Social Work and overseas charities. *Adm £2 Chd £1. Sun Aug 2 (2-6)*

■ **Church Hill Cottage, Charing Heath** ఉ✿❀ (Mr & Mrs Michael Metianu) 10m NW of Ashford. Leave M20 at junction 8 (Lenham) if Folkestone-bound or junction 9 (Ashford West) if London-bound: then leave A20 dual carriageway ½m W of Charing signed Charing Heath and Egerton. After 1m fork R at Red Lion, then R again; cottage 250yds on R. C16 cottage surrounded by garden of 1½ acres, developed & planted by present owners since 1981. Several separate connected areas each containing island beds & borders planted with extensive range of perennials, shrubs, spring bulbs, ferns and hostas. Picnic area. *Adm £1.50 Chd 50p (ACNO to Paula Carr Trust®). Open every day except Mon, from March 23 to Sept 30. For NGS Suns March 22, 29, April 5, 12, May 3, 10, 24, June 28, Aug 30; Mons April 13, May 4, 25, Aug 31 (11-5)*

▲**Cobham Hall, Cobham** ఉ✿ (Westwood Educational Trust) Next to A2/M2 8m E of junction 2 of M25, midway between Gravesend and Rochester. Beautiful Elizabethan mansion in 150 acres landscaped by Humphry Repton at end of C18. Classical garden buildings. Acres of daffodils and flowering trees planted in 1930s; grounds now being restored by Cobham Hall Heritage Trust. TEAS. *Adm House £3 OAP/Chd £2.50 Garden £1.50 (ACNO to Cobham Hall Heritage Trust®). For NGS Suns March 22, July 12 (2-5).* **Tel 01474 823371/824319**

Coldham, Little Chart, Forstal ఉ✿❀ (Dr & Mrs J G Elliott) 5m NW of Ashford. Leave M20 at junction 8 (Lenham) if Folkestone-bound or junction 9 (Ashford West) if London-bound: then leave A20 at Charing by road signposted to Little Chart, turn E in village, ¼m. 2-acre garden developed since 1970 in setting of old walls; good collection of rare plants, bulbs, alpines, mixed borders. C16 Kent farmhouse (not open). TEAS. *Adm £2 Chd 50p. Suns April 19, June 21 (2-5.30)*

Coldharbour Oast, Tenterden ఉ✿ (Mr & Mrs A J A Pearson) 300yds SW of Tenterden High St (A28), take lane signed West View Hospital, after 200yds bear R on to concrete lane signed Coldharbour, proceed for 600yds. Garden started in late 1987 from ¾-acre field in exposed position. Pond; dry stream; unusual shrubs and perennials; maintained by owners. TEA in aid of League of Friends of West View Hospital. *Adm £1.50 Acc chd free. Suns April 26, Aug 23 (1.30-5.30)*

Copton Ash, Faversham ఉ✿❀ (Mrs John Ingram & Drs Tim & Gillian Ingram) 105 Ashford Rd. On A251 Faversham-Ashford rd opp E-bound junction with M2. 1½-acre plantsman's garden developed since 1978 on site of old cherry orchard. Wide range of plants in mixed borders and informal island beds; incl spring bulbs, alpine and herbaceous plants, shrubs, young trees and collection of fruit varieties. Special interest in plants from Mediterranean-type climates. Good autumn colour. TEAS. *Adm £1.50 Acc chd free (ACNO to National Schizophrenia Fellowship, East Kent Group®). Suns April 26, May 3, 31, July 26, Aug 30, Sept 20, Oct 25; Mons May 4, Aug 31 (2-6)*

Crittenden House, Matfield ✿ (B P Tompsett Esq) 6m SE of Tonbridge. Bus: MD 6 or 297, alight Standings Cross, Matfield, 1m. Garden around early C17 house completely planned and planted since 1956 on labour-

saving lines. Featuring spring shrubs (rhododendrons, magnolias), roses, lilies, foliage, waterside planting of ponds in old iron workings, of interest from early spring bulbs to autumn colour. *Adm £2 Chd (under 12) 25p. Mons April 13, May 4 (2-6)*

25 Crouch Hill Court, Lower Halstow ✿❀ (Mrs Sue Hartfree) 5m NW of Sittingbourne. 1m W of Newington on A2, turn N to Lower Halstow; continue to T-junc, turn R, pass The Three Tuns on R, take next R (Vicarage Lane), then first R and fork R. Please park with consideration in cul de sac. Long narrow garden (300′ × 25′), landscaped on various levels with mixed borders, rock garden, small woodland area, natural stream and islands; wide range of plants, many rare and unusual. *Adm £1.50 Chd 50p. Every Sat May 16-Sept 26 (2.30-5.30); private visits also welcome, please* **Tel 01795 842426**

■ **Doddington Place, nr Sittingbourne** ఉ✿ (Mr & Mrs Richard Oldfield) 6m SE of Sittingbourne. From A20 turn N opp Lenham or from A2 turn S at Teynham or Ospringe (Faversham) (all 4m). Large garden, landscaped with wide views; trees and yew hedges; woodland garden with azaleas and rhododendrons, Edwardian rock garden; formal garden with mixed borders. New Gothic Folly. TEAS, restaurant, shop. *Adm £2.50 Chd 25p (ACNO to Kent Assoc for the Blind and Doddington Church®). May to Sept: Suns 2-6; Weds and Bank Hol Mons 11-6. For NGS Suns May 24, Sept 6; Weds June 3, 10, Sept 9*

Edenbridge House ఉ✿ (Mrs M T Lloyd) Crockham Hill Rd, 1½m N of Edenbridge, nr Marlpit Hill, on B2026. 5-acre garden of bulbs, spring shrubs, herbaceous borders, alpines, roses and water garden. House part C16 (not open). TEAS. *Adm £2 Chd 25p. Suns April 12, May 3, June 14, July 12 and Sept 27 (2-6); Weds May 20, Sept 23 (1-5) and June 17 (6.30-8.30)* **NB EVENING OPENING:** *£2.50 incl glass of wine: also private visits welcome for groups, please* **Tel 01732 862122**

Elham Gardens ✿❀ 7m from Hythe, 11m from Canterbury. Enter Elham on B2065 from Lyminge or Barham (Hythe/Canterbury). Start at The Old School House, entrance on E side of High Street between Browns (estate agent) and St Marys Road. A collection of at least four small gardens, full of colour and all very different, within easy walking distance (maps available). Village Festival, Flowers in church. TEAS. *Combined adm £2.50 Chd 50p. Sat June 27 (2-6)*

▲ **Emmetts Garden, Ide Hill** ఉ(in parts) (The National Trust) 5m SW of Sevenoaks. 1½m S of A25 on Sundridge-Ide Hill Rd. 1½m N of Ide Hill off B2042. 5-acre hillside garden. One of the highest gardens in Kent, noted for its fine collection of rare trees and shrubs; lovely spring and autumn colour. TEA. *Adm £3 Chd £1.50. For NGS Sat May 16 (11-5.30)*

Everden Farmhouse, Alkham ✿ (Martinez family) 4m W of Dover. Follow signs to Alkham Valley, turn R opp Hoptons Manor to Everden, then follow 'Garden Open' signs. Designer's garden created from field since 1990, exposed hillside, alkaline soil. Many unusual plants combined with colour and form in mind. TEA. *Adm £1.50 Chd*

50p. Sun Oct 4 (2-6); also private visits welcome, please
Tel 01303 893462

Field House, Staplehurst &⚹❀ (Mr & Mrs N J Hori)
Clapper Lane. W of A229, 9m S of Maidstone and 1½m N
of Staplehurst village centre. A 'Garden of the Mind'. Approx 2 acres designed in the tradition of contemplative
and paradise gardens. Extensive plant collection on
Wealden clay, also 2-acre, species-rich meadow with
pond. TEAS. *Adm £1.50 Chd 50p. Sun Aug 2 (2-6)*

■ **Finchcocks, Goudhurst** &⚹❀ (Mr & Mrs Richard
Burnett) Goudhurst. 2m W of Goudhurst, off A262. 4-acre
garden surrounding early C18 manor, well-known for its
collection of historical keyboard instruments. Spring
bulbs; mixed borders; autumn garden with unusual trees
& rare shrubs; recently restored walled garden on lines of
C18 pleasure garden. TEAS. *Adm £5.50 House & garden,
£2 Garden, Chd £4 & 50p. Suns Easter to Sept 28; Bank
Hol Mons; Aug every Wed, Thurs & Sun (2-6). For NGS
Suns May 10, Sept 13 (2-6)*

Forest Gate, Pluckley &⚹❀ (Sir Robert & Lady
Johnson) 8m W of Ashford. From A20 at Charing take
B2077 to Pluckley village; turn L signed Bethersden, continue 1m to garden 100yds S of Pluckley station. 2-acre
garden on heavy clay; well stocked mixed borders, laburnum tunnel, winter garden, ponds and interesting herb
collection. Many plants labelled. C17 house (not open).
TEAS in aid of Cystic Fibrosis Trust. *Adm £1.60 (£3 on
June 18 to incl glass of wine) Acc chd free. Mon May 25
(1-6); Thurs June 18 (5-8.30)* **NB EVENING OPENING**;
also groups at any time by appointment, please **Tel 0171
373 8300**

▲**Godinton Park** &⚹ (Godinton House Preservation
Trust) Entrance 1½m W of Ashford at Potter's Corner on
A20. Bus: MD/EK 10, 10A, 10B Folkestone-Ashford-Maid-
stone, alight Hare & Hounds, Potter's Corner. Formal garden designed c1900 by Reginald Blomfield, and wild
gardens. Topiary. House closed in 1998. Garden under
restoration in 1998. *Adm £1.50 Chd under 16 free. For
NGS Suns March 22, 29 (2-4)*

Godmersham Park & (John B Sunley Esq) off A28 midway between Canterbury and Ashford. Associations with Jane
Austen. Early Georgian mansion (not open) in beautiful
downland setting, 24 acres of formal and landscaped gardens, topiary, rose beds, herbaceous borders and superb
daffodils in restored wilderness. TEAS. *Adm £2 Acc chd
free (ACNO to Godmersham Church®). Sun April 19 (11-6)*

■ **Goodnestone Park, Wingham** &⚹❀ (The Lady
FitzWalter) Canterbury. Village lies S of B2046 rd from A2
to Wingham. Brown tourist signs off B2046 say Goodnestone Park gardens. 10 to 12 acres; good trees; woodland
garden, snowdrops, spring bulbs, walled garden with old-
fashioned roses. Connections with Jane Austen who
stayed here. Picnics allowed. TEAS (not in Feb, Mar).
*Adm £2.50 OAP £2.20 Chd (under 12) 20p (Disabled
people in wheelchair £1). Suns March 30 to Oct 19 (12-6);
Mons, Weds to Fris March 24 to Oct 24 (11-5). For NGS
Suns Feb 22 (snowdrops), March 22 (spring bulbs and
hellebores), Sept 13 (12-6). Closed Tues and Sats*

Goudhurst Gardens 4m W of Cranbrook on A262. TEAS
at Tara and Tulip Tree Cottage. *Combined adm £2.50 Acc
chd free. Suns May 3, June 14 (1-6)*

Crowbourne Farm House &⚹ (Mrs S Coleman) 2-
acre farmhouse garden in which replanting started in
1989. Established cottage garden; shrub roses; vegetable garden; and areas newly planted with trees and
shrubs. Former horse pond now stocked with ornamental fish

Garden Cottage &❀ (Mr & Mrs Peter Sowerby) ¾-
acre garden with small trees, shrubs, perennials and
grass, to provide year-round softly coloured fore-
ground to outstanding views of Teise valley. First laid
out in 1930s with extensive planting since 1980s

Tara &⚹❀ (Mr & Mrs Peter Coombs) 1¼ acres redesigned in 1982 into a number of linked garden areas,
including a formal herb garden, each providing a different atmosphere, using an interesting range of
plants and shrubs

Tulip Tree Cottage ⚹❀ (Mr & Mrs K A Owen) 1½
acres with sweeping lawn, established trees in herbaceous and shrub borders; 90ft *Liriodendron tulipifera*,
said to be one of finest in country, also fine *Cedrus at-
lantica glauca*. In May azalea garden of ½-acre, established 1902; *also visitors welcome by appointment,
please* **Tel 01580 211423**

■ **Great Comp Charitable Trust** &⚹❀ (R Cameron
Esq) 2m E of Borough Green. A20 at Wrotham Heath,
take Seven Mile Lane, B2016; at 1st Xrds turn R; garden
on L ½m. 7-acre garden skilfully designed for low maintenance and yr-round interest. Spacious setting of well-
maintained lawns and paths lead visitors through
plantsman's collection of trees, shrubs, heathers and herbaceous plants. Good autumn colour. Early C17 house
(not open). TEAS on Suns, Bank Hols and NGS days (2-5).
*Adm £3 Chd £1. Open Suns in March and every day April
1 to Oct 31 (11-6). For NGS (ACNO to Tradescant Trust®)
Suns March 1, 8, 15 (for hellebores, heathers and snow-
flakes); Nov 1 (for autumn colour) (11-6)*

▲**Great Maytham Hall, Rolvenden** ⚹❀ (Country Houses
Association) 4m SW of Tenterden. On A28 in Rolvenden
turn L at church towards Rolvenden Layne; Hall ½m on
R. Lutyens house (not open on NGS days) and garden, 18
acres of parkland with bluebells, daffodils and flowering
trees in spring; formal gardens incl blue and silver border, roses, hydrangeas and autumn colour. Walled garden
inspired Frances Hodgson Burnett to write her novel 'The
Secret Garden'. TEAS. *Adm £2 Chd £1 (ACNO to Country
Houses Association©). For NGS Fris May 15, July 24, Sats
April 4, Sept 19 (2-5)* **Tel 01580 241346**

Greenways, nr Downe &⚹ (Mr & Mrs S Lord) Single
Street. Gardener's garden; interesting design ideas and
plant collections; willows, jasmines, buddleias, honeysuckles and alpines; bonsai miniature garden display;
small pool, plant house and pottery. *(ACNO to Save the
Children Fund®). Private visits welcome, anytime, please*
Tel 01959 574691

■ **Groombridge Place Gardens** ⚹❀ (Andrew de Candole
Esq) Chosen by SEETB as Visitor Attraction of the Year
for 1997. 4m SW of Tunbridge Wells. Take A264 towards

E. Grinstead, after 2m take B2110: Groombridge Place entrance on L, past the church. C17 formal walled gardens with medieval moat, ancient topiary and fountains. Canal boat rides to Enchanted Forest; children's garden and birds of prey displays. Restaurant. *Adm £5.50 OAPs £4.50 Chd £3.50. Open daily April 10 to Oct 25 (10-6). For NGS Mons April 20, Oct 19 (10-6)*

Groome Farm, Egerton &*※ (Mr & Mrs Michael Swatland) 10m W of Ashford. From A20 at Charing Xrds take B2077 Biddenden Rd. Past Pluckley turn R at Blacksmiths Tea Rooms; R again, until Newland Green sign on L, house 1st on L. 1½ acres around C15 farmhouse and oast. Interesting collection trees, shrubs, roses and herbaceous plants; also water, heather and rock gardens. Picnics welcome in field. TEAS. *Adm £1.50 Acc chd free. Sun July 12 (2-6). Private visits welcome, please* **Tel 01233 756260**

115 Hadlow Road, Tonbridge ※ (Mr & Mrs Richard Esdale) Take A26 from N end of High St signed Maidstone, house 1m on L in service rd. ⅓-acre unusual terraced garden with large collection of modern roses, island herbaceous border, many clematis, hardy fuchsias, grasses and ferns, shrub borders, alpines, annuals, kitchen garden and pond; well labelled. TEA. *Adm £1.50 Acc chd free. Suns July 12, Aug 2, 30 (2-6); also private visits welcome, please* **Tel 01732 353738**

Hall Place Gardens, Leigh & (Lord Hollenden) 4m W of Tonbridge. From A21 Sevenoaks-Tonbridge, B245 to Hildenborough, then R onto B2027. Through Leigh and on R. Large outstanding garden with 11-acre lake, lakeside walk crossing over picturesque bridges. Many rare and interesting trees and shrubs. Opening for first time for 7 yrs. TEAS. *Adm £2 Chd 50p under 12 free. Sun May 24 (2-6)*

Hartlip Gardens 6m W of Sittingbourne, 1m S of A2 midway between Rainham and Newington. Parking for Craiglea in village hall car park and The Street. *Combined adm £2 Acc chd free. Sun June 14 (2-6)*
    Craiglea &*※ (Mrs Ruth Bellord) The Street. Cottage garden crammed with interesting shrubs and plants; vegetable garden; small pond
    Hartlip Place ※ (Lt-Col & Mrs J R Yerburgh) Secret garden concealed by rhododendrons, planted with old roses; shrub borders; wilderness walk; sloping lawns; pond. TEAS in aid of Kent Gardens Trust

■ **Hault Farm** &*※ (Mr & Mrs T D Willett) 7m S of Canterbury, between Petham and Waltham. From B2068 turn R signed Petham/Waltham; 2m on L. Victorian house on site of Knights Templar property once occupied by Crusader Sir Geofrey de Hautt. Plantaholic's 4 acres of woodland, bog, herbaceous, rose and scree areas. TEAS. *Adm £2 Chd £1. Suns and Bank Hols, March 29 to June 28, Aug 2 to Sept 13 (2-5). For NGS Suns March 29, May 3, Sept 13 (2-5). Groups welcome at any time by appt, please* **Tel 01227 700263**

Haydown, Great Buckland *※ (Dr & Mrs I D Edeleanu) nr Cobham, 4m S of A2. Take turning for Cobham, at war memorial straight ahead down hill, under railway bridge

to T-junc, turn R, after 200yds take L fork, follow narrow lane for 1½m. Entrance on L after riding stables. North Downs 9-acre hillside garden developed since 1980, with woodland and meadowland, incl native and unusual trees, shrubs, small vineyard, orchard, ponds, bog garden; patio with terracing; roses. TEAS on June 13. *Adm £2 (£3 on July 15 to incl glass of Haydown wine) Acc chd free (ACNO to Northfleet Rotary Club Charities). Sat June 13 (2-6); Wed July 15 (6-9)* **NB EVENING OPENING**

●**Hever Castle and Gardens** &※ (Broadland Properties Ltd) 3m SE of Edenbridge, between Sevenoaks and E. Grinstead. Signed from junctions 5 and 6 of M25, from A21 and from A264. Reinstated 120 yds of herbaceous border, also formal Italian gardens with statuary, sculpture and fountains; large lake; 'splashing' water maze; rose garden and Tudor herb and knot garden, topiary and maze. Romantic moated castle, the childhood home of Anne Boleyn, also open. No dogs in castle, on lead only in gardens. Refreshments available. *Open every day from March 1 to Nov 30 (11-6 last adm 5, March & Nov 11-4, Castle opens 12 noon). Adm Castle and gardens £7.00, Chd £3.80, gardens only £5.50, Chd £3.60*

¶■ **Higham Park, Bridge** &*※ (Mrs P Gibb) 3m SE of Canterbury take A2 Canterbury - Dover, use Bridge exit. Entrance to Higham Park top of Bridge hill (Dover side of village). The garden of 24 acres is undergoing extensive restoration by the owners. The C18 mansion (not open) was once the home of the colourful Count Louis Zborowski and his Chitty Chitty Bang Bang Cars. It is surrounded by parkland and orchards. The Edwardian terraced rose garden, Italian-style water garden and the secret garden are re-emerging. In spring there is a profusion of bulbs. TEAS. *Adm £2.50 Chd 50p. Open Suns, Weds, Bank Hol Mons April 1 to Sept 30 (12-5). For NGS Sun April 12. Private visits welcome, please* **Tel 01227 830830**

■ **Hole Park, Rolvenden-Cranbrook** &※ (Mr & Mrs D G W Barham) On B2086. 15-acre garden for all seasons set in beautiful parkland with lovely views. Extensive yew hedges a special feature amidst lawns and fine trees. Pools, walled gardens, roses and mixed borders in formal garden. In the natural parts - rhododendrons, azaleas, flowering shrubs, massed spring bulbs and a walk in the bluebell wood. Autumn colours. *Adm £2.50 Chd (under 12) 50p (ACNO to St Mary's Church, Rolvenden©). Weds April 8 to June 24 (2-6). For NGS Suns April 12, 19, May 3, 10, 24, 31, Oct 11, 18 (2-6). Private visits and parties by arrangement, please* **Tel 01580 241251**

▲**Ightham Mote, Ivy Hatch** & (in part) *※ (The National Trust) 6m E of Sevenoaks, off A25 and 2½m S of Ightham [188: TQ584535] Buses: Maidstone & District 222/3 from BR Borough Green: NU-Venture 67/8 Sevenoaks to Plaxtol passing BR Sevenoaks: alight Ivy Hatch ½m walk to Ightham Mote. 14-acre garden and moated medieval manor c.1340. Mixed borders with many unusual plants; lawns; courtyard; newly-planted orchard; water features incl small lake, leading to woodland walk with rhododendrons and shrubs. TEAS. *Adm £4.50 Chd £2.25. House and garden open as normal. Tours of garden 1.30pm, 2.30pm, 3.30pm. NT members £1 donation for tours. For NGS Wed June 24 (11.30-5.30 last admission 5pm)*

Jessups, Markbeech ❀ (The Hon Robin Denison-Pender) 3m S of Edenbridge. From B2026 Edenbridge-Hartfield rd turn L opp Queens Arms signed Markbeech, 100yds on L. Small established garden, spring bulbs and shrubs, fine views to Sevenoaks Weald. Small wood. Wildfowl pond (25 different breeds). TEAS. *Adm £1.50 Acc chd free. Sun March 29 (2-5)*

▲**Knole, Sevenoaks** ఉ ⚘ (The Lord Sackville; The National Trust) Station: Sevenoaks. Pleasance, deer park, landscape garden, herb garden. TEAS. *Adm Car park £2.50: garden £1 Chd 50p; house £5 Chd £2.50. For NGS Weds June 3, Aug 5 (11-4 last adm 3)*

¶**Knowle Hill Farm, Ulcombe** ఉ ⚘ ❀ (Hon Andrew and Mrs Cairns) 7m E of Maidstone. From M20 exit 8 follow A20 towards Lenham for 3m. R to Ulcombe. After 1½m, L at crossroads to Lenham. Take first R, past Pepper Box pub then L. 1½-acre garden planted in last 10 years with wonderful views over Weald. Described by one visitor as a controlled jungle, the intention is to create a tapestry of colour and texture which is interesting all yr. Mediterranean plants such as cistus, rosemary and lavender thrive on the warm southerly hillside with hebes, myrtles and penstemons. TEAS in aid of All Saints Church Ulcombe. *Adm £2 Acc child free. Sun Aug 30 (2-6)*

Kypp Cottage, Biddenden ⚘ ❀ (Mrs Zena Grant) Woolpack Corner. At Tenterden Rd A262 junction with Benenden Rd. Tiny woodland garden planted by owner on rough ground, now overflowing with interesting plants. Hundreds of roses and clematis intertwine, providing shady, scented nooks. Large variety of geraniums and other ground cover plants. Subject of Meridian TV programme. Morning coffee & TEAS. *Adm £1.50 Chd 30p (ACNO to NSPCC®). Suns May 24, 31; June 7, 14, 21, 28 (2-6); Mons May 25, June 1, 8, 15, 22, 29,; Tues May 26, June 2, 9, 16, 23, 30; Weds May 27, June 3, 10, 17, 24, July 1; Thurs May 28, June 4, 11, 18, 25, July 2; Fri May 22; Sat May 23 (10.30-6); also private visits welcome, please Tel 01580 291480*

Ladham House, Goudhurst ఉ ❀ (Mr & Mrs A Jessel) On NE of village, off A262. 10 acres with rolling lawns, fine specimen trees, rhododendrons, camellias, azaleas, shrubs and magnolias. Arboretum. Spectacular twin mixed borders; fountain and bog gardens. Fine view. Subject of many magazine articles. TEAS. *Adm £2.50 Chd (under 12) 50p (ACNO to Kent Association for the Blind ®). Suns May 3, 17, Oct 4 (1-5.30)*

Larksfield, Crockham Hill ఉ ❀ (Mr & Mrs P Dickinson) 3m N of Edenbridge, on B269 (Limpsfield-Oxted). Octavia Hill, a founder of the NT, lived here and helped create the original garden; fine collection of azaleas, shrubs, herbaceous plants, rose beds and woodlands; views over Weald and Ashdown Forest. **The Red House** and **Larksfield Cottage** gardens open same days. TEAS at The Red House. *Combined adm £2.50 OAPs £2 Chd 50p (ACNO to the Schizophrenia Association of Great Britain and St John Ambulance Kent.®). Suns May 17, 31 (2-6)*

Larksfield Cottage, Crockham Hill ఉ ❀ (Mr & Mrs Steven Ferigno) 3m N of Edenbridge, on B269. An enchanting garden redesigned in 1981 with attractive lawns and shrubs. Views over the Weald and Ashdown Forest. **Larksfield** and **The Red House** gardens also open same days. *Combined adm £2.50 OAPs £2 Chd 50p (ACNO to The Schizophrenia Association of Great Britain and St John Ambulance Kent®). Suns May 17, 31 (2-6)*

43 Layhams Road, West Wickham ఉ ⚘ (Mrs Dolly Robertson) Semi-detached house recognisable by small sunken flower garden in the front. Opp Wickham Court Farm. A raised vegetable garden, purpose-built for the disabled owner with easy access to wide terraced walkways. The owner, who maintains the entire 24′ × 70′ area herself, would be pleased to pass on her experiences as a disabled gardener so that others may share her joy and interest. *Collecting box. Private visits welcome all year, please Tel 0181 462 4196*

Little Combourne Farmhouse, Curtisden Green ఉ ⚘ (Mr & Mrs Grant Whytock) 5m NW of Cranbrook. Turn off A262 at Chequers Inn in Goudhurst, then 2nd R signed Blantyre House and Curtisden Green. Family garden of 1½ acres with old-fashioned roses, set in idyllic rural countryside, created by present owners around C16 farmhouse. TEAS. *Adm £1.50 Acc chd free. Sat, Sun June 20, 21 (2-6)*

Little Oast, Otford ❀ (Mrs Pam Hadrill) High Street, 3m N of Sevenoaks at W end of village, just past Horns Inn, turn R into private drive. (Please park in public car park opp Bull Inn or in Catholic church car park 80yds past Little Oast.) ½-acre garden of varied planting, designed to complement circular oast; patios, pots, a pond and 3 summer-houses. TEAS. *Adm £1.50 Acc chd free (ACNO to Hospice in the Weald®). Sun July 12 (2-6)*

Little Trafalgar, Selling ఉ ⚘ ❀ (Mr & Mrs R J Dunnett) 4m SE of Faversham. From A2 (M2) or A251 make for Selling Church, then follow signs to garden. ¾-acre garden of great interest both for its wealth of attractive and unusual plants, and its intimate, restful design. Emphasis is placed on the creative and artistic use of plants. Featured in Geoff Hamilton's Paradise Gardens. Sculpture by David Heathcote. TEAS. *Adm £1.50 Acc chd free. Suns June 7, 21, July 12, 26, Aug 9, 30, Sept 20; Mon Aug 31 (2-6); also private visits welcome, please Tel 01227 752219*

Lodge House, Smeeth ఉ ❀ (Mr & Mrs J Talbot) Between Ashford and Sellindge. 3m along A20 from M20 Junction 10, turn L signed to Smeeth. Turn R at Woolpack, continue ½m. Opposite Pound Lane turn R into entrance. 2-acre garden, with lawns sloping into sheepfields; daffodils, blossoms, flower borders and ponds in lovely setting. Plant sale in aid of Hardy Plant Society. TEAS. *Adm £2 Acc chd free. Sun April 19 (2-6)*

Long Barn, Weald ⚘ (Brandon & Sarah Gough) 3m S of Sevenoaks. Signed to Weald at junction of A21 and B245. Garden at W end of village. 1st garden of Harold Nicolson and Vita Sackville-West. 3 acres with terraces and slopes, giving considerable variety. Dutch garden designed by Lutyens, features mixed planting in raised beds. Teas in village. *Adm £2 OAP £1 Chd 50p, under 5 free (ACNO to Hospice in the Weald®). Suns June 21, July 19 (2-5)*

Longacre, Perry Wood, Selling &⅋֎ (Dr & Mrs G Thomas) 5m SE of Faversham. From A2 (M2) or A251 follow signs for Selling, passing White Lion on L, 2nd R and immediately L, continue for ¼m. From A252 at Chilham, take turning signed Selling at Badgers Hill Fruit Farm. L at 2nd Xrds, next R, L and then R. Small, ¾-acre plantsman's garden with wide variety of interesting plants, created and maintained entirely by owners. Lovely walks in Perry Woods adjacent to garden. TEAS in aid of local charities. *Adm £1 Acc chd free (ACNO to Conterbury Pilgrims Hospice®). Suns April 12, 26, May 3, 17, 24, June 7, 21, July 5, 19, Aug 30, Sept 13; Mons April 13, May 4, 25, Aug 31 (2-5); also private visits welcome, please* Tel **01227 752254**

Lullingstone Castle &⅋֎ (Mr & Mrs Guy Hart Dyke) In the Darenth Valley via Eynsford on A225. Eynsford Station ½m. All cars and coaches via Roman Villa. Lawns, woodland and lake, mixed border, small herb garden. Henry VII gateway; Church on the lawn open. TEAS. *Adm garden £2.50 OAPs/Chd £1; house 50p extra. Sun June 14 (2-6)*

Luton House, Selling ⅋ (Sir John & Lady Swire) 4m SE of Faversham. From A2 (M2) or A251 make for White Lion, entrance 30yds E on same side of rd. 5 acres; C19 landscaped garden; ornamental ponds; trees underplanted with azaleas, camellias, woodland plants. *Adm £2 Acc chd free. Sun May 10 (2-6)*

190 Maidstone Road, Chatham ⅋֎ (Dr M K Douglas) On A230 Chatham-Maidstone, about 1m out of Chatham and 7m from Maidstone. Informal ¼-acre garden; herbaceous borders on either side of former tennis court; scree garden and pool; many snowdrops and other spring bulbs. TEAS (not Feb). *Adm £1.50 Acc chd free. Suns Feb 22 (2-5) (snowdrops), March 29, May 31, Aug 2 (2-6)*

■ **Marle Place, Brenchley** &⅋֎ (Mr & Mrs Gerald Williams) 8m SE of Tonbridge, signed from Brenchley. Victorian gazebo; plantsman's shrub borders; walled scented garden, large Edwardian rockery; herbaceous borders and bog garden. Woodland walk; autumn colour. C17 listed house (not open). TEAS. *Adm £3 Chd £2.50. Every day April 1 to Oct 31 (10-5). For NGS Suns April 19, May 31, July 5 (10-6)*

Maycotts, Matfield &⅋֎ (Mr & Mrs David Jolley) 6m SE of Tonbridge. From A21, 1m S of Pembury, turn N onto B2160, turn L at Xrds in Matfield, and first L at Five Wents into Maycotts Lane. Medium-sized, partly walled garden around C16 farmhouse (not open) being developed by garden designer-owner. Herbaceous borders; old-fashioned and shrub roses; herb garden and potager; unusual perennials and foliage plants. TEAS if fine. *Adm £1.50 Acc chd free. Sun June 14 (2-6)*

Meadow Wood, Penshurst & (Mr & Mrs James Lee) 1¼m SE of Penshurst on B2176 in direction of Bidborough. 1920s garden, on edge of wood with long southerly views over the Weald, and with interesting trees and shrubs; azaleas, rhododendrons and naturalised bulbs in woods with mown walks. TEAS. *Adm £2 Chd £1 (ACNO to Relate®). Sun May 10 (2-6)*

Mere House, Mereworth &֎ (Mr & Mrs Andrew Wells) Midway between Tonbridge & Maidstone. From A26 turn N on to B2016 and then into Mereworth village. 6-acre garden with C18 lake; ornamental shrubs and trees with foliage contrast; lawns, daffodils; Kentish cobnut plat. Woodland walk. TEAS. *Adm £1.50 Acc chd free. Suns April 5, Oct 18 (2-5.30)*

Mill House &֎ (Dr & Mrs Brian Glaisher) Mill Lane, ½m N of Hildenborough, 5m S of Sevenoaks. From B245 turn into Mill Lane at Mill garage. 3-acre garden laid out in 1906; herbaceous and mixed borders; new secluded herb garden; old shrub roses and climbers; clematis and many fine trees. Formal garden with topiary; ruins of windmill and conservatory with exotics. TEAS. *Adm £2 Chd 25p. Sun June 21 (2-6)*

■ **Mount Ephraim, Hernhill** (Mrs M N Dawes and Mr & Mrs E S Dawes) Faversham. From M2 and A299 take Hernhill turning at Duke of Kent. Herbaceous border; topiary; daffodils and rhododendrons; rose terraces leading to a small lake; Japanese rock garden with pools; water garden; small vineyard. TEAS daily except Tues; lunches only Bank Hol Suns & Mons. *Adm £2.50 Chd £1. Open Easter to mid-Sept (1-6). For NGS Suns April 26 (ACNO to Karna Prayag Trust, Madras), Aug 23 (1-6)*

Nettlestead Place, Nettlestead &⅋ (Mr & Mrs Roy Tucker) 6m W/SW of Maidstone. Turn S off A26 onto B2015 then 1m on L (next to Nettlestead Church). C13 manor house set in 7-acre plantsman's garden on different levels with fine views over open countryside; many plant collections incl herbaceous and shrub island beds; formal garden with shrub and species roses; hardy geranium border; sunken pond garden; also 4 acres in course of development as pinetum and glen garden. TEAS. *Adm £2.50 Acc chd free (ACNO to Friedrich's Ataxia Group Research®). Suns June 7, Sept 13 (2-5.30)*

New Barns House, West Malling &֎ (Mr & Mrs P H Byam-Cook) Leave M20 at Exit 4 to West Malling. In High Street turn E down Waters Lane, at T-junction turn R, take bridge over by-pass, follow lane 400yds to New Barns House. 6-acre garden with fine trees and flowering cherries. Walled garden, mixed borders and shrubs. TEAS. *Adm £2 Acc chd free. Sun May 17 (2-6)*

Northbourne Court, nr Deal ⅋ (The Hon Charles James) Signs in village. Great brick terraces, belonging to an earlier Elizabethan mansion, provide a picturesque setting for a wide range of shrubs and plants on chalk soil; geraniums, fuchsias and grey-leaved plants. *Adm £3 OAPs/Chd £2.50 (ACNO to National Art Collections Fund®). Sun July 5 (2-5)*

Olantigh, Wye ⅋ (Mr & Mrs J R H Loudon) 6m NE of Ashford. Turn off A28 either to Wye or at Godmersham; ¾m from Wye on rd to Godmersham. Edwardian garden in beautiful setting; water garden; rockery; shrubbery; herbaceous border; extensive lawns. *Adm £1.80. Suns April 26, June 21 (2-5)*

Old Buckhurst, Markbeech ֎ (Mr & Mrs J Gladstone) Chiddingstone Hoath Road. 4m E of Edenbridge via

B2026, at Cowden Pound turn E to Markbeech. First house on R after leaving Markbeech on Penshurst Rd. 1-acre garden surrounding C15 farmhouse (not open). Part-walled cottage garden; shrub roses, clematis, shrubs and wide range of herbaceous plants carefully planned and maintained by owners for all year round interest, using colour, texture and shape. Teas available in Chiddingstone village. *Adm £2 Acc chd free (ACNO to St Mary's Church, Chiddingstone©). Sats May 30, Sept 5; Suns May 31, June 7, 14, Sept 6 (2-6)*

Old Place Farm, High Halden &♨❀ (Mr & Mrs Jeffrey Eker) 3m NE of Tenterden. From A28 take Woodchurch Rd (opp Chequers public house) in High Halden, and follow for ½m. 3½-acre garden, mainly designed by Anthony du Gard Pasley, surrounding period farmhouse & buildings with paved herb garden & parterres, small lake, ponds, lawns, mixed borders, cutting garden, old shrub roses, lilies & foliage plants; all created since 1969. Featured in Country Life, House & Garden and several books. TEAS in aid of St Mary's Church, High Halden. *Adm £2 Chd 50p. Sun May 3 (2-6)*

Old Tong Farm, Brenchley ♨❀ (Mr & Mrs Simon Toynbee) 1¼m S of Brenchley. Follow Horsmonden rd from Brenchley, take first R into Fairmans Lane. Medium-size garden made by owners around C15 farmhouse (not open); rose garden, pond, herb parterre, nut plat; wild woodland walk. Featured on Channel 4 Garden Party in 1997. Adj cottage with newly planted garden also open. TEAS. *Adm £2 (£3 on June 24 to incl glass of wine) Acc chd free. Suns June 28, July 12 (2-6); Wed June 24 (6-9)* **NB EVENING OPENING**

Orchard Cottage, Bickley &♨❀ (Professor & Mrs C G Wall) 1½m E of Bromley, about 400 yds from the A222. From Bickley Park Road turn into Pines Road, then 1st R into Woodlands Road, no 3 is 1st house on L. Attractive ⅓-acre garden in course of development; mixed borders with many interesting herbaceous plants and shrubs; scree beds and troughs with alpines and other small plants. TEAS. *Adm £1.50 Acc chd free (ACNO to Downs Syndrome Association: SE Branch®). Sun Aug 2 (2-5.30)*

Oswalds, Bishopsbourne (Mr & Mrs Wolfgang Kerck) 4m S of Canterbury. Turn off A2 at B2065, follow signs to Bishopsbourne, house next to church. 3-acre plantsman's garden. Year round interest includes bulbs, spring garden, mixed borders, rockeries, pools, bog garden, potager, pergola, old roses and many fruit varieties. House (not open) has interesting literary connections. *Adm £1.50 Chd 50p. By appointment only, please* **Tel 01227 830340**

Otham Gardens 4m SE of Maidstone. From A2020 or A274 follow signs for Otham 1m. Parking restricted to official car parks except for disabled people. TEAS. *Combined adm £2.50 Acc chd free (ACNO to Maidstone Mencap®). Sun June 28 (2-6)*
  ¶**The Barn** (Mrs Evelyn Catmur) A garden built around a cattle yard
  Bramley (Miss Ware) Interesting old garden on different levels; wildlife pond

Greenhill House (Dr & Mrs Hugh Vaux) Established herbaceous and shrub borders; wildflower garden; alpines
Little Squerryes & (Mr & Mrs Gerald Coomb) Established garden; herbaceous borders; interesting trees
The Limes & (Mrs John Stephens) Well-established garden with herbaceous borders and wisteria pergola
Stoneacre Special opening; NT members to pay. For garden description, see individual entry
Swallows & (Mr & Mrs Eric Maidment) Cottage garden with colourful terrace
Tulip Cottage & (Mrs Gloria Adams) Shows what can be done in a small space

▲**Owl House, Lamberhurst** &(in parts)❀ (Maureen, Marchioness of Dufferin and Ava) 1m W of A21, signposted from Lamberhurst. 16½-acre woodland garden surrounding C16 wool smuggler's cottage: water gardens, unusual roses climbing into woodland trees; daffodils, rhododendrons, azaleas, magnolias, camellias, roses, irises, good autumn colour. *Adm £4 Chd £1 (ACNO to Maureen's Oast House for Arthritics®). For NGS Suns April 5, May 17, Oct 11 (11-6)*

Oxon Hoath, nr Hadlow &♨❀ (Mrs Henry Bayne-Powell) 5m NE of Tonbridge. *Car essential.* Via A20, turn off S at Wrotham Heath onto Seven Mile Lane (B2016); at Mereworth Xrds turn W, through West Peckham. Or via A26, in Hadlow turn off N along Carpenters Lane. 10 acres, landscaped with fine trees, rhododendrons and azaleas; woodland walk; replanted cedar avenue; formal parterre rose garden by Nesfield. Large Kentish ragstone house (not shown) principally Georgian but dating back to C14; Victorian additions by Salvin. Once owned by Culpeppers, grandparents of Catherine Howard. View over C18 lake to Hadlow Folly. Picnickers welcome. *Adm £1.50 Chd 50p (ACNO to W. Peckham Church©). Sun May 24 (2-6)*

The Pear House, Sellindge ❀ (Mrs Nicholas Snowden) Stone Hill. 6m E of Ashford. Turn L off A20 at Sellindge Church towards Brabourne into Stone Hill. ⅔ acre developed by present owner. Contains smaller gardens with informal planting; bulbs, roses (over 100 different, mostly old-fashioned), shrubs, small orchard with climbing roses, pond garden, shady areas. *Adm £1.50 Chd 50p. Due to limited parking, visits by appointment welcome anytime between April 25 to July 12, please* **Tel 01303 812147**

■**Penshurst Place** &♨ (Viscount De L'Isle), S of Tonbridge on B2176, N of Tunbridge Wells on A26. 10 acres of garden dating back to C14; garden divided into series of 'rooms' by over a mile of clipped yew hedge; profusion of spring bulbs; herbaceous borders; formal rose garden; famous peony border. All yr interest. TEAS and light refreshments. *Adm House & Gardens £5.70 OAPs £5.30 Chd £3.20 Family Ticket £15: Gardens £4.20 OAPs £3.70 Chd £2.80 Family Ticket £12. Open daily March 28 to Nov 1. For NGS Wed May 6, Thurs June 4 (11-6)*

Pett Place, Charing ♨❀ (Mrs I Mills, C I Richmond-Watson Esq & A Rolla Esq) 6m NW of Ashford. From A20 turn N into Charing High St. At end turn R into Pett Lane towards Westwell. Walled gardens covering nearly 4 acres. A garden of pleasing vistas and secret places which has been featured in Country Life, House and Garden etc. A ruined C13 chapel is a romantic feature beside the manor house (not open), which was re-fronted about 1700 and which Pevsner describes as 'presenting grandiloquently towards the road'. TEAS. *Adm £2 Chd 50p (ACNO to Kent Gardens Trust®). Sats, Suns April 25, 26, June 27, 28 (2.30-5)*

Pevington Farm, Pluckley &☙ (Mr & Mrs David Mure) 3m SW of Charing. From Charing take B2077 towards Pluckley, before Pluckley turn R towards Egerton, Pevington Farm ½m on. From SW go through Pluckley, turn L for Egerton. ¾-acre garden with wonderful views over the Weald. Mixed borders with many interesting plants. Tours of garden with the owner at 12pm, 2pm and 3.30pm. TEAS for Friends of St Nicholas Church, Pluckely. *Adm £2 Chd 50p. Sun June 14 (11-5); private visits welcome in May, June, July, please* **Tel 01233 840317**

■ **The Pines Garden & The Bay Museum, St Margaret's Bay** &☙ (The St Margaret's Bay Trust) Beach Rd, 4½m NE of Dover. Beautiful 6-acre seaside garden. Water garden with waterfall and lake. Statue of Sir Winston Churchill complemented by the Bay Museum opposite. Fascinating maritime and local interest. TEAS. *Adm £1.50 Chd 35p. Gardens open daily except Christmas Day. Museum open May to end Aug (closed Mon, except Bank Hols, and Tues). For NGS Suns April 12, May 24, Aug 30 (10-5)*

Placketts Hole, Bicknor &☙☙ (Mr & Mrs D P Wainman) 5m S of Sittingbourne, and W of B2163. Owners have designed and planted 2-acre garden around charming old house (C16 with Georgian additions); interesting mix of shrubs, large borders, rose garden, a formal herb garden and sweet-smelling plants. TEAS. *Adm £1.50 Acc chd free (ACNO to Kent Gardens Trust®). Sun July 5 (2-6.30)*

Plaxtol Gardens 5m N of Tonbridge, 6m E of Sevenoaks, turn E off A227 to Plaxtol village. TEAS. Tickets and maps available at all gardens. Parking at Spoute Cottage. *Combined adm £3 Acc chd free (ACNO to Friends of Plaxtol Church©). Sun June 21 (2-6)*

   Ducks Farm ☙ (Mr & Mrs H Puleston Jones) Dux Lane. 2 acres, in course of restoration, surrounding medieval/Victorian farmhouse (not open). Mixed herbaceous borders, walled garden, vegetable garden, herb garden

   ¶**Penny Hall Cottage** (Frenie Pearce) The Street. The 1st house downhill of Papermakers Arms in High Street. Minute garden designed by owner. Low maintenance with maximum foliage interest

   Spoute Cottage &☙☙ (Mr & Mrs Donald Forbes) situated at the bottom of Plaxtol St on L side opp Hyders Forge. ¾ acre of mixed borders of contrasting flowering and foliage plants, especially for flower arranging; small pond & stream. Japanese garden. Plant nursery attached. Large car park

   Stonewold House (Mr & Mrs John Young) The Street. Situated by 2nd lamp post down the Street on R before Papermakers Arms. 4½ acres of mixed borders, vegetable plots, wisteria pergola and fruit trees. Wonderful views overlooking small lake planted to encourage wildlife

Puxted House, Brenchley &☙ (P J Oliver-Smith Esq) 6m SE of Tonbridge. From A21 1m S of Pembury turn N onto B2160, turn R at Xrds in Matfield signed Brenchley. 1½ acres with rare and coloured foliage shrubs, water and woodland plants. Alpine and rose garden all labelled. Present owner cleared 20yrs of brambles in 1981 before replanting. TEAS. *Adm £1.50 Acc chd free. Sun June 14 (2-6). Also opening with Brenchley Gardens Sun May 17*

Ramhurst Manor, Leigh & (The Lady Rosie Kindersley) Powder Mill Lane, Tonbridge. Historic property once belonged to the Black Prince and Culpepper family. Formal gardens; roses, azaleas, rhododendrons, wild flowers. TEA. *Adm £1.50 Acc chd free. Sun June 7 (2.30-6)*

The Red House, Crockham Hill &☙ (K C L Webb Esq) 3m N of Edenbridge. On Limpsfield-Oxted Rd, B269. Formal features of this large garden are kept to a minimum; rose walk leads on to 3 acres of rolling lawns flanked by fine trees and shrubs incl rhododendrons, azaleas and magnolias. Views over the Weald and Ashdown Forest. TEAS. **Larksfield** and **Larksfield Cottage gardens** also open same days. *Combined adm £2.50 OAPs £2 Chd 50p (ACNO to The Schizophrenia Assoc of Great Britain and St John Ambulance Kent®). Suns May 17, 31 (2-6)*

■ **Riverhill House, Sevenoaks** ☙ (The Rogers family) 2m S of Sevenoaks on A225. Mature hillside garden with extensive views; specimen trees, sheltered terraces with roses and choice shrubs; bluebell wood with rhododendrons and azaleas; picnics allowed. TEAS. *Adm £2.50 Chd 50p. Every Wed, Sun and Bank Hol weekends in April, May and June only (12-6). For NGS Weds April 22, May 13 (12-6)*

■ **Rock Farm, Nettlestead** ☙☙ (Mrs P A Corfe) 6m W of Maidstone. Turn S off A26 onto B2015 then 1m S of Wateringbury turn R. 2-acre garden set around old Kentish farmhouse in beautiful setting; created with emphasis on all-year interest and ease of maintenance. Plantsman's collection of shrubs, trees and perennials for alkaline soil: extensive herbaceous border, vegetable area, bog garden and plantings around two large natural ponds. Plant nursery adjoining garden. *Adm £2 Chd 50p (ACNO to St Mary's Church, Nettlestead®). Open Every Wed & Sat (11-5) & Sun (2-5) in April; Aug 1, 2, 5, 8 & 9. For NGS every Wed & Sat in May, June and July (11-5)*

Rogers Rough, Kilndown &☙☙ (Richard and Hilary Bird) 10m S of Tonbridge. From A21 2m S of Lamberhurst turn E into Kilndown; take 1st R down Chick's Lane until rd divides. Garden writer's 1½-acre garden, mainly herbaceous borders, but also rock gardens, shrubs, a small wood and pond. Extensive views. TEAS in aid of local charities. *Adm £2 Chd 50p. Suns June 21, July 19 (2-5.30); parties welcome by appointment*

Rose Cottage, Hartley &☙☙ (Mr & Mrs Crowe) Castle Hill, 3m NE of Swanley and 4m SE of Dartford. From B260 at Longfield, turn S at main roundabout, ½m up hill to Hartley Green with war memorial, where Castle Hill runs down to Fawkham Church: Rose Cottage garden is 100yds down Castle Hill on L. No parking on Castle Hill, please park on main road. 1-acre garden created from field since 1988, variety of shrubs and perennials, wild life pond, aviary and paved garden. TEA in aid of Demelza Childrens Hospice. *Adm £1.50 Acc chd free. Sun July 5 (1.30-5.30): private visits also welcome, please* **Tel 01474 707376**

St Clere, Kemsing &% (Mr & Mrs Ronnie Norman) 6m NE of Sevenoaks. Take A25 from Sevenoaks toward Ightham; 1m past Seal turn L signed Heaverham and Kemsing; in Heaverham take rd to R signed Wrotham and West Kingsdown; in 75yds straight ahead marked Private rd; 1st L and follow rd to house. 4-acre garden with herbaceous borders, shrubs, rare trees. C17 mansion (not open). TEAS. *Adm £2.50 Chd 50p. Sun June 21 (2-6)*

St Michael's Gardens Roydon Road, Seven Mile Lane, 5m NE Tonbridge, 5m SW Maidstone. On A26 at Mereworth roundabout take S exit (A228) signed Paddock Wood, after 1 ½m turn L at top of rise (signed Roydon). Gardens ¼m up hill on L. TEAS. *Combined adm £2.50 OAPs £1.50 Chd 50p. Suns April 26 (tulips)(2-6), May 17 (irises) (2-6), June 14 (roses) (5-9 wine & biscuits)*

   St Michael's House &% (Brig & Mrs W Magan) Old vicarage garden of ¾ acre enclosed by shaped yew hedge; tulips; roses, climbing roses, irises; 6-acre meadow with extensive views

   ¶**St Michael's Cottage** &% (Mr & Mrs Peter Fox) Newly planted cottage garden with rockery, arbour, ponds and wild life area

●**Saltwood Castle** (Mrs Alan Clark) 2m NW of Hythe, 4m W of Folkestone; from A20 turn S at sign to Saltwood. Medieval castle, subject of quarrel between Thomas a Becket and Henry II. C13 crypt and dungeons; armoury; battlement walks and watch towers. Lovely views; spacious lawns and borders; courtyard walls covered with roses. Picnics allowed. Saltwood Castle closed to the general public in 1998. *Private parties of 20 or more weekdays only, please write for appt*

■**Scotney Castle** &% (Mrs Christopher Hussey; The National Trust) On A21 London-Hastings, 1¼m S of Lamberhurst. Bus: (Mon to Sat) Autopoint 256, Tunbridge Wells-Wadhurst; alight Lamberhurst Green. Famous picturesque landscape garden, created by the Hussey family in the 1840s surrounding moated C14 Castle. House (not open) by Salvin, 1837. Old Castle open May-mid-Sept (same times as garden). Gift Shop. Picnic area in car park. Tea Lamberhurst. *Adm £3.80 Chd £1.90; Family ticket £9.50; Pre-booked parties of 15 or more (Wed-Fri) £2.80 Chd £1.40; April 1-Nov 1, daily except Mons & Tues, but open Bank Hol Mons (closed Good Fri). Wed-Fri (11-6), Sats & Suns 2-6 or sunset if earlier; Bank Hol Mons & Suns preceding (12-6). For NGS (ACNO to Trinity Hospice, Clapham Common®) Mon May 25 (12-6)*

Sea Close, Hythe %% (Maj & Mrs R H Blizard) Cannongate Rd. A259 Hythe-Folkestone; ½m from Hythe, signed. 21st year of opening but not much longer. An exceptional site and 1¾-acre garden overlooking the sea. Described as a gorgeous muddle, but to a carefully planned design. Created & maintained by present owners since 1966. No outside assistance. Colour throughout the year. Over 1000 varieties of plants & shrubs, many un-

usual. Cold refreshments. Teas Hythe. *Adm £1.50 Acc chd free (ACNO to Royal Signals Benevolent Fund®). Suns May 17, June 21, July 12, Aug 9 (2-5), Oct 4 (2-4)*

The Silver Spray, Sellindge &%% (Mr & Mrs C T Orsbourne) 7m SE of Ashford on A20 opposite school. 1-acre garden developed and planted since 1983 and maintained by owners. Attractively laid out gardens and wild area combine a keen interest in conservation (especially butterflies) with a love of unusual hardy and tender plants. TEAS. *Adm £1.50 Acc chd free (ACNO to St Mary's Church, Sellindge©). Suns May 24, June 14, Aug 30; Mons May 25, Aug 31; Weds June 3, July 8, Aug 26; Sats June 6, July 11 (2-5)*

■**Sissinghurst Garden, Cranbrook** &%% (Nigel Nicolson Esq; The National Trust) Station: Staplehurst. Bus: MD5 from Maidstone 14m; 297 Tunbridge Wells (not Suns) 15m. Garden created by the late V Sackville-West and Sir Harold Nicolson. Spring garden, herb garden. Tudor building and tower, partly open to public. Moat. **Because of the limited capacity of the garden, daily visitor numbers are restricted; timed tickets are in operation and visitors may have to wait before entry.** Lunches and TEAS. *Adm £6 Chd £3. Garden open April 1 to Oct 15. (Closed Mons incl Bank Hols). Tues to Fri 1-6.30 (last adm 6pm); Sats and Suns 10-5.30 (last adm 5pm); For NGS (ACNO to Charleston Farmhouse Trust®) Weds April 22, June 3, July 15, Oct 7 (1-6.30)*

Sissinghurst Place Gardens, Sissinghurst &% 2m NE of Cranbrook, E of Sissinghurst village ½m from Sissinghurst NT garden on A262. TEA. *Combined adm £2.50 (June 23 £3.50 incl wine) (ACNO to St George's Institute, Sissinghurst®). Suns, Mons, Tues April 5, 6, 7, June 21, 22 (1.30-5.30), Tues June 23 (6-9)* **NB EVENING OPENING**

   Sissinghurst Place (Mr & Mrs Simon macLachlan) Large Victorian garden of herbaceous beds, lawns, fine trees, and established yew hedges; spring woodland garden with daffodils, hellebores and pond; herbs and climbers in ruin of original house

   The Coach House (Mr & Mrs Michael Sykes) House and garden adjacent and originally part of Sissinghurst Place. In 1983, the owners designed and planted a new garden within established yew hedges. Many unusual trees, shrubs and plants

Slaney Cottage, Staplehurst % (Roger & Trisha Fermor), Headcorn Road, about 1m to E of A229 (Maidstone-Hastings). Please park in field adjoining cottage - not on road outside. Two-acre garden in the making, surrounding C18 cottage: old roses, clematis species, hardy geraniums and other herbaceous plants, both unusual and favourites: wildlife ponds and new woodland area. TEAS. *Adm £1.50 Acc chd free. Sun July 26 (2-5)*

■**Smallhythe Place, Tenterden** (Ellen Terry Museum) % (The National Trust) 2m S of Tenterden on E side of B2082 to Rye. Three acres of garden include old-fashioned roses and pinks, cottage garden borders, orchard, nuttery. Early C16 half-timbered house was home of actress Ellen Terry from 1899-1928; it contains many stage costumes and personal mementoes. *Adm £3 Chd*

1.50, Family £7. Open Sat to Weds March 28-Oct 29 (2-6 or dusk). For NGS Wed June 17 (2-5.30)

Sotts Hole Cottage, Borough Green ✕ (Mr & Mrs Jim Vinson) Crouch Lane. Crouch Lane runs SE from A25 between Esso garage and Black Horse public house, garden at bottom of 2nd hill (approx ¾m). A redundant farmer's folly. 6 acres of landscaped high maintenance cottage garden relying on annuals and half hardy perennials for colour. Probably at its best in August & September if rabbits allow it. *Adm £2 Chd £1 (ACNO to Heart of Kent Hospice®). Mon April 13, Suns June 14, Aug 2, Sept 13 (10-6)*

South Hill Farm, Hastingleigh ⬥✕❀ (Sir Charles Jessel Bt) E of Ashford. Turn off A28 to Wye, go through village and ascend Wye Downs, in 2m turn R at Xrds marked Brabourne and South Hill, then first L. Or from Stone Street (B2068) turn W opp Stelling Minnis, follow signs to Hastingleigh, continue towards Wye and turn L at Xrds marked Brabourne and South Hill, then first L. 2 acres high up on N Downs, C17/18 house (not open); old walls; ha-ha; formal water garden; old and new roses; unusual shrubs, perennials and foliage plants. TEAS. *Adm £2 Chd 25p (ACNO to Kent Association for the Blind®). Suns June 21, July 5 (2-6)*

¶**Southover, Hunton, Maidstone** ❀⬥ (Mr & Mrs David Way) 6m S of Maidstone. Via B2163 turn S down Hunton Hill and West St. By school, R into Grove Lane, parking beyond garden. 1½ acres of plant diversity, changing environments and contrasting atmospheres; a garden of gardens. Strong on internal and external vistas, herbaceous plants, wildlife habitats; good collection penstemons. Featured on TV, in 'Beautiful Borders' and in RHS Journal. TEA. *Adm £1.50 Acc chd free. Thurs June 25 (1.30-5.30); also by appt for groups, please* Tel 01622 820876

Spilsill Court, Staplehurst ⬥✕❀ (Mr & Mrs C G Marshall) Frittenden Road. Proceed to Staplehurst on A229 (Maidstone-Hastings). From S enter village, turn R immediately after Elf garage on R & just before 30mph sign, into Frittenden Rd; garden ½m on, on L. From N go through village to 40mph sign, immediately turn L into Frittenden Rd. Approx 4 acres of garden, orchard and paddock; series of gardens incl blue, white and silver; roses; lawns; shrubs, trees and ponds. Small private chapel. Jacob sheep & unusual poultry. COFFEE/TEA. *Adm £2 Chd (under 16) 50p (ACNO to Gardening for the Disabled Trust®). Suns April 5, July 26 (11-5)*

■ **Squerryes Court** (Mr & Mrs John Warde) ½m W of Westerham signed from A25. 15 acres of well-documented historic garden, C18 landscape. Part of the formal garden has been restored by the family using C17 plan. Lake, spring bulbs, azaleas, herbaceous borders, C18 dovecote, cenotaph commemorating Gen Wolfe; woodland walks. Childrens Garden Trail for Kent Gardens Trust. TEAS on NGS days for St Mary's Church, Westerham. *Adm £2.40 Chd £1.40 (House and garden £3.90 Chd £2.20) Weds, Sats, Suns from April 1 to Sept 30 (Garden 12-5.30: House 1.30-5.30). For NGS Sun July 19, Wed July 22 (12-5.30)*

■ **Stoneacre, Otham** ✕❀ (Mrs Rosemary Alexander; The National Trust) 4m SE of Maidstone, between A2020 and A274. Old world garden recently replanted. Yew hedges; herbaceous borders; ginkgo tree; unusual plants. Timber-framed Hall House dated 1480. Subject of newspaper and magazine articles. (National Trust members please note that openings in aid of the NGS are on days when the property would not normally be open, therefore adm charges apply.) TEAS. *Adm £2.50 Chd 50p. Open Weds & Sats April-Oct 31 (2-5). For NGS Suns April 19, Sept 27 (2-5). Also opening with* **Otham Gardens**. *Private visits welcome, please* Tel 01622 862871

Stonewall Park Gardens, Chiddingstone Hoath (Mr & Mrs V P Fleming) 5m SE of Edenbridge. ½-way between Markbeech and Penshurst. Large walled garden with herbaceous borders. Extensive woodland garden, featuring species and hybrid rhododendrons, azaleas; wandering paths, lakes. **North Lodge** (Mrs Dorothy Michie) traditional cottage garden full of interest. TEAS. *Adm £2.50 Acc chd free (ACNO to Sarah Matheson Trust©). Sun April 26 (2-5)*

Street Cottage, Bethersden (Mr & Mrs Timothy Stubbs) The Street. 6m SW of Ashford, 6m NE of Tenterden, turn off A28 to village centre. 1½-acre garden in lovely setting next to St Margaret's Church. Herbaceous, shrub and rose borders, vegetables and fruit with lawns and ponds; owner maintained. TEAS. *Adm £1.50 Acc chd free. Sun June 28 (2-6)*

Sutton Valence Gardens ⬥✕❀ 5m S of Maidstone on A274. Parking in Sutton Valence School. TEAS and music in gardens and village. *Combined adm £3 Acc chd free (ACNO to Sutton Valence Music Society). Sun May 24 (2-6)*

¶**Boyton Court** (Mr & Mrs Richard Stileman) From upper rd in village, go up Tumblers Hill. Take 2nd lane on R. ¼m down lane on L. Parking in field below house. A 2-acre garden with panoramic views of the Wealden landscape. 3 large mixed borders, rose borders, iris bed, small privy garden and several ornamental ponds. TEAS

The Old Parsonage (Dr & Mrs Richard Perks) From upper rd in village, climb Tumblers Hill, entrance is at top on R. A Parkng available at top of drive. 4-acre labour-saving garden with mixed borders, shrub roses and many different levels. Fine views over the Weald. The C12 keep of Sutton Valence castle is within the grounds

Shirley House ❀ (Mr & Mrs R Payne) From upper rd in village, at the beginning of Tumblers Hill, 10yds past PO on R. Parking at Sutton Valence School. A walled garden, rockeries and dry stone walls divide garden into different levels. Irises a speciality. A large collection of bearded irises on nearby allotment

¶**Sparks Hall** ❀ (Charles Day and Virginia Routh) From village, go down hill towards Headcorn (!274). At bottom of hill, turn R into Forsham Lane. ¼m down lane on L next to Oast House. Parking on verge or in field beyond house. A new garden created over past 4yrs. In front of house a formal garden enclosed in box and yew. Rose garden, wildlife pond and herbaceous borders. TEAS

¶**Tranquil Cottage** (Mrs Joy Warner) In middle of village, off courtyard beside Gulland Hall. Park at Sutton Valence School. A gem of a small, south facing village garden

Swan Oast, Stilebridge & (Mr & Mrs Bedford) Marden, 6m S of Maidstone. On A229 (Maidstone-Hastings) ½m S of Stilebridge inn, 3m N of Staplehurst. 25-year-old 1¾-acre garden, incl ¼ acre of water, landscaped with shrubberies, rockeries, with dwarf conifers and heathers, raised beds of seasonal bedding, kitchen garden; ornamental fish and small collection of waterfowl. Cream TEAS in aid of The Mike Colinwood Trust. *Adm £1.50 (eve openings £3.50 include glass of wine) Acc chd free. Suns April 19, 26, May 3, 10, June 28, July 12, 26, Aug 9, 23, 30 (2-5); Sats July 25, Aug 22 (7-10)* **NB EVENING OPENINGS** *(floodlit with classical music)*

Tanners, Brasted &❀ (Lord & Lady Nolan) 2m E of Westerham, A25 to Brasted; in Brasted turn off alongside the Green and up the hill to the top; 1st drive on R opp Coles Lane. Bus stop Brasted Green and White Hart 200yds. 5 acres; mature trees and shrubs; maples, magnolias, rhododendrons and foliage trees; water garden; interesting new planting. Plants mostly labelled. Teas in Village Tearoom, High Street, Brasted. *Adm £2 Chd 50p. Open Mons, Weds, Thurs by appointment, groups also welcome, please* **Tel 01959 563758**

2 Thorndale Close, Chatham & (Mr & Mrs L O Miles) Chatham. From A229 Chatham-Maidstone rd turn E opp Forte Posthouse into Watson Ave, next R to Thorndale Close. Minute front and rear gardens of 11' × 18' and 20' × 22'. Plantsman's garden with alpines, pool, bog garden, rockery, peat and herbaceous beds. Partly suitable for wheelchairs. *Adm £1 Acc chd under 10 free. Suns March 22, April 5, 19, May 3, 17, 31, June 14, 28 (2-5.30); also private visits welcome, please* **Tel 01634 863329**

Thornham Friars, Thurnham & (Geoffrey Fletcher Esq) Pilgrims Way, 4m NE of Maidstone. From M20 or M2 take A249, at bottom of Detling Hill turn into Detling and 1m along Pilgrims Way to garden. 2-acre garden on chalk. 12-acre park and magnificent views. Many unusual shrubs; trees; lawns with special beds for ericaceous shrubs. Tudor house. *Adm £1.50 Chd 25p. Sun May 31 (2-5.30)*

Torry Hill, Sittingbourne &❀ (Lord & Lady Kingsdown) 5m S of Sittingbourne. Situated in triangle formed by Frinsted, Milstead and Doddington. Leave M20 at junction 8 for A20, Lenham at Great Danes turn N for Hollingbourne and Frinsted (B2163). From M2 Intersection 5 via Bredgar and Milstead. From A2 and E turn S at Ospringe via Newnham and Doddington. 8 acres; large lawns, specimen trees, flowering cherries, rhododendrons, azaleas and naturalised daffodils; walled gardens with lawns, shrubs, roses, herbaceous borders, wild flower areas and vegetables. Extensive views to Medway and Thames estuaries. TEA; refreshments on July 15. *Adm £1.50 Chd (over 12) 50p (ACNO to St Dunstan's Church, Frinsted©). Suns April 19, June 14 (2-5), Wed July 15 (6.30-9).* **NB EVENING OPENING**

Town Hill Cottage, West Malling &❀ (Mr & Mrs P Cosier) 58 Town Hill. From A20 6m W of Maidstone, turn S onto A228. Top of Town Hill at N end of High St. Part walled small village garden of C16/C18 house, with many interesting plants. Hardy ferns for sale. TEAS. *Adm £1.50 Chd 75p. Sun May 17 (2-5)*

Upper Pryors, Cowden ❀ (Mr & Mrs S G Smith) 4½m SE of Edenbridge. From B2026 Edenbridge-Hartfield, turn R at Cowden Xrds and take 1st drive on R. 10 acres of country garden featuring variety, profusion of plants, water and magnificent lawns. TEAS. *Adm £2 Chd 50p. Wed June 10 (2-5)*

Walnut Tree Gardens, Little Chart &❀❀ (Mr & Mrs M Oldaker) Swan Lane. 6m NW of Ashford. Leave A20 at Charing signed to Little Chart. At Swan public house turn W for Pluckley, gardens 500yds on L. Romantic 4-acre garden set within and around walls dating from early C18. Several types of garden offering a wide range of interesting and unusual plants and shrubs. Small nursery. TEAS. *Adm £2 Acc chd free (ACNO to Green Wicket Animal Sanctuary©). Suns July 12, 19, 26, Aug 2, 9 (2-5)*

39 Warwick Crescent, Rochester &❀ (Mr & Mrs J G Sastre) Borstal. From A229 Maidstone-Chatham at 2nd roundabout turn W into B2097 Borstal-Rochester rd; turn L at Priestfields, follow Borstal St to Wouldham Way, 3rd turning on R is Warwick Cres. Small front & rear plantsperson's gardens; sinks and troughs; alpine terraces, peat & herbaceous beds; rockery with cascade & pool, bog garden, borders. Featured in NGS video 2. *Adm £1 Acc chd free. Suns April 5, May 3, June 28 (2-5.30): private visits welcome by prior arrangement, please* **Tel 01634 401636**

Waystrode Manor, Cowden &❀❀ (Mr & Mrs Peter Wright) 4½m S of Edenbridge. From B2026 Edenbridge-Hartfield, turn off at Cowden Pound. 8 acres; sweeping lawns, borders, ponds, bulbs, shrub roses, clematis and many tender plants. Orangery. All trees, plants and shrubs labelled. House C15 (not open). Last entry ½-hour before closing time. TEAS. Gift shop. *Adm £2.50 Chd 50p. Weds May 13, 27, June 24 (1.30-5.30); Suns May 24, June 28, July 5 (2-6); also open for groups of 15 or more by appt* **Tel 01342 850695**

Weald Cottage, Edenbridge &❀ (Peter & Pauline Abraham) Four Elms Road, just N of Edenbridge on B2027, opp Eden Valley School. Small garden with theme areas including French, Roman and Japanese; mixed planting of bulbs, herbaceous, shrubs and trees, vegetables and fruit trees, conservatory. TEAS. *Adm £1.50 (eve opening £2.50 incl glass of wine) Chd 25p. Suns April 12, May 3, 24, July 5; Mon April 13, May 4, 25 (2-5), Fri July 3 (7-9.30):* **NB EVENING OPENING** *(floodlit). Private visits welcome, please* **Tel 01732 863498**

Evening Openings (see also garden descriptions)	
St Michael's Gardens, Roydon	June 14 5–9pm
Edenbridge House, Edenbridge	June 17 6.30–8.30pm
Forest Gate, Pluckley	June 18 5–8.30pm
Sissinghurst Place Gardens, Sissinghurst	June 23 6–9pm
Old Tong Farm, Brenchley	June 24 6–9pm
Weald Cottage, Edenbridge	July 3 7–9.30pm
Haydown, Great Buckland	July 15 6–9pm
Swan Oast, Stilebridge	July 25, Aug 22 7–10pm
Torry Hill, Sittingbourne	July 15 6.30–9pm

Weeks Farm, Egerton, Forstal ＆⚘⚘ (Robin & Monica de Garston) Ashford, 3½m E of Headcorn. Take Smarden Road out of Headcorn, Bedlam Lane is 3rd turning on L, Weeks Farm approx 1½m on R. 2-acre garden on Wealden clay, showing varied use of badly drained site; double herbaceous borders flanking gateway, vista a feature; orchard with crocus & fritillaria. New water garden, ponds with abundance of wild life. TEAS. *Adm £1.50 Acc chd free. Suns March 8 (12-5), April 12, Sept 13 (12-6). Private visits welcome, please* **Tel 01233 756252 (evenings)**

Went House, West Malling ＆⚘ (Mrs Robin Baring) Swan Street. From A20, 6m W of Maidstone turn S onto A228. Turn E off High Street in village towards station. Queen Anne house with secret garden surrounded by high wall. Interesting plants, water gardens, woodland, parterre and octagonal potager. Concert of classical music during afternoon. TEAS. *Adm £2 Acc chd free (ACNO to St Mary's Church West Malling Bell Fund®). Suns June 14, 28 (2-6)*

West Studdal Farm, West Studdal ＆⚘ (Mr & Mrs Peter Lumsden) N of Dover half-way between Eastry and Whitfield. Take A256. Take rd signposted to Gt Mongeham at roundabout. At top of hill turn R and entrance ¼m on L. Medium-sized garden around old farmhouse set by itself in small valley; herbaceous borders, roses and fine lawns protected by old walls and beech hedges. TEAS in Dodecagonal folly. *Adm £1.50 Chd 50p. Sun Aug 23 (2-6)*

Westview, Hempstead ⚘ (Mr & Mrs J G Jackson) Spekes Rd. From M2 take A278 to Gillingham; at 1st roundabout follow sign to Wigmore, proceed to junction with Fairview Av, turn L & park on motorway link rd bridge, walk into Spekes Rd, Westview 3rd on L. ¼-acre town garden on very sloping site with many steps; good collection of plants & shrubs suitable for a chalk soil; designed by owners for all-year interest and low maintenance. Good autumn colour. TEAS. *Adm £1 Acc chd free. Weds April 22, May 13, June 3; Suns April 26, May 17, June 7 (2-5); also private visits welcome, please* **Tel 01634 230987**

Whitehill, Wrotham ⚘ (Mrs Henderson) On A20 at Wrotham, between junctions 2A (M26) and 2 (M20). 3-acre garden, incl 1½ acres with design by Gertrude Jekyll in 1919, now carefully restored from original plans. *Adm £1.50 Acc chd free (ACNO to Kent Air Ambulance©). Sun June 14 (2-5.30); private visits welcome, please* **Tel 01732 882521**

Whitehurst, Chainhurst ＆⚘ (Mr & Mrs John Mercy) 3m N of Marden. From Marden station turn R into Pattenden Lane and under railway bridge; at T-junc turn L; at next fork bear R to Chainhurst, then second turning on L. 1½ acres of trees, roses & water garden. Victorian spiral staircase leading to aerial walkway through the tree tops. Exhibition of root dwellings. TEAS. *Adm £2 Chd £1 (ACNO to Stroke Assoc®). Weds Sept 30, Oct 7 (2-5.30)*

Withersdane Hall, Wye ＆ (University of London) 3m NE of Ashford. A28 take fork signed Wye. Bus EK 601 Ashford-Canterbury via Wye. Well-labelled garden of educational and botanical interest, containing several small carefully designed gardens; flower and shrub borders; spring bulbs; herb garden. Rain-fed garden. Free guide book with map available. TEAS in Wye village. *Adm £1.50 Chd 50p. Suns March 22, May 3, June 14, Aug 30 (2-5)*

Womenswold Gardens ＆⚘⚘ Midway between Canterbury and Dover, SE of A2, take B2046 signed Wingham at Barham crossover, after about ¼m turn R at Armada beacon, follow signs for gardens. Four diverse and colourful cottage gardens within easy walking distance. St Margaret's Church will be open, with flower festival. Home-made TEAS. *Combined adm £2 Acc chd free (ACNO to St Margaret's Church®). Sat, Sun June 27, 28 (2-6)*

Worth Gardens ＆⚘⚘ 2m SE of Sandwich and 5m NW of Deal, from A258 signed Worth. A group of cottage gardens in wide variety in peaceful village setting incl a new garden, recently planted. Maps available at each garden. TEA. *Combined adm £2 Acc chd free. Sun July 5 (1-5)*

Wyckhurst, Aldington ＆⚘⚘ (Mr & Mrs C D Older) Mill Road, 4m SE of Ashford. Leave M20 at junction 10, on A20 travel S to Aldington turning; proceed 1½m to Aldington village hall, 'Walnut Tree' take rd signed to Dymchurch, after ¼m turn R into Mill Road. C16 cottage (not open) surrounded by 1-acre cottage garden; old roses; herbaceous borders; unusual perennials. Topiary and small wildflower garden. Extensive views across Romney Marsh. TEAS in aid of Bonnington Church. *Adm £2 Chd 50p. Sun June 28, Wed July 1 (11-6)*

Yalding Gardens ⚘⚘ 6m SW of Maidstone, two gardens S & W of village. *Combined adm £2.50 Chd under 12 free. Mon April 13 (2-5.30)*

  Parsonage Oasts ⚘ (Mr & the Hon Mrs Raikes) Between Yalding village and station turn off at Anchor public house over bridge over canal, continue 100yds up the lane. ¾-acre riverside garden with walls, shrubs, daffodils. TEAS in aid of The Fifth Trust for Mentally Handicapped Adults

  Rugmer Farmhouse ⚘⚘ (Mr & Mrs R Lawrence) S of village, off Benover Rd (B2162), 440yds past Woolpack Inn. 2-acre garden, surrounding C16 cottage (not open), developed by present owners since 1975; spring bulbs, mixed borders and vegetables, on Wealden clay

■ **Yalding Organic Gardens, Yalding** ＆⚘⚘ (Henry Doubleday Research Association) Benover Road. 6m SE of Maidstone, ½m S of Yalding on B2162. Yalding served by buses from Maidstone and Tonbridge, railway station 1½m. 14 individual gardens illustrating gardening through the ages, from medieval times to the present day, set in 6 beautifully landscaped acres. Incl C13 apothecary's garden, paradise garden, Tudor knot, Jekyll borders, rare heritage vegetable varieties, composting and natural pest control displays, large pergola. TEAS. *Adm £2.50 Concessions £2 Chd £1.25. Wed-Sun May to Sept; weekends only during April and Oct. Also open Easter and all Bank Hol weekends. For NGS Sat June 20; Sun Sept 13 (10-5)*

Lancashire, Merseyside & Greater Manchester

Hon County Organisers: Mr & Mrs R Doldon, Old Barn Cottage, Greens Arms Road, Turton, Nr Bolton BL7 OND Tel 01204 852139

Assistant Hon County Organiser: J Bowker Esq, Swiss Cottage, 8 Hammond Drive, Read, Burnley

DATES OF OPENING

Regular openings
For details see garden description

Catforth Gardens, Catforth
Hawthornes, Hesketh Bank

By appointment only
For telephone numbers and other details see garden descriptions. Private visits welcomed

Swiss Cottage, Read

March 29 Sunday
Weeping Ash, Glazebury
April 19 Sunday
Lindeth Dene, Silverdale
May 3 Sunday
The Ridges, Limbrick nr Chorley
May 4 Monday
The Ridges, Limbrick nr Chorley
May 17 Sunday
191 Liverpool Road South, Maghull
Woodside, Shevington

May 24 Sunday
Cross Gaits Cottage, Blacko
191 Liverpool Road South, Maghull
Loxley, Wrightington
Old Barn Cottage, Turton
May 25 Monday
Cross Gaits Cottage, Blacko
Old Barn Cottage, Turton
May 31 Sunday
Catforth Gardens, Catforth
Loxley, Wrightington
June 7 Sunday
480 Aigburth Road, Liverpool
Rufford Old Hall, Rufford, nr Ormskirk
Speke Hall, The Walk, Liverpool
June 14 Sunday
Mill Barn, Salmesbury Bottoms
June 21 Sunday
Mill Barn, Salmesbury Bottoms
The Ridges, Limbrick nr Chorley
June 28 Sunday
Catforth Gardens, Catforth
Clearbeck House, Higher Tatham
Hesketh Bank Village Gardens

South View Cottage, Treales
Windle Hall, St Helens
July 5 Sunday
Clearbeck House, Higher Tatham
July 11 Saturday
Newton Hall, nr Carnforth
July 12 Sunday
Cross Gaits Cottage, Blacko
Newton Hall, nr Carnforth
Weeping Ash, Glazebury
July 19 Sunday
Piked Edge Farm, Blacklane Ends
July 25 Saturday
Montford Cottage, Fence
July 26 Sunday
Catforth Gardens, Catforth
Montford Cottage, Fence
August 9 Sunday
Greyfriars, Walker Lane, Fulwood, Preston
August 31 Monday
Old Barn Cottage, Turton
September 6 Sunday
Windle Hall, St Helens
September 13 Sunday
Weeping Ash, Glazebury

DESCRIPTIONS OF GARDENS

¶**480 Aigburth Rd, Liverpool** &% (Mrs Bridget Spiegl) S Liverpool, on main rd (A561) between city and Runcorn bridge. Just past Liverpool Cricket Club, on LH side of rd going towards the city. Plantswoman's small town garden. Mixed herbaceous and shrubs. Some interesting and unusual plants. Spring bulbs, particularly good display of species crocus late February - early March. *Adm £1.50 Chd free (ACNO to Old Peoples' Homes Assoc®). Sun June 7 (2-5). Private visits welcome, please.* **Tel 0151 427 2344**

■**Catforth Gardens** &%❀ Leave M6 at junction 32 turning N on A6. Turn L at 1st set of traffic lights; 2m to T-junction, turn R. Turn L at sign for Catforth, L at next T-junction, 1st R into Benson Lane. Bear L at church into Roots Lane. TEAS NGS days only. *Combined adm £2 OAP £1.50 Chd 50p. Gardens and adjacent nursery open March 14 to Sept 13 (10.30-5.30). For NGS Suns May 31, June 28, July 26. Parties by appt, please* **Tel 01772 690561/690269**
    Cherry Tree Lodge (Mr & Mrs T A Bradshaw) 1-acre informal country garden, planted for yr-round interest

and colour. Wide variety of unusual shrubs; trees; rhododendrons, azaleas; rare herbaceous plants incl euphorbias, dicentras, pulmonarias; ground cover plants; national collection of hardy geraniums; 2 ponds with bog gardens, large rockery and woodland garden
    Willow Bridge Farm (Mr & Mrs W Moore) ¼-acre cottage garden with wide variety of herbaceous perennials. Also 1 acre summer flower garden with 3 natural clay-lined ponds and high banks. Large herbaceous borders and rose garden, shrubs, climbing roses intermingled with perennials

Clearbeck House, Higher Tatham &❀ (Mr & Mrs P Osborne) Signed from Wray (M6 Junction 34, A683, B6480) and Low Bentham. Partly re-landscaped garden of about 1½ acres focused on larger lake and wildlife area with increasing bird species. Traditional and formal borders near house lead out through vistas to distant views. Pyramid and symbolic garden; sculptures (some for sale); varied planting incl old-fashioned roses and wet areas. A garden to walk in, with surprises. TEAS. *Adm £1.50 Chd free. Suns June 28, July 5 (11.30-5.30). Private visits welcome (£1.50), please* **Tel 015242 61029**

LANCASHIRE, MERSEYSIDE & GREATER MANCHESTER

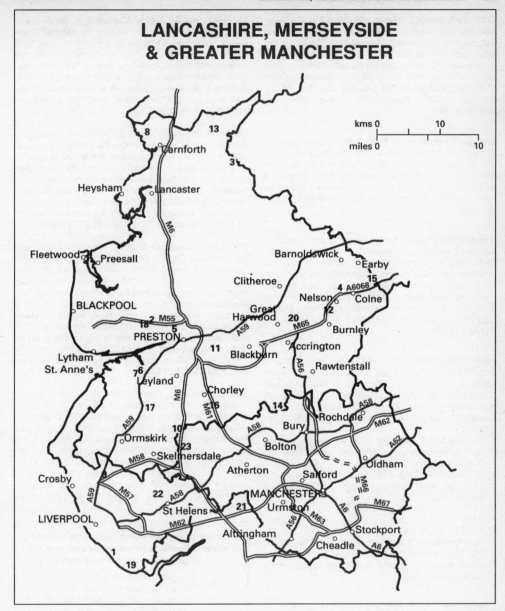

KEY

1. 480 Aigburth Road
2. Catforth Gardens
3. Clearbeck House
4. Cross Gaits Cottage
5. Greyfriars
6. Hawthornes
7. Hesketh Bank Village Gardens
8. Lindeth Dene
9. 191 Liverpool Road South
10. Loxley
11. Mill Barn
12. Montford Cottage
13. Newton Hall
14. Old Barn Cottage
15. Piked Edge Farm
16. The Ridges
17. Rufford Old Hall
18. South View Cottage
19. Speke Hall
20. Swiss Cottage
21. Weeping Ash
22. Windle Hall
23. Woodside

Cross Gaits Cottage, Blacko ⚭❀ (Mr & Mrs S J Gude) Take M65 exit junction 13. Follow Barrowford signs then Barnoldswick signs. Garden 1½m on Barnoldswick Rd opp Cross Gaits Inn. ⅔-acre walled cottage garden featured on Granada TV; shrub and herbaceous borders; 2 ornamental ponds. 700ft above sea level; fine view of Pennines. TEA. *Adm £1.50 Chd 50p. Sun, Mon May 24, 25; Sun July 12 (1-5). Private visits welcome, please* **Tel 01282 617163**

Greyfriars, Fulwood ⚭❀ (Mr & Mrs William Harrison) Walker Lane. 2m N of Preston. Junction 32 off M6 (M55); S to Preston; at Black Bull Xrds, R to Boys Lane Xrds, entrance ½m on R. 8 acres; lawns, rose beds, fuchsias; 4 greenhouses with hybrid begonias, geraniums and carnations; fountains; koi carp pond. TEAS. *Adm £2 Chd 50p. Sun Aug 9 (2-5)*

Hawthornes, Hesketh Bank ⚭❀ (Mr & Mrs R Hodson) Between Preston and Southport. Turn off A59 at Tarleton traffic lights. Head N for 2m. Turn R into Marsh Rd at end of Station Rd. 1-acre garden. Mixed borders; island beds; shrub roses; clematis. Many perennials. Pond. Nursery open daily from March 1. *Adm £1. Every Thurs, Fri May, June, July (2-5)*. Also open with **Hesketh Bank Village Gardens** *Sun June 28 (12-6). Also by appt please* **Tel 01772 812379**

Hesketh Bank Village Gardens ⚭❀ Midway between Preston and Southport. From Preston take A59 towards Liverpool, then turn R at traffic lights for Tarleton village. Straight through Tarleton to Hesketh Bank. Free vintage bus between gardens. All gardens recently featured on Granada TV. TEAS. *Combined adm £2 Chd free. Sun June 28 (12-6)*
  31 Becconsall Lane (Mr & Mrs J Baxter) Cottage style garden with pond, white and green beds and semi-woodland walk
  74 Chapel Road (Mr & Mrs T Iddon) Compact colourful garden. Wide variety of plants. Pond, arbour and gazebo. Lancashire garden winner
  11 Douglas Avenue (Mr & Mrs J Cook) Large established garden with lawns, mature trees, mixed herbaceous borders and naturalised areas
  Hawthornes (Mr & Mrs R Hodson) See separate entry
  155 Station Road (Mr & Mrs G Hale) Large and interesting garden with pond, mixed herbaceous, shrub borders and climbers

Lindeth Dene, Silverdale ⚭❀ (Mrs B M Kershaw) 38 Lindeth Rd. 13m N of Lancaster. Take M6 to junction 35, turn L (S) on A6 to Carnforth t-lights. Turn R follow signs Silverdale. After level Xing ¼m uphill turn L down Hollins Lane. At T junction turn R into Lindeth Rd. Garden is 4th gateway on L, park in rd. 1¼ acres overlooking Morecambe Bay. Limestone rock garden; troughs; pools; heathers; veganic kitchen garden, saxifrages, geraniums, Elizabethan primroses, N.Z. plants and hardy perennials. Teas and toilets available in village. *Adm £1.50 Acc chd free. Sun April 19 (2-5). Also by appt, please* **Tel 01524 701314**

191 Liverpool Rd South, Maghull ⚭❀ (Mr & Mrs D Cheetham) From A59 take turning for Maghull Town Centre. Turn L at traffic lights and veer R over canal bridge. Garden ¼m on R. ½-acre suburban garden; rhododendrons, azaleas, camellias, rockery, pool, sink gardens, primulas, a variety of trees (some unusual), shrubs, bulbs and herbaceous plants for all year colour in the smaller garden. TEAS and coffee. *Adm £1.50 Acc chd free. Suns May 17, 24 (1.30-5.30)*

Loxley, Wigan ⚭ (Mr & Mrs D J Robinson) Situated 1m from junction 27 of M6. Continue past Wrightington hospital to Xrds turn R by the garage ½m up the rd situated on L. As featured in Lancashire Life Sept '97 ¼-acre garden designed on three levels with water features and ornamental fish pond. A variety of shrubs, conifers, rhododendrons and perennials. Redesigned garden at entrance area. TEA. *Adm £1.50 Acc chd free. Suns May 24, 31 (12-5). Private visits by appt* **Tel 01257 254120**

Mill Barn, Samlesbury Bottoms ⚭❀ (Dr C J Mortimer) and **Primrose Cottage** (Mrs S Childs) Goose Foot Close, Samlesbury Bottoms, Preston. 6m E of Preston. From M6 junction 31 2½m on A59/A677 B/burn. Turn S. Nabs Head Lane, then Goose Foot Lane. 1½-acre tranquil, terraced garden along the banks of the R Darwen with many interesting and innovative features. Varied artistic planting incl some uncommon herbaceous perennials. Primrose Cottage opp is a small hillside garden with a formal but creative layout. TEAS. *Adm £1.50 Chd free. Suns June 14, 21 (2-6). Private visits of groups welcome by appt, please* **Tel 01254 853300**

Montford Cottage, Fence ⚭❀ (Craig Bullock & Tony Morris) From the M65 junction 13, take the A6068 (signs for Fence) and in 2m turn L onto the B6248 (signs for Brierfield). Proceed down the hill for ½m (past the Forest PH). Entrance to garden is on the L. Gardens within a garden. 1-acre divided into varying 'rooms'. Particular interest for the plantsman, flower-arranger and lover of foliage. Overall atmosphere of a relaxed country cottage garden, with the odd eccentric thrown in for good measure. TEAS. *Adm £2 Chd 50p. Sat, Sun July 25, 26 (2-6). No coaches*

Newton Hall, nr Carnforth ♿✿ (Mr & Mrs T R H Kimber) 12m N of Lancaster. 3m S of Kirkby Lonsdale. Exit 35. Take B6254 to Kirkby Lonsdale. 6m then through Arkholme, 2m to sign to Newton. Pass junction and cottage with round windows on L, street lamp on R. Entrance 150yds on L. Lodge at gate. Former shooting lodge 4 acres cultivated and 6 acres wild garden re-constructed, with yews from Thurland Castle. Rhododendrons and daffodils in spring, roses and herbaceous borders in summer. Superb views of Lune Valley and Ingleborough. TEAS. *Adm £2 OAPS £1.50 Chd 50p. Sat, Sun July 11, 12 (2-5)*

Old Barn Cottage, Turton ♿✿ (Ray & Brenda Doldon) Greens Arms Rd. Midway between Bolton and Darwen on B6391 off A666, or through Chapeltown Village High St (B6391). 1-acre garden on moorland site. Spring flowering trees; shrubs; azaleas, rhododendrons; water gardens; heathers; conifers, herbaceous beds; moorland views. TEAS in aid of St Ann's Church (May 25 and Aug 26), Beacon Counselling Service (May 26). *Adm £1.50 Chd free. Sun, Mon May 24, 25, Mon Aug 31 (12-5). Private visits welcome by appt (May to Aug), please* **Tel 01204 852139**

¶Piked Edge Farm, Blacklane Ends ✿✿ (Mr & Mrs R M Box) Skipton Old Rd. From roundabout on A6068 ½m E of Colne follow signs to Lothersdale. Pass Colne Golf Club, continue up hill for 1½m. Please park on L side of rd facing uphill. 1½ acres garden at 1000ft above sea level. Very hardy plants! Rockery, stone features, small pond, lawns. Large semi-organic vegetable garden with raised beds. Poultry. Short hill walks with magnificent views of Pennines. TEAS. *Adm £1.50 Chd free. Sun July 19 (1-5)*

■ The Ridges, Limbrick nr Chorley ♿✿ (Mr & Mrs J M Barlow) Cowling Rd. Approx 2m SE of Chorley. Junction 8 M61, take Cowling Rd out of Chorley towards Rivington approx 1½m on R. C17 house with 2¼-acre gardens. Incl old walled kitchen garden, cottage style, herbaceous borders, and area for growing annuals to dry. Small fish pond, laburnum arch leads to large formal lawn, surrounded by rhododendrons, and natural woodland. Ornamental centre pond. Seen on TV Border Patrol '96. TEAS in aid of Chorley Stroke Club and the Diabetic Society. *Adm £1.50 Chd 50p. Suns, Mons May 24, 25, Aug 30, 31. For NGS Suns, Mon May 3, 4, June 21 (11-5). Private visits for 5 & over welcome, please* **Tel 01257 279981**

▲Rufford Old Hall, Rufford ♿✿ (The National Trust) On A59 Liverpool to Preston rd in village of Rufford, 7m N of Ormskirk. Set in 14 acres of garden and woodland. Informal garden and walks. Spectacular in May and June for spring flowering rhododendrons and azaleas. TEAS. *Adm £1.80 Chd 90p (Garden only). For NGS Sun June 7 (12-4.30)*

¶South View Cottage, Treales ♿✿ (Pauline & Mike Coxon) Leave M55 junction 3, A585 then B5192 Kirkham at traffic lights turn L B5192 to Preston. Continue through Kirkham centre and after approx ½m, turn L (Carr Lane, signed Treales). Follow rd approx 1m, keeping Derby Arms Hotel on L. ⅓-acre garden in cottage style surrounded by open fields. Converted in 1993 from agricultural land. Large pond area, well stocked mixed herbaceous borders, lawns, containers, varied planting incl scented shrub and climbing roses. TEAS. *Adm £1.50 Chd free (ACNO to Derian House Hospice for Children, Chorley®). Sun June 28, (1-5). Private visits welcome by appt please,* **Tel 01972 686700**

▲Speke Hall, Liverpool ♿✿ (The National Trust) 8m SE of Liverpool adjacent to Liverpool Airport. Follow signs for Liverpool Airport. A formal garden with herbaceous border, rose garden; moated area with formal lawns and a recently opened stream garden. A wild wood is included. Approx size of estate 35 acres. TEAS. *Adm £1.40 Chd 70p (Garden only). Sun June 7 (12-5). Parties of 20 or over welcome, please* **Tel 0151 4277231**

Swiss Cottage, Read ✿✿ (James & Doreen Bowker) 8 Hammond Drive. 3m SE of Whalley on A671 Whalley to Burnley Road, turn by Pollards Garage, up George Lane to T junction, L into Private Rd. 1½-acre hillside garden designed on 2 levels in mature woodland setting. Variety of shrubs, trees, rhododendrons, azaleas, perennials and alpines. Stream and bog garden feature. *Adm £1.50. Private visits welcome by appt, please* **Tel 01282 774853**

Weeping Ash, Glazebury ♿✿ (John Bent Esq) ¼m S A580 (East Lancs Rd Greyhound Motel roundabout, Leigh) on A574 Glazebury/Leigh Boundary. Large garden of yr-round interest on heavy soil. A broad sweep of lawn with mixed borders of shrubs and herbaceous perennials gives way to secret areas with pools, roses and island beds, a rockery with alpines. A hot area with mediterranean planting and a further extensive lawn. Newly planted bank 100yds long. Teas 100yds N at Garden Centre. *Adm £1.50 Chd free (ACNO to Wigan/Leigh Hospice®). Suns March 29, July 12, Sept 13 (1-5). Private visits welcome, minimum 10* **Tel 01942 262066**

Windle Hall, St Helens ♿✿ (The Lady Pilkington) N of E Lancs Rd, St Helens. 5m W of M6 via E Lancs Rd, nr Southport junction. Entrance by bridge over E Lancs Rd. 200yr-old walled garden surrounded by 5 acres of lawns, rock and water garden; thatched summer house. Tufa stone grotto; herbaceous borders, pergola and rose gardens containing exhibition blooms, miniature ornamental ponies, ducks; greenhouses. TEAS. *Adm £1 Chd 50p. Suns June 28, Sept 6 (2-5)*

Woodside, Shevington ✿✿ (Barbara & Bill Seddon) M6 Exit 26 or 27. Follow to Shevington. Princes Park is small side rd off Gathurst Lane almost opp Gathurst Service Station. ⅔-acre undulating garden with several levels. Developed by owners from dense woodland and featuring rhododendrons, azalea, camellia, magnolia, acer, eucryphia, hydrangea and specimen paeonies. Lancashire garden winner. Morning coffee, afternoon TEA. *Adm £1.50 Chd free. Sun May 17 (11-5). Private visits welcome, please* **Tel 01257 255255**

Leicestershire & Rutland

Hon County Organiser:	(Leicestershire) Mr John Oakland, Old School Cottage, Oaks-in-Charnwood, nr Loughborough LE12 9YD Tel 01509 502676 or 01509 890376
Hon County Organiser:	(Rutland) Mrs Jennifer Wood, Townsend House, Morcott Road, Wing, LE15 8SE Tel 01572 737465
Assistant Hon County Organiser:	(Rutland) Mrs Rose Dejardin, Wingwell, Top Street, Wing LE15 8SE Tel 01572 737727
Hon County Treasurer:	(Rutland) Mr David Wood

DATES OF OPENING

Regular openings
For details see garden description

Barnsdale Plants and Gardens, Exton
Brooksby Agricultural College, nr
    Melton Mowbray
Long Close, Woodhouse Eaves
1700 Melton Road, Rearsby
Orchards, Walton, nr Lutterworth

March 8 Sunday
    1700 Melton Road, Rearsby
March 22 Sunday
    The Homestead, Normanton
March 24 Tuesday
    The Homestead, Normanton
April 5 Sunday
    Long close, Woodhouse Eaves
April 11 Saturday
    Paddocks, Shelbrook,
        Ashby-De-La-Zouch
April 12 Sunday
    Field Farm, Osbaston
    Paddocks, Shelbrook,
        Ashby-De-La-Zouch
April 14 Tuesday
    Whatton House, Loughborough
April 15 Wednesday
    Burbage Gardens, Burbage
April 19 Sunday
    Gunthorpe, Oakham
May 3 Sunday
    Burrough House, Burrough on the
        Hill
    Pine House, Gaddesby
May 4 Monday
    Burrough House, Burrough on the
        Hill
    Pine House, Gaddesby
May 5 Tuesday
    Whatton House, Loughborough
May 6 Wednesday
    Arthingworth Manor, Market
        Harborough
May 10 Sunday
    Burrough House, Burrough on the
        Hill
    Long Close, Woodhouse Eaves
    Preston Gardens

May 13 Wednesday
    Arthingworth Manor, Market
        Harborough
    Burbage Gardens, Burbage
May 16 Saturday
    4 Grange Cottages, Nailstone
    Holly Hayes, Birstall
May 17 Sunday
    Field Farm, Osbaston
    Holly Hayes, Birstall
    Owston Gardens, nr Oakham
    18 Park Road, Birstall
    The White Lodge, Willesley
May 18 Monday
    18 Park Road, Birstall
May 20 Wednesday
    Arthingworth Manor, Market
        Harborough
May 23 Saturday
    Paddocks, Shelbrook,
        Ashby-De-La-Zouch
May 24 Sunday
    Burrough House, Burrough on the
        Hill
    Hambleton Gardens
    The Homestead, Normanton
    Long Close, Woodhouse Eaves
    Paddocks, Shelbrook,
        Ashby-De-La-Zouch
May 25 Monday
    Burrough House, Burrough on the
        Hill
May 26 Tuesday
    Whatton House, Loughborough
May 27 Wednesday
    Arthingworth Manor, Market
        Harborough
May 31 Sunday
    Orchards, Walton, nr Lutterworth
    Wakerley Manor, Uppingham
June 3 Wednesday
    Arthingworth Manor, Market
        Harborough
    Orchards, Walton, nr Lutterworth
June 7 Sunday
    Botany Bay, Coleorton
    Burbage Gardens, Burbage
    Burrough House, Burrough on the
        Hill
    The Dairy, Coleorton

Forge Cottage, Edith Weston
Pine House, Gaddesby
Woodyton Farmhouse,
    Coalville
June 10 Wednesday
    Arthingworth Manor, Market
        Harborough
June 13 Saturday
    Paddocks, Shelbrook,
        Ashby-De-La-Zouch
June 14 Sunday
    Paddocks, Shelbrook,
        Ashby-De-La-Zouch
    Prebendal House, Empingham
June 17 Wednesday
    Arthingworth Manor, Market
        Harborough
June 20 Saturday
    Sheepy Magna Gardens
June 21 Sunday
    Field Farm, Osbaston
    Queniborough Gardens
    Sheepy Magna Gardens
    Wing Gardens
June 24 Wednesday
    Arthingworth Manor, Market
        Harborough
June 27 Saturday
    Langham Lodge, Oakham
        (Evening)
June 28 Sunday
    Beeby Manor, Beeby
    Brooksby Agricultural College, nr
        Melton Mowbray
    Clipsham House, Clipsham
    Hill House, Dunton Bassett
    Sutton Bonington Hall, Sutton
        Bonington
    Wartnaby, nr Melton Mowbray
June 30 Tuesday
    Beeby Manor, Beeby
July 1 Wednesday
    Arthingworth Manor, Market
        Harborough
July 5 Sunday
    Mill View, Shepshed
    The Priory, Ketton
July 8 Wednesday
    Arthingworth Manor, Market
        Harborough

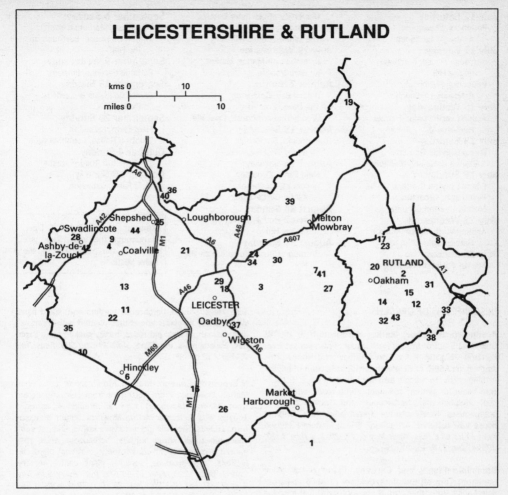

LEICESTERSHIRE & RUTLAND

KEY

1. Arthingworth Manor
2. Barnsdale Plants & Gardens
3. Beeby Manor
4. Botany Bay
5. Brooksby Agricultural College
6. Burbage Gardens
7. Burrough House
8. Clipsham House
9. The Dairy
10. Fenny Drayton Gardens
11. Field Farm
12. Forge Cottage
13. 4 Grange Cottages
14. Gunthorpe
15. Hambleton Gardens
16. Hill House, Dunton Bassett
17. Hill House, Market Overton
18. Holly Hayes
19. The Homestead
20. Langham Lodge
21. Long Close
22. Market Bosworth Gardens
23. Market Overton Gardens
24. 1700 Melton Road
25. Mill View
26. Orchards
27. Owston Gardens
28. Paddocks
29. 18 Park Road
30. Pine House
31. Prebendal House
32. Preston Gardens
33. The Priory
34. Queniborough Gardens
35. Sheepy Magna Gardens
36. Sutton Bonington Hall
37. University of Leicester Botanic Garden
38. Wakerley Manor
39. Wartnaby
40. Whatton House
41. The White House
42. The White Lodge
43. Wing Gardens
44. Woodyton Farmhouse

The maps in this book are designed to help visitors by showing the approximate locations of gardens within each county. The locations are not necessarily precise, particularly where gardens are in clusters. Detailed directions to each garden can be found in the garden descriptions.

July 11 Saturday
Paddocks, Shelbrook,
Ashby-De-La-Zouch
July 12 Sunday
Burrough House, Burrough
on the Hill
Paddocks, Shelbrook,
Ashby-De-La-Zouch
July 15 Wednesday
Arthingworth Manor, Market
Harborough
July 18 Saturday
Fenny Drayton Gardens
4 Grange Cottages, Nailstone
July 19 Sunday
Fenny Drayton Gardens
Field Farm, Osbaston
Market Overton Gardens
July 22 Wednesday
Arthingworth Manor, Market
Harborough
July 26 Sunday
Market Bosworth Gardens

University of Leicester Botanic
Garden, Oadby
The White Lodge, Willesley
July 29 Wednesday
Arthingworth Manor, Market
Harborough
August 2 Sunday
Botany Bay, Coleorton
The Dairy, Coleorton
Woodyton Farmhouse, Coalville
August 15 Saturday
Paddocks, Shelbrook,
Ashby-De-La-Zouch
August 16 Sunday
Field Farm, Osbaston
Paddocks, Shelbrook,
Ashby-De-La-Zouch
August 30 Sunday
Burrough House, Burrough
on the Hill
August 31 Monday
Burrough House, Burrough on the
Hill

September 6 Sunday
Hill House, Market Overton
The White House, Burrough on
the Hill
September 9 Wednesday
Burbage Gardens, Burbage
September 13 Sunday
Barnsdale Plants & Gardens,
Exton
September 20 Sunday
Field Farm, Osbaston
Whatton House, Loughborough
October 4 Sunday
1700 Melton Road, Rearsby
October 18 Sunday
Field Farm, Osbaston

Regular openings. Open
throughout the year. They are
listed at the beginning of the
Diary Section.

DESCRIPTIONS OF GARDENS

Arthingworth Manor, Market Harborough ✿ (Mr W
Guinness) 5m S of Market Harborough. From Market Harborough via A508 at 4m L to Arthingworth; from Northampton via A508. At Kelmarsh turn R at bottom of hill for
Arthingworth. In village turn R at church 1st L. 6 to 7-
acre beautiful garden; collection shrub roses; white garden; delphiniums, herbaceous and mixed borders;
greenhouses. Newly planted 3-acre arboretum. Original
house now restored. Art gallery, British Modern Pictures.
*Adm £1.75 Chd 50p. Weds May 6, 13, 20, 27, June 3, 10,
17, 24, July 1, 8, 15, 22, 29 (2-5)*

Barnsdale Plants and Gardens, Exton ♿✿✿ (Nick
Hamilton) Turn off Stamford/Oakham rd A606 at Barnsdale Lodge Hotel then 1m. 8 acres of individual gardens
used by Geoff Hamilton for BBC TV 'Gardeners' World'.
Wide variety of ideas and garden designs for all year interest. TEAS, light refreshments, nursery. *Adm £4.50 Chd
free (ACNO to Plant Life®). Gardens open Mar-Oct (10-5),
Nov-Feb (10-4). For NGS Sun Sept 13*

Beeby Manor, Beeby ♿✿✿ (Mr & Mrs Philip Bland) 8m
E of Leicester. Turn off A47 in Thurnby and follow signs
through Scraptoft. 3-acre mature garden with venerable
yew hedges, walled herbaceous border, lily ponds, rose
towers and box parterre, as featured in 'Homes and Gardens' 1996, 'Hunting' magazine, June 1997 and 'Surprise
Gardeners' on Central TV, Autumn 1997. C16 and C18
house (not open). TEAS. *Adm £1.80 Chd free (ACNO to
Beeby Village Funds©). Sun June 28, Tues June 30 (2-6)*

¶**Botany Bay, Coleorton** ♿✿✿ (Mr & Mrs R W Platts)
100 The Moorlands. Follow sign Sinope at Coleorton
Xrds. From A512 Ashby-Louborough Rd for ¾m. Down
drive on L. From A511 Coalville-Ashby follow sign Coleorton 400yd on R. Off road parking. Mature garden of ⅔

acre, trees, shrubs, herbaceous borders and island beds.
Wide variety of plants and shrubs planted with fragrance
in mind, viburnums, old roses, honey-suckle, lilac, daphnes, philadelphus, etc. TEAS. *Adm £1 Chd 50p. Suns June
7, Aug 2 (2-6)*

■ **Brooksby College, Melton Mowbray** ✿ 6m SW of
Melton Mowbray. From A607 (9m from Leicester or 6m
from Melton Mowbray) turn at Brooksby; entrance
100yds. Bus: Leicester-Melton Mowbray; alight Brooksby
turn, 100yds. Grounds incl extensive lawns, lake, stream,
specimen trees, shrub borders, herbaceous beds, rose
garden, topiary, wildflower meadows, national plant collections, rock gardens, pergola, plant centre/nursery.
Church built 1220. *Adm £1.50 Chd free. Every Sun July,
Aug (11-4). For NGS Sun June 28 (1-5). Private visits welcome, please Tel 01664 434291*

Burbage Gardens ✿ From M69 junction 1, take B4109
signed Hinckley. Cream TEAS and refreshments at the
Long Close only. *Combined adm £2 Chd free (ACNO to
Hinckley Hospital©) Sun June 7 (11-5). Combined adm
£1.50 Wed April 15, May 13, Sept 9 (2-5)*
  6 Denis Road ✿✿ (Mr & Mrs D A Dawkins) Sketchley
Manor Estate. From M69 junction 1 take 1409 signposted Hinkley then 1st L after roundabout. Small garden with wide range of plants, many unusual, incl
plants grown for scent, alpines in sinks. Species clematis, scree area, hellebores, spring bulbs. TEAS Weds
only. Featured in Amateur Gardening Magazine. *Private
visits welcome April to Sept 30 Tues afternoons, please
Tel 01455 230509*
  ¶**40 Duport Rd** (Mr & Mrs J Griffin) Medium terraced
garden with mixed borders and island beds containing
a wide variety of herbaceous plants and shrubs, including a small collection of hardy geraniums. *Only
open Sun June 7 (11-5)*

7 Hall Road Burbage ❀ (Mr & Mrs D R Baker) Sketchley Manor Estate. From M69 roundabout take B4109 to Hinkley at 1st roundabout L then R to Sketchley Lane. 1st R; 1st R; 1st L; into Hall Rd. Medium-sized garden; mixed borders; alpines; sink gardens; scree area; collection of hellebores and hosta; unusual plants; foliage plants. Partially suitable for wheelchairs. *Private visits welcome, please* **Tel 01455 635616**

11 Primrose Drive ❀ (Mr & Mrs D Leach) Take 2nd turning on R into Sketchley Rd. 1st L into Azalea Drive, 1st R into Marigold Drive, 1st L Begonia Drive, 1st R into Primrose Drive. No 11 is on L on bend. Small cottage garden. Spring interest camellias, clematis and hellebores, summer interest paeonies, clematis and new English roses. *Private visits welcome April to July, please* **Tel 01455 250817**

The Long Close, Bullfurlong Lane ⬥ (Mr & Mrs A J Hopewell) Burbage. 1st R onto Coventry Road 2nd R onto Bullfurlong Lane, garden on L. Limited parking, park if poss on Coventry Rd. ½-acre family garden. Mixed borders; 'natural' ponds; play area, toilets, greenhouse and cool orchid house. Organic vegetable plot. Cream TEAS, refreshments in aid of Childrens Society. *Open Sun June 7 only*

Burrough House, Melton Mowbray ⬥❀❀ (Mrs Barbara Keene) 6m W of Oakham, 5m S of Melton Mowbray. From A606 at Langham, take rd signposted to Cold Overton and Somerby, continue through Somerby to Burrough on the Hill. Approx 5 acres, with special spring interest, tulips, azaleas, rhododendrons and unique wisteria wheel. A thatched timber bower house used by the Prince of Wales and Mrs Simpson; water pools, peony, delphinium and herbaceous borders. A white and rose garden. TEAS & refreshments. *Adm £2.50 Chd free. Suns May 3, 10, 24, June 7, July 12, Aug 30, Mons May 4, 25, Aug 31 (1-6). Specialist plant fair Monday May 25. Private visits welcome, please* **Tel 01664 454226**

Clipsham House, Oakham ⬥❀ (Mr & Mrs Robert Wheatley) On B668 2m E of A1 NE of Oakham. 2 acres around early C19 former rectory; lawns, good trees, walled garden with summer house; herbaceous borders, roses, variety of shrubs, folly in small park. Featured in NGS video 1 and in The Gardener magazine. TEAS. *Adm £2 Chd free (ACNO to St Mary's Church®). Sun June 28 (2-6)*

The Dairy, Coleorton ⬥❀❀ (Mr & Mrs J B Moseley) Moor Lane off A512 W of Peggs Green Roundabout. A garden of approx ⅓-acre with mature trees and shrubs, herbaceous borders containing some unusual plants, herb garden and pergola leading to other interesting areas. TEAS. *Adm £1 Chd 50p. Suns June 7, Aug 2 (2-6)*

Fenny Drayton Gardens Situated approx 3m N of Nuneaton on the A444, crossing the A5 at The Royal Red Gate Inn and MSF Garage junction. Teas in St Michael's Church. *Combined adm £1.50 Chd free (ACNO to Mary Ann Evans Hospice Nuneaton®). Sat, Sun July 18, 19 (2-6)*

Little Froome ⬥❀ (Mr & Mrs G J Cookes) Drayton Lane. 1½-acre garden, mature trees and wide variety

of conifers. Landscaped with heathers, large pond with bridge. TEA

4 Rookery Close ❀❀ (Mr & Mrs J Dowse) Average sized garden with pond and waterfall. Abundance of hanging baskets and tubs. Very good selection of perennials and shrubs

Crofters ⬥ (Mr & Mrs G M Heaton) 16 Rookery Close. Neat tidy garden front and rear, mostly lawns and flower beds. Open views of Leicestershire countryside at rear

19 Rookery Close ⬥ (Mr & Mrs Ratcliffe) Small garden lots of colour

12 Church Lane ⬥❀ (Mr & Mrs M Ambrose) ½-acre garden, ornamental walls and borders with rockeries, pond and waterfall

Five Corners ⬥❀ (Mr & Mrs Perrin) Church Lane. ¼-acre garden, mainly lawns with mixed shrubbery borders and evergreen hedges

¶Field Farm, Osbaston ⬥❀❀ (Mr & Mrs Lee Taylor-Ryan) Off A47 nr Barleston. 5 acre garden incl lakes, ponds, arboretum. Many unusual and interesting shrubs and trees. Nature trail. TEAS. *Adm £1.50 Chd free. Suns April 12, May 17, June 21, July 19, Aug 16, Sept 20, Oct 18 (11-4.30)*

Forge Cottage, Edith Weston ⬥❀❀ (Prof J Lindesay & Dr G Hall) 5m E of Oakham off A6003. A plant lover's garden containing around 1,500 different species. Rare and unusual plants and vegetables are combined with dependable and colourful varieties. Collection of phlomis, euphorbias, hardy geraniums, brodiaeas, digitalis and oenothersas. Emphasis on drought and limestone-tolerant, hardy plants from Mediterranean. Featured on Channel 4 Garden Club 1995. *Adm £1 Chd 50p. Sun June 7 (2-6)*

¶4 Grange Cottages, Nailstone ⬥❀❀ (Hilary & Alec Duthie) From Leicester take A47 Hinckley Rd (West) after 6m turn R onto B582 signed for Desford and Ibstock. Follow B582 for about 10m at Xrds where Nailstone is signposted to the L carry straight on, the garden is ½m further on R. From Hinckley take A447 N, turn R onto B582, garden is 1m on L. A 1¼-acre registered organic smallholding with small herb nursery, herb and medicinal display gardens, kitchen garden, experimental 'Forest' garden, goats, poultry and wildlife and woodland areas. TEAS. *Adm £1 Chd 50p (ACNO to SHELTER®). Sats May 16, July 18 (10-6)*

Gunthorpe, Oakham ⬥ (A T C Haywood Esq) 2m S of Oakham. On Uppingham Rd; entrance by 3 cottages, on R going S. Medium-sized garden; spring flowers and flowering trees in good setting. TEAS. *Adm £2 Chd 50p (ACNO to Macmillan Cancer Relief). Sun April 19 (2-5.30)*

Hambleton Gardens, Hambleton ❀ 3m E of Oakham on A606 Oakham to Stamford rd. Turn R at signpost for Hambleton and Egleton. TEAS. Please do not park in village, use field adjacent to Orchard House. *Combined adm £2 Chd free. Sun May 24 (10-5)*

Orchard House (Mr & Mrs J L Cookson) Lyndon Rd. In village, church on R, immed turn R, go to bottom of hill, house is last on R, before cattle grid. Small 4-sectioned, walled and hedged gardens, mainly herbaceous and bulbs, on the edge of Rutland Water. New terrace and further gardens at rear under development. 2 acres

Stone Cottage (Malcolm Bonser & Ann Goodfellow) Ketton Rd. Opp Hambleton Hall. Approx 1-acre garden with interesting plants - shrubs, roses, herb garden and water features. Orchard underplanted with bulbs and shrubs. Views of Rutland Water

Hill House, Dunton Bassett ✾❀ (Mr & Mrs M J Rowe) The Mount, Dunton Bassett, nr Lutterworth. S of Leicester via A426 (between Leicester and Lutterworth) follow signs for Dunton Bassett, then to Leire. Grade II listed former Georgian Farmhouse. Frame Knitters workshop open to public. Small ½-acre family garden planted for yr-round interest and colour; ponds, rockery, herbs, soft fruits, ferns and large mixed herbaceous beds. Owner maintained. TEAS in aid of Dunton Bassett PTA. *Adm £1.20 Chd free. Sun June 28 (2-5)*

Hill House, Market Overton ♿❀ (Brian & Judith Taylor) Teigh Rd, Market Overton. 6m N of Oakham beyond Cottesmore, 5m from the A1 via Thistleton, 10m E from Melton Mowbray via Wymondham. ½-acre plant enthusiasts' garden consisting mainly of mixed beds designed for seasonal interest and comprising many unusual hardy and tender perennials. TEAS. *Adm £1 Chd free. Suns July 19, Sept 6 (11-5). Private group visits welcome July to Sept, please* **Tel 01572 767337**

Holly Hayes, Birstall ♿❀ (Mrs Edith A Murphy) 216 Birstall Rd, adjoining Ecology Centre. Take Birstall Rd from Redhill island. Near village hall. 4-acre garden with rhododendrons, azaleas, fine old trees incl redwoods, wisteria, pergola, flower borders and ponds. TEA. *Adm £1 Chd 20p. Sat, Sun May 16, 17 (2-6)*

The Homestead, Normanton ❀ (Mr & Mrs J E Palmer) 10m W of Grantham on A52. In Bottesford turn N, signposted Normanton; last house on R before disused airfield. ¾-acre informal plant lover's garden. Vegetable garden, small orchard, woodland area, many hellebores and single paeonies. Collections of hostas and sempervivums. TEAS. *Adm £1 Chd free (ACNO to NCCPG®). Suns March 22, May 24 (2-6)*

Langham Lodge, Oakham ♿✾❀ (Mr & Mrs H N Hemsley) ½m out of Langham on Burley Rd. 1 acre; shrubs; interesting foliage; stone walls; shrubs roses. *Adm £1 Chd free. Sat June 27 (4-9). Cheese and wine in aid of Langham Church from 6pm. Private visits welcome, please* **Tel 01572 722912**

Long Close, Woodhuse Eaves ❀ (P M Johnson) 60 Main St. S of Loughborough nr M1 Junc 23. From A6, W in Quorn B591. 5 acres spring bulbs, rhododendrons (many varieties), azaleas, flowering shrubs, camellias, magnolias, many rare shrubs, mature trees, lily ponds; terraced lawns, herbaceous borders, penstemon collection, wild flower meadow walk. TEAS and plant sales, *Adm £2 Chd 50p. Suns April 5, May 10, 24 (2-5.30). Daily Mons-Sats March-July and autumn (9.30-1 & 2-5.30) Tickets Pené Crafts Shop opp. Also private parties welcome, please* **Tel 01509 890616** *business hrs*

Market Bosworth Gardens ♿❀ 1m off A447 Coalville to Hinckley Rd, 3m off A444. Pay on Market Bosworth Market Place. Village plan available. Other gardens will also open. East Midlands in Bloom winners 1997, National finalist 1998. Free car parking. TEA. *Combined adm £2 Chd 50p. Sun July 26 (2-6)*

273 Station Road (Mrs R J Baker) Flower garden and model village

24 Northumberland Avenue (Mr & Mrs E G Watkins) Flowers, shrubs and lawns

16 Northumberland Avenue (Mr & Mrs K McCarthy) Landscape garden

¶11 Stanley Road (Mrs O Caldwell) Small mature garden with shrubs

¶Home Farm Cottage (Mr & Mrs Kitching) Farm garden with lawn, flowers, shrubs

¶13 Spinney Hill (Mrs J Bucknell) Well tended estate garden

¶Rainbow Cottage (Mr & Mrs A Clark) A cottage garden

Market Overton Gardens ✾ 6m N of Oakham beyond Cottesmore; 5m from the A1 via Thistleton; 10m E from Melton Mowbray via Wymondham. TEAS. *Combined adm £1.50 Chd free. Sun July 19 (11-5)*

Church Cottage ✾❀ (Mr & Mrs W M Cox) 6m N of Oakham beyond Cottersmore; 5m from the A1 via Thistleton. 10m E from Melton Mowbray via Wymondham. Well hidden partly walled ½ acre old fashioned garden surrounding thatched cottage, climbing and shrub roses, clematis, peonies, shrubs, perennials and lawns

Hill House see separate entry

1700 Melton Road, Rearsby ♿✾❀ (Hazel Kaye) N of Leicester on A607. In Rearsby, on L.H. side from Leicester. 1-acre garden with wide range of interesting herbaceous plants; some shrubs and trees. Extensive new water garden. Nursery. TEAS March 8 and Oct 4 only. *Adm £2 Chd 10p. Daily March to Oct (Tues to Sat 10-5, Sun 10-12). Also SPECIAL OPEN DAYS Sun March 8 (2-5) and Sun Oct 4 (2-5).* **Tel 01664 424578**

Mill View ᴥ✿ (Dr & Mrs J S G P Stableford) Tickow Lane, Shepshed. 2m W of Loughborough from junction 23 M1 on A512 for 1m take the 3rd on R; from M42 Ashby take A512 to Loughborough as entering Shepshed take first L. Victorian walled garden incl large herbaceous borders. Collection of penstemons, hosta and ferns, vegetable plot. Also a good spring garden full of bulbs etc. TEAS. *Adm £1.50 Chd free. Sun July 5 (2-5). Private visits welcome on Fris, please* Tel 01509 503202

■ **Orchards, Walton** ᴥ✿ (Mr & Mrs G Cousins) Hall Lane, Walton nr Lutterworth. 8m S of Leicester via the A50 take a R turn just after Shearsby (sign-posted Bruntingthorpe); thereafter follow signs for Walton. A garden of surprises. It is full of rare and unusual plants which are grown in colour-theme garden 'rooms'. Featured on TVs Garden Club and Garden Party. Views of countryside. TEAS. *Adm £1.50 Chd free. Open Suns June to Aug. For NGS Sun May 31, Wed June 3 (11-5). Also parties and private visits welcome June to Sept, please* Tel 01455 556958

Owston Gardens, nr Oakham ᴥ✿ 6m W of Oakham via Knossington, 2m S of Somerby. From Leicester turn L 2m E of Tilton. TEAS. *Combined adm £1.50 Chd free. Sun May 17 (2-6)*
  The Homestead (Mr & Mrs David Penny) ⅓ acre with lawn, clematis, ponds, borders, containers, alpine garden, views and photographs. Plants and sundries stalls
  Rose Cottage (Mr & Mrs John Buchanan) Undulating 1¾ acres; shrub and flower borders; spring bulbs, roses, alpines, ponds, waterfall, fine views. *(ACNO to St Andrew's Church Owston©). Private visits welcome, please* Tel 01664 454545

Paddocks, Shelbrook ᴥ✿ (Mrs Ailsa Jackson) 1½m W of Ashby-de-la-Zouch on B5003 towards Moira. A plantaholic's garden with over 2000 species and varieties in 1 acre incl snowdrops, hellebores, hardy orchids, astrantias and many less common herbaceous plants & shrubs. Plants propagated from garden for sale. NCCPG collection of old named double and single primulas. Silver medallist at Chelsea and Vincent Square. TEAS. *Adm £1.50 Chd free. Sats and Suns April 11, 12, May 23, 24, June 13, 14, July 11, 12; Aug 15, 16 (2-5). Also private visits of 10 or more welcome, please* Tel 01530 412606

Park Farm, Normanton, see Nottinghamshire

18 Park Road, Birstall ᴥ✿ (Dr & Mrs D R Ives) Turn off A6 into Park Rd at crown of the hill on Leicester side of Birstall. Local buses stop at end of Park Rd. Approx 1-acre of lawn, trees, shrubs and other mixed planting incl bluebells etc with emphasis on foliage and scent. TEAS. *Adm £1.20 Chd 30p (ACNO to LOROS®). Sun, Mon May 17, 18 (2-5.30). Private visits welcome late April to mid June, please* Tel 0116 2675118

Pine House, Gaddesby ᴥ✿ (Mr & Mrs T Milward) Rearsby Rd. From A607 Leicester-Melton Mowbray, at Rearsby turn off for Gaddesby. 2-acre garden with fine mature trees, woodland walk, with redesigned water gar-

den. Herb and potager garden and wisteria archway to a Victorian vinery. Pleached lime trees, mixed borders with unusual plants and a new rock garden, terraced garden with potted standards and a terracotta pot garden. Rare and unusual plant sale. TEAS. *Adm £1.50 Chd 20p (ACNO to Gaddesby Church©) on Sun and Bank Holiday Mon May 3, 4 (2-5). Also open Sun June 7 (2-5)*

Prebendal House, Empingham ᴥ✿ (Mr & Mrs J Partridge) Between Stamford & Oakham on A606. House built in 1688; summer palace for the Bishop of Lincoln. Recently improved old-fashioned gardens incl water garden, topiary and kitchen gardens. TEAS. *Adm £1.50 Chd 50p. Sun June 14 (2-6)*

Preston Gardens 2m N of Uppingham on A6003 between Uppingham & Oakham. Teas in Village Hall. *Combined adm £1.50 Chd free. Sun May 10 (2-6)*
  14 Main Street ᴥ (Mr & Mrs J B Goldring) ¾-acre village garden; several small borders of differing aspect; tender wall shrubs; variety of climbers incl clematis, herbaceous plants, seasonal shrubs (particularly old roses) and bulbs
  The Granary ✿ (Mr & Mrs A Morse) Delightful, peaceful ¾-acre garden intermixed with unusual and ordinary plants and bulbs. A small vegetable garden, swimming pool area surrounded with containers

The Priory, Ketton ᴥ✿ (Mr & Mrs J Acton) 3m W of Stamford. Take A6121 to Ketton, turn at Xrds in Ketton, down Church Rd, opp the churchyard. Newly created 2-acre garden; herbaceous border; water garden; alpines. Over 100 different roses. 2 courtyard gardens with mixed planting and cottage garden. TEA. *Adm £1.50 Chd 50p (ACNO to Stamford Citizens Advice Bureau®). Sun July 5 (2-6)*

Queniborough Gardens ᴥ✿ A607 N out of Leicester. 6m from Leicester. 9m from Melton Mowbray. *Combined adm £1 Chd 25p. Sun June 21 (11-5)*
  5 Barkby Road (Mr & Mrs A R B Wadd) Small cottage garden containing herbs, pond, herbaceous borders. Small orchard with greenhouse, collection of scented leaved pelargoniums
  21 Barkby Road (Mr & Mrs P Hemingray) Small, enclosed, organic, wildlife friendly garden. *Private visits welcome, please* Tel 0116 2605824
  40 The Ringway (Mr & Mrs W D Hall) Small garden with alpine scree, tufa bed, alpine house. Large pond and bog, herbaceous plants and greenhouse. *Private visits welcome, please* Tel 0116 2605908
  8 Syston Road (Mrs R A Smith) Plant enthusiasts cottage style garden; old and new English roses, small pond with frogs and newts; organic vegetable garden. TEAS. *Private visits welcome during July, please* Tel 0116 2605606

Evening Opening (see also garden descriptions)

Langham Lodge, Oakham   June 27 4–9pm

Sheepy Magna Gardens ♿✿ B4116 2½m N of Atherstone on Atherstone to Twycross Rd. Cream TEAS in aid of Sheepy Magna Church. *Combined adm £2 Chd free. Sat, Sun June 20, 21 (2-6)*

¶**Athol House, 108 Main Road** (Mr & Mrs A Brown) 108, Main Road. Next to village hall. Old garden being rejuvenated; variety of herbaceous borders, trees, shrubs, vegetable plot, natural areas, formal pond and container plants

Gate Cottage ❀ (Mr & Mrs O P Hall) Church Lane. Opp church. Approx ½-acre cottage garden; mixed herbaceous borders; greenhouse; vegetable garden; several specimen trees; lawns, patio and pond, new shrubbery

¶**Pinewood House, 64 Main Road** (Mr & Mrs P Burke) Pleasant small private garden with mature trees and mixed perennials in borders

Vine Cottage ❀ (Mr & Mrs T Clark) 26 Main Rd. Opp shop. Approx ¾-acre cottage garden; mixed herbaceous borders with many unusual plants; alpine gardens; ponds; vegetable plot with greenhouse. Cream TEAS

Sutton Bonington Hall, Sutton Bonington ♿❀ (Anne, Lady Elton) 5m NW of Loughborough; take A6 to Hathern; turn R (E) onto A6006; 1st L (N) for Sutton Bonington. Conservatory, formal white garden, variegated leaf borders. Queen Anne house (not open). Picnics. TEA. *Adm £1.50 Chd 50p (ACNO to St Michael's and St Ann's Church, Sutton Bonington®). Sun June 28 (12-5.30)*

University of Leicester Botanic Garden, Oadby ♿✿❀ Stoughton Drive South. SE outskirts of city opp race course. 16-acre garden incl grounds of Beaumont Hall, The Knoll, Southmeade and Hastings House. Wide variety of ornamental features and glasshouses laid out for educational purposes incl NCCPG collections of aubrieta, hardy fuchsia and skimmia. TEAS. *Adm £1.50 Chd free (ACNO to Rainbows Hospice®). Sun July 26 (2-5)*

Wakerley Manor, Oakham ♿❀ (A D A W Forbes Esq) 6m Uppingham. R off A47 Uppingham-Peterborough through Barrowden, or from A43 Stamford to Corby rd between Duddington and Bulwick. 4 acres lawns, shrubs, herbaceous; kitchen garden; 3 greenhouses. TEAS. *Adm £1.50 Chd free (ACNO to St Mary the Virgin Church, South Luffenham®). Sun May 31 (2-6)*

Wartnaby, Wartnaby ♿❀ (Lord & Lady King) 4m NW of Melton Mowbray. From A606 turn W in Ab Kettley, from A46 at Six Hills Hotel turn E on A676. Medium-sized garden, shrubs, herbaceous borders, newly laid out rose garden with a good collection of old-fashioned roses and others; small arboretum. Formal vegetable garden. Specialist plant fair about 20 nurseries selling a wide range of unusual plants. *Adm £2 Chd 20p (ACNO to Marie Curie Cancer Care©). Sun June 28 (11-4). Private parties welcome, please* **Tel 01664 822296 business hours**

Whatton House, Loughborough ♿❀ (Lord Crawshaw) 4m NE of Loughborough on A6 between Hathern and Kegworth; 2½m SE of junc 24 on M1. 15 acres; shrub and herbaceous borders, lawns, rose and wild gardens, pools; arboretum. Nursery open. TEAS in Old Dining Room. Catering arrangements for pre-booked parties any day or evening. *Adm £2 OAP/Chd £1. Tues April 14, May 5, 26 (2-6). Special plant sale Sun Sept 20 (2-6). Also private visits welcome, please* **Tel 01509 842268**

The White House, Main Street, Burrough on the Hill ✿❀ (Mr & Mrs D Cooper) 6m W of Oakham, 5m S of Melton Mowbray. From A606 at Langham, take rd signposted to Cold Overton and Somerby. Turn L in Somerby and follow rd through to Burrough or from B6047 at Twyford take rd signposted to Burrough on the Hill. Plantsman's garden of approx 1 acre. Formal terrace area with pond and pergola, rock garden, incl raised beds and alpine house, lawns with mixed borders, woodland walk, wild garden. Many autumn flowering bulbs and perennials. TEAS. *Adm £1 Chd 50p. (ACNO to St Mary's Church, Burrough on the Hill). Sun Sept 6 (1-6)*

¶**The White Lodge, Willesley** ✿❀ (Paul & Wendy Watson) 1m SW of Ashby-de-la-Zouch. Leave A42 at junction 12 and take B5006 N towards Ashby. 100yds beyond Golf Club entrance turn sharp L signed Willesley. Garden ½m. ⅔-acre formal garden with island beds of shrubs, roses and herbaceous plants leading to walk through 3½ acres of woodland with glades and stream with pools, island, bog garden and views. TEAS. *Adm £1.50 Chd 50p (ACNO to Leicestershire Macmillan Cancer Service®). Suns May 17, July 26 (2-6)*

¶**Wing Gardens, nr Oakham** ❀ 2m S of Rutland Water off A6003 between Oakham and Uppingham. Cream TEAS. *Combined adm £1.50 Chd free. Sun June 21 (11-6)*

Townsend House (David & Jeffy Wood) ¾ acre cottage garden with mixed borders, roses and clematis. Walled gravel garden around pool. Newly created vegetable garden

¶**Wingwell** ❀ (John & Rose Dejardin) developing garden of approx ¾ acre, mixed planting for all year interest; includes walled garden with drought resistant plants and ornamental pool. Emphasis on bold use of plants, particularly herbaceous, and interesting use of stone and paving

Woodyton Farmhouse, Grace Dieu ♿✿❀ (Mr & Mrs F A Slater) On A512, 6m E of Ashby de la Zouch, 6m W of Loughborough, 3m W of M1 junction 23. ¼-acre garden, herbaceous borders, shrub roses, hydrangeas, scree and shade. TEA. *Adm £1 Chd free. Suns June 7, Aug 2 (2-6)*

Scotland's Gardens Scheme

The National Gardens Scheme has a similar but quite separate counterpart in Scotland. Called Scotland's Gardens Scheme, it raises money for the Queen's Nursing Institute (Scotland), the Gardens Fund of the National Trust for Scotland and over 160 registered charities nominated by Garden Owners. The Handbook is available (£3.75 incl p&p) from Scotland's Gardens Scheme, 31 Castle Terrace, Edinburgh, EH1 2EL.

Lincolnshire

Hon County Organiser:	Mrs Patrick Dean, East Mere House, Lincoln LN4 2JB Tel 01522 791371 or 01476 565456
Assistant Hon County Organisers:	Lady Bruce-Gardyne, The Old Rectory, Aswardby, Spilsby PE23 4JS Tel 01790 752652
	Mrs Peter Sandberg, Croft House, Ulceby, N Lincs DN39 6SW Tel 01469 588330
	Mrs Sally Grant, Holly House, Fishtoft Drive, Boston PE22 7ES Tel 01205 750486
Hon County Treasurer:	Mrs Julian Gorst, Oxcombe Manor, Horncastle LN9 6LU Tel 01507 533227

DATES OF OPENING

Regular opening
For details see garden description

Harlaxton Manor Gardens, Grantham

By appointment only
For telephone numbers and other details see garden descriptions. Private visits welcomed

The Manor House, Bitchfield
Springtyme, Sibsey
Walnut Cottage, Careby

By appointment only
For telephone numbers and other details see garden descriptions. Private visits welcomed

February 21 Saturday
21 Chapel Street, Hacconby
25 High Street, Rippingale
Manor Farm, Keisby
February 22 Sunday
21 Chapel Street, Hacconby
25 High Street, Rippingale
Manor Farm, Keisby
March 5 Thursday
21 Chapel Street, Hacconby
April 12 Sunday
21 Chapel Street, Hacconby
Croft House, Ulceby
Little Ponton Hall, Grantham
April 13 Monday
Lincoln Gardens
April 16 Thursday
The Old Rectory, East Keal
April 19 Sunday
Grimsthorpe Castle Gdns, Bourne
April 26 Sunday
Holton-le-Moor Hall,
Holton-le-Moor
May 3 Sunday
Becklehon, Wootton
The Old Rectory, Welton le Wold

May 7 Thursday
21 Chapel Street, Hacconby
May 9 Saturday
Belton House, Grantham
May 10 Sunday
Doddington Hall, nr Lincoln
May 17 Sunday
2 School House, Stixwould
May 21 Thursday
The Old Rectory, East Keal
May 31 Sunday
83 Halton Road, Spilsby
June 4 Thursday
21 Chapel Street, Hacconby
June 7 Sunday
Holly House, Boston
Houlton Lodge, Goxhill
Lincoln Gardens
Saxby-all-Saints Gardens
Ye Olde Three Tuns, Kirkby
Underwood
June 14 Sunday
Marston Hall, Grantham
June 18 Thursday
Grimsthorpe Castle Gdns,
Bourne
June 21 Sunday
Grange Cottage, Cadney
Haconby Hall, Haconby
Harrington Hall, Spilsby
Laburnum Cottage, Cadney
The Old Rectory, East Keal
The Old Vicarage,
Holbeach Hurn
Old White House,
Holbeach Hurn
Sutton St Edmund Village
Gardens
The Villa, South Somercotes
June 28 Sunday
Heath House, Ryhall
July 2 Thursday
21 Chapel Street, Hacconby
July 5 Sunday
2 School House, Stixwould
July 12 Sunday
Gunby Hall, Burgh-le-Marsh
Heath House, Ryhall
Pinefields, Bigby

73 Saxilby Road, Sturton
by Stow
July 18 Saturday
Belton House, Grantham
July 19 Sunday
Cortadera, Nettleton
Park View, Holton-le-Moor
July 26 Sunday
Houlton Lodge, Goxhill
August 6 Thursday
21 Chapel Street, Hacconby
September 3 Thursday
21 Chapel Street, Hacconby
September 5 Saturday
Belton House, Grantham
September 6 Sunday
Croft House, Ulceby
Hall Farm, Harpswell
Heath House, Ryhall
September 20 Sunday
Aubourn Hall, Aubourn
September 27 Sunday
Harlaxton Manor Gardens,
Grantham
October 11 Sunday
21 Chapel Street, Hacconby

1999
February 20 Saturday
21 Chapel Street, Hacconby
February 21 Sunday
21 Chapel Street, Hacconby

The National Gardens Scheme is a charity which traces its origins back to 1927. Since then it has raised over £18 million for charitable purposes.

LINCOLNSHIRE

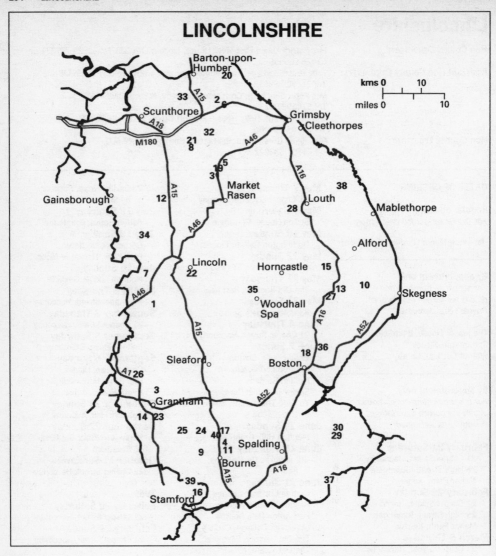

Barton-upon-Humber
20
33 A15
Scunthorpe 2
A18
M180 32
21
8
Grimsby
Cleethorpes
19 5
3 A46
Market Rasen
38
Louth
28
Mablethorpe
Gainsborough
12 A15
34
A46
Alford
7
Lincoln
22
Horncastle
15
A16
A46
35
Woodhall Spa
13
27
10
Skegness
1
A16
A52
A15
18 36
Sleaford
Boston
A1 26
3
A52
Grantham
14 23
25 24 40 17
4
9 11
Spalding
Bourne
30
29
39
A16
16
A15
37
Stamford

kms 0   10
miles 0   10

KEY

1. Aubourn Hall
2. Becklehon
3. Belton House
4. 21 Chapel Street
5. Cortadera
6. Croft House
7. Doddington Hall
8. Grange Cottage
9. Grimsthorpe Castle Gdns
10. Gunby Hall
11. Haconby Hall
12. Hall Farm
13. 83 Halton Road
14. Harlaxton Manor Gardens

15. Harrington Hall
16. Heath House
17. 25 High Street
18. Holly House
19. Holton-le-Moor Hall
20. Houlton Lodge
21. Laburnum Cottage
22. Lincoln Gardens
23. Little Ponton Hall
24. Manor Farm
25. The Manor House
26. Marston Hall
27. The Old Rectory, East Keal
28. The Old Rectory, Welton le Wold

29. The Old Vicarage
30. Old White House
31. Park View
32. Pinefields
33. Saxby-all-Saints Gardens
34. 73 Saxilby Road
35. 2 School House
36. Springtyme
37. Sutton St Edmund Village Gardens
38. The Villa
39. Walnut Cottage
40. Ye Olde Three Tuns

DESCRIPTIONS OF GARDENS

Aubourn Hall, Aubourn &♨❀ (Lady Nevile) 7m SW of Lincoln. Signposted off A606 at Harmston. Approx 3 acres. Lawns, mature trees, shrubs, roses, mixed borders. C11 church adjoining. Wheelchairs in dry weather only. TEAS. *Adm £1.50 Chd 50p (ACNO to St. Peters Church Aubourn - repairs®). Sun Sept 20 (2-5.30)*

¶**Becklehon, Wootton** ♨❀ (Robert & Pat Musgrove) 2m N of A18 at Melton Ross. Garden situated on main High St between PO and Wootton C of E School. ⅓-acre garden developed during the last four yrs. Large collection of hebes, geraniums and euphorbia. Many unusual plants. Garden divided into raised alpine bed, rockeries and Mediterranean area. Guide dogs allowed. TEAS. *Adm £1 Chd free. Sun May 3 (2-5.30)*

▲**Belton House, Grantham** &♨ (The National Trust) 3m NE of Grantham on the A607 Grantham to Lincoln rd. Easily reached and signed from the A1 (Grantham N junction). 32 acres of garden incl formal Italian and Dutch gardens, and orangery by Sir Jeffrey Wyatville. TEAS. *Adm house & garden £5 Chd £2.50. For NGS Sats May 9, July 18, Sept 5 (11-5.30). Group bookings for garden only may be booked in advance by post £3.50*

21 Chapel Street, Hacconby ♨❀ (Cliff & Joan Curtis) A15 3m N of Bourne, turn E at Xrds into Hacconby. Cottage garden overflowing with plants for yr-round interest, special interest alpines, bulbs, herbaceous. Early opening for hellebores and snowdrop collection. Asters for late opening. Featured on TV. TEAS. *Adm £1 Chd free (ACNO to Marie Curie Memorial Foundation®). Sat, Sun Feb 21, 22 (11-4) Thurs March 5 (2-6) Sun Apr 12 (11-5) Thurs May 7, June 4, July 2, Aug 6, Sept 3 (2-6), Sun Oct 11 (11-5). 1999 Sat, Sun Feb 20, 21 (11-4). Private visits and parties welcome, please* **Tel 01778 570314**

¶**Cortadera, Nettleton** &♨❀ (Mr & Mrs A T Moor) 1m SW of Caistor on the A46, just past The Salutation on opposite side. Approx ⅓-acre front and rear gardens, mixed planting with alpines, pergolas, wildlife pond and stream. TEAS. *Combined adm with* **Park View** *£1.50 Chd free. Sun July 19 (1.30-5.30)*

Croft House, Ulceby &❀ (Mr & Mrs Peter Sandberg) nr Brigg. At War Memorial from E turn L, from W turn R into Front St and then into Pitmoor Lane. 2-acre garden set within a formal design filled with informal planting. Many old favourites alongside sought-after varieties. Mixed and herbaceous borders, bulbs, meadow, gravel bed, Victorian vinery. TEAS. *Adm £1.50 Chd free. Suns April 12, Sept 6 (2-5.30). Also by appt, please* **Tel 01469 588330**

▲**Doddington Hall, Lincoln** &♨ (Antony Jarvis Esq) 5m SW of Lincoln. From Lincoln via A46, turn W on to B1190 for Doddington. Superb walled gardens; thousands of spring bulbs; wild gardens; mature trees; Elizabethan mansion. Free car park. TEAS and snacks available. *Adm garden only £2 Chd £1 (ACNO to Lincolnshire Old Churches Trust© and St Peter's Church Doddington®). For NGS Sun May 10 (2-6)*

Grange Cottage, Cadney ♨❀ (Mr & Mrs D Hoy) 3m S of Brigg. In Brigg turn L into Elwes St; follow rd to Cadney. From Market Rasen to Brigg Rd, turn L in Howsham on to Cadney Rd. ⅓-acre cottage garden; many unusual and old-fashioned plants; old roses; pond; orchard; conservatory with interesting tender plants. *Adm £1 Chd free. Sun June 21 (2-5). Private visits also welcome May to July, please* **Tel 01652 678771**

▲**Grimsthorpe Castle Gardens, Bourne** &❀ (Grimsthorpe and Drummond Castle Trust) 8m E of A1 on the A151 from the Colsterworth junction, 4m W of Bourne. 15 acres of formal and woodland gardens which incl bulbs and wild flowers. The formal gardens encompass fine topiary, roses, herbaceous borders and an unusual ornamental kitchen garden. TEAS and light meals. *Adm £3 OAP £2 Chd £1.50. Combined adm castle and garden £6 OAP £4.50 Chd £3 (ACNO to Grimsthorpe and Drummond Castle Trust®). For NGS Sun April 19, Thurs June 18 (11-6)*

▲**Gunby Hall, Burgh-le-Marsh** ❀ (Mr & Mrs J D Wrisdale; The National Trust) 2½m NW of Burgh-le-Marsh; S of A158. Free parking. 7 acres of formal and walled gardens; old roses; herbaceous borders; herb garden; kitchen garden with fruit trees and vegetables. Tennyson's 'Haunt of Ancient Peace'. House built by Sir William Massingberd 1700. Plant centre. TEAS. *Adm gardens £2.50 Chd £1. For NGS Sun July 12 (2-6) NT membership cards not valid*

Haconby Hall, nr Bourne ♨❀ (Mr & Mrs J F Atkinson) 3m N of Bourne, ¾m E of A 15 in Haconby village. A large established plantsman's garden with lawns, trees, shrubs, herbaceous borders, knot garden and ha-ha. TEAS in aid of Haconby Church. *Adm £2 Chd 50p. Sun June 21 (2-6)*

Hall Farm, Harpswell &♨❀ (Pam & Mark Tatam) 7m E of Gainsborough on A631. 1½m W of Caenby Corner. ¾-acre garden with mixed borders of trees, shrubs, roses and unusual perennials. Over 100 - mainly old - varieties of rose. Sunken garden, pond, courtyard garden and recently constructed walled gravel garden. Short walk to old moat and woodland. Free seed collecting in garden Sept 6. TEAS. *Adm £1.50 Chd 50p. Sun Sept 6 (10-6). Garden open daily with collecting box (10-5); by appt in the evenings* **Tel 0142 7668412**

83 Halton Road, Spilsby ♨❀ (Jack & Joan Gunson) In Spilsby take B1195 towards Wainfleet; garden on L. Limited parking on Halton Rd, free car park Post Office Lane, Spilsby. ¼-acre town garden and ¼-acre hardy plant nursery, divided into a series of smaller gardens featuring densely planted mixed borders, incl many unusual plants and hardy geranium collection of approx 130 varieties. Spring bulbs a feature, many unusual. Featured in 'The Times' and 'Practical Gardening'. TEAS. *Adm £1 Chd free. Sun May 31 (2-6). Garden and Nursery open Wed-Sun (10-5). March-Sept NGS collection box*

■ **Harlaxton Manor Gardens, Grantham** &❀ (University of Evansville) 1m W of Grantham off A607 Melton Mowbray rd. Historically important 110-acre formal gardens and woodland currently undergoing major restoration, spearheaded by Alan Mason. 6-acre ornate walled gardens, potager and theme gardens. Harlaxton Manor built by Gregory Gregory and with garden rivalled anything in Europe. Dutch canal, Italian gardens, French terracing, views. TEAS. *Adm £2.50 OAP £2 Chd £1.25. April 1 to Oct closed Mons except Bank Hol Mons. For NGS Sun Sept 27 (11-5)*

Harrington Hall, Spilsby &% (Mr & Mrs David Price) 6m NW of Spilsby. Turn off A158 (Lincoln-Skegness) at Hagworthingham, 2m from Harrington. Approx 5-acre Tudor and C18 walled gardens, incl recently designed kitchen garden; herbaceous borders, roses and other flowering shrubs. High terrace mentioned in Tennyson's 'Maud'. TEAS. *Adm £1.50 Chd under 14 free. Sun June 21 (2-5)*

¶**Heath House, Ryhall** &%% (Mr André Vrona) In Ryhall, 2m N of Stamford, take B1176 towards Little Bytham. After 1m turn L up Pickworth Drift (not signposted) house in ¾m. 3-acre magnificent rose garden with old roses, shrubs and climbers, sunken mown area. Autumn borders and general interest, all planted in last 5yrs by enthusiastic owners. TEAS. *Adm £1.50 Chd 50p. Suns June 28, July 12 (12-6); Sun Sept 6 (12-5)*

25 High St, Rippingale &%% (Mr & Mrs R Beddington) On A15 5m N of Bourne. Turn E at Xrds into Rippingale. No 25, Westcombe is 5th house on R. ½-acre village garden. Borders, island beds, ponds and vegetable garden. Yr-round interest. Hellebores and snowdrops in spring. TEA. *Adm £1 Acc chd free. Sat, Sun Feb 21, 22 (11-4)*

Holly House, Boston &%% (Sally & David Grant) Fishtoft Drove, nr Frithville. Fishtoft Drove is an unclassified rd approx 3m N of Boston and 1m S of Frithville on the W side of the West Fen Drain. Approx 1-acre informal gardens with mixed borders, scree beds, old sinks with alpines and steps leading down to a large pond with cascade and stream. Softly curving beds are full of unusual and interesting herbaceous plants. *Adm £1 Chd free (ACNO to Pilgrim Heart and Lung Fund®). Sun June 7 (2-6)*

Holton-le-Moor Hall, Holton-le-Moor &%% (Mr & Mrs P H Gibbons) 6m N of Market Rasen off B1434 or A46. 2½ acres well-established garden with spring bulbs and flowering trees and shrubs. Large kitchen garden and orchard. TEAS in aid of St Luke's Church. *Adm £1.50 Chd free. Sun April 26 (2-5.30)*

Houlton Lodge, Goxhill &%% (Mr & Mrs M Dearden) 6m E of Barton-on-Humber. Follow signs to Goxhill, do not go into village centre but straight on over railway bridge and take 5th turning on R. Houlton Lodge is about 100yds from junction on LH-side. Park cars outside property. A well-established very neat garden approx ¾ acre. Shrub rose and mixed borders; large island bed and rockery and conifer bed. TEAS in aid of Goxhill Methodist Church. *Adm £1 Chd free. Suns June 7, July 26 (2-6). Private visits welcome, please Tel 01469 531355*

Laburnum Cottage, Cadney &% (Colin & Jessie Lynn) 3m S of Brigg. In Brigg turn L into Elwes St, follow rd to Cadney. From Market Rasen to Brigg Rd turn L in How-sham on to Cadney Rd. 1-acre, herbaceous and mature shrub borders; island beds; smaller separate gardens within the garden; rose covered walk leading to shrub roses; small orchard; wildlife and formal pond. TEAS in aid of Cadney Church. *Adm £1 Chd free. Sun June 21 (2-5). Private parties of 10 and over welcome, please Tel 01652 678725*

Lincoln Gardens %% From bypass, take A57 signposted Saxilby. 100yds turn R onto Long Leys Rd; turn R at end onto Yarborough Rd. Free car park second turning R in Hampton St. TEAS. *Combined adm £1.50 Chd 50p. Easter Mon April 13, Sun June 7 (11-6)*

¶**Sunnyside, 144 West Parade** (Sarah & Jim Scarlett) Tiny town garden exuberantly planted for yr-round interest with a mixture of unusual herbaceous perennials, grasses, bulbs and shrubs. Pond, pebble pool with ferns. Caution narrow path round pond

Westholme, 10 Yarborough Rd % (Ian Warden & Stewart Mackenzie) Tiny town garden reflecting owners' interest in unusual herbaceous perennials and shrubs. Pond with natural plantings. Collection of hostas. Plants in containers. Unusual plants for sale. Caution - steep steps, narrow paths. Featured in 'The Garden' March '97 and 'Lincs Life' Sept '97. *Private visits welcome by parties of 10 or less, please Tel 01522 568401*

Little Ponton Hall, Grantham &% (Mr & Mrs Alastair McCorquodale) ½m E of A1 at S end of Grantham bypass. 3 to 4-acre garden. Spacious lawns with cedar tree over 200yrs old. Many varieties of old shrub roses; borders and young trees. Stream with spring garden; bulbs and river walk. Kitchen garden and listed dovecote. Adjacent to Little Ponton Hall is St Guthlacs Church which will be decorated and all visitors welcome. TEAS. *Adm £1.50 Chd 50p (ACNO to St Guthlacs Church, Little Ponton®). Sun April 12 (2-5)*

Manor Farm, Keisby %% (Mr & Mrs C A Richardson) 9m NW of Bourne, 10m E of Grantham, signed to Keisby from Lenton and Hawthorpe. ½-acre plantsman's garden. Snowdrop collection and hellebores. *Adm £1 Chd free (ACNO to Stamford and Bourne CRMF®). Sat, Sun Feb 21, 22 (11-4)*

The Manor House, Bitchfield % (John Richardson Esq) 6m SE of Grantham, close to Irnham and Rippingale. A52 out of Grantham to Spital Gate Hill roundabout; take B1176 to Bitchfield; house on R after public house. 1½ acres re-created in 1972; essentially a shrub rose garden (96 varieties) with shrubs and other perennials; 50 by 40ft pond planted spring 1985; small box hedged formal garden; ha-ha, new large garden room with fountain and over 100 plants. *Adm £2. Parties of 20 or more welcome by appointment June 1 to mid-July; no bookings accepted before May 1. Please Tel 01476 585261*

▲**Marston Hall, nr Grantham** &% (The Rev Henry Thorold) 6m N of Grantham. Turn off A1, 4½m N of Grantham; on 1½m to Marston. Station: Grantham. Notable trees; wych elm and laburnum of exceptional size. House C16 continuously owned by the Thorold family. Interesting pictures and furniture. TEAS. *Adm house & garden £2.50 Chd £1 (ACNO to Marston Church®). For NGS Sun June 14 (2-6)*

The Old Rectory, East Keal ✿ (John & Ruth Ward) 2m

SW of Spilsby on A16. Turn into Church Lane by PO. Beautifully situated, with fine views, a rambling cottage garden falling naturally into varied separate areas, and shrubs, roses, climbers, perennials and annuals. Small ponds and rock garden. TEAS Sun only TEA Thurs. *Adm £1.20 Chd free. Sun June 21 (2-5), Thurs April 16, May 21 (2-5). Private visits welcome, please* Tel 01790 752477

The Old Rectory, Welton le Wold ✿ (Mrs M L Dickinson)

3m W of Louth. The Old Rectory is on the approach rd from A157 halfway down the hill. Situated in a charming valley. Garden has been developed from an 1853 Victorian garden into the present 4 acres of woodland, mixed shrub and herbaceous borders and a water garden of 4 pools linked by a small stream. A half-walled vegetable garden, divided by a brick and timber pergola leads to a small arboretum. The adjoining park has mature trees and a young 2-acre wood with woodland walk. The nearby church is open to visitors and there are fine views. TEAS. *Adm £1.20 Chd 50p. Sun May 3 (2-5)*

The Old Vicarage, Holbeach Hurn ✿✿ (Mrs Liz Dixon-

Spain) Turn off A17 N to Holbeach Hurn, past Post Box in the middle of village, 1st turn R into Low Rd. Old Vicarage on R approx 400 yds. 2 acres of gardens incl mature trees, formal and informal areas, a croquet lawn surrounded by borders of shrubs, roses, herbaceous plants; also pond, bog garden and wild flowers; shrub roses in old paddock area. *Combined adm with Old White House £1.50 Chd free (ACNO to Hovenden House Cheshire Home®). Sun June 21 (2-6). Private visits welcome, please* Tel 01406 424148

Old White House, Holbeach Hurn ઙ✿ (Mr & Mrs A

Worth) Turn off A17 N to Holbeach Hurn, follow signs to village, go straight through, turn R after the Rose and Crown at Baileys Lane. 1½ acres of mature garden, featuring herbaceous borders, roses, patterned garden, herb garden and wild garden with small pond. TEAS. *Combined adm with The Old Vicarage £1.50 Chd free (ACNO to Hovenden House, Cheshire Home®). Sun June 21 (2-6)*

Park View, Holton-le-Moor ઙ✿✿ (David & Margaret

Jackson) 6m N of Market Rasen Turn L off A46 onto B1436 to Holton-le-Moor village. 2-acre garden started approx 6 yrs ago. Mixed shrubs, trees and herbaceous borders. TEAS. *Combined adm with Cortadera £1.50. Sun July 19 (1.30-5.30)*

Pinefields, Bigby ✿✿ (Reg & Madeleine Hill) Off A1084

between Caistor 5m and Brigg 4m. At top of Smithy Lane - junction with Main St. 4th house from Church. ¾-acre plantsperson's garden. Shrubs and herbaceous borders containing some unusual plants. Roses and clematis on pergolas and trellis. Gravelled alpine area. Wildlife pond. Arches leading to area of wild flowers. TEAS in aid of Bigby Village Hall Fund. *Adm £1.20 Chd free. Sun July 12 (1.30-5.30). Private parties welcome by appt* Tel 01652 628327

¶**Saxby-all-Saints Gardens** Between South Ferriby and Brigg on the B1204 in the centre of Saxby-All-Saints Village. TEAS. *Combined adm £1.50 Chd 50p. Sun June 7 (2-5)*

¶**Rose Cottage** ✿ (Mr & Mrs B Bearfield) A mature country garden of approx ⅓-acre to the rear of C17 cottage. Lawns, mature trees, old and modern roses. Variety of cottage garden shrubs and flowers in beds and borders. TEAS

¶**The Chestnuts** (Peter Blake) 50 Main St. Mature garden set in approx ⅓-acre. With mature trees and shrubs, lawns, herbaceous borders, pond, water feature, summer house, hostas, ferns etc

73 Saxilby Road, Sturton by Stow ઙ✿✿ (Charles &

Tricia Elliott) 9m N of Lincoln on B1241. Saxilby to Lea Rd. House on RH side entering village. Small garden and hardy plant nursery, extensively cultivated, interesting for its maximum use of available space. Ponds, gravelled areas. Beds and borders contain a broad mix of herbaceous and evergreen plants, several unusual, designed to give interest and colour throughout the year. TEAS. *Adm £1 Chd free. Sun July 12 (2-6)*

2 School House, Stixwould ✿✿ (Andrew & Sheila

Sankey) 1½m N of Woodhall Spa. ¼-acre garden, redesigned in Oct 1994 in the cottage garden style, to incl front garden with unusual perennials and shrubs, herb garden, and small turf maze. Owners are garden designers. TEAS. *Adm £1 Chd free (ACNO to Sick Children's Trust®). Suns May 17, July 5 (2-6). Private visits welcome May to Sept, please* Tel 01526 352453

Springtyme, Sibsey ઙ✿✿ (Mr & Mrs J W Lynn) Station

Rd. 5m N of Boston. From A16 at Sibsey turn R onto B1184, towards Old Leake, garden on R in 400yds. Approx ¼-acre informal garden with alpine house, scree beds, alpine troughs, densely planted mixed borders and pond. Featured in Garden Answers '97. *Adm £1 Chd free. Private visits welcome by appt only, please* Tel 01205 750438

Sutton St Edmund Village Gardens ઙ✿ Peterborough

18m, Spalding 16m, Wisbech 8m. TEAS. *Combined adm £1.50 Chd 50p (ACNO to Cystic Fibrosis Research Trust®). Sun June 21 (12-6)*

Farmers Rest (Mr & Mrs H Beaton) In Sutton St Edmund, if facing S turn L then L again onto Guanockgate, house ¼m on L, well signposted. Lovely cottage garden, flowers, vegetables, mature trees, ginko, mulberry and tulip trees. Also a life's collection of Farming Bygones will be on view

Holly Tree Farm ✿ (Mr & Mrs C Pate) In Sutton St Edmund if facing S take R turn in village onto Chapel gate. Next L onto Hallgate, farm 1st house on R. 1-acre family garden, on working 4-acre holding with mixed stock. Free range poultry. Island beds of perennials and shrubs, vegetables, fruit, scree in cottage garden style. developed over the last 9yrs

Inley Drove Farm 🏵 (Dr & Mrs Francis Pryor) N of Sutton St Edmund, 2m straight on when rd swings R, 2nd turning on R into Inley Drove. Garden 5 acres and wood 7½ acres still under construction. Double mixed borders, dry garden, herbs, natural pond, nut walk, roses, orchard and shrubs, all on land which was arable farmland until 1992

The Villa, South Somercotes 🏵 (Michael & Judy Harry) 8m E of Louth. Leave Louth by Eastfield Rd. Follow signs to S Cockerington. Take rd signposted to N & S Somercotes. House on L 100yds before church. ¼-acre densely planted in cottage style; large collection of herbs, old-fashioned and unusual perennials; orchard with interesting old varieties of fruit trees. Livestock incl flock of Lincoln Longwool Sheep. TEAS. *Adm £1 Chd free. Sun June 21 (2-6). Private visits welcome, April to end September, please* **Tel 01507 358487**

Walnut Cottage, Careby &🏵 (Roy & Sue Grundy) 6m N of Stamford on B1176. 5m E of A1 at Stretton. Situated approx ⅓m at end of Main St on L. ½-acre developing garden with interesting herbaceous borders. Herb garden, small shade and gravel areas, water garden with S facing slope leading to small woodland feature with natural pond. Featured on Channel 4 'Garden Club'. TEA. *Adm £1 Chd free. Private visits welcome by appt only Tues and Sat, May to Sept, please* **Tel 01780 410660**

Ye Olde Three Tuns, Kirkby Underwood &🏵🏵 (Ivan & Sadie Hall) A15 6m N of Bourne turn W at Xrds into Kirkby Underwood. House in centre of village. Approx ¼-acre cottage style garden developed over last 8yrs by present owners. Divided into Victorian, container and courtyard gardens. Japanese Koi carp pond, alpine trough walk, mixed borders with many unusual trees, shrubs and herbaceous plants, hostas, pulmonarias, grasses and hardy geraniums. Featured in Garden News, Lincolnshire Life. TEAS. *Adm £1 Chd free. Sun June 7 (2-6)*

Help the Hospices

Help the Hospices is a charity which supports the hospice movement throughout the country. The National Gardens Scheme is delighted to include it in its list of beneficiaries. Some facts:

- **Help the Hospices** is the only national charity helping all providers of hospice and palliative care for the terminally ill.

- **Help the Hospices'** priority is to support all measures to improve patient care for all life-threatening conditions.

- **Help the Hospices** receives no government funding.

- **Help the Hospices** principally supports the voluntary hospices as they receive relatively little government funding.

- **Help the Hospices** support is mainly in direct response to applications from voluntary hospices, usually for training.

- **Help the Hospices** funds training for the NHS and nursing home staff in patient care for the terminally ill as well as funding its own initiatives in training, research, hospice management and team leadership.

- **Help the Hospices** pays special attention to training in communication skills for staff and volunteers.

London (Greater London Area)

Hon County Organiser:	Mrs Maurice Snell, Moleshill House, Fairmile, Cobham, Surrey KT11 1BG
	Tel 01932 864532
Assistant Hon County Organisers:	Don Fuller Esq, 109 Halsbury Rd East, Northolt UB5 4PY
	Tel 0181 422 7417
	Mrs Catherine Horwood, 133 Haverstock Hill, NW3 4RU
	Tel 0171 586 0908
	Mrs Kathy Lynam, 26 Northchurch Rd, N1 4EH
	Tel 0171 254 8993
	Mrs Nancye Nosworthy, 9 Eland Rd, SW11 5JX
	Tel 0171 228 1119
	Mrs Joan Wall, Orchard Cottage, 3 Woodlands Road, Bickley, Kent
	Tel 0181 467 4190
	Mrs V West, 11 Woodlands Rd, Barnes, SW13 0JZ Tel 0181 876 7030
	Miss Alanna Wilson, 38 Ornan Road, NW3 4QB Tel 0171 794 4071
Hon County Treasurer:	Maurice Snell Esq, Moleshill House, Fairmile, Cobham KT11 1BG
	Tel 01932 864532

DATES OF OPENING

Regular Openings
For details see garden description

Chelsea Physic Garden, SW3
Myddelton House Gardens, Enfield

Special Evening Openings
May 21 Thursday
  Royal Botanic Gardens, Kew
June 4 Thursday
  13 Quen Elizabeth's Walk, N16
June 6 Saturday
  Flat 1, 1F Oval Road, NW1
June 10 Wednesday
  Little Lodge, Thames Ditton
June 11 Thursday
  Fenton House, NW3
June 17 Wednesday
  Osborne House, Long Ditton
  103 Thurleigh Road, SW12
June 18 Thursday
  Southwood Lodge, N6
June 20 Saturday
  Flat 1, 1F Oval Road, NW1
June 25 Thursday
  101 Cheyne Walk, SW10
June 27 Saturday
  125 Honor Oak Park, SE23
June 2 Thursday
  20A Seymour Buildings, W1H
June 16 Thursday
  2 Millfield Place, N6

February 22 Sunday
  Myddelton House Gardens, Enfield
March 14 Saturday
  The Elms, Kingston-on-Thames
March 15 Sunday
  The Elms, Kingston-on-Thames

March 28 Saturday
  Lambeth Palace, SE1
April 5 Sunday
  Chelsea Physic Garden, SW3
  10 Chiltern Road, Pinner
  29 Deodar Road, SW15
  29 Gilston Road, SW10
  7 The Grove, N6
  15 Lawrence Street, SW3
April 18 Saturday
  The Elms, Kingston-on-Thames
April 19 Sunday
  9 Eland Road, SW11
  The Elms, Kingston-on-Thames
  Ham House, Richmond
  16 Hillcrest Road, E18
  St Mary's Convent and Nursing
    Home, W4
  7 Upper Phillimore Gardens, W8
April 25 Saturday
  The Holme, NW1
  Trinity Hospice, SW4
April 26 Sunday
  2 Cottesmore Gardens, W8
  Eccleston Square, SW1
  109 Halsbury Road East, Northolt
  The Holme, NW1
  20A Seymour Buildings, W1H
  Trinity Hospice, SW4
  47 Winn Road, Lee
May 3 Sunday
  66 Floriston Avenue, Hillingdon
  51 Gloucester Road, Kew
  1 Grange Park, W5
  5 St Regis Close, N10
  The Watergardens,
    Kingston-on-Thames
May 6 Wednesday
  12 Lansdowne Road, W11
May 9 Saturday
  The Elms, Kingston-on-Thames

May 10 Sunday
  Chiswick Mall, W4
  The Elms, Kingston-on-Thames
  11 Hampstead Way, NW11
  37 Heath Drive, NW3
  2 Millfield Place, N6
  43 Ormeley Road, SW12
May 16 Saturday
  Highwood Ash, NW7
  1 Panmuir Road, SW20
May 17 Sunday
  39 Arundel Gardens, N21
  39 Boundary Road, NW8
  5 Burbage Road, SE24
  133 Crystal Palace Road, SE22
  5 Garden Close, SW15
  5 Greenaway Gardens, NW3
  Hall Grange, Croydon
  116 Hamilton Terrace, NW8
  117 Hamilton Terrace NW8
  Highwood Ash, NW7
  Hornbeams, Stanmore
  64 Kings Road, Richmond
  1 Panmuir Road, SW20
  43 Penerley Road, SE6
  131 Upland Road, SE22
  Well Cottage, NW3
  11 Woodlands Road, SW13
May 20 Wednesday
  Frogmore Gardens, Windsor
May 21 Thursday
  Royal Botanic Gardens, Kew
    (Evening)
May 24 Sunday
  49 & 51 Etchingham Park Road,
    N3
  109 Halsbury Road East, Northolt
  Regents College's Botany
    Garden, NW1
May 30 Saturday
  Roots & Shoots, SE11

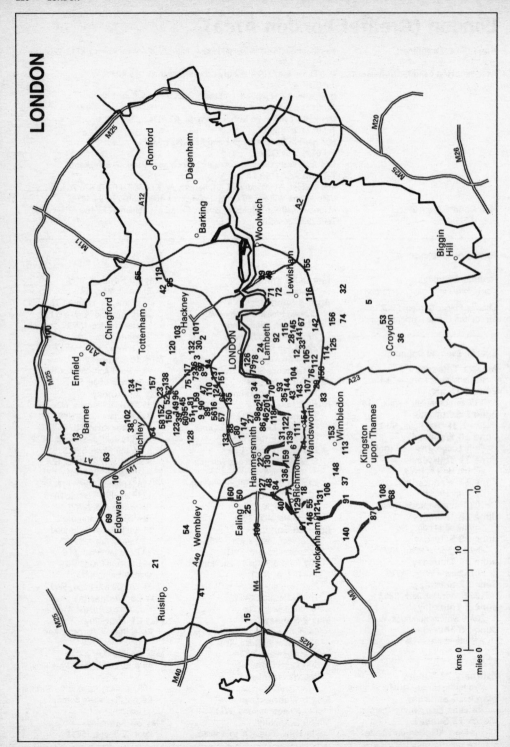

KEY

1. 29 Addison Avenue
2. Albion Square Gardens
3. 37 Alwyne Road
4. 39 Arundel Gardens
5. 1 Audrey Close
6. 33 Balmuir Gardens
7. Barnes Gardens
8. 28 Barnsbury Square
9. 39 Boundary Road
10. 25 Broadfields Avenue
11. 15a Buckland Crescent
12. 5 Burbage Road
13. 7 Byng Road
14. Carlyle's House
15. 9 Caroline Close
16. 11 Cavendish Avenue
17. 5 Cecil Road
18. 10 Charlotte Square
19. Chelsea Physic Garden
20. 101 Cheyne Walk
21. 10 Chiltern Road
22. Chiswick Mall
23. 51 Cholmeley Crescent
24. Chumleigh Multicultural Garden
25. 26 Claygate Road
26. 13 College Cross
27. 2 Cottesmore Gardens
28. 133 Crystal Palace Road
29. Culverden Road
30. De Beauvoir Gardens
31. 29 Deodar Road
32. 36 Downs Hill
33. Dulwich Gardens
34. Eccleston Square
35. 9 Eland Road
36. Elm Tree Cottage
37. The Elms
38. 49 & 51 Etchingham Park Road
39. Fenton House
40. The Ferry House
41. 66 Floriston Avenue
42. 73 Forest Drive East
43. Frankfort House
44. 5 Garden Close
45. 22 Gayton Road
46. 29 Gilston Road
47. 70 Gloucester Crescent
48. 51 Gloucester Road
49. Goldsborough
50. 1 Grange Park
51. 5 Greenaway Gardens
52. 7 The Grove
53. Hall Grange
54. 109 Halsbury Road East
55. Ham House
56. 116 Hamilton Terrace
57. 117 Hamilton Terrace
58. 11 Hampstead Way
59. 133 Haverstock Hill
60. 37 Heath Drive
61. 75 Heath Gardens
62. Highgate Village
63. Highwood Ash
64. 5 Hillcrest Avenue
65. 16 Hillcrest Road
66. The Holme
67. 125 Honor Oak Park
68. 239a Hook Road
69. Hornbeams
70. The Horticultural Therapy Demonstration Garden
71. 34 Hyde Vale
72. Hyde Vale Gardens
73. Islington Gardens
74. 26 Kenilworth Road
75. Kentish Town Gardens
76. 38 Killieser Avenue
77. 64 Kings Road
78. Lambeth Community Care Centre
79. Lambeth Palace
80. 12 Lansdowne Road
81. 10 Lawn Road
82. 15 Lawrence Street
83. 20 Lessingham Avenue
84. Leyborne Park Gardens
85. 1 Lister Road
86. 21a The Little Boltons
87. Little Lodge
88. London Lighthouse
89. 22 Loudoun Road
90. 1 Lower Merton Rise
91. 9 Lower Teddington Road
92. Lyndhurst Square Gardens
93. 4 Macaulay Road
94. Malvern Terrace
95. 2 Mansfield Place
96. 2 Millfield Place
97. 4 Mountfort Crescent
98. Museum of Garden History
99. 8 Mycenae Road
100. Myddelton House Gardens
101. 17a Navarino Road
102. 263 Nether Street
103. 15 Norcott Road
104. 2 Northbourne Road
105. 239 Norwood Road
106. Ormeley Lodge
107. 43 Ormeley Road
108. Osborne House
109. Osterley Park House
110. Flat 1, 1F Oval Road
111. 39 Oxford Road
112. 71 Palace Road
113. 1 Panmuir Road
114. 10A The Pavement
115. 174 Peckham Rye
116. 43 Penerley Road
117. 2a Penn Road
118. 35 Perrymead Street
119. 46 Preston Drive
120. 13 Queen Elizabeth's Walk
121. 3 Radnor Gardens
122. 9 Ranelagh Avenue
123. 11 Ranulf Road Gardens
124. Regents College's Botany Garden
125. 48 Rommany Road
126. Roots & Shoots
127. Royal Botanic Gardens, Kew
128. 19 St Gabriel's Road
129. 7 St George's Road
130. St Mary's Convent and Nursing Home
131. St Michael's Convent
132. 60 St Paul's Road
133. 57 St Quintin Avenue
134. 5 St Regis Close
135. 20A Seymour Buildings
136. 3 Somerton Avenue
137. South End Road
138. Southwood Lodge
139. Springfield Lodge
140. 40 Station Road
141. 26 Thompson Road
142. 27 Thorpewood Avenue
143. 103 Thurleigh Road
144. Trinity Hospice
145. 131 Upland Road
146. 15 Upper Grotto Road
147. 7 Upper Phillimore Gardens
148. The Watergardens
149. Well Cottage
150. 3 Wellgarth Road
151. 18 Westfield Road
152. 10 Wildwood Road
153. Wimbledon Gardens
154. 35 Wincanton Road
155. 47 Winn Road
156. 14A Wiverton Road
157. 27 Wood Vale
158. 66 Woodbourne Avenue
159. 11 Woodlands Road
160. 23 Woodville Road

The National Gardens Scheme is a charity which traces its origins back to 1927. Since then it has raised over £18 million for charitable purposes.

May 31 Sunday
Chiswick Mall, W4
51 Cholmeley Crescent, N6
Chumleigh Multicultural Garden, SE5
London Lighthouse, W11
22 Loudoun Road, NW8
Malvern Terrace, N1
Myddelton House Gardens, Enfield
15 Norcott Road, N16
Osterley Park House, Isleworth
Roots & Shoots, SE11
Southwood Lodge, N6
Wimbledon Gardens, SW19

June 4 Thursday
13 Queen Elizabeth's Walk, N16 (evening)

June 6 Saturday
Lambeth Community Care Centre, SE11
Flat 1, 1F Oval Road, NW1 (evening)
Trinity Hospice, SW4

June 7 Sunday
37 Alwyne Road, N1
Barnes Gardens, SW13
5 Burbage Road, SE24
26 Claygate Road, W13
13 College Cross, N1
Culverden Road, SW12
Eccleston Square, SW1
Elm Tree Cottage, South Croydon
66 Floriston Avenue, Hillingdon
70 Gloucester Crescent, NW1
133 Haverstock Hill, NW3
Kentish Town Gardens, NW5
Lambeth Community Care Centre, SE11
10 Lawn Road, NW3
Little Lodge, Thames Ditton
1 Lower Merton Rise, NW3
Lyndhurst Square, SE15
Museum of Garden History, SE1
39 Oxford Road, SW15
174 Peckham Rye, SE22
7 St George's Road, Twickenham
Trinity Hospice, SW4

June 10 Wednesday
9 Caroline Close, West Drayton
Little Lodge, Thames Ditton (evening)

June 11 Thursday
Fenton House, NW3 (evening)

June 13 Saturday
The Ferry House, Old Isleworth

June 14 Sunday
Albion Square Gardens, E8
1 Audrey Close, Beckenham
28 Barnsbury Square, N1
5 Cecil Road, N10
10 Charlotte Square, Richmond
The Ferry House, Old Isleworth
7 The Grove, N6
116 Hamilton Terrace, NW8

Highgate Village, N6
239a Hook Road, Chessington
The Horticultural Therapy Demonstration Garden, SW11
Leyborne Park Gardens, Kew
2 Mansfield Place, NW3
8 Mycenae Road, SE3
17a Navarino Road, E8
263 Nether Street, N3
2 Northbourne Road, SW4
Osborne House, Long Ditton
43 Penerley Road, SE6
60 St Paul's Road, N1
3 Somerton Avenue, Richmond
South End Road, NW3
Springfield Lodge, SW15
40 Station Road, Hampton
103 Thurleigh Road, SW12
3 Wellgarth Road, NW11
35 Wincanton Road, SW18

June 17 Wednesday
Osborne House, Long Ditton (evening)
103 Thurleigh Road, SW12 (evening)

June 18 Thursday
Southwood Lodge, N6 (evening)

June 20 Saturday
Frankfort House, SW4
9 Lower Teddington Road, Hampton Wick
Flat 1, 1F Oval Road, NW1 (evening)
St Michael's Convent, Ham

June 21 Sunday
15a Buckland Crescent, NW3
De Beauvoir Gardens, N1
Elm Tree Cottage, South Croydon
Frankfort House, SW4
5 Greenaway Gardens, NW3
5 Hillcrest Avenue, NW11
Islington Gardens, N1
38 Killieser Avenue, SW2
9 Lower Teddington Road, Hampton Wick
4 Mountfort Crescent, N1
263 Nether Street, N3
Ormeley Lodge, Richmond
71 Palace Road, SW2
7 St George's Road, Twickenham
47 Winn Road, Lee
66 Woodbourne Avenue, SW16

June 25 Thursday
101 Cheyne Walk, SW10 (evening)

June 27 Saturday
125 Honor Oak Park, SE23 (evening)

June 28 Sunday
33 Balmuir Gardens, SW15
11 Cavendish Avenue, NW8
10 Chiltern Road, Pinner
36 Downs Hill, Beckenham
5 Garden Close, SW15

22 Gayton Road, NW3
109 Halsbury Road East, Northolt
125 Honor Oak Park, SE23
26 Kenilworth Road, SE10
20 Lessingham Avenue, SW17
21a The Little Boltons, SW10
2a Penn Road, N7
9 Ranelagh Avenue, SW6
48 Rommany Road, SE27
5 St Regis Close, N10
14A Wiverton Road, SE26

July 2 Thursday
20A Seymour Buildings, W1H (evening)

July 5 Sunday
7 Byng Road, High Barnet
133 Crystal Palace Road, SE22
Dulwich Gardens, SE21
Goldsborough, SE3
1 Grange Park, W5
37 Heath Drive, NW3
75 Heath Gardens, Twickenham
Hyde Vale Gardens, SE10
46 Preston Drive, E11
3 Radnor Gardens, Twickenham
57 St Quintin Avenue, W10
15 Upper Grotto Road, Twickenham

July 11 Saturday
Carlyle's House, SW3
15 Lawrence Street, SW3
19 St Gabriel's Road, NW2

July 12 Sunday
25 Broadfields Avenue, Edgware
Carlyle's House, SW3
70 Gloucester Crescent, NW1
75 Heath Gardens, Twickenham
15 Lawrence Street, SW3
35 Perrymead Street, SW6
3 Radnor Gardens, Twickenham
27 Thorpewood Avenue, SE26
15 Upper Grotto Road, Twickenham
18 Westfield Road, NW7
10 Wildwood Road, NW11

July 16 Thursday
2 Millfield Place, N6 (evening)

July 18 Saturday
27 Wood Vale, N10

July 19 Sunday
29 Deodar Road, SW15
5 Greenaway Gardens, NW3
11 Ranulf Road, NW2
27 Wood Vale, N10
23 Woodville Road, W5

July 25 Saturday
Trinity Hospice, SW4

July 26 Sunday
29 Addison Avenue, W11
109 Halsbury Road East, Northolt
117 Hamilton Terrace, NW8
Myddelton House Gardens, Enfield
10A The Pavement, SE27

13 Queen Elizabeth's Walk, N16
48 Rommany Road, SE27
5 St Regis Close, N10
Trinity Hospice, SW4
August 1 Saturday
9 Lower Teddington Road,
Hampton Wick
August 2 Sunday
9 Lower Teddington Road,
Hampton Wick
239 Norwood Road, SE24
57 St Quintin Avenue, W10
August 9 Sunday
10 Chiltern Road, Pinner
70 Gloucester Crescent, NW1
239a Hook Road, Chessington

4 Macaulay Road, SW4
August 16 Sunday
73 Forest Drive East, E11
1 Lister Road, E11
17a Navarino Road, E8
47 Winn Road, Lee
August 22 Saturday
The Holme, NW1
August 23 Sunday
The Holme, NW1
46 Preston Drive, E11
September 5 Saturday
Trinity Hospice, SW4
September 6 Sunday
34 Hyde Vale, SE10
Trinity Hospice, SW4

September 20 Sunday
7 The Grove, N6
26 Thompson Road, SE22
October 18 Sunday
The Watergardens,
Kingston-on-Thames
October 25 Sunday
Chelsea Physic Garden, SW3

1999
February 28 Sunday
Myddelton House Gardens,
Enfield

DESCRIPTIONS OF GARDENS

29 Addison Avenue, W11 ✄ (Mr & Mrs D B Nicholson) No entry for cars from Holland Park Avenue; approach via Norland Square and Queensdale Rd. Station: Holland Park. Bus 94. Small garden packed with interesting plants, winner of many prizes and photographed over the last 10yrs for several gardening magazines. Lots of unusual wall shrubs, variegated plants and colourful perennials. Phlox paniculata (over 40 varieties) a special favourite. *Adm £1 Chd 50p (ACNO to the Museum of Garden History®). Sun July 26 (2-6)*

Albion Square Gardens, E8 ✄❀ 2m N of Liverpool St Station (BR & tube). 1m S of Dalston/Kingsland Station (BR). Buses 22, 67, 149, 243. By car approach from Queensbridge Rd northbound turning L into Albion Drive leading to Albion Square. TEAS in leafy Central Gardens winners of steel spade award from Metropolitan Gardens Association 1995/96 and Silver Certificate London Garden Square's Competition 1997. *Combined adm £4 for 4 or £1.25 each Chd £1 for 4 or 50p each. Sun June 14 (2-5.30)*
  12 Albion Square (Ann Black) Victorian gothic church provides backdrop to this 70' × 60' L-shaped garden. Brick paved herb garden leads to lawns and a terrace. Ornamental trees, shrubs and flowers. Planting is 6 yrs old and is just beginning to take shape. *(ACNO to The Peter Walker Trust®)*
  24 Albion Square (Mr David French) 80' town garden designed to unfold as a series of views and focal points divided by a yew hedge. Emphasis on foliage plants rather than flowers. Secluded seating areas, fountain and through shared summer house to No 25. *(ACNO to St Joseph's Hospice, Hackney®)*
  25 Albion Square (Sandy Maclennan) 80' informal walled garden on two levels with pond beside camomile patch and features ornamental shrubs and trees creating interest in foliage, form and colour. *(ACNO to The Peter Walker Trust®)*

The National Gardens Scheme is registered charity (No 279284). Its aim is to raise money for selected beneficiaries by opening gardens of quality and interest to the public.

---

252 Haggerston Road (Heather Wilson). 60' long, mid-terrace shady town garden. Informal, densely planted design with emphasis on unusual perennials and shrubs, incl peat bed, herbs, ferns, dry shade area, herbaceous border, fruit trees and (friendly) bee-hive. TEAS. *(ACNO to St Joseph's Hospice, Hackney®)*

37 Alwyne Road, N1 ও✄❀ (Mr & Mrs J Lambert) Station: Highbury and Islington. Bus 4, 19, 30, 43, 271. A1 runs through Canonbury Sq. Bordering the New River. Views over the river and the park would make you think you are in the country; an enclosed formal garden reminds you that you are in town. Old-fashioned roses. Unusual nicotianas for sale. TEAS. *Adm 1.50 Chd 75p (ACNO to The Whitechapel Family Centre. In memory of John Garnett®). Sun June 7 (2-6)*

¶39 Arundel Gardens, N21 ✄❀ (Michael and Julie Floyd) From Winchmore Hill BR approx 7 mins walk, turn along Hoppers Rd, Arundel Gardens 3rd on L, 39 is 1st blue door on the R. The W9 Hoppa bus runs along Hoppers Rd. from Southgate Underground. 100' × 30' town garden planted in an informal cottage style, unusual shrubs, climbers and herbaceous plants; over 30 clematis including 11 clematis alpina varieties; arbour, small water feature and conservatory with a collection of cacti and succulents. *Adm £1.00 Chd 50p (ACNO to E A Bowles of Myddelton House Society®). Sun May 17 (2-6)*

¶1 Audrey Close, Beckenham ✄❀ (David Wyatt) 2 mins from Eden Park station. By railway bridge in South Eden Park Road (where parking is available). A ¼-acre garden - with the River Beck running through - having an oriental theme. The front has a Japanese rock garden, the back includes a pond, acers and bamboos. Garden pottery made by local artist Nicoletto Savage will also be on display. TEA. *Adm £1 Chd 50p. Sun June 14 (12-5)*

33 Balmuir Gardens, SW15 ✄❀ (Mrs Gay Wilson) Putney. 5 mins walk from Putney SR Station. Off the Upper Richmond Rd on corner with Howards Lane. Bus 337, 74, 14. A designer's garden on a corner plot that is continually evolving. Secluded tiny mixed borders backed by stained beams. Pots, and a formal pond with a waterfall through moose antlers. A passionate plantswoman who tries out different colour combinations. All crammed into

80' × 38' at widest only 16' at narrowest. *Adm £2 Chd 50p (ACNO to The Robert Owen Foundation for Disability Living Accommodation®). Sun June 28 (2-7)*

Barnes Gardens, SW13 ও TEAS at 25 Castelnau. *Adm £4 for 4 gardens or £1.50 each garden, OAP £3 for 4 gardens or £1 each garden, Chd free. Sun June 7 (2-6)*
  25 Castelnau ⚹ (Dr & Mrs P W Adams) Castelnau is on the main route from Hammersmith Bridge. The garden is approx 120' × 40' designed in 1978 by Malcolm Hillier and the late Colin Hilton. The garden was planned for ease of maintenance and family living. There is a good variety of herbaceous plants, some attractive roses and a compact working vegetable area and screened swimming pool. Cream TEAS
  26 Nassau Road ও❀ (Mr & Mrs Anthony Hallett) 26 Nassau Road lies midway between the Thames and Barnes Pond and is approached via Lonsdale Rd or Church Rd. Long, slim, terraced garden with tall wisteria framed with weigela, philadelphus, pittosporum, chaemomeles, ceanothus. Borders of hebe, cistus, lilies, geranium, rose, delphiniums, potentilla and spiraea compete for colours, scents and shapes
  8 Queen's Ride ও (His Honour Sir Frank & Lady White) Train: Barnes Station, turn R down Rocks Lane, then L along Queen's Ride. Bus, 22 terminus at Putney Hospital; 3 minutes walk W along Queen's Ride. House is at the junction of Queen's Ride and St Mary's Grove. ²⁄₃-acre garden facing Barnes Common. Croquet lawn with herbaceous and mixed borders and a small history of the rose garden. Garden quiz. TEA
  12 Westmoreland Road ⚹❀ (Mr & Mrs Norman Moore) From Hammersmith take Bus 209, 33, or 72 to the Red Lion. Briefly retrace steps along Castelnau turn L into Ferry Rd then L at Xrds. Garden on two levels. Raised stone terrace planted with choisya, convolvulus, jasmine and decorative herbs. Steps down to two lower lawns, flanked by densely planted borders of flowering shrubs, lavender, larkspur and hollyhocks, and divided by pretty gazebo, with honeysuckle, roses and clematis. Beyond lies a shady circular lawn with pool and fountain, pink and white hydrangeas, ferns and hostas. *(ACNO to Viera Gray House®)*

28 Barnsbury Square, N1, ⚹ (Frank & Avril Gardner) Islington. 1¾m N of King's Cross off Thornhill Rd. Bus stop: Islington Town Hall, Upper St or Offord Rd, Caledonian Rd. Buses 4, 19, 30, 43 or 271. Tube Highbury and Islington. Small prize-winning Victorian garden; gazebo; pond; grotto; roses, shrubs, plants of interest throughout yr. *Adm £1.50 Chd 75p (ACNO to St Mary Magdalene Church®). Sun June 14 (2-6)*

39 Boundary Road, NW8 ⚹❀ (Hermoine Berton) Between Swiss Cottage and St John's Wood tube. Buses 13, 113, 82, 46, 139 down Abbey and Finchley Rd. Small walled garden 70' × 35' incl water features. Places to sit among box, camellias, roses, clematis, wisterias, rare ground-cover plants. Wildlife sanctuary, accent on foliage, texture, forms and scents. Filmed for Gardener's World, British Council and Japanese market. *Adm £1.50 Chd 50p (ACNO to London Lighthouse Aids Centre®). Sun May 17 (2-6). Private visits April to Sept. Please* **Tel 0171 624 3177**

¶25 Broadfields Avenue, Edgware ⚹ (Carol Howard) 3rd L off Hale Lane after short walk from Edgware Station. From London by car on A41 L at 1st T-lights after Apex Corner roundabout. Small colourful garden, belonging to ceramic artist, with mature trees, mixed shrubs and herbaceous border. Collection of interesting planted pots and sinks. TEAS. *Adm £1 Chd free. Sun July 12 (2-6)*

15a Buckland Crescent, NW3 ও⚹❀ (Lady Barbirolli) Swiss Cottage Tube. Bus: 46, 13 (6 mins) or Hampstead Hoppa (request stop nearby). ⅓-acre; interesting collection of shrubs and plants in well-designed garden. *Adm £1.50 Chd free (ACNO to RUKBA®). Sun June 21 (2.30-6.30). Private visits welcome for parties of 25 and over, please* **Tel 0171 586 2464**

5 Burbage Road, SE24 ⚹❀ (Crawford & Rosemary Lindsay) Nr junction with Half Moon Lane. BR Station Herne Hill, 5 mins walk. Buses 2, 3, 37, 40, 68, 196. Garden of member of The Society of Botanical Artists. 150' × 40' with large and varied range of plants. Herb garden, herbaceous borders for sun and shade, climbing plants, pots, terraces, lawns. Subject of article in 'The Garden' (RHS Journal) in April 1997. TEAS. *Adm £1.50 Chd free. Suns May 17, June 7 (2-5).* **Tel 0171 274 5610**

7 Byng Road, High Barnet ও⚹❀ (Rhian & Julian Bishop) Organic garden dominated by 3 large borders: a white garden with mainly perennials and roses; a 'cool' border of pinks, blues and mauves; and a vibrant 'hot' border incl giant dahlias, rudbeckias and other unusual plants. Also a woodland area, fountains, many pots and a collection of unusual foxgloves. TEAS. *Adm £1 Chd 25p (ACNO to Barnet Hospital Special Care Baby Unit®). Sun July 5 (12-5). Private visits welcome,* **Tel 0181 440 2042**

Capel Manor Gardens See Hertfordshire

¶Carlyle's House, SW3 ⚹ (The National Trust) Off Chelsea Embankment, between Albert and Battersea Bridges. NT sign on corner of Cheyne Row. Or via Kings Rd and Oakley St. NT sign on corner of Upper Cheyne Row. Tubes: Sloane Square and S Kensington. Buses: 11, 19, 22, 49, 239. 70' walled town garden, with restored Victorian planting theme, reflecting Thomas Carlyle's lifetime. Mature walnut and fig trees create shade. Vines on the sunny wall. Herbaceous plants, shrubs and lilies. Box edged rectangular beds and paved courtyard. *Adm £1 Chd free. For NGS Sat, Sun July 11, 12 (2-5)*

¶9 Caroline Close, W Drayton ⚹ (Sheila & Edwin White) From the Holiday Inn (M4 junc 4 Heathrow) follow signs to W Drayton/Uxbridge (A408) for 2m. At Texaco filling station take 1st L (Swan Rd B470) then 1st R (Old Farm Rd) into Caroline Close. This split-level garden (approx 180' × 35') closely follows the contours of a dried-up stream bed and its embankment now terraced and planted up for ease of maintenance with ornamental trees, shrubs and herbaceous perennials, patio roses and clematis. The extended paved areas lead to a small fruit garden (apples, plums, pears) and a vegetable/soft fruit cage. *Adm £1 Chd 50p. Wed June 10 (1.30-4) and by private appt* **Tel 01895 447795**

¶11 Cavendish Ave, NW8 ✻✿ (Renée & Theo Laub) The house is situated behind Lords Cricket Ground off Wellington Rd. 5min walk from St John's Wood tube station. Large secluded garden divided into 4 'rooms', each with its own distinct character. Interesting urns and other features, as well as unusual plants: collection of ferns, camellias, acers and hostas. Garden of yr-round interest. TEAS. *Adm £1.50 Chd free. Sun June 28 (2-6)*

5 Cecil Road, N10 ✿ (Ben Loftus Esq) Just off Alexander Park Rd between Muswell Hill and the North Circular Rd. 70' × 20' garden designer's peaceful garden; old apple trees, roses, euphorbias, masses of lilies, paeonies, hellebores, ferns, bulbs and evergreens; many scented plants, rich and varied foliage; unusual plants in containers recently much altered. Featured in Gay Search in Sainsbury's magazine. *Adm 80p Chd free. Sun June 14 (2-5)*

10 Charlotte Square, Richmond ✿ (Claire McCormack & James Cowan) 371 Bus from Richmond Station. Slug and snail resistant garden, organically cultivated. Full of herbaceous plants, fragrant climbers and shrubs (no bedding or lawns). Complete plans and plant lists available. Front 28' × 15', rear 28' × 18'. Tiny pool, hedgehogs, frogs, birds' nests. TEAS. *Adm £1 Chd free. Sun June 14 (2-6)*

■ Chelsea Physic Garden, SW3 ❧✻✿ 66 Royal Hospital Rd, Chelsea. Bus 239 (Mon-Sat). Station: Sloane Square (10 mins). Parking Battersea Park (charged). Entrance in Swan Walk (except wheelchairs). 2nd oldest Botanic Garden in UK; 3.8 acres; medicinal and herb garden, perfumery border; family order beds; historical walk, glasshouses. TEAS. *Adm £3.50 Students/Chd £1.80. Suns April 5 to Oct 25 (2-6); Weds April 8 to Oct 21 (12-5); Winter Festival Suns Feb 8, 15 (11-3) Chelsea Flower Show week Mon-Fri May 18-22 and Chelsea Festival Week Mon-Fri June 1-5 (12-5). For NGS Suns April 5, Oct 25 (2-6)*

101 Cheyne Walk, SW10 ✻✿ (Malcolm Hillier Esq) Situated to the W of Battersea Bridge. Long and narrow strongly layered with a structure of evergreen hedges and topiaries. A colonnaded Mediterranean terrace with many containers leads to a winding path set about with old roses and perennials. A romantic arbour surrounded and covered by perfumed plants surveys the whole length of the garden. *Adm £3.50 incl wine and food. Thurs 25 June (6-8). Private visits welcome for parties of 5 and over, please* Tel 0171 352 9031

10 Chiltern Road, Pinner ✻✿ (Mrs G & Mr D Cresswell) Eastcote. Off Cheney St and Barnhill/Francis Rd which link Cuckoo Hill/Eastcote High Rd (B466) with Bridle Rd/Eastcote Rd. Please park in Francis Rd. Plantswoman's garden ⅓-acre, mature trees, mixed shrubs and herbaceous plantings many propagated for sale. TEAS. *Adm £1.50 Chd free. Suns April 5, June 28, Aug 9 (2-5)*

Chiswick Mall, W4 Station: Stamford Brook (District Line). Bus: 290 to Young's Corner from Hammersmith. By car A4 Westbound turn off at Eyot Gdns S, then R into Chiswick Mall
Sun May 10 (2-6.30)
   16 Eyot Gardens ✿ (Dianne Farris) Small town garden. Front garden planted white, blue and yellow. The

back shows what can be done with a small space, by using the walls devoted to clematis. Terrace, fountain and garden art, and beds planted for yr-round interest. TEAS. *Adm £1 OAPS 50p Chd free*
Walpole House ✻✿ (Mr & Mrs Jeremy Benson) Plantsman's garden; specie and tree peonies; water garden; spring flowers. Features in 'The Englishman's Garden'. Mid C16 to early C18 house, once home of Barbara Villiers, Duchess of Cleveland. *Adm £1.50 OAP/Chd 50p (ACNO to Winchcombe Cottage Hospital®)*
Sun May 31 (2-6)
16 Eyot Gardens,
(see above)
¶Lingard House ✻✿ (Rachel Austin) A walled garden divided into a brick courtyard and terrace with a huge acacia tree; a formal lawn with miniature pond and water-spout and unusual herbaceous planting and a wire-work pergola, revealing a wild garden with ancient apple trees, climbing roses and beehive. *Adm £1 Chd free*
¶Morton House ❧✿ (Mr & Mrs Michael Manser) A ⅓-acre walled garden with lawns, yew hedges and mixed planting. Much loved but belonging to people who are rather short of time and who have enthusiastically over-planted. *Adm £1 Chd 50p (ACNO to West London Action for Children®)*
¶Staithe House ❧ (Mr & Mrs Michael Comninos) 3rd house E of Chiswick Lane South. A terrace with lovely views of R Thames curving towards Barnes. House is covered with roses and wisteria and garden surrounded by walls and trellis. Main border and small herb garden enclosed by box hedging. Various shrubs, pleached hornbeam, magnolia, paeonies, euphorbia and lavender. Two versailles boxes surmounted by trellis pyramids for old roses. *Adm £1.50 OAP/Chd 50p*
¶Swan House ❧ (Mr & Mrs George Nissen) An informal walled garden, considerably replanted 4yrs ago within an established framework. Herbaceous border, fruit trees, small vegetable garden. *Adm £1 Chd 50p*

51 Cholmeley Crescent, N6 (Ernst & Janet Sondheimer) Highgate. Between Highgate Hill and Archway Rd, off Cholmeley Park. Nearest tube Highgate. Approx ⅙-acre garden with many alpines in screes, peat beds, tufa, troughs and greenhouse; shrubs, rhododendrons, camellias, magnolias, pieris, ceanothus etc. Clematis, bog plants, roses, primulas, treeferns. Alpines for sale. TEA. *Adm £1 Chd 50p. Sun May 31 (2-6). Private visits welcome, please* Tel 0181 340 6607

Chumleigh Multicultural Garden, SE5 (Southwark Council) Situated midway along Albany Rd which runs between Old Kent Rd and Camberwell Rd. Nearest tube Elephant & Castle; buses P3, 42. Constructed around almshouses (erected in 1821 by the Friendly Female Soc) now a Parks Visitor Centre. Walled garden, nearly 1 acre divided into English, Oriental, African and Carribean, Islamic and Mediterranean styles. Many unusual plants incl tree fern, jelly palm, rice paper plant. Formal and informal water features. TEAS. *Adm £1. Sun May 31 (2-6)*

¶**26 Claygate Rd, W13** (Irena Sawyer & John Bishop) Easy walk from Northfields Station (Piccadilly Line). Buses E2 & E3. Situated between Northfield Ave and Boston Manor Rd. 3min drive from junction 2 of M4. Colourful front garden leading to imaginative small (33′ × 21′) back garden. The owners have created an oasis of calm in the midst of suburbia. An abundance of climbing roses interplanted with clematis. Fruit trees, miniature pond with goldfish, fountain, raised herb garden, a profusion of pots, window boxes, hanging baskets, small lawn and herbaceous borders. TEAS. *Adm £1 Chd free. Sun June 7 (2-6)*

13 College Cross, Islington N1 (Diane & Stephen Yakeley) A small prize-winning walled garden behind a Georgian terrace house, 5m × 17m, enclosed by evergreen climbers with bay, box, olive and fig trees. Paved areas with plants chosen for form and texture in shades of green. Large pots of white flowers incl lilies, oleander and brugmansia. *Adm £1.50 Chd 75p. Sun June 7 (2-6). Also open with* **Islington Gardens** *Sun June 21 (2-6)*

2 Cottesmore Gardens, W8 (The Marchioness of Bute) From Kensington Rd turn into Victoria Rd. Cottesmore Gardens on R. A wide range of trees, shrubs and plants concentrating on foliage shapes, fragrance and unusual plant material; many spring bulbs. *Adm £2 Chd £1 (ACNO to Winter Garden Trust®). Sun April 26 (2-5)*

133 Crystal Palace Road, SE22 (Sue Hillwood-Harris & David Hardy) East Dulwich. Buses 176, 185, 12. The addition of a pergola has subtly changed the character of this inspirational 17′ × 36′ Victorian garden created around a weathered brick terrace (once the garden wall). Roses, wisteria, clematis, shrubs, herbs and shade-loving plants combine in formality tempered by wilful indiscipline. Featured by Gay Search in Express on Sunday, European and Japanese magazines. TEAS. *Adm £1 Chd 50p (ACNO to Amnesty®). Suns May 17, July 5 (2-6). Private visits welcome, please* Tel 0181 693 3710

¶**Culverden Road SW12** Station: Balham and Tooting Bec. TEAS. *Combined adm £3 or £1.25 each garden Chd £1 or 50p each garden. Sun June 7 (2-6)*
  ¶**39 Culverden Rd** (V Warburton) Large garden, informally planted with wide range of shrubs and herbaceous plants in beds and pots, terraced area near house and magnificent willow tree with large area of decking underneath. Front garden planted with sun loving plants
  ¶**68 Culverden Rd** (Nick Ryan & Nick Branwell) Both gardens are newly designed and planted by two garden designers. Front garden: (Nick Ryan) transformed parking space, raised brick beds, seating area, circular paving in granite setts and extensive use of trelliswork. Back garden: (Nick Branwell) S facing, backing onto Tooting Bec Common, with terrace, summer house, and many unusual and architectural plants in beds and pots
  ¶**82 Culverden Rd** (E Powell) Long S facing garden which backs onto Tooting Bec Common. There are five areas in the garden: terrace and formal pond; lawn with mixed shrub and herbaceous borders; informal pond surrounded by a yew hedge; cottage garden area (herbaceous plants and vegetables); and an orchard and woodland area with large compost bins. Front garden in traditional style

De Beauvoir Gardens, N1 Islington-Hackney border. *Combined adm £2 Chd 50p. Sun June 21 (2-6)*
  51 Lawford Road (Mrs Carol Lee) Lawford Rd (formerly called Culford Rd) is a cul-de-sac with entrance for cars from Downham Rd. Parking fairly restricted. Downham Rd runs between Kingsland and Southgate Rd. Buses Kingsland Rd 149, 243, 22A/B and 67, Southgate Rd 141. A small garden 16′ × 45′ at rear of a typical Victorian terraced house. Bricked with differ-

ent levels, lots of pots and a pond with waterfalls. Hostas, ferns and anything that will grow in a pot. TEAS. *(ACNO to National Deaf Children's Soc®)*

26 Northchurch Road ✍ (Mrs Kathy Lynam) Angel tube then Buses 38, 73, 171A down Essex Rd, alight bus stop after Essex Rd Station just before Northchurch Rd. Cross over and proceed down Northchurch Rd (petrol stn on corner) to lower end near church. House on L. By car from Essex Rd. R into Halliford St past lights at Southgate Rd. Turn L 1st rd Ufton Rd, then R at bottom, house on L. Walled back garden, approx 70′ × 30′ with 2 old apple trees, greenhouse and lawn, mixed borders with clematis, roses and lots of perennials. Places to sit and ponder. TEA. *Private visits welcome, please* **Tel 0171 254 8993**

29 Deodar Road, SW15 ✍❀ (Peter & Marigold Assinder) Putney. Off Putney Bridge Rd Bus: 14, 22, 37, 74, 85, 93, 220. Tubes: Putney Bridge and East Putney. Small garden 130ft × 25ft running down to Thames with lovely view. Camellias, wide range of variegated shrubs, hardy geraniums and hydrangeas. *Adm £1 Chd 50p (ACNO to All Saints Church Putney Restoration Appeal®). Suns April 5, July 19 (2-5). Cuttings and plants and visits at other times by arrangement* **Tel 0181 788 7976**

36 Downs Hill, Beckenham ✍❀ (Janet & Marc Berlin) 2 mins from Ravensbourne Station near top of Foxgrove Rd. Long 2/3-acre E facing garden sloping steeply away from the house. Ponds and waterfalls with patio garden. Wooded area. Greenhouses. Dense planting. Varied collection of trees, shrubs and flowers. TEAS. *Adm £1 Chd free (ACNO to NSPCC®). Sun June 28 (2.30-5)*

¶**Dulwich Gardens, SE21** ✍❀ BR trains to N and W Dulwich then 15mins walk, or tube to Brixton then P4 bus passes both gardens. *Combined adm £3 Chd free. Sun July 5 (2-5)*

¶**103 Dulwich Village** ✍❀ (Mr & Mrs N Annesley) About ¼-acre country-garden-in-London. Long herbaceous border, lawn, ornamental pond, roses and many and varied other plants, plus veg patch. TEAS. Gate to next door garden

105 Dulwich Village (Andrew & Ann Rutherford) About ½-acre, mostly herbaceous with lawns and lots of old-fashioned roses. Ornamental pond, new water garden. A very pretty garden with many unusual plants

Eccleston Square, SW1 ⬦❀ (Garden Manager Roger Phillips) Off Belgrave Rd near Victoria Station, parking allowed on Suns. 3-acre square planned by Cubitt in 1828. The Garden Committee has worked over the last 18 years to see what can be created despite the inner city problems of drought, dust, fumes, shade and developers. The garden is sub-divided into mini-gardens incl camellia, iris, rose, fern, and container garden. A national collection of ceanothus incl more than 50 species and cultivars is held in the square. Featured on TV in 'The 3,000m Garden'. TEAS. *Adm £2 Chd £1. Suns April 26, June 7 (2-5)*

9 Eland Road, SW11 ✍ (Nancye Nosworthy) Battersea. Off Lavender Hill backing onto Battersea Arts Centre. G1, 345, 77 and 77a buses stop at top of st. Clapham Junction Station nearby and bus 137a Queenstown Rd. 50′ courtyard on slopes of Lavender Hill designed by Christopher Masson. Terraces with unusual shrubs; a pergola covered in vines and pool with fountain. *Adm £1 Chd free. Sun April 19 (2-5)*

Elm Tree Cottage, S Croydon ✍ (Wendy Witherick & Michael Wilkinson) 85 Croham Rd, off B275 from Croydon, off A2022 from Selsdon 64 Bus Route. A gently sloping plantsperson's garden with fine views of Croham Hurst and Valley. Cottage garden full of unusual roses, perennials, climbers and shrubs. Pond and bog garden in pots. Unsuitable for those unsteady on their feet and pushchairs. Featured on BBC Gardeners World 1997. *Adm £2 Chd free. Suns June 7, 21 (1-5). Private visits welcome, please* **Tel 0181 681 8622**

The Elms, Kingston-on-Thames ✍❀ (Prof & Mrs R Rawlings) 1m E Kingston on A308. Kingston Hospital and BR Norbiton Station 100yds. Enter via Manorgate Rd at foot of Kingston Hill. 55′ × 25′ garden owned by 'plantaholic!' Trees, shrubs, climbers, herbaceous and ground cover plants, some rare. Pool with geyser; fruit trees and soft fruits. Featured in many publications. TEAS. *Adm £1.20 Chd 50p (ACNO to Terence Higgins Trust/Home Farm Trust®). Sats, Suns March 14, 15 April 18, 19; May 9, 10 (2-5). Private groups min 10 persons welcome, please* **Tel 0181 546 7624**

49 & 51 Etchingham Park Rd, N3 ⬦✍❀ (Robert Double, Gilbert Cook and Diane & Alan Langleben) Finchley. Off Ballards Lane overlooking Victoria Park. Station: Finchley Central. 2 rear gardens. ⅝-acre; lawn, small orchard, shrubs, large selection of hostas. Sculpture by Wm Mitchell, ornamental vegetable garden as seen on TV. Exhibition and sale of water colour paintings by Robert Double. TEAS. Live music. *Adm £1 Chd free. Sun May 24 (2-5)*

▲**Fenton House, NW3** ✍ (The National Trust) 300yds from Hampstead Underground. Entrances: top of Holly Hill and Hampstead Grove. Recently created timeless 1½-acre walled garden. Laid out on three levels, garden rooms contain imaginative plantings concealed by yew hedges. The herbaceous borders have been planned to give yr-round interest while the brick-paved sunken rose garden provides a sheltered hollow of scent and colour. The formal lawn area contrasts agreeably with the rustic charm of the kitchen garden and orchard, where a waterspout trickles tranquilly in the background. A Vine House planned for 1998. *Adm £2.50 Chd 50p incl glass of wine. For NGS Thur June 11 (6.30-8.30)*

The Ferry House, Old Isleworth ⬦❀ (Lady Caroline Gilmour) By car (coaches by prior arrangement) follow signs to Syon Park parking available inside gate on L. 3 acres of mature gardens. Terrace with urns and troughs filled with unusual plants. Old-fashioned roses, climbers, shrubs and perennials edge the lawn leading down to lovely views of the Thames. Adjacent garden with herbaceous borders, avenues, groups of shrubs with backdrop of fine old trees in Syon Park. Shaded sitting areas. Vegetable and fruit cage. TEAS. *Adm £2.50 OAPs £1.50 Chd 50p. Sat, Sun June 13, 14 (2-6)*

66 Floriston Avenue, Hillingdon ◬❀ (Jean Goodall) U2 bus from Uxbridge station. From A40 at Master Brewer Motel into Long Lane (to Hillingdon) 2nd L by church (Ryefield Ave), L after shops. Pedestrian entrance to garden by lane rear of shops. Plantswoman's long narrow garden (90' × 17') with many design features, Auricula theatre, species iris and alliums, colour themed borders. Featured on Gardener's World 1997. TEAS. *Adm £1 Chd 50p. Suns May 3, June 7 (2-5). Private visits welcome, please* **Tel 01895 251036**

73 Forest Drive East, E11 ◬❀ (A J Wyllie) Leytonstone. Into Whipps Cross Rd, then SW into James Lane. 1st L into Clare Rd, 1st R into Forest Drive East. By bus to Whipps Cross Hospital or tube to Leytonstone and bus to James Lane. 20' × 65' country garden in miniature, but with full-sized plants, behind a terraced house. Small lawn with mixed borders leading to a shrub and woodland area. 2 fountains and various unusual plants. Also 20' square front garden informally planted round formal paths and centrepiece. TEA. *Adm £1 Chd 50p (ACNO to The Margaret Centre, Whipps Cross Hospital®). Sun Aug 16 (11-5)*

Frankfort House, SW4 ◬❀ (Mr & Mrs Richard Roxburgh) 82 Clapham Common, West Side. 100yds off The Avenue. South Circular Rd across grass. 10mins walk from Clapham South tube station, 20 mins walk from Clapham Junction. Close to junction with Culmstock Rd. One of the largest gardens remaining on Clapham Common. Partly walled 245' × 90'. Neglected condition when bought by present owners in 1993. Redesigned to make the most of existing mature trees incl fine cedar. Peaceful shady oasis in a busy area. Laurels, shrubs, pergola walks and large lawn. Lots of climbers, old roses, etc. Large terrace with formal box-edged beds and trellis surround new 'English' roses. Plenty of seating. TEAS. *Adm £1.50 Chd free (ACNO to Trinity Hospice®). Sat, Sun June 20, 21 (2-6)*

Frogmore Gardens, Windsor *May 20 (10.30-7 last admission 6) See Berkshire*

5 Garden Close, SW15 ◬◬ (Vivien & Tom Jestico) off Portsmouth Rd, 7-10 mins walk from the Green Man Public House, Putney Hill. ¼-acre walled garden which serves as a backdrop to architect's all glass house. Oriental inspiration with black bamboos, and swathes of box, hebe, lavender and rhododendrons. Ponds and timber decks surround the house. *Adm £1.50. Suns May 17, June 28 (11-5)*

22 Gayton Rd, NW3 ◬ (Mr & Mrs C Newman) From Hampstead underground station turn L down Hampstead High St, Gayton Rd is 1st on the L. Small victorian brick paved garden 60' × 20' with shrubs, roses, climbers, tiny pond, plants in containers. *Adm £1.50 Chd 50p. Sun June 28 (2-5)*

29 Gilston Road, SW10 ◬ (Margaret & James Macnair) Gilston Rd is a short street leading N from Fulham Rd to the Boltons. Medium sized garden (34' × 75') with large plane tree at far end. Many spring flowering bulbs and shrubs. *Adm £1.50 Sun April 5 (2-6)*

70 Gloucester Crescent, NW1 ◬ (Lucy Gent & Malcolm Turner) Nr junction Gloucester Crescent and Oval Rd 600yds SW of Camden Town Tube Station. A square in front; a triangle at the side; a wedge at the back. Strong geometry on the ground plays off against extensive plant interest. *Adm £1.50 Chd 50p. Suns June 7, July 12, Aug 9 (11-3). Private visits welcome, please* **Tel 0171 485 6906**

51 Gloucester Road, Kew ❀ (Mrs Lindsay Smith) 10 mins walk from Kew Gardens Tube Station. Travel towards S Circular along Leybourne Park Rd, cross main rd, down Forest Rd 1st L into Gloucester Rd. House ½-way down on R. A small square cottage garden. Many interesting plants and shrubs. Wallflowers and bulbs in spring. TEA. *Adm £1.50 Chd 75p. Sun May 3 (2-6)*

Goldsborough, SE3 ◬◬❀ 112 Westcombe Park Rd, Blackheath. Nearest BR Westcombe Park (10 mins walk) or Maze Hill (15 mins walk). Buses to the Standard from Central London and surrounding areas. Car parking available. Community garden for close care and nursing home residents. Approx ½ acre of landscaped gardens, incl walkways of rose-covered pergolas; fish ponds; herbaceous borders and colourful annuals. A very sheltered and peaceful garden. TEAS available. *Adm £1 Chd 50p. Sun July 5 (2-4)*

¶1 Grange Park, W5 ◬ (David Rosewarne & Margaret Gray) Off Warwick Rd at the SW corner of Ealing Common. Artists 100' × 50' woodland garden and natural planting given a strong sense of design and form with the use of paving, brick and gravel on different levels, creating a sense of both space and intimacy. Terrace with fountain well, dingley dell, twigloo, potager and gazebo. Organically gardened with an emphasis on drought tolerant planting. *Adm £1 Chd 50p. Suns May 3, July 5 (2-6)*

5 Greenaway Gardens, NW3 ◬ (Mrs Marcus) Off Frognal Lane. Tube (½ mile) Hampstead or Finchley Road Stations. Buses: Finchley Road, West End Lane stop, nos. 13, 82, 113. Large and varied garden on three levels with yr-round interest. Terrace with climbing plants; water feature and swimming pool; large lawn surrounded by over 100' of herbaceous borders, newly enlarged and replanted; wide variety of trees and shrubs; pergola, decorative urns and furniture. Partially suitable for wheelchairs. TEAS July 19 only. *Adm £1 Chd free. Suns May 17, June 21, July 19 (2-6)*

7 The Grove, N6 ◬◬ (Thomas Lyttelton Esq) The Grove is between Highgate West Hill & Hampstead Lane. Stations: Archway or Highgate (Northern Line, Barnet trains) Bus: 210, 271, 143 to Highgate Village from Archway, 214 from Camden Town. ½-acre designed for maximum all-yr interest with minimum upkeep. Water garden restructured in Autumn 1996. *Adm £1.50 OAPs/Chd £1. Suns April 5, June 14, Sept 20 (2-5.30). Private visits welcome, please* **Tel 0181 340 7205**

Hall Grange, Croydon ◬◬ (Methodist Homes) Situated in Shirley Church Rd near to junction with Upper Shirley Rd. From N leave A232 at junction of Shirley Rd and Wickham Rd. From S leave A212 at junction of Gravel Hill and Shirley Hills Rd. The garden, laid out circa 1913 by

Rev W Wilks secretary to RHS, comprises 5 acres of natural heathland planted with azaleas, rhododendrons, heathers and shrubs and is unchanged. Parking nearby. TEA. *Adm £1.30 Chd free. (ACNO to Hall Grange®). Sun May 17 (2-5)*

109 Halsbury Road East, Northolt &※ (Don Fuller) Nearest underground Sudbury Hill. L out of station, first L Cavendish Avenue. Turn L at the end, over small bridge and first R. Prize winning town garden (160' × 40') Herbaceous and mixed borders giving yr-round interest, particularly delightful in spring and summer. Many unusual plants grown and propagated for sale. TEA. *Adm £1 Chd free (ACNO to Greater Ealing Old People's Home®). Suns April 26, May 24, June 28, July 26 (2-6)*

▲Ham House, Richmond &※ (The National Trust) Mid-way between Richmond and Kingston W of A307 on the Surrey bank of the R Thames. Signposted with Tourism brown signs. Restored C17 garden, gravel terrace, paths dividing eight large grass plats; wilderness; parterre. Rose garden; C17 borders. TEAS. *Adm House and Garden £5 Chd £2.50 Family ticket £12.50 Garden only £1.50 Chd 75p. For NGS Sun April 19 (10.30-6)*

¶116 Hamilton Terrace, NW8 ※ (Mr & Mrs I B Kathuria) 5mins walk from Maida Vale tube station, next to St Marks Church. Buses 16, 16a, 98. Large formal front and back garden on different levels, yorkshire stone paving, large pots and containers, wide variety of flowering shrubs, climbers, clematis, iris, roses, hostas, hebes, lawn. Winner of Hampstead garden competition 1997. TEAS. *Adm £2 Chd 50p (ACNO to St Marks Repair Appeal®). Suns May 17, June 14 (2-6)*

117 Hamilton Terrace, NW8 &※ (Mrs K Herbert and the Tenants Association) Hamilton Terrace, where there is room for parking, is parallel with Maida Vale. Buses from Marble Arch 16, 16a, 98 go to Elgin Avenue which is near. This is a large garden, part of the back is kept wild and there is a tiny garden in memory of Dame Anna Neagle, who lived in the house. TEA. *Adm £1 Chd 20p (ACNO to the SCOPE®). Suns May 17, July 26 (2-6)*

11 Hampstead Way, NW11 ※※ (Mr & Mrs R L Bristow) Nearest tube station Golders Green, 10 min walk up North End Rd, L into Wellgarth Road, R up Hampstead Way. ¼-acre prize winning garden on two levels, unusual plants around lawns in the front; at the back, woodland garden, lawn and large patio with water features and pots. TEAS. *Adm £1.50 Chd 50p. Sun May 10 (2-6)*

133 Haverstock Hill, NW3 ※※ (Mrs Catherine Horwood) Belsize Park Tube Station turn L out of station. Buses C11, C12, 168 (Haverstock Arms stop). Prizewinning 120ft long narrow garden divided into rooms. Packed planting of old and English roses, clematis, cottage garden perennials from balconied terrace to 'secret garden'. Pond and pots with many unusual tender perennials and scented plants. Featured in Country Life and Wonderful Window-boxes. *Adm £1.50 Chd 50p. Sun June 7 (2-5.30). Private visits welcome, please* Tel 0171 586 0908

37 Heath Drive, NW3 &※※ (C Caplin Esq): Station: Finchley Rd; buses: 82, 13 & 113 Heath Drive. Many uncommon plants; lawn; pond; rockery; bamboos; ferns. Unusual treatment of fruit trees, greenhouse and conservatory. TEAS. *Adm £2 Chd 50p (ACNO to Royal Marsden®). Suns May 10, July 5 (2.30-6)*

¶75 Heath Gardens, Twickenham &※※ (Penny & Ron Pilcher) A-Z 2K 103 Train: Twickenham, turn L 10min walk. Train/tube: Richmond then bus 290, 490, H22, R70 to Heath Rd or 33, R68 to King St. From Heath Rd turn into Radnor Rd by Tamplins then R into Radnor Gardens. Access to garden in Radnor Gardens. A tiny suburban garden, 33' × 15' still being developed by present owners. Packed with interesting shrubs, many in pots, incl aralia elata, trochodendron, drimys winterii. Patio, trellis, hidden pebble fountain. TEA. *Adm 50p Chd 20p. Suns, July 5, 12 (2-6)*

Highgate Village, N6 ※※ The Grove is between Highgate West Hill and Hampstead Lane Stations: Archway or Highgate (Northern Line, Barnet trains). Bus: 210, 214, 271, 211 to Highgate Village. TEAS at 5 The Grove. *Adm £3 for 3 gardens £1.50 each garden Chd/OAP £2 for 3 gardens or £1 each garden. Sun June 14 (2-5)*

4 The Grove ※ (Cob Stenham Esq) 2-tiered with formal upper garden; view across Heath; orchard in lower garden
5 The Grove (Mr & Mrs A J Hines) Garden on 2 levels *(ACNO to local Scouts®)*
7 The Grove see separate entry

Highwood Ash, NW7 ※ (Mr & Mrs R Gluckstein) Highwood Hill, Mill Hill. From London via A41 (Watford Way) to Mill Hill Circus; turn R up Lawrence St; at top bear L up Highwood Hill; house at top on R. Stations Totteridge and Whetstone or Edgware (Northern Line). Stanmore (Jubilee Line) Arnos Grove (Piccadilly Line). Bus from all these 251. House not within walking distance of stations. 3¼-acre incl rose garden, shrub and herbaceous borders, rhododendrons, azaleas, lake with waterfall, a mixture of formal and informal. TEAS. *Adm £1.50 Chd 50p (ACNO to The North London Hospice®). Sat, Sun May 16, 17 (2-6)*

5 Hillcrest Avenue, NW11 ※※ (Mrs R M Rees) Hillcrest Ave is off Bridge Lane. By bus to Temple Fortune, Buses 82, 102, 260. Nearest Tube Golders Green or Finchley Central. Walk down Bridge Lane. Small labour saving colourful garden with many interesting features; rockery, fish pond, conservatory, tree fern. Secluded patio, auricula theatre. Cycas Revoluta, Cypressus, Sempervirens, Mediterranean front garden. TEAS. *Adm £1 Chd 50p (ACNO to ADS®). Sun June 21 (2-6) Private visits welcome, please* Tel 0181 455 0419

16 Hillcrest Road, E18 &※ (Stanley Killingback) N from London on A11 (Woodford High Rd) L into Hillcrest, last lamp on L. S from M25 or North Circular, R into Grove Hill R twice into Hillcrest. From South Woodford station (Central Line). Short walk W uphill. Small suburban garden dedicated especially to the display of 10,000 tulips in rows - 400 different varieties. Featured in Garden Answers, the Oldie and the Independent 26 April '97. *Adm £1 Chd 50p (ACNO to Emma Killingback Memorial Fund®). Sun April 19 (2-6)*

The Holme, NW1 &⚘ (Lessees of The Crown Estate Commissioners) Inner Circle, Regents Park opp Open Air Theatre. Nearest tube Regents Park or Baker St. 4-acre garden filled with interesting and unusual plants. Sweeping lakeside lawns intersected by islands of herbaceous beds. Extensive rock garden with waterfall, stream and pool. Formal flower garden with unusual annual and half hardy plants, sunken lawn, fountain pool and arbour. *Adm £2.50 Chd £1. Sats, Suns April 25, 26, Aug 22, 23 (2.30-5.30)*

125 Honor Oak Park, SE23 ⚘⚘ (Mrs Heather West) Off South Circular (A205) via Honor Oak Rd. Multifarious plant collection on 2 levels; the lower a shady, informally planted knot garden, the upper sunny with lawn, pond, pots and verandah. York stone steps flank this approx 4,000 sq.ft 'secret' retreat. Strawberry TEAS. *Adm £2.50 evening opening incl wine, Sat June 27 (6.30-8.30). Adm £1.50 Chd 50p. Sun June 28 (2-6)*

239a Hook Road, Chessington & (Mr & Mrs D St Romaine) A3 from London, turn L at Hook underpass onto A243 Hook Rd. Garden is approx 300yds on L. Parking opp in park. Bus 71, K4 from Kingston and Surbiton to North Star Pub. ¼-acre developing garden divided into 2. The flower garden contains a specimen Albizia julibrissin, a Robinia hispida, and a good mix of herbaceous plants, shrubs and climbers. Also a gravel garden, rose tunnel and pond. The potager divided by paths into small beds has many vegetables, soft fruit, fruit trees, and herbs all inter-planted with flowers. TEAS. *Adm £1.50 Chd 50p. Suns June 14, Aug 9 (2-5)*

Hornbeams, Stanmore &⚘⚘ (Dr & Mrs R B Stalbow) Priory Drive. 5m SE of Watford. Nearest underground Stanmore. Priory Drive private rd off Stanmore Hill (A4140 Stanmore-Bushey Heath Rd). ½-acre informal garden where everyday plants mingle happily with rare treasures. Kitchen garden, fruit-cage, greenhouse and conservatory shaded by Muscat grapevine. Extensive new design and planting. Unusual plants for sale. TEAS. *Adm £1.50 Chd free (ACNO to Friends of Hebrew University Botanical Gardens Group®) Sun May 17 (2.30-6) Private visits welcome, please* **Tel 0181 954 2218**

The Horticultural Therapy Demonstration Garden, SW11 &⚘ East Carriage Drive, Battersea Park, between athletics track and tennis courts. ⅓-acre; fully accessible garden with heated greenhouse, wildlife meadow and pond; vegetable and herb gardens, raised beds and containers, herbaceous beds, pergola and raised pond. Horticultural Therapy staff on hand for advice and information on accessible gardening, tools, techniques and therapeutic gardening. TEAS. *Adm £1 Chd free (ACNO to Horticultural Therapy®). Sun June 14 (11-4)*

¶**34 Hyde Vale, SE10** &⚘ (Susan & Bob Yates) From Greenwich BR station turn L towards town centre. Turn R into Royal Hill just before pelican crossing. Turn L at 4th St (Hyde Vale). Parking at top of Hyde Vale and Royal Hill car park. A large S facing mature walled garden (60' × 85'), recently redesigned. Crows foot layout with box-hedged borders and steps to shady terrace with water feature leading to developing woodland area. Shrubs,

climbers, herbaceous border. *Adm £1.50 Chd free. Sun Sept 6 (11-5)*

Hyde Vale Gardens, SE10 ⚘ Greenwich. Parking is allowed at the top of Hyde Vale and in the Royal Hill car park. From Greenwich BR station turn L towards town centre. Turn R on Royal Hill just before Pelican crossing. Turn L at 4th street (Hyde Vale). No parking outside residences. TEAS. *Combined adm £2. Sun July 5 (2-5)*
   31 Hyde Vale (Alison & John Taylor) Newly planted formal garden, with Mediterranean style terrace, accented with many pots
   51 Hyde Vale (Jane Baker) Newly designed N facing garden (20' × 60') behind terraced house. Very vertiginous steps requiring great care

Islington Gardens, N1 ⚘⚘ Station: Highbury and Islington. Bus: 4, 19, 30, 43, 104, 279 to Highbury Corner or Islington Town Hall. A1 runs through Canonbury Sq. *Combined adm £4 or £1.50 each garden Chd £2 or 75p each garden. Sun June 21 (2-6)*
   8 College Cross ⚘ (Ms Anne Weyman & Chris Bulford Esq) Walled town garden, 70' × 20' with over 400 different plants incl many unusual shrubs and herbaceous plants; walls covered with climbers. List of plants in the garden available. TEAS. *(ACNO to Family Planning Association®)*
   13 College Cross See individual entry for description
   36 Thornhill Square ⚘ (Anna & Christopher McKane) Prize-winning 120' long informal garden, with unusual herbaceous plants and shrubs in curved beds giving a country garden atmosphere. Clematis and old roses, incl a rambler covering the Wendy House. TEAS. *(ACNO to St Mary's Church®)*

¶**26 Kenilworth Rd, SE20** ⚘⚘ (Mr & Mrs S Clutson) Approx 1m from Beckenham or Crystal Palace. 5mins walk from Kenthouse BR station. Buses go along Beckenham Rd Nos 227, 176, 194, 312 & 726. Access to garden via a passageway between Nos 20 and 22 Kenilworth Rd. Kenilworth Rd is off Beckenham Rd. Small 35' × 18' back garden on two levels, designed in 1995 by present owners with ease of maintenance and young family in mind. Circular paved patio with surrounding herbaceous borders, climbers and interesting perennials in a profusion of purple, pink and white. Maximum of 15 people at any time please. *Adm 80p Chd free (ACNO to Brittle Bones Society®). Sun June 28 (2-5.30). Other times by appt* **Tel 0181 402 9035**

¶**Kentish Town Gardens, NW5** ⚘⚘ Kentish Town and Tufnell Park tube stations and buses C2, 135, 134, 214. *Combined adm £1.50 Chd £1 or Adm each garden £1 Chd 70p (ACNO to Quaker Peace and Service®). Sun June 7 (2-5.30)*
   55 Falkland Road ⚘⚘ (Carol Bateman) By car approach from Lady Margaret Rd or Montpelier Grove. Small walled garden 40' × 20' plus raised shade bed. A cottage-style garden crammed with plants
   9 Montpelier Grove ⚘⚘ (Sara Feilden & Rod Harper) Off Lady Margaret Rd. Parking in st (no restrictions). Narrow 60' garden behind terrace house. Designed for use by family with working parents. Variety of plants for interest and backdrop of greenery. Colour coordination and combination of particular interest

Kew Gardens, Richmond see entry under Royal Botanic Gardens, Kew

38 Killieser Avenue, SW2 ⓖ♨❀ (Mrs Winkle Haworth) 5 min walk from Streatham Hill BR Station. Buses 159, 137, 133 to Telford Avenue. Killieser Ave 2nd turning L off Telford Ave. Exuberantly planted 90′ × 28′ garden containing many unusual perennial plants, violas and viticella clematis. Classical rose arch, obelisk and Gothic arbour and water feature. Also L off main garden with newly planted parterre. TEAS. *Adm £1 Chd 50p. Sun June 21 (2-6). Private visits welcome for 5 or more. Please,* **Tel 0181 671 4196**

64 Kings Road, Richmond ♨❀ (Jill & Ged Guinness) Easy Sunday parking. 15 mins walk from Richmond Stn (District, N London & BR) or Buses 33, 337 to O'Casey's public house and walk up Kings Rd. Nearly ½-acre garden. Mature trees and tennis lawn from the original 1881 design. Recent planting aims for low maintenance, drought-resistance and grandchild-friendliness. TEAS. *Adm £1 Chd 50p. Sun May 17 (2.30-6)*

Lambeth Community Care Centre, SE11 ⓖ♨❀ Monkton Street. Tube or buses to Elephant and Castle, cut behind Leisure Centre to Brook Drive. Turn into Sullivan Rd at Bakery, passage to Monkton St. (or drive) to Kennington Rd buses 3, 109 159. At The Ship turn into Bishop's Terrace, 1st R to Monkton St. ⅔-acre garden. Mixed shrubs, trees, small rose garden, herbs, interesting walkways and mixed borders. Prize winner in London Hospital Gardens Competition. TEAS. *Adm £1 OAP/Chd 50p (ACNO to St. Thomas's Trustees for the garden®). Sat, Sun June 6, 7 (2-5)*

Lambeth Palace, SE1 ⓖ♨❀ (The Archbishop of Canterbury & Mrs Carey) Waterloo main line and underground, Westminster, Lambeth and Vauxhall tubes all about 10 mins walk. 3, 10, 44, 76, 77, 159, 170, 344 buses go near garden. Entry to garden on Lambeth Palace Rd (not at gatehouse) 2nd largest private garden in London. Land in hand of Archbishops of Canterbury since end C12. Work on garden carried out over last 100 years but significant renewal has taken place during last 10 years. *Adm £3 OAP/Chd 10-16 £1 (ACNO to Lambeth Palace Garden©). Sat March 28 (2-5.30)*

Evening Openings (see also garden descriptions)	
Royal Botanic Gardens, Kew	May 21 6.30—9pm
13 Queen Elizabeth's Walk, N16	June 4 6—8.30pm
Flat 1, 1F Oval Road, NW1	June 6 & 20 6—9pm
Little Lodge, Thames Ditton	June 10 6.30—9pm
Fenton House, NW3	June 11 6.30—8.30pm
Osborne House, Long Ditton	June 17 7—11pm
103 Thurleigh Road, SW12	June 17 6.30—9pm
Southwood Lodge, N6	June 18 6.30—8.30pm
101 Cheyne Walk, SW10	June 25 6—8pm
125 Honor Oak Park, SE23	June 27 6.30—8.30pm
20A Seymour Buildings, W1	July 2 6.30—9pm
2 Millfield Place, N6	July 16 5.30—9pm

12 Lansdowne Rd, W11 ⓖ (The Lady Amabel Lindsay) Holland Park. Turn N off Holland Park Ave nr Holland Park Station; or W off Ladbroke Grove ½-way along. Bus: 12, 88, GL 711, 715. Bus stop & station: Holland Park, 4 mins. Medium-sized fairly wild garden; border, climbing roses, shrubs; mulberry tree 200 yrs old. *Adm £2 Chd £1. Wed May 6 (2-6)*

10 Lawn Road, NW3 ⓖ♨❀ (Mrs P Findlay) Tube to Belsize Park or go up Haverstock Hill. Turn R at Haverstock Arms then L. House 200yds on R, with blue door. ¹⁄₁₀-acre approx; uniquely curvaceous design of intersecting circles, set in rectangular format. Organically cultured garden, very heavily stocked; many unusual and native species plants. *Adm £1 Chd 50p. Sun June 7 (2.30-6)*

15 Lawrence Street, SW3 (John Casson Esq) Between King's Rd and the river parallel to Old Church St. Nearest tubes: Sloane Square and South Kensington. Buses 11, 19, 22, 211, 319, 49. Prize-winning small Chelsea cottage garden (featured in Secret Garden Walks): 12 different camellias (April) clematis, roses, herbaceous perennials and shrubs, all yr-round interest; some unusual plants. House (built c1790), not open except for access to garden. *Adm £1 Chd 50p (ACNO to Chelsea Physic Garden®). Sun April 5, Sat, Sun July 11, 12 (2-6)*

20 Lessingham Avenue, SW17 ♨ (George Hards) Tooting Bec underground (Northern Line). Buses 155, 219. Tranquil green and white small town garden 20′ × 40′ with water feature. Closely planted to provide yr-round variety, interesting plants incl Trachelospermum jasminoides, Catalpa bungei, Auralia elata 'variegata', Romneya coulteri. TEAS. *Adm 50p (ACNO to Imperial Cancer Research Fund®). Sun June 28 (2-6)*

Leyborne Park Gardens, Kew ♨❀ 2 min walk from Kew Gardens station. Take exit signposted Kew Gardens. On leaving station forecourt bear R past shops. Leyborne Park is 1st rd on R. Bus 391, R68 to Kew Gdns station. Bus 65 to Kew Gdns, Victoria Gate. Access by car is from Sandycombe Rd. TEAS. *Combined adm £1.50 Chd free (ACNO to Arthritis and Rheumatism Council for Research®). Sun June 14 (2-5.30)*
36 Leyborne Park (David & Frances Hopwood) 120ft long mature, family garden; architect designed for minimum upkeep with maximum foliage effects; patio; imaginative children's play area; huge eucalyptus. TEAS
38 Leyborne Park ❀ (Mr & Mrs A Sandall) 120ft long almost organic garden; lawn with mixed borders; containers; long established vine; penstemons, lavenders, eryngiums, scented pelargoniums, bamboos; plants for the dry garden
40 Leyborne Park (Debbie Pointon-Taylor) 120ft long garden; lawn and mixed borders; collection of herbaceous geraniums; clematis; mature shrubs; conifers; patio with containers

1 Lister Road, E11 ♨❀ (Myles Challis Esq) Leytonstone underground station (central line). 5 mins to High Rd Leytonstone. Hills garage marks corner of Lister Rd which is directly off High Rd. Garden designer's unexpected, densely planted sub-tropical garden containing a mixture of tender plants such as daturas, gingers, cannas, tree ferns, bananas and hardy exotics incl gunneras, bamboos, cordylines, phormiums and large leaved perennials in a space unbelievably only 40' × 20'. *Adm £1 Chd 50p. Sun Aug 16 (11-4)*

21a The Little Boltons, SW10 ❀ (Mrs D Capron) Between Fulham and Old Brompton Rd off Tregunter Rd. Nearest tube Earls Court, buses 30, 14, 74. 70' × 40' prize winning herbaceous plant collection. Portrayed in House and Garden Magazine. *Adm £1 Chd 25p. Sun June 28 (2-6)*

Little Lodge, Thames Ditton ♿❀❀ (Mr & Mrs P Hickman) Watts Rd (Station 5 mins). A3 from London; after Hook underpass turn L to Esher; at Scilly Isles turn R towards Kingston; after 2nd railway bridge turn L to Thames Ditton village; house opp library after Giggs Hill Green. A cottage style informal garden. Many British native plants. An atmosphere of tranquillity, featuring plants with subtle colours and fragrance; small brick-pathed vegetable plot. TEAS. *Adm £1.50 Chd free (ACNO to Cancer Research®). Sun June 7 (11.30-6). Special evening opening Wed June 10 (6.30-9) £2.50 incl wine and light refreshments. Private visits welcome, please* **Tel 0181 339 0931**

¶London Lighthouse, 111-117 Lancaster Road, W11 ♿❀ Ladbroke Grove 1st R outside tube Hammersmith and City line. Buses 7, 23, 52, 302, 70, 295. 60' × 40' paved courtyard garden arranged on different levels comprising shaded outdoor café seating, surrounded by walls enclosed by roses; incl a pond, chamomile bed, exotic plants and scented garden. TEAS. *Adm £2 Chd 50p. Sun May 31 (2-6)*

22 Loudoun Road, NW8 ✿ (Ruth Barclay) 3 to 4 min walk to St. John's Wood tube station. Lies between Abbey Road and Finchley Rd serviced by buses, mins from bus stop. A strong emphasis on design, water, arbour garden within a garden. Back Italianate courtyard, romantic and mysterious. Interesting water features, incl grotto with water cascading down mussel shells surrounded by ferns and tree ferns. Prizewinner for 4 consecutive years. Featured in 'Town Gardens'. TEAS. *Adm £1.50 Chd 50p. Sun May 31 (2-6)*

1 Lower Merton Rise, NW3 ✿ (Mr & Mrs Paul Findlay) Between Swiss Cottage and Chalk Farm, Primrose Hill. Approx ¼-acre. Informal country cottage style garden with sunken courtyard, cascade, rose pergolas and herbaceous borders. As featured in the Evening Standard. TEAS. *Adm £1.50 Chd 50p. Sun June 7 (2-6)*

¶9 Lower Teddington Rd, Hampton Wick ✿❀ (Elsa Day) 5 mins from BR train (Waterloo) to Hampton Wick. Buses 281, 285, 111, 216, 411, 416 to High St. From A308 at roundabout take A310 (Twickenham) then R fork at 'Swan' public house. No 9 is 6th house on the L. Close to R Thames, Kingston and Hampton Court. Small walled garden designed by Cleve West and subsequently developed by owner. The garden is laid to gravel and brick on different levels with a water feature (rill) small bog area, herb bed, climbers incl roses, clematis, and vines. A variety of container grown fruits as well as numerous

perennials. TEAS. *Adm £1.50 Chd 50p (ACNO to Terence Higgins Trust®). Sats, Suns June 20, 21, Aug 1, 2 (2-6)*

¶Lyndhurst Sq Gardens, SE15 5 min walk NW from Peckham Rye station. Reduced service on Sunday. No 36 bus from Oval tube or no 171 from Waterloo. Park in nearby streets. *Combined adm £1.50 Chd 75p. Sun June 7 (2-5)*

  ¶1 Lyndhurst Sq ♿❀❀ (Josephine Pickett-Baker) Newly designed, ¹⁄₁₀-acre, walled garden. Formal layout with lawn, flower beds, gravel and flagstones. Sunken terrace with herb garden in retaining wall. Plants in terracotta containers. Evergreen, slightly tropical looking structure to planting, with perennials planted through and around. More foliage than flowers. Many unusual plants. Sitting areas in sun or shade. TEAS

  ¶3 Lyndhurst Sq ✿ (Stephen Haines & Roger Johnson) Sophisticated cottage garden approx 80' × 40', old roses, herbaceous borders, many climbers on house and in garden, sunken garden with fountain and container planting, garden surrounded by mature trees

4 Macaulay Road, SW4 ♿❀ (Mrs Diana Ross) Clapham Common Tube. Buses 88, 77, 77A, 137, 137A, 37, 345. A garden writer's prize-winning garden; appeared in House and Gardens. It currently features jungle, grotto, lots of pots and containers and an eclectic mix of shrubs, trees and herbaceous plants. 85' × 50'. *Adm £1.50 Concessions £1. Sun Aug 9 (2-6) or by appt, please* **Tel 0171 627 1137**. *Minimum charge £20 for 8 people*

Malvern Terrace, N1 ♿❀ Barnsbury. Approach from S via Pentonville Rd into Penton St, Barnsbury Rd; from N via Thornhill Rd opp Albion public House. Tube: Highbury & Islington. Bus: 19, 30 to Upper St Town Hall. Unique London terrace of 1830s houses built on site of Thos Oldfield's dairy and cricket field. Cottage-style gardens in cobbled cul-de-sac; music. Victorian plant stall. Homemade TEAS. Music. *Combined adm £1.50 Chd free (ACNO to Alzheimers Disease Society®). Sun May 31 (2-5.30)*

  1 Malvern Terrace (Mr & Mrs Martin Leman)
  2 Malvern Terrace (Mr & Mrs K McDowall)
  3 Malvern Terrace (Mr & Mrs A Robertson)
  4 Malvern Terrace
  5 Malvern Terrace
  6 Malvern Terrace (Dr B A Lynch)
  7 Malvern Terrace (Mr & Mrs Mark Vanhegan)
  8 Malvern Terrace (Mr & Mrs R Le Fanu)
  10 Malvern Terrace (Dr & Mrs P Sherwood)

2 Mansfield Place, NW3 ✿ (Matthew & Deirdre Townsend) 50yds up Heath St from Hampstead underground. At top of Back Lane, alley to Streatley Place leading to Mansfield Place. This small secret garden is divided into rooms, with the sound of water trickling from a well-shaped fountain. A mulberry tree gives shade and beauty in summer and has become the dominant feature. It is a surprisingly peaceful retreat from the bustle of Hampstead Town. 1996 winner of 'Seen from the Street' competition. TEA. *Adm £1. Sun June 14 (2-5.30)*

2 Millfield Place, N6 ♿✿ Garden is off Highgate West Hill, E side of Hampstead Heath. Buses C2, C11, C12 or 214 to Parliament Hill Fields. 1½-acre spring and summer garden with camellias, rhododendrons, many flowering shrubs and unusual plants. Spring bulbs; herbaceous borders; small orchard; spacious lawns. TEAS (May only). *Adm £1.50 Chd 50p. Sun May 10 (2-6). Adm £2.50 incl wine; Thurs July 16 (5.30-9)*

¶4 Mountfort Crescent, N1 ⟨&⟩⟨&⟩⟨※⟩ (Bridget Barker & Iain Cullen) Off Barnsbury Square (unmade rd), Islington. Garden landscaped in 1995, already surprisingly mature. 92' × 41'. Evergreen and architectural plants give yr-round interest. Hybrid musk and English roses, box edging, topiary and cistus. Phormiums and Euphorbias provide mixture of yellows and greens opp terrace. Good ground cover planting. TEAS. *Adm £1.50 Chd 50p. Sun June 21 (2-6)*

▲Museum of Garden History, SE1 ⟨&⟩⟨※⟩ (The Tradescant Trust) Lambeth Palace Road. Bus: 507 Red Arrow from Victoria or Waterloo, (C10 only on Sundays) alight Lambeth Palace. 7,450 sq ft. replica of C17 garden planted in churchyard with flowers known and grown by John Tradescant. Tombs of the Tradescants and Admiral Bligh of the 'Bounty' in the garden. Opened by HM the Queen Mother in 1983. Museum being established in St Mary-at-Lambeth. The new garden at The Ark, 220 Lambeth Road, also open. TEAS. *Adm £1 OAPs/Chd 25p (ACNO to Museum of Garden History®). For NGS Sun June 7 (10.30-5)*

¶8 Mycenae Road, SE3 ⟨※⟩⟨※⟩ (Sheila Burwash) From Westcombe Park BR station turn R onto Humber Rd almost directly opp is Mycenae Rd, some parking available outside No 8. Approx 100' L-shaped sheltered garden on a sloping site, timber decking small Japanese area, many climbers and vines, succulents and alpines a speciality. Well stocked shrub and herbaceous borders, agapanthus in pots. Shows what can be achieved on a difficult site, working on clay soil. TEAS. *Adm £1 Chd free. Sun June 14 (2-5.30). Parties of 6 or over by appt, please* **Tel 0181 858 5201**

■ Myddelton House Gardens, Enfield ⟨&⟩⟨※⟩ (Lee Valley Park) Bulls Cross. Junction 25 (A10) off M25 S towards Enfield. 1st set traffic lights R into Bullsmoor Lane, L at end along Bulls Cross. 4 acres of gardens created by E A Bowles. Gardens feature diverse and unusual plants incl national collection of bearded irises. Large pond with terrace, two conservatories and interesting historical artefacts. TEAS and plants for sale on NGS days. *Adm £1.80 Concessions £1.20 Suns and Bank hols April 12-Oct 25 (2-5). Open Mon-Fri (except Xmas hols (10-4.30). For NGS Suns Feb 22, May 31, July 26 (Feb 28 1999)*

17A Navarino Road, E8 ⟨※⟩ (John Tordoff Esq) situated between Dalston and Hackney and connects Graham Rd with Richmond Rd. Buses 38, 22A, 22B, 277, 30. Winner of the 1996 BBC Gardener's World competition to find 'the most beautiful small garden in Britain' and a finalist in the '97 Daily Mail National Gardens Competition. A formal Italian garden of clipped box and yew; rambler roses over arches and a pergola; Japanese garden, with a large informal pond, tea house, ornamental bridge, and miniature Mount Fuji. Plantings of azaleas, acers and bamboo. *Adm £1.50 Chd 50p. Suns June 14, Aug 16 (12-5). Private visits welcome, please* **Tel 0171 254 5622**

¶263 Nether Street, N3 ⟨&⟩⟨※⟩ (Judy Wiseman) Turn L from W Finchley tube. House is on the L, 2mins along the rd. Parking in rds off Nether St. House is directly facing Penstemon Close. A sculptor's garden, designed and planted as an outdoor gallery. Toes, noses and hands peep out unexpectedly between smaller plants whilst lush, dramatic foliage acts as a backdrop to life-size sculpture. Exciting water features are camouflaged to surprise unsuspecting visitors whilst mirrors, turf and mosaics are used to extraordinary effect. A garden to delight, stimulate and inspire visitors, incorporating art, horticulture and a certain amount of irreverent fun and frivolity. TEAS. *Adm £1.50 Chd 50p. Suns June 14, 21 (2-6)*

15 Norcott Road, N16 ⟨※⟩⟨※⟩ (Amanda & John Welch) Buses 73, 149, 76, 67, 243 Clapton or Stoke Newington Stations (Rectory Rd closed Suns). Largish (for Hackney) walled back garden. Pond, herbs, herbaceous plants especially irises, geraniums and campanulas. TEAS. *Adm £1 Chd 50p (ACNO to St Joseph's Hospice®). Sun May 31 (2-6)*

2 Northbourne Road, SW4 ⟨※⟩⟨※⟩ (Mr & Mrs Edward A Holmes) Clapham Common tube. Buses 137, 137A, 37. W facing, walled garden 36' × 56' with good architectural planting and rose pergola. Featured in Sainsbury's Magazine and Japanese home interest magazine. Patio extended and improved. Planting revised and 'knot' garden designed for front garden following major house renovations in 1996. Garden designed by Judith Sharpe. *Adm £1.50 OAPs/Chd 75p (ACNO to the Foundation for the Study of Infant Deaths®). Sun June 14 (2-6)*

239 Norwood Road, SE24 (Mr & Mrs J Baillie) Just off South Circular between Tulse Hill and Herne Hill BR Stations. 100' × 25'. Garden designer's romantic garden with a Mediterranean feel combined with formal English. Brick and york stone seating areas; one with Golden Hop arbour, 10' trachycarpus, large urn and 400-yr-old xanthorrhea. Formal lawn with weeping pears, weeping mulberry tree, climbing plants and painted pots. Formal topiary box garden. Finalist in Daily Mail Garden Comp 1996. *Adm £2 Chd free. Sun Aug 2 (2-6)*

Orchard Cottage, Bickley. *Sun Aug 2 (2-5.30).* See Kent

Ormeley Lodge, Richmond ⟨※⟩ (Lady Annabel Goldsmith) Ham Gate Avenue. From Richmond Park, exit at Ham Gate into Ham Gate Avenue. 1st house on R. From Richmond A307, 1½m past New Inn on R, first turning on L. House is last on L. Bus: 65. Large walled garden in delightful rural setting on Ham Common. Newly designed formal garden, wide herbaceous borders, box hedges. Walk through to newly planted orchard with wild flowers. Vegetable garden. Secluded swimming pool area, trellised tennis court with roses and climbers. TEA. *Adm £1 Chd 50p. Sun June 21 (3-6)*

43 Ormeley Road, SW12 ⟨※⟩ (Richard Glassborow & Susan Venner) Nearest tube and BR station Balham, 5 mins walk, off Balham High Rd. Big ideas in a small garden 30' × 18' approx, SW facing, full of unusual plants. *Adm £1 Chd free (ACNO to Friends of the Earth®). Sun May 10 (2-6)*

Osborne House, Long Ditton ⚘❀ (Jane & John Legate) 54 Herne Road. Off A3 at Hook Junction (no exit coming from Guildford), R towards Surbiton, L into Herne Rd before zebra crossing. Please park considerately. 100' × 50' garden with roses, clematis, herbaceous plants. Raised formal pool. Conservatory with water feature. Low level York stone terrace. New 'wild' area with informal water feature. Display of garden photography. Evening opening with lighting. TEAS. *Adm £1.50 (ACNO to Concerlink®); Sun June 14 (10-5). Adm £3.50 to include wine and light refreshments; Wed June 17 (7-11, lighting after 9)*

▲**Osterley Park House, Isleworth** ⅾ (The National Trust) Jersey Rd, Isleworth. Access is via Thornbury Rd on N side of A4 (Great West Rd) between Gillette Corner and Osterley Station. Nearest station Osterley (Piccadilly Line). Car Park £2 (NT Members free). Park with Regency-style pleasure grounds, Adam semi-circular garden house, recently restored with attractive herbaceous plantings. Private walled nursery and cut-flower garden open, with a chance to meet the gardeners. Interesting specimen trees, serpentine lakes and meadows rich in bird life. TEAS. *Adm £1 Chd free. For NGS Sun May 31 (11-4)*

Flat 1, 1F Oval Road, NW1 ⚘ (Sheila Jackson) Tube station Camden Town. Buses: any bus to Camden Town, C2 and 274 stop very near. A small side garden approaches an illustrator's very small hidden back garden approx 24ft × 20ft which abuts the Euston railway line. A great variety of plants, mainly in pots, are banked to create interesting shapes, making use of a variety of levels. This garden is the subject of the book 'Blooming Small, A City Dwellers Garden'. *Adm £1 Chd 50p. Sats June 6, 20 (6-9) or private visits welcome, please* **Tel 0171 267 0655**

39 Oxford Road, SW15 ⅾ⚘ (Jennifer Adey) 3 mins walk from E Putney Tube, off Upper Richmond Rd. Buses 14, 74 and 37. Unusual small walled garden 40' × 50'. Formal box-edged design, mainly foliage. Arched walk covered with hops, small cobbled planted areas. Interesting summerhouse and imaginative views through wrought iron gates. *Adm £1 Chd 50p. Sun June 7 (2-6)*

71 Palace Road, SW2 (Mr & Mrs Jeremy Nieboer) BR Tulse Hill, Brixton Tube. Buses 2A, 2B. By car enter Palace Rd from Norwood High St or Hillside Rd. 45' × 40' front garden formal and enclosed on a theme of blue and white. 90' × 45' rear garden laid out with herbaceous borders and brick terracing. TEAS. *Adm £1.50 Chd 50p. Sun June 21 (1-6)*

¶**1 Panmuir Road, SW20** ⚘❀ (Michael & Jenny Anderson) Easy access from A3. Nearest BR station Raynes Park, 10mins walk. Parking available by Cottenham Park on Cambridge Rd. Australian owners' interpretation of an 'English walled garden' scaled to urban size (70' × 30') which incl the Union Jack in the path layout. A new garden, hard landscaped in 1995 with planting begun in spring 1996. The compact garden incorporates a productive potager, approx 50 fruiting trees and bushes, trained in various ways, a large selection of herbs and a fragrant ornamental section. *Adm £1.50 (ACNO to MCR®). Sat, Sun May 16, 17 (11-4)*

10A The Pavement, SE27 ❀ (Brendan Byrne) Chapel Rd. Located off Ladas Rd down alleyway behind All Seasons Fish Bar. Buses 68 to Knights Hill alight at S London College. No. 2 to Norwood bus garage. BR W Norwood. Come out Knights Hill, turn L. Chapel Rd is 10 mins walk on L after passing bus garage. Smallest garden in London. A hidden oasis behind houses and shops. Country type of garden, mostly in containers. Shrubs, herbaceous, bedding and rare plants continually changing. Featured in 'The Observer' and Sainsbury's magazine. *Adm £1 Acc chd free with adult (ACNO to Horses & Ponies Protection Assoc®). Sun July 26 (10-12, 2-6)*

174 Peckham Rye, SE22 ⅾ❀ (Mr & Mrs Ian Bland) Peckham Rye Common is about 1m NE of Dulwich Village, in S London. The house overlooks Peckham Rye Common from the Dulwich side. On either side of the house are 2 side rds both called The Gardens which can be used for parking. The rear garden is reached by a side alley and is about the size of a tennis court. It was designed by Judith Sharpe to provide yr interest using mainly shrubs with varying foliage. It is an easy care, child friendly garden; best in early June when the pink and blue flowers predominate. TEAS. *Adm £1 Chd free. Sun June 7 (2.30-5.30)*

43 Penerley Rd, SE6 ⅾ⚘❀ (Mr & Mrs E Thorp) BR stations Catford, Catford Bridge (15 mins walk). Many bus routes to Catford. Off A21 just S of S Circular Rd. Plant lover's shady garden 33' × 100', with lots of interesting and unusual plants, many propagated for sale. Formal lawns, informal planting, paved areas with ferns, hostas and other foliage plants in pots. TEAS in aid of St Laurence Church. *Adm £1.50 Acc chd free. Suns May 17, June 14 (2-5.30)*

2a Penn Road, N7 ⅾ (Judy & Paul Garvey) Caledonian Rd Underground. Turn L out of station and continue N up Caledonian Rd for approx 700 yds. Penn Rd is on LHS. House is opp Penn Rd Gardens. Buses 17, 91, 259 along Caledonian Rd; 29, 253 to nearby Nags Head. 100' × 30' walled garden, plus long side-entrance border and small front garden; colourful, well-stocked borders, mature trees, containers, arches, vegetable garden. Prizewinner in local garden competition. TEA. *Adm £1 Chd free. Sun June 28 (2-6)*

35 Perrymead Street, SW6 ⚘ (Mr & Mrs Richard Chilton) Fulham. New King's Rd W from Chelsea; 1st on L after Wandsworth Bridge Rd. Stations: Fulham Broadway or Parsons Green; bus 22 from Chelsea; 28 from Kensington. Small paved garden with ornamental feature; surrounded by mature trees. Shrubs, climbers (especially clematis) interspersed with summer planting suitable for shade. *Adm £1.25 Chd 60p. Sun July 12 (2-6)*

¶**46 Preston Drive, E11** ⚘❀ (Teresa Farnham) Wanstead central line tube. Walk down A12 N side. Preston Drive 1st on L after footbridge. House opp cricket pitch. Garden designer's town garden 80' × 20'. Secluded position between cricket pitch and allotments although only 8m from Marble Arch. Constantly changing as owner experiments. Emphasis on foliage. Pond. Limited use of recycled materials. TEAS. *Adm £1 Chd 50p. Suns July 5, Aug 23 (2-6). Private visits welcome, please* **Tel 0181 530 6729**

13 Queen Elizabeth's Walk, N16 ⚹ (Lucy Sommers) From Manor House tube go S down Green Lanes, then take 2nd L off Lordship Park. 100' × 25' plantsperson's garden. Many interesting shrubs, climbers, perennials set in a series of flowing borders around pergola, arch, pond and sculpture, in both sunny and woodland areas. Created by owner to provide interest through all seasons. TEA. *Adm £1 OAP/Chd 50p. Sun July 26 (2-6). Special evening opening, Thurs June 4 (6-8.30) £2.50 incl wine. Private visits welcome, please* **Tel 0181 802 1662**

3 Radnor Gardens, Twickenham ⚹❀ (Ms Jill Payne) A-Z 2k 103. Train: Twickenham, Turn L 10 min walk. Train/tube: Richmond then bus 490, R70, H22, 290 to Heath Rd or 33, R68 to King St. From Heath Rd turn into Radnor Rd by Tamplins then R into Radnor Gardens. A narrow, green and secluded garden, 12' × 54' of a small terraced house; crammed with a wide range of plants. Tiny ponds and water features, small conservatory. *Adm 50p Chd 20p. Suns July 5, 12 (2-6)*

9 Ranelagh Avenue, SW6 ⚹ (Mrs Penny Tham) Nearest tube Putney Bridge. Approx 60' × 40'. A semi-formal two level garden featuring shade tolerant plants, incl many hostas and trees; arbutus, judas, magnolia, crab apple. Small patio with container grown plants. *Adm £1.20 Chd 50p. Sun June 28 (2-6)*

11 Ranulf Road, NW2 ⚹❀ (Mr & Mrs Jonathan Bates) 13, 82, or 113 bus to Platts Lane from Golders Green or Swiss Cottage; 28 from Golders Green or West Hampstead. Nearest stations Finchley Rd, W Hampstead and Golders Green. Take Ardwick Rd at junction of Finchley Rd and Fortune Green Rd, bear L into Ranulf Rd. No 11 is on L at brow of hill. Medium-sized garden, surrounded by trees, full of colour; herbaceous borders, roses, lilies, fuchsias, bedding plants and many geranium filled pots. Home-made TEAS. *Adm £1 Chd free. Sun July 19 (2-6)*

Regents College's Botany Garden, NW1 ❀ Regents Park. Located at the junction of York Bridge and the Inner Circle. Baker Street tube is 5 mins walk. Buses: 13, 18, 27, 30, 74, 82, 113, 139, 159, 274. Enter main gate or Garden Gate adjacent to footbridge at Clarence Gate. Described as a Secret Garden, this former Botanic Garden has been sympathetically developed so as to retain its intrinsic charm and relaxed, naturalistic atmosphere. Garden areas flow together and host a diverse selection of plants. TEA. *Adm £1.50 Concessions/Chd £1. Sun May 24 (12-5). Private visits welcome, please* **Tel 0171 487 7494**

48 Rommany Rd, SE27 ⚹ (Dr Belinda I Barnes & Mr Ronald Stuart-Moonlight). BR Gipsy Hill Stn. Buses 3, 322. Easiest access to Rommany Rd via Gipsy Rd. A luscious small 30' × 20' walled town garden created in 1995 by present owners. Ferns and hostas lead towards the York stone patio and herbaceous borders. A vine and rose covered pergola forms the entrance to the rear secret garden with fountain and trachelospernum arch. For benefit of all max 15 persons at any one time. TEAS. *Adm £1 Chd 50p (ACNO to RNLI®). Suns June 28, July 26 (1-6). Private visits by written appointment*

Roots & Shoots, SE11 ⚹❀ (Roots & Shoots Training Scheme) Vauxhall Centre, Walnut Tree Walk. Tube: Lambeth North; Buses 159, 109, 3. Just off Kennington Rd, 5 mins from War Museum. Large garden 'oasis' featured in an article in the Telegraph's Secret Gardens of England series. Mixed borders, plant nursery, ½ acre wildlife garden, large summer meadow, superb walnut tree, acacia dealbata, shrub roses and other unusual shrubs. TEAS. *Adm £1 Chd 50p (ACNO to Roots & Shoots®). Sat, Sun May 30, 31 (11-4)*

▲¶Royal Botanic Gardens, Kew ⚹❀ Easily reached via Kew Gardens station (London underground, District line and by rail from N London on Silverlink). Also from Kew Bridge station (SW Tr). Just S of Kew Bridge on A307, Kew Rd. Entry by Victoria Gate only on the Kew Rd opp Lichfield Rd. This special evening opening, during Chelsea week, provides an exclusive opportunity to enjoy the most famous of all botanic gardens. In its 300 acres Kew holds more species than any other garden worldwide. Two of the major glasshouses will be open with staff available to explain their collections and Kew's work. Refreshments. *Adm £4 Chd £2 as this is a fund raising event adm fee also applies to season ticket holders and friends of the Royal Botanic Gardens, Kew (ACNO to Friends of the Royal Botanic Gardens, Kew®). For NGS Thurs May 21 (6.30-9)*

19 St Gabriel's Road, NW2 ⚹❀ (Mrs Penelope Mortimer) St Gabriel's Rd is a short walk from Willesden Green Tube (Jubilee Line). When Penelope Mortimer moved here in 1991 she brought two van-loads of plants from her Cotswold garden. With the help of a splendid balsam poplar, a great deal of muck and hard work, what was 150ft of exhausted grass and rubbish is now a miniature country garden brimming with roses and rare herbaceous plants. 'A sanctuary!' *Adm £2 Chd under 14 free. Sat July 11 (2-6). Private visits welcome, please* **Tel 0181 452 8551**

7 St George's Rd, Twickenham ⚹❀ (Mr & Mrs Richard Raworth) St Margaret's. Off A316 between Twickenham Bridge and St Margarets roundabout. ½-acre maturing town garden backing onto private parkland. Garden divided into 'rooms'. Unusual shrubs, clematis and old English roses. Large conservatory with rare plants and climbers. Parterre, planned water feature, pergola, paved garden. Mist propagated specimens and unusual plants for sale. Featured in Penelope Hobhouse's 'Garden Style' and the The Conservatory Gardener by Anne Swithenbank. TEAS. *Adm £2 Chd 50p. Suns June 7, 21 (2-6) or private visits welcome, please* **Tel 0181 892 3713**

St Mary's Convent & Nursing Home, W4 ⚹❀ (Sister Jennifer Anne) Chiswick. Exit W from London on A4 to Hogarth roundabout. Take A316 signposted Richmond. St Mary's is 500yds down on L. Parking in Corney Rd, 1st turning L after Convent. 2½-acre walled garden with fine specimen trees; herbaceous borders and shrub borders being planted for yr-round interest, incl spring flowering shrubs and bulbs. TEAS. *Adm £1 Chd free. Sun April 19 (2-5)*

St Michael's Convent, Ham ⚘⚘ (Community of The Sisters of The Church) 56 Ham Common. From Richmond or Kingston, A307, turn onto the common at traffic lights nr the New Inn, 100 yds on the R adjacent to Martingales Close. BR trains to Richmond (also district line) or Kingston, then No 65 bus from either to Ham Common. 4-acre walled organic garden. Bible garden and circle garden of meditation. Extensive herbaceous borders, two orchards, wild life areas, working kitchen garden, vinehouse and ancient mulberry tree. Wheelchairs with difficulty. TEAS. *Collection Box. Sat June 20 (11-3)*

60 St Paul's Road, N1 ⚘⚘ (John & Pat Wardroper) Station: Highbury and Islington. Bus 4, 19, 30, 43, to Highbury Corner or Islington Town Hall. 30 bus to Clephane Rd stops outside 60 St Paul's Rd. Typical back-of-terrace town garden has been planted chiefly for shade, and to create a quiet, green enclosed atmosphere just off a busy street; designed on 3 levels with paved patios, border of flowering shrubs. *Adm £1.50 Chd 75p. Sun June 14 (2-6)*

57 St Quintin Avenue, W10 ⚘⚘ (H Groffman Esq) 1m from Ladbroke Grove/White City Underground. From Ladbroke Grove station, bus; 7 to North Pole Road, 30ft × 40ft walled garden; wide selection of plant material. Patio; small pond; hanging baskets; special features. Regular prizewinner in garden competitions. Featured on TV and in horticultural press. Special floral display tribute in memory of Princess Diana for 1998. TEAS. *Adm £1.50 Chd £1. Suns July 5, Aug 2 (2-7). Private visits welcome for parties of 10 and over, please* **Tel 0181 969 8292**

5 St Regis Close, N10 ⚘⚘ (Susan Bennett & Earl Hyde) Muswell Hill. 2nd turning on L in Alexandra Park Rd, from Colney Hatch Lane. Tube: Bounds Green/E Finchley then bus to Curzon Rd. Maureen Lipman's favourite garden. Features temple, pagodas, ponds, waterfalls. Quirky colourful containers. Planting, lawns, abundant borders, antique chimney pots. Oriental Raku-tiled mirrored enclosure created by artist owners in garden studio, conceals plant nursery. International press coverage. BBC 'Gardener's World'. TEAS. *Adm £1.50 Chd 50p. Suns May 3, June 28, July 26 (2-7)*

¶20A Seymour Buildings, W1 ⚘ (Seymour Housing Co-operative) 153/155 Seymour Place. Tube Edgware Rd, Marylebone, Baker St, Marble Arch, BR Marylebone and numerous buses. 150′ × 95′ garden completely surrounded by 4-6 storey buildings. Garden originally constructed by Westminster Council in 1982, but has since been redesigned. The sheltered central London micro-climate enables a number of marginally hardy species to survive. Large ornamental pool with waterfall, raised beds and rock garden. Dense plantings incl 8 varieties of bamboo, hardy ferns, 13 trees, musa, arbutus, yuccas, cordylines. melianthus and various species of helleborus and euphorbia. Emphasis on large evergreen shrubs and architectural plants. Chairlift in use for wheelchairs if advanced notice is given. *Adm £1.50 Chd £1 (ACNO to Terence Higgins Trust®). Sun April 26 (2-6) Thurs July 2 (6.30-9) adm £2.50 to incl wine*

3 Somerton Avenue, Richmond ⚘ (Nigel & Philippa Palmer) By junction of Clifford Ave and A316. Tiny suburban trellised garden crammed with plants, pots and scents. Conservatory, terrace, pool, 'Mediterranean' borders and miniature garden all packed into 30′ × 20′. TEAS. *Adm £1 Chd 50p. Sun June 14 (2-6)*

¶South End Rd, NW3 ⚐⚘ Hampstead tube station, Hampstead High St, bottom of Downshire Hill, South End Rd facing 'Freemason's Arms' public house. A delightful prizewinning row of cottage front gardens, facing Hampstead Heath. Also pretty walled back garden with vine, figs and other fruit trees at 101 South End Rd
  ¶83 South End Rd (Mr & Mrs Martin)
  ¶85 South End Rd (Mr & Mrs D Bramson)
  ¶89 South End Rd (Mr & Mrs C Peake)
  ¶91 South End Rd (Ms Joyce Rose)
  ¶93 South End Rd (Mr & Mrs Epstein)
  ¶95 South End Rd (Ms Deborah Moggach)
  ¶97 South End Rd (Edward Brett Esq)
  ¶101 South End Rd (Mr & Mrs P Lindsay)
Voluntary contribution for back garden
Combined adm £2 Chd £1. Sun June 14 (2-6)

Southwood Lodge, N6 ⚘⚘ (Mr & Mrs C Whittington) 33 Kingsley Place. Off Southwood Lane. Buses 210, 271, 143, 214. Tube Highgate. A romantic, hidden garden laid out last century on a steeply sloping site, now densely planted with a wide variety of shrubs, bulbs, roses and perennials. Pond, waterfall, frogs. Many unusual plants are grown and propagated for sale. Featured in Gardens Illustrated and Sunday Express Colour Magazine. *Adm £1.50 Chd 50p (ACNO to Wednesday's Child©). Sun May 31 (2-6). Special evening opening, Thurs June 18 (6.30-8.30) £2.50 incl wine. Private visits welcome, April to July please* **Tel 0181 348 2785**

¶Springfield Lodge, 348 Upper Richmond Road, SW15 ⚐⚘ (Robert & Janie Scholle) Best kept secret in Putney! One of the Captain's Houses built by Admiral Nelson. A productive garden (185′ × 75′) presented with herbaceous borders and an emphasis on rose and clematis collections. Ponds with fish, fruit trees, vegetables, soft fruit and rockery. Original conservatory now converted to keep rare breed poultry and dwarf lop rabbits. TEAS. *Adm £2 Chd free (ACNO to The Windmill Project®). Sun June 14 (2-6)*

40 Station Road, Hampton ⚘ (Marianne Cartwright) Buses 267 and 68 to Hampton Church. 1st turning on L of High St. From river end 5 mins walk. Buses 111 and 216 pass the house. Alight Police Station 100yds. Hampton BR Station 5 mins. Small secluded cottage garden romantically planted in pinks, blues and mauves. Ferns, trachelospernum jasminoides, pond. Front planted for winter and spring interest. TEA. *Adm £1 Chd 50p. Sun June 14 (2-6)*

By Appointment Gardens. These owners do not have a fixed opening day usually because they cannot accommodate large numbers or have insufficient parking space.

26 Thompson Road, SE22 ✹ (Anthony Noel Esq) A205 South Circular from Clapham Common, L into Lordship Lane. R into Crystal Palace Rd. 1st L Landcroft Rd, 1st R Thompson Rd. Anthony Noel's new garden - approx 15' × 38'. L shaped. Elegant white garden in its early stages with promise of Regency romance. Old roses, rare plants and a theatrical twist. *Adm £2, OAP £1. Sun Sept 20 (2.30-6)*

¶**27 Thorpewood Avenue, SE26** ✹✹ (Barbara & Gioni Nella) Just off the S circular (A205) turning up Sydenham Hill nr Hornimans gardens or Dartmouth Rd from Forest Hill. BR Station Forest Hill. Bus stop Thorpewood Ave nos 312, 122. Mature tree bordered ½ acre garden on a gently sloping site. Interesting mixed borders with lots of shrubs and perennials and climbers. There is a formal vegetable plot and a gravel slope growing Mediterranean plants especially thymes. The lawns and patio provide peaceful sitting areas. TEAS. *Adm £2 Chd free. Sun July 12 (2-5)*

103 Thurleigh Road, SW12 ♿✹✹ (Charles & Caroline MacKinnon) Clapham S Tube Station (Northern Line) is 5 mins walk. A 100' × 90' walled garden surrounded by limes. Formal new courtyard with box and lavender balances deep herbaceous borders and secret areas. Careful planting to minimise upkeep and to balance my dreams of Sissinghurst with our children's footballs. TEAS. *Adm £1.50 Chd 50p. Sun June 14 (1-6). Special evening opening, Wed June 17 (6.30-9) £2.50 incl wine and light refreshments (ACNO to Queen Mary's Clothing Guild®)*

●**Trinity Hospice, SW4** ♿✹✹ 30 Clapham Common North Side. Tube: Clapham Common. Bus: 37, 137, 35 stop outside. 2-acre park-like garden restored by Lanning Roper's friends as a memorial to him and designed by John Medhurst. Ricky's sculpture a feature. TEAS. *Adm £1 Chd free. Sats, Suns April 25, 26; June 6, 7; July 25, 26; Sept 5, 6 (2-5)*

131 Upland Road, SE22 ♿✹✹ (Ms G Payne & Ms P Harvey) East Dulwich. Nearest BR Peckham Rye. Buses 78, 12, 63. 78, 12 to Barry Rd. Get off 1st stop opp Peckham Rye Common. Upland Rd 50yds on L. 63 to Peckham Rye Common. Get off Forest Hill Rd. Cross over to Piermont Green leading to Upland Rd. Small garden full of surprises. Unusual, semi-oriental-style stone rear garden with ponds and waterfalls. Informal planted areas. 20' × 40' designed for effect and low maintenance. Front and side areas incl shade loving plants, bamboos, camellias, magnolias and viticellas. TEAS. *Adm £1 Chd 25p. Sun May 17 (2-5.30)*

15 Upper Grotto Road, Twickenham ✹ (Jeane Rankin) Stations Strawberry Hill or Twickenham. Buses R68, 33 to Pope's Grotto; 90B, 267, 281, 290 to Heath Rd/Radnor Rd, 2nd R into Upper Grotto Rd. Small sunny sunken courtyard garden designed and constructed with advancing age and arthritis in mind; raised borders with small shrubs, herbaceous perennials, self sown annuals; wall shrubs, other climbers; plants in pots and tiny fountain over pebbles. TEA. *Adm 75p Chd 25p. Suns July 5, 12 (2-6). Private visits welcome, please* **Tel 0181 891 4454**

7 Upper Phillimore Gardens, W8 ✹ (Mr & Mrs B Ritchie) From Kensington High St take either Phillimore Gdns or Campden Hill Rd; entrance Duchess of Bedford Walk. 100' × 35' garden; rockery, sunken garden; Italian wall fountain, ground cover planting, pergola. TEA. *Adm £1 Chd 50p. Sun April 19 (2.30-6)*

The Watergardens, Kingston-on-Thames ✹ Warren Road (Residents' Association). From Kingston take the A308 (Kingston Hill) towards London about ½m on R turn R into Warren Road. Japanese landscaped garden originally part of the Coombe Wood Nursery, approx 9 acres with water cascade features. *Adm £2 OAP £1 Chd 50p. Suns May 3, Oct 18 (2-5)*

Well Cottage, NW3 ✹✹ (Lynne & Ian Engel) 22D East Heath Rd, 5 mins walk from Hampstead station and a similar distance from the 268 and 210 bus stop at the Whitestone Pond. An interesting garden dating from the 50's within the sound of Christchurch clock chimes. One of the highest gardens in Hampstead with water, trees, and an old vine from the days when the cottage was part of a Chapel attached to a convent. Interesting new area to the side of the cottage created by Evelyn Hannah 3 yrs ago. Fenton House and Kenwood are within easy walking distance. TEAS. *Adm £1.50 Chd 50p. Sun May 17 (2-6)*

3 Wellgarth Road, NW11 ✹✹ (Mrs A M Gear) Hampstead Garden Suburb. Turning off the North End Rd. Golders Green tube 6 mins walk. Buses, 268, 210. A walk all round the house, swathe of grass with long borders of bushes, trees and climbers. Close planting, herbaceous beds, roses, heathers, lavenders: herbs, mints, some uncommon plants. Paving, pots, and old oak tree; small pond with bubbling water. Winner in Hampstead Gardens Competition and All London Championship 1996. Homemade TEAS. *Adm £1.50 (ACNO to RSPCA®). Sun June 14 (2-6)*

¶**18 Westfield Rd, NW7** ✹ (Alan Clark) From London via A41 (Watford Way) to Apex Corner Mill Hill. Turn R onto A1 and 1st R Marsh Lane. 2nd L. Small garden well planted with bedding plants and shrubs, surrounded by trees. TEA. *Adm £1. Sun July 12 (2-6)*

10 Wildwood Rd, NW11 ♿ (Dr J W McLean) Hampstead. Wildwood Rd is between Hampstead Golf Course and N end of Hampstead Heath. From North End Rd turn by Manor House Hospital into Hampstead Way, then fork R. Garden planned and maintained by owner; one of finest herbaceous borders in North London, pond, HT roses; owner-grown prize winning delphiniums and seedlings. TEA. *Adm £1.50 Chd free. Sun July 12 (2-7)*

Wimbledon Gardens, SW19 Train: BR or underground. Maps showing shortest route between the gardens will be available. Bus 93, alight at top of Wimbledon Hill and walk along Ridgeway for 1st 5 gardens, or alight on Parkside at Calonne Rd stop for Somerset Rd; route 200, alight on Ridgway at Murray Rd and walk downhill. TEAS at Somerset Rd and Murray Rd. *Combined adm for six* *gardens £3.50 or £1 per garden Chd free (ACNO to Royal Marsden Hospital, Sutton Branch®). Sun May 31 (2-6)*

9 Denmark Road ঔ (Craig & Deborah Eadie) 2 linked courtyard gardens of interesting design with raised beds, climbers, small shrubs and unusual annuals, wall fountain and dovecote

2 Denmark Avenue ✗ (John & Gillian Quenzer) Town garden (60' × 27') designed for relaxation. Small lawn dominated by a 30 yr-old magnolia tree. Informal shrub and flower beds plus annuals in season with sculptures by owner emerging from the plants and hanging on the wall by the veranda

¶**16 Hillside** ঔ (John & Monica Ellison) Formal hedging contrasts with shrubs and herbaceous planting to provide yr-round varied textures and colours designed to make the most of a sloping, dry, sunny, secluded corner site

3 Murray Road ঔ (Michael & Juliet Waugh) Corner site opp St Johns Church, a continuous narrow lawn curves round 3 sides of house bordered by informal cottage-garden planting of small shrubs, fruit trees, climbing roses, and easily grown herbaceous and ground cover plants which can survive in the dry soil. 2 small ponds. TEAS

63 Ridgway Place ঔ✗ (Alec & Carolyn Metaxa) Town garden recently redesigned by owners to incorporate a sunken patio and maximise use of beds, walls and fences around the small lawn by imaginative planting of shrubs and climbers to provide yr-round interest and privacy

21 Somerset Road ঔ✗❀ (John & Ella Perring) Early Victorian house behind beech hedge, formal front garden and drive; yr-round planting. Partly walled rear garden with 2 fine specimen cedars which pre-date the house, shrubs, herbaceous, ground cover, plants climbing over pergolas and a small herb feature around a lawn with lots of pine needles in it! TEAS served in the conservatory

35 Wincanton Rd, SW18 ❀ (Helen Faulls) Off Wimbledon Park Rd, Southfields Tube. Bus 39. Sunny garden located in a conservation area. Created by densely planting a wide variety of shrubs and herbaceous plants, incl many from the southern hemisphere, within a strong design. Colour, form and flowers yr-round. Terrace enclosed by mixed planting and fences clothed with shrubs and climbers to form a luxuriant setting for outdoor living. Featured in the Sainsbury's magazine. *Adm £1 Chd 50p (ACNO to International Spinal Research Trust®). Sun June 14 (2-6)*

47 Winn Road, SE12 ঔ❀ (Mr & Mrs G Smith) Lee. 8m SE central London. 15mins walk from either BR Lee station (Sidcup Line to Dartford) or Grove Park (Orpington Line) from Charing Cross. By car, ½m from A20 Sidcup bypass or A205 S Circular. ⅓-acre mature plantsman's garden maintained by owners. Mixed borders, alpine beds, fruit and vegetables, 3 greenhouses featuring displays of pelargoniums, fuchsias, begonias, cacti and succulents. TEAS. *Adm £1 Chd free (ACNO to The Fifth Trust©). Suns April 26, June 21, Aug 16 (2-5)*

¶**14A Wiverton Road, SE26** ✗❀ (Eric Mole Esq) Bus 75 or 194 to Newlands Pk Penge East 5mins walk train from Bromley South, or from Victoria 2 per hr to Penge E sta-

tion. Small established garden of 50' × 18' over 80 varieties of camellias, alpines, acers, some geraniums and a pool. Strictly limited numbers of people in the garden at any one time. TEA. *Adm £1 Chd free. Sun June 28 (2-5). Any day by appt March to May, please* **Tel 0181 778 9693**

27 Wood Vale, N10 ✗❀ (Mr & Mrs A W Dallman) Muswell Hill 1m. A1 to Woodman public house; signed Muswell Hill; Muswell Hill Rd sharp R Wood Lane leading to Wood Vale; Highgate tube station. ¾-acre garden with herbaceous borders; ponds; orchard and kitchen garden. Unusual layout full of surprises. Numerous shrubs, roses, trees and conifers; greenhouses. Visitors may also wander in neighbouring gardens, all of which are of high standard. TEAS. *Adm £1.50 Chd 50p under 5yrs free (ACNO to British Legion and St Georges Church®). Sat, Sun July 18, 19 (2-6)*

66 Woodbourne Avenue, Streatham ✗ (Bryan d'Alberg & Keith Simmonds) Enter from Garrads Rd by Tooting Bec Common. Easy parking. Garden designer's garden constantly evolving as featured in Sainsbury's magazine and Tessa Everleigh's book the Decorated Garden Room. Cottage style front garden 40' × 60' containing roses, irises and herbaceous plants. Rear garden approx 40' × 80' created over the last 7 yrs. Features shrubs, trees, gazebo and pool, creating a tranquil oasis in an urban setting. TEAS. *Adm £1.50 Chd 50p (ACNO to Princess of Wales Memorial Fund®). Sun June 21 (1-6)*

¶**11 Woodlands Rd, SW13** ✗❀ (Mr & Mrs Victor West) Take Vine Rd off Upper Richmond Rd to find Woodlands Rd 2nd L. A medium-sized garden with a number of beds all in early stages of development using inherited mature trees and shrubs which together with new arrivals form a densely planted area. Contrasting foliage and forms give shape with colour added by perennials. A wide variety in a limited area with experiments still taking place. TEAS. *Adm £1.50 Chd 50p. Sun May 17 (2-6)*

23 Woodville Road, W5 ✗❀ (Jill & Taki Argyropoulos) Close to Ealing Broadway Station (Central and District Lines). Bus 65 from Kingston and Richmond. 3 times prize winner in Ealing in Bloom competition. Front garden brick-paved, colourfully and densely planted borders and pots. Secluded, walled garden at rear 100' × 40' well stocked with flowering shrubs, climbers and many herbaceous plants. Alpine bed, small ornamental pond with waterfall and bog garden; also raised water trough with fish and frogs. Vegetable, herb and fruit areas. TEAS. *Adm £1. Sun July 19 (2-6)*

By Appointment Gardens. These owners do not have a fixed opening day usually because they cannot accommodate large numbers or have insufficient parking space.

Regular Openings. Open throughout the year. They are listed at the beginning of the Diary Section.

Norfolk

Hon County Organisers:	Mrs Neil Foster, Lexham Hall, King's Lynn PE32 2QJ
	Tel 01328 701 341
	Mrs David McCosh, Baconsthorpe Old Rectory, Holt NR25 6LU
	Tel 01263 577611
Assistant County Organisers:	Mrs David Mcleod, Cropton Hall, Heydon, Norfolk NR11 6RX (Publicity)
	Tel 01263 584159
	Mrs M G T Hart, Orchard House, Ringstead, Norfolk PE36 5LA
	Tel 01485 525267
Hon Treasurer:	Denzil Newton Esq OBE, Briar House, Gt Dunham, King's Lynn PE32 2LX

DATES OF OPENING

Regular openings
For details see garden description

Bradenham Hall, West Bradenham
Hoveton Hall Gardens, nr Wroxham
Mannington Hall, Norwich
Norfolk Lavender Ltd, Heacham
The Old Vicarage, East Ruston
The Plantation Garden, Norwich
Raveningham Hall, Raveningham
Sandringham Grounds

By appointment only
For telephone numbers and other details see garden descriptions. Private visits welcomed

Lawn Farm, Holt
The Mowle, Ludham

February 22 Sunday
  Rainthorpe Hall, Tasburgh
April 12 Sunday
  Gayton Hall, nr King's Lynn
  Lake House, Brundall
  Wretham Lodge, East Wretham
April 13 Monday
  Lake House, Brundall
  The Old House, Ranworth
  Wretham Lodge, East Wretham
April 19 Sunday
  Desert World, Thetford Road, Santon Downham
  The Old Vicarage, East Ruston
  The Plantation Garden, Norwich
  Stow Hall Gardens, Stow Bardolph
April 26 Sunday
  Bradenham Hall, East Dereham
  Mannington Hall, Norwich
May 3 Sunday
  Lake House, Brundall
  Wretham Lodge, East Wretham
May 4 Monday
  Lake House, Brundall

May 10 Sunday
  Hoveton House, nr Wroxham
May 17 Sunday
  Elmham House, North Elmham
  How Hill Farm, Ludham
  Rippon Hall, Hevingham, Nr Norwich
  Sheringham Park, Upper Sheringham
May 24 Sunday
  Aylsham Gardens, Litcham
  Lexham Hall, nr Litcham
  Orchard House, Ringstead
  Selborne House, Harleston
  Stow Hall Gardens, Stow Bardolph
May 31 Sunday
  Sheringham Park, Upper Sheringham
June 7 Sunday
  Alby Crafts Gardens, Erpingham
  Besthorpe Hall, Attleborough
  College Gate, Thompson
  Desert World, Thetford Road, Santon Downham
  Gillingham Hall, Nr Beccles
June 14 Sunday
  13 Drapers Lane, Ditchingham
  Felbrigg Hall, Nr Cromer
  The Garden in an Orchard, Bergh Apton
  86 Hungate Street, Aylsham
  The Old Vicarage, Carbrooke
  Rainthorpe Hall, Tasburgh
  Raveningham Hall, Raveningham
  Southacre Old Rectory, nr Swaffham
June 20 Saturday
  Wretham Lodge, East Wretham
June 21 Sunday
  Baconsthorpe Old Rectory, Holt
  Lexham Hall, nr Litcham
  Stow Hall Gardens, Stow Bardolph
  Wicken House, Castle Acre
June 27 Saturday
  Blickling Hall, Aylsham

June 28 Sunday
  Bayfield Hall, nr Holt
  Elsing Hall, nr Dereham
  Hoveton Hall Gardens, Wroxham
  Magpies, Green Lane, Mundford
  Oxburgh Hall Garden, Oxburgh
July 5 Sunday
  College Gate, Thompson
  Congham Hall Herb Gardens, Grimston, King's Lynn
  The Dutch House, Ludham
July 12 Sunday
  Congham Hall Herb Gardens, Grimston, King's Lynn
  Easton Lodge, Easton
  Hoveton House, nr Wroxham
July 19 Sunday
  Orchards, Raveningham
July 25 Saturday
  Blickling Hall, Aylsham
July 26 Sunday
  Bradenham Hall, East Dereham
  The Garden in an Orchard, Bergh Apton
  Oxburgh Hall Garden, Oxburgh
August 28 Friday
  Blickling Hall, Aylsham (Evening)
August 30 Sunday
  Oak Tree House, 6 Cotman Road, Thorpe, Norwich
September 4 Friday
  Hoveton Hall Gardens, Wroxham
September 6 Sunday
  The Plantation Garden, Norwich
September 9 Wednesday
  The Old Vicarage, East Ruston
September 20 Sunday
  Felbrigg Hall, Nr Cromer
September 27 Sunday
  Bradenham Hall, East Dereham
October 4 Sunday
  Mannington Hall, Norwich

NORFOLK

kms 0   10

miles 0   10

Hunstanton
35
30
Wells-next-the-Sea 4 25
Sheringham
Cromer
44
16
42
Fakenham
A148
Holt 3
28
A140
North Walsham
Happisburgh
6 2
34
Aylsham 23
9
King's Lynn
18
14
41
47
26
Dereham
15
Wroxham 20 21
22 29 12
32
A17
45
A47
A47
7
13
Swaffham
A10
NORWICH
38 31
24
A47
Great Yarmouth
46
Downham Market
37
A1075
33
Watton
8
17
36 40
A146
A1065
5
39
11
Bungay
19
27
Brandon
48
A11
A140
10
Thetford
Diss
43
15

KEY

1. Alby Crafts Gardens
2. Aylsham Gardens
3. Baconsthorpe Old Rectory
4. Bayfield Hall
5. Besthorpe Hall
6. Blickling Hall
7. Bradenham Hall
8. College Gate
9. Congham Hall Herb Gardens
10. Desert World
11. 13 Drapers Lane
12. The Dutch House
13. Easton Lodge
14. Elmham House Gardens
15. Elsing Hall
16. Felbrigg Hall
17. The Garden in an Orchard
18. Gayton Hall
19. Gillingham Hall

20. Hoveton Hall Gardens
21. Hoveton House
22. How Hill Farm
23. 86 Hungate Street
24. Lake House
25. Lawn Farm
26. Lexham Hall
27. Magpies
28. Mannington Hall
29. The Mowle
30. Norfolk Lavender Ltd
31. Oak Tree House
32. The Old House
33. The Old Vicarage, Carbrooke
34. The Old Vicarage, East Ruston
35. Orchard House
36. Orchards
37. Oxburgh Hall Gardens
38. The Plantation Garden

39. Rainthorpe Hall
40. Raveningham Hall
41. Rippon Hall
42. Sandringham Grounds
43. Selborne House
44. Sheringham Park
45. Southacre Old Rectory
46. Stow Hall Gardens
47. Wicken House
48. Wretham Lodge

The maps in this book are designed to help visitors by showing the approximate locations of gardens within each county. The locations are not necessarily precise, particularly where gardens are in clusters. Detailed directions to each garden can be found in the garden descriptions.

DESCRIPTIONS OF GARDENS

▲**Alby Crafts Gardens, Erpingham** &❀ (Mr & Mrs John Alston) On A140 4m N of Aylsham. Park in Alby Crafts car park. 4-acre garden with 4 ponds. Primroses, spring bulbs, wild orchids, irises, hellebores, old-fashioned roses, mixed borders, wild flower and conservation area. Observation Bee Hive during summer. TEAS. *Adm £1.50 Chd free. Open mid-March to mid-Oct, Tues to Sun (10-5). For NGS Sun June 7, with plant sale (11-5). Parties welcome, please* **Tel 01263 761226**

Aylsham Gardens *Combined adm £3 Chd free*
  5 Cromer Road & (Dr & Mrs James) Aylsham. 100yds N of Aylsham Parish Church down old Cromer Rd on LH-side. Approx 1 acre of semi-wild garden nr town centre with large willow trees and grass. Mixed borders and shrubs. Small natural pond, hostas and primulas. Vegetables. *Adm £1 Chd free. Sun May 24 (2-6)*
  10 St Michael's Close ❀❀ (M I Davies Esq) Aylsham NW on B1354 towards Blickling Hall; 500yds from market place, turn R, Rawlinsons Lane, then R again. Front gravelled area with mixed shrub and herbaceous border; small rockery. Back garden with large variety of shrubs, herbaceous plants, bulbs, small lawn, roses, azaleas. Plants, pond. Aviary, guinea pigs. TEAS. *Adm £1 Chd free. Sun May 24 (11-6). Private visits welcome, please* **Tel 01263 732174**
  West Lodge & (Mr & Mrs Jonathan Hirst) Aylsham. ¼m NW of market square on N side of B1354 (entrance in Rawlinsons Lane) Large 9-acre garden with lawns, mature trees, rose garden, herbaceous borders, ornamental pond and walled kitchen garden; Georgian House (not open) and outbuildings incl a well-stocked toolshed (open) and greenhouses. TEAS in aid of Aylsham Church. *Adm £1.50 Chd free. Sun May 24 (2-5.30)*

Baconsthorpe Old Rectory, Holt &❀❀ (Mr & Mrs David McCosh) Follow sign to Baconsthorpe from Holt bypass for 3m. Rectory is beside church at far end of village. Continuing restoration of 3-acre garden. Extensive box hedges dividing kitchen garden and newly planted herbaceous borders. 30ft conservatory. Thatched summer house, rosebeds and mulberry trees; lawns and large trees; decorative outbuildings. TEAS. *Adm £2 Chd free (ACNO to St Mary's PCC®). Sun June 21 (2-6)*

Bayfield Hall, Holt ❀ (Mr & Mrs R H Combe) 1m N of Holt, off A148. Very pretty site with medieval church ruin and magnificent view over lake and park. Part of the garden undergoing reconstruction. Wildflower centre in grounds. Mini-Antiques Road Show, Mongrel's Crufts (all dogs welcome) stalls and family entertainment, in aid of St Martins Church, Glandford. Free TEAS. *Adm £1.50 Chd 50p. Sun June 28 (2-5)*

Besthorpe Hall, Attleborough &❀❀ (John Alston Esq) 1m E of Attleborough. On Attleborough-Bunwell Rd; adjacent to Besthorpe Church. Garden with shrubs, trees and herbaceous borders within Tudor enclosures; walled kitchen garden; tilting ground. Coach parties by appt. TEAS. *Adm £2 Chd free (ACNO to Besthorpe Church®). Sun June 7 (2-5). Also private visits welcome, please* **Tel 01953 452138**

▲**Blickling Hall** &❀ (The National Trust) 1¼ miles NW of Aylsham on N side of B1354. 15m N of Norwich (A140). Large garden, orangery, crescent lake, azaleas, rhododendrons, herbaceous borders. Historic Jacobean house. Wheelchairs available. Cream TEAS and lunches. *Adm £3.50 Chd £1.75. For NGS Sats June 27, July 25 (10.30-5.30). Music and wine evening on Fri Aug 28*

■ **Bradenham Hall, West Bradenham** &❀❀ (Lt Col & Mrs R C Allhusen) Off A47 6m E of Swaffham, 5m W of East Dereham. Turn S signed Wendling and Longham. 1m turn S signed Bradenham, 2m. A garden for all seasons with massed daffodils. Arboretum of over 1000 species all labelled. Rose garden, herbaceous and mixed borders, wall shrubs and roses, fruit and vegetable garden, glasshouses. Featured in Country Life and House and Garden Tea Room. Cream TEAS. *Adm £3 Chd free (ACNO to Bradenham PCC). Open 2nd, 4th and 5th Suns of every month from April to Sept incl (2-5.30). For NGS Suns April 26, July 26, Sept 27 (2-5.30). Coaches at other times by appt only* **Tel 01362 687243**

¶**College Gate, Thompson** ❀ (Mr & Mrs J Biggs) Approx 4m S of Watton (A1075 Thetford Rd). Follow signs for Thompson, go through the village and downhill towards the Church. Round 2nd bend turn R into College Rd. 100yds on L. ⅓-acre cottage garden surrounding 300yr old thatched cottage (not open). Arranged as small 'rooms' incl rose and lavender garden, woodland area, fruit, pergola, orchard. Informal borders with 100s of varieties of plants incl shrubs, perennials, trees, conifers, roses, herbs, wild flowers etc. Teas available nearby in aid of Thompson Church Restoration Fund. *Adm £1.50 Chd free. Suns June 7, July 5 (12-5)*

■**Congham Hall Herb Gardens, Grimston** &❀❀ (Mr & Mrs Forecast) King's Lynn. From A149/A148 interchange NE of King's Lynn, follow A148 to Sandringham/Fakenham. 100yds on, turn R to Grimston. The hotel and herb garden are 2½m on L. Set in 40 acres of parkland, this working herb garden contains over 650 herbs. Cultivated gardens, 'Woodery garden' and orchards. TEAS. *Adm £1.50 Chd 50p. Open from April 1 to Sept 30 (2-4) not Saturdays. For NGS Suns July 5, 12 (2-5)*

Desert World ❀❀ (Mr & Mrs Barry Gayton) Santon Downham. On B1107. Thetford 4m, Brandon 2m. 1¼ acres landscaped plantsman's garden, specialising in tropical plants, alpines, herbaceous and spring bulbs, incl sempervivums. Glasshouses containing 12,500 cacti and succulents. Viewing of glasshouses by appt only. Featured on radio and TV. TEAS. *Adm £1.50 Chd free. Suns April 19, June 7 (1-6). Private, group visits and gardening lectures by appt. Please,* **Tel 01842 765861**

13 Drapers Lane ❀❀ (Mr & Mrs Borrett) Ditchingham. 1m Bungay off the B1332 towards Norwich. ⅓-acre plantwoman's garden containing many interesting, unusual plants incl 100 plus varieties of hardy geraniums, plus a mixture of climbers and shrubs. Herbaceous perennials a speciality. Owner maintained. TEAS. *Adm £1.50 Chd free. Sun June 14 (12-4). Also opening for Suffolk May 3, 4*

The Dutch House, Ludham ✿ (Mrs Peter Seymour) B1062 Wroxham to Ludham 7m. Turn R by Ludham village church into Staithe Rd. Gardens ¼m from village. Long, narrow garden designed and planted by the painter Edward Seago, leading through marsh to Womack Water. Approx 2½ acres. TEAS. *Adm £2 Chd free. Sun July 5 (2-5.30)*

Easton Lodge, Easton ✿ (J M Rampton Esq) 6m W Norwich. Cross the new Southern Norwich Bypass at the Easton Roundabout and take the Ringland Rd. Large garden in magnificent setting above river surrounded by fine trees; walks amongst interesting shrubs, roses, plants; herbaceous border; walled kitchen garden. Late Georgian house with Jacobean centre portion (not open). TEAS. *Adm £1.50 Chd free. Sun July 12 (2.30-5.30)*

Ellingham Hall nr Bungay. See Suffolk for details

Elmham House, North Elmham ᴑ✿✿ (Mr & Mrs R S Don) 5m N of East Dereham, on B1110. Entrance opp Church. Medium-sized garden; wild garden; C18 walled garden; view of park and lake; vineyard, tours of winery. TEAS. *Adm £2 Chd free (ACNO to St Mary's Church N Elmham®). Sun May 17 (2-6). Private visits by appt only to incl vineyard, please Tel 01362 668363*

Elsing Hall, Dereham ✿ (Mrs D Cargill) 2m E of Dereham off A47; sign to Elsing. Medieval house surrounded by moat. Over 200 varieties of old-fashioned roses; wild flower lawn, walled kitchen garden with roses, fruit trees & clematis. Many water plants by moat and fish stew. Rare and interesting trees in arboretum; formal garden with clipped box, lavender, sage, santolina and thyme. Suitable wheelchairs in places. TEAS in aid of Elsing Church. *Adm £3 Chd free. Sun June 28 (2-6). Private parties welcome, please Tel 01362 637224*

▲Felbrigg Hall, Roughton ᴑ✿ (The National Trust) 2½m SW of Cromer, S of A148; main entrance from B1436. Large pleasure gardens; mainly lawns and shrubs; orangery with camellias; large walled garden restored and restocked as fruit, vegetable, herb and flower garden; vine house; dovecote; dahlias; National colchicum collection; wooded parks. 1 Electric and 3 manual wheelchairs available. Lunches, pre booking essential. TEAS. *Adm £2.20 Chd £1. For NGS Suns June 14, Sept 20 (11-5)*

The Garden in an Orchard, Bergh Apton ᴑ✿ (Mr & Mrs R W Boardman) 6m SE of Norwich off A146 at Hellington Corner signed to Bergh Apton. Down Mill Rd 300 yds. 3½-acre garden set in an old orchard. Many rare and unusual plants set out in an informal pattern of wandering paths. ½-acre of wild flower meadows, many bamboos, specie roses, 9 species of eucalyptus. In all a plantsman's garden. TEAS. *Adm £2 Chd free. Suns June 14 (11-8), July 26 (11-6)*

Gayton Hall, King's Lynn ᴑ✿ (Mr & Mrs Julian Marsham) 6m E of King's Lynn off B1145; signs in Gayton village. 20 acres; wild woodland, water garden. Bulbs, TEAS. *Adm £2 Chd free (ACNO to NSPCC®). Easter Sun April 12 (2-6). Private visits welcome, please Tel 01553 636259*

Gillingham Hall, Beccles ᴑ✿✿ (Mr & Mrs Robin Bramley) 16m SE of Norwich, 1½m from Beccles off A146. 14-acre garden with lake, lawns, borders, rose garden, specimen plane trees, wild flower areas, bulbs; Mansion house (not open) c1600. TEAS/Plants in aid of Church Restoration Funds. *Adm £2 Chd free. Sun June 7 (2-5). Parties welcome, please Tel 01502 713294*

■ Hoveton Hall Gardens, nr Wroxham ᴑ✿✿ (Mr & Mrs Andrew Buxton) 8m N of Norwich; 1m N of Wroxham Bridge on A1151 Stalham Rd. 10-acre gardens and grounds featuring daffodils, azaleas, rhododendrons and hydrangeas in woodland. Mature, walled herbaceous garden. Water plants, lakeside walk and walled kitchen garden. Early C19 house (not open). TEAS. *Adm £3 Chd £1. Gardens open, every Wed, Fri, Sun and Bank Hols, Easter Sun to Sept 13 incl (11.30-5.30). For NGS Sun June 28, Fri Sept 4 (ACNO to Multiple Sclerosis Society Research®) (11.30-5.30)*

Hoveton House, nr Wroxham ᴑ✿ (Sir John & Lady Blofeld) 9m N Norwich, ½m Wroxham on B1062, Horning-Ludham Rd. Old-fashioned walled garden; magnificent herbaceous and other borders full of unusual plants and bulbs; rock garden. Established rhododendron grove. Kitchen garden. Park; lawns, walks with magnificent view. William & Mary House (not open.) Plants for sale May only. TEAS. *Adm £2 Chd free (ACNO to St John's Church®). Suns May 10, July 12 (2-5.30)*

How Hill Farm, Ludham ✿ (P D S Boardman Esq) 2m W of Ludham on A1062; then follow signs to How Hill; Farm Garden - S of How Hill. Very pretty garden started in 1968 with three ponds; 3-acre broad (dug as conservation project) water lilies and view over the R Ant; fine old mill. Paths through rare conifers; unusual and rare rhododendrons with massed azaleas; ornamental trees and shrubs; a few herbaceous plants; collection of English holly, ilex aquifolium (over 100 varieties). Collection of bamboos. Partly suitable for wheelchairs. TEAS. *Adm £2 Chd free (ACNO to How Hill Trust©). Sun May 17 (2-5)*

86 Hungate Street, Aylsham ✿✿ (Mrs Sue Ellis) On A140 turn L at roundabout S of Aylsham towards Stonegate, 1st R into Hungate St. Proceed for ¾m, row of white cottages on L. Small enclosed town garden 95′ × 45′ in a semi-formal style, sunken lawns, raised beds and pergolas. A plantswoman's garden, densely planted with small specimen trees/shrubs. Rhododendrons, roses, herbaceous plants, ornamental pond. *Adm £1.50 Chd free. Sun June 14 (11-5)*

Lake House, Brundall ✿ (Mr & Mrs Garry Muter) Approx 5m E of Norwich on A47; take Brundall turn at Roundabout. Turn R into Postwick Lane at T-junction. An acre of water gardens set among magnificent trees in a steep cleft in the river escarpment. Informal flower beds with interesting plants; a naturalist's paradise; unsuitable for young children or the infirm. Wellingtons advisable. 'Unusual plants for sale.' TEAS. *Adm £2 Chd free (ACNO to Water Aid®). Easter Sun & Mon April 12, 13; Sun, Mon May 3, 4 (11-5). Private parties welcome, please Tel 01603 712933*

Lawn Farm, Holt ঙ৻৻৻ (Mrs G W Deterding) Leave Holt on Cley Rd (opp. King's Head) 1m on R. 6½-acre garden with ponds and mediaeval courtyard gardens. Interesting trees and spectacular roses. Refreshments available in Holt. *Adm £2 Chd free. Open by appt April to July 31, please* **Tel 01263 713 484**

Lexham Hall, nr Litcham ঙ৻৻৻ (Mr & Mrs Neil Foster) 2m W of Litcham off B1145. Fine 17th/18th century Hall (not open); parkland with lake and river walks. Formal garden with terraces, yew hedges, roses and mixed borders. Traditional kitchen garden with crinkle-crankle wall. 3-acre woodland garden with azaleas, rhododendrons, spring bulbs and rare trees. TEAS. *Adm £2.50 Chd free (ACNO to St Andrews Church, E. Lexham® May, All Saints Church, Litcham® June). Suns May 24, June 21 (2-6). Also groups (min 20) by appt May 1 to July 31 (weekdays only), please* **Tel 01328 701288**

Magpies, Mundford ঙ৻৻৻ (Mr & Mrs Dennis Cooper) From main Mundford roundabout take A1065 to Swaffham. After ¼m turn L down Green Lane. Divided into 'rooms' giving a cottage garden effect, a 1-acre garden filled with island beds, intensively planted with unusual perennials, ornamental grasses and cottage garden plants. Ponds and planted gravel areas. A wilder margin and tree belt encourages an abundance of birds throughout the year. Featured in 'Amateur Gardening'. Wide variety of unusual plants available from adjoining nursery. *Adm £1 Chd free. Sun June 28 (12-6). Private visits welcome, please* **Tel 01842 878496**

■ **Mannington Hall** ঙ৻৻৻ (The Lord & Lady Walpole) 2m N of Saxthorpe; 18m NW of Norwich via B1149 towards Holt. At Saxthorpe (B1149 & B1354) turn NE signed Mannington. 20 acres feature roses, shrubs, lake and trees. Daffodil lined drive. Extensive countryside walks and trails. Moated manor house (not open). Saxon church with C19 follies. Lunches and TEAS in aid of Bure Valley Community Centre. *Gardens open Suns May to Sept, Weds, Thurs, Fris June to Aug. Adm £3 OAPs/students £2.50 Chd free. For NGS Sun April 26, Oct 4 (12-5)*

The Mowle, Ludham ৻৻৻ (Mrs N N Green) Ludham. B1062 Wroxham to Ludham 7m. Turn R by Ludham village church into Staithe Rd. Gardens ¼m from village. Approx 2½ acres running down to marshes. Interesting shrub borders, unusual trees etc incl tulip trees and a golden catalpa. *Adm £1.50 Chd free. Open by appt, please* **Tel 01692 678213**

●**Norfolk Lavender Ltd, Heacham** ঙ৻ On A149 13m N of King's Lynn. National collection of lavenders set in 2 acres (lavender harvest July-Aug); fragrant meadow and herb garden. Recently opened fragrant plant centre and meadow garden. TEAS. *Adm free. Collecting box. Daily to Christmas (10-5). Reopens Jan 9.* **Tel 01485 570384**

Oak Tree House, Thorpe ৻৻৻ (Will Giles Esq) 6 Cotman Rd. E of Norwich off A47 Thorpe Rd. Exotic plantsman's garden, of ½-acre on a S-facing hillside. Hardy and tender planting gives this garden a truly romantic feel. Containing palms, tree ferns, bananas, bamboos, succulents etc. Also a Grotto and vertical dripping rockery be-

decked in ferns. This garden has appeared in various TV programmes, magazines and books. TEAS. *Adm £2.50, Chd free. Sun July 12, 26, Aug 9, 23, Sept 6. For NGS Sun Aug 30 (1.30-5.30). Parties by appt, please* **Tel 01603 623167**

The Old House, Ranworth ৻৻৻ (Mr Francis & The Hon Mrs Cator) Nr S Walsham, below historic church. Attractive linked and walled gardens alongside beautiful, peaceful Ranworth inner broad. Bulbs, shrubs, potager, mown rides through recently established arboretum where dogs may be walked on leads, pond with many species of ducks and geese. ½m of woodland walk. TEA. *Adm £2 Chd free. Easter Mon April 13 (2-5)*

¶**The Old Vicarage, Carbrooke** ৻৻৻ (Lesley Kant & Stephen Cunneen) 20m W of Norwich, 3m E of Watton, off Norwich-Walton Rd (B1108). Turn into Broadmoor Rd for 2m leading to village centre. At Bridge St T junction turn L; Old Vicarage is 50yds on R. 2-acre country garden, developed and maintained by current owners. Planting incl mixed and herbaceous borders, vegetable garden, white parterre, courtyard herb garden and extensive hedging. Garden leads into small wood (2 acres) planted 12yrs ago by Woodland Trust. TEAS in aid of Carbrooke Village Millenium Green. *Adm £2 Chd free. Sun June 14 (2-5.30)*

■ **The Old Vicarage, East Ruston** ঙ৻৻৻ (Alan Gray and Graham Robeson) 3m N of Stalham on Stalham to Happisburgh/Walcott Rd (ignore all 3 signposts to East Ruston). Turn R 200 yds just N of East Ruston Church. 12-acre exotic coastal garden and grounds incl impressive herbaceous borders, autumn border, tropical border incl bananas and palms, sunken and walled gardens, Mediterranean garden and wild flower meadows and walks. TEAS. *Adm £3 Chd £1. Open every Sun and Wed from April 12 to Oct 25 incl. For NGS Sun April 19, Wed Sept 9 (2-5)*

Orchard House, Ringstead ৻ (Mr & Mrs M G T Hart) A149 13m N from King's Lynn. Turn R to Ringstead shortly after Norfolk Lavender. Follow signs to Docking. Orchard House is 3rd last on way out of village. ¾-acre shrubs and herbaceous. Mixed and themed borders and beds, small pond, water feature, herb and vegetable gardens. Sunken garden and small wild area. TEA. *Adm £1.50 Chd free (ACNO to International Glaucoma Assoc®). Sun May 24 (2-6)*

Orchards, Raveningham ঙ (Priscilla Lady Bacon) 14m SE of Norwich, 4m from Beccles off B1136. ¼-acre plantsman's garden with exceptional collection of rare and unusual plants and shrubs. Mixed herbaceous and shrub borders. *Adm £2 Chd free (ACNO to DGAA Homelife). Sun July 19 (2-5). Private visits welcome, by arrangement, please* **Tel 01508 548 322**

▲**Oxburgh Hall Garden, Oxburgh** ঙ৻ (The National Trust) 7m SW of Swaffham, at Oxburgh on Stoke Ferry rd. Hall and moat surrounded by lawns, fine trees, colourful borders; charming parterre garden of French design. Lunches. Cream TEAS. *Adm £2 Chd 50p. For NGS Suns June 28, July 26 (11-5)*

■ **The Plantation Garden, Norwich** &⚶❀ (Plantation Garden Preservation Trust) 4 Earlham Rd. Entrance between Crofters and Beeches Hotels, nr St John's R C Cathedral. 3-acre Victorian town garden created 1856-96 in former medieval chalk quarry. Undergoing restoration by volunteers, remarkable architectural features include 60ft Italianate terrace and unique 30ft Gothic fountain and newly restored rustic bridge. Surrounded by mature trees, beautifully tranquil atmosphere. *Adm £1.50 Chd free (ACNO to Plantation Garden Preservation Trust®). Suns mid April to mid Oct (2-5). For NGS TEAS Suns April 19, Sept 6 (2-5). Private visits welcome, please* Tel 01603 621868

Rainthorpe Hall, Tasburgh &❀ (Mr & Mrs Alastair Wilson) Approx 8m S of Norwich, just off the A140 - turn by garage in Newton Flotman. On 1m to red brick pillars and gates on L. Elizabethan/Victorian Country House (not open) prettily set in interesting variety of gardens, incl knot hedge (said to be as old as the house) and hazel coppice (said to be older). Fine trees and collection of bamboos. TEAS. *Adm £2.50 OAP £1.50 Chd free. Suns Feb 22 (1-4) June 14 (2-5.30). Private visits welcome, please* Tel 01508 470618

■ **Raveningham Hall, Raveningham** &❀ (Sir Nicholas Bacon) 14m SE of Norwich, 4m from Beccles off B1136. Large garden specialising in rare shrubs, herbaceous plants, especially euphorbia, agapanthus and shrub roses. Victorian conservatory and walled vegetable garden. Newly planted Arboretum. *Adm £2 Chd free. Garden open every Sunday, Bank Hols May, June, July (2-5). For NGS TEA Sun June 14 (2-5)*

Rippon Hall, Hevingham &❀ (Miss Diana Birkbeck) 8m N of Norwich. From A140 Norwich-Aylsham rd, turn R (E) at Xrds just N of Hevingham Church. Rhododendrons and azalea borders. Large herd of rare breed of British White Cattle. TEAS. *Adm £1.50 Chd 25p. Sun May 17 (2-5.30)*

● **Sandringham Grounds** &⚶❀ By gracious permission of H.M. The Queen, the House, Museum and Grounds at Sandringham will be open. 60 acres of informal gardens, woodland and lakes, with rare plants and trees. Donations are given from the Estate to various charities. For further information see p 15. TEAS. *Adm House and Grounds £4.50 OAPs £3.50 Chd £2.50; Grounds only £3.50 OAPs £3 Chd £2 April 9 to Oct 4 daily. House closed July 22 to Aug 5 incl & Grounds closed July 27 to Aug 5 incl. (Hours House 11-4.45; Grounds 10.30-5)*

Selborne House, Harleston &⚶❀ (Mr & Mrs E J Walland) Approx 5m off A140 Norwich to Ipswich Rd. Turn off to Harleston and follow one way signs or 8m from Scole A143. ¾-acre town garden, off Market Place opp Magpie Hotel. Old Wellingtonia Spruces in front garden; rock garden and pond; clematis a speciality; mixed borders; plantsman's garden. TEAS. *Adm £1.50 Chd free. Sun May 24 (2-5)*

▲**Sheringham Park, Upper Sheringham** &❀ (The National Trust) 2m SW of Sheringham. Access for cars off A148 Cromer to Holt Road, 5m W of Cromer, 6m E of Holt (signs in Sheringham Town). 50-acres of species rhododendron, azalea and magnolia. Also numerous specimen trees incl handkerchief tree. Viewing towers, waymarked walks, sea and parkland views. Special walk way and WCs for disabled. Electric wheelchairs available. TEAS. *Adm £2.50 per car. For NGS Suns May 17, May 31 (dawn to dusk).* Tel 01263 823778

Southacre Old Rectory &❀ (Mrs Clive Hardcastle) 3m NW of Swaffham off A1065 opp Southacre Church. 3-acre garden with splendid views of Castle Acre Priory. Mixed borders, shrubs, vineyard, herb garden, pool and old-fashioned rose garden. Interesting C13 church. TEAS in aid of Southacre Church Restoration Fund. *Adm £2.50 Chd free. Sun June 14 (2-5.30). Private visits welcome May, June and July, please* Tel 01760 755469

Stow Hall Gardens, Stow Bardolph &❀ (Lady Rose Hare) 2m N of Downham Market off A10. Large garden with mature trees, small secluded areas with alpines, bulbs, irises and roses. High walls and cloisters planted with scented and tender climbers. Victorian kitchen garden containing old pear and apple trees and interesting varieties of potatoes and strawberries. New architectural features on site of former Stow Hall. TEAS. *Adm £2.50 Chd free (Proceeds from plant stall for Holy Trinity Church, Stow Bardolph®). Suns April 19, May 24, June 21 (2-6)*

Wicken House, Castle Acre &⚶❀ (Lord & Lady Keith) 5m N of Swaffham off A1065; W at Newton to Castle Acre; then 2m N off the rd to Massingham. Large walled garden planted in sections with many roses and unusual herbaceous plants; gravel paths and greenhouses; swimming pool garden; spring and wild gardens. Fine views. Approx 6 acres. Rare plants for sale. Home-made cream TEAS. *Adm £2 Chd free (ACNO to the Friends of Castle Acre Church®). Sun June 21 (2-5)*

Wretham Lodge, East Wretham &⚶❀ (Mrs Anne Hoellering) A11 E from Thetford; L up A1075; L by village sign; R at Xrds then bear L. In spring masses of species tulips, hellebores, fritillaries, daffodils and narcissi; bluebell walk. In June hundreds of old roses. Walled garden, with fruit and interesting vegetable plots. Mixed borders and fine old trees. Wild flower meadows. Featured in Peter Beales' Vision of Roses and in Country Life. TEAS and plants only on May 3. *Adm £2 Chd free (ACNO to St Johns Ambulance in May®). Sun April 12, Mon April 13 (11-6) Sun May 3, Sat June 20 (2.30-5.30). Also private visits and coach parties welcome, please write or* Tel 01953 498366

By Appointment Gardens. These owners do not have a fixed opening day usually because they cannot accommodate large numbers or have insufficient parking space.

Regular openings. Open throughout the year. They are listed at the beginning of the Diary Section.

Northamptonshire

Hon County Organiser: Mrs E T Smyth-Osbourne, Versions Farm, Brackley NN13 5JY
Tel 01280 702412
Asst Hon County Organisers: Mrs John Bussens, Glebe Cottage, Titchmarsh, Kettering NN14 3DB
Tel 01832 732510
Mrs R H N Dashwood, Farthinghoe Lodge, Nr Brackley NN13 5NX
Mrs R Blake, Lodge Lawn, Fotheringhay, Peterborough PE8 5HZ
Hon County Treasurer R H N Dashwood Esq, Farthinghoe Lodge, nr Brackley NN13 5NX
Tel 01295 710377

DATES OF OPENING

Regular openings
For details see garden description

Coton Manor, Guilsborough
Cottesbrooke Hall, nr Creaton
The Menagerie, Horton nr
  Northampton
The Old Rectory, Sudborough
The Walnuts, King Cliffe
Wisteria Cottage, Maidwell Gardens

By appointment only
*For telephone numbers and other
details see garden descriptions.
Private visits welcomed*

Spring House, nr Banbury

March 29 Sunday
  The Old Rectory, Sudborough
April 5 Sunday
  Charlton, nr Banbury
  The Nursery Gardens,
    Geddington
April 13 Monday
  Great Addington Manor, nr
    Kettering
April 19 Sunday
  Finedon Gardens, nr
    Wellingborough
  Maidwell Hall, Northampton
May 3 Sunday
  The Haddonstone Show Garden,
    nr Northampton
May 4 Monday
  The Haddonstone Show Garden,
    nr Northampton
May 10 Sunday
  Great Brington Gardens,
    Northampton
  Holdenby House, Garden and
    Falconry Centre
  Mill House, Stoke Doyle, nr
    Oundle
May 17 Sunday
  Bulwick Rectory & Hollyberry
    Bank, Bulwick

Deene Park, nr Corby
Falcutt House, Brackley
Guilsborough & Hollowell Gardens
Newnham Hall, Daventry
May 24 Sunday
  4 Elmington Cottages, Oundle
  Lois Weedon House, Weedon
    Lois, nr Towcester
  Newnham Gardens, nr Daventry
  The Old Barn, Weedon Lois
May 25 Monday
  Titchmarsh Gardens, nr
    Thrapston
May 31 Sunday
  Glendon Hall, Kettering
  Sholebroke Lodge, Whittlebury,
    Towcester
June 6 Saturday
  Canons Ashby House, Daventry
June 7 Sunday
  Litchborough Gardens, Towcester
  The Nursery Gardens,
    Geddington
  The Old Glebe, Brackley
  Preston Capes Gardens,
  Versions Farm, nr Brackley
June 9 Tuesday
  Coton Manor, Guilsborough
June 10 Wednesday
  Badby Gardens, nr Daventry
June 13 Saturday
  Evenley Gardens, Brackley
June 14 Sunday
  Badby Gardens, nr Daventry
  Evenley Gardens, Brackley
  Kilsby Gardens, nr Rugby
  Maidwell Gardens
  Stoke Park, Stoke Bruerne,
    Towcester
June 16 Tuesday
  Evenley Gardens, Brackley
June 17 Wednesday
  Maidwell Gardens
  The Old Barn, Weedon Lois
June 20 Saturday
  Flore Gardens, nr Northampton
June 21 Sunday
  Cottesbrooke Hall, nr Creaton
  Flore Gardens, nr Northampton

Gamekeepers Cottage, nr
  Creaton
The Old Rectory, Sudborough
June 23 Tuesday
  Evenley Gardens, Brackley
    (Evening)
June 27 Saturday
  The Walnuts, Kings Cliffe
June 28 Sunday
  Aynho Gardens, nr Banbury
  Easton Neston, Towcester
  Great Harrowden Gardens, nr
    Wellingborough
  Harpole Gardens, Northampton
  The Menagerie, Horton nr
    Northampton
  The Walnuts, Kings Cliffe
July 1 Wednesday
  The Old Barn, Weedon Lois
July 5 Sunday
  Park House, Norton
  West Haddon Gardens, nr
    Northants
July 11 Saturday
  The Prebenal Manor House,
    Nassington
July 12 Sunday
  Cranford Gardens, nr Kettering
  Ravensthorpe Gardens
July 15 Wednesday
  The Old Barn, Weedon Lois
  Ravensthorpe Nursery,
    Ravensthorpe Gardens
    (Evening)
July 19 Sunday
  Castle Ashby House, nr
    Northampton
  1 The Green, Kingsthorpe Village
July 22 Wednesday
  1 The Green, Kingsthorpe Village
August 2 Sunday
  Bulwick Gardens, nr Corby
August 9 Sunday
  Cottesbrooke Hall, nr Creaton
  Gamekeepers Cottage, nr Creaton
August 16 Sunday
  4 Elmington Cottages, Oundle
September 6 Sunday
  Canons Ashby House, Daventry

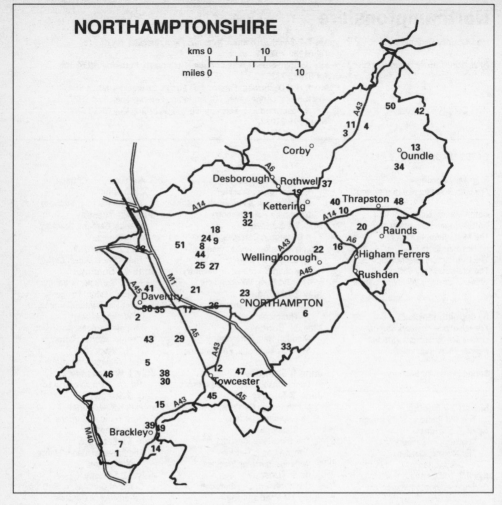

NORTHAMPTONSHIRE

kms 0   10
miles 0   10

KEY

1. Aynho Gardens
2. Badby Gardens
3. Bulwick Gardens, Corby
4. Bulwick Rectory, Bulwick
5. Canons Ashby House
6. Castle Ashby House
7. Charlton
8. Coton Manor
9. Cottesbrooke Hall
10. Cranford Gardens
11. Deene Park
12. Easton Neston
13. 4 Elmington Cottages
14. Evenley Gardens
15. Falcutt House
16. Finedon Gardens
17. Flore Gardens
18. Gamekeepers Cottage
19. Glendon Hall
20. Great Addington Manor
21. Great Brington Gardens
22. Great Harrowden Gardens
23. 1 The Green
24. Guilsborough & Hollowell
     Gardens
25. The Haddonstone Show
     Garden
26. Harpole Gardens
27. Holdenby House
28. Kilsby Gardens
29. Litchborough Gardens
30. Lois Weedon House
31. Maidwell Gardens
32. Maidwell Hall
33. The Menagerie
34. Mill House
35. Newnham Gardens
36. Newnham Hall
37. The Nursery Gardens
38. The Old Barn
39. The Old Glebe
40. The Old Rectory
41. Park House
42. The Prebendal Manor
     House
43. Preston Capes Gardens
44. Ravensthorpe Gardens
45. Sholebroke Lodge
46. Spring House
47. Stoke Park
48. Titchmarsh Gardens
49. Versions Farm
50. The Walnuts
51. West Haddon Gardens

The Haddonstone Show Garden,
   nr Northampton
The Nursery Gardens, Geddington
The Old Rectory, Sudborough
September 8 Tuesday
   Coton Manor, Guilsborough

September 13 Sunday
   Deene Park, nr Corby
September 27 Sunday
   Evenley Gardens, Brackley
October 4 Sunday
   Bulwick Rectory, Bulwick

October 11 Sunday
   Park House, Norton

DESCRIPTIONS OF GARDENS

Aynho Gardens, nr Banbury & 6m SE of Banbury on B4100. Teas in Village Hall. *Combined adm £2 Chd free (ACNO to St Michael's Church, Aynho®). Sun June 28 (2.30-6)*

Aynhoe Park ⊗ (County Houses Association) 14 acres of parkland surround the house (not open to visitors). Sweeping lawns, contrast with woodland left in its natural state to provide a rich habitat for wildlife and plants, incl small leafed ivy. Seasonal flower beds, herbaceous borders and graceful groupings of trees and limewalk

Catton House ⊗ (Mrs C H Harmer) Well established small walled garden with mature trees, various shrubs and specialising in roses and clematis; sunken walled rose garden

1 Charlton Road (Mr & Mrs C J Brownhall) Medium-sized garden with some mature trees, herbaceous borders and shrubs, small rockery and fish pond

Friars Well (Mr & Mrs T R Sermon) 3-acre garden on top of hill with magnificent views; divided into sections with mixed hedges and stone wall; pleached limes and hornbeams, unusual shrubs and roses

Hansel House (Mrs S Belcher) Cottage garden with roses, mixed borders and small pond

Puente Sierra ⊗ (Mr and Mrs R Sawbridge) 1 Cartwright Gardens. ½-acre walled garden with interesting mature evergreens, shrubberies and deciduous trees, bulbs, lilies, palms and hibiscus. Also a fruit and vegetable area

¶Rose Cottage (Mr & Mrs D F Watkins) Garden with many different features incl a large natural pond

16 Roundtown (Miss A Bazin) Old-fashioned cottage garden with inner walled section, herbaceous borders, roses, shrubs and fruit trees

Badby Gardens, nr Daventry ⊗❀ 3m S of Daventry on E side of A361. TEAS at Church Hill. *Combined adm £2 (ACNO to St Mary's Church®). Wed June 10, Sun June 14 (2-6)*

Church Hill ⊗ (Dr & Mrs C M Cripps) Close to Badby Woods and Fawsley Park (suitable for walks and picnics). Medium-sized country garden on an irregular sloping site, parts of which have been recently redesigned. Yew hedges, mixed borders thickly planted in colour groups. Some interesting plants, shady border, greenhouse and conservatory

The Old House & (Dr & Mrs C Rose) A medium-sized open garden overlooking Badby Woods. Mostly stone raised beds recently designed and planted with a good variety of traditional herbaceous plants, featuring many David Austin roses as a speciality

Stone Way (Mr & Mrs C Howes) ⅝-acre open-plan family garden containing: flower beds, bushes, annual and perennial plants; gazebo and patio with rockeries,

small orchard, greenhouse, vegetable plot; aviary with canaries

Bulwick Gardens, nr Corby 7m NE of Corby, 10m SW of Stamford, ½m off A43. TEAS. *Combined adm £2 Chd free (ACNO to Multiple Sclerosis®). Sun Aug 2 (2-5.30)*

Bulwick Hall & (Mr & Mrs G T G Conant) Formal terraced 8-acre walled garden leading to river and island. 50 metre double herbaceous borders. 100 metre holly walk ending at attractive C18 wrought iron gates. C19 orangery and arcade; large kitchen garden; fine mature trees; peacocks. TEAS

Hollyberry Barn &❀ (Colin McAlpine) A cottage garden with curved herbaceous borders; arches; raised vegetable beds; greenhouses; cold frames; gravelled area with alpine plants and pots. *Sun May 17 with* **Bulwick Rectory**

The Shambles ⊗ (Mr & Mrs M R Glithero) Herbaceous plants, many containers, vegetable garden with fruit and an original village well

Bulwick Rectory, Bulwick &⊗❀ (Revd & Mrs Mervyn Wilson) 8m NE of Corby; 13m NE of Kettering; next to Bulwick Church. Old rectory garden retaining some orginal featues. Largely replanted with a notable collection of apple, pear and plum trees. This is an unusual, self supporting garden developed and worked by the present rector to basic organic principles with vegetables, free range poultry and bees. TEAS and plants May only inc **Hollyberry Barn** in aid of Bulwick Parish Church. *Adm £1.50 Chd free. Suns May 17, Oct 4 (2-5). Private visits welcome, please* **Tel 01780 450249**

▲**Canons Ashby House, Daventry** &⊗❀ (The National Trust) Formal gardens enclosed by walls. Gate piers from 1710; fine topiary; axial arrangement of paths and terraces; wild flowers, old varieties of fruit trees, newly planted gardens. Home of the Dryden family since C16, Manor House 1550 with contemporary wall paintings and Jacobean plasterwork. TEAS. *Adm £3.60 Chd £1.80 (includes house). Reduced party rate. For NGS Sat June 6, Sun Sept 6 (12-5.30)*

▲**Castle Ashby House, nr Northampton** &❀ (The Marquis of Northampton) 6m E of Northampton. 1½m N of A428; turn off between Denton and Yardley Hastings. Parkland incl avenue planted at suggestion of William III in 1695; lakes etc by Capability Brown; Italian gardens with orangery; extensive lawns and trees. Nature trail. Elizabethan house (not open). TEA. *Adm £2.50 Chd/OAPs £1. For NGS Sun July 19 (11-5)*

Charlton, nr Banbury & 7m SE of Banbury, 5m W of Brackley. From A41 turn off N at Aynho; or from A422 turn off S at Farthinghoe. Home-made TEAS **The Cottage**. *Combined adm £2 Chd £1 (ACNO to Friends of*

Charlton Primary School©). Sun April 5 (2-6)
The Cottage (Lady Juliet Townsend) Flowering shrubs, spring bulbs, roses, lawns, woodland walk, stream and lakes. House in village street
Holly House (The Hon Nicholas Berry) Walled garden with beautiful views. C18 house (not open)

■**Coton Manor, Guilsborough** ⬥✿❀ (Mr & Mrs Ian Pasley-Tyler) 10m N of Northampton. 11m SE of Rugby nr Ravensthorpe Reservoir. From A428 & A50 follow Tourist signs. C17 stone manor house with old yew and holly hedges, extensive herbaceous borders, rose garden, water garden, herb garden, woodland garden, famous bluebell wood (early May) and newly planted wildflower meadow. Home-made Lunches and TEAS. *Adm £3 OAPs £2.50 Chd £1.50. Open daily Weds to Suns & Bank Hols Easter to end Sept. For NGS Tues June 9, Sept 8 (12-5.30). Private parties welcome, please* **Tel 01604 740219**

■**Cottesbrooke Hall Gardens, nr Creaton** ⬥✿❀ (Captain & Mrs J Macdonald-Buchanan) 10m N of Northampton, nr Creaton on A5199 and Brixworth on A508. (A14 link rd A1/M1). Notable gardens of great variety incl fine old cedars and specimen trees, herbaceous borders, water and wild gardens. TEAS. *Adm House & Gardens £4 Gardens only £2.50 Chd half price. Open Easter to end Sept. House and Gardens open afternoons of Thursdays and Bank Hol Mons plus all Sun afternoons in Sept (2-5). Garden only also open on Tues, Wed and Fri afternoons. For NGS Combined adm with* **Gamekeepers Cottage** *£2.50 Chd £1.25 (ACNO to All Saints Church®). Suns June 21, Aug 9 (2-6). House NOT open on these days.* **Tel 01604 505808**

Cranford Gardens, nr Kettering 4½m E of Kettering. A14 Kettering-Thrapston. TEAS, Station House, Oakrise. Car parking available. *Combined adm £2 Chd 50p (ACNO to Kettering Hospital Centenary Appeal®). Sun July 12 (2-6)*
16 Duck End (Miss Margaret Thomson) Very small cottage garden overlooking the church. Borders of perennials and shrubs
45 High Street (Mr & Mrs M Naylor) A flower arranger's garden consisting of many herbaceous plants, fernery, herb garden, ponds and fruit and vegetables
Oakrise ⬥ (Mr & Mrs G T Oakes) 5 The Green. ½-acre with variety of shrubs, perennials, dwarf conifers; Japanese water garden with Koi Carp and water plants; lovely view
Station House ⬥❀ (Mr & Mrs A Bates) Garden created from the original railway station. Old platform now a walled patio with fish pond and rockery. Many varieties of trees, new planting of shrubs, herbaceous perennials. Natural wildlife pond
Also 2 small cottage gardens – "Over the garden wall"
4 The Green
8 The Green

Deene Park, nr Corby ⬥✿ (Edmund Brudenell Esq) 5m N of Corby on A43 Stamford-Kettering Rd. Large garden; long mixed borders, old-fashioned roses, rare mature trees, shrubs, natural garden, large lake and waterside walks. Parterre designed by David Hicks echoing the C16 decoration on the porch stonework. Interesting Church

and Brudenell Chapel with fine tombs and brasses. TEAS. *Adm £2 Chd 50p. Suns May 17, Sept 13 (2-5)*

Easton Neston, Towcester ⬥ (The Lord & Lady Hesketh) Entrance on Northampton Rd (old A43). Hawksmoor's only Private house. Large formal garden; ornamental water, topiary; walled garden; woodland walk with C14 church (not open) in grounds. TEAS. *Adm £2.50 Chd 50p. Sun June 28 (2-6)*

4 Elmington Cottages, Elmington ✿❀ (Mr & Mrs D L Welman) Proceed N along A605 from Oundle, garden ½m on R. 4 acres started 1992. Herbaceous border, shrubbery, orchard, native and ornamental trees, kitchen garden, lavender and yew walks. *Adm £1.50 Chd free. Suns May 24 (11-6), Aug 16 (11-4)*

Evenley Gardens, Brackley From Brackley 1m S on A43. Teas at Evenley Hall. *Combined adm £2 (June) £1.50 (Sept) Chd 50p. Sat, Suns June 13, 14, Sept 27 (2-6). Evenings Tues June 16, 23 (5-9)*
15 Church Lane (Mr & Mrs K O'Regan) ⅓-acre garden with pond, mixed borders and vegetables. Terrace and herb garden on S side of house *(Not open June 16, 23, Sept 27)*
Five Gables ✿❀ (Mr & Mrs M Bosher) Constantly developing plantsman's garden of 1½ acres sloping to pond. Old-fashioned roses, mixed borders, masses of pots. *Also Tues June 16, 23 (5-9), Sun Sept 27 (2-6)*
¶**33 The Green** (Mr & Mrs A Bullock) A young garden, developing with a young family, with an accent on design. *(Not open June 16, 23 or Sept 27)*
Hill Grounds ⬥❀ (Mr & Mrs C F Cropley) Garden designer and lecturer's mainspring of inspiration. Plantsman's garden of 2 acres sheltered by 200yds C19 yew hedge. Many rare plants. *Also Tues June 16, 23 (5-9), Sun Sept 27 (2-6)*
The Manor House (Mr & Mrs H Bentley) Established garden on ½-acre sloping site; topiary and an ambience in harmony with fine Elizabethan Manor House (not open). *(Not open June 16, 23, Sept 27)*

Falcutt House, Brackley ⬥✿❀ (Paul & Charlotte Sandilands) Falcutt, Helmdon. 4m N of Brackley, 2m to the W of A43 off the B4525. 3-acre garden in secluded rural setting; fine hedges incl yew topiary; mixed borders; lilacs, ancient mulberry tree; garden in process of being restored; young tree plantation. TEAS in aid of St Mary Magdalen, Helmdon. *Adm £1.50 Chd free. Sun May 17 (1.30-5). Private visits welcome by prior appt, please* **Tel 01280 850204**

Finedon Gardens, Wellingborough ✿ 2m NE of Wellingborough on the A510, 6m SE Kettering on the A6. Teas in aid of Finedon Church, at Finedon Antique Centre. *Combined adm £1.50 Chd free. Sun April 19 (2-6)*
1 Grove Way ⬥ (Mr & Mrs P J Sibley) Small recently established plantsman's garden
4 Harrowden Lane ⬥ (Mr & Mrs D J West) ½-acre garden on a steep slope, created since 1982 from waste land; lawns, rose and flower beds; ornamental fish pond, aviary and greenhouses
23 Regent Street ✿ (Mr & Mrs G Perkins) ½-acre garden, organically cultivated, 2 large ponds, aviaries and numerous pets. Large collection of containers

Flore Gardens, nr Northampton 7m W of Northampton, 5m E of Daventry on A45. Flower Festival at All Saints Church and U.R Chapel incl light lunches, Teas, plants, etc. *Combined adm £2 Chd free (ACNO to Flore Flower Festival®). Sat, Sun June 20, 21 (11-6)*

Beech Hill ✱ (Dr & Mrs R B White) 1 acre facing S over the Nene Valley. Lawns, herbaceous and shrub borders with mature trees. There is a vegetable garden, an orchard, alpine house, cool greenhouse. Hanging baskets and tubs

The Croft (John & Dorothy Boast) ⅓-acre cottage garden with mature trees, shrubs, lawns, interesting perennials, climbers and herbs

38 High Street ✱❀ (Mr & Mrs P Harrison) ¾-acre informal garden with views over the Nene valley. Incl mature trees, pond, vegetable garden and perennials

The Manor House ✱ (Richard & Wendy Amos) 1-acre garden with established lawns and herbaceous border surrounded by mature trees. Formal pond and walled kitchen garden

The Old Manor ✱ (Mr & Mrs Keith Boyd) Medium-sized garden of early C18 house comprising lawn, herbaceous border, rose garden, vegetables, fruit and paddock with pond and shrubs

6 Thornton Close ❀ (Mr & Mrs D L Lobb) Medium-sized garden; trees, shrubs, herbaceous plants, conifers and alpines. 2 fish ponds

Gamekeepers Cottage Garden, Cottesbrooke ♿✱❀ (Mr & Mrs D R Daw) 10m W of Northampton, nr Creaton on A50; nr Brixworth on A508. Cottage garden featuring unusual herbaceous plants, flowers for drying, fruit, vegetables, native plants with a difference. Strictly organic. Featured on Ch4 Garden Club and in various publications. *For NGS only Combined adm £2.50 Chd £1.25 with* **Cottesbrooke Hall**. *Suns June 21, Aug 9 (2-6)*

¶Glendon Hall, Kettering ♿✱❀ (Rosie Bose & Mr & Mrs J Chippindale) 3m NW of Kettering. Take A6003 to Corby off roundabout W of Kettering, turning L onto Glendon Rd, signposted Rothwell, Desborough, Rushton. Entrance 1½m on L. Approx 2 acres Victorian gardens. Mature specimen trees, topiary, box hedges, herbaceous borders stocked with many unusual plants, large walled kitchen garden. TEAS. *Adm £2. Sun May 31 (2-6). Private visits welcome, please* **Tel 01536 711732**

Great Addington Manor, Great Addington (Mr & Mrs G E Groome) 7m SE of Kettering, 4m W Thrapston, A510 exit off A14 signed Finedon and Wellingborough. Turn 2nd L to the Addingtons. 4½-acre manor gardens with lawns, mature trees, mulberry, yew hedges, pond and spinney. Spring daffodils. Teas in Village Hall. *Adm £2 Chd over 5yrs 50p (ACNO to Great Addington Church Maintenance Fund®). Mon April 13 (2-5.30)*

Great Brington Gardens, Northampton ✱ 7m NW of Northampton off A428 Rugby rd. 1st L turn past main gates of Althorp. Tickets/maps at church. Gardens signed in village. Parking facilities. Lunches, TEAS. Exhibition and plant stall at various village venues in aid of St Mary's Church. *Combined adm £2 Chd free (ACNO to St Mary's Church®). Sun May 10 (11-5)*

Beard's Cottage ❀ (Capt & Mrs L G Bellamy) Designed and planted by Ann and Bill Bellamy, formerly at Folly House. 2nd yr in this garden, mainly shrubs and herbaceous borders

Brington Lodge ♿❀ (Mr & Mrs P J Cooch) An old garden on the edge of the village, approx ¾ acre, partially walled with a number of spring flowering trees and shrubs

30 Great Brington ♿ (Mr & Mrs John Kimbell) Interesting small garden attached to old stone cottage, well-stocked with shrubs, climbers and perennials. Small pond with bog area, secret garden

New Cross ♿ (R J Kimbell) ½-acre old country garden surrounding a mellow Northamptonshire stone house. Mature trees and shrubs with many spring flowering bulbs

The Old Rectory ♿ (Mr & Mrs R Thomas) 3-acre garden with mature trees, yew hedging, formal rose garden, vegetable and small herb gardens. ½-acre orchard

Ridgway House (Mr & Mrs John Gale) 1½ acres with lawns, herbaceous borders and many spring-flowering shrubs and bulbs

Rose Cottage ♿ (Mr David Green) 2yr-old estate cottage garden designed, built and planted by owner. Variety of fan fruit trees, rockery and brick terrace with pagoda

Great Harrowden Gardens, nr Wellingborough On A509 2m N of Wellingborough on the L. 5m S of Kettering on the R. TEA. *Combined adm £2 Chd free. Sun June 28 (2-dusk)*

Dolphins ♿✱❀ (Mr & Mr R C Handley) 2-acre country garden surrounding old stone house. Many old roses grown among interesting trees, shrubs and a wide range of hardy perennials

Great Harrowden Lodge ♿❀ (Mrs J & Mr R M Green) Situated ¾m from Great Harrowden Church on the lane to Finedon. 1¼-acre garden on a dry exposed site, recently extended. Wide variety of herbaceous perennials

Remember that every time you visit a National Gardens Scheme garden you are helping to raise money for:

The Queen's Nursing Institute
County Nursing Associations
The Nurses' Welfare Service
Macmillan Cancer Relief
Marie Curie Cancer Care
Help the Hospices
Crossroads
The Gardens Fund of the National Trust
The Gardeners' Royal Benevolent Society
The Royal Gardeners' Orphans Fund

Additional Charities Nominated by Owners
Other charities as decided from time to time by Council

1 The Green, Kingsthorpe Village ✿✿ (Mrs D Nightingale) 2m N of Northampton Town Centre. Turn off A508 into Mill Lane at Cock Hotel Junction, taking 2nd turn R. ⅓-acre well-established garden on steep slope, partly terraced. Planned for yr-round interest with a variety of shrubs, herbaceous and climbing plants; to be explored with many surprises. TEAS. *Adm £1.20 Chd 50p. Sun July 19 (12-5), Wed July 22 (2-6)*

Guilsborough and Hollowell Gardens 10m NW of Northampton between A5199 (formerly A50) - A428. 10m E of Rugby. Cream TEAS at **Dripwell House** by Guilsborough WI. Teas at Hollowell Village Hall. *Combined adm £2 Chd free. Sun May 17 (2-6). Private visits welcome for parties of 12 and over*

    Dripwell House, Guilsborough ✿✿ (Mr & Mrs J W Langfield, Dr C Moss, Mr & Mrs P G Moss) 2½-acre mature garden; many fine trees and shrubs on partly terraced slope. Rock garden, herbaceous border, herb garden. Some unusual shrubs and many rhododendrons and azaleas in woodland garden. Cream TEAS in garden. **Tel 01604 740140**

    Gower House ✿ (Peter & Ann Moss) Small garden evolving since 1991 on part of Dripwell vegetable garden. A plantsman's garden with herbaceous alpine, climbing plants and shrubs. **Tel 01604 740755**

    Rosemount, Hollowell ✿✿✿ (Mr & Mrs J Leatherland) In centre of village, up hill behind bus shelter towards Church, entrance 100yds on R. ½-acre plantsman's garden reconstructed in 1982, unusual plants and shrubs, alpine garden, fish pond, small collections of clematis, conifers, camellias, daphne and abutilons. Partly suitable for wheelchairs. Car parking and Teas at village hall behind Church, **Tel 01604 740354**

The Haddonstone Show Garden, East Haddon Manor, nr Northampton ✿✿✿ (Mrs J Barrow) 10m N of Northampton, 12m S of Rugby, from A428. Walled garden on different levels, old shrub roses, ground cover plants, conifers, climbers; swimming pool surrounded by Haddonstone Colonnade, over 30 planted pots and containers. TEAS. Refreshments. Specialist plant stands and exhibition of flower paintings (May). *Adm £2.50 Chd free (ACNO to NSPCC®). Garden Festival Weekend Sun, Mon May 3, 4 (10-5). Early Autumn opening Sun Sept 6 (2-5)*

Harpole Gardens, Northampton 4m W Northampton on A45 towards Weedon. Turn R at The Turnpike Hotel into Harpole. TEAS and stalls at The Close. The Gardens below are varied, incl an old-fashioned country garden, cactus and succulents, water gardens and unusual plants. *Combined adm £2 Chd free. Sun June 28 (12-6)*

    The Close ✿✿ (Mr & Mrs M Orton-Jones) 68 High St. Old-fashioned English country garden with large lawns, herbaceous borders and mature trees, stone house

    The Cottage (Angie & John Roan) 23 Park Lane. An informal cottage garden transformed from a rubbish tip

    Thorpe House (Mr & Mrs R Fountain) A walled cottage garden with many unusual plants and sunken water feature created by the present owners

33 High Street (Mr S Orton-Jones) A thatched cottage with walled garden featuring many unusual plants

47b High Street (Mr & Mrs Peter Rixon) An enclosed ⅙-acre garden consisting of cottage borders, a rockery, pond, rose and herb areas; a Japanese style feature and a large collection of cacti and succulents

74 Larkhall Lane (Mr & Mrs J Leahy) A medium-sized informal garden with a wide variety of plants, shrubs, some mature trees, climbers, alpines, pond and small vegetable plot. Becoming more established after many changes

19 Manor Close (Mr & Mrs E Kemshed) 40yds × 10yds flower arranger's garden on an estate, cultivated by present owners since 1975

Millers (Mr & Mrs M Still) 56 Upper High St. Old stone farmhouse with about an acre of lawns and mixed borders mainly shrubs; some mature trees; good views overlooking the farm and strawberry field

▲**Holdenby House, Garden and Falconry Centre** ✿ (Mr & Mrs James Lowther) 7m NW of Northampton. Signposted from A50 and A428. Impressive house and garden built from the Elizabethan remains of what was the largest house in England and former prison of Charles 1; Elizabethan garden reproduced in miniature by Rosemary Verey; fragrant and silver borders. Children's farm; museum; falconry centre; working armoury; C17 farmstead and rare breeds of farm animals bring this historical garden to life. TEAS and shop (on Suns) *Adm £2.75 (groups of 25 or more £2.25) OAP £2.75 Chd £1.75. For NGS Sun May 10 (2-6)*

Kilsby Gardens, nr Rugby 5m SE of Rugby on A428 turn R on B4038 through village. 6m N of Daventry on A361. Teas in village hall in aid of Village Hall. *Combined adm £2 Chd free. Sun June 14 (2-6)*

    ¶**Carrillon** ✿✿ (Mr & Mrs R Yabsley) Curves are the order for this small garden of approx 100sq m. The curved, raised, well stocked flower beds are complemented by the shaped path leading to a patio. Small fish pond set into a rock garden. The garden benefits from the mature trees in the adjacent garden which soften the high walls that surround it

    ¶**Danetre House** ✿✿ (Mr & Mrs D Topliss) A mature garden of ⅓-acre trees and lawns surrounded by beds and shrubs, some specimen plants incl hibiscus, magnolia, clematis, wisteria, roses, acer, new spiral herbal parterre at its peak in June

    ¶**Manor Cottage** ✿ (Madam Cheng) A small, partly stone walled cottage garden adjacent to a C17 thatched cottage. Borders designed for easy maintenance. Small vegetable plot and fruit trees, water feature utilising reclaimed natural materials

    ¶**The Rickyard** ✿ (Dr & Mrs N Gostick) A small walled garden, under development, in a former farmyard. Some original features are retained but to maximise the space emphasis is on 'vertical gardening' and the use of containers. An irrigation system reduces watering. Organic. There are many foliage plants as this is a flower arranger's garden, a pergola and formal fishpond links the house and garden, creating the effect of outside rooms

The Old Vicarage රිෂ (Mr & Mrs P G B Jackson) On A5 opp George Hotel. 1-acre; lawns, mature trees, shrubs, herbaceous border, small water garden, vegetable garden

Pytchley House ර්ෂ (Mr & Mrs T F Clay) 14 Main Rd. 1-acre mature garden; lawns; trees; island beds; vegetables; new cottage garden; ponds; wild area

The White House ර (John & Lesley Loader) Chapel St. ½-acre partly walled garden with ponds and stream, heather bed, herbaceous border, vegetable garden with raised beds

Litchborough Gardens, nr Towcester ෂ Litchborough village is mid-way between Northampton and Banbury. Teas in WI Hall. *Combined adm £2.50 Chd free (ACNO to St Martin's Church®). Sun June 7 (2-6)*

Bruyere Court ර (Mr R Martin) Farthingstone Rd. 4 acres of landscaped garden featuring lawns; 2 ornamental lakes with rock streams and fountain; shrub borders; rhododendron and azalea borders; herbaceous border; old-fashioned rose hedge; ornamental trees and conifers

The Hall ර (Mr & Mrs A R Heygate) Large garden with open views of parkland; laid to lawns and borders with clipped hedges around the house; the extensive woodland garden has large numbers of specimen trees and shrubs; walks wind through this area and around the lakes

Orchard House ❀ (Mr & Mrs B Smith) Banbury Rd. Landscape architects country garden designed for low maintenance; orchard, pools, conservatory and working pump. *Private visits welcome by parties of less than 5, please* **Tel 01327 830144**

The House on the Green (Mr & Mrs K E Ellis) 1 Ivens Lane. ¼-acre cottage garden which includes well, summerhouse, water feature, rockery, variety of trees, shrubs, roses and bulbs; unusual garden foliage, flowering plants, herbs, soft fruit

2 Kiln Lane (Anna Steiner) Semi-wild garden originally built over a farmyard; features include artists studio and bog garden

Lois Weedon House, Weedon Lois (Sir John & Lady Greenaway). 7m from Towcester on the edge of Weedon Lois village. Pass through village going E towards Wappenham; as you leave village entrance on R. Large garden with terraces and fine views; lawns; pergola; water garden; mature yew hedges; pond. TEAS. *Combined adm with* **The Old Barn** *£2 Chd free (ACNO to Lois Weedon PCC®). Sun May 24 (2-6)*

Maidwell Gardens ෂ 8m N of Northampton on A508, 6m S of Market Harborough. TEAS. *Adm £2.50 Chd free. Sun June 14 (2-6), Wed June 17 (10-6)*

The Old Bake House (Ken & Angela Palmer) Small walled garden with herbaceous borders and shrubs

The Old Barn ර්ෂ (Mr & Mrs John Groocock) ¾-acre garden developed around an old stone barn. Mixed herbaceous and shrub borders, clematis and roses

School Farmhouse ර (Mr & Mrs D J Carter-Johnson) ¾-acre walled cottage garden brimful of traditional mid-summer flowering perennials

Wisteria Cottage ෂ❀ (Mr & Mrs P J Montgomery) A plantsman's cottage garden, approx ½-acre. Compris-

ing a series of rooms in themed colours; featured in 'The English Garden'. *Open daily for NGS April 12 to Sept 27 (2-6)* **Tel 01604 686308**

Maidwell Hall ර❀ (Mr & Mrs P R Whitton, Maidwell Hall School) A508 N from Northampton, 6m S of Market Harborough, entrance via gate on S fringe of Maidwell village. 45 acres of lawns, playing fields, woodland. Colourful display of spring bulbs, magnolias and early flowering shrubs; mature rose garden; lake and arboretum. TEA. *Adm £2.50 Chd free (ACNO to St Mary's Church, Maidwell®). Sun April 19 (2-5). Private visits welcome April to July, Sept to Oct, please* **Tel 01604 686234**

■ **The Menagerie** ර්ෂ❀ (Mr Mark Jackson-Stops) On B526, 6m S of Northampton, 1m S of Horton, turn E at lay-by, across field. These newly developed gardens are set around an C18 folly. Most recently completed is the exotic bog garden to complement the native wetland garden. Also rose garden, shrubberies, herbaceous borders and wild flower areas. TEAS. *Adm £3 Chd £1.50. Thurs (10-4) April to Sept incl and last Sun of the month (2-6). House, garden and shell grotto open to parties by written appt. For NGS Sun June 28 (2-6)*

Mill House, Stoke Doyle ෂ (Mr & Mrs H Faure Walker) 1½m SW of Oundle. Walled garden, vegetable and fruit garden; small gravel garden. Former field area with continuous planting since 1989 of trees, shrubs and roses. *Adm £1.50 Chd free. Sun May 10 (11-5)*

Newnham Gardens ර 1m E of Daventry on B4037. Teas in Village Hall. *Combined adm £2 Chd free. Sun May 24 (2-6)*

The Cross ❀ (M Dawkins) Manor Lane. A cottage garden incl wall plants, perennials, a few unusual plants and pond. Overall winner of local gardens competition

Newnham Grounds (Mr & Mrs Roy Hodges) Approx 3 acres mature garden mostly planted in late 20's on 3 levels with lovely views. Developing new areas. Lime avenue. Interesting shapes and paths

Newnham Fields ❀ (Mr & Mrs E R Mobbs) Church St. Mature garden with many unusual and rare plants, climbers and conifers, next to church with valley view and small pond

Newnham Hall, Daventry (Mr & Mrs David Barrie) Newnham on B4037 1½m S of Daventry. 4-acre garden and parkland. Beautiful views, topiary walk, walled kitchen and herbaceous garden. Woodland walk around informal pond. TEAS. *Adm £2 Chd free. Suns May 17 (2-6)*

The Nursery Gardens, Geddington ර❀ (Christine Sturman) 3m N of Kettering on A43. Turn into village. Follow brown tourist signs for 'Boughton House'. Nursery gardens approx ½m on R. 1-acre garden, set in 2½ acres which incl a spinney, paddock and nursery. New owners presently restoring the garden to incl shrub and herbaceous borders, sunken garden, pergola walk and orchard. Featuring a cottage garden, mediterranean area and display beds. TEAS. *Adm £2 Chd free. Suns April 5, June 7, Sept 6 (2-5)*

The Old Barn, Weedon Lois ✷❀ (Mr & Mrs John Gregory) Small plantsman's garden designed by the owners to compliment converted C18 barn; with interesting selection of hardy perennials, incl collections of euphorbia, hardy geraniums and violas. Unusual plants for sale. *Combined adm £2 with* **Lois Weedon House.** *Sun May 24 Adm £1 incl TEA. Weds June 17, July 1, 15 (2-6)*

¶**The Old Glebe, Brackley** ᕕ (Richard Watson) 1½m N from Brackley town centre on the Radstone rd. Garden developed from 6 acres of farmyard and paddocks over 7 yrs. Avenue leads to pond with varied planting and stone features. Formal area recently laid out. Teas at **Versions Farm.** *Adm £1.50 Chd 50p. Sun June 7 (2-6)*

■ **The Old Rectory, Sudborough** ᕕ✷ (Mr & Mrs A P Huntington) exit 12 off A14. Village just off A6116 between Thrapston & Brigstock. Classic 3-acre country garden with rare and unusual plants surrounding a fine Georgian Rectory (not open). Features incl mixed shrub and herbaceous borders; formal rose garden; newly planted pond area alongside Harper's Brook; woodland walk; spring bulbs and hellebore collection a specialty. Potager originally designed by Rosemary Verey and developed by the owners with Rupert Golby. Quantity of containers with emphasis on summer half-hardies. TEAS. *Adm £2.50 Chd free (ACNO to All Saints Church, Sudborough®). Suns March 22, 29, Sun, Mon April 12, 13, May 24, 25, Suns June 14, 21, July 5, Sept 6. For NGS Suns March 29, June 21, Sept 6 (2-6). Private visits welcome, please* **Tel 01832 733247**

¶**Park House, Norton** ✷ (Mr & Mrs J H Wareing Russell) Daventry 2½m. Northampton 11m. 3½m N of Weedon (A5) 2nd Norton/Daventry turn on L. Garden entrance L before village. Approx 5 acres. Lawns leading down to lakes. Large variety of trees and shrubs, herbaceous borders, heather beds, azalea, roses and ¼m lakeside walk. TEA. *Adm £2 Chd free. Suns July 5, Oct 11 (2-6). Private visits welcome by appt, please* **Tel 01327 702455**

The Prebendal Manor House Gardens, Nassington ᕕ✷ (Mrs J Baile) Church Street, off c14 Wansford to Oundle Rd. 6m N of Oundle, 8m W of Peterborough, 6m S of Stamford. Designed by Michael Brown and unique to E Anglia are the 6 acres of recreated mediaeval gardens set within the grounds of an early C13 manor house. Incl are the mediaeval fish ponds, rose arbour, herber, trellised raised herb beds, turf seat and mediaeval garden historical display in the tithe barn. TEAS. *Adm £2.50 Chd £1. Sat July 11 (2-5.30)*

Preston Capes Gardens ✷ Approx 7m S of Daventry, 3m N of Canon's Ashby. Homemade TEAS at **Old West Farm.** TEAS and plants in aid of St Peter's & St Paul's Church. *Combined adm £2.50 Chd free. Sun June 7 (2-6)*

    The Folly (Mrs M Gee & Mr A Carlisle) Approx ½-acre garden, with outstanding views. Lawns with specimen shrubs, herbaceous borders and ornamental fish pond. Sloping plot, with pond, marginal plants and berry-bearing trees and shrubs

    City Cottage ᕕ❀ (Mr & Mrs Gavin Cowen) A mature garden in the middle of an attractive village, with a walled herbaceous border, rose beds, flowering shrubs, wisteria and a newly planted garden with unusual shrubs

    Fernlea ✷❀ (Mr & Mrs B Firmin) Small garden designed by RHS for easy maintenance and yr-round interest. Pergola and water feature

    Old West Farm ᕕ❀ (Mr & Mrs Gerard Hoare) Little Preston. 2-acre garden re-designed since 1980. Woodland area underplanted with shrubs and bulbs. Roses and borders designed for yr-round interest

Ravensthorpe Gardens Halfway between Rugby and Northampton. Signposted Ravensthorpe 1½m from the A428. TEAS in aid of Guilsborough School PTA. *Combined adm £2 Chd free. Sun July 12 (2-6)*

    32 The High St ᕕ✷ (Mr & Mrs J Patrick) Moderate size garden planted over the last 8yrs. Mostly perennials but some shrubs and roses; also greenhouse and vegetables

    Ravensthorpe Nursery ᕕ❀ (Mr & Mrs Richard Wiseman) Approx 1-acre new show garden being developed to display plants; wide range of shrubs, trees and hardy perennials, incl shrub rose and mixed borders with fine views; also private ¼-acre owners' plantsman's garden. *Also open Wed July 15 (6.30-9).* **Tel 01604 770548**

    Wigley Cottage ᕕ✷ (Mr & Mrs Dennis Patrick) Small flower arrangers' and plantsman's garden with many interesting and unusual plants, shrubs and trees; water features, greenhouse and gravel terrace with outstanding view over Ravensthorpe Reservoir

    Woodslea ᕕ✷ (Mr & Mrs L Highton) Small neat garden planted with many colourful bedding plants, hanging baskets; planted pots and containers, pond with koi carp

Sholebroke Lodge, Whittlebury ᕕ❀ (A B X Fenwick Esq) 3m S of Towcester. Turn off A413 Towcester end of Whittlebury village. 5-acre informal garden. Many interesting plants and walks through flowering shrubs. Pond planting and wall plants. Garden shop in old barn. Homemade TEAS. *Adm £2 Chd free. Sun May 31 (1-6)*

The Spring House, Chipping Warden ✷ (Mr & Mrs C Shepley-Cuthbert) Mill Lane, on A361 between Banbury and Daventry. Garden originally laid out by Miss Kitty Lloyd Jones in the thirties and now mature. Approx 3 acres app through a 16' tapestry hedge. April-May spring flowers, bulbs and blossom. June-Sept bog and water garden at its most colourful. Other times unconventional borders, shrub roses and specimen trees with many new plantings. Ploughmans lunches and Teas available for groups & clubs by arrangement. *Private visits welcome April to Oct, please* **Tel 01295 660261**

▲**Stoke Park, Stoke Bruerne** ᕕ (A S Chancellor Esq) Towcester. 1m off A508 between Northampton and Stony Stratford. Stoke Park is down a private road ¾m, 1st turning L, ¼m beyond village. Approx 3 acres. Terraced lawn with ornamental basin, orchard, herb garden, shrub and other borders, as setting to two C17 pavillions and colonnade. TEA. *Adm £2 Chd £1. For NGS Sun June 14 (2-6)*

Titchmarsh Gardens 2m N of Thrapston, 6m S of Oundle on A605, Titchmarsh signposted as turning to E. TEAS. *Combined adm £2 Chd free (ACNO to St Marys Church, Titchmarsh©). Mon May 25 (2-6)*

  Glebe Cottage ﾖﾀ (Mrs J Bussens) ⅓ acre; NE aspect; informal herbaceous and shrub borders and beds. Clematis in a variety of situations
  16 Polopit ﾀ (Mr & Mrs C Millard) ½ acre. Developed since 1984; rockeries, ornamental and herbaceous borders; fruit decorative shrubs
  Titchmarsh House ﾖﾀ (Mr & Mrs Ewan Harper) 4 acres extended and laid out since 1972; cherries, magnolias, herbaceous irises; shrub roses, clematis, range of wall shrubs, walled borders. *Private visits welcome, please Tel 01832 732439*

Versions Farm, Brackley ﾖﾀﾐ (Mrs E T Smyth--Osbourne) 2m N of Brackley on the Turweston Rd. 3-acres plantsman's garden; wide-range of unusual plants; shrubs and trees; old stone walls; terraces; old-fashioned rose garden; iris border; pond. Conservatory. Cream TEAS. *Adm £2 Chd free (ACNO to Whitfield Church®). Sun June 7 (2-6). Parties welcome by appt May to July, please Tel 01280 702412*

■ **The Walnuts, King's Cliffe** (Mr & Mrs Martin Lawrence). 7m NE of Oundle, 7m SW of Stamford, 4m W of Wansford from A1 and A47; last house on L leaving King's Cliffe on rd to Apethorpe. 2½-acre country garden with lawns, mature trees and hedges, mixed herbaceous and shrub borders, sunken rose garden. Mown pathway through meadow to pond, R Willowbrook and woodland walk. Ornamental vegetable garden. TEAS in aid of All Saints Church. *Adm £1.50 Chd free. Every Wed April to July. For NGS Sat, Sun June 27, 28 (2-6). Private visits welcome, please Tel 01780 470312*

West Haddon Gardens The village is on the A428 between Rugby and Northampton and lies 4m E of M1 exit 18. Lunches/Teas in village hall. *Combined adm £2.50 Chd free (ACNO to West Haddon Parish Church and West Haddon Baptist Church®). Sun July 5 (12-6)*

  Beech Trees ﾀ (Gerald & Daphne Kennaird) Small partially walled garden with views over rolling Northamptonshire countryside. Terrace, lawns, mixed borders and small pond
  Hardays House ﾖ (Guy & Anne Ballantyne) 1½ acres, lawns and shrubbery on sloping ground with S-facing views, pond, vegetable garden, flower beds
  Lime House ﾀ (Lesley and David Roberts) ½-acre of walled garden with rockeries, herbaceous borders, walk-through shrubbery, rose beds; croquet lawn. Summerhouse and patio with greenhouse
  The Mews ﾀ (Rob and Jane Dadley) ½-acre of secluded walled garden including lawns, secret garden, herbaceous border, formal and informal ponds, statuary and pergolas
  Wesleyan Cottage (Stephanie & Paul Russell) Small walled garden with walkways and paved sitting areas. Colourful borders and containers and newly built pond
  West Cottage (Geoff & Rosemary Sage) 1 acre of mixed borders and lawns; informal ponds; lawn tennis court; kitchen garden and greenhouses; many containers and baskets

---

Evening Openings (see also garden descriptions)

Evenley Gardens, Brackley	June 16, 23 5–9pm
Ravensthorpe Nursery, Ravensthorpe Gardens	July 15, 6.30–9pm

Marie Curie Cancer Care

Marie Curie Cancer Care is a charity which cares for people with cancer. The National Gardens Scheme is delighted to include it in its list of beneficiaries. Some facts and figures:

- More than 250,000 people in Britain develop cancer every year. Almost 160,000 people die from the disease annually, the second biggest killer after heart disease.

- **Marie Curie Nurses** provide over 1.3 million hours a year of practical nursing care at home. The service is available day or night, 365 days a year, to patients and their families without charge.

- **Marie Curie Centres** cared for more than 4,600 patients in 1996/97.

- **Marie Curie Cancer Care** operates a research institute which investigates the underlying causes of cancer.

Northumberland & Tyne and Wear

Hon County Organiser:	Mrs G Baker Cresswell, Preston Tower, Chathill, Northumberland NE67 5DH Tel 01665 589210
Assistant Hon County Organisers:	Mrs T Sale, Ilderton Glebe, Ilderton, Alnwick, Northumberland NE66 4YD Tel 01668 217293
	Mrs Susan White, Hexham Herbs, Chesters Walled Garden, Chollerford, Hexham NE46 4BQ Tel 01434 681483

DATES OF OPENING

Regular Openings
For details see garden description

Northumbria Nurseries, Ford

By appointment only
For telephone numbers and other details see garden descriptions. Private visits welcomed

Beauclerc Lodge, Riding Mill

April 25 Saturday
Bide-a-Wee Cottage, Stanton
May 3 Sunday
Preston Tower, Chathill
May 10 Sunday
66 Darras Road, Ponteland
Wallington, Cambo

May 17 Sunday
Hexham Herbs, Chesters Walled Garden, Chollerford
May 27 Wednesday
Bide-a-Wee Cottage, Stanton
Loughbrow House, Hexham
June 7 Sunday
Ashfield, Hebron
Lilburn Tower, Alnwick
Meldon Park, Morpeth
June 14 Sunday
66 Darras Road, Ponteland
June 18 Thursday
Herterton House, Hartington
June 24 Wednesday
Loughbrow House, Hexham
June 28 Sunday
Chillingham Castle, Chillingham
Mindrum, Cornhill on Tweed
July 5 Sunday
Berryburn, Ancroft

Kirkwhelpington Village Gardens
Ravenside, East Heddon
July 12 Sunday
Kirkley Hall College, Ponteland
July 16 Thursday
Herterton House, Hartington
July 19 Sunday
Cragside, Rothbury
July 22 Wednesday
Loughbrow House, Hexham
July 28 Tuesday
Kiwi Cottage, Scremerston
July 29 Wednesday
Bide-a-Wee Cottage, Stanton
August 6 Thursday
Herterton House, Hartington
August 16 Sunday
66 Darras Road, Ponteland
Wallington, Cambo

DESCRIPTIONS OF GARDENS

Ashfield, Hebron &✿✿ (B & R McWilliam) 3m N of Morpeth, Hebron is ½m E of A1. The 5-acre garden is developing with a further herbaceous border, more woodland plantings and tree and shrub groupings. The area closest to the house has many bulbs, a collection of alpines, dwarf conifers, herbaceous and mixed borders. The woodland garden stretches along the W boundary incl collections of sorbus, acer and betula. TEAS. *Adm £1.50 Chd free. Sun June 7 (1-5) Private visits welcome, please* **Tel 01670 515616**

¶**Beauclerc Lodge, Riding Mill** ✗ (Mrs M A Seymour) From Styford roundabout on A69 (Brockbushes Farm location). Follow signs to Riding Mill go through village take L turn (opp small residential estate) signposted Slaley and Shepards Dene 1¾. Follow Rd up the hill to top on sharp bend house is situated just there on the L handside. Look for yellow garage doors. Mixed garden, water features incl wildlife pond herbaceous borders, shrubs, evergreens, mature trees. Victorian greenhouse, woodland area. TEAS. *Adm £1.50 Chd 25p. Weekends by appt,* **Tel 01434 682293**

Berryburn, Ancroft ✗✿ (Mr & Mrs W J Rogers-Coltman) 5m S of Berwick. Take Ancroft Mill Rd off A1 for 1m;

drive entrance 2nd turn on R beside council bridge. 4 acres created from wilderness since 1981. Mixed borders; shrubs; shrub roses; woodland walk alongside burn with developing wood garden. Partially suited for wheelchairs. TEA. *Adm £2 Chd free. Sun July 5 (2-5). Private visits welcome, please* **Tel 01289 387332**

Bide-a-Wee Cottage, Stanton ✗✿ (M Robson) 7m NNW of Morpeth. Turn L off A192 out of Morpeth at Fairmoor. Stanton is 6m along this road. Both a formal and informal garden developed out of a small stone quarry as well as some surrounding higher land. Natural rock is featured as are water and marsh areas. Garden contains mixed planting with a large number of perennial species. *Adm £1.75. Sats April 25 (1.30-4), Weds May 27, July 29 (2-5)*

▲**Chillingham Castle, Chillingham** ✗✿ (Sir Humphry Wakefield) Approx 16m N of Alnwick. Signposted from A1 and A697. Romantic grounds laid out by Sir Jeffrey Wyatville, fresh from his triumphs at Windsor Castle. Command views over the Cheviots and incl topiary gardens and woodland walk. Parkland and lake. TEAS. *Adm Castle and Grounds £3.90 Grounds only £2.80 Chd free. For NGS Sun June 28 (12-5)*

▲**Cragside, Rothbury** ✗✿ (The National Trust) 13m SW of Alnwick (B6341); 15m NW of Morpeth (B6344).

NORTHUMBERLAND

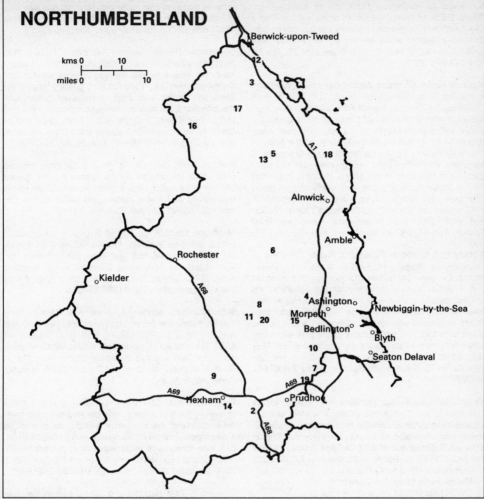

kms 0 — 10
miles 0 — 10

Berwick-upon-Tweed

12

3

17

16

13 5

A1

18

Alnwick

Amble

6

Rochester

Kielder

A68

8

11 20

1

4 Ashington

Morpeth

15

Bedlington

Newbiggin-by-the-Sea

Blyth

10

Seaton Delaval

9

7

A69 19

Hexham 14

2 Prudhoe

A68

KEY

1. Ashfield	7. 66 Darras Road
2. Beauclerc Lodge	8. Herterton House
3. Berryburn	9. Hexham Herbs
4. Bide-a-Wee Cottage	10. Kirkley Hall College
5. Chillingham Castle	11. Kirkwhelpington
6. Cragside	Village Gardens

12. Kiwi Cottage	18. Preston Tower
13. Lilburn Tower	19. Ravenside
14. Loughbrow House	20. Wallington
15. Meldon Park	
16. Mindrum	
17. Northumbria Nurseries	

Formal garden in the 'High Victorian' style created by the 1st Lord Armstrong with special features incl fully restored orchard house, carpet bedding, dahlia walk and fernery. 3½ acres of rock garden. Extensive grounds of over 1000 acres famous for rhododendrons and beautiful lakes. Restaurant. Shop. Grounds, Power Circuit and Armstrong Energy Centre. TEAS. *Adm House, Garden & Grounds £5.80; Garden & Grounds £3.80 Chd £1.90. Family ticket House, Garden & Grounds (2 adults & 2 chd) £15. For NGS Sun July 19 (10.30- 6.30). Large parties by appt, please* **Tel 01669 620150/620333**

66 Darras Road, Ponteland &❀ (Mr & Mrs D J Goodchild) SW of A696 at Ponteland. Turn L after crossing the R Pont. Travelling W, signposted Darras Hall. 1m on R. Medium-sized garden, owner designed and maintained, with herbaceous and shrub borders incl some unusual varieties. Conifers, kitchen garden, water garden and greenhouses. Bulbs in spring. TEA. *Adm £1.50 Chd free. Suns May 10, June 14, Aug 16 (2-6)*

▲**Herterton House, Hartington** ⋠❀ (Frank Lawley Esq) Cambo, Morpeth. 2m N of Cambo on the B6342 signposted to Hartington. (23m NW of Newcastle-on-Tyne). 1 acre of formal garden in stone walls around a C16 farmhouse. Incl a small topiary garden, physic garden, flower garden and a nursery garden. Planted since 1976. *Adm £2 Chd free. For NGS Thurs June 18, July 16, Aug 6 (1.30-5.30)*

Hexham Herbs, Chesters Walled Garden, Chollerford &⚘❀ 6m N of Hexham, off the B6318. ½m W from Chollerford by Chesters Roman Fort, take L turning signposted Fourstones and immed L through stone gateposts. 2-acre walled garden containing a very extensive collection of herbs. Raised thyme bank, home to the National Thyme Collection, Roman garden; National Collection of Marjoram. Elizabethan-style knot garden, gold and silver garden and collection of dye plants. Herbaceous borders contain many unusual plants and old-fashioned roses. Woodland walk with wildflowers and pond. Featured on BBC2's 'Gardener's World' and Channel 4's 'Over the Garden Wall'. Shop sells herbal gifts, honey and dried flowers. *Adm £1.50 Chd under 10 free. Sun May 17 (1-5)*

Kirkley Hall Gardens, Ponteland &⚘❀ 2½m NW of Ponteland on Morpeth rd. Turn L at main college entrance. Car park. These beautiful gardens and Victorian walled garden form a showcase for the gardening enthusiast. Walled garden with climbers, wall-trained fruit trees, borders and unusual and colourful herbaceous plants all grouped and labelled. Grounds contain shaped island beds following the contours of the land each composed for variety of profile and continuity of colour. TEA. *Adm £1.50 OAPs 70p family £3 Chd under 8 free. Sun July 12 (10-4). Private visits welcome, please* **Tel 01661 860808**

Kirkwhelpington Village Gardens ⚘❀ On A696 approx 10m N of Belsay. Turn R into village. A number of small gardens in an attractive village. Each garden entirely different with something of interest for everyone. Teas in village hall. *Combined adm £2 Chd free tickets at village hall (ACNO to Village Hall Fund®). Sun July 5 (1.30-5.30)*
   Cliff House (Mr & Mrs I Elliot)
   Middle Farm (Mr & Mrs T Lawson)
   The School House (Mr & Mrs F Young)
   Sike View (Prof & Mrs D Kinniment)
   Welburn (Prof D Wise)
   West House (Mr & Mrs C Scott)
   Whitridge House (Mr & Dr C Keating)

Kiwi Cottage, Scremerston &⚘❀ (Mrs D Smail) Kiwi Cottage is in the village of Scremerston, about 2½m due S of Berwick-upon-Tweed. It is the 1st house on the R hand side of the village, off the A1 rd coming from the S and the last house on the L hand side of the village when travelling S from Berwick-upon-Tweed. Entrance through gateway next to War Memorial. Please drive in and do not park on the rd. 3-acre garden with lawns, annuals, herbaceous plants, providing colour and interest throughout the year. Shrubs, orchard and large vegetable garden. *Adm £2 Chd 50p. Sun July 28 (2.30-5)*

Lilburn Tower, Alnwick ⚘❀ (Mr & Mrs D Davidson) 3m S of Wooler on A697. 10 acres of walled and formal gardens incl conservatory and large glass house. About 30 acres of woodland with walks and pond garden. Also ruins of Pele Tower and C15 Chapel. Rhododendrons and azaleas. TEAS. *Adm £2 Chd 50p under 8 free. Sun June 7 (2-6)*

Loughbrow House, Hexham &❀ (Mrs K A Clark) Take B6303 from Hexham, signed Blanchland, after ¼m take R hand fork, after a further ¼m you come to another fork, the lodge gates are in intersection. Garden ½m up the drive. Bog garden with pond. A woodland garden with rhododendrons and azaleas. Old-fashioned roses and a long bed of hybrid teas, 3 herbaceous borders, large area of lawns. An extensive kitchen garden and a paved courtyard. *Adm £2 Chd free. Weds May 27, June 24, July 22 (12-3)*

Meldon Park, Morpeth ⚘ (M J B Cookson) Situated 6½m W of Morpeth on B6343. Approx 8 acres, garden and woodland walks. Mature trees, rhododendrons, shrub borders and herbaceous borders and walled kitchen garden. TEA *Adm £2 Chd free. Sun June 7 (2-5)*

Mindrum, Cornhill on Tweed ❀ (Hon P J Fairfax) On B6352, 4m from Yetholm, 5m from Cornhill on Tweed. Old-fashioned roses; rock and water garden; shrub borders. Wonderful views along Bowmont Valley. Approx 3 acres. TEAS. *Adm £2 Chd 50p. Sun June 28 (2-6). Private visits welcome, please* **Tel 01890 850246**

■ **Northumbria Nurseries, Ford** &❀ Berwick upon Tweed. Follow the flower signs on the brown Ford Etal Heritage signs to Ford village, 10m N of Wooler, off A697. 1¾-acre walled garden incl display beds and growing areas. Teas available in village. *Open all year Mon to Fri (8-6, or dusk), March to Oct Sat, Sun (10-6, or dusk). Donations for NGS*

Preston Tower, Chathill &⚘❀ (Maj & Mrs T Baker Cresswell) 7m N of Alnwick, take the turn signed to Preston and Chathill. Preston Tower is at the top of a hill, in 1¼m. Mostly shrubs and woodland; daffodils and azaleas. C14 Pele Tower with great views from the top. TEAS. *Adm £2 Chd 50p (ACNO to local church®). Mon May 3 (2.30-5). Parties by appt, please* **Tel 016655 89210**

Ravenside, East Heddon ⚘❀ (Mrs J Barber) 9m from Newcastle on the A69 take the Heddon on the Wall B6528 turn off, at end of slip rd turn R under bridge then L to East Heddon. 3rd house on R. ⅓-acre plantswoman's garden filled with shrubs, shrub roses, herbaceous borders, alpine, many in troughs and pond with bog area. TEAS. *Adm £2 Chd free. Sun July 5 (2-5). Private visits welcome, please* **Tel 01661 825242**

▲**Wallington, Cambo** &❀ (The National Trust) From N 12m W of Morpeth (B6343); from S via A696 from Newcastle, 6m W of Belsay, B6342 to Cambo. Walled, terraced garden with fine shrubs and species roses; conservatory with magnificent fuchsias; 100 acres woodland and lakes. House dates from 1688 but altered, interior greatly changed c.1740; exceptional rococo plasterwork by Francini brothers; fine porcelain, furniture, pictures, needlework, dolls' houses, museum, display of coaches. Tearoom. Shop. *Adm to Walled garden, garden and grounds £2.80 Chd £1.40. Last admission (5). For NGS Suns May 10, Aug 16 (10-7). Free guided walk at 2pm*

Nottinghamshire

Hon County Organisers: Mr & Mrs A R Hill, The White House, Nicker Hill, Keyworth NG12 5EA
Tel 0115 9372049
Assistant Hon County Organisers: Mr & Mrs J Nicholson, 38 Green Lane, Lambley, Nottingham NG4 4QE
Tel 0115 9312998
Hon County Treasurer: Mr J Gray, 43 Cliffway, Radcliffe-on-Trent NG12 1AQ
Tel 0115 9334272

DATES OF OPENING

Regular openings
For details see garden description

Felley Priory, Underwood
Hodsock Priory, Blyth
Holme Pierrepont Hall, Nottingham

March 22 Sunday
Hodsock Priory, Blyth
March 29 Sunday
Woodpecker Cottage, Girton
April 1 Wednesday
Woodpecker Cottage, Girton
April 5 Sunday
Morton Hall, Retford
Skreton Cottage, Screveton
April 12 Sunday
Felley Priory, Underwood
April 13 Monday
Gateford Hill Nursing Home
Holme Pierrepont Hall,
Nottingham
Mill Hill House, East Stoke
The Old Rectory, Kirkby in
Ashfield
April 26 Sunday
37 Loughborough Road,
Ruddington
May 3 Sunday
Southwell, Bishops Manor
14 Temple Drive, Nuthall
May 4 Monday
Mill Hill House, East Stoke
May 10 Sunday
Gringley on the Hill Gardens
(some)
Morton Hall, Retford
May 17 Sunday
7 Barratt Lane, Attenborough
Brackenhurst College,
Southwell
Roselea, Newark
May 18 Monday
7 Barratt Lane, Attenborough
May 19 Tuesday
7 Barratt Lane, Attenborough
Hodsock Priory, Blyth
May 20 Wednesday
The Beeches, Milton, Tuxford

Hodsock Priory, Blyth
May 21 Thursday
Hodsock Priory, Blyth
May 23 Saturday
The Beeches, Milton, Tuxford
May 24 Sunday
Laurel Farm,
Stanton-on-the-Wolds
Rose Cottage, 82 Main Road,
Underwood
The White House, Keyworth
May 27 Wednesday
Mill Hill House, East Stoke
May 30 Saturday
Hucknall Gardens
May 31 Sunday
Epperstone Gardens (some)
Hucknall Gardens
Papplewick Hall, Papplewick
Park Farm, Normanton
June 7 Sunday
7 Barratt Lane, Attenborough
June 8 Monday
7 Barratt Lane, Attenborough
June 9 Tuesday
7 Barratt Lane, Attenborough
June 14 Sunday
Canal Turn, Retford
Epperstone Gardens (some)
Gardeners Cottage, Papplewick
Gringley-on-the Hill Gardens
Manor House, Gonalston
Upton & Headon Gardens
Woodbine Cottage, Granby
June 21 Sunday
Askham Gardens
Baxter Farm, Willoughby on the
Wolds
Park Farm, Normanton
Rose Cottage, 82 Main Road,
Underwood
June 25 Thursday
Holme Pierrepont Hall,
Nottingham
June 28 Sunday
Felley Priory, Underwood
Mill Hill House, East Stoke
Norwell Gardens
July 5 Sunday
Sutton Bonington Hall, Sutton
Bonington

Thrumpton Hall, Nottingham
Woodpecker Cottage, Girton
July 8 Wednesday
Woodpecker Cottage, Girton
July 12 Sunday
Brackenhurst College,
Southwell
Burton Joyce Gardens
Roselea, Newark
14 Temple Drive, Nuthall
July 19 Sunday
Canal Turn, Retford
The Old Rectory, Kirkby in
Ashfield
Rose Cottage, 82 Main Road,
Underwood
July 26 Sunday
The White House, Keyworth
August 9 Sunday
Rose Cottage, 82 Main Road,
Underwood
August 23 Sunday
Hucknall Gardens
August 31 Monday
Mill Hill House, East Stoke
September 6 Sunday
Rose Cottage, 82 Main Road,
Underwood
September 23 Wednesday
Mill Hill House, East Stoke
October 18 Sunday
Morton Hall, Retford

Regular openings. Open
throughout the year. They are
listed at the beginning of the
Diary Section.

By Appointment Gardens.
These owners do not have a fixed
opening day usually because they
cannot accommodate large numbers or have insufficient parking
space.

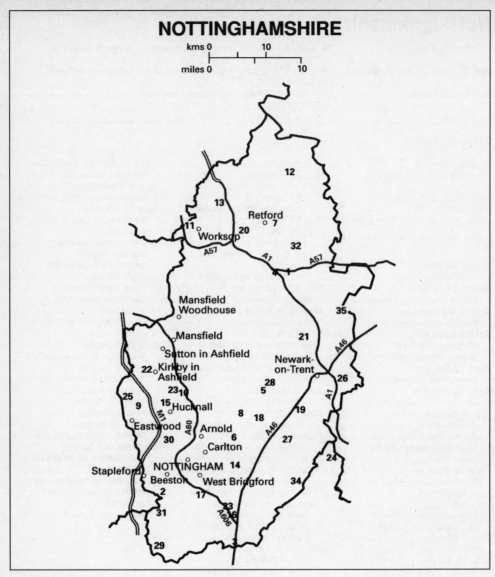

NOTTINGHAMSHIRE

kms 0   10
miles 0   10

12

13

Retford 7

11 Worksop 20

A57   A1   A57

32

4

Mansfield
Woodhouse

35

Mansfield

21

A46

Sutton in Ashfield

Newark-
on-Trent

22 Kirkby in
Ashfield

26

A1

23 10

28

5

25

9 15 Hucknall

8 18

19

Eastwood

A60

Arnold

A46

30

6

27

Carlton

24

Stapleford

NOTTINGHAM 14

Beeston West Bridgford

34

2

17

33

31

A606

16

29

3

KEY

1. Askham Gardens
2. 7 Barratt Lane
3. Baxter Farm
4. The Beeches
5. Brackenhurst College
6. Burton Joyce Gardens
7. Canal Turn
8. Epperstone Gardens
9. Felley Priory
10. Gardeners Cottage
11. Gateford Hill Nursing Home
12. Gringley-on-the Hill Gardens

13. Hodsock Priory
14. Holme Pierrepont Hall
15. Hucknall Gardens
16. Laurel Farm
17. 37 Loughborough Road
18. The Manor House
19. Mill Hill House
20. Morton Hall
21. Norwell Gardens
22. The Old Rectory
23. Papplewick Hall
24. Park Farm

25. Rose Cottage
26. Roselea
27. Skreton Cottage
28. Southwell, Bishops Manor
29. Sutton Bonington Hall
30. 14 Temple Drive
31. Thrumpton Hall
32. Upton & Headon
       Gardens
33. The White House
34. Woodbine Cottage
35. Woodpecker Cottage

DESCRIPTIONS OF GARDENS

Askham Gardens, Markham Moor &⚭ On A638 between Markham Moor and Gamston, in Rockley village turn E to Askham. Wide variety of pleasant English village gardens. TEAS at Manor Lodge. *Combined adm £2 Chd free (ACNO to Askham Church®). Sun June 21 (2-6)*
   Nursery House (Mr & Mrs D Bird)
   Stone Lea (Mr & Mrs J Kelly)
   Villosa ✿ (Mr T Townrow)
   Manor Lodge (Mr & Mrs Kelly Bloom)

7 Barratt Lane, Attenborough &✿ (Mrs D Lucking & Mr & Mrs S J Hodkinson) Beeston, 6m SW of Nottingham. Off A6005 nr Attenborough Station. ¾-acre established plantsman's garden. Mature trees, unusual flowering shrubs, bulbs, hostas, bearded irises and clematis. Children welcome. *Adm £1.20 Chd 40p (ACNO to St Mary's Church®). Suns May 17, June 7 (11-6), Mons May 18, June 8 (3-8), Tues May 19, June 9 (3-8)*

Baxter Farm, Willoughby on the Wolds &✿ (Dr & Mrs Peter Tatham) 10m S of Nottingham, 12m N of Leicester. About ½m off A46 at the E end of Main St. Old farmhouse and barns. 1-acre garden planted last 20 yrs. Conservatory, old cattle drinking pond now planted, herbaceous borders, informal plantings of old roses, irises, hardy geraniums and many climbers. Pergola in beech and yew hedged walks. Kitchen garden. TEAS. *Adm £1.20 Chd free. Sun June 21 (2-6)*

The Beeches, Milton, Tuxford &⚭✿ (Margaret & Jim Swindin) 12m N of Newark. Off A1 at Markham Moor roundabout take Walesby sign into village (1m). Garden for all seasons developed organically from a wilderness with wild life in mind. 1 acre with 2-acre hay meadow. Mature trees, shrubs, herbaceous, climbing and alpine plants. Pond, small woodland with bulbs and shade loving plants. Vegetables in raised beds and tunnel. Top and soft fruit. Adj Mausoleum grounds also open. TEAS. *Adm £1.20 Chd free. Wed, Sat May 20, 23 (2-5.30)*

Brackenhurst College, Southwell &✿ (The Secretary) Brackenhurst 1m S of Southwell on A612. Ornamental shrubs, lawns, rose, sunken, and walled gardens, glasshouses, views. Organic vegetable plot. Wheelchair users please notify in advance. TEAS. *Adm £1.50 Chd 50p. Suns May 17 (12-4.30) July 12 (12-5)*

Burton Joyce Gardens, Burton Joyce ✿ In Burton Joyce turn N off A612, Nottingham to Southwell Rd, into Lambley Lane, Bridle Rd ½m on R, an impassable looking rd. *Combined adm £1.80 Chd 50p. Sun July 12 (2-6)*
   Dumbleside, 17 Bridle Road &✿ (Mr & Mrs C P Bates) 1-acre mixed borders, woodland slopes, stream and water garden wth naturalised ferns, primulas, hostas and moisture loving plants. Terrace and orchard with spring and summer bulbs. *Private visits welcome, please* Tel 0115 9313725
   61 Lambley Lane ✿ (Mr & Mrs R B Powell) Approx ⅔-acre of spring flowering plants; shrubs, azaleas; bulbs and trees; mixed borders

Canal Turn, Retford &⚭✿ (Mr & Mrs H M Healey) Welham Rd. A620 Retford to Gainsborough Rd, nearly opp 'Hop Pole' public house 1m Retford roundabout. True plantsman's garden 3¼ acres. Developing arboretum 1,000 trees, shrubs, many rare and unusual. Several water features incl large wildlife pond. Shrubberies, rockeries, herb, rose and conifer beds. Gazebo, pergola, trellis, many honeysuckle, clematis, grasses, bamboo. Large fruit and veg area. TEA in aid of Notts Wildlife Trust. *Adm £1.50 Chd 50p. Suns June 14, July 19 (2-5). Private visits welcome, please* Tel 01777 711449

Epperstone Gardens 8m NE Nottingham off A6097 between Lowdham and Oxton. Parking opp Cross Keys. *Combined adm £1.50 Chd free (ACNO to Epperstone Church Organ Fund©). Hazelwych and White Gates, Sun May 31 (2-6) and The Old Rectory and Hill House, Sun June 14 (2-6)*
   Hazelwych (Mr P J Clark) ½-acre, trees, shrubbery, pond and alpine terrace
   White Gates &✿ (Mrs V Pilsworth) 2 acre rhododendrons, azaleas, heathers, shrubbery, herbs and orchard. Parking in field opp White Gates
   The Old Rectory ✿ (Mr & Mrs Cedric Coates) Enter from churchyard. Approx 2 acres mature garden in superb setting incl lawns, borders, herbaceous, mature yews forming 'The Dark Walk'. Lovely sculptured large box hedge. New enclosed herb and salad garden
   Hill House (Mrs J M Sketchley) 1½ acres incl herbaceous border; formal rose garden; shrub roses and herb garden

■ **Felley Priory, Underwood** &✿ (The Hon Mrs Chaworth Musters) 8m SW Mansfield, off A608 ½m W M1 junction 27. Old-fashioned garden round Elizabethan house. Orchard of daffodils, herbaceous borders, pond. Topiary, rose garden. Unusual plants and shrubs for sale. Refreshments. Teas in aid of Marie Curie Cancer Care. *Adm £1.50 Chd free. Weds March 11, 25, April 8, 22, May 13, 27, June 10, 24, July 8, 22, August 12, 26, Sept 9, 23, Oct 14, 28 (9-4). For NGS Sundays April 12, June 28 (11-4). Private visits welcome except Mondays, for parties of 15 min, please* Tel 01773 810230

Gardeners Cottage, Papplewick &&❀ (Mrs J Hildyard) Nr Papplewick Hall. 6m N of Nottingham off A60. Interesting old-fashioned garden of 1½ acres with 150yd long border, shrub and rhododendrons; shrub roses. Large rockery and water feature. *Adm £1.50 Chd 25p. Sun June 14 (2-6)*

Gateford Hill Nursing Home, Worksop &❀ 1m N of Worksop on A57. Nursing home is well signed from main rd. Impressive house built 1860. Large walled garden. Spectacular display of daffodils with many varieties. A fine collection of mature, native and evergreen trees. Cream TEAS and plants. *Adm £1.20 Chd 50p. Mon April 13 (1-5)*

Gringley on the Hill Gardens, Bawtry 6m E of Bawtry, 5m W of Gainsborough on A631. Cream teas in aid of Gringley Church. *Combined adm £2 Chd 50p. Gringley Hall and Honeysuckle Cottage open Suns May 10 and June 14 (2-5). The Old Vicarage Sun June 14 only (2-5)*
    Gringley Hall &&❀ (Mr & Mrs I Threlfall) 2-acre walled English country garden, several mixed borders - different colour themes. Large rose collection; dry/Mediterranean and water gardens. Attractive potager. *Private visits welcome Weds and Suns, please* Tel **01777 817262**
    Honeysuckle Cottage &❀ (Miss J E Towler) Approx ¼-acre traditional small terraced cottage garden with mixed borders. Interesting loose laid chevron brick wall; paths of river boulders and brick
    ¶**The Old Vicarage** ❀ (John and Helena Simmonds). Interesting 3-acre garden, partly Victorian with rising terraced formal rose garden. Orchard and paddock. Views. (*only open June 14*)

■**Hodsock Priory, Blyth** && (Sir Andrew & Lady Buchanan) Off B6045, Blyth-Worksop rd approx 2m from Al. Share the beauty and peace of a traditional 5-acre private garden on the historic Domesday site. Sensational snowdrops, massed daffodils, bluebell wood, fine trees, mixed borders, roses, lilies, ponds. *Adm £2.50 Chd free and visitors in wheelchairs. Open daily for 4 weeks Feb/March (10-4). Dates depend on weather, check by tel first. Hot refreshments. Every Tues, Wed & Thurs April to Aug (1-5). For NGS Sun March 22, Tues, Wed, Thurs May 19, 20, 21 (1-5). All enquiries to Lady Buchanan* Tel **01909 591204**

■**Holme Pierrepont Hall** &❀ (Mr & Mrs Robin Brackenbury) From A52 Nottingham/Grantham rd follow signs to National Water Sports Centre for 1½m. Formal listed Courtyard Garden (1875) enclosed by early Tudor house incls lawns, flower beds, elaborate box parterre, possibly influenced Nesfield. Contemporary planting of shrub roses, herbs, herbaceous plants fit into authentic early framework. E of house clipped yews, shrubs and long June border of old-fashioned roses. TEAS. *Adm £1.50 Chd 50p (ACNO to ADA Sarah Matheson Trust®). Every Sun June, July, Aug; Tues Aug, Thurs July, Aug, Fridays Aug. For NGS Mon April 13, Thurs June 25 (2-5.30)*

¶**Hucknall Gardens, Hucknall** ❀ Approx 1m N of Hucknall market place on A611 Annesley Rd turn opp Jet Service Station into Victoria St. Two 80' long narrow

gardens, one with Japanese influences and a pebble sun design inspired by Zeneca Garden Chelsea, showing differing ways of making full use of available space. Ponds, variety of climbers, unusual plants and patio. *Combined adm £1.90 Chd 10p. Sat, Sun May 30, 31, Sun Aug 23 (1-5)*
    ¶**32 Victoria St** (Perri Morton)
    ¶**32a Victoria St** (Louise Hickman)

¶**Laurel Farm, Stanton-on-the-Wolds** (Mrs Val Moffat) Browns Lane. Approx 7m SE of Nottingham. From A606 turn at Fina Garage onto Browns Lane; ½m on RHS. Peaceful country garden of about ⅔ acre. Re-developed over last 4yrs. Pond, bog, gravel areas and raised beds. Gunnera, Gingko and many rare and unusual shrubs and plants. Courtyard area. TEAS, cake stall in aid of Stanton Church. *Adm £1.20 Chd free. Sun May 24 (2-5)*

37 Loughborough Road, Ruddington (Mr & Mrs B H C Theobald) 4m S of Nottingham via A60 Loughborough Rd, cross A52 Ring Rd at Nottingham Knight. Take 1st L 400yds beyond roundabout and immed L again up Old Loughborough Rd. 1-acre garden with many unusual varieties of spring bulbs, perennials, shrubs and trees in borders, island beds, shady walk and walled patio. Featured ITV Surprise Gardeners 1997. *Adm £1.50 Chd free. Sun April 26 (2-5). Private visits welcome by appt, please* Tel **0115 984 1152**

The Manor House, Gonalston &❀ (Mr & Mrs John Langford) ⅛m on the N-side of A612 between Lowdham and Southwell. Walled C17 farmhouse in centre of village. ¾-acre garden made from farmyard over past 25yrs by present owners. Pergolas, terraces, obelisks, Irish yews, box hedges, ponds used to give formality and to divide garden into separate areas. Enthusiasm for herbaceous plants, climbers, shrubs and their propagation. TEAS and plants in aid of Amnesty International (British Section). *Adm £1.50 Chd 50p. Sun June 14 (2-5)*

Mill Hill House, East Stoke &❀ (Mr & Mrs R J Gregory) Elston Lane. 5m S of Newark on A46 turn to Elston. Garden ½m on R. Entrance through nursery car park. ½-acre country garden close to the site of the Battle of East Stoke (1487). A series of small gardens closely planted with many unusual hardy/half hardy plants provide yr-round interest and a tranquil atmosphere. Featured on TV. Teas in Newark. *Adm £1.20 Chd free. Weds May 27, Sept 23, Sun June 28, Mons April 13, May 4, Aug 31 (10-6). Private visits welcome, please* Tel **01636 525460**

Morton Hall, Retford &❀ (Lady Mason) 4m W of Retford. Entrance on Link Rd from A620 to S bound A1. Spring woodland garden, flowering shrubs, rhododendrons, azaleas, specimen trees; pinetum in park, cedars and cypresses. Bulbs, autumn colour. Picnics. Partly suitable for wheelchairs. TEAS in aid of Ranby Church. *Adm £2.50 per car or £1.50 per person whichever is least. Suns April 5, May 10, Oct 18 (2-6). Also groups by appt, please* Tel **01777 701142**

Norwell Gardens & 6m N of Newark off A1 at Cromwell turning. Gardens incorporating colourful planting schemes, unusual climbers, plantsman's garden, well

stocked ponds, aviary. Vintage bus between gardens. TEAS in aid of Beaumond House Hospice. *Combined adm £1.80 Chd free. Sun June 28 (2-5.30)*
  Norwell Nurseries ❀ (Andrew Ward)
  1 Marston Cottage (Mr & Mrs B Shaw)
  Climsland (C Read)
  The Beeches (Mrs Edna Batty)

The Old Rectory, Kirkby in Ashfield &❀ (Mr & Mrs M F Brown) Adjacent to St Wilfrids Church on B6018, 1½m W of Kirkby town centre. Ample parking. 2½-acre garden restored, constantly evolving. New scented garden and 'outside living' area being developed. Mature trees, many new varieties of plants; spring flowers. Hosta haven. Teas in Church Hall in aid of St Wilfrids Church. *Adm £1.50 Chd free. Easter Mon April 13, Sun July 19 (2-5)*

Papplewick Hall, Papplewick (Dr & Mrs R B Godwin-Austen) North end of Papplewick Village on B683, 7m N of Nottingham off the A60. Parking at Hall. Woodland garden of approx 8 acres underplanted with rhododendrons; spring bulbs and hostas. *Adm £2 Chd £1 (ACNO to St James Church, Papplewick®). Sun May 31 (2-5)*

Park Farm, Normanton &❀❀ (Mr & Mrs John E Rose) Bottesford. Half way between Bottesford and Long Bennington on A1 side of Normanton village on old Normanton Airfield. 3-acre garden, developed since 1987; formal and mixed borders; natural and formal ponds; small lakes seeded with wild flowers scree gardens and small woodland area. Mature trees moved to flat open field prior to the creation of garden. Large scented, colour co-ordinated herb garden. TEAS. *Adm £1.50 Chd free. Suns May 31, June 21 (2-6)*

Rose Cottage, 82 Main Rd, Underwood ❀❀ (Mr & Mrs Allan Lowe) 1½m from junction 27 M1. Take B608 to Heanor. Join B600; after about 200-300yds turn R into Main Rd by large sign for 'the Hole in the Wall' Inn. Flower arranger's cottage garden with ponds; shrubs; small secret garden. Rear garden of approx 1,000 sq yds with surprise features, partly developed from a field over last few years; goat and other animals. Various flowers for showing; greenhouses; aviary. TEAS. *Adm £1.20 Chd free. Suns May 24, June 21, July 19, Aug 9, Sept 6 (2-6)*

¶**Roselea, Newark** ❀❀ (Bruce & Marian Richmond) Old Newark Road, Coddington. 1½m E of Newark. Leave A1 signed Coddington. 100yds from junction N; 300yds from junction S. Medium-sized cottage style closely planted plantsmans garden. Colour all year round. Many unusual plants, esp clematis, 150 hardy geraniums. Pots and alpines. Plants propagated from garden for stall. *Adm £1.20 Chd free. Suns May 17, July 12 (2-6). Private visits welcome, please* **Tel 01636 76737**

Skreton Cottage, Screveton &❀ (Mr & Mrs J S Taylor) 8m SW of Newark, 12m E of Nottingham. From A46 Fosse Rd turn E to Car Colston; L at green and on for 1m. 1¾-acre mature garden, created during the last 30yrs to be a 'garden for all seasons' with separate areas of different character. Fine display spring bulbs old and English roses, wide variety of trees, shrubs herbaceous plants; spacious lawns, pool, orchard, kitchen garden, green-

houses and many interesting design features. TEAS and plants in aid of St Wilfrid's Church, Screveton. *Adm £1.50 Chd free. Sun April 5 (2-6)*

Southwell, Bishops Manor ♿ (The Rt Rev the Lord Bishop of Southwell & Mrs Harris) End of Bishops Drive on S side of Minster. The house is built into a part of the old medieval Palace of the Archbishops of York. The ruins form a delightful enclosed garden, lawns, 4 seasons tree garden, orchard and vegetable garden. Rockery, attractive borders in an unusual setting. Herb knot garden and other features under development. TEAS in aid of Mirasol Charitable Trust. *Adm £1.50 Chd free. Sun May 3 (2-5)*

Sutton Bonington Hall &❀ (Anne, Lady Elton) 5m NW of Loughborough, take A6 to Kegworth, turn R (E) onto A6006. 1st L (N) for Sutton Bonington into Main St. Approx 5 acres highly individual formal garden. Strong design informally planted with restricted colour palette (white, yellow, green). Topiary, long variegated leaf border. Queen Anne House (not open) Conservatory (1810) planted in white. Plant stall. Picnics. TEA. *Adm £1.50 Chd 50p (ACNO to St Michael's & St Ann's Church, Sutton Bonington®). Sun July 5 (12-5.30). Also open for Leicestershire*

14 Temple Drive, Nuthall &❀ (Tom & Margaret Leafe) 4m NW of Nottingham. From M1 leave at junction 26, A610 towards Nottingham. Circle 1st roundabout in A6002 then Nottm Rd lane, leave on minor rd. From Nottingham take A610, turning at Broxtowe Inn, Cinderhill. Parking restricted, use Nottingham rd. ⅓-acre garden with herbaceous borders; island beds, ornamental trees, shrubs; troughs; old-fashioned roses; clematis. Fruit, vegetable garden. TEAS, cake stall in aid of The Cats Protection League. *Adm £1.20 Chd 50p. Suns May 3, July 12 (2-5.30). For private visits* **Tel 0115 9271118**

Thrumpton Hall, Nottingham &❀ (The Hon Mrs Rosemary Seymour) 8m SW of Nottingham. W of A453; 3m from M1 at Exit 24. Large lawns; massive yew hedges; rare shrubs; C17 larches, cedars, planted to commemorate historic events since George III. Lake. Early Jacobean house shown. NO DOGS in house. TEA. *Adm to Garden £1 Chd 50p; House £2 extra Chd £1 (ACNO to Museum of Garden History®). Sun July 5 (2.30-6)*

Upton & Headon Gardens &❀ On A638 S of Retford turn L to Grove or in Eaton Village turn L to Upton. Adjoining villages, varied cottage gardens, incl wild flower meadow, specialist herb garden. TEAS. *Combined adm £1.50 Chd free. Sun 14 June (2-6)*
Headon
  Greenspotts (Mr & Mrs Dolby)
  The Homestead (Mr & Mrs Brailsford)
Upton
  Manor House (Mr & Mrs Walker) Plants in aid of Headon Church
  Willowholme Herb Farm (Mr & Mrs Farr) *Private visits welcome, please* **Tel 01777 248053**

The White House, Keyworth ❀❀ (Mr & Mrs Tony Hill) Nicker Hill. Approx 8m SE Nottingham. From A6006 at Stanton-on-the-Wolds, by Fina Garage, turn into Browns

Lane; follow road into Nicker Hill. ¾-acre overlooking fields. Semi-walled paved area, many pots. Brick pergola, water/bog garden. Rich colour coordinated informal packed planting; rare trees, shrubs, climbers, herbaceous, especially clematis, geraniums, grasses. Tender plants many unexpectedly thriving outside in E midlands. Large plant stall. Teas available nearby. *Adm £1.20 Chd free. Suns May 24, July 26 (2-5). Also private visits welcome, please* Tel 0115 9372049

Woodbine Cottage, Granby ✗ (Erika & Stuart Humphreys) 14m E of Nottingham on A52 Nottingham-Grantham. Turn S 1m E of Bingham signed Granby 2½m. Small, de-veloping, traditional cottage garden, closely planted, un-usual plants. *Adm £1.20 Chd free. Sun June 14 (1.30-5.30)*

Woodpecker Cottage, Girton ⅗✗❀ (Mr & Mrs Roy Hill) 6m N of Newark W off A1133. 1st cottage on R in village. Approx 1 acre interestingly designed and de-veloped by owners, many unusual plants, trees, shrubs, water garden. Delphiniums and roses feature in summer, gravel and grass paths lead to secluded areas. French potage garden, field with indigenous trees, wild flowers. TEAS in aid of St Cecilia's Church, Girton. *Adm £1.20 Chd free. Suns, Weds March 29, April 1, July 5, 8 (2-5.30). Private group visits welcome, please* Tel 01522 778759

SYMBOLS USED IN THIS BOOK (See also Page 17)

¶   Opening for the first time.

❀   Plants/produce for sale if available.

⅗   Gardens with at least the main features accessible by wheelchair.

✗   No dogs except guide dogs.

●   These gardens advertise their own dates in this publication although they do not nominate specific days for the NGS. Not all the money collected by these gardens comes to the NGS but they do make a guaranteed contribution.

■   These gardens nominate specific days for the NGS and advertise their own dates in this publication.

▲   These gardens open regularly to the public but they do not advertise their own dates in this publication. For further details, contact the garden directly.

Crossroads

Crossroads is a charity which cares for carers. The National Gardens Scheme is delighted to include it in its list of beneficiaries. Some facts and figures:

- One in 7 of the adult population is caring for a relative or friend.

- Most of the carers are women.

- 20% of carers say they never get a break and 65% of carers say their health has suffered as a result of caring responsibilities.

- **Crossroads** employs over 4,000 staff who support and provide respite care for the carers.

- **Crossroads** supports 28,000 carers and provides nearly 3 million care hours per year.

- The contribution of carers saves tax payers over £30 billion per year.

Oxfordshire

Hon County Organisers:	Col & Mrs J C M Baker, Hartford Greys, Sandy Lane, Boars Hill, Oxford, OX1 5HN Tel 01865 739360
Hon County Treasurer:	Col J C M Baker
Assistant Hon County Organisers:	
Vale of the White Horse & SW Oxon (Abingdon, Bampton, Faringdon & Wantage areas)	Mrs D J Faulkner, Haugh House, Longworth, Abingdon OX13 5DX Tel 01865 820286
N Oxon (Banbury, Charlbury and Chipping Norton areas)	Mr & Mrs B A Murphy, Hundley Cottage, Hundley Way, Charlbury OX7 3QU Tel 01608 810549
S Oxon (Didcot, Goring, Henley and Wallingford areas)	Mr & Mrs R J Baldwin, Northfield Cottage, High Street, Long Wittenham OX14 4QJ Tel 01865 407258
E Oxon (Headington, Iffley, Bicester, Kidlington, Steeple Aston & Thame areas)	Mr & Mrs J Lankester, Park Wall, Otmoor Lane, Beckley, Oxford OX3 9TB Tel 01865 351312
W Oxon (Witney, Burford & Woodstock areas), Central Oxford & Colleges	Mrs M Curtis, Bradwell, Blackditch, Stanton Harcourt, Witney OX8 1SB Tel 01865 881957
Editor & Advertising Manager:	Mrs P G Pinney, Pond House, Pyrton, Watlington OX9 5A1 Tel 01491 612638

DATES OF OPENING

Regular openings

For telephone number and other details see garden descriptions. Private visits welcomed.

Brook Cottage, Alkerton, nr Banbury
The Clock House, Coleshill
Kingston Bagpuize House, Abingdon
4 Northfield Cottages, Water Eaton
Old Church House, Wantage
Stansfield, Stanford-in-the-Vale
Stanton Harcourt Manor, Stanton Harcourt
Waterperry Gardens, nr Wheatley

By appointment only

For details see garden descriptions

23 Beech Croft Road, Summertown
Clematis Corner, Shillingford
14 Lavender Place, Carterton
Mount Skippet, Ramsden
Yeomans, Tadmarton

February 22 Sunday
Broadwell House, nr Lechlade
March 8 Sunday
Greystone Cottage, Kingwood Common
March 12 Thursday
Greystone Cottage, Kingwood Common

March 19 Thursday
Greystone Cottage, Kingwood Common
March 22 Sunday
Ashbrook House, Blewbury
Magdalen College, Oxford
Wadham College, Oxford
April 4 Saturday
Blenheim Palace, Woodstock
April 5 Sunday
Blenheim Palace, Woodstock
Broughton Poggs & Filkins Gardens
Buckland, nr Faringdon
The Mill House, Sutton Courtenay
25 Newfield Road, Sonning Common
Pettifers, Wardington
Shotover House, nr Wheatley
Tadmarton Gardens
April 9 Thursday
Greystone Cottage, Kingwood Common
April 12 Sunday
Bignell House, Chesterton
The Manor House, Clifton Hampden
Town Farm Cottage, Kingston Blount
April 13 Monday
Broadwell Gardens, nr Lechlade
Brook Cottage, Alkerton, nr Banbury
Epwell Mill, nr Banbury

Kencot Gardens, nr Lechlade
April 16 Thursday
Greystone Cottage, Kingwood Common
April 19 Sunday
Holywell Manor, Oxford
Lime Close, Drayton
The Mill House, Stadhampton
The Old Rectory, Coleshill
April 25 Saturday
Garsington Manor. nr Oxford
April 26 Sunday
Kingston Bagpuize House, nr Abingdon
Shellingford House, nr Faringdon
Stanton Harcourt Manor, Stanton Harcourt
Troy & Gould's Grove Farmhouse, Ewelme
Wick Hall & Nurseries, Radley
May 3 Sunday
Adderbury Gardens
May 4 Monday
Brook Cottage, Alkerton, nr Banbury
May 10 Sunday
Greystone Cottage, Kingwood Common
The Manor House, Sutton Courtenay
Stansfield, Stanford-in-the-Vale
May 14 Thursday
Greystone Cottage, Kingwood Common

OXFORDSHIRE

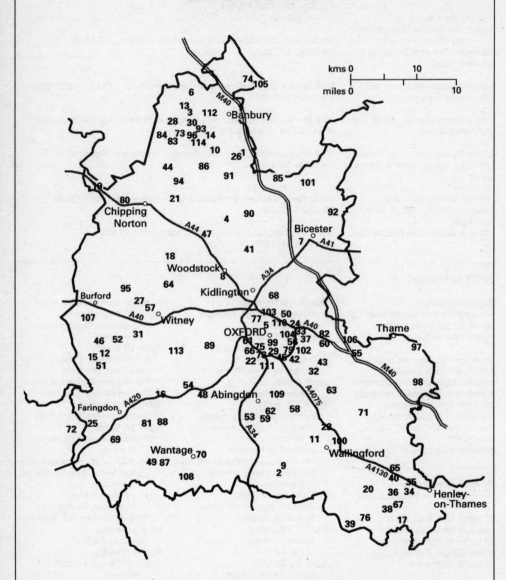

kms 0   10

miles 0   10

74 105

6

13
3   112
28   30
84 73 96 93   14
83   114
10   26 1
M40
Banbury

44   86
94   91
85   101
19
80   21
Chipping
Norton   A44
4   90   92
47
Bicester
41   7   A41
18
64   8   A34
Woodstock
95   Kidlington   68
Burford   27   57
107   A40
Witney   103   50
77   5   110 24 A40
OXFORD   104   82   106   Thame
46   52   31   61   33   37   60
15   12   89   99   56   102   55   97
51   113   66 75 29 79
22   111   96 42   43
54   16   32
Faringdon   A420   48   Abingdon   109   63
72   25   81   88   53   62   58   71   98
69   59
Wantage   28   11   100
49   87   70   Wallingford
108   9   A4130   65
2   40   35
20   36   34   Henley-
38   67   on-Thames
39   76   17

The maps in this book are designed to help visitors by showing
the approximate locations of gardens within each county. The
locations are not necessarily precise, particularly where gardens
are in clusters. Detailed directions to each garden can be found
in the garden descriptions.

KEY

1. Adderbury Gardens
2. Ashbrook House
3. Balscote Gardens
4. Barton Abbey
5. 23 Beech Croft Road
6. Bellevue
7. Bignell House
8. Blenheim Palace
9. Blewbury Gardens
10. Bloxham Gardens
11. Brightwell-cum-Sotwell Gardens
12. Broadwell House
13. Brook Cottage
14. Broughton Castle
15. Broughton Poggs & Filkins
    Gardens
16. Buckland
17. Chalkhouse Green Farm
18. Charlbury Gardens
19. Chastleton Glebe Gardens
20. Checkendon Court
21. Chivel Farm
22. Christ Church
23. Clematis Corner
24. Corpus Christi
25. Clock House
26. Colegrave Seeds Ltd
27. Dundon House
28. Epwell Mill
29. Exeter College
30. Fiveways Cottage
31. Friars Court
32. Garsington Manor
33. Green College
34. Green Place
35. Greys Court
36. Greystone Cottage
37. Headington Gardens
38. Hearns House
39. Heron's Reach
40. Highmoor Hall
41. Hill Court
42. Holywell Manor
43. Home Close
44. Hook Norton Manor
45. Iffley Gardens
46. Kencot Gardens
47. Kiddington Hall
48. Kingston Bagpuize House
49. Kingstone Lisle Park
50. Lady Margaret Hall
51. Langford Gardens
52. 14 Lavender Place
53. Lime Close
54. Longworth Gardens
55. Lower Chilworth Farm
56. Magdalen College
57. Manor Farm
58. The Manor House, Clifton
    Hampden
59. The Manor House, Sutton
    Courtenay
60. The Manor House, Wheatley
61. Merton College
62. The Mill House, Sutton
    Courtenay
63. The Mill House,
    Stadhampton
64. Mount Skippett
65. Nettlebed Gardens
66. New College
67. 25 Newfield Road
68. 4 Northfield Cottages
69. Nutford Lodge
70. Old Church House
71. The Old Rectory, Brightwell
    Baldwin
72. The Old Rectory, Coleshill
73. Partway House
74. Pettifers
75. Queen's College
76. Querns
77. Rewley House
78. St Hilda's College
79. St John's Home
80. Salford Gardens
81. Shellingford House
82. Shotover House
83. Sibford Ferris Gardens
84. Sibford Gower Gardens
85. Souldern Gardens
86. South Newington Gardens
87. Sparsholt Manor
88. Stansfield
89. Stanton Harcourt Manor
90. Steeple & Middle Aston
    Gardens
91. Stonewalls
92. Stratton Audley Gardens
93. Swalcliffe Lea House
94. Swerford Park
95. Swinbrook House
96. Tadmarton Gardens
97. Towersey Manor
98. Town Farm Cottage
99. Trinity College
100. Troy & Gould's Grove
     Farmhouse
101. Tusmore Park
102. University Arboretum
103. Upper Wolvercote
     Gardens
104. Wadham College
105. Wardington Manor
106. Waterperry Gardens
107. Westwell Manor
108. White's Farm House
109. Wick Hall & Nurseries
110. Wolfson College
111. Wood Croft
112. Wroxton Gardens
113. Yelford Gardens
114. Yeomans

May 17 Sunday
The Clock House, Coleshill
Headington Gardens, Oxford
Kingstone Lisle Park, nr
    Wantage
Longworth Gardens
Pettifers, Wardington
Upper Wolvercote Gardens
Wardington Manor,
    Wardington
May 20 Wednesday
Towersey Manor, nr Thame
May 21 Thursday
Greystone Cottage, Kingwood
    Common
May 23 Saturday
Hearns House, Gallows Tree
    Common

May 24 Sunday
Barton Abbey, Steeple Barton
Bellevue, Hornton
Hearns House, Gallows Tree
    Common
Nutford Lodge, Longcot
St John's Home, Oxford
Wood Croft, Boars Hill
May 25 Monday
Brook Cottage, Alkerton, nr Banbury
Epwell Mill, nr Banbury
Hearns House, Gallows Tree
    Common
Lower Chilworth Farm, Milton
    Common
Nutford Lodge, Longcot
Sparsholt Manor, nr Wantage
Swerford Park, nr Chipping Norton

Wroxton Gardens
May 26 Tuesday
Nutford Lodge, Longcot
May 27 Wednesday
Nutford Lodge, Longcot
May 28 Thursday
Nutford Lodge, Longcot
May 29 Friday
Nutford Lodge, Longcot
May 30 Saturday
Greys Court, Rotherfield Greys
Nutford Lodge, Longcot
May 31 Sunday
Charlbury Gardens
Checkendon Court, Checkendon
Nettlebed Gardens
Nutford Lodge, Longcot
Partway House, Swalcliffe

June 1 Monday
Gothic House, Charlbury Gardens
June 2 Tuesday
Gothic House, Charlbury Gardens
June 3 Wednesday
Gothic House, Charlbury Gardens
June 4 Thursday
Greystone Cottage, Kingwood
Common
June 7 Sunday
Balscote Gardens, nr Banbury
Bloxham Gardens, nr Banbury
Friars Court, Clanfield
Sibford Ferris Gardens
South Newington Gardens, nr
Banbury
Stansfield, Stanford-in-the-Vale
University Arboretum, Nuneham
Courtenay
Waterperry Gardens, nr Wheatley
Wolfson College, Oxford
June 13 Saturday
Hill Court, Tackley
June 14 Sunday
Chalkhouse Green Farm, Kidmore
End
The Clock House, Coleshill
Hill Court, Tackley
The Manor House, Wheatley
The Mill House, Sutton
Courtenay
Sibford Gower Gardens
Stratton Audley Gardens
June 17 Wednesday
Sibford Gower Gardens
June 21 Sunday
Broughton Castle, nr Banbury
Green College, Oxford
Iffley Gardens, S Oxford
Kiddington Hall, Woodstock
Langford Gardens, nr Lechlade
Lime Close, Drayton
Lower Chilworth Farm, Milton
Common (Evening)
St Hilda's College, Oxford
Salford Gardens, nr Chipping
Norton
Souldern Gardens
Stanton Harcourt Manor, Stanton
Harcourt

White's Farm House, Letcombe
Bassett
Yelford Gardens
June 24 Wednesday
Towersey Manor, nr Thame
June 28 Sunday
Blewbury Gardens
Exeter & New Colleges, Oxford
Green Place, Rotherfield Greys
Kencot House, Kencot, nr
Lechlade
Manor Farm, Old Minster Lovell
Manor Farm, Kencot, nr Lechlade
New College, Oxford
Querns, Goring Heath
Steeple & Middle Aston
Gardens
July 4 Saturday
Nutford Lodge, Longcot
July 5 Sunday
Dundon House, Minster Lovell
Nutford Lodge, Longcot
Swalcliffe Lea House
Westwell Manor, nr Burford
July 12 Sunday
Brightell-cum-Sotwell Gardens, nr
Wallingford
Chastleton Glebe Gardens
Headington Gardens, Oxford
Heron's Reach,
Whitchurch-on-Thames
Lady Margaret Hall, Oxford
25 Newfield Road, Sonning
Common
The Old Rectory, Brightwell
Baldwin
Sibford Gower Gardens
Town Farm Cottage, Kingston
Blount
July 18 Saturday
Highmoor Hall, Nettlebed
July 19 Sunday
Balscote Gardens, nr Banbury
Fiveways Cottage, Shutford
Queen's & Wadham Colleges,
Oxford
Rewley House, Oxford
Stonewalls, Hempton, nr
Deddington
Swinbrook House, nr Burford

White's Farm House, Letcombe
Bassett
July 26 Sunday
Ashbrook House, Blewbury
Tusmore Park, Bicester
August 2 Sunday
Broughton Castle, nr Banbury
Chivel Farm, Heythrop
Home Close, Garsington
Shotover House, nr Wheatley
August 9 Sunday
Christ Church, Corpus Christi &
Merton College, Oxford
Headington Gardens, Oxford
Trinity College, Oxford
Waterperry Gardens, nr Wheatley
August 16 Sunday
Chalkhouse Green Farm,
Kidmore End
Colegrave Seeds Ltd, West
Adderbury
August 23 Sunday
Friars Court, Clanfield
August 30 Sunday
Salford Gardens, nr Chipping
Norton
August 31 Monday
Broadwell Gardens, nr Lechlade
Brook Cottage, Alkerton, nr
Banbury
Kencot Gardens, nr Lechlade
September 5 Saturday
Nutford Lodge, Longcot
September 6 Sunday
Epwell Mill, nr Banbury
Nutford Lodge, Longcot
September 13 Sunday
The Clock House, Coleshill
The Old Rectory, Coleshill
September 20 Sunday
Tadmarton Gardens
September 27 Sunday
Kingston Bagpuize House, nr
Abingdon
Pettifers, Wardington
October 4 Sunday
The Clock House, Coleshill
Garsington Manor. nr Oxford
Hook Norton Manor, Banbury
The Mill House, Sutton Courtenay

Scotland's Gardens Scheme

The National Gardens Scheme has a similar but quite separate counterpart in Scotland. Called Scotland's Gardens Scheme, it raises money for the Queen's Nursing Institute (Scotland), the Gardens Fund of the National Trust for Scotland and over 160 registered charities nominated by Garden Owners. The Handbook is available (£3.75 incl p&p) from Scotland's Gardens Scheme, 31 Castle Terrace, Edinburgh, EH1 2EL.

DESCRIPTIONS OF GARDENS

Adderbury Gardens J10 M25 S of A423 on A4260, 3m S of Banbury. A large village with many quaint lanes and a beautiful church. TEAS at Church House. *Combined adm £2.50 Chd free. Sun May 3 (2-6)*

    Berry Hill House &⚘&❀ (Mr & Mrs J P Pollard) Berry Hill Rd, off A4260 signed Milton, Bloxham, W Adderbury. 2-acre garden reclaimed since 1982. Mature trees; lawns; shrubbery; mixed herbaceous and shrub borders. Kitchen garden

    Sorbrook Manor (Mr & Mrs R Thistlethwayte) 3 acres, lawns with mature trees and shrubs running down to the bridge over the Sorbrook

    ¶**The Old Vicarage** &❀ (Mr & Mrs Peter Job) Georgian House in 2 acres of mature gardens and meadows. Newly created lake beyond

Arboretum See Oxford University Gardens under University Arboretum

Ashbrook House, Blewbury &❀ (Mr & Mrs S A Barrett) 4m SE of Didcot on A417; 3½-acre chalk garden with small lake, stream, spring bulbs herbaceous borders. TEAS. *Adm £1.50 Chd free. Suns March 22, July 26 (2-6)*

Balscote Gardens, nr Banbury Pretty hill village ½m off A422 5m W of Banbury. TEAS June 7 in Balscote in aid of Church (C14 St Mary Magdalene), July 19 at Shutford. *Combined adm (3 gdns) £2.50 Chd free. Suns June 7, July 19 (2-6)*

    Colbar ❀ (Mr & Mrs C Neville) Small terrace with prolifically planted pots. Water cascade with pool, shrubs, herbaceous plants, alpines and lawn. Well stocked vegetable garden

    Home Farm &❀ (Mr & Mrs G C Royle) C17 house and barn with attractive views from ½-acre closely planted elevated garden designed for yr-round interest with unusual plants, contrasting foliage, flowering shrubs, bulbs and perennials. Featured in The Garden, Sunday Express Magazine, A Guide to Garden Visits and Homes and Antiques Dec '97. *Adm £2. Private visits also welcome by appt, please* **Tel 01295 738194**

    Manor Cottage (Mrs P M Jesson) This is both a ⅓-acre garden crafted from a steep slope using local stone and treated timbers and a ⅔-acre woodland scheme. Variety of decorative trees and shrubs. 250 broad-leaved indigenous trees

Barton Abbey, Steeple Barton &❀ (Mrs R Fleming) On B4030; 1m Middle Barton; ½m from junction of A4260 and B4030. 4 acres lawns & garden under restoration; 3 acres of lake; fine trees; kitchen garden and glasshouses. Plants and home produce stall. TEAS. *Adm £2 Chd free. Sun May 24 (2-5)*

23 Beech Croft Road, Summertown ⚘ (Mrs A Dexter) Oxford. A 23yd by 7yd, south-facing, plant lover's paved garden of a terraced house has been made secluded by planting evergreen shrubs, roses and clematis all round the brick walls; the 2 herbaceous, 2 alpine, 2 shady beds all contain many unusual plants, shrubs, ferns; troughs filled with small alpines. NO push-chairs. *Adm £3. Private visits welcome April to Sept 30* **Tel 01865 56020**

Bellevue, Hornton ⚘❀ (Mr & Mrs E W Turner) Bell St. 6m NW of Banbury. Between A422 and B4100. Approx 1½-acre hillside garden of many aspects. Bordered walks; a 'surprise' garden leading to water falling to pools, flower beds and the finest views of Hornton Village. Added attraction miniature windmill ⅓ scale of original at Hornton. TEAS in aid of Cubs and Brownies. *Adm £2 Chd free. Sun May 24 (2-6). Private group visits welcome, please* **Tel 01295 670304**

Bignell House, Chesterton ❀ (Mr & Mrs P J Gordon, Lord & Lady of Bignell) On A4095 2m SW of Bicester, 12m Oxford. 16-acre traditional English country house landscape garden; lawns leading to lake system with rock pool; stone arches; bridge to daffodil island; moat walk; fine mature trees; aconites, primroses, variety of wild species and woodland plants. House (not open) designed by William Wilkinson mid C19 (one wing only remains). TEAS. *Adm £1.50 Chd free (ACNO to BBONT®). Easter Sun April 12 (2-6)*

▲**Blenheim Palace, Woodstock** &⚘ (His Grace the Duke of Marlborough) 8m N of Oxford. Bus: 20 Oxford-Chipping Norton-Stratford, alight Woodstock. Original grounds and garden plan by Henry Wise. Park landscaped and lake created by 'Capability' Brown in late C18. Maze. Lavender and herb garden; formal gardens by Achille Duchêne; Butterfly house. Restaurant, Cafeteria. Adventure Play Area. *Adm charge not available on going to press. For NGS Sat, Sun April 4, 5 (10.30-4.45)*

¶**Blewbury Gardens** &⚘❀ Located on A417 between Streatley and Wantage. 6 gardens in a charming downland village, the majority of which are cottage gardens surrounding beautiful old properties. Lime tolerant, unusual and climbing plants are much in evidence. Colour co-ordinated herbaceous borders stocked with perennials for all yr-round interest are also featured. A village opening for plantsman, artists and browsers. TEAS in village hall. *Combined adm £3 Acc chd free. Sun June 28 (2-6)*

    ¶**Carpenters** &⚘ (Nick & Melanie Longhurst) TEAS in aid of The Amenity Fund for the George Schuster Ward of the Fairmile Hospital

    ¶**Green Bushes** &⚘❀ (Phil & Rhon Rogers)

    ¶**Hall Barn Close** &⚘ (Richard & Lindy Farrell)

    ¶**Nottyngham Fee House** &⚘ (Patricia Weaver) Teas in aid of Westminster Childrens Hospital

    ¶**The Old Malt House** &⚘ (Ervin & Mary Seibold)

    ¶**Stocks** &⚘ (Richard & Norma Bird)

Bloxham Gardens, nr Banbury ⚘ A large village near Banbury on A361 to Chipping Norton. Has a fine church with a 198ft spire. TEAS in village by WI. *Combined adm £2.50 Chd free. Sun June 7 (2-6)*

    25 The Avenue (Miss E Bell-Walker) A small informal garden with emphasis on small shrubs; sub shrubs and herbaceous plants

    113 Courtington Lane (Mr P C Bury) Sheltered garden with emphasis on herbaceous borders, shrubs and tubs. Winding paths giving attractive rural views

    71 Courtington Lane (Mr P Sheasby) About ¼ acre with herbaceous borders, shrubs, rockeries and small peat beds; there is a small pond and a series of alpine troughs; the greenhouse contains cacti and a large succulent collection especially Lithops, Haworthia and Echeveria; a wide range of herbaceous species are grown

Frog Lane Cottage (Mr & Mrs R Owen) An artist's and a plantsman's garden. Steeply terraced on many levels, extending to the brook. Mixture of shrubs, herbaceous plants, and mature trees, wonderful views across valley (approx ⅔ acre)

Brightwell-cum-Sotwell Gardens, nr Wallingford Off A4130 between Didcot (4m) and Wallingford (2m). Ancient village with many timber-framed cottages. Parking in village centre. Teas at Sotwell House. *Combined adm £2 Chd free. Sun July 12 (2-6)*

¶**Fairthorne Cottage** & (Mr & Mrs W P Chilton) Cottage garden with small stream and water feature

The Priory &⚘ (Mr & Mrs C Scroggs) Walled garden, C16 farmhouse, 200 plantings in shrubbery; herbaceous border and rose bed. Brick paved vegetable garden

Sotwell House &⚘ (Mr & Mrs D Dobbin) 3-acre mature garden set in the centre of the village with a moat surrounding the perimeter which provides an ideal habitat for water fowl. The borders consist mainly of roses and herbaceous plants with a few specimen trees

Spring Cottage ⚘ (Mr & Mrs M C Dix) Small pretty cottage garden featuring shrubs, roses, clematis and perennials

Sunnyside &⚘ (Mr D Batten) 1-acre garden featuring annuals, mixed borders and 2 fishponds

Broadwell Gardens, nr Lechlade 5m NE Lechlade, E of A361 to Burford. Delightful Cotswold village with interesting church. TEAS. *Combined adm with* **Kencot Gardens** *£3 Chd free. Mon April 13 (2-6). Mon Aug 31 (2-6). Adm* **Broadwell House** *£2 Chd free. Sun Feb 22 (2-4)*

Broadwell House &⚘ (Brigadier & Mrs C F Cox) Mature 2-acre garden planted for colour throughout the year. Many interesting trees and shrubs incl wellingtonia, ginkgo, acers, aralias, salix, clematis. Topiary, rare plants, many golden, silver and variegated; unusual grasses, penstemons and osteospermums, also many hardy geraniums. Featured in 'Over the Hills from Broadway'. Listed house and old barn. Gardening clubs welcome. *Adm £2 Chd free. Suns Feb 22 (2-4); Mon April 13 (2-6), Mon Aug 31 (2-6). Private parties welcome by prior arrangement*

Broadwell Old Manor &⚘ (Mr & Mrs M Chinnery) 1-acre garden with listed house. Shrub borders, courtyard and topiary garden. Pleached lime hedge, old mulberry tree, young tulip and sorbus trees. *April 13 only (2-6)*

●**Brook Cottage, Alkerton** ⚘ (Mr & Mrs D Hodges) Well Lane. 6m W of Banbury. ¾m off A422. Follow signs in village. 4-acre hillside garden formed since 1964. Wide variety of trees, shrubs and perennials in areas of differing character. Water garden; alpine scree; one-colour borders. Over 200 shrub and climbing roses. Many clematis. Interesting throughout season. DIY Tea & Coffee. Refreshments for groups by arrangement. *Adm £2.50 OAPs £2 Chd free. Mon to Fri incl Bank Hols (9-6) 13 April to 30 Oct. Evenings, weekends and all group visits by appt* **Tel 01295 670303** *or* **670590**

▲**Broughton Castle, nr Banbury** &⚘ (Lord Saye & Sele) 2 ½m W of Banbury on Shipston-on-Stour rd (B4035). 1-acre shrub, herbaceous borders, walled garden, roses, climbers against background of C14-C16 castle surrounded by moat in open parkland. House also open, extra charge. TEAS. *Adm Garden only £2 Chd £1. For NGS Suns June 21, Aug 2 (2-5)*

Broughton Poggs & Filkins Gardens &⚘ Enchanting limestone villages between Burford and Lechlade, just E of A361. A number of gardens varying in size from traditional cottage garden to over 2 acres, growing wide variety of plants. TEAS. *Combined adm £2 Chd free. Tickets from* **The Court House, Broughton Hall** *or* **Little Peacocks** *(ACNO to Broughton & Filkins Church Funds®). Sun April 5 (2-5.30)*

Broughton Poggs:

Broughton Hall (Mr & Mrs C B S Dobson)

Corner Cottage (Mr & Mrs E Stephenson)

The Court House ⚘ (Richard Burls Esq)

The Garden Cottage (Mr & Mrs R Chennells)

Manor Farm Cottage (Mr & Mrs E R Venn)

Rose Cottage (Mr & Mrs R Groves)

Filkins:

St Peter's House (John Cambridge Esq)

Little Peacocks (Colvin & Moggridge, Landscape Consultants)

Buckland, nr Faringdon ⚘ (Mrs Richard Wellesley) Signposted to Buckland off A420, lane between two churches. Beautiful lakeside walk; fine trees; daffodils; shrubs. Norman church adjoins garden. *Adm £2 Chd free (ACNO to Richard Wellesley Memorial Transport Fund®). Sun April 5 (2-7). Private visits welcome Tues and Thurs, please* **Tel 01367 870235**

Chalkhouse Green Farm, Kidmore End &⚘ (Mr & Mrs J Hall) Situated 2m N of Reading between A4074 and B481. Approx 1.5m SE of Kidmore End. 1-acre garden and traditional farmstead. Herbaceous borders, herb garden, shrubs, old-fashioned roses, trees incl medlar, quince and mulberries. Farm animals ranging from an ancient breed of British White cattle, donkey, pigs, piglets and ducks, to a ferret. Farm trail rides. TEAS and swimming in covered pool in aid of 'Music for disabled children appeal', Friends of Ormerod School. *Adm £1.50 Chd under 16 and wheelchairs free. Suns June 14, Aug 16 (2-6)*

Charlbury Gardens, Charlbury &⚘ Large historic village on B4022 Witney-Enstone. Teas at the Church. *Combined adm £2 Chd 50p (ACNO to Wytham Hall Sick Bay for Homeless, Medical Care®). Sun May 31 (2-6)*

Gothic House (Mr & Mrs Andrew Lawson) Nr Bell Hotel. ⅓-acre walled garden, planted for sculpture display and colur association. False perspective, pleached lime walk with bulbs, trellis, alpine pyramid, terrace pots. *Also open Mon, Tues, Wed June 1, 2, 3 (2-4.30). Adm £1.50 Chd 50p*

The Priory (Dr D El Kabir & Others) Adjacent Church. Formal terraced topiary gardens with Italianate features, incl foliage colour schemes, parterres, specimen trees and shrubs, water features and over 3 acres of recently planted arboretum

Chastleton Glebe Gardens, nr Moreton-in-Marsh &® 3m SE of Moreton-in-Marsh and W of Chipping Norton off A44. TEAS in aid of Chastleton Church. *Combined adm £2.50 Chd free. Sun July 12 (2-6)*
> **Chastleton Glebe** (Prue Leith) 5 acres, old trees, terraces (one all red); small lake, island; Chinese-style bridge, pagoda; formal vegetable garden; views; rose tunnel
> **Gardeners Cottage** (Ray Pearse) Plantsman's garden, small herbaceous; pool; patio; tubs, baskets and organic vegetable patch. All-yr-round colour with alpines

Checkendon Court, Checkendon &® (Sir Nigel Broackes) NW of Reading. 2m NE of Woodcote off A4074 nr Checkendon church. 15 acres, attractively laid out with yew hedges, herbaceous borders, roses, kitchen garden. New rhododendrons and azalea planting and new laburnum pergola walk now complete. Teas on Checkendon Village Green in aid of Checkendon School Assoc. *Adm £2 Chd free. Sun May 31 (2-5)*

Chivel Farm, Heythrop &®® (Mr & Mrs J D Sword) 4m E of Chipping Norton, off A44 or A361. High and open to extensive view, medium-sized garden designed for continuous interest. Colour schemed borders with many unusual shrubs, roses, herbaceous plants; small formal white garden, conservatory. TEAS in aid of St Nicholas Church, Heythrop. *Adm £2 Chd free. Sun Aug 2 (2-6)*

Christ Church see Oxford University Gardens

Clematis Corner, Shillingford & (Mike & Dorothy Brown) 15 Plough Close. At Shillingford roundabout (10m S of Oxford on A4074), take A329 towards Warborough and Thame. Clematis Corner is 200yds from roundabout, 1st on L inside Plough Close, just round sharp L bend. ¼ acre garden specialising in clematis (over 200 varieties) grown in a variety of ways, within mixed flower beds. Beautiful views of the Chilterns. TEAS. *Adm £1.50 Chd 50p (ACNO to ICRF®). Private visits welcome by appt April 1 to Aug 31, please Tel 01865 858721*

Clock House, Coleshill &®® (Denny Wickham & Peter Fox) 3½m SW of Faringdon on B4019. Garden at top of village. Planted around site of Coleshill House, which was burnt down in the 50s. The main floor plan has also been laid out and is planted as a memorial to this famous house. Walled garden in old laundry drying ground; with big greenhouse, unusual plants with emphasis on foliage, vegetables and herbs; good views across Vale of the White Horse and parkland. Toilets not suitable disabled. TEAS. *Adm £1.50 Chd free. Open every Thurs April to Oct (2-5). Suns May 17, June 14, Sept 13, Oct 4 (2-6). Private visits welcome, please Tel 01793 762476*

Colegrave Seeds Ltd, West Adderbury & Milton Rd. Off A4260 Banbury-Oxford rd. From M40 travelling S leave at junction 11: travelling N leave at junction 10. In Adderbury head for Milton and Bloxham. Trial grounds ½m on R. Seed trial grounds and patio display gardens containing thousands of summer flowering annuals and perennials. Many new items in trial prior to introduction. A festival of colour unique in Oxfordshire. Covered display. TEAS. *Adm £2.50 Chd £1 (ACNO to The David Colegrave Foundation®). Sun Aug 16 (10-5)*

Corpus Christi College see Oxford University Gardens

Dundon House, Minster Lovell &®® (Mr & Mrs W Pack) Off B4047 opp White Hart, sign to Minster Lovell Hall and Leafield. First drive on R. Parking in field on L. Disabled parking at house. Mainly C16 house rebuilt on old quarry site in 1930s, not open. Views across Windrush valley. 4-acre part terraced garden. Flower, shrub rose and wild gardens enclosed by yew hedges and stone walls, created in 1980s. Newly planted woodland. TEAS by WI. *Adm £2 OAPs £1.50 Chd free. Sun July 5 (2-6). Groups welcome by appt, please Tel 01993 775092*

Epwell Mill, nr Banbury &® (Mrs William Graham & Mrs David Long) Epwell, 7m W of Banbury, between Shutford and Epwell. Medium-sized garden, interestingly landscaped in open country, based on former water-mill; terraced pools; bulbs; azaleas. Home-made TEAS. *Adm £1.50 Chd free (ACNO to Epwell Parochial Church Council®). Mons April 13, May 25, Sun Sept 6 (2-6)*

Exeter College see Oxford University Gardens

Fiveways Cottage, Shutford &® (Dr & Mrs M R Aldous) 5m W of Banbury between A422 to Shutford & B4035 to Shipston on the Tadmarton Rd. Just over ½ acre, started 1986. Essentially cottage garden style, with shrubs, roses, small woodland areas, herbaceous borders and ponds. Many clematis varieties grown. Teas in Shutford Village Hall. *Adm £2 (ACNO to Rangapara Hospital Trust®). Sun July 19 (2-6)*

Friars Court, Clanfield & (Mr J H Willmer) On A4095 Farindon to Witney, S of Clanfield [OS 285009]. C16 part moated farmhouse. New/mature gardens, woodland walks and nature trail. Working displays on alternative energy, museum and shop. TEAS. *Adm £2 Chd under 12 free. Suns June 7, Aug 23 (2-6). Gardens open at other times by appt only, Tel 01367 810206*

Garsington Manor, nr Oxford &® (Mr & Mrs L V Ingrams) SE of Oxford N of B480. House C17 of architectural interest (not open). Monastic fish ponds, water garden, dovecot c.1700; flower parterre and Italian garden laid out by Philip and Lady Ottoline Morrell; fine trees and yew hedges. Free car park. TEAS in aid of local churches. *Adm £2 Chd free. Sat April 25, Sun Oct 4 (2-5)*

Green College see Oxford University Gardens

Green Place, Rotherfield Greys &®® (Mr & Mrs R P Tatman) 3m W of Henley-on-Thames next to Greys War Memorial. Extensive views towards the E from secluded 1-acre garden containing a pergola walk of fragrant climbers, herbaceous borders, rose beds and containers of hostas, fuchsias and annuals. Sale of excellent plants, home-made cakes and preserves. Teas in village hall in aid of WI. *Adm £1 Chd free. Sun June 28 (2-6)*

▲Greys Court, Rotherfield Greys ®® (Lady Brunner; The National Trust) 3m W of Henley-on-Thames on rd to Peppard. 8 acres amongst which are the ruined walls and buildings of original fortified manor. Rose, cherry, wisteria and white gardens; lawns; kitchen garden; ice house; Archbishop's maze. Jacobean house open with C18 alterations on site of original C13 house fortified by Lord Grey in C14. Donkey wheel and tower. TEAS. *Adm garden £3 Chd £1.50 House & Garden £4 Chd £2. For NGS Sat May 30 (2-5.30)*

Greystone Cottage, Kingwood Common &&& (Mr & Mrs W Roxburgh) Colmore Lane. Signposted from B481 Nettlebed-Reading rd. 2-acre plantsman's garden in woodland setting. Featuring hellebores, ponds, wildflower meadow and pinetum. Many unusual plants and bulbs providing continual interest. Entry in 'RHS Gardeners Year Book'. TEAS in aid of Oxfam (March 8), Peppard C of E School (May 10). *Adm £2 Chd free. Suns March 8, May 10 (2-6), Thurs March 12, 19, April 9, 16, May 14, 21, June 4 (11-5). Private visits and groups very welcome, please* **Tel 01491 628559**

Headington Gardens East Oxford, off London Road, ¾m inside ring road. Teas in Parish Hall, Dunstan Rd in aid of WI. *Combined adm £2 Chd free. Suns May 17, July 12, Aug 9 (2-6)*

  2 Fortnam Close & (Mr & Mrs D Holt) Off Headley Way, follow signs to John Radcliffe Hospital. Multi-award winner, featured on TV and radio. ¼-acre garden on 3 levels, trees, shrubs, heathers, azaleas and a large wisteria. Roses, bearded iris and other herbaceous plants in a planned layout which incl a pond and pergola. Watercolour paintings and pressed flower arrangements to view if you wish

  40 Osler Road && (Mr & Mrs N Coote) After traffic lights in centre of Headington shopping centre, 2nd turn on R opp Royal Standard public house. ⅔-acre secret garden on dry soil on the edge of Old Headington. Pots, exotic plants, design, and house create a Mediterranean fantasy in a cold climate. Featured in many publications. *Private visits for groups welcome, please* **Tel 01865 767680 (after dark)**

  Pumpkin Cottage &&& (Mr & Mrs M Davis) 6 St Andrew's Lane, Old Headington, off St Andrew's Rd, nr to Church. Small garden, 20m × 16m, enclosed within stone walls situated at rear of Grade II listed cottage. Small pool and rockery; mixed planting; paved areas with some container grown plants. Small cobble paved front garden. Wheelchair access possible by arrangement

  1 Stoke Place && (Mr & Mrs M Carrington) Off St Andrew's Rd. The garden (just short of an acre) takes its shape from a network of old stone walls which have survived in the area. Trees and stone work provide a framework for a linked series of paths and flower beds which gives an atmosphere of seclusion. Small pools and many contrasting shrubs and plants. *Open May 17 only (ACNO to RSPCA®)*

Hearns House, Gallows Tree Common && (Mr & Mrs J Pumfrey) 5m N of Reading, 5m W of Henley. From A4074 turn E at The Fox, Cane End. Architects house in 2-acre garden in woodland setting. Designed for maintenance by two people with full time careers. Emphasis on design, good foliage and single colour areas with paved courtyard and shady walks. Redesigned and much expanded water feature. Wide variety of hardy plants incl for example 40 named Euphorbia. TEAS or coffee in aid

of Oxfam. *Adm £2 Chd free. Sat, Sun, Mon May 23, 24, 25 (10-12; 2-5)*

Heron's Reach, Whitchurch-on-Thames & (Mr B Vorhaus) Eastfield Lane. From Pangbourne take Toll-bridge rd over Thames to Whitchurch-on-Thames. At The Greyhound turn R into Eastfield Lane. 1-acre in beautiful Thames-side setting with views to the Chilterns; woodland garden with pond, stream, shrubs and herbaceous borders. TEAS. *Adm £2 Chd free. Sun July 12 (2-6). Private visits also welcome in July, please* **Tel 01734 843140**

Highmoor Hall, Nettlebed &&& (Mr & Mrs P D Persson) Highmoor. 1m S of Nettlebed on B481 to Reading. 6-acre garden in a peaceful setting: open views across ha-ha; secluded areas; mature trees; water garden; walled kitchen garden; shrubberies and herbaceous borders with an accent on colour blending. Arts Centre within the grounds. TEAS. *Adm £2 Chd free (ACNO to TEAR Fund®). Sat July 18 (2-6)*

Hill Court, Tackley &&& (Mr & Mrs Andrew Peake) 9m N of Oxford. Turn off A4260 at Sturdy's Castle. Walled garden of 2 acres with yew cones at top of terrace as a design feature by Russell Page in the 1960s. Terraces incl silver, pink and blue plantings, white garden, herbaceous borders, shrubberies, orangery. Many rare and unusual plants. Entry incl History Trail with unique geometric fish-ponds (1620), C17 stables, pigeon house, C18 lakes, ice-house etc (stroll of 1hr (not suitable for wheelchairs)). TEAS. Pied Pipers recorder group (Sun only). *Adm £1.50 Chd free (ACNO to Tackley Youth Club & Tackley Newsletter®). Sat, Sun June 13, 14 (2-6)*

Holywell Manor see Oxford University Gardens

Home Close, Garsington && (Dr P Giangrande and Miss M Waud) Southend. SE of Oxford, N of B480. 2-acre garden with listed house and granary. Interesting trees, shrubs and perennials planted for all-yr-interest. Terraces, walls and hedges divide the garden into ten distinct areas. *Adm £1.50 Chd free. Sun Aug 2 (2-6). Private visits welcome April 1 to Sept 30, please* **Tel 01865 361394**

Home Farm, Balscote see Balscote Gardens

Hook Norton Manor, Banbury & (Mr & Mrs Nicholas Holmes) SW of Banbury. From A361, 1m from Chipping Norton turn N and follow signs. 2½-acres terraced lawns leading down to streams; trees, shrubs and bog garden. TEAS in aid of St Peter's Church. *Adm £1.50 Chd free. Sun Oct 4 (2-5.30)*

Iffley Gardens, S Oxford && Secluded old village within Oxford's ring road, off A4158 from Magdalen Bridge to Littlemore roundabout. Renowned Norman church, featured on cover of Pevsner's Oxon guide. Short footpath from Mill Lane leads to scenic Iffley Lock and Sandford to Oxford towpath. Teas from 3-5 at thatched village hall, Church Way. Two plant stalls, one in aid of NGS, the other for The White House Nursery. *Combined adm £2 OAPs £1.50 Chd free. Sun June 21 (2-6)*

8 Abberbury Road &. (F S Tordoff Esq) Off Church Way. ½-acre plantsman's garden developed since 1971. Mature trees, shrubs, coloured and variegated foliage, many old and modern shrub roses and climbers. *Private visits welcome, please* **Tel 01865 778644**

24 Abberbury Road &. (Mr & Mrs E Townsend-Coles) ½-acre family garden with fruit, flowers and vegetables

65 Church Way ✿ (Mrs J Woodfill) Small cottage garden planted with shrubs, perennials and herbs, many of them grown for their historical associations. *Private visits welcome, please* **Tel 01865 770537**

71 Church Way (Mrs M L Harrison) A small, low maintenance professionally designed, front garden with mixed shrubs and herbaceous plantings. *Private visits welcome, please* **Tel 01865 718224**

122 Church Way (Sir John & Lady Elliott) Small secluded cottage style garden with trees, shrubs, roses and herbaceous plants behind listed house with view of church tower

11 Iffley Turn &. (Ann & Matthew Ellett) A well established garden of ½-acre containing many mature trees, a vegetable plot, herbaceous borders and a pond

The Mill House (Mrs P A Lawrence) 30 Mill Lane. A terraced garden dropping westwards to the river at the old mill-race

Rosedale ✿ (Mrs T Bennett) Mill Lane, off Church Way. ½-acre garden on different levels, hidden behind walls. A mixture of trees, shrubs, roses and herbaceous plants with a large rockery and tiny woodland garden. *Private visits welcome, please* **Tel 01865 714151**

Kencot Gardens, nr Lechlade 5m NE of Lechlade, E of A361 to Burford. A most charming Cotswold village with interesting church. TEAS. *Combined adm with* **Broadwell Gardens** *£3 Chd free. Mon April 13; Mon Aug 31. Also* **Kencot House** *and* **Manor Farm** *open Sun June 28. Combined adm £2 Chd free*

De Rougemont &. (Mr & Mrs D Portergill) ½-acre garden with very varied planting: over 350 named plants; beds for perennials, conifers, fuchsias, herbs and roses; spring bulbs; vegetables and fruit trees; soft fruit cage; greenhouse with vine; well

The Gardens &. (Lt-Col & Mrs J Barstow) ¼-acre cottage garden featuring spring bulbs, iris, roses, herbaceous, rock plants, old apple trees and a well

Ivy Nook (Mr & Mrs W Gasson) Cottage garden; rockeries, lawns, mixed borders. *Mons April 13, Aug 31*

Kencot Cottage ✿ (Mrs M Foster) Very small garden with spring bulbs and bedding, also bonsai trees

Kencot House ✿ (Mr & Mrs A Patrick) 2-acre garden with lawns, trees, borders; quantities of daffodils and other spring bulbs; roses and over 50 different clematis; notable ginkgo tree. Interesting carved C13 archway. *Also open Sun June 28*

Manor Farm (Mr & Mrs J R Fyson) 2-acre garden with lawns and herbaceous borders; naturalised spring bulbs; incl long-established fritillaries; clipped yew, pleached lime walk, pergola with rambling and gallica roses. Mature orchards. C17 listed farmhouse. *Mon April 13, Sun June 28 only*

Kiddington Hall, Woodstock ✿✿ (Hon Maurice & Mrs Robson) 4m NW of Woodstock. From A44 Oxford-Stratford, R at Xrds in Kiddington and down hill; entrance on L. Partly suitable for wheelchairs. Large grounds with lake, parkland designed by Capability Brown; terraced rose garden and orangery beside house designed by Sir Charles Barry; C12 church, C16 dovecote and large walled kitchen garden. Fete and TEAS in aid of St Nicholas Church, Kiddington. *Adm £2 Chd free. Sun June 21 (2-6)*

■ **Kingston Bagpuize House, nr Abingdon** &.✿✿ (Mr & Mrs Francis Grant) The gardens contain a notable collection of unusual trees, shrubs, perennials and bulbs. House not suitable for wheelchairs. TEAS. *Adm garden only £1.50. House and garden £3.50 OAP's £3 Chd £2.50 (under 5's free to garden, not admitted to the house). Open Bank Hol weekends Sat, Sun, Mon, also March 8, April 5, 25, 26; June 13, 14; July 15, 18, 19; Aug 5, 8, 9 and Sept 9, 12, 13, 23, 26, 27; Oct 11 (2.30-5.30) last adm 5pm. Plants NGS days only. For NGS Suns April 26, Sept 27. Groups welcome by written appt Feb to Nov, please* **Tel 01865 820259**

▲**Kingstone Lisle Park, nr Wantage** &. (Mr & Mrs J L S Lonsdale) 5m W of Wantage along B4507. 12 acres of gardens incl a shrubbery, pleached limes, an avenue leading up to an ornamental pond. 3 acres of lakes. TEAS. *Adm for NGS garden only £2.50 Chd free (ACNO to St John the Baptist Church, Kingstone Lisle®). Sun May 17 (2-5)*

Lady Margaret Hall see Oxford University Gardens

Langford Gardens, nr Lechlade &.✿ E of A361 Burford-Lechlade; W of A409 Burford-Faringdon. Mixture of cottage and formal gardens in old limestone village which makes a feature of roses. Saxon church decorated with flowers. Large free car park. TEAS in aid of St Matthew's church. *Combined adm £2.50 Chd free. Sun June 21 (2-6)*
  Bakery Cottage (Miss R Amies)
  The Barn (Mr & Mrs D E Range)
  ¶**2 Church Lane** (Mr A Keating)
  ¶**5 Church Lane** (Mr D Carden)
  ¶**1 Cooks Farm Cottages** (Mr H Davies)
  Cotswold Bungalow (Mr & Mrs J Dudley)
  Dunford House (Mr & Mrs H Catlin)
  26 The Elms (Mr R Stacey)
  Lime Tree Cottage (Dr & Mrs M Schultz)
  Lockey House (Mrs A Kemp & Mr & Mrs N Gardner)
  Lower Farm (Mr & Mrs T Brown)
  ¶**Moss Cottage** (Mr Mark Thomas)
  The Old School & Barn (Sir Hardy Amies) Collection of 60 old English roses & clematis
  The Old Vicarage (Mr & Mrs A Radcliffe)
  ¶**Peevish Corner** (Mr & Mrs D Kirby)
  Rectory Farm (Mr & Mrs R J Kirby)
  Rosefern Cottage (Mr & Mrs J Lowden)
  Stonecroft (David Apperley & Christine Romanek)
  Threeways (Mrs R G Wilson)
  Wellbank (Mr & Mrs Reid-Purvis)

14 Lavender Place, Carterton ✿✿ (Mrs Angela Chambers) Off Upavon Way (B4020). Plant enthusiast's tiny 35 ft square garden behind small modern bungalow. Clematis and other climbers provide secluded setting for densely packed collection of about 300 unusual and exotic shrubs and perennials. With all-yr-interest. *Adm £1 Chd free (ACNO to Association for International Cancer Research®). Private visits welcome by appt June 1 to Aug 31, please* **Tel 01993 843216**

Lime Close, Drayton &® (M-C de Laubarede) 35 Henleys Lane. 2m S of Abingdon. 3-acre mature garden with very rare trees, shrubs, perennials and bulbs. New unusual topiary; raised beds; rock garden and sinks with alpines. Newly reclaimed border planted with interesting shade lovers. Pond, ornamental kitchen garden with pergola. Herb garden designed by Rosemary Verey. Listed C16 house (not open). Unusual plants for sale from Green Farm Plants. TEAS. *Adm £2 Chd free. Suns April 19, June 21 (2-6)*

Longworth Gardens & Longworth is N of A420 between Kingston Bagpuize and Faringdon. TEAS at Longworth Manor in aid of St Marys Church Longworth. *Combined adm £2 Chd free. Sun May 17 (2-6)*

   Longworth Manor &® (Col & Mrs John Walton) A medium-size garden with roses, borders, shrubs and ornamental ponds. C17 house (not open) with good views over R Thames. Special features are wild flower meadow and a new formal garden

   Haugh House (Mrs David Faulkner) Medium-size garden divided into distinct areas. Willow house

Lower Chilworth Farm, Milton Common &®® (Mr & Mrs Michael Hedges) On A329 Thame to Wallingford rd by junction 7 & 8 off M40 and signposted off A418 Thame to Oxford rd. The farm is ½m NW of village on old A40 (line of poplar trees down drive). 1-acre informal plantsmans garden in a lovely setting, incl walled, sunken and courtyard gardens, scree, herbaceous and shrub borders; water feature. Nature trail incl 2-acre lake and old railway track. Dogs welcome on trail only. TEAS. Plants May only. *Adm £1.50 Chd free. Mon May 25 (2-6). Sun June 21 (6-9)*

Magdalen College see Oxford University Gardens

Manor Farm, Old Minster Lovell &® (Sir Peter & Lady Parker) Off B4047 Witney-Burford rd; turn R at sign to Old Minster Lovell and Leafield; in ¼m cross Windrush bridge, turn R at Old Swan; no parking in village, follow signs to large free car park. Adjoining churchyard and ruins of Minster (open); C14 dovecote. Owner is author of book about her garden: 'Purest of Pleasures'. TEAS by WI. *Adm £2 Chd free. Sun June 28 (2-5)*

The Manor House, Clifton Hampden &® (Mr C Gibbs) 4m E of Abingdon on A415. 4-acre romantic C19 garden above R Thames with statuary and far-reaching views; long pergola, lime tunnel, herbaceous borders, bulbs, wild riverside walks, much new planting in progress. TEAS in aid of St Michael's and All Angels Church. *Adm £2 Chd free. Sun April 12 (2.30-5.30). Parties welcome, please* **Tel 01865 407720**

The Manor House, Sutton Courtenay &®® (The Hon David Astor) 4m S of Abingdon. Out of Abingdon on the A415. Turn off to Culham -Sutton Courtenay. From A34

going N come into Milton Village take last rd on R to Sutton Courtenay. 10 acres of garden approx 35 acres of land. ½m R Thames Bank. TEAS. *Adm £1.50 Chd 50p. Sun May 10 (2-6)*

The Manor House, Wheatley &®® (Mr & Mrs T G Hassall) 26 High St, Wheatley. Off A40 E of Oxford. 1½-acre garden of Elizabethan manor house; formal box walk; herb garden, cottage garden with rose arches and a shrubbery with old roses. A romantic oasis in this busy village. TEAS in aid of Wheatley Windmill Restoration Society. *Adm £1.50 Acc chd free. Sun June 14 (2-6)*

The Mill House, Stadhampton &® (Mr & Mrs F A Peet) A329/B480, 8m SE of Oxford. 1-acre family garden with old mill and stream. Mill not working but machinery largely intact and wheel turning with pumped water. Parking on green; parking for disabled only at house. TEAS in aid of Stadhampton Church Restoration Fund. *Adm £1 Chd free. Sun April 19 (2-5.30)*

The Mill House, Sutton Courtenay &®® (Mrs J Stevens) Abingdon, Oxon, OX14 4NH. Approx 8½ acres; R Thames runs through garden which is on several islands with mill pond and old paper mill. TEAS. *Adm £2 Chd £1, under 4 free. Suns April 5, June 14, Oct 4 (2-6). Parties of 10 and over also welcome on other days by appt in writing*

Mount Skippet, Ramsden &® (Dr & Mrs M A T Rogers) 4m N of Witney. At Xrds turn E towards Finstock; after 30yds, turn R (sign-post Mount Skippet). After 400yds turn L (No Through Way sign) for 75yds. 2 acres; 2 rock gardens; alpine house; stone troughs; shrubs; herbaceous beds; tufas; conservatory; many rare plants. Fine views. Cotswold stone house largely C17. Teas for groups by prior arrangement. *Adm £1 Chd free (ACNO to Finstock Church®). Private visits welcome April 1 to Sept 30, please* **Tel 01993 868253**

Nettlebed Gardens On A4130, some 5m NW of Henley-on-Thames. Take B481 towards Reading and after 200yds turn R into Sue Ryder Home where there is ample parking. Teas and Plant sales in aid of Sue Ryder Home. *Combined adm £2 Chd free. Sun May 31 (2-5.30)*

   Red Lion House &® (Mr & Mrs G Freeman)

   Sue Ryder Home &®® (The Sue Ryder Foundation) 26-acre garden surrounding large Edwardian house (not open). Fine rhododendrons and rare trees. Large lawns, pond and Italian terrace. The dell and secret garden are in the course of replanting

New College see Oxford University Gardens

25 Newfield Road, Sonning Common &® (Joyce & David Brewer) 5m N of Reading on B481 Nettlebed Rd, on leaving village turn L past Catholic Church, Shiplake Bottom then immed L into Newfield Rd. Free car parking available behind village hall Wood Lane. Garden 5 mins walk N. Small interesting garden of ¼ acre. In excess of 110 varieties of clematis; shrubs, spring bulbs, annuals and containers; mature trees and vegetable garden. TEAS. *Adm £1.50 Chd under 16 free (ACNO to Action Against Breast Cancer®). Suns April 5, July 12 (2-6). Private visits welcome, April to Sept please* **Tel 0118 9723611**

4 Northfield Cottages, nr Kidlington ♿✿❀ (Miss S E Bedwell) Water Eaton. From Sainsbury Roundabout S of Kidlington on A4260 take exit for A34 N. Take 1st R Water Eaton lane opp Kings Arms. Then 1st L following signs for Northfield Farm. Over 2nd bridge to 4th cottage on L. Approx ¼-acre designed over last 7-8 yrs. Mainly herbaceous, unusual plants, fruit, vegetables and greenhouse extending into two further gardens, woodland garden. *Adm £1. Every Tues, Fri, Sat, March 21 to Aug 29 (2-5). Private visits welcome all year, please* **Tel 01865 378910**

Nutford Lodge, Longcot ♿❀ (Mr & Mrs K Elmore) In Longcot Village next to The King & Queen public house. S of A420 between Faringdon and Shrivenham. 1½-acre sculpture garden with accent on fragrance, for the blind. Ponds, rockeries, colour schemed borders, potager, views to White Horse; indoor gallery. *Adm £1 Chd free (ACNO to Headway in Oxford®). May 24 to May 31 (2-8) daily; Sats, Suns July 4, 5, Sept 5, 6 (2-6). Also private visits welcome, please* **Tel 01793 782258**

Old Church House, Wantage ♿ (Dr & Mrs Dick Squires). At the crossway of A417 and A338. Situated next to Parish Church nr the Wantage market square. An unusual town garden running down to the Letcombe brook. Much interest with different levels, follies, water, mature trees and many special plants. Tickets and teas at Vale & Downland Museum close by in Church St. *Adm £1 Chd free (ACNO to Vale & Downland Trust®). Tues to Sun. Private visits also welcome, please* **Tel 01235 762785**

The Old Rectory, Brightwell Baldwin ♿❀ (Mr & Mrs Donald Chilvers) 2m W of Watlington via Cuxham (B480). 1½-acre garden and parkland surrounding beautiful Georgian rectory. Open views to S over ha-ha. Formal garden layout with herb, rose and herbaceous beds, terracing and walls. Designed by owners and planted 1990 yet mature; rare breed of sheep. TEAS and plant sales in aid of village hall appeal. *Adm £2 Chd free. Sun July 12 (2.30-6)*

The Old Rectory, Coleshill ♿ (Sir George & Lady Martin) 3m W of Faringdon. Coleshill (NT village) is on B4019 midway between Faringdon and Highworth. Medium-sized garden; lawns and informal shrub beds; wide variety shrubs, incl old-fashioned roses, 40-yr-old standard wisteria. Distant views of Berkshire and Wiltshire Downs. House dates from late C14. TEAS. *Adm £1 Chd free. Suns April 19 (2-6), Sept 13 (2-5)*

The Old Rectory, Farnborough, nr Wantage see Berkshire

Oxford see also 23 Beech Croft Road, East Oxford, Headington, Iffley

Oxford University Gardens

  Christ Church ✿ **Masters' Garden** Entrance on Christ Church Meadow (through War Memorial garden on St Aldate's). Created in 1926, has herbaceous borders and a new border with some unusual shrubs. A walk through the newly designed and replanted Pocock Garden, past Pocock's plane, an oriental plane

planted in 1636, leads to the Cathedral Garden. *Adm £1 Chd free. Combined adm £2.50 with* **Corpus Christi** *and* **Merton gardens.** *Sun Aug 9 (2-5)*
  Corpus Christi ♿✿ Entrance from Merton St or **Christ Church Fellows' garden.** Several small gardens and courtyards overlooking Christchurch meadows. Fellows' private garden not normally open to the public. TEAS in aid of 'Breakthrough Breast Cancer'. *Adm £1. Combined adm £2.50 with* **Christ Church** *and* **Merton.** *Sun Aug 9 (2-5)*
  Exeter College, Rector's Lodgings ✿ The Turl, between High & Broad Sts, Oxford. Small enclosed garden, herbaceous and shrubs, especially clematis. Fellows' Garden and Chapel also open. *Combined adm with* **New College** *£1.50 Chd free. Sun June 28 (2-5)*
  Green College ♿✿ Woodstock Rd, next to Radcliffe Infirmary. 3 acres; lawns, herbaceous borders, medicinal garden with notes on traditional usage of plants. Radcliffe Observatory (Tower of the Winds) open for views of Oxford and TEAS. *Adm £1 Chd free (incl Observatory). Sun June 21 (2-6)*
  Holywell Manor ✿❀ (Balliol College) Central Oxford at corner of Manor Rd & St Cross Rd on L of St Cross Church opp law library. College garden of about 1 acre, not normally open to the public. Imaginatively laid out 50 yrs ago around horse chestnut to give formal and informal areas. Mature ginkgo avenue, spinney with spring flowers and bulbs. *Adm £1 Chd free. Sun April 19 (2-6). Private visits welcome, please* **Tel 01865 271501**
  Lady Margaret Hall Norham Gardens, 1m N of Carfax from Banbury Rd into Norham Rd, 2nd R into Fyfield Rd. 8 acres of formal and informal gardens; mixed herbaceous and shrub borders and walk by R Cherwell. College 110 yrs old includes listed buildings. TEAS. *Adm £1.50 Chd free. Sun July 12 (2-6)*
  Magdalen College, Fellows' Garden and **President's Garden** (not normally open to the public) ♿✿ Entrance in High St. 60 acres incl deer park, college lawns, numerous trees 150-200 yrs old, notable herbaceous and shrub plantings; Magdalen Meadows are surrounded by Addison's Walk, a tree-lined circuit by the R Cherwell developed since the late C18. An ancient herd of 40 deer is located in the grounds. Light lunch and TEAS. *Adm £2 Chd £1. Sun March 22 (1-5). Private visits welcome by arrangement with Home Bursar* **Tel 01865 276050**
  Merton College, Oxford ♿✿ **Fellows' Garden** Merton St, parallel to High St. Ancient mulberry said to have associations with James 1; specimen trees incl sorbus and malus vars; long mixed herbaceous border; view of Christ Church meadow. *Adm £1 Chd free. Combined adm £2.50 with* **Christ Church** *and* **Corpus Christie.** *Sun Aug 9 (2-5)*
  New College, Oxford ♿✿ **Warden's Garden** Entered from New College Lane, off Catte St. Secret walled garden, replanted 1988 with interesting mix of herbaceous and shrubs. *Adm £1 Acc chd free. Combined adm with* **Exeter College** *£1.50. Sun June 28 (2-5)*
  Queen's College, Provost's, Fellows' and Nuns' Gardens ✿ High Street. ½-acre with splendid herbaceous borders, rose garden, high old stone walls; large ilex tree. Magnificent statues set in wall of Hawksmoor's

library (viewed from Provost's garden). *Combined adm with* **Wadham College** *£1.50. Sun July 19 (2-5)*

Rewley House &✿ (Oxford University Dept for Continuing Education) Wellington Sq., St John Street. Courtyard gardens, originally planted by townscaper, Jeanne Bliss, with variegated shrubs, climbers, trailing plants in mobile boxes on wheels. Landscaped gardens designed and maintained by Walter Sawyer, head of the University Parks. TEA. *Adm £1 Chd free. Sun July 19 (2-5). Private visits welcome, please* **Tel 01865 270375**

St Hilda's College &✿✿ Approx 15 mins walk E from city centre. Cross Magdalen Bridge and turn R at roundabout into Cowley Place. College Lodge at end on R. Or park in public car park at St Clements. Approx 5 acres laid to lawns and flower beds with flood plain meadow containing interesting wild flowers. TEAS. *Adm £1 Chd under 12 free. Sun June 21 (2-5)*

Trinity College, Oxford &✿✿ **President's Garden** Entrance in Broad St. Surrounded by high old stone walls, has mixed borders of herbaceous, shrubs and statuary. Historic Main College Gardens with specimen trees incl 250-yr-old forked catalpa, fine long herbaceous border and handsome garden quad originally designed by Wren. **Fellows' Garden** Small walled terrace, herbaceous borders; water feature formed by Jacobean stone heraldic beasts. TEAS in aid of Sobell House Hospice Charity. *Adm £1.50 Chd free. Sun Aug 9 (2-5)*

▲**University Arboretum, Nuneham Courtenay** &✿✿ 6m S of Oxford on A4074 (formerly A423), 400yds S of Nuneham Courtenay. 55 acres incl informal rhododendron walks, camellia, bamboo and acer collections, natural woodland and oak woodland, meadow with pond and associated aquatics and marginals; fine collection of mature conifers; many 150 yrs old. Staff available to answer queries. Plant stall in aid of Oxford University Botanic Garden. *Adm £1 Chd under 12 free. Sun June 7 (2-5)*

Wadham College &✿ **Fellows' Private Garden & Warden's Garden** Parks Rd. 5 acres, best known for trees and herbaceous borders. In Fellows' main garden, fine ginkgo and Magnolia acuminata, etc; in Back Quadrangle very large Tilia tomentosa 'Petiolaris'; in Mallam Court white scented garden est 1994; in Warden's garden an ancient tulip tree; in Fellows' private garden Civil War embankment with period fruit tree cultivars, recently established shrubbery with unusual trees and ground cover amongst older plantings. *Adm £1 Chd free. Sun March 22. Combined adm with* **Queen's College** *£1.50. Sun July 19 (2-5)*

Wolfson College &✿ End of Linton Rd, off Banbury Rd, between city centre and Summertown shops. 9 acres by R Cherwell; garden developed in recent years with comprehensive plant collection tolerant of alkaline soils, grown in interesting and varied habitats both formal and informal, around a framework of fine mature trees; award winning building designed by Powell & Moya; President's garden. TEAS. *Adm £1 free. Sun June 7 (2-6)*

¶**Partway House, Banbury** &✿✿ (Mr & Mrs M Brown) ¾m from Swalcliffe on Shipston Rd at the Sibford Ferris fork. 2 acres of mature shrubs and herbaceous plants. Distant views. Exceptional for the area is acid soil condi-

tions, azaleas and rhododendrons. TEAS. *Adm £2 Chd free. Sun May 31 (2-6)*

Pettifers, Lower Wardington &✿✿ (Mr J & the Hon Mrs Price) 5m NE of Banbury. C17 village house. 13 yr-old 1½-acre plantsman's garden frames an exceptional view of sheep pastures and wooded hills. New Autumn border, with some areas reaching maturity. Unusual plants for sale. TEAS. *Adm £1.50 Chd free. Suns April 5, Sept 27 (2-6). Also open with* **Wardington Manor** *Combined adm £2.50 Chd free. Sun May 17 (2-6). Private visits welcome by appt*

Queen's College see Oxford University Gardens

Querns, Goring Heath &✿✿ (Mr M & the Hon Mrs Whitfeld) 3m NE of Pangbourne. Take B4526 from A4074 Reading-Oxford Rd. After ½m follow signs. 2-acre garden: shrub and herbaceous borders, rose garden, shrub rose garden, courtyard and formal pond. Listed house dating from early C16 with large thatched C17 barn. TEAS. *Adm £2 Chd free. Sun June 28 (2-6)*

Rewley House see Oxford University Gardens

St Hilda's College see Oxford University Gardens

St John's Home, Oxford &✿✿ St Mary's Rd, off Leopold St S of Cowley Rd. 1m E from the Plain. Limited parking. 3-acre grounds of All Saints Convent and St John's Home for the Elderly. Mature trees, lawns, secluded prayer garden and vegetable garden. Comper chapel open. TEAS. *Adm £1.50 OAPS £1 Chd free (ACNO to Society of All Saints Sisters of the Poor®). Sun May 24 (2-5)*

Salford Gardens, nr Chipping Norton ✿ 2m W of Chipping Norton. Off A44 Oxford-Worcester. TEAS. *Combined adm £1.50 Chd free. Suns June 21, Aug 30 (2-6)*

    Old Rectory &✿ (Mr & Mrs N M Chambers) 1½-acre garden mainly enclosed by walls. A garden of yr-round interest with unusual plants in mixed borders, many old roses, orchard and vegetable garden

    Willow Tree Cottage ✿ (Mr & Mrs J Shapley) Small walled twin gardens; one created by owners since 1979 with shrub and herbaceous borders, many clematis; other created 1985 from old farmyard with large alpine garden. Featured in 'Successful Gardening'

¶**Shellingford House, Faringdon** & (Mr & Mrs Nicholas Johnston) In Shellingford village off Faringdon to Wantage rd. 2 acres with eccentric features, stream, fritillarias, spring flowers and bulbs. Orchard, gnome garden and childrens entertainments. TEAS. *Adm £2 Chd 50p (ACNO to Shellingford Church®). Sun April 26 (2-6)*

Shotover House, Wheatley &✿ (Lt-Col Sir John Miller) 6m E of Oxford on A40. Bus: Oxford to Thame or Oxford to High Wycombe to London; alight Islip turn. Large unaltered landscape garden with ornamental temples, lawns and specimen trees. Also small collection of rare cattle, sheep and birds. *Adm £1.50 Chd free. Suns April 5, Aug 2 (2-6)*

Sibford Ferris Gardens ⚘ Nr the Warwickshire border, S of B4035 (Banbury 6½m, Shipston-on-Stour 7½m). TEAS in aid of Sibford Primary School PTA. *Combined adm £2 Chd free. Sun June 7 (2-6)*

    Back Acre ❀ (Mr & Mrs F A Lamb) Almost an acre, much of which is wild woodland and rough grass with wild flowers; rockery and pond, constructed about 100 years ago and restored over the last few years

    Maria's House ♿ (Mr & Mrs B R Mills) ¼-acre old cottage garden, surrounded and subdivided by low stone walling. Features incl box hedge porch, small pond, rockeries and herbaceous borders

    Sibford School ❀ (The Manor Walled Gardens) 1½ acres of walled gardens, completely reconstructed and replanted since 1984. Designed with central pergola covered pathways, with many varieties of climbing roses and clematis. The garden is subdivided to provide vegetable plots, soft fruit, greenhouses and herb garden. The gardens are used for the teaching of horticulture and are maintained by students at the school

Sibford Gower Gardens Nr the Warwickshire border, S of B4035 (Banbury 7m, Shipston-on-Stour 7m) Superlative views and numerous intriguing tucked away lanes are features of this village. TEAS in aid of Sibford Primary School. **Handy Water Farm** & **Meadow Cottage** *Combined adm for 2 gardens £2 Chd free Sun, Wed June 14, 17 (2-6);* **The Manor House, Temple Close, Meadow Cottage** *Combined adm for 3 gardens £2 Acc chd free. Sun July 12 (2-6)*

    Handywater Farm ⚘❀ (Mr & Mrs W B Colquhoun) ½m N of Sibford Gower on rd to Epwell; 1½-acre family garden in process of creation since 1980. Lovely setting in open rolling countryside. Westerly sloping lawns, stream and ponds, shrub and herbaceous beds

    The Manor House ♿ (Mr & Mrs Roger Garner) Opp Wykeham Arms. Completely reconstructed May 1989, the gardens (under 1 acre) are already well established and compliment the romantic atmosphere of this recently renovated rambling thatched manor house

    Meadow Cottage ♿⚘❀ (Mr & Mrs Roger Powell) 6 The Colony. At S end of village. A 1.3-acre garden started from a field in 1988. Large 'shrubaceous' borders; over 1300 different plants; many unusual. Conifers; shrub roses and alpines in raised beds; budding arboretum and series of waterfalls leading to stream. Views. *Also by appt June and July*

    Temple Close ♿❀ (Mrs Vera Jones) E of Wykham Arms. 1¼ acres with rockery, various beds of shrubs, roses, perennials and herbs; paved stream-side walk running through extensive water garden between two ponds with fountains; pets paddock; good view

Souldern Gardens Between Banbury (8m) and Bicester (7m) off B4100. 4 gardens in picturesque 'Best Kept' prizewinning village. TEAS. *Combined adm £2 Chd free (ACNO to Souldern Trust®). Sun June 21 (2-6)*

    Great House Close ♿❀ (Mrs C E Thornton) Long, varied garden and orchard framed by old farm buildings

    The Old Forge (Mr & Mrs D Duthie) Resourceful, densely planted cottage garden with stone walling

    Park Lodge ♿⚘ (Mrs J Bellinger) Garden retrieved from woodland with pond and flower borders

Souldern Manor ♿⚘ (Mr & Dr C Sanders) 25 acres of C17 house with much fresh development. Linked ponds, rock garden, waterfall, fountains, temple, pavillions and view of Cherwell valley are enhanced by many newly planted mature trees. Children's play area

South Newington Gardens, nr Banbury A small village 1½m from Bloxham, nr Banbury on A361 to Chipping Norton. It has a fine church, with superb mediaeval wall paintings. TEA at the village hall with stalls. 3 gardens within easy walking distance. *Combined adm £2 Chd free (ACNO to Ken Butcher Memorial Birth Centre Appeal®). Sun June 7 (2-6)*

    Applegarth ⚘❀ (Mr & Mrs Andrew Edgar) ¾-acre cottage garden with a rose walk featuring old-fashioned roses and lavenders; herbaceous borders and mixed gardens with some unusual shrubs and young trees; small water garden and ponds

    The Barn ♿⚘ (Mrs Rosemary Clark) Green Lane. 1 acre of lawns and mixed borders with outdoor chess game, croquet lawn, trompe l'oeil, vine walk and vegetable patch

    The Little Forge ♿ (Mr M B Pritchard) Small garden with shrubs; trees and vegetable patch

Sparsholt Manor, nr Wantage (Sir Adrian & Lady Judith Swire) Off B4507 Ashbury Rd 3 ½m W of Wantage. Summer borders, lakes and wilderness. Teas in village hall in aid of Sparsholt Church. *Adm £1.50 Chd free (ACNO to St John Ambulance, Wantage Division®). Mon May 25 (2-6)*

Stansfield, Stanford-in-the-Vale ⚘❀ (Mr & Mrs D Keeble) 49 High St. 3½m SE of Faringdon. Park in street. Plantsman's 1¼-acre garden on alkaline soil. Wide range of plants, many uncommon. Scree bed, sinks and troughs, damp garden, herbaceous borders, ornamental grasses. Copse underplanted with hellebores and shade loving plants. Aromatic plants. Unusual trees and shrubs. Yr-round interest. Wide range of plants for sale. TEAS. *Adm £1 Chd free. Every Tues April 7 to Aug 25 (10-4); Suns May 10, June 7 (2-6). Garden clubs and private visits also welcome, please* **Tel 01367 710340**

■ **Stanton Harcourt Manor, Stanton Harcourt** ♿❀ (Mr Crispin & The Hon Mrs Gascoigne) W of Oxford on B4449. Picturesque stone manor house with unique C15 Great Kitchen, Chapel and Pope's Tower. Formal gardens leading to woodland area with remains of moat and medieval stew ponds. TEAS. *Adm House and garden £4 Chd/OAP's £2. Garden only £2.50 Chd/OAP's £1.50. Thurs April 23, May 14, June 4, 18, July 2, 16, 30; Aug 13, Sept 10, 24; Suns April 12, 26, May 3, 17, 24, June 7, 21, July 5, 19, Aug 2, 16, 30, Sept 13, 27, Bank hol Mons April 13, May 4, 25, Aug 31. For NGS Suns April 26, June 21 (2-6)*

Evening Opening (see also garden descriptions)

Lower Chilworth Farm, Milton Common

                                 June 21 6–9pm

Steeple & Middle Aston Gardens Beautiful stone villages midway between Oxford & Banbury, ½m off A4260. Villages bordering Cherwell valley; interesting church and winding lanes with a variety of charming stone houses and cottages. Map available at all gardens. TEAS and lunchtime barbecue at Canterbury House (in Village Hall if wet) ⅓rd in aid of local scout group. *Combined adm £2.50 Chd free. Sun June 28 (1-6)*

Canterbury House & ⚘ (Mr & Mrs M G Norris) Former rectory in 2-acre garden with mature trees and intersected by walls. The garden is continually being redeveloped for ease of maintenance, interest and attraction of wildlife. *(ACNO to Specialcare Baby Unit, John Radcliffe®)*

Home Farm House ⚘ (Mr & Mrs T J G Parsons) ¾m N of Steeple Aston, opp Middle Aston House. 1-acre informal garden surrounding C17 farmhouse, fine view. Mixed planting, incl unusual perennials, shrubs and roses. *Private visits welcome May to Oct, please* **Tel 01869 340666**

Kralingen (Mr & Mrs Roderick Nicholson) 2-acre informal garden designed for low maintenance without professional help. Great variety of interesting trees and shrubs. Water garden and wild flower area

The Longbyre (Mr & Mrs V Billings) Hornton stone house in ¼ acre. Garden constructed out of old orchard. Water feature, mixed perennials, shrubs, tubs on different levels

¶Oak Ridge, Steeple Aston ⚘ (Mr & Mrs M J Simmonds) Small, redeveloped cottage garden designed for low maintenance, botanical interest and quiet relaxation

Rowans & ⚘ (Mr & Mrs M J Clist) The Dickredge, opp White Lion. An acre of orchard and mixed garden, incl shrubs, herbaceous borders, alpines, vegetables

Stonewalls, Hempton & ⚘ (Mr & Mrs B Shafighian) 1½m W of Deddington on B4031. A plantsman's garden of 1½ acres divided into many interesting areas, incl shrubbery, herbaceous border, conifer and heather bed, nearly 200 clematis and climbers. Sunken pool. TEAS in aid of St John's Church, Hempton. *Adm £1.50 Chd free. Sun July 19 (2-6)*

Stratton Audley Gardens 3m NE of Bicester, off A421 to Buckingham. Village dates from Roman times. Church is largely mediaeval with spectacular late C17 tomb. TEAS at Stratton House. *Combined adm £2 Chd free (ACNO to Helen House Hospice®). Sun June 14 (2-6)*

1 Church Cottages & ⚘ (Mr & Mrs L Sweetman) About ½-acre. A proper country cottage garden with rockery, pools and stonework, vegetables, seasonal bedding, orchids

Mallories & ⚘ (Mr P Boyd) Mainly walled garden of ¾ acre behind row of C17 cottages converted to house. Sunny and shady herbaceous borders, bearded irises, old roses and other shrubs, wall plants and climbers, small conservatory. Plant stall in aid of Stratton Audley Church

Stratton House & ⚘ (Mr & Mrs P J Bailey) A quiet and peaceful walled garden, set in ¾-acre with terraces, paved area with fountain, herbaceous border, shrubs, heathers, ornamental pond, topiary, a black walnut tree and a yew, said to be over 400 yrs old

Swalcliffe Lea House, Swalcliffe Lea ⚘ (Jeffrey & Christine Demmar) Situated between Tadmarton and Shutford The garden has been developed during the last 10 yrs. It covers 7 acres with lawns, flower beds, informal ponds, herb garden, pergola, kitchen garden, orchard and woodland walk. There is a wide range of young trees, shrubs and plants. TEAS. *Adm £2 Chd free. Sun July 5 (2-5.30). Private visits welcome by appt, please* **Tel 01295 788278**

Swerford Park, nr Chipping Norton (Mr & Mrs J W Law) 4m NE of Chipping Norton, just off A361 to Banbury, ½m W of Swerford Church. In extensive parkland setting with lakeside walks, garden of Georgian house overlooks spectacular wooded valley with series of lakes linked by waterfalls. Approach along front drive where signed; parking at rear only, may not be very close. TEAS. *Adm £2 Chd free (ACNO to Swan Lifeline, Windsor®). Mon May 25 (2-6)*

Swinbrook House, nr Burford & ⚘ (Mrs J D Mackinnon) 1½m N of Swinbrook on Shipton-under-Wychwood Rd. Large garden; herbaceous border; shrubs; shrub roses; large kitchen garden; fine views. Picnics allowed. TEA. *Adm £1.50 Chd free. Sun July 19 (2-6)*

Tadmarton Gardens 5m SW of Banbury on B4035. Refreshments at village hall in aid of St Nicholas Church, Tadmarton. *Combined adm £2.50 Chd free. Suns April 5, Sept 20 (1.30-5)*

The Arches & ⚘ (Mr & Mrs J Bolland) ⅕-acre garden designed and created by present owners since 1983. Lovingly adapted for disabled occupant. Open air 'rooms' incl Japanese, William Kent and Mediterranean gardens, summer houses. A garden for sitting in

Buxton House & ⚘ (Mr & Mrs J Steele) Small garden created in last 10 yrs incl a waterfall and two fountains

Tadmarton Manor & ⚘ (Mr & Mrs R K Asser) Old established 2½-acre garden; beautiful views of unspoilt countryside; fine trees, great variety of perennial plants and shrubs; hardy cyclamen, tunnel arbour; C15 barn and C18 dovecote

Tile Cottage (Mr & Mrs D Woodward) Traditional country garden. Flowers, vegetables and orchard

Towersey Manor, Towersey & ⚘ (Mr & Mrs U D Barnett) 1½m SE of Thame, 300yds down Manor Rd from Xrds in middle of village. Main garden of 2 acres lies behind house. Within the last 23 yrs this once open and flat site has been transformed by the present owners. Formal hornbeam hedges frame smaller informal areas incorporating many shrubs, trees and old-fashioned and modern shrub roses. *Adm £1.50 Chd free. Weds May 20, June 24 (2-6). Private visits welcome on weekdays May to July, please* **Tel 01844 212077**

Town Farm Cottage, Kingston Blount & ⚘ (Mr & Mrs J Clark) 4m S of Thame. 1½m NE of junction 6, M40 on B4009. 1¼-acre colourful garden bursting with many unusual plants. Totally developed over last 10 yrs by present 'plantaholic' owners. Features large rockery and herbaceous borders, scree beds full of 'little treasures'.

Rare English mature black poplar trees by small lake, full of fish. Red Kites frequently seen overhead. TEAS. *Adm £1.50 Chd under 14 free. Suns April 12, July 12 (2-6). Private visits also welcome, please Tel 01844 352152*

Trinity College see Oxford University Gardens

Troy & Gould's Grove Farmhouse, Ewelme ፚ❀ (Mr & Mrs D Ruck Keene & Mr T Ruck Keene) 3m NE of Wallingford. From roundabout on A4074/A4130 take exit signed Ewelme, RAF Benson (Clacks Lane). Approx 1½m turn R at T-junction towards Henley. 1½-acre garden featuring grey and herb gardens, daffodils; summer houses used by Jerome K Jerome (former owner). Small flocks of Jacob and Hebridean sheep with lambs. Small garden adjacent with interesting shrubs and fine views of The Chilterns. TEAS in aid of Marie Curie Foundation. *Adm £2.50 Chd free. Sun April 26 (2-6)*

Tusmore Park, Bicester ፚ❀ (Tusmore Park Holdings) Off A43. 3½m S of Brackley. Approx 20 acres of lawns, herbaceous borders, woodland garden and terraces. 6-acre lake, 3 greenhouses; walled garden. TEAS. *Adm £1.50 Chd free. Sun July 26 (2-6)*

Upper Wolvercote Gardens ፚ❀ N Oxford. Secluded old village within Oxford's ring rd. From Oxford take first turn L off Woodstock Rd; park at Plough Inn or beside village green. Teas at Plough. Walk up Church Lane (unmetalled) from green. Cluster of old houses by church, with hillside gardens overlooking Port Meadow and Wytham woods. *Combined adm £2 Chd free. Sun May 17 (2-5)*
  The Close ፚ❀ (Dr & Mrs H G Reading) ¾-acre terraced front garden with spectacular views framed by trees. Orchard at rear
  1 Cyprus Terrace ❀ (Mrs H Coyte) End cottage of Victorian terrace; tiny garden with spring bulbs, even smaller woodland bank
  Church Farm House ፚ❀ (Mr & Mrs S Franks) C17 house with ½-acre garden. Fruit trees and roses bordered by low box hedges; Cotswold stone walls, marble statue among lime trees, courtyard garden with raised pond
  19 First Turn (Mr J Powis & Ms A Munro) C16 cottage with secluded small garden, densely planted with perennials, shrubs and fruit trees
  Old Church House ❀ (Mr & Mrs E M Loft-Simson) C17 vine-covered cottage with small walled 'hortus conclusus', with fountain
  1 Osborne Close ❀ (Dr A W McDonald) Small enclosed sloping informal garden with water feature
  Uplands ፚ❀ (Dr & Mrs M J M Leask) Secluded ¼-acre garden on a slope surrounded by trees

Wadham College see Oxford University Gardens

Wardington Manor, Wardington ፚ (The Lord & Lady Wardington) 5m NE of Banbury. 5-acre garden with topiary, rock garden, flowering shrub walk to pond. Carolean manor house 1665. TEAS. *Combined adm with Pettifers £2.50 Chd free. Sun May 17 (2-5.30). Private visits by parties also welcome adm £2, please Tel 01295 750202*

■ **Waterperry Gardens** ፚ❀ 2½m from Wheatley M40 Junction 8. 9m E of Oxford. Gardens well signed locally with Tourist Board 'rose' symbol. 20 acres; ornamental gardens with many interesting plants; shrub, herbaceous and alpine nurseries; glasshouses and comprehensive fruit section. High quality plant centre, garden shop (**Tel 01844 339226**). TEA SHOP. Saxon church with famous glasses and brasses in grounds. *Adm Gardens & Nurseries £3 OAPs £2.50 Chd £1.50 under 10 free.* **OPEN DAILY** *except Christmas and New Year hols and July 16 to 19. Coach parties by appt only Tel 01844 339254 . For NGS (ACNO to NCCPG®). Suns June 7, Aug 9 (9-5.30)*

Westwell Manor, nr Burford ❀❀ (Mr & Mrs T H Gibson) 2m SW of Burford, from A40 Burford-Cheltenham, turn L after ½m on narrow rd signposted Westwell. Unspoilt hamlet with delightful church. 6 acres surrounding old Cotswold manor house, knot and water gardens, potager, shrub roses, herbaceous borders, topiary, moonlight garden. *Adm £2 Chd 50p (ACNO to St Mary's Church Westwell®). Sun July 5 (2-6.30)*

White's Farm House, Letcombe Bassett ፚ❀ (Dr & Mrs M Shone) 3m SW of Wantage. Take B4507 signed Ashbury, then through Letcombe Regis. 2½ acres; mixed borders; wild garden with 35 yrs growth of chalk-tolerant trees, shrubs, unusual herbaceous plants, summer bulbs. Gravel scree bed, plants in pots and tubs, pond, playground and monster adventure walk. Wood and willow features. New minimalist shingle garden with roses and alpines. TEAS in C18 barn. *Adm £2 Chd free. Suns June 21, July 19 (2-6)*

Wick Hall & Nurseries, Radley ፚ❀ (Mr & Mrs P Drysdale) Between Abingdon & Radley on Audlett Drive. Parking for disabled at house, some off-street parking. Approx 10 acres lawns and wild garden; topiary; pond garden; rockeries; walled garden enclosing knot garden; young arboretum. Early C18 house (not open), barn and greenhouses, large display of old horticultural and agricultural tools. TEAS in aid of Radley WI. *Adm £1.50 Chd free. Sun April 26 (2-5)*

Wolfson College see Oxford University Gardens

Wood Croft, Boars Hill ❀ (St Cross College) Foxcombe Lane, S of Oxford. From ring rd follow signs to Wootton and Boars Hill. From junction at top Hinksey Hill, house 1st on L. 1½ acres designed and planted by the late Prof G E Blackman FRS. Rhododendrons, camellias, azaleas, many varieties primula in woodland and surrounding natural pond; fine trees. TEA. *Adm £1 Chd free (ACNO to Royal Marsden Hospital Development Appeal®). Sun May 24 (2-6)*

Wroxton Gardens ፚ❀ 3m NW of Banbury off A422. Grounds of Wroxton Abbey open free. Teas at village fete May. *Combined adm £2 Chd free. Mon May 25 (1-6)*
  6 The Firs Stratford Rd (Mr & Mrs D J Allen) Approx ⅓-acre family garden with island beds, shrubs, herbaceous perennials incl large collection of cranesbill geraniums
  Laurels Farm (Mr & Mrs R Fox) ½-acre with island beds, shrubs, old roses and herbaceous perennials

Yelford Gardens &⚬❀ From Witney 2m from A40 take A415. 1m S towards Standlake or Abingdon just past Cokethorpe School at Hardwick Xrd turn R. Single track rd with passing places. TEAS. *Combined adm £3 Chd free (ACNO to St Nicholas & St Swithun's, Yelford® and Springfields School Witney©). Sun June 21 (2-6)*

Broad Leas House (Mr & Mrs Rogers) 1-acre plantsman's garden started 18 years ago. Herbaceous borders, shrubberies, lawns, spindle apple trees, vegetable garden with soft fruit area and small formal rose garden

Yelford Manor &⚬❀ (R Rosewell Esq) 3-acre garden surrounding C15 timber framed manor house (not open). Knot gardens, clipped yews, shrubs, borders moat garden and lawns

Yeomans ❀ (Mrs M E Pedder) Tadmarton 5m SW of Banbury on B4035. Small garden on 4 levels, featured in 'Easy Plants for Difficult Places' by Geoffrey Smith; C16 thatched cottage. Colourful from spring to autumn; wide variety annuals, perennials, shrubs; many climbers incl roses, clematis; shrub roses with hips. *Adm £1 Chd free (ACNO to Katharine House Hospice Trust®). Private visits welcome for 2 and over, by appt, please. April to Sept* **Tel 01295 780285**

The *National Gardens Scheme* is pleased to invite you to
a special Evening Opening at

The Royal Botanic Gardens, Kew
during Chelsea Week
Thursday, May 21st, 6.30–9pm

Enjoy the glorious late spring at Kew at an exclusive Evening Opening. Two of the major glasshouses will be open, with staff available to explain their collections and Kew's work.

Admission: £4 Adults, £2 Children,
in aid of the National Gardens Scheme

(as this is a fund-raising event, admission fee also applies to Season Ticket holders and Friends of the Royal Botanic Gardens, Kew) Refreshments available

Kew is easily reached via the Kew Gardens station (London Underground District Line, and by rail from North London on Silverlink). Also from Kew Bridge station (South West Trains). By road the Gardens are located just south of Kew Bridge on the A307, Kew Road.

Entry by Victoria Gate Only, on the Kew Road, opposite Lichfield Road.

Powys

See separate Welsh section beginning on page 396

Shropshire

Hon County Organisers: Mrs J H M Stafford, The Old Rectory, Fitz, Shrewsbury SY4 3AS
Tel 01743 850555
Mr James Goodall, Rectory Cottage, Chetton, Bridgnorth, Shropshire
WV16 6UF
Mrs A Cooke, Harnage Farm, Cound, Shropshire SY5 6EJ

Hon County Treasurer: Mrs P Trevor-Jones, Preen Manor, Church Preen, nr Church Stretton SY6 7LQ

DATES OF OPENING

Regular openings
For details see garden description

Burford House Gardens, Tenbury
Wells
Hawkstone Hall, Shrewsbury
Hodnet Hall Gardens, nr Market
Drayton
Weston Park, Shifnal
Wollerton Old Hall, Wollerton

By appointment only
*For telephone numbers and other
details see garden descriptions.
Private visits welcomed*

Ashford Manor, Ashford Carbonel
Fairfield, Oldbury, Bridgnorth
Farley House, Much Wenlock
Haye House, Eardington

March 28 Saturday
   Attingham Park, nr Shrewsbury
March 29 Sunday
   Attingham Park, nr Shrewsbury
April 5 Sunday
   Chyknell, Bridgnorth
April 7 Tuesday
   Radnor Cottage, Clun
April 12 Sunday
   Badger Farmhouse, Badger
April 13 Monday
   Hundred House Hotel, Norton
April 19 Sunday
   Astley Abbotts House,
      Bridgnorth
   Brownhill House, Ruyton XI
      Towns
April 21 Tuesday
   Radnor Cottage, Clun
April 25 Saturday
   Benthall Hall, Broseley
April 26 Sunday
   Morville Gardens, nr
      Bridgnorth
May 2 Saturday
   Field House, Clee St Margaret
May 3 Sunday
   Field House, Clee St Margaret

May 4 Monday
   Millichope Park, Munslow
May 10 Sunday
   Gatacre Park, Six Ashes
   Preen Manor, Church Preen
May 11 Monday
   Mawley Hall, Cleobury Mortimer
May 12 Tuesday
   Radnor Cottage, Clun
May 15 Friday
   Cruckfield House, Ford
May 17 Sunday
   Adcote School, Little Ness
   Brownhill House, Ruyton XI
      Towns
   Cricklewood Cottage, Plox Green
   Gatacre Park, Six Ashes
   Ridgway Wood, Edgton
   Thornfield, Twmpath, Gobowen
May 24 Sunday
   Gate Cottage, nr Ellesmere
   Hatton Grange, Shinral
   Longnor Hall, Longnor
   Peplow Hall, Hodnet
   Ridgway Wood, Edgton
   Walcot Hall, Lydbury North
   Willey Park, Broseley
May 25 Monday
   Dudmaston, Quatt
   Hundred House Hotel, Norton
   Longnor Hall, Longnor
   Oteley, Ellesmere
   Ridgway Wood, Edgton
   Walcot Hall, Lydbury North
May 26 Tuesday
   Radnor Cottage, Clun
May 30 Saturday
   Brownhill House, Ruyton XI
      Towns
May 31 Sunday
   Adcote School, Little Ness
   Bitterley Court, Ludlow
   Brownhill House, Ruyton XI
      Towns
   The Lyth, Ellesmere
   Triscombe, Wellington
June 5 Friday
   Wollerton Old Hall, Wollerton
June 7 Sunday
   Adcote School, Little Ness
   The Old Rectory, Fitz

   The Old Vicarage, Cardington
   The Patch, Acton Pigot
June 8 Monday
   Brownhill House, Ruyton XI
      Towns
June 11 Thursday
   Preen Manor, Church Preen
June 12 Friday
   Wollerton Old Hall, Wollerton
June 14 Sunday
   Adcote School, Little Ness
   Brownhill House, Ruyton XI
      Towns
   Chyknell, Bridgnorth
   Cricklewood Cottage, Plox Green
   Gate Cottage, nr Ellesmere
   The Old Vicarage, Cardington
   The Patch, Acton Pigot
June 15 Monday
   Mawley Hall, Cleobury Mortimer
June 16 Tuesday
   Weston Park, Shifnal
June 19 Friday
   Cruckfield House, Ford
   Wollerton Old Hall, Wollerton
June 20 Saturday
   Hartshill Gardens, Oakengates
   Moortown, nr Wellington
June 21 Sunday
   Glazeley Old Rectory, Nr
      Bridgnorth
   Harnage Farm, Cound
   Hartshill Gardens, Oakengates
   Lower Hall, Worfield
   Madeley New Gardens, Telford
   Millichope Park, Munslow
   Moortown, nr Wellington
June 22 Monday
   Brownhill House, Ruyton XI
      Towns
June 25 Thursday
   Preen Manor, Church Preen
June 26 Friday
   Wollerton Old Hall, Wollerton
June 27 Saturday
   Whittington Village Gardens, nr
      Oswestry
June 28 Sunday
   Bitterley Court, Ludlow
   David Austin Roses, Albrighton
   Triscombe, Wellington

SHROPSHIRE

KEY

1. Acton Round
2. Adcote School
3. Ashford Manor
4. Astley Abbotts House
5. Attingham Park
6. Badger Farmhouse
7. Benthall Hall
8. Bitterley Court
9. Brownhill House
10. Burford House Gardens
11. Church Bank
12. Chyknell
13. Cricklewood Cottage
14. Cruckfield House
15. David Austin Roses
16. Dudmaston
17. Fairfield
18. Farley House
19. Field House
20. Gatacre Park

21. Gate Cottage
22. Glazeley Old Rectory
23. Harnage Farm
24. Hartshill Gardens
25. Hatton Grange
26. Hawkstone Hall
27. Haye House
28. Hodnet Hall Gardens
29. Hundred House Hotel
30. Limeburners
31. Linley Hall
32. Longnor Hall
33. Lower Hall
34. The Lyth
35. Madeley New Gardens
36. Mawley Hall
37. The Mill Cottage
38. Millichope Park
39. Moortown
40. Morville Gardens

41. Nordybank Nurseries
42. The Old Rectory
43. The Old Vicarage
44. Oteley
45. The Patch
46. Peplow Hall
47. Preen Manor
48. Radnor Cottage
49. Ridgway Wood
50. Ruthall Manor
51. Stottesdon Village Gardens
52. Thornfield
53. Triscombe
54. Walcot Hall
55. Weston Park
56. Whittington Village Gardens
57. Willey Park
58. Wollerton Old Hall

Whittington Village Gardens, nr
Oswestry

June 29 Monday
Brownhill House, Ruyton XI
Towns

July 5 Sunday
Linley Hall nr Bishops Castle
The Mill Cottage, Cound
The Old Vicarage, Cardington

July 7 Tuesday
Radnor Cottage, Clun

July 8 Wednesday
Burford House Gardens, Tenbury
Wells

July 9 Thursday
Preen Manor, Church Preen

July 10 Friday
Cruckfield House, Ford

July 11 Saturday
Field House, Clee St Margaret

July 12 Sunday
Cricklewood Cottage, Plox Green
Field House, Clee St Margaret
Hundred House Hotel, Norton

The Old Vicarage, Cardington

July 13 Monday
Mawley Hall, Cleobury Mortimer

July 14 Tuesday
Weston Park, Shifnal

July 19 Sunday
Acton Round, Morville
Astley Abbotts House, Bridgnorth
Church Bank, Rowley
Nordybank Nurseries, Clee St
Margaret

July 23 Thursday
Preen Manor, Church Preen

July 26 Sunday
Brownhill House, Ruyton XI
Towns

July 28 Tuesday
Radnor Cottage, Clun

August 1 Saturday
Hodnet Hall Gardens, nr Market
Drayton

August 2 Sunday
Limeburners, Ironbridge
Ruthall Manor, Ditton Priors

August 5 Wednesday
Hawkstone Hall, Shrewsbury

August 6 Thursday
Hawkstone Hall, Shrewsbury

August 8 Saturday
Hodnet Hall Gardens, nr Market
Drayton

August 12 Wednesday
Burford House Gardens, Tenbury
Wells

August 23 Sunday
Madeley New Gardens, Telford

August 30 Sunday
Stottesdon Village Gardens

August 31 Monday
Stottesdon Village Gardens

September 6 Sunday
Brownhill House, Ruyton XI
Towns

September 11 Friday
Cruckfield House, Ford

October 4 Sunday
Preen Manor, Church Preen

DESCRIPTIONS OF GARDENS

Acton Round, Morville &⚘❀ (Mr & Mrs Hew Kennedy) 6m W of Bridgnorth. A458 Morville-Shrewsbury, 2m after Morville turn L (W). 1½-acre garden with yew hedges; rose herbaceous and newly planted borders; various follies; attractive church and beautiful early Georgian house (not open). TEAS. *Adm £2 Chd £1 (ACNO to Acton Round Church®). Sun July 19, (2-6.30). Garden also open by appt* **Tel 01746 714203**

Adcote School, Little Ness ⚘ (Adcote School Educational Trust Ltd) 8m NW of Shrewsbury via A5, turn off NE follow signs to Little Ness. 20-acres; fine trees incl beeches, tulip trees, oaks (American and Evergreen); atlas cedars, Wellingtonia etc; rhododendrons, azaleas; small lake; landscaped garden. House (part shown) designed by Norman Shaw RA; Grade I listed building; William Morris wallpapers; de Morgan tiles. TEAS. *Adm £1.50 Acc chd free. Suns May 17, 31, June 7, 14 (2-5). Other times strictly by appt only* **Tel 01939 260202**

Ashford Manor, Ashford Carbonel & (Kit Hall Esq) 2¾m S of Ludlow. E of A49 Ludlow-Leominster. Garden of 2 acres, herbaceous foliage and shrubs grown in the hope of maintaining interest through the entire year, hence very few flowers. Worked entirely by owner. Picnic area - Dogs welcomed. Reasonably level ground. *Adm 50p. Private visits welcome all year, please* **Tel 01584 872100**

Astley Abbotts House, Bridgnorth ❀ (Mrs H E Hodgson) 2m NW of Bridgnorth. B4373 from Bridgnorth turn R at Cross Lane Head. 10 acres, 5 acres PYO lavender, bee village; herbs; wild woodland garden; fine trees; lawns; rhododendrons. Only partly suitable for wheelchairs. TEAS. *Adm £1.50 Chd free (ACNO to Wolverhampton Eye Infirmary®). Suns April 19 (2-6), July 19 (11-6)*

▲**Attingham Park, nr Shrewsbury** (The National Trust) 4m SE of Shrewsbury on B4380. Parkland landscaped by Leggett and Repton, offering choice of walks. Swathes of naturalised narcissi along the river bank. Tearoom (2-4). Park open (12-6). House closed. *Adm £1.50 Chd 75p (NT members free). For NGS Sat, Sun March 28, 29 (12-6)*

Badger Farmhouse, Badger &❀ (Mr & Mrs N J D Foster) From A464 Shifnal to Wolverhampton Rd turn S to Burnhill Green. In Burnhill Green turn W to Beckbury. At T junction in Beckbury turn S, ¾m on R. 3-acre garden. Over 300 varieties of daffodils and narcissi in a mature setting. Mainly in three orchards, one of apple one pear and plum and one of cherry. Also fine trees, shrubs and roses. TEAS. *Adm £1.50 Chd free (ACNO to Riding for the Disabled, Brockton Group®). Easter Sun April 12 (2-6). Private visits welcome, please* **Tel 01746 783222**

▲**Benthall Hall, Broseley** &⚘ (The National Trust) 1m NW of Broseley, 4m NE of Much Wenlock (B4375); turning up lane marked with brown sign. Garden 3 acres; shrub roses; rockery banks; lawns; former kitchen garden; wild garden. Interesting plants and fine trees. C16 house also open. *Adm £2 Chd £1. For NGS Sat April 25 (1.30-5.30)*

Bitterley Court, Ludlow &❀ (Mr & Mrs J V T Wheeler) Next to Bitterley Church. Follow A4117 E from Ludlow and turn off to Bitterley after about 2m. 5m from Ludlow altogether. A 6-acre garden featuring specimen and rare trees, shrubs, woodland walks, ornamental kitchen garden and herbaceous borders. TEAS in aid of Marie Curie Nurses and Imperial Cancer Research. *Adm £2 Chd free. Suns May 31, June 28 (2-6)*

Brownhill House, Ruyton XI Towns ⚘❀ (Roger & Yoland Brown) 10m NW of Shrewsbury on B4397. Park at

Bridge Inn. Unusual and distinctive hillside garden (over 500 steps) bordering River Perry featured on TV and in magazines. Great variety of plants and styles from laburnum walk and formal terraces to woodland paths plus large kitchen garden. 200 varieties of plants for sale, proceeds to NGS. TEAS. *Adm £1.50 Chd free. Suns April 19, May 17; Sat, Sun May 30, 31, Suns June 14, July 26, Sept 6 (1.30-5.30) Mons June 8, 22, 29 (6.30-8.30). Also by appt May-Aug please* **Tel 01939 261121. Website www.eleventowns.demon.co.uk**

■ **Burford House Gardens, Tenbury Wells** &&& (Treasures of Tenbury) 1m W of Tenbury Wells on A456. 4 acres of sweeping lawns and serpentine borders, set in beautiful surroundings in the Teme Valley, around an elegant Georgian house. National Clematis Collection and over 2,000 other kinds of plants in wonderful combinations of colours and textures. Nursery offers over 200 varieties of clematis and comprehensive range of usual and unusual plants. Fine church, gallery and gift shop. DOGS on lead, nursery only. TEAS. *Adm £2.50 Chd £1. Open every day, all yr-round 10-5. For NGS Weds July 8, Aug 12 (10-5)*

Church Bank, Rowley && (Mr & Mrs B P Kavanagh) 12m SW of Shrewsbury on B4386 Montgomery Rd continuing through Westbury. After ⅓m turn R for Rowley. After 3½m turn L at Xrds for Brockton. Church Bank is on L after 120yds. A S-facing, steeply sloping garden; packed with interesting and unusual plants, predominantly perennial, with a large area of young woodland and 'natural' planting which incl 2 pools - one newly made and a bog garden. *Adm £1.50 Chd free (ACNO to Action Aid®). Sun July 19 (2-6); also private visits welcome May to Sept, please* **Tel 01743 891661**

Chyknell, Bridgnorth && (Mr & Mrs Simon Kenyon-Slaney) 5m E of Bridgnorth between Claverley and Worfield. Signed off A454 and A458. 5-acre garden designed by Russell Page. TEAS. *Adm £1.50 Chd 50p (ACNO to The County Air Ambulance Trust®). Suns April 5, June 14 (2-6)*

Cricklewood Cottage, Plox Green &&& (Paul & Debbie Costello) On A488 1m SW of Minsterley. Park on grass verges, not on rd. Delightful ⅓-acre cottage garden in attractive setting. Mature borders packed with shrubs and perennials, walks alongside trout stream, waterfalls, flourishing bog garden. Imaginative use of long narrow garden with a surprise round every corner. Featured in books and magazines. TEAS. *Adm £1.50 Chd free (ACNO to Holy Trinity Church Minsterley®). Suns May 17, June 14, July 12 (2-6). Private visits also welcome, please* **Tel 01743 791229**

¶**Cruckfield House, Ford** &&& (Mr & Mrs G M Cobley) 5m W of Shrewsbury A458, turn L towards Cruckton. 4 acre garden with backdrop of mature trees. The romantic S garden, formally designed, is informally and intensively planted with an extensive range of unusual herbaceous plants. Nick's garden, with many specie trees and shrubs, surrounds a large pond with bog and moisture loving plants. Ornamental kitchen garden with pretty outbuildings. Rose and peony walk. TEAS. *Adm £2.50 Chd 50p. Fris May 15, June 19, July 10, Sept 11 (2-6)*

▲**David Austin Roses, Albrighton** && (Mr & Mrs David Austin) Bowling Green Lane, 8m NW of Wolverhampton. 4m from Shifnal (A464) L into Bowling Green Lane; or junction 3, M54 to Albrighton, R at sign 'Roses & Shrubs', Bowling Green Lane 2nd R. Breeders of the famous English roses. Gardens; 900 varieties old roses, shrub, species and climbing roses; herbaceous display garden. Semi-wild private garden, trees and water garden with many plants. Variety of plants for sale. Sculpture by Pat Austin. TEAS. *Adm £2 Chd free. For NGS Sun June 28 (2-6)*

▲**Dudmaston, Quatt** && (The National Trust; Sir George Labouchere) 4m SE of Bridgnorth on A442. Bus stop at gates ½m. 8 acres with fine trees, shrubs; lovely views over Dudmaston Pool and surrounding country. Dingle walk. TEAS. *Adm £2.50 Chd £1. For NGS Mon May 25 (2-6)*

Fairfield, Oldbury, Bridgnorth && (Mr & Mrs G P Beardsley) Take B4363 from Bridgnorth to Cleobury Mortimer Rd 100 yds from SVR railway bridge - over bypass turn L. Informal landscaped garden of approx 3½ acres, containing sweeping lawns, many interesting trees and shrubs, water garden and woodland area. *Adm £1.50 Chd free. April to end July Mon to Fri incl (2-6), strictly by appt please,* **Tel 01746 763291**

Farley House, Much Wenlock & (Mr & Mrs R W Collingwood) From A458 at Much Wenlock turn N on to A4169 signed Ironbridge; house 1m on L. 1-acre garden made since 1980 by owners; alpines, herbaceous island beds, shrubs and trees. Coach parties welcome. *Adm £2 Chd free. Open by appt April to Oct, please* **Tel 01952 727017**

Field House, Clee St Margaret &&& (Dr & Mrs John Bell) 8m NE of Ludlow. Turning to Stoke St Milborough and Clee St Margaret. 5m from Ludlow, 10m from Bridgnorth along B4364. Through Stoke St Milborough to Clee St Margaret. Ignore R turn to Clee Village. Field House on L. Parking. 1-acre garden created since 1982 for yr-round interest. Mixed borders; rose walk; pool garden; herbaceous borders; spring bulbs and autumn colours. TEAS in aid of Village Hall Fund. *Adm £1.50 Chd 50p. Sats, Suns May 2, 3, July 11, 12 (12-6). Private visits welcome, please* **Tel 01584 823242**

Gatacre Park, Six Ashes && (Lady Thompson) 6m SE of Bridgnorth on A458. Stourbridge-Bridgnorth Rd. 8 acres. Originally a Victorian garden partly redeveloped over the last 56 years by present owner. Flowering shrubs, fine trees, incl 100ft tulip tree and manna ash; topiary walk; large woodland garden with pieris, azaleas, rhododendrons incl many interesting species now fully grown. Lovely views over Park. TEAS. *Adm £2 Chd free (ACNO to Tuck Hill Church, Six Ashes®). Suns May 10, 17 (2-6)*

Gate Cottage, nr Ellesmere && (G W Nicholson & Kevin Gunnell) 10m N of Shrewsbury on A528. At village of Cockshutt take rd signposted English Frankton. Garden is 1m on R. Parking in adjacent field. A developing garden at present about 2 acres. Informal mixed plantings of trees, shrubs, herbaceous of interest to flower arrangers and plantsmen. Pool and rock garden; informal pools. Large collection of hostas; old orchard with roses. TEA. *Adm £1.50 Chd 50p. Suns May 24, June 14 (1-5). Parties by appt at other times, please* **Tel 01939 270606**

Glazeley Old Rectory, nr Bridgnorth &⌀❀ (Mr & Mrs R Arbuthnott) 3m S of Bridgnorth on B4363 Bridgnorth-Cleobury Mortimer rd. 2-acre garden in beautiful natural setting. Herbaceous borders, bulbs, alpines, old-fashioned roses, shrubs and trees. Paved, heather and bog gardens. TEAS. *Adm £1.50 Chd 50p. Sun June 21 (2-6). Private visits welcome, please* **Tel 01746 789443**

Harnage Farm, Cound &⌀❀ (Mr & Mrs Ken Cooke) 8m SE of Shrewsbury on A458. Turn to Cound 1m S of Cross Houses. Harnage Farm 1m, bearing L past church. ½-acre farmhouse garden; well stocked with herbaceous plants, shrubs and climbers and a collection of old roses. Extensive views over beautiful Severn Valley. TEAS. *Adm £2 (ACNO to Ward 21, Nurses Fund, Shrewsbury Hospital©). Sun June 21 (2-6)*

Hartshill Gardens, Oakengates &⌀❀ E of Shrewsbury. Once within the Telford/Wrekin district. Follow local signs to Oakengates. TEAS. *Combined adm £1 Chd free. Sat, Sun June 20, 21 (2-5.30)*
  Longmede (Mr & Mrs D J Steele) 13 Hartshill Road. Approx ½-acre ornamental garden with specimen trees, shrubs and raised alpine beds. Yr-round interest. Very easy access for the disabled. *Private visits welcome (April-Oct), please* **Tel 01952 612710**
  Northcote (Mr & Mrs R A Woolley) 15 Hartshill Road. ¼-acre garden with vegetables, flowers and shrubs. *Private visits welcome (April-Oct), please* **Tel 01952 613644**

Hatton Grange, Shifnal &❀ (Mrs Peter Afia) Lodge gate entrance on A464, 2m S of Shifnal. 1m up drive. Large dingle with pools, rhododendrons, azaleas, fine old trees; shrubbery; roses; lily pond garden. TEAS. *Adm £2 Chd free (ACNO to BACUP®). Sun May 24 (2-7). Parties by appt, please* **Tel 01952 460415**

■ **Hawkstone Hall, Marchamley** (Redemptorist Study Centre) 13m NE of Shrewsbury. 6m SW of Market Drayton on A442. Entrance from Marchamley. Spacious, mid-Victorian garden (20 acres) with recent varied plantings in many different areas. Pools, rockery, large thatched arbour, herbaceous border etc. Extensive walks among splendid trees. Wide range of climbing plants incl 50 climbing rose cvs. Georgian mansion (open) with courtyard garden and winter garden. TEAS. *Adm garden only £1.50 Chd £1. Open Aug 5 to 31. For NGS Wed, Thurs Aug 5, 6 (2-5)*

Haye House, Eardington &⌀❀ (Mrs Paradise) 2m S of Bridgnorth, sign Highley B4555. 1m through village Eardington. 1-acre garden especially planted by the owner, for her work as a National & International flower demonstrator. Grade 2 listed house (not open). TEAS. *Adm £2.50 Chd free. Private visits welcome, April to Oct (10-6), also open in the evening by appt, please* **Tel 01746 764884**

■ **Hodnet Hall Gardens, nr Market Drayton** &❀ (Mr & the Hon Mrs A Heber-Percy) 5½m SW of Market Drayton; 12m NE Shrewsbury; at junc of A53 and A442. 60-acre landscaped garden with series of lakes and pools; magnificent forest trees, great variety of flowers, shrubs providing colour throughout season; featured on TV and Radio. Unique collection of big-game trophies in C17 tea-rooms. Gift shop and kitchen garden. TEAS and light lunches. Free parking. *Adm £3 OAP £2.50 Chd £1.20. April to end of Sept (Tues to Sat 12-5; Suns & Bank Hols 12-5.30). Reduced rates for organised parties of 25 or over* **Tel 01630 685 202**. *For NGS Sats Aug 1, 8 (12-5)*

Hundred House Hotel, Norton ⌀❀ (Sylvia & Henry Phillips) Situated on the A442 in the village of Norton. Midway between Bridgnorth and Telford. Large cottage garden created by Sylvia Phillips since 1986. Unusual stone placements, recently completed memorial garden, herbaceous borders, bulbs, old-fashioned roses and climbers, young acers and betulas. Also features a working herb garden for the hotel. Teas and lunches in hotel. *Adm £2 Chd £1. Mons April 13, May 25, Sun July 12 (12-5)*

Limeburners, Ironbridge &⌀ (Mr & Mrs J E Derry) Lincoln Hill. On outskirts of Ironbridge, Telford. From Traffic Island in Ironbridge take Church Hill and proceed up hill for ½m, garden on L 300yds below The Beeches Hospital. Prize-winning garden formerly site of a rubbish tip developed by owners as a Nature garden to attract wildlife. Many unusual shrubs giving year round interest. Featured on TV Channel 4, Garden Club. TEAS in aid of Arthritis & Rheumatism Council for Research. *Adm £2 Chd free. Sun Aug 2 (2-6). Private visits also welcome April to Sept, please* **Tel 01952 433715**

Lingen Nursery, Lingen Village See Herefordshire

Linley Hall, nr Bishops Castle &❀ (Justin Coldwell Esq) 3m NE of Bishops Castle. Turn E off A488 nr Lydham. Parkland; lawns, walled kitchen garden; lake; temple. Plants and produce for sale. TEAS. *Adm £1.50 Chd free. Sun July 5 (2-6)*

Longnor Hall, Longnor &⌀ (Mr & Mrs A V Nicholson) Longnor. Take A49 S of Shrewsbury to Longnor. Entry to Longnor Hall garden through grounds of Longnor Church. 70-acre garden and parkland. Interesting varieties of trees; herbaceous borders, yew and beech hedges; walled kitchen garden; stable yard and C17 house (not open); sheep and deer; Cound Brook; views of The Lawley and Caer Caradoc hills. Adjacent C13 Longnor Church. TEAS. *Adm £1.50 Chd 50p (ACNO to St. Mary's Church, Longnor®). Sun, Mon May 24, 25 (2-6)*

Lower Hall, Worfield &❀ (Mr & Mrs C F Dumbell) E of Bridgnorth. ½m N of A454 in village centre. 4 acres on R Worfe. Garden developed by present owners. Courtyard with fountain, walled garden with old-fashioned roses, clematis and iris. Water garden with pool, primula island and rock garden. Woodland garden incl rare magnolias and paper bark trees. Plant sales to local charity. WI TEAS. *Adm £2.50 Chd free. Sun June 21 (2-6). Private visits welcome. Coach and evening parties by appt, local catering can be arranged.* **Tel 01746 716607**

The Lyth, Ellesmere ♿️✿❀ (Mr & Mrs L R Jebb) 1m SE of Ellesmere; entrance between Whitemere and junction of A528/A495. 2-acre garden, rhododendrons, azaleas; good outlook on parkland; heath bed, shrub borders. Regency colonial house (not open), birthplace of founder of Save The Children, Eglantyne Jebb. Meres nearby worth a visit. TEAS by local Save the Children Fund. *Adm £1.75 Chd 50p. Sun May 31 (2-6)*

Madeley New Gardens, Telford ✿❀ (% Dr & Mrs G Richards) From Ironbridge up steep hill towards Madeley (B4373) R at roundabout into Glendinning Way. Group of gardens of various sizes up to 1¼ acres. Differing styles and planting incl water features, herbaceous borders and vegetables. Also woodland walk with views across Ironbridge Gorge. TEAS. *Adm £2 Chd 50p. Suns June 21, Aug 23 (2-6).* **Tel 01952 587417**

Mawley Hall, Cleobury Mortimer ♿️❀ (Mr & Mrs R A Galliers-Pratt) 2m NE of Cleobury Mortimer. On A4117 Bewdley-Ludlow Rd. Bus: X92, alight at gate. A natural garden in beautiful country with magnificent views; designed for wandering amongst roses, herbs, flowering shrubs; fine old trees. TEAS. *Adm £1.50 OAPs £1 Chd under 15, 50p. Mons May 11, June 15, July 13 (2-6)*

The Mill Cottage, Cound ♿️✿❀ (Mrs A J Wisden & Miss J M Hawkes) 8m SE of Shrewsbury on A458. Turn to Cound 1m S of Cross Houses. Mill Cottage 300yds on L ¼-acre cottage garden. Unusual and lovely herbaceous plants. Good and varied collection of hostas and ferns and a variety of clematis, plus a collection of plants in pots, conservatory and outdoor. TEAS. *Adm £2 Chd 50p (ACNO to Shrewsbury League of Friends®). Sun July 5 (2-6)*

Millichope Park, Munslow (Mr & Mrs L Bury) 8m NE of Craven Arms. From Ludlow (11m) turn L off B4368, ¾m out of Munslow. 13-acre garden with lakes; woodland walks; fine specimen trees, wild flowers; herbaceous borders. TEAS. *Adm £2 Chd 50p. Mon May 4, Sun June 21 (2-6). Private visits welcome, please* **Tel 01584 841234**

Moortown, nr Wellington ✿❀ (David Bromley Esq) 5m N of Wellington. Take B5062 signed Moortown 1m between High Ercall and Crudgington. Approx 1-acre plantsman's garden. Here may be found the old-fashioned, the unusual and even the oddities of plant life, in mixed borders of 'controlled' confusion. *Adm £2 Chd 50p. Sat, Sun June 20, 21 (2-5.30)*

Morville Gardens, nr Bridgnorth ♿️❀ Nine gardens in and around Morville Hall. 3m NW of Bridgnorth on A458 at junction with B4368. TEAS. *Combined adm £3 Chd 50p (ACNO to Morville Church®). Sun April 26 (2-5)*
    Morville Hall (Dr & Mrs J C Douglas and National Trust) 4-acre garden in fine setting, incl box parterre, mature shrub borders, pond garden, medieval stewpond
    ¶**South Pavilion** (Mr & Mrs B Jenkinson) Stylish formal courtyard garden
    The Vineyard (Mr I J S Rowe) Prize-winning small vineyard
    ¶**The Cottage** (Mr & Mrs J Begg) Pretty walled garden with good climbers

¶**Top Pool Barn** (Mrs J I Bolton) ⅓ acre family garden, begun 1992, built to survive children and dogs
▲**The Dower House** (Dr Katherine Swift) 1.5 acre sequence of gardens in various historical styles, incl turf maze, medieval garden, Elizabethan knot garden, formal veg garden, C17 canal garden, wild garden. *Parties also welcome,* **Tel 01746 714407**
Nos 1 & 2 The Gatehouse (Mr & Mrs F A Rowe & Judie Mennell) Two colourful cottage gardens, with woodland and formal areas
¶**Poplar Cottage Farm** (Elizabeth Bacon) ¾m N of Morville on A458. ⅓-acre flower arranger's garden; yr-round interest, many unusual plants

▲**Nordybank Nurseries, Clee St Margaret** ❀ (P Bolton) 7½m NE of Ludlow. Turning to Stoke St Milborough and Clee St Margaret 5m from Ludlow, 10m from Bridgnorth along B4364, through Stoke St Milborough on the Lane to Clee St Margaret. 1-acre cottage garden on sloping site. Informal plantings of trees, shrubs and unusual herbaceous, incl herbs and wildflowers. Also 'Rose Garden' with over 60 varieties of old roses and 'Field Garden' with 700 varieties of herbaceous plants. TEAS. *Adm £1.50 Chd free. For NGS Sun July 19 (12-6)*

The Old Rectory, Fitz ✿❀ (Mrs J H M Stafford) A5 NW of Shrewsbury; turn off at Montford Bridge, follow signs; from B5067 turn off at Leaton, follow signs. 1¼-acre botantist's garden; shrubs, vegetables; water garden. Partially suitable for wheelchairs. TEAS. *Adm £2 Chd 50p. Sun June 7 (12-6)*

The Old Vicarage, Cardington ♿️ (W B Hutchinson Esq) 2m N of B4371 Church Stretton/Much Wenlock rd, signed, or turn off A49 Shrewsbury-Ludlow rd at Leebotwood, 2½-acre scenic garden; trees, shrubs, roses, primulas, alpines, water and bog garden. Picnics allowed; on site parking. *Adm £2 Chd free. Suns June 7, 14; July 5, 12 (12-5.30). Private visits welcome, June, July, Aug, please* **Tel 01694 771354**

Oteley, Ellesmere ❀ (Mr & Mrs R K Mainwaring) Entrance out of Ellesmere past Mere, opp Convent nr to A528/495 junction. 10 acres running down to Mere, incl walled kitchen garden; architectural features many interesting trees, rhododendrons and azaleas, views across Mere to Ellesmere Church. Wheelchairs only if dry. TEAS in aid of NSPCC. *Adm £2 Chd 50p. Mon May 25 (2-6). Private visits also welcome, please* **Tel 01691 622514**

The Patch, Acton Pigot ♿️✿❀ (Mrs J G Owen) 8m SE of Shrewsbury between A49 and A458. Take Cressage Rd from Acton Burnell. Turn L after ½m, signpost Acton Pigot. A garden for the plant connoisseur in excess of ½ acre. June early herbaceous, shrubs and trees. Plants in aid of St. Anthony's Cheshire Home. TEAS. *Adm £1.50 Chd free. Suns June 7, 14 (2-6). Coach parties welcome by arrangement, please* **Tel 01743 362139**

Peplow Hall, Hodnet ♿️❀ (The Hon & Mrs R V Wynn) 3m S of Hodnet via A442; turn off E. 10-acre garden with lawns, azaleas, rhododendrons, etc; roses, herbaceous borders; walled kitchen garden; 7-acre lake. TEAS. *Adm £2.50 Chd 50p. Sun May 24 (2-5.30)*

Preen Manor, Church Preen ✿❀ (Mr & Mrs P Trevor-Jones) nr Church Stretton; signposted from B4371 Much Wenlock-Church Stretton Rd. 6-acre garden on site of Cluniac monastery and Norman Shaw mansion. Kitchen; chess; water and wild gardens. Fine trees in park; woodland walks. Featured in NGS video 1. Replanning still in progress. TEAS. *Adm £2.50 Chd 50p. Sun May 10, Thurs June 11, 25, July 9, 23 (2-6); Sun Oct 4 (2-5) 4.30 Harvest Thanksgiving. Private visits and coach parties by appt June & July only (min 15)* Tel 01694 771207

Radnor Cottage, Clun ✿❀ (Pam and David Pittwood) 8m W of Craven Arms, 1m E of Clun on B4368 midway between Clunton and Clun. 2 acres S-facing slope, overlooking Clun Valley. Developed since 1988 for all-year-round interest. Daffodils; cottage garden borders; dry stone wall and terracing with herbs and alpines; stream and bog garden with willow collection; native trees, orchard, wild flower meadow. TEAS. *Adm £1.50 Chd 50p (ACNO to Clun Memorial Hall®). Tues April 7, 21, May 12, 26, July 7, 28 (2-6). Private visits welcome, please* Tel 01588 640451

Ridgway Wood, Edgton ✿❀ (Mr & Mrs A S Rankine) 4m NW of Craven Arms. Turn W off A49 on to A489, 2½m, then left towards Edgton ¾m, drive on right. Informal 2½-acre garden created and maintained for all yr round colour and set in 20 acres of mixed woodland. Mixed borders, heather beds, woodland garden, azaleas, shrubs and trees. Woodland walks. TEAS. *Adm £2 Chd 50p (ACNO to Shropshire and Mid Wales Hospice®). Suns May 17, 24; Mon May 25 (11-6)*

Ruthall Manor, Ditton Priors ♿✿ (Mr & Mrs G T Clarke) Bridgnorth. Ruthall Rd signed nr garage. 1-acre garden with ha-ha and old horse pond planted with water and bog plants. Rare specimen trees. Designed for easy maintenance with lots of ground-covering and unusual plants. TEAS in aid of Village Hall by Committee. *Adm £2 Chd free. Sun Aug 2 (2-6). Parties welcome April to Sept, please* Tel 01746 712608

Stottesdon Village Gardens ♿✿❀ (Stottesdon Garden Committee). 7m from Bridgnorth on B4363 turn R 3m. From Kidderminster 11m on A4117 turn R 4m. A village community in unspoilt countryside. A variety of gardens, new and old; cottage flowers; unusual plants; vegetables; bedding displays. TEAS in aid of St Mary's Church. *Combined adm £2 Chd £1. Sun, Mon Aug 30, 31 (2-6)*

¶Thornfield, Twmpath, Gobowen ♿ (Mrs Gillian M Walker) About 2m N of Oswestry. Turn off the A5 (Oswestry by-pass) at the Gobowen roundabout towards the Orthopaedic Hospital. 2nd R just over the railway bridge opp hospital car park. Garden of approx 2 acres. Large borders informally planted with a mixture of trees, shrubs and herbaceous plants to provide interest and colour over many months. Pool containing goldfish and planted with waterlilies. TEAS. *Adm £1.50 Chd 50p. Sun May 17 (2-6)*

Triscombe, Wellington ✿❀ (Dr & Mrs J Calvert) Roslyn Rd is close to Wrekin College which is well signposted. Approx ¾-acre town garden with access via

steps. Features well stocked herbaceous and shrub borders, pond and bog garden, pergolas, alpine house, rockery and container plants. TEAS in aid of Shropshire & Mid Wales Hospice, Telford Day Centre. *Adm £1.50 Chd 50p. Suns May 31, June 28 (1.30-5)*

Walcot Hall, Lydbury North ♿❀ (The Hon Mrs E C Parish) Bishops Castle 3m. B4385 Craven Arms to Bishops Castle, turn L by Powis Arms, in Lydbury N. Arboretum planted by Lord Clive of India's son. Cascades of rhododendrons, azaleas amongst specimen trees and pools. Fine views of Sir William Chambers' Clock Towers, with lake and hills beyond. TEAS. *Adm £2 Chd 15 and under free. Sun, Mon May 24, 25 (2-6). Also by appt for parties, please* Tel 01588 680232

■ **Weston Park, Shifnal** ♿ (The Weston Park Foundation) 7m E of Telford on the A5 A1 Weston-under-Lizard. Access junction 12 M6 and junction 3 M54. Free car/coach park. Capability Brown landscaped gardens and parkland, incl fine collection, rhododendrons and azaleas. Formal gardens restored to original C19 design, rose garden and long border together with colourful adjacent Broderie Garden. TEAS and light meals available in The Old Stables restaurant. Park and garden. *Adm £3.50, OAP's £2.50, Chd £2, reduced rates for parties of 20 or more. Open Easter to September (enquiries for dates and times,* Tel 01952 850207*). For NGS Tues June 16, July 14 (11-5)*

Whittington Village Gardens, nr Oswestry ♿❀ Daisy Lane Whittington. 2½m NE of Oswestry. Turn off B5009 150yds NW of church into Top St then into Daisy Lane. Car parking at Whittington Castle and Top St. A group of 10-12 adjacent border village gardens. Interesting and varied water features. A genuine cottage garden, complete with hens. One specializing in unusual perennials, some rare, and a chance to see the runner up of the 1997 Shrops Star Garden Competition, Westbourne House. TEAS at **The Bramleys**; Top St. *Adm £2.25 Chd free. Sat, Sun June 27, 28 (1-5.30)*

Willey Park, Broseley ✿❀ (The Lord & Lady Forester) 5m NW of Bridgnorth. Turn W off B4373. Much Wenlock 4m. 6-acre formal garden set in extensive parkland. Fine views. 10-acre woodland rhododendron/azalea walk. Magnificent mature trees. Recently planted herbaceous borders. Spectacular azalea bed near house. TEAS. *Adm £2 Chd/OAP £1 (ACNO to Willey & District Village Hall®). Sun May 24 (2-6)*

■ **Wollerton Old Hall, Wollerton** ♿✿❀ (John & Lesley Jenkins) Nr Market Drayton on A53 between Hodnet and A53/A41 junction and follow brown signs. Award-winning 3-acre garden created around C16 house (not open). Featured on BBC2, Granada TV, NGS video 1, various publications. A combination of formal design and intensive cultivation of perennials. A painter's garden using planting combinations with an emphasis on colour and form. Lunches, TEAS. *Adm £2.50 Chd 50p. Every Fri and Sun May 1 to Aug 30 (12-5). For NGS, every Fri in June. Parties, min 25, by appt, please* Tel 01630 685760

Somerset (incorporating South Avon)

Hon County Organiser:	Miss P Davies-Gilbert, Coombe Quarry, West Monkton, Taunton TA2 8RE Tel 01823 412187
Assistant Hon County Organisers:	Mrs B Hudspith, Rookwood, West St, Hinton St George, TA17 8SA Tel 01460 73450
	Mrs Judy Kendall, Barle House, 17 High St, Chew Magna, BS40 8PR Tel 01275 332459
	Mrs Shirley Gyles, Rose Cottage, Flax Bourton, BS48 3QE Tel 01275 462680
Somerset Leaflet:	Richard D Armitage Esq, Dormers, Park Lane, Carhampton, TA24 6NN Tel 01643 821386
Publicity:	Mrs Alison Kelly, The Mount, Wincanton, Tel 01963 32487
Tour Advisor and Talks:	Mrs Lyn Spencer-Mills, Hooper's Holding, Hinton St George, TA17 8SE Tel 01460 76389
Treasurer:	John A Spurrier Esq, Tudor Cottage, 19 Comeytrowe Lane, Taunton TA1 5PA Tel 01823 333827

DATES OF OPENING

Regular openings
For details see garden description

Church Farm and The Gables,
    Stanton Prior
Clapton Court Gardens, Wellington
Cothay Manor
Elworthy Cottage, Elworthy
Greencombe, Porlock
Hadspen Garden, nr Castle Cary
Hatch Beauchamp Gardens, Taunton
Hestercombe Gardens
Lower Severalls, Crewkerne
Milton Lodge, Wells
Sherborne Garden, Litton
The Time-Trail of Roses

By appointment only
*For telephone numbers and other
details see garden descriptions.
Private visits welcomed*

Benchmark, Wells
Littlecourt, West Bagborough
The Mill, Henley Lane, Wookey

February 17 Tuesday
    Tone Dale House, Wellington
March 15 Sunday
    Elworthy Cottage, Elworthy
    Langford Court, Langford
March 17 Tuesday
    Hestercombe Gardens
March 22 Sunday
    Harptree Court, East Harptree
March 29 Sunday
    Elworthy Cottage, Elworthy
April 4 Saturday
    Stowleys,Bossington Lane,
    Porlock

April 5 Sunday
    Coley Court & Widcombe Lodge
    Glencot House, Wookey Hole
    Smocombe House, Enmore
April 10 Friday
    Beryl, Wells
April 12 Sunday
    Fairfield, Stogursey
    Greencombe, Porlock
    Higher Luxton Farm,
        Churchingford
    Wayford Manor, Crewkerne
April 13 Monday
    Elworthy Cottage, Elworthy
    Higher Luxton Farm,
        Churchingford
April 18 Saturday
    Montys Court, Norton Fitzwarren
    The Mount, West Hill, Wincanton
April 19 Sunday
    Barrington Court, Ilminster
    Cobbleside, Milverton
    Crowe Hall, Widcombe
    Hangeridge Farm, Wellington
    Montys Court, Norton Fitzwarren
    The Mount, West Hill, Wincanton
    The Time-Trail of Roses
April 25 Saturday
    Brackenwood Garden Centre,
        Portishead
    Kingsdon, Somerton
April 26 Sunday
    Brackenwood Garden Centre,
        Portishead
    Kingsdon, Somerton
    The Old Rectory, Limington
    Vellacott, Lawford
May 3 Sunday
    Chinnock House, Middle Chinnock
    Dial House, Catcott
    Holt Farm, Nr Bristol
    Ilminster Gardens

Manor Farm, Middle Chinnock
    Pear Tree Cottage, Stapley
    Thatch End, Bridgwater
    Wayford Manor, Crewkerne
May 4 Monday
    Clapton Court Gardens
    Holt Farm, Nr Bristol
    Ilminster Gardens (Evening)
    Pear Tree Cottage, Stapley
    Telconia, Axbridge
May 6 Wednesday
    Leigh Farm, Halstock
May 9 Saturday
    Kingsdon, Somerton
May 10 Sunday
    Court House, East Quantoxhead
    Hadspen Garden, nr Castle Cary
    Kingsdon, Somerton
    Milton Lodge, Wells
    West Bradley House,
        Glastonbury
May 11 Monday
    Telconia, Axbridge
May 16 Saturday
    Parsonage Farm, Publow
May 17 Sunday
    Cannington College Gardens
    Forge House, Oake
    Hangeridge Farm, Wellington
    7 Little Keyford Lane, Frome
    Parsonage Farm, Publow
    Smocombe House, Enmore
    Vellacott, Lawford
    Wayford Manor, Crewkerne
May 18 Monday
    Telconia, Axbridge
May 22 Friday
    Hapsford House, Great Elm
May 23 Saturday
    Greencombe, Porlock
    The Mill, Cannington
    Perridge House, Pilton

May 24 Sunday
Ash House, Rimpton
Chinnock House, Middle
   Chinnock
Dial House, Catcott
Elworthy Cottage, Elworthy
Hinton St George Gardens,
   Crewkerne
The Mill, Cannington
The Mill House, Castle Cary
Milton Lodge, Wells
The Mount, West Hill, Wincanton
Stone Allerton Gardens, nr
   Wedmore
Thatch End, Bridgwater
The Time-Trail of Roses
Telconia, Axbridge
Windmill Cottage, Backwell
Woodborough, Nr Minehead

May 25 Monday
Chinnock House, Middle Chinnock
Hinton St George Gardens,
   Crewkerne
The Mill House, Castle Cary
The Mount, West Hill, Wincanton
Stone Allerton Gardens, nr
   Wedmore
Telconia, Axbridge

May 27 Wednesday
Vellacott, Lawford

May 29 Friday
Blackwithies, Langport
Hapsford House, Great Elm

May 30 Saturday
Blackwithies, Langport
Pendower House, Taunton

May 31 Sunday
Blackwithies, Langport
Kites Croft, Westbury-sub-Mendip
7 Little Keyford Lane, Frome
Pendower House, Taunton
Wayford Manor, Crewkerne

June 1 Monday
Telconia, Axbridge

June 3 Wednesday
Kites Croft, Westbury-sub-Mendip
Leigh Farm, Halstock

June 5 Friday
Hapsford House, Great Elm

June 7 Sunday
Elworthy Cottage, Elworthy
Gaulden Manor, Tolland
The Mount, Chelston
Pear Tree Cottage, Stapley
Sherborne Garden, Litton
Thurloxton Gardens

June 8 Monday
Telconia, Axbridge

June 9 Tuesday
Hestercombe Gardens
Tone Dale House, Wellington

June 10 Wednesday
Withey Lane Farmhouse, Barton
   St David

June 12 Friday
Hapsford House, Great Elm

June 13 Saturday
190 Goldcroft, Yeovil
Pendower House, Taunton
Wellesley Park Gardens,
   Wellington

June 14 Sunday
Church Farm and The Gables,
   Stanton Prior
Cobbleside, Milverton
Crowe Hall, Widcombe
Darkey Pang Too Gang, Oakhill
Goblin Combe, Cleeve
190 Goldcroft, Yeovil
Middle Farmhouse, Little Weston
Milton Lodge, Wells
Pendower House, Taunton
Sherborne Garden, Litton
The Spinney, Bristol
The Time-Trail of Roses
8 Trossachs Drive, Bathampton
Vellacott, Lawford
Wellesley Park Gardens,
   Wellington

June 15 Monday
Telconia, Axbridge

June 17 Wednesday
Wellesley Park Gardens,
   Wellington
Windmill Cottage, Backwell
Withey Lane Farmhouse, Barton
   St David

June 19 Friday
Hapsford House, Great Elm

June 21 Sunday
Abbey Farm, Montacute
Brewers Cottage, Taunton
Greencombe, Porlock
Hangeridge Farm, Wellington
Lydeard House, Bishops Lydeard
Montys Court, Norton Fitzwarren
The Old Rectory, Swell
Sherborne Garden, Litton
Stogumber Gardens, Taunton
Sunnyside, Wells
Walnut Farm, Yarley, Nr Wells

June 22 Monday
Telconia, Axbridge

June 24 Wednesday
Vellacott, Lawford

June 26 Friday
Hapsford House, Great Elm

June 27 Saturday
Holt Farm, Nr Bristol
Stowleys,Bossington Lane, Porlock

June 28 Sunday
Cothay Manor, Wellington
Dodington Hall, Nether Stowey
Hatch Beauchamp Gardens,
   Taunton
Holt Farm, Nr Bristol
Montacute House, Montacute
The Old Rectory, Limington

Rose Cottage, Templecombe
Sherborne Garden, Litton

June 29 Monday
Telconia, Axbridge

July 1 Wednesday
Leigh Farm, Halstock

July 2 Thursday
2 Old Tarnwell, Upper Stanton
   Drew

July 5 Sunday
Barford Park, nr Bridgwater
7 Little Keyford Lane, Frome
Milton Lodge, Wells
Sherborne Garden, Litton

July 6 Monday
Telconia, Axbridge

July 8 Wednesday
2 Old Tarnwell, Upper Stanton
   Drew

July 11 Saturday
Pondarosa, Crewkerne

July 12 Sunday
Barrington Court, Ilminster
Brewers Cottage, Taunton
Fernhill, Nr Wellington
Pondarosa, Crewkerne
Popinjays & Little Norton Mill
Sherborne Garden, Litton
Sutton Hosey Manor, Long Sutton
Vellacott, Lawford
Wall House, Taunton

July 13 Monday
Telconia, Axbridge

July 14 Tuesday
2 Old Tarnwell, Upper Stanton
   Drew
6 Tirley Way

July 15 Wednesday
Fernhill, Nr Wellington
Popinjays & Little Norton Mill
6 Tirley Way
Windmill Cottage, Backwell

July 19 Sunday
Braglands Barns, Stogumber
Brent Knoll Gardens, Highbridge
Greencombe, Porlock
Hangeridge Farm, Wellington
7 Little Keyford Lane, Frome
Sherborne Garden, Litton
Teleconia, Axbridge
Tintinhull House, nr Yeovil

July 20 Monday
Telconia, Axbridge

July 22 Wednesday
Oare Manor Cottage, Oare
Vellacott, Lawford

July 26 Sunday
Cothay Manor, Welllington
Oare Manor Cottage, Oare
Sherborne Garden, Litton

July 27 Monday
Telconia, Axbridge

August 1 Saturday
The Mill, Cannington

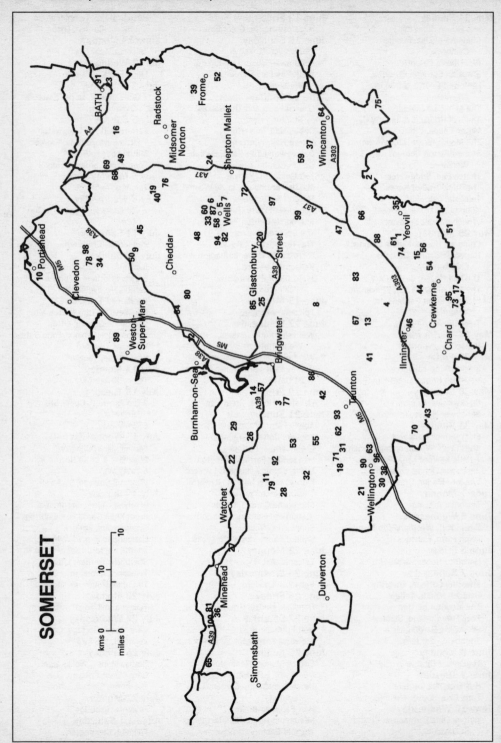

SOMERSET

kms 0   10   10
miles 0

BATH 91
23

Radstock
16

Frome 52
39

Midsomer
Norton

Shepton Mallet
24

Wincanton 64
37
59
A303

75

2

69
68 49
76
40 19

48
33 60 6
58 87 5 7
94 82 Wells
620
97
99
A37
47
66

35
Yeovil
61 1
74 15 56
88
54

51

10 Portishead

Cheddar

Glastonbury
85 Street
25
A39

8

83
4
44
Crewkerne 95
73 17

Clevedon
78 98
34
50 9
80

67 13

Ilminster 46
Chard

Weston-
Super-Mare

89

41
70
43

Bridgwater
86

Burnham-on-Sea
14
57
A39
3
77
42 Taunton

29
26

53 55
62 93
90 96
63
38

22
92
18 71 31
21 30

79 11
28
32

Watchet

27

Minehead
100 81
36

65

Simonsbath

Dulverton

A4
A38
M5
A38
M5
M5
A39
A303
A39

KEY

1. Abbey Farm
2. Ash House
3. Barford Park
4. Barrington Court
5. Benchmark
6. Beryl
7. Birdwood
8. Blackwithies
9. Bourne House
10. Brackenwood Garden Centre
11. Braglands Barns
12. Brent Knoll Gardens
13. Brewers Cottage
14. Cannington College Gardens
15. Chinnock House
16. Church Farm and The Gables
17. Clapton Court
18. Cobbleside
19. Coley Court & Widcombe Lodge
20. Coombe House
21. Cothay Manor
22. Court House
23. Crowe Hall
24. Darkey Pang Too Gang
25. Dial House
26. Dodington Hall
27. Dunster Castle
28. Elworthy Cottage
29. Fairfield
30. Fernhill
31. Forge House
32. Gaulden Manor
33. Glencot House
34. Goblin Combe
35. 190 Goldcroft
36. Greencombe
37. Hadspen Garden

38. Hangeridge Farm
39. Hapsford House
40. Harptree Court
41. Hatch Beauchamp Gardens
42. Hestercombe Garden
43. Higher Luxton Farm
44. Hinton St George Gardens
45. Holt Farm
46. Ilminster Gardens
47. Kingsdon
48. Kites Croft
49. Lady Farm
50. Langford Court
51. Leigh Farm
52. 7 Little Keyford Lane
53. Littlecourt
54. Lower Severalls
55. Lydeard House
56. Manor Farm
57. The Mill, Cannington
58. The Mill, Wookey
59. The Mill House
60. Milton Lodge
61. Montacute House
62. Montys Court
63. The Mount, Chelston
64. The Mount, Wincanton
65. Oare Manor Cottage
66. The Old Rectory, Limington
67. The Old Rectory, Swell
68. 2 Old Tarnwell
69. Parsonage Farm
70. Pear Tree Cottage
71. Pendower House
72. Perridge House
73. Pondarosa

74. Popinjays & Little Norton Mill
75. Rose Cottage
76. Sherborne Garden
77. Smocombe House
78. The Spinney
79. Stogumber Gardens
80. Stone Allerton Gardens
81. Stowleys,Bossington Lane
82. Sunnyside
83. Sutton Hosey Manor
84. Teleconia
85. Thatch End
86. Thurloxton Gardens
87. The Time-Trail of Roses
88. Tintinhull House
89. 6 Tirley Way
90. Tone Dale House
91. 8 Trossachs Drive
92. Vellacott
93. Wall House
94. Walnut Farm
95. Wayford Manor
96. Wellesley Park Gardens
97. West Bradley House
98. Windmill Cottage
99. Withey Lane Farmhouse
100. Woodborough

The maps in this book are designed to help visitors by showing the approximate locations of gardens within each county. The locations are not necessarily precise, particularly where gardens are in clusters. Detailed directions to each garden can be found in the garden descriptions.

August 2 Sunday
Coombe House, Glastonbury
The Mill, Cannington
Sherborne Garden, Litton
August 5 Wednesday
Leigh Farm, Halstock
August 6 Thursday
Dunster Castle, nr Minehead
August 9 Sunday
Hangeridge Farm, Wellington
Sherborne Garden, Litton
August 16 Sunday
Birdwood, Wells
Fernhill, Nr Wellington
Sherborne Garden, Litton
Windmill Cottage, Backwell
August 19 Wednesday
Fernhill, Nr Wellington
August 23 Sunday
Lady Farm, Chelwood
Leigh Farm, Halstock

Sherborne Garden, Litton
August 30 Sunday
Kites Croft, Westbury-sub-Mendip
Sherborne Garden, Litton
August 31 Monday
Beryl, Wells
September 2 Wednesday
Kites Croft, Westbury-sub-Mendip
September 6 Sunday
Fernhill, Nr Wellington
Sherborne Garden, Litton
September 9 Wednesday
Fernhill, Nr Wellington
September 12 Saturday
Perridge House, Pilton
September 13 Sunday
Bourne House, Burrington
Harptree Court, East Harptree
7 Little Keyford Lane, Frome
Sherborne Garden, Litton
Vellacott, Lawford

September 16 Wednesday
Leigh Farm, Halstock
Vellacott, Lawford
September 19 Saturday
The Mount, West Hill, Wincanton
September 20 Sunday
Elworthy Cottage, Elworthy
The Mount, West Hill, Wincanton
Sherborne Garden, Litton
Windmill Cottage, Backwell
September 27 Sunday
7 Little Keyford Lane, Frome
Sherborne Garden, Litton
October 3 Saturday
Holt Farm, Nr Bristol
October 4 Sunday
Holt Farm, Nr Bristol
October 7 Wednesday
Leigh Farm, Halstock
October 11 Sunday
Elworthy Cottage, Elworth

DESCRIPTIONS OF GARDENS

Abbey Farm, Montacute ও৯ (Mr & Mrs G Jenkins) 4m from Yeovil follow A3088, take slip road to Montacute, turn L at T-junction into village. Turn R between Church and Kings Arms (no through Rd). 2½-acre of mainly walled gardens on sloping site provide setting for mediaeval Priory gatehouse. Roses; herbaceous borders. Clematis, white garden. Parking available. TEAS in aid of St Catherine Church Fund®. *Adm £2 Chd free. Sun June 21 (2-5.30). Private visits welcome, please* **Tel 01935 823572**

Ash House, Rimpton ও৯ (Mr & Mrs Malcolm Shennan) 3m from Sherborne turn off B3148 at White Post Inn down hill to Rimpton. 1st house on L after ½m. Garden planted in 1988/89. 1½ acres, mixed borders, small pond, collection of ornamental garden trees. Many rare and interesting plants. TEAS. *Adm £2 Chd free. Sun May 24 (2-6). Private visits welcome May to Sept, please* **Tel 01935 851179**

Barford Park, Spaxton ও (Mr & Mrs M Stancomb) 4½m W of Bridgwater, midway between Enmore and Spaxton. 10 acres including woodland walk. Formal garden, wild garden and water garden, surrounding a Queen Anne house with park and ha ha. TEAS. *Adm £2 Chd free (ACNO to Somerset Garden Trust®). Sun July 5 (2-5.30)*

▲**Barrington Court, Ilminster** ও৯৯ (The National Trust) NE of Ilminster. Well known garden constructed in 1920 by Col Arthur Lyle from derelict farmland (the C19 cattle stalls still exist). Gertrude Jekyll suggested planting schemes for the layout; paved paths with walled rose and iris, white and lily gardens, large kitchen garden. Licensed restaurant, plant sales and garden shop. Lunches and TEAS. *Adm £4.20 Chd £2.10. Suns April 19, July 12 (11-5.30)*

Benchmark, Wells ৯৯ (Mr & Mrs Terence Whitman) 99 Portway. On A371 Cheddar Rd out of Wells, ½m from city centre on L. ¾-acre mature garden with mixed borders and potager, interesting perennials incl more than 100 varieties of penstemon. *Adm £1. Private visits and groups welcome, please* **Tel 01749 677155**

Beryl, Wells ও৯ (Mr & Mrs E Nowell) 1m N of Wells off B3139 to Bath. Left at Hawkers Lane. Victorian park created in 1842. Walled vegetable garden broken into quadrangles with box hedging and double flower picking borders. More recent planting of trees and shrubs and creation of walks and vistas. Morning coffee and TEAS. *Adm £1 OAP/Chd 50p. Fri April 10, Mon Aug 31 (11-5.30).* **Tel 01749 678738**

Birdwood, Wells ৯৯ (Mr K & Mrs S Crane) 1½m NE Wells on B3139. Last house in Wells on edge of Mendip Hills nr double bend sign. House has long stone garden wall close to Rd. Traditional Victorian garden with stone walls, lawns, herbaceous border, organic vegetable garden and terraces. There is a small wood and wild area with conservation in mind. TEAS. *Adm £1 Chd 50p. Sun Aug 16 (11-5.30)*

¶**Blackwithies, Langport** ও৯ (Mr & Mrs Jack Ward) 2½m NW of Langport on A372 between villages of Aller and Othery. ½m N of Aller. Parking. A developing 1¼-acre garden with extensive views of the levels and ancient woodlands. Plantings designed to provide vistas and hidden places with yr-round form and colour. Wide borders; large pond, canals, water lilies, marginal plants; long curving pergola, summer house (still under construction); copse with specimen trees and apiary; vegetable, fruit garden; incl espaliers; greenhouses. TEAS. *Adm £2 Chd £1 (ACNO to St Andrew's Aller PCC® (for bell restoration fund)). Fri, Sat, Sun May 29, 30, 31 (11-5)*

Bourne House, Burrington ও৯৯ (Mr & Mrs Christopher Thomas) 12m S Bristol. N of Burrington. Turning off A38 signposted Blagdon-Burrington; 2nd turning L. 4 acres, and 2 paddocks. Stream with waterfalls & lily pond; new pergola; mature trees, and shrubs. Large area Autumn cyclamen. Mixed borders; new rose bed. TEAS in aid of St Peters Hospice, Bristol. *Adm £1.50 Chd free. Sun Sept 13 (2-6). Private visits welcome by appt, please* **Tel 01761 462494**

▲**Brackenwood Garden Centre Woodland Garden, Portishead** ৯৯ (Mr & Mrs John Maycock) 131 Nore Rd. From Bristol A369 (10m). M5 Junc 19. 1m from Portishead on coast rd to Clevedon. 8-acre woodland garden. Rhododendrons, camellias, Japanese maples and pieris; secluded woodland pools with waterfowl; many rare trees and shrubs. Magnificent coastal views. Japanese maples in full colour in the Autumn. Restaurant and Tea Room open every day. *Adm £1.50 OAPs £1.25 Chd 60p. For NGS Sat, Sun April 25, 26 (9-5),* **Tel 01275 843484**

¶**Braglands Barn, Taunton** ও৯৯ (Simon & Sue Youell) 12m NW of Taunton. Follow A358 towards Minehead. Turn L towards Stogumber, just past Bee World turn R, parking in field. 1-acre garden started in 1995. Mixed herbaceous and shrub borders with many unusual plants, large rose bed, pond and bog garden. Additional 1-acre field with trees. Teas available at Bee World. *Adm £1.50 Chd free. Sun July 19 (2-6)*

Brent Knoll Gardens, Highbridge ৯ off A38 2m N of Highbridge and M5 exit 22. A mixture of 3 colourful country gardens. TEAS at Copse Hall in aid of Parish Hall. *Combined adm £2.50 Chd free. Sun July 19 (2-6)*

   Copse Hall ৯ (Mrs S Boss & A J Hill Esq) Terraced gardens, crinkle crankle kitchen garden wall. Pond area now established with a surprise. Partly suitable for wheelchairs. *Private visits welcome, please* **Tel 01278 760301** *evenings*

   Pen Orchard (Major & Mrs J Harper) Still a busy people's garden

   ¶**Pound Orchard** (Mr & Mrs J F Tucker) A beginners garden from a paddock in 2 years

Brewers Cottage, Isle Brewers ও৯৯ (Mr & Mrs J A Clements) 9m ESE of Taunton. 1½m from A378 at Fivehead. ¾-acre garden hidden behind a pretty cottage. Newly designed over the last few years, features incl a formal herb garden, pergola with old roses, and colour themed borders around old apple trees. Further areas of woodland, 'secret' yew enclosed garden and iris walk still being developed. TEAS in aid of Village Church. *Adm £1.50 Chd free. Suns June 21, July 12 (2-6.30) Private visits welcome,* **please Tel 01460 281395**

▲**Cannington College Gardens** &*⊘*❀ Cannington, 3m NW of Bridgwater. On A39 Bridgwater-Minehead Rd. Old College: Benedictine Priory 1138; fine Elizabethan W front; 7 old sandstone walled gardens protect wide range of plants, incl many less hardy subjects. Ceanothus, Fremontias, Wistarias etc. New College (built 1970); magnificent views to Quantocks; tree and shrub collections; ground cover plantings; lawn grass collection and trials; one of the largest collections of ornamental plants in SW England incl 4 national plant collections. TEA. *Adm for both College grounds £2 Chd (& organised parties of OAPs) £1. Special rates for party bookings. For NGS Sun May 17 (2-5)*

Chiffchaffs, Chaffeymoor see Dorset

Chinnock House, Middle Chinnock &*⊘*❀ (Guy & Charmian Smith) Off A30 between Crewkerne and Yeovil. 2-acre walled gardens, silver, scented and herbaceous; recently redesigned. TEAS in aid of West Chinnock Primary School. *Adm £1.50 Chd free. Sun, Mon May 24, 25 (2-6). Also open May 3 (2-6) with* **Manor Farm.** *Combined adm £2.50 Chd free. Private visits welcome for parties of 2 or over, please* **Tel 01935 881229**

■ **Church Farm & The Gables, Stanton Prior** &*⊘*❀ 6m from Bath on A39 Wells Rd; at Marksbury turn L to Stanton Prior; gardens set in beautiful countryside in unspoilt village. Ploughman's lunches & cream teas, June 14 in aid of St Lawrence Church. *Combined adm £2 Chd free. 1st and 2nd Weds May to Sept (11-5). For NGS Sun June 14 (11-6). Open by appt all year, please* **Tel 01761 470384/472690**
> **Church Farm** (Mr & Mrs Leslie Hardwick) Herbaceous borders, rock garden, scree garden; shrub roses, many unusual plants, wild area with ¼-acre pond
> **The Gables** (Mr & Mrs Alistair Hardwick) Newly created cottage garden

■ **Clapton Court Gardens** *⊘* (Mr & Mrs P Giffin) 3m S of Crewkerne on B3165 to Lyme Regis in Clapton village. 10 acres of beautiful gardens. Woodland garden with streams, the largest Ash tree in Gt Britain. Many rare and interesting plants. Terraced formal gardens with ornamental lily pond, white border, yellow border, mixed herbaceous and rose garden, rockery and fine collection of narcissus and other bulbs. *Adm £3 Chd free. Tues, Weds, Thurs April to Sept incl (2-5). For NGS Mon May 4 (2-5) Coach parties by appt, please* **Tel Mike & Penny Cox 01460 73220**

Cobbleside, Milverton &*⊘* (Mr & Mrs C Pine) 7m W of Taunton on B3227 L at roundabout to Milverton. ¾-acre walled garden incl herb garden and potager. Completely redesigned, with photographs illustrating the old layout. *Adm £1.50 Chd free. Suns April 19, June 14 (2-5.30)*

> **The National Gardens Scheme** is a charity which traces its origins back to 1927. Since then it has raised over £18 million for charitable purposes.

Coley Court & Widcombe Lodge, South Widcombe. East Harptree. *Combined adm £1.50 Chd free. Sun April 5 (2-6)*
> **Coley Court** (Mrs M J Hill) East Harptree, 8m N of Wells from A39 at Chewton Mendip take B3114 for 2m. Well before East Harptree turn R at sign Coley and Hinton Blewitt. 1-acre garden, stone walls, spring bulbs; 1-acre old mixed orchard. Early Jacobean house (not open)
> ¶**Widcombe Lodge** (Mr & Mrs P M Walker) From W Harptree take B114 (Chewton Mendip rd), turn L at East Harptree Xrds for about 1m. Garden on R. Old walled garden, mature shrubs and massed bulbs

Coombe House, Bove Town &*⊘*❀ (Colin Wells-Brown & Alan Gloak) Bove Town is at the top of Glastonbury High St it is a hill and the garden is near the top approx ¼m. Please park in town and take the 'Tor Bus' from St Dunstans car park. No parking near or at house. Approx 1½ acres. A garden for an old house on an ancient site. Walled formal and romantic shrub and herbaceous garden with delightful views and some unusual plants. Vegetable garden, 2 orchards, nut walk, water features, pergolas and grass garden. TEAS. *Adm £2 Chd 50p (ACNO to Aled Richards Trust®). Sun Aug 2 (2-6)*

■ **Cothay Manor, Greenham** &*⊘*❀ (Mr & Mrs A H B Robb) 5m W of Wellington. From A38 at Beambridge Hotel turn R signposted Thorne St Margaret. Go straight for 1½m turn R signposted Cothay. 1½m keep L, entrance on L. Laid out in the 1920s by Reginald Cooper, a close friend of Harold Nicholson of Sissinghurst, and Lawrence Johnston of Hidcote, this jewel of a garden has been completely restored over the last 4 years. Plantsman's paradise, yew walk, courtyards, garden rooms, ox bow bog garden, river, medieval house (not open). Cream TEAS. *Adm £3 Chd free. Every Thurs and 1st Sun May to Sept incl and by appt. For NGS Suns June 28, July 26 (2-6)*

Court House, East Quantoxhead &❀ (Sir Walter & Lady Luttrell) 12m W of Bridgwater off A39; house at end of village past duck pond. Lovely 5-acre garden; trees, shrubs, roses and herbaceous. Woodland garden started 1992. Views to sea and Quantocks. Partly suitable for wheelchairs. Teas in Village Hall. *Adm £2 Chd free. Sun May 10 (2-5.30)*

▲**Crowe Hall, Widcombe** & (John Barratt Esq) 1m SE of Bath. L up Widcombe Hill, off A36, leaving White Hart on R. Large varied garden; fine trees, lawns, spring bulbs, series of enclosed gardens cascading down steep hillside. Italianate terracing and Gothic Victorian grotto contrast with park-like upper garden. Dramatic setting, with spectacular views of Bath. New trellis and water garden created in 1995. Featured in NGS gardens video 2. Dogs welcome. TEAS. *Adm £2 Chd £1. For NGS Suns April 19, June 14 (2-6).* **Tel 01225 310322**

Darkey Pang Tso Gang, Oakhill *⊘*❀ (Graham & Chrissy Price) 3m N of Shepton Mallet off A367 in Oakhill High St opp converted chapel. ¾-acre. Creatively designed and landscaped by owner since 1981. Crammed with trees, shrubs, herbaceous and climbers, with a lushness of greens and leaf combinations. Winding paths link wild and cultivated areas with grotto, pergola, wildlife pond and bog garden. As featured on TV and in Homes and Gardens. TEAS. *Adm £1.50 Chd 50p (ACNO to Aswick and Oakhill Playgroup®). Sun June 14 (2-6). Private visits welcome Weds only June 24 to July 22 (9.30-dusk), please* **Tel 01749 840795**

¶**Dial House, Bridgwater** &*&&* (Mrs Peter Strallen) Turn N off A39 between Bridgwater (8m) and Street to Catcott. Continue straight into village. Turn L at T junction. Fork R at War Memorial and immed L at cul de sac sign. No parking at house. Informal partly walled garden surrounding C14 house (not open) wisteria, rambling roses, herbaceous borders. Catcott is a regular winner of Britain in Bloom. TEAS in aid of village charities. *Combined adm with* **Thatch End** *£2 Chd free. Suns May 3, 24 (2-6). Private visits welcome by appt, please* **Tel 01278 722008**

Dodington Hall, Nether Stowey *&&* (Grania & Paul Quinn) A39 Bridgwater-Minehead. 2m W of Nether Stowey turn at signpost opp Castle of Comfort. ¼m turn R. Entrance through churchyard. Reclaimed 1½-acre terrace garden; clematis, shrub roses, bulbs; Tudor house (part open). TEAS in aid of Life. *Adm £2 Chd free. Sun June 28 (2.30-5.30). Private visits welcome, please* **Tel 01278 741400**

▲**Dunster Castle, Dunster** &*&* (The National Trust) 3m SE of Minehead. NT car park approached direct from A39. Terraces of sub-tropical plants, shrubs and camellias surrounding the fortified home of the Luttrell family for 600 yrs; fine views. Self-drive battery operated car available. Teas in village. *Adm Garden Only £2.80 Chd £1.30. Family ticket £6.70. For NGS Thurs Aug 6 (10-5)*

■ **Elworthy Cottage, Elworthy** *&&* (Mike & Jenny Spiller) 12m NW of Taunton on B3188. 1-acre garden. Many unusual herbaceous plants. Large collection of hardy geraniums (over 200 varieties); hellebores, pulmonarias, campanulas, penstemons, violas, grasses and plants for foliage effect. Wide selection of plants from the garden for sale. *Adm £1 Chd free. Nursery and Garden open Tues, Thurs and Fri (11-5) mid March to mid Oct. For NGS Suns March 15, 29, May 24, June 7, Sept 20, Oct 11; Mon April 13 (2-5.30). Parties welcome, please* **Tel 01984 656427**

Fairfield Court, Lower Failand see Bristol and South Glos

Fairfield, Stogursey &*&* (Lady Gass) 11m NW of Bridgwater 7m E of Williton. From A39 Bridgwater-Minehead turn N; garden 1½m W of Stogursey. Woodland garden with bulbs and shrubs; paved maze. Views of Quantocks. Dogs in park and field only. TEA. *Adm £2 Chd free (ACNO to Stogursey Church®). Easter Sun April 12 (2-5.30)*

Fernhill, nr Wellington *&&* (Peter & Audrey Bowler) White Ball Hill. W on A38 from Wellington. Past Beam Bridge Hotel and at top of Hill follow signs into garden. Mature wooded garden in approx 2 acres with rose, herbaceous, shrub, and mixed borders all unique in colour and content. Interesting octagonal pergola; alpine and bog garden with waterfalls and pools leading to shady arbour. TEAS on terrace with fine views over ha-ha to Black

Downs and Mendips. Good plant collection. *Adm £1.50 Chd free. Suns, Weds July 12, 15, Aug 16, 19, Sept 6, 9 (2-6). Private visits welcome* **Tel 01823 672423**

Forge House, Oake &*&&* (Peter & Eloise McGregor) On A38 midway between Taunton & Wellington. Take signpost for Oake. 1st house on R entering village. 1-acre informal country garden with emphasis on colour, bee and butterfly plants and fragrance. Unmanaged wildlife area and pond. Please park in village. TEA if fine. *Adm £2 Chd free. Sun May 17 (2-6). Disabled & parties welcome week-ends April to June,* **Tel 01823 461 500 after 7**

Gaulden Manor, Tolland &*&&* (Mr & Mrs J Le G Starkie) Nr Lydeard St Lawrence. 9m NW Taunton off A358. Medium-sized garden made by owners. Herb; bog; scent and butterfly gardens. Bog plants, primulas and scented geraniums. Partly suitable for wheelchairs. Cream TEAS. *Adm house & garden £3.80, garden only £1.80, Chd £1.80. Sun June 7 (2-5)*

Glencot House, Wookey Hole *&&* (Mrs Jenny Attia) ½m SW of Wells. From Wells follow the signs to Wookey Hole. Through the village, past the Wookey Hole Caves and take 1st turning L into Titlands Lane. Proceed for approx ½m and the entrance to Glencot Cricket field is on LH-side. Drive across field and park to L of bridge. 18 acres of parkland of which approx 4 acres are formal gardens with frontage to R Axe. Herbaceous borders, rose walk and terraced walk with a water feature. TEAS. *Adm £1.50 Chd 50p. Sun April 5 (2-5)*

Goblin Combe, Cleeve *&&* (Mrs H R Burn) 10m S of Bristol on A370, turn L onto Cleeve Hill Rd just before Lord Nelson Inn. After 300 yds turn L onto Plunder St, first drive on R. Car parking near the bottom of the drive just beyond the Plunder St turning. 2 acre terraced garden with interesting collection of trees, shrubs and borders, surrounded by orchards, fields and woodlands. Magnificent views. TEAS. *Adm £1.50 Chd free (ACNO to The Music Space Trust®). Sun June 14 (2-5.30)*

190 Goldcroft, Yeovil &*&&* (Mr & Mrs E Crate) Take A359 from roundabout by Yeovil College, then 1st R. ¼-acre. Colour-themed shrub and herbaceous borders and island beds, rose garden, raised ponds, vegetable garden designed for the visually impaired. As seen on BBC 2 Gardeners' World. TEAS in aid of Somerset Association for the blind. *Adm £1.50 Chd 50p. Sat, Sun June 13, 14 (2-5). Groups welcome by appt* **Tel 01935 475535**

■ **Greencombe, Porlock** &*&&* (Miss Joan Loraine, Greencombe Garden Trust) ½m W of Porlock, L off road to Porlock Weir. 52-yr-old garden on edge of ancient woodland, overlooking Porlock Bay. Choice rhododendrons, azaleas, camellias, maples, roses, hydrangeas, ferns, small woodland plants and clematis. National collections of Polystichum, (the 'thumbs up' fern), Erythronium (dog's tooth violets), Vaccinium (blue berries) and Gaultheria. Completely organic, with compost heaps on show. TEA. *Adm £3 Chd under 16 50p. Sats, Suns, Mons, Tues, April, May, June, July (2-6); private visits, please* **Tel 01643 862363**. *For NGS Sats, Suns, April 12, May 23, June 21, July 19 (2-6)*

● **Hadspen Garden, Castle Cary** ♿✿❀ (N & S Pope) 2m SE of Castle Cary on A371 to Wincanton. 5-acre Edwardian garden featuring a 2-acre curved walled garden with extensive colourist borders of shrub roses and choice herbaceous plants; woodland of fine specimen trees. National Rodgersia Collection. Lunches, TEAS. *Adm £2.50 Chd 50p (ACNO to Friends of the Earth®). Garden and Nursery open Thurs, Fri, Sat, Sun & Bank Hol Mon (10-5); private visits welcome, March 5 to Sept 27 (10-5) please* **Tel 01749 813707** *(after 6pm). For NGS Sun May 10 (9-6)*

Hangeridge Farm, Wrangway ♿✿❀ (Mrs J M Chave) Wellington, 1m off A38 bypass signposted Wrangway. 1st L towards Wellington Monument over motorway bridge 1st R. 1-acre garden, herbaceous borders, flowering shrubs and heathers, raised rockeries, spring bulbs. Lovely setting under Blackdown Hills. Selection of plants available from garden. TEAS. *Adm £1 Chd free. Suns April 19, May 17, June 21, July 19, Aug 9 (2-7). Parties by appt* **Tel 01823 662339**

Hapsford House, Great Elm (Mrs Enthoven) ½m out of Frome on A362 to Radstock. 1st rd on L to Great Elm, Hapsford and Wells. Approx ½m house on L 8-acre C19 Grade II listed garden runs from Regency house (not open) to island on River Wells. Woodland, riverside and meadow walks. Extensive laburnum walk to main house. Sensitive restoration since 1990 and replanting incl many species and shrub roses. *Adm £2.50 Chd £1. Fris from May 22 to June 26. Parties by appt* **Tel 01373 463557**

Harptree Court, East Harptree ♿❀ (Mr & Mrs Richard Hill) 8m N of Wells via A39 Bristol Rd to Chewton Mendip, then B3114 to East Harptree, gates on L. From Bath via A368 Weston-super-Mare Rd to West Harptree. Large garden in beautiful setting. Many exotic plants and newly designed herbaceous borders in walled garden. Fine trees, 18C stone bridge, subterranean passage, lily pond, paved garden. TEAS. *Adm £1.50 Chd free. Suns March 22, Sept 13 (2-6)*

Hatch Beauchamp Gardens 5m SE of Taunton (M5 junction 25) off A358 to Ilminster. Turn L in village of Hatch Beauchamp at Hatch Inn. Parking at Hatch Court. TEAS. *Combined adm £2.50 Chd £1 under 12 free. Sun June 28 (2.30-5.30)*
● **Hatch Court** ♿✿❀ (Dr & Mrs Robin Odgers) Hatch Beauchamp. 5-acre garden with 30 acres of parkland and deer park surrounding a perfect 1750 Palladian mansion. Extensive, recent and continuing restoration redesign and replanting. Magnificent walled kitchen garden, fine display of roses, shrubs, clematis and many young trees. Glorious views and a lovely setting. 1995 Historic Garden Restoration Award. TEAS June 11-Sept 10. *Adm £3.50 House open Thurs (2.30-5) June 11-Sept 10. Adm £2.50 Garden open daily April 13-Sept 30 (10-5.30). For NGS Sun June 28 (2.30-5.30)*
Hatch Court Farm ♿✿ (John Townson Esq) ⅓-acre walled garden with mixed borders created over recent yrs from derelict farm buildings. Also wild area with mediaeval pond surrounded by wood and parkland. Woodland walk

■ **Hestercombe Gardens** ❀ (SCC/Hestercombe Gardens Project) 4m N of Taunton. Follow Tourist Information 'Daisy' symbol. Encompasses over 3 centuries of garden history in 50 acres of formal gardens and parkland. Famous Edwardian gardens designed by Sir Edwin Lutyens and planted by Gertrude Jekyll created 1904-6. The terraces and borders are based on Jekyll's original planting scheme and are considered the supreme example of their famous partnership. Landscape Garden opened in 1997 for the first time in over 125 yrs designed by Coplestone Warre Bampfylde in the 1750's. Georgian pleasure grounds comprise 40 acres of lakes, temples and woodland walks. TEAS. *Combined adm £3.25 Chd £1 under 5 free (ACNO to Hestercombe Gardens Trust®). Open every day (10-5). For NGS Tues March 17, June 9 (10-5)*

Higher Luxton Farm, Churchingford ✿ (Mr & Mrs Peter Hopcraft) 1½m out of Churchingford on Honiton Rd. Over county boundary into Devon past thatched farmhouse on R; next turning on L before Xrds. 9m S of Taunton, 9m N of Honiton. Approx 1 acre with species trees and bulbs; walls with clematis; ponds with primula; lovely views. Pony stud. Partly suitable for wheelchairs. TEAS in aid of Churchstanton Church. *Adm £1 Chd free. Sun, Mon April 12, 13 (2-6)*

Highview, Portishead see Bristol and South Glos

Hinton St George Gardens, Crewkerne 2m NW of Crewkerne. N of A30 Crewkerne-Chard; S of A303 Ilminster Town Rd, at roundabout signed Lopen & Merriott, then R to one of Somerset's prettiest villages. TEAS in aid of Cats Protection League, dog park provided at Hooper's Holding. *Combined adm £3 Chd free. Sun, Mon May 24, 25 (2-6)*
Fig Tree Cottage ♿✿ (Mr & Mrs Whitworth) Old walled cottage garden and courtyard of stables made from kitchen garden of neighbouring rectory, over the past 18 years by owners inspired by Margery Fish. Ground cover, shrubs, old-fashioned roses. Three giant fig trees, all perennials. *Private visits welcome, please* **Tel 01460 73548**
Hooper's Holding ♿❀ (Ken & Lyn Spencer-Mills) ⅓-acre garden, in a formal design; lily pool; dwarf conifers, rare herbaceous and shrubby plants; NCCPG National Collection of Hedychiums; fancy cats and poultry. (Hedychiums flowering Sept and Oct). *Private visits welcome, Adm £1.50, please* **Tel 01460 76389**
Rookwood (Ian & Betty Hudspith) ¼-acre, modern garden, herbaceous borders, pond, greenhouse, vegetable garden and fruit cage
Springfield House ♿❀ (Capt & Mrs T Hardy) 1½-acres; semi-wild wooded dell, mature trees framing view to Mendips, shrubs, herbaceous plants, bulbs
¶**End House** ♿ (Helen Ford) In corner of what was 200 yr old walled kitchen garden, ½-acre being reshaped and renovated. Trees, shrubs, herbaceous perennials, climbers, and new courtyard area

Holt Farm, Blagdon ✿❀ (Mrs Sarah Mead) Approx 12m S of Bristol, located off the A368 Weston-Super-Mare to Bath Rd, between the villages of Blagdon and Ubley. The entrance to Holt Farm is approx ½m outside Blagdon, on the L-hand side. A developing farmhouse garden bordering Blagdon lake with wild flower meadow, stream, woodland walk and sunken walled garden. Extensive herbaceous planting throughout the 3-acre site, with several new projects underway. Cream TEAS. *Adm £1.50 Chd free (ACNO to The Home Farm Trust®). Sun, Mon May 3, 4, Sats, Sun June 27, 28, Oct 3, 4 (2-6)*

Ilminster Gardens &*❀* TEA. *Combined adm £1.50 Chd free. Sun May 3 (2-5), Mon May 4 (6-8)*

¶**Hermitage** &*❀* On B3168 (old A303) on W side of Ilminster, next to Shrubbery Hotel. 2½-acres garden with mixed borders on various levels. Rockeries, ponds, vegetable garden and woodland. TEA in aid of St Mary's Parish Hall Fund. *(ACNO to Action for ME®)*
15 Summerlands Park Avenue (Christine Akhurst) Wedge shaped, rear cottage style garden, 85' long. Slopes towards the S with heavy clay soil. Interesting shrubs and many tubs, mature fruit trees and a particularly fine quince. TEA in aid of Children's Hospice
5 Summerlands Park Avenue (Katherine Saunders) 90' long sloping suburban back garden, designed and built by owner from bare plot since 1990. Railway sleeper and gravel terraces, shrubs, tulips, alliums, aquilegias, living willow fence and arch, camomile walk, salad bed

Iford Manor, nr Bradford-on-Avon see Wiltshire

Jasmine Cottage, Clevedon see Bristol and South Glos

Kingsdon, Somerton &*❀* (Mrs Charles Marrow) 2m SE of Somerton off B3151 Ilchester Rd. From Ilchester roundabout on A303 follow NT signs to Lytes Cary; left opp gates ½m to Kingsdon. 2-acre plantsman's garden and nursery garden. Over 500 varieties of unusual plants for sale. Teas in Village Hall. *Adm £2 Chd free. Sats, Suns April 25, 26, May 9, 10 (2-7). Private visits welcome, please* **Tel 01935 840232**

Kites Croft, Westbury-sub-Mendip *❀* (Dr & Mrs W I Stanton) 5m NW of Wells. On A371 follow signs from Westbury Cross. 2-acre garden planted for colour throughout season with fine views to Glastonbury Tor. Winding paths lead from the terrace to different levels; lawn, ponds, rockery, herbaceous borders, shrubs and wood. Some unusual plants from garden for sale. *Adm £1.50 Chd free. Sun May 31, Wed June 3, Sun Aug 30, Wed Sept 2 (2-5). Private visits and groups welcome, please* **Tel 01749 870328.**

Lady Farm, Chelwood &*❀* (Mr & Mrs M Pearce) On the A368 ½m E of Chelwood roundabout (A37 & A368) 8m S of Bristol and 8m W of Bath. Recently planted garden of 6 acres incl spring fed watercourse flowing into 2 lakes with adjacent large rock features. Large herbaceous borders. Rambling and new English roses. Large area of new style 'prairie' and 'steppe' planting as shown on HTV Oct '97. About 60 different species of grasses. Not recommended for children under 14. TEAS in aid of Chelwood Church. *Adm £2 Chd free. Sun Aug 23 (2-6). Private parties always welcome, plenty of parking, please* **Tel 01761 490770**

Langford Court, Langford &*❀* (Sir John & Lady Wills) 150yds S of A38 Bristol-Bridgwater rd. 11½m S of Bristol. 1½m N of Churchill traffic lights. Signpost marked Upper Langford. 3½ acres. Lawns and trees, good display of daffodil and crocus. Topiary. Pleasant setting and outlook. New water garden. TEAS. *Adm £1.50 Chd free (ACNO to Somerset St John®). Sun March 15 (2-6)*

10 Linden Road, Clevedon see Bristol and South Glos

¶■ **Leigh Farm, Halstock** *❀* (Mr & Mrs L J Lauderdale) Leave the A37 Yeovil-Dorchester Rd 2m S of Yeovil, signposted to Sutton Bingham and Halstock. Continue for 3½m to Halstock. Turn R at the village post office/shop. Continue for 1¾m Leigh Farm is on the R, down a short concrete drive. A young and expanding plantsman's garden of 1 acre being developed by the owners who created the garden at Ashtree Cottage, Kilmington. Ponds, herbaceous borders, trees, shrubs and roses in beautiful rural setting. Garden and nursery open on Tues and Weds March-Oct. TEAS on Sun Aug 23 only. *Adm £2 Chd 50p (ACNO to Woodgreen Animal Shelters®). For NGS Weds May 6, June 3, July 1, Aug 5 (10-5), Sun Aug 23 (2-6), Weds Sept 16, Oct 7 (10-5)*

7 Little Keyford Lane, Frome *❀* (Duncan Skene) Approach Frome on B3092. Take 1st L on outskirts. 10 yr-old garden full of colour and surprise. Herbaceous perennials predominate with good collections of iris, daylilies, monardas, crocosmias, michaelmas daisies etc. Organic cultivation is progressively encouraging animal life. At the limits of the possible for a solo gardener. New features for 1998. Unusual plants for sale. Refreshments. *Adm £1.50 Chd free (ACNO to Amnesty International®). Suns May 17, 31, July 5, 19, Sept 13, 27 (2-5). Private visits welcome,* **Tel 01373 472879**

Littlecourt, West Bagborough &*❀* (Jane Kimber & John Clothier) 7m N of Taunton signed from A358. 6-acre garden in fine setting with woodland and water; spectacular new borders, interesting and extensive planting; wonderful views. *Adm £2. Private visits very welcome any time, please* **Tel 01823 432281**

● **Lower Severalls, Crewkerne** &*❀* (Howard & Audrey Pring) 1½m NE of Crewkerne. Turning for Merriott off A30; or Haselbury from A356. 2½-acre plantsman's garden beside early Ham stone farmhouse. Herbaceous borders and island beds with collections of unusual plants, shrubs and interesting features. Herb gardens. Garden and nursery (open daily March 1 to Oct 20 10-5, Suns 2-5. Closed all day Thurs.) Nursery sells herbs, herbaceous plants and half-hardy conservatory plants. *Adm £1.50 Chd free. Coaches and groups welcome by appt.* **Tel 01460 73234**

Lydeard House, Taunton &*❀* (Mr & Mrs T S Faun) Take A358 from Taunton to Bishops Lydeard, turn L at Bishops Lydeard church. House 500yds on R. A garden of 4 acres with large water garden, parterre, fernery, shrubs, herbaceous borders. *Adm £2.50. Sun June 21 (2-5.30)*

Manor Farm, Middle Chinnock ☒ (Simon & Antonia Johnson) Off A30 between Crewkerne and Yeovil. Garden of 'rooms', created over the last seven years; incl formal areas, mixed borders, pond garden, herb garden, vegetable and cutting garden, and orchard. *Combined adm with* **Chinnock House** *£2.50 Chd free Sun May 3 (2-6)*

The Manor House, Walton-in-Gordano see Bristol and South Glos

The Mill, Cannington ☒☀ (Mr & Mrs J E Hudson) 21 Mill Lane. 4m W of Bridgwater on A39. Turn opposite Rose & Crown. ¼-acre cottage type plantsman's garden with waterfall and pond, over 80 clematis and National Caltha Collection. Featured in NGS video 1. TEA in aid of Cannington W.I. *Adm £1.50 Chd free (ACNO to NCCPG®). Sats May 23, Aug 1 (2-5), Suns May 24, Aug 2 (11-5). Private visits welcome by appt, please* **Tel 01278 652304**

The Mill, Wookey ☒☒☀ (Peter & Sally Gregson) 2m W from Wells off A371. Turn L into Henley Lane, driveway 50yds on L. 2½ acres beside R Axe. Traditional and unusual cottage plants informally planted in formal beds with roses, pergola, lawns and 'hot red border'. Ornamental kitchen garden. Wide selection of plants seen in garden for sale in nursery. TEA for pre-arranged groups. *Adm £1 Chd free. Please* **Tel 01749 676966**

The Mill House, Castle Cary ☒☒☀ (Jenny & Peter Davies) Do not go into Castle Cary Town Centre, but follow signs to Torbay Rd Industrial Estate (W). Entrances to Trading Estate on L proceed E along Torbay Rd about 200yds. Garden on the R. Approx 1-acre terraced sloping garden, with stream and waterfalls. Emphasis on Natural look. Many interesting plants mingled with native flora. Bog garden; and vegetable plot. TEAS and plants in aid of Oncology Centre BRI Bristol. *Adm £1.50 Chd free. Sun, Bank Holiday Mon May 24, 25 (2-6).* **Tel 01963 350842**

●**Milton Lodge, Wells** ☒☀ (D C Tudway Quilter Esq) ½m N of Wells. From A39 Bristol-Wells, turn N up Old Bristol Rd; car park first gate on L. Mature Grade II listed terraced garden with outstanding views of Wells Cathedral and Vale of Avalon. Mixed borders; roses; fine trees. Separate 7-acre arboretum. TEAS. *Adm £2 Chd under 14 free. Open daily (2-6) ex Sats, Good Friday to end Oct; parties by arrangement. For NGS Suns May 10, 24, June 14, July 5 (2-6). Private visits welcome, please* **Tel 01749 672168**

▲**Montacute House, Montacute** ☒☒☀ (The National Trust) NT signs off A3088 4m W of Yeovil and A303. Magnificent Tudor House with contemporary garden layout. Fine stonework provides setting for informally planted mixed borders and old roses; range of garden features illustrates its long history. Lunch and TEAS. *Adm Garden only £2.90 Chd £1.30. For NGS Sun June 28 (11-5.30)*

¶**Montys Court, Norton Fitzwarren** ☒☒☀ (Major & Mrs A Mitford-Slade) 4m W of Taunton on B3227. 1m W of Norton Fitzwarren on LH side. 2-acre garden in parkland setting with views to the Quantock and Blackdown Hills. Formal rose garden filled with tulips in spring. Numerous shrubs, mature trees, extensive lawns and her-

baceous border. Cream TEAS Sun June 21 only. *Adm £1.50 Chd free (ACNO to Multiple Sclerosis® (April) All Saints Church Norton Fitzwarren (June)). Sat, Sun April 18, 19 (2-5), Sun June 21 (2-6)*

The Mount, Chelston ☒☀ (Jim & Gilly Tilden) Off M5 1m NW of junction 26. At A38 Chelston roundabout take Wellington rd. After 200yds turn R to Chelston. 1st house on R. Enclosed garden with herbaceous borders and shrubs; trees, old roses, more shrubs and small bog garden outside. 1 acre altogether. TEAS in aid of Wellington Stroke Club. *Adm £1 Chd free. Sun June 7 (2-6)*

The Mount, Wincanton ☒☀ (Alison & Peter Kelly) Follow one-way system round lower half of town, bear L at signposted Castle Cary, on up hill, house on L. 1¼-acre. Plantswoman's garden with hidden surprises. Speciality an alpine lawn and garden, half terraced shrub borders, gravel bed, rock garden and pond. Cream TEAS Suns in aid of Friends of Verrington Hospital. *Adm £2 Chd free. Sat, Sun April 18, 19, Sun, Mon May 24, 25, Sat, Sun Sept 19, 20 (2-5.30). Private visits welcome at weekends, April 18 to end June, please* **Tel 01963 32487** *after sundown*

Oare Manor Cottage, Oare ☒ (Mr & Mrs J Greenaway) 6m W of Porlock off A39. 50yds from Oare Church immortalized in R D Blackmore's 'Lorna Doone'. Sheltered cottage garden in the romantic Oare Valley. Old-fashioned herbaceous borders, tall hedges. Featured on ITV West Country. Fine views of the moor. Parking in lower field. TEAS. *Adm £1.50 Chd 50p (Share to Anti-Slavery International©). Wed July 22, Sun July 26 (2-6). Private visits welcome, please* **Tel 01598 741242**

The Old Rectory, Limington ☒☒☀ (David Mendel & Keith Anderson) 5m N of Yeovil. From A303 or A37 turn off at Ilchester. Follow signpost to Limington; in centre of village next to church. Approx 1-acre. Recently replanted garden surrounding Georgian Rectory. Mixed borders containing some unusual plants, shrub roses, small knot and ornamental kitchen gardens are set within existing old walls, fruit trees and box hedges. *Adm £1.50 Chd free. Suns April 26, June 28 (2-6). Private visits welcome, please* **Tel 01935 840035**

The Old Rectory, Swell ☒☒☀ (Cdr & Mrs J R Hoover) Fivehead. 4m W of Langport on A378, signposted Swell. ½m S of A378. Mature, informal garden of approx. 1½ acres. Good trees; natural pond with water and bog plants. Old-fashioned roses. Stone belfry from ancient church of St Catherine. TEAS. *Adm £2. Sun June 21 (2-5.30)*

2 Old Tarnwell, Upper Stanton Drew ☒☀ (Ken & Mary Payne) Lies 6m S of Bristol between the B3130 and A368 just W of Pensford. Detailed directions given when appt. is made. A quart of good plants poured into a quarter pint sized plot featuring colour themed borders, ornamental grasses, clematis and a well stocked "puddle"! Possibly the smallest, most intensively planted garden in the Yellow Book (total 0.02 acres). Plenty of ideas for small gardeners! Regret not suitable for children. Featured on HTV and in The English Garden. *Adm £1.50. Only by appt. Thurs July 2, Wed July 8, Tues July 14 (10-8), please* **Tel 01275 333146**

Parsonage Farm, Publow ✻❀ (Mr & Mrs Andrew Reid) 9m S of Bristol. A37 Bristol-Wells; at top of Pensford Hill, almost opp B3130 to Chew Magna, take lane which runs down side of row of houses; 250yds on R. 3½-acre woodland garden with large collection of trees and shrubs incl rhododendrons, azaleas and conifers; tuffastone rockery. Partly suitable for wheelchairs. TEAS in aid of All Saints, Publow. *Adm £1.50 Chd free. Sat, Sun May 16, 17 (2-5)*

Pear Tree Cottage, Stapley ❀ (Mr & Mrs Colvin Parry) 9m S of Taunton nr Churchingford. Charming cottage garden leading to 2½-acre newly made park; well planted with interesting trees and shrubs leading to old leat and mill pond. Cream TEAS. *Adm £1.50 Chd 50p. Sun, Mon May 3, 4, Sun June 7 (2-6)*

Pendower House, Hillcommon ♿✻ (Mrs O M Maggs) 5m W of Taunton off B3227 (old A361) turn R at Oake Xrds. 1st on R, parking on L verge. 1-acre landscaped garden created since 1980 on fairly level site. Shrub and herbaceous borders, collection of ceonothus. Fine display of roses, incl old-fashioned. Lge variety of young specimen and mature trees incl acers. Cream TEAS. *Adm £1.50 Chd free. Sats, Suns May 30, 31, June 13, 14 (2-6)*

¶Perridge House, Pilton ✻ (Richard & Jennifer Sheldon) Shepton Mallet 3m. Pilton ½m to E. Coming from Shepton Mallet turn R off B3136 (Pilton shop on R) for N Wootton. ½m to 1st turning L. 200yds to 1st entrance on L. Grounds are approx 20 acres of which ½ is Beech Wood and garden (3 acres) S facing slope offering a wide range of trees and shrubs many of which are unusual. The best times of year are May or Sept/Oct. TEAS in aid of Pilton Church. *Adm £2 Chd 50p. Sats May 23, Sept 12 (2-5.30)*

Pondarosa, Wayford ✻❀ (Gordon & Pearl Brown) Approx 2½m S of Crewkerne off the B3165 Lyme Regis Rd Dunsham Lane. Approx 2-acre garden being transformed from field. Water garden. Mixed borders. Collection of ornamental water fowl. TEA. *Adm £1.50 Chd free. Sat, Sun July 11, 12 (2-6)*

Popinjays & Little Norton Mill, Little Norton. 6m W of Yeovil. From A303 take A356. L to Norton-sub-Hamdon. Through village and follow signs. *Combined adm £2.50 Chd free. Sun July 12, Wed July 15 (2-6)*

Popinjays (Eric & Jean Dunkley) Hamstone house with courtyard and ½-acre sloping garden. Herbaceous planting, water features, seating areas; fruit, vegetables and orchard, plus paddock with views from Ham Hill treeline across Little Norton valley and beyond. No parking: use field as for Little Norton Mill

Little Norton Mill (Tom & Lynn Hart) 3 acres of landscaped gardens, meadow and orchard. Mill pond, ornamental ponds, marsh garden. Many mature rare trees and shrubs

Rose Cottage, Henstridge ♿❀ (Mr & Mrs J A Perrett) Church St. Approx 7m between Sherborne and Shaftesbury on A30. Turn into village at traffic lights and take second R into Church St and Rose Cottage is on R. ¼-acre cottage garden, edged by stream, planted to create a romantic mood full of evocative scents, in threads of gentle colour combinations. TEAS in aid of British Red Cross. *Adm £1 Chd free. Sun June 28 (2-6)*

■ Sherborne Garden, Litton ♿❀ (Mr & Mrs John Southwell) 15m S of Bristol 15m W of Bath, 7m N of Wells. On B3114 Litton to Harptree, ½m past Ye Olde Kings Arms. 4½ acre landscaped garden of horticultural interest. Wide selection of trees, shrubs and herbaceous plants; collection of hollies (150), hardy ferns (250); hostas, rose species, grasses and hemerocallis - well labelled. Ponds, pinetum. Picnic area. Tea, coffee and biscuits. *Adm £1.50 Chd free. Every Mon June to end of Sept. For NGS every Sun June to end Sept (11-6). Private visits and groups welcome throughout year, please* **Tel 01761 241220**

Silton House, Silton see Dorset

Smocombe House, Enmore ✻❀ (Mr & Mrs Dermot Wellesley Wesley) 4m W of Bridgwater take Enmore Rd, 3rd L after Tynte Arms. 5-acres S facing in Quantock Hills. Lovely woodland garden; views down to stream and pool; waterside stocked with interesting plants for spring/summer display; arboretum designed by Roy Lancaster; charming old kitchen garden. Garden not really suitable for wheelchairs or those who have difficulty in walking. TEAS in aid of Enmore Parish Church. *Adm £1.50 Chd free. Suns April 5, May 17 (2-6)*

¶The Spinney, Brockley ♿✻❀ (John & Felicity Ford) 9m SW of Bristol on the A370 towards Weston. 100yds past Brockley fruit stall turn R into St Nicholas Way, follow the signs to park and then walk 5 mins across a field to the spinney. Very limited parking at house for those unable to walk far, please phone for directions. Set in the middle of a small wood beginning to recover from the ravages of the storms and dutch elm disease. A peaceful 3-acre garden, fairly newly planted with the aim of keeping its rural charm. A good variety of unusual plants. TEAS and plant sale in aid of multiple sclerosis. *Adm £1.50 Chd free. Sun June 14 (2-6).* **Tel 01275 462425**

Stogumber Gardens ❀ A358 NW from Taunton for 11m. Sign to Stogumber W near Crowcombe. Six delightful gardens of interest to plantsmen in lovely village at edge of Quantocks. TEAS. *Combined adm £2.50 Chd free. Sun June 21 (2-6)*

Brook Cottage ♿✻ (Mrs M Field) Good plants incl lilies in a lovely setting; small pond for added interest

¶Hill Farm (Mr & Mrs A Jeans) A large garden on three levels with herbaceous plants, shrubs and roses

¶Pitts Cottage (Mr & Mrs B Young) Pretty cottage garden with interesting herbaceous plants. Redeveloped rear garden with vegetables and herb bed

Butts Cottage (Mr & Mrs J A Morrison) Cottage garden with old roses, old-fashioned perennials, alpines, pond, small vine house and vegetable garden

Manor Mill (Mr G E A Dyke) Delightful gardens of interest to plantsmen

Cridlands Steep (Mrs A M Leitch) Large and interesting garden with collection of trees and wildlife pond

Stone Allerton Gardens 11m NW of Wells, 2m from A38, signposted from Lower Weare. TEAS. *Combined adm £2 Chd free. Sun, Mon May 24, 25 (2-6)*

Fallowdene ❀ (Prof & Mrs G H Arthur) ½-acre of walled garden. Rose and honeysuckle pergola, mixed shrub and herbaceous borders. Splendid views over levels to Quantocks

Greenfield House (Mr & Mrs D K Bull) ½-acre walled garden, mixed planting. Colour garden. Farmyard fowls

Stowleys, Porlock &❀ (Rev R L Hancock) Bossington Lane. NE of Porlock off A39. 6m W of Minehead. Medium-size garden, approx 2 acres with magnificent views across Porlock Bay and Bristol Channel. Daffodils, roses, unusual tender plants incl leptospermum, drimys and embothrium. Parking in paddock next door to garden. TEAS. *Adm £1.50 Chd free. Sats April 4, June 27 Plants June only (2-6)*

¶**Sunnyside, Wells** ✂❀ (Nigel Cox & Patsy Koeb) W from Wells (2m) along B3139 to Wedmore Rd. After Pheasant Inn at Wookey reach village sign for Yarley 100yds beyond turn L up Yarley Hill, house 200yds on L. ½-acre cottage garden with large variety of plants, some rare. Organic vegetable plot. Large collection of asiatic and oriental lilies and also many varieties of salvia. *Combined adm with* **Walnut Farm** *£2 Chd 50p. Sun June 21 (2-6)*

Sutton Hosey Manor, Long Sutton &✂❀ (Roger Bramble Esq) On A372 just E of Long Sutton. 2-acres; ornamental kitchen garden, lily pond, pleached limes leading to amelanchier walk past duck pond; rose and juniper walk from Italian terrace; Judas tree avenue; new ptelea walk. TEA. *Adm £2 Chd over 3 yrs 50p. Sun July 12 (2.30-6)*

¶**Telconia, Biddisham** &✂❀ (Mr & Mrs Weber) Biddisham is 4m S of Axbridge on the A38. Take no through rd into village, ½m on R, just after church. Just under ⅓-acre of colourful, sweeping borders and lawns. Mixed plantings of shrubs and perennials, many unusual, grasses and over 150 varieties of hemerocallis (day lilies). Selection of plants for sale propagated from the garden. TEAS Sun July 19 only. *Adm £1.50 Chd free (ACNO National Animal Welfare Trust, Heavens Gate®). Mons May to Aug (2-6), Sun July 19 (2-6)*

¶**Thatch End, Catcott** &✂❀ (Mrs Rita Williams) Turn N off A39 between Bridgwater and Street to Catcott. Continue straight into village turn L at T junction. Fork R at War Memorial and immed L at cul de sac sign. No parking at house. Typical small cottage garden. Wide variety of plants and vegetable garden on three levels. Wheelchairs lowest level only. For teas see Dial House, Catcott. Catcott is a regular winner of Britain in Bloom. TEAS. *Combined adm with* **Dial House** *£2 Chd free. Suns May 3, 24 (2-6). Private visits also welcome by appt Tel* **01278 722 327**

Thurloxton Gardens A38 between Taunton & Bridgwater. Well signed. Ample parking available. Picnics welcome and bicycles. TEAS in aid of St Giles, Thurloxton.

Combined adm £2 Chd free. Sun June 7 (2-6)

Coombe Mill ✂ (Mr & Mrs Hugh Pollard) Newly created gardens situated around a C17 Mill in an area of outstanding natural beauty. The total area of approx. 2 acres incl a newly planted lime walk, an avenue of ornamental pears set in the formal section of the garden and a woodland walk through the quarry from which stone was obtained for the Mill and other buildings in the area. The latest project is a water garden now in its 3rd yr

Coombe Quarry (Patricia Davies-Gilbert) Cottage garden with quarry walk. Roses, shrubs, vegetables and animals

¶**The Old Manor** & (Mr & Mrs Ryan Cove) 1 acre of lawns, good trees and Victorian walled garden

■ **The Time-Trail of Roses, Wells** ✂ (Mrs Susan Lee) No on-site parking. Use car park in Tucker St and walk to entrance at top of Westfield Rd. Magnificent collection of 1500 different roses, planted in ½-acre garden in date order of their introduction to show their beauty, diversity and evolution; plus NCCPG collection of 250 miniatures. Also many spring bulbs, lilies, fruit and herbs. TEA Suns Easter to Oct 18 also Weds, Thurs, Fris, Sats May, June and July (2-6). Closed Aug. *For NGS Suns April 19 (bulbs), May 24 (species roses), June 14 (old roses). Adm £2.50 May, June, July, £1.50 other times Chd free. Parties by appt Tel* **01749 674677**

▲**Tintinhull House, Yeovil** ✂ (The National Trust) NW of Yeovil. Tintinhull Village, Yeovil. Signs on A303, W of Ilchester. Famous 2-acre garden in compartments, developed 1900-1960, influenced by Gertrude Jekyll and Hidcote; many good and uncommon plants. C17 & C18 house (not open). TEAS in aid of St Margaret's Church. *Adm £3.70 Chd £1.80. For NGS Sun July 19 (12-6)*

¶**6 Tirley Way, Weston-Super-Mare** ❀ (Aileen Birks) A370 into WSM turn R into Baytree Rd. At top of hill turn R then immed L into Milton Hill. 2nd L into Ashbury Drive then 2nd R. 2000 varieties shoe horned into small suburban garden incl 100 plus fuchsia varieties and some exotics. Pond and water feature, pergola, large greenhouse. TEAS. *Adm £1 Chd free (ACNO to Free Wheelers Emergency Volunteer Service®). Tues, Wed July 14, 15 (11-5)*

Tone Dale House, Wellington (Victoria & Ben Fox) Just outside Wellington on the Milverton to Wellington Rd. 3-acre garden first planned in early C18 beside a millstream. Many interesting trees and various plantings. Parking limited. TEA. *Adm £2.50 Chd free. Tues Feb 17, June 9 (2-5.30)*

Tranby House, Whitchurch, Bristol see Bristol and South Glos

¶**8 Trossachs Drive, Bathampton** ✂❀ (Sheila Batterbury) Take A36 S out of Bath (signposted Warminster). ¼m up the hill from the city, then R into Trossachs Drive (opp sign marked Bathampton and copper beech). ⅔-acre of terraced garden on a hillside. Created 3yrs ago from an old orchard. Many interesting and unusual plants brought from London (and happier in the West Country!). Lots of colour. TEA. *Adm £1.50. Sun June 14 (2.30-6)*

University of Bristol Botanic Garden see Bristol and South Glos

¶**Vellacott, Taunton** ⚲✿ (Kevin & Pat Chittenden) Off A358 9m NW of Taunton signed Lawford. ½-acre garden on S facing slope with splendid views. Profusely stocked with a very wide range of plants and trees. Ponds, fruit garden and potager. TEAS if fine. *Adm £1.50 Chd under 14 free. Suns, Weds April 26, May 17, 27, June 14, 24, July 12, 22, Sept 13, 16 (2-6). Private visits welcome by appt, please* **Tel 01984 618249**

Wall House, Staplegrove ♿⚲ (Mr & Mrs I Polley) On the outskirts of Taunton on the A358 Staplegrove Rd towards Norton Fitzwarren. ½-acre garden with trees, shrubs, perennials, roses and mediterranean plants in borders, beds and containers for yr-round colour. *Adm £1 Chd 50p. Sun July 12 (2-6)*

Walnut Farm, Yarley ⚲✿ (Angela & John Marsh) 3m W of Wells. On B3139 turn L at Yarley Cross. Island site 200yds up Yarley Hill. ⅔-acre garden with many unusual perennials mixed with shrubs, roses and climbers. 2 ponds and bog garden. Yr-round interest. Splendid views of Mendips. Conservatory. Small conservation area in adjoining field. Cream TEAS and plants in aid of Coeliac Society. *Combined adm with* **Sunnyside** *£2 Chd 50p. Sun June 21 (2-6). Private visits welcome, please* **Tel 01749 676942**

Wayford Manor, Crewkerne ✿ (Mr & Mrs Robin L Goffe) SW of Crewkerne. Turning on B3165 at Clapton; or on A30 Chard-Crewkerne. 3 acres, noted for magnolias and acers. Bulbs; flowering trees, shrubs; rhododendrons. Garden redesigned by Harold Peto in 1902. Fine Elizabethan manor house (not open). TEAS in aid of local charities. *Adm £2 Chd 50p. Suns April 12, May 3, 17, 31 (2-6); also private parties welcome, but please* **Tel 01460 73253**

Wellesley Park Gardens, Wellington ♿⚲ ½m from centre of Wellington on S side, or can be found by turning down Hoyles Rd off the Wellington Relief Rd and taking 3rd rd L. 3 gardens situated just below the brow of the hill. TEAS. *Combined adm £2 Chd free. Sat, Sun, Wed June 13, 14, 17 (2-6)*
> **Greenlands, 46 Wellesley Park** ✿ (Jack & Pat Kenney) A ½-acre 1930's town garden planted in cottage garden style with herbaceous plants and shrubs. Small wildlife pond. TEA and plants
> **Miraflores, 49 Wellesley Park** (Dr & Mrs R W Phillips) ½-acre garden of mixed herbaceous planting with over 60 varieties of old roses. Pond and orchard
> **48 Wellesley Park** (John & Julie Morton) A ⅕-acre garden with pond, pergola and vegetable garden designed to be seen from the house to give an illusion of more space. Many specimen plants and containers

West Bradley House, nr Glastonbury (Mr & Mrs E Clifton-Brown) 2½m due E of Glastonbury. Turn S off A361 (Shepton Mallet/Glastonbury Rd) at W Pennard. C17 octagonal stone house in 3-acre open garden next to church. 3 old carp ponds at different levels, with waterfall between 2. Range of unusual perennials and waterside

plants. 70 acres of apple orchards around house, hopefully in full blossom when garden open. Visitors welcome to walk (or even drive) through orchards. Parking available. TEAS in aid of W Bradley Church. *Adm garden and orchards £2 Chd free (ACNO to The Listening Library®). Sun May 10 (2-6)*

Weston House, Buckhorn see Dorset

Windmill Cottage, Backwell ⚲✿ (Alan & Pam Harwood) Hillside Rd. 8m SW of Bristol. Take A370 Backwell. Parking available in Backwell and New Inn (10 min walk). Hillside Rd is single track lane with no parking (unless for special reasons). Into a 2-acre plot put a plentiful variety of plants, add to this a pinch of knowledge and a sprinkling of wildflowers, together with a reasonable amount of ground cover; blend in some colour and a generous dash of fragrance. Bind the whole thing together with a large collection of clematis. TEAS. *Adm £1.50 Chd free. Suns May 24, Aug 16, Sept 20, Wed June 17, July 15 (2-5.30). Groups welcome by appt, please* **Tel 01275 463492**

Withey Lane Farmhouse, Barton St David ⚲✿ (Sqn Ldr & Mrs H C Tomblin) 4m E of Somerton, turn off B3153 in Keinton Manderville. Turn R in Barton 100yds past Barton Inn. 200yds turn L at Manor House. 300yds turn R into small lane; farmhouse 300yds on right. ½-acre enthusiast's garden with many unusual and interesting plants; herbaceous beds with shrubs; raised alpine beds; old roses; climbing plants; 1½-acre cider orchard. *Adm £1 Chd 50p. Open Weds June 10, 17 (2-5). Private visits and groups welcome April to Sept, please* **Tel 01458 850875**

Woodborough (R D Milne) Porlock Weir. From Porlock proceed towards Porlock Weir. After West Porlock take the very first turning L opposite the gates of Porlock Vale House & Equitation Centre. Woodborough is the only house up this lane. 70yr old garden of 2-3 acres on a steep slope with a wide variety of shrubs, mainly ericaceous, and an excellent collection of Ghent azaleas and loderi rhododendron. Water features and magnificent views over Porlock Bay. Open for charities each weekend in May or by appt. TEAS. *Adm £2 Chd under 12 free (ACNO to NGS and British & International Sailors' Soc®). Sun May 24 (12-5.30)*

Remember that every time you visit a National Gardens Scheme garden you are helping to raise money for:

The Queen's Nursing Institute
County Nursing Associations
The Nurses' Welfare Service
Macmillan Cancer Relief
Marie Curie Cancer Care
Help the Hospices
Crossroads
The Gardens Fund of the National Trust
The Gardeners' Royal Benevolent Society
The Royal Gardeners' Orphans Fund

Staffordshire & part of West Midlands

Hon County Organisers: Mr & Mrs D K Hewitt, Arbour Cottage, Napley, Market Drayton, Shropshire
TF9 4AJ Tel & Fax 01630 672852

DATES OF OPENING

Regular openings
For details see garden description

The Covert, Burntwood Loggerheads
Manor Cottage, Chapel Chorlton

By appointment only
For telephone numbers and other
details see garden descriptions.
Private visits welcomed

Eastfield House, Kings Bromley

March 14 Saturday
202 Rising Brook, Stafford
April 2 Thursday
The Covert, Burntwood
Loggerhead
April 10 Friday
Arbour Cottage, Napley
April 13 Monday
Manor Cottage, Chapel Chorlton
April 15 Wednesday
The Old Doctors House,
Loggerheads
38 Park Avenue, Rising Brook,
Stafford
202 Rising Brook, Stafford
April 17 Friday
Arbour Cottage, Napley
April 24 Friday
Arbour Cottage, Napley
May 1 Friday
Arbour Cottage, Napley
May 2 Saturday
The Old Doctors House,
Loggerheads
May 5 Tuesday
Grapevine, Kings Bromley
May 10 Sunday
Bleak House, Bagnall
May 15 Friday
Arbour Cottage, Napley
May 17 Sunday
Little Onn Hall, Church Eaton
Wightwick Manor, Compton
May 24 Sunday
Heath House, nr Eccleshall
Stanley House Farm, nr Milwich
May 26 Tuesday
Grapevine, Kings Bromley
May 27 Wednesday
26 Lapley Avenue, Stafford

The Old Doctors House,
Loggerheads
38 Park Avenue, Rising Brook,
Stafford
May 29 Friday
Arbour Cottage, Napley
May 31 Sunday
Stonehill, Hollington
The Wombourne Wodehouse
June 7 Sunday
The Garth, Milford
The Hollies Farm, Pattingham
June 10 Wednesday
38 Park Avenue, Rising Brook,
Stafford
Thornfold, Leek
June 12 Friday
Arbour Cottage, Napley
June 13 Saturday
The Old Doctors House,
Loggerheads
June 14 Sunday
12 Darges Lane, Great Wyrley
Flashbrook Lodge, Flashbrook
Little Onn Hall, Church Eaton
Thornfold, Leek
Westward Ho, Rugeley
June 17 Wednesday
Grapevine, Kings Bromley
Strawberry Fields, Hill Ridware
Thornfold, Leek
Woodside House,
Barton-under-Needwood
June 20 Saturday
The Covert, Burntwood
Loggerheads (**Evening**)
Lower House, Sugnall Parva,
Eccleshall
June 21 Sunday
Bankcroft Farm, Tatenhill,
Burton-on-Trent
Flashbrook Lodge, Flashbrook
Lower House, Sugnall Parva,
Eccleshall
Stanley House Farm, nr Milwich
Woodside House,
Barton-under-Needwood
June 24 Wednesday
38 Park Avenue, Rising Brook,
Stafford
202 Rising Brook, Stafford
June 26 Friday
Arbour Cottage, Napley
June 28 Sunday
Biddulph Grange Garden, Biddulph

The Covert, Burntwood
Loggerheads
The Garth, Milford
Grafton Cottage,
Barton-under-Needwood
July 1 Wednesday
The Old Doctors House,
Loggerheads
July 5 Sunday
The Beeches, Rocester
12 Darges Lane, Great Wyrley
Moseley Old Hall, Fordhouses
98 Walsall Road, Aldridge
July 8 Wednesday
38 Park Avenue, Rising Brook,
Stafford
July 12 Sunday
Bankcroft Farm, Tatenhill,
Burton-on-Trent
Bleak House, Bagnall
Stonehill, Hollington
Strawberry Fields, Hill Ridware
July 15 Wednesday
Strawberry Fields, Hill Ridware
July 18 Saturday
The Old Doctors House,
Loggerheads
July 19 Sunday
Brookside, Abbots Bromley,
Heath House, nr Eccleshall
Strawberry Fields, Hill Ridware
Woodside House,
Barton-under-Needwood
July 21 Tuesday
Grapevine, Kings Bromley
July 25 Saturday
Inglenook, Tamworth
July 26 Sunday
Woodside House,
Barton-under-Needwood
July 29 Wednesday
Brookside, Abbots Bromley,
26 Lapley Avenue, Stafford
38 Park Avenue, Rising Brook,
Stafford
August 2 Sunday
Inglenook, Tamworth
August 5 Wednesday
The Old Doctors House,
Loggerheads
August 9 Sunday
Brookside, Abbots Bromley,
Grafton Cottage,
Barton-under-Needwood
The Willows, Trysull

STAFFORDSHIRE
AND PART OF THE
WEST MIDLANDS

Biddulph
4

Kidsgrove

A52   A53

29 Leek

A50

A34

5

STOKE-ON-TRENT

Newcastle-
under-Lyme

27

3 Rocester

1   A51   21

23   7

Stone

A50

26 Uttoxeter

20

M6

15

6

Burton
upon Trent

11

Stafford

2

25   24

12

31

Rugeley
28

A51

14   35
9   13

19

A34

A38

A5

Cannock

Lichfield

A5

A51

M54   22

M6

30

Tamworth
17

16   32

Wolverhampton

33   34

10

kms 0   10

miles 0   10

KEY

1. Arbour Cottage
2. Bankcroft Farm
3. The Beeches
4. Biddulph Grange Garden
5. Bleak House
6. Brookside
7. The Covert
8. 12 Darges Lane
9. Eastfield House
10. Edgewood House
11. Flashbrook Lodge
12. The Garth

13. Grafton Cottage
14. Grapevine
15. Heath House
16. The Hollies Farm
17. Inglenook
18. 26 Lapley Avenue
19. Little Onn Hall
20. Lower House
21. Manor Cottage
22. Moseley Old Hall
23. The Old Doctors House
24. 38 Park Avenue

25. 202 Rising Brook
26. Stanley House Farm
27. Stonehill
28. Strawberry Fields
29. Thornfolld
30. 98 Walsall Road
31. Westward Ho
32. Wightwick Manor
33. The Willows
34. The Wombourne
    Wodehouse
35. Woodside House

August 11 Tuesday
Grapevine, Kings Bromley
August 16 Sunday
The Covert, Burntwood
Loggerheads
Edgewood House,
Stourton

August 27 Thursday
The Covert, Burntwood
Loggerhead
August 31 Monday
Manor Cottage, Chapel Chorlton
September 1 Tuesday
Grapevine, Kings Bromley

September 15 Tuesday
Grapevine, Kings Bromley
September 20 Sunday
Wightwick Manor, Compton
September 27 Sunday
Biddulph Grange Garden, Biddulph

DESCRIPTIONS OF GARDENS

Arbour Cottage, Napley ᵭ⚲❀ (Mr & Mrs D K Hewitt)
4m N of Market Drayton on Staffs/Shrops border. Take
A53 then B5415 signed Woore, turn L 1¾m at telephone
box. Country garden 2 acres with alpine screes, mixed
perennials, shrub roses and many paeonias, bamboos etc.
Colour all yr from shrubs and trees of many species.
TEAS. *Adm £2 Chd free. Fris April 10, 17, 24, May 1, 15,
29, June 12, 26 (2-5). Private visits welcome, please* Tel
01630 672852

¶Bankcroft Farm, Tatenhill ⚲ (Mrs Penelope Adkins)
Take Tatenhill road off A38 Burton flyover. 1m, 1st house
on left approaching village. Parking on farm. 1 acre developing organic country garden with winding paths and
well established shrubs and trees. Herbaeous borders,
ponds, orchard and large vegetable garden. New woodland and wildlife walk. TEAS. *Adm £1.50 (ACNO Burton
Cats Protection League®). Suns June 21, July 12 (11-5).
Private visits welcome June and July* Tel 01283 546715

¶The Beeches, Rocester ᵭ⚲❀ (Mr & Mrs K Sutton)
Mill Street 5m north of Uttoxeter on B5030, turn right
into village by J.C.B. factory. By Red Lion public house
take road for Marston Montgomery. A plant lover's garden of about ¾ acre, herbaceous borders, box garden,
many varieties of shrubs, rhododendrons and azaleas.
Pools, roses, fruit trees, climbing plants, an all year round
garden. 3 times winner of East Staffs Borough in Bloom
competition. TEA. *Adm £1.50 Chd free. Sun July 5 (2-5)*

▲Biddulph Grange Garden, Biddulph ⚲❀ (The
National Trust) 3½m SE of Congleton, 7m N of Stoke-on-
Trent on A527. An exciting and rare survival of a high
Victorian garden extensively restored since 1988. Con-
ceived by James Bateman, the 15 acres are divided into a
number of smaller gardens designed to house specimens
from his extensive plant collection. An Egyptian Court;
Chinese Pagoda, Willow Pattern Bridge; Pinetum and Ar-
boretum combine to make the garden a miniature tour of
the world. TEAS. *Adm £4 Chd £2 Family £10. April 1 to
Nov 1, Wed to Fri (12-6), Sat to Sun (11-6). For NGS
Suns June 28, Sept 27 (11-6)* Tel 01782 517999

Bleak House, Bagnall ⚲❀ (Mr & Mrs J H Beynon)
A5009 to Milton Xrds turn for Bagnall. 2m up hill past
golf course to corner opp Highlands Hospital. 1-acre
plantswoman's garden on 3 levels with roses, herbaceous
borders. Terraces leading to informal garden incl stone
quarry with pool and waterfall. TEAS. *Adm £2 Chd free.
Suns May 10, July 12 (1-5). Parties welcome, please* Tel
01782 534713

Brookside, Abbots Bromley ⚲ (Mr & Mrs L Harvey) Approach village from Uttoxeter or Rugeley via B5013; from
Burton via B5017. Turn opp Bagot Arms Inn situated in
the main st. Village garden comprising shrubs, herbaceous and bedding plants, rose and herb gardens, water
features with brook running along the Northern Boundary. TEAS in nearby C17 hall. *Adm £1.50 Chd free. Suns
July 19, Aug 9, Wed July 29 (1.30-5.30)*

The Covert, Burntwood Loggerheads ᵭ⚲❀ (Mr &
Mrs Leslie Standeven) On Staffs/Shrops borders. Turn off
A53 Newcastle-Market Drayton Rd onto Kestrel Drive, The
Burntwood nr Loggerheads Xrds, adjacent hotel. Plantper-
son's garden featuring many rare and unusual plants. Mediterranean scree, tuffa, peat and mixed beds. Alpine
house. Featured Gardeners World magazine 1996. TEAS.
*Adm £2 Chd 50p. Suns June 28, Aug 16 (2-5.30). TEA.
Thurs April 2 to Aug 27 incl (2-5). Sat June 20 (7-9) adm
£3 incl wine. Private visits welcome, please* Tel 01630
672677

12 Darges Lane, Great Wyrley ⚲❀ (Mr & Mrs K Hackett)
From A5 take A34 towards Walsall. Darges Lane is 1st
turning on R (over brow of hill). House on R on corner of
Cherrington Drive. ¼-acre well stocked plantsman's and
flower arranger's garden. Foliage plants a special feature.
Mixed borders incl trees, shrubs and rare plants giving yr-
round interest. Features constantly changing. National
collection of lamiums. TEAS. *Adm £1.50 Chd 50p. Suns
June 14, July 5 (2-6). Also private visits welcome, please*
Tel 01922 415064

Eastfield House, Kings Bromley ᵭ (Mr & Mrs A Rogers)
Kings Bromley lies 5m N of Lichfield on A515 Lichfield to
Ashbourne rd and 3m W of the A38 on the A513 Tamworth to Rugeley rd. Eastfield House is ½m E of the village centre on the A513. 2-acre garden surrounding a
Victorian House, shrubs, lawns herbaceous plants, pond
and bog garden. *Adm £1.50 Chd 50p. Private visits welcome June to Sept, please* Tel 01543 472315

Edgewood House, Stourton ❀ (Mr & Mrs G E Fletcher)
4m W of Stourbridge 11m E of Bridgnorth. Take A458
from Stew Poney Junction on A449 (Wolverhampton/Kid-
derminster) towards Bridgnorth. 1st lane on R (Greens-
forge Lane). ¾m along lane on L. 12 acres of woodland
with winding paths and cultivated natural garden with
small pools. Rhododendrons and azaleas. TEAS. *Adm £2
Chd free. Sun Aug 16 (2-6)*

Flashbrook Lodge, Flashbrook ⚲ (Mrs Minnie A Mansell)
On A41 4m N of Newport, take rd signed Knighton. A garden established in 1992 from green field site of approx 1
acre. Features large pool, rockery, waterfall, pergola,

gazebo, arbour, trees, shrubs, old-fashioned shrub roses and herbaceous perennials with all yr interest. TEAS. *Adm £1.50 Chd 50p (ACNO St Michael and All Angels Church, Adbaston®). Suns June 14, 21 (2-6)*

The Garth, Milford ❀ (Mr & Mrs David Wright) 2 Broc Hill Way, 4½m SE of Stafford. A513 Stafford-Rugeley Rd; at Barley Mow turn R (S) to Brocton; L after ½m. ½-acre; shrubs, rhododendrons, azaleas, mixed herbaceous borders, naturalized bulbs; plants of interest to flower arrangers. Rock hewn caves. Fine landscape setting. Coach parties by appt. TEAS. *Adm £1.50 Chd 50p. Suns June 7, 28 (2-6). Private parties welcome, please* **Tel 01785 661182**

Grafton Cottage, Barton-under-Needwood ❀❀ (Mr & Mrs P Hargreaves) Bar Lane. Bar Lane is ½m W of Top Bell public house off B5016 to Yoxall. ¾m along lane. A plant lover's cottage garden. ¼-acre. Trellises covered with many old roses, over 50 varieties of clematis; wide range of unusual perennials with all-summer interest, stream. Winner of E Staffs Borough in Bloom competition. Featured in Aug 96 Practical Gardening and May 97 Amateur Gardener. TEAS. *Adm £2 Chd free (ACNO Arthritis Rheumatism Council for Research®). Suns June 28, Aug 9 (1.30-5.30). Parties welcome,* **Tel 01283 713639**

Grapevine, Kings Bromley ❀❀ (Mr & Mrs B Harber) 37 Leofric Close. A513 5m N of Lichfield. An artist's prize-winning small garden. Perennials, shrubs, roses, climbers and bulbs combine with water features, containers, conservatories and statuary to provide colour, form and scent throughout the summer. Please park at village hall approx 350 yds. TEA. *Adm £1.50. Tues May 5, 26, Wed June 17, Tues July 21, Aug 11; Sept 1, 15 (12-4). Private parties welcome, please* **Tel 01543 472762**

Heath House, nr Eccleshall ❀❀ (Dr & Mrs D W Eyre-Walker) 3m W of Eccleshall. Take B5026 towards Woore. At Sugnall turn L, after 1½m turn R immediately by stone garden wall. After 1m straight across Xrds. 1½-acre garden. Borders, bog garden, woodland garden new (1997) peat bed and alpine bed. Many unusual plants. Car parking limited and difficult if wet. TEAS. *Adm £2 Chd free (ACNO Parish Church®). Suns May 24, July 19 (2-6). Also private visits welcome, please* **Tel 01785 280318**

The Hollies Farm, Pattingham ❀❀ (Mr & Mrs J Shanks) From Wolverhampton A454 W, follow signs to Pattingham. Cross t-lights at Perton, 1½m R for Hollies Lane. From Pattingham take Wolverhampton Rd 1m turn L to Hollies Lane. 2-acre plantsman's landscaped garden with interesting trees and shrubs in lovely countryside setting. TEAS in aid of NSPCC. *Adm £2 Chd free. Sun June 7 (2-6)*

Inglenook, Tamworth ❀❀❀ (Mr & Mrs J Sippitts) 25 Clifford St, Glascote. From new A5 bypass, take B5440 signed Glascote to B5000 approx ½m. Follow sign for town centre at roundabout for 300yds. Clifford St 1st R opp Glascote WMC. Extra parking opp WMC. ¼-acre garden of mixed borders, shrubs and trees; small wildlife pond, ornamental pond. Arbours and gazebo. 'Garden

News' and Thompson & Morgan Gardeners of the Year 1996. TEA. *Adm £1 Chd 25p. Sat July 25; Sun Aug 2 (1-5)*

¶26 Lapley Avenue, Stafford ❀ (Mrs D Parker) 2m NW of Stafford Town. Off junction 14 on M6. On to Eccleshall Rd towards Stafford. First right into Creswell Farm Drive. Straight on to end of road to car park and signed short walk to 26 Lapley Ave. Small town garden completely landscaped by owners since 1990. With a few surprises! Pond with a bridge, pergola, specimen trees although young, wide variety of plants. TEA. *Adm £1.50 Chd free. Weds May 27, July 29 (2-6)*

Little Onn Hall, Church Eaton ❀ (Mr & Mrs I H Kidson) 6m SW of Stafford. A449 Wolverhampton-Stafford; at Gailey roundabout turn W on to A5 for 1¼m; turn R to Stretton; 200yds turn L for Church Eaton; or Bradford Arms-Wheaton Aston and Marston 1¼m. 6-acre garden; herbaceous lined drive; abundance of rhododendrons; formal paved rose garden with pavilions at front; large lawns with lily pond around house; old moat garden with fish tanks and small ruin; fine trees; walkways. Paddock open for picnics. TEAS. *Adm £2 Chd 50p. Suns May 17, June 14 (2-6)*

Lower House, Sugnall Parva, Eccleshall ❀❀ (Mr & Mrs J M Treanor) 2m W of Eccleshall. On B5026 Loggerheads Rd turn R at sharp double bend. House ½m on L. Large cottage garden with all yr colour and interest, mixed borders, shrubs, pond and rockery in rural setting. TEAS. *Adm £2 Chd free. Sat, Sun June 20, 21 (1-6). Also private visits welcome, please* **Tel 01785 851 378**

Manor Cottage, Chapel Chorlton ❀❀ (Mrs Joyce Heywood) 6m S of Newcastle-U-Lyme. On A51 Nantwich to Stone Rd turn behind Cock Inn at Stableford; white house on village green. The garden is full of interesting and unusual plants especially fern, euphorbias, grasses and geraniums. TEAS. *Adm £1.50 Chd 50p. Every Mon April 13 to Aug 31 (2-5). Also private visits welcome, please* **Tel 01782 680206**

▲Moseley Old Hall, Fordhouses ❀❀ (The National Trust) 4m N of Wolverhampton, between A460 & A449 south of M54 motorway; follow signs. Small modern reconstruction of C17 garden with formal box parterre; mainly includes plants grown in England before 1700; old roses, herbaceous plants, small herb garden, arbour. Late Elizabethan house. TEAS. *Adm Garden £1.80 Chd 90p. For NGS Sun July 5 (1.30-5.30)*

The Old Doctors House, Loggerheads ❀❀❀ (Mr & Mrs David Ainsworth) The Burntwood. On Staffs/ Shrops border. Turn off A53 Newcastle to Market Drayton rd onto Kestrel Drive/The Burntwood nr Loggerheads Xrds, adjacent hotel. ¾-acre garden with a strong sense of peace and tranquility. Woodland plantings of Barnhaven primulas, hellebores, meconopsis, ferns. Mixed beds of over 30 Penstemon, Euphorbia, Salvia etc. Pool, waterfall. Wide selection of plants propagated for sale. TEAS in aid of Shropshire Hospice. *Adm £1.50 Chd 50p. Weds Apr 15, May 27, July 1, Aug 5, Sats May 2, June 13, July 18 (1-5). Group visits 10 or more, please* **Tel 01630 673363**

38 Park Avenue, Rising Brook, Stafford ⚘❀ (Mr & Mrs Eric Aspin) Leave M6 at junction 13, A449 towards Stafford, approx 2m, past Royal Oak on R, past Westway on L, next turn L. From Stafford take A449 over railway bridge, 4th turn on R. ⅛-acre small town garden with interesting design features and varied planting. 'Every corner's a mini masterpiece', Express and Star, June 1996. Secluded white garden, good selection of old roses and clematis. TEA. *Adm £1.50 Chd free. Weds April 15, May 27, June 10, 24, July 8, 29 (2-6). Private visits welcome, please* **Tel 01785 212762**

¶202 Rising Brook, Stafford ⚘ (Mr Adrian E Hubble) From junction 13 on M6 head towards Stafford town centre on A449. After passing right hand bend with guard rail, house located on left between Park Avenue and Highfields Grove. Park with consideration in either of those streets. A plantsman's small town garden (⅓ acre) packed with over 500 varieties of choice plants to provide all year interest. Hellebores, snowdrops, woodland anemones, epimediums and species irises form the backbone of the spring collection. *Adm £1.50 Chd 50p. Sat March 14 (12-4), Weds April 15, June 24, open with* **38 Park Avenue** *(2-6)*

¶Stanley House Farm, Milwich ⚘❀ (Mr & Mrs J Lockwood) On B5027 between Milwich and Uttoxeter approx 2m Milwich and 4m Uttoxeter. A new garden of 3 acres started from scratch in 1994. Features include a wild flower orchard; walled garden; laburnum tunnel; ponds; shrubs; trees and herbaceous borders. Trees are a special feature and an arboretum is being planted. TEAS in aid of Uttoxeter NSPCC. *Adm £2 Chd free. Suns May 24, June 21 (2-6)*

Stonehill Quarry Garden, Hollington ♿⚘❀ (David and Caroline Raymont) Great Gate. 6m NW Uttoxeter. A50 to Uttoxeter. Take B5030 to JCB Rocester, L to Hollington. Third R into Keelings Lane and Croxden Abbey. At Gt Gate, L to Stonehill [SKO53402]. 6 acre pickaxe development started 1992. All year interest. Woodland walk, azaleas, rhododendrons, wild flowers and spring bulbs. Herbaceous borders, shrubs, alpines, pond and rock garden (newly extended for 1998). Teas in aid of St Giles Church. *Adm £1.50 Chd 50p. NGS Suns May 31, July 12 (2-6). Group visits welcome by arrangement, please* **Tel 01889 507202**

Strawberry Fields, Hill Ridware ⚘ (Mr & Mrs T Adams) 5m N of Lichfield. B5014 Lichfield/Abbots Bromley. At Hill Ridware turn into Church Lane by Royal Oak Inn, then 1st R. This delightful ⅓-acre award winning garden has a water trail and a succession of focal points that draw you round this plant person's paradise. Pleasing country views. TEAS. *Adm £1.50 Chd free. Suns July 12, 19; Weds June 17, July 15 (11-5). Group visits welcome, please* **Tel 01543 490516**

Thornfold, Leek ⚘❀ (Mrs Patricia Machin) A523. 1m from Leek. L at hospital Moorland Rd, 2nd R Thornfield Ave, Arden Close on R. Please park with consideration in the Avenue. New small cottage garden, yr-round colour from mixed herbaceous borders, trellises with roses and clematis. Pond, unusual plants. TEA. *Adm £1.50 Chd free. Weds June 10, 17, Sun June 14 (1.30-5)*

98 Walsall Road, Aldridge ⚘❀ (Mr & Mrs T Atkins) 3m NW of Walsall on A454, 300yds past White House Inn. ⅓-acre well stocked small town garden, mostly shrubs and perennials with informal pond. *Adm £1.50 Chd 50p. Sun July 5 (2-6)*

Westward Ho, Rugeley ♿⚘❀ (Mr & Mrs A Hargreaves) Kingsley Wood Rd. From N: Proceed from junction A513 and A51 towards Rugeley. After 1m turn R into Bower Lane, after 1.8m turn R into Kingsley Wood Rd. From S: At large island in Rugeley take N A51 to Stone/Stafford. After 300yds turn L at t-lights towards Penkridge after 1.7m turn R into Stafford Brook Rd, 1st L into Kingsley Wood Rd. Large garden in heart of Cannock Chase with places to sit and enjoy herbaceous beds, shrubs, trees, pool, pagoda, pergola and woodland walk. TEAS. *Adm £1.50 Chd free (ACNO Chadsmoor Methodist Church®). Sun June 14 (1-5.30)*

▲Wightwick Manor, Compton ♿ (The National Trust) 3m W of Wolverhampton A454, Wolverhampton-Bridgnorth, just to N of rd, up Wightwick Bank, beside Mermaid Inn. Partly suitable for wheelchairs. 17-acre, Victorian-style garden laid out by Thomas Mawson; yew hedges; topiary; terraces; 2 pools; rhododendrons; azaleas. House closed. TEAS. *Adm £2 Chd £1. For NGS Suns May 17, Sept 20 (2-6)*

The Willows, Trysull ♿⚘❀ (Mr & Mrs Nigel Hanson) 7m SW of Wolverhampton. From A449 at Himley B4176 towards Bridgnorth, 2¼m turn R to Trysull. ¾m on L. 2-acre plant lover's garden created and maintained by garden designers Nigel and Jane since 1981. Natural pool, hostas, gunnera etc. Shrub rose garden, tropical beds with dramatic flowers and foliage. Colour theme borders with a extensive range of interesting and unusual plants. Teas in village hall in aid of Trysull Church. *Adm £2 Chd free. Sun Aug 9 (2-6). Private parties welcome, please* **Tel 01902 897557**

The Wombourne Wodehouse, Wolverhampton ♿⚘❀ (Mr & Mrs J Phillips) 4m S of Wolverhampton just off A449 on A463 to Sedgley. 18-acre garden laid out in 1750. Mainly rhododendrons, herbaceous and iris border, woodland walk, water garden. TEAS. *Adm £2 Chd free. Sun May 31 (2-5.30); also private visits welcome in May, June, July, please* **Tel 01902 892202**

Woodside House, Barton-under-Nedwood ⚘❀ (Mr & Mrs R C Webster) Take B5016 out of Barton-under-Needwood. Turn R at Top Bell public house, 300yds turn R. 1-acre garden of rare and unusual plants including 70 varieties of salvias; Japanese garden with stream, waterfalls and lily pond; rose walk; cottage garden. Large Koi pond with rockery and waterfall. TEAS. *Adm £2 Chd free (ACNO RNIB®). Wed June 17, Suns June 21, July 19, 26 (1.30-6). Private visits welcome by appt June 7 to Aug 31 (1.30-6), please* **Tel 01283 716046**

Evening Opening (see also garden descriptions)

The Covert, Burntwood Loggerheads June 20 7–9pm

Suffolk

Hon County Organisers:

(East) Mrs Robert Stone, Washbrook Grange, Washbrook, Nr Ipswich IP8 3HQ
Tel 01473 730244

(West) Lady Mowbray, Hill House, Glemsford, Nr Sudbury CO 10 7PP
Tel 01787 281930

Asst Hon County Organiser: (East) Mrs T W Ingram, Orchard House, Chattisham Lane, Hintlesham IP8 3NW
Tel 01473 652 282

Mrs R I Johnson, 13 Trinity St, Bungay NR35 1EH Tel 01986 895226

Asst Hon County Organiser: (West) Mrs M Pampanini, The Old Rectory, Hawstead, Bury St Edmunds IP29 5NT
Tel 01284 386 613

Mrs A Kelsey, The Priory, Church Road, Little Waldingfield CO10 OSW
Tel 01787 2477335

Hon County Treasurer: (West) Sir John Mowbray

DATES OF OPENING

Regular openings
For details see garden description

Blakenham Woodland Garden, Little
  Blakenham
Euston Hall, nr Thetford
Somerleyton Hall, Lowestoft
Woottens, Wenhaston

By appointment only
*For telephone numbers and other
details see garden descriptions.
Private visits welcomed*

Battlies House, Rougham
Garden House, Nr Newmarket
Grundisburgh Hall, Woodbridge
Rumah Kita, Bedfield

March 29 Sunday
  East Bergholt Place, East
    Bergholt
April 5 Sunday
  Barham Hall, Barham, Ipswich
  The Beeches, Walsham-le-Willows
  Great Thurlow Hall, Haverhill
April 13 Monday
  East Bergholt Place, East Bergholt
April 19 Sunday
  Holly Cottage, Long Melford
April 26 Sunday
  Tollemache Hall, Offton
May 3 Sunday
  13 Drapers Lane, Ditchingham
  The Old Hall, Barsham
  The Rookery, Eyke
  Stour Cottage, East Bergholt
May 4 Monday
  13 Drapers Lane, Ditchingham
  Horringer House, Horringer
  The Old Hall, Barsham
  Stour Cottage, East Bergholt

May 10 Sunday
  Somerleyton Hall, Lowestoft
  Thrift Farm, Cowlinge, nr
    Newmarket
May 17 Sunday
  Blakenham Woodland Garden,
    Little Blakenham
  The Priory, Stoke by Nayland
May 20 Wednesday
  Blakenham Woodland Garden,
    Little Blakenham
May 24 Sunday
  Clipt Bushes, Cockfield
  Moat Cottage, Great Green,
    Cockfield
  Rosedale, Colchester Road,
    Bures, nr Sudbury
  Thrift Farm, Cowlinge, nr
    Newmarket
  Washbrook Cottage, Ipswich
  Windmill Cottage, Capel St Mary
May 25 Monday
  Thrift Farm, Cowlinge, nr
    Newmarket
  Washbrook Cottage, Ipswich
May 31 Sunday
  Aldeburgh Gardens
June 7 Sunday
  Bedfield Hall
  Bungay Gardens
  Elmsett Manor, Elmsett, Ipswich
  Hengrave Hall, Hengrave
  Ruma Kita, Bedfield
  Windmill Cottage, Capel St Mary
June 13 Saturday
  Wyken Hall, Stanton
June 14 Sunday
  Bedford House Stables,
    Newmarket
  2 Brook Farm Cottage, Walsham
    Le Willows
  Gable House, Redisham
  The Lawn, Walsham Le Willows
  Rosemary, East Bergholt

  Stour Cottage, East Bergholt
June 20 Saturday
  Sun House, Long Melford
June 21 Sunday
  13 Drapers Gardens, Ditchingham
  Old Manor House, Kelsale,
    Saxmundham
  2 Factory Cottages, Cowlinge
  Sun House, Long Melford
  Thrift Farm, Cowlinge
June 28 Sunday
  Boxted Hall, Nr Bury St Edmunds
  Ely House, Long Melford
  Euston Hall, nr Thetford
  Garden House Farm, Drinkstone
  The Hill House, Glemsford
  Mildenhall Gardens
  North Cove Hall, Beccles
  Reydon Grove House, Reydon
  Rosedale, Colchester Road,
    Bures, nr Sudbury
July 4 Saturday
  The Barn, Lavenham
  Salisbury House, Lavenham
  Thumbit, Walsham-le-Willows
July 5 Sunday
  Bildeston Hall, Bildeston
  The Old Hall, Barsham
  Thumbit, Walsham-le-Willows
  Treaclebenders, Drinkstone
July 12 Sunday
  2 Factory Cottages, Cowlinge
  Highfields Farm, Bures
  Redisham Hall, Beccles
July 19 Sunday
  Clipt Bushes, Cockfield
  Moat Cottage, Great Green,
    Cockfield
  Riverside House, Stoke Road,
    Clare
July 22 Wednesday
  Highfields Farm, Bures
July 26 Sunday
  Highfields Farm, Bures

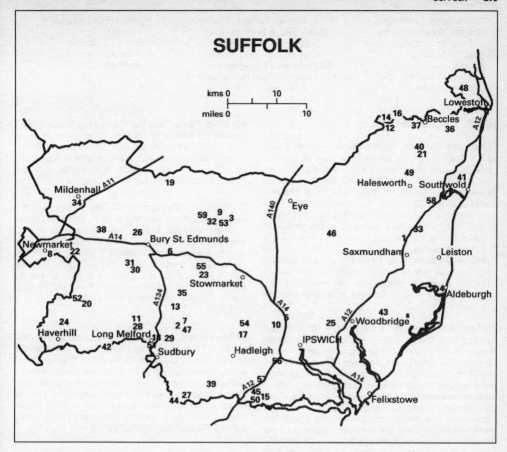

SUFFOLK

kms 0   10

miles 0   10

Lowestoft

48

14 16
12 37 Beccles
36

40
21

49
Halesworth

Southwold

41

58

Mildenhall
34

19

A140

Eye

46

33

1

38 26
Newmarket   A14   Bury St. Edmunds
8   22
6

59 9 3
32 53

Saxmundham

Leiston

31
30

55
23
Stowmarket

52
20

35

13

2 7
47

54
17

10

25

43
Woodbridge

Aldeburgh

24
Haverhill   Long Melford
11
28
29
42
51
Sudbury

Hadleigh

IPSWICH

56

39   51

44 27   45
50 15

Felixstowe

KEY

1. Old Manor House
2. The Barn
3. 2 Brook Farm Cottage
4. Aldeburgh Gardens
5. Barham Hall
6. Battlies House
7. Bedfield Gardens
8. Bedford House Stables
9. The Beeches
10. Blakenham Woodland Garden
11. Boxted Hall
12. Bungay Gardens
13. Clipt Bushes
14. 13 Drapers Lane
15. East Bergholt Place
16. Ellingham Hall
17. Elmsett Manor
18. Ely House
19. Euston Hall
20. 2 Factory Cottages
21. Gable House
22. Garden House
23. Garden House Farm

24. Great Thurlow Hall
25. Grundisburgh Hall
26. Hengrave Hall
27. Highfields Farm
28. The Hill House
29. Holly Cottage
30. Horringer House
31. Ickworth House
32. The Lawn
33. Magnolia House
34. Mildenhall Gardens
35. Moat Cottage
36. North Cove Hall
37. The Old Hall
38. Porters Lodge
39. The Priory
40. Redisham Hall
41. Reydon Grove House
42. Riverside House
43. The Rookery
44. Rosedale
45. Rosemary
46. Rumah Kita

47. Salisbury House
48. Somerleyton Hall
49. St Stephens Cottage
50. Stour Cottage
51. Sun House
52. Thrift Farm
53. Thumbit
54. Tollemache Hall
55. Treacle Benders
56. Washbrook Grange
57. Windmill Cottage
58. Woottens
59. Wyken Hall

The maps in this book are designed
to help visitors by showing the
approximate locations of gardens
within each county. The locations
are not necessarily precise,
particularly where gardens are in
clusters. Detailed directions to each
garden can be found in the garden
descriptions.

Porters Lodge, Cavenham
Rosedale, Colchester Road,
Bures, nr Sudbury
August 30 Sunday
Ellingham Hall, nr Bungay
Rosedale, Colchester Road,
Bures, nr Sudbury

St Stephens Cottage, Spexhall
September 6 Sunday
Euston Hall, nr Thetford
Holly Cottage, Long Melford
September 13 Sunday
Ickworth House, Park & Gardens,
Horringer

Magnolia House, Yoxford
The Old Hall, Barsham
October 17 Saturday
East Bergholt Place, East
Bergholt

DESCRIPTIONS OF GARDENS

¶**Aldeburgh Gardens, Aldeburgh** ❀ From A12 take A1094 to Aldeburgh. On approach to town go over 1st roundabout then almost immed R into Park Rd. At tennis courts on the R turn R into Priors Hill Rd. TEAS and tickets at Stanford House. *Combined adm £3.50 Chd free. Sun May 31 (2-5.30)*
Heron House (Mr & Mrs J Hale) 1¾ acres with views over coastline, river and marshes. Unusual trees, herbaceous beds, many shrubs, ponds and a waterfall in a large rock garden
Stanford House (Lady Cave) 1½ acres of terraced garden with waterfall, water garden and wide variety of rare plants and specimen shrubs luxuriating in a mild maritime climate. Beautiful views over riverside and sea

Barham Hall, Barham ✿✿❀ (Mr & Mrs Richard Burrows) From Ipswich A45 W. 4m sign Great Blakenham to roundabout. Leave by 3rd turning to Claydon. Through Claydon, after decontrolled signs turn R up Church Lane to Barham Green. ½m up Church Lane. 7 acres of undulating gardens mainly recreated during the last 5yrs. 3 herbaceous borders, lake surrounded by azaleas and bog plants, woodland shrub garden full of spring flowers; very considerable collection of victorian roses set in well kept lawns with mature trees; a water garden and many other interesting features. St Mary's and St Peter's Church open with famous Henry Moore sculpture. TEA. *Adm £2 OAPs £1.50 Chd 25p (ACNO to St Mary's & St Peters Church Barham®). Sun April 5 (2-5)*

¶**The Barn, Lavenham** ✿ (Mr & Mrs Ronald Hayes) Barn St off the Market Place. Very pretty small informal garden with roses and clematis and a wide variety of other plants. 'Food for Thought' will provide home made teas. Also open **Salisbury House**, Church St. *Adm £2 Chd free. Sat July 4 (2-6)*

Battlies House, Bury St Edmunds ✿✿ (Mr & Mrs John Barrell) Turn N off A14 at GT Barton and Rougham industrial estate turning, 3m E of Bury St Edmunds. In ½m turn R by lodge. 8-acre garden, lawns; shrubberies, woodland walk with a variety of old trees; rhododendrons; elms and conifers. *Adm £2 Chd free. Private visits welcome, please Tel 01284 787397*

¶**Bedfield Hall, Woodbridge** (Timothy & Christine Easton) Bedfield is situated 2½m NW of the A1120 on secondary rd turning between Earl Soham and Saxted Green. 2 acre moated gardens around house C15-C17 (not open). Formal yew hedges and topiary with potager. Shrub roses, iris beds, woodland area. Courtyard for teas, plants and cards. *Combined adm with Rumah Kita £3. Sun June 7 (2-5)*

¶**Bedford House Stables, Newmarket** ✿✿❀ (Mrs S Cumani) On Bury Rd (A11) out of Newmarket from the clock tower, 2nd big house on L behind wood panelling fence. 3 acre garden with many roses and herbaceous plants, well planted vegetable plot, wildlife area and pond. *Adm £2 Chd free. Sun June 14 (2-5)*

The Beeches, Walsham-le-Willows ✿ (Dr & Mrs A J Russell) 10m NE of Bury St Edmunds; signed Walsham-le-Willows off A143. At Xrds in village pass Church on L, after 50yds turn L along Grove Rd. Pink house behind Church. 3 acres; lawns, herbaceous border, mature and newly-planted trees. Potager, thatched summer house with ornamental pond, gazebo and wild garden by stream. TEAS. *Adm £2 Chd under 14 free (ACNO to St Mary's Church, Walsham-le-Willows®). Sun April 5 (2-5.30)*

¶**Bildeston Hall, Ipswich** (Mr & Mrs Christopher Woods) 4m from Hadleigh on Stowmarket Rd, B1115. House is next to Baptist Church in Duke St off Market Square (clock tower). 8yr old 1½-acre walled garden formally derelict and empty for 10yrs. Has stream and weir with bridges. Much statuary incl 'Eternal Meeting' of 1933 by Gilbert Ledward. Kitchen garden with summer house. Croquet lawn, gypsy caravan, and many places to sit. *Adm £2 Chd free. Sun July 5 (2-6)*

■ **Blakenham Woodland Garden, Little Blakenham** ✿ 4m NW of Ipswich. Follow signs from 'The Beeches' at Lt Blakenham, 1m off the old A1100, now called B1113. 5-acre bluebell wood densely planted with fine collection of trees and shrubs; camellias, magnolias, cornus, azaleas, rhododendrons, roses, hydrangeas. *Adm £1 Chd £1. Open daily (1-5) except Sats, March 1 to June 30. For NGS Sun Wed May 17, 20 (1-5). Parties welcome by appt, please Tel 0171 911 5487*

Boxted Hall, Boxted, Bury St Edmunds ✿✿ (Mrs Weller-Poley) Boxted Hall is approached by a drive off the B1066 Bury St Edmunds-Long Melford back of ½m S of Boxted Village. Moated House (not open) with 4 acres of grounds, extensive lawns, trees and roses in outstanding setting. Strawberry TEAS. *Combined adm with Hill House, Glemsford £3 Chd free. Sun June 28 (2-6)*

¶**2 Brook Farm Cottage, Walsham-le-Willows** (John Folkard) A143 E from Bury St Edmunds at Ixworth turn R at 2nd roundabout approx 4m. Cottage on L. Pretty ¼-acre cottage garden; with interesting vegetable plot, fruit cage and small fish pond. Teas at The Lawn just across rd. *Combined adm with The Lawn £3 Chd free. Sun June 14 (2.30-6)*

¶**Bungay Gardens, Bungay** *&* Car park in Church St in centre of Bungay. TEAS, map and plants at Castle House. *Comb adm £3 Chd £1. Sun June 7 (2-5.30)*

¶**Foundry Cottage** *&&* (Mrs Mary Moire) Two level site of former small foundry. Interesting use of limited space sheltered by castle wall, old buildings, garden room, veranda, lawns terrace and small pond, rockery and orderly potager. Many shrubs, container and climbing plants

¶**Castle House** (Mrs J D Mason) Lovely small garden under the 40' walls of Bigod Castle keep in Bungay. Formal and informal plantings of herbaceous, alpines and climbers. Special features, semi-circular walkway and newly planted mediterranean garden

¶**13 Trinity Street** *&* (Sara Johnson) Tiny floral walled garden. Box edged beds with mixed planting, climbers and pond

Clipt Bushes, Cockfield *&&* (Mr & Mrs H W A Ruffell) Just off the A1141 8m S of Bury St Edmunds and 3m N of Lavenham. Ample parking. Approx 3 acres designed for easy maintenance. Shrubberies, extensive lawns, specimen trees and old roses. Cream TEAS. *Combined adm with* **Moat Cottage** *£3 OAP £1.50 Chd free. Suns May 24, July 19 (2-6)*

13 Drapers Lane, Ditchingham *&&* (Mr & Mrs Borrett) 1¼m Bungay off the B1332 towards Norwich. ⅓-acre plantswoman's garden containing many interesting, unusual plants including 100 plus varieties of hardy geraniums, plus a mixture of climbers and shrubs. Herbaceous perennials a speciality. Owner maintained. TEAS. *Adm £1.50 Chd free. Sun, Mon May 3, 4 (12-4) also open on Sun June 21 under Ditchingham Gardens, Norfolk*

East Bergholt Place, East Bergholt *&&&* (Mr & Mrs Rupert Eley) On the B1070 towards Manningtree, 2m E of A12. 15-acre garden originally laid out at the beginning of the century by the present owner's great Grandfather. Full of many fine trees and shrubs some of which are rarely seen in East Anglia. Particularly beautiful in spring when the rhododendrons, magnolias and camellias are in full flower, and in Autumn, with newly cut topiary and Autumn colours. TEAS. *Adm £2 Chd free. Mon, Suns March 29, April 13, Oct 17 (2-5.30)*

Ellingham Hall, nr Bungay *&&&* (Col & Mrs H M L Smith) On A143 between Beccles 3m and Bungay 2m. Georgian house set in parkland. The 2-acre garden, designed by Sue Gill (see Great Campston, Gwent) is planted in deep borders with a wide and unusual variety of plants and trees. The recently planted 'Terracotta Garden' has a Mediterranean atmosphere. The walled garden includes fan trained fruit trees and a nuttery. TEAS. *Adm £2.50 Chd under 12 free. Sun Aug 30 (2-6)*

¶**Elmsett Manor, Elmsett, Ipswich** *&* (Mr & Mrs O Cooper) Situated 1m N of the village in Manor Rd. 2.5 acres. Won the Strutt and Parker Garden Award for Suffolk. Open to the public for the first time the garden comprises of several distinct areas. Mediterranean walled swimming pool area; orchard and wild area; informal water garden; lily pond and kitchen garden. Linked by brick paths, Victorian arches smothered in roses with yew and lavender walks. Planting is characterised by an exuberant use of cottage style on a large scale. Garden 'romps and rambles with glorious enthusiasm'. TEAS. *Adm £2 Chd free. Sun June 7 (2-6)*

Ely House, Long Melford *&* (Miss J M Clark) Church Walk N end of village opp top green. 3½m N of Sudbury on A134. Interesting small-walled garden with mixed borders. Home of potter making fountains and garden pots. Adjacent orchard. *Adm £2. Sun June 28 (2-6)*

● **Euston Hall, Thetford** *&* (The Duke & Duchess of Grafton) on the A1088 12m N of Bury St Edmunds. 3m S of Thetford. Terraced lawns; herbaceous borders, rose garden, C17 pleasure grounds, lake and watermill. C18 house open; famous collection of paintings. C17 church; temple by William Kent. Craft shop. Wheelchair access to gardens, tea-room and shop only. TEAS in Old Kitchen. *Adm house & garden £3 OAPs £2.50 Chd 50p Parties of 12 or more £2.50 per head (ACNO to NGS®). Thurs June 4 to Sept 24; Suns June 28 & Sept 6 (2.30-5)*

2 Factory Cottages, Cowlinge *&* (Ms Annie Hayes) Situated on the main rd through Cowlinge village, 7m from Haverhill, 10yds from turning to Hobbles Green. Small country garden set in ⅓-acre with pond, pavilion and many interesting plants. TEAS. *Adm £1.50 Chd free. Suns June 21, July 12 (2-6)*

Gable House, Redisham *&&&* (Mr & Mrs John Foster) 3½m S of Beccles. Mid-way between Beccles and Halesworth on Ringsfield-Ilketshall St Lawrence Rd. 1-acre garden containing wide range of interesting plants, alpines and bulbs in newly created scree and woodland area under construction during the last year. Greenhouses with many unusual plants. Home-made TEAS. *Adm £2 (ACNO to St Peters Church Redisham®). Sun June 14 (2-5.30)*

Garden House, Brookside, Moulton *&&&* (Mr & Mrs John Maskelyne) 3m due E of Newmarket on B1085. The garden is close to the Pack Horse Bridge and faces the village green. Interesting ¾-acre plantsman's garden, roses, small woodland area, alpines and mixed borders. Small water feature, pergola: large number of clematis. Past chairman of British Clematis Society; maintained by owners. *Adm £2 Chd free. Open by appt April to Aug, private visits welcome, please Tel 01638 750283*

Garden House Farm, Drinkstone *&&* (Mr & Mrs Seiffer) A14 turn off at Woolpit, go through village and follow signs to Drinkstone and then Drinkstone Green, past Cherry Tree Inn sign then 1st L, Rattlesden Rd. After ¾m turn L down lane and drive to end. 3m from Woolpit. Formerly the gardens of Barcock's Nursery. Woodland garden with many camellias, magnolias and spring flowers. Newly created summer garden. Plantsman's garden with many rare and unusual plants, trees and shrubs. 11 acres incl pond and lake. TEAS and plant stall in aid of NACC. *Adm £2 Chd free. Sun June 28 (2-5.30). Private visits welcome, please Tel 01449 736434*

Regular openings. Open throughout the year. They are listed at the beginning of the Diary Section.

Great Thurlow Hall, Haverhill & (Mr & Mrs George Vestey) N of Haverhill. Great Thurlow village on B1061 from Newmarket; 3½m N of junction with A143 Haverhill-Bury St Edmunds rd. 20 acres. River walk and trout lake with extensive and impressive display of daffodils and blossom. Spacious lawns, shrubberies and roses. Walled kitchen garden. Inspired gardener. TEA. *Adm £2 Chd free. Sun April 5 (2-5)*

Grundisburgh Hall, Woodbridge & & (Lady Cranworth) 3m W of Woodbridge on B1079, ¼m S of Grundisburgh on Grundisburgh to Ipswich Rd. Approx 5 acres walled garden with yew hedges; wisteria walk and mixed borders. Old rose garden; lawns and ponds. *Adm £2.50 Chd free (ACNO to St Marys Grundisburgh, St Botolphs Culpho®). Private visits welcome May 20 to July 20, please* **Tel 01473 735 485**

Hengrave Hall, Hengrave & & & 3½m NW Bury St Edmunds on A1101. Tudor mansion (tours available). Lake and woodland path. 5-acre formal garden with spacious lawns. Mixed borders with some unusual plants. Kitchen garden. TEAS in aid of Hengrave Bursary Fund. *Adm £2 OAPs £1 Chd free. Sun June 7 (2-6)*

Highfields Farm, Bures & & & (Mr & Mrs John Ineson) 6m SE of Sudbury. From Bures Church take Nayland Rd. In 2m turn L signposted Assington. Take 1st R Tarmac Drive. From other directions take Assington-Wormingford rd. Approx 1½-acre plantsman's garden started in 1984 with mixed borders, shrubs, chamomile lawn and herbaceous beds. Various features incl lily pond, wildlife pond and folly. No WCs. TEAS. *Adm £2 Chd free. Suns July 12, 26, Wed July 22 (2-6). Private visits welcome in July and August, please* **Tel 01787 227136**

The Hill House, Glemsford & & (Sir John and Lady Mowbray) 100yds N of village of Glemsford on the back rd to Hawkedon and Boxted. Lately renovated garden of 1 acre with interesting mixed borders and conservatory. Strawberry teas at Boxted Hall. *Combined adm with* **Boxted Hall** *£3 Chd free. Sun June 28 (2-6)*

¶**Holly Cottage, Long Melford** & & (Mrs Barbara Segall) Coming from Sudbury roundabout take A134 travelling N towards Bury St Edmunds. Take 1st R turn off A134 Long Melford bypass. 4th house on L 250yds along rd, Mills Lane. Garden writer's ½-acre country garden of ½ acre features long, mixed herbaceous borders, vegetables and herb gardens with unusual vegetables. Old roses, small bog garden, shade garden and arbours. Good spring colour as well as late summer, early autumn interest. Was featured in Gardens without Borders in January '97. TEAS. *Adm £2 Chd free. Suns April 19, Sept 6 (2-6)*

¶**Horringer House, Horringer** & & (Mrs Lawson) 3½m from Bury St Edmunds on A143. SW of Bury. Garden entrance 1st drive on L, after Sharpe's Lane. (1m from church, last house in village). Approx 5 acres, of which the walled kitchen garden is about ½ acre. The latter is cultivated organically and has many Victorian features such as a sunken hot-house, box hedges, very ancient apple trees and espaliers. The main garden has a fine stand of redwoods, thuyas etc plus a vibrant pond and

many beds and borders. TEAS. *Adm £2 Chd free. Mon May 4 (2-6)*

▲**Ickworth House, Park & Gardens, Horringer** & & (The National Trust) 3m SW of Bury St. Edmunds on W side of A143 [155:TL8161] 70 acres of garden. South gardens restored to stylized Italian landscape to reflect extraordinary design of the house. Fine orangery, agapanthus, geraniums and fatsias. North gardens informal wild flower lawns with wooded walk; the Buxus collection, great variety of evergreens and Victorian stumpery. New planting of cedars. The Albana Wood, a C18 feature, initially laid out by Capability Brown, incorporates a fine circular walk. Restaurant TEAS. *Adm £4.75 (house, park and garden) Chd £2. £1.75 (park and garden) Chd 50p. For NGS Sun Sept 13 (10-5.30). Private visits of 15 and over welcome, please* **Tel 01284 735270**

The Lawn, Walsham-le-Willows & (Mr & Mrs R Martineau) NE from Bury St Edmunds on A143 about 6m to Ixworth bypass R at 2nd roundabout to Walsham-le-Willows. 3½m house on R, ½m short of village. About 3½ acres of lawns, herbaceous borders, roses and shrubs overlooking parkland. Also a woodland walk around an 8-acre wood. TEAS. *Combined adm with* **Brook Farm Cottage** *£3 Chd free. Sun June 14 (2.30-6)*

Magnolia House, Yoxford & (Mr Mark Rumary) On A1120 in centre of Yoxford. Small, completely walled village garden. Mixed borders with flowering trees, shrubs, climbers, bulbs, hardy and tender plants. Featured in UK and foreign gardening books and magazines. TEA. *Adm £2 Chd free. Sun Sept 13 (2-6)*

¶**Mildenhall Gardens** From Fiveways roundabout at Barton Mills follow signs to Mildenhall and at 2nd mini roundabout take 2nd exit L along Queensway (signposted West Row), then 2nd L down Wamil Way. Parking at Riverside Middle School car park in Wamil Way. Teas at The Priory Churchyard. *Combined adm £3 Chd free. Sun June 28 (2-6)*

¶**61A Church Walk** & (Mr & Mrs D G Reeve) Walled garden surrounding modern bungalow. Sunken paved area, raised bed with pond and waterfall. Patio with water feature. New planting in front garden and established rockery. Many herbaceous plants and shrubs

¶**12 Churchyard** (Mr & Mrs D L Frape) Part of C18 workhouse overlooking church, with walled cottage garden and an informal area of ½-acre with trees and shrubs

¶**15 Mill Street** (Mr & Mrs J Child) An elegant walled garden, approx ½ acre, newly landscaped but looking well established. River frontage with pergolas, a pond and perennial borders. Large walled vegetable garden

¶**Tiggywinkle Cottage** (Mrs Marion Turner) Designed and created over 6 yrs, the small secluded garden contains pillar, shrub and patio roses, flowering shrubs and many unusual perennials and alpines. Statues and containers complement the borders and paved areas

Moat Cottage, Great Green, Cockfield & (Stephen & Lesley Ingerson) Take A134 S from Bury St Edmunds. After Sicklesmere village turn sharp L for Cockfield Green and R at 1st Xrds. Follow winding rd through Bradfield St

Clare. At Great Green fork L Moat Cottage is opp garage at far end. 1 acre of enchanting cottage garden created over the last 11yrs and forever changing. The garden is divided into smaller areas incl white, herb, herbaceous borders and water features, with a kitchen garden that provides the owners with all year round vegetables. Teas at Clipt Bushes (1½m). *Combined adm with* **Clipt Bushes** *£3 OAPs £1 Chd free. Sun May 24, July 19 (2-6)*

North Cove Hall, Beccles &❀ (Mr & Mrs B Blower) Just off A146 3½m E of Beccles on Lowestoft Rd. Take sign to North Cove. 5 acres of garden; large pond; new water feature; mature and interesting young trees. Walled kitchen garden; shrub roses; herbaceous borders; woodland walks. Home-made TEAS. *Adm £2 Chd free. Sun June 28 (2-5.30)*

The Old Hall, Barsham &❀ (Maurice & Janet Elliott) Off B1062 1½m W of Beccles. Recently restored C16 Hall, Civic Trust Award 1994. Young garden, many unusual trees, shrubs and climbers. 85 clematis, recently enlarged herb garden (over 400 different grown); greenhouse. Small nursery specialising in herbs. TEAS. *Adm £2 Chd free. Suns, Mons May 3, 4, July 5, Sept 13 (2-5). Private visits welcome, please* **Tel 01502 717475**

¶**Old Manor House, Kelsale** &✗ (Mr & Mrs J Cowie) Turn off A12 taking B1121 signposted Kelsale, Saxmundham, at Xrds take L signposted Kelsale village centre, into Bridge St, follow signs to parking and garden. Gertrude Teryllesque garden laid out originally in 1908. 6 acres with a potager, old English rose garden, large herbaceous border, pond and moat. TEAS. *Adm £2 Chd free. Sun June 21 (2-6)*

Porters Lodge, Cavenham & (Mr Craig Wyncoll) 5m W of Bury St Edmunds; 1m SW of Cavenham on the rd to Kentford. 2 acres of woodland walks surrounding and linked into an acre of semi-formal lawns with mixed borders and ponds. An unusual and interesting garden designed as a series of interlinked spaces enlivened by fountains, statutary and architectural 'follies'. TEAS. *Adm £2 Chd free. Sun July 26 (2-6)*

The Priory, nr Stoke-by-Nayland &❀ (Mr & Mrs H F A Engleheart) 8m N of Colchester, entrance on B1068 rd to Sudbury. Interesting 9-acre garden with fine views over Constable countryside, with lawns sloping down to small lakes & water garden; fine trees, rhododendrons & azaleas; walled garden; mixed borders & ornamental greenhouse. Wide variety of plants; peafowl. Homemade TEAS. *Adm £2 Chd free. Sun May 17 (2-6)*

Redisham Hall, Beccles &✗ (Mr Palgrave Brown) From A145 1½m S of Beccles, turn W on to Ringsfield-Bungay Rd. Beccles, Halesworth or Bungay, all within 6m. 5 acres; parkland and woods 400 acres. Georgian house C18 (not shown). Safari rides. TEAS. *Adm £2 Chd free (ACNO to East Suffolk Macmillan Nurses®). Sun July 12 (2-6)*

Reydon Grove House, Reydon &❀ (Cmdr & Mrs J Swinley) Situated ½m N of Reydon Church. Turnings off the Wangford-Southwold rd. 1½-acre mature garden.

Large herbaceous borders, many interesting and unusual shrubs and plants, old-fashioned roses. Large vegetable garden. TEAS in aid of Reydon Church. *Adm £2 Chd free. Sun June 28 (2-5.30) Private visits welcome June to Sept, please* **Tel 01502 723655**

Riverside House, Clare ✗ (Mr & Mrs A C W Bone) On the A1092 leading out of Clare, towards Haverhill. A peaceful walled garden, bordering the R Stour, with lawns, trees, mixed herbaceous beds and shrubs. Awarded first prize in 1997 for the best garden in Suffolk under 1 acre. TEAS. *Adm £2 Chd free. Sun July 19 (2-5.30)*

The Rookery, Eyke &✗❀ (Captain & Mrs Sheepshanks) 5m E of Woodbridge turn N off B1084 Woodbridge-Orford Rd when sign says Rendlesham. 10-acre garden; planted as an arboretum with many rare specimen trees and shrubs; landscaped on differing levels, providing views and vistas; the visitor's curiosity is constantly aroused by what is round the next corner; ponds, bog garden, shrubbery, alpines, garden stream, bulbs, herbaceous borders and a 1-acre vineyard. Wine tastings and farm shop. Home-made TEAS. *Adm £2 Chd 50p. Sun May 3 (2-5.30). Private visits welcome for parties of 10 and over, please* **Tel 01394 460271**

Rosedale, Bures ✗❀ (Mr & Mrs Colin Lorking) 40 Colchester Rd. 9m NW of Colchester on B1508. As you enter the village of Bures, garden is on the L or 5m SE of Sudbury on B1508, follow signs through village towards Colchester, garden is on the R as you leave village. Approx ⅓-acre, plantsman's garden; many unusual plants, herbaceous borders, pond, woodland area. Featured in Daily Mail Weekend Magazine. TEA. *Adm £1.50 Acc chd free. Suns May 24, June 28, July 26, Aug 30 (12-6). Private visits welcome, please* **Tel 01787 227619**

Rosemary, Rectory Hill &✗❀ (Mrs N E M Finch) Turn off the A12 at East Bergholt and follow rd round to church. Rosemary is 100yds down from the church on L. Mature 1-acre garden adapted over 26yrs from an old orchard loosely divided into several smaller gardens; mixed borders; herb garden; over 90 old roses, unusual plants. TEAS. *Adm £2 Chd free. Sun June 14 (2-6) and private visits welcome June and July, please* **Tel 01206 298241**

Rumah Kita, Bedfield & (Mr & Mrs I R Dickings) 2½m NW of the A1120 on secondary rd turning between Earl Soham and Saxted Green. 1½-acre garden designed and planted by owners; mixed borders of many unusual plants. Parterre, scree, peat and raised alpine beds. *Adm £2 Chd free (Combined adm with* **Bedfield Hall** *June 7 £3). Private visits welcome, individual or parties, please* **Tel 01728 628401**

St Stephens Cottage, Spexhall ✗❀ (Sheila & Brian Gibbs-Pitman) 2m from Halesworth off A144 Halesworth to Bungay Rd take signposted lane to Spexhall Church. 1-acre cottage garden with island beds surrounding mature trees, natural pond, unusual plants. New 3 acres which incl formal scented garden, rosary, potager and newly planted arboretum. Featured in national journals. TEAS. *Adm £2 Chd free. Sun Aug 30 (2-5). Parties welcome by appt May-Aug, please* **Tel 01986 873394**

¶**Salisbury House, Lavenham** ✗ (Peter Coxhead) Centre of Lavenham opp the Swan Hotel. Also open **The Barn**. Attractive partly walled garden of 1 acre with many roses and shrubs and herbaceous plants, pergolas. *Adm £2 Chd free. Sat July 4 (2-6)*

■ **Somerleyton Hall, Lowestoft** ও✗ (The Lord & Lady Somerleyton) 5m NW of Lowestoft. Off B1074. Large garden; famous maze, beautiful trees and borders. House C16 150 yrs old lavishly remodelled in 1840's. Grinling Gibbons' carving, library, tapestries. Mentioned in Domesday Book. Miniature railway. Light lunches & TEAS. *Adm £4.50 OAP £4.20 Chd £2.20 Family £12.60. House open 1.30-5 Gardens 12.30-5.30: Easter Sun to end Sept, Thurs, Suns, Bank Hol Mons; in addition Tues, Weds, July and Aug; miniature railway will be running on most days. For NGS Sun May 10. Group private visits welcome by prior arrangement (Min 20)*

Stour Cottage, East Bergholt ✗ (Mr J H Gill) From A12, turn to E Bergholt, follow rd around to the R towards the village centre. Car parking in the centre of the village. Take the lane to the R by the post office and Stour Cottage Garden entrance is the first large gate on the L side of lane. ⅓-acre walled garden with strong design elements and extensive range of herbaceous perennials informally planted. Many unusual half-hardy shrubs and climbers. Fountain, water garden and conservatory. Collection of tender plants. Runner up in the Strutt and Parker Country Garden awards for Suffolk (under 1 acre category) 1997. *Adm £2 Chd free. Sun, Mon May 3, 4 Sun June 14 (2-6)*

Sun House, Long Melford ও✗❀ (Mr & Mrs John Thompson) Centre of village, 3½m N of Sudbury on A134 opp Cock & Bell Inn. 2 attractive adjacent walled gardens with roses, shrubs, hostas, ferns and many rare herbaceous plants - over 100 clematis, water and architectural features, folly and paved courtyards. Runner up Daily Mail /RHS Garden Competition 1995 - Winner Best Garden in East Anglia - Look East TV - BBC Gardeners World. *Adm £2 Chd free. Sat, Sun June 20, 21 (2-6)*

Thrift Farm, Cowlinge ও✗❀ (Mrs J Oddy) 7m SE of Newmarket, centrally between Cowlinge, Kirtling and Gt Bradley. On the Gt Bradley rd from Kirtling. Picturesque thatched house set in a cottage style garden extending to approx 1½ acres. Forever changing island beds filled with herbaceous plants amongst shrubs and ornamental trees in great variety. It is a garden which encourages you to walk round. Owner maintained. Featured on Channel 4 Garden Party. TEA. *Adm £2. Suns, Mon May 10, 24, 25, June 21, (2-7) All yr Wed (11-4). Private visits welcome please Tel 01440 783274*

Thumbit, Walsham-le-Willows ও (Mrs Ann James) 10m NE of Bury St Edmunds. Leave A143 at Walsham-le-Willows sign and continue through Xrds by church on Badwell Rd to outskirts of village (½m). House is part of thatched C16 one-time inn. Shared driveway - (please do not drive in). Small informal garden with emphasis on design and plant association. Pergola, pool, topiary. 500 choice plants, shrubs, roses and climbers. 'Country Garden' award winner and featured on TV. TEA, lunches by

arrangement. *Adm £2 OAP £1 Chd free. Sat, Sun July 4, 5 (2-6). Private visits welcome, please Tel 01359 259 414*

Tollemache Hall, Offton ও✗ (Mr & Mrs M Tollemache) Nr Ipswich S of the B1078 opp the Ringshall turning. 4 acres of recently renovated garden in a lovely rural setting. Shrubs, rose and knot gardens. A large walled garden with interesting herbaceous borders. Also woodland walk planted with many conifer species. Suffolk punches, TEAS. *Adm £2 Chd free. Sun April 26 (2-6)*

¶**Treaclebenders, Drinkstone** ✗❀ (Mrs Maureen Ridge) 10m E of Bury St Edmunds. Leave A14 at Woolpit, L at village pump, R opp Plough public house. R at T junction with grass triangle, L beside railings at Xrds into Drinkstone. After 1m turn L opp phone box into Rattlesden Road. 200yds and L into Cross St. Garden on R of lane. Park in Rattlesden Rd. Plantsman's garden of about 1 acre surrounding thatched Tudor cottage. All yr colour with many interesting plants, incl many winter and spring bulbs and autumn and winter cyclamen. Owner maintained. Plant stall in aid of ARC. *Adm £2 Chd free (ACNO to The Arthritis and Rheumatism Council®). Sun July 5 (2-6). Private visits welcome, please Tel 01449 736 226*

Washbrook Grange, Ipswich ✗❀ (Mr & Mrs Robert Stone) From Ipswich take A1071 to Hadleigh. L at 1st roundabout and then 1st R to Chattisham. ½m on L. 5 acres with small lake, ornamental vegetable garden, maple walk, herbaceous borders, roses, iris, shrubs and trees both old and new; woodland walk and river garden. TEAS. *Adm £2 Chd free. Sun, Mon May 24, 25 (2-6)*

Windmill Cottage, Capel St Mary ✗❀ (Mr & Mrs G A Cox) Approx 3m S of Ipswich. Turn off at Capel St Mary. At far end of village on R after 1.2m. ½-acre plantsman's cottage style garden. Island beds, pergolas with clematis and other climbers. Many trees and shrubs, iris bed, ponds and vegetable area. Filmed for Anglia TV 1998 'Great Little Gardens'. TEAS. *Adm £2 Chd free. Suns May 24, June 7 (2-6)*

Woottens, Wenhaston ও✗❀ (M Loftus) Blackheath Rd. Woottens is situated between A12 and B1123 follow signposts to Wenhaston. Woottens is a small romantic garden with attached plantsman nursery, in all about 1-acre; scented leafed pelargoniums, violas, cranesbills, lilies, salvias, penstemons primulas, etc. Featured in Gardens Illustrated and RHS Journal. *Adm £1.50 OAPs 50p Chd 20p. Weds May to Sept (9.30-3)*

Wyken Hall, Stanton ও❀ (Sir Kenneth and Lady Carlisle) 9m NE from Bury St Edmunds along A143. Follow signs to Wyken vineyards on A143 between Ixworth and Stanton. 4-acre garden much developed recently; with knot and herb gardens; old-fashioned rose garden; wild garden; nuttery, gazebo and maze, herbaceous borders and old orchard. Woodland walk, vineyard. Wine and TEAS. *Adm £2 OAPs £1.50 Chd free. Sat June 13 (2-6)*

The National Gardens Scheme is a charity which traces its origins back to 1927. Since then it has raised over £18 million for charitable purposes.

Surrey

Hon County Organiser:	Lady Heald, Chilworth Manor, Guildford GU4 8NL Tel 01483 561414
Assistant Hon County Organisers:	Miss C Collins, Knightsmead, Rickman Hill Rd, Chipstead CR5 3LB Tel 01737 551694
	Mrs J Foulsham, Vale End, Albury, Guildford GU5 9BE Tel 01483 202296
	Mrs J M Leader, Stuart Cottage, East Clandon GU4 7SF Tel 01483 222689
	Mrs D E Norman, Spring Cottage, Mannings Hill, Cranleigh GU6 8QN Tel 01483 272620
	Mrs J Pearcy, Far End, Pilgrims Way, Guildford GU4 8AD Tel 01483 563093
	Mrs J Trott, Odstock, Castle Square, Bletchingley RH1 4LB Tel 01883 743100
Hon County Treasurer:	Mr Ray Young, Paddock View, 144 Dorking Road, Chilworth, Guildford GU4 8RJ Tel 01483 569597

DATES OF OPENING

Regular openings
For details see garden description

Crosswater Farm, Churt
Ramster, Chiddingfold
Titsey Place Gardens
Walton Poor, Ranmore Common

By appointment only
For telephone numbers and other details see garden descriptions. Private visits welcomed

Pinewood House, Heath House Road, Woking
Rise Top Cottage, Mayford

February 22 Sunday
9 Raymead Close
March 11 Wednesday
High Meadow, Churt
March 29 Sunday
Albury Park Garden, Albury
Compton Lodge, Moor Park, Farnham
April 4 to 8 Saturday to Wednesday
Chilworth Manor, Guildford
April 8 Wednesday
High Meadow, Churt
April 12 Sunday
Coverwood Lakes and Gardens, Ewhurst
High Meadow, Churt
Lodkin, Hascombe
April 13 Monday
High Meadow, Churt
April 14 to 18 Tuesday to Saturday
Vann, Hambledon
April 15 Wednesday
The Coppice, Reigate
Knightsmead, Chipstead

April 18 Saturday
Vann, Hambledon
Woodside, Send
April 19 Sunday
Coverwood Lakes and Gardens, Ewhurst
Vann, Hambledon
Woodside, Send
April 22 Wednesday
Hookwood Farm House
41 Shelvers Way, Tadworth
April 26 Sunday
Coverwood Lakes and Gardens, Ewhurst
Munstead Wood, nr Godalming
Street House, Thursley
Winkworth Arboretum, Hascombe
May 2 to 6 Saturday to Wednesday
Chilworth Manor, Guildford
Saturday 2 May
The Old Croft, South Holmwood
May 3 Sunday
Coverwood Lakes and Gardens, Ewhurst
Feathercombe nr Hambledon
22 Knoll Road, Dorking
The Old Croft, South Holmwood
May 4 Monday
Crosswater Farm, Churt
Feathercombe nr Hambledon
Vann, Hambledon
Walton Poor, Ranmore Common
May 5 to 10 Tuesday to Sunday
Vann, Hambledon
May 6 Wednesday
22 Knoll Road, Dorking
May 9 Saturday
Vann, Hambledon
May 10 Sunday
Polesden Lacey, Bookham
87 Upland Road, Sutton
Vann, Hambledon
Wintershall Manor, Bramley

May 13 Wednesday
Brook Lodge Farm Cottage, Blackbrook
High Meadow, Churt
Hookwood Farm House
May 17 Sunday
Arden Lodge, Limpsfield
Ashcombe Cottage, Nr Dorking
Coverwood Lakes and Gardens, Ewhurst
Halnacker Hill, Bowlhead Green
Hethersett, Littleworth Cross
Snowdenham House, Bramley
May 20 Wednesday
Dunsborough Park, Ripley
Unicorns, Farnham
May 24 Sunday
Copt Hill Shaw, Kingswood, Tadworth
Coverwood Lakes and Gardens, Ewhurst
Crosswater Farm, Churt
Feathercombe nr Hambledon
High Meadow, Churt
Postford House, Chilworth
Windlesham Park, nr Bagshot
May 25 Monday
Brockhurst, Chiddingfold
Crosswater Farm, Churt
Feathercombe nr Hambledon
High Meadow, Churt
May 27 Wednesday
Coverwood Lakes and Gardens, Ewhurst
May 31 Sunday
The Copse Lodge, Burgh Heath
Lodkin, Hascombe
Moleshill House, Cobham
Munstead Wood, nr Godalming
Postford House, Chilworth
June 1 to 7 Monday to Sunday
Vann, Hambledon
June 3 Wednesday
Hookwood Farm House

June 6 Saturday
Vann, Hambledon
June 7 Sunday
Alderbrook, Cranleigh
Claremont Landscape Garden,
Esher
Dovecote, Cobham
Ridings, Tadworth
Vann, Hambledon
Walton Poor, Ranmore Common
June 10 Wednesday
High Meadow, Churt
Sutton Place, Guildford
Walton Poor, Ranmore Common
June 11 Thursday
Chilworth Manor, Guildford
(Evening)
**June 13 to 17 Saturday to
Wednesday**
Chilworth Manor, Guildford
June 14 Sunday
Brook Lodge Farm Cottage,
Blackbrook
Halnacker Hill, Bowlhead Green
Haslehurst, Haslemere
High Hazard, Blackheath
Loseley Park, Guildford
Red Oaks, Redhill Common
6 Upper Rose Hill, Dorking
Yew Tree Cottage, Haslemere
June 17 Wednesday
Unicorns, Farnham
June 20 Saturday
Thanescroft, Shamley Green
June 21 Sunday
Four Aces, Pirbright
Hatchlands Park, East Clandon
Redlands House, Capel
Spring Cottage, Cranleigh
Street House, Thursley
Thanescroft, Shamley Green
Vale End, Albury
June 22 Monday
Four Aces, Pirbright
June 24 Wednesday
Shepherds Lane Gardens,
Guildford (also Evening)
Spring Cottage, Cranleigh
June 27 Saturday
Brookwell, Bramley
Knightsmead, Chipstead
June 28 Sunday
Addlestone Gardens
Arden Lodge, Limpsfield
Brockhurst, Chiddingfold (also
Evening)
Brookwell, Bramley
Chinthurst Lodge, Wonersh
Knightsmead, Chipstead
The Pottery, Brickfields, Compton
Ridings, Tadworth
**June 29 to July 5 Monday to
Sunday**
Vann, Hambledon

July 1 Wednesday
Shepherds Lane Gardens,
Guildford
July 4 Saturday
Tanyard Farmhouse, Horley
Vann, Hambledon
July 5 Sunday
Four Aces, Pirbright
Narrow Water, Cobham
Tanyard Farmhouse, Horley
Vann, Hambledon
Woodbury Cottage, Reigate
July 6 Monday
Four Aces, Pirbright
July 8 Wednesday
Brook Lodge Farm Cottage,
Blackbrook
High Meadow, Churt
July 9 Thursday
Chilworth Manor, Guildford
(Evening)
High Meadow, Churt
**July 11 to 15 Saturday to
Wednesday**
Chilworth Manor, Guildford
July 11 Saturday
Little Mynthurst Farm, Norwood
Hill
Stuart Cottage, East Clandon
July 12 Sunday
Brockhurst, Chiddingfold
Heathfield, Albury Heath
Little Mynthurst Farm, Norwood
Hill
Redlands House, Capel
Stuart Cottage, East Clandon
July 14 Tuesday
41 Shelvers Way, Tadworth
(Evening)
July 15 Wednesday
The Coppice, Reigate
The Copse Lodge, Burgh Heath
(Evening)
41 Shelvers Way, Tadworth
Shepherds Lane Gardens,
Guildford
69 Station Road, Chertsey
July 19 Sunday
Ashcombe Cottage, Nr Dorking
Brook Lodge Farm Cottage,
Blackbrook
Compton Lodge, Moor Park,
Farnham
The Copse Lodge, Burgh Heath
Munstead Wood, nr Godalming
73 Ottways, Ashstead
Tanhouse Farm, Newdigate
July 22 Wednesday
Brook Lodge Farm Cottage,
Blackbrook
July 23 Thursday
73 Ottways, Ashstead
July 26 Sunday
47 Harvest Road, Englefield Green

50 Milton Avenue, Sutton
Pathside, Cheam
Red Oaks, Redhill Common
Vale End, Albury
July 28 Tuesday
RHS Garden, Wisley (Evening)
July 29 Wednesday
9 Raymead Close
**August 1 to 5 Saturday to
Wednesday**
Chilworth Manor, Guildford
August 1 Saturday
South Cheam Gardens
August 2 Sunday
Odstock, Bletchingley
South Cheam Gardens
August 9 Sunday
Brook Lodge Farm Cottage,
Blackbrook
47 Harvest Road, Englefield
Green
Loseley Park, Guildford
August 12 Wednesday
Brook Lodge Farm Cottage,
Blackbrook
High Meadow, Churt
August 15 Saturday
The Old Croft, South Holmwood
August 16 Sunday
105 Fairway, Chertsey
The Old Croft, South Holmwood
August 19 Wednesday
69 Station Road, Chertsey
August 23 Sunday
Brook Lodge Farm Cottage,
Blackbrook
41 Shelvers Way, Tadworth
August 30 Sunday
Haslehurst, Haslemere
High Meadow, Churt
Stuart Cottage, East Clandon
August 31 Monday
High Meadow, Churt
September 6 Sunday
Moleshill House, Cobham
Woodbury Cottage, Reigate
September 9 Wednesday
High Meadow, Churt
Knightsmead, Chipstead
September 13 Sunday
Dunsborough Park, Ripley
September 20 Sunday
Claremont Landscape Garden,
Esher
October 4 Sunday
Albury Park Garden, Albury
Winkworth Arboretum,
Hascombe
October 11 Sunday
9 Raymead Close
Walton Poor, Ranmore Common
October 18 Sunday
Coverwood Lakes and Gardens,
Ewhurst

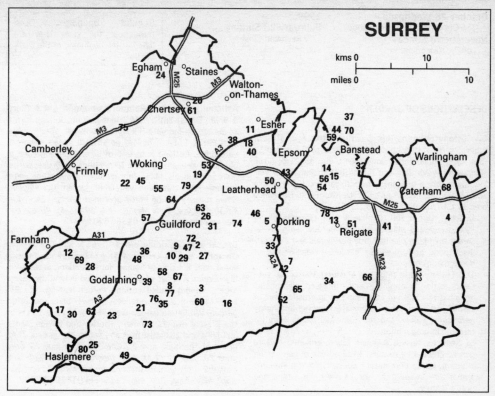

SURREY

kms 0   10
miles 0   10

Egham 24
Staines
Walton-on-Thames
Chertsey 20 61
Esher 11
Camberley
Frimley
Woking
M3 75
M25
A3 38 18 40
Epsom
Banstead 32
Warlingham
37
44 70
59
Leatherhead
53
19
79
50 43
14
56 15
54
Caterham 68
M25
22 45
55
64
63
26 31
74
46
5 Dorking
78 13 51
Reigate 41
4
57
Guildford
72 2
9 47
10 29 27
71
33
7
A24
42
M23
A22
Farnham
A31
12
69 28
36
48
58 67
8
77
3
60
16
65
52
34
66
Godalming 39
A3
17 30 62
23
21
73
76 35
6
80 25
Haslemere
49

KEY

1. Addlestone Gardens
2. Albury Park Garden
3. Alderbrook
4. Arden Lodge
5. Ashcombe Cottage
6. Brockhurst
7. Brook Lodge Farm Cottage
8. Brookwell
9. Chilworth Manor
10. Chinthurst Lodge
11. Claremont Landscape Garden
12. Compton Lodge
13. The Coppice
14. The Copse Lodge
15. Copt Hill Shaw
16. Coverwood Lakes and Gardens
17. Crosswater Farm
18. Dovecote
19. Dunsborough Park
20. 105 Fairway
21. Feathercombe nr Hambledon
22. Four Aces
23. Halnacker Hill
24. 47 Harvest Road
25. Haslehurst
26. Hatchlands Park
27. Heathfield

28. Hethersett
29. High Hazard
30. High Meadow
31. Hookwood Farm House
32. Knightsmead
33. 22 Knoll Road
34. Little Mynthurst Farm
35. Lodkin
36. Loseley Park
37. 50 Milton Avenue
38. Moleshill House
39. Munstead Wood
40. Narrow Water
41. Odstock
42. The Old Croft
43. 73 Ottways
44. Pathside
45. Pinewood House
46. Polesden Lacey
47. Postford House
48. The Pottery
49. Ramster
50. 9 Raymead Close
51. Red Oaks
52. Redlands House
53. RHS Garden

54. Ridings
55. Rise Top Cottage
56. 41 Shelvers Way
57. Shepherds Lane Gardens
58. Snowdenham House
59. South Cheam Gardens
60. Spring Cottage
61. 69 Station Road
62. Street House
63. Stuart Cottage
64. Sutton Place
65. Tanhouse Farm
66. Tanyard Farmhouse
67. Thanescroft
68. Titsey Place Gardens
69. Unicorns
70. 87 Upland Road
71. 6 Upper Rose Hill
72. Vale End
73. Vann
74. Walton Poor
75. Windlesham Park
76. Winkworth Arboretum
77. Wintershall Manor
78. Woodbury Cottage
79. Woodside
80. Yew Tree Cottage

October 28 Wednesday
The Old Croft, South Holmwood
November 8 Sunday
Lodkin, Hascombe

1999
February 28 Sunday
9 Raymead Close

Regular openings. Open throughout the year. They are listed at the beginning of the Diary Section.

DESCRIPTIONS OF GARDENS

Addlestone Gardens ✗✿ Situated within ½m of each other, 5m NE of Woking off B3121. From M25 junction 11 take A320 signposted Woking then L into B3121 or A317 signposted Weybridge and R into B3121 and follow yellow signs. Maps available at each garden. Light snacks and TEAS in aid of St Paul's Church Roof Fund. *Combined adm £2 Chd free. Sun June 28 (11-5)*

Charton, Ongar Hill (Daphne & John Clarke-Williams) ⅓-acre upward sloping mature garden, with trees, shrubs, climbing plants, hardy perennials and sink gardens, pond and vegetable garden. Extensive use of home-made compost

106 Liberty Lane (Mrs Ann Masters) 100′ × 30′ suburban garden belonging to self confessed 'plantaholic' imaginatively laid out containing an interesting mix of shrubs, grasses, hardy perennials, climbers and hardy geraniums, a pond and some unusual plants. Very interested in propagation

St Keverne (Lynne & Julian Clarke-Willams) ⅓-acre garden created by owners. Inspired use of companion planting. Hardy perennials - specialising in geraniums and alliums; many trees, shrubs and roses. Gravel and pots a feature

Albury Park Garden, Albury ᕕ✗✿ (Trustees of Albury Estate) 5m SE of Guildford. From A25 take A248 towards Albury for ¼m, then L up New Rd, entrance to Albury Park immediately on L. 14-acre pleasure grounds laid out in 1670s by John Evelyn for Henry Howard, later 6th Duke of Norfolk. ¼m terraces, fine collection of trees, lake and river. The gardens of Albury Park Mansion also open (by kind permission of Country Houses Association Ltd) (house open). TEAS. *Adm £2 Chd 50p. Suns March 29, Oct 4 (2-5)*

Alderbrook, Smithwood Common (Mr & Mrs P Van den Bergh) Cranleigh. A281 from Guildford turn L 1m out of Bramley. Turn R at roundabout then immediately L. Drive on L just beyond far end of Smithwood Common. Approx 8 acres of woodland walks with azaleas and rhododendrons. Terraces with magnificent views to S Downs. TEA. *Adm £1.50 Chd free. Sun June 7 (2-6)*

¶**Arden Lodge, Limpsfield** ᕕ✗ (Mr & Mrs C Bruce-Jones) 1m E of Oxted. From A25 take B269 Edenbridge rd for 200 yds. R down Brick Kiln Lane. Pastens rd 2nd turning L, house at end of road. 2-acre greensand garden with extensive views of Weald. Triangular herbaceous border; rhododendrons, azaleas and much formal and informal mixed planting with interesting trees, shrubs, roses and containers. TEAS. *Adm £2 Chd free. Suns May 17 (3-6), June 28 (3-7)*

Ashcombe Cottage, Ranmore Common ᕕ✗✿ (Beryl & Bryan Davis) 2m NW of Dorking. From Dorking turn R at the top of Ranmore Hill signed Bookham, Westhumble. Pass Parish Church. In ½m go straight ahead down private drive. Cottage is at end of lane. ¾-acre garden of old game-keeper's cottage. Mixed beds of shrubs, perennials and annuals. Many unusual plants. Interesting water feature. Fruit trees and vegetable garden. Greenhouse. Small nursery selling hardy perennial plants. TEAS. *Adm £1.50 Chd free. Suns May 17, July 19 (10-5). Private parties welcome, please Tel 01306 881599*

Brockhurst, Chiddingfold ✿ (Prof & Mrs C F Phelps) On the Green at Chiddingfold A283. Entrance through small gate RH-side of Manor House. Parking around Village Green. A series of gardens, tucked behind the village green. An old walled cottage border leading into 2½ acres of lawns, shrubs, walkways, flower beds and watergarden. Within the garden created over the last 13 yrs by the present owners are many species and foliage plants, incl lilies and clematis; fruit and vegetable garden. TEAS in aid of charities. *Adm £2 Chd 25p. Mon May 25, Suns June 28, July 12 (2-5). Also June 28 (6-7.30) with wine available. Private visits welcome for parties of 10 and over April, May, June, July, Aug, please Tel 01428 683092*

Brook Lodge Farm Cottage, Blackbrook ᕕ✗✿ (Mrs Basil Kingham) 3m S of Dorking. Take L-hand turning for Blackbrook off A24, 1m S of Dorking 500yds past Plough Inn. 3½-acre 50-yr-old plantsman's garden made by present owner. Hardy and tender plants, especially flowering shrubs, herbaceous, shrub roses, climbers, conifers and bulbs. Emphasis on foliage and plant association. Large kitchen garden and fruit cage, attractive herb garden and large heated greenhouse leading to smaller gardener's cottage garden. Featured in various magazines. TEAS. *Adm £2 Chd free (ACNO to St Catherine's Hospice, Crawley®). Weds May 13, July 8, 22, Aug 12, Suns June 14, July 19, Aug 9, 23 (2-5)*

Brookwell, Bramley ᕕ✗✿ (Mr & Mrs P R Styles) 1½m S of Bramley on A281; turn R into private road-bridleway in Birtley Green. 2-acre garden with lake and woodland. Mixed borders, sunken garden and knot garden planted with scented flowers and herbs. Collection of old roses, fruit tunnel and vegetable garden; greenhouses and conservatory. *Adm £1.50 Chd 25p. Sat June 27, Sun June 28 (2-6). Private visits welcome by appointment. June, July and September, please Tel 01483 893423 (evenings)*

Chilworth Manor ᕕ✗ (Lady Heald) 3½m SE of Guildford. From A248, in centre of Chilworth village, turn up Blacksmith Lane. House C17 with C18 wing on site of C11 monastery recorded in Domesday Book; monastic stewponds in garden. C18 walled garden added by Sarah, Duchess of Marlborough; spring flowers; flowering shrubs; herbaceous border. Flower decorations in house (Sats, Suns): April; Michael Kemp, May; Haslemere Flower Club, June; Chobham Floral Club, July; St Catherine's Flower Arrangement Group, August; Guildford Floral Decoration Society. Attractive car park open from 12.30 for picnicking. TEAS (Sat, Sun, only). *Adm to garden £2 Chd free. Adm to house £1 Sat & Sun only (ACNO to Marie Curie Foundation Guildford Branch®); Open Sats to Weds April 4 to 8, May 2 to 6, June 13 to 17, July 11 to 15, Aug 1 to 5 (2-6). Evenings Thurs June 11, July 9 (6-8) Adm £2.50 (glass of wine) also private visits welcome, please* **Tel 01483 561414**

Chinthurst Lodge, Wonersh ♿✿❀ (Mr & Mrs M R Goodridge) 4m S Guildford, A281 Guildford-Horsham. At Shalford turn E onto B2128 towards Wonersh. Just after Wonersh rd sign, before village, garden on R. 1-acre yr-round garden, herbaceous borders, white garden, large variety specimen trees and shrubs; kitchen garden; fruit cage; two wells; ornamental pond. TEAS. *Adm £1.50 Chd free (ACNO to Guildford Branch Arthritis & Rheumatism Council®). Sun June 28 (12-6)*

▲**Claremont Landscape Garden, Esher** ♿ (The National Trust) 1m SE of Esher; on E side of A307 (No access from A3 by-pass). Station: Esher. Bus GL 415, alight at entrance gates. One of the earliest surviving English landscape gardens; begun by Vanbrugh and Bridgeman before 1720; extended and naturalized by Kent; lake; island with pavilion; grotto and turf amphitheatre; viewpoints and avenues. TEAS 11-5. *Adm £3 Chd £1.50. For NGS Suns June 7, Sept 20 (10-7)*

Compton Lodge, Farnham ✿❀ (Mr & Mrs K J Kent) 2m E of Farnham along A31 Hogs Back (new rd) follow signs Runfold. Turn S down Crooksbury Rd at Barfield School signposted Milford & Elstead. 1m on R Compton Way, Compton Lodge 2nd house on R. 1¼-acre S-facing sloping mixed garden. Mature rhododendrons, heather bed, azaleas. TEAS. *Adm £1.50 Chd 50p. Suns March 29, July 19 (11-5)*

Cooksbridge, Fernhurst (See Sussex)

The Coppice, Reigate ❀ (Mr & Mrs Bob Bushby) M25 to junction 8. A217 (direction Reigate) down Reigate Hill, immediately before level Xing turn R into Somers Rd cont as Manor Rd. At very end turn R into Coppice Lane. Please park carefully. 'The Coppice' approx 200yds on L. Partly suitable wheelchairs. 6½ acres redeveloped in last 10yrs. Mixed borders with interesting and unusual plants giving yr-round interest. Pergola, 2 large ornamental ponds. Thousands of fritillarias and spring bulbs, April. Cream TEAS. *Adm £1.50 Chd 50p (ACNO to Winged Fellowship®). Weds April 15; July 15 (2-5)*

The Copse Lodge, Burgh Heath ♿✿❀ (Marian & Eddie Wallbank) 6m S of Sutton on A217 dual carriageway. Heathside Hotel car park 200yds on L from traffic lights at junction A217 with Reigate Rd. Please park in overflow car park at rear of hotel (our thanks to Heathside Hotel). Garden 60yds on L from hotel. ¾-acre architectural garden featuring yuccas, palms and grasses; large tender specimens in pots; Japanese garden with bamboos, acers

and Tea House; ornamental pond with waterfalls, rock garden, conservatory with specimen palms. Featured in the Daily Mail. TEAS. *Adm £2 Chd free. Suns May 31, July 19 (10.30-5). Evening opening Wed July 15 (7-10)*

Copt Hill Shaw ♿✿❀ (Mr & Mrs M Barlow) Alcocks Lane, Kingswood. 6m S of Sutton off the A217. 1st turn on L after Burgh Heath traffic lights, Waterhouse Lane. Alcocks Lane 1st on L. Parking in Furze Hill, courtesy of Legal and General. A formal garden of 1½ acres laid out in 1906. Fine yew hedges and topiary with azaleas, mature trees and pergola of old roses and clematis. Spring bulbs, alliums, small collection of unusual plants. Vegetable garden. TEAS. *Adm £2 Chd free (ACNO to National Asthma Campaign®). Sun May 24 (2-5.30)*

● **Coverwood Lakes and Gardens, Ewhurst** ♿✿❀ (Mr & Mrs C G Metson) Peaslake Rd. 7m SW of Dorking. From A25 follow signs for Peaslake; garden ½m beyond Peaslake. Landscaped water, bog garden and cottage gardens (in lovely setting between Holmbury Hill and Pitch Hill); with rhododendrons, azaleas, primulas, fine trees. 3½-acre Arboretum planted March 1990. Featured in NGS video 1. Marked farm trail to see pedigree cattle and flock of sheep. (Mr & Mrs Nigel Metson). Home-made TEAS. *Adm £2.50 Chd £1 car park and Chd under 5 free (Shore to NGS®). Suns April 12, 19, 26 May 3, 17, 24; Wed May 27 (2-6); Sun Oct 18 hot soup and sandwiches (11-4.30). Also private visits welcome, please* **Tel 01306 731103/1**

■ **Crosswater Farm, Churt** ♿✿❀ (Mr & Mrs E G Millais) Farnham and Haslemere 6m, from A287 turn E into Jumps Road ½m N of Churt village centre. After ¼m turn acute L into Crosswater Lane and follow signs for Millais Nurseries. 6-acre woodland garden surrounded by NT heathland. Plantsman's collection of rhododendrons and azaleas including many rare species collected in the Himalayas, and hybrids raised by the owners. Ponds, stream and companion plantings. Specialist Rhododendron nursery also open. TEAS on NGS days only. *Adm £1.50 Chd free. Daily May 1 to June 6. For NGS Mon May 4, Sun, Mon May 24, 25 (10-5) + 25% other receipts. Private parties welcome, please* **Tel 01252 792698**

Dovecote, Cobham ✿❀ (Mr & Mrs R Stanley) Off A307 Esher to Cobham rd near A3 bridge. Turn R from Cobham, L from Esher into Fairmile Lane. Then 4th L into Green Lane. ⅓-acre plot surrounding extended bothy. Secluded plant lovers yr-round garden with natural boundaries of mature trees, shrubs and hedges developed by present owners to incl many hardy plants on light sandy soil. TEA. *Adm £1.50 Chd free. Sun June 7 (10.30-5.30)*

■ **Dunsborough Park, Ripley** ✿❀ (Baron & Baroness Sweerts De Landas Wyborgh) Entrance across Ripley Green. Bus GL 715 alight Ripley village. Extensive walled gardens redesigned by Penelope Hobhouse; herbaceous borders; 70ft gingko hedge, ancient mulberry tree, water garden. Edwardian wooden glasshouses (under restoration). Part suitable for wheelchairs. TEAS in aid of charities. *Adm £2.50 Chd £1.25. Thur July 2, (12-6). For NGS Wed May 20, Sun Sept 13 (12-6). Private vistors welcome by appt,* **Tel 01483 225366**

The Elms Kingston-on-Thames (see London)

Elm Tree Cottage, South Croydon (see London)

105 Fairway, Chertsey ✿✾ (Tony Keating) Junction 11 M25 to Chertsey. Off Free Prae Rd. Opp. RC School. Sub-tropical garden containing palms, bananas, tree ferns, cannas, cacti, hardy exotics, passion flowers in a front and rear garden of semi-detached house. TEA. *Adm £1 Chd 50p. Sun Aug 16 (11-5)*

Feathercombe, Hambledon ✿ (Wieler & Campbell families) S of Godalming. 2m from Milford Station off Hambledon Rd, between Hydestile Xrds and Merry Harriers. 12-acre garden of mature rhododendrons, azaleas, shrubs and topiary. Fine views of Blackdown, Hindhead and Hogs Back. House by Ernest Newton. Garden designed and made from 1910 by Surrey author and journalist Eric Parker and his wife Ruth (neé Messel) of Nymans. Now maintained by his grandchildren. *Adm £1.50 Chd 10p (ACNO to St Peter's Church, Hambledon®). Suns, Mons May 3, 4; 24, 25 (2-6)*

Four Aces, Pirbright ✾✿ (Mr & Mrs R V St John Wright) 5m NW of Guildford on A322 Bagshot Road. Just before Brookwood arch, directly opp West Hill Golf Club, turn L into Cemetery Pales. After 9/10m turn sharp L after village sign into Chapel Lane. Four Aces is 5th house on R. Overflow parking in village green car park, 250yds. Approx ⅔-acre 13yr-old garden with 2 ponds, terraces with pergolas, loggias and pots; mixed borders with shrubs, perennials, herb garden and old roses planted in informal cottage garden style. Appeared in 'Country Homes'. TEAS. *Adm £1.50 Chd 50p. Suns, Mons June 21, 22, July 5, 6 (11-5). Private visits welcome May to July, please* **Tel 01483 476226**

Hall Grange, Croydon (see London)

Halnacker Hill, Bowlhead Green ✾✿ (Mr & Mrs C N Daubeny) From A3 southbound turn L signposted Bowlhead Green (opp Thursley exit); at Xrds turn R and go 0.7m. From A286 turn off just S of Brook into Park Lane; after 2m turn R signposted Bowlhead Green. 1-acre terraced cottage garden designed as series of small informal plantsman's gardens maintained by the owners. Large variety of trees, shrubs, perennials, old roses and many tender and less common plants. 5 acres of woodland with walks and fine views. TEAS. *Adm £1.50 Chd free (ACNO to Meath Home©). Suns May 17, June 14 (1-5)*

47 Harvest Road, Englefield Green ✾ (Mr Tony Faulkner) Directly opp Royal Holloway College on A30. Nearest BR station is Egham. Car parking facilities are a short walk away in Victoria Street. Small cottage garden, shrubs, mixed borders and ornamental trees; gazebo and small pond. Now features a Japanese style garden. TEAS. *Adm £1 Chd free. Suns July 26, August 9 (2-6)*

Haslehurst, Haslemere ✾✿ (Mrs W H Whitbread) Bunch Lane. Turn off High St into Church Lane, leave church on L, carry on to T-junction, turn R, Hazelhurst 2nd on L. 2½ acres; lawns, superb trees, rhododendrons, azaleas; various shrubs; paved rose garden, double herbaceous border; woodland rockery & waterfall. C15 Barn. TEAS. *Adm £1.50 Chd 50p (ACNO to Queen Mary's Clothing Guild®). Suns June 14 (also* **Yew Tree Cottage**), *Aug 30 (2.15-6). Private visits welcome, please* **Tel 01428 643471**

▲**Hatchlands Park, East Clandon** ♿✾ (The National Trust) Situated near East Clandon, off A246. If using A3 from London direction, follow signposts to Ripley to join A247 and proceed via West Clandon to A246. If coming from Guildford take A25 and then A246 towards Leatherhead at West Clandon. The garden and park were designed by Repton in 1800 and there are 3 newly restored walks in the park. On the S side of the house is a small parterre, now restored, designed by Gertrude Jekyll in 1913 to flower in May/June. The house is open to the public on this day. TEA. *Adm £1.50 Chd 75p gardens only. For NGS Sun June 21 (11.30-5.30)*

¶**Heathfield, Albury Heath** ✿ (Mr & Mrs M.E. Demetriadi) 5½m SE of Guildford and 1m SE of Albury. From Albury take A248 E for ¼m and turn 1st R up New Road. Follow signs to car park in Heath Lane. 1-acre garden, larger part of which was landscaped by Mrs Demetriadi in 1996. It slopes with different levels and contains many unusual plants. Running water/bog garden and rockery; herb, vegetable and fruit gardens, gravel garden, mixed borders and attractive courtyard. Morning coffee and home-made TEAS in aid of the Guildford Macmillan Day Care Centre Appeal. *Adm £2.50 Chd free Sun July 12 (10-5)*

Hethersett, Littleworth Cross ✾✿ (Lady Adam Gordon) S of Hog's Back (A31) 1½m from Seale Church on Elstead rd or 1m N from B3001 Milford-Farnham rd. A unique opportunity to enjoy this historic woodland garden created at the end of C19 by H J Mangles, an early hybridiser of rhododendrons. In the 25-acre wood are many mature trees and shrubs incl many of his hybrids, species from the earliest expeditions to the Himalayas, as well as large drifts of azaleas. *Adm £2 Chd under 12 free. Sun May 17 (2-6)*

High Hazard, Blackheath ♿✿✾ (Mr & Mrs P C Venning) 4½m SE of Guildford on A281, at Shalford turn E on B2128 towards Wonersh, at entry to Wonersh, turn L into Blackheath Lane, straight on at Xrds in village. Access to garden is 300yds on R. Park in Heath car park a further 150yds up lane. (No access to front of house (cricket ground in use). ½-acre garden designed and laid out by the present owners. Herbaceous and mixed borders containing interesting and some unusual herbaceous perennial plants, a large number of which are for sale on the premises. TEAS in aid of St Martin's Church, Blackheath. *Adm £1.50 Chd free Sun June 14 (2-6)*

High Meadow, Churt ✾✿ (Mr & Mrs J Humphries) Tilford Rd. From Hindhead A3 Xrds A287 signposted Farnham. After ½m R fork to Tilford. 1.9m to Avalon PYO. Park here, short walk to garden. Disabled parking in drive. Approx 1 acre maintained by owners. Rare and unusual plants attractively planted to provide all-year interest; large collection of old and David Austin roses; pergola walk, sunken garden with pond, colour co-ordinated borders, alpines and troughs; featured in Channel 4 Garden

Party. TEAS, Bank Hols only. *Adm £2 Chd free (ACNO to G.U.T.S. at Royal Surrey County Hospital). Every 2nd Wed March to Sept. Bank Hols April 12, 13, May 24, 25, Aug 30, 31 (2-5). Groups welcome, please* Tel 01428 606129

239a Hook Road, Chessington (see London)

Hookwood Farmhouse, West Horsley &⚘❀ (Eric & Sarah Mason) From Guildford A246 turn R into Staple Lane (signposted Shere). At top turn L then first L into Shere Rd and first L into Fullers Fm Rd. From Leatherhead turn L into Greendene, after approx 2.5 miles turn R into Shere Rd then first L. The 1.5 acre garden made by the owners is on S facing slope of N Downs. Wide range of plants and large collection of hardy Geraniums. Walled garden in old farmyard. TEAS in aid of The Rainbow Trust 50%. *Adm £2 Chd free. Weds April 22, May 13, June 3 (11-5). Private visits April-June, please* Tel 01483 284760

Knightsmead, Chipstead ⚘❀ (Mrs Jones & Miss Collins) Rickman Hill Rd, Chipstead. From A23 in Coulsdon turn W onto B2032. Through traffic lights, L fork into Portnalls Rd. Top of hill at Xrds, R into Holymead Rd. R into Lissoms Rd. R into Bouverie Rd. ½-acre plantsman's garden, owner designed and maintained. Wide variety of shrubs, perennials for yr-round interest; hellebores, spring bulbs, woodland plants; pond; scented roses; raised alpine and peat beds, clematis, hardy geraniums etc. Small craft exhibition. Appropriate refreshments throughout, in aid of Surrey Wildlife Trust. *Adm £1.50 Chd 50p. Weds April 15, Sept 9 (10-4) Sat, Sun June 27, 28 (2-5.30). Private visits welcome, please* Tel 01737 551694

22 Knoll Road, Dorking &⚘❀ (David & Anne Drummond) From one way system after May's Garage turn L up the Horsham rd (A2003 which runs to N Holmwood roundabout A24). Knoll Road is on R just beyond The Bush Inn. ⅓-acre town garden with many interesting and unusual plants. Mixed borders, raised beds, sinks, mini-meadow and peat bed, fern alley and some fruit and vegetables, a surprising front garden; conservatory. (Mostly suitable for wheelchairs if driven to front door.) Refreshments in aid of Amnesty. *Adm £1.50 Chd free. Sun, Wed May 3, 6 (10.30-5.30). Private visits welcome, please* Tel 01306 883280

Little Lodge, Thames Ditton (see London)

Little Mynthurst Farm, Norwood Hill &⚘❀ (Mr & Mrs G Chilton) Between Leigh (2m) and Charlwood (3m); from Reigate take A217 to Horley; after 2m turn R just after river bridge at Sidlowbridge; 1st R signed Dean Oak Lane; then L at T junction. 12-acre garden; walled, old-fashioned roses, herbaceous borders and shrubs around old farm house (not open), rose beds and lake setting; Tudor courtyard and orchard; bird and butterfly garden; rose walk. Kitchen garden with greenhouses and secret garden. TEAS in aid of Leigh and District Cottage Garden Society and NGS. *Adm £2 Chd free. Sat, Sun July 11, 12 (12-5). Coach parties welcome on NGS days only by prior arrangement please contact Head Gardener Mark Dobell* Tel 01293 862639 or 863318

Lodkin, Hascombe ❀ (Mr & Mrs W N Bolt) Lodkin Hill. 3m S of Godalming. Just off B2130 Godalming-Cranleigh, on outskirts of Hascombe; take narrow lane off signposted Thorncombe Street. Country garden of 5½ acres incl woodland, stream, 4 Victorian greenhouses rebuilt to produce fruit, flowers and vegetables. Much of the old cast staging etc has been retained. In parts suitable for wheel chairs. TEAS. *Adm £1.50 Chd 20p. Suns April 12, May 31 (2-6). Sun Nov 8 (2-4) Adm £1 Chd free (No TEAS). Private parties welcome, please* Tel 01483 208 323

▲**Loseley Park, Guildford** &⚘ (Mr & Mrs M G More-Molyneux) Leave A3 at Compton, S of Guildford, on B3000 for 2m. Signposted. Guildford Station 2m, Godalming Station 3m. 2½-acre walled garden transformed from an organic vegetable garden to a formal garden. Features a rose garden with over 1,000 bushes, mainly old-fashioned varieties. Herb garden with sections for culinary, medicinal, ornamental and dyeing. A flower garden and newly planted white garden. Moat walk, terrace, herbaceous borders and ancient wisteria. TEAS. *Adm £2.25 Chd £1.25. For NGS Suns June 14, Aug 9 (1-5)*

¶**50 Milton Avenue, Sutton** ⚘❀ (Mr & Mrs D Wright) 1m E of Sutton Stn, off Westmead Rd. 154 bus to Westmead Rd/Ringstead Rd. At bottom of Ringstead Rd turn into Kingsley Ave, 1st R, then 1st L. Or bus to Wrythe Green, turn into Brookfield Ave, then 2nd turn on L. Award winning Sutton and London in bloom front garden planted for maximum colour with special theme. Small rear garden 30' × 80'. Planted to capacity with hardy and tender perennials, shrubs with interesting foliage, summer bedding, grasses and hostas around a small pond, patio with hanging baskets and a large collection of fuchsias. Winner of 3 gold medals & Banksian Award from London Gardens Society. TEA. *Adm £1.30 Acc chd 50p. Sun July 26 (11-5)*

Moleshill House, Cobham &⚘❀ (Mr & Mrs M Snell) House is on A3043 Esher to Cobham Rd next to free car park by A3 bridge. Flower arranger's walled romantic garden. Topiary and garlanded cisterns around house; circular lawn surrounded by informal borders; gravel bed; dovecote; bee alcoves; sorbus lutescens avenue, bog garden, paving and pots. TEAS. *Adm £1.50 Chd free. (ACNO to St Mary's Stoke D'Abernon, Fabric Fund®). Suns May 31, Sept 6 (2.30-5.30).*

Munstead Wood, Godalming &❀ (Sir Robert & Lady Clark) Take B2130 Brighton Rd out of Godalming towards Horsham. After 1m church on R, Heath Lane just thereafter on L. 400yds on R is entrance to Munstead Wood. Parking on L of Heath Lane. 10 acres of rhododendrons, azaleas, woods and shrub and flower beds. Home until 1931 of Gertrude Jekyll and recently restored to her plans. The architect for the house (not open) was Edwin Lutyens. TEAS. *Adm £2 OAPs £1 Chd free (ACNO to Pestalozzi Children's Village Trust®). Suns April 26, May 31, July 19 (2-6)*

¶**Narrow Water, Cobham** ⚘❀ (Roger & Debbie Atkinson) Knipp Hill. Turn off A307 Portsmouth Road, Esher to Cobham into Fairmile Lane. Turn L into Miles Lane. Follow road which narrows into Knipp Hill and pass house drive on right. Park in Pony Chase at bottom of Knipp Hill. Garden designers own garden. Formal terrace with herbs, circular lawn surrounded by mixed borders, vegetable area and summer border, terracotta pots. Home made cakes. TEAS. *Adm £1.50 Chd free. Sun July 5 (11-4)*

Odstock, Bletchingley &✿❀ (Mr & Mrs J F H Trott) Between Godstone 2m and Redhill 3m on A25, at top of village nr Red Lion pub. Parking in village, no parking in Castle Square. ⅔ of an acre maintained by owners and developed for all-yr interest. Special interest in climbers. Variety of plants and shrubs with imaginative complementary and contrasting groupings of form and colour. Japanese features; dahlias. No dig, low maintenance vegetable garden. TEAS. *Adm £2 Chd free (ACNO to St Mary's Church, Bletchingley®). Sun Aug 2 (1-5.30). (Disabled welcome – please telephone first* **01883 743100)**

The Old Croft, South Holmwood ❀ (David and Virginia Lardner-Burke) 3m S of Dorking. From Dorking take A24 S for 3m. Turn L at sign to Leigh-Brockham into Mill Road. ¾m on L, 2 free car parks in NT Holmwood Common. Follow signs for 400yds along woodland walk. 5-acre parkland garden with lake, stream, ponds, woodland, wild and formal areas, herb garden, wide variety of specimen trees and shrubs; more new developments. Garden designed by owner. TEAS. *Adm £2 Chd free (ACNO to St Catherine's Hospice, Crawley®). Sats, Suns May 2, 3; Aug 15, 16 (2-6). Wed Oct 28 (11-4)*

73 Ottways Lane, Ashtead &✿❀ (Mr & Mrs Peter Gray) From A24 Ashtead to Leatherhead rd turn into Ottways Lane just S of Ashtead Village or into Grange Rd at traffic lights N of M25 by Downsend School. Approx ⅓-acre. Large herbaceous border, shrubs and fuchsias. Patio with pergola, hanging baskets and troughs. New water feature planned for 1998. TEAS in aid of Family Focus. *Adm £1.50 Chd free. Sun July 19 (11-5.30), Thurs July 23 (2-5.30)*

Pathside, 70 York Road, Cheam ✿❀ (Mr & Mrs F Wood) York Rd runs between Cheam Rd and towards Dorset Rd which is a turning off Belmont Rise (A217). Mature garden with good range of trees, shrubs, herbaceous plants, lawn, ponds etc. A footpath pattern has been laid round the garden forming views, vistas and planted 'rooms' with landscaping. Interesting sunken dell garden, which has been rebuilt, featuring stone walls, arches and raised beds. Exhibition of paintings. TEAS in aid of Salvation Army. *Adm £1. Sun July 26 (10-4)*

Pinewood House &✿ (Mrs J Van Zwanenberg) Heath House Rd. 3m Woking, 5m Guildford off A322 opp Brookwood Cemetery Wall. 4 acres. Walled garden and arboretum; water garden; bulbs in April. Interesting house finished in Dec '86 with indoor plants. *Adm house & gardens £2. Private visits welcome for parties of 2-30 April to Oct, please* **Tel 01483 473241**

▲**Polesden Lacey, Bookham** &✿❀ (The National Trust) nr Dorking. 1½m S of Great Bookham off A246 Leatherhead-Guildford rd. 60 acres formal gardens; walled rose garden, winter garden, lavender garden, iris

garden, lawns; magnificent views. Regency villa dating early 1820's, remodelled after 1906 by the Hon Mrs Ronald Greville, King George VI and Queen Elizabeth (now the Queen Mother) spent part of their honeymoon here. For wheelchair details **Tel 01372 452048.** Plants in aid of NT. Lunch and TEAS in licensed restaurant in grounds (11-5). *Adm garden and grounds £3, Chd £1.50; family ticket £7.50. For NGS garden only Sun May 10 (11-6)*

Postford House, Chilworth &✿ (Mrs R Litler-Jones) 4m SE Guildford Route A248 Bus LC 425 Guildford-Dorking alight nr entrance. 25 acres woodland; bog garden; stream; rose garden; vegetable garden; rhododendrons, azaleas and shrubs; swimming pool open. Home-made TEAS. Morning coffee in aid of RSPB. *Adm £2 Chd free. Suns May 24, 31 (11-5). Private visits welcome, please* **Tel 01483 202657**

¶**The Pottery, Brickfields, Compton** &✿ (Mrs M Wondrausch) From Guildford leave A3 on B3000 to Compton thru' village 2nd R into Binscombe Lane. This is an artist's wild organic garden growing round a C17 cottage. Mowed paths lead to strange sculptures and fountains. Large brick-raised mature herb garden. Miniature flowering meadow under a giraffe. Historic hedge and fruit tree planting. Small garden by working pottery and shop with grouped terracotta pots unusually planted, inventive galvanized fountain. Decorated pots for sale. *Adm £2 Chd free Sun June 28 (10.30-5). Private visits by appointment, please* **Tel 01483 414097**

●**Ramster, Chiddingfold** &✿ (Mr & Mrs Paul Gunn) On A283, 1½m S of Chiddingfold; large iron gates on R. Mature 20-acre woodland garden of exceptional interest with lakes, ponds and woodland walks. Laid out by Gauntlett Nurseries of Chiddingfold in early 1900s. Fine rhododendrons, azaleas, camellias, magnolias, trees and shrubs. New bog garden. Picnic area. Special sale of 'plants and pots' May 9-25. TEAS daily in May. *Adm £2.50 Chd under 16 free (Share to NGS®). Daily from April 18 to July 12 (11-5.30). Parties welcome, please* **Tel 01428 654167**

9 Raymead Close, Fetcham ✿❀ (Mrs Susan Kirkby) Take A245 out of Cobham, through Stoke D'Abernon on Cobham rd over motorway, through Fetcham, then L at Raymead Way, then 2nd L. From B2122 Gt Bookham to Leatherhead rd, turn L into Cobham Rd, R into Raymead Way then 2nd L. ⅓-acre plantsman's garden of unusual design with narrow paths, small sunken garden, ponds and cosy secluded corners. Trees, shrubs, perennials and annuals with an emphasis on yr-round colour. Also interesting berries and winter bark. TEAS. *Adm £1.50 Chd £1. Sun Feb 22 (1-4), Wed July 29 (2-5.30), Sun Oct 11 (1-4), Sun Feb 28 1999 (1-4), or* **Tel 01372 373728**

¶**Red Oaks, Redhill** ✿❀ (Mr & Mrs B Moray) A25 from Reigate E towards Redhill, after 1m turn R at war memorial (just after Toyota garage) into Hatchlands Rd. Then immed L for 25yds, cross Whitepost Hill junction into Blackstone Hill and park hereabouts. Walk up hill to Red Oaks following signs, approx 300yds. This ⅔ acre pleasant garden incl cobbled courtyard, burgeoning conservatory, new sunken garden, wide lawn with mixed borders and a view to Reigate Hill. Developed and maintained by the owners. TEAS. *Adm £1.50 Chd 50p. Suns June 14, July 26 (11-5)*

¶**Redlands House, Capel** &⚘ (Mrs V Jefferys) A24 S of Dorking for 6m. Take turn to Capel village. On R before church. Park on roadside or village hall car park. 1.5 acres of varied planting with colour themed herbaceous borders, shrubs, ornamental gazebo, pergola walk, wildlife pond and copse. Homemade teas at Capel Church. *Adm £2 Chd free. Suns June 21, July 12 (2-5)*

▲**RHS Garden Wisley** &⚘ (Royal Horticultural Society) 1m from Ripley, W of London on A3 and M25 (Junction 10). Follow signs with flower logo. The primary garden of the RHS and centre of its scientific and educational activities. Arboretum, alpine and wild garden, rock garden, mixed borders, model gardens, fruit and vegetable garden, rose garden, glasshouses, orchard, formal gardens, canal, woodland garden and trial grounds. *Ticket prices (incl RHS members): £3. For NGS special evening opening with music, Tues July 28 (6.30-9)*

Ridings, Tadworth &⚘⚘ (Mr & Mrs K Dutton) A217 to large roundabout 6m S of Sutton and 3m N of junction 8 on M25 take B2220 sign posted Tadworth. Take 2nd R into Tadorne Rd; L into Cross Rd. House on corner of Epsom Lane S. ¾-acre informal garden planted by present owners over 21yrs, to provide all yr round interest. Unusual trees, shrubs and herbaceous plants, with emphasis on shape, texture and colour harmony. Collection of shrub roses a feature in summer. Vegetable plot. TEAS. *Adm £1.50 Chd free. Suns June 7, 28 (2-5.30). Private visits welcome (May to July), please Tel 01737 813962*

Rise Top Cottage, Mayford ⚘⚘ (Trevor Bath) Midway between Woking and Guildford, off A320. On entering Maybourne Rise, take immed L. At top of Rise turn L along rough track about 100yds. Please park tactfully in Maybourne Rise. ⅓-acre approx. Profusely planted in a cottage garden style with both old and new varieties. Special interests incl aquilegias, pulmonarias, herbs, old roses, white flowers and particularly hardy geraniums. TEAS. Not suitable for wheelchairs. *Adm £1.50 Chd free. Private visits welcome, please Tel 01483 764958*

Royal Botanic Gardens, Kew (see London)

41 Shelvers Way, Tadworth ⚘⚘ (Mr & Mrs K G Lewis) 6m S of Sutton off the A217. 1st turning on R after Burgh Heath traffic lights heading S. 400yds down Shelvers Way on L. ⅓-acre plantsman's garden as featured in 'Your Garden' magazine. Attractive cobbled area leading to a wide variety of herbaceous and other plants. Many spring bulbs followed by azaleas and old roses. Designed and developed by owners. Coffee and TEAS. *Adm £1.50 Chd free. Weds April 22, July 15, Sun Aug 23 (10.30-5). Evening (Adm £3 incl wine and snacks). Tues July 14 (6-9) Private visits welcome, please Tel 01737 210707*

¶**Shepherds Lane Gardens, Guildford** ⚘⚘ From Guildford, 1m W from A3 on A322 Worplesdon Rd. Turn L at traffic lights at Emmanuel Church, Stoughton into Shepherds Lane. Gardens are L on brow of hill. Alterna-

tively, via A323 Aldershot Rd and Rydes Hill Rd, Shepherds Lane is 2nd R. TEAS. *Combined adm £1.50 Chd free (ACNO to Abbeyfield®). Weds June 24 (2-5) and (7-9), July 1, 15 (11-5)*

    67 Shepherds Lane (Mr & Mrs C Graham) ¼-acre suburban garden with mixed borders, lawn, specimen small trees, pond, alpine bed, fruit garden with dwarf trees. Featured by Daily Express for 1997 yellow book launch. *Private visits welcome, please Tel 01483 566445*

    ¶**69 Shepherds Lane** & (Mrs J Hall) Suburban garden 35' × 100'. Newly created in 1996 on circular theme. All seasons garden with mixed shrubs, herbaceous and tree planting in silver, pink and blue shades. Linked by ornamental gates with No 67 to appear as one garden

Snowdenham House, Bramley &⚘ (The Hon Lady Hamilton) Snowdenham Lane. S of Guildford A281 from Guildford, R at Bramley mini-roundabout. House is ½m on L. Georgian house, outbuildings and water mill (not open). 9 acres of water, woodland, formal and walled gardens. Wide range of rhododendrons, azaleas and specimen trees and shrubs in woodland garden bordering stream. TEAS in aid of Bramley Church. *Adm £2.50 Chd free. Sun May 17 (11.30-5)*

South Cheam Gardens ⚘⚘ Situated approx 1m S of Cheam village. *Combined adm £2 Chd 50p. Sat, Sun Aug 1, 2 (11-5)*

    87 Sandy Lane (Mr & Mrs L West) ⅓-acre garden featuring sub-tropical plants, incl palm trees, several tree ferns, bananas, agaves, bamboos and acers. Large collection of cannas; rockery with small water feature. Fruit trees, dahlia borders, vegetable garden and three greenhouses. TEAS

    89 Sandy Lane (Mr & Mrs Jeff Jones) ⅓-acre with a lower, middle and upper garden. Lower garden features conifers, bedding plants and pots; the middle garden has a pond, rockery, dahlia and sweet pea beds and herbaceous border. The upper garden is devoted to all vegetables with 30 feet of greenhouse space. Plants in aid of Shere & Peaslake Cubs & Venture Scouts

Spring Cottage, Cranleigh &⚘⚘ (Mr & Mrs D E Norman) A281 from Guildford turn L 1m out of Bramley. Turn R at roundabout then immed L, into Smithwood Common Rd; garden 1m on R just N of Cranleigh School. Easy parking. 1-acre garden with lovely view; cottage garden; small woodland garden, old roses, pond and new greenhouse area. TEAS. *Adm £2 Chd free. Sun, Wed June 21, 24 (11.30-5.30); private visits welcome, please Tel 01483 272620*

Spur Point, nr Fernhurst (See Sussex)

¶**69 Station Road, Chertsey** ⚘ (Stephanie Grimshaw) Junction 11 M25 to A317, L at roundabout, L Eastworth Rd. 1st L Highfield Rd into Station Rd. Green house on R, ¼ down Station Rd. Small garden with informal planting of unusual shrubs and trees. With gazebos, pond, folly and hidden surprises. *Adm £1.50 Chd free. Weds July 15, Aug 19 (12-4)*

Street House, Thursley &⚘ (Mr & Mrs B M Francis) From London take A3. 8m past Guildford turn R at sign Thursley/Churt/Frensham, 50yds past Three Horseshoes inn, bear L at fork signed The Street and No through road. Garden ahead. From Portsmouth/Petersfield turn L from A3 into Thursley village. Parking on recreation ground 100yds past house. Please park carefully in wet weather. Street House (not open), a listed Regency building and childhood home of Sir Edwin Lutyens where he first met Gertrude Jekyll. Garden of 1¼ acres divided into three. Astrological garden. Specimen Cornus kousa; rare old roses; special rhododendrons and camellias; rubus tridel. Home-made TEAS. *Adm £1.50 Chd 50p. Suns April 26, June 21 (2-6)*

Stuart Cottage, East Clandon &⚘ (Mr & Mrs J M Leader) Situated 4m E of Guildford on the A246 or from A3 via Ripley turning L in centre of Ripley, Rose Lane, then 2nd R. East Clandon is 4m. ½-acre partly walled cottage garden with well-stocked herbaceous beds, containing some unusual planting. Rose and clematis walk, water features and paved areas with planting. Victorian chimney pots used as planters add to the charm of this C16 cottage. Home-made TEAS share to Cherry Trees and Church Fund. *Adm £1.50 Chd free. Sat, Sun July 11, 12 (2-6) Sun Aug 30, (11-6). Groups welcome by prior arrangement. Please* **Tel 01483 222689**

▲**Sutton Place, Guildford** &⚘ (Sutton Place Foundation) From A320 (Guildford-Woking) turn into Clay Lane. At Xrds take Blanchards Hill towards Sutton Green. Lodge gates approx ¼m on R. 60 acres, around Tudor Manor House. A series of individual gardens each with its own theme and interest. A woodland garden which runs down to the R Wey. Many of the gardens were designed by Sir Geoffrey Jellicoe and the more recently established gardens were designed by Patrick Bowe. Light lunches and TEAS. *Adm £5 Chd £2. For NGS Wed June 10 (10-4) Suitable for wheelchairs in parts. NO COACH PARTIES ON JUNE 10. Private visits welcome by prior appt. for parties of 12-40 please* **Tel 01483 504455**

¶**Tanhouse Farm, Newdigate** &⚘ (Mrs N Fries) Midway between Dorking and Horsham. On A24 turn L at roundabout at Bearegreen. R at T junction in Newdigate 1st farm on R approx ⅔m. C16 listed farmhouse (not open) in informal 1-acre garden developing since 1987 with herbaceous borders, rose garden, small lake, stream, short farm walk, picnic area. TEAS. *Adm £1.50 Chd 50p. Sun July 19 (2-6)*

Tanyard Farmhouse, Langshott, Horley &⚘ (Mr & Mrs E Epson) At edge of Horley on A23. Travelling from Redhill turn L into Ladbroke Rd at Chequers Hotel roundabout. Continue ½m, garden on L. Park in Lake Lane. ⅓-acre 4-yr-old garden designed, planted and still being developed by owners, around a C15/17 Wealden farmhouse. Formal layout, with informal planting, incl small white garden with pond, scented rose garden with lavender and clematis, rustic trellises and arches. Mixed borders with shrubs and perennials, some unusual. Terrace with pots and baskets containing herbs, perennials and annuals. TEAS. *Adm £1.50 Chd free. Sat, Sun July 4, 5 (2-6)*

Thanescroft, Shamley Green &⚘⚘ (Mr & Mrs Peter Talbot-Willcox) 5m S of Guildford, A281 Guildford-Horsham rd, at Shalford turn E onto B2128 to Wonersh and Shamley Green. At Shamley Green Village sign turn R to Lord's Hill, ¾m on L. 4-acres. Pool garden with shrubberies and Rowan avenue. Lower level kitchen garden integrated with roses, mixed borders, yew and box hedges. Orchard with shrub roses. Lawns and fine old trees. Rhododendrons and primula walk. Ice house. TEAS. *Adm £2 Chd free. Sat, Sun June 20, 21 (2-6)*

●**Titsey Place and Gardens, Oxted** ⚘ (The Trustees of the Titsey Foundation) On A25 between Oxted and Westerham, turn L into Limpsfield Village down High St, turn L (on sharp bend) into Bluehouse Lane and R into Water Lane. Follow road under M25 and through park to walled garden car park. An ancestral home of the Greshams since 1534. Splendid walled kitchen garden, lakes, rose gardens and fountains in 15 acres. *Adm £4 House and garden (Adults) £2, Chd £1 (under 16) garden only. Weds and Suns May 20 to Sept 27 (1-5) Easter Mon April 13, Mon May 4. Private visits welcome if pre-booked, please* **Tel 01273 475411**

Unicorns, Farnham ⚘ (Mr & Mrs Eric Roberts) Long Hill, The Sands. Approx 4½m E of Farnham take A31 towards Guildford. 1st slip rd to Runfold turn R, then L into Crooksbury Rd through 's' bend then L turn to The Sands through village past Barley Mow public house on R. Park tactfully in Littleworth Rd. Long Hill 1st turning on R. Partly woodland garden on a sloping site, rhododendrons, azaleas, ferns, plants for ground cover and many other interesting and unusual plants and shrubs. Teas at Manor Farm, Seale. *Adm £1 Chd free. Weds May 20, June 17 (2-5). Private visits welcome from mid April to end of August please* **Tel 01252 782778** *after 6pm*

87 Upland Road, Sutton &⚘⚘ (Mr & Mrs David Nunn) 50yds S Carshalton Beeches station into Waverley Way, at shops into Downside Rd, then 1st on L. 0.4-acre secluded suburban plantsman's garden overlaying chalk. Shrubs; herbaceous; orchard; fruit and vegetable garden. Developed and maintained by owners. Exhibition of botanical watercolour paintings. TEAS. *Adm £1.50 Chd free. Sun May 10 (2-6)*

6 Upper Rose Hill, Dorking ⚘⚘ (Peter & Julia Williams) From roundabout at A24/A25 junction follow signs to town centre and Horsham. ½m S of town centre turn L after Pizza Piazza and 2nd R at top of hill. Parking available in rd and in large car park behind Sainsbury's (5 min walk). ½-acre informal suburban terraced garden on dry sand. Planted for yr round interest with foliage and form; fruit and vegetables; some unusual plants. TEAS in aid of Mole Valley Crossroads. *Adm £1.50 Chd free. Sun June 14 (2-6). Private visits welcome, please* **Tel 01306 881315**

Vale End, Albury ⚘ (Mr & Mrs John Foulsham) 4½m SE of Guildford. From Albury take A248 W for ¼m. 1-acre walled garden on many levels in beautiful setting; views from terrace across sloping lawns to mill pond and woodland; wide variety herbaceous plants and old roses; attractive courtyard. Fruit, vegetable and herb garden.

Morning coffee and home-made TEAS in aid of Guildford Macmillan Day Care Centre Appeal. *Adm £2 Chd free. Suns June 21, July 26 (10-5)*

Vann, Hambledon ✍️❀ (Mr & Mrs M B Caroe) 6m S of Godalming. A283 to Wormley. Follow yellow 'Vann' signs for 2m. An English Heritage registered garden of 4½ acres surrounding Tudor/William & Mary house with later additions and alterations by W D Caröe. Old cottage garden, pergola, ¼-acre pond, Gertrude Jekyll water garden 1911, azaleas, spring bulbs and woodland. New South End and double vegetable garden borders. Featured on TV Great English Gardens and many magazines. Maintained by family with 2 days help per week. Private groups and guided garden tours welcome. Lunches, home-made teas, and refreshments by prior arrangement **Tel 01428 683413**. WC and plant sales weekends only. *Adm £2.50 Chd 50p (ACNO to Hambledon Village Hall®). Tues to Sat April 14 to 18 (10-6), Sun April 19 (10-6) TEAS. Bank Hol Mon May 4 (2-6) TEAS. Tues May 5 to Sun May 10 (10-6), Mon June 1 to Sun June 7, Mon June 29 to Sun July 5 (10-6)*

■ **Walton Poor, Ranmore** ♿❀ (Mr & Mrs Nicholas Calvert) 4m W of Ranmore. From N and W off A246 on outskirts of East Horsley turn R to Greendene, 1st fork L Crocknorth Rd. From E take A2003 to Ranmore Rd from Dorking to E Horsley. Approx 3 acres; tranquil, rather secret garden; paths winding between areas of ornamental shrubs; dell; pond; herb garden. Autumn colour. Extensive range of foliage, scented plants and herbs for sale; garden nr forest paths leading to North Downs with fine views over Tillingbourne valley. TEAS (May and June) (from 3pm). *Adm £2 Chd 50p (ACNO to Leukaemia Research®). Herb garden open daily Wed to Sun Easter to Sept 30. For NGS Mon May 4, Sun, Wed June 7, 10 (11-6) Sun Oct 11 (11-5). Private visits of 10 and over welcome to the main garden, please* **Tel 01483 282273**

Windlesham Park, nr Bagshot ♿✍️ (Mr & Mrs Peter Dimmock) Woodlands Lane. 2m E of Bagshot. S of Sunningdale, NW of Chobham; from Windlesham Church S to T-junction, turn L into Thorndown Lane becoming Woodlands Lane over M3; entrance 100yds on R, white pillars. 9-acre parkland setting with many and varied well established azaleas and rhododendrons. Fine cedars and mature trees; wet areas. WC not suitable for wheelchairs. TEAS. *Adm £2 Chd 50p (ACNO to St John the Baptist Church®). Sun May 24 (2-6)*

▲**Winkworth Arboretum, Hascombe** (The National Trust) Godalming. Entrances with car parks - Upper, 3m SE of Godalming on E side of B2130; Lower, 2¼m S of Bramley on Bramley-Hascombe rd, turn R off A281 from Guildford at Bramley Xrds, up Snowdenham Lane. Coaches (by written arrangement) should use Upper car park on B2130. Station: Godalming 3m. 95 acres of hillside planted with rare trees and shrubs; 2 lakes; many wild birds; view over N Downs. Tours on both days with Eric Barrs, Head of Arboretum from kiosk. 2.30pm; £2 extra, chd free. Limited suitability for wheelchairs. Disabled visitors use lower car park. Disabled WC. TEAS 11-

5.30. *Adm £2.70 Chd 5-16 £1.35 Family ticket £6.75. All NT members donation please. For NGS Suns April 26, Oct 4 (daylight hrs)*

Wintershall Manor ✍️ (Mr & Mrs Peter Hutley) 3m S of Bramley village on A281 turn R, then next R. Wintershall drive next on L. Bus: AV 33 Guildford-Horsham; alight Palmers Cross, 1m. 2-acre garden and 200 acres of park and woodland; bluebell walks in spring; wild daffodils; rhododendrons; specimen trees; lakes and flight ponds; path to Chapel of St Mary has Stations of Cross by contemporary sculptors. Rosary Walk and St Francis Chapel by lakes. Superb views. Music and verse by the Guildford School of Acting. Partially suitable for wheelchairs. TEA from 3.30 pm. *Adm £2 OAPs £1.50 Chd 4-14 50p (ACNO to Wintershall Charitable Trust®). Sun May 10 (2-5). Private parties welcome, please* **Tel 01483 892167**

Wisley see RHS Garden Wisley

¶**Woodbury Cottage, Reigate** ✍️❀ (Shirley & Robert Stoneley) Colley Lane 1m W of Reigate. M25 junction 8, A217 (direction Reigate). Immed before level Xing turn R into Somers Rd., cont as Manor Rd. At very end turn R into Coppice Lane and follow signs to car park. Garden is 300yds walk from car park. Cottage garden just under ¼-acre made and maintained by owners. The garden is stepped on a a slope with mixed harmonious planting, enhanced by its setting under Colley Hill. Still attractive in September. TEAS. *Adm £1.50 Chd free. Suns July 5 (10-5) Sept 6 (10-4)*

Woodside, Send ✍️❀ (Mr & Mrs J A Colmer) Send Barns Lane, nr Ripley, 4m NE of Guildford; on A247 (Woking/ Dorking Rd) 200yds west (Send side) at junction with B2215. If travelling via M25 leave at junction 10. ⅓-acre garden; main feature rock garden and alpine house; many shrubs incl rhododendrons, ericaceous species etc; herbaceous planting; specialist collection of alpines. *Adm £1.50 Chd free. Sat, Sun April 18, 19 (2-6). Private visits welcome in May, please* **Tel 01483 223073**

Yew Tree Cottage, Haslemere ✍️❀ (Mr & Mrs E E Bowyer) Bunch Lane. Turn off High St into Church Lane, leave church on L, carry on to T junction, turn L, 1st house on L. 2-acre garden created by owners since 1976 on hillside. Large variety of trees and shrubs, water garden, kitchen garden, Jacob and Shetland sheep, rare breed poultry, Shetland pony in paddock beyond garden. Partially suitable wheelchairs. See **Haslehurst**. Tea at Haslehurst. *Adm £1.50 Chd 50p. Sun June 14 (2-6). Coach parties by prior arrangement. Private visits welcome, please* **Tel 01428 644130**

Evening Openings (see also garden descriptions)	
Chilworth Manor, Chilworth	June 11, July 9 6–8pm
Shepherds Lane Gardens, Guildford	June 24 7–9pm
Brockhurst, Chiddingfold	June 28 6–7.30pm
41 Shelvers Way, Tadworth	July 14 6–9pm
The Copse Lodge, Burgh Heath	July 15 7–10pm
RHS Garden, Wisley	July 28 6.30–9pm

Sussex

Hon County Organisers:	(East & Mid-Sussex)
	Mrs Janet Goldsmith, Sunnymead, Tapsells Lane, Wadhurst TN5 6RS
	Tel 01892 783264
	(West Sussex)
	Mrs Consie Dunn, Wildham, Stoughton, Chichester PO18 9JG
	Tel 01243 535202
Assistant Hon County Organisers:	(East & Mid-Sussex)
	Mrs Miriam Book, Appledore, 50 Hill Drive, Hove BN3 6QL
	Mrs Anne Bramall, Lea Farm, Peasmarsh, Rye TN31 7ST
	Mrs Rosemary Collins, Windwhistle, Faircrouch Lane, Wadhurst TN5 6PP
	Mrs Judy Emrich, Old Mill Barn, Argos Hill, Rotherfield TN6 3QF
	Mrs Sophie Neal, Legsheath Farm, nr East Grinstead RH19 4JN
	Mrs Lynn Neligan, Old School House, Church Lane, Northiam TN31 6NN
	Mrs Jan Newman, Graywood House, Graywood, East Hoathly BN8 6QP
	Mrs Nikola Sly, Lilac Cottage, High Hurstwood, Uckfield,
	Mrs Carolyn Steel, Beeches, Cuckfield Lane, Warninglid RH17 5UB
	(West Sussex)
	Mrs Nigel Azis, Coke's Barn, West Burton, Pulborough RH20 1HD
	Mrs Jane Burton, Church Farmhouse, Lavant, nr Chichester PO18 0AL
	Mrs Louise Pollard, 6 Holbrook Park, Northlands Rd, Horsham RH12 5PW
	Mrs Claudia Pearce, 12 Belsize Rd, Worthing BN11 4RH
	Mrs Jenny Woodall, Nyewood House, nr Petersfield, Hants GU31 5JL
Hon County Treasurers:	(East & Mid-Sussex)
	D C Goldsmith Esq, Sunnymead, Tapsells Lane, Wadhurst TN5 6RS
	(West Sussex)
	W M Caldwell Esq, The Grange, Fittleworth, Pulborough RH20 1EW

DATES OF OPENING

Regular openings
For details see garden description

Borde Hill Garden, nr Haywards
   Heath
Great Dixter, Northiam
High Beeches Gardens, Handcross
Moorlands, Friar's Gate, nr
   Crowborough
West Dean Gardens, nr Chichester

By appointment only
*For telephone numbers and other
details see garden descriptions.
Private visits welcomed*

Cedar Tree Cottage, Washington
Combehurst, Frant
The Old Chalk Pit, Hove
The Old Rectory, Newtimber
64 Old Shoreham Road, Hove
Rosemary Cottage, Rotherfield
Spur Point, nr Fernhurst
46 Westup Farm Cottages, Balcombe
Whitehouse Cottage, Staplefield
Yew Tree Cottage, Crawley Down

March 15 Sunday
   Champs Hill, Coldwaltham, nr
      Pulborough

March 18 Wednesday
   Champs Hill, Coldwaltham, nr
      Pulborough
March 22 Sunday
   Berri Court, Yapton
   Champs Hill, Coldwaltham, nr
      Pulborough
   Orchards, Rowfant
March 23 Monday
   Berri Court, Yapton
March 25 Wednesday
   Champs Hill, Coldwaltham, nr
      Pulborough
March 28 Saturday
   Manor of Dean, Tillington
March 29 Sunday
   Champs Hill, Coldwaltham, nr
      Pulborough
   Manor of Dean, Tillington
   Penns in the Rocks, Groombridge
March 30 Monday
   Manor of Dean, Tillington
April 4 Saturday
   Rymans, Apuldram, nr Chichester
April 5 Sunday
   Bates Green, Arlington
   High Beeches Gardens, Handcross
   New Grove, Petworth
April 6 Monday
   Bates Green, Arlington
   Little Thakeham, Storrington

April 7 Tuesday
   Little Thakeham, Storrington
April 8 Wednesday
   The Hawthorn, Lower Beeding
April 12 Sunday
   Bignor Park, nr Pulborough
   Chidmere House, Chidham
   The Hawthorn, Lower Beeding
   Merriments Gardens, Hurst Green
   Orchards, Rowfant
April 13 Monday
   Bignor Park, nr Pulborough
   Chidmere House, Chidham
   Stonehurst, Ardingly
April 14 Tuesday
   Northwood Farmhouse,
      Pulborough
April 15 Wednesday
   Northwood Farmhouse,
      Pulborough
April 18 Saturday
   King Edward VII Hospital,
      Midhurst
   Manor of Dean, Tillington
April 19 Sunday
   Church Farm, Aldingbourne
   Cooke's House, West Burton
   Ghyll Farm, Sweethaws,
      Crowborough
   Hurst Mill, Petersfield
   Manor of Dean, Tillington

Newtimber Place, Newtimber
April 20 Monday
Cooke's House, West Burton
Manor of Dean, Tillington
April 21 Tuesday
Cooke's House, West Burton
Coombland, Coneyhurst
April 22 Wednesday
Houghton Farm, Arundel
Little Dene, Chelwood Gate
April 23 Thursday
Little Dene, Chelwood Gate
April 25 Saturday
Coombland, Coneyhurst
April 26 Sunday
Cooke's House, West Burton
Offham House, Offham
Stonehurst, Ardingly
Warren House, Crowborough
April 27 Monday
Cooke's House, West Burton
April 28 Tuesday
Cooke's House, West Burton
April 30 Thursday
Borde Hill Garden, nr Haywards
Heath
May 1 Friday
Borde Hill Garden, nr Haywards
Heath
May 2 Saturday
Duckyls, Sharpthorne
May 3 Sunday
Champs Hill, Coldwaltham, nr
Pulborough
Duckyls, Sharpthorne
Gaywood Farm, Pulborough
Ghyll Farm, Sweethaws,
Crowborough
Malt House, Chithurst
The White Magpie, Lamberhurst
May 4 Monday
Duckyls, Sharpthorne
Highdown Gardens, Goring-by-Sea
Malt House, Chithurst
Warren House, Crowborough
May 6 Wednesday
Champs Hill, Coldwaltham, nr
Pulborough
Nyewood House, Nyewood, Nr
Rogate
May 7 Thursday
Bates Green, Arlington
May 9 Saturday
New Grove, Petworth
May 10 Sunday
Berri Court, Yapton
Champs Hill, Coldwaltham, nr
Pulborough
Hammerwood House, Iping
Malt House, Chithurst
New Grove, Petworth
Selehurst, Lower Beeding, nr
Horsham
Stonehurst, Ardingly

Three Oaks, West Broyle
Wadhurst Park, Wadhurst
May 11 Monday
Berri Court, Yapton
May 12 Tuesday
Sheffield Park Garden, nr Uckfield
Three Oaks, West Broyle
May 13 Wednesday
Champs Hill, Coldwaltham, nr
Pulborough
Little Dene, Chelwood Gate
May 14 Thursday
Bates Green, Arlington
Little Dene, Chelwood Gate
Stone House Hotel, Rushlake
Green
May 16 Saturday
Manor of Dean, Tillington
May 17 Sunday
Ansty Gardens
Ashdown Park Hotel, Wych Cross
Champs Hill, Coldwaltham, nr
Pulborough
Cowdray Park Gardens, Midhurst
Ghyll Farm, Sweethaws,
Crowborough
Hammerwood House, Iping
1 & 6 Holbrook Park
Legsheath Farm, nr Forest Row
Manor of Dean, Tillington
Mayfield Cottage Gardens,
Mayfield (also Evening)
Merriments Gardens, Hurst Green
Mountfield Court, nr
Robertsbridge
Standen, East Grinstead
Trotton Old Rectory, nr Rogate
Trotton Place, nr Rogate
Warren House, Crowborough
May 18 Monday
Manor of Dean, Tillington
Mountfield Court, nr
Robertsbridge
May 20 Wednesday
Houghton Farm, Arundel
May 21 Thursday
Bates Green, Arlington
May 24 Sunday
Baker's Farm, Shipley
Chidmere House, Chidham
Cookscroft, Earnley
Fishers Farm, Etchingham
Hurston Place, Pulborough
Moorlands, Friar's Gate, nr
Crowborough
Rose Cottage, Hadlow Down
May 25 Monday
Chidmere House, Chidham
Cookscroft, Earnley
Highdown Gardens, Goring-by-Sea
Orchards, Rowfant
Warren House, Crowborough
May 28 Thursday
Duckyls Holt, West Hoathly

The Priest House, West Hoathly
May 30 Saturday
Coombland, Coneyhurst
Five Oaks Cottage, West Burton
Gaywood Farm, Pulborough
Newhaven Botanic Gardens
Roundhill Cottage, East Dean
Sennicotts, Nr Chichester
(Evening)
94 Wepham, Burpham
The White House, Burpham, Nr
Arundel
May 31 Sunday
Cobblers, Crowborough
Cowbeech Farm, Cowbeech
Fitzhall, Iping, nr Midhurst
Five Oaks Cottage, West Burton
Gaywood Farm, Pulborough
Ghyll Farm, Sweethaws,
Crowborough
Newhaven Botanic Gardens
Nymans, Handcross
Pembury, Clayton
Priesthawes Farm, Polegate
Roundhill Cottage, East Dean
June 1 Monday
Cowbeech Farm, Cowbeech
(Evening)
June 3 Wednesday
Cabbages and Kings Garden,
Wildernesss Farm, Hadlow Down
June 6 Saturday
King John's Lodge, Etchingham
Somerset Lodge, North St,
Petworth
June 7 Sunday
Hailsham Grange, Hailsham
King John's Lodge, Etchingham
Kingston Gardens, nr Lewes
Little Hutchings, Etchingham
Moorlands, Friar's Gate, nr
Crowborough
Neptune House, Cutmill
North Manor, Flansham, Bognor
Regis
Nyewood House, Nyewood, Nr
Rogate
Offham House, Offham
Somerset Lodge, North St,
Petworth
Warren House, Crowborough
June 8 Monday
Little Thakeham, Storrington
Somerset Lodge, North St,
Petworth
June 9 Tuesday
Coombland, Coneyhurst
Little Thakeham, Storrington
Somerset Lodge, North St,
Petworth
June 10 Wednesday
Ashburnham Place, Battle
Lilac Cottage, Duncton
Little Dene, Chelwood Gate

North Manor, Flansham, Bognor
 Regis
Nyewood House, Nyewood, Nr
 Rogate
Somerset Lodge, North St,
 Petworth
June 11 Thursday
Ashburnham Place, Battle
Little Dene, Chelwood Gate
Somerset Lodge, North St,
 Petworth
Uppark, South Harting
West Dean Gardens, nr Chichester
June 12 Friday
Ashburnham Place, Battle
Somerset Lodge, North St,
 Petworth
June 13 Saturday
Chantry Green House, Steyning
Coombland, Coneyhurst
Lilac Cottage, Duncton
Manvilles Field, Fittleworth
 (Evening)
Reynolds Kitchen Court, Petworth
Somerset Lodge, North St,
 Petworth
June 14 Sunday
Ashburnham Place, Battle
Berri Court, Yapton
Chantry Green House, Steyning
Clinton Lodge, Fletching
Cobblers, Crowborough
Dyke Road Avenue Gardens,
 Brighton
Frith Hill, Northchapel
 (Evening)
Frith Lodge, Northchapel
 (Evening)
The Grange, Fittleworth
Hurston Place, Pulborough
Knabbs Farmhouse, Fletching
Lilac Cottage, Duncton
Manvilles Field, Fittleworth
New Barn, Egdean, nr Petworth
Reynolds Kitchen Court, Petworth
Sands, Warnham
Somerset Lodge, North St,
 Petworth
Tinkers Bridge Cottage, Ticehurst
June 15 Monday
Berri Court, Yapton
Clinton Lodge, Fletching
Hurston Place, Pulborough
Knabbs Farmhouse, Fletching
New Barn, Egdean, nr Petworth
June 16 Tuesday
Coombland, Coneyhurst
New Barn, Egdean, nr Petworth
June 17 Wednesday
Clinton Lodge, Fletching
June 18 Thursday
Doucegrove Farm, Northiam
Frith Hill, Northchapel
Frith Lodge, Northchapel

June 19 Friday
Doucegrove Farm, Northiam
Down Place, South Harting
June 20 Saturday
Bankton Cottage, Crawley Down
Coombland, Coneyhurst
Down Place, South Harting
Frith Hill, Northchapel (Evening)
Frith Lodge, Northchapel (Evening)
Manor of Dean, Tillington
Winchelsea Gardens, Rye
June 21 Sunday
Bankton Cottage, Crawley Down
Down Place, South Harting
Framfield Gardens
Ketches, Newick
Manor of Dean, Tillington
Merriments Gardens, Hurst Green
Moat Mill Farm, Mayfield
The Old Vicarage, Firle
Town Place, Freshfield, nr
 Sheffield Park
Trotton Old Rectory, nr Rogate
Trotton Place, nr Rogate
June 22 Monday
Manor of Dean, Tillington
Northwood Farmhouse,
 Pulborough
June 23 Tuesday
Northwood Farmhouse,
 Pulborough
June 24 Wednesday
Bateman's, Burwash
Clinton Lodge, Fletching
Houghton Farm, Arundel
June 25 Thursday
Town Place, Freshfield, nr
 Sheffield Park
June 27 Saturday
Coombland, Coneyhurst
Five Oaks Cottage, West Burton
Long House, Cowfold
South Harting Gardens
June 28 Sunday
Baker's Farm, Shipley
12 Belsize Road, Worthing
Casters Brook, Cocking
Cobblers, Crowborough
Five Oaks Cottage, West Burton
72 Grand Avenue, Worthing
Mayfield Gardens, Mayfield
Perryhill, Hartfield
Pheasants Hatch, Newick
Rose Cottage, Hadlow Down
Sherburne House, Eartham
South Harting Gardens
June 29 Monday
Pheasants Hatch, Newick
Rose Cottage, Hadlow Down
June 30 Tuesday
Sands, Warnham (Evening)
July 1 Wednesday
Clinton Lodge, Fletching
Parham Gardens, nr Pulborough

July 2 Thursday
Parham Gardens, nr
 Pulborough
July 4 Saturday
Gaywood Farm, Pulborough
July 5 Sunday
Bosham, Hambrook and
 Nutbourne Gardens
Casters Brook, Cocking
The Garden In Mind, Stansted
 Park
Gaywood Farm, Pulborough
Hailsham Grange, Hailsham
The Lodge Garden, Westfield
The Patched Gloves, Broad Oak
Priesthawes Farm, Polegate
Town Place, Freshfield, nr
 Sheffield Park
Westerleigh, Wadhurst
8 Wimblehurst Road, Horsham
July 6 Monday
The Lodge Garden, Westfield
Westerleigh, Wadhurst
July 8 Wednesday
Bosham, Hambrook and
 Nutbourne Gardens
Grandturzel Farm, Burwash
Ringmer Park, Lewes
July 9 Thursday
Duckyls Holt, West Hoathly
Grandturzel Farm, Burwash
The Priest House, West Hoathly
July 10 Friday
Berri Court, Yapton (Evening)
Five Oaks Cottage, West Burton
 (Evening)
July 11 Saturday
Buckhurst Park, Withyham
Crown House, Eridge
Manor of Dean, Tillington
Palmer's Lodge, West Chiltington
 Village
July 12 Sunday
Ambrose Place Back Gardens,
 Worthing
Ansty Gardens
Bates Green, Arlington
Cobblers, Crowborough
Crown House, Eridge
Five Oaks Cottage, West Burton
Manor of Dean, Tillington
Nyewood House, Nyewood, Nr
 Rogate
Nymans, Handcross
Palmer's Lodge, West
 Chiltington Village
Town Place, Freshfield, nr
 Sheffield Park
July 13 Monday
Bates Green, Arlington
Manor of Dean, Tillington
July 15 Wednesday
12 Belsize Road, Worthing
 (Evening)

72 Grand Avenue, Worthing
(Evening)
Nyewood House, Nyewood, Nr
Rogate
July 17 Friday
Pashley Manor, Ticehurst
Wakehurst Place, Ardingly
July 18 Saturday
Bumble Cottage, West Chiltington
Palmer's Lodge, West Chiltington
Village
July 19 Sunday
Bumble Cottage, West Chiltington
Fitzhall, Iping, nr Midhurst
Kings Hill House, Hurst Green
Merriments Gardens, Hurst Green
Moorlands, Friar's Gate, nr
Crowborough
Orchards, Rowfant
Palmer's Lodge, West Chiltington
Village
Wadhurst Gardens
July 20 Monday
Wadhurst Gardens
July 22 Wednesday
Houghton Farm, Arundel
Little Dene, Chelwood Gate
July 23 Thursday
Ebbsworth, Nutbourne
Little Dene, Chelwood Gate
July 24 Friday
Ebbsworth, Nutbourne
Rye Gardens, Rye
July 25 Saturday
Bumble Cottage, West Chiltington
July 26 Sunday
12 Belsize Road, Worthing
Brickwall House, Northiam
Bumble Cottage, West Chiltington
Cobblers, Crowborough
72 Grand Avenue, Worthing
July 31 Friday
Denmans, Fontwell, nr Arundel
August 1 Saturday
Neptune House, Cutmill (Evening)
August 2 Sunday
Ashdown Park Hotel, Wych Cross
Champs Hill, Coldwaltham, nr
Pulborough
August 5 Wednesday
Cabbages and Kings Garden,
Wilderness Farm, Hadlow
Down
Champs Hill, Coldwaltham, nr
Pulborough
August 7 Friday
Five Oaks Cottage, West Burton
(Evening)
St Marys House, Bramber
August 8 Saturday
St Marys House, Bramber
August 9 Sunday
Champs Hill, Coldwaltham, nr
Pulborough

Cobblers, Crowborough
Five Oaks Cottage, West Burton
August 12 Wednesday
Champs Hill, Coldwaltham, nr
Pulborough
August 14 Friday
Latchetts, Dane Hill
August 15 Saturday
Latchetts, Dane Hill
Manor of Dean, Tillington
August 16 Sunday
2 Adelaide Cottages, Halnaker
Champs Hill, Coldwaltham, nr
Pulborough
Manor of Dean, Tillington
Perryhill, Hartfield
August 17 Monday
Manor of Dean, Tillington
August 22 Saturday
Bignor Park, nr Pulborough
August 23 Sunday
Bignor Park, nr Pulborough
Cobblers, Crowborough
Merriments Gardens, Hurst Green
August 26 Wednesday
Little Dene, Chelwood Gate
August 27 Thursday
Little Dene, Chelwood Gate
August 30 Sunday
Chidmere House, Chidham
Cooksbridge, Fernhurst
Newtimber Place, Newtimber
Round Oak, Old Station Road,
Wadhurst
Warren House, Crowborough
August 31 Monday
Chidmere House, Chidham
Cooksbridge, Fernhurst
Highdown Gardens, Goring-by-Sea
New Barn, Egdean, nr Petworth
Penns in the Rocks, Groombridge
Round Oak, Old Station Road,
Wadhurst
September 2 Wednesday
Cabbages and Kings Garden,
Wilderness Farm, Hadlow
Down
September 5 Saturday
Rymans, Apuldram, nr Chichester
September 6 Sunday
The Hawthorn, Lower Beeding
High Beeches Gardens, Handcross
The Lodge Garden, Westfield
Merriments Gardens, Hurst Green
September 7 Monday
The Lodge Garden, Westfield
September 9 Wednesday
Cobblers, Crowborough
September 12 Saturday
Manor of Dean, Tillington
Standen, East Grinstead
September 13 Sunday
Bates Green , Arlington
Cowbeech Farm, Cowbeech

Manor of Dean, Tillington
September 14 Monday
Bates Green, Arlington
Cowbeech Farm, Cowbeech
(Evening)
Manor of Dean, Tillington
September 17 Thursday
8 Wimblehurst Road, Horsham
September 18 Friday
Denmans, Fontwell, nr Arundel
Ringmer Park, Lewes
September 26 Saturday
Five Oaks Cottage, West Burton
September 27 Sunday
Five Oaks Cottage, West Burton
The Garden In Mind, Stansted
Park
October 3 Saturday
Manor of Dean, Tillington
October 4 Sunday
Manor of Dean, Tillington
October 5 Monday
Manor of Dean, Tillington
October 13 Tuesday
Sheffield Park Garden, nr
Uckfield
October 18 Sunday
Coates Manor, Fittleworth
October 19 Monday
Coates Manor, Fittleworth
October 24 Saturday
Berri Court, Yapton
October 25 Sunday
Berri Court, Yapton
Orchards, Rowfant

**Remember that every time
you visit a National
Gardens Scheme garden
you are helping to raise
money for:**

The Queen's Nursing Institute
County Nursing Associations
The Nurses' Welfare Service
Macmillan Cancer Relief
Marie Curie Cancer Care
Help the Hospices
Crossroads
The Gardens Fund of the
National Trust
The Gardeners' Royal
Benevolent Society
The Royal Gardeners' Orphans
Fund
Additional Charities
Nominated by Owners
Other charities as decided
from time to time by Council

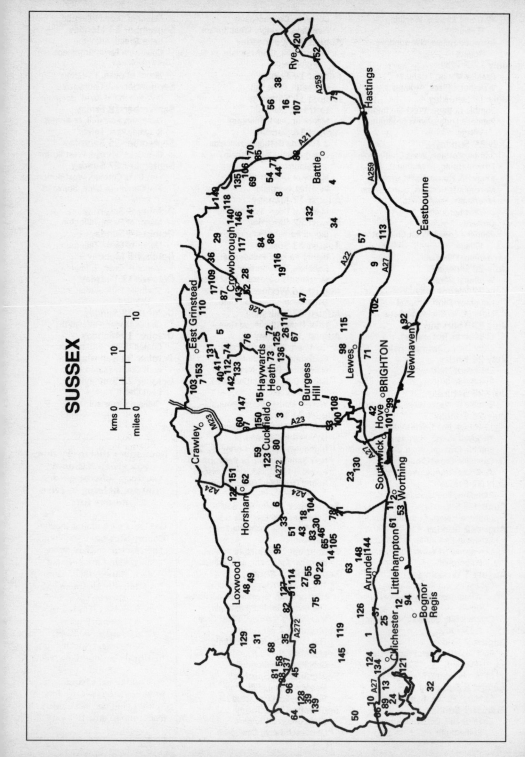

SUSSEX

Rye 120
152
38
56   16   107   Hastings
A259
A21
70   80   Battle
85   106 77   4
135   69   54   44
140 118   8   132
Crowborough 140   146   141   34
29   117   57
36   84   86   113
17109   28   116   A22   9   A27
87 143   52   19   47   102   Eastbourne
110   A26   26 11   115   92
East Grinstead   5   72   67   Newhaven
131   125   98   71
153   74   136 73   BRIGHTON
103   40 41 112 133   15 Haywards   108   Hove 99
7   142   Heath   Burgess   42   101
147   Cuckfield 3   Hill   100   Southwick
60   150   A23   93   Worthing
59 80   27   2
123   23 130   53
151   A272   78   Littlehampton 61
Crawley   62   6   33   104   25   94
Horsham   18   65   Bognor
95   51   43 83 30 46   105   126   57   12   Regis
114   14   63   144   Chichester   121
48 49   55 22   148   1   32
Loxwood   127 81   90   Arundel   124
82   75   145 119   134
129   31   35   20   13
68   10 A27   24
81 58 137   89
96   45   50
128
139
64

kms 0   10   10
miles 0   10

KEY

1. 2 Adelaide Cottages
2. Ambrose Place Back Gardens
3. Ansty Gardens
4. Ashburnham Place
5. Ashdown Park Hotel
6. Baker's Farm
7. Bankton Cottage
8. Bateman's
9. Bates Green
10. Bay Tree Cottage
11. 12 Belsize Road
12. Berri Court
13. 4 Berrymead Cottages
14. Bignor Park
15. Borde Hill Garden
16. Brickwall House
17. Buckhurst Park
18. Bumble Cottage
19. Cabbages and Kings Garden
20. Casters Brook
21. Cedar Tree Cottage
22. Champs Hill
23. Chantry Green House
24. Chidmere House
25. Church Farm
26. Clinton Lodge
27. Coates Manor
28. Cobblers
29. Combehurst
30. Cooke's House
31. Cooksbridge
32. Cookscroft
33. Coombland
34. Cowbeech Farm
35. Cowdray Park Gardens
36. Crown House
37. Denmans
38. Doucegrove Farm
39. Down Place
40. Duckyls
41. Duckyls Holt
42. Dyke Road Avenue Gardens
43. Ebbsworth
44. Fishers Farm
45. Fitzhall
46. Five Oaks Cottage
47. Framfield Gardens
48. Frith Hill
49. Frith Lodge
50. The Garden In Mind
51. Gaywood Farm
52. Ghyll Farm

53. 72 Grand Avenue
54. Grandturzel Farm
55. The Grange
56. Great Dixter
57. Hailsham Grange
58. Hammerwood House
59. The Hawthorn
60. High Beeches Gardens
61. Highdown Gardens
62. 1 & 6 Holbrook Park
63. Houghton Farm
64. Hurst Mill
65. Hurston Place
66. Jacaranda
67. Ketches
68. King Edward VII Hospital
69. King John's Lodge
70. Kings Hill House
71. Kingston Gardens
72. Knabbs Farmhouse
73. Latchetts
74. Legsheath Farm
75. Lilac Cottage
76. Little Dene
77. Little Hutchings
78. Little Thakeham
79. The Lodge Garden
80. Long House
81. Malt House
82. Manor of Dean
83. Manvilles Field
84. Mayfield Gardens
85. Merriments Gardens
86. Moat Mill Farm
87. Moorlands
88. Mountfield Court
89. Neptune House
90. New Barn
91. New Grove
92. Newhaven Botanic Gardens
93. Newtimber Place
94. North Manor
95. Northwood Farmhouse
96. Nyewood House
97. Nymans
98. Offham House
99. The Old Chalk Pit
100. The Old Rectory
101. 64 Old Shoreham Road
102. The Old Vicarage
103. Orchards

104. Palmer's Lodge
105. Parham Gardens
106. Pashley Manor
107. The Patched Gloves
108. Pembury
109. Penns in the Rocks
110. Perryhill
111. Pheasants Hatch
112. The Priest House
113. Priesthawes Farm
114. Reynolds Kitchen Court
115. Ringmer Park
116. Rose Cottage
117. Rosemary Cottage
118. Round Oak, Old Station Road
119. Roundhill Cottage East Dean
120. Rye Gardens
121. Rymans
122. Sands
123. Selehurst
124. Sennicotts
125. Sheffield Park Garden
126. Sherburne House
127. Somerset Lodge
128. South Harting Gardens
129. Spur Point
130. St Mary's House
131. Standen
132. Stone House Hotel
133. Stonehurst
134. Three Oaks
135. Tinkers Bridge Cottage
136. Town Place
137. Trotton Old Rectory
138. Trotton Place
139. Uppark
140. Wadhurst Gardens
141. Wadhurst Park
142. Wakehurst Place
143. Warren House
144. 94 Wepham
145. West Dean Gardens
146. Westerleigh
147. 46 Westup Farm Cottages
148. The White House
149. The White Magpie
150. Whitehouse Cottage
151. 8 Wimblehurst Road
152. Winchelsea Gardens
153. Yew Tree Cottage

Evening Openings (see also garden descriptions)

Mayfield Cottage Gardens, Mayfield	May 17 5–7.30pm	
Sennicotts, nr Chichester	May 30 5–8pm	
Cowbeech Farm, Cowbeech	June 1, Sept 14 5–8pm	
Manvilles Field, Fittleworth	June 13 6–8pm	
Frith Hill, Northchapel	June 14 & 20 5–8pm	
Frith Lodge, Northchapel	June 14 & 20 5–8pm	
Sands, Horsham	June 30 6–8.30pm	
Berri Court, Yapton	July 10 6–8.30pm	
Five Oaks Cottage, West Burton	July 10, Aug 7 5–8pm	
72 Grand Avenue, Worthing	July 15 5.30–8pm	
12 Belsize Road, Worthing	July 15 5.30–8pm	
Neptune House, Cutmill	August 1 5–8pm	

DESCRIPTIONS OF GARDENS

¶2 Adelaide Cottages, Halnaker ⅋ (Mrs Joan Mezulis) 3½m NE of Chichester on A285. 200yds on L after Anglesey Arms public house. Off street parking. An unexpected hidden garden of ½ acre at the end of a path. A blaze of summer colour in herbaceous borders, vegetables from unusual seeds brought from Latvia. Wide variety of trees and shrubs. TEAS. *Adm £1.50 Chd 50p. Sun Aug 16 (2-6)*

Ambrose Place Back Gardens, Richmond Rd ⅋❀ Worthing. Take Broadwater Rd into town centre, turn R at traffic lights into Richmond Rd opp Library; small town gardens with entrances on left; parking in rds. TEAS. *Combined adm £1.50 Chd 50p (ACNO to Christ Church and St Paul's Worthing®). Sun July 12 (11-1, 2-5)*
    No 1 (Mrs M M Rosenberg) Walled garden; shrubs, pond, climbing plants
    No 3 (Mr & Mrs M Smyth) Paved garden with climbing plants, lawn and pond
    No 4 (Mrs J Green) Paved garden raised herbaceous borders, lawn & flowering summer plants
    No 5 (Mr & Mrs P Owen) Paved with borders
    No 6 (Mrs Leslie Roberts) Attractive garden with conservatory
    No 7 (Mr & Mrs M Frost) Patio garden, with conservatory
    No 8 (Mr & Mrs P McMonagie) Summer flowering plants and lawn
    No 11 (Mrs M Stewart) Roses, summerhouse, flowering plants
    No 12 (Mr & Mrs P Bennett) Original paved small garden with trees
    No 13 (Linda Gamble) Discrete courtyard with design studio
    No 14 (Mr & Mrs A H P Humphrey) Roses, flowering plants, greenhouse and bonsai collection
    Ambrose Villa (Mr & Mrs Frank Leocadi) Italian style small town garden

Ansty Gardens ⅋❀ On A272. 3m W of Haywards Heath. 1m E of A23. Start in car park signposted in Ansty village. Coffee, Ploughmans, TEAS & plants in aid of Riding for the Disabled, St Catherines Hospice, St James & St Peters Hospice, Ansty Village Hall Trust. *Combined adm £2.50 Chd free. Suns May 17, July 12 (11-6)*
    Apple Tree Cottage (Mr & Mrs Longfield) Cottage garden, herbaceous borders, mature trees
    Brenfield (Dr & Mrs Mace) Major private collection of cacti and succulents
    Greenacre (Mr & Mrs Owen) 2½-acre mixed garden
    Netherby (Mr & Mrs Gilbert) Cottage garden
    Whydown Cottage (Mr & Mrs Gibson) 1-acre woodland garden

Ashburnham Place, Battle ⅋⅋❀ (Ashburnham Christian Trust) 5m W of Battle on A271 (formerly B2204). 220 acres of beautifully landscaped gardens, with glorious views over 3 lakes, designed by George Dance and Capability Brown. Recent restoration work includes scented Prayer Garden and kitchen gardens within the 4-acre walled garden. Work in progress on C19 winter garden. Peaceful woodland walks. Features from several centuries. Cream TEAS in C18 orangery. *Adm £2.50 Chd*
50p (ACNO to Ashburnham Christian Trust®). Wed, Thurs, Fri, Sun June 10, 11, 12, 14 (2-5.30)*

Ashdown Park Hotel, Wych Cross ⅋ 6m S of E Grinstead. Take A22, 3m S of Forest Row, turn L at Wych Cross by garage, 1m on R. From M25 take M23 S and leave at junction 10 taking A264 to E Grinstead. Approach from S on A22, turn R at Wych Cross. 186 acres surrounding Ashdown Park Hotel. Parkland setting, mixture of woodland walks, water gardens and walled garden with glasshouse. Fine mature specimen trees, terraced lawns leading to carp filled lake. Restored 'Secret Garden' due to open Spring 1998. A peaceful oasis in the heart of Ashdown Forest. Gardens and grounds under 7yr restoration plan. TEA. *Adm £2.50 Chd free. Suns May 17, Aug 2 (2-6)*

Baker's Farm, Shipley ⅋❀ (Mr & Mrs Mark Burrell) 5m S of Horsham. Take A24 then A272 W, 2nd turn to Dragon's Green, L at George and Dragon then 300yds on L. Large Wealden garden; lake; laburnum tunnel; shrubs, trees, rose walks of old-fashioned roses; scented knot garden and bog gardens. TEAS. *Adm £2 Chd free (ACNO to St Mary the Virgin, Shipley®). Suns May 24, June 28 (2-6). Parties by appt, please Tel 01403 741215*

Bankton Cottage, Crawley Down ⅋⅋❀ (Mr & Mrs Robin Lloyd) 4m W of East Grinstead. 2½m E of M23 (J.10). On B2028 1m N of Turners Hill Xrds. 3½-acre partially walled cottage garden, herbaceous borders, shrub and climbing roses, small lake and pond with bog gardens. Enormous number of terracotta pots planted up, many seconds for sale. TEAS in aid of Cheshire Homes. *Adm £1.50 Chd free. Sat, Sun June 20, 21 (2-6). Large parties welcome by appt only May to July, please Tel 01342 718907 or 714793*

▲Bateman's, Burwash ⅋⅋ (The National Trust) ½m S (A265). From rd leading S from W end of village. Home of Rudyard Kipling from 1902-1936. Garden laid out before he lived in house and planted yew hedges, rose garden, laid paths and made pond. Bridge to mill which grinds local wheat into flour. LUNCHES & TEAS. *Adm £4.80 Groups 15 or more £4 Chd £2.40. For NGS Wed June 24 (11-5.30) last entry 4.30. Parties welcome by appt on open days, please Tel 01435 882302, Fax 882811*

Bates Green, Arlington ⅋⅋❀ (Mr & Mrs J R McCutchan) 2½m SW of A22 at Hailsham and 2m S Michelham Priory, Upper Dicker. Approach Arlington passing the 'Old Oak Inn' on R continue for 350yds then turn R along a small lane. [TQ5507] Follow Bluebell walk signs for May openings. Plantsman's tranquil garden of over 1 acre gives yr-round interest; extensive refurbished rockery; natural pond, mixed borders with colour themes, and shaded foliage garden. TEAS. *Adm £2 Chd free. Suns April 5, July 12, Sept 13 (2.30-5). Mons April 6, July 13, Sept 14; Thurs May 7, 14, 21 (10-5) Private visits welcome, please Tel 01323 482039*

12 Belsize Rd, Worthing ⅋❀ (Claudia & Peter Pearce) 10m W of Brighton, 6m E of Littlehampton, off A259. From Brighton follow signs for Worthing town centre then A259 at traffic lights (Richmond Rd). Continue for approx 1m to traffic lights/junction with Heene Rd. Carry straight on and take 2nd turning on R for Belsize Rd. Ornamental garden with large variety of perennials, shrubs and climbers, some unusual. Many pots and hanging baskets. TEAS. *Adm £1.50 Chd free. Suns June 28, July 26 (2-6). Weds July 15 (5.30-8)*

Berri Court, Yapton &❀ (Mr & Mrs J C Turner) 5m SW of Arundel. In centre of village between PO & Black Dog public house. A2024 Littlehampton-Chichester rd passes. Intensely planted 2-acre garden of wide interest; trees, flowering shrubs, heathers, eucalyptus, daffodils, shrub roses, hydrangeas and lily pond. TEAS for afternoon openings. *Adm £1.50 Chd free. Suns, Mons March 22, 23, May 10, 11; June 14, 15, (2-5); Sat, Sun Oct 24, 25 (12-4.30); Fri July 10 (6-8.30) with a glass of wine. Private visits welcome for 4 and more, please* **Tel 01243 551663**

Bignor Park, Pulborough (The Viscount & Viscountess Mersey) 5m from Petworth on West Burton rd. Nearest village Sutton (Sussex). 11 acres of trees, shrubs, flowers and magnificent views of the South Downs, from Chanctonbury Ring to Bignor Hill. Music in the temple. Bring a picnic. TEAS and plants in aid of British Red Cross. *Adm £2 Chd free. Easter Sun, Mon April 12, 13, Sat, Sun Aug 22, 23 (12-6)*

Bohunt Manor, Liphook see Hampshire

■ **Borde Hill Garden, Haywards Heath** &❀ 1½m N of Haywards Heath on Balcombe Rd. 200 acres of Sussex parkland with spring displays of rhododendrons, camellias, magnolias and azaleas. Summer planting incl new rose and herbaceous garden designed by Robin Williams. Autumn displays of crocuses and shrubs, woodland walks with nature trails, 120 champion trees, 2 coarse lakes and children's trout pond for fishing, picnic area and adventure playground. New Bressingham plant centre and shop. Garden tours. Open daily all year 10-6. *Adm £3 Chd £1.50 Family day £8, season £19. For NGS Thurs, April 30, Fri May 1* **Tel 01444 450326, Fax 440427 www.bordehill.co.uk.**

¶**Bosham, Hambrook and Nutbourne Gardens, Chichester** &✗ 4m W of Chichester on A259, past White Swan roundabout Berrymead. 1½m further W on A259 to Barleycorn public house. Jacaranda just beyond. Parking St Wilfred's Church 100yds on R in Broad Rd opp public house. Continue N in Broad Rd, 2nd L Priors Leaze Lane, 1st R Hambrook Hill South. Bay Tree Cottage 150yds on L. Parking adjacent. *Combined adm £2 Sun July 5 (2-6), Wed July 8 (2-5)*
¶**Jacaranda** (Barbara & Ian Corteen) In an area of ½ acre are shrubs, hanging baskets, containers, herbaceous borders and show quality vegetables all meticulously maintained by an enthusiast
¶**Bay Tree Cottage** ✗ (Nick & Pauline Hill) Small cottage garden divided into 'rooms' which are a riot of roses, climbers, shrubs, pots and mixed beds, A little gem
¶**4 Berrymead Cottages** &✗ (David & Betty Martin) Garden of 1 acre, 2 lawn areas, herbaceous borders, trees and shrubs. Old fruit trees give informality and character. TEA

Brickwall House, Northiam & (Frewen Charitable Trust) 8m NW of Rye on B2088. Tudor home of Frewen family since 1666. Featured in the filming of 'Cold Comfort Farm'. Gardens and walls built and laid out by Jane Frewen c1680; chess and knot gardens; arboretum. Cream TEAS (scones & cream only). *Adm £2 Chd £1 under 10 free. Sun July 26 (2-5). Parties welcome of 30 to 50, please* **Tel 01797 223329**

Buckhurst Park, Withyham ✗ (Earl & Countess De La Warr) On B2110 between Hartfield and Groombridge. Drive adjacent to Dorset Arms public house. Historic garden undergoing complete restoration. Repton park, large lake with woodland walk and ornamental waterfall and rocks created by James Pulham. Terraces, lily pond and pergolas designed by Lutyens and originally planted by Jekyll. Shetland pony stud. TEAS. *Adm £3 Chd £1.50 (ACNO to Sussex Historic Churches©). Sat July 11 (2-5.30). Private visits possible, please* **Tel 01892 770790 or 770220**

Bumble Cottage, West Chiltington ✗ (Mr & Mrs D Salisbury-Jones) 2m E of Pulborough, 2m N of Storrington. From Pulborough turn off A283 E of Pulborough into West Chiltington Rd then R into Monkmead Lane (signed Roundabout Hotel) follow yellow signs. From Storrington take B2139. L into Greenhurst Lane, R at T Junction 100yds fork L into Monkmead Lanel. Charming 'all seasons' garden of 1 acre created from a sandy slope. Wide variety of interesting trees, shrubs and plants combined with ponds all set off by very fine lawn. Featured on Grassroots TV programme. *Adm £1.50 Chd 25p. Sats, Suns July 18, 19, 25, 26 (2-6)*

■ **Cabbages & Kings, Hadlow Down** ✗❀ (Andrew & Ryl Nowell) Wilderness Farm. ½m S of A272 centre Hadlow Down. A former windswept farmyard transformed by designer Ryl Nowell into a magical haven rich with inspiration for planting and design. The garden opens to spectacular views of the High Weald and is now run organically by Joss Nowell and Nancy Saunders to demonstrate the practicalities of maintaining a beautiful organic garden. TEAS. *Adm £2.50 OAPs £2. Sat, Sun Bank Hols, Easter to Oct (10-6). For NGS Weds June 3, Aug 5, Sept 2 (2-6). Group visits welcome by appt, please* **Tel 01825 830552**

Casters Brook, Cocking &✗ (Mr & Mrs John Whitehorn) 3m S of Midhurst at Cocking PO on A286 take sharp turn E; garden is 100yds to right. Ponds, with islands, fountains, trout and a small bridge distinguish this 2-acre site, sloping past lawns and rose beds down to the ponds with a hugh gunnera under a massive plane tree. Near the house are a fig court and a herb garden, by the churchyard a secret garden and a shady walk. Dramatic sculptures by Philip Jackson on loan add the finishing touch. TEAS. *Adm £2 Chd free (ACNO to Cocking Church®). Suns June 28, July 5 (2-6). Private visits welcome, please* **Tel 01730 813537**

Cedar Tree Cottage, Washington ✗❀ (Mr & Mrs G Goatcher) Rock Rd. Turn W off A24 ¼m N. of Washington Roundabout. Park in 'Old Nursery' Car Park. Mixed borders with many unusual shrubs and perennials, leading into newly developing 5 acre arboretum with many rare subjects and also some fine mature trees and shrubs dating from early C20. Good views of S Downs. *Adm £2 Chd free. By appointment only, parties welcome,* **Tel 01903 892030**

Champs Hill, Coldwaltham க்&❀ (Mr & Mrs David Bowerman) S of Pulborough. on A29, turn R to Fittleworth; garden 400yds. 27 acres of acid-loving plants around sand pits and woodland. Superb views. Featured in The Garden Magazine Sept '97. TEAS. *Adm £2 Chd free. Suns, Weds March 15, 18, 22, 25, 29; May 3, 6, 10, 13, 17; Aug 2, 5, 9, 12, 16 Suns (2-6), Weds (11-4). Private visits welcome for parties of 10 and over, please* **Tel 01798 831868**

Chantry Green House, Steyning ❀❀ (Mr R S Forrow & Mrs J B McNeil) 5m N of Worthing, 10m NW of Brighton off A283. Turn into Church St from High St opp White Horse Inn. Garden 150yds down on LH-side. Parking on Fletchers Croft car park, entrance opp church. An interesting 1-acre garden, recently redesigned by Jack Grant White. Features incl a wall fountain, herbaceous borders and extensive shrub borders with a predominance of colourful evergreens providing interest throughout the year. There is also a small arboretum and rock and water garden. TEAS and plants in aid of NSPCC. *Adm £1.50 Chd 50p. Sat, Sun June 13, 14 (2-5)*

Chidmere House, Chidham க் (Thomas Baxendale Esq) 6m W of Chichester. A259 1m Bus: SD276/200 Chichester-Emsworth. Interesting garden; subject of article in 'Country Life' and other magazines; yew and hornbeam hedges; bulbs, and flowering shrubs bounded by large mere, now a private nature reserve. C16 house (not open). TEAS Suns only. *Adm £2 Chd free under 12 (ACNO to Chidham Parish Church®). Suns, Mons April 12, 13, May 24, 25 (2-6) Aug 30, 31 (2-7). Parties welcome, please* **Tel 01243 572287 or 573096**

Church Farm, Aldingbourne க்& (Mr & Mrs Jerome O'Hea) 4¼m E of Chichester. Take B2233 off A27. Turn R into Oving Rd. Entrance 250yds on L. 4 acres designed by John Brookes in 1980. Spring garden with massed bulbs. Shrubs and mixed borders. New walled garden, and field pond. Conservatory. TEAS. *Adm £1.50 Chd 50p. Sun April 19 (2-5)*

Clinton Lodge, Fletching க்&❀ (Mr & Mrs H Collum) 4m NW of Uckfield; from A272 turn N at Piltdown for Fletching, 1½m. 6-acre formal and romantic garden, overlooking parkland, with old roses, double herbaceous borders, yew hedges, pleached lime walks, copy of C17 scented herb garden, medieval-style potager, vine and rose allee, wild flower garden. Carolean and Georgian house (not open). Plant Stall on June 14, 15. TEAS. *Adm £3 Chd £2 (ACNO to Fletching Church Fabric Fund®). Sun June 14; Mon June 15, Weds June 17, 24, July 1 (2-6). Parties over 20 welcome, please* **Tel 01825 722952**

Coates Manor, Fittleworth ❀❀ (Mrs G H Thorp) ½m S of Fittleworth; turn off B2138 at signpost marked 'Coates'. 1 acre, mainly shrubs and foliage of special interest. Small walled garden with tender and scented

plants. Often featured in UK and foreign gardening magazines. Elizabethan house (not open) scheduled of historic interest. TEAS in aid of Children's Society *Adm £1.50 Chd 20p. Sun, Mon, Oct 18, 19 (11-5). Private visits by arrangement, please* **Tel 01798 865356**

Cobblers, Crowborough க்&❀ (Mr & Mrs Martin Furniss) Mount Pleasant, Jarvis Brook. A26, at Crowborough Cross take B2100 towards Crowborough Station. At 2nd Xrds turn into Tollwood Rd. 2-acre sloping site designed by present owners to display great range of herbaceous and shrub species. Famous water garden. Colour all season. 9 different, unique owner-made garden seats. Subject of many articles and TV programmes. *Adm £3.50 Chd £1 (incl home-made TEAS). Suns May 31, June 14, 28, July 12, 26, Aug 9, 23 (2.30-5.30). Groups welcome by appt, please* **Tel 01892 655969**

Combehurst, Frant ❀ (Mrs E E Roberts) 3m S of Tunbridge Wells off A267, 400yds S of B2099. 2½-acre beautifully laid out garden; shrubs, trees, plants. TEA. *Adm £2 Chd free. Private visits and small coach parties welcome by appt, April to Sept (2-5). Please* **Tel 01892 750367**

Cooke's House, West Burton க்& (Miss J B Courtauld) 5m SW of Pulborough. Turn off A29 at White Horse, Bury, ¾m. Old garden with views of the Downs, Elizabethan house (not open); varied interest, spring flowers, topiary, herbaceous borders, herbs. TEA. *Adm £1.50 Chd free under 14. Suns, Mons, Tues April 19, 20, 21, 26, 27, 28 (1-5). Private visits welcome, please* **Tel 01798 831353**

Cooksbridge, Fernhurst & (Mr & Mrs N Tonkin) On A286 between Haslemere and Midhurst, ¾m S of Fernhurst Xrds. 6 acres, and adjoining bluebell wood beside the R Lodd. This is a plantsman's garden for all seasons. Features incl the herbaceous border, vine and ornamental plant houses, lily pond and lake with waterfowl. TEAS. *Adm £2 Chd 50p 5 and under free (ACNO to Sussex Wildlife Trust®). Sun, Mon Aug 30, 31 (2-6). Private visits and groups welcome by appt, please* **Tel 01428 652212**

Cookscroft, Earnley க்❀ (Mr & Mrs John Williams) 6m S of Chichester. At end of Birdham Straight take L fork to E Wittering. 1m on, before sharp bend turn L into Bookers Lane. 2nd house on L. 5-acre garden started from fields 9yrs ago. Many trees grown from provenance seeds or liners. Collections of eucalyptus, birch, snake bark maples and unusual shrubs. 3 ponds with waterfalls and a Japanese garden. An interesting and developing garden, incl a woodland area. TEAS in aid of St Wilfrids Hospice. *Adm £1.50 Chd free. Sun, Mon May 24, 25 (2-6). Private visits welcome by appt, please* **Tel 01243 513671**

Coombland, Coneyhurst ❀❀ (Neville Lee Esq) In Billingshurst turn off A29 onto A272 to Haywards Heath approx 2m. In Coneyhurst, turn R for further ¾m. 5-acres undulating site, heavy clay. Old shrub roses, species roses and ramblers scrambling up ageing fruit trees; extensive plantings of hardy geraniums; interesting herbaceous borders; oak woodland and copse; large water area planted in iris and other water plants; water wheel. National collection hardy geraniums. TEAS on terrace. *Adm*

£1.50 Chd 50p (ACNO to NCCPG® May 30 only). Sats, Tues April 21, 25, May 30 June 13, 20, 27 (10-5) June 9, 16 (2-5), please **Tel 01403 741727**

Cowbeech Farm, Cowbeech ⚘⚘⚘ (Lady Shawcross) 4m NE of Hailsham. A271 to Amberstone, turn off N for Cowbeech. 5-acre garden with knot herb garden and water feature. Bog garden with many unusual plants, Japanese garden with bridge, moongate and waterfall - carp and koi carp. Beautiful colours in spring and autumn. Yellow and red borders. Farmhouse TEAS Suns only. *Adm £3.50 Chd £1.25. Suns May 31, Sept 13 (2-5), Mons June 1, Sept 14 (5-8) wine. Private visits welcome by appt for minimum of 10 May to Oct, please* **Tel 01323 832134**

Cowdray Park Gardens, Midhurst ⚘ (The Viscount Cowdray) S of A272. 1m E of Midhurst. Entrance by East Front. Avenue of Wellingtonias; rhododendrons, azaleas; sunken garden with large variety trees and shrubs, Lebanon cedar 300 yrs old; pleasure garden surrounded by ha-ha, new water garden. TEA. *Adm £2 Chd free. Sun May 17 (2-6)*

Crown House, Eridge ⚘⚘⚘ (Maj L Cave) 3m SW of Tunbridge Wells. A26 Tunbridge Wells-Crowborough rd (229, 729 bus route); in Eridge take Rotherfield turn S, then take 1st R, house 1st on L, short walk from bus stop. 1½ acres with pools; rose garden and rose walk; herbaceous border; herb garden. Full size croquet lawn. Prize winner in Sunday Express garden of the year competition. Plant and produce stalls. TEAS. *Adm £1.50 Chd under 14 free (ACNO to Multiple Sclerosis®). Sat, Sun July 11, 12 (2-6). Private visits welcome May to Oct, please* **Tel 01892 864389** *or* **864605**

▲**Denmans, Fontwell** ⚘⚘⚘ (Mr John Brookes) Chichester and Arundel 5m. Turn S on A27 at Denmans Lane, W of Fontwell Racecourse. Renowned gardens extravagantly planted for overall, all-year interest in form, colour and texture; areas of glass for tender species. TEAS. *Adm £2.80 OAPs £2.50 Chd £1.50 child rate 4-16yrs. For NGS Fris July 31, Sept 18 (9-5)* **Tel 01243 542808**

Doucegrove Farm, Northiam ⚘ (Mr P M Camp) 9m N Hastings, 9m W Rye. From Northiam take A28 S 1½m to Horns Cross ¼m S turn L at sign to Catholic Church, 100 yds turn L, on R. Park in church car park before gates to Private Rd. 2 acres of formal garden incl four ponds, two rose gardens and many interesting varieties of trees, shrubs and plants. *Adm £3 Chd £1. Thurs, Fri June 18, 19 (10-4)*

Down Place, South Harting ⚘⚘⚘ (Mr & Mrs D M Thistleton-Smith) 1m E of South Harting. B2124 to Chichester, turn L down unmarked lane below top of hill. This large hillside, chalk garden is surrounded by woodlands, with fine views of surrounding countryside. The garden sweeps down through terraced herbaceous, shrub and rose borders to a natural meadow containing many wild flowers incl several species of orchid. Woodland walks and interesting kitchen and cottage gardens. TEAS. *Adm £1.50 Chd 50p (ACNO to Harting Parish Church®). Fri, Sat, Sun June 19, 20, 21 (2-6). Private visits welcome by appt, April-July* **Tel 01730 825374**

Duckyls, Sharpthorne ⚘ (Lady Taylor) 4m SW of E Grinstead. 6m E of Crawley. At Turners Hill take B2028 S 1m fork left to W Hoathly, turn L signed Gravetye Manor. Interesting old 12-acre woodland garden. Partly suitable for wheelchairs. TEAS. *Adm £3 Chd £1 (ACNO to Elizabeth Fitzroy Homes®). Sat, Sun, Mon May 2, 3, 4 (12-6). Parties welcome by appt, please* **Fax/Tel 01342 811038**

Duckyls Holt, West Hoathly ⚘ (Mr & Mrs Kenneth Hill) 4m SW of E Grinstead. 6m E of Crawley. At Turners Hill take B2028 S 1m fork left to W Hoathly, 2m on R. A surprisingly intimate cottage garden of about 2 acres on many different levels. Small herb garden, formal and informal plantings. Herbaceous borders and rose border. Heated swimming pool, which visitors are welcome to use. TEAS. *Adm £1.50 Chd free. Thurs May 28, July 9 (11-5.30) Also open within walking distance* **The Priest House**

¶**Dyke Road Avenue Gardens, Brighton** Approaching from A27T Brighton bypass S into Brighton at Devil's Dyke roundabout junction into Dyke Road Avenue. *Combined adm £1.50 Chd 50p. Sun June 14 (2-6)*

> **93 Wayland Avenue** ⚘⚘⚘ (Brian & Sylvia Jackson) L into Tongdean Lane, R into Wayland Ave. Creatively designed small garden, with emphasis on dense, informal planting incl unusual plants, shrubs, grasses, clematis, tender perennials and climbers. Focal points provided by rose arch and water features in rockery and bog garden areas. Designed to encourage wildlife. *Private visits by appt, welcome mid May to mid Aug. Please* **Tel 01273 501027.** *Also group visits with* **64 Old Shoreham Rd**

> ¶**Appledore, Hove** ⚘ (Tony & Miriam Book) 50 Hill Drive. R off Dyke Rd Ave into Hill Brow. L into Hill Drive. Sloping family garden. Part carefully tended by plant-loving parents, part flattened by football-loving children. Colourful drought resistant bank. Sunny tea terrace. TEAS. *(ACNO Family Holiday Assn®)*

Ebbsworth, Nutbourne ⚘⚘⚘ (Mrs F Lambert) nr Pulborough. Take A283 E from junction with A29 (Swan Corner) 2m with 2 L forks signposted Nutbourne. Pass Rising Sun and follow signs to garden. Charming, well-planted, owner maintained cottage garden, surrounding old cottage. Roses and lilies, together with herbaceous borders. Man-made stream and ponds planted with water plants. TEAS. *Adm £2 Chd free. Thurs, Fri July 23, 24 (2-5)*

¶**Fishers Farm, Etchingham** ⚘⚘⚘ (Mr & Mrs David Pettman) Take A265 to Etchingham from A21 at Hurst Green. 1st turning L after level crossing. After ½m turn R into Fontridge Lane, continue for 1m. 3 acres incl walled garden, pond with golden orfe, formal rose garden and mixed borders with azaleas, acers and old-fashioned shrub roses. TEAS. *Adm £2 Chd free. Sun May 24 (11-5)*

▲**Fitzhall, Midhurst** ⚘⚘⚘ (Mr & Mrs G F Bridger) Iping, 3m W of Midhurst. 1m off A272, signposted Harting Elsted. 9 acres; incl herb garden; herbaceous and shrub borders; vegetable garden, woodland walks. Farm adjoining. House (not open) originally built 1550. TEAS. *Adm £2 Chd £1. For NGS Suns May 31, July 19 (2-6). Private visits welcome, please* **Tel 01730 813634**

¶**Five Oaks Cottage, West Burton** ✿❀ (Jean & Steve Jackman) From the A29 4m S of Pulborough, take the B2138 signposted to Fittleworth and Petworth. Turn immediately L and L again at the T-junction. 1m on the L. An artist's garden where wild and cultivated flowers intermingle. Disorderly by design to attract insects and birds. May and June opening for foliage contrasts; July, August and September for seedheads. Always lots of specials in pots. Not suitable for children due to small pond and many poisonous plants. *Adm £1.50 Chd free. Sats, Suns May 30, 31, June 27, 28 (2-5); Fridays July 10, Aug 7 (5-8); Suns July 12, Aug 9 (2-5); Sats, Suns Sept 26, 27 (2-5)*

Framfield Gardens, Uckfield ☖ From Uckfield, take B2102 E to Framfield or approaching from A22 leave at Peartree junction S end of bypass. *Combined adm £2 Chd 25p. Sun June 21 (11-6)*

  Hailwell House, Uckfield (Lady Elizabeth Baxendale) On B2102 1m E of Uckfield or from Framfield ½m N of Church. 3-acre garden with shrub borders, mixed borders, roses and lakeside walk

  Hobbs Barton (Mr & Mrs Jeremy Clark) At T-junction by church in Framfield, continue ⅓m along The Street, L into Gatehouse Lane for ½m, L up unsigned road. 2½ acres of informal gardens with undulating lawns, mixed borders, shrubberies, roses etc; specimen trees, several water features; part walled vegetable and fruit garden. Ploughmans and TEAS in C17 barn room

Frith Hill, Northchapel ✿❀ (Mr & Mrs Peter Warne) 7m N of Petworth on A283 turn E in centre of Northchapel into Pipers Lane. ¾m on L. 1-acre garden, comprising walled gardens with herbaceous borders; shrubbery; pond; old-fashioned rose garden and arbour. Herb garden leading to white garden with gazebo. Outstanding views of Sussex Weald. *Adm £2.50 eve with glass of wine, £1.50 afternoon teas Chd free (ACNO to 1st Northchapel Scouts®). Sun June 14 (5-8), Thurs June 18 (2-6), Sat June 20 (5-8)*

Frith Lodge, Northchapel (Mr & Mrs Geoffrey Cridland) 7m N of Petworth on A283 turn E in centre of Northchapel into Pipers Lane ¾m into bridleway. 1-acre cottage style garden created around pair of Victorian gamekeepers cottages. Undulating ground with spectacular roses, informal planting with paved and hedged areas; outstanding views of Sussex Weald. Featured on Sky TV, finalist Daily Mail Garden Competition, Period Living, '97. *Adm £2 Chd £1. Sun June 14 (5-8) Thurs June 18 (2-6), Sat June 20 (5-8). Parties welcome by appt only, please write to Frith Lodge, Northchapel, W Sussex, GU28 9JE*

The Garden in Mind, Stansted Park ✿ (Mr & Mrs Ivan Hicks - Stansted Park Foundation) The Lower Walled Garden. Stansted Park, Rowlands Castle. Follow brown signs. Stansted is 3m NE of Havant, 7m W of Chichester. A surreal symbolic ½-acre walled garden. Extravagant planting combined with sculpture, assemblage, found objects, mirrors and chance encounters. Wide range of plants; sequioa to sempervivum, marigolds to melianthus grasses, foliage plants, topiary and tree sculpture. Featured in numerous publications, Garden Party, TV and C4. Come with an open mind. *Adm £2 Chd donation. Suns July 5, Sept 27 (2-6)*

Gaywood Farm, nr Pulborough ☖✿ (Mrs Anthony Charles) 3m S of Billingshurst turn L off A29 into Gay Street Lane. After railway bridge at 2nd junction fork L and at T junction turn L signed 'no through rd'. 3-acre garden, surrounding ancient farm house, built between C14 and C18. Fine weeping Ash, black Mulberry, Irish yews and extravagantly planted borders with interesting plant assoc. Large pond surrounded by good planting. TEAS. *Adm £2 Chd free. Sats, Suns May 3, 30, 31, July 4, 5 (2-5). Private visits welcome groups only, please* Tel **01798 812223**

Ghyll Farm, Sweethaws Lane ❀ (Mr & Mrs I Ball) Crowborough. 1m S of Crowborough centre on A26. L into Sheep Plain Lane immed R Sweethaws Lane ½m. 'The Permissive Garden' planted by the late Lady Pearce. 1-acre, azaleas, camellias, woodland bluebell walk; spectacular views. TEAS. *Adm £2 Chd 50p. Suns April 19, May 3, 17, 31 (2-5.30) Private visits welcome, please* Tel **01892 655505** *for appt*

72 Grand Ave, Worthing ✿❀ (Mr & Mrs D E Marshall) 10m W of Brighton, 6m E of Littlehampton, off A259. From Brighton follow signs for Worthing town centre then A259 at traffic lights (Richmond Rd). Continue for approx 1m to traffic lights/junction with Heene Rd. Carry straight on and take 5th turning on L for Grand Avenue. Medium-size part walled town garden. Begun in 1976. Cottage garden feel, closely planted with old roses, clematis, perennials, decorative foliage trees and shrubs, pots and statuary. Competition winner Hillier Garden Centres 1997. *Adm £1.50 Chd free. Suns June 28, July 26 (2-6). Weds July 15 (5.30-8)*

¶**Grandturzel Farm, Etchingham** ☖✿ (Sir Frank & Lady Sanderson) S off A265 at Etchingham towards Robertsbridge. R at top of next hill (approx ½m) into Fontridge Lane. 1½m on R. Pretty farmhouse and cottage gardens with informal mixed beds. Some newly established, and surrounded by pasture land grazed by horses and sheep. Walks down to the River Dudwell. The resident bassets and labradors would be delighted to escort. TEAS. *Adm £2 Chd under 16 free (ACNO St Bartholomew's, Burwash). Wed, Thur July 8, 9 (2-6)*

The Grange, Fittleworth ☖✿ (Mr & Mrs W M Caldwell) A283 midway Petworth-Pulborough; in Fittleworth turn S onto B2138 then turn W at Swan. Car parking available. 3-acre garden sloping to the R Rother. Spring flowering shrubs, specimen trees, herbaceous borders; pond and stream. Walled garden with old roses and clematis; small formal vegetable and cutting garden. TEAS in aid of St Wilfrid's Hospice, Chichester. *Adm £1.50 Chd free. Sun June 14 (2-6)*

● **Great Dixter, Northiam** ✿❀ (Christopher Lloyd) ½m N of Northiam, off A28 8m NW of Rye. For bus information call 01797 223053. A garden with many features topiary, meadow plantings, mixed borders and exotic garden. Many exciting and constantly changing uses of annuals and bedding plants in enclosed spaces around late C15 mediaeval manor house open (2-5). *Adm house & gardens £4 Chd £1 gardens only £3 Chd 50p. April 1 to Oct 25 daily except Mons but open on Bank Hols (2-5)*

Hailsham Grange, Hailsham &♠♣ (Noel Thompson Esq) Turn off Hailsham High St into Vicarage Rd, park in public car park. Formal garden designed and planted since 1988 in grounds of former C17 Vicarage (not open). A series of garden areas representing a modern interpretation of C18 formality; Gothic summerhouse; pleached hedges; herbaceous borders; romantic planting in separate garden compartments. Featured in Country Living and Grass Roots. Teas in adjacent church in aid of The Hailsham Church Clock Restoration Fund. *Adm £1.50 Chd free. Suns June 7, July 5 (2-5.30)*

Hammerwood House, Iping &♣ (The Hon Mrs J Lakin) 1m N of A272 Midhurst to Petersfield Rd. Approx 3m W of Midhurst. Well signposted. Large informal garden; fine trees, rhododendrons, azaleas, acers, cornus, magnolias; wild garden (¼m away), bluebells, stream. TEAS. *Adm £2 Chd free (ACNO to King Edward VII Hospital, Midhurst®). Suns May 10, 17 (2-5.30)*

¶The Hawthorn, Lower Beeding &♠♣ (Ian & Elizabeth Gregory) 4m S of Horsham on the A281 turn L in Lower Beeding into Sandygate Lane, (B2115 signposted Crawley/London/Gatwick) at Cisswood House Hotel. 1½ acres planted since 1990 by the owners from a larger paddock to provide all-yr-round interest. Interesting plants incl trees and shrubs, perennials and spring bulbs. The garden has various areas based on colour themes or specific plants and there are woodland and winter areas, pond and bog garden, an herbaceous bed, fruit and vegetables and a newly completed modern knot garden. TEAS. *Adm £1.50 Chd free. Wed April 8 (2-5); Sun April 12 (1-5); Sun Sept 6 (2-5)*

■ High Beeches Gardens, Handcross ♠ (High Beeches Gardens Conservation Trust) Situated on B2110 1m E of A23 at Handcross. 20-acres of enchanting landscaped woodland and water gardens; spring daffodils; bluebell and azalea walks; many rare and beautiful plants; wild flower meadows, glorious autumn colours. Picnic area. Car park. *Daily April, May, June, Sept, Oct (1-5) closed on Weds. In July & Aug Mons & Tues only. TEA. Adm £3.50 Acc chd free (ACNO to St Mary's Church, Slaugham®). For NGS Suns April 5, Sept 6 (1-5). Also by appt for organised groups at any time, please* **Tel 01444 400589**

▲Highdown, Goring-by-Sea &♠ (Worthing Borough Council) Littlehampton Rd (A259), 3m W of Worthing. Station: Goring-by-Sea, 1m. Famous garden created by Sir F Stern situated in chalk pit and downland area containing a wide collection of plants. Spring bulbs, paeonies, shrubs and trees. Many plants were raised from seed brought from China by great collectors like Wilson, Farrer and Kingdon-Ward. *Collecting box. For NGS Mons May 4, 25, Aug 31 (10-8). Parties by appt, please* **Tel 01903 239999 ext 2544**

1 & 6 Holbrook Park, &♠♣ (Mr & Mrs Paul Leithsmith & John & Louise Pollard) From Horsham take A24 Dorking direction. At roundabout take A264 signposted Gatwick. Follow dual carriageway then 2nd lane on L marked Old Holbrook. 10 acres Victorian parkland garden with fine trees, azaleas and rhododendrons. Informal

areas provide colour and interest throughout the year, shrub and herbaceous walk, two ponds, conservatory, Pergola, recently planted Bamboo walk. Coffee, Ploughman's Lunches, TEAS. *Adm £2 Chd free. Sun May 17 (11-5). No 6 only Plantswoman and designer's garden, private visits welcome Thurs April - end October (1-4) please* **Tel 01403 252491**

Houghton Farm, Arundel ♠♣ (Mr & Mrs Michael Lock) Turn E off A29 at top of Bury Hill onto B2139 or W from Storrington onto B2139 to Houghton. 1-acre garden with wide variety of shrubs and plants, interesting corners and beautiful views. Tea Houghton Bridge Tea Gardens. *Adm £1.50 Chd free. Weds April 22, May 20, June 24, July 22 (2-5)*

Hurst Mill, Hurst ♠ 2m SE of Petersfield on B2146 midway between Petersfield and S Harting. 8-acre garden on many levels in lovely position overlooking 4-acre lake in wooded valley with wildfowl. Waterfall and Japanese water garden beside historic mill. Bog garden; large rock garden with orientally inspired plantings; acers, camellias, rhododendrons, azaleas, magnolias, hydrangeas and ferns; shrubs and climbing roses; forest and ornamental trees. TEAS. *Adm £1.50 Chd free. Sun April 19 (2-5)*

Hurston Place, Pulborough (Mrs David Bigham) Off the A283 between Pulborough and Storrington approx 3m. From Pulborough going towards Storrington at 2 cottages turn L. Straight down lane, over small bridge round to R and garden on L behind mature yew hedge. A garden divided into 2 parts: One a walled, semi formal garden with boxed edged beds, vegetables and borders. Two herbaceous wall beds, planted mainly in the cottage garden style. Orchard and wild part of garden has good daffodils and narcissi in April. TEAS in aid of Parham Church. *Adm 1.50 Chd 50p. Suns May 24, June 14, Mon June 15 (2-6)*

Ketches, Newick &♣ (David Manwaring Robertson Esq) 5m W of Uckfield on A272. Take Barcombe Rd S out of Newick, house is on right opp turning to Newick Church. 3 acres; lovely old-fashioned roses; specimen trees; shrub and herbaceous borders. TEAS. *Adm £2 Chd under 12 free. Sun June 21 (2-6). Parties welcome by appt, mid May to mid July, please* **Tel 01825 722679**

King Edward VII Hospital, Midhurst & 3m NW of Midhurst. Hospital built early this century, stands in grounds of 152 acres elevated position of great natural beauty; extensive views across Downs. Gardens by Gertrude Jekyll. Aspect over gardens and pine woods little changed. TEAS. *Collecting box. Sat April 18 (10-4)*

King John's Lodge, Etchingham &♠♣ (Mr & Mrs R A Cunningham) Burwash to Etchingham on the A265 turn L before Etchingham Church into Church Lane which leads into Sheepstreet Lane after ½m. L after 1m. 3-acre romantic garden surrounding a listed house. Formal garden with water features, wild garden, rose walk, large herbaceous borders, old shrub roses and secret garden. Garden statuary for sale. TEAS. *Adm £2 Chd free. Sat June 6 (2-6), Sun June 7 (11-6). Also private visits welcome, please* **Tel 01580 819232**

¶Kings Hill House, Hurst Green ✻❀ (Mr & Mrs M Marceau) Take A229 signposted Hawkhurst E off A21 (Coopers Corner). ⅓m R into Merriments Lane. A mature garden of approx 4 acres set in 25 acres of rolling countryside on the border of East Sussex and Kent. Originally laid out in 1930 this nicely balanced garden features roses, herbaceous borders, rhododendrons, herb garden and pond. There are additional walks; avenue of specimen trees and old woodland copse. TEAS. *Adm £2 Chd free (ACNO Hawkhurst Cottage Hospital League of Friends®). Sun July 19 (2-5.30)*

Kingston Gardens, nr Lewes ❀ 2½m SW of Lewes. Turn off A27 signposted Kingston at roundabout; at 30 mph sign turn R. Home-made TEAS **Nightingales.** *Combined adm (payable at* **Nightingales** *only) £2 Chd free. Sun June 7 (2-6)*

Nightingales (Geoff & Jean Hudson) The Avenue. Informal sloping ¾-acre garden for all-year interest; wide range of plants incl shrub roses, hardy geraniums, perennials, ground cover. Mediterranean plants, conservatory. Childrens' play area. Short steep walk or drive, parking limited, to:-

The White House (John & Sheila Maynard Smith) Kingston Ridge. ½-acre garden on a chalk ridge. Shrubs, roses, herbaceous borders, alpines, greenhouse. Unusual plants

Knabbs's Farmhouse, Fletching ♿❀ (Mrs W G Graham) 4m NW of Uckfield; from A272 turn N at Piltdown for Fletching, 1 ½m. Garden at N end of village and farm. ½-acre informal garden; mixed beds and borders; shrubs, roses, perennials, foliage plants. Good views over ha-ha. Teas at Clinton Lodge. *Adm £1.50 Chd 20p. Sun, Mon June 14, 15 (2-6)*

Latchetts, Danehill ✻❀ (Laurence & Rebeka Hardy) 5m NE Haywards Heath. SW off A275 into Freshfield Lane. 1m on R. Parking in mown field. 3-4 acre colourful, well maintained country garden still being developed bordering fields and woods, overlooking lake. NEW water garden. Terraces, pergolas, lawns, shrubs, mixed borders, cutting and vegetable garden. 'Something interesting round every corner'. 'Well worth visiting'. 'We'll be back next year'. Cream TEAS. *Adm £2 Chd 50p. Fri, Sat Aug 14, 15 (2-5.30)*

Legsheath Farm, nr Forest Row ♿❀ (Mr & Mrs Michael Neal) Legsheath Lane. 2m W of Forest Row, 1m S of Weirwood Reservoir. Panoramic views over reservoir. Exciting 10-acre garden with woodland walks, water gardens and formal borders. Of particular interest, clumps of wild orchids, a fine davidia, acers, eucryphia and rhododendrons. TEAS. *Adm £2 Chd free. Sun May 17 (2-6)*

Lilac Cottage, Duncton ✻❀ (Mrs G A Hawkins) Willet Close. 3m S of Petworth on the W side of A285 opp entrance to Burton Park. Park in Close. ¼-acre village garden on several levels with shrubs, small trees and approx 100 varieties of shrub and climbing roses and herb garden. TEAS. *Adm £1. Wed, Sat, Sun June 10, 13, 14 (2-6). Private visits welcome, please* **Tel 01798 343006**

Little Dene, Chelwood Gate ✻❀ (Prof & Mrs D Anderson) 8m S of East Grinstead. Take A275 off A22 at Wych Cross, then 1st L and 2nd R. Plantsman's garden yr-round interest. Many unusual shrubs and climbers, over 100 clematis, raised alpine bed. Wheelchairs if dry. *Adm £1.50. Weds, Thurs April 22, 23 May 13, 14 June 10, 11 July 22, 23 Aug 26, 27 (11-4.30). Also evening visits. Private visits and parties welcome, please* **Tel 01825 740657**

Little Hutchings, Etchingham ♿✻❀ (Mr P Hayes) Fontridge Lane. [TQ 708248.] Take A265 to Etchingham from A21 at Hurst Green. 1st turning L after level crossing. R after ½m. Colourful 1½-acre old-fashioned cottage garden laid out over 22 years. At least 300 different roses, over 100 metres of tightly packed herbaceous borders full of many different perennials. Large collection of clematis. Shrubberies containing specimen trees and shrubs. Kitchen garden. TEAS. *Adm £2.20 Chd free. Sun June 7 (11-5). Also group visits by appt, please* **Tel 01580 819374 (evenings)**

Little Thakeham, Storrington ✻❀ (Mr & Mrs T Ractliff) From Storrington take B2139 to Thakeham. After 1m turn R into Merrywood Lane and garden is 400yds on L. 4-acre garden with paved walks, rose pergola, flowering shrubs, specimen trees, herbaceous borders and carpets of daffodils in spring. The garden laid out to the basic design of Sir Edward Lutyens in 1902 and planted by his client Ernest Blackburn. No toilet fac. House closed to public. Partially suitable for wheelchairs. TEAS. *Adm £2 Chd £1. Mons, Tues April 6, 7, June 8, 9 (2-5)*

The Lodge Garden, Westfield ✻❀ (Sandra Worley & Danny Butler) Between Westfield & Sedlescombe. From Hastings take A28 Ashford Rd to Westfield Village. Just past car showroom turn L into Cottage Lane past post office approx 2m on L adjacent to Westfield Place. Redesigned over the last 5 yrs into a plantsman's cottage style garden with pond, arches, gazebo and 1860 working hand pump. Boasting a wide range of unusual herbaceous plants and shrubs completely surrounded by deciduous woodland. TEAS. *Adm £1.50. Nursery open Wed to Sun. For NGS Suns, Mons July 5, 6, Sept 6, 7 (10.30-5) Parties welcome by appt, please* **Tel 01424 870186**

Long House, Cowfold ❀ (Mr & Mrs V A Gordon Tregear) 1m N of A272, Cowfold-Bolney rd; 1st turning L after Cowfold. Fine walled gardens and ponds (4½ acres) with further expansion into fields and woodland with restored and new ponds, new broadwalk. New structures and courtyards designed in 1988 by Tom Hancock. Beautiful house dating from early C16 (not open). TEAS. *Adm £2 Chd free (ACNO to British Diabetic Assoc®). Sat June 27 (11-5)*

Malt House, Chithurst ❀ (Mr & Mrs Graham Ferguson) Rogate. From A272, 3½m W of Midhurst turn N signposted Chithurst then 1½m; or at Liphook turn off A3 onto old A3 for 2m before turning L to Milland, then follow signs to Chithurst for 1½m. 5 acres; flowering shrubs incl exceptional rhododendrons and azaleas, leading to 50 acres of lovely woodland walks. TEA. *Adm £2 Chd 50p (ACNO to Friends of King Edward VII Hospital Midhurst®). Suns May 3, 10, Mon May 4 (2-6); also private visits welcome for parties or plant sales, please* **Tel 01730 821433**

The Manor of Dean, Tillington ⚘❀ (Miss S M Mitford) 2m W of Petworth. Turn off A272 N at NGS sign. Flowers, shrubs, specimen trees, bulbs in all seasons. 2 pigmy goats, Vietnamese pigs, tame lambs. House (not open) 1400-1613. TEA 50p. *Adm £1 Chd over 5 50p. Sats, Suns, Mons March 28, 29, 30, April 18, 19, 20, May 16, 17, 18, June 20, 21, 22, July 11, 12, 13, Aug 15, 16, 17, Sept 12, 13, 14, Oct 3, 4, 5 (2-6). Private visits welcome, please* Tel 01798 861247

Manvilles Field, Fittleworth ⚘❀❀ (Mrs P J Aschan & Mrs J M Wilson) 2m W of Pulborough take A283 to Fittleworth, turn R on sharp L-hand bend. 2 acres of garden with orchard, many interesting shrubs, clematis, roses, other herbaceous plants. Beautiful views surrounding garden. TEAS. Wine June 13. *Adm £1.50 Chd free. Sat June 13 (6-8), Sun June 14 (2-6)*

Mayfield Cottage Gardens, Mayfield ⚘❀ 8m S of Tunbridge Wells. At N end of Mayfield turn off A267 at Marchants Garage into Fletching St signposted Witherenden. *Combined adm £2.50 incl glass of wine Chd 30p. Sun May 17 (12-2) and (5-7.30)*
> **Courtney Cottage** (Mr & Mrs Don Clark) opp Carpenters Arms ¼ acre steep sloping S facing garden with views. Range of interesting cottage garden plants and artefacts. Medieval house (not open)
> **The Oast** (Mr & Mrs Bob Henderson) Bottom of hill opp Rose and Crown. Charming ½-acre sloping garden with S views, field walk and vegetable garden

Mayfield Gardens ⚘ 8m S of Tunbridge Wells on A267. *Combined adm £2 Chd 20p. Sun June 28 (2-5.30)*
> ¶**Berkley Cottage** (Mrs B Walsh Atkins) Old Lane. N off Station Rd (near RC Church). ½-acre sloping garden, roses and herbaceous border
> **Maryhill** ⚘ (Mr & Mrs I A D Lyle) Knowle Park, off West Street (S of High St at Barclays Bank). Approx 1 acre formal garden with pergola
> **The Oast** ❀ As in Mayfield Cottage Gardens above
> **The Vicarage** St Dunstans Church (Fr Grant Holmes) High St. ¼-acre terraced. TEAS in aid of St Dunstan's Church

■ **Merriments Gardens, Hurst Green** ⚘ (Mark & Mandy Buchele & Mr David Weeks) Hawkhurst Rd. Situated between Hawkhurst & Hurst Green. 4-acre garden with richly planted mixed borders in country setting. Ponds, streams and rare plants give beautiful display all season. TEAS. *Adm £2.50 Chd £1. Open daily Easter Weekend to Oct. For NGS Suns April 12, May 17, June 21, July 19, Aug 23, Sept 6 (12-5). Parties welcome by appt, please* Tel 01580 860666

Moat Mill Farm, Mayfield ❀ (Mr & Mrs C Marshall) Newick Lane. 1m S on Mayfield-Broadoak Rd. 8 acres, formal rose garden, walled garden and woodland garden surrounded by farmland pasture. Picnic area (12.30-2). TEAS and ice creams. *Adm £1.50 Chd 50p. Sun June 21 (2-5.30)*

Moorlands, Friar's Gate, nr Crowborough ❀ (Dr & Mrs Steven Smith) 2m N of Crowborough. St Johns Rd to Friar's Gate. Or turn L off B2188 at Friar's Gate. 4 acres set in lush valley adjoining Ashdown Forest; water garden with ponds and streams; primulas, rhododendrons, azaleas, many unusual trees and shrubs. New river walk. TEAS. *Adm £2 Chd free. Every Wed April to Oct 1 (11-5). Suns May 24, June 7, July 19 (2-6). Private visits welcome, please* Tel 01892 652474

Mountfield Court, nr Robertsbridge ⚘❀ (Mr & Mrs Simon Fraser) 2m S of Robertsbridge. On A21 London-Hastings; ½m from Johns Cross. 2-3-acre wild garden; flowering shrubs, rhododendrons, azaleas and camellias; fine trees. Homemade TEAS. *Adm £2 Chd free (ACNO to All Saints Church Mountfield®). Sun, Mon May 17, 18 (2-6)*

Neptune House, Cutmill ⚘❀ (The Hon & Mrs Robin Borwick) From Chichester take A259 to Bosham roundabout, after ½m R into Newells Lane. 150yds on L. Garden extends to 6 acres incl a lake. The R Cut runs through the garden feeding 3 ponds. Planting is being increased, particularly around the lake which is home to various waterfowl. TEAS June 7 (2-6) only. *Adm £2 Chd £1; Sun June 7 (2-6) Evening party Adm £2.50 Chd £1; Sat Aug 1 (5-8) Wine and sausage barbeque or bring a picnic. Live classical music on both occasions. Private visits and coach tours welcome April 4 to Sept 30, please* Tel 01243 576900

New Barn, Egdean ⚘❀❀ (Mr & Mrs Adrian Tuck) 1m S of Petworth turn L off A285, at 2nd Xrds turn R into lane or 1m W of Fittleworth take L fork to Midhurst off A283. 200yds turn L. 2 acres, owner maintained all yr-round garden. Converted C18 barn in beautiful peaceful farmland setting. Large natural pond and stream, water irises, roses, shrubs and herbaceous; woodland area with swing. Seats in garden, picnic area, Autumn colour. Refreshments. *Adm £1.50 Chd 20p. Sun, Mon, Tues June 14, 15, 16; Bank Hol Mon Aug 31 (12-6). Private visits welcome all-yr minimum 4 visitors, please* Tel 01798 865502

New Grove, Petworth ⚘❀ (Mr & Mrs Robert de Pass) 1m S of Petworth turn L off A285 and take next L. Follow signs. From the N at Xrds in Petworth straight across into Middle Street then L into High Street follow signs. A mature garden of about 3 acres. Mainly composed of shrubs with all year interest incl a small parterre; magnolias, camellias, azaleas, cornuses, roses etc. lovely views to the South Downs. TEAS in aid of King Edward VII Hospital, Midhurst. *Adm £2 Chd free. Sat, Suns April 5, May 9, 10 (2-6)*

¶**Newhaven Botanic Gardens, Newhaven** ⚘❀❀ (Mr J Tate) On B2109 (Avis Rd) off A26 from Lewes or off A259 from S. Specialist gardens include ¼-acre glasshouse complex exhibiting worldwide flora collection, cacti/succulents, fernery, orangery, insectivorous plants, Australasian and S American flowering plants, tropical house, Italian garden, bromeliads and alpines. 2 acre leisure garden creatively landscaped with shrub borders, water features and Sussex modelled in miniature. Picnic facilities. TEAS. *Adm £2.99 OAP £2.85 Chd £2.25. Sat May 30 (10-5.30), Sun May 31 (9-6)*

Newtimber Place, Newtimber ⚘❀ (Andrew Clay Esq) 7m N of Brighton off A281 between Poynings and Pyecombe. Beautiful C17 moated house. Wild garden, roses, mixed borders and water plants. TEAS in aid of Newtimber Church. *Adm £1.50 Chd 50p. Suns April 19, Aug 30 (2-5.30)*

North Manor, Flansham &⚘❀ (Mr & Mrs Derek Bingley) Hoe Lane is a turning off the NW side of the A259 and is approx 2½m E of Bognor Regis and 4m W of Littlehampton. A small old English garden ¼-acre, with box and yew hedges, oriental poppies, herbaceous borders with special attention to blending of colours. TEAS. *Adm £1.50. Sun, Wed June 7, 10 (2-6)*

Northwood Farmhouse, Pulborough &⚘ (Mrs P Hill) 1m N of Pulborough on A29. turn NW into Blackgate Lane and follow lane for 2m then follow the signs. Cottage garden with bulbs, roses, pasture with wild flowers and pond all on Wealded clay surrounding Sussex farmhouse dating from 1420. TEA. *Adm £2 Chd £1. Tues, Wed April 14, 15, Mon, Tues June 22, 23 (2-5)*

Nyewood House, Nyewood &❀ (Mr & Mrs Timothy Woodall) From A272 at Rogate take rd signposted Nyewood, S for approx 1¼m. At 40 mph sign on outskirts of Nyewood, turn L signposted Trotton. Garden approx 500yds on R. 3-acre S facing garden recently renovated, colour planted borders, 100 varieties of roses, knot garden, pleaching, rose walk, water feature, and potager. TEAS. *Adm £1.50 Chd free. Weds May 6, June 10, July 15; Suns June 7, July 12 (2-5.30)*

▲**Nymans, Handcross** &⚘❀ (The National Trust) On B2114 at Handcross signposted off M23/A23 London-Brighton rd, SE of Handcross. Bus: 137 from Crawley & Haywards Heath [TQ265294]. One of the great gardens of the Sussex Weald. The walled garden with its fountain, the hidden sunken garden, rose garden, romantic ruins and woodland walks. A few rooms in Nymans House are open. Bring your own picnic and enjoy the garden. Tea rooms (11-5), shop (11-6). *Adm £5 Chd £2.50. For NGS Suns May 31 (11-6), July 12 (11-9)*

Offham House, Offham &❀ (Mr & Mrs H N A Goodman) 2m N of Lewes on A275. Cooksbridge station ½m. Fountains; flowering trees; double herbaceous border; long paeony bed. Queen Anne house (not open) 1676 with well-knapped flint facade. Recently planted herb garden. Featured in George Plumptre's Guide to 200 Gardens in Britain. Home-made TEAS. *Adm £2 Chd 25p (ACNO to Lewes Victoria Hospital®). Suns April 26, June 7 (2-6)*

The Old Chalk Pit, Hove &⚘❀ (Mr & Mrs Hugo Martin) 27 Old Shoreham Road, Hove, E Sussex BN3 6NR. A270. Unexpected, romantic oasis for chalk loving plants, old roses and climbers forming different informal areas incl white garden, ponds, wildlife and shady spots. TEA by arrangement for groups. *Adm £1.50 Chd 50p. Private and group visits, welcome* **Tel 01273 564807**

The Old Rectory, Newtimber & (Lambert & Rosalyn Coles) 7m N of Brighton off A281 between Poynings and Pyecombe. 2 acres with views of South Downs and Newtimber Church. Pond garden, fine tulip tree, perennial borders; combined kitchen and flower garden. *Adm £1.50 Chd 50p. Parties welcome by appt, please* **Tel 01273 857288**

64 Old Shoreham Road, Hove &❀ (Brian & Muriel Bailey) A270. Mainly walled garden 12.6 metres by 33.6 metres on flint and chalk. Alpine bed, arches, bog garden, conservatory, fruit bushes and trees, herb parterre, 2 ponds with fountain and waterfall, pergola, rose arbour, trellises, vegetables. Over 800 different varieties of plants - all named. 100 pots, many containing chalk hating plants. *Adm £1 or £2 with owner as guide Chd 50p. Private visits by appt welcome evenings and weekends, please* **Tel 01273 889247.** *Also group visits with* **93 Wayland Avenue, Dyke Road Avenue Gardens**

The Old Vicarage, Firle &❀ (Arabella & Charlie Bridge) 5m SE Lewes on A27 towards Eastbourne. Sign to Firle. 3½-acre garden with downland views. Walled garden with mixed vegetable and flower borders. Recent new pond area. Partially suited for wheelchairs. TEAS. *Adm £1.50 Chd free. Sun June 21 (2-5)*

Orchards, Rowfant ❀❀ (Penelope S Hellyer) From Turners Hill Xrds N on B2028 for 1½m, L into Wallage Lane, ½m turn R or from A264 turn S at Duke's Head roundabout for 2m. Woodland garden created by the late renowned horticulturist Arthur Hellyer and his wife Gay. 7-acre woodland garden, mature trees, herbaceous and mixed borders, orchards, bluebell wood, wild orchid meadow, heather/conifer garden, rhododendrons and camellias. Yr-round interest. Continuing restoration and replanting by their daughter. Owners nursery. TEA. *Adm £2 Acc chd free. Suns March 22 (2-4), April 12 (2-5), July 19 (2-6), Oct 25 (1-4), Mon May 25 (2-5).* **Tel 01342 718280**

Palmer's Lodge, West Chiltington Village ❀ (R Hodgson Esq) At Xrds in centre of West Chiltington Village opp Queens Head. 2m E of Pulborough 3m N Storrington. A charming plantsman's ½-acre garden with herbaceous and shrub borders. TEAS, Sunday only in aid of Motor Neurone. *Adm £1.50 Chd free. Sats, Suns July 11, 12, 18, 19, (2-6). Private visits welcome following written application (July only)*

▲**Parham Gardens, nr Pulborough** &⚘❀ 4m SE of Pulborough on A283 Pulborough-Storrington Rd. In the heart of an ancient deer park, below the South Downs. 4 acres of walled garden; 7 acres pleasure grounds with lake. 'Veronica's Maze' a brick and turf maze designed with the young visitor in mind. Picnic area. Suitable for wheelchairs on dry days. Cream TEAS. *Adm £3 Chd 50p. For NGS Wed, Thurs July 1, 2 (12-6)* **Tel 01903 744888**

▲ **Pashley Manor, Ticehurst** ❀❀ (Mr & Mrs J Sellick) 1½m SE Ticehurst Pashley Manor is a grade 1 Tudor house standing in a well timbered park with magnificent views across to Brightling Beacon. The 9 acres of formal garden, dating from the C18, were created in true English romantic style, have many ancient trees and fine shrubs. New plantings add interest and subtle colouring throughout the year. Water features, a classical temple, walled rose garden and new herbaceous borders. Refreshments in aid of Macmillan. *Adm £4.50 OAPs £4. For NGS Fri July 17 (11-5).* **Tel 01580 200692**

¶**The Patched Gloves, Broad Oak** campfire (Howard Norton) Nr Rye. On Chitcombe Road B2089, 4m E of A21, ¾m W of A28. A 3-acre garden largely created in last 5yrs filled with extensive collection of interesting plants in 4 contrasting areas. A Mediterranean garden; traditional garden; semi-wild pond garden and reclaimed field with Jekyll-style herbaceous border, roses and specimen trees. TEAS. *Adm £1.50 Chd free. Sun July 5 (2-6)*

Pembury, Clayton campfire (Nick & Jane Baker) Nr Hassocks. 6m N of Brighton. On B2112, 100yds from A273. Parking on village green; disabled parking only at garden. Owner maintained 2-acre garden on clay soil. Winding paths give the visitor a choice of walks through mixed borders, paved areas and woodland, with views to the South Downs and surrounding countryside. Jack and Jill windmills (Jill open pm), Saxon church with restored wall paintings and children's play area nearby. Light refreshments in village hall in aid of Clayton Church Fund. *Adm £2 Chd free. Sun May 31 (11-6)*

Penns in the Rocks, Groombridge campfire (Lord & Lady Gibson) 7m SW of Tunbridge Wells on Groombridge-Crowborough Rd just S of Plumeyfeather corner. Bus: MD 291 Tunbridge Wells-East Grinstead, alight Plumeyfeather corner, ¾m. Large wild garden with rocks; lake; C18 temple; old walled garden. House (not open) part C18. Dogs under control in park only (no shade in car park). TEAS. *Adm £2.50 Up to two chd 50p each, further chd free. Sun March 29, Mon Aug 31 (2.30-5.30). Parties welcome, please* **Tel 01892 864244**

¶**Perryhill, Hartfield** campfire (John & Elspeth Whitmore) Midway between East Grinstead and Tunbridge Wells. 1m N of Hartfield on B2026. Turn into unmade lane just S of Perryhill Nurseries. 1½ acres, set below C15 Hall house (not open), with stunning views onto Ashdown Forest. Mixed borders, formal rose garden, ornamental shrubs and trees, newly planted parterre, water garden, fruit and vegetables. TEAS. *Adm £2 Chd 50p. Suns June 28, Aug 16 (2-6)*

Pheasants Hatch, Piltdown campfire (Mrs G E Thubron) 3m NW of Uckfield on A272. 2 acres, rose gardens with ponds and fountains; beautiful herbaceous borders; foliage; wild garden; peacocks. TEAS. *Adm £1.50 Chd free. Sun, Mon June 28, 29 (2-6.30). Parties welcome June to July, please* **Tel 01825 722960**

▲**The Priest House, West Hoathly** campfire (Sussex Archaeological Society) 4m SW of East Grinstead, 6m E Crawley. At Turners Hill take B2028 S, 1m fork L to West Hoathly, 2m S turn R into North Lane. C15 timber-framed house with small cottage garden. Features large selection of herbs in formal garden plus mixed herbaceous borders with long established yew topiary, box hedges and espalier fruit trees. TEAS. *Adm £1 Chd free. For NGS Thurs May 28, July 9 (11-5.30). Also open within walking distance* **Duckyls Holt Tel 01342 810479**

Priesthawes Farm, Polegate campfire (Mr & Mrs A Wadman) On B2104 2½m. S Hailsham 4m N Eastbourne. 1m N of Stone Cross. C15 listed house of historical interest (not open) surrounded by 2½ acres. Walls used to full advantage with large clematis collection, climbers, old roses, herbaceous borders and pergola. Mainly replanted in the last 15 yrs. Lovely views over farmland. TEAS in aid of St Lukes Church. *Adm £2 Chd free (ACNO to St Wilfreds Hospice®). Suns May 31, July 5 (2-5). Private visits also welcome mid May to July, please* **Tel 01323 763228**

¶**Reynolds, Kitchen Court, Petworth** campfire (Michael & Alison Follis) NE exit from Town Car Park up Rosemary Lane. An elegant, yet profusely planted, quiet small town garden in the centre of Petworth. It has been meticulously designed for all yr interest with a large number of specimen plants. It has a number of features including a raised pond and an extensive collection of clematis. TEAS. *Adm £1.50 Chd free. Sat, Sun June 13, 14 (2-6)*

Ringmer Park, Ringmer campfire (Mr & Mrs Michael Bedford) Situated on A26 1½m NE of Lewes and 5m S of Uckfield. 6-acre garden with extensive rose gardens incl 100ft pergola and substantial mixed border featuring many old-fashioned roses. 100ft double herbaceous border. White garden, hot garden, incl dahlia display, Autumn border under development. Mature trees and lawns, kitchen and fruit garden. *Adm £2 Chd free. Wed, Fri July 8, Sept 18 (2-5.30)*

Rose Cottage, Hadlow Down campfire (Ken & Heather Mines) Uckfield. Off A272 6m NE of Uckfield & 4m NW of Heathfield. A new garden created from ½ acre of wilderness. Shoestring budget requires imaginative use of reclaimed materials to leave sufficient funds to satisfy a confirmed plantaholic's passion for interesting and unusual plants. Tiny woodland and gravel gardens, pond, mouldering carvings from a demolished Victorian church and organic vegetable garden. TEAS in aid of 'Breakthrough'. *Adm £1.50 Chd 50p. Suns May 24, June 28, Mon June 29 (2-6). Groups by appt* **Tel 01825 830314**

Rosemary Cottage, nr Rotherfield campfire (Mr & Mrs D R Coe) Bletchinglye Lane. From Mark Cross on the A267, 9m S of Tunbridge Wells, turn W on the B2100 towards Crowborough, after 1m turn L into Bletchinglye Lane signed as no through rd. 150yds on R. ⅓-acre informal garden with mixed borders, herbs, ponds and paved pathways. The garden is managed following organic principles and incl planting for beneficial insects and wildlife. Interesting vegetable garden based on 4 ft beds with extensive compost area. TEAS. *Adm £1 Chd 50p. Open by appt May to Sept, please* **Tel 01892 852584**

Round Oak, Wadhurst campfire (Mr & Mrs B J Mitchell) 6m SE Tunbridge Wells. At Lamberhurst take B2100 off A21. ⅓m after Wadhurst sign turn R at 30mph sign, L into Gloucester Rd, turn R, 200yds on R. 1-acre garden in the early yrs of restoration. Designed to provide all season interest. Wide variety of shrubs, roses and perennials with interesting features incl a secret garden, rockeries and pond. TEAS. Ploughmans lunches Mon only. *Adm £1.50 Chd free. Sun Aug 30 (2-5), Mon Aug 31 (10.30-4.30)*

Roundhill Cottage, East Dean campfire (Mr Jeremy Adams) Take A286 Chichester-Midhurst. At Singleton follow signs to Charlton/East Dean. In East Dean turn R at Hurdlemakers Inn and Roundhill is approx 100yds on R. 1-acre country garden of surprises set in tranquil fold of the South Downs, designed in 1980 by Judith Adams whose inspiration came from French impressionists. *Adm £1.50 Chd free. Sat, Sun May 30, 31 (2-6)*

Rye Gardens, Rye ☒ 3 gardens in the centre of Rye. Cars must be left in public car parks. TEAS at 11 High Street. *Combined adm £2.50 Chd free. Fri July 24 (12.30-5)*
    11 High Street (Mr & Mrs C Festing) One way street on RH-side next to Midland Bank. ⅓-acre old walled garden, many trees incl gingko by pond. Vinery and vine covered pergola
    Lamb House (The National Trust) West Street nr church. 1-acre walled garden; variety of herbaceous plants, shrubs, trees, herbs. Home of Henry James 1898-1916 and E F Benson 1918-1940
    The Old House (Rev'd & Mrs W Buxton) 45 The Mint; continuation of High Street. A modest-sized well stocked colourful cottage garden on different levels adjoining C15 cottage. *Private visits welcome, please* Tel 01797 223191

Rymans, Apuldram ☒ (Suzanna Gayford) Take Witterings Rd out of Chichester; at 1½m SW turn R signposted Apuldram; garden down rd on L. Walled and other gardens surrounding lovely C15 stone house (not open); bulbs, flowering shrubs, roses. New water feature. Sandwiches and drinks in aid of Leukemia Research Fund. *Adm £1.50 Chd 50p. Sats April 4, Sept 5 (12-4)*

▲St Mary's House, Bramber ☒☒ (Mr Peter Thorogood) Bramber. 10m NW of Brighton in Bramber Village off A283 or 1m E of Steyning. Medium-sized formal gardens with amusing topiary, large example of living-fossil Gingko tree and Magnolia Grandiflora; pools and fountains, ancient ivy-clad 'Monk's Walk', all surrounding listed Grade I C15 timber framed medieval house, once a monastic inn. New for 1998, The Secret Gardens. Rediscover the lost Victorian Walled and Pleasure Gardens, hidden for over half a century, rescued last year, now under restoration. TEAS. *Adm £2 Chd 50p. For NGS Fri, Sat Aug 7, 8 (2-5.30)* Tel 01903 816205

¶Sands, Horsham ☒☒ (Professor & Mrs R P Dales) 3½m NW of Horsham. From A24 enter Warnham and follow signposts to Northlands and Ockley. Country garden of approx 1 acre on Wealden clay, surrounding C15 farmhouse. Various areas from grassy orchard to pond, kitchen garden and charming herb garden are separated by hedges. Borders and beds contain mainly shrubs and herbaceous perennials, incl a collection of hardy geraniums. TEAS. *Adm £1.50 Chd free; Sun June 14 (2-6). £2.50 Chd free; to incl glass of wine, Tues June 30 (6-8.30)*

Selehurst, Lower Beeding ☒☒ (Mr & Mrs M Prideaux) 4½m S of Horsham on A281 opp Leonardslee. Woodland garden in romantic valley. Sham-Gothic tower on the skyline above a pebblework waterfall, chain of five ponds, further waterfalls, pretty bridge. Fine trees, tree-like rhododendrons, eucryphias, azaleas, camellias, stewartias. Formal features incl walled garden with borders semi-circular arbour of cytissus battandieri, 60' rose and laburnum tunnel underplanted with ferns, artichokes, grasses

and hostas. Newly planted box and herb parterre. Fine views of the South Downs. TEAS. *Adm £2 Chd free (ACNO to St. John's Church, Coolhurst®). Sun May 10 (1-5)*

Setters Green, Rowlands Castle see Hampshire

Sennicotts, nr Chichester ☒☒ (John Rank Esq) From Chichester take B2178 signed to Funtington for 2m. Entrance on R. Long drive ample parking near house. From Fishbourne turn N marked Roman Palace then straight on until T junction. Entrance opp. 6-acre mature garden with intriguing spaces, lawns, rhododendrons and azaleas. Large walled kitchen and cutting garden, greenhouses and orchard. *Adm £3 to incl glass of wine Chd free. Sat May 30 (5-8)*

▲Sheffield Park Garden, Uckfield ☒☒ (The National Trust) Midway between E Grinstead and Lewes, 5m NW of Uckfield; E of A275. The garden, with 4 lakes, was laid out by Capability Brown in C18, greatly modified early in the C20. Many rare trees, shrubs and fine waterlilies; the garden is beautiful at all times of year. TEAS Oak Hall (not NT). *Adm £4.20 Chd £2.10. For NGS Tues May 12, Oct 13 (11-6) last adm 5*

Sherburne House, Eartham ☒☒☒ (Mr & Mrs Angus Hewat) 6m NE of Chichester, approach from A27 Chichester-Arundel Rd or A285 Chichester-Petworth Rd, nr centre of village, 200yds S of church. Chalk garden of about 2 acres facing SW. Shrub and climbing roses; lime-tolerant shrubs; herbaceous, grey-leaved and foliage plants, pots; water feature; small herb garden, kitchen garden potager and conservatory. TEAS. *Adm £1.50 Chd 50p. Sun June 28 (2-6) or by appt in June* 01243 814261

Somerset Lodge, Petworth (Mr & Mrs R Harris) North St. On A283 and A272 100yds N of church. Parking in town car park. Charming ½-acre town garden with ponds and walled kitchen garden, small collection of old roses and wildflower garden. Cleverly landscaped on slope with beautiful views. TEAS in aid of Petworth Parish Church. *Adm £1.50 Chd 50p. Sats, Suns, Mon, Tues, Wed, Thurs, Fri June 6, 7, 8, 9, 10, 11, 12, 13, 14 (12-6). Parties by appt, please* Tel 01798 343842

South Harting Gardens 4m SE of Petersfield on B2146. Cream TEAS at Pyramids. *Combined adm £1.50 Chd 50p. Sat, Sun June 27, 28 (2-5.30)*
    Ivy House ☒ (Mr & Mrs David Summerhayes) At S end of village opp Harting Church on B2136. 1½-acre terraced village garden, sloping down to brook with orchard and paddock beyond, Specimen trees, shrubs and roses. Views to Harting Down
    The Old House (Captain & Mrs Duncan Knight) Next to the White Hart Inn. Small village walled garden. Herbaceous borders, pond, roses and delphiniums. Some unusual plants
    Pyramids ☒☒ (Mrs S J Morgan) 200yds on R up North Lane. ½-acre with mainly chalk loving plants; old-fashioned roses, rose arbour; pool; uniquely shaped old apple trees. Interesting modern house (designed 1965 by Stout & Lichfield) linked to garden by paved areas. Fine views

Spur Point, Kingsley Green &❀ (Mr & Mrs T D Bishop) Marley Heights. Plantsman's garden created by owners since 1970. 3 acres of S facing terraces containing rhododendrons, azaleas, roses, mixed borders and scree beds. Not suitable for children. *Adm £2. Private visits welcome May and June by individuals, and parties of no more than 20, please* **Tel 01428 643050**

▲**Standen, East Grinstead** ✄ (The National Trust) 1½m from East Grinstead. Signed from B2110 and A22 at Felbridge. Approx 12 acres of hillside garden, packed with surprises. Features include quarry and bamboo gardens and three summer houses. Lovely views over the Medway and Ashdown Forest. Partly suitable for wheelchairs. TEAS in aid of NT Enterprises. *Adm Garden £3 Chd £1.50. For NGS Sun May 17, Sat Sept 12 (12.30-6 Last adm 5pm)*

¶**Stone House Hotel, Rushlake Green** &✄❀ (Mr & Mrs Peter Dunn) 4m E of Heathfield. Take B2096 towards Battle. 4th R to Rushlake Green. At green, turn L keeping green on R. Entrance far L at Xrds. A Georgian and Tudor Manor House set in parkland owned by Roberts Dunn family since 1495. 5 acre garden consisting of 1728 walled kitchen garden with herb garden and newly established yew hedged fruit garden with apple walk. Rose garden with old-fashioned roses and fountain. 100' herbaceous hot border and smaller white, yellow and blue border. Garden renovated in last 3 yrs. Lakes. *Adm £2.50 Chd £1. Thurs May 14 (10-12.30 & 2-4.30)*

Stonehurst, Ardingly ❀ (Mr D R Strauss) 1m N of Ardingly. Entrance 800yds N of S of England showground, on B2028. 30-acre garden set in secluded woodland valley. Many interesting and unusual landscape features; chain of man made lakes and waterfalls; natural sandstone rock outcrops and a fine collection of trees and shrubs. TEAS. *Adm £2.50 Chd £1 (ACNO to Homelife®). Mon April 13, Suns April 26, May 10 (11-5)*

Three Oaks, West Broyle &✄ (Mr & Mrs J C A Mudford) From roundabout N of Chichester take B2178 (Funtington) rd NW for about 1½m. Turn L into Pine Grove and after 100yds R into West Way. Small cottage garden with unusual plants in beds and borders that just happened. Vegetable garden. TEAS. *Adm £1.50. Sun May 10, Tues May 12 (1.30-6)*

Tinkers Bridge Cottage, Ticehurst ❀ (Mrs Michael Landsberg) From B2099 1m W Ticehurst; turn N to Three Leg Cross for 1m; R after Bull Inn. House at bottom of hill. 12 acres attractively landscaped; stream garden nr the house leading to herbaceous borders, newly planted trees and shrubs, pond, wild flower meadow and woodland walk. *Adm £2 to incl TEA Chd 50p. Sun June 14 (2.30-5.30)*

Town Place, Freshfield &✄❀ (Mr & Mrs A C O McGrath) 3m E Haywards Heath. From A275 turn W at Sheffield Green into Ketches Lane for Lindfield. 1¾m on L. 3 acres with sunken rose garden, 150' herbaceous border, walled herb and shrub rose gardens, shrubbery, ancient hollow oak, orchard and spring-cabbage patch. C17 Sussex farmhouse (not open). TEAS. *Adm £2.50 Chd*

free (ACNO to St Peter & St James Hospice®). Thurs June 25, Suns June 21, July 5, 12 (2-6)

Trotton Old Rectory, nr Petersfield ✄❀ (Captain & Mrs John Pilley) 3m W of Midhurst on A272. This typical English garden with its rose beds designed by Hazel Le Rougetel, framed in box and yew, has 2 levels with beautiful and interesting trees and shrubs running down to a lake and the R Rother. Newly planted pleached limes with formal planting. Featured Meridian TV Aug '97. Plants for sale in the adjoining vegetable garden. *Adm £2 Chd free. Suns May 17, June 21 (2-6)*

Trotton Place, nr Rogate &✄ (Mr & Mrs N J F Cartwright) 3½m W of Midhurst on A272. Entrance next to church. Garden of over 4 acres surrounding C18 house (not open). Walled fruit and vegetable garden; C17 dovecote. Fine trees; mature borders with shrub roses; lake and woodland walk. TEAS in aid of Trotton Church PCC. *Adm £2 Chd free. Suns May 17, June 21 (2-5.30)*

▲**Uppark, South Harting** &✄ (The National Trust) 5m SE of Petersfield on B2146, 1½m S of S Harting. Fine late C17 house situated high on the South Downs with magnificent views towards the Solent. Reptonian garden replanned and replanted since major fire in 1989. Woodland walk. House open (1-5). **Gardener Guided Tours** hourly from 11.30. Post Fire Restoration Exhibition. Tearoom and shop open. *Collection for NGS Adm £2.50 Chd £1.25. Thurs June 11 (11.30-5.30)*

Wadhurst Gardens ✄❀ 6m SE of Tunbridge Wells. 2 gardens created by present owners. TEAS at Sunnymead. *Combined adm £2 Chd free. Sun, Mon July 19, 20 (2-5.30)*

 Sunnymead (Mr & Mrs D Goldsmith) On B2099 ¾m SE Wadhurst Station at junction of Tapsells Lane. 1¼-acre landscaped garden imaginatively designed for the sporting family, small kitchen garden
 Millstones (Mr H W Johnson) next door to Sunnymead. ½-acre plantsman's garden featuring an exceptionally wide range of shrubs and perennial plants

Wadhurst Park, Wadhurst ✄❀ (Dr & Mrs H Rausing) 6m SE of Tunbridge Wells. Turn R along Mayfield Lane off B2099 at NW end of Wadhurst. L by Best Beech public house, L at Riseden Rd. This magnificent garden was re-created on C19 site with restored conservatories and is situated within an 800-acre park, stocked with 7 species of deer. Trailer rides into park at 3 and 4pm. Partly suitable for wheelchairs. TEAS. *Adm £2 Chd 50p. Sun May 10 (2-5.30). Sorry no video or photography*

▲**Wakehurst Place, Ardingly** &✄ (National Trust & Royal Botanic Gardens, Kew) 5m N of Haywards Heath on B2028. National botanic garden noted for one of the finest collections of rare trees and flowering shrubs amidst exceptional natural beauty. Walled gardens, heath garden, Pinetum, scenic walks through steep wooded valley with lakes, attractive water courses and large bog garden. Guided tours 11.30 & 2.30 most weekends, also pre-booked tours. Administration **Tel 01444 894067.** Restaurant. *Adm £4.50 Concessions £3 Chd £2.50 under 5's free. For NGS Fri July 17 (10-7)*

Warren House, Crowborough ✿❀ (Mr & Mrs M J Hands) Warren Rd. From Crowborough Cross take A26 towards Uckfield. 4th turning on R. 1m down Warren Rd. Beware speed ramps. Beautiful house steeped in history with 9-acre garden and views over Ashdown Forest. Series of gardens old and new, displaying a wealth of azaleas, rhododendrons, impressive variety of trees and shrubs. Sweeping lawns framed by delightful walls and terraces, woodlands, ponds and ducks. Planted and maintained solely by owner. TEAS. *Adm £2 Chd free. Suns April 26, May 17, June 7, Aug 30, Mons May 4, 25 (2-5). Groups welcome by appt, please* **Tel 01892 663502**

¶**94 Wepham, Burpham** ❀ (S Atterton) 2m from A27 E of Arundel station. Past Warningcamp. Lane to the L goes to Burpham, carry straight on to No 94. Park in field, disabled spaces opp ⅓-acre garden. 'Typical cottage garden'. Roses round the door, hollyhocks, aquilegias, foxgloves, violas, pansies and poppies from seed collected around the world. Plants labelled. Home of Mervyn Peake in 1940. TEAS in aid of Village Hall and Church. *Adm £1 Chd free. Sat May 30 (2-6)*

●**West Dean Gardens** &✿❀ (Edward James Foundation) On A286, 5m N of Chichester. 35-acre historic garden in tranquil downland setting. 300ft long Harold Peto pergola, mixed and herbaceous borders, rustic summerhouses, water garden and specimen trees. Restored 2½-acre walled garden contains fruit collection, 13 Victorian glasshouses, apple store, large working kitchen garden, tool and mower collection. Circuit walk (2¼m) climbs through parkland to 45-acre St Roches Arboretum. *Adm £3.50 OAP £3 Chd £1.50. Open daily March 7 to Oct 25 (11-5). For NGS Wed June 11 (11-5)* **Tel 01243 818210**

Westerleigh, Wadhurst &✿ (Mr M R Toynbee) Mayfield Lane ⅔m on R on B2100 going SW to Mark Cross from junction with B2099. Opp main gate Bellerby's College. About 5 acres, lawns, herbaceous border and shrub borders. Kitchen garden, formal pool garden and beautiful views. TEAS. *Adm £2 Chd free. Sun July 5 (2-5.30), Mon July 6 (2-5)*

46 Westup Farm Cottages, Balcombe ✿❀ (Chris & Pat Cornwell) Midway Cuckfield and Crawley. 1¼m Balcombe Station off B2036. Telephone for further directions. Well stocked cottage garden, designed to provide yr-round interest in idyllic setting. *Adm £1 Chd free. Private visits incl parties welcome all yr, please* **Tel 01444 811891**

The White House, Burpham ✿ (Elizabeth Woodhouse) Turn off A27 Arundel-Worthing Rd ½m S of Arundel. Proceed through Wepham to Burpham for 2m. Charming garden planned and planted by practicing garden designer artist. Great attention to plant forms and colour associations. Small very 'wild' garden with pond, not suitable for children. *Adm £1.50 (ACNO to Arundel Cathedral Organ Fund®). Sat May 30 (2-6). Private visits welcome, please write for appt*

The White Magpie, Lamberhurst ❀ (Mr Ronald J Wootton) From Lamberhurst, on B2100 signposted Wadhurst 1m approx turn R (Hog Hole Lane) for ½m. A small

estate with some 5 acres of garden, surrounded by farmland, valley views, series of interlinking ponds, walled garden. All to the memory of Mrs J P Wootton. TEAS. *Adm £1.50 Chd free (ACNO to The Hodgkins Disease Association®). Sun May 3 (1-6)*

Whitehouse Cottage, Staplefield (Barry Gray Esq) Staplefield Lane. 5m NW of Haywards Heath. Garden is ⅓m. E of A23; and 2m S of Handcross. In Staplefield at Xrds by cricket pavilion take turning marked Staplefield Lane for 1m. 4-acre woodland garden with mixed shrubs, old roses; paths beside stream linked by ponds; interesting paved and planted areas around house. TEAS. *Adm £1.50 Chd 50p. Open most days, please telephone first, individuals or groups welcome* **Tel 01444 461229**

8 Wimblehurst Road, Horsham &✿❀ (Dr & Mrs S J Dean) ½m N of town centre. From A24 Horsham Bypass take B2237 Warnham Rd into Horsham. Turn L at 1st set of traffic lights. Please park in side rds. Disabled park in drive. ⅓-acre walled town garden with a backdrop of mature trees. A plantswoman's garden with deep herbaceous borders incorporating plants for year interest. Secluded areas. Brick terrace with many containers luxuriantly planted. Greenhouse vegetable and cut flower garden. TEAS in aid of The Church of St Mary The Virgin Restoration Appeal. *Adm £1.50 Chd free. Sun, Thurs July 5, Sept 17 (11-5). Private visits, small groups welcome by appt, please* **Tel 01403 268166**

Winchelsea Gardens, Rye ✿ S of Rye. TEAS in aid of local charity at Old Castle House. *Combined adm £2 Chd 75p. Sun June 20 (2-6)*

¶**Alards Plat** (Mrs Cynthia Feast) 1 High St. A paved cottage garden

¶**Little Plat** (Dr David Dewhirst) German St. A cottage garden

Nesbit (Mr & Mrs G Botterell) High St. Formal enclosed ½-acre garden, many and varied plants

Old Castle House (Mr & Mrs R Packard) Castle St. Walled garden with roses, varied trees and shrubs

Periteau House (Mr & Mrs Lawrence Youlten) High St. A walled garden

Tower Cottage (Dr & Mrs Ben Chishick) Barrack Square. A cottage garden with views

No 1 Trojans Plat (Mr Norman Turner) Back Lane. Grade 2 listed archway providing access to small garden of great variety

¶**Winchelsea Cottage** (Mr & Mrs Colin Spencer) High Street. A walled town garden of interest

Yew Tree Cottage, Crawley Down ❀ (Mrs K Hudson) 4m W of East Grinstead. 2½m E of M23 (J10). On B2028 N of Turners Hill. ¼-acre garden planted for yr round interest and easy management, new gravel gardens with grasses. Featured on BBC2 Gardeners World in 1997 with Gay Search. *Adm £1.50 OAPs £1 Chd free. Parties welcome May to Aug (10-6), please* **Tel 01342 714633**

The National Gardens Scheme is a charity which traces its origins back to 1927. Since then it has raised over £18 million for charitable purposes.

Warwickshire & part of West Midlands

Hon County Organiser:	Mrs D L Burbidge, Cedar House, Wasperton, Warwick CV35 8EB
Assistant Hon County Organiser:	Mrs C R King-Farlow, 8 Vicarage Road, Edgbaston, Birmingham B15 3EF
	Mrs Cynthia Orchard, Honington Glebe, Honington, Shipston-on-Stour Warwickshire CV36 5AA
	Mr P Pashley, 14 Mayfield Aveune, Stratford-on-Avon Warwickshire CV37 6XB
Hon County Treasurer:	Michael Pitts, Hickecroft, Mill Lane, Rowington, Warwickshire CV35 7DQ

DATES OF OPENING

Regular openings
For details see garden description

Arbury Hall, Nuneaton
89 Harts Green Road, Harborne
The Master's Garden, Lord Leycester
   Hospital, Warwick
The Mill Garden, Warwick
Ryton Organic Gardens

By appointment only
For telephone numbers and other details see garden descriptions. Private visits welcomed

Parham Lodge, Alveston
Woodpeckers, Bidford-on-Avon

March 28 Saturday
   Elm Close, Welford-on-Avon
March 29 Sunday
   Elm Close, Welford-on-Avon
March 30 Monday
   Elm Close, Welford-on-Avon
April 4 Saturday
   Elm Close, Welford-on-Avon
April 5 Sunday
   Elm Close, Welford-on-Avon
   Greenlands, Wellesbourne
April 6 Monday
   Elm Close, Welford-on-Avon
April 18 Saturday
   Baddesley Clinton
   Castle Bromwich Hall Garden
      Trust
April 19 Sunday
   Ilmington Manor, nr
      Shipston-on-Stour
   Ivy Lodge, Radway
   The Master's Garden, Lord
      Leycester Hospital, Warwick
   The Mill Garden, Warwick
   Moseley Gardens, Birmingham
   Parham Lodge, Alveston
   52 Tenbury Road, Kings Heath,
      Birmingham
April 26 Sunday
   The Hiller Garden & Dunnington
      Heath Farm, Alcester

Pereira Road Gardens,
   Birmingham
Wheelwright House, Long
   Compton
April 29 Wednesday
   89 Harts Green Road, Harborne
May 1 Friday
   Avon Cottage, Ashow, nr
      Kenilworth
May 4 Monday
   55 Elizabeth Road, Moseley
May 10 Sunday
   The Mill Garden, Warwick
May 13 Wednesday
   Arbury Hall, Nuneaton
   The Folly Lodge, Halford
May 17 Sunday
   Compton Scorpion Farm, nr
      Ilmington
   Ilmington Manor, nr
      Shipston-on-Stour
   Pear Tree Cottage, Ilmington
   52 Tenbury Road, Kings Heath,
      Birmingham
May 23 Saturday
   Elm Close, Welford-on-Avon
May 24 Sunday
   Ashover, 25 Burnett Road,
      Streetly
   Elm Close, Welford-on-Avon
   Hunningham Gardens
May 25 Monday
   Elm Close, Welford-on-Avon
   Hunningham Gardens
May 27 Wednesday
   89 Harts Green Road, Harborne
May 31 Sunday
   Barton House,
      Barton-on-the-Heath
   Maxstoke Castle, nr Coleshill
   172 Stonor Road, Hall Green
   52 Tenbury Road, Kings Heath,
      Birmingham
   Warwickshire Constabulary HQ
June 7 Sunday
   Avon Cottage, Ashow, nr
      Kenilworth
   Dorsington Gardens,
      Stratford-on-Avon
   Packington Hall, Meriden, nr
      Coventry

June 10 Wednesday
   The Folly Lodge, Halford
June 14 Sunday
   Idlicote Gardens
   Pereira Road Gardens,
      Birmingham
June 17 Wednesday
   52 Tenbury Road, Kings Heath,
      Birmingham (Also Evening)
June 20 Saturday
   Compton Scorpion Farm, nr
      Ilmington
   Hickecroft, Rowington
   Packwood House, nr Hockley
      Heath
June 21 Sunday
   Compton Scorpion Farm, nr
      Ilmington
   Foxgloves, Dunchurch, Rugby
   Hickecroft, Rowington
   Holywell Gardens, nr Claverdon
   Ilmington Gardens, nr
      Shipston-on-Stour
   The Mill Garden, Warwick
   Paxford, Princethorpe
   50 Wellington Rd, Edgbaston
   Whichford & Ascott Gardens,
      Shipston-on-Stour
June 24 Wednesday
   The Folly Lodge, Halford
   89 Harts Green Road, Harborne
   52 Tenbury Road, Kings Heath,
      Birmingham (Also Evening)
June 27 Saturday
   Alscot Park, nr Stratford-on-Avon
   Coughton Court, Alcester
   Ryton Organic Gardens, nr
      Coventry
June 28 Sunday
   Alscot Park, nr Stratford-on-Avon
   The Earlsdon Gardens, Coventry
   The Hiller Garden & Dunnington
      Heath Farm, Alcester
   Honington Village Gardens
   Roseberry Cottage, Fillongley
July 4 Saturday
   Upton House, nr Banbury
July 5 Sunday
   Balsall Common Gardens, Balsall
      Common
   Greenlands, Wellesbourne

WARWICKSHIRE

KEY

1. Alne View
2. Alscot Park
3. Arbury Hall
4. 4 Arnold Villas
5. Ashover
6. Avon Cottage
7. Avon Dassett Gardens
8. Baddesley Clinton
9. Balsall Common Gardens
10. Barton House
11. Ilmington Gardens
12. Castle Bromwich Hall Gardens Trust
13. Cedar House
14. Charlecote Park
15. Compton Scorpion Farm
16. Coughton Court
17. Dorsington Gardens
18. The Earlsdon Gardens
19. Earlsdon Gardens
20. 55 Elizabeth Road
21. Elm Close

22. The Folly Lodge
23. Foxgloves
24. Greenlands
25. Hall Green Gardens Hall Green
26. 89 Harts Green Road
27. Hickecroft
28. The Hiller Garden & Dunnington Heath Farm
29. Holywell Gardens
30. Honington Village Gardens
31. Hunningham Gardens
32. Idlicote Gardens
33. Ilmington Gardens
34. Ilmington Manor
35. Ivy Lodge
36. 78 Marsham Road
37. The Master's Garden
38. Maxstoke Castle
39. The Mill Garden
40. Moseley Gardens
41. 100 Oldbury Road
42. Orchard Cottage

43. Packington Hall
44. Packwood House
45. 2 Paddox House
46. Parham Lodge
47. Paxford
48. Pear Tree Cottage
49. Pereira Road Gardens
50. Roseberry Cottage
51. Hall Green Gardens
52. Ryton Organic Gardens
53. 172 Stonor Road
54. 26 Sunnybank Road
55. 52 Tenbury Road
56. Tysoe Manor
57. Upton House
58. 8 Vicarage Road
59. Warmington Village Gardens
60. Warwickshire Constabulary HQ
61. 50 Wellington Rd
62. Wheelwright House
63. Whichford & Ascott Gardens
64. Woodpeckers

July 8 Wednesday
Arbury Hall, Nuneaton
The Folly Lodge, Halford
July 11 Saturday
Charlecote Park, Warwick
Elm Close, Welford-on-Avon
Orchard Cottage, Hurley
July 12 Sunday
Ashover, 25 Burnett Road,
Streetly
Avon Dassett Gardens
Elm Close, Welford-on-Avon
Ilmington Manor, nr
Shipston-on-Stour
78 Marsham Road, nr Kingsheath
Moseley Gardens, Birmingham
Orchard Cottage, Hurley
8 Vicarage Road, Edgbaston
July 13 Monday
Elm Close, Welford-on-Avon
July 15 Wednesday
8 Vicarage Road, Edgbaston
(Evening)
July 19 Sunday
Hall Green Gardens, Hall Green
The Mill Garden, Warwick
100 Oldbury Road, Greets Green

Parham Lodge, Alveston
Paxford, Princethorpe
Warmington Village Gardens
July 26 Sunday
26 Sunnybank Road, Wylde Green
August 2 Sunday
Alne View, Pathlow
Avon Cottage, Ashow, nr
Kenilworth
172 Stonor Road, Hall Green
August 9 Sunday
Ashover, 25 Burnett Road,
Streetly
The Mill Garden, Warwick
August 12 Wednesday
The Folly Lodge, Halford
August 16 Sunday
The Hiller Garden & Dunnington
Heath Farm, Alcester
100 Oldbury Road, Greets
Green
August 23 Sunday
4 Arnold Villas, Rugby
2 Paddox House, Hillmorton
September 6 Sunday
Cedar House, Wasperton, nr
Warwick

September 9 Wednesday
The Folly Lodge, Halford
September 13 Sunday
52 Tenbury Road, Kings Heath,
Birmingham
Tysoe Manor, Warwick
Wheelwright House, Long
Compton
September 20 Sunday
The Mill Garden, Warwick
Ryton Organic Gardens, nr
Coventry
September 26 Saturday
Castle Bromwich Hall Garden
Trust
Elm Close, Welford-on-Avon
September 27 Sunday
Elm Close, Welford-on-Avon
October 4 Sunday
The Hiller Garden & Dunnington
Heath Farm, Alcester
October 11 Sunday
The Mill Garden, Warwick

DESCRIPTIONS OF GARDENS

Alne View, Pathlow &⚭❀ (Mrs E Butterworth) 5m from Henley-in-Arden; 3m N of Stratford on the A3400. Approx ⅓-acre. Shrubs, perennials, 2 small ponds and rockery. Aviary, collection of fuchsia, greenhouses. TEAS. *Adm £1.50 Chd free (ACNO to Wilmcote CE J & I School©). Sun Aug 2 (2-5)*

Alscot Park, nr Stratford-on-Avon &❀ (Mrs James West) 2½m S of Stratford-on-Avon A3400. Fairly large garden; extensive lawns, shrub roses, new lavender parterre planted in 1995. fine trees, orangery, with C18 Gothic house (not open), river, deer park, lakes. TEAS in aid of Warwickshire Assoc of Boys Clubs. *Adm £1.50 Chd free. Sat, Sun June 27, 28 (2-6)*

■ **Arbury Hall, Nuneaton** & (Rt Hon The Viscount Daventry) 3m SW of Nuneaton off the B4102 (Junction 3 M6/A444). Free Car Park. Delightful 10-acre garden with a sense of peace. Bulbs at start of season, followed by rhododendrons, azalea and wisteria, then roses in June and autumn colours from trees and shrubs. Formal rose garden. Lakes with wildfowl. Bluebell woods. Pollarded limes and arboretum in old walled garden. *Adm to Hall & Gardens £4.50 Chd £2.50 Gardens only £3 Chd £2. Easter Sun to last Sun in Sept. Hall, Suns and Bank Hol Mons. For NGS Weds May 13, July 8 (2-5.30). Last admission 5pm.*

4 Arnold Villas, Rugby ⚭ (Patrick Pratt) From Paddox House, Dunsmore Avenue continue along A428 towards Rugby for approx 1¼m. After roundabout take 1st L into Horton Crescent. For Parking cross A428 and follow signs to Church Walk. Arnold Villas on R. Small town garden containing a wide variety of shrubs, tender climbers and unusual plants. Exotics, mediterranean plants framed by mature palms. *Combined adm with* **2 Paddox House** *£2 Chd free. Sun Aug 23 (2-5.30)*

Ashover, Streetly ⚭❀ (Jackie & Martin Harvey) 25 Burnett Rd. 8m N of Birmingham. Take A452 towards Streetly, then B4138 alongside Sutton Park. Turn L at shops into Burnett Rd. ⅓-acre well stocked plant lovers' garden. Cottage-style mixed plantings planned for yr round interest with the use of bulbs, shrubs and herbaceous plants. Garden constantly changing. Particular emphasis in May with azaleas and other late spring colour, also in summer with shrubs, roses, climbers and a wide range of perennials, many unusual. New water feature being established. Cream TEAS. *Adm £1.50 Chd 50p. Suns May 24, July 12, Aug 9 (1.30-5.30)*

¶**Avon Cottage, Ashow nr Kenilworth** ⚭❀ (Neil Collett) 1½m E of Kenilworth. From A452 Kenilworth to Leamington Rd turn into B4115 (signposted Ashow and Stoneleigh). Proceed for ¼m and there is a R hand turn into Ashow. Cottage at the far end of the village adjacent to Church (driveway opp village club). Limited parking only, please park outside village and walk in to avoid any congestion. Charming cottage garden surrounding picturesque C18 grade II listed building. 1½-acres with extensive R Avon frontage. Diverse and interesting plantings for yr-round appeal. Newly-planted orchard area with free-range domestic and waterfowl. *Adm £1.50 Chd 50p (ACNO to Ashow Parish Church®). Fri May 1, Suns June 7, Aug 2 (1-6)*

Avon Dassett Gardens &⚘ 7m N of Banbury off B4100 (use Exit 12 of M40). Car parking in the village and in car park at top of hill. TEAS at **Old Mill Cottage**. *Combined adm £2.50 Chd free (ACNO to Myton Hamlet Hospice®). Sun July 12 (2-6). Coaches welcome, please* **Tel 01295 690643**

Hill Top Farm ⚘ (Mrs N & Mr D Hicks) 1-acre garden. Display of bedding plants, perennials and roses. Conifers and heathers. Extensive kitchen garden. Greenhouses

Old Mill Cottage (Mr & Mrs M Lewis) Conservation garden of ½ acre with shrubs, perennial borders and rockeries. Collection alpines and herbs. Two ponds and kitchen garden. Newly planted tropical garden

Old Pumphouse Cottage (Mrs W Wormell) Cottage garden with mixed borders featuring varieties of pinks and shrub roses and clematis. Kitchen garden and greenhouse

The Old Rectory (Mrs L Hope-Frost) 2-acre garden surrounding listed building mentioned in Doomsday Book (not open). Large variety of fine trees and shrubs. Small wood

The Coach House, Bitham Hall (Mr & Mrs G J Rice) 2-acre plantsman's garden, part of former Victorian garden overlooking Edge Hill. Walls give shelter and support for many climbers and more tender perennials and shrubs. Woodland area, orchard and fruit and vegetable garden. *Private visits by individuals and or groups welcome by appt, please* **Tel 01295 690255**

¶**Avon House** (Mr & Mrs E H Dunkley) Interesting village garden with mature trees, roses and herbaceous borders

¶**4 Lower End** (Mr & Mrs M J Edgington) Interesting contrasts between the cottage garden, the courtyard and the vegetable garden

▲**Baddesley Clinton** &⚏ (The National Trust) ¾m W off A4141 Warwick-Birmingham rd near Chadwick End. 7½m NW of Warwick. Mediaeval moated manor house little changed since 1633; walled garden and herbaceous borders; natural areas; lakeside walk. Lunches and TEAS. *Adm Grounds only £2.40 Chd £1.20. Shop and restaurant open from noon. For NGS Sat April 18 (12-5)*

Balsall Common Gardens &⚏⚘ Balsall Common. 5m S of M42/M6 intersection, 6m W of Coventry, 10m N of Warwick, junction of A452 and B4101. From traffic lights of this intersection go W along B4101 towards Knowle for ¾m. Map available for each garden. TEAS at **White Cottage and Silver Trees Farm**. *Combined adm £2 Chd 50p (ACNO to The Helen Ley Home®). Sun July 5 (1.30-6). Private visits welcome May & June, please* **Tel 01676 533143**

The Bungalow (Mr & Mrs G Johnson) Table Oak Lane, Fen End. 2 acres mixed borders, pond and lawn. New areas developing

Firs Farm (Mr & Mrs C Ellis) Windmill Lane. ½-acre garden, courtyard with tubs, walled garden, formal garden with rose bed and mixed borders

Meriglen (Mr & Mrs J Webb) Windmill Lane, Balsall Common. ¾-acre mixed borders, small woodland

The Pines (Mr & Mrs C Davis) Hodgetts Lane. 1½-acre formal garden. Avenue of flowering trees, series of small gardens, vegetable, herb garden and rose walk

Silver Trees Farm (Mr & Mrs B Hitchens) Balsall Street. 1½ acres, mixed borders, orchard, bog area, woodland garden. Large formal pond

Fen End House (Mr & Mrs W Husselby) Fen End. 1-acre garden, with lawns interspersed with borders containing formal and informal planting schemes

White Cottage Farm (Mr & Mrs J Edwards) Holly Lane. 1½ acres cottage garden, mixed borders, pond, sunken garden

32 Wootton Green Lane (Dr & Mrs Leeming) Balsall Common. Lawns, water features, greenhouses

Barton House, Barton-on-the-Heath &⚏⚘ (Mr & Mrs I H B Cathie) 2m W of Long Compton on the A3400 Stratford-upon-Avon to Oxford Rd. 5-acre garden with mature trees, species and hybrid rhododendrons and azaleas, magnolias and moutan paeonies. Japanese garden, catalpa walk, rose garden, secret garden and many rare and exotic plants. Manor House by Inigo Jones. TEAS. *Adm £2 Chd £1 (ACNO to St Lawrence Church®). Sun May 31 (2-6). Private visits for groups by appt only, please* **Tel 01608 674303**

▲**Castle Bromwich Hall Garden Trust, Chester Rd** &⚘ 4m E of Birmingham. 1m from junction 5 of the M6 (exit Northbound). An example of the Formal English Garden of the C18. The restoration, started in 1985 provides visitors, academics and horticulturalists opportunity of seeing a unique collection of historic plants, shrubs, medicinal and culinary herbs and a fascinating vegetable collection. Guided tours Weds, Sats & Suns. Shop. Refreshments available; meals by arrangement. TEAS. *Adm £2 OAPs £1.50 Chd 50p. For NGS Sats April 18, Sept 26 (2-6)*

Cedar House, Wasperton &⚏ (Mr & Mrs D L Burbidge) 4m S of Warwick on A429, turn R between Barford and Wellesbourne, Cedar House at end of village. 3-acre mixed garden; shrubs, herbaceous borders, ornamental trees, woodland walk. TEAS. *Adm £1.50 Chd free (ACNO to St John's Church, Wasperton®). Sun Sept 6 (2-6)*

▲**Charlecote Park, Warwick** &⚏ (The National Trust) 1m W of Wellesbourne signed off A429. 6m S of Warwick, 5m E of Stratford upon Avon. Landscaped gardens featuring clipped yews and terraces with urns, contain a C19 orangery; a rustic thatched summer house by the cedar lawn; a River Parterre and a Wilderness garden under development. A 1m walk follows a route round the park along the banks of the R Avon, giving fine vistas to two churches. Water feature in the wilderness garden. TEAS in Orangery. *Adm £4.80 Chd £2.40. For NGS Sat July 11 (12-6)*

Compton Scorpion Farm, nr Ilmington ⚏ (Mrs T M Karlsen) As for Ilmington Manor then fork L at village hall; after 1½m L down steep narrow lane, house on L. Garden designed and created by owners in 1989 from meadow hillside, aiming at Jekyll single colour schemes. Wild garden and cherry walk established. Dew pond created in '97. *Adm £1.25 Chd free. Sun May 17, Sat, Sun June 20, 21 (2-6)*

▲**Coughton Court, Alcester** &✿❀ (Mrs C Throckmorton) On A435 2m N of Alcester. 12 acres of garden designed by Christina Birch with a courtyard containing an Elizabethan knot garden; beyond are lime walks and a yew rotunda with views of parkland; a new walled garden, continuing by the lake a new rose labyrinth. There are a series of 'rooms' culminating in an herbaceous garden; a walk planted with willows and native shrubs and trees beside the River Arrow; a new bog garden and a formal orchard. TEAS. *Adm £3.90 Chd £1.95 (ACNO to Coughton Catholic Church Restoration Appeal®). For NGS Sat June 27 (11-5.30)*

Dorsington Gardens &✿ 6m SW of Stratford-on-Avon. On B439 from Stratford turn L to Welford-on-Avon, then R to Dorsington. TEAS. *Combined adm £2.50 Chd free (ACNO to St Peter's Church, Dorsington®). Sun June 7 (2-5.30)*

    Aberfoyle (Mr & Mrs B Clarke) Well established cottage garden, fine trees and shrubs

    Knowle Thatch (Mr & Mrs P Turner) Large garden, mature trees, shrubs and herbaceous borders

    Whitegates (Mrs A Turner) Shrubs, mature trees and shrub roses

    The Moat House (Mr & Mrs I Kolodotschko) 6-acre moated garden incl walled vegetable garden, conservatory with mediterranean plants

    The Old Manor (Mr F Dennis) 3 acres with fairy walk, herb garden, fish pond. Nearby, the Welshman's Track with arboretum and Udde Well. Marquee TEAS

    ¶**The Welshman's Barn** (Mr F Dennis) 5 acres with Japanese garden, Oz maze, statue garden of heroes, wildflower garden and stream

    The Old Rectory (Mr & Mrs N Phillips) 2-acre Victorian garden with mature trees incl old espalier fruit trees, box hedges, herbaceous borders, many old roses, large pool, small wood

    Windrush (Mrs M Mills) Country garden with shrubs, cottage plants and roses

The Earlsdon Gardens, Coventry ❀ Turn towards Coventry at the A45/A429 traffic lights. Take 3rd L turn into Beechwood Ave, to St Barbara's Church. Maps available. Plus other gardens also open and an Allotments Trail. TEAS. *Combined adm £1.50 Chd free. Sun June 28 (1.30-5)*

    ¶**105 Beechwood Avenue** (Margaret & Mick Atkins) Large, varied, mature garden

    40 Hartington Crescent (Viv and George Buss) An unusually large garden with interest for all ages, new water feature

    114 Hartington Crescent (Liz Campbell and Dennis Crowley) Large, mature, pretty garden

    ¶**12 Palmerston Road** (Harold Eldrige) Restful shady garden

    22 Radcliffe Road (Sondra and John Halliday) Plantswoman's continually evolving garden

    ¶**87 Rochester Road** (Edith Lewin) Peaceful, mature cottage garden

    ¶**39 Palmerston Road** (Joan Miles) Secluded, pretty garden

    15 Shaftsbury Road (Elaine Tierney) Plantaholic's small garden shared with young children

    ¶**10 St Andrew's Road** (Peter Turnbull) Interesting evergreen and shrub garden

55 Elizabeth Road, Moseley ✿❀ (Rob & Diane Cole) 4m S of Birmingham City centre, halfway between Kings Heath Centre & Edgbaston Cricket Ground. Off Moor Green Lane. Plantsman's garden 100' × 30' on 3 levels, with scree area and mixed borders of alpines, rhododendrons, primulas and perennials, many unusual. Alpine House, and tubs. *Adm £1 Chd free. Mon May 4 (2-5)*

Elm Close, Welford-on-Avon &✿❀ (Mr & Mrs E W Dyer) Binton Rd. 5m from Stratford off A4390. Elm Close is between Welford Garage and The Bell Inn. ⅔-acre plantsman's garden designed and maintained by owners and stocked for yr-round effect. Bulbs, alpines, clematis and hellebores a particular speciality. Listed in The Good Gardens Guide. TEAS Suns only in aid of Red Cross. *Adm £1.50 Chd free. Sats, Suns, Mons March 28, 29, 30, April 4, 5, 6, May 23, 24, 25, July 11, 12, 13 Sept 26, 27 (2.30-5.30). Parties welcome by appointment, please* **Tel 01789 750793**

The Folly Lodge, Halford ✿❀ (Mike & Susan Solomon) On A429 (Fosse Way) 9m NE Moreton in Marsh. 9m SE Stratford on Avon. In Halford take turning opp PO to Idlicote. House is 300yds down on R. Softly curving beds overflowing with plants enhance the fine views. A wide range of interesting plants, incl grasses, give yr-round interest. Come to sit, and enjoy the peace and beauty of our garden. TEA. *Adm £1.50 Chd free. Weds May 13, June 10, 24, July 8, Aug 12, Sept 9 (2-5). Group visits welcome by appt, please* **Tel 01789 740183**

Foxgloves, Dunchurch &❀ (Eve Hessey & George Andrews) 35 Rugby Rd. On A426 nr village centre. Small gardens with ornamental potager, fruit cage, cordon fruit trees, grapes, figs, kiwi fruit, herb garden, lawn with colour themed herbaceous borders, ornamental shrubs, climbing roses and collections of foxgloves and hardy geraniums, nut tunnel. TEA. *Adm £1 Chd free. Sun June 21 (2-5). Private visits also welcome, please* **Tel 01788 817643**. *Other village gardens may be open ring for details*

Greenlands, Wellesbourne &❀ (Mr Eric T Bartlett) Leave Statford-upon-Avon due E on the B4086. Garden on Xrds at Loxley/Charlecote by airfield. An acre of mature trees; shrubs; shrub roses and herbaceous borders. TEAS. *Adm £1.50 Chd free. Suns April 5, July 5 (11-5). Parties welcome, please* **Tel 01789 840327**

Hall Green Gardens &❀ *Combined adm £1.20 Chd free (ACNO to local Hospices & REAP®). Sun July 19 (2-5). Also by appt*

    120 Russell Rd ❀ (Mr D Worthington) Turn off A34 E at Reg Vardy Motors, Hall Green, down York Rd then L into Russell Rd. Small suburban garden designed by owner; shrubs, herbaceous, climbers, old roses and fountain; tubs, hanging baskets and window boxes. TEAS. **Tel 0121 624 7906**

    63 Green Road (Mrs M Wilkes) Green Rd is W off A34, Hall Green Parade (nr Hall Green Station). Narrow suburban garden; 4 pools, bedding plants, herbaceous, shubs, several distinctive features made by owner. Recently partially remodelled. **Tel 0121 624 6716**

■ **89 Harts Green Road, Harborne** &⚶❀ (Mrs Barbara Richardson) 3m Birmingham City Centre [A-Z A2 p88] off Fellows Lane/War Lane. ½-acre split level informal garden with troughs, scree, rockery and mixed borders of unusual plants, shrubs and climbers. Pond and vegetable garden. Adjoining orchard contains small nursery offering wide range of plants, many propagated from garden. *Adm £1 Chd free. Open every Wed in April, May, June, July and Sept. For NGS Weds April 29, May 27, June 24 (2-5). Private visits and groups welcome, please* **Tel 0121 427 5200**

Hickecroft &⚶ (Mr & Mrs J M Pitts) Rowington. 6m NW of Warwick, 15m SE of Birmingham on B4439 between Hockley Heath and Hatton. Turn into Finwood Rd (signed Lowsonford); at Rowington Xrds 1st L into Mill Lane. 2-acre garden reaching maturity following redesigning and replanting. Interesting plants, mixed borders. Home to part of the NCCPG Digitalis collection. TEAS. *Adm £2 Chd 50p (ACNO to St Laurence Church®). Sat, Sun June 20, 21 (2-5.30). Private visits welcome, please* **Tel 01564 782384**

▲**The Hiller Garden & Dunnington Heath Farm, Alcester** &⚶❀ (Mr & Mrs R Beach) On B4088 (was A435), 7m N Evesham, 2m S Ragley Hall. 2-acre garden of all-yr interest displaying unusual herbaceous perennials, old-fashioned and species roses; and English roses. Cream TEAS. *Adm by donation. Open all yr. For NGS Suns April 26, June 28, Aug 16, Oct 4 (10-4). Private gardens of Dunnington Heath Farm (adjacent) also open on NGS days. Adm £1 Chd free*

Holywell Gardens &⚶❀ 5m E of Henley-in-Arden, nearest village Claverdon. Coffee and TEAS in aid of Myton Hospice. *Combined adm £2 Chd free. Sun June 21 (11-6)*

  Holywell Farm (Mr & Mrs Ian Harper) 2½-acre natural garden; lawn, trees, shrubs. Laid out in 1963 for easy maintenance, surrounding C16 half timbered house

  Manor Farm (Mr & Mrs Donald Hanson) Cottage type garden surrounding C16 farmhouse with natural duck pond, yew and box hedges, herb garden; white and grey border

Honington Village Gardens &⚶❀ 1½m N of Shipston-on-Stour. Take A3400 towards Stratford then R signed Honington. TEAS **Honington Hall**. *Combined adm £2.50 Chd free (ACNO to All Saints Church, Honington®). Sun June 28 (2.15-5.30)*

  Feldon Cottage (Mr & Mrs H James)

  Honington Glebe (Mr & Mrs John Orchard) Over 2 acres of informal garden interesting ornamental trees; shrubs and foliage. Parterre and raised lily pool recently laid out in old walled garden

  Honington Hall (B H E Wiggin) Extensive lawns; fine trees. Carolean house (not open); Parish Church adjoining house

  Honington Lodge (Lord & Lady Tombs)

  The Old House (Mr & Mrs R S Smith)

  Old Mullions (Mr & Mrs R Lawton)

Hunningham Village Gardens, Hunningham &⚶❀ From Leamington Spa B4453 to Rugby. Signposted Hunningham R after Weston-under-Wetherley. Or A425 to Southam at Fosseway (B4455) turn L. At Hunningham Hill turn L then follow signs to church (open). Teas at Vicarage in aid of St Margarets Church. *Adm £2 Chd free. Sun, Mon May 24, 25 (2-5)*

  High Cross (Mr & Mrs T Chalk) Secluded garden with small wildlife pool

  ¶**The Old Hall** (Mr & Mrs N W Horler) Large old garden with walled areas, listed building

  The Olde School House (Mr & Mrs G Longstaff) 1 acre of borders, shrubs, pond and wildlife paddock area

  Sandford Cottage (Mr & Mrs A Phillips) Village cottage garden

  ¶**Hunningham Croft** (P Taylor) Interesting garden with large collection of clematis

  ¶**The Bungalow** (O Rouse) Cottage garden with large vegetable plot

Other gardens may open

Idlicote Gardens &❀ 3m NE of Shipston-on-Stour. TEAS. *Combined adm £2 OAPs £1 Chd free (ACNO to Parish Church of St James the Great®). Sun June 14 (2-6)*

  Idlicote House (Mrs R P G Dill) About 4 acres. Fine views. Small Norman church in grounds. House C18 (not open) listed Grade II

  Badgers Farm (Sir Derek & Lady Hornby)

  1 Bickerstaff Cottages (Mr & Mrs C Balchin)

  Bickerstaff Farm (Sir John & Lady Owen)

  Home Farm (Mr & Mrs G Menzies-Kitchen)

  The Old Rectory (Mr & Mrs G Thomson)

  Stone Cottage (Mr & Mrs C Rosser)

  Woodlands (Capt & Mrs P R Doyne)

  ¶**2 Bickerstaffs Cottages** (Mrs S Hopkinson)

  ¶**3 Bickerstaffs Cottages** (Miss A Cummins)

  ¶**Badgers Cottage** (Dr & Mrs D Custance)

Ilmington Gardens, nr Shipston-on-Stour ❀ 8m S of Stratford-on-Avon, 4m NW of Shipston-on-Stour. Ilmington traditional Morris dancers. Teas in the Village Hall. Start anywhere, all gardens well signed and within walking distance. Free map supplied at the Manor. *Combined adm £3 Chd free (ACNO to Shipston Home Carers®). Sun June 21 (2-6)*

  The Manor (D Flower) (see next entry)

  The Bevingtons (N & F Tustain)

  Foxcote Hill (M & S Dingley)

  Foxcote Hill Cottage (A Terry)

  Crab Mill (Mr & Mrs Sherringham)

  Pear Tree Cottage (Dr & Mrs A F Hobson)

  Frog Orchard (M Naish)

  ¶**Puddocks** (Mr & Mrs R Newey)

  ¶**Ilmington Grange** (Mr & Mrs A Butcher)

Ilmington Manor &❀ (Mr D & Lady Flower) 4m NW of Shipston-on-Stour, 8m S of Stratford-on-Avon. Daffodils in profusion (April). Hundreds of old and new roses, ornamental trees, shrub and herbaceous borders, rock garden, pond garden, topiary, fish pond with Koi. House (not open) built 1600. TEAS. *Adm £2 Chd free (ACNO to Ilmington Village Hall®). Suns April 19, May 17, July 12 (2-6). Also open Sun June 21 with* **Ilmington Gardens**. *Private visits welcome, please* **Tel 01608 682230**

Ivy Lodge, Radway & (Mrs M A Willis) 7m NW of Banbury via A41 and B4086, turn R down Edgehill; 14m SE of Stratford via A422. L below Edgehill. 4-acres; spring bulbs and blossom; wildflower area; climbing roses; site Battle of Edgehill. TEAS. *Adm £1.50 OAP £1 Chd free (ACNO to the Katherine House Hospice Trust®). Sun April 19 (2-6). Also parties welcome April to July and throughout Oct (Autumn colours), please* **Tel 01295 670371** *or* **670580**

¶78 Marsham Road, Kingsheath ✿❀ (Phil & Amy Harding) Off the Alcester Rd between Kingsheath and the Maypole. Turn off into Meadfoot Ave, Marsham Rd leads off A-Z 4A 106. Approx 150′ leading down to Stratford canal. Specialist collection of geraniums, stone troughs, lawns, koi pool, fountain. Perennials and annuals. TEAS. *Adm £1. Sun July 12 (2-6)*

■ **The Master's Garden, Lord Leycester Hospital, Warwick** ✿ (Susan Rhodes for the Patron and Governors) High Street. Town centre beside West Gate. C14 Guildhall, Chapel, courtyard, Great Hall and Museum of the Queen's Own Hussars also open to public. Historic walled garden, incl Norman arch and ancient finial of Nilometer. Civic Trust Award 1997, visited by H M The Queen. TEAS. *Adm £1 Chd free. Open daily except Mons, Easter to Sept 30 (10-4.30). For NGS Sun April 19 (11-5). Parties welcome, please* **Tel 01926 491422**

Maxstoke Castle &✿❀ (Mr & Mrs M C Fetherston-Dilke) nr Coleshill, E of Birmingham, 2½m E of Coleshill on B4114 take R turn down Castle Lane; Castle Dr 1¼m on R. 4 to 5 acres of garden and pleasure grounds with flowers, shrubs and trees in the immediate surroundings of the castle and inside courtyard; water-filled moat round castle. *Adm £2.50 OAP/Chd £1.50 under 6 free. Sun May 31 (2-5)*

■ **The Mill Garden, Warwick** &✿❀ (Mr A B Measures) 55 Mill St. Off A425 beside castle gate. 1 acre; series of informal, partially enclosed areas, on river next to castle. Superb setting; herb garden; raised beds; small trees, shrubs, cottage plants and some unusual plants. Use St Nicholas Car Park. Tea in Warwick. *Adm £1 Chd free (ACNO to Lord Leycester Hospital®). Open daily 9 till dusk, Easter to mid Oct. Open for NGS Suns April 19, May 10, June 21, July 19, Aug 9, Sept 20, Oct 11. Parties welcome by appt, please* **Tel 01926 492877**

Moseley Gardens, Birmingham ✿❀ Approx 3m from Birmingham City Centre halfway between Kings Heath Centre & Moseley Village. TEA April 19. TEAS July 12. *Combined adm £1.50 Chd free. Suns April 19, July 12 (2-6)*

   7 Ashfield Rd (Mr & Mrs Bartlett) Small garden with secluded, cottage feel. Attractive pond with rockery, waterfall and shingle bank

   No 16 Prospect Rd ❀ (Mrs S M & Mr R J Londesborough) Small garden with wide range of plants. Large collection of containers. Small conservatory. Featured on ITV 'Our House' and channel 4 'Garden Party' and in 'Good Housekeeping' magazine. *Also private visits welcome all year, please* **Tel 0121 449 8457**

   No 19 Prospect Rd (Mr A White) Well planted spring suburban garden. *April 19 only*

   No 20 Prospect Rd (Martin Page & Annie Sofiano) Large town garden on 3 levels. *July 12 only*

   No 30 Prospect Rd (Mrs J Taylor) South-facing terraced garden incorporating rockery-covered air-raid shelter. Featured on 'Garden Party'

   No 33 School Rd (Ms J Warr-Arnold) Mixed garden containing plants with interesting histories. *Sun July 12 only*

   No 65 School Rd (Mrs W Weston) Small shady garden with patio, pergola and pond.Featured on 'Garden Party. *Sun July 12 only*

¶100 Oldbury Rd, Greets Green &✿ (Harry Green) West Bromwich or Oldbury nearest towns. Junction 9 M6, junction 1 or 2 M5. The jewel in the town. ¾-acre garden. Colourful Japanese water garden with two large pools and numerous bridges and waterfalls. Features incl bird scarer, water basins and many japanese Ornaments, lanterns and torogate. Featured on many tv programmes incl Central News, Gardeners World, Gardening Time and Wish You Were Here. Best water garden, best unusual garden, best overall garden and gardening family of the year. Also featured in many magazines incl Water Gardener and Koi Carp. TEA. *Adm £1 Chd 20p. Suns July 19, Aug 16 (10-6)*

Orchard Cottage, Hurley &❀ (Mr & Mrs G Roberts) M42, junction 9, take A4097 to Kingsbury. 2nd island, R to Coventry, 1st L to Hurley. Approx 1½m, R into Dexter Lane cottage at end of lane. C17 property in ¾ acre. Cottage garden with informal plantings of mixed beds and borders containing many interesting plants, original water feature, evolving meadow orchard. A 10-yr-old garden that thinks it's 50! TEAS. *Adm £1 Chd under 12 free. Sat, Sun July 11, 12 (2-6)*

Packington Hall &✿ (Lord & Lady Guernsey) Meriden. On A45, towards Coventry, after Stonebridge Roundabout. Packington's pleasure grounds were laid out in 1750 by Capability Brown. The lawns run down to the 18 acre Hall Pool and are studded with clumps of azaleas and rhododendrons, together with specimen trees. The more formal area around the House has recently been replanted. TEAS. *Adm £2.50 Chd £1.50 (ACNO to Assoc for Brain Damaged Children, Coventry®). Sun June 7 (2-5.30)*

▲**Packwood House** &✿❀ (The National Trust) 11m SE of Birmingham. 2m E of Hockley Heath. Carolean yew garden representing the Sermon on the Mount. Tudor house with tapestries, needlework and furniture of the period. Teas at Baddesley Clinton (NT) Henley in Arden or Knowle. *Adm House and garden £4.20, garden only £2.10 Chd £1.05 For NGS June 20 (1.30-5.30)*

2 Paddox House, Hillmorton ✿❀ (Anne Sutton) From Rugby take A428 to Hillmorton signed Northampton M1. Approx 1½m from town centre turn R opposite garage into Rainsbrook Avenue, which leads to Dunsmore Ave. Garden on R. From Motorway junction 18 follow signs to Rugby. Small town garden designed by the owner for peace and tranquility. Informal pond and ivy mound for wildlife. Hidden corners, gravel, pots and containers, some unusual plants. *Combined adm with* **4 Arnold Villas** *£2 Chd free. Sun Aug 23 (2-5.30)*

Parham Lodge, Alveston ♿❀❀ (Mr & Mrs K C Edwards) 2m E of Stratford upon Avon off B4086. 1-acre country garden, celebrating its 21st birthday. Designed by owners for colour, texture and scent at all seasons, large pond and terraces. Island beds, spring and summer bulbs. Wild flower apple orchard. Old cedars, copper beech and hornbeams. Rose, herb and cutting gardens etc. Beehives so no sprays for 20 years. TEAS in aid of Macmillan Cancer Relief. *Adm £1 Chd 50p. Suns April 19, July 19 (12-6). Private visits welcome, please* **Tel 01789 268955**

Paxford, Princethorpe ♿❀❀ (Mr & Mrs A M Parsons) 7m SE of Coventry, on B4453 Leamington Rd approx 200yds from junction with A423. A flower arranger's garden with heathers and fuchsias which has been designed and maintained by the owners as a series of rooms. Parking on road on one side only please. TEA. *Adm £1 (ACNO to Stretton-on-Dunsmore Parish Church®). Suns June 21, July 19 (2-6)*

Pear Tree Cottage, Ilmington ❀ (Dr & Mrs A F Hobson) 8m S of Stratford-on-Avon, 4m NW of Shipston-on-Stour. Cottage garden with many interesting plants and bulbs. Designed and maintained by owners; rock garden and terrace. Partially suitable for wheelchairs. Teas at Ilmington Manor May 17. *Adm £1 Chd free. Sun May 17 (2-6). Also open Sun June 21 (2-6) with* **Ilmington Gardens**

Pereira Road Gardens ❀❀ Birmingham A-Z 1c p.88 between Gillhurst Rd and Margaret Grove, ¼m from Hagley Rd or ½m Harborne High St. TEAS June 14 at **No. 84** in aid of St Mary's Hospice. *Adm £1; combined adm £2 OAPS £1 Chd 30p. Suns April 26, June 14 (2-5)*
> **No. 45** (Mrs Wyn White) 'Alf's garden'; on 5 levels, with spring bulbs, rhododendrons, roses, shrubs, herbaceous borders and fruit trees in formal and informal areas. Harborne Nature Reserve and Bird Sanctuary can be visited. *(ACNO to The Liver Foundation Trust, Queen Elizabeth Hospital®). June 14 only*
> **No. 48** (Liz Hurst) A dog-friendly garden with 2 long raised borders, pond with rock garden and koi, and patio with many pots. *June 14 only*
> **No. 50** ❀ (Prof Peg Peil) ¼ acre on several levels, with about 1000 shrubs; perennials, alpines and herbs for all seasons, fruit and vegetables. Large bed of plants with African connections, seen on Central TV. (Plants sold in aid of Catholic Fund for Overseas Development.)
> **No. 55** (Emma Davis & Martin Comander) A young, child-friendly garden with deck and gravel area and informal beds with a variety of trees and shrubs. *June 14 only*
> **No. 84** (Mrs R E Bennett) ⅕ acre with 30 degree sloping concreted bank, now extensive rockery, interesting shrubs, herbaceous borders. *June 14 only*

Roseberry Cottage, Fillongley ♿❀❀ (Mr & Mrs Richard G Bastow) 6m N of Coventry on B4098 Tamworth Road. Go under motorway bridge to top of hill, take Woodend Lane, sign on R. Turn L into Sandy Lane, opp triangle of beech trees. 1st house on R in Sandy Lane.

Please use one way system due to restricted parking. Garden of 1¾ acres incl herbaceous border, rock garden, pool, peat and bog area, scree and small herb garden. Stone troughs, orchard with wild flowers, organically grown fruit and vegetables. Herbs for sale, thymes a speciality. TEA. *Adm £1.50 Chd 50p (ACNO to NCCPG®). Sun June 28 (2-5)*

■ **Ryton Organic Gardens** ♿❀❀ 5m SE of Coventry (off A45 to Wolston). Headquarters of the Henry Doubleday Research Association, the UK showcase for organic gardening. As seen on TV, thirty practical and attractive demonstration gardens incl flowers, roses, herbs, shrubs, top and soft fruit, forest garden, plus Heritage vegetables, composting, pest and disease control and gardening without digging displays. New for 1998 - herbaceous perennials and grasses in landscaping and a Cooks' Garden. Award-winning restaurant and speciality shop. TEAS. *Adm £2.50 concessions £2, Chd £1.25. Open daily except Christmas period. For NGS Sat June 27, Sun Sept 20 (10-5)*

Sheepy Magna Gardens, nr Atherstone see Leicestershire

¶**172 Stonor Road, Hall Green** ❀❀ (Mrs O Walters) Just off the Robin Hood roundabout on the A34 B'ham to Stratford Rd. Take the Baldwins Lane exit from the roundabout. Stonor Rd is 2nd L. Very small plantswoman's garden (approx 20m × 7m) wide variety of plants some not usually considered hardy in this area. Scree containers, shade beds, ferns, climbers, conservatory. TEAS. *Adm £1 Chd 50p (ACNO to St Mary's Hospice®). Suns May 31, Aug 2 (2-5.30)*

26 Sunnybank Road ❀❀ (Chris & Margaret Jones) Wylde Green. ¾m S of Sutton Coldfield. Turn off A5127 towards Wylde Green Station then; 2nd L. Medium-sized town garden on sandy soil, redesigned by present owners as a series of 'rooms'. Yr-long interest achieved by use of bulbs, shrubs and herbaceous plants. Includes pond, scree, bog area, and dry shaded areas. Featured on Garden Club Aug 93 (Channel 4), Secret Gardens (BBC) Spring 96, and in 'Your Garden' magazine. TEAS in aid of John Willmott School PTA. *Adm £1 OAPs 50p Chd free. Sun July 26 (2-6)*

52 Tenbury Road, Kings Heath ♿❀❀ (Mr G & Mrs V Grace Darby) 5m S of city centre off A435 (Alcester Rd). 4¾m from junction 3 off M40. ⅛ of an acre suburban garden in cottage garden style. Informal plantings of mixed beds and borders with interesting and unusual plants, shrubs, climbers. Filmed for BBC and ITV. Minimum use of chemical pest control. TEAS in aid of South Birmingham Talking Newspaper (for the Blind) April 19, May 10, 31 and Muscular Dystrophy Wed June 17, 24, Sun Sept 13 (2-5). *Adm £1.50 Chd free. Suns April 19, May 17, 31 (2-5), Wed June 17, 24 (2-5 & 6-8.30). Private and group visits welcome April to Sept Weds preferred, please* **Tel 0121 444 6456**

Evening Openings (see also garden descriptions)

8 Vicarage Road, Edgbaston   July 15 6.30–8.30pm

Tysoe Manor, Tysoe ৬෴ (Mr & Mrs W A C Wield) 5m NE of Shipston-on-Stour. Take the 4035 to Banbury. In Brailes turn L to Tysoe. The Manor is the 1st house on the L after reaching Upper Tysoe. 4-acre garden, large lawns with stone walls, herbaceous and flower borders; shrubs and mature ornamental and fruit trees. TEAS in aid of Tysoe Church. *Adm £2 Chd free. Sun Sept 13 (2-6)*

▲**Upton House** ෴ (The National Trust) 7m NW of Banbury on A422; 2m S of Edgehill. Terraced garden, rockeries, herbaceous borders, roses, water gardens, lawns. House contains a connoisseur's collection of porcelain, tapestries and paintings. Partially suitable for wheelchairs. Coaches by appt. TEAS. *Adm garden only £2.50 Chd £1.25. For NGS Sat July 4 (2-6 last adm 5.30)*

8 Vicarage Rd ৬෴ (Charles & Tessa King-Farlow) Edgbaston, 1½m W of City Centre off A456 (Hagley Rd). ¾-acre retaining in part its Victorian layout but informally planted with mixed borders of interesting and unusual plants; shrub rose border; walled potager and conservatory. Featured in House and Garden Sept 1995 and Sainsbury Magazine June 1997. TEAS in aid of St George's Church. *Adm £1.50 Chd free. Sun July 12 (2-5.30). Special evening opening Adm £2.50 to include a glass of wine, Wed July 15 (6.30-8.30) Private visits very welcome, please Tel 0121 455 0902*

Warmington Village Gardens ৬෴ 5m NW of Banbury on B4100. Teas at **The Village Hall**. *Combined adm £2 Chd free (ACNO to Warmington PCC Restoration Fund®). Sun July 19 (2-6) Car park; coaches welcome, please Tel 01295 690 318*
   Berka (Mr & Mrs B J Castle) Chapel Street
   3 Court Close (Mr & Mrs C J Crocker)
   The Glebe House (Mr & Mrs G Thornton) Village Road
   Holly Cottage (Dr & Mrs T W Martin) The Green
   ¶**Lilac Tree Cottage** (Mr & Mrs D M Pittaway) Chapel St
   The Manor House (Mr & Mrs G Lewis) The Green
   The Old Rectory (Sir Wilfred & Lady Cockcroft) The Green
   Rotherwood (Miss M R Goodison) Soot Lane
   Sunnyside (Mr & Mrs M Borlenghi) Chapel Street
   Underedge (Mr & Mrs J Dixon) 1 Church Hill
   Woodcote (Mr & Mrs K W Mellor) School Lane

Warwickshire Constabulary, Police HQ, Leek Wootton ❀ Mid-way between Warwick and Kenilworth, 1m N of the Gaveston Island, on the Kenilworth Rd, off the A46 Warwick to Coventry by-pass. From Warwick, turn L after Anchor Public House in centre of village, signposted Police Headquarters. Approx 6 acres of mixed garden, large and small shrubs, Chinese garden, walk around lakes. TEAS. *Adm £1.50 Chd free (ACNO to Victim Support®). Sun May 31 (1.30-5)*

50 Wellington Rd, Edgbaston ৬෴ (Mrs Anne Lee) Corner of Ampton Rd and Wellington Rd. 1-acre walled town garden. York stone paving, brick paths and architectural features. 100-yr-old rhododendrons and mature trees with woodland walk. Two long mixed borders, shrub roses, fountain, croquet lawn. TEAS. *Adm £1.50 Chd free. Sun June 21 (2-6). Private visits also welcome April to Oct, please Tel 0121 440 1744*

Wheelwright House, Long Compton ৬❀ (Richard & Suzanne Shacklock) 6m S of Shipston-on-Stour on A3400; at S end of Long Compton village take rd signed to Little Compton; Wheelwright House is 300yds on L. 1-acre garden surrounding C18 house. Stream with attractive bridges forms centrepiece. Bog garden, shade gardens, colourful mixed borders with wide variety of traditional and unusual plants. Formal lily pool with rose pergola. Mediterranean garden. TEAS in aid of Long Compton Church. *Adm £1.50 Chd free. Sun April 26, Sept 13 (2-5.30). Private visits welcome, please Tel 01608 684478*

Whichford & Ascott Gardens, Shipston-on-Stour ෴ 6m SE of Shipston-on-Stour. Turn E off A3400 at Long Compton for Whichford. Cream TEAS (Teas in aid of St Michaels Church). Car park and picnic area. *Combined adm £2.50 Chd free. Sun June 21 (2-6)*
   Ascott Lodge (Charlotte Copley) Garden with beautiful views, lawns sloping to pond, well stocked borders, plus courtyard garden
   The Old Rectory (Mr & Mrs P O'Kane) Established family garden with lawns, water garden and ponds, with some interesting new tree and shrub planting
   Pine Tree Cottage (Mr & Mrs W Pinfold) Colourful cottage garden with unusual plants, planting and features. Bird aviary and small pool
   Brook Hollow (Mr & Mrs J A Round) Terraced hillside garden with a large variety of trees, shrubs and plants. Stream and water features
   Combe House (Mr & Mrs D C Seel) Hidden garden surrounding house; mature fine trees
   The Gateway (Mrs M W Thorne) Large garden in attractive setting with magnificent trees and small stream. Lawn enclosed with fine box hedges
   The Old House (Mr & Mrs T A Maher) Undulating garden. Natural ponds, trees and shrubs
   Roman Row (Mr & Mrs S C Langdon) Beautiful well kept cottage garden
   Stone Walls (Mrs J Scott-Cockburn) Walled garden; paved garden in foundations of old stable
   The Whichford Pottery (Mr & Mrs J B M Keeling) Secret walled garden, unusual plants, large vegetable garden and rambling cottage garden. Adjoining pottery

Woodpeckers, nr Bidford-on-Avon ৬෴ (Dr & Mrs A J Cox) The Bank, Marlcliff, 7m SW of Stratford-on-Avon. Off the B4085 between Bidford-on-Avon and Cleeve Prior. 2½-acre plantsman's country garden designed and maintained by owners; colour-schemed borders, old roses, meadow garden, small arboretum, alpines in troughs and gravel, pool, knot garden, potager. Featured on BBC2 'Gardener's World' and in 'The English Garden' and 'The Garden'. *Adm £2.50. Private visits by Societies or individuals welcome at all seasons, please Tel 01789 773416*

The National Gardens Scheme is a charity which traces its origins back to 1927. Since then it has raised over £18 million for charitable purposes.

Wiltshire

Hon County Organiser: Brigadier Arthur Gooch, Manor Farmhouse, Chitterne, Warminster BA12 OLG
Assistant Hon County Organisers: Mrs David Armytage, Sharcott Manor, Pewsey SN9 5PA
Mrs Anthony Heywood, Monkton House, Monkton Deverell, Warminster BA12 7EX
Mrs Colin Shand, Ashton House, Worton, Devizes SN10 5RU

DATES OF OPENING

Regular openings
For details see garden description

The Abbey House, Malmesbury
Bowood House & Gardens, nr
  Chippenham
Heale Gardens & Plant Centre,
  Middle Woodford
Iford Manor, nr Bradford-on-Avon
Lackham Gardens, Lacock
Long Hall Gardens & Nursery,
  Stockton
The Mead Nursery, Brokerswood
Pound Hill House, West Kington
Stourton House, Stourton

By appointment only
*For telephone numbers and other
details see garden descriptions.
Private visits welcomed*

Bryher, Bromham
Mevagissy, Burbage

February 14 Saturday
Lacock Abbey, Chippenham
February 15 Sunday
Lacock Abbey, Chippenham
February 21 Saturday
Lacock Abbey, Chippenham
February 22 Sunday
Lacock Abbey, Chippenham
March 15 Sunday
Lower House, Whiteparish
March 29 Sunday
Corsham Court, nr Chippenham
April 1 Wednesday
Sharcott Manor, nr Pewsey
April 5 Sunday
Crudwell Court Hotel, Malmesbury
Great Chalfield Manor, nr
  Melksham
Manor House Farm, Hanging
  Langford
Sharcott Manor, nr Pewsey
April 12 Sunday
The Abbey House, Malmesbury
East Stowell Gardens
Upper Chelworth Farm, nr
  Cricklade
April 13 Monday
The Abbey House, Malmesbury

Conock Manor, Chirton
Hyde's House, Dinton
April 19 Sunday
Baynton House, Coulston
Fonthill House, nr Tisbury
Long Hall Gardens & Nursery,
  Stockton
The Old Rectory, Corsley
April 26 Sunday
Iford Manor, nr Bradford-on-Avon
Oare House, nr Pewsey
Ridleys Cheer, Mountain Bower
May 3 Sunday
Little Durnford Manor, nr
  Salisbury
Spye Park, nr Chippenham
May 4 Monday
Home Covert, Roundway
May 6 Wednesday
Sharcott Manor, nr Pewsey
May 9 Saturday
Upper Chelworth Farm, nr
  Cricklade
May 10 Sunday
Luckington Court, Luckington
Waterdale House, Milton
May 16 Saturday
Stourton House, Stourton
May 17 Sunday
7 Norton Bavant, nr Warminster
Ridleys Cheer, Mountain Bower
Stourton House, Stourton
May 30 Saturday
Mompesson House, Salisbury
The Wardrobe, Salisbury
May 31 Sunday
Bowood Rhododendron Walks, nr
  Chippenham
The Close, Pewsey
Inwoods, Farleigh Wick
June 3 Wednesday
Sharcott Manor, nr Pewsey
June 7 Sunday
Dauntsey Gardens
13 Kingsdown Road, Stratton St
  Margaret
Mallards, Chirton
Martins, Whitehill
Stourhead Garden, Stourton
Upper Chelworth Farm, nr
  Cricklade
June 14 Sunday
Ark Farm, Tisbury

Avebury Manor Garden,
  Avebury
Corsham Court, nr Chippenham
Edington Gardens
Faulstone House, Bishopstone
Foscote Gardens, Grittleton
Landford Lodge, nr Salisbury
Manor Farm, Monkton Deverill
The Old Rectory, Stockton
Pertwood Manor, Hindon
38 & 40 Sherford Road, Haydon
  Wick
June 20 Saturday
Hazelbury Manor, Wadswick, nr
  Box
June 21 Sunday
Alton Gardens
Bolehyde Manor, Allington
Bratton Gardens
Chisenbury Priory, East
  Chisenbury
Coulston Gardens, Coulston
The Courts, Holt
Goulters Mill Farm, Burton
Great Durnford Gardens
Guyers House, Corsham
Hazelbury Manor, Wadswich, nr
  Box
Hillbarn House, Great Bedwyn
June 28 Sunday
Foresters House, Sherston
Hyde's House, Dinton
Little Durnford Manor, nr
  Salisbury
Long Hall Gardens & Nursery,
  Stockton
The Old Rectory, Corsley
Pound Hill House, West
  Kington
Ridleys Cheer, Mountain Bower
Sharcott Manor, nr Pewsey
Yew Tree Farm, Hankerton
July 1 Wednesday
Sharcott Manor, nr Pewsey
July 5 Sunday
Upper Chelworth Farm, nr
  Cricklade
Yew Tree Farm, Hankerton
July 11 Saturday
Great Somerford Gardens
July 12 Sunday
Crudwell Court Hotel, nr
  Malmesbury

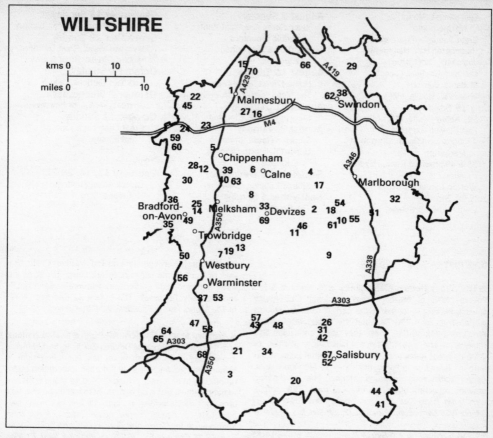

WILTSHIRE

kms 0   10

miles 0   10

KEY

1. The Abbey House
2. Alton Gardens
3. Ark Farm
4. Avebury Manor Garden
5. Bolehyde Manor
6. Bowood Rhododendron Walks
7. Bratton Gardens
8. Bryher
9. Chisenbury Priory
10. The Close
11. Conock Manor
12. Corsham Court
13. Coulston Gardens
14. The Courts
15. Crudwell Court Hotel
16. Dauntsey Gardens
17. East Kennett Manor
18. East Stowell Gardens
19. Edington Gardens
20. Faulstone House
21. Fonthill House
22. Foresters House
23. Foscote Gardens
24. Goulters Mill Farm

25. Great Chalfield Manor
26. Great Durnford Gardens
27. Great Somerford Gardens
28. Guyers House
29. Hannington Hall
30. Hazelbury Manor
31. Heale Gardens & Plant
    Centre
32. Hillbarn House
33. Home Covert
34. Hyde's House
35. Iford Manor
36. Inwoods
37. Job's Mill
38. 13 Kingsdown Road
39. Lackham Gardens
40. Lacock Abbey Gardens
41. Landford Lodge
42. Little Durnford Manor
43. Long Hall Gardens &
    Nursery
44. Lower House
45. Luckington Court
46. Mallards

47. Manor Farm
48. Manor House Farm
49. Martins
50. The Mead Nursery
51. Mevagissy
52. Mompesson House
53. 7 Norton Bavant
54. Oare House
55. The Old Bakery
56. The Old Rectory, Corsley
57. The Old Rectory, Stockton
58. Pertwood Manor
59. Pound Hill House
60. Ridleys Cheer
61. Sharcott Manor
62. 38 & 40 Sherford Road
63. Spye Park
64. Stourhead Garden
65. Stourton House
66. Upper Chelworth Farm
67. The Wardrobe
68. Waterdale House
69. Worton Gardens
70. Yew Tree Farm

East Kennett Manor, nr
  Marlborough
Great Somerford Gardens
Hannington Hall, Hannington
Job's Mill, Crockerton
Lackham Gardens, Lacock
Mallards, Chirton
Waterdale House, Milton

July 19 Sunday
The Abbey House, Malmesbury
East Stowell Gardens
13 Kingsdown Road, Stratton St
  Margaret
38 & 40 Sherford Road, Haydon
  Wick
Worton Gardens, Devizes

July 26 Sunday
Oare House, nr Pewsey

August 2 Sunday
Heale Gardens & Plant Centre,
  Middle Woodford
The Old Bakery, Milton
  Lilbourne

August 16 Sunday
Home Covert, Roundway
The Mead Nursery, Brokerswood

August 22 Saturday
Stourton House, Stourton

August 23 Sunday
Stourton House, Stourton
Upper Chelworth Farm, nr
  Cricklade

September 2 Wednesday
Sharcott Manor, nr Pewsey

September 6 Sunday
The Courts, Holts

September 13 Sunday
Avebury Manor Garden, Avebury

September 20 Sunday
Swaynes Mead, Great Durnford
Hillbarn House, Great Bedwyn

October 4 Sunday
Lackham Gardens, Lacock

October 7 Wednesday
Sharcott Manor, nr Pewsey

October 11 Sunday
Great Chalfield Manor, nr
  Melksham

1999
February 13, 14, 20 21
Lacock Abbey Gardens,
  Chippenham

DESCRIPTIONS OF GARDENS

■ **The Abbey House, Malmesbury** ✿❀ (Barbara & Ian Pollard) NNE of Market Cross adjoining C12 Abbey Church. Parking in long stay car park N of town (adjoins gardens). As seen BBC TV 'Meet the Ancestors'. Gardens developing around C16 house (not open) built upon C13 remains of The Abbott's house. Millennium planting of 2000 different roses and 2000 herbs. Formal gardens, laburnum tunnel, woodland, river and St Aldhelm's pool. Spring bulbs, rhododendrons, maples, bog garden and growing collection of rare shrubs and trees. TEA on NGS days. *Adm £2.80 Chd £1. Tues, Weds, Suns Easter to Oct 14. For NGS Easter Sun, Mon April 12, 13, Sun July 19 (10-6)*

¶**Alton Gardens** ✿ 7m SW of Marlborough, where Lockeridge/Woodborough-Upavon rd crosses Devizes/Pewsey rd, 6m Devizes, 4m Pewsey. Three gardens in Alton Priors and Alton Barnes, with short, partly field, walks between or car park for each. TEAS in aid of Save the Children Fund. *Combined adm £2.50 Chd £1. Sun June 21 (2-6)*

  ¶**Chandlers House** ❀ (Mr & Mrs A Hibbert-Hingston) ½-acre partly walled garden created since 1989, yew hedges, pleached limes, low walls and climbers. Interesting herbaceous and shrub borders, small formal old-rose garden with arches and tiny fountain pool, summer-house, paving and gravel plantings, iris bed
  ¶**The Priory** & (Cdm & Mrs J W Soames) ¾-acre surrounding house of medieval origins, set in the heart of the Wiltshire downs. Features incl herbaceous and shrub borders with decorative trees and many roses and climbers
  ¶**Yew Tree Cottage** ❀ (Mr & Mrs R Partis) ½-acre garden surrounding C18 thatched cottage. Colour themed well stocked herbaceous borders with clipped box and yew hedges. Thatched lattice-work summer house, ornamental kitchen garden, with espalier and cordon fruit, brick-edged beds and clipped box

Ark Farm, Tisbury ✿ (Mr & Mrs Edmund Neville-Rolfe) 9m from Shaftesbury. 2½m from Tisbury. From Tisbury follow English Heritage signs to Old Wardour Castle. Private rd from Castle car park to Ark Farm. 1¼ acres incl water and woodland gardens, as featured in Country Life and the Daily Telegraph. TEAS. *Adm £2 Chd free (ACNO to The Mental Health Foundation®). Sun June 14 (2-6)*

▲**Avebury Manor Garden, Avebury** ✿❀ (The National Trust) On A4361 9m N of Devizes 2m from Beckhampton roundabout on A4. Use main car park and follow signs to Manor. 5-acres. Ancient walled garden undergoing restoration on site of former priory, divided by stone walls and topiary hedges, incl rose garden, herbaceous border, new orchard, topiary garden. Italian walk and half moon garden. Late mediaeval manor house (open). Plant sales Sept only. *Adm House and Garden £3 Chd £1.50; Garden only £2.25 Chd £1. For NGS Suns June 14, Sept 13 (Garden 11-5) (House 2-5)*

Bolehyde Manor, Allington &❀ (Earl and Countess Cairns) 1½m W of Chippenham on Bristol Rd (A420). Turn N at Allington Xrds. ½m on R. Parking in field. A series of gardens around C16 Manor House; enclosed by walls and topiary, densely planted with many interesting shrubs and climbers, mixed rose and herbaceous beds; inner courtyard with troughs full of tender plants; wild flower orchard, vegetable, fruit garden and greenhouse yard. TEAS. *Adm £2 Chd 50p (ACNO to Kingston St Michael Church©). Sun June 21 (2.30-6). Also private groups welcome, please* Tel 01249 652105

■ **Bowood Rhododendron Walks, nr Chippenham** ✿ (The Earl of Shelburne) Entrance off A342 between Sandy Lane and Derry Hill villages. A breath-taking display of rhododendrons and azaleas from the minute detail of the individual flower to the grand sweep of colour formed by hundreds of shrubs, surrounded by a carpet of bluebells. *Open mid April to mid June, depending on the flowering season. For NGS Adm £3 Chd free. Sun May 31 (11-6).* Tel 01249 812102. *Also open* Bowood House & Gardens Luncheon and Teas. Garden centre. *Adm £5.20 OAP £4.30 Chd £3. April 1 to Nov 1 (11-6)*

¶**Bratton Gardens** 2m E of Westbury on B3098; Court Lane on N side leads to Lower Rd. Best parking nr to village green, footpaths lead to gardens. Teas on green in aid of village hall. *Combined adm £2.50 Acc chd free. Sun June 21 (2-6)*

¶**Court Lane Farm** ✿❀ (Lt Col & Mrs Anthony Hyde) A 2-acre country garden established in the past 23 yrs, with varied, mostly informal, planting; fruit and vegetables; surrounded by wildlife areas

¶**Merrydown** (Sqn Ldr & Mrs A Thompson) A flower arranger's garden with borders planted for colour and variety, incl shrubs, herbaceous and roses; small terrace garden and an unusual bamboo hedge; ⅕-acre with views over fields beyond

¶**Peach Tree Cottage** ✿ (Mr & Mrs C Little) Recently established ½-acre garden, planted with many unusual shrubs and conifers. Extensive use of mulching to reduce maintenance. Wild area and wildlife pond, no-dig vegetable beds, mixed borders and fruit

Bryher, Bromham ර✿ (Mr & Mrs Richard Packham) Yard Lane. 4m N of Devizes on A342 to Chippenham turn R into Yard Lane at Xrds. Compact level garden, approx 1 acre created around bungalow home. Borders planted mainly for foliage effect using wide range of red, gold, silver and variegated plants, with many unusual varieties; wildlife garden with short walks; display greenhouse. Views of Roundway Hill. *Adm £1. Private visits welcome, May to October, please* **Tel 01380 850455**

Chisenbury Priory, East Chisenbury ර✿❀ (Mr & Mrs John Manser) 6m SW of Pewsey, turn E from A345 at Enford then N to E Chisenbury, main gates 1m on R. Mediaeval Priory with Queen Anne face and early C17 rear (not open) in middle of 5-acre garden on chalk; mature garden with fine trees within clump and flint walls, herbaceous borders, shrubs, roses. Moisture loving plants along mill leat and carp pond, orchard and wild garden, many unusual plants. TEAS. *Adm £2 Chd free. Sun June 21 (2-6)*

The Close, Pewsey ර✿❀ (Mr & Mrs Simon Courtauld) 6m S of Marlborough, S end of Pewsey, off A345. Turn L at builders yard, then R before R Avon. 7 acres, informal herbaceous borders, shrubs, climbers, river walk and water meadow. TEAS in aid of Pewsey Church. *Adm £2 Chd free. Sun May 31 (2-6)*

Conholt Park, Chute See Hants

Conock Manor, Chirton ර✿❀ (Mr & Mrs Bonar Sykes) 5m SE of Devizes, off A342. Mixed borders, flowering shrubs; extensive replanting incl new arboretum and woodland walk; collection of eucalyptus trees. C18 house in Bath stone (not shown). TEA. *Adm £2 OAP/Chd £1 under 16 free (ACNO to St John the Baptist Church). Mon April 13 (2-6)*

▲**Corsham Court, nr Chippenham** ර✿ (James Methuen-Campbell Esq) 4m W of Chippenham. S of A4. Park and gardens laid out by Capability Brown and Repton. Large lawns with fine specimens of ornamental trees; rose garden; lily pond with Indian bean trees; spring bulbs; young arboretum; C18 bath house; Elizabethan mansion with al-

terations. TEAS. *Adm gardens £2 OAP £1.50 Chd £1. For NGS Suns March 29, June 14 (2-5.30)*

Coulston Gardens, Coulston ✿❀ TEAS in aid of Coulston Church and village hall. *Combined adm £3 Chd free. Sun June 21 (2-6)*

Baynton House 4m E of Westbury on B3098. 8 acres on green sand, incl two spring fed lakes, spring bulbs. Developing water garden, roses, herbaceous garden. Good variety of specimen trees. Garden much expanded in 86/87 and still expanding. Ample parking in deer park. C17 Georgian house (not open). *Adm £2 Chd free. Also open Sun April 19*

Font House (Mr & Mrs R S Hicks) 1½m E of Edington on B3098 take 1st L to Coulston, 1st house on L. 1-acre garden in rural surroundings which has been restored from a wilderness over past 30yrs and is still evolving; on 2 levels with courtyard, herbaceous/mixed borders, shrubs, herbs and trees

▲**The Courts, Holt** ර✿❀ (National Trust) Holt, 2m E of Bradford-on-Avon, S of B3107 to Melksham. In Holt follow National Trust signs, park at Village Hall. 3½-acres formal gardens divided by yew hedges and raised terraces. Features incl conservatory, lily pond, colour-themed herbaceous borders, pleached limes, venetian gates and stone ornaments. 3½ acres wildflower and arboretum; many fine trees. NT C15 House (not shown). Plant sales in Sept in aid of Bath Cancer Research Unit. Teas in church hall in aid of Church Hall Fund. *Adm £3 Chd £1.50. For NGS Suns June 21, Sept 6 (1.30-5.30)*

Crudwell Court Hotel, nr Malmesbury ර❀ (Nicholas Bristow Esq) On A429 Cirencester/Malmesbury rd. 2½-acre garden surrounding former C17 Rectory. Fine specimen 'rivers' beech, blue atlas cedar, magnolias, C12 dovecote surrounded by ancient yew hedges; Victorian sunken pond. Rose garden with spectrum and pastel coloured herbaceous border. Spring colour border outside conservatory. Herb garden; climbing roses; espaliered fruit trees and an Edwardian wooded walk. Swimming pool available in July. Coffee, lunch TEAS. *Adm £1.50 Chd free. Suns April 5, July 12 (11-5). Private visits welcome, please* **Tel 01666 577194**

¶**Dauntsey Gardens** ර✿ 5m SE of Malmesbury, 8m NW of Chippenham. Approach via Dauntsey Rd from Gt Somerford, 1¼m from Volunteer Inn. TEAS. *Combined adm £2.50 Chd 50p (ACNO to St James Church®). Sun June 7 (2-6)*

¶**Garden Cottage Dauntsey Park** (Miss Ann Sturgis) Continuing restoration of 5-acre garden, incl restored walled kitchen garden organically run; greenhouses; formal garden; orchard and woodland walks

¶**Idover House** (Mr & Mrs Christopher Jerram) Medium-sized mature garden in established setting with many mature trees incl two large wellingtonias, spacious lawns, herbaceous borders, formal rose garden; swimming pool garden, duck pond; yew walk to kitchen garden and woodland garden

East Kennet Manor, nr Marlborough ර✿❀ (Mrs C B Cameron) 5m W of Marlborough, ½m S of A4. 3-acre sarsen stone walled garden, featuring long herbaceous border; shrubs; herbs and several small gardens divided by hedges. C18 house (not open) with stable block and dovecote. *Adm £1.50 Chd free. Sun July 12 (2-6)*

¶**East Stowell Gardens** Turn W off A345 2m N of Pewsey; immed R, gardens 1m on L. Car park, East Stowell Farmhouse. TEAS July 19 only. *Combined adm £1.50 Chd free (ACNO to Oare School Building Fund©). Suns April 12, July 19 (2-6)*

¶**East Stowell Farmhouse** ✿❀ (Mrs Rosalind Adams) Mature country garden. Long mixed herbaceous border, shrubs, wild area, trees, hedges and open views to fields and Downs

¶**One New Cottage** (Tony Inwood) New garden started 2yrs ago. Spring and summer garden with bulbs and old roses with later flowering herbaceous borders. Many unusual plants, small vegetable garden, incl trellis and arches

¶**North Lodge** ✿ (Peter & Tracey Ranger) An enjoyable colourful display of mix shrub and perennial with containers and hanging baskets set in an orchard garden. *Only open July 19*

Edington Gardens 4m Westbury on B3098 halfway between Westbury and West Lavington. Follow signs and park outside The Monastery Garden for the Priory or in Church car park, and for The Old Vicarage walk up hill to B3098. Teas in Parish Hall. *Combined adm £3.50 Chd free (ACNO to Wiltshire Garden Trust®). Sun June 14 (2-6)*

Bonshommes Cottage (Michael Jones Esq) Through Old Vicarage garden. ¼-acre garden with mixed herbaceous, roses, shrubs. There is renewed effort to reduce the dominant Japanese knotweed, long established in this part of the former Vicarage garden

Edington Priory ঙ (Mr & Mrs Rupert Cooper) 4-acre gardens with medieval well, walls and carp lake. Herbaceous borders, kitchen garden and extensive lawns with shrubs and roses

The Monastery Garden ঙ (Mr & Mrs Allanson-Bailey) 2½-acre garden with many varieties of spring bulbs; orchard and shrub roses; mediaeval walls of national importance

The Old Vicarage ঙ✿❀ (J N d'Arcy Esq) A 2-acre garden on greensand situated on hillside with fine views; intensively planted with herbaceous borders; newly built wall borders, gravel garden; shrubs; a small arboretum with a growing range of trees; woodland plants; bulbs; lilies and recently introduced species from abroad. NCCPG National Collection of Evening primroses, over 20 species

Faulstone House, Bishopstone ঙ✿❀ (Miss Freya Watkinson) Take minor rd W off A354 at Coombe Bissett 3m SW of Salisbury, after 2m turn S into Harvest Lane 300yds E of White Hart Inn. Separate smaller gardens in large garden surrounding Old Manor House. C14 Defence Tower converted to pigeon loft in C18. Many old-fashioned roses, herbaceous plants (some unusual), large vegetable garden. Meadow with river frontage set in rural surroundings. TEAS in aid of Bishopstone Church. *Adm £1.50 Chd free. Sun June 14 (2-6)*

Fonthill House, nr Tisbury ❀ (The Lord Margadale) 3m N of Tisbury. W of Salisbury via B3089 in Fonthill Bishop.

Large woodland garden; daffodils, rhododendrons, azaleas, shrubs, bulbs; magnificent views; formal garden, limited for wheelchairs. TEAS. *Adm £1.50 Chd 30p. Sun April 19 (2-6)*

Foresters House, Sherston ঙ✿❀ (R Creed Esq) High Street. 5m from Malmesbury on B4040. Fascinating geometric design by the modernist Preben Jakobsen with subtle planting. All in an average size Cotswold stone walled village garden. Featured in 'Landscape Design' and 'Great Planting'. Garden grown plants for sale and TEAS in aid of Sherston Parish Church. *Adm £1.50 Chd free. Sun June 28 (2-6)*

Foscote Gardens, Grittleton ✿❀ 5m NW of Chippenham. A420 Chippenham-Bristol; after 2m turn R onto B4039 to Yatton Keynell, fork R for Grittleton; in village for 2m, just over motorway turn R at Xrds; house on right. Home-made TEAS. *Combined adm £1.50 Chd 30p. Sun June 14 (2-6)*

Foscote Stables (Mr & Mrs Barry Ratcliffe) 2½-acres; many clematis; shrub roses; unusual shrubs, trees; small collection ornamental ducks

Foscote Stables Cottage (Mrs Beresford Worswick) This adjoining garden has been re-designed and re-planted but still retains its cottage character. Unusual and some rare plants for sale

Goulters Mill Farm, Burton ✿❀ (Mr & Mrs Michael Harvey) The Gibb. On B4039 5m W of Chippenham; 2m NW of Castle Combe, through the Gibb. Park at top of 300 metre drive and walk down to garden. Approx ¾-acre cottage garden; mixed perennials, eremurus, old-fashioned roses; water garden and woodland walk. Home-made cream TEAS in aid of Russian Immigrants to Israel. *Adm £1.50 Chd 20p. Sun June 21 (2-5)*

▲**Great Chalfield Manor, nr Melksham** ✿❀ (The National Trust; Mr & Mrs Robert Floyd) 4m from Melksham. Take B3107 from Melksham then 1st R to Broughton Gifford follow sign for Atworth, turn L for 1m to Manor. Park on grass outside. Garden and grounds of 7 acres laid out 1905-12 by Robert Fuller and his wife. Garden paths, steps, dry walls relaid and rebuilt in 1985 and roses replanted; daffodils, spring flowers; topiary houses, borders, terraces, gazebo, orchard, autumn border. C15 moated manor (not open) and adjoining Parish Church. TEAS. *Adm £2.50 Chd free (ACNO to All Saints Church®). For NGS Suns April 5, Oct 11 (2-5)*

Great Durnford Gardens ঙ✿ Midway between Salisbury and Amesbury off the A345. Turn W at High Post Petrol Station to Woodfords. After 1m take 1st R to Great Durnford. Into village turn L and park next to Black Horse Inn (as signed). Lunches and Teas at Black Horse. *Combined adm £2.50. Sun June 21 (2-6)*

Old Hall ❀ (Mr & Mrs M Snell) Established part cob walled 2-acre village garden with lawns, herbaceous borders, featured vegetable patch and conservatory. Staddle barn, thatched barn, chickens and Herdwick sheep

Swaynes Mead (Major & Mrs Simon Poett) 1-acre of intensive garden established over last 30yrs. C17 thatched cottage with climbing roses. Many unusual plants, shrubs and trees for yr-round interest. **Swaynes Mead** *only, Adm £2. Sun Sept 20 (2-6)*

Great Somerford Gardens &*&❀* 2m N of M4 between junctions 17 and 18; 2m S of B4042 Malmesbury Wootton Bassett rd; 3m E of A429 Circencester-Chippenham rd. TEAS. *Combined adm £3, Chd under 13 free (ACNO to Parkinson's Society®). Sat, Sun July 11, 12 (1.30-6)*
  Old Church School (Cdr & Mrs Peter Neate) ¾-acre garden created over the last 5yrs from school playing field. Centred around formal yew-hedged area containing flourishing pool, parterre and shrubs, surrounded by herbaceous, hebe and rose beds, pergolas and arches, rockery and heathers and a good collection of trees and shrubs. TEAS
  The Old Maltings (Dr & Mrs S Jevons) Front garden recently designed with extensive and interesting herbaceous and shrub borders. Behind house is walk down to and across R Avon into conservation area with plantations of young native trees and shrubs
  The Mount House (C Kirkham-Sandy) 3 acres of lawns, shrubs. Large traditional fruit and vegetable garden. Approx 100 roses. Mainly creation of late Ann Phillips. The Mount area and new Coach House garden also open
  White Lodge, Startley *&* (Major & Mrs Jonathan Oliphant) Partially-walled garden, developed gradually over last 25 yrs. Old-fashioned roses, clematis, herbaceous borders, incl unusual plants. Topiary, catalpa tree. TEAS

Guyers House, Corsham &*&❀* (Mr & Mrs Guy Hungerford) Pickwick. Guyers Lane directly off A4 opp B3109 Bradford-on-Avon turning. Garden has been recently restored and is being extended. 5 acres of herbaceous borders, new yew walks, lawns, pond, walled garden, rose hoops, climbing and shrub roses; walled garden; kitchen garden. TEA. *Adm £1.50 Chd free. Sun June 21 (2-5.30)*

Hannington Hall, Hannington &❀ (Mrs A F Hussey-Freke) 5m N of Swindon. 2m NW of Highworth, from B4019 Highworth-Blunsdon, at Freke Arms, turn N for Hannington. 3 acres. Interesting trees and shrubs. Walled kitchen garden. Well preserved ice house. Very interesting house built in 1653. TEAS. *Adm £1.50 Chd free. Sun July 12 (2-5.30)*

▲**Hazelbury Manor Gardens, Wadswick, nr Box** &*&* 5m SW of Chippenham; 5m NE of Bath. From A4 at Box, A365 to Melksham, L onto B3109; 1st L; drive immed on R. 8 acres Grade II landscaped gardens around C15 fortified manor. Impressive yew topiary and clipped beeches around large lawn; herbaceous and mixed borders blaze in summer; laburnum and lime walkways. Other features incl rose garden, stone ring, enchanting fountain and rockery. TEAS. *Adm gardens only £2.80 OAP £2 Chd £1. For NGS Sat, Sun June 20, 21 (2-6). Private visits welcome, please* **Tel 01225 812952/812088**

■ **Heale Gardens & Plant Centre, Middle Woodford** &❀ (Guy Rasch Esq) 4m N of Salisbury on Woodford Valley Rd between A360 and A345. 8 acres beside R Avon; interesting and varied collection of plants, shrubs; roses in formal setting of clipped hedges and mellow stone-

work surrounding C17 manorhouse where Charles II hid after battle of Worcester. Water garden with magnolia and acer frames, authentic Japanese Tea House and Nikko bridge. Well stocked plant centre. Gift shop. Open all year. TEAS in house on NGS Sun pm only. *Adm £2.75 Acc chd under 14 free (ACNO to Salisbury Hospice®). For NGS Sun Aug 2 (10-5).* **Tel 01722 782504**

Hillbarn House, Great Bedwyn *&❀* (Mr & Mrs A J Buchanan) SW of Hungerford. S of A4 Hungerford-Marlborough. Medium-sized garden on chalk with hornbeam tunnel, pleached limes, herb garden; some planting by Lanning Roper; a series of gardens within a garden. Swimming pool may be used (under 12). Topiary. TEA. *Adm £2 Chd 50p. Suns June 21, Sept 20 (2-6). Private visits of 10 and over welcome, please* **Tel 01672 870207**

Home Covert, Roundway &❀ (Mr & Mrs John Phillips) 1m N of Devizes on minor rd signed Roundway linking A361 to A342, 1m from each main rd. Extensive garden on greensand created out of ancient woodland since 1960. Situated below the Downs with distant views. Formal borders around the house contrast with water gardens in the valley below. Planting is of wide botanical interest. TEAS on May 4 in aid of Wilts Wildlife Trust, Aug 16 in aid of St James Church Repair Fund. *Adm £2 Chd free. Mon May 4, Sun Aug 16 (2-6). Open at other times by prior arrangement, please* **Tel 01380 723407**

Hyde's House, Dinton ❀ (George Cruddas Esq) 5m W of Wilton, off B3089, next to church. 2 acres of wild and formal garden in beautiful situation with series of hedged garden rooms. Numerous spring bulbs and blossom. Open in June hopefully to catch the roses. Large walled kitchen garden, herb garden and C13 dovecote (open). Charming C16/18 Grade 1 listed house (not open), with lovely courtyard. NT walks around park and lake. TEAS in adjacent thatched 'old school room'. *Adm £2 Chd under 16 free (ACNO to St Mary's Church, Dinton®). Mon April 13, Sun June 28 (2-5). Private visits of 20 and over welcome, please* **Tel 01722 716203**

■ **Iford Manor, nr Bradford-on-Avon** (Mr & Mrs Hignett) Off A36 7 miles S of Bath – sign to Iford 1m or from Bradford-on-Avon/Trowbridge via Lower Westwood village (brown signs). Entrance and free parking at Iford Bridge. Very romantic Italian-style terraced garden, listed Grade 1, home of Harold Peto 1899-1933. House not shown. TEAS May to Sept, Sats, Suns and Bank Hol Mons. *Adm £2.50 OAPs/Student/Chd 10+ £1.90. Open daily May to Sept (except Mons & Fris), April & Oct Suns only. For NGS Sun April 26 (2-5). Private visits welcome at other times for groups, please* **Tel 01225 863146, 862364 messages and Fax**

Inwoods, Farleigh Wick &❀ (Mr & Mrs D S Whitehead) 3m NW of Bradford-on-Avon. From Bath via A363 towards Bradford-on-Avon; at Farleigh Wick, 100yds past Fox & Hounds, R into drive. 5 acres with lawns, borders, flowering shrubs, wild garden, wild flower wood. TEAS in aid of Muscular Dystrophy. *Adm £1.50 Chd 50p. Sun May 31 (2-6)*

Job's Mill, Crockerton ❀ (Virginia, Marchioness of Bath) 1½m S of Warminster. Bus: Salisbury-Bath, alight Warminster. Medium-sized garden; small terraced garden, through which R Wylye flows; swimming pool; kitchen garden. TEAS. *Adm £1.50 Chd 50p (ACNO to WWF®). Sun July 12 (2-6)*

13 Kingsdown Road, Stratton St Margaret ⚮❀ (Mr & Mrs Kenneth Tomlin) Approach from S on A419. L at Kennedys Garden Centre (signposted Upper Stratton). ½m turn L at t-lights and park opp Kingsdown inn. Long and narrow garden on edge of town closely planted with shrubs and herbaceous plants. Vegetable garden. Unusual plants with some for sale. Example of maximum use of space available. TEA. *Adm £1 Chd free. Suns June 7, July 19 (2-6)*

■ **Lackham Gardens, Lacock** ♿❀ (Lackham College Principal D E Williams) 2m S of Chippenham on A350. Few mins S of junction 17 on M4. Walled garden with greenhouses, lawn paths separating plots, labelled with variety of interesting shrubs, unusual vegetables, herbaceous plants, fruit. Pleasure gardens with historical collection of roses, mixed borders, lawns; woodland walks down to river. Museum of Agricultural/Horticultural Equipment, animal park. Adventure playground. Coffee shop; TEAS Bookable menu (11-4). *Adm £3 Chd £1 (ACNO to Horticultural Therapy of Frome, Somerset®). For NGS Suns July 12, Oct 4 (2-5)*

▲**Lacock Abbey Gardens, Chippenham** ♿⚮❀ (National Trust) Off A350 between Melksham-Chippenham. Follow National Trust signs. Use public car park just outside Abbey. Victorian woodland garden with a pond and exotic tree specimens. Display of early spring flowers with carpets of aconites; snowdrops; crocuses and daffodils. C13 Abbey with C18 gothic additions. (Mediaeval cloisters and Fox Talbot Museum open on NGS days, house closed until April). Teas in village. *Adm £1.80 Chd free. For NGS Sats, Suns Feb 14, 15; 21, 22 (2-5) 1999 Sats, Suns Feb 13, 14; 20, 21 (2-5). Parties welcome, please* Tel 01249 730227/730459

Landford Lodge, nr Salisbury ♿❀ (Mr & Mrs Christopher Pilkington) 9m SE of Salisbury turn W off A36; garden ½m N of Landford. C18 House (not open) in lovely parkland overlooking lake; many fine trees. Special feature 3-acre wood with rhododendrons and azaleas. Herbaceous; ornamental terrace and swimming pool (open). Tree nursery. 500 varieties of trees planted in alphabetical order in walled garden. TEAS. *Adm £1.50 Chd 50p (ACNO to Salisbury Mencap Horticultural Trust®). Sun June 14 (2-5). Private parties of 10 and over welcome, please* Tel 01794 390247

Little Durnford Manor, nr Salisbury ♿❀ (Earl & Countess of Chichester) 3m N of Salisbury, just beyond Stratford-sub-Castle. Extensive lawns with cedars; walled gardens, fruit trees, large vegetable garden; small knot and herb gardens, terraces, borders, gravel garden, water garden, lake with islands, river walks. Cottage Garden also on view. Home-made TEAS. *Adm £1.50 Chd 50p (ACNO to Wessex Medical School Trust®). Suns May 3, June 28 (2-6)*

■ **Long Hall Gardens & Nursery, Stockton** ♿⚮❀ (Mr & Mrs N H Yeatman-Biggs) 7m SE of Warminster; S of A36; W of A303 Wylye interchange. 4-acre mainly formal; series of gardens within a garden; clipped yews; flowering shrubs, fine old trees; masses of spring bulbs; fine hellebore walk. C13 Hall (not open). TEAS. *Adm £2 Chd free (ACNO to Stockton Church®). 1st Sat of the month from May 2 to Aug 1 (2-6). Private visits welcome, please* Tel 01985 850424. *Adjacent nursery specialising in chalk tolerant plants, all organically grown, many uncommon varieties and new introductions. Wed (9.30-5.30) to Sat (9.30-7), March 18 to Sept 26. For NGS Suns April 19, June 28 (2-6).*

Lower House, Whiteparish ♿⚮❀ (Mr & Mrs D J Wood) On A27 between Salisbury and Romsey (7m). Garden is N side of A27, Salisbury end of village, opp Newton Bungalows. Informal garden of 1 acre containing part of National Collection of Hellebores. *Adm £1.50 Chd free. Sun March 15 (2-4) Private visits welcome by appt Mon to Sat, March 9 to 24 (10-12 and 2-4), please* Tel 01794 884306

Luckington Court, Luckington ♿❀ (The Hon Mrs Trevor Horn) 10m NW of Chippenham; 6m W of Malmesbury. Turn S off B4040 Malmesbury-Bristol rd. Medium-sized garden, mainly formal, well-designed, amid exquisite group of ancient buildings; fine collection of ornamental cherries; other flowering shrubs. House much altered in Queen Anne times but ancient origins evident; Queen Anne hall and drawing-room shown. TEAS in aid of Luckington Parish Church. *Collecting box. Sun May 10 (2.30-6)*

Mallards, Chirton ♿⚮❀ (Mr & Mrs T Papé) 4½m SE of Devizes just N of A342. Through village and garden is on R. 1-acre garden with several distinct areas: hot sunny borders, rose garden, woodland glades and bog garden. All informally planted and tucked into woodland on the banks of the upper R Avon. Also a woodland walk. TEAS in aid of Chirton & Marden Parish Churches. *Adm £1.50 Chd free. Suns June 7, July 12 (2-6)*

Manor Farm, Monkton Deverill ♿❀ (W G M Wood) 5m S of Warminster. Take Mere rd off A350 at Longbridge Deverill. Monkton Deverill 2m. C18 and C19 village farmhouse garden. Walled kitchen garden. New orchards and hedging, formal and informal planting. Box nursery. Picnics welcome. TEAS. *Adm £1 Chd free. Sun June 14 (12-6)*

Manor House Farm, Hanging Langford ♿ (Miss Anne Dixon) 9m NW of Salisbury S of A36 Salisbury-Warminster. 3m SE of A303 Wylye interchange. Follow signs from Steeple Langford. Series of walled gardens with masses of bulbs, herbaceous plants, many shrubs, old-fashioned roses, collection of clematis, peonies and delphiniums. Ornamental pond, secret garden in walls of shearing barn, superb walnut, C14/16 Wiltshire manor house (not open). Teas Hanging Langford Village Hall in aid of Village Hall Fund. *Adm £2 Chd free. Sun April 5 (2-6)*

March End, Sherfield English See Hants

Martins, Whitehill ⚘❀ (Mrs Diana Young) Bradford-on-Avon. The top of Whitehill is off New Rd (N side of town) and Martins is the 4th house down from the top. Whitehill is 200yds from Castle Inn and Christ Church. No Parking at garden. Parking in nearby streets and town centre car parks. Surprisingly spacious garden on several levels with magnificent S facing views. Restful but full of colour and character, incl small orchard and meadow, ancient lime and mulberry. TEAS in aid of Dorothy House Foundation. *Adm £1.50 Chd free. Sun June 7 (2-6)*

■ **The Mead Nursery, Brokerswood** ⚘❀ (Mr & Mrs S Lewis-Dale) Equidistant Frome and Westbury E of Rudge. Follow signs for Woodland Park. Halfway between Rudge and Woodland Park. 1¼-acre nursery with over 1,000 varieties of herbaceous perennials, alpines and bulbs, many unusual. Display beds for colour and design ideas. Raised beds, sink garden, and bog bed. TEAS on NGS day only. *Adm £1.50 Chd £1 to incl teas. Nursery open Feb 1 to Oct 31 Wed to Sat (9-5), Sun (12-5). For NGS Sun Aug 16 (12-5), please* Tel 01373 859990

¶**Mevagissy, Burbage** ⚘❀ (Mrs Pamela Mitchell) 6m SE of Marlborough off A346. Garden 20 metres from Burbage Royal British Legion Hall. Large cottage garden with vegetables, fruit, flowers, many rare plants; water feature; glasshouses incl unusual succulents and cacti. *Adm £1.50 OAP £1 Chd 50p. Open by appt, April to Sept,* Tel 01672 810026

▲**Mompesson House, Salisbury** ⚘❀ (The National Trust) The Close. Enter Salisbury Cathedral Close via High St Gate and Mompesson House is on the R. The appeal of this comparatively small but attractive garden is the lovely setting in Salisbury Cathedral Close and with a well-known Queen Anne House. Planting as for an old English garden with raised rose and herbaceous beds around the lawn. Climbers on pergola and walls; shrubs and small lavender walk. TEAS. *Adm £1 Chd free. For NGS Sat May 30 (11-5)*

7 Norton Bavant, nr Warminster ⚘❀ (Mr & Mrs J M Royds) 2m E of Warminster on A36 turn W to Sutton Veny on Cotley Hill roundabout at Heytesbury, then R to Norton Bavant. Turn R in village, 1st house on R after tall conifer hedge. Alpine plant collector's garden with numerous varieties (many rare). Spring bulbs, alpine house, many troughs, borders, dwarf conifers and specialised collection of daphnes. Members of AGS especially welcome. TEAS in aid of Norton Bavant Church. *Adm £1.50 Chd free. Sun May 17 (2-5). Private visits and parties welcome March to June, please* Tel 01985 840491

Oare House, nr Pewsey ⚘ (Henry Keswick Esq) 2m N of Pewsey on Marlborough Rd (A345). Fine house (not open) in large garden with fine trees, hedges, spring flowers, woodlands; extensive lawns and kitchen garden. TEA. *Adm £2 Chd free (ACNO to The Order of St John®). Suns April 26, July 26 (2-6)*

The Old Bakery, Milton Lilbourne ⚘❀ (Joyce, Lady Crossley) E of Pewsey on B3087. Turn down village st by garage at Xrds. The Old Bakery opp churchyard. Fairly intensive 1-acre garden. Mixed shrub and herbaceous plantings. 3 small glasshouses; small rock garden; some rare

plants. Home-made TEAS. *Adm £1.50 Chd free. Sun Aug 2 (2-6). Private parties welcome, please* Tel 01672 562716

The Old Rectory, Corsley ⚘❀ (Mr & Mrs L N Lacey) Midway Frome/Warminster. Take A3098 (Frome) off A36. ½m turn L signposted Corsley. Also accessible from A361. A C16 Rectory with Georgian facade added 1827 in 3½ acres of pleasure gardens. During past centuries each occupier has progressively developed garden. Continued by present owners, who have re-established many older areas, made their own contribution to overall pattern. Mixed shrub and herbaceous planting, rose and water gardens, vegetable garden, orchard, woodland walks. Many unusual plants and trees, over 80 varieties of clematis. TEAS. *Adm £2 Chd 50p (ACNO to Imperial Cancer Research Fund®). Suns April 19, June 28 (2-6)*

The Old Rectory, Stockton ⚘❀ (Mr & Mrs David Harrison) 7m SE of Warminster, S of A36 W of A303 Wylye interchange. 2-acre garden surrounds C18 house, with lawns and fine old trees incl a cedar and a beech. To the S it splits into several smaller gardens; entirely walled herb garden with variety of herbs, with climbers, fine roses and vines. The orchard, dominated by stunning walnut tree, leads to 3 smaller walled gardens with a variety of plants incl roses and peonies. Featured on TV and in the recently published 'A guide to garden visits', by Judith Witching. TEAS. *Adm £1.75 Chd free. Sun June 14 (2-6). Private visits welcome, please* Tel 01985 850607

Pertwood Manor, Hindon ⚘❀ (Mr & Mrs James Giles) Off A350 (1m N of A303) 7m Shaftesbury, 8m Warminster. Take signs marked Pertwood Manor farm. 1½-acre part walled garden surrounding manor house (not open) in elevated position with lovely views. Herbaceous borders, various trees and shrubs. Sunken rose garden. Short woodland walk, small vegetable garden. Recently restored Church of St Peter. Home-made TEAS. *Adm £1.50 Chd free (ACNO to NSPCC®). Sun June 14 (2-6)*

■ **Pound Hill House, West Kington** ⚘❀ (Mr & Mrs P Stockitt) From A420 Chippenham-Bristol rd turn R by Shoe garage, then 2nd L, 2nd R into village, entrance at nursery. Series of small gardens, set around C15 Cotswold house, to provide interest throughout yr. Old-fashioned rose garden with clipped box, small Victorian vegetable garden, old shrub roses, herbaceous borders, water garden, courtyard garden with planted pots and containers. Planted paved area, also buxus, taxus, topiary. Connoisseur plants available in retail plant area. TEAS in aid of West Kington Church. *Adm £2. Open 7 days a week (2-6) Feb to Dec. Adm £2. For NGS Sun June 28 (2-6). Parties welcome,* Tel 01249 782781

Ridleys Cheer, Mountain Bower ⚘❀ (Mr & Mrs A J Young) N Wraxall. At 'The Shoe' on A420 8m W of Chippenham turn N then take 2nd L and 1st R. 1½-acre informal garden with unusual trees and shrubs; incl acers, liriodendrons, magnolias, oaks, salix and zelkova. Some 75 different shrub rose varieties incl hybrid musks, albas and species roses; planted progressively over past 22 yrs; also potager and 2-acre arboretum planted 1989. Cream TEAS in aid of N Wraxall Church and Dorothy House Foundation. *Adm £2 Chd under 14 free. Suns April 26,*

May 17, June 28 (2-6). Private visits welcome, please **Tel 01225 891204**

Sharcott Manor, nr Pewsey &✿❀ (Capt & Mrs David Armytage) 1m SW of Pewsey via A345. 5-acre garden with water planted for yr-round interest. Many young trees, bulbs, climbers and densely planted mixed borders of shrubs, roses, perennials and unusual plants, some of which are for sale in the small garden nursery. TEAS in aid of IFAW and Wiltshire Air Ambulance appeal. *Adm £2 Chd free. First Weds in every month from April to Oct (Except Aug) (11-5). Suns April 5, June 28 (2-6) all for NGS. Also private visits welcome, please* **Tel 01672 563485**

¶38 & 40 Sherford Rd, Haydon Wick ✿❀ (Mr & Mrs Barry Furness & Mr & Mrs Arnold Mack) Swindon. From A419 Turnpike roundabout take A4311. Turn R at the Moonrakers Inn (B4006) and follow for 1m turning R into Thames Avenue. Pass through traffic calming scheme, turn L into Avonmead follow for ½m turning L into Sherford Rd. Fine examples of packing large selection of plants into small urban gardens approx 100' long. Both are planted with many unusual varieties (shrubs, conifers, climbers, herbaceous, tender and annuals). No 38 is 2yrs into development while no 40 has a 15 yr history, and contrasts the development and maturity of gardening. Range of plants and permanent features eg ponds, pergolas, give inspiration to those who wish to develop their own small plot. TEA. *Adm £1.50 Chd free. Suns June 14, July 19 (11-5)*

Spye Park, nr Chippenham ❀ (Mr & Mrs Simon Spicer) Take A342 Chippenham and Devizes rd, turn W at Sandy Lane opp 'The George' public house. Turn S after ½m at White Lodge. Follow signs to car park. Exit only through the village of Chittoe. 25-acre woodland walk through carpets of bluebells with paths cut through the wood. Some fine old trees mostly oak and beech, survivors of the 1989 hurricane, incl the remnants of 1000-yr-old King Oak with the 900-yr-old Queen still alive. TEAS. *Adm £1 Chd free (ACNO to Southmead Hospital Special Care Baby Unit©). Sun May 3 (11-5). Private parties welcome when bluebells are out, please* **Tel 01249 730247**

▲Stourhead Garden, Stourton &✿ (The National Trust) 3m NW of Mere on B3092. One of earliest and greatest landscape gardens in the world; creation of banker Henry Hoare in 1740s on his return from the Grand Tour, inspired by paintings of Claude and Poussin; planted with rare trees, rhododendrons and azaleas over last 240yrs. Open every day of year. Lunch, tea and supper Spread Eagle Inn at entrance. NT shop. Teas (Buffet service Village Hall). *Adm March to Oct £4.40 Chd £2.40 parties of 15 or over £3.70. Nov to Feb £3.40 Chd 1.50. For NGS Sun June 7 (9-7)*

■ Stourton House, Stourton &✿❀ (Mrs Anthony Bullivant) 3m NW of Mere (A303) on rd to Stourhead. Park in NT car park. 4½-acres informal gardens; much to attract plantsmen and idea seekers. Interesting bulbs, plants and shrubs, through all seasons. Speciality daffodils, delphiniums and hydrangeas. Well known for 'Stourton Dried Flowers' whose production interest visitors. Coffee, lunch, TEAS in Stourton House Garden. *April 1 to end Nov, Sun, Wed, Thurs and Bank Hol Mons. Adm £2.50 Chd 50p*

(ACNO to St Peters Church, Stourton®). For NGS Sats, Suns May 16, 17; Aug 22, 23 (11-6). Private visits welcome for parties of 12 and over any day, please **Tel 01747 840417**

Upper Chelworth Farm, nr Cricklade &✿❀ (Mr & Mrs Hopkins) Take B4040 off A419, through Cricklade, L at 1st Xrds, 1st house on L. Approx ½-acre garden of mixed perennials, shrubs and water garden. Small nursery. TEAS. *Adm £1 Chd free. Sun April 12, Sat May 9, Suns June 7, July 5, Aug 23 (2-6)*

2 Warren Farm Cottages, West Tytherley See Hants

¶▲The Wardrobe, Salisbury &✿ (Wardrobe & Museum Trustees) 58 The Close. Enter via High St gate. The Wardrobe is along West Walk. Bounded by original walls and R Avon, redesigned garden incl herbaceous borders, shrubs, mature trees and lawn. TEAS. *Adm incl entrance to house and military museum £2 Chd 50p (ACNO to Wardrobe and Museum Trust®). Sat May 30 (10-5).* **Tel 01722 414536**

Waterdale House, Milton ❀ (Mr & Mrs Julian Seymour) East Knoyle. North of East Knoyle on A350 turn W signed Milton, garden signed from village. 4-acre mature woodland garden with rhododendrons, azaleas, camellias, maples, magnolias, ornamental water redesigned with new terrace, bog garden; herbaceous borders. Gravelled pot garden. TEAS if fine. *Adm £1.50 Chd free. Suns May 10, July 12 (2-5). Private visits welcome April to July, lunches for parties up to 20 if required, please* **Tel 01747 830262**

Worton Gardens, Devizes &✿ Devizes-Salisbury A360 turn W in Potterne or just N of West Lavington. From Seend turn S at Bell Inn, follow signs to Worton. TEAS at Ivy House. *Combined adm £2 Chd free. Sun July 19 (2-6)*

> **Ashton House** ❀ (Mrs Colin Shand) ½-acre garden in 3 sections with herbaceous borders, many shrubs and birch grove; walled courtyard and raised vegetable garden; lovely views across Avon Vale
>
> **Brookfield House** &✿ (Mr & Mrs Graham Cannon) A new 1-acre garden owned since 1993, and being developed with small children in mind. Part-walled garden with mixed borders and separate fruit and vegetable garden
>
> **Ivy House** (Lt Gen Sir Maurice and Lady Johnston) 2-acre series of gardens separated by yew hedges and walls; herbaceous borders; shrubs; pond garden with maples and many fine trees incl swamp cypress, holm and red oak, medlar and mulberry; interesting vegetable garden and large greenhouse
>
> **Oakley House** ❀ (Mr & Mrs Michael Brierley) ½-acre village garden with herbaceous borders, roses, many shrubs; small pond and bog garden within a rockery; planted by owners since 1974

¶Yew Tree Farm, Hankerton ✿❀ (E I & Mrs C H Grierson) Off the B429 at Malmesbury take B4040 to Cricklade, turn L at E end of Charlton to Hankerton, approx 1m on L. Approx 1 acre developed over the last 10yrs, mixed herbaceous and shrub borders, with pergolas and arches, two ponds and vegetable garden. *Adm £1.50 Chd 50p. Suns June 28, July 5 (2-6)*

Worcestershire

Hon County Organiser:	Mrs Barbara Phillips, Cedar Lodge, Blakeshall, Wolverley, nr Kidderminster DY11 5XR Tel 01562 850238
Assistant County Organisers:	Mrs Jeanie Neil, Viewlands, Blakeshall, Wolverley, nr Kidderminster DY11 5XL Tel 01562 850360
	Mrs Jane Carr, Conderton Manor, nr Tewkesbury, Glos GL20 7PR Tel 01386 725389
Hon County Treasurer:	Mrs Lorraine Purcell, 73 Worcester Road, West Hagley, Stourbridge, West Midlands DY9 OLF Tel 01562 885936

DATES OF OPENING

Regular openings
For details see garden description

Barn House, Broadway
Barnards Green House, Malvern
Bodenham Arboretum,
 Wolverley
The Cockshoot, Castlemorton
Eastgrove Cottage Nursery, nr
 Shrawley
The Elms, Lower Broadheath
Kyre Park, Tenbury Wells
The Manor House, Birlingham
The Priory, Kemerton
Red House Farm, Bradley Green, nr
 Redditch
Spetchley Park, nr Worcester
Stone House, Cottage Gardens,
 Stone
White Cottage, Stock Green nr
 Inkberrow

By appointment only
*For telephone numbers and other
details see garden descriptions.
Private visits welcomed*

Conderton Manor, nr Tewkesbury
Impney Park, Droitwich Spa
Keepers Cottage, Alvechurch
Overbury Court, nr Tewkesbury
Shuttifield Cottage, Birchwood

February 19 Thursday
 Dial Park, Chaddesley Corbett
March 18 Wednesday
 The Cottage, Broughton Green,
 nr Hanbury
March 22 Sunday
 Little Malvern Court, nr Malvern
March 29 Sunday
 Kyre Park, Tenbury Wells
 White Cottage, Stock Green, nr
 Inkberrow
April 1 Wednesday
 The Elms, Lower Broadheath

April 2 Thursday
 Barnard's Green House, Malvern
April 5 Sunday
 Ripple Hall, nr Tewkesbury
April 10 Friday
 Spetchley Park, nr Worcester
April 12 Sunday
 Eastgrove Cottage Garden
 Nursery, nr Shrawley
 White Cottage, Stock Green, nr
 Inkberrow
 Whitlenge House Cottage,
 Hartlebury
April 13 Monday
 Stone House Cottage Gardens,
 Stone
 Whitlenge House Cottage,
 Hartlebury
April 15 Wednesday
 The Cottage, Broughton Green,
 nr Hanbury
 Holland House, Cropthorne
April 19 Sunday
 Astley Horticultural Society
 Barbers, Martley, nr Worcester
 Barnard's Green House,
 Malvern
April 22 Wednesday
 The Elms, Lower Broadheath
April 26 Sunday
 Eastgrove Cottage Garden
 Nursery, nr Shrawley
April 29 Wednesday
 St Egwins Cottage, Norton,
 Evesham
April 30 Thursday
 Dial Park, Chaddesley Corbett
May 3 Sunday
 Arley House, Upper Arley, nr
 Bewdley
 The Cockshoot, Castlemorton
 The Cottage Herbery, Boraston,
 Tenbury Wells
 The Manor House, Birlingham, nr
 Pershore
 Stone House Cottage Gardens,
 Stone
 Windyridge, Kidderminster

May 4 Monday
 The Cockshoot, Castlemorton
 The Manor House, Birlingham, nr
 Pershore
 Stone House Cottage Gardens,
 Stone
May 6 Wednesday
 Monsieurs Hall, Bromsgrove
May 7 Thursday
 Barnard's Green House, Malvern
 Monsieurs Hall, Bromsgrove
May 10 Sunday
 Eastgrove Cottage Garden
 Nursery, nr Shrawley
 St Egwins Cottage, Norton,
 Evesham
 Spetchley Park, nr Worcester
 Windyridge, Kidderminster
May 13 Wednesday
 St Egwins Cottage, Norton,
 Evesham
May 14 Thursday
 The Manor House, Birlingham, nr
 Pershore
May 17 Sunday
 24 Alexander Avenue, Droitwich
 Spa
 The Cottage Herbery, Boraston,
 Tenbury Wells
 Priors Court, Long Green
 White Cottage, Stock Green, nr
 Inkberrow
May 18 Monday
 Ivytree House, Clent
May 20 Wednesday
 The Cottage, Broughton Green,
 nr Hanbury
 The Elms, Lower Broadheath
 Ivytree House, Clent
 Red House Farm, Bradley Green
May 24 Sunday
 Astley Towne House
 The Cockshoot, Castlemorton
 The Cottage Herbery, Boraston,
 Tenbury Wells
 The Manor House, Birlingham, nr
 Pershore
 The Priory, Kemerton

Stone House Cottage Gardens,
Stone
White Cottage, Stock Green, nr
Inkberrow
Whitlenge House Cottage,
Hartlebury
May 25 Monday
The Cockshoot, Castlemorton
The Manor House, Birlingham, nr
Pershore
Stone House Cottage Gardens,
Stone
Whitlenge House Cottage,
Hartlebury
May 27 Wednesday
Holland House, Cropthorne
May 28 Thursday
Barnard's Green House, Malvern
The Priory, Kemerton
May 31 Sunday
Cedar Lodge, Blakeshall, nr
Wolverley
The Cockshoot, Castlemorton
Woodmancote, Wadborough
June 3 Wednesday
St Egwins Cottage, Norton,
Evesham
June 7 Sunday
The Cockshoot, Castlemorton
The Cottage Herbery, Boraston,
Tenbury Wells
Eastgrove Cottage Garden
Nursery, nr Shrawley
Glenclyne, Cropthorne
Madresfield Court, nr Malvern
Pershore College of Horticulture
St Egwins Cottage, Norton,
Evesham
White Cottage, Stock Green, nr
Inkberrow
June 11 Thursday
The Manor House, Birlingham, nr
Pershore
The Priory, Kemerton
June 13 Saturday
White Cottage, Stock Green, nr
Inkberrow
June 14 Sunday
24 Alexander Avenue, Droitwich
Spa
Bell's Castle, Kemerton
Charlton House, Lulsley,
Knightwick
The Cockshoot, Castlemorton
Hanbury Hall, nr Droitwich
Orchard Bungalow, Bishops
Frome
Pershore Gardens, Pershore
Stone House Cottage Gardens,
Stone
Upper Court, Kemerton
Woodmancote, Wadborough
June 15 Monday
Ivytree House, Clent

June 17 Wednesday
The Cottage, Broughton Green,
nr Hanbury
Ivytree House, Clent
Monsieurs Hall, Bromsgrove
Red House Farm, Bradley Green
June 18 Thursday
Dial Park, Chaddesley Corbett
Monsieurs Hall, Bromsgrove
June 21 Sunday
Birtsmorton Court, nr Malvern
Broadway Church Street Gardens
Eastgrove Cottage Garden
Nursery, nr Shrawley
Eldersfield Court, Eldersfield
The Priory, Kemerton
White Cottage, Stock Green, nr
Inkberrow
June 24 Wednesday
The Elms, Lower Broadheath
June 25 Thursday
Barnard's Green House, Malvern
June 28 Sunday
The Cockshoot, Castlemorton
The Cottage Herbery, Boraston,
Tenbury Wells
Eldersfield Court, Eldersfield
Woodmancote, Wadborough
July 5 Sunday
Broadway, Snowshill Road
Gardens
Spetchley Park, nr Worcester
Yew Tree House, Ombersley
July 9 Thursday
Monsieurs Hall, Bromsgrove
July 12 Sunday
Arley Cottage, Upper Arley, nr
Bewdley
Eastgrove Cottage Garden
Nursery, nr Shrawley
Orchard Bungalow, Bishops
Frome
The Priory, Kemerton
Woollas Hall, Eckington, nr
Pershore
July 13 Monday
Ivytree House, Clent
July 15 Wednesday
The Cottage, Broughton Green,
nr Hanbury
Ivytree House, Clent
Red House Farm, Bradley Green
St Egwins Cottage, Norton,
Evesham
July 16 Thursday
Barnard's Green House, Malvern
The Manor House, Birlingham, nr
Pershore
July 18 Saturday
Abberley Gardens, Nr Worcester
July 19 Sunday
Abberley Gardens, Nr Worcester
24 Alexander Avenue, Droitwich
Spa

The Cottage Herbery, Boraston,
Tenbury Wells
Glenclyne, Cropthorne
July 26 Sunday
Eastgrove Cottage Garden
Nursery, nr Shrawley
St Egwins Cottage, Norton,
Evesham
July 28 Tuesday
The Elms, Lower Broadheath
August 2 Sunday
The Priory, Kemerton
August 5 Wednesday
St Egwins Cottage, Norton,
Evesham
August 6 Thursday
Barnard's Green House, Malvern
August 9 Sunday
Orchard Bungalow, Bishops Frome
August 18 Tuesday
The Elms, Lower Broadheath
August 19 Wednesday
The Cottage, Broughton Green,
nr Hanbury
August 23 Sunday
The Priory, Kemerton
August 30 Sunday
Barnard's Green House, Malvern
Stone House Cottage Gardens,
Stone
Whitlenge House Cottage,
Hartlebury
August 31 Monday
Stone House Cottage Gardens,
Stone
Whitlenge House Cottage,
Hartlebury
September 6 Sunday
The Priory, Kemerton
September 10 Thursday
The Manor House, Birlingham, nr
Pershore
September 15 Tuesday
The Elms, Lower Broadheath
September 16 Wednesday
The Cottage, Broughton Green,
nr Hanbury
September 27 Sunday
Bodenham Arboretum, Wolverley
Eastgrove Cottage Garden
Nursery, nr Shrawley
White Cottage, Stock Green, nr
Inkberrow
September 30 Wednesday
The Elms, Lower Broadheath
October 4 Sunday
Kyre Park, Tenbury Wells
October 18 Sunday
Nerine Nursery, Welland

1999
February 18 Thursday
Dial Park, Chaddesley Corbett

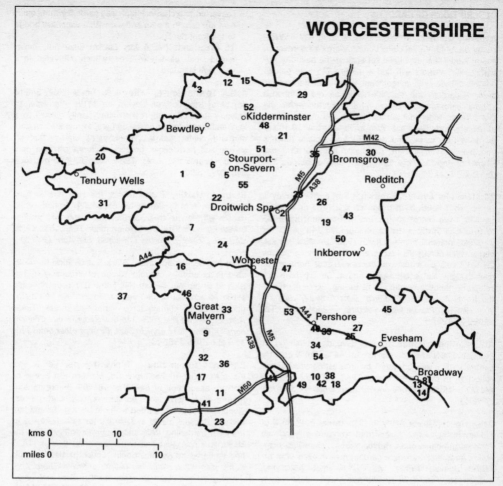

WORCESTERSHIRE

KEY

1. Abberley Gardens
2. 24 Alexander Avenue
3. Arley Cottage
4. Arley House
5. Astley Horticultural Soc
6. Astley Towne House
7. Barbers
8. Barn House
9. Barnard's Green House
10. Bell's Castle
11. Birtsmorton Court
12. Bodenham Arboretum
13. Broadway Church Street Gardens
14. Broadway, Snowshill Road
15. Cedar Lodge Blakeshall Gardens
16. Charlton House
17. The Cockshoot
18. Conderton Manor
19. The Cottage, Broughton Green

20. The Cottage, Herbery
21. Dial Park
22. Eastgrove Cottage Garden Nursery
23. Eldersfield Court
24. The Elms
25. Glenclyne
26. Hanbury Hall
27. Holland House
28. Impney Park
29. Ivytree House
30. Keepers Cottage
31. Kyre Park
32. Little Malvern Court
33. Madresfield Court
34. The Manor House
35. Monsieur's Hall
36. Nerine Nursery
37. Orchard Bungalow

38. Overbury Court
39. Pershore College of Horticulture
40. Pershore Gardens
41. Priors Court
42. The Priory
43. Red House Farm
44. Ripple Hall
45. St Egwins Cottage
46. Shuttifield Cottage
47. Spetchley Park
48. Stone House Cottage Gardens
49. Upper Court
50. White Cottage
51. Whitlenge House Cottage
52. Windyridge
53. Woodmancote
54. Woollas Hall
55. Yew Tree House

DESCRIPTIONS OF GARDENS

Abberley Gardens, nr Worcester ❀ 12m NW of Worcester on A443. Varied collection of approx 13 gardens in and around Abberley Village set against the beautiful Abberley Hills. Visitors will find a mature 2½ acre garden on the hillside with magnificent views and herbaceous beds; a garden with lakeside walk; an old farmhouse scented garden, and a 5-acre garden created within the last 5 years. Individual garden details and map provided at gardens and village hall. Also available from 10.30 onwards will be coffee and delicious home-made lunches and teas in Village Hall. *Combined adm £2 Chd free (ACNO to Abberley Parochial Church Council®). Sat, Sun July 18, 19 (11.30-5)*

24 Alexander Avenue, Droitwich Spa ও ✿❀ (Malley & David Terry) South from Droitwich Spa towards Worcester A38, town centre approx 1m. Or from junction 6 M5 to Droitwich Town centre. A new garden 140' × 40' for yr-round interest, planted April 1996. Unusual shrubs, herbaceous perennials, ferns and shade loving plants. Clematis, and pillar roses in the herbaceous borders; alpine troughs and small alpine house. Superb lawn developed without re-seeding or re-turfing. Scree garden at the front. *Adm £1.50 Chd free. Suns May 17, June 14, July 19 (2-6). Private visits welcome by appt, please* **Tel 01905 774907**

Arley Cottage, Upper Arley ও (Woodward family) nr Bewdley. 5m N of Kidderminster off A442. Small country garden with lawns bordered by interesting shrubs and collection of rare trees. Cream TEAS. *Adm £1 Chd free (ACNO to Motor Neurone disease Association®). Sun July 12 (2-5)*

Arley House, Upper Arley ✗ (R D Turner Esq) 5m N of Kidderminster. A442. Arboretum containing specimen conifers and hardwoods, rhododendrons, camellias, magnolias, heathers; Italianate garden; greenhouses with orchids, alpines. Aviary with ornamental pheasants, budgerigars. TEA. *Adm £2 Chd free (ACNO to St Peter's, Upper Arley®). Sun May 3 (2-7)*

Astley Horticultural Society ও❀ Astley village 3m W of Stourport-on-Severn. On B4196 to Worcester, start the trail at the Parish Room, map provided. Selection of gardens of very different sizes and styles. Craft stalls and teas at Parish Room. *Combined adm £2 Chd free (ACNO to local charities). Sun April 19 (1-5.30).* **Tel 01299 826540**

  The Sytche (Mr & Mrs Kilby) Well cared for garden with a good selection of spring flowers and a fine vegetable garden

  The White House (Mr & Mrs Tidmarsh) Eccentric garden with follies, water features and pergolas. Long herbaceous border inspired by Christopher Lloyd. Wild flower bank

  Little Yarhampton (Mr & Mrs Walley) Beautiful views from pretty garden. Arboretum and lovely woodland walk round lake

  Astley Towne House (Mr & Mrs Tim Smith) See separate entry below

  Koi Cottage (Mr & Mrs Raybold) Small village garden converted to a classical Japanese garden with magnificent Koi carp in a pool bridged with a Japanese bridge to the front door

  15 Riverlands (Mr & Mrs Clarke) Beautifully maintained small garden with every inch cultivated to a very high standard

Astley Towne House, Astley ও❀ (Tim & Lesley Smith) 3m W of Stourport on Severn on B4196 Worcester to Bewdley Road. Recently constructed family garden to a very ambitious design of the owners, formal kitchen garden with central fountain, grass paths winding through shrubs and herbaceous borders, children can see pets corner. Approx 2½ acres. TEAS. *Adm £2 Chd free. Sun May 24 (1-5.30)*

Barbers, Martley ও✗❀ (Mr & the Hon Mrs Richard Webb) 7m NW of Worcester on B4204. Medium-sized garden with lawns, trees, shrubs, pools and wild garden. Cowslip and fritillary lawn. Home-made TEAS. *Adm £1.50 Chd free (ACNO to Martley Church®). Sun April 19 (2-6)*

Barn House, Broadway ও (Mark & Jane Ricketts) Situated in beautiful Cotswold village of Broadway in the High St nr bottom of Fish Hill. Large C17 country house set in 16 acres of garden and paddocks. The well maintained gardens contain large variety of shrubs. TEAS. *Adm £1.50 Chd free (ACNO to Sue Ryder Home, Cheltenham®). Open daily April to Sept. By appt other times (10-6).* **Tel 01386 858633**

Barnard's Green House, Malvern ও✗❀ (Mr & Mrs Philip Nicholls) 10 Poolbrook Rd, Malvern. On E side of Malvern at junction of B4211 and B4208. 3-acre garden, mature trees, herbaceous border, rockery, heather beds, woodland, vegetable garden with old brick paths and box hedges. Unusual plants and shrubs for sale. Featured in Practical Gardening 1996 and Inspirations 1997. Mrs Nicholls is a specialist and writer on dried flowers. 1635 half-timbered house (not open). Coach parties by appt. TEAS. *Adm £2 Acc chd free (ACNO to SCF®). Suns April 19, Aug 30 and every Thursday April to Sept incl. (2-6). Also private visits welcome, please* **Tel 01684 574446**

Bell's Castle, Kemerton ❀ (Lady Holland-Martin) NE of Tewkesbury. 3 small terraces with battlements; wild garden outside wall. The small Gothic castellated folly was built by Edmund Bell (Smuggler) c1820; very fine views. TEAS and gift stall. *Adm £1 Chd free. Sun June 14 (2-6). Parties welcome, please* **Tel 01386 725333**

Birtsmorton Court, nr Malvern ও✗ (Mr & Mrs N G K Dawes) 7m E of Ledbury on A438. Fortified manor house (not open) dating from C12; moat; Westminster pool, laid down in Henry V11's reign at time of consecration of Westminster Abbey; large tree under which Cardinal Wolsey reputedly slept in shadow of ragged stone. Newly planted white garden. Topiary. Motor Museum extra. TEAS in aid of Birtsmorton Church. *Adm £2 Chd 50p. Sun June 21 (2-6)*

■ **Bodenham Arboretum and Earth Centre, Wolverley** ❀ (Mr & Mrs J D Binnian) Situated 5m from Kidderminster, 2m N of Wolverley off the B4189. Follow signs from Wolverley Church Island. Award winning arboretum landscaped in 134 acres during the last 25 yrs, contains over 2000 species of trees and shrubs; 2 chains of lakes and pools; woods and glades; grove of dawn redwoods and laburnum tunnel. Bring wellingtons or strong shoes. Partly suitable for wheelchairs. Refreshments in Earth Centre Rotunda Restaurant. *Adm £2.50 Chd £1 under 5 free (ACNO to Kew Gardens Millennium Seed Bank Appeal©). Open daily May-Oct 31 (11-5). For NGS Sun Sept 27, (2-5).* **Tel 01562 852444**

Broadway, Church Street Gardens ✿ Rd from the Green towards Snowshill. Public car park nearby, via Church Close. Cream TEAS and home-made cakes at **Bannits**. *Combined adm £2 Chd free. Sun June 21 (2-5.30)*
>   **Bannits** (Dr & Mrs R Juckes) C18 Cotswold stone house. 1-acre of formal terraced garden with herbaceous borders and lavender walk. 1½ acres old orchard and 1½ acres wild garden with path to stream
>   **St Michael's Cottage** (Mr & Mrs K R Barling) Thatched cottage with approx ⅓-acre intensively planted cottage style and herbaceous garden planned in colour groups, incl a small white sunken garden

Broadway, Snowshill Road Gardens ⚥✿ All six gardens are on Snowshill Rd. TEAS at **Far Bunchers**. *Combined adm £2 Chd free (ACNO to Lifford Hall, Broadway®). Sun July 5 (2-6)*
>   **Far Bunchers** (Mrs A Pallant) A recently developed mixed garden of about 1 acre. Emphasis on shrub roses and organic vegetable growing
>   **Meadowside** (Mrs P Bomford) A very pleasing and compact cottage garden that slopes down to the stream
>   **The Mill** (Mr & Mrs H Verney) A 2½-acre paddock, bounded by 2 streams has been transformed since 1975 into an attractive garden that will support a variety of wildlife. Informal planting of trees, shrub roses and other shrubs, moisture loving plants and bulbs
>   **Mill Hay Cottage** (Dr & Mrs W J A Payne) The 2-acre garden is of relatively recent origin and is still being developed. A special feature is the number of unusual trees, incl many fruiting species
>   **Mill Hay House** (Mr & Mrs H Will) The large mill pond is a centre for attention in a well laid out and interesting garden
>   **The Old Orchard** (Major & Mrs I Gregory) A cottage garden that slopes down to the stream together with an old orchard and shrub rose garden adjacent to the rd

Cedar Lodge, Blakeshall, Wolverley ⚥✿ (Malcolm & Barbara Phillips) 4m N of Kidderminster off A449 (B4189) midway between villages of Wolverley and Kinver. Award winning garden 1997. Designed by the owner with an eye to plant associations and the complementary textures, shapes and colours of a wide range of shrubs and trees, in keeping with the country setting. The ¾-acre incl pools and gravel gardens. TEAS. *Adm £2 Chd free. Sun May 31 (2-5.30). Private visits welcome,* **Tel 01562 850238**

Charlton House, Lulsley, Knightwick ⚥ (Mr & Mrs S Driver-White) 9m W of Worcester via A44, turn 1st L after Knightsford Bridge towards Alfrick, 1st L after Fox &

Hounds signed Hill Rd, Lulsley; 1m at end of lane. ⅔-acre intimate garden of shrubs, shrub roses created by owner since 1970. Fine barns. No children. *Adm £1.50. Sun June 14. Coach parties and private visits by appt, please* **Tel 01886 821220**

The Cockshoot, Castlemorton ✿ (Clive & Elizabeth Wilkins) 7m S of Malvern. [OS map ref: S0773379]. B4208 turn into New Rd opp Robin Hood pub. Take 1st L (½m). At 200yds bear L at fork. Keep on narrow rd until track. Straight along track. ¾-acre country garden set in common land below Malvern Hills. Surrounds a Georgian cottage built about 1721. Herbaceous borders, shrubs, trees. Also many hostas. TEAS. *Adm £1.50 Chd 50p. Every Sun, Mon, Tues May 3 to June 30 (11-8)*

Conderton Manor, nr Tewksbury ⚥⚥ (Mr & Mrs William Carr) 5½m NE of Tewkesbury. 7-acre garden with magnificent views of Cotswolds; many trees and shrubs of botanical interest. Formal terrace with parterre. 100yd long shrub border, rose arches and borders in former kitchen garden. Teas available at the Silk Shop in the village. *Adm £2. Visits by appt only, yr-round, please* **Tel 01386 725389**

The Cottage, Broughton Green ⚥✿ (Mr Terry Dagley) nr Hanbury Hall (Nat Trust). 3½m E of Droitwich. Via B4090, turn R at sign, 1m junction. Park on side of rd. The Cottage 250yds up farm track. ½-acre plantsman's country garden, stocked with extensive range of hardy perennials, bulbs, shrubs and trees to give yr-round interest. The quiet rural setting encourages abundant wildlife. *Adm £1.50 Chd free. Weds March 18, April 15, May 20, Sept 16 (11-5), June 17, July 15, Aug 19 (11-8). Private visits welcome, please* **Tel 01905 391670**

The Cottage Herbery, Boraston, nr Tenbury Wells ⚥✿ (Mr & Mrs R E Hurst) On A456, turn for Boraston at Peacock Inn, turn R in village, signposted to garden. 1-acre organic true cottage garden with a mix of herbs, herbaceous perennials, old roses, vegetables and native plants, a wildlife haven. The Cornbrook runs through the garden creating areas for bog and moisture loving plants. Featured on ITV, BBC2 'Paradise Gardens', C4 'Wild gardens'. Gold Medal winners at major shows. TEAS weekdays by appt. *Adm £1.50 Chd free. Suns May 3, 17, 24, June 7, 28, July 19 (11-5). Groups welcome by appt, please* **Tel 01584 781575**

Dial Park, Chaddesley Corbett ⚥✿ (Mr & Mrs David Mason) 4½m from Kidderminster, 4½m from Bromsgrove on A448. 150yds towards Kidderminster from turn into Chaddesley Corbett village. Approx ¾-acre garden developed since 1990 containing interesting and unusual plants with yr-round interest. Incl collections of snowdrops, sambucus and hardy ferns. Also small collection of country bygones. TEA. *Adm £1.50 Chd free. Thurs Feb 19 (1-5) April 30 (2-6) June 18 (2-8). 1999 Feb 18 (1-5). Private visits welcome, please* **Tel 01562 777451**

●**Eastgrove Cottage Garden Nursery, Sankyns Green, Shrawley** ⚥⚥✿ (Malcolm & Carol Skinner) 8m NW of Worcester on rd between Shrawley (B4196) and Great Witley (A443). Unique country cottage flower garden, 28 yrs in the making so far, though situated deep in the countryside attracts worldwide interest. A plantsman's paradise yet a joy for all; everchanging inspired planting, meticulously maintained, developing arboretum. Home-made ice cream. *Adm £2 Chd free. Thurs, Fri, Sat, Sun, Mon April 2 to July 31; Thurs, Fri, Sat Sept 3 to Oct 10 and Sun Sept 27 (2-5)*

Eldersfield Court, Eldersfield ⚶ ❀ (Mr & Mrs E C Watkins) Opp the church. 6m W of Tewkesbury A438/B4211 or 12m S of Malvern B4208 past Pendock. Queen Anne house (not open). 2 acres mostly created by present owners since 1984 with formal borders, classic English rose garden, ridge walk with views, steps, slopes. Cream TEAS. *Adm £2 Chd free. Suns June 21, 28 (2-6)*

The Elms, Lower Broadheath ⚶❀ (Mr & Mrs Marshall Stewart) 4m W of Worcester, B4204 turn opp school into Frenchlands Lane. Through farm gate, lane becomes track (drive with care). Isolated, peaceful setting. 1½-acre evolving garden surrounding late Georgian farmhouse. Mixed colour-themed garden 'rooms', lily pool, rose walk, ornamental kitchen garden created from old fold yard. Nursery specialising in unusual hardy plants. Rare breed sheep. Farming bygones. TEAS. *Adm £2 Chd free. Tues, Weds April 1 - Sept 30 (2-5). Private visits welcome, please* **Tel 01905 640841**

¶**Glenclyne, Cropthorne** ❀ (Sue & Mike Waller) Brook Lane. Just off A44, 3m W of Evesham. From Evesham turn R after New Inn; from Pershore, L after Bell Inn, then 150yds on L. Some parking on small private rd; otherwise, Brook Lane. ⅔-acre cottage garden extensively developed over past 5yrs and laid out to give a range of views and perspectives. Wide variety of herbaceous perennials; unusual 'recycled' statuary, view to Bredon Hill. TEAS. *Adm £ 1 Chd free (ACNO to Canine Friends©). Suns June 7, July 19 (11-6)*

▲**Hanbury Hall, Hanbury** ⚶⚶❀ (The National Trust) 3m NE of Droitwich, 6m S of Bromsgrove. Signed off B4090. Recreation of C18 formal garden by George London incl sunken parterre, fruit garden and wilderness. Victorian forecourt with detailed planting. William & Mary style house of 1701; contemporary Orangery and Ice House. TEAS. *Adm garden only £2.50 Chd £1. For NGS Sun June 14 (2-6)*

Holland House, Cropthorne (Warden: Mr Peter Middlemiss) Main St, Pershore. Between Pershore and Evesham, off A44. Car park at rear of house. Gardens laid out by Lutyens in 1904; thatched house dating back to 1636 (not open). TEAS. *Adm £1 Chd free (ACNO to USPG®). Weds April 15, May 27 (2.30-5)*

¶**Impney Park, Droitwich** (Sir Geoffrey Dear) On A38 Droitwich/Bromsgrove Rd. 1m W of junction 5. M5 (next door to Chateau Impney). 3-acre garden, set in 7 acre parkland. Facing SW with views of Severn Vale, across to Malverns. Formal terracing sweeps down into lawns, herbaceous borer and into informal shrubberies, massed with bulbs and hardy geraniums. Formal rose garden. Surrounded by mature trees, encouraging abundant wildlife. TEA. *Adm £2 Chd free. Open by appt only for clubs*

and societies from mid-March until October, excluding August.* **Tel 01905 773309**

Ivytree House, Clent ❀ (Mrs L Eggins) [OS139 91.79] Bromsgrove Rd. 3m SE of Stourbridge and 5m NW of Bromsgrove, off A491 Stourbridge to Bromsgrove dual carriageway. Car parking next door behind the Woodman Hotel. Over 1,000 varieties of small trees, shrubs and herbaceous plants in approx ½-acre plantsman's cottage garden; tree ivies and ivytrees, collection of aucubas, small conservatory with fuchsia trees, pond garden, fruit and vegetables, bantams and bees. *Adm £1.50 Chd free. Mons, Weds May 18, 20, June 15, 17, July 13, 15 Mons (2-5), Weds (2-5 & 7-9). Also private visits welcome, please* **Tel 01562 884171**

Keepers Cottage, Alvechurch ⚶❀ (Mrs Diana Scott) Take main rd through Alvechurch towards Redditch. Turn opp sign to Cobley Hill and Bromsgrove for 1m over 2 humpback bridges. 3-acre garden at 600ft with fine views towards the Cotswolds; rhododendrons, camellias; old-fashioned roses; unusual trees and shrubs; rock garden; 2 alpine houses and new potager; paddock with donkeys. *Adm £2 Chd £1. Private visits welcome in May, please* **Tel 0121 445 5885**

■ **Kyre Park, Kyre** ⚶❀ (Mr M H Rickard & Mr & Mrs J N Sellers) 4m S of Tenbury Wells or 7m N of Bromyard. Follow signs to Kyre Church off B4214. Approx 29 acre Georgian shrubbery walk under restoration, 5 lakes, waterfalls, hermitage, picturesque views, mature trees and Norman dovecote. Stout shoes advised. Ferns for sale at Rickards Hardy Fern Nursery. RHS gold medal winners since 1992. TEAS, light lunches. *Adm £1.50 Chd 50p. Open daily Easter to Oct. For NGS Suns March 29, Oct 4 (11-6). Coach parties by appt, please* **Tel 01885 410282**

Little Malvern Court, Malvern ⚶❀ (Mrs T M Berington) 4m S of Malvern on A4104 S of junction with A449. 10 acres attached to former Benedictine Priory, magnificent views over Severn valley. An intriguing layout of garden rooms, and terrace round house. Water garden below, feeding into chain of lakes. Wide variety of spring bulbs, flowering trees and shrubs. Notable collection of old-fashioned roses. TEAS. *Adm £3 Chd 50p (5-14) (ACNO to SSAFA®). Sun March 22 (2-5). Other opening times please,* **Tel 01684 892988**

Madresfield Court ⚶ (Sir Charles & Lady Morrison) Nr Malvern. 60 acres formal and parkland garden incl rare species of mature trees, Pulhamite rock garden, maze, majestic avenues and a mass of wild flowers. TEAS. *Adm £2 Chd 50p (ACNO to Madresfield Primary School©). Sun June 7 (2-5.30)*

The Manor House, Birlingham ⚶❀ (Mr & Mrs David Williams-Thomas) nr Pershore off A4104. Very fine views of Bredon Hill with short walk to R Avon for picnics. Walled white and silver garden, gazebo and many herbaceous borders of special interest to the plantsman. Many plants for sale, all propogated from the garden. Featured in 'House & Garden' and 'Sunday Express'. TEAS. *Adm £1.50 Chd free. May every Thurs and Suns 3 and 24 also*

Mons 4 and 25 and Fri 8, June and July every Wed and Thurs up to and incl July 16 Aug closed, Sept every Thurs (11-5.30). Private visits welcome, please **Tel 01386 750005**

Monsieurs Hall, Bromsgrove ✿✿ (Tony & Jane Cowan) A448 1½m W Bromsgrove. L into Monsieurs Hall Lane. 400yds on L. Hilltop acre with extensive views. Newly created herb garden and parterre in keeping with C16 house. Brick pergola. Informal mixed borders and rockeries with many unusual plants, leading to hazel grove and spinney. Conservatory. Featured on Central TV. TEA. *Adm £1.50 Chd free. Wed, Thurs May 6, 7 (2-6), June 17, 18 (2-5 & 7-9); Thurs July 9 (2-6). Private visits welcome, please* **Tel 01527 831747**

Nerine Nursery, Welland ✿✿ (Mr & Mrs I L Carmichael) Brookend House, ½m towards Upton-on-Severn from Welland Xrds (A4104 × B4208). Internationally famous National Collection of Nerines, 30 species and some 800 named varieties in 5 greenhouses and traditional walled garden with raised beds, hardy nerines. Coaches by appt only. TEAS. *Adm £1.50 Chd free. Sun Oct 18 (2-5). Private visits welcome, please* **Tel 01684 594005**

Orchard Bungalow, Bishops Frome ✿✿ (Mr & Mrs Robert Humphries) Bishops Frome. 14m W of Worcester. A4103 turn R at bottom of Fromes Hill, through village of Bishops Frome on B4214. Turn R immediately after deregulation signs along narrow track for 250yds. Park in field 200yds from garden. ½-acre garden with conifers, trees, shrubs and herbaceous borders. Over 400 roses incl many old varieties, 4 ponds, small stream, 3 aviaries and dovecote. 1997 competition winners. TEAS. *Adm £1.50 Chd free. Suns June 14, July 12, Aug 9 (2-6). Private visits welcome, please* **Tel 01885 490273**

Overbury Court, nr Tewkesbury ✿ (Mr & Mrs Bruce Bossom) 5m NE of Tewkesbury, village signed off A46. Georgian house 1740 (not open); landscape gardening of same date with stream and pools. Daffodil bank and grotto. Plane trees, yew hedges. Shrub, cut flower, coloured foliage, gold and silver, shrub rose borders. Norman church adjoins garden. *Adm £1.50 Chd free. Private visits welcome minimum charge £10 following written application or* **Fax 01386 725528**

Pershore College of Horticulture ✿✿✿ 1m S of Pershore on A44, 7m from M5 junction 7. 180-acre estate; ornamental grounds; arboretum; fruit, vegetables; amenity glasshouses; wholesale hardy stock nursery. RHS Regional Centre at Pershore. Plant Centre open for sales and gardening advice. TEA. *Adm £1 Chd 50p. Sun June 7 (2-4)*

Pershore Gardens ✿ Charming cross-section of gardens behind the Georgian houses. These vary from the large formal gardens, Pershore House and Stanhope House, the communal gardens developed at Ganderton Court to delightful well-stocked small gardens, an example of which is in Priest Lane, a prize winner on several occasions in the Pershore in Bloom competition. Those who want a good walk can visit Mount Pleasant, off Station Rd to see not only interesting gardens but fabulous views. Refresh-

ments at St Andrews Visitors' Centre and The Brandy Cask in Bridge St. *Adm £2 Chd free will allow access to all gardens. Sun June 14 (2-6)*

Priors Court, Long Green ✿✿✿ (Robert Philipson-Stow) From Tewkesbury A438 to Ledbury. Exactly 5m pass under M50. Garden on hill on L of A438. From Ledbury, Worcester or Gloucester aim for Rye Cross (A438 and B4208) then take A438 for Tewkesbury. Priors Court is approx 3m from Rye Cross on R. 3-acre garden established in 1920s. C15 house (not open). Rock, herb and vegetable gardens, mature trees and shrubs, herbaceous and rose borders; stunning views. Nearby Norman church open. TEAS. *Adm £2 (ACNO to Berrow & Pendock Parish Church®). Sun May 17 (2-6). Private visits by appt for parties of less than 20, please* **Tel 01684 833221**

The Priory, Kemerton ✿✿ (The Hon Mrs Peter Healing) NE of Tewkesbury B4080. Main features of this 4-acre garden are long herbaceous borders planned in colour groups; stream, fern and sunken gardens. Many unusual plants, shrubs and trees. Featured in BBC2 'Gardeners' World', 'The Garden magazine', Channel 4 Garden Party 1996. Small nursery. TEAS Suns only. *Adm £1.50 May and June, £2 July to Sept Chd free. (ACNO to St Nicholas Church, Kemerton® Aug 2, St Richard's Hospice® Aug 23, SSAFA® Sept 6). Every Thurs May 28 to Sept 24, Suns May 24, June 21, July 12, Aug 2, 23, Sept 6 (2-6) Thurs May 28, Sept 24, Oct by appt only. Private visits by appt for 20 and over, please* **Tel 01386 725258**

Red House Farm, Bradley Green, nr Redditch ✿✿ (Mrs M M Weaver) Flying Horse Lane, Bradley Green. 7m W of Redditch on B4090 Alcester to Droitwich Spa. Ignore signpost to Bradley Green. Turn opp The Red Lion. Approx ½-acre plant enthusiast's cottage garden containing wide range of interesting herbaceous perennials; roses; shrubs; alpines. Garden and small nursery open daily offering wide variety of plants mainly propagated from garden. *Adm £1 Chd free. Weds May 20, June 17, July 15 (11-5). Private visits welcome, please,* **Tel 01527 821269**

Ripple Hall, nr Tewkesbury ✿ (Sir Hugo Huntington-Whiteley) Off A38 Worcester-Tewkesbury (nr junction with motorway); Ripple village well signed. 6 acres; lawns and paddocks; walled vegetable garden; cork tree and orangery. TEAS. *Adm £1.50 Acc chd free (ACNO to St John Ambulance®). Sun April 5 (2-5)*

St Egwins Cottage, Norton ✿✿ (Mr & Mrs Brian Dudley) 2m N of Evesham on B4088. Park in St Egwins Church car park not Church Lane. Walk through churchyard to Church Lane (50yds). ⅓-acre plantsman's garden, many unusual plants; mainly perennials incl hardy geraniums, campanulas and salvias. Featured in 'Your Garden' and 'Home and Country' Magazines 1997. Small thatched cottage next to C12 church (open). TEAS Suns only. TEA Weds only. *Adm £1.50 Chd free. Suns, May 10, June 7, July 26; Weds April 29, May 13, June 3, July 15; Aug 5 (2-5). Also private visits welcome May, June and July, please* **Tel 01386 870486**

¶**Shuttifield Cottage, Birchwood** ✿☙ (Mr & Mrs D Judge) 8m W of Worcester on A4103 to Hereford. Turn R opp Storridge Church to Birchwood. Turn L down steep tarmaced drive. Large natural 2 acre mixed garden extending into old woodland. Woodland walk with anenomies, bluebells, rhododendrons and azaleas. Extensive old rose garden and mixed borders of unusual shrubs, trees and perennials. Adjoining the garden is small deer park incorporating natural wild areas with ponds and shrubs. Veg garden. TEA. *Adm £1.50. By appt only, coaches welcome by arrangement,* **Tel 01886 884243**

■ **Spetchley Park, nr Worcester** ☖☙ (R J Berkeley Esq) 2m E of Worcester on A422. 30-acre garden containing large collection of trees, shrubs and plants, many rare and unusual. New garden within kitchen garden. Red and fallow deer in nearby park. TEAS. *Adm £2.90 Chd £1.40. Open Tues-Fri (11-5), Bank Hol Mons (11-5) Suns (2-5). For NGS Fri April 10 (11-5), Suns May 10, July 5 (2-5)*

●**Stone House Cottage Gardens** ☖✿☙ (James and Louisa Arbuthnott) Stone, 2m SE of Kidderminster via A448 towards Bromsgrove next to church, turn up drive. 1-acre sheltered walled plantsman's garden with towers; rare wall shrubs, climbers and interesting herbaceous plants. In adjacent nursery large selection of unusual shrubs and climbers for sale. Featured in The Garden, Country Life and Hortus. Coaches by appt only. *Adm £2 Chd free. Suns May 3, 24; June 14; Aug 30; Mons April 13, May 4, 25; Aug 31; also open March 1 to Oct 17 every Wed, Thurs, Fri, Sat (10-5.30). Private visits welcome Oct 18 to March 1, please* **Tel 01562 69902**

Upper Court, Kemerton ☖ (Mr & Mrs W Herford) NE of Tewkesbury B4080. Take turning to Parish Church from War Memorial; Manor behind church. Approx 13 acres of garden and grounds incl a 2-acre lake where visitors would be welcome to bring picnics. The garden was mostly landscaped and planted in 1930s. TEAS. *Adm £2 Chd free. Sun June 14 (2-6)*

■ **White Cottage, Stock Green, nr Inkberrow** ☖✿☙ (Mr & Mrs S M Bates) Earls Comon Rd. A422 Worcester to Alcester, turn at Red Hart public house. 1½m to T-junction, turn L. 2 acres, herbaceous and shrub beds, stream and spring wild flower area, large specialist collection of hardy geraniums, nursery, plants available. *Adm £1.50 OAPS £1. Open Mar 28 to Sept 27 (10-5). [Closed Apr 5, 19, May 8 to 12 incl. June 14, 28, July 12, 26. All Aug. Sept 6, 20 and every Wed and Thurs.] Open for NGS Mar 28, 29, April 4, 11, 12, 18, 25, 26, May 2, 3, 16, 17, 23, 24, 30, 31, June 6, 7, 13, 20, 21, 27, July 4, 5, 11, 18, 19, 25, Sept 5, 12, 13, 19, 26, 27. Please* **Tel 01386 792414**

Whitlenge House Cottage, Hartlebury ☖✿☙ (Mr & Mrs K J Southall) Whitlenge Lane. S of Kidderminster. Take A442 (signposted Droitwich) over small island, ¼m, 1st R into Whitlenge Lane. Follow signs. Home of Creative Landscapes, RHS medal winners. Professional landscaper's garden with over 600 varieties of trees, shrubs etc. Water features, twisted pillar pergola, gravel gardens, rockeries. 2 acres of plantsman's garden with adjacent nursery specialising in large specimen shrubs.

TEAS. *Adm £2 Chd free. Suns, Mons April 12, 13, May 24, 25, Aug 30, 31 (10-5). Private visits welcome, parties of 10 and over, please* **Tel 01299 250720**

Windyridge, Kidderminster ✿☙ (Mr P Brazier) Turn off Chester Rd N (A449) into Hurcott Rd, then into Imperial Avenue. 1-acre spring garden containing azaleas, magnolias, camellias, rhododendrons, mature flowering cherries and davidia. Please wear sensible shoes. *Adm £1 Chd free. Suns May 3, 10 (2-6). Private visits welcome, please* **Tel 01562 824994**

Woodmancote, Wadborough ☖✿ (Ila & Ian Walmsley) 1½ m S of Stoulton, which is on A44 between Worcester and Pershore. ¾-acres acquired and developed in stages over the last 10yrs. 2 ponds lawn and wide variety of shrubs and herbaceous plants. Please park considerately at The Mason Arms (400yds). Bar meals available. TEAS in aid of St Peter's Church, Pirton. *Adm £1.50 Chd free. Suns May 31, June 14, 28 (11-5)*

Woollas Hall, Eckington (Mr & Mrs Clive Jennings) On Bredon Hill, off B4080 Bredon to Pershore rd. From Eckington take the rd to the Combertons and Woollas Hall. Drive past farm over cattle grid, up drive marked private and park in field, before 2nd cattle grid, no cars past this point please. The Jacobean Manor house (not open) is the setting for the 1-acre garden on several levels, created and maintained by owners, since 1984. Numerous walkways featuring separate enclosures with fine trees, shrubs, mixed and herbaceous borders. Fine views over Bredon Hill and surrounding countryside. *Adm £2 Chd 50p. Sun July 12 (2-6)*

Yew Tree House, Ombersley ☖ (Mr & Mrs W D Moyle) Turn off A449 up Woodfield Lane R at T-junction. 2½-acre garden with many rare herbaceous plants and shrubs. Pretty walled garden with alpines and lily pond, numerous old-fashioned roses. Mature plantings of blue, pink and white borders around tennis court and other yellow and white beds. Orchard, copse and lawns with lovely views set around c1640 timber framed house. TEA. *Adm £2 OAPs £1.50 Chd free. Sun July 5 (2-6)*

Yorkshire

Hon County Organisers:

(N Yorks - Districts of Hambleton, Richmond, Ryedale, Scarborough & Cleveland)

Mrs William Baldwin, Riverside Farm, Sinnington, York YO6 6RY Tel 01751 431764

(West & South Yorks & North Yorks Districts of Craven, Harrogate, Selby & York)

Mrs Roger Marshall, The Old Vicarage, Whixley, York YO5 8AR Tel 01423 330474 Fax 01423 331215

(E Yorks)

Mrs Philip Bean, Saltmarshe Hall, Howden, Goole, Yorkshire DN14 7RX Tel 01430 430199 Fax 01430 431607

DATES OF OPENING

Regular openings
For details see garden description

Ampleforth College Junior School, Gilling East
Burton Agnes Hall, Driffield
Castle Howard, nr York
Constable Burton Hall, nr Leyburn
Harewood House, nr Leeds
Harlow Carr, Harrogate
Land Farm, nr Hebden Bridge
Newby Hall Gardens, Ripon
Parcevall Hall Gardens, Skyreholme
Plants of Special Interest Nursery, Braithwell
Shandy Hall, Coxwold
Stockeld Park, Wetherby

By appointment only
For telephone numbers and other details see garden descriptions. Private visits welcomed

Evergreens, Bilton
Holly Cottage, Leas Gardens, Scholes
30 Latchmere Road, Leeds
Les Palmiers, Barnsley
Ling Beeches, Scarcroft
Tan Cottage, Cononley

March 11 Wednesday
Joan Royd House, Penistone
April 5 Sunday
Acorn Cottage, Boston Spa
Harlow Carr Botanical Gardens, Harrogate
Joan Royd House, Penistone
Victoria Cottage, Stainland
April 8 Wednesday
Acorn Cottage, Boston Spa
April 12 Sunday
Netherwood House, Ilkley
April 15 Wednesday
Acorn Cottage, Boston Spa
April 19 Sunday
Acorn Cottage, Boston Spa
Bolton Percy Gardens

Hillcrest, Whitgift
April 26 Sunday
Hallgarth, Ottringham
Oxenber House, Austwick
Sinnington Gardens
The White Cottage, Halsham
April 29 Wednesday
Oxenber House, Austwick
May 3 Sunday
Il Giardino, Bilton
54a Keldgate, Beverley
The Old Vicarage, Whixley
Shandy Hall, Coxwold
May 4 Monday
The Chimney Place, Bilton Grange
Old Sleningford, nr Ripon
May 10 Sunday
Blackbird Cottage, Scampston
Hemble Hill Farm, Guisborough
Maspin House, Hillam
The Spaniels, Hensall
Victoria Cottage, Stainland
May 17 Sunday
Hillbark, Bardsey
Joan Royd House, Penistone
Stillingfleet Lodge, nr York
Woodlands Cottage, Summerbridge
May 19 Tuesday
Beacon Hill House, nr Ilkley
May 23 Saturday
Nawton Tower Garden, Nawton
May 24 Sunday
High Farm, Bilton
Il Giardino, Bilton
Nawton Tower Garden, Nawton
Old Sleningford, nr Ripon
Shandy Hall, Coxwold
Three Gables, Markington
8 Welton Old Road, Welton
May 25 Monday
The Chimney Place, Bilton Grange
Nawton Tower Garden, Nawton
Old Sleningford, nr Ripon
May 27 Wednesday
Oxenber House, Austwick
May 30 Saturday
Pennyholme, Fadmoor

May 31 Sunday
East Wing, Thorp Arch
Oxenber House, Austwick
Park House, nr York
Pennyholme, Fadmoor
June 6 Saturday
Burton Agnes Hall, Driffield
Pennyholme, Fadmoor
Sleightholme Dale Lodge, Fadmoor
York Gate, Leeds 16
June 7 Sunday
Burton Agnes Hall, Driffield
Elvington Gardens, nr York
Hunmanby Grange, Wold Newton
Joan Royd House, Penistone
Kelberdale, Knaresborough
Norton Conyers, nr Ripon
Pennyholme, Fadmoor
Plants of Special Interest Nursery, Braithwell
55 Rawcliffe Drive, York
Secret Garden, York
Sleightholme Dale Lodge, Fadmoor
Snilesworth, Northallerton
Springfield House, Tockwith
Victoria Cottage, Stainland
York Gate, Leeds 16
June 13 Saturday
The Chimney Place, Bilton Grange
Helmsley Gardens
June 14 Sunday
Brookfield, Oxenhope
Derwent House, Osbaldwick
Hillcrest, Whitgift
Littlethorpe Gardens, Nr Ripon
Parcevall Hall Gardens, Skyreholme
Parkview, South Cave
Saltmarshe Hall, Saltmarshe
Sinnington Gardens
8 Welton Old Road, Welton
June 17 Wednesday
Brookfield, Oxenhope
Kelberdale, Knaresborough
June 21 Sunday
Blackbird Cottage, Scampston

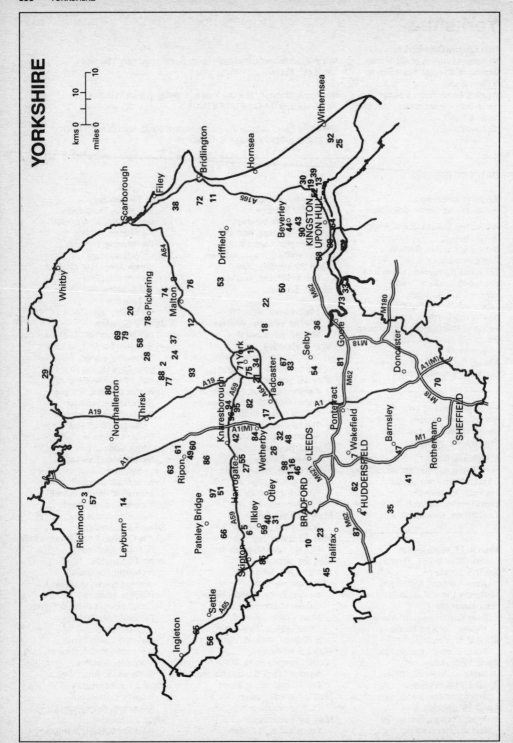

YORKSHIRE

kms 0
miles 0

Withernsea
92
25

Bridlington
Hornsea

Filey
Scarborough
38
72
11

A165
Beverley
90 43
44
KINGSTON
UPON HULL
30
19 39
13
89
64
68

Whitby
Driffield
A64
53
50
73 33
M62
M180

Pickering
74
76
Malton
12
78
20
22
18
Selby
36
54
81
Goole
Doncaster
M18
A1(M)
70
M18

69
79
58
28 2
24 37
93
88
77
York
71
75 34 15
34
67
83
9

29
80
Thirsk
A19
Northallerton
A59
A19
94 95
86
82
17
1
A1
Pontefract
M62
Wakefield
Barnsley
M1
Rotherham
SHEFFIELD

Richmond 3
57
Leyburn 14
Knaresborough
42
84
A1(M)
55
27
26 32
48
Wetherby
98
91 16
46
M621
LEEDS
BRADFORD
62
4 HUDDERSFIELD
35
41
47

Ripon
61
49 60
63
97
51
Harrogate
Otley
Pateley Bridge
66
5
59 40
31
Ilkley
23
10
Halifax
M62
87
45

Settle
A65
65
Ingleton
56
Skipton
85

KEY

1. Acorn Cottage	34. 32 Holly Bank Road	67. Park House
2. Ample Forth College Junior School	35. Holly Cottage, Scholes	68. Parkview
3. Aske	36. Holly Cottage, Wressle	69. Pennyholme
4. Bankfield	37. Hovingham Hall	70. Plants of Special Interest
5. Beacon Hill House	38. Hunmanby Grange	Nursery
6. Beamsley Hall	39. Il Giardino	71. 55 Rawcliffe Drive
7. Bishops Lodge	40. Inglemere Lodge	72. Rudston House
8. Blackbird Cottage	41. Joan Royd House	73. Saltmarshe Hall
9. Bolton Percy Gardens	42. Kelberdale	74. Scampston Hall
10. Brookfield	43. 54a Keldgate	75. Secret Garden
11. Burton Agnes Hall	44. 80 Lairgate	76. Settrington House
12. Castle Howard	45. Land Farm	77. Shandy Hall
13. The Chimney Place	46. 30 Latchmere Road	78. Sinnington Gardens
14. Constable Burton Hall Gardens	47. Les Palmiers	79. Sleightholme Dale Lodge
15. Derwent House	48. Ling Beeches	80. Snilesworth
16. 8 Dunstarn Lane	49. Littlethorpe Gardens	81. The Spaniels
17. East Wing	50. Londesborough Cross	82. Springfield House
18. Elvington Gardens	51. Low Hall	83. Stillingfleet Lodge
19. Evergreens	52. Lullaby	84. Stockeld Park
20. Fernwood	53. Manor Farm	85. Tan Cottage
21. Goddards	54. Maspin House	86. Three Gables
22. Great Givendale	55. The Mews Cottage	87. Victoria Cottage
23. Grey Shaw Syke Cottage	56. Middle Birks	88. Wass Gardens
24. Grimston Gardens	57. Millgate House	89. 8 Welton Old Road
25. Hallgarth	58. Nawton Tower Garden	90. 26 West End
26. Harewood House	59. Netherwood House	91. 5 Wharfe Close
27. Harlow Carr Botanical Gardens	60. Newby Hall & Gardens	92. The White Cottage
28. Helmsley Gardens	61. Norton Conyers	93. The White House
29. Hemble Hill Farm	62. The Old Rectory	94. Whixley Gardens
30. High Farm	63. Old Sleningford	95. Croft Cottage
31. Highfield House	64. Oliver Lodge	96. The Old Vicarage
32. Hillbark	65. Oxenber House	97. Woodlands Cottage
33. Hillcrest	66. Parcevall Hall Gardens	98. York Gate

Croft Cottage, Green
  Hammerton
Hallgarth, Ottringham
Holly Cottage, Wressle
54a Keldgate, Beverley
Shandy Hall, Coxwold
Victoria Cottage, Stainland
The White Cottage, Halsham
Whixley Gardens

June 24 Wednesday
  32 Holly Bank Road, York
    (Evening)
  Oxenber House, Austwick
  Wass Gardens

June 28 Sunday
  Aske, Richmond
  Bankfield, Huddersfield
  Bishops Lodge, Wakefield
  Bolton Percy Gardens
  High Farm, Bilton
  Hillbark, Bardsey
  Hovingham Hall, Hovingham
  Kelberdale, Knaresborough
  80 Lairgate, Beverley
  Lullaby, Hull
  Oxenber House, Austwick

Scampston Hall, Malton
Stillingfleet Lodge, nr York

July 1 Wednesday
  Rye Hill, Helmsley
  Low Hall, Darce

July 5 Sunday
  8 Dunstarn Lane, nr York
  Fernwood, Cropton
  Grimston Gardens, Gilling East
  Hunmanby Grange, Wold Newton
  Londesborough Cross,
    Shiptonthorpe
  Millgate House, Richmond
  The Old Rectory, Mirfield
  26 West End, Walkington

July 8 Wednesday
  East Wing, Thorp Arch
  Shandy Hall, Coxwold
  The White House, Husthwaite

July 9 Thursday
  Grimston Gardens, Gilling East

July 11 Saturday
  The Chimney Place, Bilton Grange

July 12 Sunday
  Beamsley Hall, nr Skipton
  Great Givendale, Pocklington

Lullaby, Hull
Manor Farm, Thixendale
Middle Birks, Clapham
Shandy Hall, Coxwold
Victoria Cottage, Stainland

July 15 Wednesday
  Middle Birks, Clapham
  Sinnington Gardens

July 18 Saturday
  Sleightholme Dale Lodge,
    Fadmoor

July 19 Sunday
  8 Dunstarn Lane, Leeds 16
  Goddards, York
  Grey Shaw Syke Cottage, Ogden
  32 Holly Bank Road, York
  Joan Royd House, Penistone
  Low Hall, Darce
  Plants of Special Interest
    Nursery, Braithwell
  Rudston House, Rudston
  Sleightholme Dale Lodge,
    Fadmoor
  5 Wharfe Close, York

July 26 Sunday
  55 Rawcliffe Drive, York

Secret Garden, York
July 29 Wednesday
The Mews Cottage,
Harrogate
August 2 Sunday
Inglemere Lodge, Ilkley
The Spaniels, Hensall
August 9 Sunday
8 Dunstarn Lane, Adel
Highfield House, Ilkley
5 Wharfe Close, Adel
Woodlands Cottage,
Summerbridge

August 19 Wednesday
Three Gables, Markington
August 23 Sunday
Oliver Lodge, Hessle
Settrington House, nr Malton
Stockeld Park, Wetherby
Three Gables, Markington
August 26 Wednesday
Oxenber House, Austwick
August 30 Sunday
Oxenber House, Austwick
September 2 Wednesday
Oxenber House, Austwick

September 6 Sunday
East Wing, Thorp Arch
September 13 Sunday
Hillbark, Bardsey
Plants of Special Interest
Nursery, Braithwell
September 20 Sunday
Hallgarth, Ottringham
Maspin House, Hillam
The White Cottage, Halsham
October 4 Sunday
Harlow Carr Botanical Gardens,
Harrogate

DESCRIPTIONS OF GARDENS

Acorn Cottage, Boston Spa ✸ (Mr & Mrs C H Froggatt) 50 Church Street. A659 1m SE of Wetherby. Off A1 Church St opp Central Garage. Small walled alpine garden of outstanding quality, alpine plant collection established over 75yrs, two generations, good range of small flowering bulbs, alpine flowers March to May attractively planted in local limestone formations. *Adm £1.50 Chd 50p incl coffee/tea and homemade biscuits and scones. Sun, Wed April 5, 8. (ACNO to Northern Horticultural Society®)   Wed, Sun April 15, 19 (ACNO to Martin House Hospice®) (11-4). Also by appt March to May, coaches or individuals very welcome,* **Tel 01937 842519**

Ampleforth College Junior School, Gilling East ✸ (Fr Abbot and Community) The Castle, Gilling East, 18m N of York. Medium-sized terraced garden with steep steps overlooking golf course. Unsuitable for handicapped or elderly. *Adm £1.50 Chd free. For NGS July & Aug daily dawn to dusk. Large parties welcome, please* **Tel 01439 766874 (Fr Kevin)**

Aske, Richmond ✿✸ (Marquess & Marchioness of Zetland) Aske is between the town of Richmond and village of Gilling West on the B6274. Capability Brown park with lake. Wonderful trees. Large walled garden, lovely woodland walks. Brand new formal terraced gardens designed by Martin Lane Fox. TEAS. *Adm £2 Chd under 12 £1. Sun June 28 (2-6)*

Bankfield, Huddersfield ✸✿ (Norma & Mike Hardy) Queens Rd, Edgerton. From Huddersfield ring rd follow A629 to Halifax for ½m. Cross traffic lights at Blacker Rd, turn R after 100yds. From M62, turn S at junction 24 to Huddersfield on A629. After ¾m pass 30mph sign, turn L after 200yds. ⅔-acre cottage style garden which has evolved over 15yrs from a neglected Victorian town garden. Large number of perennials incl many unusual and rare of interest to plant collectors. Rambling paths, informal beds, pond, gazebo, conifer arch, terraced beds around lawn. TEAS. *Adm £2 Chd free. Sun June 28 (11-5). Private visits also by appt, please* **Tel 01484 535830**

Beacon Hill House, nr Ilkley ✸✿ (Mr & Mrs D H Boyle) Langbar 4m NW of Ilkley. 1¼m SE of A59 at Bolton Bridge. Fairly large garden sheltered by woodland 900' up, on the southern slope of Beamsley Beacon. Several fea-

tures of interest to garden historians survive from the original Victorian garden. Early flowering rhododendrons, large shrub roses, mixed borders, unusual hardy and half-hardy shrubs and climbers making use of south facing walls. Natural wildlife pond and greenhouse with established tender plants. TEAS. *Adm £2 Chd free. Tues May 19 (2-6.30)*

Beamsley Hall, nr Skipton ✿✸ (Marquess & Marchioness of Hartington) Beamsley. 5m E of Skipton. 6-acre traditional English garden with new plantings; incl extensive herbaceous border and kitchen garden. Minor restrictions for wheelchairs. TEAS. Also at Bolton Abbey or at Devonshire Arms. *Adm £2 OAPs £1.50 Chd under 15 free. Sun July 12 (1.30-5)*

Bishop's Lodge, Wakefield ✿ (Bishop of Wakefield & Mrs McCulloch) Sandal 3m S of Wakefield (A61 Barnsley). Turn L opp Walnut Tree Inn (Woodthorpe Lane) towards Wakefield Golf Club. Recently re-ordered well-established 8-acre garden, maintained as a place of peace in an urban Diocese. Mixed plantings of trees, shrubs, roses and herbaceous borders. Old orchard, meadow and woodland. Secluded Chapel garden and area for quiet contemplation. TEAS. *Adm £1.50 Chd free (ACNO to The African Dioceses of Mara, Soroti and Karamoja©). Sun June 28 (2-6)*

Blackbird Cottage, Scampston ✿✸ (Mrs Hazel Hoad) 5m from Malton off A64 to Scarborough through Rillington turn L signposted Scampston only, follow signs. ⅓-acre plantswoman's garden made from scratch since 1986. A great wealth of interesting plants, with shrub, herbaceous border. Alpines are a speciality. Please visit throughout the day to ease pressure on a small but inspirational garden. Unusual plants for sale. Morning coffee and TEAS in aid of Scampston Village Hall & Church. *Adm £1.50 Chd free. Sun May 10, June 21 (10-5). Private visits welcome, please* **Tel 01944 758256**

Bolton Percy Gardens ✿✸✿ 5m E of Tadcaster 10m SW of York. Follow Bolton Percy signs off A64. Light lunches/TEAS in aid of Church. *Combined adm £3 OAP £2.50 Chd free. Suns April 19, June 28 (1-5)*
    Bolton Percy Cemetery An acre of old village churchyard gardened by Roger Brook, in which garden plants are naturalised. Featured on TV
    Betula (Roger Brook) Unusual plants, some alpines and the National Dicentra Collection

The White House (Mr & Mrs Martin Nulty) Family garden lovingly created on a strict budget by enthusiastic plantswoman. Mixed borders of continuous interest, gravel in shade, water feature and small productive vegetable garden

Windy Ridge (Mr & Mrs J S Giles) Large collection of Barnhaven and Elizabethan primroses; Hose-in-Hose, Jack-in-the-Green, etc. Wild and unusual hardy plants grown in an attractive cottage garden style, sloping down to the Ings, greatly influenced by Margery Fish. Featured on TV

Brookfield, Oxenhope ✿❀ (Dr & Mrs R L Belsey) 5m SW of Keighley, take A629 towards Halifax. Fork R onto A6033 towards Haworth. Follow signs to Oxenhope. Turn L at Xrds in village. 200yds after P O fork R, Jew Lane. A little over 1 acre, intimate garden, incl large pond with island and mallards. Many varieties of candelabra primulas and florindaes, azaleas, rhododendrons. Unusual trees and shrubs; screes; greenhouse and conservatory. TEA 50p. *Adm £1.50 Chd free. Sun, Wed June 14, 17 (2-6). Also by appt, please* **Tel 01535 643070**

●**Burton Agnes Hall, Driffield** craft ❀ (Mrs S Cunliffe-Lister) Burton Agnes is on A166 between Driffield & Bridlington. 8 acres of gardens incl lawns with clipped yew and fountains, woodland gardens and a walled garden containing a potager, herbaceous and mixed borders; maze with a thyme garden; jungle garden; campanula collection garden and coloured gardens containing giant games boards also collections of hardy geraniums, clematis, penstemons and many unusual perennials. 'Gardeners Fair' *Adm £2.50 Chd £1 Sat, Sun June 6, 7; specialist nurseries; gardening advice; dried flower & herb craft.* TEAS. *Adm £2 Chd £1. April 1 to Oct 31 (11-5)*

●**Castle Howard, nr York** craft ❀ (Castle Howard Estate Ltd) 15m NE of York off the A64. 6m W of Malton. Partially suitable for wheelchairs. Formal grounds laid out from C18 to present day, incl fountains, lakes, cascades and waterfalls. The woodland garden, Ray Wood, has a very important collection of rhododendron species and hybrids amounting to 600 varieties, also a notable collection of acers, nothofagus, arbutus, styrax, magnolia and a number of conifers. Two formal rose gardens planted in the mid 1970's include a large assembly of old roses, china roses, bourbon roses, hybrid teas and floribunda. Plant centre by the car park. *Adm Grounds and Gardens £4.50 Chd £2. Every day March 13 to Nov 1 (10-4.30)*

The Chimney Place, Bilton Grange ✿❀ (Mrs Paddy Forsberg) 23 Parthian Road, E Hull. Take Holderness Rd, R into Marfleet Lane, R at roundabout into Staveley Rd, L into Griffin Rd, Parthian Rd 1st on R. A small secluded, hedge enclosed, 30-yr-old garden, designed and maintained by owner, for the welfare of birds, fish, frogs and butterflies. Containers for alpines and rockery plants, new crockpot gardens. Allium avenue, summerhouse and rockery pool cascade. *Adm £1 Acc chd free. Mons May 4, 25, Sats June 13, July 11 (1.30-4.30). Private visits welcome, please* **Tel 01482 783804**

●**Constable Burton Hall Gardens, nr Leyburn** craft (Charles Wyvill Esq) 3m E of Leyburn on A684, 6m W of

A1. Large romantic garden, with terraced woodland walks; garden and nature trails. An array of naturalized daffodils set amidst ancient trees. Rock garden with choice plants. Fine John Carr house (not open) set in splendour of Wensleydale countryside. *Adm £2 OAPs £1.50 Chd 50p. March 22 to Oct 20 daily (9-6). Guided tours of gardens by appt, please* **Tel 01677 460225**

¶**Croft Cottage, Green Hammerton** craft ✿ (Alistair & Angela Taylor) Between York and Harrogate. 3m E of A1 adjacent to A59. Opp village green, next to Social Club. Secluded ½-acre cottage garden developing into a number of 'garden rooms'. Conservatory, clipped yew, old brick, cobbles and pavers used for formal areas leading to developing water feature, mixed borders and orchard with wild flowers. *Adm £1 Chd free (Combined adm with* **Whixley Gardens** *£3). Sun June 21 (12.30-5)*

Derwent House, Osbaldwick craft ✿❀ (Dr & Mrs D G Lethem) On village green at Osbaldwick. 2m E of York city centre off A1079. Approx ¾ acre, a most attractive village garden extended in 1984 to provide a new walled garden with yew hedges and box parterres. Conservatories, terraces, rose garden and double herbaceous borders leading to meadow with plantings of Eucalyptus. TEAS. *Adm £1.50 Chd free. Sun June 14 (1.30-5)*

8 Dunstarn Lane, Leeds 16 craft (Mr & Mrs R Wainwright) Adel. From Leeds ring rd A6120 exit Adel, up Long Causeway. 4th junction R into Dunstarn Lane. 28 bus from Leeds centre stops near gate. Garden formerly known as The Heath. 2 acres of long herbaceous and rose borders of exceptional quality. 60 varieties of delphiniums and wide range of August blooming plants giving a magnificent display of summer colour. *Adm £1.50 Chd free. Suns July 5, 19, Aug 9 (2-6)*

¶**East Wing, Thorp Arch Hall** ✿❀ (Fiona Harrison & Chris Royffe) Thorp Arch 1m S of Wetherby take A659 into Boston Spa centre. Turn L to Thorp Arch, Thorp Arch Hall at end of main street. A ¾-acre garden surrounding the East Wing of an C18 John Carr house, being imaginatively developed by new owners (previously at Fieldhead, Boston Spa). An inspiring garden arranged to link spaces and emphasize views. Newly designed courtyards, water features, potager, earth sculpture and dry garden. Dramatic combinations of plants, unusual bamboos and climbers. Photographic exhibition and small nursery. TEAS. *Adm £1.50 Chd 50p. Suns May 31, Sept 6 (11-5) Wed July 8 (3-7). Private visits welcome,* **Tel 01937 843513**

Elvington Gardens, nr York craft ❀ 8m SE of York. From A1079, immed after leaving York's outer ring road turn S onto B1228 for Elvington. Light lunches and Teas in Village Hall in aid of village hall. *Combined adm £3 Chd free. Sun June 7 (11-5)*

    Brook House (Mr & Mrs Christopher Bundy) Old established garden with fine trees; herb garden with rustic summer house; kitchen garden and new pond garden

    Elvington Hall (Mr & Mrs Pontefract) 3-4-acre garden; terrace overlooking lawns with fine trees and views; sanctuary with fish pond

    Eversfield (David & Helga Hopkinson) Modest sized garden with a wide variety of unusual perennials;

grasses and ferns divided by curved lawns and gravel beds. Small nursery. **Tel 01904 608332**

Red House Farm (Dr & Mrs Euan Macphail) Entirely new garden created from a field 12 years ago. Fine collection of hardy perennials shrubs and roses. Courtyard with interesting plantings and half-acre young wood

Evergreens, Bilton &✿❀ (Phil & Brenda Brock) 119 Main Rd. 5m E of Hull. Leave city by A165. Exit B1238. Bungalow ¼m on L nearly opposite the Asda Store. Over 1 acre developed since 1984. Features incl mosaics and sundials; tower; raised beds; rockeries and landscaped pond; Japanese garden; conifer, heather and mixed beds. Collection of dwarf conifers, many labelled. Photographs showing development of garden; small conifer/plant nursery open. *Adm £1 Acc chd free. Private visits and parties welcome by appt. Buffet or light refreshments may be booked May to Sept,* **Tel 01482 811365**

Fernwood, Cropton (Dick & Jean Feaster) 4m NW of Pickering. From A170 turn at Wrelton signed Cropton. 1-acre garden created by the owners in the last 10yrs, containing a series of individual gardens, herbaceous borders, a large collection of species and old roses, a wide variety of interesting and unusual plants, with a view of the N Yorkshire moors beyond. Morning coffee & TEAS. *Adm £1.50 Chd free. Sun July 5 (11-5)*

▲Goddards, York ✿❀ (The National Trust Yorkshire Regional Office) 27 Tadcaster Rd. 2m from York centre on A64, next to Swallow Chase Hotel. 1920s garden designed by George Dillistone, herbaceous borders, yew hedges, terraces with aromatic plants, rock gardens, pond. Guided tours. TEAS. *Adm £3 Chd free incl NT members. Sun July 19 (1-5). Large parties by appt May to Sept, please* **Tel 01904 702021**

¶Great Givendale, Pocklington (Mr & Mrs J H Goodhart) 12m E of York. Go to the top of Garrowby Hill and turn R where sign says Pocklington. Approaching Great Givendale from Pocklington follow the brown signs designating 'Scenic Drive'. This takes you to Givendale. Garden is situated on the edge of the Yorkshire Wolds at 400ft with good views over the Vale of York. Scented, water and wild butterfly gardens, as well as shrubs and lawns. Cymbidium and phalenopis orchids are kept in the greenhouses, but the former will not be in flower. TEAS. *Adm £2 Chd free. Sun July 12 (10-6)*

Grey Shaw Syke Cottage, Ogden ✿❀ (John & Cynthia Wareing). 4m N of Halifax on A629. Please park in Ogden Water car park. Pretty ⅓-acre cottage garden with many attractive features developed from a field and maintained by present owners. Good collection of old roses, wide range of herbaceous perennials, wildlife pond and small vegetable plot. The garden is set within magnificent moorland scenery at over 1000'. TEAS. *Adm £1.50 Chd free. Sun July 19 (10-4). Private visits welcome summer weekends, please* **Tel 01422 240148**

Grimston Gardens, Gilling East ❀ The hamlet of Grimston is 1m S of Gilling East 7m S of Helmsley 17m N of York on B1363. Follow sign 1m S of Gilling East. TEA.

Adm £2 Chd free. Sun, Thurs July 5, 9 (1.30-5.30)

Bankside House (Clive & Jean Sheridan) ½-acre garden established some thirty years ago. Mature plantings together with newer developments, incl semi-formal beds, Japanese area, shaded walk and recently created parterre

Grimston Manor Farm (Richard & Heather Kelsey) ½-acre garden with recent extension. The intricate design is profusely planted with a wide collection of herbaceous plants; trees and shrubs incorporating fine country views and old farm buildings

Hallgarth, Ottringham &✿❀ (Mr & Mrs John Hinchliffe) Turn N in Otteringham on A1033 Hull to Withernsea rd, signed Halsham. ¾m 1st L over former railway crossing. 1-acre informal country garden developed and maintained by owners from an initial design for part by John Brookes. Large and unusual trees, shrubs and plants, many for use by flower arrangers. New pond garden, flowering cherries, dwarf rhododendrons, bush roses, flower borders etc. Cakes and preserves stall. Tea by Ottringham Church. *Also open* **The White Cottage,** *Halsham. Adm £1.50 Chd free. Suns April 26, June 21, Sept 20 (2-5)*

●Harewood House, nr Leeds &❀ (Harewood House Trust) 9m N of Leeds on A61. 80 acres of gardens within 1000 acres of Lancelot 'Capability' Brown landscaped parkland, formal terraces restored to original Sir Charles Barry design, 2m of box edging surrounding a Victorian formal garden, enhanced by Italianate fountains and statues, charming informal walks through woods around the lake to the cascade and rock garden with collections of hosta and rhododendrons. TEAS Cafeteria. *Adm gardens, grounds, Bird Garden and Terrace Gallery Adults £5.50 OAP £4.50 Chd £3. Open daily March 17 to Oct 25 (10-5). Weekends Nov to Dec. For NGS private groups by appt, please* **Tel Trevor Nicholson 0113 288 6331**

■ Harlow Carr Botanical Gardens, Harrogate ✿❀ (Northern Horticultural Society) On B6162 (Harrogate - Otley) 1m W of town centre. 68 acres developed over past 50yrs as a Botanic garden ("A Wisley for the North") incl 5 national collections. Landscaped to incl heather, bulb, rock, scented and foliage gardens, herbaceous borders, vegetable, fruit and flower trials, alpine houses. Extensive woodland and streamside plantings, winter garden and wild flower meadow. Museum of Gardening, library and model village. Restaurant. Plant and Gift Shop. *Adm £3.50 OAP £2.60 Chd free. Open all year. For NGS Suns April 5, Oct 4 (9.30-6)*

Helmsley Gardens &❀ Teashops in Helmsley. *Adm £1 each gdn. Chd free. Sat June 13 (2-6)*

Ryedale House (Dr & Mrs J A Storrow) 41 Bridge Street. On A170, 3rd house on R after bridge into Helmsley from Thirsk and York. ¼-acre walled garden; varieties of flowers, shrubs, trees, herbs. *Private visits welcome, please* **Tel 01439 770231**

Rye Hill ✿❀ (Dr & Mrs C Briske) 15 Station Rd. Follow yellow signs from bridge on A170. ¼-acre site interestingly divided into compartments. Intensely planted with many unusual varieties of flowering shrubs, roses, clematis and perennials. Baskets, containers, pond and well stocked conservatory. TEAS. *Also open Wed July 1 (2-6). Private visits welcome: please write*

Hemble Hill Farm, Guisborough ♿❀ (Miss S K Edwards) On A171 between Nunthorpe and Guisborough opp the Cross Keys Inn. Dogs welcome, 7-acre garden facing the Cleveland Hills with formal and informal areas incl lake; young arboretum; heather, rhododendrons, large conservatory. TEAS. *Adm £1.50 Chd free. Sun May 10 (2-5.30). Private visits welcome June to Sept, please* **Tel 01287 632511**

High Farm, Bilton ❀❀ (Mr & Mrs G R Cooper) 5m E of Hull City Centre, take A165 Brid Rd, turn off at Ganstead Lane, onto B1238 to Bilton. Turn L opp Church. High Farm is at the bottom of Limetree Lane. Drive straight up the drive past the house, where parking is available in paddock. A mature garden of approx 1½ acres, harmoniously created and maintained by its present owners around a Georgian farmhouse. Many trees, shrubs, old species and climbing roses, herbaceous plants. Flower arrangers will find much to interest them in the many unusual and rare plants. TEAS. *Adm £1.50 Chd free (ACNO to RBL®). Suns May 24, June 28 (1-5)*

¶Highfield House, Ilkley ♿❀❀ (Mr & Mrs David Garnett) Burley Woodhead. Above Burley-in-Wharfedale, between Hawksworth and Ilkley, opp the Hermit Inn. A large beautifully maintained, established, yet still developing garden with lovely plantings using a wide variety of flowering shrubs, rhododendrons and azaleas creating secluded areas. Water from the moors feeds natural ponds; an extremely long pergola supports many unusual climbing plants and provides outstanding views up Wharfedale. Terraces and paths lead to a hidden herbaceous walkway full of colour and interest. TEAS. *Adm £2 Chd free. Sun Aug 9 (1-5.30)*

Hillbark, Bardsey ❀❀ (Malcom Simm & Tim Gittins) 4m SW of Wetherby, turn W off A58 into Church Lane. The garden is on L before Church. Car parking at village hall (Woodacre Lane). 1-acre country garden started in 1987. Past winner Sunday Express 'Large Garden of the Year'. Shrubs, perennials, and some annuals provide year round colour. Lively plantings across terraces, descending to ponds and stream with ducks and marginal plants. Some unusual garden ceramics. TEAS. *Adm £1.50 Chd 50p (ACNO to Cookridge Hospital Cancer Research®). Suns May 17, June 28, Sept 13 (11-5). Private visits welcome by appt May to July, please* **Tel 01937 572065**

¶Hillcrest, Whitgift ❀❀ (Mrs Stella Grieve) 6m E of Goole. Follow 'RSPB Blacktoft Sands Nature Reserve' signs from M62 or Scunthorpe, turning L past garage on A161 at Swinefleet, and R onto unclassified rd (also RSPB signposted). Garden is on main st of village of Whitgift approx 1m before nature reserve. (on rd parking). ¾-acre of country garden and paddock on edge of R Ouse. Created 10 yrs ago from field, with spring border, 100ft of raised rockery, ponds and colour-schemed summer borders of herbaceous perennials and shrubs. The wide collection is also designed to encourage wildlife. *Adm £2 Chd free (ACNO to Royal Society for Protection of Birds (RSPB)®). Suns April 19, June 14 (1-5)*

32 Holly Bank Road, York ❀ (Mr & Mrs D Matthews) Holgate. A59 (Harrogate Rd) from York centre. Cross iron bridge, turn L after Kilima hotel (Hamilton Drive East). Fork slightly L (Holly Bank Rd) after 400yds. Garden designer's small town garden planted for yr-round interest. Shrubs, small trees, climbers, clematis and container plants. Cobbled fountain, 4 separate patio areas, small pond. Finalist in Daily Mail National Gardens Competition. *Adm £1.50 incl tea Chd free. Evening opening Wed June 24 (6.30-9.30), Sun July 19 (11-5). Private visits for parties of 6-10 by appt, please* **Tel 01904 627533**

Holly Cottage, Leas Gardens, Scholes (Mr & Mrs John Dixon) 8m S of Huddersfield on A616. Turn W at signpost to Scholes. ½-acre sloping garden of interest created from a field in 1988 with raised alpine bed and paved area with troughs; pond with small bog garden, rockery and herbaceous borders with good selection of plants. *Adm £2 Chd free. Private visits welcome Feb to end Oct, please* **Tel 01484 684083/662614**

Holly Cottage, Wressle ♿❀❀ (Maureen Read) 1m N of the A63 between Howden and Selby. A ¾-acre country garden of intriguing design. Interesting 'gardens' within the garden are distinctive feature. Densely planted beds and borders incl many uncommon plants. Meandering grass walks and informal planting add to the peaceful atmosphere. TEA. *Adm £1.50 Chd free. Sun June 21 (2-5)*

Hovingham Hall, Hovingham ♿❀ (Sir Marcus & Lady Worsley) 8m W of Malton. In Hovingham village, 20m N of York; on B1257 midway between Malton and Helmsley. Medium-sized garden; yew hedges, shrubs and herbaceous borders. C18 dovecote and riding school; cricket ground. TEAS in aid of Hovingham Church. *Adm £2.50 Chd free. Sun June 28 (2-5). Enquiries* **Tel 01653 628206**

Hunmanby Grange, Wold Newton ♿❀❀ (Mr & Mrs T Mellor) Hunmanby Grange is a farm 12½m SE of Scarborough, situated between Wold Newton and Hunmanby on the rd from Burton Fleming to Fordon. The garden has been created from exposed open field, on top of the Yorkshire Wolds near the coast. Foliage colour, shape and texture have been most important in forming mixed borders, a gravel garden, pond garden, orchard and laburnum tunnel. TEAS in aid of St Cuthbert's Church, Burton Fleming. *Adm £1.50 Chd free. Suns June 7, July 5 (11-5). Private visits welcome,* **Tel 01723 891636**

Il Giardino, Bilton ♿❀❀ (Peter & Marian Fowler) 5m E of Hull City Centre. Take A165 Hull to Bridlington Rd. B1238 to Bilton Village. Turn L opp. St Peter's Church. Once neglected garden approx ⅓ acre redesigned and revived over last 10yrs by present owners. Features incl mixed borders and island beds stocked with unusual plants, shrubs and trees. Attractive beech hedge, herb garden, orchard of apple; pear; plum; cherries; and filberts; entwined with many types of clematis. Greenhouse with a collection of named pelargoniums; potted citrus; fig tree and other less common plants. TEAS. *Adm £1 Chd free. Suns May 3, 24 (12-5)*

Inglemere Lodge, Ilkley ✿✿ (Mr & Mrs Peter Walker-Sharp) Easby Drive. From Ilkley centre A65 towards Skipton, after ¾m turn L opp post box. Owner built and maintained ¼ acre colourful flower garden surrounding L-shaped bungalow approached by attractive, well planted drive. Naturally divides into areas of differing styles - cottage and more formal with pond. Many interesting plants, mostly labelled. TEAS in aid of Guide Dogs for the Blind. *Adm £1.50 Chd free. Sun Aug 2 (1.30-5). Private visits by appt, please* **Tel 01943 607333**

Joan Royd House, Penistone ✿✿ (Mrs M Griffiths & Dr A Owen Griffiths) Cubley. 13m NW of Sheffield. M1 junction 37 A628 (Manchester), into Penistone, turn L at lights. 1st R at derestriction sign. 'All yr' plantsman's garden of 1½ acres at 900′ close to Peak Park and Holmfirth (Last of the Summer Wine). It offers styles from formal to wild and wooded. Various gardens incl old, single and English roses. Topiary, interesting borders incl many varieties of hosta, hedera, campanula, hardy geranium, hardy fuchsia and the genus polypodiaceae. Greenhouses, shady garden room and small pinetum. The dell has large species and shrub roses by a small stream. Seats and gazebos abound. TEA. *Adm £2.50 Chd £1. Suns April 5, May 17, June 7, July 19. Wed March 11 (2-5)*

Kelberdale, Knaresborough ✿✿ (Stan & Chris Abbott) 1m from Knaresborough on B6164 Wetherby rd. House on L immed after new ring rd roundabout. Attractive owner-made and maintained, medium-sized plantsman's garden with river views. Full of yr-round interest with large herbaceous border, conifer and colour beds. Alpines and pond. Vegetable and wild gardens. Winner 1997 RHS/Daily Mail National Garden Competition. TEA. *Adm £1.50 Chd free. Suns June 7, 28 (11-6) Wed June 17 (2-8). Group visits welcome, please* **Tel 01423 862140**

54a Keldgate, Beverley ✿✿✿ (Lenore & Peter Greensides) Half-way between the double mini roundabout at SW entrance to Beverley on the B1230 and Beverley Minster. No private parking. ½-acre 'secret' garden within the charming town of Beverley. Largely created and solely maintained by the present owners over the last 18yrs. Clematis in variety, herbaceous plantings and shrubs, an inner garden of old roses, underplanted with peonies and geraniums; kitchen garden, fruit trees and irises, spring bulbs in season. TEAS in aid of Shelter on June 21 only. *Adm £1.20 Chd free. Suns May 3, June 21 (2-5). Group visits welcome, please* **Tel 01482 866708**

80 Lairgate, Beverley ✿✿ (Mary & David Palliser) In town centre on 1-way system. Enclosed ⅓-acre garden developed and maintained since 1986 by present owners, with many plants of interest to flower arrangers. Shrubs, climbers, old roses, bulbs, herbaceous and tender perennials, to provide yr-round and horticultural interest. *Adm £1 Acc chd free. Sun June 28 (2-5)*

●**Land Farm, nr Hebden Bridge** ✿✿ (J Williams Esq) Colden. From Halifax at Hebden Bridge go through 2 sets traffic lights; take turning circle to Heptonstall. Follow signs to Colden. After 2¾m turn R at 'no thru' road, follow signs to garden. 4 acres incl alpine; herbaceous, heather, formal and newly developing woodland garden.

Elevation 1000ft N facing. Has featured on 'Gardeners' World'. C17 house (not open). Art Gallery. *Adm £2 Chd free. May to end Aug; Open weekends and Bank Hols (10-5). By appt parties welcome evenings during week. Adm £3 incl refreshments, please* **Tel 01422 842260**

30 Latchmere Rd, Leeds 16 ✿✿ (Mr & Mrs Joe Brown) Moor Grange. A660 from City Centre to Lawnswood Ring Rd roundabout; turn sharp left on to ring rd A6120 for ⅓m to 3rd opening on left Fillingfir Drive; right to top of hill, turn right at top by pillar box, then left almost opposite into Latchmere Road, 3rd house on left. Cars and coaches to park in Latchmere Drive please. A small garden always full of interest; fern garden; herbaceous borders; alpine garden; glade; 2 pools; patio built of local York stone; sink gardens; collection of 80 clematis. *Adm £2. Tours, groups and private parties are welcome by written appt*

'Les Palmiers' Barnsley ✿✿ (Richard Darlow & Christine Hopkins) 106 Vaughan Road. From M1 junction 37 take A628 towards Barnsley. Turn L at major Xrds to hospital. Turn L at hospital Xrds into Gawber Rd, after ½m turn L into Vernon Way. 1st cul-de-sac on R. Rear Mediterranean garden with tender and exotic subjects permanently planted eg palms, cordylines, yuccas, cacti and eucalyptus; exotic plants in pots. Featured in BBC Gardeners World and magazines/journals. TEA. *Adm £1.50 OAP £1. Open by appt only, weekends all yr, also evenings mid summer please* **Tel 01226 291474**. *Not suitable for young children due to many spiky plants!*

Ling Beeches, Scarcroft ✿✿✿ (Mrs Arnold Rakusen) Ling Lane, 7m NE of Leeds. A58 mid-way between Leeds and Wetherby; at Scarcroft turn W into Ling Lane, signed to Wike on brow of hill; garden ⅓m on right. 2-acre enchanting woodland garden designed by owner emphasis on labour-saving planting; unusual trees and shrubs; ericaceous plants, some species trees, conifers, ferns, interesting climbers. Featured in The English Woman's Garden other publications and TV. *Private visits welcome by appt, please* **Tel 01132 892450**

Littlethorpe Gardens, nr Ripon ✿✿✿ Littlethorpe lies 1½m SE of Ripon indicated by signpost close to Ripon Racecourse on the B6265 twixt Ripon and the A1. Teas at Littlethorpe Village Hall (nr Church). *Combined adm £3 Chd free. Sun June 14 (1.30-5.30)*

> **Deanswood** (Mrs J Barber) Garden of approx 1½ acres created during the last 11 yrs. Herbaceous borders; shrubs; special features streamside garden; 3 ponds with many unusual bog/marginal plants. Adjacent nursery open. *Private visits also welcome, please* **Tel 01765 603441**

> **Field Cottage** (Mr & Mrs Richard Tite) A 7yr-old 1-acre plantsman's garden with walled garden, small pond, raised sleeper beds, gravel garden, vegetable plot, herbs, Victorian style greenhouse and extensive range of unusual plants in containers

> **Littlethorpe House** (Mr & Mrs James Hare) 2 acres with many beautiful varieties of old-fashioned roses; extensive established mixed herbaceous and shrub borders

¶**Londesborough Cross, Shiptonthorpe** ✎❀ (Mr & Mrs J W Medd) A1079 Hull to York rd 2m from Market Weighton 5m from Pocklington. Turn off in Shiptonthorpe down the side of church Londesborough Cross is at bottom of town st. In 13yrs nearly 1 acre of derelict railway goods yard has been transformed and maintained by the owners into a delightful garden. The old railway platforms are still intact. The garden comprises herbaceous borders, island beds, pools, bog garden, scree and rock gardens. TEAS in aid of British Diabetic Association. *Adm £1.50 Chd free. Sun July 5 (1-5)*

¶**Low Hall, Dacre** ❀✎❀ (Mrs P A Holliday) 4m S of Pateley Bridge on B6451 between Dacre and Dacre Banks. Large romantic garden in keeping with character of C17 family home, designed and developed by owner since 1980s. Neutral to acid soil provides ideal conditions for especially fine shrubs, trees, roses; hardy and tender plants festoon house and old dry-stone walls. Lovely blending of colours and winter interest. Yew and beech hedges give frost and wind protection. Differing levels incorporate orchard, pond and vegetable with cutting flower garden. TEAS. *Adm £1.50. Wed July 1, Sun July 19 (1-5)*

Lullaby, Hull ✎❀ (Michael Whitton) From the A165 (Holderness Rd), take Salthouse Rd towards Sutton Village. Turn R into Dunvegan Rd, R into Barra Close and R again. Developed over the last 10yrs into a peaceful retreat with planting to attract wildlife. Architectural features incl obelisks, a summerhouse, courtyard garden, water and pergolas, all in 40' × 60'. Evergreens provide yr-round interest. TEA in conservatory. *Adm £1 Acc chd free. Suns June 28, July 12 (2-5). Private visits welcome, please* Tel 01482 783517

Manor Farm, Thixendale ❀✎❀ (Charles & Gilda Brader) 10m SE of Malton, unclassified rd through Birdsall, ½m up hill, turn L at Xrds for Thixendale - 3m, 1st farm on R. 17m E of York, turn off A166 rd at the top of Garrowby Hill follow signs for Thixendale, 4m turn into village, drive through to end, farm on L. Created in the last 8yrs, nestling in a frost pocket and wind tunnel! 1-acre garden featuring 2 pergolas, rose garden, alpine area, courtyard, small knot garden and large lawns surrounded by mixed beds. TEA. *Adm £1.50 Chd free. Sun July 12 (11-5)*

Maspin House, Hillam ❀✎❀ (Dr & Mrs H Ferguson) Hillam Common Lane. 4m E of A1 on A63. Turn R in Monk Fryston after Thrust Garage. L at T junction. Continue for 1m. Ample parking in adjacent field. Garden of 1½ acres started in 1985. Created and maintained by enthusiastic plant collector and handy husband. Beautiful and unusual plants plus many interesting features incl ponds, gravel garden and woodland area. TEAS in aid of Monk Fryston School. *Adm £1.50 Chd free. Suns May 10, Sept 20 (1-5). Private visits welcome, by appt please,* Tel 01977 684922

The Mews Cottage, Harrogate ✎❀ (Mrs Pat Clarke) 1 Brunswick Drive. W of town centre. From Cornwall Rd, N side of Valley Gardens, 1st R (Clarence Dr), 1st L (York Rd), first L (Brunswick Dr). A small garden on a sloping

site of particular interest to hardy planters. Full of unusual and familiar plants but retaining a feeling of restfulness. A courtyard with trompe l'oeil and a gravelled area enclosed by trellising, provide sites for part of a large collection of clematis. Winner Daily Mail/RHS National Garden Competition 96. TEAS. *Adm £1.50 Chd 50p. Wed July 29 (2-5.30). Private visits for groups, societies and parties welcome, please* Tel 01423 566292

¶**Middle Birks, Clapham** ✎❀ (The Sanderson Family) At Clapham turn S off A65 to Keasden. Pass Clapham Station, take R fork, continue for approx 2m. Large dairy farm at 625' with wonderful panoramic views of three peaks from the drive. A 1-acre family garden developing with imagination and enthusiasm, sheltered by buildings and new plantings. Colour themed herbaceous borders, mixed beds with shrubs and old roses. Garden structures, gravelled area and small water features. TEAS by Newby WI. *Adm £1.50 Chd free. Sun July 12, Wed July 15 (2-5)*

Millgate House, Richmond ✎❀ (Austin Lynch & Tim Culkin) Market Place. House is located at bottom of Market Place opp Barclays Bank. SE walled town garden overlooking the R Swale. Although small the garden is full of character, enchantingly secluded with plants and shrubs. Foliage plants incl ferns, hostas; old roses and interesting selection of clematis, small trees and shrubs. Featured in The English Garden 1997 and Garden Design 1997. Full of ideas for small gardens. *Adm £1.50 Chd 50p. Sun July 5 (8am-8pm). Parties welcome, please* Tel 01748 823571

Nawton Tower Garden, Nawton ❀❀ (Douglas Ward Trust No. 4) 5m NE of Helmsley. From A170, between Helmsley and Nawton village, at Beadlam turn N 2½m to Nawton Tower. Large garden; heathers, rhododendrons, azaleas, shrubs. Tea Helmsley and Kirbymoorside. *Adm £1.50 Chd 50p. Sat, Sun, Mon May 23, 24, 25 (2-6); private visits welcome, please* Tel 01439 771218

Netherwood House, Ilkley ❀❀ (Mr & Mrs Peter Marshall) 1m W of Ilkley on A65 towards Skipton; drive on L, car parking adjacent to house. Large natural garden with magnificent trees. Daffodils, spring flowering shrubs, duck pond; rockery, and woodland stream. Lovely views up Wharfedale. TEAS. *Adm £2 Chd free. Easter Sun April 12 (2-5.30)*

●**Newby Hall & Gardens, Ripon** ❀✎❀ (R E J Compton Esq) 40-acres extensive gardens laid out in 1920s; full of rare and beautiful plants. Winner of HHA/Christie's Garden of the Year Award 1987. Formal seasonal gardens, stunning double herbaceous borders to R. Ure and National Collection holder Genus Cornus. Miniature railway and adventure gardens for children. Lunches & TEAS in licensed Garden Restaurant. Newby shop and plant stall. *Adm Gardens only £4.30, OAPs £3.70, Disabled/Chd £2.90. Easter/April to Sept daily ex Mons (Open Bank Hols) (Gardens 11-5.30; House 12-5). Group bookings and further details from Administrator* Tel 01423 322583

▲**Norton Conyers, nr Ripon** ❀❀ (Sir James & Lady Graham) 4m NW of Ripon. Take Melmerby and Wath sign off A61 Ripon-Thirsk. Large C18 walled garden of interest to garden historians. Interesting borders and orangery;

some hardy plants for sale. House which was visited by Charlotte Bronte, and is an original of 'Thornfield Hall' in 'Jane Eyre', is also open. TEAS. *Adm £1.50 Chd free. For NGS Sun June 7 (2-5)*

The Old Rectory, Mirfield &⚤✿ (G Bottomley Esq) Exit 25 of M62; take A62 then A644 thru Mirfield Village; after approx ½m turn L up Blake Hall Drive, then 1st L, Rectory at top of hill. Attractive 1-acre garden surrounding half timbered Elizabethan Rectory, colourful mixed beds and borders, Mulberry tree dating from C16; well, pergola and small ornamental pond. TEA. *Adm £1.50 Chd free. Sun July 5 (2-5)*

Help the Hospices

Help the Hospices is a charity which supports the hospice movement throughout the country. The National Gardens Scheme is delighted to include it in its list of beneficiaries. Some facts:

- **Help the Hospices** is the only national charity helping all providers of hospice and palliative care for the terminally ill.

- **Help the Hospices'** priority is to support all measures to improve patient care for all life-threatening conditions.

- **Help the Hospices** receives no government funding.

- **Help the Hospices** principally supports the voluntary hospices as they receive relatively little government funding.

- **Help the Hospices** support is mainly in direct response to applications from voluntary hospices, usually for training.

- **Help the Hospices** funds training for the NHS and nursing home staff in patient care for the terminally ill as well as funding its own initiatives in training, research, hospice management and team leadership.

- **Help the Hospices** pays special attention to training in communication skills for staff and volunteers.

Old Sleningford, nr Ripon &✿ (Mr & Mrs James Ramsden) 5m W of Ripon, off A6108. After North Stainley take 1st or 2nd L, follow sign to Mickley for 1m. Lovely early C19 house and garden with original layout of interest to garden historians. Many acres with magnificent trees; woodland walk and Victorian fernery; exceptionally romantic lake with islands; watermill and walled kitchen garden; long herbaceous border; yew, huge beech hedges. Flowers, grasses grown for drying. Several plant and other stalls. Homemade TEAS. *Adm £2.50 Chd 50p (ACNO to N of England Christian Healing Trust®). Bank Hol Mon May 4, Sun May 24, Mon May 25 (1-5). Groups catered for, also private visits by appt, please* **Tel 01765 635229**

The Old Vicarage, Whixley ⚤✿ (Mr & Mrs R Marshall) Between York and Harrogate. ¾m from A59 3m E of A1. A delightful ¾-acre walled flower garden with mixed borders, unusual shrubs, climbers, roses, hardy and half-hardy perennials, bulbs. Paths and garden structures leading to new vistas using the gardens natural contours. Courtyard with small herb garden. Lunches and TEAS. *Adm £1.50 Chd free. Sun May 3 (12.30-5) Combined adm with* **Whixley Gardens** *£3. Sun June 21 (12.30-5.30)*

Oliver Lodge, Hessle &⚤ (Mrs M Beaulah) 10 Heads Lane. ¼m from Humber Bridge roundabout, take exit marked A1105 signposted Hessle. 2nd turning on L, Lodge 100yds on L. The garden site is an old chalk pit, approx 1½ acres, with large trees and lawns. Planned in the C18 style with gazebo, mount and statuary. The banks are planted with shrubs chosen for their leaf colour and form. *Adm £1.50 Chd free. Sun Aug 23 (11-5). Private visits welcome, please* **Tel 01482 648032**

Oxenber House, Austwick ✿ (Kath Robinson & Patrick Pickford) 4m N of Settle A65. From village main st pass public house and school on L. Town Head Lane next L. ¾-acre planted for yr-round colour and interest. Gravel garden, scree, small pond and waterfall with alpines, ornamental grasses, foliage plants, ferns, spring bulbs, herbaceous and hardy perennials. Wild flower and vegetable area. Lovely views. TEA April 26 for Action Research. *Adm £1.50 Chd free. Suns April 26, May 31, June 28, Aug 30, Weds April 29, May 27, June 24, Aug 26, Sept 2 (11-5.30). Private visits welcome, please* **Tel 015242 51376**

■ **Parcevall Hall Gardens, Skyreholme** ✿ (Walsingham College (Yorkshire Properties) Ltd) 9m N of Skipton signs from B6160 Burnsall rd or off B6265 Grassington-Pateley Bridge rd. 20-acres in Wharfedale; shelter belts of mixed woodland, fine trees; terraces; fishponds; rock garden; tender shrubs incl desfontainea; crinodendron; camellia; bulbs; rhododendrons; orchard for picnics, old varieties of apples; autumn colour; birds in woodland; splendid views. TEA. *Adm £2 Chd (5-12 yrs) 50p. Good Friday to Oct 31 daily (10-6), winter by appt. For NGS Sun June 14 (10-5)*

Park House, nr York &✿ (Mr & Mrs A T Preston) Moreby 6m S of York. Between Naburn and Stillingfleet on B1222. Approx ½-acre, gardened since 1988, set within a 2-acre walled garden using some of the 16′ walls to display a wide variety of wall shrubs and climbers. Some herbaceous and mixed shrub borders. Large conservatory.

TEAS. *Adm £1.50 Chd free (ACNO to Asthma Research Campaign®). Sun May 31 (2-5.30)*

Parkview, South Cave ᕫ⚘⚘ (Mr & Mrs Christopher Powell) 45 Church Street. 12m W of Hull on A63 turn N to S Cave on A1034. In centre of village turn L by chemists, 250yds on L black gates under arch. ⅓-acre sheltered garden of perennial and shrub packed beds, pond and bog bed. Rose/honeysuckle pergola underplanted with 70+ varieties of hosta. Organic fruit and vegetable garden. TEAS. *Adm £1 Chd free if on reins. Sun June 14 (2-5). Private visits welcome, please* **Tel 01430 423739**

Pennyholme, Fadmoor (Mr C J Wills) 5m NW of Kirkbymoorside. From A170 between Kirkbymoorside and Nawton, turn N, ½m before Fadmoor turn L, signed 'Sleightholmedale only' continue N up dale, across 3 cattlegrids, to garden. No Buses. Large, wild garden on edge of moor with rhododendrons, azaleas, primulas, shrubs. TEAS in aid of All Saints, Kirkbymoorside. *Adm £2 Chd £1 (ACNO to All Saints, Kirkbymoorside®). Sat, Suns May 30, 31, June 6, 7 (11.30-5)*

■ **Plants of Special Interest Nursery, Braithwell** ᕫ⚘ (Mr & Mrs Peter Dunstan) A1(M) junction 36 through Old Edington. From M18 Junction 1 take A631. Turn L in Maltby to Braithwell. Nursery in centre of village. ¼-acre Mediterranean-style garden with patio and water feature adjacent to recently planted raised beds in small walled cottage garden. Nursery with excellent unusual plants and bulbs. From August a colourful display of ornamental gourds, squashes and pumpkins growing behind the nursery. Tea-room. Lunches/TEAS. *Adm £1 Chd 50p. Nursery open March to Nov Tues to Sats (9-5.30). Suns and Bank Hol Mons (10-5). For NGS Suns June 7, July 19, Sept 13 (10-5).* **Tel 01709 812328**

55 Rawcliffe Drive, York ⚘⚘ (Mr & Mrs J Goodyer) Clifton. A19 from York centre, turn R at Clifton Green traffic lights (Water Lane). Rawcliffe Drive is 1st L after Clifton Hotel. A 30yd by 10yd suburban garden on 2 levels. Planted for yr-round interest with excellent use of foliage and colour. Many unusual shrubs, herbaceous plants and bulbs; around 90 clematis. *Adm £1.50 Chd free incl TEA. Suns June 7, July 26 (11-5). Also private visits welcome April to July, please* **Tel 01904 638489**

Rudston House, Rudston (Mr & Mrs Simon Dawson) nr Driffield. On B1253 5m W of Bridlington. S at Bosville Arms for approx 300yds. Birthplace of authoress Winifred Holtby. Victorian farmhouse (not open) and 2 acres of garden with fine old trees, lawns, paths with clipped box hedges, interesting potager with named vegetable varieties, roses, hosta bed and short woodland walk, with a pond. Plenty of seats. Cream TEAS in aid of Rudston Church. *Adm £1.50 Chd free. Sun July 19 (11-5)*

Rye Hill (Dr & Mrs C Briske) see Helmsley Gardens

Saltmarshe Hall, Saltmarshe ᕫ⚘⚘ (Mr & Mrs Philip Bean) Howden. From Howden (M62, Jct 37) follow signs to Howden, Howdendyke and Saltmarshe. House in park W of Saltmarshe village. Large lawns, fine old trees, R Ouse and a Regency house with courtyards provide a set-

ting for shrubs, climbers, herbaceous plants and roses. Of special interest to plantsmen and garden designers are a pond garden, a walled garden and a large herbaceous border. Approx 10 acres. TEAS in aid of Laxton Church. *Adm £2 Acc chd free. Sun June 14 (2-5.30). Private visits welcome, please* **Tel 01430 430199**

Scampston Hall, Malton ᕫ⚘⚘ (Sir Charles & Lady Legard) 5m E of Malton off A64 Leeds to Scarborough rd. Through Rillington turn L signed 'Scampston Only'. Follow signs. 8 acres of garden in process of refurbishment; includes woodland walk by lakes and Palladian Bridge created by Capability Brown. Restored walk-in rock garden built in C19 and part of a Walled Garden with glass houses, herbaceous borders, formal rose garden. *Adm £2.50 Chd under 12 free. Sun June 28 (1-5)*

Secret Garden, York ⚘⚘ (Mr & Mrs A C Downes) 10 Sherwood Grove, Acomb. From York on A59, turn L into Beckfield Lane opp Manor School, ¼m before Western Ring Rd. Take 1st R, 2nd L. ¾-acre garden hidden behind suburban semi, developed and extended over 20 yrs. Features rockeries, pond, fruit cage but primarily extensive mixed plantings incl many unusual plants. 5 greenhouses with vines, cactus, succulent & tender plant collections. Small Nursery. TEA. *Adm £1 Chd free. Suns June 7, July 26 (10-5). Also private visits welcome, please* **Tel 01904 796360**

Settrington House, nr Malton ᕫ (Sir Richard Storey BT) 4m SE of Malton. Turn off A64 at Scagglethorpe. Settrington House 2m, next to medaeval village church. Late C18 garden with creative lawns, herbaceous borders, woodland and lakeside walks; herb garden. TEA. *Adm £1 Chd free (ACNO to Settrington Church®). Sun Aug 23 (2-5.30)*

■ **Shandy Hall, Coxwold** ⚘⚘ (The Laurence Sterne Trust) N of York. From A19. 7m from both Easingwold and Thirsk turn E signed Coxwold. Home of C18 author Laurence Sterne. 2 walled gardens, 1 acre of tulips, unusual perennials, old roses in low walled beds. Another acre in old quarry of trees, shrubs, bulbs, climbers and wild flowers. Season long interest. Featured in the Good Garden Guide, Country Life and Period Living. Shop. Unusual plants for sale. Wheelchairs with help. Teas in Coxwold (School House Tea Room; home baking). *Adm £2 Chd £1 (ACNO to Laurence Sterne Trust®). Gardens open daily except Sats from May 1. House open Wed & Sun (2-4.30) June 1 to Sept 30. Groups by appt. For NGS Suns May 3, 24, June 21, July 12, Wed July 8 (2-5).* **Tel 01347 868465**

Sinnington Gardens ⚘⚘ 4m W of Pickering on A170. Tickets on village green. TEAS June 14 only. *Combined adm £2.50 Chd free. Suns April 26, June 14, Wed July 15 (12-5)*

   Friars Hill (Mr & Mrs James Baldwin) 1¾-acre with extensive herbaceous beds. Delphiniums, old roses and alpine troughs

   Riverside Farm (Mr & Mrs William Baldwin) 1½-acre with cottage garden, old roses, interesting plants; shrubs and conservatory

Sleightholme Dale Lodge, Fadmoor ❀ (Mrs Gordon Foster; Dr & Mrs O James) 3m N of Kirkbymoorside. 1m from Fadmoor. Hillside garden; walled rose garden; herbaceous borders. *Not* suitable for wheelchairs. No coaches. TEAS (Teas and plants not available May 31, June 1). *Adm £2 Chd 50p. Sat, Sun June 6, 7 (11.30-5) Sat, Sun July 18, 19 (2-7)*

Snilesworth, Northallerton ௵❀ (Viscount Ingleby) Halfway between Osmotherley and Hawnby. From Osmotherley bear L sign posted Snilesworth, continue for 4½m across the moor. 4½m from Hawnby on Osmotherley Rd. Turn R at top of hill. Garden created from moorland in 1957 by present owners father; rhododendrons and azaleas in a 30 acre woodland setting with magnificent views of the Hambleton and Cleveland hills; snowgums grown from seed flourish in a sheltered corner. TEAS. *Adm £1.50 Chd 50p (ACNO to Hawnby Church®). Sun June 7 (2-5)*

The Spaniels, Hensall ௵❀❀ (Janet & Dennis Tredgett) 2m N of M62, 5m S of Selby. Turn E off A19 to Hensall. Field Lane is last turn on R in Hensall Village. A new ⅔-acre garden planted over the last 5yrs on previous farmland. Long mixed borders in colour themes, incl young conifers, trees and shrubs, divided by curved lawns with island beds. Small wildlife pond. TEAS. *Adm £1 Chd 50p. Suns May 10, Aug 2 (12-5). Private visits welcome, please Tel 01977 661858*

Springfield House, Tockwith ௵❀❀ (Mr & Mrs S B Milner) 5m E of Wetherby; 1m off B1224. Garden at W end of village. 1½ acres. Well established walled garden with herbaceous borders, water and rock gardens. Rose and conifer garden; shrub walk. Wide variety of plants. TEA. *Adm £1.50 Chd free. Sun June 7 (2-5)*

Stillingfleet Lodge, nr York ௵❀❀ (Mr & Mrs J Cook) 6m S of York, from A19 York-Selby take B1222 signed Sherburn in Elmet. ½-acre plantsman's garden subdivided into smaller gardens, each one based on a colour theme with emphasis on the use of foliage plants. Wild flower meadow and natural pond; new 50 metre double herbaceous borders, holders of National Collection of Pulmonaria. Adjacent nursery will be open. Homemade Teas in village hall in aid of local church. *Adm £1.50 Chd over 5yrs 50p. Suns May 17, June 28 (1.30-5.30)*

■ **Stockeld Park, Wetherby** ௵❀❀ (Mr & Mrs P G F Grant) 2m NW of Wetherby. On A661 Wetherby-Harrogate Rd; from Wetherby after 2m entrance 2nd lodge on left. Bus: Wetherby-Harrogate, alight Stockeld lodge gates (¼m drive). 4-acres with lawns, grove and flowers, fine trees and roses. House built 1758 for Col Middleton by James Paine (listed Grade 1). C18 pigeon cote. Chapel 1890. TEAS. *Gardens only Adm £2 Chd £1 (2-5). Open Thurs only April 2 to Oct 8 (2-5). For NGS Sun Aug 23 (2-5)*

Tan Cottage, Cononley ❀ (Mr & Mrs D L Shaw) West Lane. Take A629; turn off to Cononley 2¾m S of Skipton; top of village turn R onto Skipton rd. ¾-acre plantsman's garden, featured twice on TV, adjoining C17 house (not open). Interesting plants, many old varieties; national

collection of primroses. *Adm £2. Private visits by appt only, please Tel 01535 632030*

Three Gables, Markington ௵❀ (Jack Muirhead Esq) The Barrows, nr Harrogate. 7m N of Harrogate (A61 to Ripon) L at Wormald Green. R at village shop. If from Ripon, R at 'Monkton Moor' Xrds on A61 (approx 3m) 1st house on R past 'Markington' sign. ¾-acre garden set in woodland, approached over bridge of chinoiserie design crossing trout stream. Herbaceous border with streamside plantings. Terrace garden with many container plants and pergola. Steep bank garden to rear. Choice trees, shrubs; many unusual plants, sculptures and wood carvings. TEAS. *Adm £2 Chd free. Suns May 24, Aug 23, Wed Aug 19 (1-5). Private visits by groups and societies welcome, please Tel 01765 677481*

Victoria Cottage, Stainland ❀ (John Bearder Esq) Beestonley Lane. 6m SW of Halifax. From Halifax (A629 - Huddersfield) fork R B6112 (Stainland). Turn R at 2nd set traffic lights (B6114), after 1m fork L (Branch Rd), after 1m turn L by mills continue up hill. From A640 Huddersfield (M62 junction 23) follow signs to Sowood. Just before Stainland take L Barkisland fork passing Black Horse Garage. Continue for 1m down Beestonley Lane. ¾-acre plantsman garden, created by the owner from a NE sloping field since 1950. Daffodils; flowering shrubs, trees and roses; some are unusual, in a hilly and wild part of the Pennines. Scenic setting. *Adm £1.50 Chd 30p. Suns April 5, May 10, June 7, 21; July 12 (10-5). Private visits welcome and parties by appt only, please Tel 01422 365215/374280*

Wass Gardens, nr Coxwold ❀❀ ¼m from Byland Abbey on Coxwold-Ampleforth rd. 6m SW of Helmsley turning from A170. 9m E of Thirsk; turn from A19 signed Coxwold. A variety of gardens in a picturesque village set amid a broad cleft of deep wooded slopes. TEAS in aid of Wass Village Institute. *Adm £2 Chd free. Wed June 24 (12-5)*

8 Welton Old Road, Welton ❀ (Dr & Mrs O G Jones) In village of Welton 10m W of Hull off A63. Coming E turn L to village. Past church turn R along Parliament St. and up hill. House 50yds on R opp Temple Close. From E take A63 and turn off at flyover to Brough; turn R for Welton and follow above instructions. Roadside parking in village. Informal 1-acre garden developed by owners over 30yrs. Imaginative planting with unusual shrubs, plants and less common trees; natural pond and lily pond. TEAS. *Adm £1.50 Chd free. Suns May 24, June 14 (2-5). Private visits welcome Tel 01482 667488*

Regular openings. Open throughout the year. They are listed at the beginning of the Diary Section.

By Appointment Gardens. These owners do not have a fixed opening day usually because they cannot accommodate large numbers or have insufficient parking space.

The Old Vicarage, East Ruston is a Norfolk garden near the sea that opens for the Scheme in both spring and autumn
Photograph by Brian Chapple

The new rose garden at **Borde Hill Garden**, **Haywards Heath**, **Sussex**, which has opened for the National Gardens Scheme for over 60 years *Photograph courtesy of Borde Hill Garden*

Right: Vegetable gardens are increasingly popular with visitors. **Glebe House, Llanvair Kilgeddin** is the home of the County Organiser for **Gwent**
Photograph by Clive Boursnell

Below: At **Lady Farm, Chelwood** in **Somerset**, a spring fed watercourse runs through the garden, which includes prairie and steppe plants and a variety of grasses
Photograph by Nada Jennett

Left: **Holme Pierrepont Hall** in **Nottinghamshire** is a formal, listed garden dating from 1875 but including contemporary planting
Photograph by Clive Boursnell

Below: An herbaceous border and summer house at **Kelberdale, Knaresborough, Yorkshire**
Photograph by Rosalind Simon

A box parterre at **Beeby Manor**, **Beeby**, in **Leicestershire**
Photograph by Clive Boursnell

The Gardeners' Royal Benevolent Society, one of the National Gardens Scheme beneficiaries, assists many gardeners during their retirement *Photograph by courtesy of GRBS*

Right: Part of the double herbaceous
border close to the ancient stew-ponds at
Cadhay, Ottery St Mary in **Devon**
Photograph by Eric Crichton

Below: Roses in abundance in the 12-acre
garden at **Coughton Court, Alcester,
Warwickshire**
Photograph by Clive Boursnell

Left: Many village gardens open together on the same day: **Hill Grounds** is part of the **Evenley Gardens** in **Northamptonshire**
Photograph by Brian Chapple

Below: Among world-famous gardens which open for the National Gardens Scheme are the **Royal Horticultural Society's Gardens** at **Wisley** in **Surrey**
Photograph by Nada Jennett

26 West End, Walkington ✗ (Miss Jennifer Hall) 2m from Beverley on the B1230, 100yds beyond Xrds in centre of village on the R. Interesting ½-acre cottage garden opening into an old wooded gravel pit still being developed by the owner single-handedly. Many rare plants collected over 16yrs. TEA. *Adm £1.50 Chd free. Sun July 5 (1.30-5)*

5 Wharfe Close, Leeds 16 ✗❀ (Mr & Mrs C V Lightman) Adel. Signposted off Leeds ring rd A6120 (¼m E of A660 Leeds-Otley rd). Follow Long Causeway into Sir George Martin Drive. Wharfe Close adjacent to bus terminus. Please park on main rd. Medium-sized well stocked garden created from sloping site incorporating pools, rock gardens and mixed borders, small woodland walk. Unusual plants grown on predominantly acid soil. TEAS. *Adm £1 Chd free. Suns July 19, Aug 9 (2-5)*

The White Cottage, Halsham ⅙✗❀ (Mr & Mrs John Oldham) 1m E of Halsham Arms on B1362, Concealed wooded entrance on R. Ample parking. The garden was created by its owners 25yrs ago. Delightful specialised and unusual planting in island beds. Natural pond and water feature; small woodland area, vegetable and herb garden; architect designed sunken conservatory. Traditional pergola. Teas in aid of Halsham Church (April only). *Adm £2 Chd free (ACNO to Halsham Church Restoration Fund®). Suns April 26, June 21, Sept 20 (2-5). Private group visits welcome by appt, please* **Tel 01964 612296**

The White House, Husthwaite ⅙✗❀ (Dr & Mrs A H Raper) 3m N of Easingwold. Turn R off A19 signposted Husthwaite 1½m to centre of village opp parish church. Come and meet the gardener, an enthusiastic plantswoman, exchange ideas and visit a 1-acre country garden, herb garden, conservatory, gardens within the garden; herbaceous, particularly a hot summer border; shrubs; borders and many fascinating unusual plants. New landscaping and planting in the old orchard. *Adm £2. Wed July 8 (2-6)*

¶**Whixley Gardens** ❀ 3m E of A1 off A59 York/Harrogate. Follow signs to Whixley. Light lunches, TEAS at The Old Vicarage. *Combined adm £3 Chd free (incl* **Croft Cottage, Green Hammerton)** *Sun June 21 (12.30-5.30)*
  ¶**Ash Tree House** (Mr & Mrs E P Moffitt) A well designed unusual garden of approx 0.2 acre with extensive rockeries making full use of the sloping site. Established excellent plantings of heathers, alpines, hardy plants, climbers and shrubs
  ¶**Cobble Cottage** (John & Oliver Hawkridge and Barry Atkinson) An imaginatively designed, constantly changing, small cottage garden full of decorative architectural plants and old family favourites. Interesting water garden, containers and use of natural materials
  ¶**Croft Cottage** see separate entry
  The Old Vicarage (Mr & Mrs Roger Marshall) See separate entry

Windy Ridge (Mr & Mrs J S Giles) see Bolton Percy Gardens

Woodlands Cottage, Summerbridge ❀ (Mr & Mrs Stark) ½m W of Summerbridge on the B6165 (Ripley-Pateley Bridge). 1-acre country garden constructed and developed over the past 12yrs by the owners from a sloping site incorporating part of the existing woodland edge, field and natural stone outcrops with an attractive enclosed cottage style garden; herbaceous, formal herb garden, unusual hardy plants and separate vegetable area. Small nursery. TEAS in aid of Martin House Hospice. *Adm £1.50 Chd 50p. Suns May 17, Aug 9 (1.30-5). Private visits welcome by appt* **Tel 01423 780765**

York Gate, Leeds 16 ✗❀ (GRBS) Back Church Lane, Adel. Behind Adel Church ½m from A660. A garden created by the Spencer family and bequeathed to The Gardeners' Royal Benevolent Society. 1-acre plantsman's garden, divided into 8 individual gardens, each with unique architectural features. TEA. *Adm £2.50 Chd free (ACNO to GRBS®). Sat, Sun June 6, 7 (2-6). Private visits welcome, please* **Tel 0113 2678240**

WALES

Carmarthenshire & Pembrokeshire

Hon County Organiser: Mrs Duncan Drew, Cwm-Pibau, New Moat, Clarbeston Road, Haverfordwest, Pembrokeshire SA63 4RE Tel 01437 532454

Hon County Treasurer: Mr N Edmunds, Parc-y-Robert, New Moat, Clarbeston Road, Haverfordwest, Pembrokeshire SA63 4RY

DATES OF OPENING

Regular Openings
For details see garden description

Cilwern, Talley
The Dingle, Crundale
Hilton Court Nurseries, Roch
Picton Castle, The Rhos
Saundersfoot Bay Leisure Park

By appointment only
For telephone numbers and other details see garden descriptions. Private visits welcomed

Blaengwrfach Isaf, Bancyffordd
Cwm Pibau, New Moat
The Forge, Landshipping
The Swallows, Grove Hill

April 12 Sunday
   Llysnewydd, Llangadog
April 13 Monday
   Llysnewydd, Llangadog
May 3 Sunday
   Llysnewydd, Llangadog
May 4 Monday
   Llysnewydd, Llangadog
May 9 Saturday
   Colby Woodland Garden, Narberth
May 10 Sunday
   Brynsifi, Llanelli
May 17 Sunday
   Great Griggs, Llanteg
   Picton Castle, The Rhos
May 24 Sunday
   Ffynone, Boncath
   Hean Castle, Saundersfoot
June 7 Sunday
   Le Bocage Bryngoleu. Llannon
   Living Garden, Bryn

Llysnewydd, Llangadog
June 14 Sunday
   Cwm Cottage, Tycroes
June 21 Sunday
   Cilwern, Talley
July 5 Sunday
   Great Griggs, Llanteg
   Llysnewydd, Llangadog
July 11 Saturday
   Maesyrynn, Nantycaw
July 12 Sunday
   Maesyrynn, Nantycaws
July 26 Sunday
   Picton Castle, The Rhos
August 2 Sunday
   Llysnewydd, Llangadog
   Maesyrynn, Nantycaws

DESCRIPTIONS OF GARDENS

Blaengwrfach Isaf, Bancyffordd ✿❀ (Mrs Gail M Farmer) 2m W of Llandysul. Leaving Llandysul on Cardigan rd, by Half Moon pub fork L; continue on this rd; approx 1½m, after village sign Bancyffordd farm track on R. ¾-acre garden incorporating woodland, wild and cottage garden aspects within a secluded and sheltered area. Areas specially created with bees, butterflies and birds in mind; new pathway bordered by wild-flower meadow. Incl in 'English Private Gardens'. *Adm £1 Chd free. Private visits welcome April, May, June, Oct (10-4), please* **Tel 01559 362604**

Brynsifi, Llanelli ✿❀ (A C & B Grabham) 3m W of Llanelli on B4308 Llanelli to Trimsaran rd. Signed off main rd. Medium-sized organic garden created on shale bank with natural stone retaining walls planted to give yr-round interest. Extension to garden currently being undertaken to include wildlife pond. TEA. *Adm £1.50 Chd free (ACNO to Cats Protection League®) Sun May 10 (2-6). Also private visits* **Tel 01554 810294** *after 8pm*

■ **Cilwern, Talley** ♿✿❀ (Mrs Anne Knatchbull-Hugessen) 6m NE of Llandeilo off B4302. Turn L by large sign on main rd. Garden on L 200yds down lane. Tranquil 1½-acre garden in valley. Created over 17yrs by owner from marshy scrubland. Wide range young and mature trees, shrubs and perennials; also new plantings. Hardy geraniums in variety. Collection of grasses being established. Newly planted hardy geranium 'walk' to display the 90+ varieties now grown. Pond, stream and small woodland area. Adjoining nursery. TEAS. *Adm £1 Chd free. Open daily (11-6) donation to NGS. For NGS Sun June 21 (2-6)*

▲**Colby Woodland Garden, Narberth** ❀ (The National Trust) ½m inland from Amroth and 2m E of Saundersfoot. Sign-posted by Brown Tourist Signs on the coast rd and the A477. 8-acre woodland garden in a secluded and tranquil valley with a fine collection of rhododendrons and azaleas. Tea rooms and gallery. Walled garden open by kind permission of Mr & Mrs A Scourfield Lewis. TEAS. *Adm £2.80 Chd £1.40. For NGS Sat May 9 (10-5). Large parties by appt, please* **Tel 01834 811885**

¶**Cwm Cottage, Tycroes** ❀ (Mr & Mrs A Ruthen) 4m NE from M4 Pont Abraham and 16m from Llandeilo in SW direction. Cwm Cottage lies behind the Mountain Gate Inn, Tycroes on the A483, Pont Abraham-Llandeilo Rd. Car parking available on top car park of Mountain Gate Inn. 3½ acres, incorporating a woodland and river walk, wild and cottage gardens, areas created for wildlife habitat, wild flower meadow and ponds. Plants and crafts for

CARMARTHENSHIRE & PEMBROKESHIRE

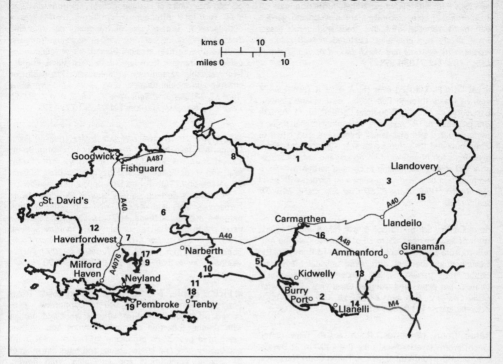

kms 0   10
miles 0   10

KEY

1. Blaengwrfach Isaf
2. Brynsifi
3. Cilwern
4. Colby Woodland Garden
5. Cwm Cottage
6. Cwm Pibau
7. The Dingle
8. Ffynone
9. The Forge
10. Great Griggs
11. Hean Castle
12. Hilton Court Nurseries
13. Le Bocage Bryngoleu. Llannon
14. Living Garden
15. Llysnewydd
16. Maesyrynn
17. Picton Castle
18. Saundersfoot Bay Leisure Park
19. The Swallows

sale. Rescued animals and birds in garden. TEA and coffee. Lunches available at Mountain Gate. *Adm £1.50 Chd 50p. (ACNO to World Wildlife Fund®) Sun June 14 (10-4). Also private visits welcome, please* **Tel 01269 593340**

Cwm Pibau, New Moat (Mrs Duncan Drew) 10m NE of Haverfordwest. 4-acre garden bordered by streams and created since 1978; mainly young rare shrubs on a hillside. *Adm £1 Chd free. Private visits welcome, please* **Tel 01437 532 454**

●**The Dingle, Crundale** 占♨❀ (Mrs A J Jones) On approaching Haverfordwest from Carmarthen on A40, take R turn at 1st roundabout signed Fishguard & Cardigan. At next roundabout take R turn on to B4329. ½m on fork R opp General Picton; then 1st right into Dingle Lane. 3-

acres plantsman's garden; rose garden and rose walk, vast selection of beautiful and unusual shrubs and herbaceous water garden; woodland walk. Extensive wildlife. A garden of many 'rooms', secret, peaceful and romantic. Peacocks. Nursery adjoining, specializing in old roses, clematis and herbaceous. Tearoom. *Adm £1 Chd 50p (ACNO to MCR®). Weds to Suns March 15 to Oct 18 (10-6)*

Ffynone, Boncath (Earl & Countess Lloyd George of Dwyfor) From Newcastle Emlyn take A484 to Cenarth, turn L on B4332, turn L again at Xrds just before Newchapel. Large woodland garden in process of restoration. Lovely views, fine specimen trees, rhododendrons, azaleas. Ask for descriptive leaflet. House by John Nash (1793), not shown. Later additions and garden terraces by F Inigo Thomas c1904. TEAS in aid of Fishguard Sea Cadets. *Adm £1.50 Chd under 14 free. Sun May 24 (2-6)*

The Forge, Landshipping & (Mrs S Mcleod-Baikie) Nearest town Narbeth. Landshipping well sign posted. Pass New Park with pillar box; 200yds further on, gate on R. Approx 2½ acres recently planted woodland garden with many varieties of bulbs, trees and shrub roses. Small, pretty very charming. Featured in NGS video 2. *Private visits welcome mid-March to mid-April and also in June, please* **Tel 01834 891279**

Great Griggs, Llanteg & (M A & W A Owen) A477 from St Clears through Red Roses, next village Llanteg. Signposted on L 'Colby Woodland Garden', turn L immed; 2nd entrance on R. Approx 1-acre plantsman's organic garden created and maintained by owners, consisting of lawns bounded by shrub borders and interspersed with scree beds full of alpines. Two ponds, and natural stonework incl seating; all leading to cottage garden with summerhouse, in turn leading to semi-wild garden with pond and shrubs. TEAS. *Adm £1.50 Chd 50p. Suns May 17, July 5 (2-6)*

Hean Castle, Saundersfoot & (Mr & Mrs T Lewis) 1m N of Saundersfoot. 1½m SE of Kilgetty. Take the Amroth rd from Saundersfoot or the Sardis rd from Kilgetty. 2-acres; mixed borders with some unusual plants and shrubs; rose garden; walled garden and greenhouse; conifers; pot plants and troughs. Good view. TEAS. *Adm £1.50 Chd free. Sun May 24 (11-5). Also private visits welcome, please* **Tel 01834 812222**

Hilton Court Nurseries, Roch & (Mrs Cheryl Lynch) From Haverfordwest take the A487 to St Davids. 6m from Haverfordwest signs L to Hilton Court Nurseries. 4 acres of garden with superb setting overlooking ponds and woodlands. Spectacular lily ponds in July and August; wild flower walks; unusual trees and shrubs giving colour throughout the year. Nursery adjoining. TEAS. *Collecting box. Daily March to October 1 (9.30-5.30), October (10.30-4).* **Tel 01437 710262**

Le Bocage Bryngoleu, Llannon & (Mr & Mrs Ivor Russell) 13m from Swansea, 7m from Llanelli. From junction 49 (Pont Abraham) on M4 take A48(T) in the direction of Cross Hands. Turn L after approx 3kms towards Village of Llwyn Teg. At [map ref SN 56 E on OS 159.] 1-acre garden with converted stable block, leading to extensive choice of walks each about ½m long in mature and newly develop-ing woodlands and alongside natural streams. 15 acres overall incl 2 lakes; fine views of the surrounding countryside. Ample seating. TEA. *Adm £1.50 Chd 50p. Sun June 7 (2-6). Open all year by appt and private parties welcome, please* **Tel 01269 842343**

Living Garden, Bryn & (Alan & Justine Clarke) 4a Brynmorlais, Llanelli; 2½m NE of town on B4297. Parking in lay-by on main rd please. Long, slender plantsman's garden subdivided for interest. Rare and attractive collection of plants, containers, water features and pools, one under redevelopment. TEAS. *Adm £1 Chd 25p. Sun June 7 (2-5); also private visits welcome, please* **Tel 01554 821274** *April to Sept*

Llysnewydd, Llangadog & (Jan Jones & Nick Voyle) Midway between Llandeilo and Llandovery. Turn off A40 into centre of Llangadog. Bear L in front of village shop. Turn 1st R. After approx ½m turn R. Garden approx 600yds on R. 1 acre oasis of tranquility set in scenic Towy Valley. Quiet, relaxing garden evolving from the need to prevent river erosion. Planted for yr-round interest in areas ranging from full sun to deep shade. Productive vegetable garden with greenhouses. Unsuitable for children and mobile phones. TEAS. *Adm £1. Suns, Mons April 12, 13, May 3, 4. Suns June 7, July 5, Aug 2, (11-5). Private visits welcome, please* **Tel 01550 777432**

Maesyrynn, Nantycaws & (Mr & Mrs Thomas) From Carmarthen take A48 dual carriageway E towards Swansea. After approx 3m turn L for Nantycaws. From Swansea, sign reads Police HQ and Nantycaws. Drive 300yds BP garage on L. Turn R into lane opp; 2nd bungalow on L. Plantsman's cottage garden approx ½ acre. Mainly herbaceous beds and shrubs. Pond and water feature, pergolas and raised beds. Highly productive vegetable garden with greenhouses. Lovely views in rural setting. TEAS. *Adm £1 Chd free (ACNO to the British Heart Foundation®). Sat, Sun July 11, 12, Sun Aug 2 (10-6). Parties welcome June to Sept, please* **Tel 01267 234198**

■ **Picton Castle, The Rhos** & (Picton Castle Trust) 3m E of Haverfordwest on A40 to Carmarthen, signposted off main rd. Mature 40-acre woodland garden with unique collection of rhododendrons and azaleas, many bred over 35yrs producing hybrids of great merit and beauty; rare and tender shrubs and trees like magnolia, myrtle, embothrium and eucryphia. Wild flowers abound. Walled garden with roses, fernery, herbaceous and climbing plants and large clearly labelled collection of herbs. Restaurant, shop, craft shop gallery and garden nursery. *Adm £2.50 Chd £1, under 5 free. Open daily except Mons, April to Sept and Bank Hols. For NGS Suns May 17, July 26 (10.30-5).* **Tel 01437 751326**

Saundersfoot Bay Leisure Park & (Gavin Steer Esq) Broadfield, Saundersfoot. On B4316, ¾m S from centre of Saundersfoot. Interesting layout of lawns, shrubs and herbaceous borders with many plants of botanical interest in 20-acre modern holiday leisure park. Large rock garden and water feature; laburnum walk; Japanese Garden. Holders of a National collection of Pontentilla fruticosa. Tea Saundersfoot. *Adm free. April 1 to Oct 28 daily (10-5)*

¶**The Swallows, Pembroke** & (Mrs Moore) One-way system through Pembroke main st to roundabout. Keep R. Down hill. Up Grove Hill. The 'Swallows' is on the R. A haven on the edge of the town. Garden sub-divided to give interest. Trees, shrubs, phormiums, cordylines, bamboos to give a Mediterranium feel. Hosta walk. Pergolas, ponds and water features. Wildlife haven. A plantsman's garden. *Adm £1 Chd 50p. June, July, August (2-5). Private visits welcomed. Parties by arrangement (15-20).* **Tel 01646 682248**

Ceredigion/Cardiganshire

Hon County Organiser: Mrs Joy Neal, Llwyncelyn, Glandyfi, Machynlleth, SY20 8SS
Tel 01654 781203

Treasurer: Mrs Sheila Latham, Garreg, Glandyfi, Machynlleth, SY20 8SS

DATES OF OPENING

Regular openings
For details see garden description

Farmyard Nurseries, Llandysul
The Walled Garden at Pigeonsford,
  Llangranog
Winllan, nr Lampeter
Ynyshir Hall Hotel, Eglwysfach,
  Machynlleth

By appointment only
For telephone numbers and other details see garden descriptions. Private visits welcomed

Coetmor, Talybont, nr Aberystwyth
The Mill House, Glandyfi
Old Cilgwyn Gardens, Newcastle
  Emlyn

March 29 Sunday
Farmyard Nurseries, Llandysul

April 26 Sunday
Pant-yr-Holiad, Rhydlewis
May 10 Sunday
Llwyncelyn, Glandyfi
The Mill House, Glandyfi
Pant-yr-Holiad, Rhydlewis
May 17 Sunday
Cae Hir, Cribyn
May 23 Saturday
Dyffryn, Pennant, Llannon
Glanarthen Stores, Cross Inn,
  Aberystwyth
May 24 Sunday
Dyffryn, Pennant, Llannon
Glanarthen Stores, Cross Inn,
  Aberystwyth
May 31 Sunday
Crynfryn Penuwch & Tynewydd
  Bwlchllan
June 7 Sunday
Cae Hir, Cribyn
The Walled Garden at
  Pigeonsford, Llangranog

June 14 Sunday
Glangwenffrwd, Llangeitho
June 21 Sunday
Llanllyr, Talsarn
June 28 Sunday
Farmyard Nurseries, Llandysul
Plas Llidiardau, Llanilar
July 5 Sunday
Crynfryn Penuwch & Tynewydd
  Bwlchllan
July 11 Saturday
Felindre, Aberarth, Aberaeron
July 12 Sunday
Cae Hir, Cribyn
July 19 Sunday
The Walled Garden at
  Pigeonsford, Llangranog
July 26 Sunday
Farmyard Nurseries, Llandysul
August 30 Sunday
Llanaerchaeron, Ciliau Aeron,
  Aberaeron

DESCRIPTIONS OF GARDENS

▲**Cae Hir, Cribyn** ⚲❀ (Mr Wil Akkermans) W on A482 from Lampeter. After 5m turn S on B4337. Cae Hir is 2m on L. A remarkable and fascinating creation with lovely view of many garden enclosures divided into a bonsai 'room', separate blue, gold, white and red gardens on a hillside leading down to the valley where large ponds form a water and wild garden created by a Dutch plantsman. As featured on radio and national and regional TV. TEA. *Adm £2 Chd 50p. For NGS Suns May 17, June 7, July 12 (1-6)*

Coetmor, Talybont ❀ (Dr & Mrs G Hughes) From Aberystwyth take A487 towards Machynlleth, 7m N to Talybont. 2nd turn L after shop on village green. House visible in the trees 300yds straight up lane. 2-acre garden extended and planted during last 10yrs with interesting trees and shrubs incl embothrium, styrax japonica, ptelea aurea, zelkova, rhododendrons, azaleas, acers and a range of sorbus. Also an increasing collection of less common conifers. *Collecting box. Private visits and parties welcome April to June and Sept to Nov, please* **Tel 01970 832365**

Crynfryn & Tynewydd ⚲❀ TEAS. *Combined adm £2 Chd free. Suns May 31, July 5 (10.30-6)*
  Crynfryn, Penuwch (Mr & Mrs Tom Murton) On B4576 between Penuwch and Bwlchllan, 8m Aberaeron, 8m Tregaron. 1-acre woodland garden with mature trees, pond, bog plants, meconopsis and primulas, herbaceous borders and collection of old shrub roses in glorious position overlooking Cambrian Mts
  Tynewydd, Bwlchllan (Mr & Mrs Robin Edwards) 1m S of Crynfryn. 2-acre garden, 2 large ponds, massive herbaceous plantings, pergola, maturing trees and shrubs, alpine house. Extensive mountain views

Dyffryn, Pennant ⚲❀ (Mr & Mrs O P J Richards) SN 521, 637. From Aberarth, continue 100yds up hill, turn R, B4577 to Pennant. Xrds at centre of village turn L. Follow rd up hill past school. R fork, 250yds turn R. ⅔-acre partly woodland; many shrubs for flower arranging; small ponds; small Japanese garden; open perennial border; interesting plants, local bird life. TEAS. *Adm £1.50. Sat, Sun May 23, 24 (12-6)*

¶■ **Farmyard Nurseries, Llandysul** ❀ Off Carmarthen rd (B4336) 2nd L opp Valley Garage. Approx 1m follow signs. TEA. *Combined adm £1.50 Chd free (ACNO to British Diabetic Assoc.®) For NGS Suns March 29 (9-6), June 28, July 26 (9-7)*
  ¶**Farmyard Nurseries** (Mr Richard Bramley) Interesting 1-acre shade garden; woodland walks lead to natural water feature, sunken walled area, large hellebore, fern and hosta plantings and magnificent view. Adjoining specialist hellebore and herbaceous 3-acre nursery. *Open daily*

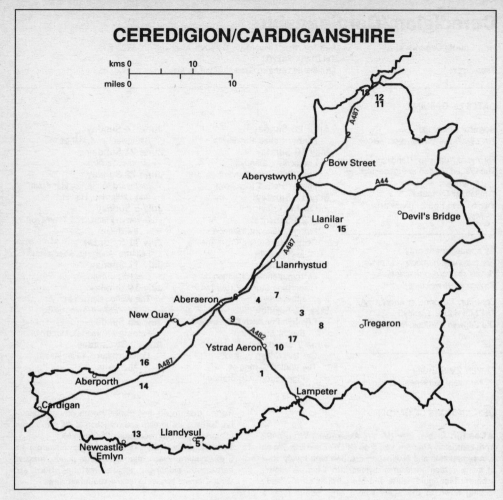

CEREDIGION/CARDIGANSHIRE

kms 0   10

miles 0   10

KEY

1. Cae Hir
2. Coetmor
3. Crynfryn & Tynewydd Gardens
4. Dyffryn
5. Farmyard Nurseries
6. Felindre
7. Glanarthen Stores
8. Glangwenffrwd
9. Llanaerchaeron
10. Llanllyr
11. Llwyncelyn
12. The Mill House
13. Old Cilgwyn Gardens
14. Pant-yr-Holiad
15. Plas Llidiardau
16. The Walled Garden at Pigeonsford
17. Winllan
18. Ynyshir Hall Hotel

¶**Cottage Garden** (Mrs G M Bramley) Winding stepped paths around beds packed with unusual and interesting plants. Masses of colour, wide general range, old roses, herbaceous, shrubs and climbers

Felindre, Aberarth, Aberaeron ✿❀ (Mr & Mrs Peter Davis) 1m N of Aberaeron on A487. Turn L towards sea after bridge. 1-acre informal garden, 200 yds from sea, partly rough hillside. Salt-hardy coastal shrubs, pines, eu-calyptus, mulberry. Wide variety of herbaceous plants in-cluding geraniums, primulas, euphorbia and salvias, growing in sun and shade on dry stone walls and pave-ment, and damp pond edges. Productive vegetable gar-den. TEA in old stable. *Adm £1.50. Sat July 11 (10-5)*

¶**Glanarthen Stores, Cross Inn** ❀✿❀ (Dr & Mrs David Shepherd) 4m NE of Aberaeron, Xrds B4577 with B4337 centre of village. Small but exquisite garden, behind village shop, overflowing with the best cultivars of herbaceous plants and compact shrubs, full of interesting features including mini vegetable garden all designed for ease of maintenance. *Adm £1 Chd 50p (ACNO to Breast Test Wales©). Sat May 23, Sun May 24 (2-5)*

¶**Glangwenffrwd, nr Tregaron** &⚘⚘ (Mr & Mrs John Escott) 10m NNW of Lampeter on B4342 Talsarn-Llangeitho Rd. Picturesque 5-acre garden sheltered by mature woodland. Extensive lawns, stream and pretty bridge. Meadow walk. Mixed borders with range of roses, primulas, herbaceous plants and shrubs leading to woodland area and recently planted arboretum. TEAS. *Adm £1.50 Chd 50p. Sun June 14 (11-5)*

▲**Llanerchaeron, Ciliau Aeron, Aberaeron** &⚘⚘ (The National Trust) 2m inland from Aberaeron, N of the A482 to Lampeter. 12-acre gardens of Nash house undergoing restoration. 2 walled gardens contain original rose parterre, fruit, vegetables etc. Volunteers will now concentrate on pleasure grounds and shrubberies with very limited resources. The lake and most farm buildings are yet to be restored. TEA. *Adm £2 Chd free. For NGS Sun Aug 30 (11-5)*

Llanllyr, Talsarn &⚘⚘ (Mr & Mrs Robert Gee & Mr Matthew Lewes Gee) 6m NW of Lampeter on B4337 to Llanrhystud. Garden of about 4 acres, originally laid out in 1830s, renovated, replanted and extended since 1989. Mixed borders, lawns, bulbs, large fish pond with bog and water plants. Formal water garden. Shrub rose borders; foliage, species and old-fashioned plants. TEAS. *Adm £1.50 Chd 50p (ACNO to Llanfihangel Church Restoration Fund®). Sun June 21 (2-6). Private visits welcome April to Oct. Please* Tel 01570 470900 or 470788

Llwyncelyn, Glandyfi ⚘⚘ (Mr & Mrs Stewart Neal) On A487 Machynlleth (6m). From Aberystwyth (12m) turn R just before Glandyfi sign. 8-acre hillside garden/arboretum alongside Dyfi tributary, collections of hybrid/specie rhododendrons, azaleas, camellias, bluebells in oak woodland, hydrangeas, fernery and unusual plants. TEAS. *Adm £2 Chd 50p includes entrance to Mill House garden. Sun May 10 (1-6)*

The Mill House, Glandyfi ⚘ (Prof & Mrs J M Pollock) On main A487 Machynlleth 5½m. From Aberystwyth 12m; turn R up lane almost directly opp sign for Glandyfi (on L). 2nd house up lane, approx 150yds. Picturesque garden of a former watermill, with millstream, millpond, and several waterfalls in woodland setting, about 1½ acre. Azaleas, rhododendrons and Spring colour enhance waterside vistas, and new tree planting continues a programme of woodland development and rejuvenation. *Open daily by appointment during May,* Tel 01654 781342. *Collecting box*

Old Cilgwyn Gardens & (Mr & Mrs Edward Fitzwilliams) Situated 1m N of Newcastle Emlyn on the B4571, turn R into entrance. A mixed garden mainly woodland of 14 acres set in 900 acres of parkland, 53 acres of which are Sites of Special Scientific Interest; snowdrops, daffodils,

bluebells, rhododendrons, a large tulip tree, well trained fremontodendron, crinodendron and many hydrangeas make this a plantsman's garden of great interest. *Adm £1.50 Chd free. Private visits welcome all year, please* Tel 01239 710244

▲**Pant-yr-Holiad** ⚘⚘ (Mr & Mrs G H Taylor) Rhydlewis, 12m NW Llandysul. NE Cardigan. From coast rd take B4334 at Brynhoffnant S towards Rhydlewis; after 1m turn left; driveway 2nd L. 5-acres embracing walled garden housing tender plants, alpine beds, water features, rare trees and shrubs in woodland setting; extensive collection rhododendron species; fancy water-fowl. Collections of birch and unusual herbaceous plants. Home of 'Holiad' rhododendron hyrids. Featured on regional TV and radio. TEA. *Adm £2 Chd £1. For NGS Suns April 26, May 10 (2-5)*

Plas Llidiardau, Llanilar &⚘⚘ (L A Stalbow & G Taylor) 7m SE of Aberystwyth. Turn off A487 3m S of Aberystwyth onto A485 to Tregaron and Llanilar. From Llanilar take B4575 to Trawsgoed. Plas Llidiardau is ¾m on R. 7-acre country house garden redeveloped and planted since 1985. Wide selection of unusual plants and environments. Double herbaceous borders, formal pond, gravel garden, walled garden, organic raised beds, wooded areas, stream, wildlife pond. TEAS. *Adm £1.50 Chd 50p. Sun June 28 (1-6). Private visits welcome May to July, please* Tel 01974 241434

■ **The Walled Garden at Pigeonsford, nr Llangranog** ⚘ (Mr David & Dr Hilary Pritchard) On A487 14m from Cardigan, at Pentregat turn N on B4321 for Pontgarreg. ¾m past Pontgarreg turn L at Xrds. (Ski slope is R turn). Entrance signposted R 1½ acres of natural woodland, river walks and 2 acres of ambitious new planting of trees and shrubs. On S-facing slope, now a working nursery garden with 1 acre of pre-Victorian walled garden, with botanical collections of choice herbaceous, shrubs, fruit and vegetables. TEAS. *Adm £1.50. Open Wed to Sun April 10 to Sept 27 (10-6). For NGS Sun June 7, July 19 (10-6)*

Winllan, Talsarn (Mr & Mrs Ian Callan) 8m NNW of Lampeter on B4342, Talsarn-Llangeitho rd. 6-acres wildlife garden owned by botanists happy to share their knowledge with visitors. The garden includes a large pond, herb-rich meadow, small woodland and 600 yds of river bank walk. Over 200 species of wildflowers with attendant butterflies, dragonflies and birds. Limited suitability for wheelchairs. *Adm £1.50 Chd 50p (under 12 free). Open May & June daily (12-6). Also private visits welcome July & Aug, please* Tel 01570-470612

Ynyshir Hall Hotel, Machynlleth (Mr & Mrs R J Reen) Situated off main A487 in Eglwysfach Village, Ynyshir Hall has 14-acre landscaped gardens; mature ornamental trees. The mild climate allows many tender and unusual trees and shrubs; fine collection of specie and hybrid rhododendrons and azaleas built up over many decades. TEAS. *Adm £1.50 Chd 50p. May 1 to 31 (9-5)*

Denbighshire & Colwyn

Hon County Organiser: Mrs Susan Rathbone, Bryn Celyn, Ruthin LL15 1TT Tel 01824 702077
Assistant Hon County Organiser: Miss Marion MacNicoll, Trosyffordd, Ystrad Rd, Denbigh LL16 4RL Tel 01745 812247
Hon County Treasurer: Mr Alan Challoner, 13, The Village, Bodelwyddan LL18 5UR Tel 01745 583451

DATES OF OPENING

By appointment only
For telephone numbers and other details see garden descriptions. Private visits welcomed.

17 Broclywedog, Rhewl
Bryn Celyn, Llanbedr
Merlyn, Abergele
Tal-y-Bryn Farm, Llannefydd
Trosyffordd, Ystrad
Tyn Yr Odyn, Llannefydd

February 1 Sunday
Caereuni, Godre'r Gaer
February 15 Sunday
Plas Draw, Llangynhafal
March 1 Sunday
Caereuni, Godre'r Gaer
April 5 Sunday
Caereuni, Godre'r Gaer
May 3 Sunday
Caereuni, Godre'r Gaer

May 10 Sunday
Bryniau Gardens
May 17 Sunday
Rhagatt Hall, Carrog
Tyn-y-Graig, Llandrillo
May 30 Saturday
Dolhyfryd, Denbigh
May 31 Sunday
33 Bryn Twr, Abergele
Dolhyfryd, Denbigh
June 7 Sunday
Berth and The Cottage, Llandbedr
Caereuni, Godre'r Gaer
June 12 Friday
Dibleys Nurseries, Cefn-rhydd
June 13 Saturday
Dibleys Nurseries, Cefn-rhydd
June 14 Sunday
Castanwydden, Llandyrnog
Dibleys Nurseries, Cefn-rhydd
Gwysaney Hall, Mold
June 21 Sunday
Nantclwyd Hall, Ruthin

July 5 Sunday
Caereuni, Godre'r Gaer
July 11 Saturday
Cerrigllwydion Hall, Llandyrnog
July 12 Sunday
The Coach House, Bodfari
July 19 Sunday
Bodrhyddan, Rhuddlan
Glan-yr-Afon, Clocaenog
Henllan Village Gardens
July 26 Sunday
Cygnet, Llangynhafal
August 2 Sunday
Caereuni, Godre'r Gaer
September 6 Sunday
Caereuni, Godre'r Gaer
Gwysaney Hall, Mold
October 4 Sunday
Caereuni, Godre'r Gaer
November 1 Sunday
Caereuni, Godre'r Gaer

DESCRIPTIONS OF GARDENS

Berth and The Cottage, Llanbedr ✿❀ (Mr & Mrs C Davey & Mrs F Davey) From Ruthin take A494 towards Mold. After 1½m at the Griffin Inn turn L on to B5429. After 1m turn R at Xrds. Garden 1st L. 2½-acre established garden; mixed borders, shrubs, vegetable garden, cottage garden; stream and water garden. Refreshments. *Adm £2 Chd free (ACNO to St Peters Organ Fund®). Sun June 7 (2-6)*

Bodrhyddan, Rhuddlan ✿❀ (The Lord & Lady Langford) From Rhuddlan take the A5151 to Dyserth. The garden is on the L. Parterre garden in the French style; formal garden, clipped yew hedges; water garden; woodland walk leading to St Mary's Well. TEAS. *Adm £2 Chd 50p (ACNO to ST Kentigern's Hospice®). Sun July 19 (2-6)*

17 Broclywedog, Rhewl ✿❀ (Mel Royles) Ruthin. From Ruthin take A525 to Denbigh. Turn R in Rhewl onto Llandyrnog Rd. 2nd rd on R. A small attractive plantsmans garden packed with unusual varieties of geranium, erodium, hellebores, alpine and others yr-round interest. TEA. *Adm £1.50 Chd 25p. Private visits welcome, please* Tel 01824 702139

Bryn Celyn, Llanbedr ♿✿❀ (Mr & Mrs S Rathbone) Ruthin. [OS Ref SJ 133 603]. From Ruthin take A494 towards Mold. After 1½m at the Griffin Inn turn L onto B5429. 1½m house and garden on R. 1-acre garden; mixed borders; walled garden; old-fashioned roses. *Adm £2 Chd 25p. Private visits welcome June and July, please* **Tel 01824 702077**

Bryn Meifod, Graig Glen Conwy see Gwynedd gardens

33 Bryn Twr, Abergele ✿❀ (Mr & Mrs C R Knowlson) (To incl adjoining garden, **'Lynton'**) A55 W take slip rd to Abergele. Turn L at roundabout then over traffic lights; 1st L signed Llanfair T H. 3rd rd on L, no. 33 is on L. There are 2 connected gardens (Lynton) of approx ¾ acre in total, containing patio and pond areas; mixed herbaceous and shrub borders. TEAS. *Combined adm £2.50 OAPs £2 Chd free (ACNO to St Michaels, Abergele Scout Group©). Sun May 31 (2-6). Also by appt, please* **Tel 01745 828201**

Bryniau Gardens ✿ 2m from Dyserth on A5151 towards Trelawnyd. 1st L out of Dyserth after lay-by on R. TEAS at Craig-y-Castell. *Combined adm £2.50 OAPs £1 Chd free. Sun May 10 (1-5.30)*
Appletree Cottage (Mr & Mrs R L Owen) Approx 1½

DENBIGHSHIRE & COLWYN

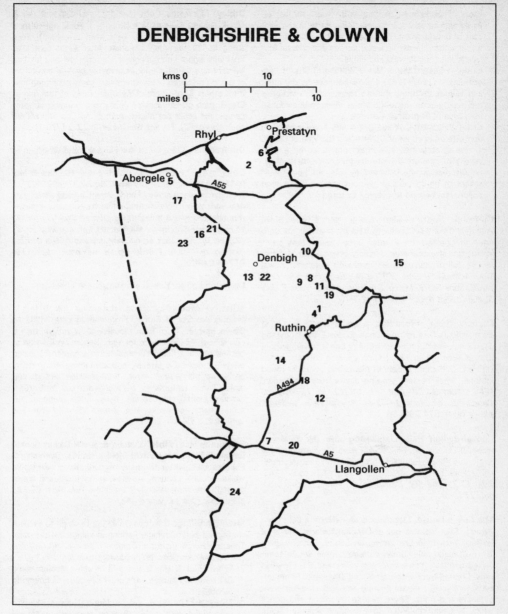

KEY

1. Berth and The Cottage
2. Bodrhyddan
3. 17 Broclywedog
4. Bryn Celyn
5. 33 Bryn Twr
6. Bryniau Gardens
7. Caereuni
8. Castanwydden
9. Cerrigllwydion Hall
10. The Coach House
11. Cygnet
12. Dibleys Nurseries
13. Dolhyfryd
14. Glan-yr-Afon
15. Gwysaney Hall
16. Henllan Village Gardens
17. Merlyn
18. Nantclwyd Hall
19. Plas Draw
20. Rhagatt Hall
21. Tal-y-Bryn Farm
22. Trosyffordd
23. Tyn Yr Odyn
24. Tyn-y-Graig

acres of landscaped gardens with trees; shrubs; alpines and herbaceous plants. Some parts in the process of development. Gardener's retreat. Features incl a rock quarry garden, a water garden and natural hillside with spring flowers and bulbs

Craig-y-Castell (Mr & Mrs D Watchorn) Site of Dyserth Castle (1241/1263) 4 acres bounded by dry moat and vallum, featuring mature trees, shrubs, rockeries and rose garden. Beautiful views towards Snowdonia. ¾m beyond **Appletree Cottage**

Craig-y-Castell Cottage (Mr & Mrs A Williams) Garden with open views of Dyserth and the Vale of Clwyd. 1 acre of reclaimed wilderness populated by a wide variety of conifers and shrubs that can withstand ignorant malpractice. Planted by the 'ad hoc Topsy' school of garden design without the aid of squared paper. ¾m beyond **Appletree Cottage**

Caereuni, Godre'r Gaer ৬ঔ❀ (Mr & Mrs Steve Williams) Take A5 Corwen to Bala rd. R at t-lights onto A494 to Chester. 1st R after layby; house ¼m on L. Microcosm of exotic styles, mainly oriental and Mediterranean, full of unusual plants and with wonderful views. TEA. *Adm £1.50 Chd 25p (ACNO to Melin-y-Wig Chapel©). Suns Feb 1, March 1, April 5, May 3, June 7, July 5, Aug 2, Sept 6, Oct 4, Nov 1 (2-5)*

Castanwydden, Fforddlas, Llandyrnog ৬❀ (A M Burrows Esq) Take rd from Denbigh due E to Llandyrnog approx 4m. From Ruthin take B5429 due N to Llandyrnog. [OS ref 1264 (sheet 116).] Approx 1-acre cottage garden with a considerable variety of plants and bulbs. Yr-round interest. Small nursery growing plants from the garden. TEAS. *Adm £1.50 Chd £1 (ACNO to Llangynhafal Church®). Sun June 14 (2-6). Private visits welcome, please Tel 01824 790404*

Cerrigllwydion Hall, Llandyrnog ঔ❀ (Mr & Mrs D Howard) Llandyrnog. B5429 ½m from Llandyrnog village on Ruthin Road. Extensive grounds with mature trees; herbaceous borders; vegetables and greenhouses. TEAS. *Adm £1.75 Chd 50p (ACNO to Llanynys Church®). Sat July 11 (2-6)*

The Coach House, Llandyrnog ঔ❀ (Mrs F A Bell) Llandyrnog. Take Mold rd out of Denbigh towards village of Bodfari. Turn R to Llandyrnog on B5429. House approx 1m on L-hand side. Small cottage garden set in semi-walled garden with views of the valley and the Clwydian Hills. Created from rough farm land 10yrs ago. Some unusual herbaceous plants thriving amongst an assortment of ducks and hens. Short walk to woodland and ponds which is being replanted to encourage wildlife. TEAS. *Adm £1 Chd 50p. Sun July 12 (2-6)*

¶**Cygnet, Llangynhafal** (Gwilym & Sandra Edwards & Margaret Houston) Take road from Denbigh due E to Llandyrnog roundabout straight on 2m. From Ruthin take B5429 ½m turn R, garden 2½m opp the Golden Lion. 1 acre newly designed garden, with herbaceous borders and young azalea bed, small vegetable plot and rose terrace panoramic views of the vale of Clwyd. TEAS. *Adm £1.50 Chd 25p. Sun July 26 (2-6)*

Dibleys Nurseries, Cefn-rhydd, Llanelidan ঔ❀ (Mr & Mrs R Dibley) Take A525 to Xrds by Llysfasi Agricultural College (4m from Ruthin, 14m from Wrexham). Turn along B5429 towards Llanelidan. After 1½m turn L at Xrds with houses on the corner. Continue up lane for 1m. Nursery and gardens on L. 9 acres arboretum consisting of a wide selection of unusual trees, some becoming mature, others newly planted. Beautiful views of the Vale of Clwyd. Also glasshouses of gold medal winning streptocarpus and other pot plants. *Adm £1.50 Chd 50p (ACNO to Action Aid®). Fri, Sat, Sun June 12, 13, 14 (10-5)*

Dinbren Isaf, Llangollen, see Flintshire and Wrexham

Dolhyfryd, The Lawnt, Denbigh ৬ঔ❀ (Captain & Mrs H M C Cunningham) 1m from Denbigh on B5401 to Nantglyn. Several acres of park, woodland and shrub garden with river; magnificent native trees, many azaleas, rhododendrons and bulbs. TEAS *Adm £2 Chd 50p (ACNO to Henshaw's Society for the Blind®). Sat, Sun May 30, 31 (2.30-6.30). Crocuses on a sunny day end of Feb and beginning of March. Private parties welcome, please Tel 01745 814805*

Donadea Lodge, Babell see Flintshire & Wrexham

¶**Glan-yr-Afon, Clocaenog, Ruthin** ঔ (Mr & Mrs J Draper) 4m SW of Ruthin. From Ruthin take B5105 to Clawddnewydd. Turn R to Clocaenog. In village, turn L opp school. Follow this rd for ½m. Garden on RH side at bottom of hill. A delightful small cottage garden bordered on two sides by a stream, and containing many richly perfumed plants incl roses, honeysuckles and garden pinks. Other features to be found are old fruit trees, densely planted herbaceous beds, huge standard fuschias, hens and ducks. TEA. *Adm £1.50 Chd 25p. Sun July 19 (11-5)*

Gwysaney Hall, Mold (Captain & Mrs P Davies-Cooke) Entrance on R, ½m out of Mold on A541, Denbigh rd. Picturesque park with many mature trees; extensive walks through gardens, shrubberies, pinetum and water garden; fine views. Plants if available. TEA. *Adm £2 Chd 50p. Suns June 14, Sept 6 (2-6)*

¶**Henllan Village Gardens** On B5382 Denbigh to Henllan rd. Signed before village. Parking in village inn car park. Teas in Church Institute. *Combined adm £2.50 Chd free (ACNO to Samaritans/WI Henllan®). Sun July 19 (2-6)*
　¶**Hen Efail** ৬ (Mr & Mrs J M Mostyn) Medium-sized flat rambling garden with good selection of flowering plants
　Maes-y-Ffynnon ৬ (Mr & Mrs I Hodson) ¾-acre redesigned with varied planting areas using natural contours. Roses, shrubs, alpines, overflowing tubs of flowers
　¶**Tycrwn** ঔ (Mrs M Burns) Small garden planted on incline with waterfalls and ponds incl rockery, herb garden, bog garden and meadow

Merlyn, Moelfre, Abergele ঔ (Drs J E & B E J Riding) Leave A55 (Conwy or Chester direction) at Bodelwyddan Castle, proceed uphill by castle wall 1m to Xrds. 0.1m to T-junction. (white bungalow) R B5381 towards Betws yn

Rhos for 2m, then fork L (signed Llanfair TH) after telephone box garden 0.4m on R. 2-acre garden developed from a field since 1987. Long mixed border; damp and gravel garden; many shrubs and old roses; rhododendrons and azaleas; spring garden. Views of sea. Year round interest. *Adm £1.50 Chd 25p. Private parties welcome Feb to Nov incl by prior arrangement, please* **Tel 01745 824435**

Nantclwyd Hall, Ruthin *&* (Sir Philip & Lady Isabella Naylor-Leyland) Take A494 from Ruthin to Corwen. The garden is 1½m from Pwllglas on L. Approx 3 acres of formal gardens and further grounds. Temples and follies by Sir Clough Williams-Ellis. Grotto by Belinda Eade. New rustic bridge over the river Clwyd. *Adm £2 Chd 50p. Sun June 21 (2-6). Private visits welcome following written application*

Pen-y-Bryn, Llangollen, see Flintshire and Wrexham

Plas Draw, Llangynhafal *&* (Mr Graham Holland) 3m NE of Ruthin and 2m N of Llanbedr, turn R off B5429 [OS re SJ134 623]. 4-acre garden to C18 house, mature woodland and pools; drifts of snowdrops, crocus and early daffodils in the beauty of the vale of Clwyd. 14-acre park with specimen trees; formal planting; old photographs on show. TEA. *Adm £2 Chd 50p (incl tea and biscuits) (ACNO to Llangynhafal Parish Church®). Sun Feb 15 (1-4)*

Rhagatt Hall, Carrog *&&* (Cdr & Mrs F J C Bradshaw) 1m NE of Corwen. A5 from Llangollen, 3m short of Corwen, turn R (N) for Carrog at garage, cross R Dee and keep bearing L. 1st opening on R after Carrog and seeing river again. 5-acre garden with azaleas, rhododendrons, trees, rare magnolia, bluebell wood; extensive views. Georgian house. TEAS. *Adm £1 Chd 50p. Sun May 17 (2-6)*

Tal-y-Bryn Farm, Llannefydd *&&* (Mr & Mrs Gareth Roberts) From Henllan take rd signed Llannefydd. After 2½m turn R signed Bont Newydd. Garden ½m on L. Newly designed working farmhouse garden planted to make best use of existing buildings and features framing wonderful views. *Adm £1.50 Chd 25p. Private visits welcome by appt, please* **Tel 01745 540 256**

Trosyffordd, Ystrad *&&&* (Miss Marion MacNicoll) From A525 to Denbigh, turn by swimming pool. Ystrad Rd sign Prion and Saron 1½m on R after 1st hill. Medium-sized, old established garden. Unusual plants, some for sale. *Adm £2 Chd 25p (incl tea). Private visits welcome April to Sept, please* **Tel 01745 812247**

Tyn-y-Graig, Llandrillo *&&* (Maj & Mrs Harry Robertson) 1½m from Llandrillo towards Bala, R off the B4401 Corwen to Bala Rd. Developed over 30yrs, a hillside garden approx 2 acres, incorporating 6 descending landscaped pools. TEA. *Adm £2 Chd 50p (ACNO to Christie Hospital NHS Trust®). Sun May 17 (2-5.30)*

Tyn yr Odyn, Llannefydd *&&* (Mr & Mrs J S Buchanan) 8m from Denbigh. B5382 signed Henllan and Llansannan. In Bryn Rhyd yr Arian, turn sharp R signed Llannefydd and Aled Plants. Garden ½m on L. Approx ⅔-acre cottage garden on the bank of R Aled, with stream, ponds and alpine garden; conifers, heathers, roses, shrubs, greenhouses and alpine house. Small nursery adjacent. *Adm £1.50 Chd 50p. Private visits welcome any day April to September, please* **Tel 01745 870394**

Crossroads

Crossroads is a charity which cares for carers. The National Gardens Scheme is delighted to include it in its list of beneficiaries. Some facts and figures:

- One in 7 of the adult population is caring for a relative or friend.
- Most of the carers are women.
- 20% of carers say they never get a break and 65% of carers say their health has suffered as a result of caring responsibilities.
- **Crossroads** employs over 4,000 staff who support and provide respite care for the carers.
- **Crossroads** supports 28,000 carers and provides nearly 3 million care hours per year.
- The contribution of carers saves tax payers over £30 billion per year.

Flintshire & Wrexham

Hon County Organiser:	Mrs J R Forbes, Pen-y-Wern, Pontblyddyn, nr Mold CH7 4HN
	Tel 01978-760531
Assistant Hon County Organiser:	Mrs Gwen Manuel, Tir-y-Fron, Llangollen Rd, Ruabon, LL14 6RW
	Tel 01978 821633
Hon County Treasurer:	Mr Peter Manuel, Tir-y-Fron, Llangollen Rd, Ruabon, LL14 6RW
	Tel 01978 821633

DATES OF OPENING

Regular openings
For details see garden description

Dolwen, Cefn Coch

By appointment only
For telephone numbers and other details see garden descriptions. Private visits welcomed

Alyn View, Rhydymwyn nr Mold
Cartref, Babell
Donadea Lodge, Babell
Pen-y-Wern, Pontblyddyn

March 15 Sunday
Erddig Hall Garden, Wrexham
April 5 Sunday
Hawarden Castle, Hawarden
April 19, Sunday
Hartsheath, Pontblyddyn

April 22 Wednesday
Hartsheath, Pontblyddyn
April 26 Sunday
Hartsheath, Pontblyddyn
May 3 Sunday
Tir-y-Fron, Ruabon
May 4 Monday
Tir-y-Fron, Ruabon
May 17 Sunday
Hawarden Castle, Hawarden
Three Chimneys, Rhostyllen
May 19 Tuesday
Chirk Castle, nr Wrexham
May 24 Sunday
Argoed Cottage, nr Overton
May 31 Sunday
Brambles, Garth, Trevor
Tri Thy, Pontybodkin, nr Mold
June 3 Wednesday
Pen-y-Bryn, Llangollen
June 7 Sunday
The Garden House, Erbistock
Tri Thy, Pontybodkin, nr Mold

June 14 Sunday
Bryn Tirion, Pen-y-Felin, Nannerch
Pen-y-Bryn, Llangollen
June 21 Sunday
The Garden House, Erbistock
June 28 Sunday
Dolwen, Cefn Coch
July 5 Sunday
The Garden House, Erbistock
July 15 Wednesday
Bryn Tirion, Pen-y-Felin, Nannerch
July 18 Saturday
Welsh College of Horticulture, Northop
July 19 Sunday
The Garden House, Erbistock
September 13 Sunday
The Garden House, Erbistock
September 27 Sunday
Dolwen, Cefn Coch
October 18 Sunday
Three Chimneys, Rhostyllen

DESCRIPTIONS OF GARDENS

Alyn View, Rhydymwyn, nr Mold ✗ (Mr & Mrs Smith) Directions on appointment. A cottage garden of 1 acre. A shady private garden and a very sunny open garden. Both areas full of established trees, shrubs and herbaceous borders. *Adm £1.50 Chd 50p. Private visits welcome, please* Tel 01352 741771

Argoed Cottage, Overton &✿ (Mr & Mrs C J Billington) App Overton from Wrexham on A528 cross over Overton Bridge and in about ¾m on brow of hill turn L into Argoed Lane. 1¾-acre garden. Interesting trees and shrubs. Herbaceous beds; roses; vegetable garden and water feature. TEAS. *Adm £1.50 Chd free. Sun May 24 (2-5).*

Brambles, Garth, Trevor ✿ (Tony & Deb Jones) Wrexham to Llangollen A483, A539. Turn R in Trevor at Australia Arms Inn. ½m on R. ¾-acre tiered garden on hillside. Mixture of shrubs, conifers and rhododendrons; pond, aviary and featuring dry-stone walls. TEAS. *Adm £1.50 Chd free (ACNO to Garth C P School®). Sun May 31 (1-5)*

Bryn Tirion, Pen-y-Felin, Nannerch ✗✿ (Julia White) 6m W of Mold, off A541 (Mold to Denbigh rd) into Nannerch Village. Turn opp Cross Foxes Inn into Pen-y-Felin Rd. 7/10m along rd. Small picturesque country garden on SW-facing hillside. Steps lead down through terraced areas which have been densely planted in cottage style with many varieties of old fashioned plants and herbs. TEAS. *Adm £1.50 Chd 50p (ACNO to Capricorn Animal Rescue®). Sun June 14, Wed July 15 (11-6).* Tel 01352 741498

Cartref, Babell &✗✿ (Mrs D Jones) Caerwys Rd. Turn off A541 Mold to Denbigh rd at Afonwen signposted Babell. At T-junction turn R, Black Lion Inn turn L, 1st L. 4th house. From Holywell old A55, turn L for Gorsedd then L again. L at Gorsedd Church for Babell, 2m down that rd turn R at Babell Chapel which is now Chapel House, 4th house. Very attractive well-stocked cottage garden; clematis, climbers, vegetables and roses. *Adm £1 Chd 25p (ACNO to Cancer Research®). June and July by appt, please* Tel 01352 720638

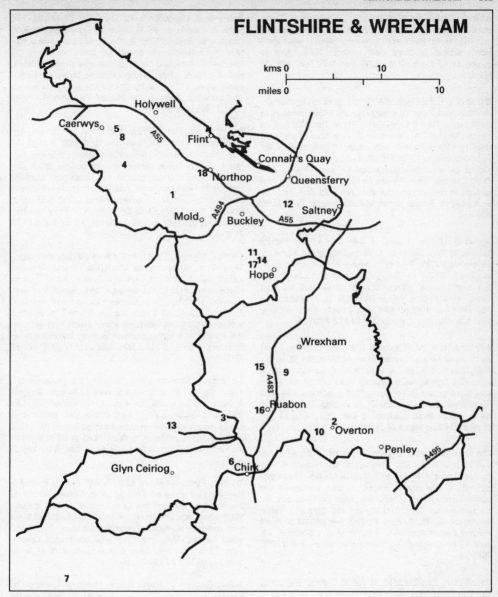

FLINTSHIRE & WREXHAM

kms 0   10

miles 0   10

Holywell

Caerwys   5   8   A55   Flint

4

Connah's Quay

18   Northop   Queensferry

1

Mold   A494   Buckley   12   A55   Saltney

11

17   14

Hope

Wrexham

15   9

A483

16   Ruabon

13   3   10   2   Overton

Glyn Ceiriog   6   Chirk   Penley   A495

7

KEY

1. Alyn View nr Mold
2. Argoed Cottage
3. Brambles
4. Bryn Tirion
5. Cartref
6. Chirk Castle
7. Dolwen
8. Donadea Lodge
9. Erddig Hall Garden
10. The Garden House

11. Hartsheath
12. Hawarden Castle
13. Pen-y-Bryn
14. Pen-Y-Wern
15. Three Chimneys
16. Tir-y-Fron
17. Try Thy
18. Welsh College of
     Horticulture

The maps in this book are designed to help visitors by showing the approximate locations of gardens within each county. The locations are not necessarily precise, particularly where gardens are in clusters. Detailed directions to each garden can be found in the garden descriptions.

▲**Chirk Castle, nr Wrexham** ᚛ (The National Trust) Chirk 7m SE of Llangollen. Off A5 in Chirk by War Memorial. 4½ acres trees and flowering shrubs, rhododendrons, azaleas, rockery, yew topiary. TEAS. *Adm to garden £2.40 OAPs/Chd £1.20. For NGS Tues May 19 (11-5)*

■ **Dolwen, Cefn Coch** ⚹❀ (Mrs F Denby) Llanrhaeadr-ym-Mochnant. From Oswestry take the B4580 going W to Llanrhaeadr. Turn R in village at Three Tuns Inn and up narrow lane for 1m. Garden on R. 14m from Oswestry. 4 acres of hillside garden with pools, stream, small wood and many different types of plant and unusual annuals all backed by a stupendous mountain view. TEAS. *Adm £1.50 Chd free. Every Fri and last Sun in month from May to Sept in aid of local charities. For NGS Sun June 28, Sept 27 (2-5). Private parties welcome, please* **Tel 01691 780 411**

Donadea Lodge, Babell ᚛⚹❀ (Mr & Mrs Patrick Beaumont) Turn off A541 Mold to Denbigh at Afonwen, signposted Babell; T-junction turn L. A55 Chester to St Asaph take B5122 to Caerwys, 3rd turn on L. Shady garden with unusual plants, shrubs; shrub and climbing roses; clematis; pink, yellow and white beds. Featured on S4C 1996. *Adm £1.50 Chd 30p. Private visits welcome from May 1 to Aug 1, please* **Tel 01352 720204**

▲**Erddig Hall, nr Wrexham** ᚛⚹ (The National Trust) 2m S of Wrexham. Signed from A483/A5125 Oswestry Road; also from A525 Whitchurch Road. Garden restored to its C18 formal design incl varieties of fruit known to have been grown there during that period and now incl the National Ivy Collection. NT shop open. TEA. Tours of the garden by Head Gardener at 1pm, 2pm. *Adm £2 Chd £1. For NGS Sun March 15 (12-3) Garden only*

The Garden House, Erbistock ᚛❀ (Mr S Wingett) 5m S of Wrexham on A528 Wrexham to Shrewsbury. Follow signs at Overton Bridge to Erbistock Church. Shrub and herbaceous plantings in monochromatic, analogous and complementary colour schemes. Rose pergolas and hydrangea avenue (over 200 species and cultivars). Victorian dovecote. TEAS. *Adm £1 Chd free (ACNO to Frank Wingett Cancer Appeal©). Suns June 7, 21, July 5, 19, Sept 13 (2-6) Private visits welcome, please* **Tel 01978 780958**

Hartsheath, Pontblyddyn ⚹ (Dr M C Jones-Mortimer) ¾m E of intersection with A541, stone lodge on S side of A5104. Large woodland garden; many varieties of flowering cherries and crab apples. Tidy picnic lunchers welcomed. Lunch & Tea at Bridge Inn, Pontblyddyn. *Adm £1.50 Chd £1 (ACNO to Pontblyddyn Church©). Sun April 19 (12-5) Wed April 22 (2-5) Sun April 26 (12-5). Also private visits welcome weekdays Feb-May, Sept-Oct, please* **Tel 01352 770 217**

Hawarden Castle, Hawarden ᚛⚹ (Sir William & Lady Gladstone) On B5125 just E of Hawarden village. Large garden and picturesque ruined castle. *Adm £1.50 Chd/OAPs £1. Suns April 5, May 17 (2-6)*

Pen-y-Bryn, Llangollen ᚛⚹❀ (Mr & Mrs R B Attenburrow) Signs at t-lights on A5 in centre of Llangollen. Walking distance or field parking. 2-acre garden on wooded plateau overlooking town; panoramic views; on site of old hall with established trees, shrubs and rhododendrons, walled garden, water feature, extensive lawns and herbaceous borders. TEAS. *Adm £2 Chd free (ACNO to Friends of Llangollen International Musical Eisteddfod®). Wed June 3, Sun June 14 (2-6)*

Pen-y-Wern, Pontblyddyn ᚛⚹ (Dr & Mrs Forbes) 5m SE of Mold, 7m NW of Wrexham. On E side of A541, ½ way between Pontblyddyn and Caergwrle. 2½-acre terraced country-house garden incl interesting small gardens. Shrubs, conifers, grasses and herbaceous borders; rose garden spectacular in June/July. Magnificent copper beech with canopy circumference of 250ft and other splendid trees. *Adm £1.50 Chd 50p (ACNO to Hope Parish Church®). Private visits welcome, please* **Tel 01978 760531**

Three Chimneys, Rhostyllen ⚹❀ (Mr & Mrs Hollington) 3m SW of Wrexham via Rhostyllen. From Wrexham A5152 fork R at Black Lion onto B5097. From Ruabon B5605 turn L onto B5426 signed Minera. Turn R ½m over bridge, L at Water Tower. Garden ¼m on L opp post box. Forester's garden of 1 acre; maples, conifers, cornus and sorbus species and varieties. Many small trees used in the manner of a herbaceous border. Very unusual and interesting. *Adm £1.50 Chd 50p. Suns May 17 (2-6) Oct 18 (1-5)*

Tir-y-Fron, Ruabon ᚛⚹❀ (Mr & Mrs P R Manuel) Llangollen Rd. 5m from Wrexham, take A539 from Ruabon By-Pass, signed Llangollen, turn R on brow of hill after 200yds. 1¾-acre garden with shrubs and herbaceous plants surrounded by mature trees with quarry. Offa's Dyke separates garden from drive. TEAS in aid of Llangollen Canal Boat Trust. *Adm £2 Chd free. Sun, Mon May 3, 4 (2-6)*

Tri Thy, Pontybodkin nr Mold ᚛⚹❀ (Norma Restall & Daughters) Signposted off Chester to Corwen A5104 at Pontybodkin. Follow Craft Centre signs. ⅓-acre garden 500ft above sea level. Created within old farm buildings and surrounding land. Shrubs, herbaceous, roses and water feature. TEAS in aid of Cyma Community Centre. *Adm £1.50 Chd 50p. Suns May 31, June 7 (2-6) or by appt* **Tel 01352 771359**

Welsh College of Horticulture, Northop ᚛ Village of Northop is 3m from Mold and close to the A55 expressway. Mature gardens incorporating many national award winning features. Commercial sections. Garden Centre and retail sections where produce and garden sundries can be purchased. A Golf Course is being constructed for the teaching of Greenkeeping Skills. Car parking. TEA. *Adm £1 OAPs & Chd 50p. Sun July 18 (12-5)*

By Appointment Gardens. These owners do not have a fixed opening day usually because they cannot accommodate large numbers or have insufficient parking space.

Glamorgan

Hon County Organiser: Mrs L H W Williams, Llanvithyn House, Llancarfan, South Glamorgan CF62 3AD
Tel 01446 781232

DATES OF OPENING

By appointment only
*For telephone numbers and other
details see garden descriptions.
Private visits welcomed*

11 Arno Road, Little Coldbrook
7 St Peters Terrace, Cockett,
Swansea
19 Westfield Road, Glyncoch,
Pontypridd

April 5 Sunday
Merthyr Mawr House, Bridgend
April 26 Sunday
Trehedyn House,

Peterston-super-Ely
May 17 Sunday
Llanvithyn House,
Llancarfan
9 Willowbrook Gardens, Mayals,
Swansea
May 30 Saturday
Cwmpennar Gardens
May 31 Sunday
Cwmpennar Gardens
June 7 Sunday
Springside, Pen-y-Turnpike, Dinas
Powys
June 21 Sunday
The Clock House & St Mary's,
Llandaff

June 28 Sunday
11 Eastcliff, Southgate,Swansea
Fonmon Castle, nr Barry
July 4 Saturday
Pontygwaith Farm, Edwardsville
July 5 Sunday
Pontygwaith Farm, Edwardsville
July 19 Sunday
The Rise, Pentyrch
July 26 Sunday
57 Heol Bryncwils, Sarn
August 9 Sunday
6 Alma Road, Penylan, Cardiff
Maes-y-Wertha Farm, Bryncethin

DESCRIPTIONS OF GARDENS

6 Alma Road, Penylan, Cardiff ✗❀❀ (Mr Melvyn Rees)
N from city centre, off Marlborough Rd. Take Cardiff E
junction 29 from M4, Llanedeyrn exit from Eastern Avenue, then towards Cyncoed and down Penylan Rd. Redesigned S-facing terraced house garden 30' × 15' with
many species from the S and E hemispheres, incl Dickso-
nia Antarctica; some redesign this yr. Generally Japanese
look; railway sleepers used as paving material with gravel
infill. TEAS. *Adm £1 Chd 50p (Share to Alzheimers Disease
Society®). Sun Aug 9 (2-6). Private visits welcome, please
Tel 01222 482200*

11 Arno Road, Little Coldbrook, Barry ✗ (Mrs D
Palmer) From A4050 Cardiff to Barry, take roundabout
marked Barry Docks and Sully. Then 2nd R into Coldbrook
Rd, 2nd L into Langlands Rd, then 6th R into Norwood
Cresc; 1st L into Arno Rd. 40ft × 30ft informal planta-
holic's garden with ponds, herbaceous plants, scree gar-
den planted with low growing alpines. As featured on
Radio Wales 'Gardening Matters' Aug '95. TEAS. *Adm £1.
Limited parking. Private visits and small groups welcome,
Mar to Oct please Tel 01446 743642*

The Clock House, Llandaff ♿✗❀ (Prof & Mrs Bryan
Hibbard) Cathedral Close, 2m W of Cardiff. Follow signs
to Cathedral via A4119. Bus: Cardiff alight Maltsters
Arms. Small walled garden; fine old trees; wide variety of
shrubs and plants; important collection of shrub, species
and old roses. TEA. *Combined adm with St Mary's £2
Acc chd free. Sun June 21 (2-6)*

Cwmpennar Gardens ✗❀ Mountain Ash 1m. From
A4059 turn R 100yds N of the traffic lights; follow sign to
Cefnpennar, uphill for ¾m. Car park 100yds past bus

shelter in Cwmpennar. Two of the gardens are contigu-
ous, the third at entrance to Cwmpennar 100yds from
others. Gardens high on mountain side in one-time coal
mining village in rural surroundings. Tynewydd awarded
1st prize in gdn competition for Rhondda-Cynon-Taff.
Gardens with variety of features, landscapes and unusual
plants. TEAS. Glamorgan Wildlife Trust Sales stall. *Combined adm £2 Chd £1 (Share to St Illtyd's Church Restoration Fund®). Sat, Sun May 30, 31 (2-6)*
   Ivy Cottage (Mr & Mrs D H Phillips)
   Tynewydd (Mr & Mrs B Davies)
   Woodview (Miss A & Miss R Bebb)

11 Eastcliff, Southgate ♿✗❀ (Mrs Gill James) Take
the Swansea to Gower road and travel 6m to Pennard. Go
through the village of Southgate and take the 2nd exit off
the roundabout. Garden 200yds on the L. Seaside garden
approx ⅓ acre and developed in a series of island and
bordered beds for spring and summer interest. A large
number of white, blue-green unusual plants. Shown on
Gardener's World Feb '97. TEAS. *Adm £1.50 Chd free.
Sun June 28 (2-5). Also private visits welcome, please Tel
01792 233310*

Fonmon Castle, nr Barry ♿✗❀ (Sir Brooke Boothby)
Take rd Cardiff-Llantwit Major, marked for Cardiff Airport.
Take turning W of Penmark for Fonmon village, bear R
round pond. Gate ¼m on. Medium-sized garden. Walled
kitchen garden; flowering shrubs; good trees; fuchsias.
Ancient castle (shown Tues & Weds April to Sept (2-5)).
TEAS. *Adm £1.50 Chd 50p. Sun June 28 (2-6). Tel
01446 710206*

¶57 Heol Bryncwils, Sarn ✗❀ (Mr & Mrs P J Thomas)
Approx 2½m from Bridgend Town. Garden approx 2½mins
from junction 36 M4. Take rd signposted Maesteg A4063,

GLAMORGAN

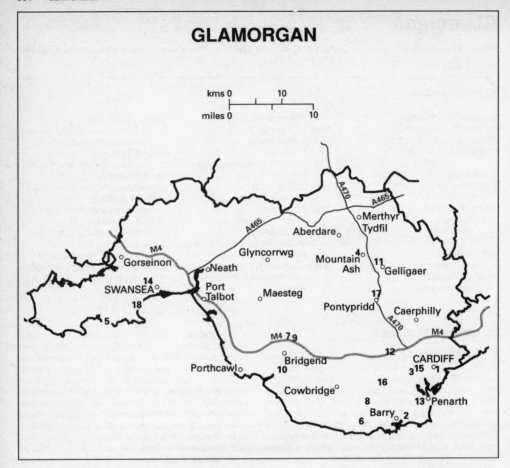

kms 0   10

miles 0   10

KEY

1. 6 Alma Road
2. 11 Arno Road
3. The Clock House & St Mary's
4. Cwmpennar Gardens
5. 11 Eastcliff
6. Fonmon Castle
7. 57 Heol Bryncwils
8. Llanvithyn House
9. Maes-y-Wertha Farm
10. Merthyr Mawr House
11. Pontygwaith Farm
12. The Rise
13. Springside
14. 7 St Peters Terrace
15. The Clock House & St Mary's
16. Trehedyn House
17. 19, Westfield Road
18. 9 Willowbrook Gardens

100yds after lights turn R signposted Sarn, next R then 2nd R house at centre of close. Owners are uncontrollable plant enthusiasts. Garden is very intensively planted with huge collection of interesting and unusual plants. Abies Koreana etc. Pergola, arbour, herbaceous and mixed borders, shade area. Garden approx 90′ × 70′. *Adm £1.50 Chd 50p. Sun July 26 (2-6)*

Llanvithyn House, Llancarfan ✍❀ (Mr & Mrs L H W Williams) 1.8m S off A48 at Bonvilston, sign for Llancarfan 100yds W of Bonvilston Garage, 1m N of Llancarfan. Medium-size garden on site of C6 monastery. C17 gate-house. Lawns, interesting trees, shrubs, borders. TEAS if fine. *Adm £1.50 Chd 25p. Sun May 17 (2-6)*

¶Maes-y-Wertha Farm, Bryncethin ♿❀ (Mrs S Leyshon) 3m N of Bridgend. Follow sign for Bryncethin and turn R at Masons Arms. Follow sign for Heol-y-Cyw garden about 1m outside Bryncethin on the R. A new 3-acre garden. Informal mixed beds with large selection of perennial plants, shrubs, conifers and trees. Water garden fed by natural spring. Large grass area under new planting. TEA. *Adm £1.50 Chd 25p (ACNO to Sandville Self Help Foundation®). Sun Aug 9 (2-6)*

Merthyr Mawr House, Merthyr Mawr ✗❀ (Mr & Mrs Murray McLaggan) 2m SW of Bridgend. Large garden with flowering shrubs, magnolias, scree and walled vegetable garden; bluebell wood with ruined C14 chapel; swallow hole. TEA. *Adm £1.50 Chd £1. Sun April 5 (2-6)*

Pontygwaith Farm, Edwardsville ᕷ❀ (Mr & Mrs R J G Pearce) Take A470 towards Merthyr. At roundabout take R hand turn to join A4054 Old Cardiff to Merthyr Rd towards Aberfan. Travel N for approx 3m through Quaker's Yard and Edwardsville. 1m out of Edwardsville turn sharp L by old bus shelter. Garden at bottom of hill. Medium-sized garden; surrounding C17 farmhouse adjacent to Trevithick's Tramway; situated in picturesque wooded valley; fish pond, lawns, perennial borders and lakeside walk. TEAS. *Adm £1.20 Chd 50p. Sat July 4, Sun July 5 (2-6)*

¶The Rise, Heol-y-Parc, Pentyrch ✗ (Joy & Chris Lyddon) 7m NW of Cardiff. Take Llantrisant Rd A4119, turn R at Rhyddlafar hospital, L at Church into Penuel Rd and L after ⅓m. Approx ¾-acre garden of mixed shrub and herbaceous borders with some unusual plants. Good open views towards Vale of Glamorgan, weather permitting! TEAS. *Adm £1.50 Chd 50p (ACNO to NSPCC®). Sun July 19 (2-6)*

¶1 St Mary's Llandaff ✗ (Dr & Mrs Michael Smith) Cathedral Green. 2m W of Cardiff. Follow signs to Cathedral via A4119. Bus: Cardiff alight Malsters Arms. Small, natural garden approx 100' × 50'. Mixed planting incl herbaceous perennials and herbs, a silver bed and shrubs. *Combined adm with* **The Clock House** *£2 Acc chd free. Sun June 21 (2-6)*

7 St Peters Terrace, Cockett ✗ (Mr & Mrs Tony Ridler) Cockett. 4m W of Swansea behind Cockett Rd (A4216) between railway bridge and church. Young, ⅓-acre designers garden divided into series of formal enclosed areas. TEA. *Adm £1. Private visits welcome April 1-Aug 31, please* **Tel 01792 588217**

Springside, Dinas Powys ✗❀ (Prof & Mrs Michael Laurence) From Cardiff take B4055 to Penarth and Dinas Powys as far as the Leckwith (Cardiff Distributor Rd) roundabout. Then take B4267 to Llandough, up Leckwith Hill past Leckwith Village, take R-hand fork in rd into Pen-y-Turnpike as far as the 30mph sign. Turn R immed into Springside. Undulating 2-acre garden recently rescued after 30yrs of wilderness. Spacious, with views and newly planted trees; small ponds and old village water supply returned to nature, where children must be supervised; vegetable garden. Parking in the grounds only available in dry weather. TEA. *Adm £2 Chd 50p (ACNO to Dinas Powys Orchestra©). Sun June 7 (2-6)*

Trehedyn House, Peterston-Super-Ely ᕷ (Mr & Mrs Desmond Williams) A148 Cardiff to Cowbridge. Turn R at Sycamore Cross (½way between St Nicholas and Bonvilston). Take 2nd L. Garden ½m on L. Medium-sized garden. Interesting trees, shrubs, borders, bulbs and spring planting. TEA. *Adm £1.50 Chd 50p. Sun April 26 (2-6)*

19 Westfield Road, Glyncoch Pontypridd ✗❀ (Mr & Mrs Brian Dockerill) From Pontypridd travel 1.5m N along B4273. Take L turn by school. At top of hill follow rd to L. Take first R and R again into Westfield Rd. Enthusiasts collection of over 2,500 different varieties of plants, many unusual, grown in ½-acre garden designed as a series of interlinked enclosures each of different character. Featured on BBC Gardener's World '97. TEA. *Adm £1 Chd 50p. Prevented by limited parking from having specific open day, we welcome visitors by appt through the yr, please* **Tel 01443 402999**

9 Willowbrook Gardens, Mayals, Swansea ✗ (Dr & Mrs Gallagher) 4m W of Swansea on A4067 (Mumbles) rd to Blackpill; take B4436 (Mayals) rd; 1st R leads to Westport Ave along W boundary of Clyne Park; 1st L into cul-de-sac. ½-acre informal garden designed to give natural effect with balance of form and colour between various areas linked by lawns; unusual trees suited to small suburban garden, esp conifers and maples; rock and water garden. TEAS. *Adm £1.50 Chd 30p. Sun May 17 (2-6); also private visits welcome, please* **Tel 01792 403268**

SYMBOLS USED IN THIS BOOK
(See also Page 17)

¶   Opening for the first time.

❀   Plants/produce for sale if available.

ᕷ   Gardens with at least the main features accessible by wheelchair.

✗   No dogs except guide dogs.

●   These gardens advertise their own dates in this publication although they do not nominate specific days for the NGS. Not all the money collected by these gardens comes to the NGS but they do make a guaranteed contribution.

■   These gardens nominate specific days for the NGS and advertise their own dates in this publication.

▲   These gardens open regularly to the public but they do not advertise their own dates in this publication. For further details, contact the garden directly.

Gwent (Monmouthshire, Newport and Caerphilly)

Hon County Organiser: Mrs Joanna Kerr, Glebe House, Llanfair Kilgeddin, Abergavenny NP7 9BE
Tel 01873 840422
Asst Hon County Organiser: Mrs Catriona Boyle, Penpergwm Lodge, Abergavenny NP7 9AS
Tel 01873 840208

DATES OF OPENING

Regular openings
For details see garden description

The Nurtons, Tintern
Penpergwm Lodge, nr Abergavenny
Plas Cwm Coed, Tredunnock
Tredegar House & Park, Newport
Veddw House, Devauden

April 12 Sunday
Hill Place, Llanishen
April 19 Sunday
Veddw House, Devauden
May 3 Sunday
Glebe House, Llanvair
Kilgeddin
May 10 Sunday
Great Campston, Llanfihangel
Crucorney
May 17 Sunday
The Nurtons, Tintern
Veddw House, Devauden
May 24 Sunday
Wyndcliffe Court, St Arvans,
Chepstow
May 31 Sunday
Chwarelau, Llanfapley, nr
Abergavenny
The Volland, Lower Machen

June 7 Sunday
Clytha Park, nr Abergavenny
The Graig, nr Raglan
Trostrey Lodge, Bettws
Newydd
June 14 Sunday
Great Killough, Abergavenny
June 20 Saturday
Lower House Farm, Nantyderry
June 21 Sunday
Lower House Farm, Nantyderry
June 27 Saturday
Castle House, Usk
June 28 Sunday
Castle House, Usk
Tredegar House & Park, Newport
July 4 Saturday
Great Campston, Llanfihangel
Crucorney
July 5 Sunday
Bryngwyn Manor, Raglan
Court St Lawrence, Usk
Great Campston, Llanfihangel
Crucorney
July 12 Sunday
Gilwern and Llangrwyney Gardens
Orchard House, Coed Morgan, nr
Abergavenny
July 19 Sunday
The Graig, nr Raglan

The Nurtons, Tintern
Plas Cwm Coed, Tredunnock
July 26 Sunday
Veddw House, Devauden
August 2 Sunday
Charters, Nantyderry
August 9 Sunday
Caerleon Campus Gardens,
Caerleon
August 23 Sunday
The Nurtons, Tintern
Veddw House, Devauden
August 24 Monday
Llan-y-Nant, Coed Morgan,
Abergavenny
September 6 Sunday
Castle House, Usk
The Nurtons, Tintern
September 12 Saturday
Lower House Farm, Nantyderry
September 13 Sunday
Lower House Farm, Nantyderry
October 18 Sunday
Llanover, Abergavenny
October 25 Sunday
Great Campston, Llanfihangel
Crucorney

DESCRIPTIONS OF GARDENS

Bryngwyn Manor, Raglan &❀ (Mr S Inglefield) 2m W of Raglan. Turn S off old A40 (Abergavenny-Raglan rd) at Croes Bychan (Raglan Garden Centre); house ¼m up lane. 3 acres; good trees, mixed borders. TEAS. Dogs on leads. *Adm £2 Chd under 10 free. Sun July 5 (2-6)*

¶**Caerleon Campus Gardens, Caerleon** &❀ M4 junction 26, follow signs for Caerleon, through one way system. Next L past Caerleon Endowed school and Lodge Rd. ¼m campus on the L hand side. Formal bedding schemes to the main building, shrubberies, small arboretum, large expanse of grass. Formal clipped yew hedgerows. TEA. *Adm £2 Chd free. Sun Aug 9 (10-5)*

Castle House, Usk &❀ (Mr & Mrs J H L Humphreys) 200yds from Usk centre; turn up lane opp fire station. Medium-sized garden of orderly disorder with herb garden and vegetables set around ruins of Usk Castle. TEAS. *Adm £2 Chd free. Sat, Sun June 27, 28 as part of Usk Gar-*

dens Day (donation to NGS) (10-6). For NGS Sun Sept 6 (2-6). Private visits also welcome, please Tel 01291 672563

Charters, Nantyderry &❀ (Mr & Mrs Peter W Lang) 5m in each direction to Abergavenny, Pontypool and Usk. From B4598 Usk to Abergavenny turn off at Chain Bridge. 1m to garden opp Foxhunter Inn. Abergavenny/Pontypool Rd turn at Nantyderry sign, approx 1m to garden. Approx 2½-acre garden. Mixed borders, shrubs and herbaceous. Interesting rockery. Kitchen garden, vegetables organically grown. Dried flower arrangements and bunches for sale. Plants and vegetables for sale. TEAS. *Adm £2 Chd free. Sun Aug 2 (2-6)*

Chwarelau, Llanfapley, nr Abergavenny ❀ (Mr & Mrs Maurice Trowbridge) On B4233 3½m E of Abergavenny. Medium-sized garden with magnificent views, approached down 200yd drive fringed by ornamental trees and shrubs. TEAS. *Adm £1.50 Chd free. Sun May 31 (2-6)*

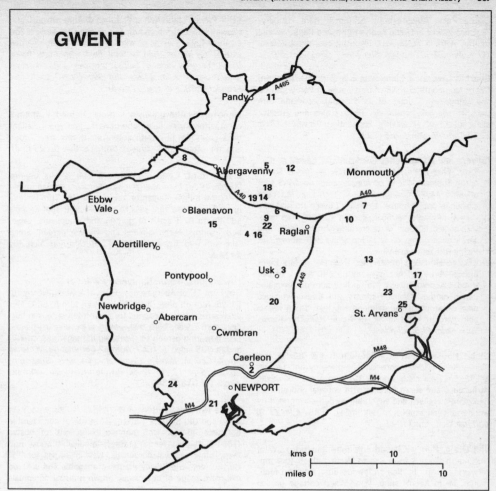

GWENT

KEY

1. Bryngwyn Manor
2. Caerleon Campus Gardens
3. Castle House
4. Charters
5. Chwarelau Farm
6. Clytha Park
7. Court St Lawrence
8. Gilwern and Llangrwyney Gardens
9. Glebe House
10. The Graig
11. Great Campston
12. Great Killough
13. Hill Place
14. Llan-y-Nant
15. Llanover
16. Lower House Farm
17. The Nurtons
18. Orchard House
19. Penpergwm Lodge
20. Plas Cwm Coed
21. Tredegar House & Park
22. Trostrey Lodge
23. Veddw House
24. The Volland
25. Wyndcliffe Court

Clytha Park, Abergavenny & (Sir Richard Hanbury-Tenison) ½ way between Abergavenny and Raglan on old rd (not A40). 5 acres; C18 layout; trees, shrubs; lake. TEAS. *Adm £1.50 Chd 50p. Sun June 7 (2-6)*

Court St Lawrence, Llangovan &※ (Mrs G D Inkin) 6m SW of Monmouth, 5m NE of Usk, between Pen-y-Clawdd and Llangovan. 5 acres of garden and woodland with trees, shrubs, lake, roses etc. TEAS, plants and produce stalls in aid of St David's Foundation, Newport. *Adm £1.50 Chd 50p. Sun July 5 (2-6)*

Gilwern and Llangrwyney Gardens *Sun July 12 (2-6)*
¶**The Five Bells, Llanelli Church** ※ (Mr & Mrs P Aeron-Thomas) 4m W of Abervagenny on A465 turn off onto A4077 through Gilwern. Turn L at the Corn Exchange public house. 1½m up Church Rd and opp Church. ⅔ acre terraced garden created 8yrs ago, with mixed borders of interesting shrubs, roses and herbaceous plants on N facing slope 740′ above Usk Valley with extensive views
¶**Forge House, Llangrwyney** &※ (Mr & Mrs Peter Bishop) 4m W of Abergavenny on A40 turn L at Bell Hotel, Llangrwyney. Garden on R. 1-acre owner-maintained garden. Unusual shrubs and trees. Extensive planting around large millpond and leat. Small vegetable garden. TEAS in aid of Nevill Hall Thrombosis Fund. *Adm £1.50 Chd free*

Glebe House, Llanvair Kilgeddin &※※ (Mr & Mrs Murray Kerr) Midway between Abergavenny and Usk on B4598, 5m from each. Approx 1½-acre garden of mixed herbaceous and shrub borders with unusual and interesting plants, orchard and vegetable garden surrounded by wonderful rural aspects of Usk Valley. TEAS. *Adm £1.50 Chd free. Sun May 3 (2-6)*

The Graig, Pen-y-Clawdd &※ (Mrs Rainforth) SW of Monmouth. Turn S from Raglan-Monmouth rd (not motorway) at sign to Pen-y-Clawdd. Bus: Newport-Monmouth, alight Keen's shop, ½m. Mixed cottage garden with interesting shrubs and roses and kitchen garden. TEAS. *Adm £1.50 Chd free. Suns June 7, July 19 (2-6). Private visits welcome, please Tel 01600 740270*

Great Campston, Llanfihangel Crucorney &※ (Mr & Mrs A D Gill) 7m NE of Abergavenny; 2m towards Grosmont off A465 at Llanfihangel Crucorney. Drive on R just before brow of hill. Pretty 2-acre garden set in wonderful surroundings. Designed and planted from scratch by Mrs Gill, a garden designer; wide variety of interesting plants and trees enhanced by lovely stone walls, paving and summer house with fantastic views. The house stands 750ft above sea level on S facing hillside with spring fed stream feeding 2 ponds. TEAS. *Adm £1.50 Chd 50p (ACNO to 'Mind'®). Sun May 10, Sat, Sun July 4, 5, Sun Oct 25 (2-6). Private visits welcome, please Tel 01873 890633*

Great Killough, Llantilio Crosseny &※※ (Mr & Mrs John F Ingledew) 6m E of Abergavenny. S of B4233. 3-acre garden created in the 1960s to complement mediaeval house. TEAS. *Adm £1.50 Chd free (ACNO to Barnardo's®). Sun June 14 (2-6)*

¶**Hill Place, Llanishen** ※※ (Sean & Anne Dixon-Child) Midway between Monmouth (12m) and Chepstow (12m) on the B4293. 3 acres of wildlife friendly hillside garden with lovely views. Wild daffodil field with many trees. Mixed borders, spring bulbs, terraces and container grown plants. *Adm £1.50 Chd 50p (ACNO to Rescue Foundation®). Sun April 12 (2-6)*

Llanover, nr Abergavenny & (Robin Herbert, Esq) 4m S of Abergavenny. Bus: Abergavenny-Pontypool, alight drive gates. Large water garden; many rare trees, good autumn colour. TEAS. *Adm £2 Chd 50p. Sun Oct 18 (2-6)*

Llan-y-Nant, Coed Morgan &※ (Mr & Mrs Charles Pitchford) 4m from Abergavenny, 5m from Raglan on old A40 (now B4598) Raglan to Abergavenny rd. Turn up lane opp 'Chart House' inn; pass Monmouthshire Hunt Kennels 500yds on R. 3 acres of garden and woodlands. Lawn, beds, shrubs, herbs, alpines and kitchen garden. Small lake with wild life. TEAS. *Adm £1.50 Chd 50p. Mon Aug 24 (2-6)*

Lower House Farm, Nantyderry ※※ (Mr & Mrs Glynne Clay) 7m SE of Abergavenny. From Usk-Abergavenny rd, B4598, turn off after Chain Bridge. ¼m turn R, on L. Medium-sized garden designed for all-yr interest; mixed borders, fern island, herb bed, paved area, unusual plants. Late flowering perennials. Featured in magazines, on T.V. and in NGS video 1. TEAS. *Adm £2 Chd free (ACNO to All Saints Church, Kemeys Commander©). Sats, Suns June 20, 21, Sept 12, 13 (2-6). Private visits also welcome, please Tel 01873 880257*

■ **The Nurtons, Tintern** ※※ (Adrian & Elsa Wood) On A466 opp Old Station, Tintern. 2.5-acres of considerable botanical interest with notable collections of hostas (100+), salvias, ferns, grasses, medicinal herbs and many other unusual perennials. New plantings for '98. Our nursery 'Wye Valley Plants' propagates and sells an extensive range of organically grown unusual perennials and herbs, many from the garden. Nursery and garden open Wed-Mon (10.30-5) March to end Oct. TEAS. *Adm £1.50 Chd free (ACNO to Gwent Wildlife Trust®). For NGS Suns May 17, July 19, Aug 23, Sept 6 (10.30-5). Group visits also welcome, please Tel 01291 689253*

Orchard House, Coed Morgan &※※ (Mr & Mrs B R Hood) 1½m N of old Raglan-Abergavenny rd. Approx 6m from Abergavenny. Turn opp King of Prussia or The Charthouse. A garden of approx 1½ acres with mixed borders of unusual herbaceous plants and shrubs, rosebeds and lawn. TEAS in aid of St David's Church. *Adm £1.50 Chd 50p. Sun July 12 (2-6). Private visits welcome April to Sept, please Tel 01873 840289*

● **Penpergwm Lodge, nr Abergavenny** &※ (Mr & Mrs Simon Boyle) 3m SE of Abergavenny. On B4598 towards Usk, after 2½m turn L opp King of Prussia Inn. Entrance 150yds on L. 3-acre formal garden with mature trees, hedges & lawns; interesting potager, mixed unusual plants & vegetables; apple & pear pergola and S-facing terraces with sunloving plants. Nursery specialising in unusual hardy perennials. Home of Catriona Boyle's School of Gardening, now in its 12th yr. *Adm £1.50 Chd free. Thurs, Fris, Sats, Suns March 26 to Oct 4. Private visits and parties welcome, please* Tel 01873 840208

¶**Plas Cwm Coed, Tredunnock** ♿❀❀ (John & Eliana Humphries) N from Caerloen village towards Usk for 3m, then signed Plas Cwm Coed, L 150yds; or S from Usk for 4m, immed after Cwrt Bleddyn Hotel. 5-acre garden in wooded valley beside brook, with ponds, herbaceous borders backed by yew hedges, rose and shrub gardens, rockery, laburnum walk, dry stone walls. Victorian terrace created by John Humphries, gardens correspondent, the Western Mail. TEAS and plants NGS day. *Adm £1.50 Chd 50p (over 5). Sats, Suns from May 9 to Sept 13 (10-5). For NGS Sun July 19 (2-6). Groups by arrangement, please* Tel 01633 450373

■ **Tredegar House & Park, Newport** ♿❀❀ (Newport County Borough Council) 2m SW of Newport Town Centre. Signposted from A48 (Cardiff rd) and M4 junction 28. Series of walled formal gardens dating from the early C18 surrounding one of the most magnificent late C17 houses (also open). Orangery Garden recently restored to early C18 appearance with coloured mineral parterres, espaliered fruit trees, box hedging etc. TEAS. *Adm £2 Chd 50p (ACNO to The Friends of Tredegar House and Park®). For NGS Sun June 28 (11-6). House, Gardens etc open Easter to end of Oct, for details, please* Tel 01633 815880

Trostrey Lodge, Bettws Newydd ❀ (Mr & Mrs Roger Pemberton) Half way between Raglan and Abergavenny on old road (not A40). Turning to Bettws Newydd opposite Clytha gates, 1m on R. 'Another Eden, demi-paradise'

commented one observer about this walled garden. High concentration of interesting old-fashioned flowers, roses, vines and herbs, all bordered by rosemary, box, lavender and rugosas. It is set within a decorative orchard, surrounded by fine landscape in one of the prettiest parts of the Usk Valley. Local dairy ice creams and teas. *Adm £1.50 Chd free. Sun June 7 (11-6)*

■ **Veddw House, Devauden** ❀❀ (Anne Wareham & Charles Hawes) Between Chepstow and Monmouth on B4293. Signed from public house on the green. 4 acres; emphasis on good garden pictures with colour harmonies and contrasts. Formal vegetable garden with old roses and clematis; hardy geranium walk; small themed gardens; ruin, wild garden; conservatory. Unique ornaments of wood and enamel. Lovely views, woodland walks. *Adm £2 Chd 50p (ACNO to Heart Research Foundation for Wales®). Every Sun April 12 to Sept 20 incl (2-5). For NGS Suns April 19, May 17, July 26, Aug 23 (2-6). Parties welcome by appt, please* Tel 01291 650836 *(pm only)*

The Volland, Lower Machen ♿❀❀ (Mr & Mrs William Graham) Between Newport and Caerphilly, 10mins from junction 28 (M4) W of Lower Machen Village, 1st R before county boundary. 1½-acres of interesting shrubs, trees, herbaceous plants and fern rockery. TEAS. *Adm £1.50 Chd free. Sun May 31 (2-6)*

Wyndcliffe Court, St Arvans ♿❀ (HAP Clay Esq) 3m N of Chepstow, turn at Wyndcliffe signpost. Bus: Chepstow-Monmouth; alight St Arvans, Wyndcliffe stop, ¼m. Medium-sized garden; herbaceous borders; views, topiary, shrubs. Mentioned in The Historic Gardens of Wales. TEA. *Adm £1.50 Chd free. Sun May 24 (2-6). Private visits welcome, please* Tel 0129162 2352

Marie Curie Cancer Care

Marie Curie Cancer Care is a charity which cares for people with cancer. The National Gardens Scheme is delighted to include it in its list of beneficiaries. Some facts and figures:

- More than 250,000 people in Britain develop cancer every year. Almost 160,000 people die from the disease annually, the second biggest killer after heart disease.

- **Marie Curie Nurses** provide over 1.3 million hours a year of practical nursing care at home. The service is available day or night, 365 days a year, to patients and their families without charge.

- **Marie Curie Centres** cared for more than 4,600 patients in 1996/97.

- **Marie Curie Cancer Care** operates a research institute which investigates the underlying causes of cancer.

Gwynedd

Hon County Organiser:
Anglesey, North Caernarfonshire
Aberconwy

Mrs B S Osborne, Foxbrush, Port Dinorwic, Felinheli, Gwynedd LL56 4JZ
Tel 01248 670463

Hon County Organiser:
South Caernarfonshire &
Merionethshire

Mrs Roessa Chiesman, Crud-yr-Awel, Llwyngwril, Gywnedd LL37 2UZ
Tel 01341 250736

Assistant County Organiser:

Mrs W N Jones, Waen Fechan, Islaw'r Dref, Dolgellau LL40 1TS
Tel 01341 423479

DATES OF OPENING

Regular openings
For details see garden description

Bryn Meifod, Glan Conwy
Farchynys Cottage, Bontddu
Plas Muriau, Bettws-y-Coed
Plas Penhelig, Aberdovey

By appointment only
For telephone numbers and other details see garden descriptions. Private visits welcomed

Bryn-y-Bont, Nantmor
Cefn Bere, Dolgellau
Gwyndy Bach, Llandrygarn
Haulfryn, Llanberis
Hen Ysgoldy, Llanfrothen
Llys-y-Gwynt, Llandegai
Pencarreg, Glyn Garth, Menai Bridge

March 15 Sunday
Bryniau, Boduan
March 22 Sunday
Foxbrush, Aber Pwll, Port Dinorwic
April 12 Sunday
Arch Noah, Tywyn
Bont Fechan Farm, Llanystumdwy
Bryniau, Boduan
Crug Farm, nr Caernarfon
April 13 Monday
Arch Noah, Tywyn
April 19 Sunday
Foxbrush, Aber Pwll, Port Dinorwic
April 26 Sunday
Gilfach, Rowen, nr Conwy

May 2 Saturday
Penrhyn Castle, nr Bangor
May 3 Sunday
Bryniau, Boduan
Haul-a-Gwynt, Wylfa, Anglesey
Tyr Gawen, Llanegryn
May 4 Monday
Glan-y-Morfa, Bryncrug
Tyr Gawen, Llanegryn
May 7 Thursday
Plas Newydd, Anglesey
May 17 Sunday
Bont Fechan Farm, Llanystumdwy
May 24 Sunday
Bryn Golygfa, Bontddu
Bryniau, Boduan
Crug Farm, nr Caernarfon
Glandderwen, Bontddu
Maenan Hall, Llanrwst
Pen-y-Parc, Beaumaris
Rhyd, Trefor
St John the Baptist & St George
Tyn-y-Cefn, Dolwen, nr Festiniog
May 25 Monday
Arch Noah, Tywyn
Bryn Golygfa, Bontddu
Crug Farm, nr Caernarfon
Glandderwen, Bontddu
May 31 Sunday
Bryn Eisteddfod, Glan Conwy
Trysglwyn Fawr, Amlwch
June 7 Sunday
Gilfach, Rowen, nr Conwy
June 13 Saturday
Bronclydwr, Rhoslefain
June 14 Sunday
Bryniau, Boduan
Glan-y-Morfa, Bryncrug
Henllys Lodge, Beaumaris
June 20 Saturday
Marian, Talwrn

June 21 Sunday
Foxbrush, Aber Pwll, Port Dinorwic
June 28 Sunday
Tyn-y-Cefn, Dolwen, nr Festiniog
July 5 Sunday
Afallon, Bontddu
Braich-y-Foel, Bwlch Derwin
Bryniau, Boduan
Glandderwen, Bontddu
July 6 Monday
Afallon, Bontddu
Glandderwen, Bontddu
July 12 Sunday
Glan-y-Morfa, Bryncrug
Henllys Lodge, Beaumaris
July 18 Saturday
6 Llewellyn Road, Tywyn
July 19 Sunday
Crug Farm, nr Caernarfon
Rhyd, Trefor
July 26 Sunday
Haul-a-Gwynt, Wylfa, Anglesey
Tyn-y-Cefn, Dolwen, nr Festiniog
August 9 Sunday
Glan-y-Morfa, Bryncrug
Pentre Bach, Llwyngwril
August 16 Sunday
Bont Fechan Farm, Llanystumdwy
Gilfach, Rowen, nr Conwy
August 23 Sunday
Maenan Hall, Llanrwst
August 30 Sunday
Bryniau, Boduan
Crug Farm, nr Caernarfon
Tyn-y-Cefn, Dolwen, nr Festiniog
October 3 Saturday
Bryn Meifod, Glan Conwy
October 4 Sunday
Bryn Meifod, Glan Conwy
Bryniau, Boduan

DESCRIPTIONS OF GARDENS

Afallon, Bontddu ✗ (Mr & Mrs Edward O Williams) 5m W of Dolgellau. Take A496 to Bontddu. Garden is N, 50yds past Bontddu Hall Hotel. 1-acre cottage garden. Summer flowers, clipped yew hedges, variety of trees and shrubs. *Adm £1 Chd free. Sun, Mon July 5, 6 (11-6)*

¶**Arch Noah, Tywyn** ❀ (Mr & Mrs J Fisher) A few minutes from Tywyn centre, by Tallyllyn narrow gauge railway station, turn into Neptune Rd, over bridge and 1st L into Faenol Isaf. A garden created to suppress the winds from the sea. Many beautiful trees creating a wind barrier. Woodlands, trees and shrubs in a garden made by the owners for easy maintenance over 20yrs ago.

GWYNEDD

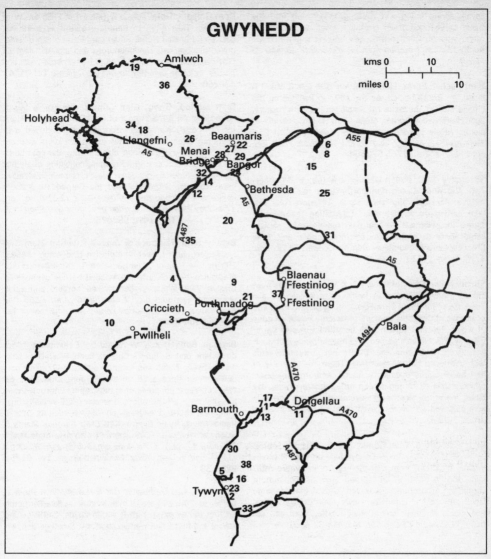

kms 0   10

miles 0   10

Amlwch
19
36
Holyhead
34 18
Llangefni   26   Beaumaris
A5
Menai   27 22
Bridge   28 29
32   Bangor
14   24
12   Bethesda
A5
20
A487
35
4
9
Criccieth   21
10   3   Porthmadog
Pwllheli
6
8
A55
15
25
31
A5
Blaenau
Ffestiniog
37   Ffestiniog
A494   Bala
A470
17
7 1
Barmouth   13   Dolgellau
11   A470
30
38
A487
5
16
Tywyn   23
2
33

KEY

1. Afallon
2. Arch Noah
3. Bont Fechan Farm
4. Braich-y-Foel
5. Bronclydwr
6. Bryn Eisteddfod
7. Bryn Golygfa
8. Bryn Meifod
9. Bryn-y-Bont
10. Bryniau
11. Cefn Bere
12. Crug Farm
13. Farchynys Cottage

14. Foxbrush
15. Gilfach
16. Glan-y-Morfa
17. Glandderwen
18. Gwyndy Bach
19. Haul-a-Gwynt
20. Haulfryn
21. Hen Ysgoldy
22. Henllys Lodge
23. 6 Llewellyn Road
24. Llys-y-Gwynt
25. Maenan Hall
26. Marian

27. Pen-y-Parc
28. Pencarreg
29. Penrhyn Castle
30. Pentre Bach
31. Plas Muriau
32. Plas Newydd
33. Plas Penhelig
34. Rhyd
35. St John the Baptist &
     St George
36. Trysglwyn Fawr
37. Tyn-y-Cefn
38. Tyr Gawen

Lovely spring bulbs and roses growing high into the trees, shrubs and trees closely planted to provide yr round interest. Quiet setting encouraging wildlife. TEAS. *Adm £1.50 Chd free. Sun April 12, Mons April 13, May 25 (12-5)*

Bont Fechan Farm, Llanystumdwy &̊※ (Mr & Mrs J D Bean) 2m from Criccieth on the A497 to Pwllheli on the L-hand side of the main rd. Small garden with rockery, pond, herbaceous border, steps to river, large variety of plants. Nicely planted tubs. TEAS. *Adm 75p Chd 25p. Suns April 12, May 17, Aug 16 (11-5). Private visits welcome, please* **Tel 01766 522604**

¶**Braich-y-Foel, Bwlch Derwin** ⚭※ (Mrs E M Cooper) Take the A487 Caernarfon/Porthmadog rd. Leave the A487 at Pant Glas and follow signs. A remote rural cottage garden on former farm. Interesting features designed for eventual 'old age' easy maintenance. ⅓-acre cared for with enthusiasm by Mrs Cooper and Sally Crookes, extra vegetable garden Mr Cooper. TEAS. *Adm £1. Sun July 5 (12-6)*

¶**Bronclydwr, Rhoslefain** ⚭ (Mr & Mrs Michael Bishton) Take the A493 Dolgellau to Tywyn rd at Rhoslefain take Tonfanau rd for about ½m. Fork L along private rd to end of tarmac rd then take unmade rd to large house on edge of wood. Peaceful garden with beautiful views of Cardigan Bay. Plantsman's garden with a wide range of camellias, shrubs and herbaceous plants. Set in informal beds with a wooded hillside backdrop. There are a variety of half hardy plants; cannas, echiums, embothrium, phormium, acacia etc. A bog garden with gunnera, arums, day lillies, iris etc is also being developed. Garden about 1-acre plus wild and wooded area. *Adm £1.50 Chd free. Sat June 13 (10-6)*

Bryn Eisteddfod, Glan Conwy &̊※ (Dr Michael Senior) 3½m SE Llandudno 3m W Colwyn Bay; up the hill (Bryn-y-Maen direction) from Glan Conwy Corner where A470 joins A55. 8 acres of landscaped grounds incl mature shrubbery, arboretum, old walled 'Dutch' garden, large lawn with ha-ha. Extensive views over Conwy Valley, Snowdonia National Park, Conwy Castle, town and estuary. TEAS. *Adm £1 Chd 50p. Sun May 31 (2-5)*

Bryn Golygfa, Dolgellau ⚭※ (Miss C M Ellis) 5m W of Dolgellau. Take A496 to Bontddu; garden is N 100yds past Bontddu Hall Hotel. Small garden on steep hillside; mixed planting incl rhododendrons and alpines. *Adm £1 Chd free. Sun, Mon May 24, 25 (11-6). Private visits and parties welcome mid-May to mid-Aug, please* **Tel 01341 430260**

Bryn Meifod, Graig, Glan Conwy ⚭※ (Dr & Mrs K Lever) Just off A470 1½m S of Glan Conwy. Follow signs for Aberconwy Nursery. ¾-acre garden developed over 25yrs but extensively replanted in the last 10yrs. Unusual trees, shrubs and woodland plants, scree and peat beds. Good autumn colours. Wide ranging collection of alpines especially autumn gentians and cyclamen. Extensive views towards Snowdonia and the Carneddau. Nursery adjacent. *Collection Box. Fri afternoons (2-5) from April 17 to May 29 inclusive. Gentian open days Sat, Sun Oct 3, 4, (2-5) please* **Tel 01492 580875**

Bryn-y-Bont, Nantmor ※ (Miss J Entwisle) 2½m S of Beddgelert, turn L over Aberglaslyn Bridge into A4085, 500yds turn L up hill, 2nd house on R. Small garden created since 1978 on S facing wooded hillside overlooking Glaslyn Vale. Water garden, mixed borders and small woodland. Featured on TV and Radio. *Adm £1.50 Chd free. Private visits and small parties welcome, please* **Tel 01766 890448**

Bryniau, Boduan ※ (P W Wright & J E Humphreys) ½m down lane opp. St Buan's Church, Boduan, which is halfway between Nefyn and Pwllheli on the A497. New garden created since 1988 on almost pure sand. Over 80 types of trees; hundreds of shrubs, many unusual, showing that with a little effort, one can grow virtually anything anywhere. Broadcast on BBC Gardeners World, Radio Wales, Radio Cymru, S4C Clwb Garddio. Plants & woodcraft for sale. TEAS. *Adm £1 Chd free. Suns March 15, April 12, May 3, 24, June 14, July 5, Aug 30, Oct 4 (11-6) and private visits welcome, please* **Tel 01758 7213 38**

Cefn Bere, Cae Deintur ⚭ (Mr & Mrs Maldwyn Thomas) Dolgellau. Turn L at top of main bridge on Bala-Barmouth Rd (not the by-pass); turn R within 20yds; 2nd R behind school and first L half way up short hill. Small garden; ex-

---

SYMBOLS USED IN THIS BOOK (See also Page 17)

¶   Opening for the first time.

※   Plants/produce for sale if available.

&̊   Gardens with at least the main features accessible by wheelchair.

⚭   No dogs except guide dogs.

●   These gardens advertise their own dates in this publication although they do not nominate specific days for the NGS. Not all the money collected by these gardens comes to the NGS but they do make a guaranteed contribution.

■   These gardens nominate specific days for the NGS and advertise their own dates in this publication.

▲   These gardens open regularly to the public but they do not advertise their own dates in this publication. For further details, contact the garden directly.

tensive collection of alpines, bulbs and rare plants. Tea Dolgellau. *Collecting box. Individuals and parties of up to 25 welcome, spring, summer and autumn months, please* **Tel Dolgellau 01341 422768**

Crug Farm, Griffiths Crossing ⚘🌸 (Mr & Mrs B Wynn-Jones) 2m NE of Caernarfon ¼m off main A487 Caernarfon to Bangor Road. Follow signs from roundabout. ⅔-acre; grounds to old country house. Gardens filled with choice, unusual collections of climbers, and herbaceous plants; over 300 species of hardy geraniums. Featured in 'The Garden' and on BBC TV Gardeners World. Only partly suitable wheelchairs. TEAS in aid of local charities. *Thurs to Suns & Bank Hols Feb 22 to Sept 28 (10-6). Adm £1 Chd free. Natural Rock garden only open Suns April 12, May 24, July 19, Aug 30, Mon May 25 (10-6). Private parties welcome, please* **Tel 01248 670232**

Farchynys Cottage, Bontddu ⚘ (Mrs G Townshend) On A496 Dolgellau-Barmouth rd; well-signed W of Bontddu village. 4 acres; informal country garden on steep wooded hillside; unusual shrubs and trees; azaleas, over 75 species of rhododendron, giant Liriodendron tulipifera. Best mid-May, mid-June. *Adm £1 Chd free. Open daily except Sats, May 1st to Sept 30. Parties welcome, please* **Tel 01341 430245**

Foxbrush, Felinheli ♿⚘ (Mr & Mrs B S Osborne) On Bangor to Caernarfon Road, entering village opp layby with Felinheli sign post. Fascinating 3-acre country garden created around winding river; ponds and small wooded area. Rare and interesting plant collections incl rhododendrons, ferns, primula, clematis and roses; 45ft long pergola; fan-shaped knot garden; coaches welcome. Featured BBC Anchors Away and Period Living magazine and on S4C Club Garddio. TEAS. *Adm £1 incl C16 cottage museum Chd free. Suns March 22, April 19, June 21 (12-5). Also private visits and parties welcome, please* **Tel 01248 670463**

Gilfach, Rowen ♿⚘ (James & Isoline Greenhalgh) At Xrds 100yds E of Rowen (4m S of Conwy) S towards Llanrwst, past Rowen School on L; turn up 2nd drive on L, signposted. 1-acre country garden on S-facing slope overlooking Conwy Valley; set in 35 acres farm and woodland; mature shrubs; herbaceous border; small pool. Partly suitable wheelchairs which are welcome. Magnificent views of River Conwy and mountains. TEAS. *Adm £1 Chd free. Suns April 26, June 7, Aug 16 (11-5)*

¶**Glan-y-Morfa, Tywyn** ⚘🌸 (J Aldridge & D Collins) [Grid ref SH135 612040]. From Bryncrug on A493 nr Tywyn. Take lane by the church signposted Craig-y-Deryn and Abertrinant (Bird Rock) for ½m. Glan-y-Morfa next building on L past the farm. Cottage garden. Sympathetic to wildlife divided into several small areas with trees and shrubs. Kitchen garden. Ancient stone barn. *Adm £1.50 Chd free. Mon May 4, Suns June 14, July 12, Aug 9 (11-5)*

Glandderwen, Bontddu (A M Reynolds Esq) 5m W of Dolgellau. Take A496 to Bontddu. Garden is on S 100yds past Bontddu Hall Hotel. ½-acre on N bank of Mawddach Estuary facing Cader Idris; set amid large oaks; shrubs; trees; steep and rocky nature. *Adm £1 Chd free. Suns,*

Mons May 24, 25; July 5, 6 (11-6). Private visits and parties welcome May 1 to Sept 30, please **Tel 01341 430229**

Gwyndy Bach, Llandrygarn ♿⚘🌸 (Keith & Rosa Andrew) From Llangefni take the B5109 towards Bodedern, the cottage is exactly 5m out on the L. A ¾-acre artist's garden set amidst rugged Anglesey landscape. Romantically planted in intimate 'rooms' with interesting plants and shrubs, old roses and secluded lily pond. Studio attached. *Open by appt May, June and July, please* **Tel 01407 720651**

Haul-a-Gwynt, Wylfa ♿⚘ (Mark & Wendy Markwald) Off A5025 2m from Cemaes Bay travelling towards Holyhead. Turn R at Magnox Power Station sign. At main gate turn R for ¼m to Nature Trail car park on R. Please park here unless disabled. Opp car park is Tyn-y-Maes and Haul-a-Gwynt House sign. Private lane 100yds to house. ¾ acre of walled garden, sheltering 200 varieties of flowering shrubs, climbers and trees, the majority named. Fish pond and waterfall, greenhouse and alpine rockery. TEA in restored farm labourer's cottage. *Adm £1 Chd free. Suns May 3, July 26 (11-5). Private visits welcome, please* **Tel 01407 710058**

Haulfryn, Llanberis ♿⚘ (Adrian & Diane Anthoine) Church Lane. 5 min walk from centre of Llanberis, up lane between garage and church. Garden approx 1 acre. Commenced 1987 from rough sheep pasture at foot of Snowdon. Numerous tree plantings, natural rock outcrop; variety of ericaceous shrubs, old roses and mixed herbaceous borders bounded by a natural mountain stream. Partly suitable wheelchairs. TEAS. *Adm £1 Chd free. Private visits welcome, please* **Tel 01286 870446**

Hen Ysgoldy, Llanfrothen ⚘ (Mr Brian Archard) From Garreg via B4410, after ½m L; garden 200yds on R. Natural garden with streams and established trees, incl magnolias, eucalyptus and embothrium. Shrubs incl a variety of azaleas and rhododendrons, mixed borders planted for colour and interest all-yr. *Adm £1.50 Chd free. Private visits and parties welcome April 1 to Aug 31, please* **Tel 01766 771231**

Henllys Lodge, Beaumaris ♿⚘🌸 (Mr & Mrs K H Lane) Past Beaumaris Castle, ½m turn L, 1st L again. Lodge at entrance to Henllys Hall Hotel drive. Approx 1-acre country garden, planted in traditional cottage style using perennials, shrubs, old roses and featuring extensive collection of hardy geraniums. Small woodland area. Stunning views across Menai Straits. TEAS. *Adm £1 Chd free. Suns June 14, July 12 (12-5.30). Private visits and parties welcome, please* **Tel 01248 810106**

¶**6 Llewellyn Road, Tywyn** ⚘ (Mr & Mrs P I Askey) From Dolgellau follow A493 coast rd to Fairbourne to Rhoslefain to Bryncrug, turn R at Little Bridge to Tywyn (signposted). Follow main rd through Tywyn till you arrive at main railway bridge, go under bridge turn L, 3rd bungalow on L. A small town garden with a mixture of annual and perennials flowers. Roses, clematis, pond, greenhouse also small vegetable garden. Vegetables grown to a fairly high standard. TEAS. *Adm £1. Sat July 18 (1.30-6.30)*

Llys-y-Gwynt, Llandegai &⊛ (Jennifer Rickards & John Evans) 3m S of Bangor and 300yds from Llandygai Roundabout on expressway. Follow signs to Llanberis off A5 and 100yds from entrance to Esso Service Station and Travel Lodge. 2-acre rambling garden; well established trees and shrubs and magnificent views; pond, N-facing rockery; large Bronze Age burial cairn. Planting with emphasis on wind resistance, yr-round interest and encouraging wild life. *Adm £1 Chd free. Private visits welcome, please* **Tel 01248 353863**

Maenan Hall ⊛ (The Hon Mr & Mrs Christopher McLaren) Exactly 2m N of Llanrwst on E side of A470, ¼m S of Maenan Abbey Hotel. Gardens created since 1956 by the late Christabel, Lady Aberconway and then present owners; 10 acres; lawns, shrub, rose and walled gardens; rhododendron dell; many species of beautiful and interesting plants, shrubs and trees set amongst mature oaks and other hardwoods; fine views across Conway valley. Home-made TEAS. *Adm £2 Chd 50p (ACNO to St David's Hospice Foundation® May 24; Hope House Children's Respite Hospice® Aug 23). Suns May 24, Aug 23 (10-5). Last entry 4pm*

¶**Marian, Talwrn** &⊗ (Dr & Mrs I R Gwynedd Jones) Stone farmhouse situated on R, 2m from Pentraeth on Pentraeth-Talwrn Rd. Take Amlwch exit from Britannia Bridge, L-hand turn for Llangefni at Pentraeth, opp Panton Arms. Look out for church in the field on R-hand side Marian is the next farmhouse. ¼m along the rd. Woodland garden of approx ¾ acre. Shrubs and perennials. Newly constructed vegetable garden with box edging, gravel paths and pergolas. TEAS. *Adm £1 (ACNO to Llanffinan Church Fund®). Sat June 20 (2-5)*

Pen-y-Parc, Beaumaris (Mrs E E Marsh) A545 Menai Bridge-Beaumaris rd; after Anglesey Boatyard 1st L; after Golf Club 1st drive on L. NOT easy for wheelchairs. 6 acres; beautiful grounds, magnificent views over Menai Strait; azaleas, rhododendrons and heathers; interesting terrain with rock outcrops used to advantage for recently planted conifer and rock gardens; small lake in natural setting; 2 further enclosed gardens. We would like to share the pleasure of this garden. TEA. *Adm £1 Chd 50p. Sun May 24 (11-5)*

Pencarreg, Glyn Garth & (Miss G Jones) 1½m on A545 Menai Bridge towards Beaumaris, turn R in front of a lodge set back from the rd, Pencarreg is 100yds on R down the drive. Parking in lay-by on main rd, parking on courtyard for small cars and disabled. Planted for all-yr interest and colour with common and unusual shrubs. Small stream. Garden terminates at cliff edge and this has been skilfully planted. Views to the Menai Straits and the Carneddi Mountains in the distance. Featured in 4 television programmes. *Collecting Box (ACNO to Snowdonia National Park Society©). Private visits welcome all year, please* **Tel 01248 713545**

▲**Penrhyn Castle** & (The National Trust) 3m E of Bangor on A5122. Buses from Llandudno, Caernarvon. Betwsy-Coed; alight: Grand Lodge Gate. Large gardens; fine trees, shrubs, wild garden, good views. Castle rebuilt in 1830 for 1st Lord Penrhyn, incorporating part of C15

building on C8 site of home of Welsh Princes. Exhibition of National Trust Countryside; museum of locomotives and quarry rolling stock. NT Shop. TEAS and light lunches. *Adm £3 Chd £1.50 (Garden and Exhibition only). For NGS Sat May 2 (11-5). Last adm ½ hr prior to closing. Private visits welcome, please* **Tel 01248 353084**

¶**Pentre Bach, Llwyngwril** ⊗⊛ (Mr & Mrs N Smyth) [Grid ref E591N095]. Entrance is 40yds S of stone bridge in centre of Llwyngwril, 12m from Dolgellau, on A493 coast rd. Public car park 100yds from entrance. 1-acre cultivated organically. Walled kitchen garden with glasshouse. No-dig raised bed system. Small 'woodland garden' with soft fruit and herbs, using permaculture principles, composting, shrubs, free range hens. Magnificent sea views. TEAS. *Adm £1 Chd 50p. Sun Aug 9 (10-5)*

Plas Muriau, Betws-y-Coed ⊗⊛ (Lorna & Tony Scharer) On A470 approx ¼m N of Waterloo Bridge, Betws-y-Coed; entrance by minor junction to Capel Garmon. A large garden dating from the 1850s recently restored. About 1 acre open to visitors. A structured garden within a woodland setting, with magnificent views. Unusual perennials and herbs, wild flowers, bulbs and roses. Many unusual plants for sale at adjacent nursery, Gwydir Plants. *Adm £1. Fri and Sats Easter to July incl (11-5) or by arrangement at nursery or by appt. Please* **Tel 01690 710201**

▲**Plas Newydd** &⊗ (The Marquess of Anglesey; The National Trust) Isle of Anglesey. 1m SW of Llanfairpwll and A5, on A4080. Gardens with massed shrubs, fine trees, and lawns sloping down to Menai Strait. Magnificent views to Snowdonia. C18 house by James Wyatt contains Rex Whistler's largest wall painting; also Military Museum. TEAS and light lunches. *Adm garden only £2, Chd £1. For NGS Thurs May 7 (11-5.30) last entry 5pm*

Plas Penhelig, Aberdovey (Mr & Mrs A C Richardson) Between 2 railway bridges. Driveway to hotel by island and car park. 14 acres overlooking estuary, exceptional views. Particularly lovely in spring: bulbs, daffodils, rhododendrons, azaleas; rock and water gardens, mature tree heathers, magnolias, euphorbias; herbaceous borders, rose garden; wild and woodland flowers encouraged in large orchard; formal walled garden with herbaceous borders, large range of greenhouses, peaches, herbs. TEAS. *Adm £1.50 Chd 50p. Wed to Sun incl: April 1 to mid-Oct (2.30-5.30). Collecting box*

Rhyd, Trefor &⊗⊛ (Ann & Jeff Hubble) nr Holyhead. From Bodedern 2¼m along B5109 towards Llangefni, turn L. 2½ acres of gardens etc with many facets, herbaceous beds with some rare and unusual plants; many varieties of rhododendron, clematis and climbing roses, trees and shrubs; conservatory, ponds, rockery, pergola and nature walk (good footwear needed). Garden bordered by stream. Partly suitable wheelchairs. TEAS. *Adm £1 Chd free. Suns May 24, July 19 (11-5). Private visits welcome, please* **Tel 01407 720320**

Regular openings. Open throughout the year. They are listed at the beginning of the Diary Section.

St John the Baptist & St George, Carmel (Bishop Abbot Demetrius) On the A487 to Groeslon follow signs to Carmel. At village centre turn L and L again at Xrds. Holy community in the making under the authority of The Orthodox Catholic Church of America. This is not a garden in the traditional sense but a spiritual retreat from the stresses and strains of modern life, surrounded on all sides by space and rural tranquillity. We are privileged to share a glimpse of a more contemplative life. TEA. *Adm £1 Chd free. Sun May 24 (2-5)*

Trysglwyn Fawr, Rhosybol ዿ (Lord & Lady Stanley of Alderley) Take the road S from Amlwch to Llanerchymedd. After 2m having passed the Parys Mountain mine shaft on your R, turn L, Trysglwyn Fawr is 1,000yds down that rd on your L. 1-acre garden overlooking farm land to fine view of Snowdonia. Mixed flower and shrub beds; vegetable garden, fruit garden and conservatory; farm walk showing amenity woodland and ponds, and wind farm. TEA. *Adm £1 Chd free. Sun May 31 (1-5)*

Tyn-y-Cefn, Ffestiniog ዿ✿ (Robert & Sheila Woodier) On the A496 3m from Maentwrog, 2m from Tanygrisiau [OS 695439]. Scenic setting in Snowdonia National Park for large garden with cottage garden atmosphere. Informal plantings of mixed beds and borders incl trees, shrubs, old-fashioned roses, climbers and many unusual plants. TEAS. *Adm £1. Suns May 24, June 28 July 26, Aug 30 (11-6). Private visits welcome, please* Tel 01766 831810

¶Tyr Gawen, Llanegryn ዿ✿ (Jane Whittle) 4m NE of Tywyn (Merioneth). Leave A493 through Llanegryn, 1½m beyond village, up farm track on L. A garden teased from S facing ½-acre of mountainside, with spring and idyllic views to provide enchantment and peaceful places to sit, inspired book 'Somewhere to Grow'. Water, flowers, shrubs, lawn, semi-wild areas, bulbs, trees from the Celtic Tree Calender, quartz pebble maze, dens, fruit and vegetables; ducks, geese, chickens - organic, permaculture principles, re-cycled materials. TEAS. *Adm £1.50 Chd free. Sun, Mon May 3, 4 (2-5.30)*

The *National Gardens Scheme* is pleased to invite you to
a special Evening Opening at

The Royal Botanic Gardens, Kew

during Chelsea Week
Thursday, May 21st
6.30–9pm

Enjoy the glorious late spring at Kew at an exclusive Evening Opening. Two of the major glasshouses will be open, with staff available to explain their collections and Kew's work.

Admission: £4 Adults, £2 Children,
in aid of the National Gardens Scheme
(as this is a fund-raising event, admission fee also applies to Season Ticket holders and Friends of the Royal Botanic Gardens, Kew)
Refreshments available

Kew is easily reached via the Kew Gardens station (London Underground District Line, and by rail from North London on Silverlink). Also from Kew Bridge station (South West Trains). By road the Gardens are located just south of Kew Bridge on the A307, Kew Road.

Entry by Victoria Gate Only, on the Kew Road, opposite Lichfield Road.

Powys

Hon County Organisers:

(North – Montgomeryshire)   Captain R Watson (Retired), Westwinds, Kerry, Newtown, Powys
Tel 01686 670605

(South – Brecknock & Radnor)   Miss Shan Egerton, Pen-y-Maes, Hay on Wye, Hereford HR3 5PP
Tel 01497 820423

Assistant County Organiser:
(South)   Lady Milford, Llanstephan House, Llanstephan, Brecon. Powys LD3 0YR
Tel 01982 560693

Hon County Treasurer: (North)   Captain R Watson (Retired)
Hon County Treasuer: (South)   Lady Milford

DATES OF OPENING

Regular openings
For details see garden description

Ashford House, Brecon
Mill Cottage, Abbeycwmhir
The Walled Garden, Knill

By appointment only
*For telephone numbers and other
details see garden descriptions.
Private visits welcomed*

Maenllwyd Isaf, Abermule
The Millers House, Welshpool
Llangorse Gardens

April 5 Sunday
Hill Crest, Brooks, Welshpool
April 14 Tuesday
Diamond Cottage, Buttington,
Welshpool
April 19 Sunday
Crossways, Newcastle on Clun
Hill Crest, Brooks, Welshpool
April 26 Sunday
Crossways, Newcastle on Clun
Llansantffraed House & Scethrog
House nr Brecon
April 28 Tuesday
Diamond Cottage, Buttington,
Welshpool
April 29 Wednesday
Llansantffraed House, nr Brecon
May 2 Saturday
Glansevern, Berriew, Welshpool
Tan-y-Llyn Nurseries, Meifod
May 3 Sunday
8 Baskerville Court, Clyro
Crossways, Newcastle on Clun
Hill Crest, Brooks, Welshpool
Tan-y-Llyn Nurseries, Meifod
May 9 Saturday
Glansevern, Berriew, Welshpool
May 10 Sunday
Crossways, Newcastle on Clun

Gliffaes Country House Hotel,
Crickhowell
May 12 Tuesday
Diamond Cottage, Buttington,
Welshpool
May 17 Sunday
Crossways, Newcastle on Clun
Glanwye, Builth Wells
Hill Crest, Brooks, Welshpool
May 24 Sunday
Bronhyddon,
Llansantffraid-ym-Mechain
Crossways, Newcastle on Clun
Garth House, nr Buith Wells
Maesllwch Castle,
Glasbury-on-Wye
May 25 Monday
Llysdinam, Newbridge-on-Wye
May 26 Tuesday
Diamond Cottage, Buttington,
Welshpool
May 27 Wednesday
Powis Castle Gardens,
Welshpool
May 31 Sunday
Ashford House, Talybont on
Usk
Bodynfoel Hall, Llanfechain
Crossways, Newcastle on Clun
Gregynog, Tregynon
June 2 Tuesday
Diamond Cottage, Buttington,
Welshpool
June 6 Saturday
Tan-y-Llyn Nurseries, Meifod
June 7 Sunday
Crossways, Newcastle on Clun
Llanstephan House, Llyswen
Tan-y-Llyn Nurseries, Meifod
June 14 Sunday
Crossways, Newcastle on Clun
Hill Crest, Brooks, Welshpool
Pen-y-Maes, Hay-on-Wye
Point Farm, Newtown
June 16 Tuesday
Diamond Cottage, Buttington,
Welshpool

June 21 Sunday
Abernant, Fron
Crossways, Newcastle on Clun
Tretower House, Crickhowell
Welsh Border Gardens in the
Hindwell Valley
June 27 Saturday
Belan-yr-Argae, Welshpool
June 28 Sunday
8 Baskerville Court, Clyro
The Bushes, Berriew
Crossways, Newcastle on Clun
Hill Crest, Brooks, Welshpool
Llys-y-Wen, Carno
Treberfydd, Nr Bwlch
June 30 Tuesday
Diamond Cottage, Buttington,
Welshpool
July 4 Saturday
Tan-y-Llyn Nurseries, Meifod
July 5 Sunday
Crossways, Newcastle on Clun
Penmyarth, Glanusk Park
Tan-y-Llyn Nurseries, Meifod
July 12 Sunday
Crossways, Newcastle on Clun
Hill Crest, Brooks, Welshpool
Parc Gwynne, Glasbury-on-Wye
Gilwern and Llangrwyney
Gardens
July 14 Tuesday
Diamond Cottage, Buttington,
Welshpool
July 19 Sunday
Coity Gardens, Talybont-on-Usk
Crossways, Newcastle on Clun
Fraithwen, Tregynon, Newtown
July 28 Tuesday
Diamond Cottage, Buttington,
Welshpool
August 1 Saturday
Tan-y-Llyn Nurseries, Meifod
August 2 Sunday
Tan-y-Llyn Nurseries, Meifod
August 9 Sunday
Llysdinam, Newbridge-on-Wye
Point Farm, Newtown

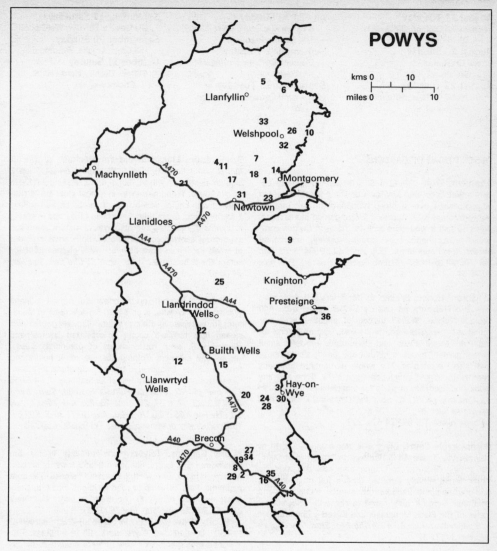

POWYS

kms 0   10
miles 0   10

Llanfyllin○   5   6

33
Welshpool○ 26 10
32

4 11   7
17   18   14
1   Montgomery

31   23
Newtown

Machynlleth○

A470
21

Llanidloes○

A44

A470

9

25   Knighton

A470   A44   Presteigne

Llandrindod
Wells○   36

22

Builth Wells

12   15

○Llanwrtyd
Wells

A470   20   3 Hay-on-
24   30 Wye
28

A40 Brecon○

A470   27
19 34
8
29 2   35
16   A40
13

KEY

1. Abernant
2. Ashford House
3. 8 Baskerville Court
4. Belan-yr-Argae
5. Bodynfoel Hall
6. Bronhyddon
7. The Bushes
8. Coity Gardens
9. Crossways
10. Diamond Cottage
11. Fraithwen
12. Garth House
13. Gilwern and Llangrwyney
    Gardens
14. Glansevern
15. Glanwye
16. Gliffaes Country House
    Hotel
17. University of Wales
18. Hill Crest
19. Llansantffraed House &
    Scethrog House nr
    Brecon
20. Llanstephan House
21. Llys-y-Wen
22. Llysdinam
23. Maenllwyd Isaf
24. Maesllwch Castle
25. Mill Cottage
26. The Millers House
27. Llangorse Gardens
28. Parc Gwynne
29. Penmyarth
30. Pen-y-Maes
31. Point Farm
32. Powis Castle Gardens
33. Tan-y-Llyn Nurseries
34. Treberfydd
35. Tretower House
36. Welsh Border Gardens in the
    Hindwell Valley

August 11 Tuesday
Diamond Cottage, Buttington, Welshpool
August 23 Sunday
Hill Crest, Brooks, Welshpool
August 25 Tuesday
Diamond Cottage, Buttington, Welshpool

August 30 Sunday
8 Baskerville Court, Clyro
The Bushes, Berriew
September 1 Tuesday
Diamond Cottage, Buttington, Welshpool
September 15 Tuesday
Diamond Cottage, Buttington, Welshpool

September 19 Saturday
Glansevern, Berriew, Welshpool
September 20 Sunday
Hill Crest, Brooks, Welshpool
October 11 Sunday
Gliffaes Country House Hotel, Crickhowell

DESCRIPTIONS OF GARDENS

Abernant, Fron ⚹❀ (J A & B M Gleave) Midway between Welshpool and Newtown on the A483. The garden is approached over a steep humpback bridge; straight ahead through gate. Approx 2.5 acre garden incl orchard. There is also a woodland area to the rear. Garden comprises lawns, pond, rose garden, rockery, ornamental shrubs, trees and ferns. TEA. *Adm £1.50 OAP's £1 Chd free (ACNO to Welsh Historic Gardens Trust®). Sun June 21 (2-5)*

■ **Ashford House, Brecon** ❀ (Mr & Mrs D A Anderson) ¾m E of Talybont on Usk on B4558 signed from A40 through village. Walled garden of about 1 acre surrounded by woodland and wild garden approx 4 acres altogether. Mixed shrub and herbaceous borders; small formal garden; meadow garden and pond; alpine house and beds; vegetables. The whole garden has gradually been restored and developed since 1979. Bring and buy plant stall. Suitable in parts for wheelchairs. TEAS. *Adm £2 Chd free (ACNO to Save the Children®). Open Wed April 1 to Sept 30 (2-6). For NGS Sun May 31 (2-6). Also by appt, please* **Tel 01874 676 271**

8 Baskerville Court, Clyro ⚹❀ (Mr & Mrs S Smith) nr Hay-on-Wye. Leave A438 Hereford to Brecon rd at Clyro. Baskerville Court is nr church and behind Baskerville Arms. Small steeply terraced garden full of interesting and unusual plants imaginatively planted, incl alpines and heathers. Pergola and conservatory with magnificent views of the Black Mountains and Kilvert's Church. Teas at Baskerville Arms. *Adm £2 Chd free. Suns May 3, June 28, Aug 30 (11-5)*

Belan-yr-Argae, Cefn-Coch ⚹(part) (Ivy Pritchard Evans) 14m SW of Welshpool via Llanfair Caereinion and Cefn Coch and 11m NW of Newtown via Tregynon and Adfa. Garden attached to an old-fashioned farm comprising formal and wild gardens with pools, unusual plants, shrubs and trees, all set in approx ½ acre. Yr-round interest. TEA. Raffles. *Adm £1 Chd free (ACNO to ADFA CM Chapel©). Sat June 27 (3 onwards). Private visits welcome May 25 onwards, please* **Tel 01938 810658**

Bodynfoel Hall, Llanfechain ⚹❀ (Maj Bonnor-Maurice) 10m N of Welshpool. Via A490 to Llanfyllin. Take B4393 to Llanfechain, follow signs. Approx 3½ acres; gardens and woodland; lakes; young and mature trees; shrub roses and heather bank. TEAS. *Adm £1 OAPs 50p Chd 50p. Sun May 31 (2-6)* **Tel 01691 648486**

Bronhyddon, Llansantffraid-ym-Mechain ❀ (Mr & Mrs R Jones-Perrott) 10m N Welshpool on A495 on E side in centre of village. Long drive; parking in fields below house. Wood having been almost clear felled now planted with choice young trees & shrubs on acid soil on S facing slope. Grass rides have been made and in spring is a mass of bluebells and foxgloves; a mature stand has anemones, snowdrops & primroses. Both areas lead out of small garden in front of house with elegant Regency verandahs & balconies. TEAS. *Adm £1 Chd free. Sun May 24 (2-6)*

The Bushes, Pantyfridd, Berriew ⚹❀ (Hywel & Eileen Williams) 8m Welshpool on B4390 Berriew (3m) to Manafon. In picturesque Rhiew Valley. ⅔-acre garden designed into terraced colour co-ordinated 'rooms' and planted with over 700 varieties of perennials, roses, shrubs and climbers clothing the old stone house and farm buildings. Imaginative use of local stone in attractive patios and water features. TEAS Sun only. *Adm £1.50 Chd free (ACNO to Cystic Fibrosis Trust®). Suns, Mons April 12, 13; May 24, 25; June 28, 29; July 26, 27; Aug 30, 31. For NGS Suns June 28, Aug 30 (1.30-5.30). Private parties day or evening, please* **Tel 01686 650338**

¶**Coity Gardens, Talybont-on-Usk** ⚹❀ Brecon 6m Crickhowell 6m. Leave village on B4558 towards Brecon. Approx ½m at pink cottages take L signed Talybont reservoir, then 1st R up to road junctions turn L to Coity Mawr and Dan-y-Coity at top. Refreshments. *Combined adm £3.50 Chd free. Sun July 19 (11-5)*
  ¶**Coity Mawr** (Mr & Mrs W Forwood) 4-acre garden at 850'. Created over 4 yrs, work still in progress. Terraced with spectacular view of black mountains across Usk valley. Mature trees, unusual plants and shrubs, rose and water gardens, parterre, willow arbour. Unusual plants for sale
  ¶**Dan-y-Coity** ⚹❀ (P H Barker & E Dowman) 1-acre terraced, walled garden at 850' with good mountain views. Interesting variety of plants, some rare. Stream and pond feature with bog garden. Collections of sorbus, ferns, hostas and camelias, fruit trees

■ **Crossways, Newcastle on Clun, Shropshire** ⚹❀ (Mr & Mrs R Smith) B4368 4m W of Newcastle turn R at Xrds signposted Crossways. 1m cottage at top of T-junction. [Map ref. 205 859]. 1-acre cottage garden and nursery 1400ft on Shropshire/Welsh border. Ponds, wildlife and woodland area, unusual and rare herbaceous plants. Small nursery, open Suns April 1 to Sept 30 (2-6). Garden open for NGS. *Adm £1. Suns April 19, 26, May 3, 10, 17, 24, 31, June 7, 14, 21, 28, July 5, 12, 19. Private visits welcome, please* **Tel 01686 670890**

Diamond Cottage, Buttington, Welshpool ❀❀ (Mr & Mrs D T Dorril) From Welshpool on A458 3m turn R into Heldre Lane. From Shrewsbury, turn L past 'Little Chef' Trewern into Sale Lane. Then follow signs. 1.7-acre garden on steep N facing slope at 700ft. Unusual herbaceous plants and shrubs; wooded dingle with stream; vegetable garden, patio and pools. Extensive views to Berwyn Mountains. TEAS. *Adm £1.20 Chd free. Tues April 14, 28; May 12, 26; June 2, 16, 30; July 14, 28; Aug 11, 25; Sept 1, 15 (2-6). Other times and groups April to Sept, please* **Tel 01938 570570**

Fraithwen, Tregynon ❀❀ (Mr & Mrs David Thomas) 6m N of Newtown on B4389 midway between villages of Bettws Cedewain and Tregynon. 1-acre garden created in the last 10yrs; herbaceous borders, rockeries and ponds packed with interesting, unusual and rare plants and shrubs for colour throughout the year. Also on display antique horse-drawn machinery and house implements. Partially suitable for wheelchairs. TEAS. *Adm £1.50 Chd free (ACNO to Bettws Community Hall®). Sun July 19 (2-6). Private parties welcome, please* **Tel 01686 650307**

¶**Garth House, Garth** ❀❀ (Mr & Mrs F A Wilson) Garth on A483 6m W of Builth Wells. Drive gates in village of Garth by Garth Inn. Large wood with azaleas and rhododendrons; water and shrub garden; herbaceous garden; fine views. Historic connection with Charles Wesley and the Gwynne family. TEAS. *Adm £2 Chd free. Sun May 24 (2-6)*

¶**Gilwern & Llangrwyney Gardens** *Sun July 12 (2-6)*
 ¶**Forge House** ❀❀ (Mr & Mrs Peter Bishop) 4m W of Abergavenny on A40 turn L at Bell Hotel, Llangrwyney. Garden on R. 1-acre owner maintained garden. Unusual shrubs and trees. Extensive planting around large millpond and leat. Small vegetable garden. TEAS in aid of Nevill Hall Thrombosis Fund. *Adm £1.50 Chd free*
 ¶**The Five Bells** ❀ (Mr & Mrs P Aeron-Thomas) Llanelli Church. 4m W of Abergavenny on A465 turn off onto A4077 through Gilwern. Turn L at the Corn Exchange public house. 1½m up Church Rd and opp Church. ⅔-acre terraced garden created 8yrs ago, with mixed borders of interesting shrubs, roses and herbaceous plants on N facing slope. 740' above Usk valley with extensive views. *Adm £1.50 Chd free*

■ **Glansevern Hall Gardens, Berriew** ❀❀ (Mr & Mrs R N Thomas) 4m SW of Powis Castle, Welshpool, on A483 at Berriew. 13-acre mature garden situated nr banks of R Severn. Centred on Glansevern Hall, a Greek Revival house of 1801. Noted for variety of unusual tree species; much new planting; lake with island; woodland walk; large rock garden and grotto. Walled rose garden; water features. TEAS. Free car/coach park. *Adm £2 Chd free. Fris, Sats and Bank Hol Mons, May to Sept. For NGS Sats May 2, 9, Sept 19 (12-6)*

Glanwye, Builth Wells ❀❀ (Mr & Mrs David Vaughan, G & H Kidston) 2m E Builth Wells on A470. Large garden, rhododendrons, azaleas; herbaceous borders, extensive yew hedges, lawns, long woodland walk with bluebells and other woodland flowers. Magnificent views of upper Wye Valley. Illustrated in 'Some Borderland Gardens' by B & A Palmer. TEAS. *Adm £2 Chd free (ACNO to Llanddewi Cwm and Alltmawr Church®). Sun May 17 (2-5)*

■ **Gliffaes Country House Hotel, Crickhowell** ❀ (Mr & Mrs Brabner) 3m W of Crickhowell on A40. Large garden; spring bulbs; azaleas & rhododendrons, new ornamental pond; heathers; shrubs; ornamental trees; fine maples; autumn colour; fine position high above R Usk. Cream Teas available at hotel. *April to Dec. For NGS Adm £2 Chd free (collecting box). Suns May 10, Oct 11 (2-5)*

Gregynog, Tregynon ❀ (University of Wales) 7m N of Newtown. A483 Welshpool to Newtown Rd, turn W at B4389 for Bettws Cedewain, 1m through village gates on left. Large garden; fine banks, rhododendrons and azaleas; dell with specimen shrubs; formal garden; colour-coded walks starting from car park. Descriptive leaflet available. Early C19 black and white house; site inhabited since C12. TEAS. *Adm £1.50 Chd 50p 12/16 yrs. Sun May 31 (2-6)*

Hill Crest, Brooks ❀ (Mr J D & Mrs P Horton) 9m SW of Welshpool. Turn R to Berriew, then L by Lion Hotel, through village towards Bettws Cedewain. Turn R after 3m to Brooks then 1m up hill on L. 8m NE from Newtown. Through Bettws Cedewain. Take Brooks Rd, after 3m turn L. House at top of hill on L. Approx 1 acre of mixed shrub borders, alpine sinks and pool; hillside arboretum with daffodils and rhododendron walk. *Adm £1 Chd 10p. Suns April 5, 19, May 3, 17, June 14, 28, July 12, Aug, 23, Sept 20 (1-5). Group visits welcome all year, please* **Tel 01686 640541**

Llangorse Gardens ❀ Llangorse is on B4560 4m off A40 at Bwlch, 6½m from Brecon and 4½m from Talgarth. Park in village. TEAS in aid of Llangorse Church. *Adm £1.50 Chd free*
 The Neuadd (Mr & Mrs P Johnson) Informal garden of approx 1 acre with mixed borders of interesting trees, shrubs and herbaceous plants, emphasis on good foliage and unusual forms of cottage garden and native plants; small vegetable and fruit garden, meadow gardens and copse. Maintained by owners on organic lines to encourage wild life. *Private visits welcome, please* **Tel 01874 658 670**
 The Old Vicarage ❀❀ (Major & Mrs J B Anderson) Small family garden maintained by owners with interesting herbaceous and shrub borders; lawns, trees and vegetables. Plants usually for sale in aid of NGS. *Private visits welcome Spring to Oct, please* **Tel 01874 658639**

Llansantffraed House Bwlch, nr Brecon ❀❀❀ (Mrs A Inglis) On A40 at junction to Talybont-on-Usk, 6m E of Brecon, 2m W of Bwlch next to Llansantffraed Church. ½-acre sloping lawns, shrubs and trees with huge yew hedges. Masses of spring bulbs; old-fashioned wall of aubretia, alyssum and alpines. TEA in conservatory overlooking the Usk and Brecon Beacons. *Combined adm with* **Scethrog House** *£1.50 Chd free. Sun, Wed April 26, 29 (2-5)*

¶**Scethrog House** ✿❀ (Mr & Mrs V Bennett) 5m E of Brecon on A40 turn L for Scethrog. 1 acre garden. Mixed borders, spring bulbs and clipped yews. Tea at Llansantffraed House. *Only open April 26*

Llanstephan House, Llyswch ♿✿❀ (Lord & Lady Milford) Off small rd between Boughrood and Erwood Bridge on opp side of R Wye to A470 (Brecon-Builth Wells rd). Large garden with rhododendrons, azaleas, shrubs, old-fashioned roses, walled kitchen garden. Managed with emphasis on natural surroundings providing scope for a variety of wildlife. Beautiful views of Wye Valley and Black Mountains. TEAS. *Adm £2 Chd free. Sun June 7 (2-5)*

Llysdinam, Newbridge-on-Wye ♿❀ (Lady Delia Venables-Llewelyn & Llysdinam Charitable Trust) SW of Llandrindod Wells. Turn W off A479 at Newbridge-on-Wye; right immed after crossing R Wye; entrance up hill. Large garden. Azaleas; rhododendrons, water garden and herbaceous borders; shrubs; woodland garden; kitchen garden; fine view of Wye Valley. TEAS in aid of NSPCC. *Adm £2 Chd free. Mon May 25, Sun Aug 9 (2-6). Private parties welcome, please* **Tel 01597 860 200**

¶**Llys-y-Wen, Carno** ♿❀ (Mr & Mrs A J Avery) On A470 immed on L when entering village from Newtown (11m) Machynleth 17m. 1-acre garden. Large mature trees enclosing borders with wide variety of plants and shrubs. Wildlife pond. TEAS. *Adm £1.50 Chd free. Sun June 28 (10-5). Other times by appt, please* **Tel 01686 420643**

Maenllwyd Isaf, Abermule ♿✿ (Mrs Denise Hatchard) 5m NE of Newtown & 10m S of Welshpool. On B4368 Abermule to Craven Arms, 1½m from Abermule. 3 acres; unusual shrubs and plants; goldfish pool; 'wild' pool; R Mule. C16 listed house. *Adm £1 Chd free (ACNO to Winged Fellowship Trust®). Private visits welcome all year. Gardening clubs etc welcome, please* **Tel 01686 630204**

TAKEN, AUGUST BANK HOLIDAY **1993** from LLANTHONY, Brecon Beacons National Park. Bedlington/Lurcher cross, all white except for a grey head and grey splodge high on left side. Still missed by family, reward for information leading to his return. G ELLIOTT, The Smithy, Llanthony NP7 7NN 01873 890781

Maesllwch Castle, Glasbury-on-Wye ❀ (Walter de Winton Esq) Turn off A438 immed N of Glasbury Bridge. Through Glasbury, ½m turn R at church. Medium-sized, garden owner maintained. Exceptional views from terrace across R Wye to Black Mountains. Woodland walk to old walled garden now used for young trees. Fine trees, C18 gingko tree. TEA. *Adm £2 Chd free (ACNO to All Saints Church, Glasbury®). Sun May 24 (2-5)*

Mill Cottage, Abbeycwmhir ❀ (Mr & Mrs B D Parfitt) 8m N of Llandrindod Wells. Turning L off A483, 1m N of Crossgates Roundabout, then 3½m on L, signposted Abbeycwmhir. ⅓-acre garden of unusual and rare shrubs, small trees and climbers. Numerous ericaceae. Narrow paths and steps; limited parking. TEA. *Adm £1 Chd 50p. Sat to Sun incl, May 30 to June 7, July 4 to 12, August 1 to 9 (mid-day to dusk)*

The Millers House, Welshpool ♿❀ (Mr & Mrs Mark Kneale) About 1¼m NW of Welshpool on rd to Guilsfield A490; turn R into Windmill Lane; 4th cottage on L. 1½-acre country garden begun in 1988. Superb views. Mixed shrub and herbaceous borders, roses, climbers; pool. Ornamental and fruit trees incl a planting of 12 hardy eucalyptus. *Adm £1.25 Chd free. Private visits welcome, please* **Tel 01938 555432**

Parc Gwynne, Glasbury on Wye ♿❀ (Mr & Mrs W Windham) From Brecon towards Hereford on A438 cross Glasbury Bridge, 1st L signposted Boughrood and 1st l at War Memorial. Entrance across green. Small riverside garden, mainly herbaceous, incl white border. TEAS and bring and buy plant stall. *Adm £2 Chd free (ACNO to Queen Mary's Clothing Guild® and All Saints Church Glasbury®). Sun July 12 (2-5)*

Penmyarth, Glanusk Park ♿ (Mr & The Hon Mrs Legge-Bourke) 2m W of Crickhowell. A40, 12m from Brecon, 8m from Abergavenny. 11-acre rose, rock and wild garden. TEAS. *Adm £2. Sun July 5 (2-5)*

Pen-y-Maes ♿❀ (Miss S Egerton) 1m W of Hay on Wye on B4350 towards Brecon. Entrance on L. 2-acre garden, mainly herbaceous. Walled kitchen garden with geometric beds of herbs, vegetables and flowers. Shrub roses, irises, paeonies and espaliered pear trees. TEAS. *Adm £2 Chd free. Sun June 14 (2-5)*

Point Farm ♿✿❀ (Mr & Mrs F Podmore) Bryn Lane, Newtown. Head N across river from town centre. Take R-hand rd into Commercial St off roundabout. L at fork into Llanfair Rd L at hospital for 1½m along Bryn Lane. At 750' the ½-acre garden set in unspoilt views of the countryside. Patio, pergola, herbaceous plants and shrub beds, colour co-ordinated for yr-round interest. Soft fruits, raised vegetable garden with 15' × 25' greenhouse with peach and apricot trees, vegetables and tender plants. TEAS. *Adm £1 Acc chd free and raffle by Aberhafesp WI and Happy Circle. Suns June 14, Aug 9 (2-6). Private visits welcome, please* **Tel 01686 625709**

▲**Powis Castle Gardens** ⚘✿ (The National Trust) Welshpool. Turn off A483 ¾m out of Welshpool, up Red Lane for ¼m. Gardens laid out in 1720 with most famous hanging terraces in the world; enormous yew hedges; lead statuary, large wild garden. Part of garden suitable for wheelchairs, top terrace only. Wheelchairs available free of charge. TEA in tea rooms. *Adm (garden only) £4 Chd £2. For NGS Wed May 27 (11-6) last entry 5.30*

Tan-y-Llyn, Meifod ⚘✿ (Callum Johnston & Brenda Moor) From Oswestry on the A495 turn L in village, cross R Vyrnwy and climb hill for ½m bearing R at Y-junction. [Map ref 167125]. 3-acre sheltered garden and orchard in Montgomeryshire hills. Informally terraced; laid out to complement the proportions of existing hillside. Thorn grove, herb garden; extensive collection of container plants. Nursery specialising in alpines, herbaceous plants and herbs. TEAS. Events, demonstrations and exhibitions. *Adm £1 Chd free. Sats, Suns May 2, 3, June 6, 7, July 4, 5, Aug 1, 2 (2-5)*

Treberfydd, Bwlch & (Lt Col & Mrs D Garnons Williams) 2¼m W of Bwlch. From A40 at Bwlch turning marked Llangorse then L for Pennorth. From Brecon, leave A40 at Llanhamlach. 2¼m to sign Llangasty Church but go over cattle grid to house. Large garden; lawns, roses, trees, rock garden. Plants for sale at commercial nursery. TEAS. *Adm £2 Chd free (ACNO to Llangasty Church®). Sun June 28 (2-6)*

¶**Tretower House, Tretower** &✿ (Lt Col & Mrs P K Cracroft) Leave Crickowell on A40 towards Brecon. Take R fork for Builth Wells. Garden 1m in Tretower village. 2½-acre family garden maintained by owners. Mainly herbaceous. Views of Black Mountains and Tretower Castle. TEAS. *Adm £2 Chd free. Sun June 21 (2-5)*

¶**Welsh Border Gardens in the Hindwell Valley** On the R 1½m from Presteigne going towards Kington on the B4355. TEAS at The Rodd. *Combined adm £3.50 Chd free. Sun June 21 (2-5)*

¶**The Rodd** ✿ (Lady Nolan) Topiary, mature shrubs and old apple trees enclose this Elizabethan house, old shrub roses and a gnarled medlan add to the atmosphere of romance and wildness within a formal setting. Teas in aid of Sidney Nolan Trust

¶**Little Rodd** &✿ (Mr & Mrs Brian Boobbyer) Cottage garden, planted with an emphasis on fragrance; mainly shrubs interspersed with perennials which are allowed to seed. Over 60 varieties of shrub and climbing roses

¶**Ricketts Castle** (Mr H Evans) Unique small garden created by local craftsman from strip of roadside land. Immaculately clipped hedges divide the garden areas

The Walled Garden, Knill & (Miss C M Mills) 3m from Kington and Presteigne. Off B4362 Walton-Presteigne rd to Knill village; right over cattle grid; keep right down drive. 4 acres; walled garden; river; bog garden; primulas; shrub and climbing roses. Nr C13 Church in lovely valley. Featured in the Water Gardener and in various books on gardens in the area. *Private visits and garden clubs welcome any day (10-7) Adm £1.50, please Tel 01544 267411*

Crossroads

Crossroads is a charity which cares for carers. The National Gardens Scheme is delighted to include it in its list of beneficiaries. Some facts and figures:

- One in 7 of the adult population is caring for a relative or friend.
- Most of the carers are women.
- 20% of carers say they never get a break and 65% of carers say their health has suffered as a result of caring responsibilities.
- **Crossroads** employs over 4,000 staff who support and provide respite care for the carers.
- **Crossroads** supports 28,000 carers and provides nearly 3 million care hours per year.
- The contribution of carers saves tax payers over £30 billion per year.

The *National Gardens Scheme* is pleased to invite you
to a special Evening Opening at

The Royal Horticultural Society's Garden
at
Wisley

on the occasion of the first evening of the
Wisley Flower Show
Tuesday, July 28th, 6.30–9pm

Enjoy an exclusive evening stroll through this renowned
garden, greeted by the music of the Corelli String Quartet; then
savour a midsummer supper, entertained by the remarkable
Guildford Barbershop Harmony Club

The Wisley Flower Show marquee open for public view 7–9pm,
with plant sales by Show Exhibitors 7–8pm

Admission: £3 (excluding refreshments) in aid of the National
Gardens Scheme (admission fee also applies to RHS members)

Coach parties must pre-book two weeks in advance,
Telephone (01483) 224234

The Terrace Restaurant will open for pre-booked
dinner reservations on Telephone (01483) 225329
The Conservatory Cafe will open for drinks and
self-service buffet

RHS Garden, Wisley is located near the A3/M25 intersection at Junction 10

Index to Gardens

This index lists all gardens alphabetically and gives the counties in which they are to be found. Refer to the relevant county pages where the garden and its details will be found, again in alphabetical order. The following unorthodox county abbreviations are used: B & SG—Bristol & South Gloucestershire; C & W—Cheshire and Wirral; G, N&C—Gloucestershire (North & Central); G, S&B—Gloucestershire (South) & Bristol; L & R—Leicestershire and Rutland; L, M & GM—Lancashire, Merseyside and Greater Manchester; W & WM—Warwickshire & part of West Midlands; C/C—Ceredigion/Cardiganshire; C & P—Carmarthenshire & Pembrokeshire; D & C—Denbighshire & Colwyn; F & W—Flintshire & Wrexham. An * denotes a garden which will not be in its normal alphabetical order as it is a group garden and will be found under the Group Garden name but still within the county indicated.

G

Guildhall, The*   Cambs
Guilsborough and
   Hollowell Gardens   Northants
Gunby Hall   Lincs
Gunthorpe   L & R
Guyers House   Wilts
Gwyndy Bach   Gwynedd
Gwysaney Hall   D & C

H

Haconby Hall   Lincs
Haddonstone Show
   Garden   Northants
115 Hadlow Road   Kent
Hadspen Garden   Somerset
252 Haggerston Road*   London
Hailsham Grange   Sussex
Hailwell House*   Sussex
Halecat   Cumbria
Halewell*   G, N&C
Half Moon House   Devon
Halfpenny Cottage*   G, N&C
Halfpenny Furze*   Bucks
Hall, The*   Northants
Hall Barn   Bucks
Hall Barn Close*   Oxon
Hall Farm   Lincs
Hall Grange   London
Hall Green Gardens   W & WM
Hall Place Gardens   Kent
7 Hall Road Burbage*   L & R
Hallgarth   Yorks
Hallowarren   Cornwall
Halnacker Hill   Surrey
109 Halsbury Road East   London
83 Halton Road   Lincs
Ham Gate*   Dorset
Ham House   London
Hambledon House   Hants
Hambleton Gardens   L & R
Hamblyn's Coombe   Devon
116 Hamilton Terrace   London
117 Hamilton Terrace   London
Hammerwood House   Sussex
11 Hampstead Way   London
Hamstead Grange   IoW
Hanbury Hall   Worcs
286 Handley Road   Derbys
Handywater Farm*   Oxon
Hangeridge Farm   Somerset
Hannington Hall   Wilts

Hansel House*   Northants
Hapsford House   Somerset
Harcombe House   Hants
Hardays House*   Northants
Hardwick Hall   Derbys
Hardwicke House*   Cambs
Hare Hill Gardens   C & W
Harewood   Bucks
Harewood House   Yorks
Harfield Farm House   Hants
Harlaxton Manor Gardens   Lincs
Harlow Carr Botanical
   Gardens   Yorks
Harnage Farm   Shropshire
Harpole Gardens   Northants
Harptree Court   Somerset
Harrington Hall   Lincs
Harris Garden & Experimental
   Grounds, The   Berks
4 Harrowden Lane*   Northants
Hartland Abbey   Devon
40 Hartington Crescent*   W & WM
144 Hartington Crescent*   W & WM
Hartlip Gardens   Kent
Hartlip Place*   Kent
89 Harts Green Road   W & WM
Hartsheath   F & W
Hartshill Gardens   Shropshire
47 Harvest Road   Surrey
Haslehurst   Surrey
Haslingfield Gardens   Cambs
14 Haslingfield Road*   Cambs
Hatch Beauchamp Gardens   Somerset
Hatch Court*   Somerset
Hatch Court Farm*   Somerset
Hatchlands Park   Surrey
Hatherways*   Bucks
Hatton Grange   Shropshire
Haugh House*   Oxon
Haughton Hall   C & W
Haul-a-Gwynt   Gwynedd
Haulfryn   Gwynedd
Hault Farm   Kent
133 Haverstock Hill   London
Hawarden Castle   F & W
Hawkesbury Gardens   B & SG
Hawkesbury Home Farm*   B & SG
Hawkstone Hall   Shropshire
Hawthorne, The   Sussex
Hawthornes   L, M & GM
Hayden Barn Cottage   Hants
Haydown   Kent
Haye House   Shropshire
Hayling Island Gardens   Hants

Hayne Old Manor   Devon
Haynstone Orchard   Hereford
Hazel Cottage   G, S&B
Hazelbury Manor Gardens   Wilts
Hazelmount   Cumbria
Hazelwych*   Notts
Headington Gardens   Oxon
Headland   Cornwall
Heale Gardens & Plant
   Centre   Wilts
Hean Castle   C & P
32 Heanor Road   Derbys
274 Heanor Road   Derbys
Hearns House   Oxon
37 Heath Drive   London
75 Heath Gardens   London
Heath House
—Eccleshall   Staffs
—Ryhall   Lincs
Heatherwood   Dorset
Heathfields   Surrey
Heathlands   Hants
Heddon Hall   Devon
Heligan Gardens   Cornwall
Helmsley Gardens   Yorks
Hemble Hill Farm   Yorks
Hemingdale*   Cambs
Hen Efail*   D & C
Hen Ysgoldy   Gwynedd
Henbury Hall   C & W
Heneage Court   B & SG
Hengrave Hall   Suffolk
Henllan Village Gardens   D & C
Henllys Lodge   Gwynedd
Heol Bryncwils   Glams
Hergest Croft Gardens   Hereford
Hermitage*   Somerset
Heron House*   Suffolk
Heron's Reach   Oxon
Herterton House   Northumb
Hesketh Bank Village
   Gardens   L, M & GM
Hestercombe Gardens   Somerset
Hethersett   Surrey
Hever Castle and Gardens   Kent
Hexham Herbs, Chesters
   Walled Garden   Northumb
35 Heyes Lane   C & W
Hickecroft   W & WM
Hidcote Manor Garden   G, S&B
High Beckside Farm   Cumbria
High Beeches Gardens   Sussex
High Cleabarrow   Cumbria
High Cross*   W & WM

The *National Gardens Scheme* is pleased to invite you to
a special Evening Opening at

The Royal Botanic Gardens Kew

during Chelsea Week
Thursday, May 21st
6.30–9pm

Enjoy the glorious late spring at Kew at an exclusive
Evening Opening.

Two of the major glasshouses will be open, with staff
available to explain their collections and Kew's work.

Admission: £4 Adults, £2 Children,
in aid of the National Gardens Scheme
(as this is a fund-raising event, admission
fee also applies to Season Ticket holders and
Friends of the Royal Botanic Gardens, Kew)

Refreshments available

Kew is easily reached via the Kew Gardens station (London
Underground District Line, and by rail from North London on
Silverlink). Also from Kew Bridge station (South West Trains).
By road the Gardens are located just south of Kew Bridge on
the A307, Kew Road.

Entry by Victoria Gate Only
on the Kew Road, opposite Lichfield Road.

Y

Index to Advertisers

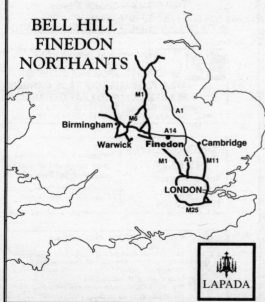

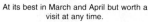

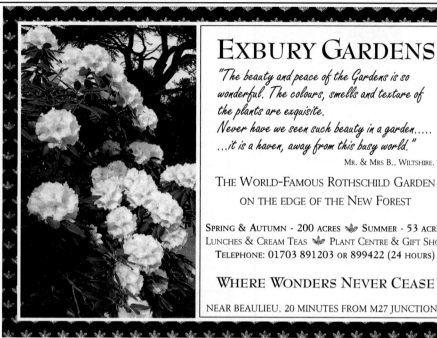

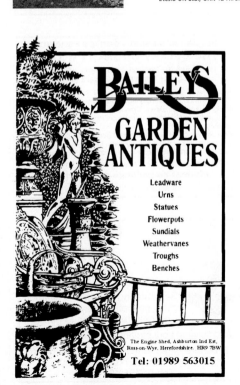

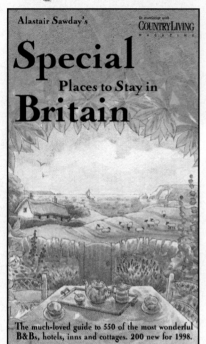